Encyclopedia of
Urban America
The Cities and Suburbs

Encyclopedia of
Urban America
The Cities and Suburbs

Volume 1
A–L

Neil Larry Shumsky
Editor

ABC-CLIO

Santa Barbara, California
Denver, Colorado
Oxford, England

Library of Congress Cataloging-in-Publication Data

Encyclopedia of urban America : the cities and suburbs / Neil Larry Shumsky,
    editor
        p.   cm.
      Includes bibliographical references and index.
      Contents: vol. 1. A–L — vol. 2. M–Z.
        1. Cities and towns—United States—Encyclopedias.   2. Suburbs—
    United States—Encyclopedias.   3. Cites and towns—United States—History.
    4. Suburbs—United States—History. I. Shumsky, Neil L., 1944– .
      HT123.E5   1998   98-11698
      307.76'0973'03—dc21   CIP

ISBN 0-87436-846-4 (alk. paper)

04 03 02 01 00 99 98   10 9 8 7 6 5 4 3 2 1

ABC-CLIO, Inc.
130 Cremona Drive, P.O. Box 1911
Santa Barbara, California 93116-1911

This book is printed on acid-free paper ∞.

Dedicated to:

E
R
M I C H A E L
C

Contents

Encyclopedia of Urban America
The Cities and Suburbs

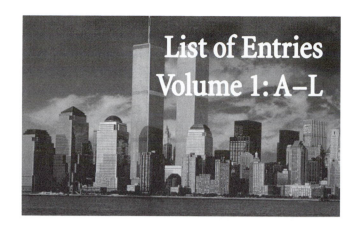

List of Entries
Volume 1: A–L

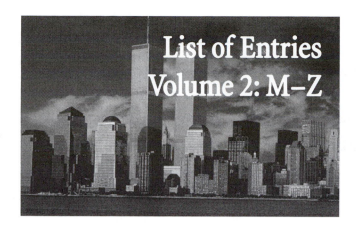

List of Entries
Volume 2: M–Z

Contributors

Abadinsky, Howard
Department of Criminal Justice
St. Xavier University

Abbott, Carl
Department of Urban Studies and Planning
Portland State University

Abbott, Mark
Department of Urban Specializations
Harris-Stowe State College

Achor, Shirley
Emerita, Department of History
East Texas State University

Adams, Annmarie
School of Architecture
McGill University

Adams, Bluford
Department of English
University of Iowa

Adler, Jeffrey S.
Department of History
University of Florida

Ahouse, John
Special Collections, Doheny Library
University of Southern California

Albright, Alex
Department of English and Journalism
East Carolina University

Allen, Robert C.
James Logan Godfrey Professor of American Studies,
    History, and Communication Studies
University of North Carolina, Chapel Hill

Allswang, John
Department of History
California State University, Los Angeles

Alperovich, Gershon
Department of Economics
Bar-Ilan University
Ramat-Gan, Israel

Archer, John
Department of Cultural Studies and
    Comparative Literature
University of Minnesota, Twin Cities Campus

Arnold, Joseph L.
Department of History
University of Maryland, Baltimore County

Arnott, Richard
Department of Economics
Boston College

Bachin, Robin F.
Charlton W. Tebeau Assistant Professor of History
University of Miami (Florida)

Balmori, Diana
Balmori and Associates
New Haven, Connecticut

Barnes, Elsie M.
School of Social Sciences
Norfolk State University

Barr, Terry F.
Department of English
Presbyterian College

Barrow, Mark V., Jr.
Department of History
Virginia Polytechnic Institute and State University

Barrows, Robert G.
Department of History
Indiana University–Purdue University at Indianapolis

Bauerlein, Mark
Department of English
Emory University

Bauman, John F.
Department of History
California University of Pennsylvania

Beard, Rick
Executive Director
Atlanta Historical Society

Beito, David
Department of History
University of Alabama

Bennett, Larry
Political Science Department
DePaul University

Benton, J. Edwin
Department of Government and International Affairs
University of South Florida

Bethel, Elizabeth Rauh
Division of Behavioral Sciences
Lander University

Bianco, Martha J.
Center for Urban Studies
Portland State University

Biles, Roger
Department of History
East Carolina University

Binder, John J.
Department of Business Administration
University of Illinois, Chicago

Binford, Henry
Department of History
Northwestern University

Black, Brian
Liberal Studies Program
Skidmore College

Blackmar, Elizabeth
Department of History
Columbia University

Blackwelder, Julia Kirk
Department of History
Texas A & M University

Blair, Karen J.
Department of History
Central Washington University

Blau, Judith R.
Department of Sociology
University of North Carolina, Chapel Hill

Blee, Kathleen M.
Department of Sociology
University of Pittsburgh

Bluestone, Daniel
School of Architecture
University of Virginia

Blumin, Stuart
Department of History
Cornell University

Borchert, James
Department of History
Cleveland State University

Bottles, Scott
Capital Markets Group, Wells Fargo Bank
Los Angeles, California

Bouman, Mark J.
Department of Geography, Economics, and History
Chicago State University

Bowman, Sylvia P. H.
Department of English
University of Houston, Downtown

Brasch, Walter M.
Department of Mass Communications
Bloomsburg University

Bratt, Rachel G.
Department of Urban and Environmental Policy
Tufts University

Bringhurst, Newell G.
Department of History and Political Science
College of the Sequoias

Broaddus, Billie
Medical Heritage Center
University of Cincinnati

Brody, M. Kenneth
Department of Sociology and Anthropology
Central College

Buenker, John D.
Department of History
University of Wisconsin, Parkside

Burgess, Patricia
Levin College of Urban Affairs
Cleveland State University

Burke, Thomas E.
Division of the Budget
New York State

Burton, Joseph A.
Department of Architectural Studies
Clemson University

Cain, Louis P.
Department of Economics
Loyola University Chicago

Campbell, Hilbert
Department of English
Virginia Polytechnic Institute and State University

Caputo, David A.
President
Hunter College of the City University of New York

Chappelka, Art
School of Forestry
Auburn University

Choldin, Harvey
Department of Sociology
University of Illinois, Urbana-Champaign

Chudacoff, Howard P.
University Professor, Department of History
Brown University

Cocks, Catherine
History Department
State University of New York, Oswego

Contosta, David R.
Department of History
Chestnut Hill College

Cranz, Galen
Department of Architecture
University of California, Berkeley

Cromley, Elizabeth
Department of Art & Architecture
Northeastern University

Crooks, James B.
Department of History, Philosophy and Religious Studies
University of North Florida

Cross, Bradley
Department of History
University of Cincinnati

Curtis, Susan
Department of History
Purdue University

Cutler, William
Department of History
Temple University

Cybriwsky, Roman
Department of Geography and Urban Studies
Temple University

Danbom, David B.
Department of History
North Dakota State University

Daniels, Roger
Charles Phelps Taft Professor of History
University of Cincinnati

Darden, Joe T.
Urban Affairs Programs
Michigan State University

Davies, Edward J., II
Department of History
University of Utah

Davis, Donald F.
Department of History
University of Ottawa

Davis, James L.
Department of Geography
Western Kentucky University

Day, Jared N.
Department of History
Carnegie-Mellon University

DeLyser, Dydia
Department of Geography and Anthropology
Louisiana State University

Dent, Gary
Social Science/Public Service Technology Division
Virginia Western Community College

Dewey, Scott Hamilton
California State University, Los Angeles
Los Angeles, California

Diamond, Etan
Department of History
Carnegie-Mellon University

DiCiccio, Carmen
Department of History
University of Pittsburgh

Dicke, Thomas S.
Department of History
Southwest Missouri State University

DiGirolamo, Vincent
Department of Interdisciplinary Writing
Colgate University

Dilger, Robert Jay
Institute for Public Affairs
West Virginia University

Diner, Steven J.
Department of History
George Mason University

Dizikes, John
Cowell College
University of California, Santa Cruz

Doezema, Marianne
Mount Holyoke College Art Museum
Mount Holyoke College

Doherty, Maura
Department of History
Illinois State University

Dolce, Philip C.
Social Sciences/Communications Arts
Bergen Community College

Domosh, Mona
College of Liberal Arts
Florida Atlantic University

Dougherty, James
Department of English
University of Notre Dame

Downey, Dennis
Dean of Graduate Studies
Millersville University of Pennsylvania

Eaton, Leonard
Independent Scholar
Otter Creek, Oregon

Ebner, Michael
A.B. Dick Professor of History
Lake Forest College

Eisinger, Peter
College of Urban, Labor, and Metropolitan Affairs
Wayne State University

Eldot, Paula
Emerita, Department of History
California State University, Sacramento

Emlen, Robert
American Civilization
Brown University

Emmons, David M.
Department of History
University of Montana

Evensen, Bruce J.
Department of Communication
DePaul University

Fairbanks, Robert B.
Department of History
University of Texas, Arlington

Fairfield, John D.
History Department
Xavier University

Farmer, Rod
History and Education
University of Maine, Farmington

Farrar, Haywood
Department of History
Virginia Polytechnic Institute and State University

Feagin, Joe R.
Department of Sociology
University of Florida

Felson, Marcus
School of Criminal Justice
Rutgers University, Newark

Ferdinand, Theodore N.
Center for the Study of Crime, Delinquency and Corrections
Southern Illinois University, Carbondale

Figone, Albert J.
Department of Health and Physical Education
Humboldt State University

Fine, Lisa M.
Department of History
Michigan State University

Fine, Sidney
Emeritus, Department of History
University of Michigan

Fisher, Glenn W.
Emeritus, Hugo Wall School for Urban and Public Affairs
Wichita State University

Flanagan, Maureen A.
Department of History
Michigan State University

Foster, Mark S.
Department of History
University of Colorado, Denver

Fraser, Walter J., Jr.
Department of History
Georgia Southern University

Fredericksen, Patricia J.
Department of Political Science
Washington State University

French, Roderick S.
University Seminars
George Washington University

Fried, Lewis
Department of English
Kent State University

Gabaccia, Donna
Charles H. Stone Professor of American History
University of North Carolina, Charlotte

Galishoff, Stuart
Department of History
Georgia State University

Garcia, John A.
Department of Political Science
University of Arizona

Garner, John S.
School of Architecture
University of Illiniois, Urbana-Champaign

Gerber, Philip
Department of English
State University of New York, College at Brockport

Giamo, Benedict
Department of American Studies
University of Notre Dame

Gilfoyle, Timothy J.
Department of History
Loyola University Chicago, Lake Shore Campus

Gilje, Paul A.
Department of History
University of Oklahoma

Gillette, Howard, Jr.
American Studies Program
George Washington University

Glasmeier, Amy
Department of Geography
Pennsylvania State University

Gold, Christina Sheehan
Department of History
University of California, Los Angeles

Goldfield, David
Robert Lee Bailey Professor of History
University of North Carolina, Charlotte

Goldin, Milton
Milton Goldin Company
Tarrytown, New York

Goodsell, Charles
Center for Public Administration and Policy
Virginia Polytechnic Institute and State University

Gough, Robert
Department of History
University of Wisconsin, Eau Claire

Green, Norma F.
Department of Journalism
Columbia College Chicago

Greenberg, Amy S.
Department of History
Pennsylvania State University

Grenier, Guillermo J.
Department of Sociology and Anthropology
Florida International University

Griffin, Joseph
Emeritus, Department of English
University of Ottawa

Grossman, Barbara W.
Mary Ingraham Bunting Institute
Radcliffe College

Grossman, James
Newberry Library
Chicago, Illinois

Groth, Paul
Department of Architecture
University of California, Berkeley

Haas, Edward F.
Department of History
Wright State University

Hakim, Simon
Department of Economics
Temple University

Hale, Jason
Bradley Department of Electrical Engineering
Virginia Polytechnic Institute and State University

Hanes, Jeffrey Eldon
Department of History
University of Oregon

Hardy, Stephen H.
Department of Kinesiology
University of New Hampshire

Harm, Nancy J.
School of Social Work
University of Arkansas, Little Rock

Harmon, Sandra D.
Department of History
Illinois State University

Harris, Richard
Department of Geography
McMaster University

Hawes, Joseph
Department of History
University of Memphis

Haywood, C. Robert
Emeritus, Department of History
Washburn University

Hempstead, Katherine
Office of Population Research
Princeton University

Henderson, A. Scott
Independent Scholar
Aiken, South Carolina

Hennesey, James
Jesuit Residence
Le Moyne College

Henslin, James
Department of Sociology and Social Work
Southern Illinois University, Edwardsville

Herscovici, Steve
Senior Economist, Analysis Group/Economics
Cambridge, Massachusetts

Hill, Patricia Evridge
Department of Social Science
San José State University

Hilton, George W.
Emeritus, Department of Economics
University of California, Los Angeles

Hirsch, Arnold R.
Department of History
University of New Orleans

Hoffman, Steven J.
Department of History
Southeast Missouri State University

Holli, Melvin J.
Department of History
University of Illinois, Chicago

Holloran, Peter
Independent Scholar
Cambridge, Massachusetts

Holtzclaw, Robert P.
Department of English
Middle Tennessee State University

Hood, Clifton
Department of History
Hobart and William Smith Colleges

Hoover, Dwight W.
Emeritus, Department of History
Director Emeritus, Center for Middletown Studies
Ball State University

Howe, Deborah
Department of Urban Studies and Planning
Portland State University

Hudnut-Beumler, James
Dean of Faculty
Columbia Theological Seminary

Hunt, Michael E.
Environment, Textiles, and Design
University of Wisconsin

Hunter, Albert
Department of Sociology
Northwestern University

Hutcheson, John D., Jr.
College of Public Administration and Urban Studies
Georgia State University

Hyman, Harold M.
Emeritus, William P. Hobby Professor of History
Rice University

Issel, William
Department of History
San Francisco State University

Isserman, Maurice
Department of History
Hamilton College

Jensen, Richard
Department of History
University of Illinois, Chicago

Johanningsmeier, Edward L.
University Parallel Program
University of Delaware

Johnson, David A.
College of Architecture and Planning
University of Tennessee, Knoxville

Johnson, David R.
Division of Behavioral and Cultural Sciences
University of Texas, San Antonio

Johnson, Marilynn
Department of History
Boston College

Johnson, Victoria
School of Cinema-Television
Division of Critical Studies
University of Southern California

Jones, Kathleen W.
Department of History
Virginia Polytechnic Institute and State University

Kantor, Paul
Department of Political Science
Fordham University

Karr, Ronald Dale
O'Leary Library
University of Massachusetts, Lowell

Kaufman, Burton I.
Department of History and Center for Interdisciplinary Studies
Virginia Polytechnic Institute and State University

Keating, Ann Durkin
Department of History
North Central College

Keller, Mollie
Department of Archives and Records
Bridgeport, Connecticut

Kemp, John R.
Office of Public Information and Publications
Southeastern Louisiana University

Kennedy, Lawrence W.
Department of History and Political Science
University of Scranton

Kennedy, Rick
Department of History and Government
Point Loma Nazarene College

Kerson, Toba Schwaber
Graduate School of Social Work and Social Welfare
Bryn Mawr College

Kerstein, Robert
Department of History, Political Science and Psychology
University of Tampa

Kilar, Jeremy W.
Department of History
Delta College

King, Leslie J.
Department of Geography
McMaster University

Kirk, Gordon W., Jr.
Department of History
Western Illinois University

Kirschner, Don S.
Emeritus, Department of History
Simon Fraser University

Klaus, Susan
Past Imperfect, Consultants in Historical Research
Washington, D.C.

Klebaner, Benjamin J.
Department of Economics
City College of the City University of New York

Kleinberg, S. J.
American Studies
Brunel University, London

Klink, William R.
Department of Languages and Literature
Charles County Community College

Knepper, Cathy D.
Independent Scholar
Kensington, Maryland

Knobel, Dale T.
President, Denison University
Granville, Ohio

Knox, Paul L.
Dean, College of Architecture and Urban Studies
Virginia Polytechnic Institute and State University

Kornwolf, James D.
Department of Art and Art History
College of William and Mary

Krinsky, Carol Herselle
Department of Fine Arts
New York University

Krynicki, Dorothy
Department of Political Science
Fordham University

Kuhn, Sarah
Department of Regional Economic and Social Development
University of Massachusetts, Lowell

Kujawa, Richard Stephen
Department of Geography
Saint Michael's College

Lane, James B.
Department of History and Philosophy
Indiana University Northwest

Lane, Roger
Department of History
Haverford College

Lazarus, Barry
Doctor of Medicine
West Hartford, Connecticut

Lees, Andrew
Acting Dean of the Graduate School
Rutgers University, Camden

Leggett, John C.
Department of Sociology
Rutgers University

Leonard, Stephen J.
Department of History
Metropolitan State College of Denver

Lewis, Carol W.
Department of Political Science
University of Connecticut

Leyendecker, Liston E.
Department of History
Colorado State University

Linden, Blanche M. G.
Independent Scholar
Fort Lauderdale, Florida

Lindstrom, Diane
Department of History
University of Wisconsin

Liscombe, R. Windsor
Department of Fine Arts
University of British Columbia

Loeb, Carolyn
Department of Art
Central Michigan University

Loviscek, Anthony L.
Department of Economics
Seton Hall University

Luckingham, Bradford
Department of History
Arizona State University

Lui, Adonica
Department of Sociology
Harvard University

MacLachlan, Ian
Department of Geography
University of Lethbridge

Magliari, Michael
Department of History
California State University, Chico

Mahoney, Timothy R.
Department of History
University of Nebraska, Lincoln

Maland, Charles
Department of English
University of Tennessee, Knoxville

Malino, Sarah S.
Department of History
Guilford College

Manzo, Joseph T.
Department of Geography
Concord College

Maranto, Robert
Department of Government and Law
Lafayette College

Marlais, Michael
Department of Art
Colby College

Marling, Karal Ann
Department of Art History and American Studies
University of Minnesota

Marsh, Margaret
Department of History
Temple University

Marston, Sallie
Department of Geography and Regional Development
University of Arizona

Martin, Michel
Department of History
Temple University

Martone, Michael
Department of English
University of Alabama

Masteller, Richard N.
Division of Humanities and Arts
Whitman College

McComb, David G.
Department of History
Colorado State University

McMullin, Thomas A.
Department of History
University of Massachusetts, Boston

McNickle, Chris
Independent Scholar
New York, New York

Mehrhoff, W. Arthur
Local and Urban Affairs Program
St. Cloud State University

Melosi, Martin V.
Department of History
University of Houston

Mergen, Bernard
American Studies Program
George Washington University

Miller, Donald L.
John Henry MacCracken Professor of History
Lafayette College

Miller, Randall M.
Department of History
Saint Joseph's University

Miner, Curtis
Pennsylvania Historical and Museum Commission
State Museum of Pennsylvania

Moogk, Peter N.
Department of History
University of British Columbia

Morgan, H. Wayne
Department of History
University of Oklahoma

Morgan, Keith
Art History Department
Boston University

Mormino, Gary R.
Department of History
University of South Florida

Moss, Richard
Department of History
Colby College

Muccigrosso, Robert
Department of History
Brooklyn College of the City of New York

Murphy, Russell D.
Department of Government
Wesleyan University

Namorato, Michael
Department of History
University of Mississippi

Nanry, Charles
School of Management and Labor Relations
Rutgers University

Nellis, Eric G.
Department of History
Okanagan University College

Nelson, Arthur C.
City Planning, Public Policy and International Affairs
Georgia Institute of Technology

Nelson, Joel I.
Department of Sociology
University of Minnesota

Nelson, Kristine E.
Graduate School of Social Work
Pennsylvania State University

Newell, Charldean
Department of Public Administration
University of North Texas

Nice, David C.
Department of Political Science
Washington State University

Nord, David Paul
Journalism and American Studies
Indiana University

Nowak, David J.
Northeastern Forest Experiment Station
Forest Service, United States Department of Agriculture

Nye, David
Center for American Studies
Odense University, Denmark

Ochsner, Jeffrey Karl
Department of Architecture
University of Washington

O'Connor, Carol
Department of History
Utah State University

Ogilvie, Philip
Office of Public Records
Washington, D.C.

O'Hara, James
Department of English
Pennsylvania State University, York Campus

O'Kane, James
Department of Sociology
Drew University

Orser, W. Edward
American Studies Department
University of Maryland, Baltimore County

Orum, Anthony M.
Department of Sociology
University of Illinois, Chicago

Pacyga, Dominic A.
Liberal Education Department
Columbia College

Parry, Sally E.
Department of English
Illinois State University

Pascoe, Craig
Department of History
University of Tennessee

Peterson, Jon A.
Department of History
Queens College of the City University of New York

Pierannunzi, Carol
Department of Political Science
Kennesaw State College

Pike, Burton
Comparative Literature and German
Graduate Center of the City University of New York

Pike, Robert M.
Department of Sociology
Queen's University

Pisciotta, Alexander W.
Department of Criminal Justice and Social Work
Kutztown University

Power, Garrett
School of Law
University of Maryland

Prestamo, Felipe J.
School of Architecture
University of Miami

Prinz, Andrew K.
Urban Studies Program
Elmhurst College

Rainey, Reuben M.
Department of Landscape Architecture
University of Virginia

Ramirez, Jan Seidler
Associate Director
Museum of the City of New York

Rappaport, Theodore S.
Bradley Department of Electrical Engineering
Virginia Polytechnic University and State University

Rayfield, Jo Ann
Department of History
Illinois State University

Reed, James W.
Department of History
Rutgers University, New Brunswick

Reilly, Edward C.
Department of English
Arkansas State University

Rich, Wilbur C.
Department of Political Science
Wellesley College

Riess, Steven A.
Department of History
Northeastern Illinois University

Robertson, Kent A.
Local and Urban Affairs Program
St. Cloud State University

Rock, Howard A.
Department of History
Florida International University

Rodriguez, Joseph A.
Department of History
University of Wisconsin, Milwaukee

Rorabaugh, W. J.
Department of History
University of Washington

Rosenzweig, Roy
Department of History
George Mason University

Rosner, David
Graduate School and University Center
City University of New York

Ruchelman, Leonard
Department of Urban Studies
Old Dominion University

Rury, John
School of Education
DePaul University

Sánchez-Jankowski, Martín
Department of Sociology
University of California, Berkeley

Sautter, Udo
Seminar für Zeitgeschichte
Professur für nordamerikanische Geschichte
Eberhard-Karls Universität Tübingen

Sawislak, Karen
Department of History
Stanford University

Scharnhorst, Gary
Department of English Language and Literature
University of New Mexico

Scherzer, Kenneth A.
Department of History
Middle Tennessee State University

Schlereth, Thomas J.
Department of American Studies
Department of History
University of Notre Dame

Schneider, John C.
Corporate and Foundation Relations
Tufts University

Schwartz, Joel
Department of History
Montclair State University

Scott, Pamela
Papers of Pierre Charles L'Enfant
Washington, D.C.

Sculle, Keith A.
Head, Research and Education
Illinois Historic Preservation Agency

Shachmurove, Yochanan
Department of Economics
University of Pennsylvania

Shapiro, Herbert
Department of History
University of Cincinnati

Shaw, Ronald E.
Department of History
Miami University (Ohio)

Sies, Mary Corbin
Department of American Studies
University of Maryland

Singer, Stan
Film Studies
Arizona State University

Skaburskis, Andrejs
School of Urban and Regional Planning
Queen's University

Slayton, Robert A.
Department of History
Chapman University

Smith, Preston
Department of Political Science
Mount Holyoke College

Soden, Dale E.
Department of History
Whitworth College

Sonenshein, Raphael J.
Department of Political Science
California State University, Fullerton

Soper, Barlow
Behavioral Sciences
Louisiana Tech University

Spaeth, David A.
College of Architecture
University of Kentucky

Spillane, Joseph
Department of History
Center for Studies in Criminology and Law
University of Florida

Spinney, Robert G.
Department of History
Trinity International University

Sprague, Paul E.
Emeritus, Department of History
University of Wisconsin, Milwaukee

Squires, Gregory D.
Department of Sociology
University of Wisconsin, Milwaukee

Stansfield, Charles A., Jr.
Department of Anthropology and Geography
Rowan University of New Jersey

Starr, Raymond G.
Department of History
San Diego State University

Steinberg, Allen
Department of History
University of Iowa

Stelter, Gil
Department of History
University of Guelph

Stempel, Tom
Department of Radio-TV-Cinema
Los Angeles City College

Stepenoff, Bonnie
Historic Preservation Program
Southeast Missouri State University

Stevens, John D.
Department of Communication
University of Michigan

Stinson, Robert
Department of History
Moravian College

Sutherland, John F.
Director, Institute of Local History
Manchester Community College

Takagi, Dana Y.
Adlai E. Stevenson College
University of California, Santa Cruz

Tarr, Joel A.
Richard S. Caliguiri Professor of Urban and Environmental
    History and Policy
Carnegie Mellon University

Teaford, Jon C.
Department of History
Purdue University

Tenenbaum, Susan
Department of Political Science
Baruch College of the City University of New York

Tenzer, Morton J.
Department of Political Science
University of Connecticut

Thomas, June Manning
Urban and Regional Planning Program and
    Urban Affairs Programs
Michigan State University

Thompson, Gregory L.
Department of Urban and Regional Planning
Florida State University

Thorp, Daniel
Department of History
Virginia Polytechnic Institute and State University

Tischauer, Leslie
Division of Social Science
Prairie State College

Toll, William
Department of History
University of Oregon

Trolander, Judith Ann
Department of History
University of Minnesota, Duluth

Tucker, C. Jack
Department of Sociology
Winthrop University

Tunbridge, John E.
Department of Geography
Carleton University

von Hoffman, Alexander
Joint Center for Housing Studies
Harvard University

Wach, Howard M.
Department of History
Bronx Community College

Wallenstein, Peter
Department of History
Virginia Polytechnic Institute and State University

Wallis, Allan D.
Graduate School of Public Affairs
University of Colorado, Denver

Weber, Michael P.
Department of History
Duquesne University

Weigold, Marilyn E.
Department of History, Political Science and Economics
Pace University, White Plains Campus

Weingarden, Lauren S.
Department of Art History
Florida State University

Weinstein, Raymond M.
Department of Sociology
University of South Carolina, Aiken

Weisbrot, Robert S.
Department of History
Colby College

Weisenberger, Carol A.
Department of History
University of Northern Iowa

Weiss, Ellen
School of Architecture
Tulane University

West, Graham
Chartered Geologist
United Kingdom

White, John H., Jr.
Department of History
Miami University (Ohio)

Wikstrom, Nelson
Department of Political Science
Virginia Commonwealth University

Williams, Bruce B.
Fletcher Jones Professer of Sociology
Mills College

Williams, Marilyn Thornton
Department of History
Pace University

Wilson, Leslie
Department of History
Montclair State University

Wilson, Lucy
Department of English
Loyola Marymount University

Winkler, Allan M.
Department of History
Miami University (Ohio)

Winter, Robert
Arthur G. Coons Professor of the History of Ideas
Occidental College

Winteregg, Steven L.
Department of Music
Wittenberg University

Wohlenberg, Ernest H.
Department of Geography
Indiana University

Wolner, Edward
Department of Architecture
Ball State University

Wood, Joseph S.
Office of the Provost
George Mason University

Woodard, J. David
Department of Political Science
Clemson University

Woods, Mary
Department of Architecture
Cornell University

Worthington, William
National Museum of American History
Smithsonian Institution

Wright, Charles L.
Senior Economist, Projects
Interamerican Development Bank

Wyly, Elvin
Department of Geography
Rutgers University

Yagoda, Ben
Department of English
University of Delaware

Young, Terence
Department of History
Clemson University

Zonderman, David
Department of History
North Carolina State University

Preface and Acknowledgments

These two volumes are eclectic and idiosyncratic at the same time. They are eclectic because more than 300 people from many disciplines—ranging from history to sociology to political science to architecture to art to criminology—wrote about 500 entries for this encyclopedia. At the same time, the volumes are idiosyncratic because one individual—me—selected the topics to be included, contacted potential authors to write the entries, and then accepted, modified, or rejected the articles that were submitted. Thus, in a strange way, the project represents an extraordinary collective effort, but it is also an individual undertaking. It reflects the accumulated knowledge of all the contributors, but it also delineates what is important to me.

This extraordinary degree of collaboration was essential, but also desirable, because few people, if anyone at all, have the knowledge, ability, or interest to write anything consequential about approximately 500 separate, although related, topics—even a few hundred words about many of them. Other than conducting the enormous (sometimes overwhelming) amount of bureaucratic and administrative record-keeping that such a joint project entails, one of the editor's major responsibilities is locating, persuading, cajoling, and occasionally arm-twisting colleagues, friends, and a few former friends into writing entries.

But before an editor can undertake that task, he or she must decide how to organize and what to include in an encyclopedia like this one; what entries should be contained, and what is the basis for their selection. When I began conceptualizing this project, it seemed to me that there were two possible kinds of design. The encyclopedia could be organized around specific places, and each entry would be a particular city, suburb, or urban place. The other possibility was to include some specific places but generally to include entries relating to specific urban phenomena, people, places, and events.

I chose the latter kind of framework for several reasons. First (but not necessarily most important), and to make no bones about it, that type of organization was more interesting to me and offered a greater amount of intellectual stimulation to a sometimes routine activity. Second, I was aware that other encyclopedias were being prepared about individual cities, and I didn't want to duplicate what they were already doing or compete with their editors for authors. Finally, my understanding with the publisher was that this encyclopedia was to concern urban America, not specific urban places in the United States. To a large degree, but not exclusively, I was supposed to include information about subjects that was relevant to urban places in general, not to specific locales or sites.

Easier said than done. Trying to compose a list of every "urban" topic seemed insuperable, never-ending, and afforded the unpleasant potential of producing an infinite list of subjects for entries. Enter the first form of eclecticism. Trying to find some consensus about what was "significant" and therefore worth including in the encyclopedia, I merged the indexes of a number of well-known and highly regarded general books about urban America. Books as old as *A History of Urban America* by Charles Glaab and A. Theodore Brown to books as recent as Joel Garreau's *Edge City*. Books as wide-ranging as Kenneth Jackson's *Crabgrass Frontier* to more narrowly focused books such as Margaret Marsh's *Suburban Lives*. Merging the indexes of all these books allowed me to see how many scholars thought a topic important enough to mention in their own general books. Was it one, two, or many? From this list, I constructed an initial list of topics I would like to include in the encyclopedia. Generally, but not always, I included those subjects mentioned in more than one of the books; and, generally, but not always, I excluded those topics mentioned in only a single book. My rationale was simple; if more than one scholar thought an item worth mentioning in a general work, I thought it important enough to include in this encyclopedia. But if only one of the authors considered a topic worth mentioning, I attributed that to an individual idiosyncrasy and rejected the topic from my list.

After deciding on a preliminary list of topics, an editor needs to locate others willing to write the entries. Preferably, places largely on the basis of the relationship between their populations and their political boundaries. But because the bureau has changed these definitions frequently, because it has also changed its terminology often, and because its terminology has rarely, if ever, become part of everyday speech, its various explanations of "urban" and different kinds of urban places have been difficult to understand and to apply.

The Census Bureau first reported the "urban population" of the United States in 1870, and that year it counted the urban population as the number of people living in cities and towns larger than 8,000 people. But for the next three censuses, the bureau defined urban places differently, in some censuses including cities or towns having populations of 4,000 or more, and in other years those with populations of 8,000 or more. In a supplementary report to the twelfth census (1900), published in 1906, the bureau tried to make sense of the different numbers. It finally concluded that "the meaning popularly attached to urban, namely, pertaining to a city, has been found inapplicable to census purposes, owing to the different meanings of 'city' in the different parts of the United States." As a result, that year, and in subsequent censuses up to and including the sixteenth (1940), the population required for an incorporated place to be considered "urban" was reduced to 2,500; New England towns of the same size were considered "urban" even if they did not contain an incorporated place.

The 1940 census also contained a statistical time series of the urban population since 1790. Using the contemporary definition of "urban" (essentially 2,500 people living in an incorporated place), it revealed the number of urban places in each of nine size groups ranging from fewer than 2,500 to more than 1 million. At least until the middle of the twentieth century, then, the Census Bureau implicitly acknowledged that the meaning of the word "urban" rested heavily on population, but it provided no clear explanation of the minimum population required for a place to be considered "urban," and it failed to explain how the nine different kinds of urban had been determined. Interestingly, it never used the words "town" or "city" when describing the population, perhaps suggesting either that the definitions were unclear, that the bureau was unable to define them satisfactorily, and that the relationship between "town," "city," and "urban" could not be determined.

The seventeenth census, taken in 1950, substantially redefined "urban." The urban population now included all people who lived in (1) incorporated cities, villages, and boroughs larger than 2,500 people, (2) incorporated towns larger than 2,500 except in New England, New York, and Wisconsin, where a "town" was simply a minor subdivision of a county (and also challenging the equation of the word "town" with "city" and "urban"), (3) the densely settled urban fringe of both incorporated and unincorporated areas around cities that had a population of 50,000 or more, and (4) unincorporated places larger than 2,500 outside of the urban fringe. Thus, the definition of "urban" used in 1950 distinguished among places on the basis of their legal status (incorporated or not), geographic status (located outside or inside of New England, New York, or Wisconsin), and political status (part of the urban fringe or not). According to the 1950 *Census of Population,* this new definition did not "exclude a number of equally large and densely settled places, merely because they were not incorporated." Even though the bureau was trying to define "urban" more precisely and usefully in order to include the entire urban population and exclude the entire rural population, it probably confused things even more. After explaining why the new definition was superior to the old, the bureau acknowledged that, "although the urban population under the old definition was exactly the population living in urban places . . . the new definition includes persons living outside urban places." Remarkable—some towns were not urban, but it was possible for a person to be part of the urban population without living in an urban place.

At the same time, and for the first time, the census of 1950 set forth a new kind of place, the "urbanized area." The 157 urbanized areas it identified in the United States each included one city of at least 50,000 people and its "urban fringe," the contiguous area consisting of (1) incorporated places with a population of at least 2,500, (2) incorporated places smaller than 2,500 but containing at least 100 dwelling units and a density of 500 dwelling units per square mile, (3) unincorporated places with a density of 500 dwelling units per square mile, and (4) "territory devoted to commercial, industrial, transportational, recreational, and other purposes functionally related to the central city." In establishing this new classification, the "major objective" of the bureau was "to provide a better separation of urban and rural population in the vicinity of our cities than was possible under the old definition."

Although the category of "urbanized area" may not have actually provided a "better separation" of urban and rural, it certainly provided a different definition. Its major effect was to include within the urban population an additional 6,203,596 people who lived "under distinctly urban conditions in the immediate environs of our larger cities." This increase of almost 10 percent in the number of people living in "urbanized areas" seems to have rested on no objective criteria, standards, or measurements. Instead, the boundaries of "urbanized areas" were determined "after careful examination of all available maps, aerial photographs, and other sources of information."

But the difficulty of defining "urban" continued. The Census Bureau continued to shy away from the words "city" and "town," perhaps recognizing their imprecision and lack of clear meaning. Instead, it reported the population of two other kinds of places—"standard metropolitan areas" and "central cities." The Federal Committee on Standard Metropolitan Areas, composed of representatives from various interested agencies and sponsored by the Bureau of the Budget, created the "standard metropolitan area" (SMA) to establish comparability among the data gathered and presented by different agencies of the federal government, including the Census Bureau itself, as well as the metropolitan districts used in the *Census of Population,* the industrial areas used in the *Census of Manufactures,* and the labor market areas used by the Bureau of Employment Security. To be an SMA, a county (or group of adjacent counties) had to satisfy several conditions. It had to have at least one city with 50,000 people; moreover, the whole area had to have a "metropolitan" character, which meant that it was "socially and economically integrated with the central city."

To establish metropolitan character, a county (1) needed either to contain 10,000 nonagricultural workers, or to contain 10 percent of the nonagricultural workers of the entire SMA, or to have at least 50 percent of its population living in an area contiguous to the central city and have a population density of at least 150 people per square mile, and (2) needed to have a work force that was at least two-thirds nonagricultural.

In addition, to be considered part of an SMA, (1) at least 15 percent of the workers living in a contiguous county had to work in the county containing the largest city in the SMA, or (2) 25 percent of the people working in a contiguous county had to reside in the county containing the largest city in the SMA, or (3) the number of monthly telephone calls made to the largest city in the SMA from a contiguous county had to be at least four times the number of telephone subscribers in the county. Suddenly, and with no apparent warning, where an area's labor force worked and the destination of its telephone calls had become a distinguishing factor in the definition of "metropolitan."

At the same time that the Census Bureau established the existence of SMAs, it also designated some cities as "central cities." In fact, an SMA could have more than one "central city," certainly an unusual use of the word "central." The largest was known as the "principal central city," but other cities with populations greater than 25,000 and at least one-third as large as that of the principal central city could also be designated a "central city." At the time of the 1950 census, several SMAs possessed more than one "central city."

The terminology that the bureau used to describe the population in 1950 says several things about its concept of urban places. For one thing, the bureau distinguished between an "urban place" and the "urban population." A person did not have to live in an "urban place" in order to be counted as part of the "urban population." In addition, the Census Bureau differentiated not only between "urban place" and "urban population," but also among different kinds of urban places, and not just towns and cities. There were "urban places," "urbanized areas," "standard metropolitan areas," and "central cities," as well as "principal central cities." As would be expected, each had its own definition and each suggested different counts of the urban population of the United States.

However, the new definitions of 1950 did not satisfy the Census Bureau for long, and it tried refining them in 1970. That year, it modified them in several significant ways. It noted that between 1960 and 1970, something quite new had occurred in the United States. In annexing surrounding territory (an old process), cities such as Chesapeake, Virginia, and Oklahoma City, Oklahoma, had incorporated areas that would otherwise have been considered "rural." This created a real dilemma if the bureau were to continue using political boundaries in defining "urban." If everyone who lived in those newly incorporated areas was classed as "urban," then the "urban population" would include "persons whose environment is primarily rural in character." In order to avoid this possibility, the Census Bureau created still another new category, the "extended city." An "extended city" was legally a "city," but one that had both an "urban" part and a "rural" part. It contained at least five square miles with a population density of fewer than 100 people per square mile; moreover, this area (the incorporated rural extension to the city) had to constitute at least 25 percent of the total land area of the legal city. Implicitly, the bureau was again suggesting a distinction between "urban" and "city." A "city," or at least parts of one, was not necessarily "urban."

Ironically, at the same time that the bureau was excluding this group of rural people from the urban population, it was nevertheless including the entire population of "urbanized areas" within the urban population. While it was removing from the urban population some people who lived in cities established by a government, it was adding others in areas it considered rural, or putting it another way, it was refining the meanings of "urbanized area," "central city," and "urban fringe" in contradictory ways. As just mentioned, everyone who lived in an "urbanized area" became part of the "urban population." But a particular city's name now had to be incorporated into the name given an "urbanized area" for that city to be considered a "central city." Even this was not precise enough, and the names given to "urbanized areas" were restricted to three cities. The largest city was generally listed first, followed by the next two, but each of them had to have a population of at least 250,000. Yet even that wasn't exactly adequate, and four exceptions were made: the "urbanized areas" of New York, New York–Northeastern New Jersey, which contained New York City and Newark, Jersey City, Paterson,

Clifton, and Passaic, New Jersey; Chicago, Illinois–Northwestern Indiana, which included Chicago, Illinois, and Gary, Hammond, and East Chicago, Indiana; Los Angeles–Long Beach, which encompassed Los Angeles, Long Beach, Anaheim, Santa Ana, and Garden Grove; and San Francisco–Oakland, which incorporated San Francisco, Oakland, and Vallejo. Finally, in the census of 1970, the bureau changed the term used for metropolitan areas from Standard Metropolitan Area (SMA) to Standard Metropolitan Statistical Area (SMSA), and it decided that everyone who lived in an SMSA was part of the "metropolitan population." Going even farther, it classed the entire population of the United States as "inside central city or cities" and "outside central city or cities." Everyone who lived outside of an SMSA was classed as part of the "nonmetropolitan population."

Fearing that all of these distinctions might be confusing, in 1970 the bureau tried to explain the relationships among the different kinds of urban places. "Urbanized areas" could be seen as physical cities rather than legal cities or metropolitan communities. They were usually smaller than SMSAs and were contained within an SMSA. But, in some cases, because the boundaries of an SMSA were determined by political boundaries, and the boundaries of an "urbanized area" followed patterns of urban land use, an "urbanized area" could be interpreted as "the thickly settled core" of an SMSA, reflecting the "existence of considerable rural areas in metropolitan counties."

In both the census of 1980 and the census of 1990, the bureau changed its terminology once again. For 1980, it devised the "Standard Consolidated Statistical Area." This new term reflected the fact that, in some parts of the United States, contiguous SMSAs themselves had become so economically and socially integrated with each other that some concept linking them together and reflecting their relationship needed to be created. And, in 1990, the bureau attempted to rationalize both usage and definition. It made only minor changes in the definitions of "urban," "extended city," and "urbanized area." It made its greatest modifications in considering the "metropolis." It loosely defined the "metropolitan area" (MA) as a place with a large population nucleus and any adjacent communities highly integrated with it socially and economically. To be an MA, an area required either a single place whose population was at least 50,000 or an urbanized area as defined by the Census Bureau that had a population of 100,000 (only 75,000 in New England). An MA also contained one or more central counties that had close economic and social ties with the central county city, that had a specified level of commuting, and that met certain standards concerning population density, urban population, and population growth. The bureau classed an MA as either a Metropolitan Statistical Area (MSA) or a Consolidated Metropolitan Statistical Area (CMSA). To be considered an MSA, a place had to be relatively freestanding and not associated with other MSAs. But, if an MSA had a population exceeding 1 million people, the bureau could divide it into Primary Metropolitan Statistical Areas (PMSAs). In this case, the bureau considered the MSA to be a CMSA, and it recognized subordinate PMSAs that it defined as a "large urbanized county or cluster of counties that demonstrates very strong internal and social links, in addition to close ties to other portions of the larger area."

Perhaps this ongoing refinement of terms, concepts, and definitions by the Census Bureau reflects nothing more than the knowledge that "urban" places have grown larger over time. This is certainly true. But the changed—and constantly changing—vocabulary and usage reflects more. For one thing, it indicates the recognition that as "urban" places grew larger and became more populous, they overflowed their political boundaries, and this created serious problems as the bureau tried to count the "urban" and the "rural" population and distinguish between them. When the problem began, some states did not use the words "town" or "city" in the same way as other states. In some, the word "town" or "township" did not necessarily denote an urban place. According to the bureau, some of those localities obviously belonged in any reporting of the urban population, but others did not. In other instances, population that clearly seemed to be part of an urban place functionally, and was contiguous to that urban place, was positioned beyond its legal, political borders. Clearly, this population was not "rural" in the sense of "living a rural life," but neither did these people live in a legal town or city. Should that place be considered urban? Sometimes, a place clearly existed and functioned within a particular urban realm but lay beyond a city's boundaries and did not even adjoin it. Was that place "urban" or not?

All of these questions arose from more than a deeper comprehension of cities. The Census Bureau was essentially recognizing and acknowledging that political boundaries did not necessarily contain the entire urban population, and it was trying to resolve this dilemma by recognizing new kinds of places and devising new terms that permitted the inclusion of the residents of these places within the total urban population. However, there was more to it than that. The number of terms created, and the attempt at precise definitions, seem to imply the recognition of functional differences between "urban" areas of different sizes. Even more, while the technically precise, narrow definitions that the Census Bureau used never entered the common vocabulary, an alternative set of words and phrases crept into everyday speech and also the vocabulary used by students of cities—words like "suburb," "megalopolis," "multicentered metropolis," or, most recently, "edge city." The development of this added vocabulary made the very definition of the word "city" itself more nebulous and vague, especially for urbanists. For example, if a "metropolis" somehow differed from a "city," then both words needed defining in a way that communicated the differences clearly, otherwise the distinction meant little. When people heard about or read about or analyzed New York City or Boston or Chicago, or especially Phoenix or Houston or some of the newer locations in the Sunbelt, it was necessary to know if the subject being considered was the whole "metropolitan region" or only the place contained within the political boundaries of an incorporated city. To use the terminology of the census, was one referring to an "urbanized area," "a metropolitan area," "a central city," or "a consolidated metropolitan area"? To use the more common terms, was one referring to the political city, the metropolitan area, or the whole megalopolis?

To some degree, but in a rather simplistic way, the more commonly used words and phrases constitute little more than a hierarchy of size. From smallest to largest, the pecking order of size ranges from hamlet to village to town to city to metropolis to megalopolis. Merriam-Webster's WWWebster Dictionary on the World Wide Web defines "hamlet" as "a small village," a "village" as "a settlement usually larger than a hamlet but smaller than a town," a "town" as "a compactly settled area usually larger than a village but smaller than a city," a "city" as "an inhabited place of greater size, population, or importance than a town or village," a "metropolis" as "a large important city," and a "megalopolis" as "a very large important city."

But to contend that the only, or even that the most significant, distinction among these words (or the ones devised by the Census Bureau) and the places they denote is size overlooks significant factors and traits. For one thing, basing a hierarchy on size alone disregards other important words or phrases—terms like "suburb" or "multicentered metropolis" or "edge city" that don't fit quite as neatly. These words can be squeezed into the same hierarchy as the others only if some distinguishing characteristic or characteristics other than size is admitted.

Moreover, claiming that a hierarchy of these terms is based exclusively on size ignores striking differences among places that are designated differently. While any place called a city is probably larger than a town, is greater size its only, or even its primary, distinguishing feature? Perhaps cities have one or more highways running through or around them, but major expressways come nowhere near towns. How significant is that difference? Enough to differentiate a "city" from a "town"? Or is it simply a fortuitous or secondary condition, less important than population in determining if a place is a "city" or a "town"? Turning the tables for a moment, while a large proportion of the people who live in a village might practice agriculture, most residents of a town are not at all likely

to engage in farming. Is that economic difference less important than population in making a place a "village" rather than a "town"? Can a town possibly have an agricultural economy? If not, is the nature of the economic base a defining characteristic of different kinds of places, both small and large, including the "megalopolis" or (to use the census term) the "consolidated metropolitan statistical area"?

Perhaps these questions seem silly and headed nowhere. It would be easy to ask what difference it makes if a place is called a "village" rather than a "town." Who cares if a place is termed a "city" rather than a "metropolis"? Why does it matter if a place is a "metropolitan statistical area" or a "primary metropolitan statistical area"? What difference could there possibly be if the entire "urbanized" population actually lives in "urbanized areas"? To some extent, it matters very little. In everyday conversation, it probably doesn't make much difference at all if someone calls Camden, New Jersey, just across the Delaware River from Philadelphia, Pennsylvania, with a population greater than 500,000 in 1990, a city, a suburb of Philadelphia, a part of the Philadelphia metropolitan area, or part of the East Coast megalopolis that extends from Washington, D.C., to the south to Boston, Massachusetts, to the north.

But it is also true that each of these terms has different connotations and implies something very different about Camden, its functioning, its relationship to Philadelphia, and how it connects to the entire population of the region. Perhaps more important, each terminology suggests something quite different about the life of Camden and the lives of the people who live there. The way in which a place is described determines how that place is perceived by an audience.

Equally important, if not more so, is the issue of government policy. If different kinds of urban places actually have different characteristics and different natures other than their population, it is critical for officials at every level of government to know those traits and whether any particular place is more properly a "city" or a "metropolis," for example. If officials do not understand those characteristics and those natures, then any attempt to create effective policies and programs must fail. If a policy is to succeed, what can or cannot be done or undone must be shaped, at least in part, by whether a particular condition or state or problem (whatever it might be) is inherently an integral part of a place being a "city," a "town," or a "suburb" or if that status is irrelevant to the issue. Without that understanding, a policy may well be misguided and a total waste of time, energy, and resources. It might even have serious, negative consequences.

Our vocabulary contains words and phrases that identify and refer to many different kinds of urban places that are recognized as being distinct. The very creation and usage of that broad terminology strongly attests to the perception of variations among those places. But, the differences have yet to be explained clearly and effectively, certainly not by compilers of dictionaries or by the Census Bureau. When people say "Los Angeles," it is frequently not at all clear whether they mean a particular city, a county, a metropolitan area, a large part of southern California (whatever that might mean), or if they are just using the name of the city figuratively and symbolically. Many people who live in Orange County, just east of Los Angeles and adjacent to it, understand this very well. They hate being called Angelenos and being said to live in Los Angeles. Many of them detested having the local professional baseball team called the California Angels and applauded the recent change to the Anaheim Angels. While the name of a baseball team might not be very consequential, if policymakers attempt to confront traffic problems, or the increasing number of "dysfunctional" families, or the extent of drug abuse, or any other perceived problem in a populous place, they need to be quite sure if the specific condition that troubles them has developed from "city-ness," "metropolitan-ness," "megalopolitan-ness," or if it has just developed because a particular group of people happen to live there. Does a specific place have a certain need or problem because Anaheim exists? Because Irvine belongs to the Los Angeles–Long Beach Metropolitan Region? Because Santa Ana is part of the southern California megalopolis? What is the crucial variable that determines whether a place is part of an "urban area," an "urbanized area," a "metropolitan statistical area," a "primary metropolitan statistical area," or a "consolidated metropolitan statistical area"? These distinctions must matter. If they do not, it is very difficult, if not impossible, to understand why so much effort has been expended on developing them.

This encyclopedia attempts to, at least, confront all these questions and offer a few tentative answers. But as much as this work tells about the cities and suburbs of the past and the present, it reveals equally well the tremendous amount still unknown and waiting to be learned. For example, what exactly is a suburb? The WWWebster Dictionary says that it is "an outlying part of a city or town" or "a smaller community adjacent to or within commuting distance of a city" or "the residential area on the outskirts of a city or large town." These definitions suggest peripheral location, subordinate status, and economic dependence. But is that true? Is a suburb just a place on the edge of a city that is "functionally" connected to that city? Or does a suburb have some nature and set of characteristics independent of the city itself? Can all suburbs over time be considered comparable and be compared to each other? Does the same word accurately describe Beverly Hills, completely surrounded by Los Angeles in the 1990s, and Brookline, on the outskirts of Boston in the 1850s? Is the "suburb" of 31,971 in 1990 and located in the midst of a sprawling megalopolis so similar to a "suburb" of 5,164 on the outskirts of a city in 1860 that the same term describes both satisfactorily? Is Beverly Hills subordinate to Los Angeles? How many residents of that independent city think that they are dependent on Los Angeles or understand the relationship between Beverly Hills and Los Angeles? What percentage of the population of that much smaller city commute to work in Los Angeles? Is driving two miles across the boundary along Santa Monica Boulevard to Century City really commuting?

These questions, and countless others like them, have rarely been asked, much less answered. But in order to understand urban civilization and urban society, it is critical to know about a whole panoply of urban forms, about the recently discovered "edge city" and about the "metropolis" and "megalopolis," for example. What are the most significant characteristics of those latter two places? How does either of them differ from a city, or from the other? Are they simply descriptive words that characterize places on the basis of the size of their populations, geographic extent, and crossing of urban borders? Or is there something analytically and functionally different about them that actually shapes their nature, determines the lives of the people who live in them, and has crucial implications for the development and formulation of policy? Are their institutions significantly different from those of traditional cities?

But before those questions can be answered, perhaps even before they should be asked, other queries need to be posed and resolved. More histories of individual cities and suburbs are needed, especially of contemporary cities and suburbs. As of 1997 no scholarly histories had been published on several of the 25 largest cities in the United States and of countless smaller but nevertheless important ones. This absence is perhaps related to the fact that many of these cities are in the Southwest, West, or other parts of the Sunbelt. There are almost no scholarly histories of the most important or largest (not at all the same) "suburbs" in the United States today. Most of these cities, and almost all of the suburbs, developed more recently; Boston has certainly been studied far more than Seattle or El Paso. Perhaps newer places have evolved in ways that seem different from the cities and suburbs that developed in the eighteenth century or the first half of the nineteenth century, and they have not had time to attract the interest of a substantial number of scholars. Maybe that will change as a new generation of scholars emerges.

Furthermore, it is almost impossible to think of these younger cities and suburbs without immediately thinking of the entire metropolitan, or even megalopolitan, region, not just the traditional "central" city and its surrounding or outlying suburbs. But that very fact, then, raises significant questions about what should and should not be studied. If one is trying to understand Los Angeles in the late twentieth century, should an author consider or not consider the communities of the Antelope Valley (north of the political boundaries of Los Angeles) as a part of the study? If one is writing about San Francisco, should an author include or not include the many independent municipalities of Marin County, the San Francisco Peninsula, Silicon Valley to the south, and the East Bay, including Berkeley and Oakland? What are the relationships among all of these places, and how have they been mutually related over time, especially the last 50 years? As early as 1964, James E. Vance, Jr., pointed out the difference between San Francisco and the San Francisco Bay area and the need to study the entire Bay area and not just the single well-known city. He pointed out the hazards of thinking that San Francisco had the same importance to everyone in the area and to every part of the area. Just in passing, it seems worth pointing out that the rapid decline and almost complete disappearance of "urban biography" as a distinct genre occurred at about the same time that these new urban forms began to be recognized and that few urban biographies extend beyond the time when issues of new urban forms—the metropolis, the megalopolis, and the edge city—truly became relevant. Perhaps the time has come to resurrect that benighted form of scholarly investigation in order to understand the new processes better.

Asking questions about urban places that are neither city nor suburb implies other subjects that also need exploration. Have these various kinds of urban places produced unique institutions or types of institutions that should be considered separately and regarded as distinct from each other? For example, it is universally conceded that the automobile has had tremendous effects on American cities. But to say that does not consider if "the machine" has functioned differently in, and had different effects on, the city, the suburb, or the metropolis. In the second half of the twentieth century, when almost every member of the American urban middle class has had access to automotive travel, have people in different kinds of urban places used cars differently? Has their particular pattern of automobile use distinguished the lives of people in these different kinds of places and changed the places themselves? While the automobile in the urban setting has only recently begun to be studied and analyzed in depth, the automobile has never been specifically studied with regard to the metropolitan world. One could ask similar questions about any of the institutions that seem so common to the entire society, such as the family, the church or temple, the public school, the country club, or the shopping mall, just to name a few. What is the precise relationship among the Cub Scout pack, the drive-in church, and the modern metropolis? How do these metropolitan institutions differ from earlier urban ones? Do they differ from traditional suburban ones? What do they reveal about the nature of contemporary urban society and the nature of many contemporary places called simply, but imprecisely, "urban"?

Many of the few people who have studied those questions have been set off—or set themselves off—into a separate, scholarly world, a specialized world that approaches urban places in a somewhat roundabout way. They have examined cities from the vantage point of regional planning. And a fundamental problem results. To many people (most especially to those outside the field), the word "region" is ambiguous, and there is a tendency to think that "region" inevitably includes some rural area. To other people, a "region" is either wholly rural, or it is an urban place and any surrounding rural area or areas that it dominates or strongly influences. Therefore, those who conduct regional studies are often thought not to be students of cities.

Of course, people in the field realize that this is false, and that there is a strong link between regional planning and city planning. But perhaps the concept of "region" needs rethinking and should be acknowledged to include "urban" and "urbanized." Perhaps the links between regional planning and city planning need to be strengthened and broadened so that all kinds of links between cities and regions become more evident. If that happened, then perhaps regions like the Atlantic seaboard from Washington, D.C., to Boston; the area around Philadelphia including places like Camden, New Jersey; the San Francisco Bay area; or the Los Angeles–Long Beach Metropolitan Region would be studied in their entirety, and we would understand them more easily. Doing so might be an overwhelming scholarly task, but if it happened, important phenomena might not be overlooked, subjects might not be conceived as narrowly as they have been, and analysis might not be shaped and limited by a vocabulary that hides as much as it discloses.

Hopefully, this encyclopedia provides insight and understanding into where we have been, and where we are, and what we already know about the urban world. If it does that successfully, perhaps it will also tell us where we still need to go and what we still need to learn.

References

Oxford English Dictionary, http://etext.virginia.edu/oed.html, 1997. At Electronic Text Center, University of Virginia Library.

Tisdale, Hope. "The Process of Urbanization." *Social Forces* 20 (1942): 311–316.

U.S. Bureau of the Census. *Historical Statistics of the United States, Colonial Times to 1970.* 2 vols. Vol. I, 2. Washington, DC: Government Printing Office, 1975.

———. *Nineteenth Census of the United States (1970). Census of Population,* Vol. 1, part A, sec. 1, page x. Washington, DC: Government Printing Office, 1970.

———. *Seventeenth Census of the United States (1950). Census of Population: Number of Inhabitants,* Vol. I, xvii. Washington, DC: Government Printing Office, 1950.

————. *Twelfth Census of the United States (1900). Special Reports of the Census Office.* Supplementary Analysis, 20. Washington, DC: Government Printing Office, 1900.

————. *Twentieth Census of the United States (1980). Census of Population, Characteristics. Chapter B. General Population Characteristics,* part I, A-5. Washington, DC: Government Printing Office, 1980.

————. *Twenty-first Census of the United States (1990). Census of Population, General Population Characteristics,* vol. 1, A-8–A-9. Washington, DC: Government Printing Office, 1990.

Vance, James E., Jr. *Geography and Urban Evolution in the San Francisco Bay Area.* Berkeley, CA: Institute of Governmental Studies, 1964.

Weber, Adna Ferrin. *The Growth of Cities in the Nineteenth Century: A Study in Statistics.* New York: Macmillan Company for Columbia University Press, 1899.

WWWebster Dictionary, http://www.m-w.com/dictionary, 1997.

Encyclopedia of
Urban America
The Cities and Suburbs

Abrams, Charles (1902–1970)

Charles Abrams was a lawyer, public official, activist, author, and teacher who significantly influenced the course of public housing and urban studies in the United States as well as in developing countries of Africa, Asia, and South America. Emigrating from Poland in 1904, Abrams received his LL.B. from Brooklyn Law School in 1922. In 1933 he coauthored the New York Municipal Housing Authorities Law, which became the model for subsequent federal and state housing legislation. As counsel for the New York City Housing Authority (NYCHA) from 1934 to 1937, Abrams successfully argued *NYCHA v. Muller,* establishing the legality of using eminent domain proceedings to clear slums and build public housing.

In 1955 Abrams became New York State Rent Administrator, and from 1956 to 1959 he chaired the New York State Commission against Discrimination. As chairman, he successfully drafted legislation to include housing financed by the Federal Housing Administration (FHA) and the Veterans Administration (VA) under the New York State Law against Discrimination. From 1961 to 1965, Abrams was president of the National Committee against Discrimination in Housing, an organization that led the fight for an executive order barring discrimination in federally subsidized housing.

A participant in more than 20 overseas missions, Abrams helped establish housing authorities and planning schools throughout the world. He held teaching positions at the New School for Social Research, the University of Pennsylvania, Massachusetts Institute of Technology, and Columbia University. Throughout his career, Abrams passionately supported public housing and homeownership for the poor, and he criticized discrimination and what he called the "business welfare state." In addition to writing or delivering countless speeches, articles, and reports, Abrams wrote seven books, including *Revolution in Land* (1939); *The Future of Housing* (1946); *Forbidden Neighbors* (1955); and *The City Is the Frontier* (1965). Often written for a general audience, Abrams's works informed public debate on urban issues for almost four decades.

—*A. Scott Henderson*

References

Abrams, Charles. "Charles Abrams: A Biography," 7–12. Papers and Files. Ithaca, NY: Cornell University Press, 1975.

———. "Reminiscences." Oral History Interview (April 26, May 10, 1964). New York: Columbia University Oral History Collection.

Henderson, A. Scott. "Housing and the Democratic Ideal: The Life and Thought of Charles Abrams." Ph.D. dissertation, State University of New York, Buffalo, 1996.

Taper, Bernard. "A Lover of Cities." *The New Yorker* (February 4, 11, 1967).

Addams, Jane (1860–1935)

One of the most famous women in American history, settlement house leader Jane Addams was born to Sarah (Weber) Addams and John Huy Addams, businessman and state senator, in Cedarville, Illinois. When Jane was two years old, her mother died. Her stepmother, Anna Haldeman Addams, was a woman of wealth, culture, and social refinement. Jane spent her childhood in Cedarville, then graduated from Rockford Seminary (later Rockford College) in 1881. Her father died shortly thereafter, leaving her financially independent. For six months, she attended Philadelphia's Woman's Medical College, then dropped out. She also made two extensive tours of Europe, on the second visiting the first settlement house in the world, Toynbee Hall, in London. Returning home, a single woman in her late twenties, she was faced with the question of what to do with her life.

Her answer was to establish Hull House in Chicago in 1889. At the time, she thought she was establishing the first settlement in the United States, but it was, in fact, the third, the other two being in New York. A college friend, Ellen Gates Starr, joined her in this enterprise. The two women successfully appealed to other college-educated, well-to-do women in Chicago to volunteer to teach classes and lead clubs, as well as to donate money.

Addams was a pragmatist; if a project didn't accomplish its purpose, even if it was a good idea, she would drop it and move on to something else. An example was the restaurant featuring nutritious food that the settlement opened. Its purpose was to improve her immigrant neighbors' diet, but when they failed to patronize the restaurant she closed it. The settlement also featured lectures by prominent men like Frank Lloyd Wright and John Dewey, but her neighbors found more immediate benefit in English and citizenship classes. In addition, she made the settlement a social meeting ground for the neighborhood with large-group activities, such as receptions, a band, plays, concerts, and speeches along with smaller clubs and classes. As such, Addams may have intended to superimpose small-town social interaction on a low-income urban neighborhood.

Addams was also an effective reformer. A talented writer and speaker, she was a superb publicist for her causes. Her best-known work, *Twenty Years at Hull House* (1910), became a classic. She also published a sequel in 1930 plus other books and articles, including *Democracy and Social Ethics* (1902), *The Spirit of Youth and the City Streets* (1909) about juvenile delinquency, and *A New Conscience and an Ancient Evil* (1911) about prostitution. She participated actively in the labor movement, helping to mediate the Pullman Strike in 1894 plus other strikes, making Hull House available to women trying to unionize, and supporting the labor activities of Florence Kelley, a Hull House resident who was chief factory inspector for Illinois. Addams worked to improve her neighborhood in other ways, even serving as garbage inspector. She took a political approach by serving as a school board member and backing a reform candidate for alderman from her ward. When the infant National Association for the Advancement of Colored People listed her name as one of its founders in 1909, the organization gained instant national credibility. Although she failed to change the politics of her neighborhood, she was active as a suffragist and seconded Theodore Roosevelt's nomination by the Bull Moose Party for the presidency in 1912 because he favored votes for women.

In addition, Addams resisted militarism and struggled to promote peace. That activity diminished her almost saintly public image during World War I, but she later received the Nobel Peace Prize in 1931 for her leadership of the Women's International League for Peace and Freedom.

—*Judith Ann Trolander*

See also
Henry Street Settlement; Hull House; Kelley, Florence; Settlement House Movement; Wald, Lillian D.

References
Davis, Allen F. *American Heroine: The Life and Legend of Jane Addams.* New York: Oxford University Press, 1973.
Farrell, John C. *Beloved Lady: A History of Jane Addams' Ideas on Reform and Peace.* Baltimore: Johns Hopkins University Press, 1967.
Levine, Daniel. *Jane Addams and the Liberal Tradition.* Madison: State Historical Society of Wisconsin, 1971.

African-American Towns

Between 1865 and 1905, African-American entrepreneurs established several racially exclusive towns in Oklahoma, Kansas, and other nearby states. Nicodemus, Kansas (established in 1879), Mound Bayou, Mississippi (1897), Langston, Oklahoma (1891), and Boley, Oklahoma (1904), are among the best known, although many smaller (and often short-lived) all-black towns also developed in the South and West during these years. Informed by African-American community building in the South after the Civil War, these towns and communities also reflected the general optimism and local boosterism that swept across the United States at the end of the century.

Throughout the South during the 1860s, the possibility of acquiring land held resonant promise for a people emerging from bondage. The former slaves repeatedly insisted to both members of the Union Army and to administrators of the Freedman's Bureau that "we would rather live by ourselves than scattered among the whites" and that "the great cry of our people is to have land." But the amount of land available for sale on the open market never matched their hunger for land. In addition, all during Reconstruction, public and private opinion in the white South vigorously opposed land ownership by African Americans. As a result, their acquisition of land in the South and West, particularly after 1877, resulted more often from development projects planned, organized, and executed by black entrepreneurs than it did from private transactions between individuals.

The all-black communities established during the final decades of the nineteenth century initially prospered in the near West, where land was more readily available than it was in the former Confederacy, although some of these towns did grow in the South. Nicodemus, Kansas, Mound Bayou, Mississippi, Langston, Oklahoma, and Boley, Oklahoma, typify the developments planned by and for African Americans during this period. All four communities initially prospered, their growth stimulated by an influx of black migrants from Alabama, the Carolinas, Georgia, and Tennessee who were drawn west by the promise of cheap, affordable land, economic self-sufficiency, and personal security.

William Smith and Thomas Harris, two African-American ministers from Tennessee, and W. R. Hill, an African-American Kansas land speculator, established Nicodemus, Kansas. Once the trio had secured the land in 1877, they began recruiting settlers from the congregations of rural black churches in Tennessee and Mississippi. Those bound for Nicodemus—the community numbered approximately 700 people by 1897—were joined by other African Americans in a widespread movement from the South and into a number of Kansas locations after they were literally driven from parts of Louisiana and Mississippi.

These settlements provided the model on which subsequent towns were organized; they also provided a training ground for community leaders and builders such as Isaiah T. Montgomery, who later established Mound Bayou, Mississippi, and Edward P. McCabe, who subsequently founded Langston, Oklahoma, and inspired Boley, Oklahoma.

Montgomery, born a slave, initially joined the exodus to Kansas, but by 1885 he had returned to Mississippi. There, probably inspired by the example he had seen in Kansas, he struck a deal with the Louisville, New Orleans, and Texas Railroad to settle African-American farmers along its line in Bolivar County, Mississippi. Forty-seven families immediately settled in the area, and Mound Bayou emerged as the mercantile center of the county. The town was incorporated in 1898 with 183 residents. By 1904, its population exceeded 400, and an additional 2,500 farmers lived in the surrounding township.

In contrast to Montgomery, Edward P. McCabe was born in Troy, New York, and worked at a variety of jobs before he moved to Illinois in 1875. There, he entered Republican politics before finding his way to Kansas in 1878. McCabe was elected auditor of the state in 1882 and reelected in 1884. Insinuations of improper behavior drove him from public office, and in 1889 he joined the land rush into Indian Territory. By 1890, he was promoting the development of Langston (about 40 miles northeast of Oklahoma City) as a town for African Americans. His promotional advertisements attracted farmers from Arkansas, Texas, and other southern states to a site that McCabe probably intended to be a springboard for the development of a separate African-American state, with himself as its governor. Boley, in southeastern Oklahoma, had stronger ties to Mound Bayou than to the more western towns, and its growth and prosperity matched Langston's during the early years of the twentieth century, although neither town provided McCabe with the political power base he had originally envisioned.

Like Mound Bayou and the Kansas towns, those in Oklahoma initially prospered, but the local economies of all of these planned communities relied on cotton as a cash crop. By the second decade of the twentieth century, the ravages of the boll weevil combined with the chaos of local politics and the larger climate of racial discrimination to erode the early prosperity and community stability. Town leaders, once so optimistic, saw political institutions weakening. Local business failures compounded the problems caused by growing political powerlessness. Scarcity of capital, vastly unequal distributions of income, and an inability to provide residents with marketable, nonagricultural skills eventually doomed the once-promising developments. For these black towns, boosterism at the turn of the century proved to be an empty promise.

—*Elizabeth Rauh Bethel*

References

Bethel, Elizabeth Rauh. *Promiseland, A Century of Life in a Negro Community.* Columbia: University of South Carolina Press, 1997.

Crockett, Normal L. *The Black Towns.* Lawrence: Regents Press of Kansas, 1979.

Du Bois, W. E. B. *Black Reconstruction.* New York: Russell and Russell, 1935.

Magdol, Edward. *A Right to the Land.* Westport, CT: Greenwood Press, 1977.

Oubre, Claude. *Forty Acres and a Mule.* Baton Rouge: Louisiana State University Press, 1978.

Painter, Nell Irvin. *The Exodusters.* New York: Knopf, 1977.

African Americans in Cities

The African-American experience in American cities is as complex as the differences among the millions of people and the several centuries involved, among New York, New Orleans, Chicago, Richmond, and Los Angeles. But one ironic generalization may be applied to all of it: the major theme in black history has been the struggle for equal status, and a closely related strain has been that migration to the city, among what was originally an overwhelmingly rural people, traditionally promised hope and progress, for both individual and community. Hope was of course never fully realized, and progress often denied by the actual conditions of urban living. Black history may be divided into many periods, each having both betterment and setbacks. But the crowning irony is the fact that just as the centuries-long hegira from country to city had reached a climax, at virtually the same moment as the drive for legal status and political power seemed within reach, the city itself began sliding into a decline that has overshadowed all the other gains made by African Americans.

The record of black origins in colonial North America is murky, but it is clear that within no more than a generation of the famous shipment of Africans to Jamestown in 1619, African Americans were being brought to Boston, and then to Dutch Manhattan, as personal or household slaves. And from the beginning, the lives of urban blacks, in both the North and the South, differed from the existence of those left locked in the countryside.

For people without land, agricultural labor has always been brutal, especially so for Africans and their descendants in America. For objects of racial prejudice and, as the seventeenth century progressed, subjects of a kind of slavery uniquely harsh in its hereditary nature and depersonalization, life in town or city offered at least the hope of freedom, however limited in practice, added to the universal attractions of variety. Black men and women in towns often worked at crafts requiring skills, giving them value and economic leverage; household servants, too, whether objects of sexual exploitation or paternal affection, had their own kinds of leverage. And the large number who worked as sailors or longshoremen in early port towns enjoyed at least movement, opportunity, and exposure to a wider world.

Some of these Africans had been freed as a gift; in southern settlements, the great majority of freedmen and freedwomen were the lighter-skinned children of slaveowners. Others managed to buy their freedom, or simply to seize it by escaping. The town, and later city, offered refuge as attractive to escaped slaves in the Americas as to escaped serfs in medieval Europe. But whether slave or free, the growing numbers of African Americans in cities faced white inhabitants with problems familiar ever since: job competition, fear, and racism.

White artisans early complained about skilled slaves who threatened to undercut their own wages as blacksmiths, leather workers, teamsters, or sailors. Their resentments surely contributed to a special black reputation for the kind of petty crime always common among the urban poor. Fierce racism, too, from the beginning, centered around black male sexuality, and in a few northern and most southern colonies punishments for violating white women called for castration or, in a few cases, death by fire. Deep fears were revealed in 1712 when slaves in New York were convicted of murdering nine whites. By 1741, when the slave population approached one-fifth of the total, an alleged "Negro Conspiracy" to burn down the city caused hundreds to flee, while nearly 100 blacks were transported, hanged, or burned at the stake.

Such fears gave rise to slave codes, similar in virtually all of the colonies except those in New England, which were modeled on Mosaic law. These typically prohibited slaves from testifying in court against whites, buying liquor, or bearing arms; laws forbidding assembly in number were clearly aimed at city dwellers. As the freed class grew through the late seventeenth and early eighteenth centuries—and from very early on freed African Americans overwhelmingly lived in cities—other laws were passed to distinguish them from whites. Again, these differed by region, even by colony, but African Americans everywhere but New England were denied the vote, and in most places were forbidden to marry whites or to serve in the militia, thus preventing them from owning guns.

But this uneven color line, rarely fully drawn in law or completely enforced in practice, was gradually offset in the later eighteenth century in the North by amelioration and emancipation, as some white colonials began to justify their grievances against Great Britain by appealing to principles of human rights that were obviously incompatible with human slavery. Until then, humane treatment had been inspired almost wholly by religion, in Boston by the felt need to include Africans as at least secondary members of the Christian community and in Philadelphia by a quiet Quaker campaign against slavery itself. When these religious convictions were joined by secular principles, the trickle of emancipations became a stream. With the start of the American Revolutionary War, both sides promised freedom to slaves who joined them if they were victorious, and many blacks served among the patriots with distinction. The stream became a river of freedom in the urban North. In Philadelphia, for example, there had been 1,400 slaves and 100 free blacks in 1765; by 1783, just 400 were enslaved, over 1,000 free.

The first famous African Americans date from these years: Phyllis Wheatley, the poet; Crispus Attucks, first to die in the Boston Massacre; Benjamin Banneker, the mathematician and astronomer. During the Revolutionary Era, too, the first enduring community organizations were founded: Prince Hall organized the African-American branch of the Masonic Lodge in Cambridge, Massachusetts, in 1775 and Absalom Jones established the Free African Society in Philadelphia in 1787. Both groups emphasized mutual aid, religious uplift, and racial betterment, and they inspired others across the North.

Masons and Free Africans also joined white groups in the first political attacks on slavery. As courts and legislatures pushed the new northern states to end slavery, and as the logic of the Revolution joined economic depression to inspire thousands of manumissions even in the plantation South, it appeared that African Americans, led by their own urban elite, were on the way to full citizenship in the new nation.

But between the American Revolution and the Civil War, the high hopes of the 1780s eroded. To the extent that black men and women controlled their own destinies, they were able to strengthen their community institutions. But at the same time, white working-class resentments were fueled by the very success and growth in the number of urban blacks. Beyond that, blacks were affected by economic and political developments far beyond their control—the revival of plantation slavery based on cotton, the economic cycle, European immigration, and finally the tensions threatening the new national union.

During the 1790s, the fraternal and mutual aid societies were joined by the third of the great triad of formal African-American institutions, the church. A group of Philadelphians, rebelling against segregated seating, established their own church, soon known as the African Methodist Episcopal (AME) denomination. From then on, as soon as their numbers allowed, free people throughout the urban North founded their own churches; whatever their denominational affiliation, these most assimilated of American blacks typically included the word "African" in their titles. And for the next century and more, these churches were nurseries of leadership for both men and women. Schools, especially in the South, were run by churches or lodges if they existed at all, while the buildings themselves provided meeting places for a whole range of community associations, from literary clubs to fraternities, that marked the life of urban African America.

One focus of these institutions was always the abolition of slavery. For several decades, the stream of manumissions kept flowing. But most northern states provided for only gradual emancipation over time, the federal constitution sanctioned slavery, and in 1793 Congress passed a Fugitive Slave Act. Great slave revolts in Santo Domingo, followed by the revolutionary conspiracies of two artisans, Gabriel Prosser near Richmond in 1800 and Denmark Vesey in Charleston in 1822, inspired fearful southern states to make manumission almost impossible and to restrict those already freed. Simple racism in the North was aggravated by black émigrés from the Caribbean, and as southern plantation slavery was firmly reestablished by the new economic importance of cotton, black petitioners and their allies were forced on the defensive.

But even in the South, white fears were often relaxed. New Orleans brought more complex racial traditions with it when Louisiana joined the union, and the business of community building was unstoppable. Although in Richmond or Charleston, the "free" half of the black population was not far from slavery, the slave half was not far from free in the indiscriminate bustle of the city. Despite the poverty of most victims of racist exclusion, wider opportunities in the North allowed men like the sea captain Paul Cuffe, sail maker James Forten, and a host of other artisans and businessmen to gain some economic success. Their families established an enduring class structure based partly on shades of color, respectable reputation, as well as wealth, and a social system based on unusual economic and social opportunities for women. But even at the top, few were safe from fears of kidnapping and reenslavement, and none could escape the discrimination that hedged them in almost everywhere.

The great paradox was always that, especially before great segregated "ghettos" were formed, white urban workingmen were both their closest associates and their bitterest enemies, as the two groups rarely lived far apart. To the extent that blacks and whites intermarried legally, drank, watched dogfights and cockfights, played, and worked together, they typically did so near the waterfronts, brickyards, and neighborhoods where poor people lived. At the same time, economic competition and status anxieties afflicted the working class more than richer whites. One result of increasing democracy for white males, then, in the antebellum decades, was the passage of more racist legislation. Some northern states adopted "black codes" much like the South's, allowing a kind of semislavery—denying the vote, forbidding in-migration, and requiring passes and official registration. In most of the Northeast outside of New England, the vote, granted in the Revolutionary Era, was revoked, and black youngsters were either segregated or completely excluded from the new public schools.

Black men and women continued to fight back. One timeless method was to help fugitive slaves find refuge. Another, beginning in 1830, was to bring together leaders, mostly from northern cities, in annual conventions that protested slavery and discrimination and, then as later, urged the majority to embrace moral and economic self-improvement in an effort to combat racial stereotypes. A third was to join a newly militant abolition movement within which they debated a variety of strategies, criticized the racism of white allies within the abolition movement, and largely rejected plans, first broached in the Revolutionary Era, to flee slavery and racism by returning to Africa.

But whatever their efforts, social, economic, and political developments combined to push down blacks in northern cities. Irish immigration brought unskilled, hungry, often violent peasant competitors into an economy not yet ready to absorb them. During the painful beginnings of the new urban industrial economy, workingmen seized on race and ethnicity as principles of association and helped shrink the number of skilled jobs available. In custom, even more than in law, segregation in public places came to rule. And as whites of all classes came to dread the approach of a war over the proper place of African Americans in the fragile national union, it was easy to make scapegoats of African Americans themselves. Riots became increasingly familiar features of antebellum cities, and no group was more frequently targeted than blacks.

Pogroms may be a better term than *race riots* to describe these affrays in which white gangs invaded black neighborhoods on a variety of pretexts to beat, burn out, or kill their politically helpless inhabitants. After the spurt in the 1790s, the growth of free black communities slowed, while the pace of European immigration pushed down their proportion of the urban population as a whole. The official census has always been a poor measure—African Americans had no reason to trust white inquisitors and many reasons to hide—but it does appear that in Philadelphia, for example, the largest black community in the North, there may actually have been a net loss of black population during the violent 1840s. In short, however better off than their cousins on the plantation, the black residents of American cities, battered and insecure, were losing ground in the era before the Civil War.

Between the onset of the Civil War and the end of World War I, the lives of the growing number of African Americans living in cities developed partly along lines already drawn. Mutual benefit societies, masonic lodges, and above all churches nurtured other associations and helped define class differences within black communities. White racism and working-class resentments still plagued efforts to win skilled jobs, and crime and vice continued to beset black neighborhoods. Differences between the North and the South—as well as between the small urban population and the great southern agricultural majority—remained. But dramatic economic and political changes ensured that the black urban history of these years had a shape of its own.

Great political change occurred as the Civil War transformed the lives of the urban minority as well as the newly freed millions of the South. Once the war became a crusade to end slavery, with black troops recruited to help, wholly new leadership opportunities opened for those with education and sophistication. In the North itself, such opportunities were delayed for some years. The riots of the antebellum decades actually peaked in the middle of the war in the New York Draft Riot of 1863, in which largely Irish protesters lynched, beat, and burned out the city's black population. This outburst had lesser echoes in smaller cities. No northern state, either, voluntarily granted blacks the right to vote. But in the hopeful early years of Reconstruction, as the freedmen looked to new institutions to help them cope with their new condition, the vote was granted by congressional fiat.

Although it was the potential power of the agricultural millions that drove Reconstruction, it was disproportionately the old free urban elite who spoke for them and who took new jobs as political officeholders with Reconstruction agencies or as civil servants. Northerners—fugitives rejoining family, soldiers who took root, or simply men and women eager to join the new order—often participated directly, and the suspect census returns for 1870 register a net outflow from Philadelphia, the city with the largest black population north of the old slave states. The community infrastructure, built upon independent church, lodge, and benefit association, that was long familiar in northern cities quickly blossomed once southern blacks were allowed to meet with no whites present. The AME denomination, for example, had reached no more than 20,000 members before the war; but during the next two decades missionaries sent south from its Philadelphia headquarters pushed this up twentyfold, to about 400,000 by 1880. The message was secular as well as spiritual; the messengers, like those of other denominations, helped establish schools and organize political parties as well as churches.

True equality was never fully won in any southern city, certainly in no state, and the urban political agenda, modest by northern standards but fiercely contested in places such as Richmond or Charleston, was no more than gaining segregated access to such services as the new schools, hospitals, and streetcar systems that opened after the war. The successful white assault on Reconstruction, signaled dramatically in the bloody New Orleans "race riot" of 1866, never fully turned back the clock in this respect. But while the black population of southern cities continued to grow, the number of voters began to shrink in the late 1870s. Jobs as clerks, policemen, and firemen were lost, and as segregation tightened there was no pretense that separate was truly equal. As northerners returned home, and the more outspoken southerners fled or were driven out (as in the Wilmington, North Carolina, pogrom of 1899), the political life of blacks in the urban South turned moribund.

Developments in northern cities were dramatically different, as passage of the Fifteenth Amendment to the Constitution in 1870 guaranteed the vote, and the vote provided leverage, however small the number of people who voted. Black men and women had begun to protest discrimination during the war, in Philadelphia using nonviolent direct action to desegregate horsecars, in Chicago successfully petitioning for repeal of the state's "black codes." A combination of public protests, political agitation, and individual lawsuits under the federal Civil Rights Law of 1875 helped open places of public accommodation; and, when the Supreme Court ruled the law unconstitutional in 1883, state legislatures passed their own, if weaker, versions. By the mid-1880s, virtually all northern and western cities had outlawed legal discrimination. Although some schools remained segregated, public education was available everywhere.

Education was the great success story of the era. Partially inspired by the promise of full citizenship, the black population of Philadelphia, with an estimated literacy rate of 20 percent in the 1850s, pushed that figure over 90 percent by the 1890s. Black men and women regularly scored higher than European immigrants on written examinations of all kinds, and the first African-American political demand in that city was to put all positions under the new civil service system and make all appointments dependent on test scores. The political issue of the era was less civil rights than civil service: black voters, sometimes city councilors, in a few places legislators, pushed for jobs as policemen, clerks, and schoolteachers. Under Republican rule, Washington, D.C., was a Mecca for many: it was the source of patronage jobs in the Post Office, Frederick Douglass served as city marshal, and members of the black elite received diplomatic posts in Haiti or Liberia.

A new urban professional and white-collar class arose. Missionary colleges had mushroomed across the South during Reconstruction, and in the North the number of doctors educated at major universities soared. Full legal citizenship allowed African Americans to practice law for the first time, many educated at Washington's new Howard University Law School. Literacy and ambition multiplied weekly newspapers; Philadelphia alone produced 23 between 1870 and 1900. The AME's long-running *Christian Recorder* and others papers served, like denominational and lodge membership themselves, to unite urban leadership across the nation with "letters from" other cities filled with news of jobs, politics, and social events.

In this expansive era, city wages seemed high, and against the oppressive background of southern agriculture, the vitality of city life was continually on display in the form of soaring new Gothic church spires, parading bands, fancy balls, organized sports, and all-black theatrical troupes. In contrast to the antebellum era, black urban growth outpaced the white. But except in the declining port cities of the old South, and along the borders, as in Baltimore and Washington, the result of starting from a low base was that the percentages in expanding manufacturing centers remained low. Although rural black fertility was higher than the white average, urban fertility was far lower. Even in Philadelphia, with the largest community in the North, the 85,000 residents of 1910 were only 5.5 percent of the city's total. More important than raw numbers was the fact that outside the civil service, the new white-collar armies of typists, salesclerks, and phone operators demanded by the new high-rise urban economy excluded African Americans almost entirely. Except during the brief heyday of the Knights of Labor in the 1880s, unions were at best segregated, and black artisans were driven out; all over the country, the number and variety of skilled jobs held by black men and women declined dramatically. It was even easier to wall off the new manufacturing sector; with limited exceptions, as in the new Birmingham steel mills and Henry Ford's Detroit, factory jobs were reserved for whites only, except for temporary black strikebreakers.

The fact that black men and women were largely confined to domestic and unskilled jobs undermined the new urban professional class except for teachers and civil servants. Whites would not go to black doctors, and blacks could not afford them; not a single black attorney in Philadelphia, during this era, was able to earn a living by practicing law alone. Just as the desperate turned to theft, the ambitious turned to such criminal enterprises as gambling, prostitution, and operating speakeasies, although here, too, they typically answered to white overlords.

In his pathbreaking study *The Philadelphia Negro*, W. E. B. Du Bois showed that however victimized they were by discrimination, the great majority of urban blacks were not merely churchgoers but members of major denominations, and most children were born to two-parent families. Proportionally more blacks than whites, too, held jobs in the money economy, in part because most married women worked. African Americans were also noted for the strength of their self-help associations, and they had less trouble than whites with alcohol, then the prevailing drug. Rates of violent crime, while not low, were lower than those of the immigrant Irish in the mid-nineteenth century, far lower than those of Italians in the early twentieth. But while residential patterns remained somewhat mixed, the growing size of black neighborhoods made it easy for politicians to "zone" them

as vice centers, trapping both the elite and the working class in an atmosphere that bred trouble.

It was in this era of retreat from earlier hopes and increasing segregation that the National Association for the Advancement of Colored People (NAACP) was born in 1909. The demand for full civil rights was in many respects the revolt of a frustrated urban minority against those who spoke for the rural southern majority. The shift to urban leadership received an economic and demographic boost during the next decade. Manufacturers, following Henry Ford, were already beginning to experiment with black workers when the outbreak of World War I multiplied the demand for labor. With hopeful trainloads daily leaving the Deep South in a "Great Migration" northward into Detroit, Chicago, Cleveland, Philadelphia, and New York, it was clearer than ever that the city was the future. And America's 1917 entry into a war "to make the world safe for democracy" seemed to promise a new day.

At least one promise of the World War I Era was fulfilled: although the majority still lived in the South, it was those in the city, and especially the North, who drew the most attention and made the most news. During and just after the war itself, that news was often bad. Army and navy were segregated, and so was the nation's capital, under Democratic administration for the first time in decades. Urban race riots returned in force as whites resented black newcomers who shared shop or yard, moved into previously restricted areas, and strained public facilities. The difference this time was that blacks fought back, however defensively. East St. Louis was the first, in 1917; demobilization in 1919 was marked by scores of others, as African Americans were largely driven from their new factory jobs. The Chicago Riots of that year, which killed 23 blacks and 15 whites, were especially notable for inspiring a massive official report that described in detail for the first time the life of what would come to be known as the "ghetto."

One of the clearest results of the "Great Migration" in shifting the black center of urban gravity north and west of the older border cities was to create new spatial patterns. Population was now highly concentrated, segregated by real estate arrangements, custom, and fear. The political and economic results, long in the making, were by then clear. The biggest northern ghettos, Chicago's and then New York's, elected not only local officials but also the first black congressmen since Reconstruction and helped assure at least some civil service jobs as garbage collectors, clerks, policemen, and teachers. The earlier business enterprises—those run by skilled artisans or originating in domestic service such as caterers—continued to decline as fearful white patrons would not enter black neighborhoods or allow blacks into their homes. This loss was partially offset by businesses that depended on segregation for their success—barber and beauty shops, undertakers, and real estate and insurance agencies. And while these generated few jobs, and drew no outside money into the community, they could be lucrative, and a few entrepreneurs had money to show and spend.

Popular enthusiasm for jazz in the 1920s gave the era its name, and the nightlife of Harlem and the South Side of Chicago became a cachet among visiting whites. But the underside of the stories of Bessie Smith and Louis Armstrong was that the entertainment business, as it had been earlier in New Orleans and Memphis, was tied to gambling, prostitution, and illegal liquor sales; madams and numbers sellers, servants of white bosses, and allies of politicians elbowed legitimate businessmen and professionals unable to escape their neighborhoods. Still, the success not only of the popular culture, but also of the high culture that grew out of it—as in the famous Harlem Renaissance of Langston Hughes and Zora Neale Hurston—had another effect: respect for African-American achievement helped urban liberals, many of them Jewish, place black issues back on the national reform agenda for the first time since Reconstruction. And as the 1920s ended in the Great Depression, these allies were badly needed.

The precarious urban population was especially hard hit by the Great Depression. Chicago's blacks were two to five times more likely to lose their jobs than whites; more than half of the African Americans in Philadelphia were unemployed in 1933, and only 1 percent of the young men held factory jobs. New Deal agricultural policy compounded urban problems by helping to shove southern tenants and sharecroppers off the land; while the pace slowed some, hundreds of thousands of desperate men and women still flocked into cities to compete for scarce jobs.

But the outlook was not completely hopeless. Without directly attacking segregation, the New Deal generally provided equal pay and benefits in a variety of jobs and programs that helped the urban poor get through hard times, and black urban voters responded with a historic shift to the reigning Democratic Party. The successor to Du Bois's classic study of Philadelphia, St. Clair Drake and Horace Clayton's angry *Black Metropolis,* the climax of a generation of Chicago sociology, describes a Depression Era city full of poverty, crime, and frustration but also with a rich associational life, good times, and vitality. And as another European war broke out, with another labor shortage and another burst of official idealism about democracy and equality, the end of the 1930s promised another round of hope.

Major wars had always helped urban African Americans. So, decidedly, did World War II and its aftermath, a time when the long trek out of agriculture accelerated. By the early 1940s, more than half the black population was living in cities, and by 1960, proportionally more blacks than whites. The dominance not only of the city but of the North was confirmed in

these years. Migrants going north were typically young, married, childless, and ambitious. Contrary to conventional wisdom, they were statistically better educated than urbanities already in place, white as well as black. And as earlier, while southern metropolitan areas usually attracted men and women from nearby rural areas, they often moved again, to New York, Chicago, or Los Angeles after they had learned new skills.

The dual goals were more freedom and better jobs. During the war itself, the need for labor opened office and factory jobs to blacks, often for the first time. This time, victory in war did not slam the doors shut again; the gains were held, the foothold expanded, until the same 1960 census that registered the decisive shift to city living noted that proportionally more blacks than whites were also working in factories.

Nothing came easy. Southern and working-class whites, especially in the early years, still resented the advances of black Americans, and in 1943 Detroit witnessed a virtual replay of the Chicago Riot of 1919. But the Congress of Industrial Organizations (CIO), born in the Depression, far larger and more aggressive than previous umbrella unions, recruited African Americans, who then quit their traditional role as industrial strikebreakers. And with the opposition of organized labor added to the sheer size of urban ghettos, the Detroit riot was the last in which white gangs raided or fought border wars with their black counterparts.

Politically, civil rights never left the national agenda during this period, as the Republican Party still honored its older traditions and the Democrats were increasingly liberal. Only southern congressional power blocked new legislation. Still, President Harry S. Truman was able to desegregate the military by executive order in 1948. And as the NAACP, based largely in the urban North, peaked in size and influence, Thurgood Marshall and other lawyers won a series of court battles culminating in the great 1954 Supreme Court decision that demanded that Topeka, Kansas, desegregate its schools. Although the white South resisted and fought back bitterly, and actual progress was slow, black women and men took direct action, as when Martin Luther King, Jr., led the Montgomery, Alabama, bus boycott of 1957.

Virtually every economic index pointed up during these years. The number of skilled artisans doubled, from just 3 percent to 6 percent of the African-American workforce; white-collar office workers moved up even faster, from 6 percent to 13 percent. Domestic work plummeted as factory work soared, while at the other end of the scale doctors and especially lawyers (who had lost ground steadily since 1910) staged a strong comeback, increasingly led by women professionals. The most important falling indices were unemployment, which for the black population reached an all-time low of 4.5 percent during the Korean War, and homicide.

The black homicide rate, the most reliable criminal index, had not only been climbing steadily since the late nineteenth century but diverging even more sharply from the overall rate. The urban Industrial Revolution, with its promise of good wages for steady work and its demand for orderly, rational behavior, had been driving down disorderly behavior and individual violence in most of the developed world. Among American whites, these indices had been declining since the Civil War. Although some immigrant groups had high rates for a short time after they arrived, these often fell with dramatic speed once their young men had been absorbed into the workforce. Urban African Americans, long denied factory and office jobs and segregated into criminal neighborhoods, did not experience the same effect until after 1940, but by 1960 the black death rate from homicide, at 23 per 100,000 annually, was dropping faster than the white.

Segregation still ruled in most places, and no black person could escape bitter experiences with white racism. But legal segregation was clearly doomed, certainly in cities with growing numbers of black voters. Every year broke new ground, as Jackie Robinson led a parade of pioneers into professional sports, Billy Eckstine and Nat "King" Cole crossed a hidden line by joining Ella Fitzgerald and Lena Horne in singing love songs to white teenagers over the radio, B. O. Davis, Jr., earned his stars as an Air Force general, and Gwendolyn Brooks won a Pulitzer Prize and Ralph Bunche a Nobel Peace Prize. With the urban industrial revolution at its peak, the 1940s and 1950s were the "good old days" of city living. The schools and trolleys worked, the streets were safe (at least in retrospect), and an expanding America dominated the world economy. But peak suggests a downturn, and in terms of the prospects of urban black America, there was another side to the era.

Although the movement toward civil rights never slowed, the underlying demographic and economic progress of these two crucial decades slowed measurably during the 1950s. The very growth of the black urban population, the basis of so much hope, helped spur a white exodus to nearby suburbs. After reaching their peak size in the census of 1950, the older American cities of the North and Midwest began to bleed population. And if this seemed the golden age of the city, in terms of sheer explosive growth it was actually the golden age of the suburbs, as federal and local governments both promoted new forms of residential segregation by race and income.

The effect of federal housing policy, begun under the New Deal with no direct reference to race, was twofold. One expanding set of programs underwrote the home mortgages that financed suburban development. But mortgage policy was set by private bankers who made these developments racially exclusive by denying loans to blacks. Other programs provided for "slum clearance" and then "public housing" in older cities. But low-cost housing never matched the loss to "clearing," and the result of building "projects" only in marginal urban areas, without protection against discrimination, was to create bleak new all-black enclaves.

The result of these policies was to encourage the racial division of major metropolitan areas, with a bedroom ring of white suburbs surrounding increasingly black central cities. And for young African Americans inside the rings, there were signs of serious disaffection. One was the growth of the separatist Nation of Islam, an almost exclusively northern urban phenomenon, headquartered in Chicago. The other, defying all the hopeful economic and social indicators, was a tripling of the birthrate among unwed teenagers. Both suggested trouble ahead.

One convenient date to begin the modern era of urban black history is August 28, 1963, when Martin Luther King, Jr., told the March on Washington and the entire nation that "I Have a Dream." For African Americans in general, the decades since have brought many successes in the form of political power, economic gain, and international recognition. But the dream of racial harmony has not advanced much. And for the first time, the nation's cities have represented not progress but trouble and even despair.

A Civil Rights Bill, the immediate object of the March, won quick support. But the federal government then launched two campaigns that Americans never fully accepted. First, the war in Vietnam, although fought with record numbers of black combat troops, was the only major international war that promised nothing for the race as a whole. Bitterly denounced by political and spiritual leaders, its escalating cost also helped gut appropriations for the War on Poverty, which had been launched by the Economic Opportunity Act of August 1964, just days after Congress authorized fighting in Vietnam.

The many programs of the expanding War on Poverty, while colorblind in both intent and action, were soon identified with the urban black poor. Success stories such as Medicare were often overshadowed by well-publicized scandals involving welfare and the actions of low-level administrators. By decade's end, the military was spending $100 billion a year in Vietnam alone, while a tripling of antipoverty programs reached $30 billion. But only a small fraction of this (including social security) ever reached the ghetto. And while the proportion of African Americans living in poverty declined from 55 percent to 39 percent during the decade, and government programs helped propel many into the middle class, life for those left behind was better measured by climbing rates of unemployment, murder, and children born out of wedlock.

Even while civil rights faded from the national agenda, partly because of its successes, the issue of race grew ever more important. Life in the urban South was improved by a new surge of political power, a product of the Voting Rights Act of 1965, and in time Atlanta and Birmingham joined Newark and Detroit in electing black mayors. But the historic shift to the Democratic Party a generation earlier was balanced and then overridden as first white southerners and then blue-collar northerners defected to the Republicans, who reasserted their control of national elections beginning in 1968. Stereotypes about sexual and working habits contributed to this realignment. So, most dramatically, did the latest redefinition of the term *race riot.*

Whatever progress had been made by the mid-1960s, it had not closed the gap between white suburbanites and blacks in inner cities; and it was certainly not enough to satisfy angry young men in the ghettos. As the movement for justice and equality moved from South to North, from small towns and cities to great ones, it grew strident and more violent. The call for "black power" was never well defined, but the sight of young men on street corners shaking their fists and chanting in unison was calculated to terrify the majority. And nothing made more spectacular television news than the roughly 100 "race riots" that swept cities of every size and region between 1964 and 1968. In practice, both riots and casualties were confined almost entirely to black communities, and whites were rarely involved except for the police, whose much resented activities often sparked the outbursts. Dozens died in the Watts area of Los Angeles in 1965, while the National Guard shot up parts of Newark in 1967, and U.S. Army paratroopers were required to pacify Detroit in 1967 after 43 killings, mostly by local officers. Scholarly contributors to the Kerner Commission, shortly after the fact, noted that the riots were rooted in long-term frustration and that the rioters were typically young men of long residence who had jobs and educations slightly better than average. But television viewers saw only cities looted and burning, sometimes for days on end. By 1968, both the assassination of King and the riotous reaction to it symbolized a revolution in attitudes in just five years.

Beneath this turmoil, and at first unnoticed because of it, was an economic shift that had enormous consequences for all Americans, but especially for poor blacks in cities. Beginning at mid-century, older cities had begun to bleed not only white people but also manufacturing jobs. And if the legacy of the politics and policies of the 1960s is still in dispute, the result of the accelerating shift from a manufacturing to a service economy is not. African-American employment in the urban industrial sector, late in coming, arrived just as that sector was decaying. And as urban voting power continually increased, as whites tossed the keys to the city back over their shoulders as they left, winning more jobs in municipal government was undercut by the fact that municipal government was unable to stem the economic decline.

Since the early 1970s, the fate of African Americans as a group has polarized along class lines. The history is familiar. A variety of programs such as affirmative action, combined with their own innate abilities, has helped millions move into the middle class, and beyond that for a few stars into national and even international recognition. One ironic result of the civil rights movement is that members of the black middle and working classes may now move almost anywhere and have far less need for black community organizations—church and lodge, newspaper, and NAACP. Such people may live in, but are frequently not identified with, the city; in some cases they have effectively left the black community.

The few local businesses left in the ghetto have served not as centers of neighborhood life but as foci of jealous resentment when taken over by new Asian immigrants, widely praised as "the model minority." As educational requirements for even modest jobs have steadily risen, blacks left behind have sunk deeper into dependency and crime, aggravated by the "crack cocaine" epidemic of the 1980s. For casual television observers (the American majority), it is only the black "underclass" that remains in, and is identified with, the city.

The result is that the city has lost its historic meaning for African Americans. Its life is not celebrated, as by a Langston Hughes, but inspires only lyrics of despair. By the 1980s many, and in the 1990s more, were fleeing to suburbs or even returning to the rural and small-town South. The most popular book about black urban life published in the 1980s, Nicholas Lemann's *The Promised Land,* concluded that real salvation lies not in Chicago but back in the Mississippi Delta. The most influential scholarly study has been William Julius Wilson's *The Truly Disadvantaged: The Inner City, the Underclass, and Public Policy;* in contrast to the vitality shown by his predecessors, from Du Bois in the 1890s through Drake and Clayton in the 1940s, Wilson sketches a kind of anticity: a city not of movement but stagnation, not of variety but monotony, not a dream but a nightmare, of whole census tracts in which virtually no one has a legitimate job and married men are an endangered species.

In reality, neither the city nor the African-American communities that stretch from New York to Los Angeles are fairly represented by their most desperate neighborhoods. But it is no accident that in public discourse the adjective "urban" is often used as a synonym or a code word for "black" and too often modifies the noun "problems." As a result of economic transformation compounded by shortsighted public policies, American cities are in deep trouble. The ills of the African Americans who live in them, from family instability to the lack of modern job skills, represent in extreme form the ills of all Americans. There is no way to rescue the cities—civilization—without addressing these ills.

—*Roger Lane*

See also

African Americans in Suburbs; Desegregation of Education; Desegregation of Housing; Ghetto; Great Migration; Harlem; Housing Segregation; Public Housing; Race Riots; Slavery in Cities; South Side of Chicago.

References

Drake, St. Clair, and Horace Clayton. *Black Metropolis: A Study of Negro Life in a Northern City.* New York: Harcourt, Brace, 1945.

Du Bois, W. E. B. *The Philadelphia Negro: A Social Study.* Reprint ed. Millwood, NY: Kraus-Thompson, 1973.

Jaynes, Gerald David, and Robin M. Williams, Jr. *A Common Destiny: Blacks and American Society.* Washington, DC: National Academy Press, 1989.

Kerner, Otto, et al. *Report of the National Advisory Commission on Civil Disorders.* Washington, DC: Government Printing Office, 1968.

Lane, Roger. *Roots of Violence in Black Philadelphia, 1860–1900.* Cambridge, MA: Harvard University Press, 1986.

———. *William Dorsey's Philadelphia and Ours: On the Past and Future of the Black City in America.* New York: Oxford University Press, 1991.

Lewis, David Levering. *When Harlem Was in Vogue.* New York: Oxford University Press, 1979.

Meier, August, and Elliot Rudwick. *From Plantation to Ghetto.* 3d ed. New York: Hill and Wang, 1976.

Nash, Gary. *Forging Freedom: The Formation of Philadelphia's Black Community 1720–1840.* Cambridge, MA: Harvard University Press, 1980.

Wilson, William Julius. *The Truly Disadvantaged: The Inner City, the Underclass, and Public Policy.* Chicago: University of Chicago Press, 1987.

African Americans in Suburbs

Although the fact is often ignored in the traditional literature, African Americans have participated in the outward migration that has shaped American cities in the twentieth century. Harlan Paul Douglass's *The Suburban Trend,* published in 1925, offered a preliminary analysis. In a brief section entitled "Foreign and Negro Suburbs," he examined black settlements in the New York and Chicago metropolitan areas. "No Northern city," he wrote, "has massed so large a portion of the Negro population as some of the Northern suburbs." Within this framework he cited Evanston, Illinois, and East Orange, Englewood, and Montclair, New Jersey, as examples of black movement outward. Yet, Douglass sharply distinguished between white and black suburbanites. The latter, he concluded, were primarily domestics and service workers imported to serve the larger white community.

Nearly 30 years passed before others considered the issue of blacks in the suburbs. The majority of scholars who followed Douglass failed to test his thesis; rather, they debated the question of African-American suburbanization on a statistical battlefield. The studies of Donald Bogue, Avery Guest, William Pendleton, Leo Schnore, Harry Sharp, Reynolds Farley, and others defined the subject largely by the numerical presence of blacks outside the core. Their efforts were either statistical comparisons of aggregate census data or case studies noting demographic changes in particular metropolitan areas.

More recently, Harold Connolly, Philip Clay, Robert Lake, Harold Rose, Andrew Weise, Henry Louis Taylor, Jr., and others have broadened the definition of African-American suburbanization. Each has provided a more analytical view of African-American settlement, and Clay has identified six different types of black suburbs. Taken together, all their efforts have complemented the earlier numerical data by examining the nature of society and community.

As a result of this collective research, African-American suburbanization can be defined as the process of settlement by blacks in outlying sections of the city or in regions beyond the urban fringe. Similar to the movement of other ethnic groups, black outward migration has had a historical dimension. African Americans have entered suburbia by establishing or relocating in parts of cities far from urban core locations and, more recently, by spilling across city borders into integrated communities as well as racially separate enclaves.

It seems likely that African-American suburbanization extends well back into the colonial era. Certainly, pioneer suburbanites resided there during the Revolutionary Era. Slavery was responsible for the largest number of this group in the hinterland, but smaller numbers of blacks affected by urban prejudice also sought residence on the metropolitan rim.

Northern emancipation during the antebellum period represented the next step as freed slaves and freemen remained outside of central cities. Southwark and Northern Liberties abutting central Philadelphia, Lawnside in southern New Jersey, Skunk Hollow in northern New Jersey, Sandy Ground on Staten Island, Seneca Village in Manhattan's Central Park, and Brooklyn's Weeksville all illustrate this trend. Most of the African Americans who lived in these suburbs did not commute on a daily basis; however, some did frequent the city for leisure and social activities. In general, blacks, like their white counterparts, made their livelihoods by laboring and farming.

By the time of the Civil War, black suburbanization was occurring in the old West. Kinloch, outside of St. Louis, was the Midwest's best-known all-black enclave, but Chicago, Cincinnati, Cleveland, and Pittsburgh were among the cities that either had separate black enclaves or integrated settlements along their outer rings.

Southern suburbanization followed different paths, but it too became visible at the time of the Civil War and Reconstruction. All-black enclaves, influenced by the placement of Freedmen's Bureau outposts, existed outside of Richmond, Atlanta, Raleigh, Nashville, and Savannah before they were annexed in the late 1880s and 1890s. In smaller southern cities, a network of black towns resisted urban expansion and achieved complete independence. Mound Bayou, Mississippi

A middle-class African-American family in front of their suburban home in Georgia in the 1890s.

(outside of Jefferson's Bend), is one example of these permanent communities.

By the turn of the century, the movement of African Americans into suburbs was occurring in the Far West. It was especially visible in southern California where urbanization and suburbanization occurred simultaneously; in fact, they were hard to distinguish. Although there were few attempts at developing separate black suburbs, most African Americans intermingled among whites in the suburbs and satellite cities of Los Angeles.

Between 1900 and 1930, the North, Midwest, and Far West witnessed the first significant increase in the number of black suburbanites. Owning one's own house became a national symbol of racial independence and achievement. Pronouncements by black leaders, word of mouth, and colorful advertisements in African-American periodicals encouraged blacks to purchase property on both sides of the urban boundary. For a significant few, suburbia was an alternative to the fast pace of the city and an improvement over the rural South.

While ghettos began forming in major cities, a different process occurred on their rims. In contrast to the stereotype of affluent suburban living, African Americans experienced a myriad of living conditions. The range of their suburban dwellings reflected both their needs and also their options. Shacks, cottages, bungalows, chicken farms, small ranches, and a few mansions were all part of the picture, and most African Americans did not realize the suburban dream of open space and a beautiful home. Southern migrants and former city dwellers sought different goals—especially greater opportunities for better housing and employment. And while many settlements contained elite physicians, attorneys, and educators, their numbers were few. Laborers, laundresses, and skilled, semiskilled, and service workers made up the majority of suburbia's black residents.

Many of them could not afford property and opted to rent or board with others, and overcrowding was not uncommon. The more fortunate purchased small plots of land where they built homes after work using scrap materials. They used their yards to plant vegetables and raise animals rather than to grow flowers. The wealthier settlers bought either existing housing or new homes constructed by companies that could be either white or black. But far too often, while not forced to use their yards for survival, they needed the additional income to make ends meet.

Although living near or among whites, black residents were considered a shadow on the suburbs. Whenever they could, whites tried to ignore them despite knowing that African Americans were essential to the existing social order. However, whites refused to accept blacks as social equals and tried to limit their visibility. Prejudice and hostility led to the development of restrictive covenants, the formation of protective associations, and sporadic violence. The dominant society threatened new black residents, refused to hire minorities for municipal positions, and restricted restaurants, theaters, schools, roller rinks, amusement parks, beaches, pools, scouting troops, and YMCAs to whites. In many instances, physical barriers—sanitary canals, waterways, railroad tracks, walls, even highways—were used to separate black territories from areas inhabited by whites.

Dissatisfaction with these conditions led to a new wave of all-black communities. Unlike settlements formed in the antebellum North or the South during Reconstruction, these communities developed from failed white ventures as well as from cries for self-reliance. Robbins, Illinois, Lincoln Heights and Chargin Falls, Ohio, and Eight Mile-Wyoming, Michigan—all established between 1915 and 1930—demonstrated a different kind of "black" suburbia.

Throughout the first half of the twentieth century, black suburban growth, while masked by the tremendous white flight, did not go unnoticed. It was strongly contested, and many civic policies and court decisions sided with angry white residents. By 1930, with blacks already feeling the grip of the Great Depression, white resistance seemed victorious. The first wave of black outward movement had declined. Despite the presence of local branches of national organizations like the Urban League and the National Association for the Advancement of Colored People (NAACP), black suburbanites faced many of their challenges without substantial assistance as these organizations could not overcome the strong white hostility. Problems increased within communities as newcomers outnumbered the original settlers, and local leaders could not resolve the conflicts that occurred as part of the ongoing loss of community. Yet, this small "Great Migration" left its mark, and some 20 suburbs had black populations that exceeded 10 percent of the total.

Social and legal action renewed migration after World War II, and with it came greater numerical and percentage growth. In 1948 the Supreme Court declared restrictive covenants illegal in *Shelley v. Kraemer,* and it rejected damages in *Jackson v. Barrows* four years later. Meanwhile, the GI Bill of Rights enabled thousands of black veterans to purchase homes, and the Federal Housing Administration, long an ally of protective associations, outlawed its own racially motivated practices.

In 1970 the suburbanization of America peaked when the urbanized population outside of cities surpassed the rural and urban populations for the first time. Civil rights activism, the growth of a larger black middle class, and a supportive administration in Washington greatly contributed to black urban deconcentration. An important aspect of this shift was the fact that more blacks moved outward than ever before. Roughly one out of every five African Americans became suburbanites between 1960 and 1970. Virtually overnight, the national black suburban population doubled, and by 1980 nearly 20 percent of all blacks lived in suburbs.

As more African Americans tried to achieve the American dream of homeownership in the suburbs, only the poorest members of the black community failed to leave the inner city. Federal and state initiatives clearly assisted this outward movement. The 1975 *Mount Laurel* decisions by the New Jersey Supreme Court, for example, effectively opened suburbs to both minorities and the working classes by declaring that a clear exclusionary ordinance violated the state constitution and then, in 1983 announcing remedial measures to assist in the construction of low- and moderate-cost housing.

Finally, suburbia began to offer something other than low-paying, frequently menial service jobs to African Americans who sought more than token compensation and demanded a full role in suburban affairs. Black political empowerment, thwarted since the 1920s, began to flourish, and during the 1980s suburbia elected its first black councilmen, mayors, and congressmen.

However, despite the gains, suburbia is still not integrated. Few African Americans reside farther than 30 miles from a city. The majority of them live in older and often decaying inner suburbs that have experienced increased levels of white flight. Many once prominent communities are now over 30 percent black, and these face dwindling resources as their most established residents are white and aging, and the newcomers, usually minorities, are less prosperous than those who departed.

A woman and a man sit in their back yard with their dog in Cairo, Illinois, 1985.

Still, new trends reveal the uniqueness of the black suburban experience. Washington's Beltway has given rise to new and more affluent predominantly black communities. Prince George's County, Maryland, offers an example of more prosperous blacks disregarding race as the primary factor in suburban settlement. Its residents have demonstrated that black suburbs can thrive.

While Atlanta, New York, and Chicago have many suburbs with African-American residents, Los Angeles has the largest number of examples. Although some blacks do nestle in elite Beverly Hills and Palos Verdes, the majority live in much more modest locations. Baldwin Hills, a predominantly black bedroom suburb of professionals, has survived increasing crime and a devastating fire; it represents both the struggles and also the successes of an inner-city enclave. In contrast, Compton symbolizes the black suburban dream gone astray. Once a working-class bedroom suburb, it was transformed in the aftermath of the Watts riots of 1965. Predominantly white before then, it is currently more than 90 percent minority. With no major industry to enrich city coffers, Compton has grown increasingly poor. The city is trapped in a cycle as the perception persists that this is a community filled with poverty and crime, and businessmen are wary of investing there. It is no surprise that Compton ranks tenth among the nation's poorest suburbs.

Unfortunately, race remains a critical factor in homeownership and community development. Even as some African Americans become the socioeconomic equals of their white counterparts, they still encounter daily hostility and discrimination. However, suburbia still represents the American dream. It holds the promise of space and opportunity. One day, the realities of the suburban experience for African Americans may match those of whites.

—*Leslie Wilson*

See also

African-American Towns; African Americans in Cities; Great Migration.

References

Connolly, Harold. "Black Movements into the Suburbs: Suburbs Doubling Their Black Population during the 1960s." *Urban Affairs Quarterly* 9 (1973): 91–111.

DeGraaf, Lawrence B. "City of Black Angels: The Emergence of the Los Angeles Ghetto, 1890–1930." *Pacific Historical Review* 39 (1970): 323–352.

Douglass, Harlan Paul. *The Suburban Trend.* Reprint ed. New York: Arno Press, 1970.

Jackson, Kenneth. *Crabgrass Frontier: The Suburbanization of the United States.* New York: Oxford University Press, 1985.

Rose, Harold. *Black Suburbanization.* Cambridge, MA: Ballinger, 1976.

Sternlieb, George, and Robert Lake, "Aging Suburbs and Black Home-Ownership." *Annals of the American Academy of Political and Social Science* 422 (1975): 105–117.

Taylor, Henry L. "The Building of a Black Industrial Suburb: The Lincoln Heights, Ohio Story." Ph.D. dissertation, State University of New York, Buffalo, 1979.

Wiese, Andrew. *A Place of Our Own: The Chagrin Falls Park Story from 1921 to 1950.* Iowa City, IA: Self-published, 1986.

Wilson, Leslie. "Dark Spaces: An Account of Afro-American Suburbanization, 1890–1950." Ph.D. dissertation, City University of New York, 1992.

Agglomeration

Agglomeration refers to the colocation of economic activities, and its benefits are experienced as economies of scale external to the firms involved. There are two primary types of agglomeration economies, urbanization and localization. Urbanization economies refer to benefits resulting from the size of a metropolitan area and the diversity of its local industrial base. The larger a metropolitan area, presumably, the more diverse its economy and therefore the availability of larger markets for a firm's products and a greater variety of suppliers. If markets are larger, the costs of market transactions are reduced, and if the variety of suppliers is greater, the costs of acquiring inputs are decreased.

Localization economies are associated with dense concentrations of firms in the same industry. In this case, economic benefits result from the existence of specialized infrastructure and suppliers. When this happens, firms can specialize intensively with confidence that critical quantities of skilled labor and technical ability will be locally available. Once again, costs of obtaining information decline.

—*Amy Glasmeier*

References

Chinitz, Benjamin. "Contrasts in Agglomeration: New York and Pittsburgh." *American Economic Review* 51 (1961): 279–289.

Glasmeier, Amy. "Flexible Districts, Flexible Regions? The Institutional Limits to Districts in an Era of Globalization and Technological Paradigm Shifts." In Ash Amin and Nigel Thrift, eds., *Globalization, Institutions, and Regional Development in Europe,* 118–146. Oxford, England: Oxford University Press, 1994.

Hoover, Edgar. *The Location of Economic Activity.* New York: McGraw-Hill, 1948.

Malmberg, Anders. "Industrial Geography: Agglomeration and Local Milieu." *Progress in Human Geography* 20 (1996): 392–403.

Agricultural Revolution

Urban growth is closely connected to agricultural productivity. Nowhere has this been more the case than in the United States, whose most valuable natural resource is its vast expanse of fertile land.

In the seventeenth and eighteenth centuries U.S. agricultural productivity increased not because of changes in methods, mechanization, or the application of scientific techniques to farming, but because of increased inputs of fertile land and labor. The increasing reliance on the labor of slaves, who did not enjoy the legal or customary protections enjoyed by hired labor or indentured servants, was especially important in increasing productivity.

Foreign observers generally considered American agriculture lacking in both art and skill. While English farmers applied increasingly sophisticated irrigation, drainage, fertilization, and crop-rotation schemes, American farmers practiced long-fallow agriculture, clearing the land of vegetation and deserting it for a few years, and frequently abandoned degraded lands entirely. Their extensive farms reflected the relative cheapness of land and dearness of labor in America.

American farmers became more attentive to the potential benefits of innovation between the Revolutionary War and the Civil War. Mechanization played a crucial role in altering agriculture during this period. The cotton gin, invented by Eli Whitney in 1793, made cotton the most important southern crop and the preeminent American export. The mechanical reaper, developed in the 1830s by Cyrus McCormick, dramatically altered the small grain harvest, and by 1860, 70 percent of wheat was being cut by mechanical reapers. Improved plows, harrows, seed drills, and threshing machines further increased the productivity of farmers who grew wheat and other small grains.

Some farmers also became more attentive to improved crops, animal breeds, and agricultural methods during this period. Farmers in long-settled regions used systematic rotational plans and manure management to restore worn-out soils. The first American agricultural scientists, some trained in Germany, the world leader in the study of soil chemistry, also appeared in this period. Among the most prominent were Edmund Ruffin, an advocate of calcareous manure for acidic soils, and Yale soil chemist Samuel Johnson. Farmers shared agricultural information through farm newspapers, agricultural societies, and county fairs, all of which proliferated after 1815.

During the second half of the nineteenth century, the federal government developed and implemented a systematic plan to make agriculture more productive. In 1862 Congress passed the Morrill Land Grant College Act, which provided support for agricultural colleges in each of the states. The Morrill Act was based at least partially on the premise that agriculture was an enterprise demanding the sophistication and scientific knowledge that higher education could provide. Under the 1862 legislation and the Second Morrill Act of 1890, nearly 70 land-grant colleges were established by the states. Also in 1862, the U.S. Department of Agriculture (USDA), which had been a part of the Patent Office, achieved independence, but it lacked cabinet status and was headed by a commissioner. The department, which received cabinet status in 1889, quickly became the main repository of scientific expertise in agriculture in the United States. Building on efforts undertaken in a few states, Congress passed the Hatch Act in 1887. This legislation provided

$15,000 per year to states to create "experiment stations" that would conduct scientific research on agricultural problems.

None of these endeavors was desired, welcomed, or hardly even noticed by most farmers. Almost no farmers sent their children to land-grant colleges, and the scientific findings of the USDA and the experiment stations went unheeded by most farmers, who scoffed at the impracticality of "book farming." Farmers' apparent backwardness and resistance to change seemed to many urban observers in the early twentieth century to imperil the country. The population of the United States grew by 40 percent between 1900 and 1920, while agricultural productivity barely increased, with the result that food prices doubled. One reaction to the backwardness of farming was the Country Life Movement, which included among its goals improved rural education and the inculcation of better farming and business techniques. Another reaction was the Smith-Lever Act of 1914, which provided federal matching funds to states to create a network of county extension agents who would carry principles of agricultural science and sound farming practice directly into the countryside.

The first signs of the sweeping agricultural revolution that continues even today can be seen in the 1920s, when agricultural mechanization began in earnest. Between 1920 and 1930, the number of gasoline-powered tractors on American farms nearly quadrupled, from 246,000 to 920,000. While these early tractors could not perform all field operations for all farmers, they did allow those who possessed them to become much more efficient, and they were the main reason one person on a farm could feed 9.8 people in 1930, up dramatically from 8.3 a decade earlier.

Greater individual productivity means superfluous population. In the decade of the twenties, 6,250,000 people moved from farms to cities, helping to fuel the economic boom enjoyed by urban America. The 1920s also witnessed the first great triumph of modern plant breeding, with the introduction of hybrid corn, which returned yields that were 20 percent or more higher than open-pollinated varieties.

While rural out-migration slowed in the thirties, the trend toward greater agricultural productivity, especially through mechanization, continued. By lavishing benefits on the largest and most productive producers of commodities, New Deal agricultural programs rewarded and encouraged further mechanization. The effects of these programs were especially evident in the cotton-growing South, where the tractors landlords purchased with government crop loans combined with acreage-reduction subsidy payments put sharecroppers off the land.

The most dramatic phase of the agricultural revolution took place during World War II and the years immediately following. The mechanization of agriculture continued and accelerated. The number of tractors on American farms increased from 1.45 million in 1940 to 2.35 million five years later as the demand for food increased dramatically. Practical self-propelled combine harvester-threshers for small grains, along with corn and cotton pickers, were either introduced or significantly improved. Rural electrification, initiated with the creation of the Rural Electrification Administration by the federal government in 1935, revolutionized dairy farming and accelerated the mechanization of other enterprises as well. Improved crop and animal breeds further enhanced productivity in virtually every kind of agriculture.

The most dramatic element that contributed to increased productivity during and after World War II was a new generation of chemicals. DDT, developed in the 1890s and rediscovered on the eve of World War II by Swiss chemists, controlled a wide range of pests far better than any previous insecticides. In 1945, 2,4-D, a broad-leafed weed herbicide developed by scientists at the University of Chicago, became available to farmers. Also introduced at the end of the war was anhydrous ammonia, a gas that liquefies when it comes in contact with the air; it provided an easy and effective means of nitrogen fertilization. While these chemicals transformed the production of cultivars, animal raising was altered dramatically by the introduction of antibiotics and growth hormones.

No branch of agriculture was unaffected by machinery, hybrids, and chemicals, but some were revolutionized. In no area was change more dramatic than in the cotton-growing South. There, landlords who had replaced sharecroppers with tractors in the planting phase could now do without laborers to chop cotton by using 2,4-D on weeds, and they could replace pickers by using mechanical cotton harvesters. The development of varieties in which the bolls ripened uniformly further facilitated mechanization. These developments interacted with one another in such a way as to doom sharecropping. As late as 1935, there were nearly 1.5 million sharecroppers in the South; by 1960 there were fewer than 200,000, and the Census Bureau announced it would no longer bother to count them.

Machines, chemicals, and improved breeds and varieties led to an unprecedented surge in productivity. In 1940 one worker on a farm fed 10 people, and just five years later, 15. By 1970 one person on the farm fed 45, and 90 in 1990. This surge in agricultural productivity resulted in cheap food for urban consumers. In 1945 the average consumer spent about one-third of his or her income on food and beverages. By 1990, only about one-sixth of the average consumer's income went for food and beverages.

The revolution in agricultural productivity also led to an unprecedented rural-to-urban migration. Between 1945 and 1970, 21 million people left American farms for towns and cities. Usually they participated in and helped advance the postwar economic boom the United States enjoyed, but sometimes, especially when they lacked education and skills, they became part of an urban underclass that took on aspects of permanence.

While the agricultural revolution continues, with biotechnology playing an increasingly prominent role, we have already seen most of its significant effect on urban America. Food prices are unlikely to fall dramatically, and fewer than 4.5 million people now live on farms. As far as urban America is concerned, the agricultural revolution is effectively over.

—David B. Danbom

References

Danbom, David B. *Born in the Country: A History of Rural America.* Baltimore: Johns Hopkins University Press, 1995.

Drache, Hiram M. *History of U.S. Agriculture and Its Relevance to Today.* Danville, IL: Interstate Publishers, 1996.

Fite, Gilbert C. *American Farmers: The New Minority.* Bloomington: Indiana University Press, 1981.

Hurt, R. Douglas. *American Agriculture: A Brief History.* Ames: Iowa State University Press, 1994.

Schlebecker, John T. *Whereby We Thrive: A History of American Farming, 1607–1972.* Ames: Iowa State University Press, 1975.

Shover, John L. *First Majority—Last Minority: The Transforming of Rural Life in America.* DeKalb: Northern Illinois University Press, 1975.

Air Pollution

Air pollution first became a visible problem in the United States after the Civil War, when northern cities, swollen by demographic and industrial growth, began experiencing persistent smoke palls. Smoke and odors were not new, but the wind had previously dispersed emissions from smaller populations that used less fuel. However, industrialization, the replacement of firewood with coal, and the huge increase in per capita fuel use at the same time that America's population was exploding led cities' smoke and soot to accumulate rapidly in amounts that swamped normal atmospheric dilution. Industrialization increased all traditional air pollution sources, such as those in the home, while introducing major new ones such as factories, blast furnaces, smelters, locomotives, and steamships. Smoke problems first surfaced in heavily industrialized cities like Pittsburgh and Chicago but later appeared in other population centers such as Philadelphia and New York City, especially as easterners shifted from anthracite to cheaper, dirtier bituminous coal.

Public concern over smoke soon followed; despite their pride about urban and industrial growth, many Americans shared earlier English fears of the "Big Black Smoke" of new industrial centers, connoting evil and immorality along with smoke and squalor. Civic reform or-

A motorcycle rider emerges from a haze of smog in Los Angeles, 1958.

ganizations, often women's groups, crusaded against smoke, citing suspected health risks and proven ugliness and damage. Chicago passed America's first smoke-control ordinance in 1881 and other cities soon followed. But often these laws were not enforced due to pressure for unlimited economic growth and production, especially during wartime. Into the 1950s, most sporadic urban smoke abatement campaigns accomplished little, with drives during the 1940s in St. Louis and Pittsburgh as notable exceptions.

After World War II, America saw change as unprecedented affluence, new lifestyle expectations, and health concerns led citizens to demand relief from the air pollution problems that had grown with the nation's cities and industrial capacity. Smoke and soot lessened as natural gas and oil increasingly replaced coal. New research and monitoring technology uncovered dangerous, invisible, gaseous air pollutants such as sulfur dioxide, carbon monoxide, and ozone after dramatic air pollution incidents killed people in Donora, Pennsylvania (1948), and London, England (1952). Los Angeles gained fame for photochemical smog and for leading the nation's fight against air pollution; there, scientists first discovered the automobile's major role (1950). Citizens' groups organized to fight smog as air pollution became one of the nation's foremost environmental concerns.

Even determined postwar local abatement efforts proved inadequate for conurbations and air pollution problems stretching across county and state boundaries, while state and local governments feared losing polluting industries (and jobs and revenue) to less polluted areas by demanding cleanup. Consequently, the federal government assumed increasing responsibility for the problem. Early federal legislation (1955, 1963, 1965, and 1967) sought to preserve state and local responsibility while offering limited federal scientific, technical, and financial assistance. When this approach failed, the federal government took overall responsibility for national air quality under the Clean Air Act of 1970, administered by the new Environmental Protection Agency. Air pollution remains a problem for America's cities, though some progress has been made.

Air pollution, a by-product of modern urban industrial culture, helped create America's suburbs, for suburbanites fled contaminated air along with other urban problems. Wealthier suburbs often were built upwind of industrial districts. Later, as urban air pollution increased and spread over the suburbs, suburbanites expressed much of the public demand for air pollution control: historically, environmental issues have primarily concerned relatively affluent, educated citizens like those found in middle-class suburbs. Ironically, as with other urban problems they hoped to escape, suburbanites gradually brought air pollution with them through their consumption and their means of commuting to and from the city—most notoriously, the now-entrenched automobile culture, perhaps the greatest polluter of the air.

—*Scott H. Dewey*

See also
Land Pollution; Water Pollution.
References
Ayres, Robert U. "Air Pollution in Cities." In Walt Anderson, ed., *Politics and Environment: A Reader in Ecological Crisis*, 78–100. Pacific Palisades, CA: Goodyear Publishing Company, 1970.
Davies, J. Clarence. *The Politics of Pollution.* New York: Pegasus, 1970.
Grinder, Robert Dale. "The Battle for Clean Air: The Smoke Problem in Post–Civil War America." In Martin V. Melosi, ed., *Pollution and Reform in American Cities, 1870–1930*. Austin: University of Texas Press, 1980.
Krier, James E., and Edmund Ursin. *Pollution and Policy: A Case Essay on California and Federal Experience with Motor Vehicle Air Pollution, 1940–1975*. Berkeley: University of California Press, 1977.
Lipfert, Frederick W. *Air Pollution and Community Health: A Critical Review and Data Sourcebook.* New York: Van Nostrand Reinhold, 1994.
Snyder, Lynne Page. "'The Death-Dealing Smog over Donora, Pennsylvania': Industrial Air Pollution, Public Health Policy, and the Politics of Expertise, 1948–1949." *Environmental History Review* 18 (1994): 117–139.

Airports

Not only have airports been a major force in urban growth strategies, but they have also profoundly affected the spatial development of metropolitan areas. A close relationship has existed between cities and their airports since the early twentieth century. Although many cities had private airstrips by World War I, the development of municipal airports usually occurred in the 1920s, particularly after 1926 when the government first awarded airmail contracts to commercial airlines. Viewed as another tool to boost urban growth, cities across the nation bought land and developed airports or purchased already established airstrips and turned them into municipal airports. Chicago, which developed Midway Airport in 1927, planned to become the "Detroit of Aviation." Dallas voters approved a $400,000 bond issue that same year to purchase Love Field from a private corporation, again hoping to become a major player in aviation. By 1938, municipalities or county governments had constructed 1,833 airfields at a cost of about $340 million.

Significant federal government funding for municipal airports came later. New Deal programs during the Depression poured about $139 million into airport construction, although much of that went to develop smaller airports, many of which did not survive. As new and larger planes appeared, additional financial aid for airport development proved necessary, which helps explain passage of the Civil Aeronautics Act of 1938. Under this act, Congress established a six-year program of improvements for the nation's airports and provided funds specifically for that purpose—the first time in the nation's history. The U.S. Conference of Mayors played a significant role in securing this legislation.

World War II impacted the development of municipal airports to an even greater extent. The Development of Landing Acres for National Defense Programs helped create and improve a whole series of airports near major cities. Chicago's O'Hare International Airport began as a military airfield and was developed for the city only after the military sold it as surplus in 1946. Love Field in Dallas, although a municipal field before the war, maintained that status when the fighting ceased only because of the army's decision to spend $6 million to improve it for wartime use.

World War II marks a watershed in airport history in another way, too. During and after the war, cities made a sustained effort to plan for future aviation development. Several comprehensive city and metropolitan plans for the 1940s provided separate volumes about airport development and its relationship to urban growth. Cincinnati devised a ten-year plan for airport development in 1948, while air-conscious Dallas planned for a 21-airport system. Congress participated in this new planning emphasis and passed the Federal Airport Act of 1946, which for the first time made the federal government the chief developer of the nation's airport system. Federal funding for airport construction was to be matched by local funds, so many cities increased spending on airport development. That act also required the formulation of a national airport plan to provide an adequate airport system for civilian needs.

The growing involvement of the federal government in airport construction for major metropolitan centers has had benefits but has not been without some problems. Federal funding has not always been available, and red tape has stalled more than one city. Furthermore, federal government priorities of a safe and efficient air system have sometimes conflicted with local urban goals of convenience and growth. This was especially the case after World War II when the federal government started pushing for the decentralization of airports and supported regional airfields.

During the early years of airport development, many argued the importance of keeping airports accessible to downtown businessmen, the chief users of the service. By the 1950s, most airports still remained within 10 miles of the central business district. Indeed, after the war, airport boosters placed great emphasis on making airports more accessible through superhighway development between airport and city. The federal government, however, concerned with noise and safety, encouraged the construction of airports further out. The development of Willow Run as Detroit's municipal airport located 30 miles from the central business district, and Baltimore's Friendship Airport, midway between that city and Washington, are examples of this new tendency. Such placement of airports has accelerated the decentralization of metropolitan America and often has produced business, commercial, and residential development to rival that of the incorporated city it was built to serve. When developed in the 1970s, locals called the Dallas–Fort Worth International Airport the largest real estate speculation in the area's history and saw it play a critical role in further decentralizing both Dallas and Fort Worth.

—*Robert B. Fairbanks*

References

Barrett, Paul. "Cities and Their Airports: Policy Formation, 1926–1952." *Journal of Urban History* 14 (1987): 112–137.

Braden, Betsy, and Paul Hagan. *A Dream Takes Flight; Hartsfield International Airport and Aviation in Atlanta.* Athens: University of Georgia Press, 1989.

Fairbanks, Robert B. "A Clash of Priorities: The Federal Government and Dallas Airport Development, 1917–1964." In Joseph F. Rishel, ed., *American Cities and Towns: Historical Perspectives,* 164–184. Pittsburgh: Duquesne University Press, 1992.

Noel, Thomas J. "Unexplored Western Skies: Denver International Airport." *Journal of the West* 30 (1991): 90–100.

Alger, Horatio, Jr. (1832–1899)

The novelist Horatio Alger, Jr., was born in Chelsea, Massachusetts, to Horatio Alger, a Unitarian minister and farmer, and Olive Augusta Fenno, his wife. After graduating from Harvard in 1852, Alger worked as a teacher and journalist while contributing poems, essays, and stories to such literary weeklies as *True Flag, American Union,* and *Gleason's Pictorial.* He entered Harvard Divinity School in 1857, completed the ministerial course there in 1860, and spent ten months traveling through Europe in 1860 and 1861. Ordained minister of the Unitarian society in Brewster, Massachusetts, in 1864, he resigned 15 months later after he was accused of sexually molesting boys in his congregation—a charge he did not deny—and he moved to New York City in April 1866 to begin his literary career in earnest.

Over the next 30 years, before he retired in 1896, Alger wrote nearly 100 juvenile books, many of them novels set in New York. These followed a basic story pattern in which a young hero, morally equipped to resist the temptations of the big city and thrown unexpectedly upon his own resources, struggles to gain economic independence and social respectability. In order to color these sentimental stories with a few gritty details, Alger frequented such institutions as the Newsboys' Lodging House and the Five Points Mission as well as the docks and other sites where "friendless urchins could be found." His conversations with the orphans or so-called "street Arabs" he met when he arrived in New York gave him "first hand knowledge of street-boys and their mode of life," he later

remembered. "My interest was excited, and led me a few months later to undertake the story of 'Ragged Dick.'"

This juvenile novel, the first that Alger wrote after he arrived in the city, was his only best-seller. The *Boston Transcript* commended the book upon its publication for portraying "the courage, the ambition, the struggling nobility" of the "street Arabs." In 1947 the Grolier Club of New York named it one of the 100 most influential American books published before 1900. The Ragged Dick series (1867–1870) included a total of six novels thematically devoted to depicting the plight of New York street children. In its notice of *Mark the Match Boy* (1869), the third novel in the series, the *New York Evening Post* remarked that "his sketches of the little Arabs of our streets are very life-like and effective, and there is a pathos in some of his descriptions that goes directly to the heart."

In a later novel, *Phil the Fiddler* (1871), Alger presumed to write a social exposé of the plight of Italian street children in the tradition of Charles Dickens and Harriet Beecher Stowe. Through A. E. Cerqua, superintendent of the Italian school at the Five Points, and G. F. Secchi de Casale, editor of the weekly *Eco d'Italia,* Alger "obtained full and trustworthy information" that he incorporated into his text.

Alger's didactic formula evolved over the course of his career, especially after the late 1870s, as he spiced it with sensation and violence to compete with the more popular dime novelists. To supplement his income from writing, until the late 1870s Alger tutored the children of some prominent Jewish families in New York, including Benjamin Cardozo, later an Associate Justice of the U.S. Supreme Court, and E. R. A. Seligman, later Professor of Political Economy at Columbia University. He traveled to Europe a second time in 1873 and to the West in 1877, 1878, and 1890. He died in declining circumstances in Natick, Massachusetts, in 1899.

—*Gary Scharnhorst*

References

Cawelti, John G. *Apostles of the Self-Made Man.* Chicago: University of Chicago Press, 1965.

Scharnhorst, Gary. *Horatio Alger, Jr.* Boston: Twayne, 1980.

Scharnhorst, Gary, with Jack Bales. *The Lost Life of Horatio Alger, Jr.* Bloomington: Indiana University Press, 1985.

Weiss, Richard. "Horatio Alger, Jr., and the Response to Industrialism." In Frederick C. Jaher, ed., *The Age of Industrialism in America.* New York: Free Press, 1968.

Zuckerman, Michael. "The Nursery Tales of Horatio Alger." *American Quarterly* 24 (1972): 191–209.

Almshouses

Almshouses were established in the larger towns of the United States in the seventeenth and eighteenth centuries to house and minimally sustain the most dependent parts of the population. Generally, their financial support and maintenance were the responsibility of local government. Known in different parts of the United States as almshouses, poorhouses, or county infirmaries, homes, or asylums, they were originally genuine attempts to create safe, reasonably comfortable havens for the worthy poor. As Alexander Johnson's *The Almshouse,* published in 1911, begins, "So long as there shall be poor people to be cared for by public charity, a place of refuge, an asylum for worn out and feeble men and women, will probably be a necessity." However, soon after such facilities had been instituted, the occupants were blamed for achieving this ignominious condition as a result of their own immoral or depraved behavior related to drink, prostitution, or other kinds of habitual indulgences. As the last resort for the most helpless in society, those who had no one to care for them or who had been abandoned by family or employer, almshouses were so spare and stigmatized that almost no one entered them voluntarily. To enter meant social degradation and disgrace even if the cause was unavoidable injury or illness. Undifferentiated facilities, they housed the town's dependent populations—the destitute, the orphaned, the marginally criminal, the insane, the blind, the alcoholic, the syphilitic, the crippled, and the otherwise incapacitated—with almost no distinctions made among kinds of population on the basis of age, sex, or reason for entry. Simply put, almshouses were centers of misery. Like the inhabitants of prisons and insane asylums, residents were called inmates.

Often, almshouses were also workhouses in which the inhabitants were expected to contribute to their own support. It was common for almshouses to run farms where carefully supervised inmates grew their own food and sold any surplus to support the enterprise. Almshouses were managed and operated by trustees or overseers of the poor who differed greatly from the inmates in social class, education, religion, and ethnic background. While the overseers were respectable and influential citizens, and visitors were from the charitable middle class, superintendents were often political appointees. Service was provided by a master or matron and scant numbers of attendants, and later, by nursing and medical students.

Toward the end of the eighteenth century, these institutions had become the municipal hospitals of seaport cities, even if their names remained the same. In the nineteenth century, industrialization and urbanization resulted in increased poverty, unemployment, and sickness. The growing numbers of people living in almshouses underscored the precariousness of urban life, and the very sick were separated from the destitute or permanently incapacitated. So-called almshouses encompassed smallpox hospitals, lunatic asylums, children's asylums, birthing units, nurseries, general wards for medical and surgical cases, units for venereal disease and alcoholism, and facilities for "incurables." By this time, the workhouse component of almshouses had all but disappeared, and the seriously ill made up the great majority of occupants.

—*Toba Schwaber Kerson*

See also
Workhouses.
References
Johnson, A. *The Almshouse: Construction and Management.* New York: Russell Sage Foundation, 1911.
Katz, M. B. *Poverty and Policy in American History.* New York: Academic Press, 1983.
Lawrence, C. *History of the Philadelphia Almshouses and Hospitals from the Beginning of the Eighteenth to the Ending of the Nineteenth Centuries.* Philadelphia: Charles Lawrence, 1905.
Rosenberg, Charles E. *Explaining Epidemics and Other Studies in the History of Medicine.* New York: Cambridge University Press, 1992.
Rothman, David J. *The Almshouse Experience: Collected Reports.* New York: Arno Press, 1971.

Amusement Parks

In nineteenth-century America, outdoor amusement (defined as public activities held in open spaces for recreation or entertainment) occurred in a number of different locales. There were the public parks that arose in response to increasing urban populations and the desire of reformers to counteract the negative effects of overcrowding. Fairmont Park in Philadelphia and Central Park in New York, for instance, provided the opportunity for leisurely pastimes. More boisterous activities, often sponsored by fraternal associations, were confined to picnic groves. Parker's Grove near Cincinnati and Jones' Wood in New York entertained people with swings and merry-go-rounds, target shootings, footraces, donkey rides, music and dancing, and bowling matches. There were also carnivals and traveling circuses to amuse the public with trained animal acts, human freak shows, acrobatic performances, and equestrian exhibitions. Another locale for amusement was seaside resorts. With improvements in water and rail transportation, numerous towns along the New England, New York, and New Jersey shores became fashionable vacation spots. Upper- and middle-class clienteles enjoyed the resort's ocean bathing, hunting, fishing, and sailing facilities or were entertained with musical concerts and dramatic plays.

The development of New York's Coney Island exceeded that of other resorts since it could be reached by a larger population in less time at a lower price. In the late nineteenth century, a new dimension was added to outdoor amusement as technological advances brought about the construction of various mechanical devices. The most impressive of these were built at or moved to Coney Island because, even at 5 or 10 cents a ride, the profit potential was enormous. For example, the Sawyer Observatory from the Philadelphia Centennial Exposition of 1876, a 300-foot iron tower with two steam elevators, was reerected there. In 1884 the Switchback

Railway, America's first roller coaster, was introduced at Coney Island, attracting 10,000 patrons on opening day alone. Built during the next decade were the Shoot-the-Chutes, the first large-scale water amusement ride; the Flip Flap, the first vertical looping roller coaster; and a Ferris Wheel half the size of the one at the Columbian Exposition in Chicago.

In the 1890s other amusement devices, albeit not as grand, popped up in nearly every city, large and small, that was served by electricity. The traction companies responsible for streetcar lines often paid a flat monthly fee for the electricity to operate the trolleys. To reduce their costs and to induce the public to ride streetcars on Saturdays and Sundays, many companies placed mechanical rides and attractions at the end of a trolley line, usually near a body of water. The term *trolley park* thus entered the vocabulary. At Coney Island, the nickel trolley brought this seaside resort within reach of New York's multitudes.

The modern amusement park was born in Coney Island at the turn of the century. At that time, Coney's West Brighton section housed the largest collection of entertainments in the world. In an area only twelve blocks wide and two blocks deep, there were hundreds of amusement stands, restaurants, saloons, sandwich counters, sideshows, mechanical rides, pavilions, bathhouses, and so on. West Brighton also achieved notoriety for its cheap hotels, brothels, gambling dens, fakir booths, and girlie shows. Coney's reputation for immorality, vulgarity, vice, crime, and public disorder stimulated reform efforts to "clean up" the area. Local businessmen and showmen, eager to capitalize on American workers' increased leisure time and spending power, were able both to satisfy the demands of reformers and reap huge profits. They fenced in hitherto independent rides, sideshows, and games, excluded gambling and prostitution, charged admission, and employed guards to keep the riffraff out. The new "amusement parks," as they were called, catered primarily to a middle-class clientele, enjoyed great popularity, and contributed to Coney's moral and cultural renaissance.

The first of these amusement parks was Sea Lion Park, built in 1895 by Paul Boyton on a large plot of land that enclosed various aquatic exhibitions, water rides, trained animal acts, and a ballroom. In 1897 George C. Tilyou opened Steeplechase, named for the mechanical racetrack with eight wooden horses that circled the 15-acre park. In his park, Tilyou designed and introduced a number of mechanical rides, fun houses, gaming devices, and sideshow practices— amusement ideas and innovations that can be seen at any of today's parks and that look to be just as popular now as a century ago.

Tilyou was also instrumental in bringing back to Coney Island and incorporating into Steeplechase novel and interesting entertainment attractions developed by other show-men. One such initiative resulted in the creation of yet another amusement park. In 1901 Tilyou visited the Pan-American Exposition in Buffalo, New York, and was captivated by an illusion ride named A Trip to the Moon, conceived by Frederick A. Thompson and operated in partnership with Elmer S. Dundy. The following year the financially successful ride was presented at Steeplechase on a concession basis and continued to draw large crowds. After the 1902 season, Thompson and Dundy broke with Tilyou over a contract dispute and built a rival park. They bought Boyton's unsuccessful Sea Lion Park, razed most of the attractions, and in 1903 created Luna Park, named for Dundy's sister and not, as most people thought, for their famous illusion ride. Luna's impressive success—with its emphasis on cultural themes, building design, spectacle, and ambiance—spawned the construction of Dreamland, the last of the Coney Island amusement parks, right across the street on 15 acres of oceanfront property. Dreamland, built by politicians and not by showmen, copied and expanded Luna's original ideas, stressed architectural grandeur, and was dubbed the "Gibraltar of the Amusement World."

Steeplechase is considered the prototype of modern amusement parks. Its amusement formula was based on different principles than either Luna Park or Dreamland. Advertised as "the Funny Place," Steeplechase had no exotic villages, reenactments of natural disasters, architectural styles, or thematic forms. Tilyou built and patented his own mechanical devices in Steeplechase—the Human Roulette Wheel, Earthquake Floor, Razzle-Dazzle, Blow Hole, Electric Seat, and dozens more. He also appealed to a more working-class audience, had decidedly sexual overtones in many rapid-motion rides (e.g., the Wedding Ring, Barrel of Love, Dew Drop): and offered less well-to-do patrons a convenient way of temporarily breaking with Victorian standards. The pattern forged at Steeplechase (mechanical rides, a midway, sideshows, fun houses, audience participation, voyeurism, interaction with strangers) was applied to other amusement parks Tilyou operated in a number of cities, some with the same name. So successful were these parks that their style of entertainment soon became the industry standard, copied by virtually every other park operator for decades.

Coney Island's improved reputation and commercial success led to a dramatic increase in the number of amusement parks throughout the United States in the first decade of the twentieth century. From Maine to California nearly every shorefront city and town had some assortment of mechanical rides, food and game concessions, and sideshows at one or more trolley park or public park midway. Americans were caught up in the outdoor amusement craze. Local promoters around the country built imitator parks structured around "novelties" or entertainment innovations developed at Coney

Island. Some made fortunes while others lost heavily when they attempted to attract the wrong class of people or misread the public's taste in amusement. Most of these new parks—e.g., Riverview Park in Chicago, Willow Grove Park in Philadelphia, and Euclid Beach in Cleveland—presented a variety of attractions that appealed to all classes, reaped steady profits, and achieved a considerable degree of permanence. So strong was Coney's influence on the outdoor amusement industry that many promoters unabashedly affixed names like Coney Island, Steeplechase, Luna Park, or Dreamland to their park names.

The second decade of the twentieth century witnessed a steady increase in both the number of amusement parks being built and their attendance figures. During the summer of 1911, for example, Kansas City's five parks counted almost 2 million visitors. Many of the staples of today's amusement parks, such as the penny arcade and various skill games, were popularized in this period. So too were the amusement park piers at coastal cities, with roller coasters and other mechanical rides on wooden or steel platforms extending hundreds of feet over the water. One important development was the invention of the underfriction roller coaster, changing this device from a scenic gravity ride to an undulating thrill ma-

chine. By 1919, there were more than 1,500 amusement parks in American cities.

Amusement parks reached their zenith in the 1920s, a time of strong economic growth. Engineers and designers of amusement devices created faster and higher roller coasters, bumper cars, and vertigo-inducing rides. The widespread use of the automobile paved the way for the construction of parks unrelated to mass transit lines. Existing parks were refurbished according to middle-class tastes and had a family orientation. Playland near New York City, for example, presented itself in 1928 as a beautifully designed park—with a tree-lined mall, beach, picnic grounds, and children's ride area separated from the major amusements—while Coney Island Park near Cincinnati, explicitly named after the famous park in New York and originally a nineteenth-century picnic grove, stressed cleanliness and improved its image each time the park was renovated.

However, many parks closed in this decade or began a long period of deterioration. Lack of adequate parking for automobiles curtailed the patronage of urban parks. Transit companies sold their parks to private individuals and former trolley parks became hangouts for local rowdies and were no longer known as places for family enter-

Crowds pack Morey's Pier amusement park on the Wildwood, New Jersey, boardwalk in 1992.

tainment. Several successive summers of bad weather forced smaller parks out of business.

With the onset of the Depression, the amusement industry declined precipitously. Money for capital improvements and new promotions dried up. People turned to the movies, now with sound, for a cheap fantasy. Increased reliance on automobiles sounded the death knell for trolley parks. By the end of the decade there were fewer than 300 amusement parks, and attendance was down as well.

The only bright spot at this time was the development of major new amusement devices that would play an important role in traditional and newer theme parks in years to come. At the 1933 Chicago World's Fair, the first cable Sky Ride in America was introduced. Two decades later Disneyland's cable car ride served to transport people from one location to another and entertain them with a bird's-eye view of the park. A 250-foot Parachute Jump opened at the 1939 New York World's Fair was moved to Steeplechase a year later and became the most visible symbol of Coney Island. Many parks today have parachute rides half as tall.

During World War II new parks were not built, and in the late 1940s, with the advent of television, people entertained themselves more at home. New parks seldom got off the drawing boards as the novelty of amusement parks had worn thin. The white, middle-class exodus to the suburbs and the influx of poor and minority populations to cities further adversely affected the amusement park industry. With the start of the baby boom, America was changing, and many traditional amusement parks managed to survive by adding dance bands, swimming pools, picnic facilities, and children's rides.

A whole new era in amusement park history started with Disneyland in 1955. Walt Disney's creation, now called a "theme park," appealed primarily to middle-class, suburban, travel-oriented, national audiences, the kind of people who shunned traditional amusement parks with bad reputations in their local communities. In the 1960s and 1970s, many theme parks in the Disney mold were built throughout the country by large corporations or conglomerates such as Six Flags, Taft Broadcasting, Anheuser-Busch, Marriott, and Bally Manufacturing. Other theme parks were sponsored by smaller companies or individual investors for regional markets. The success of national and regional theme parks stimulated a renewed interest in, and financial commitment to, many older traditional amusement parks. Despite earlier neglect and deterioration, Kennywood Park (Pittsburgh), Cedar Point Park (Sandusky, Ohio), Elitch Gardens (Denver), Dorney Park (Allentown), Hershey Park (Hershey), and Playland (Rye, New York) survive to this day via renovation and expansion to compete with the new theme parks. The building of longer, taller, faster, and curvier roller coasters, or "scream machines," also helped sustain traditional amusement parks.

Unfortunately, closings of urban amusement parks in the 1960s and 1970s were all too common. Many became sites for gang violence and racial tensions as they found themselves in the middle of deteriorating neighborhoods. Riverview Park (Chicago), Olympic Park (Irvington, New Jersey), Euclid Beach Park (Cleveland), Palisades Park (Fort Lee, New Jersey), and Glen Echo Park (Washington, D.C.) could not survive the social and economic problems typical of the times. Also contributing to park closings were natural disasters such as fires and floods, deaths of original owners without family members able to take over, prohibitive insurance costs, and skyrocketing land values. Steeplechase itself, the harbinger of all amusement parks, closed in 1964, its demise due mainly to the urban decay of Coney Island outside its gates.

In the 1980s and 1990s, however, it is apparent that theme parks did not, and probably never will, replace traditional amusement parks. Traditional parks have lower admission costs and shorter lines, contain classic mechanical rides and amusement devices no longer manufactured, and provide local residents the opportunity for one-day excursions. Sites and carousels have been declared historic landmarks, and there is a great deal of nostalgia for the cultural products and behavioral styles of traditional parks. Indeed, as theme parks look for new attractions to get the public to return, many are installing models of turn-of-the-century thrill rides—e.g., Shoot-the-Chutes, Bobsled, and Virginia Reel—while others are developing areas designed to re-create the look and feel of a traditional park. Disney World's new Boardwalk of food and game concessions, modeled on Coney Island, is a prime example of this latter trend, ironic in light of Disney's well-known dislike for that seaside resort. Americans, and profit-minded theme park owners, have rediscovered traditional amusement parks and the culture they generated.

—*Raymond M. Weinstein*

See also

Coney Island; Disneyland; Theme Parks.

References

Adams, Judith A. *The American Amusement Park Industry: A History of Technology and Thrills.* Boston: Twayne, 1991.

Griffin, Al. *"Step Right Up, Folks!"* Chicago: Henry Regnery, 1974.

Hildebrandt, Hugo John. "Cedar Point: A Park in Progress." *Journal of Popular Culture* 15 (1981): 87–107.

Kyriazi, Gary. *The Great American Amusement Parks: A Pictorial History.* Secaucus, NJ: Citadel Press, 1976.

Mangels, William F. *The Outdoor Amusement Industry: From Earliest Times to the Present.* New York: Vantage Press, 1952.

National Amusement Park Historical Association. "Amusement Park Chronology." *National Amusement Park Historical News* 8 (1986): 3–27.

Nye, Russell B. "Eight Ways of Looking at an Amusement Park." *Journal of Popular Culture* 15 (1981): 63–75.

Onosko, Tim. *Fun Land U.S.A.* New York: Ballantine Books, 1978.

Weinstein, Raymond M. "Disneyland and Coney Island: Reflections on the Evolution of the Modern Amusement Park." *Journal of Popular Culture* 26 (1992): 131–164.

Anderson, Sherwood (1876–1941)

Although best known as the author of *Winesburg, Ohio* (1919), a fictional treatment of small-town life in the American Midwest, Sherwood Anderson also wrote "urban" novels and short stories. Anderson spent much of his young adult life in Chicago, and here his impressions of urban life, its problems and possibilities, were formed. Reared in a small Ohio town, he first saw Chicago as a common laborer, later as a successful advertising copywriter, and then as a contributor to the "Chicago Renaissance" in literature.

Perhaps in part because his harness-maker father failed to adapt, much of Anderson's work concerns the shift in America from an agricultural society to an urbanized, industrial one. In early "Chicago" novels like *Windy McPherson's Son* (1916) and *Marching Men* (1917), he dealt with the plight of individuals in the face of vast and rapid industrialization, with the accompanying sudden and unruly growth of both towns and cities in the Midwest and with the depersonalization and isolation that could result.

Anderson's interest in the change to industrialism spanned his career. *Winesburg, Ohio* deals with the essential sterility of the old order; *Poor White* (1920) explores the process and effects of urban manufacturing; and *Perhaps Women* (1931) analyzes the impact of a machine-based economy on American men and women. But Anderson's portrayal of the urban differs in several ways from that of some of his more pessimistic contemporaries. He stressed love as a humanizing force in the face of futility and isolation; he sometimes presented the city nonrealistically through impressions, moods, and ideas; he acknowledged a fascination with the vast energy and sense of possibility that the machine age represented; and, finally, he clearly recognized, in his own experience, the greater opportunities for cultural development afforded by large cities like Chicago, New York, New Orleans, or Paris. Anderson thus moved from an early, specific use of Chicago to a concern with the urban in general that continued to develop throughout his career.

—*Hilbert Campbell*

References

Jones, Howard M., and Walter B. Rideout, eds. *Letters of Sherwood Anderson.* Boston: Little, Brown, 1953.

Modlin, Charles E., ed. *Sherwood Anderson: Selected Letters.* Knoxville: University of Tennessee Press, 1984.

Townsend, Kim. *Sherwood Anderson: A Biography.* Boston: Houghton Mifflin, 1987.

Williams, Kenny J. *A Storyteller and a City: Sherwood Anderson's Chicago.* DeKalb: Northern Illinois University Press, 1988.

Annexation

One of the major themes of American urban history is rapid growth. Frontier outposts have burgeoned into major cities within a few short decades. Faced with such growth, municipalities repeatedly needed to redraw their boundaries to absorb the population spilling over into suburban fringes. Annexation is the procedure by which municipalities acquired this new territory and extended their limits. Yet, in some cases the annexation process has been more of an obstacle to change than an aid. For a number of municipalities, this procedure has too often reinforced existing boundaries and frustrated plans for urban expansion.

Since municipalities are creations of states, municipal boundary adjustment has always been a state responsibility. Consequently, there has never been a single American annexation procedure but, instead, different procedures in various states. The earliest municipal boundary adjustments were accomplished through special acts of the state legislature. A municipality petitioned the state legislature for a boundary change, and that body decided whether to accede. Thus, in 1804 the Massachusetts legislature attached South Boston to Boston through a special act; 12 years later Maryland's state lawmakers expanded Baltimore's territory from less than 1,000 acres to more than 8,000; and in 1841, through state legislative fiat, the area of St. Louis increased sixfold. In none of these cases was there a local referendum that permitted residents of the area annexed to approve or veto the boundary extension.

During the second half of the nineteenth century, however, growing opposition to special laws applying to a single locality resulted in state constitutional provisions prohibiting such legislation. Faced with these new constitutional mandates, state legislatures adopted general procedures for municipal annexation that shifted responsibility for boundary adjustment from the state capital to local officials and the electorate. Under these laws, the property holders or residents in the area to be annexed, or the city council of the annexing municipality, generally initiated the process by petitioning county officials for a boundary change. In a number of states, a referendum was then held, and annexation depended on the approval of a majority of the voters in the territory to be absorbed.

Some states, especially in the Northeast, continued to rely on special legislation, but even in those states there was increasing deference to the opinion of residents in the areas to be annexed. For example, in the late 1860s and early 1870s, the Massachusetts legislature enacted a series of special laws merging Roxbury, Dorchester, Charleston, Brighton, and West Roxbury with the city of Boston. But the legislature required popular referenda prior to any annexation. If a majority of voters in any of the communities to be absorbed opposed annexation, then their community would not become part of Boston.

Though in most states residents of outlying districts gained a stronger voice in the boundary adjustment process, some jurisdictions still permitted forced annexation. For example, in 1918 Maryland's legislature enacted special legislation that added 49 square miles to Baltimore without a popular referendum. In both Missouri and Texas, cities could annex unilaterally by passing an ordinance defining the area to be annexed. Residents of outlying areas had no voice in the process. However, such forced procedures were the exception rather than the rule in the United States.

Before 1920, the requirement for voter approval did not necessarily prove an insuperable barrier to annexation. Eager for the superior services available to city residents, voters in fringe areas repeatedly opted for absorption. For example, in 1889 residents in outlying towns voted to join Chicago, thereby almost quadrupling the city's domain. Between 1895 and 1920, a series of annexation elections increased the area of Los Angeles from 29 to 364 square miles. Southern Californians needed water, and Los Angeles had an ample supply. Consequently, they voted to join the city.

By the second and third decades of the twentieth century, however, annexation victories were becoming less frequent. Independent suburban municipalities were improving services, so residents viewed annexation to the central city as less advantageous. Moreover, America's large cities had a reputation for corrupt government dominated by political machines catering to immigrant groups. For thrifty, native-born, middle-class Americans along the suburban fringe, the prospect of boss rule in a polyglot municipality was unappealing, especially since the central city could no longer necessarily provide superior services. Between 1909 and 1914, annexation by Chicago was rejected by voters in Evanston, by residents of Oak Park on two occasions, and by Cicero's electorate in four separate referenda. Boston annexed its last new territory in 1912, Detroit's expansion ended in 1926, and Minneapolis extended its boundaries for the last time in 1927. By the 1920s and 1930s, in one metropolitan area after another, voter approval seemed an insuperable obstacle to annexation of the suburban fringe.

After World War II, however, Americans witnessed a resurgence of territorial expansion. The number of cities over 5,000 in population that annexed territory rose from 152 in 1945 to 712 in 1960. During the 1950s, 62 percent of all places larger than 2,500 changed their boundaries; in the 1960s, 63 percent did so; and in the 1970s and 1980s, the respective figures were 68.5 percent and 66.5 percent.

Annexations were most common in the South but relatively rare in the Northeast. Between 1950 and 1970, the area of the 63 northeastern municipalities defined as central cities by the Census Bureau increased only 6.8 percent, whereas the area of the 101 southern central cities soared 200.2 percent. Older northeastern hubs such as Boston, New York City, Buffalo, Philadelphia, and Pittsburgh annexed no territory.

Surrounded by suburban municipalities with no desire to consolidate with troubled core cities, these traditional urban centers had no opportunity to expand. Many newer Sunbelt centers, however, annexed vigorously and blocked the rise of suburban municipalities that could choke their growth. During the late twentieth century annexation was increasingly a regional phenomenon, of little significance in the Northeast but a major fact of metropolitan life in the South and West.

The rash of new annexations led to a growing number of clashes among adjacent municipalities as each vied for tax-rich tracts of land. In order to avoid such conflicts and make the annexation process less of a free-for-all, some states created administrative agencies to supervise boundary adjustments. In 1959 Minnesota pioneered this reform, and California followed suit in 1963, establishing a Local Agency Formation Commission in each county. Alaska, Washington, Oregon, and Wisconsin were among the other states to opt for this procedure between 1959 and 1969. Under the various state laws, a proposed annexation was submitted to the supervisory agency, which considered the wisdom of the boundary adjustment and either ruled in its favor or vetoed it. If the recommendation was positive, the proposal generally had to be submitted to the voters of the area to be annexed. Administrative supervision supplemented, but did not eliminate, the long-standing tradition of popular determination.

Thus, at the close of the twentieth century, annexation proceedings remained common in much of the United States, and voter approval was still a vital element in the process of boundary change. A number of states had sought to impose some order on the procedure, but conflict continued as municipalities attempted land grabs, outlying residents fought them off, and adjoining cities prepared their own plans of territorial acquisition.

—Jon C. Teaford

See also
Consolidation.
References
Bigger, Richard, and James D. Kitchen. *How the Cities Grew: A Century of Municipal Independence and Expansionism in Metropolitan Los Angeles.* Los Angeles: Haynes Foundation, 1952.
Sengstock, Frank S. *Annexation: A Solution to the Metropolitan Area Problem.* Ann Arbor: University of Michigan Law School, 1960.
Teaford, Jon C. *City and Suburb: The Political Fragmentation of Metropolitan America, 1850–1970.* Baltimore: Johns Hopkins University Press, 1979.

Anti-Semitism

Anti-Semitism is the belief that Jews are different and inferior. In the nearly 350 years since Jews first emigrated to America, anti-Semitism has taken both ordinary and extraordinary forms. Ordinary anti-Semitism is the conviction that

Jews are different in their creed, inner nature, and appearance, and that they possess distinctive traits and attitudes such as aggressiveness, materialism, and clannishness that separate them from other people and groups of people. Extraordinary anti-Semitism is the willingness of individuals, groups, or an entire society to blame Jews for political, social, or economic change. The Jew becomes the displacement substitute, the scapegoat, for those who feel and express frustration or deprivation.

Anti-Semitism is behavior as well as belief; both ordinary and extraordinary anti-Semitism can and have been expressed as overt aggressive behavior. The Red Scare, Ku Klux Klan, Great Depression, and political upheaval in Europe intensified and heightened the pervasive anti-Semitism after World War I, and in 1944 nearly 25 percent of Americans named Jews as a threat to the nation.

After World War II, anti-Semitism appeared to wane. Jews began to shift their residential center from urban ghettos to suburbs where their appearance and aspirations resembled their gentile neighbors. Restrictive covenants, neighborhood redlining, university quotas, employment restrictions, and blackballing from clubs and social organizations eased though they did not disappear. In 1962 only 1 percent of the population perceived Jews as a threat to the nation, and only 3 percent said they would dislike having Jewish neighbors.

In the last four decades, living in suburbs has transformed Jewish life. In cities, Jews tended to live with other Jews; and there was less need to worry about living as Jews. In the suburbs, at least initially, Jews lived mostly with non-Jews. They needed to confront, define, and institutionalize being Jewish. Secularization of Jewish institutional life followed. Synagogues and temples became social centers as much as the focus of religious life. As parents climbed the socioeconomic ladder, they shifted the responsibility of providing their children with a Jewish identity to the synagogue, the community center, and the Jewish day school. By the early 1980s, Jews had seemingly created "gilded ghettos" free from oppression where they reaped the rewards of an open-class society while they enjoyed fulfillment of the American dream.

Complete assimilation, intermarriage, and the loss of Jewish identity, not anti-Semitism, have become today's chief concern for Jewish leaders. Whereas fewer than 5 percent of Jewish men and women married non-Jews in 1960, today the number is more than 50 percent, and the percentage is trending upward steeply. Fully 40 percent of the Jewish population is ambivalent about the escalating loss of Jewish identity.

But ordinary and extraordinary anti-Semitic activity is increasing, too. The data from 1993 show that anti-Semitic attacks against individuals have risen 245 percent since 1986, and the number of anti-Semitic incidents on college campuses has increased sharply. In 1993 more than 50 percent of Jews under 35 said that they had experienced some form of anti-Semitism. Jews who previously felt comfortable in suburban enclaves find their institutions and homes increasingly under assault from youthful vandals, skinheads, and neo-Nazi groups.

Most contemporary suburban and urban Jews are committed to cultural tolerance in a society that promises to accept a wide range of attitudes and behaviors as well as religious and ethnic diversity. But American Jewry is less secure than its prosperity and prominence suggest. In a recent broad-based community survey, 20 percent of Jews had experienced anti-Semitism. Nearly 30 percent of the general population, the same as 30 years ago, believe that Jews are more loyal to Israel than the United States. Ambivalence about their own identity has caused college-age Jews of the New Left to link arms with groups of color who view Zionism and Jews in pejorative terms. In their view Jews and Zionism are tied together as examples of colonialism, racism, and imperialism. Black anti-Semitism has risen to a vitriolic pitch among African-American leadership, fully 50 percent of whom refuse to disassociate themselves from the pronouncements of Louis Farrakhan and his followers. Holocaust education and revisionism are spiraling upward in tandem. Assaults on the barrier separating church and state, the insertion of school prayer, and themes of Christianizing America by the Fundamentalist Right are not merely constitutional issues for Jews but suggest the destruction of religious and cultural pluralism.

Some Jews believe that concerns about rising anti-Semitism are exaggerated. They suspect that anti-Semitism has kept them a people and that its absence will dissolve their will to survive as a distinct group. Furthermore, the emergence of a genuine multiethnic and multireligious society will protect Jewish interests and prevent anti-Semitism from intruding into public life.

The rise in anti-Semitic activity in the 1980s and 1990s has coincided with the decline in social civility and the increasing coarseness of modern life. Mass culture, the submergence of the individual within groups, an apparent disappearance of public manners and politeness, and hostility toward women and minorities have made it "hip" to hate. Some Jews worry that anti-Semitic incidents may be more tolerated as society becomes hardened to crime, murder, and drugs.

At the start of a new century, urban and suburban Jews need to emerge from the cocoon of the "gilded ghetto." Jews need to enhance public awareness of anti-Semitic activity and support legislation against hate crimes. They must attack anti-Semitism and marginalize it. Holocaust education must be supported and revisionism combated. Jews must exercise political influence and build coalitions with all groups.

—Barry Lazarus

See also
Skokie, Illinois.
References
Anti-Defamation League. *Audit of Anti-Semitic Incidents.* New York: Anti-Defamation League, 1979–1993.

Bayor, Ronald H. *Neighbors in Conflict: The Irish, Germans, Jews, and Italians of New York City, 1929–1941.* Baltimore: Johns Hopkins University Press, 1979.

Belth, Nathan C. *A Promise to Keep: A Narrative of the American Encounter with Anti-Semitism.* New York: Times Books, 1979.

Gerber, David A. "Anti-Semitism and Jewish-Gentile Relations in American Historiography and the American Past." In David A. Gerber, ed., *Anti-Semitism in American History,* 3–54. Urbana: University of Illinois Press, 1986.

Higham, John. *Send These to Me: Jews and Other Immigrants in Urban America.* New York: Atheneum, 1975.

Rose, Peter I., ed. *The Ghetto and Beyond: Essays of Jewish Life in America.* New York: Random House, 1969.

Silberman, Charles E. *A Certain People: American Jews and Their Lives Today.* New York: Summit Books, 1985.

Sklare, Marshall, ed. *The Jewish Community in America.* New York: Behrman House, 1974.

Synnott, Marcia G. *The Half-Opened Door: Discrimination and Admissions of Harvard, Yale, Princeton, 1900–1970.* Westport, CT: Greenwood Press, 1979.

Tobin, Garry A. *Jewish Perceptions of Anti-Semitism.* New York: Plenum Press, 1988.

Apartment Buildings

Apartment buildings are places to live in which several households each have independent dwelling units while sharing a roof, a front door, a lobby, and perhaps additional facilities and services. They make possible a higher density of population on a given land area than private house development. Apartment buildings bring an increased level of activity and architectural presence, an urban intensity, to the street.

The term *apartment* was usually used in the nineteenth century to distinguish middle-class buildings from their predecessors, tenements built for the working class. Yet, apartment buildings have always carried meanings antithetical to American home-owning ideals: the units are usually rented instead of owned, the buildings are shared instead of private, and strangers are brought into intimate contact with family quarters. Perhaps this is why these buildings are often called "apartment houses" but never "apartment homes."

Apartment buildings bring into focus many issues related to American urbanism, class structure, and family life, as well as the topic of architectural design. These buildings were the first to declare middle-class values on a large scale in U.S. cities of the 1860s and 1870s. Their size and level of architectural embellishment rivaled earlier public buildings, such as churches and governmental buildings, for visual and physical prominence in the cityscape. Although the self-contained nuclear family was recognized as the ideal household form, apartment-house life presented alternatives: bachelor flats, buildings for single women, and units without

kitchens were all tried in the early years of apartment-house development. Apartment houses also created opportunities for women's independence through easy access to urban transportation and proximity to attractions such as department stores and restaurants. Apartments fostered ease of housekeeping through the smaller size of household units, and because they made available prepared meals in apartment-building dining rooms, roof gardens, rooms for social events, and maid services.

In the larger American cities of the mid-nineteenth century, there was a shortage of respectable housing for people who considered themselves middle class rather than working class and who shared the values of privacy, propriety, and family self-containment. The possibilities for middle-class dwelling space in the 1850s and 1860s did include single-family houses, but these were increasingly priced beyond the means of middle-class urban families and were affordable only in out-of-town locations. The housing pressures first felt in Boston in the 1850s and New York in the 1860s had spread to Chicago and Washington, D.C., by the 1870s and 1880s. Unable to afford a entire private house, families had to rent smaller spaces—half of a house, or one floor in a house that had been subdivided into flats. Some chose boarding arrangements, where they had a private room, but shared meals, the dining room, and living rooms with other boarders and the family who owned the house. For well-to-do families who were unwilling to undertake the expense of a whole private house, a hotel suite was not an uncommon choice for permanent dwelling space. This was an especially popular answer to the housing problem in Washington, where the population of government officials was particularly mobile and welcomed the flexibility of a hotel home.

Designers raised the question of how the middle class should live in the city and produced plans for apartment houses first in newspapers and popular magazines. The first apartments were constructed in Boston in the 1850s, then in New York, Chicago, and Washington. Although many people had lived in multiple dwellings—boarding houses, hotels, or subdivided houses—still, the first buildings constructed deliberately as apartment houses seemed like something new. Boston's Hotel Pelham by Arthur Stone has long been cited as America's first, erected in 1857 (and demolished in 1916). Boston's second apartment house was built in 1869, the same year as New York's Stuyvesant Apartments. Designed by Richard Morris Hunt, the Stuyvesant (demolished in the 1950s) is usually mentioned as New York's first. In Washington, D.C., the 1880 Portland Flats on Thomas Circle was that city's first proper apartment house; Chicago followed with the Mentone Flats in 1882.

As the early experiments cautiously developed, designers and their clients struggled to arrive at suitable forms for the new middle-class multiple dwelling. Clients had to be convinced that they could retain their "home values" while living in close proximity to others. These home values might shift in meaning from one client group to the next or from one city to the next, and they might find their best guarantee in interior planning or in exterior expression. Designers (both architects and developers) had to find both exterior styles and interior layouts that could sustain their clients' needs for the symbolic meanings attached to "home." In addition, they needed to ensure the health of homes in the industrial city by providing sunlight and fresh air, establish the privacy of the home from incursions by other families, and maintain privacy for individual family members, from each other and from servants.

In addition, designers in these cities worked toward a variety of goals in designing the new buildings. For example, in New York pressure was felt to design domestic styles that offered some sort of individuation to those who dreamed of private single-family houses but could not afford them because of high land prices on crowded Manhattan Island. Chicago's designers felt a special obligation to make the new apartment houses fit into Chicago's changing image of itself as a town, then a city, then a metropolis; buildings' exterior forms changed in response to this evolving city image. Washington's apartment designers sometimes worked for a special kind of client—the legislator whose family might live in Iowa or Maine and who needed a Washington residence for only part of the year. Another sort of Washington client was socially prominent, moving in international business or diplomatic circles, with a need for a commensurably impressive dwelling space.

In the mid-nineteenth century, where would architects seek precedents as they designed the first apartment houses? There were several models available for multifamily dwellings, but none of them satisfied middle-class demands for privacy and self-containment in a home. The multifamily type most familiar to mid-century New York was the working-class tenement building, a precedent that represented everything unhealthy and unhomelike to middle-class families. Another possible source of design inspiration was the apartment tradition in Paris, where families of all classes had lived comfortably in apartment buildings since the Renaissance. However, Parisian apartments alarmed Americans who did not like the idea of being sandwiched between households of strangers above and below. The Paris apartment type afforded too little privacy with its mix of social classes and a "nosy" concierge who was said to spy on the residents and even read their mail.

The remaining kind of building deliberately intended to provide dwelling space for multiple families was the hotel. Before the Civil War hotels allowed a middle-class family to reside at a fashionable address for less expense than running an independent household. But within a decade, writers were complaining that hotels ruined family life because they threw strangers into close proximity, exposed children to unfamiliar behaviors and values, and tempted wives to stray from marital virtue with the man next door.

The model for arranging interior space that seemed to provide the best organizational principles for apartment designers was the private house, but to translate its forms into a one-floor unit in a large, shared apartment house was a serious challenge. Houses possessed several valued characteristics. They visibly proclaimed their separateness and independence with architectural devices such as roof and cornice details and strongly articulated front entrances. Houses also possessed a kind of "natural" zoning of space, in which the different functions of the house occupied separate floors. In the later nineteenth century, these functions were described as zones of publicity, privacy, and service.

These models of multifamily dwellings were available to architects and their clients, but none of them satisfied American standards. Furthermore, the ideal for planning satisfying interior spaces was the multistory house, whose features had to be reallocated to a single floor in the typical apartment or "flat." Because the models failed to match American home ideals, apartment-house designers had to invent new solutions.

In the first years of apartment construction, buildings tended to be small; "walk-ups," or buildings without elevators, were erected everywhere. Three to six stories high, these first apartments of the 1850s to 1870s did not capitalize on the available elevator technology that commercial structures were already using. Unlike the experimental metal framing of commercial structures, brick or stone structural techniques satisfied builders of housing, and it was not until the turn of the century that metal structural systems began to influence the appearance and height of apartment houses. Low height combined with exterior materials and ornament to make the first apartment houses resemble single-family row houses, a type familiar to city dwellers in the 1870s.

In the 1880s, and especially in the 1890s, as taller apartment buildings with elevators appeared in several cities, their height and scale were already familiar from the commercial buildings of the preceding decades. Ten- or twelve-story apartment houses in the early 1880s established a new typical scale in New York, and made apartments visually prominent on city streets. While the same scale was noticeable in Chicago, apartment-house designers there eschewed the flamboyant ornament of the French-inspired Manhattan style, preferring more restraint in keeping with the developing Chicago aesthetic. In Washington, the new height and public presence of apartment houses were always tempered by the city's building height restriction—no structure was to exceed the Capitol in height.

The planning of individual apartment units, while responding to different lot shapes in Washington or Chicago or Boston, still shows similarities from one city to the next, changing with the decades. In the 1860s and 1870s, there was no standard layout for apartments, so many different room layouts were tried. Early designers laid out rooms according to the rank of their occupants: in Hunt's Stuyvesant Apartments of 1869, for example, the more public, entertainment rooms—parlor, library, dining room—were linked to the "master bedroom," these spaces all being identified with the heads of the household; meanwhile, remaining family bedrooms were juxtaposed to service spaces. This intermingling of service, private, and public spaces would, in retrospect, appear to be bad planning once design principles based on function had matured. Twentieth-century architects defined the spaces of the apartment on the basis of function rather than rank, clustering together rooms with similar uses.

In the early years, long hallways were a common feature of apartment plans; in Washington's early flats this feature preserved row house planning, where rooms were strung along a corridor from front to rear. However, by the first decade of the twentieth century, planning practices converged on a generally respected set of organizational principles. Replacing the long hallway with a foyer, anteroom, or reception room made all the public spaces of the apartment accessible from the entrance door. This clustering made it possible to develop a grand entertainment suite. Chicago, Washington, and New York plans all exhibit this tendency—one that would be even more fully explored in the high-priced apartments between the world wars. Likewise, a national tendency to clarify and separate private spaces into one zone, and service spaces into another, can be seen in architectural journals.

The success of apartment buildings encouraged their spread to more cities in the United States, but the forms began to diversify. Duplex and even triplex apartments appeared at the high-rent end of development—apartments with two or three floors of rooms in one unit—sometimes with a double-height salon or studio combined with single-story bedrooms and service rooms. The Gainsborough on Central Park South in New York opened in 1908, providing artists with double-height, well-lit salons for their studios along with a full complement of rooms for family life and entertaining. At the 1921 Marguery on Park Avenue, two-story apartments provided wealthy residents with as many rooms as a good-sized house plus numerous servants' rooms, individual elevators, and even wine cellars.

In cities, apartment houses grew to 20 and 30 stories by the 1920s. These tall buildings created a new residential skyline along the borders of Central Park in New York or on Chicago's lakeshore (called the "Gold Coast" for its expensive apartment buildings), complementing the contemporary commercial skyline in the central business district.

Garden apartments became popular in developing city real estate further from the urban core. In Washington, apartment building spread out along Connecticut Avenue into areas where land was less expensive. Lower-height buildings were placed on bigger lots, available for decorative landscaping. Easy access to private grounds made these apartment houses urban in density and living style, yet rural in their connection to nature. In more crowded districts, such as upper Manhattan, where real estate was too expensive for park-like settings, apartment buildings with generous courtyards could still provide tenants with a private landscape and paths, greenery, or fountains.

The 1920s saw the expansion of client groups for apartment houses. Well-understood design principles based on function enabled architects to arrange even very small or very large apartments according to convenient groupings of functions. This knowledge, in turn, resulted in apartment houses designed for a very wide range of middle- and upper-class audiences, each aimed at a specific niche in the real estate development of a city. Apartments could be found with none or with several servants' rooms; with a modest living room or a suite of half a dozen entertainment rooms; with one or two bedrooms, or ten. Exterior ornament, entrance expression, and the furnishing of lobbies aided in making class distinctions visible to residents and passersby.

Some cities, such as Buffalo, New York, never developed a taste for grand apartment houses—only three or four were built there in the 1920s—but many five-story units complemented single- and two-family houses to provide homes for the middle class. Likewise, four- to six-story apartment blocks proved popular in Chicago, Philadelphia, the Bronx, and San Francisco, creating a dense neighborhood texture surrounding the downtown core. Unlike the elite artists' studio apartments of the first decade, a new form of studio apartment also became popular in the 1920s. In these studios, most functions were arranged in a single room, with kitchen equipment along one wall and perhaps a fold-up bed in a closet, particularly well suited to the needs of single tenants. Frank Lloyd Wright's design for the 1929 Elizabeth Noble Apartments in Los Angeles is a model of the modern studio apartment.

In some architect-designed communities of the 1910s and 1920s, apartments were used as an element of the commercial strip in communities of otherwise single-family houses. Forest Hills Gardens in Queens, New York, was designed as a commuter residential space, a suburb within the city; in buildings flanking the railroad station in the center of town, apartments were located above storefronts and office spaces. The apartments were thus contained and not allowed to disturb the rest of a landscape reserved for single-family houses. The same pattern was used in 1929 in Radburn, New Jersey; apartments were associated with commerce, a step down from the American dream of a separate household in a freestanding house.

At the end of World War II, clients for residential architecture evidenced an even stronger preference for private houses. The parents of the "baby boom" generation bought newly built freestanding single-family houses in record numbers. Apartments seemed to many a remnant of an earlier life without cars and lawns, back in the crowded city. While serious city dwellers continued to live in prewar apartments, for most of the American population, apartments lost their luster. During the triumphant suburbanization of America in the 1950s, only the socially or economically marginal elected apartment life outside of cosmopolitan settings.

At this time, the federal government entered residential construction on a large scale. For families in the suburbs, the government provided several kinds of mortgage subsidies and tax reductions. For the poor, the government built high-rise apartment blocks in "urban renewal" areas, land cleared of aging or decayed nineteenth-century housing, too close to business and manufacturing sites to appeal to the new suburbanites. These apartment dwellings were often called "projects" to distinguish them from middle-class dwellings, but they were designed internally with the same modern spaces and facilities as those in middle-class apartments. One of these publicly commissioned "projects," Pruitt-Igoe in St. Louis (opened in 1955 and demolished by 1975), comprised 33 apartment towers, each 11 stories tall, set on land that had been reshaped by the removal of traditional streets into an enormous undifferentiated field. When these apartments were occupied by thousands of people struggling in poverty, the apartment tower proved to be unworkable.

In the 1970s, new understandings of the relationships between a fulfilling domestic life and smaller-scale buildings, streets, and landscaping led to a change in housing policy. Apartments intended for the poor began to be constructed closer to the ground, like garden apartments from the 1920s and 1930s . As suburban life became more familiar and the suburban population older, the 1970s also saw a reevaluation of older urban apartments. Shifts in real estate practice enabled people to purchase their apartment units in buildings financially restructured as cooperatives or condominiums.

Shifting demographics in the 1970s and 1980s brought some new ideas to apartment-building designers. Growth in the number of aging parents unable to care for a whole house led to a demand for "in-law" apartments—small but independent apartments attached to the suburban houses of their married children. On the West Coast, very high rents coupled with a high number of single people led to the appearance of apartment units specifically designed for two unrelated individuals to share. At either end of the unit was a bedroom/dressing room/bathroom suite; in the middle was a shared kitchen and living room. This arrangement gave each party privacy while allowing them to save on rent and the costs of furnishing.

The apartment form has proved to be flexible over its life span: adaptable to high-rise or low-building configurations, urban or more open suburban settings, arranged for nuclear family life or for singles or unrelated groups, for the wealthy or the poor, the multiple dwelling affords opportunities for the future. Perhaps some of the nineteenth-century experiments in collective dining, shared social spaces, or housekeeping services will be revived as both designers and clients continue searching for economy of space, adequate privacy, and ease of housekeeping.

—*Elizabeth Cromley*

See also
Condominiums; Tenement.
References
Alpern, Andrew. *Apartments for the Affluent.* New York: McGraw-Hill, 1975.
Cromley, Elizabeth. *Alone Together: A History of New York's Early Apartments.* Ithaca, NY: Cornell University Press, 1990.
Goode, James. *Best Addresses: A Century of Washington's Distinguished Apartment Houses.* Washington, DC: Smithsonian Institution Press, 1988.
Plunz, Richard. Plunz, Richard. **History of Housing in New York City. New York: Columbia University Press, 1990.** New York: Columbia University Press, 1990.

Apprenticeship

The origins of apprenticeship—learning an occupational craft (usually by a boy or young man from a master craftsman)—lie deep in medieval England. They stem from combining artisanal control of "mysteries" (crafts, trades, or mechanical arts) through guilds and the common practice of employment by servitude. Guilds did not develop in the English colonies, and apprenticeships were usually part of neighborly relations in the intimate communities of colonial society. Apprenticeship for girls consisted simply of learning household work and economy, and young women were sent into service mostly for their labor. In colonial society, even male apprentices were generally servants first and trainees second, and the conventional length of preindustrial apprenticeships corresponded to the indentures of voluntary servants, three to seven years. Usually it was parents who volunteered indentures; they were eager for their sons to learn some useful calling, and they also wanted to socialize their boys away from the immediate family. These practices reflected the Tudor Statute of Artificers of 1563, which required parents to bind out their sons to either a trade or agriculture.

The word *apprentice* itself was as likely to be associated with servitude as with training, and the "duty boys" who were indentured into early Virginia were also shown as apprentices in contemporary records. Public officials also indentured large numbers of orphans for terms as long as 15 years and expected them to be brought up in civility, to serve a family, and to learn a trade or occupation. For example, Isaiah Thomas, the great printer-patriot, was indentured in 1756 when he was a seven-year-old orphan. His master, a printer, was given control of him for 13 years and was expected to teach the boy his trade and raise him within the government of a family. In the colonies, apprentices received education in the fullest sense of the word, learning obedience, cooperation, and literacy, as well as a trade.

Apprenticeship has never been a specifically urban phenomenon in American history, but in the last century and a half its relationship to organized labor in cities has given it a metropolitan cast. Less than 10 percent of the colonial population lived in cities such as Boston, Philadelphia, New York, Newport, or Charleston, but even there apprentices invariably lived with their masters. A small but significant percentage of urban slaves were also brought up to practice a trade, and some free blacks acquired journeyman status. Usually, urban apprentices went on to practice their craft full time, but their rural counterparts also had to be capable of farming. The useful rural crafts were limited to a few vital trades such as blacksmithing, carpentry, weaving-tailoring, shoemaking, and masonry. An eighteenth-century rural blacksmith, for example, needed to be experienced as a forgeman, nail maker, and plowwright, in addition to being a farmer. Rural apprentices, therefore, received a grounding in agriculture as well as artisanship. In the port cities, more sophisticated apprenticeships existed in entrepreneurial crafts such as silversmithing, wig making, printing, and distilling. In preindustrial America, there was a hierarchy of crafts, ranging from the simple like tailoring to the complex like printing, and apprenticeships existed in all of them.

A second phase in the history of apprenticeship began during the Revolutionary Era and coincided with the industrial, technological, and market revolutions of the late eighteenth and early nineteenth centuries. This meant wage labor. It also meant that businessmen determined the skills that their workers needed, and new employers focused more on the final product than on the process of production or the older values of comprehensibility, initiative, and talent.

Steam power and the production of textiles and steel implements with machines produced standardized training of apprentices. And, as white male servitude lost legitimacy in the new republic, apprentices were increasingly paid. By the middle and end of the nineteenth century and the advent of trade unions, the standards, terms, and conditions of apprenticeship no longer pretended to socialize apprentices, and the process of losing the highly personal relation between masters and servants/apprentices had begun.

At the same time, distinctions between "skilled" workers, who learned specialized tasks at the hand of a master, and "tradesmen," who continued to learn highly specialized crafts under increasingly regimented programs of accreditation, began to blur. Also, as new and increasingly profitable trades in tool and die making, plumbing, and electricity appeared, most wage earners in industrial America were not apprenticed to their work. Mechanics Institutes flourished as socioeducational enclaves and to protect trades. By 1900, serving an apprenticeship had become something of a privileged rite of passage for a minority of white American men in the increasingly urban, industrial, capitalistic United States.

As the Gilded Age gave way to Progressivism, and as government became directly involved in every facet of economic and industrial regulation, vocational education, trade schools, and technical schools replaced, competed with, or coordinated the older systems of shop apprenticeships. As state and federal regulation of the economy increased, and as national standards were developed for every activity from engineering to automobile repair, the government began to set formal requirements for apprenticeships; it began doing this in 1917 as government and labor unions grew together in importance during World War I.

After a break in the 1920s, the sequence of crises beginning with the Great Depression, extending into World War II, and culminating with the Cold War further enlarged the role of government in domestic as well as in foreign affairs. Still, the control of their own membership by trade unions meant that these organizations could influence who was admitted to apprenticeship programs. The National Apprenticeship Act of 1937 and the Bureau of Apprenticeship that it established had marked a significant redesign of apprenticeship; by the 1960s one of the chief means of maintaining national security was guaranteeing the existence of a well-educated and technically trained workforce. Two generations of the military draft, the "military-industrial complex," and the space race nourished the greatest expansion of institutional education in American history, its most visible result being the explosion in university populations. But vocational, technical, and trades education affected a great many more young people. The great economic boom after World War II demanded vocational skills attuned to highly technical but increasingly standardized performances. Statistically, the population after 1945 was the best trained and best educated in history; but that had less to do with apprenticeship in the older sense and more to do with the specialized, task-determined skills demanded by automobile, chemical, textile, and electronics manufacturing, service, and repair.

And what of the present state of apprenticeship in America, and the future? For a start, apprenticeship today is narrowly job related and has nothing to do with socialization or education. Also, it is steadily shrinking in importance as tasks become more simplified and specialized, even in more complex technologies. As tasks themselves become redundant, the people performing them are interchangeable. Today, apprentice plumbers, electricians, and auto mechanics still sign formal "indentures," and while their employers and unions are still involved in transferring qualifications, public vocational schools and the government's regulatory agencies are just as significant in determining the end result. Apprenticeship, as socialization, tutelage, and mentoring, and as mastery of an applied craft or art, has undergone great changes in its application and meaning over the last three centuries in ways that reflect significant transformations in the country's social, economic, and vocational conditions and values.

—Eric G. Nellis

See also
Artisans.
References
Bailyn, Bernard. *Education in the Forming of American Society.* Chapel Hill: University of North Carolina Press, 1960.
Dubofsky, Melvyn. *Industrialism and the American Worker, 1865–1920.* 2d ed. Arlington Heights, IL: Harlan Davidson, 1995.
Kursh, Harry. *Apprenticeships in America: A Report on Golden Opportunities in Industry for Students, Parents, Teachers, Guidance Counselors, and Leaders.* Rev. ed. New York: W. W. Norton, 1965.
Lipset, Seymour Martin, ed. *Unions in Transition: Entering the Second Century.* San Francisco: ICS Press, 1986.
Rorabaugh, W. J. *The Craft Apprentice: From Franklin to the Machine Age in America.* New York: Oxford University Press, 1986.
Seybolt, Robert. *Apprenticeship and Apprenticeship Education in Colonial New England and New York.* Reprint ed. New York: Arno Press, 1969.

Architecture

Because of their concentrations of wealth, population, and talent, along with their need for powerful symbols, urban areas have been the major settings for significant architecture throughout the world. American cities and suburbs are no exceptions.

During the earliest decades of settlement, American colonists adapted vernacular styles from the Old World to the requirements of the local climate and the availability of building materials in the various regions. Throughout most of New England, for example, the absence of any readily obtainable limestone (a crucial ingredient in making mortar) forced its inhabitants to build with wood, giving rise to the familiar New England clapboard house. At the same time, they discovered that thatched roofs and half-timber construction, with wattle and daub filler, would not withstand the extremes of temperature—hard freezes in winter and intense heat (at least compared to England) during the summer. Houses built in this manner were thus sheathed in clapboards very soon after settlement, a second reason for this distinctive, regional flavor.

By contrast, an abundance of both clay and lime (largely from oyster shells) in the tidewater areas of the upper South allowed for widespread brick construction in this area. In the Middle Atlantic colonies, ample supplies of wood, stone, clay, and lime deposits permitted a much greater variety of construction textures and techniques.

The initial structures in colonial New England especially, but also in Virginia, often exuded a vague medieval flavor, which was also typical of late sixteenth- and early seventeenth-century building in England. Characteristics included steeply pitched roofs, massive chimneys (in some cases with clustered flues), and casement windows (swinging outward and hinged on one side), with small panes of leaded glass.

Regional influences were pervasive far beyond the East Coast. In the Deep South, both wide central hallways and open porches were devices to capture cool summer breezes. In Louisiana, French and Spanish influences are even now reminders of the once colossal struggle among the Western European powers to control North America.

Early structures in the Midwest frequently reflected the eastern origins of its settlers. For example, as New Englanders poured across the upper reaches of the Midwest, they recreated familiar community patterns, complete with village greens and white-steepled churches. The southern portions of the midwestern states, on the other hand, received most of their population from the upper South. There residents erected square, hipped-roof courthouses, a style that may have been inspired by the Governor's Palace at Williamsburg, Virginia. Wealthier southern migrants into the Midwest continued to create spacious homes with open galleries and wide central hallways. Those from Pennsylvania, who generally settled between the New Englanders and the southerners in midwestern regions, preferred stone houses (whenever they could find suitable building stone) or plain, utilitarian structures of brick or wood. These reflected the simple tastes of both the Quakers and the Pennsylvania Dutch (i.e., Pennsylvania Germans), who have had a powerful effect on the physical culture of Pennsylvania.

In the West and Southwest, there are unmistakable Spanish influences. The early mission churches in particular are an attractive blend of late Baroque motifs (often quite colorful and elaborate) and native adobe construction. In the early twentieth century, this Spanish Colonial style enjoyed a revival, lending an unmistakable flavor to this section of the

United States, which lingers as the twentieth century ends. Spanish motifs were also applied lavishly in Florida during the first decades of this century.

It was back on the East Coast, however, that wealthy colonists in the mid-eighteenth century began importing high architectural styles from England, though often after a lag of several years—or even decades. The Georgian style (named for the English kings who reigned during the eighteenth century) was thus widely used in American cities like Boston, New York, Philadelphia, and Charleston. As a late Renaissance motif, with numerous gestures to classical antiquity, the Georgian style had a powerful appeal to the colonial bourgeoisie whose members valued the order, symmetry, and rationality of Georgian design, as did their counterparts in the Old World.

The principal elements of Georgian construction were balanced treatments of windows, doors, and building wings, the use of pilasters and triangular pediments, and decorative elements such as dentile moldings. Casement windows, associated with late medieval design, were now replaced by sash windows (which moved up and down in tracks instead of swinging out on hinges). The Georgian style also owed a great debt to the sixteenth-century Venetian architect Andrea Palladio, as translated through English designers and their pattern books. From Palladio came the five-part scheme, made up of a central structure, flanked by identical appendages, which were then connected to the main building by covered walkways, or arcades. Also stemming from Palladio was the so-called Palladian opening, made up of a large round-headed window—or archway—flanked by rectangular side windows, shutters, or panels.

Although Georgian forms survived the American Revolution, particularly in remote areas of the United States, they were gradually replaced by the Federal style, so named because it flourished during the early years of the American federation. Nevertheless, its roots were in Great Britain, where Americans continued to look for current standards of culture and taste. The originators of this new style were the Adam brothers, especially Robert, who was in turn indebted to eighteenth-century archaeological expeditions to Italy, where digs revealed that Roman domestic building had been far freer and more delicate than Renaissance architects had realized, having based their designs largely on Roman temples and other public buildings.

The principal characteristics of Federal design in the United States were plainer facades than in the Georgian period, with exterior decoration confined almost wholly to the doorway, where elliptical fan lights were often featured above entrances. Columns and pilasters were also narrower and more delicate than in the Georgian style. Interior rooms were sometimes rendered in oval or hexagonal shapes, with ceiling and mantel decorations in the form of swags, garlands, urns, and other motifs that had been discovered in the Italian excavations, particularly in homes unearthed at Pompeii and Herculaneum.

Federal architecture, largely used in domestic construction, had a counterpart in public buildings that was known as the Roman Revival style. It combined elements from Roman public buildings as well as Roman homes. The most important proponent of this style was Thomas Jefferson, who used it in his plans for the University of Virginia and the state capitol in Richmond. He also proposed Roman styles for the nation's new capitol in Washington, where they were supposed to symbolize both the power and virtue of the new republic. But Roman motifs could easily lend themselves to imperial interpretations, as evidenced in the monuments erected all over Paris by Napoleon Bonaparte.

Greek forms, on the other hand, seemed more appropriate to American democracy. Newer, more accurate drawings of Greek ruins, combined with American sympathy for Greek revolutionaries in the early nineteenth century, intensified the passion for Greek models. Accordingly, banks, hospitals, churches, and schools came forth cloaked in Greek columns, acanthus leaves, and severe triangular pediments. These elements were less bold in residential construction, where rows of freestanding columns were a rarity in cities (though not on antebellum plantation houses). The use of Greek Revival by wealthy southern planters, who frequently compared themselves to Greco-Roman aristocrats and whose wealth had likewise derived from slavery, also demonstrated that this style did not always reflect democratic sentiments and was open to various symbolic uses.

Although starkly classical in inspiration, the Greek Revival was part of the larger romantic movement. Central to understanding the romantic thrust in architecture is the concept of *associationalism:* that is to say, a given structure was supposed to make the beholder associate with certain times, places, or feelings. This was especially true of the Gothic Revival that flourished in the pre–Civil War period but that continued to inspire architects well into the early twentieth century.

These Gothic forms were supposed to recall the mysteries of medieval Christianity at a time when religious revivals were eschewing the more rationalistic forms of certain eighteenth-century religions. In addition, Gothic lines were thought to be more in harmony with the curvaceous and irregular lines of organic nature. In cities, the Gothic was most often employed in ecclesiastical architecture, but it found sympathetic clients among American colleges and universities that wanted to associate themselves with the oldest universities in England and Europe, founded in the Middle Ages. Many art museums, seen as sanctuaries of beauty and good taste, likewise opted for Gothic designs. However, in the early suburbs of nineteenth-century America, Gothic villas and cottages made powerful anti-urban statements, with designs rooted in a preindustrial past and organic lines echoing the forest or rural countryside. Furthermore, certain writers about the family believed that the Gothic habitation could help its occupants connect more strongly with Christian values and even make the home into a private chapel of sorts.

Coexisting with the Gothic Revival was a resurgence of Romanesque styles, which similarly recalled the Middle Ages. Romanesque designs, most noted for their use of rounded vaults and arches, as opposed to the pointed Gothic, were most often found in churches and public buildings.

Sympathetic to Romanesque forms was the Italianate style, which also featured rounded shapes, especially in doors and windows, and was used most often in domestic design. The Italianate was supposed to recall country villas outside northern Italian towns. It competed successfully with the Gothic style by the 1840s and was particularly favored for suburban villas. Superseding the Italianate in the post–Civil War period was the Mansard style, taken from the Mansard Revival of Napoleon III's Second French Empire and associated by many with the high culture of Paris. Its most distinguishing feature was a steeply pitched, trapezoidal, hipped roof, from which protruded dormer windows in various sizes and shapes. In suburbs, the Mansard house, frequently combined with Italianate motifs, was a common sight, while some spectacular public buildings were rendered in a flamboyant Mansard design, most notably the State, War, and Navy building in Washington, D.C. (later known as the Old Executive Office Building).

The floor plans of these romantic buildings were often far more irregular than those used in the eighteenth and early nineteenth centuries, reflecting the romantic interest in irregular lines, as well as in individual feeling and expression. Tower rooms, bay windows, porches, alcoves, and private bed chambers were all calculated to give privacy and opportunity for individual reflection. The number and variety of rooms also demonstrated the growing wealth of middle- and upper-class Americans.

During the latter third of the nineteenth century, new technologies and building materials began to transform American architecture. The railroad, for example, allowed more affluent metropolitan dwellers to escape the crime, noise, dirt, and disease of the city at the end of the day by commuting to suburban enclaves that might lie within—or even outside—the municipal boundaries. It was here that romantic villas in Gothic, Italianate, and Mansard dress flourished in the mid-nineteenth century, followed in the 1880s and 1890s by the Queen Anne house.

Originated by British architects, and so labeled by them, the Queen Anne had little to do with architectural design during the reign of this English monarch except for supposedly representing a transition from late Gothic to early Renaissance architecture, a process well under way when Anne assumed the throne in 1702. However inappropriate its name may have been, the Queen Anne was known in the United States for its eclecticism, including contrasts of textures and colors with frequent combinations of brick, stone, stucco, shingles, and half timbering on the same exterior walls. The use of towers, porches, galleries, and overhanging gable ends also gave Queen Anne houses a feeling of exuberance that echoed the tremendous energy and growth of the United States during the Gilded Age.

Meanwhile such innovations as structural steel, electric elevators, telephones, and other communication devices made tall buildings both possible and practical. First in Chicago and then in New York, skyscrapers began thrusting upward in a seeming proclamation of the country's arrival as the world's commercial juggernaut. Although designed to reflect internal functions, most early skyscrapers had exteriors covered with elaborate, nonfunctional decoration, particularly on their towers and street-level facades.

By the 1890s, a reaction against the chaos and excesses of rapid industrialization and urbanization helped to produce a new classical revival, which was more Roman than Greek in inspiration. This movement received a tremendous boost from the Columbian Exposition, held in Chicago in 1893, where the main exhibit halls, designed in colossal Roman Revival motifs, were placed around a classical court of honor. Many large cities in the United States embraced this arrangement of grand boulevards lined with classical libraries, museums, and public buildings, in what came to be called the City Beautiful movement. Banks, railroad stations, and business establishments likewise embraced this latest wave of classical design. Continuing to be influenced by romantic, associationalist theories of art and architecture, proponents of the City Beautiful movement believed that such a display of rational yet elegant form could somehow make inroads against the poverty, squalor, crime, homelessness, and political corruption that continued to afflict big cities. The persistence of these conditions showed that art and architecture alone would not—and could not—lead to urban renewal and political reform.

Complimenting this more formal classicism was the Colonial Revival movement in the United States as the twentieth century began. It stemmed from a number of factors, including a heightened sense of American patriotism, a nostalgia for what many citizens wanted to believe was a simpler and better time, and from uneasiness among old-stock Americans about massive immigration from southern and

Eastern Europe. Although the Colonial Revival was most evident in suburbs and country houses, simplified elements of it even appeared in urban row houses. Schools also embraced the style as a way of inculcating patriotism and assimilating immigrant children, and some Protestant denominations adopted it as a means of symbolizing their rejection of elaborate ritual and conveying their allegiance to a country that had strong roots in the Protestant Reformation.

The most prominent features of the Colonial Revival style were similar to original colonial structures, with simple rectangular lines, balanced doors, windows, and wings, and the use of such decorative elements as small-paned windows, triangular pediments, fluted pilasters, and lots of red brick and white paint. (In places like eastern Pennsylvania, where there was abundant building stone, many Colonial Revival structures were rendered in that material, particularly those intended to give a more informal country look.) The Colonial Revival had two main differences from its eighteenth-century model—Colonial Revival structures were likely to be larger and more spacious than their prototypes and they were frequently embellished with details, such as pilasters, urns, and doorway pediments that were much larger than existed in eighteenth-century originals.

Competing with the Colonial Revival around the turn of the century were late medieval English styles, which ranged from formal Tudor or Jacobean designs to more vernacular cottage motifs. Universities, clubs, libraries, and large suburban houses were most likely to appear in Tudor or Jacobean dress, while the cottage style was typically found in smaller though usually prosperous suburban areas. Tudor and Jacobean structures featured stucco and half timbering, nearly horizontal Gothic archways, and clear, leaded-glass windows. English-style cottages were identifiable by their steep roofs and gable ends, casement windows, and rough, undressed stone exteriors. These English styles can be linked to the same upper-class and often anti-urban sentiments that had given rise to the Colonial Revival. Many old-stock Americans who embraced these English revivals were also strong Anglophiles.

While some designers looked to the alleged order and simplicity of the past, others during the early twentieth century turned to science, technology, and efficiency studies for inspiration. Such emphases appealed to middle-income families in particular. The detached single-family dwelling was still the ideal for them, but modest means and the lack of servants called for a dwelling that was compact and easy to clean. The latest theories in domestic hygiene also demanded that households dispense with fancy, overstuffed furniture, dreamy alcoves, and irregular floor plans, which often collected dust and germs. At the same time, the high cost of modern appliances meant that the homeowner had to spend as much for plumbing, electrical wiring, central heating, and other amenities as for the basic shell of the house itself.

For many, the bungalow offered the best possible solution. The typical bungalow was a one-and-a-half story rectangular structure, often with a dormered room (running the entire length of the upper half-story), seldom exceeding 800 square feet overall. Bedrooms were small and used only for sleeping. The kitchen was equally functional, equipped with all the latest appliances for the housewife who was now considered, at least by the more advanced women's magazines, a "domestic scientist." One large room on the first floor commonly functioned as a combined living and dining area. Although the bungalow had been adapted from small cottages in India (from whence the name derived), the American version took on a variety of regional looks—from white wooden siding in the Midwest, to stucco walls and red tile roofs (Spanish Colonial) on the West Coast, to vague English Colonial treatments in the East.

The double crises of the Great Depression and World War II resulted in a long hiatus for building in the United States, first as the lack of funds and then as the paucity of building materials (during the war) made construction of any sort difficult unless it was commissioned by the government. Not until 1946 could Americans begin to replace their deteriorated building stock on a wide scale, and for the first time in the country's history, government policy played a major role in the real estate market. With the exception of public housing and resettlement projects during the Depression (and the construction of housing for the military and war workers), governments at every level had historically pursued a laissez-faire policy toward housing—or had been content with zoning ordinances and perfunctory building codes.

Toward the end of World War II, and just after it, federal legislation such as the GI Bill of Rights and the Federal Housing Act stimulated new construction through federally guaranteed mortgages. Passage of the Interstate Highway Act in 1956, coupled with federal, state, and local decisions to deemphasize mass transit, also left a tremendous imprint on housing patterns. Because federal guidelines for subsidized loans favored new construction in relatively undeveloped areas, the nation's suburbs benefited far more than its cities from these government programs. Indeed, such policies, combined with the decline of mass transit and the construction of interstate highways into and out of cities, gave a tremendous boost to suburbanization.

During this suburban boom, all but the most expensive housing had fairly uniform styles. Typical suburban dwellings thus appeared in one-story, horizontal ranch designs or along vaguely colonial lines (which had not fallen out of favor since the advent of the Colonial Revival a half-century or so before). Both the "rancher" and the colonial model were well suited for relatively cheap housing, with their simple floor plans and plain exterior lines. Both were also associated in many buyers' minds with the "authentic" American landscape during the frightening years of the Cold War, when both patriotism and assimilation into the mainstream of middle-class American life were widely touted as essential for national survival. Glaringly absent from these developments were the corner grocery store and other nearby institutions of urban neighborhoods, as most suburban communities banned all commercial establishments in residential blocks and as the automobile became the primary means of transportation for the middle class. Shopping centers and drive-in facilities of every sort developed to meet this need, from banks and beverage stores to churches and fast-food restaurants.

Meanwhile, during the postwar period, the tall office building was stripped of virtually all exterior decoration as it became a series of glass boxes stacked on top of one another. Known as the international style, this building form was thought to be independent of both time and place, and infinitely adaptable for use anywhere in the world—hence international. Within 20 years after World War II, the centers of large American cities came to resemble a series of glass-lined canyons whose walls reflected one another endlessly. Liberating at its debut, this glass and glistening metal format grew boring and predictable in the hands of second-rate architects, who seemed oblivious to playfulness, innovation, and novelty, and who treated older structures with obvious contempt. By the early 1970s a handful of designers began to recognize the human needs of the public, as well as the merits of the earlier-built environment. It was as if the era's counterculture, with its emphases upon individual expression and the surrounding environment, combined with a vigorous neoromanticism, had found an echo in the nation's newest wave of architecture.

By the end of the twentieth century a growing nostalgia for town-scale architecture, along with fears about the breakdown of the family and community, has led to a revival of porches, towers, alcoves, and bay windows, with houses themselves set close to sidewalks and streets, most notably in suburbs that had long prided themselves on privacy and distance from thoroughfares. There has also been a return to Victorian styles like the Mansard and Queen Anne, much simplified and often combined—however incongruously—with Colonial Revival motifs. As in the previous 50 years, most of this construction took place in suburbs while inner cities continued to decay and much of their older housing stock fell into ruin.

At the same time, some city governments have tried to renew their commercial centers by encouraging a new wave of tall office-building construction, commercial centers, symphony halls, and ballparks to proclaim a sense of wealth, playfulness, and exuberance that cities, at their best, have always offered visitors and more affluent residents. However attractive these new structures have been, they have been able to do little to solve the massive human suffering and antisocial behavior that continues to afflict cities, or to staunch the seemingly unending exodus of more prosperous Americans into ever more distant suburbs.

—*David R. Contosta*

See also

Balloon Frame Construction; Broadacre City; Bulfinch, Charles; Burnham, Daniel H.; Chicago School of Architecture; Jenney, William Le Baron; Kahn, Louis I.; Landscape Architecture and Urban Design; Pattern Books; Perry, Clarence Arthur; Richardson, Henry Hobson; Stein, Clarence S.; Sullivan, Louis H.

References

Andrews, Wayne. *Architecture, Ambition, and Americans*. New York: Free Press, 1978.

Baker, John Milnes. *American House Styles: A Concise Guide*. New York: W. W. Norton, 1994.

Blumenson, John J-G. *Identifying American Architecture: A Pictorial Guide to Styles and Terms, 1600–1945*. Nashville, TN: American Association for State and Local History, 1977.

Fitch, James Marston. *American Building: The Historical Forces That Shape It*. Boston: Houghton Mifflin, 1966.

Handlin, David P. *American Architecture*. New York: Thames and Hudson, 1985.

Katz, Peter. *The New Urbanism. Toward an Architecture of Community*. New York: McGraw-Hill, 1994.

McAlester, Virginia, and Lee McAlester. *A Field Guide to American Houses*. New York: Knopf, 1984.

Poppeliers, John, et al. *What Style Is It?* Washington, DC: Preservation Press, 1977.

Pratt, Dorothy, and Richard A. Pratt. *A Guide to Early American Homes*. New York: McGraw-Hill, 1956.

Roth, Leland M. *A Concise History of American Architecture*. New York: Harper & Row, 1979.

Smith, G. E. Kidder. *A Pictorial History of Architecture in America*. New York: American Heritage, 1976.

Stern, Robert A. M. *Pride of Place: Building the American Dream*. Boston: Houghton Mifflin, 1986.

Wright, Gwendolyn. *Building the Dream: A Social History of Housing in America*. New York: Pantheon, 1981.

Armory Show

The International Exhibition of Modern Art, held at the 69th Infantry Regiment Armory in New York City in 1913 and known ever since as the Armory Show, was one of the pivotal events in the spread of modernism in art. While modern European art would certainly have come to the United States without the exhibition, it served to jump-start interest in abstraction in what was, to all intents and purposes, a provincial scene.

The Armory Show, like any major art exhibition, was intimately tied to the urban environment. In a very basic way, it introduced the artistic products of one city, Paris, to the inhabitants of three American urban centers, New York, Chicago, and Boston. Without the leisure-class audiences in each city, without the cultural energy inherent to big city art districts, like Montmartre in Paris or Greenwich Village in New York, the Armory Show would not have happened.

The exhibition was organized by Arthur B. Davies, second president of the Association of American Painters and Sculptors, which had been formed in 1912 with the specific idea of putting on "national and international exhibitions of the best examples procurable of contemporary art." In the fall of 1912, Davies and the painter Walt Kuhn traveled to Europe to select work for the international contingent of the exhibition. They were aided by American artists living in Paris, especially Walter Pach, who led them on a frantic tour of Parisian studios. In a remarkably short period of time—Kuhn was in Europe for just under two months, Davies less than a month—they assembled a strong sampling of the modern art of the period.

There were gaps, to be sure. The international section of the Armory Show had a decidedly French bias with modernist innovations in Germany and Russia greatly underrepresented, while Italian Futurism and Dutch De Stijl were not represented at all. And there were inconsistencies. Much of the international section could hardly be called contemporary in 1913. Courbet, Corot, Daumier, Delacroix, and Ingres were all included, as were many of the French impressionists, at a time when Impressionism, though respected, was passé in Paris. But the Armory Show introduced Americans to father figures of modernism like Cézanne, Gauguin, Munch, Redon, Seurat, and Van Gogh, to new movements like Cubism and Fauvism, and to the latest work of the Parisian avant garde, including Constantin Brancusi, Georges Braque, Marcel Duchamp, Fernand Leger, Henri Matisse, and Pablo Picasso. It was in all respects a major event.

However, the Armory Show was neither exclusively nor primarily an exhibition of European art. Nearly two-thirds of the artists in the exhibition were Americans, and some 60 percent of the works shown were by Americans. There was, in fact, a real disparity between the contemporary French and American work represented. "Modern" art in New York in 1913 meant either Impressionism or the gritty realism of "Ash Can School" painters like Robert Henri, John Sloan, and George Bellows. It is singularly ironic that many of the impressionists and realists who made up the Association of American Painters and Sculptors would themselves be eclipsed and dated by the modern European art they helped bring to this country.

Attendance figures for the exhibition are disputed, but both New York, where at least 90,000 passed through the show, and Chicago, where 200,000 saw it, drew extremely large crowds for art events in 1913. Only the Boston run, which attracted under 13,000 visitors, was a disappointment in terms of attendance. The Armory Show was designed to appeal to young, "radical" intellectuals, and it garnered much more criticism than praise. Conservative critics like Royal Cortissoz and conservative artists of the National Academy of Design like Kenyon Cox lampooned the show. Even Theodore Roosevelt, who passed for a progressive in other times and situations, mercilessly ridiculed the exhibition. Although the show had intelligent and sensitive supporters such as the photographer Alfred Stieglitz, it was by and large a success by scandal. People came to the exhibition to see such outrageous works as Marcel Duchamp's Nude Descending a Staircase, labeled "an explosion in a shingle factory" by one critic. But scandal was the Armory Show's major achievement. Never before had an exhibition in America drawn such violent attention. In Chicago there were questions of obscenity and an attempt to hang Matisse in effigy. For one brief moment, modern art served as shock therapy to a sleepy bourgeois culture. Art challenged accepted values in a direct way that made it matter to a number of people who had not thought about it much at all before. If it did nothing else, the Armory Show still would have been important because it put art in the headlines of three major American urban centers.

—*Michael Marlais*

See also
Bellows, George; Sloan, John.
References
Brown, Milton W. *The Story of the Armory Show.* New York: Joseph H. Hirshhorn Foundation, 1963.
Green, Martin. *New York, 1913: The Armory Show and the Paterson Strike Pageant.* New York: Scribners, 1988.
Schapiro, Meyer. "The Introduction of Modern Art in America: The Armory Show." In *Modern Art 19th & 20th Centuries,* 135–178. New York: G. Braziller, 1978. Originally published as "Rebellion in Art." In Daniel Aaron, ed., *America in Crisis.* New York: Knopf, 1952.

Armour, Philip Danforth (1832–1901)

Philip Armour, American agro-industrialist and commodity speculator, founded Armour and Company in 1870. In an age of industrialization and in a region that was becoming a hotbed of innovative mechanization, Armour integrated a series of key industrial technologies in grain storage and meat processing to create the modern meatpacking industry.

Armour's first business success occurred during the California gold rush. He then moved to Milwaukee to invest in a grain elevator business and later in pork processing to supply westbound settlers. Armour moved to Chicago in 1875, the same year as Gustavus Swift, his main corporate rival. Philip and his brother Simeon entered the fresh beef industry in 1882, and in 1883 the brothers were the first to introduce mechanical refrigeration and later to use a laboratory to process meat by-products into chemical compounds such as pepsin. They incorporated their business in 1884 and led the industry in expanding outside Chicago with a beef plant in Kansas City. By 1886 Armour and Company was second only to Swift among Chicago-based meatpackers with one-quarter of total meat output.

Armour and Company was more vertically integrated and diversified than most packers. In addition to fresh beef and pork, it also manufactured a wide range of processed meats such as sausage, and it converted by-products to lard, oleomargarine, fertilizer, gelatin, and glue. Armour also expanded into the shipment and marketing of grain and California citrus fruit. By 1891, he owned six grain elevators and controlled nearly one-third of Chicago's grain trade.

The strength of Armour was in logistics, not the manufacturing process itself; Armour once claimed that he had never held a knife in his hand. "If you showed me a piece of meat I could not tell you what part of the bullock it came from." The key to success in Chicago's nascent packing industry lay in controlling transportation and distribution. Like other big packers, Armour owned hundreds of refrigerator cars for the eastbound shipment of fresh carcasses. In addition, he built a network of "branch houses" to wholesale the full line of fresh and processed meats in major urban centers. Armour also inaugurated "peddler cars" in 1887, which were essentially branch houses on rails to service smaller centers.

Famed for petty philanthropy (he gave away dollar bills) and more substantial charitable initiatives (Armour Mission and Armour Institute of Technology), Philip Armour was no friend of organized labor. In reaction to the advent of the eight-hour day in meatpacking, and following Chicago's 1886 Haymarket Riot, he was a leader in organizing the National Independent Meatpackers Association, which soon forced a return to the ten-hour working day.

Armour is significant as one of the vanguard of merchant capitalists turned industrialists and financiers who created the enterprise and employment that drove the growth of the Midwest's manufacturing heartland. He had a span of control over his business empire that was new to the agro-industrial sector, a full half-century prior to the recognition of the hegemony of the multinational corporation. One nineteenth-century magazine writer marveled over Armour's global span of control, market intelligence, and use of state-of-the-art communication technology (the telegraph) in the strategic management of his enterprise.

Toward the end of his life, the ethics and sanitation of Armour's meat enterprise were brought into question by the "embalmed beef scandal," which concerned the quality of meat served to American troops during the Spanish-American War. Complaints about price fixing by a series of cartels led to government scrutiny and a review of competitive practices. Public outcry and the ensuing political furor set the stage for unprecedented regulation of private enterprise in the form of the Meat Inspection Act and the Sherman Antitrust Act (1890). Five years after Philip Armour's death in 1901, Armour and Company became the principal corporate villain in Upton Sinclair's classic muckraking novel, *The Jungle*. Armour Meats remained a significant player in the industry until 1970 when it was acquired by the Greyhound conglomerate and gradually disintegrated.

—*Ian MacLachlan*

References

Cronon, William. *Nature's Metropolis: Chicago and the Great West.* New York: W. W. Norton, 1991.

Davenport, Cora Lillian. "The Rise of the Armours, an American Industrial Family." M.A. thesis, University of Chicago, 1930.

Leech, Harper, and John Charles Carroll. *Armour and His Times.* Freeport, NY: Books for Libraries Press, 1938.

Skaggs, Jimmy M. *Prime Cut: Livestock Raising and Meatpacking in the United States, 1607–1983.* College Station: Texas A & M University Press, 1986.

Wade, Louise Carroll. *Chicago's Pride: The Stockyards, Packingtown, and Environs in the Nineteenth Century.* Urbana: University of Illinois Press, 1987.

Warren, Arthur, "Philip D. Armour." *McClure's Magazine* 2 (1894): 260–280.

Armstrong, Louis (1900–1971)

Louis Armstrong, American's leading virtuoso jazz trumpeter, was born in New Orleans. He learned to play cornet in the Colored Waifs' Home, a reform school to which he was sent for firing a gun at the New Year's Day parade of 1913. He led the boys' band there, and after he was released Joseph "King" Oliver, his idol, gave him cornet lessons.

At that time, jazz had an unsavory reputation as the music played in the New Orleans red light district, Storyville. But musicians like Armstrong brought jazz north to Kansas City, Chicago, Detroit, and New York in the 1920s. Jazz put the roar in Roaring Twenties, and it gained respectability when popular singers like Bing Crosby and big bands and swing orchestras adopted the style.

In 1917 Armstrong's career expanded when he joined Kid Ory's band and then exploded in 1922 when he connected up with King Oliver's Creole Jazz Band in Chicago. Known as "Dippermouth" and "Satchelmouth" (or "Satchmo"), he introduced scat singing by using his husky voice as an emotive musical instrument to sing nonsense words in place of lyrics. By 1925, he had joined Erskine Tate's orchestra as a trumpeter and formed his own band, first called the Hot Five and then the Hot Seven, making popular records with the best jazz and blues singers of the era. Armstrong's instinctive musical talent led him to mellow the jazz brass sound and to use improvisation in delicate melodies and solo riffs with his sure tones, joyous quality, and comic stage sense.

Louis Armstrong belting it out in the 1944 motion picture Atlantic City.

By 1930, his appearances in movies had expanded his reputation as a comic, and on a tour of Europe he played for England's King George VI. By 1947 he was accepted as an American genius, even playing at Boston's prestigious Symphony Hall, later releasing a recording of the concert, "Satchmo at Symphony Hall" (Decca, 1951). In 1956 he again toured Europe and also Africa. His best-known songs include "Savoy Blues," "Chinatown Tiger Rag," "Tight Like That," "Potato Head Blues," "When It's Sleepy Time Down South," "I Can't Give You Anything But Love," "Ain't Misbehavin'," "C'est si bon," "I'll Walk Alone," "Do You Know What It Means to Miss New Orleans," "Hello Dolly," and his own compositions, "Sister Kate" and "If We Never Meet Again."

Armstrong's movies include *Pennies from Heaven* (1936), *Satchmo the Great* (1956), *The Five Pennies* (1959), and *Hello, Dolly* (1969). Satchmo was a goodwill ambassador bringing American music around the world, and his career spanned the music of Scott Joplin, Jelly Roll Morton, Bessie Smith, and Robert Johnson. Although his movie appearances and stage persona eclipsed his role as an innovative jazz musician, Armstrong was the Joe Louis of music, a champion to African Americans and a hero to millions around the world. When he died in New York City in 1971, he was a beloved figure in the international entertainment industry and an influential American trumpeter and singer of the first caliber.

—*Peter C. Holloran*

See also
Jazz; New Orleans, Louisiana.
References
Armstrong, Louis. *Satchmo: My Life in New Orleans.* New York: Prentice-Hall, 1954.
Bergreen, Laurence. *Louis Armstrong: An Extravagant Life.* New York: Broadway Books, 1997.
Collier, James Lincoln. *Louis Armstrong: An American Genius.* New York: Oxford University Press, 1983.
Giddins, Gary. *Satchmo.* New York: Doubleday, 1988.
Jones, Max. *Louis: The Louis Armstrong Story.* Boston: Little, Brown, 1971.
Meryman, Richard. *Louis Armstrong—A Self-Portrait.* New York: Eakins Press, 1971.

Artisans

Artisans in America date back to the first settlement at Jamestown in 1607 as the London Company expected that the riches it would find in America would require the services of goldsmiths, perfumers, and the like. While the company never found treasure, artisans remained an integral part of American society from the early seventeenth century to the mid- or late nineteenth century. Nor have they, of course, disappeared, as can be seen from both local craft shows and the variety of handmade goods available to contemporary consumers.

Artisans also went by the names of *mechanic* and *craftsman.* If retailers, they would also be known as tradesmen, though this distinction had disappeared by the eighteenth century in America. The most common definition of an artisan was a skilled handicraftsman who owned his own tools and worked for himself or as a foreman for a merchant or contractor (in which case he was a master craftsman) or who worked for a wage (in which case he was a journeyman). Those in training to become mechanics were apprenticed to masters and worked from age 13 to 21 in return for learning the "mystery" of the craft as well as for room and board, clothing, and some general education.

The American artisan emerged from a strong English tradition in which artisans occupied a position above the large number of tenant farmers but well below that of gentlemen. The necessity of working with one's hands lowered a man's standing in British society to a level requiring deference to the better bred, better educated, and more wealthy. Samuel Johnson's famed dictionary, for example, characterized mechanic as "mean, servile, of mean occupation."

From the colonial era on, American artisans could be found in both rural and urban settings in both the North and South. Those in rural settings often did other jobs as well, including agriculture, practicing their craft largely during the winter. They also tended to be generalists, doing various tasks with wood or iron that would be divided in a city.

Artisans were most noticeable in urban settings. They composed the bulk of the urban population, generally between

50 and 60 percent. They occupied a middling position in both social and economic status, below merchants and professionals and above unskilled laborers, free blacks, and slaves. They wore distinct dress, most notably the leather aprons that symbolized artisan standing. They belonged to their own societies, had their own work hours (usually 12 to 14 hours a day with meal breaks), and maintained a unique identity at least as strong as ethnic or religious affiliation.

Mechanics worked in a panoply of different occupations that had their own standing within the craft community. At the top were such elite professions as silversmithing, goldsmithing, and watchmaking. These required exquisite skills and catered to the very top of society. In the middle were the many crafts that formed the lifeblood of the city: construction trades (carpenters, masons), shipbuilding (shipwrights, riggers, rope makers), food and tobacco processing (butchers, bakers, tobacconists), furniture making (chair makers, upholsterers), forging (blacksmiths, coppersmiths), and transportation (cart men). At the bottom were two of the most populous trades, shoemaking and tailoring.

The colonial era has generally been thought of as the "golden age" of the craftsman. That is, the number in each city was adequate but not greater than the need. Mobility was thus common, and an apprentice could expect to earn journeyman standing, perhaps traveling like Benjamin Franklin to another city, in no more than five to ten years. Then he would open his own shop and practice his trade, assisted by one or two apprentices and journeymen and his wife and family, for the rest of his working life. He would generally own his dwelling, with the store in the front and living quarters in the back facing a yard and an alley where he kept his cow and pig and privy. As an independent entrepreneur, he would make an adequate living, enough to be able to retire at the end of his working days in a modest competence. Moreover, he was able to make goods of high skill "to order," working at his own pace. However, for the poorer trades, this was not likely by the mid-eighteenth century, as many tailors and shoemakers could not often become master craftsmen and even those who did lived near poverty.

The situation worsened after the American Revolution. While financial horizons brightened with the lifting of British mercantile restrictions, the opening of international markets, and the expansion of national markets, this "business revolution" also meant that masters had to orient themselves to the issue of profit and loss. The craft shop became less a family enterprise than a modern business. Journeymen and even apprentices were less likely to live with the master; apprentices left their indentures before they expired. Fewer journeymen achieved master craftsman status in the larger trades, including printing, construction (which employed about two-fifths of the journeymen in American cities), and

furniture making, along with shoemaking and tailoring. With the influx of immigrant labor during the Jacksonian Era, the journeyman's position deteriorated into sweatshop conditions as intense competition among manufacturers, along with the expanding labor pool, forced artisans into the position of semiskilled laborers.

Nevertheless, some American artisans played significant roles in the development of urban business, labor, and politics. As entrepreneurs, they were highly inventive in the use of advertisement, aggressively sought banking capital from often reluctant merchants, founded their own banks, formed joint stock companies and cooperatives to purchase supplies in the building and forging crafts, and were adept at workshop organization. Too, they organized to lobby for tariff protection and other governmental support. The more aggressive and ambitious tradesmen saw the American Revolution as providing not only political but also economic independence.

Artisans originated the American labor movement. Particularly after the Revolution, when they found the road to advancement increasingly more difficult, journeymen organized into craft societies. These were different from traditional English societies that were organized by masters to control prices and market conditions and gain prestige and social security (which some American masters did attempt to form), but rather they were intended to allow journeymen to maintain their place in the new market. By demanding that all members of a craft belong to their society, they attempted to negotiate as a unit with master craftsmen, threatening to walk out on any master who did not meet their wage demands or who employed nonsociety craftsmen. The early nineteenth century was replete with labor actions by journeymen, including strikes and attempts by journeymen to open their own shops. Journeymen societies were intensely democratic, with detailed constitutions as well as provisions for death and disability benefits. They also provided recreation and prestige.

Artisans were active in politics from the colonial era on. With suffrage granted to craftsmen who operated their own business, candidates for colonial assemblies had to appeal to artisan concerns, and their votes could make the difference as to which faction prevailed. During the Revolution the mechanic interest came into its own. Through mechanics' committees, as the journeymen societies were now known, artisans fully shared in the governance of New York and Philadelphia and were active in Charleston. In Boston, they were at the heart of the Sons of Liberty. They were far more radical than the merchant community both in the demand for immediate independence and for democratic provisions in new state constitutions. They remained active after the Revolution as strong supporters of the federal government and its ability to implement tariff protection and strengthen the union of states.

Following independence, artisans became a pillar of the new Jeffersonian Democratic-Republican Party even though artisans sometimes seemed to favor policies, like the protective tariff, pressed by the Federalists. The Jeffersonians prevailed in large part because of their ability to recognize and address artisan needs. These included economic concerns, but equally important, recognition of craftsmen as full-fledged citizens. Unlike the opposition Federalists, who demanded deference and did not expect mechanics to run for office or oppose their policies, Jeffersonians put artisans on their tickets and reversed the centuries-long tradition of the mechanic as a second-class citizen.

A large majority of craftsmen accounted for Jefferson's victory in New York and thus his election to the presidency in 1800. Political activity remained strong thereafter as artisans generally stayed loyal to the Democratic Party. After the election of 1828, a number split off into workingmen's parties, reflecting their loss of standing with the advent of large-scale immigration and harsh working conditions. While these parties had brief lives because of internal divisions, as the largest single voting bloc mechanics remained central to urban politics. Craftsmen developed an ideology of "artisan republicanism" that stressed the central role of the producer in the well-being of the state. They emphasized the cooperative yet independent spirit of the workshop as a model for the new nation. At the same time that they held on to classical republican ideals of a cooperative society, mechanics were equally at home with the liberal ideals of capitalist independence or the right of journeymen to organize freely in the marketplace to secure their economic standing.

At least until the Civil War, artisans were the most critical political and economic force in American cities. They were fundamental in the development of American politics, American labor, and American business.

—Howard Rock

See also
Apprenticeship.
References
Bridenbaugh, Carl. *The Colonial Craftsman*. Chicago: University of Chicago Press, 1950.
Rock, Howard B. *Artisans of the New Republic: The Tradesmen of New York City in the Age of Jefferson*. New York: New York University Press, 1979.
Smith, Billie G. *"The Lower Sort:" Philadelphia's Laboring People, 1750–1800*. Ithaca, NY: Cornell University Press, 1990.
Stott, Richard B. *Workers in the Metropolis: Class, Ethnicity and Youth in Antebellum New York*. Ithaca, NY: Cornell University Press, 1990.
Wilentz, Sean. *Chants Democratic: New York City and the Rise of the American Working Class, 1788–1850*. New York: Oxford University Press, 1984.

Asian Americans in Cities

Asian immigrants, like other immigrants in modern America, have been more concentrated in cities than most Americans. In addition, urban Asians have tended to settle in distinctive neighborhood clusters or enclaves. What has made Asian urban patterns somewhat different from those of other immigrants has been the long persistence of some of those neighborhoods, once established. No other ethnic neighborhood in America has lasted as long as San Francisco's Chinatown, which is still centered where Chinese settled in the 1850s. Yet, just as there are clear distinctions to be made between different groups of European immigrants—or immigrant groups from the Western Hemisphere or Africa for that matter—similar kinds of distinctions can be made between the settlement patterns of the various Asian immigrant and ethnic groups from the mid-nineteenth century right up to the end of the twentieth.

These ethnic groups will be considered in two different ways—by ethnic group and by period. Given the variety of Asian-American urban experiences, it is appropriate to treat the major ethnic groups separately, although patterns similar to all immigrants and to all or most Asian immigrants will be noted. Given the great changes in American immigration law, many groups need to be examined twice, once for the period before World War II and then for the postwar era. In the latter period there are more Asian-American groups, and their incidence in the population has increased sharply.

Chinese Americans to 1940

Numerically significant immigration of Chinese to the United States began shortly after the United States annexed California in 1848. At the time of the Chinese Exclusion Act of 1882, there were probably about 125,000 Chinese in the United States, some two-thirds of them in California and more than 90 percent in the American West. During this period, the Chinese, like many other immigrant groups, became not only predominantly urban, but large-city urban. But, unlike most other urban-centered ethnic groups, the Chinese moved to large cities after first settling in small towns and rural areas. In 1880, for example, only 21.7 percent of Chinese lived in cities of over 100,000; this percentage increased with every census. By 1910 almost half of Chinese Americans lived in such cities, and by 1940 more than 70 percent did. Initially, large city meant San Francisco, which the Chinese called *dai fou* or big city. By 1940, however, only about a third of large-city Chinese Americans lived in San Francisco (17,782 of 55,030), with another 3,201 across the bay in Oakland. Seven other large cities had more than 1,000 Chinese that year: there were 12,203 in New York, nearly 5,000 in Los Angeles, and just over 2,000 in Chicago. Seattle, Portland, Oregon, Sacramento, and Boston each had between 1,000 and 2,000 Chinese.

Much that has been written about the early Chinese-American community assumes that all Chinese were common laborers, but in reality the community was highly structured and class-differentiated from its earliest days. This may best be seen by examining San Francisco. During much of the pre–World War II era, about every fifth Chinese American called San Francisco home. The bay city's supremacy was not just numerical. It was the cultural, economic, and administrative center of Chinese America, the entrepot through which goods and services were distributed, the communication center not only for the spreading Chinese diaspora within America, but also between the New World and the Old.

The merchants and entrepreneurs who dominated San Francisco's Chinatown developed a whole range of activities. As early as 1876, the city directory contained nine double-columned pages of what it called Chinese business houses, followed by an alphabetical list arranged by types of businesses. These included an asylum, bakers, barbers, butchers, carpenters, carvers and engravers, a cheese manufacturer, clothing manufacturers, drug stores, dry goods stores, employment offices, grocery stores, hotels, interpreters, Japanese and Chinese fancy goods, watchmakers and jewelers, many laundries spread all over town, lodging houses, merchants, a purveyor of opium, a painter, pawnbrokers, a photographer, physicians, restaurants, a shirt manufacturer, shoemakers, a silk factory, slipper manufacturers, tailors, two theaters, tinsmiths, umbrella and fan makers, variety stores, and wood and lumber dealers.

The merchants who ran Chinese San Francisco organized what came to be called the Chinese Consolidated Benefit Association—the so-called Six Companies—which had branches all over Chinese America. The CCBAs had two distinct sides. On the one hand, they performed truly benevolent functions, and that aspect of their activities may properly be compared to the myriad immigrant protective associations that flourished all over ethnic America. On the other hand, they operated not only to enhance the economic gains of the merchants but also to exercise significant social control over most Chinese Americans.

In the first capacity, the organized merchants acted as the voice of the community. As early as 1853, the heads of the companies testified before a hostile committee of the California legislature. Later, they hired prominent Caucasian attorneys to speak for them. Company agents met incoming ships from China, arranged to house and employ the newcomers, provided medical care for the sick, and sent the bones of the dead to China for burial. In an age before the social service state, the Six Companies and the benevolent organizations of other ethnic groups all over America performed many of its functions.

But parallel to this benevolence was the self-serving function. There were no free lunches in Chinese America. The merchants were entrepreneurs with fingers in many pies. The most successful of them probably came with significant amounts of capital and had ties to established mercantile houses in China. Merchants' income came from a wide variety of sources, including normal international trade, purveying exotic and indigenous commodities to the Chinese community, importing opium both before and after it became illegal, advancing money to would-be immigrants under the "credit ticket" system, and acting as labor contractors. One group of merchants not only provided up to 10,000 laborers at a time to the Union and Central Pacific Railroads—reportedly at a rate of $1 a man per month—but also profited from contracts to provide rice and other commodities to those workers. The merchants also used the associations to ensure that individuals settled their debts and paid their share of the cost of the welfare system. Every Chinese who returned to China was supposed to be checked at the dock to make sure that he owed nothing to his Chinese creditors. While the system was certainly not 100 percent efficient, its continuance over decades suggests that it was more than marginally effective. And, since the overwhelming number of Chinese in America thought of themselves as sojourners and wanted to return to China, any system that could affect that return was an ideal mechanism for social control.

By 1940, the largely metropolitan Chinese-American population had not been replenished by sizable new legal immigration for more than half a century. In that year's census, for the first time, citizen Chinese outnumbered aliens, who, like other Asians, were ineligible for naturalization, and the gender ratio, which had been as high as 26 males for every female in 1890, had dropped below 3 males for every female.

Japanese Americans to 1940

Japanese immigrants began to come to the United States in significant numbers in the 1890s, and even though immigration was curtailed by the Gentlemen's Agreement of 1907–1908 and stopped by the Immigration Act of 1924, the Japanese-American population continued to grow steadily because of the relatively large number of women and high rate of family formation. By 1920, more than one-third of the Japanese-American population was female (34.5 percent); consequently, by 1940 more than three-fifths were native born (62.7 percent).

Although by 1940 a slight majority of Japanese Americans (54.8 percent) lived in cities, the real locus of Japanese America was agrarian as many city dwellers were involved in market gardening and in the distribution and sale of the produce of Japanese agriculture. This had not always been the case. The first enduring Japanese-American communities were small urban enclaves in West Coast cities. In 1896 the perhaps 100 Japanese in Los Angeles ran at least 16 restaurants serving 10- and 15-cent meals to workingmen. Even after the economic focus of Japanese America had shifted to agriculture, West Coast cities continued to be the community's cultural centers. Although most of the important ethnic organizations were centered in San Francisco, Los Angeles soon became the largest city of Japanese America, and Seattle took second place. These and other West Coast cities were home to thriving enclaves with a very large number of petty entrepreneurs called Japan towns—*nihonmachi* in Japanese. (The American-born Nisei would later refer to them as "J-towns.")

Much of the lucrative foreign trade was in the hands of the so-called *kaisha,* the overseas branches of large Japanese trading companies, such as Mitsubishi and Company (*Mitsubishi Shoji Kaisha*). Japanese immigrant-labor contractors functioned as their Chinese predecessors had done. Shinzaburo Ban (1854–1926), a college graduate and former employee of the Japanese foreign office, established S. Ban and Company in Portland in 1891. He provided workers to railroads and other enterprises; opened a general store with branches in Denver, Sheridan, Wyoming, and Tokyo; and operated a shingle company and a lumber mill. At one time he had 3,000 employees.

Most Japanese entrepreneurs, like their counterparts in other contemporary ethnic groups, were small-scale operators. In Seattle, for example, Japanese operated hundreds of small businesses, most of which served a regional ethnic population of some 14,000 in the 1930s. The great exception was the hotel business; a survey conducted in 1935 showed 183 Japanese-owned hotels, most of them near Seattle's Skid Road, that catered to white workingmen. Los Angeles's "Little Tokyo," an area centering around East First Street in the city's downtown, was the nation's largest *nihonmachi.* Most of the city's Japanese residents lived within a three-mile radius.

Yet the ethnic economy of Los Angeles was predominantly agricultural, centering on the marketing of Japanese-grown produce. The most impressive operations were in the City Market, where the largest ethnic produce houses grossed over $1 million annually. Daily market sheets and radio broadcasts of market prices were published and aired in Japanese.

The key organization of the immigrant generation was the San Francisco–based Japanese Association of America, which had local branches wherever there were significant Japanese populations. The impetus for its formation had come from the Japanese government, and Japanese consuls and consuls-general played key roles in its organization, operation, and finances. Immigrants who needed to do business with the Japanese government usually did so through the nearest association; the most crucial service they provided was getting passports for family members, including the famous "picture brides." Like the Chinese Six Companies, the associations were an effective instrument for social control.

By 1940, Japanese Americans, still mainly centered on the Pacific Coast, seemed to be making a transition from a largely immigrant community of aliens to one that would be led by a native-born generation—from the first generation, or Issei, to the second generation, or Nisei.

Other Asians in Prewar America

Significant numbers of three other Asian ethnic groups were present in the continental United States before 1940—about 5,000 each of Koreans and Asian Indians, and 45,000 Filipinos. Only the latter group had a noticeable urban presence. Some two-thirds of Filipinos (67.4 percent) lived in California, with only about 6 percent of them female. Most worked as migrant laborers in California's "factories in the fields," or as casual urban laborers. Few followed entrepreneurial pursuits, although ethnic enclaves, often called "Little Manilas," developed in such agricultural centers as Stockton, California, and there were small Filipino communities in Los Angeles, San Francisco, and Seattle.

Tiny Filipino communities also developed in a few midwestern cities. Most notable was Chicago, where many Filipinos worked as Pullman porters and in the post office. These tended to be young men who had come to the United States to go to college but who had never managed to graduate; many formed families with second-generation European women.

The Impact of World War II

The most obvious and immediate impact of the war was the destruction and dispersion of the West Coast Japanese-American community, most of whose residents were incarcerated in concentration camps. The war returned prosperity to the United States and also, although it was difficult to recognize at the time, began the reversal of the racist immigration policies that had excluded all Asian immigrants (except Filipinos) after 1924 and prevented all of them from being naturalized. The change began with the repeal of the Chinese Exclusion Acts in 1943, which not only gave Chinese a small quota of immigrants annually but made them eligible for naturalization. Similar legislation was enacted for Filipinos and Asian Indians in 1946, and in 1952 the otherwise nativist McCarran-Walter Act dropped all ethnic and racial barriers to naturalization. The earlier changes can be categorized as good behavior prizes stemming from World War II; the 1952 action was an offshoot of the Cold War, as even most nativists realized that the United States could hardly claim "leadership of the Free World" when the country's immigration policy barred so many of the world's peoples. Major immigration reform, following postwar recommendations made by President Harry S. Truman, came only as part of Lyndon Johnson's Great Society in 1965.

Postwar Asian America

The first large-scale postwar Asian-American migration was the return to the West Coast of most of the Japanese Americans incarcerated in "internment camps" somewhat inland, but many never went back. In 1940, 88.5 percent had lived in the three Pacific states; in 1950, only 69.3 percent did. Almost all of the 30,000 Japanese who then lived east of the mountain states were urban Americans; but even in their largest new center, Chicago, where some 11,000 now lived, there was nothing even resembling a "J-town." Of those who returned to the West Coast, more lived in cities than before, as many had lost their land. In 1940, 41.4 percent of West Coast Japanese Americans had been employed in agriculture; by 1950 this had fallen to 32.5 percent, and by 1960, in California, only 20.9 percent were so employed.

Postwar Japanese Americans were thus highly urban, but their residences were now much more widely dispersed. Most did not live in the remaining Japan towns, although a minority did begin to form suburban clusters, as in Gardena, a sub-urb of Los Angeles. The core of Los Angeles's old Little Tokyo is still Japanese, but it now features a luxury hotel and the Japanese American National Museum, and it is more of a tourist attraction than an ethnic enclave. Although there has been some immigration from Japan, most of the growth in the Japanese-American population—from 126,000 in 1940 to 847,000 in 1990—stems from one of two factors, the inclusion of the Hawaiian population after statehood in 1959 or natural increase. Hawaii is the only state without a Euro-American majority; Honolulu is about 60 percent Asian/Pacific American, and many of Hawaii's smaller cities and rural areas have even higher concentrations. The addition of Hawaii's Japanese Americans more than doubled the Japanese-American population figure in 1960.

But the vast majority of the more than 7 million Asian Americans reported in the 1990 census, when Asian Americans constituted nearly 3 percent of the total population, is predominantly the result of post–World War II and Cold War immigration patterns. Immigration from Asia, both absolute and relative, has grown steadily during this period. In the 1960s, it amounted to about 12 percent of all legal immigration and 34 percent in the 1970s. During the period 1981 to

A newsstand in New York displays Chinese- and English-language papers.

1889, 42 percent of all legally admitted immigrants to the United States came from Asia, another 42 percent came from Latin America, and only 11 percent came from Europe. There is every reason to believe that the Asian component of our immigration will shrink, at least in the foreseeable future, but it has been the major factor in Asian-American population growth since 1965.

Nearly two-thirds (65.6 percent) of the 7.3 million Asian Americans enumerated in the 1990 census were born in Asia, and, of the native-born third, more than half are the children of postwar immigrants. It is important to compare the 3 percent of the population that the 1990 Asian Americans represented with the 0.7 percent of the population they represented as recently as 1970, a fourfold increase in just two decades. Were the same thing to happen in the next 20 years—it almost certainly will not—Asian Americans would be nearly 12 percent of the population in 2010. Today, almost all Asian Americans live in urban or suburban areas, and most are still concentrated in the Far West, although there are members of most Asian-American groups in every state in the union and some Asian Americans in almost every county.

In 1990 nearly two-fifths (39.1 percent) of all Asian Americans lived in California, as one would expect, but the second state in its number of Asians was New York, followed by Hawaii, Texas, Illinois, New Jersey, Washington, Virginia, Florida, Massachusetts, Maryland, Pennsylvania, and Michigan. Those thirteen states, only three of them "traditional" homes of Asian Americans, accounted for 84.6 percent of all Asian Americans. For all of the groups, save Asian Indians, about one-third or more lived in California and at least two-fifths in the Far West. All of the Southeast Asian refugee groups were highly concentrated in California.

As is to be expected from their growing number, many of the post–World War II immigrants have had visible impacts on American cities. Chinese immigrants have expanded existing Chinatowns, particularly in San Francisco and New York. In the latter city, a second Chinatown has been created in the borough of Queens, once almost exclusively the home of white ethnics. Even more striking has been the development of what Timothy Fong has called "the first suburban Chinatown" in Monterey Park, California, in the San Gabriel Valley just east of Los Angeles. This community, which had just 1,113 Asian residents (2.9 percent) in 1960, had 34,022 Asians (56 percent) in 1990. And while Chinese Americans were the largest single group of Asians (63 percent), Monterey Park also had a sizable Japanese-American community of 6,081 (17.4 percent) and significant numbers of other Asian-American ethnic groups. These inhabitants were largely middle-class professionals and entrepreneurs. Similar patterns can be seen all over the San Gabriel Valley; at least nine other suburban entities have, in the last dozen years or so,

achieved percentages of Asian-American residents ranging from 16.3 to 37.4.

This suburban pattern, first established by the movement of Japanese Americans to Gardena (near Los Angeles) after they returned from the camps, is being repeated today by other ethnic groups. Filipino Americans, for example, are flocking to Daly City, just south of San Francisco; between 1983 and 1990, 4,036 persons from the Philippines told the Immigration and Naturalization Service that their destination was zip code 94015, and many others found their way there later. In the same period, 3,688 Vietnamese reported an intention to emigrate to two Orange County zip codes. This pattern has been repeated in many other places.

This interesting new pattern of suburban enclaves filled with well-educated and relatively prosperous immigrants should not obscure the fact that most Asian immigrants do not fit this model. The majority still go to large cities, and many of them are the traditional exploited proletarians, like the women Chinese garment workers of whom Xiaolan Bao has written. The large cities, too, are the home of many prosperous and not so prosperous entrepreneurs. The most visible example of this pattern is the Koreatown that sprawls along Olympic Boulevard near downtown Los Angeles, not too far from Little Tokyo and Chinatown. This area contained, just before the disastrous "Rodney King" riots of 1991, perhaps 10,000 businesses of all kinds that catered both to the Korean-American community and, more and more, to the blacks and Hispanics who constitute the majority of the population in the area and the immediately surrounding vicinity. Highly publicized conflicts between Korean storekeepers and their underclass customers have occurred not only in Los Angeles but also in New York, Philadelphia, and Chicago. In those cities, Korean Americans have specialized as greengrocers, filling a useful niche. Less conflict ridden, and also somewhat less prosperous, is the Vietnamese "Little Saigon" that has developed in Westminster in Orange County near Los Angeles.

Most of the immigrants from Southeast Asia fit a third model; they are refugees, a by-product of the misbegotten American war there. (Thais, who numbered 91,360 in 1990, are the major exception to this generalization.) While some, such as the former South Vietnamese leader, Nguyen Cao Ky, came with significant assets—he now operates a thriving liquor store–delicatessen in Alexandria, Virginia—most are ill-prepared for success in modern America. In 1989, for example, 23.8 percent of Vietnamese families, 32.2 percent of Laotian families, 42.1 percent of Cambodian families, and 61.8 percent of Hmong families lived below the poverty line. These grim statistics belie the "success" stories—like that of the Vietnamese girl who wins a spelling bee—which the American media, conditioned to Horatio Alger and the melting pot, delight in airing. Using family and household income data, many have hailed the Asian-American success story, but if one looks at per capita income, it is clear that Asian Americans earn a little below the national norm. Data show that per capita income for all Asian Americans averaged $13,806 as opposed to $14,444 for all other Americans. Income for individual ethnic groups ranged from $19,373 for Japanese individuals to $17,777 for Asian Indians, $14,877 for Chinese, $13,616 for Filipinos, $11,970 for Thais, $11,178 for Koreans, $9,033 for Vietnamese, $5,597 for Laotians, $5,121 for Cambodians, and an almost incredible $2,692 for Hmong.

Many critics of the new, multicultural America deplore the tendency of immigrant/ethnic groups to cluster in enclaves where they rub shoulders with what they regard as their own kind, forgetting that this has always been the case. The reasons for this have not changed. If we listen to Chinese Americans over the years we find them saying the same thing. In Chicago, in the 1920s, for example, an immigrant told Ching-Chao Wu that:

> Most of us can live a warmer, freer and a more human life among our relatives and friends than among strangers. . . . Chinese relations with the population outside Chinatown are likely to be cold, formal and commercial. It is only in Chinatown that a Chinese immigrant has society, friends and relatives who share his dreams and hopes, his hardships, and adventures. Here he can tell a joke and make everyone laugh with him; here he may hear folktales told which create the illusion that Chinatown is really China.

Similarly, a recent Chinese immigrant woman who went to an American university and works for the state of California explained to Timothy Fong:

> Monterey Park is a good place for new immigrants. . . . Chinese stores and restaurants make this place so convenient for Chinese people. . . . It's just like their own home. . . . You don't have to speak English to live here.

—*Roger Daniels*

See also
Chinatown.
References
Chan, Sucheng. *Asian Americans: An Interpretive History.* Boston: Twayne, 1991.
Daniels, Roger. *Asian America: Chinese and Japanese in the United States since 1850.* Seattle: University of Washington Press, 1988.
Kim, Illsoo. *New Urban Immigrants: The Korean Community in New York.* Princeton, NJ: Princeton University Press, 1981.
Kitano, Harry H. L., and Roger Daniels. *Asian Americans: Emerging Minorities.* 2d ed. Englewood Cliffs, NJ: Prentice-Hall, 1992.
Modell, John. *The Economics and Politics of Racial Accommodation: The Japanese of Los Angeles, 1900–1942.* Urbana: University of Illinois Press, 1969.
Posadas, Barbara, and Roland L. Guyotte. "Aspiration and Reality: Occupational and Educational Choice among Filipino Migrants to Chicago, 1900–1935." *Illinois Historical Journal* 85 (1992): 89–104.
Takaki, Ronald. *Strangers from a Different Shore: A History of Asian Americans.* Boston: Little, Brown, 1989.
Taylor, Quintard. "Blacks and Asians in a White City: Japanese Americans and African Americans in Seattle, 1890–1940." *Western Historical Quarterly* 22 (1991): 401–429.
Yu, Renqui. *To Save China, to Save Ourselves: The Chinese Hand Laundry Alliance of New York.* Philadelphia: Temple University Press, 1992.
Yung, Judy. *Unbound Feet: A Social History of Chinese Women in San Francisco.* Berkeley: University of California Press, 1995.

Attitudes toward Cities

The founding of new cities in the New World, the explosive growth of the urban sector during the nineteenth and early twentieth centuries, and the interplay between processes of urban decay and efforts at renewal in subsequent decades have given rise to a wide range of commentary and reflection. From their inception, cities have elicited from contemporary observers a multitude of intellectual efforts to make sense of social and cultural changes, which, though by no means confined to the urban milieu, could be detected more clearly there than anywhere else, and American cities have aroused at least as much interest as cities in any other country.

It would be misleading in the extreme to suggest that there has been a basic attitude toward cities in America. The attitudes that have been expressed have often conflicted with one another, reflecting not only the differing professions and politics of those who have held them but also differences among specific places about which they have written and differences between particular periods. There has certainly been a good deal of anxiety about and disaffection from urban ways of life. But such sentiments have found expression in a dialectical relationship, not only with urban growth itself and all the challenges that have resulted from it but also with a variety of opinions according to which it was less these problems than a whole host of urban opportunities that most merited attention. Like modernity in general, for which it has frequently stood as an emotionally potent symbol, the (big) city has been the subject of continuing controversy and disagreement.

During roughly the first two centuries of the American experience, when the overwhelming majority of Americans still lived in small villages and on the land, there were only faint stirrings of interest in urban themes—few of which even began to approach the levels of intensity and generality that characterized urban discourse in later years. Throughout the colonial period and well beyond, American cities had not yet become large enough or problematic enough to engender widespread debates about the virtues and vices of urbanization or about the relative merits of city and countryside as places in which to live the good life.

The voices that were raised were on the whole more positive than negative. Precisely because the urban sector was still so underdeveloped, many men emphasized the advantages of establishing new towns. According to the main proprietor of the Carolinas, in a communication of 1671 to his agents there, "the Planting of People in Townes" was "the Cheife thing that [had] given New England soe much the advantage over Virginia," and he urged them to foster urban development. Subsequent arguments for legislation designed to promote "cohabitation" in Virginia and Maryland emphasized the likelihood of commercial benefits, but they also referred to expected advances in the areas of religion and education. A future president, John Adams, expressed annoyance after a visit to Boston in 1758 as a result of the noise, the filth, and the confusion he had encountered there. But he also voiced pleasure at having been able to hear "the greatest men in America" plying their trade in the law courts and to experience the "joys of serene sedate conversation" as well as the company of attractive young women. Another political intellectual, Benjamin Franklin, described with quiet but evident pride the evolution of city services in Philadelphia, in which he had played no small part.

The man most frequently cited as an American enemy of the city is Thomas Jefferson. In an often quoted passage in his *Notes on the State of Virginia* (1784), anti-urban sentiments that were usually implicit in his defenses of agriculture came clearly to the fore. "The mobs of great cities," he wrote, "add just so much to support of pure government as sores do to the strength of the human body." He reiterated this view later, but it must also be pointed out that after his presidency he displayed an increasing awareness of the need for manufacturing and of the concomitant need for urban development if America was to assert itself effectively on the international scene.

About 1820, as urban growth intensified, cities began to come to the forefront of American as well as European consciousness, and for well over a century urban commentaries occupied central positions in the broader discourses about society and culture. The decades between the early nineteenth century and World War II constituted the "golden" age of urban-centered thought, which can best be treated in a brief overview of a series of preeminent themes that recur repeatedly in the literature of the period.

According to many commentators, urban growth was leading to potentially disastrous breakdowns of physical health, personal morality, social stability, and cultural quality. All of these developments appeared to be linked to one another in a downward spiral of general decline.

Much of the sharpest criticism pertained to the physical and the physiological hardships that stemmed from the excessive crowding of too many inhabitants into too little space in the areas inhabited by ordinary city folk. Beginning in the 1830s and 1840s, medical doctors who specialized in the newly emerging science of public health, such as Thomas Griscom in New York, began to produce a steady stream of complaints about the ways in which urban conditions led to high rates of disease. Overcrowded housing and poor drainage of contaminated water were seen quite rightly as primary causes of cholera and other life-threatening illnesses, including typhus and tuberculosis.

Later in the century, the concern with urban death rates declined somewhat, but there was a continuing, and indeed a growing, realization that the upsurge of immigrants had in fact exacerbated the problem of poor housing and other forms of physical deprivation that were memorably portrayed by the journalist Jacob Riis in *How the Other Half Lives* (1890). Riis documented, in pictures as well as in words, the ways in which the slum environment stunted and deformed those who lived there, contributing to a process that was coming to be known on both sides of the Atlantic as "degeneration." There was also growing anxiety over the decline of urban birthrates, particularly among the middle classes, who seemed to be permitting themselves to be outnumbered by more prolific immigrants, yet another aspect of the perceived urban threat to the demographic and physiological health of the American nation.

Many critics voiced the belief that life in big cities was not only physically unhealthy but also morally unsound. They complained that urban conditions undermined stable families and other forms of primary social control and that city dwellers were responsible for far more than their fair share of vice, crime, and resistance to the existing order of society and government.

Clergymen played an especially important part in voicing this complaint against the urban milieu. Both individually and collectively, they were keenly aware of being confronted by a rising population of men and women who were less and less likely to go to church and to accept the moral as well as the spiritual guidance that the clergymen were prepared to offer. But they expressed a sense of unease that went well beyond the matter of religiosity per se. For example, in the 1880s, the Protestant minister Josiah Strong portrayed the American city as a hotbed of moral dangers that necessitated constant vigilance and vigor on the part of all right-thinking citizens. In a widely read book called *Our Country* (1885), Strong bemoaned a number of interrelated "perils" that ostensibly menaced the stability and future progress of the American republic, among them, immigration, Roman Catholicism, secularism, intemperance, socialism, and the concentration of great wealth, all of which were intensified by the final peril, the American city. The city was full of "social dynamite." It was a place where—untouched by the right kind of religion (namely, Protestantism)—"roughs, gamblers, thieves, robbers, lawless and desperate men of all sorts" came together, made their evil plans, and did their wicked deeds.

Clergymen were by no means the only critics of urban morals. In this connection, it is useful to cite the example of Jane Addams, who was not only the key figure in the rise of the American settlement house movement but also a formative influence in the early history of urban sociology. In *The Spirit of Youth and City Streets* (1909), Addams drew on her many years of direct experience with slum children at Hull House in Chicago in order to depict one sector of the urban population that was especially at risk of becoming involved in deviant behavior. Describing the big city as a place in which young people suffered constant exposure to temptations that almost inevitably proved too strong for them to resist, she added an empirical foundation—and a more pointedly environmentalist explanation—to denunciations of the sort uttered by Strong and others. Later, in the 1920s and 1930s, the continuing problem of deviant behavior in urban settings was pointed out again and again in the writings of various members of the so-called Chicago School of Sociology, led by Robert E. Park. Louis Wirth argued that urban life led to "personal disorganization, mental breakdown, suicide, delinquency, crime, corruption, and disorder," and many other sociologists voiced similar views.

Another set of worries had to do with culture and aesthetics. Not only conservative antimodernists but also novelists, poets, literary essayists, and architects and city planners were deeply offended by the visual ugliness, monotony, and mediocrity that seemed to surround them. This point can be most readily illustrated via the works of men of letters, who, even though they themselves thrived in urban centers, generally displayed bitter contempt for big cities. In a manner suggestive of Charles Dickens's denunciation of the fictional city of Coketown (actually modeled on Manchester) in *Hard Times* (1854), Dickens's American contemporary, Herman Melville, in *Pierre* (1852), contrasted the city and the countryside by referring to rural America as "the most poetical and philosophical . . . part of this earth" and describing urban America as "the more plebeian portion [with a] dirty unwashed face." Similar sentiments appear repeatedly in the writings of other representatives of the Transcendentalist movement, including Nathaniel Hawthorne, Ralph Waldo Emerson, and Henry David Thoreau. Half a century later, when he returned to the United States after a long stay in England, the novelist Henry James recoiled from New York. In his *The American Scene,* James denounced the American metropolis for its "monotonous commonness," its lack of history, and the preoccupation of its inhabitants with the pursuit of wealth instead of beauty.

It must be pointed out that although much of the critical commentary does indeed reveal an anti-urban mentality, criticism of urban problems was by no means synonymous with opposition to cities per se. Henry James, for instance, recoiled not from the big city as such but from the *American* city, which he implicitly contrasted with a more refined urbanism that he believed clearly characterized many older cities in Europe.

Moreover, many other critics argued that the only sensible way of responding to the many problems the big cities posed was to seek solutions for them within the urban milieu itself. Large numbers of moderate conservatives, "new" liberals, and socialists advocated a wide range of measures designed to change cities so that their component parts would operate properly and their numerous inhabitants could live happily. In their thinking, discontent with one or another facet of the contemporary big city went hand in hand with accepting the big city as such and the determination to make the best of it. It was very much in this spirit, for instance, that Jane Addams undertook her efforts to rescue a certain portion of the lower classes from the streets of Chicago.

Such strategies for dealing with urban problems were strongly encouraged by a number of considerations that pointed toward the basic benefits of urban development. There was a widespread awareness that big cities had come to stay whether one liked them or not and that their presence was vital to the functioning of a prosperous economy. There was also a great deal of genuine affection for urban life, pride in urban accomplishment, and confidence in urban progress. The growth of big cities was clearly accompanied by an urban ethos that manifested itself not only in expressions of hope by urban reformers but also in countless paeans of praise by writers whose contemplation of past and ongoing developments led them to believe that their wishes could indeed be fulfilled.

Complaints about the poverty and poor health that afflicted some urbanites were countered by frequent celebrations of the urban economy and the wealth it produced. In the 1850s many boosters of relatively new cities in the South, the Midwest, and the West strongly supported the commercial development of places such as New Orleans, Chicago, and San Francisco. The statistician Adna Weber, in *The Growth of Cities in the Nineteenth Century* (1899), amplified such arguments at a more theoretical level. He pointed out that the economic growth of modern society as a whole depended heavily on a division of labor that was unthinkable without the geographic concentration of productive forces in and around cities. He also incorporated into his discourse a wide range of social and political concerns. Clearly echoing the sentiments of earlier thinkers such as John Adams, he asserted happily that the urban environment stimulated "liberal and progressive thought." In his view, "the variety of occupations, interests and opinions" fostered "a broader and freer judgment," which he and other progressives heartily welcomed. Agreeing with conservative critics that urban life acted as a solvent of many sources of social restraint, he took heart from what they deplored. In a similar vein, the sociologist Robert E. Park, despite all of his documented awareness of urban pathologies, celebrated in the urban environment a "moral climate" that both permitted and promoted ambition, diversity, and innovation.

The city's champions, ever mindful of their opponents' charge that urban freedom to be oneself could quickly degenerate into living without due regard for one's fellow city dwellers, hastened to offer another defense. In steadily growing numbers, they argued that the urban milieu could nourish not only liberty but also cooperation and thus community. They insisted on the crucial role that cities played in generating and supporting collective efforts to ameliorate their own worst problems. Henry Tappan, the chancellor of the University of Michigan, in a lecture titled "The Growth of Cities," made this point in the 1850s. "There can be no question," he stated, "that the association of men in cities is favorable to the highest development of humanity." The lesson both of ancient history and of more recent European history was that "the same causes which make cities the centers of intelligence, enterprise, and education, must go to make them, also, the centers of religious and benevolent influence."

Subsequently, this perspective was reiterated in the works of men who called their readers' attention less to the achievements of religious and other voluntary groups than to those of municipal governments. It was in the numerous and enthusiastic celebrations of the good works emanating from city halls that the belief in urban betterment through mutuality and organization found its clearest and most triumphant expression. Much of this sentiment was nourished by the example of the German Empire, where urban administrators set enviable examples of foresight and competence as they made their cities more attractive places in which to live—examples many Americans sought to emulate. Referring to such efforts, Charles Zueblin (a former professor of sociology at the University of Chicago) looked back in the second edition of his *Municipal Progress* (1916) to what he regarded as a spectacular record of recent improvement. After listing a whole host of measures designed to improve the physical, social, and cultural well-being of city dwellers, he concluded exuberantly that "the progressive satisfaction of the wants of all the people has ceased to be a utopian ideal; it is the only reasonable municipal program."

City boosters praised the urban scene with a view to offsetting cultural criticism in two ways. On the one hand, they pointed to the flowering of cultural institutions, many of them sponsored or assisted by local governments. Frederic C. Howe, a Cleveland-based reformer, wrote in his widely read *The City: The Hope of Democracy* (1905) that in urban areas "night schools, art exhibitions, popular lectures and concerts, college settlements . . . a cheap press, labor organizations [and] the church" were all "bringing enlightenment at a pace never before dreamed of."

Other authors placed greater emphasis on the ways in which the urban panorama itself provided a stimulating spectacle that could greatly enrich the works of creative artists—including those artists who chose to portray what they saw around them in somewhat somber tones. Theodore Dreiser, best known as a commentator on the city for his depiction of urban degradation in *Sister Carrie* (1901), celebrated the city elsewhere in no uncertain terms. In a series of often lyrical vignettes about New York written between 1900 and 1915 and later published as *The Color of a Great City* (1930), he depicted "the beauty of life itself . . . a shifting, lovely, changeful thing ever." The glory of the city lay in its variety, which yielded dramatic contrasts between extremes—contrasts that the observant author would find endlessly fascinating. Such attitudes continued to manifest themselves in the 1920s and 1930s, not only in the essays in which the noted journalist H. L. Mencken applauded the "infinitely grand and gorgeous spectacle" of the American metropolis but also in writings by numerous other observers, who discerned in New York, in Chicago, and elsewhere a colorful dynamism that transcended good and evil.

On the eve of World War II, Charles Merriam, a professor of political science at the University of Chicago, wove together many elements of a pro-urban discourse in an essay titled "Urbanism" that appeared in the *American Journal of Sociology* (1939). He argued that the faults of modern cities were "not those of decay and impending decline but of exuberant vitality crowding its way forward under tremendous pressure." The assets of an urban-industrial civilization, which included not only "the vast expansion of productive power" but also "the growth of centers of science, medicine, education, invention, and religion," were, in his view, very real and very great. The municipal history of the past generation pointed toward "a day of hope," when still better "patterns of community structure" would lead to "wiser plans and programs of action and higher levels of material and spiritual prosperity."

Although statements such as Merriam's indicate the persistence, even during the Great Depression, of certain elements of a city-centered optimism, the high tide of those sentiments had already begun to ebb by the end of the Progressive Era around 1920; and it ebbed still further after 1945. As many cities not only stopped growing but also began to shrink, modes of discourse in which the urban scene had appeared as a locus of opportunity that brought out the best in its residents were increasingly supplanted by newer discourses of decay and decline. To be sure, ongoing support for cities was clearly evident, especially in the 1950s and early 1960s, in the growing revulsion among many intellectuals against the rise of suburbia. In *The Exploding Metropolis* (1958), William Whyte, Jr., and other writers decried the "assault on urbanism" as a process that militated against diversity and produced instead a dull conformity. In a similar vein, Jane Jacobs, in *The Death and Life of Great American Cities* (1963), articulated an eloquent plea for relatively compact urban areas, which she valued in large measure for their vital heterogeneity. But it became increasingly apparent in the later 1960s and 1970s that writers such as Whyte and Jacobs were fighting a rearguard action.

The sense of almost cosmic doom with regard to modern urban development expressed by Lewis Mumford in *The City in History* (1961) was reinforced not only by ongoing suburbanization but also by trends within the cities themselves—most notably, vehicular congestion, pollution, poverty, crime, and racial rioting. Collections of essays such as James Q. Wilson's *The Metropolitan Enigma: Inquiries into the Nature and Dimensions of America's "Urban Crisis"* (1968), Nathan Glazer's *Cities in Trouble* (1970), and William Gorham and Nathan Glazer's *The Urban Predicament* (1976) were filled with scholarly essays that laid bare the roots and magnitude of urban problems without evincing very much confidence that these problems were likely to be solved.

In 1990, toward the end of their *Urban America: A History,* David R. Goldfield and Blaine A. Brownell took stock of the metropolitan present. They offered a balanced view that emphasized the "anomalous" quality of big city life in our time. "Gleaming downtowns" that had sprung back to life during the booming 1980s might compete successfully with office parks and malls on the cities' peripheries, but "hope-lost people crouch[ed] in the shadows of decaying neighborhoods." America, they asserted, was "no closer to solving the social fallout from American urbanization than ... when cities were mere clusters huddled around the waterfront," and all they could say with confidence about the future was that cities would somehow change and somehow survive. Although their affection for cities was clearly evident, their analysis did not inspire a great deal of hope. If there was a prevailing attitude toward the city at the end of the period treated in this entry, they expressed it as well as anyone could.

—*Andrew Lees*

See also
Chicago School of Sociology; Mumford, Lewis; Park, Robert Ezra; Riis, Jacob August; Wirth, Louis.
References
Bender, Thomas. *Toward an Urban Vision: Ideas and Institutions in Nineteenth-Century America.* Lexington: University Press of Kentucky, 1975.
Boyer, Paul S. *Urban Masses and Moral Order in America, 1820–1920.* Cambridge, MA: Harvard University Press, 1978.
Bremner, Robert H. *From the Depths: The Discovery of Poverty in the United States.* New York: New York University Press, 1956.
Hamer, David. *New Towns in the New World: Images and Perceptions of the Nineteenth-Century Urban Frontier.* New York: Columbia University Press, 1990.
Lees, Andrew. *Cities Perceived: Urban Society in European and American Thought, 1820–1940.* New York: Columbia University Press, 1985.
Matthews, Fred H. *Quest for an American Sociology: Robert E. Park and the Chicago School.* Montreal: McGill-Queens University Press, 1977.
Still, Bayrd, ed. *Mirror for Gotham: New York as Seen by Contemporaries from Dutch Days to the Present.* New York: New York University Press, 1956.
———. *Urban America: A History with Documents.* Boston: Little, Brown, 1974.
White, Morton, and Lucia White. *The Intellectual versus the City: From Thomas Jefferson to Frank Lloyd Wright.* Cambridge, MA: Harvard University Press, 1962.

Automobiles

From prehistoric times, humans have yearned to improve the speed, ease, and comfort of traveling and transporting goods. They also improved litters and sedan chairs to enhance the comfort of passengers; any benefits to slaves and servants carrying the devices were incidental. Historians have traced the development of improved wheeled vehicles, from the crudest oxcarts and wagons to the finest carriages, over thousands of years. The parallel challenges of developing adequate streets and roads challenged civilizations around the world for many centuries. Some, like the Romans, developed remarkable road systems, remnants of which are still evident today. However, until the development of steam and electric power, beginning in the late eighteenth century, humans made little progress in any area of travel. A seaman from biblical times might be impressed by the sheer size of a late-eighteenth-century British frigate, but he would have instinctively understood its operation. The same would hold true for a medieval peasant magically set down on a roadway in nineteenth-century Russia; he would not have been startled by the appearance of modern wagons or carts.

In the first century A.D., a Greek engineer, Hero, invented a hollow sphere, with two protruding spouts pointed in opposite directions. When filled with water and heated by fire, the sphere whirled rapidly on an axle. Hero had harnessed steam power, but for many centuries its potential for replacing animal or human power was undeveloped. Only in the late eighteenth and early nineteenth centuries did scientists and engineers, by then armed with the knowledge of Sir Isaac Newton's laws of dynamics, begin to apply steam power to larger devices. Benjamin Franklin experimented with electricity in the late eighteenth century. The development of batteries and, eventually, the dynamo in the 1870s symbolized the fact that scientists familiar with electricity were poised for major breakthroughs.

The late eighteenth century marked a period of intense ferment as intellectuals explored new political, social, and economic horizons. It was the age of Adam Smith, Jean Jacques Rousseau, Thomas Jefferson, and a host of other inspired thinkers intent on challenging accepted conventions. It is hardly surprising that this period also marked the initial stages of mechanically powered conveyances over both water and land.

Many historians have advanced arguments claiming that one individual or another was *the* inventor of the automobile. Further complicating the issue is debate over the definition of the device and the degree to which experimental models operated successfully. Americans first witnessed cumbersome, steam-powered wagons lumbering over urban streets in scattered locations at the turn of the nineteenth century. Some authorities claim that one Apollos Kinsey drove a steam carriage in Hartford, Connecticut, in 1797. Other inventors had applied for and received patents even earlier. In 1787 Oliver Evans received a patent for a steam-powered vehicle, but this unknown millwright put off serious experimentation for more than a decade. Meanwhile, Harvard professor Nathan Read sought a U.S. patent, but he evidently produced nothing. Evans finally began working on a steam-powered device in earnest. Hired by the city of Philadelphia to build a steam dredge in 1805, Evans saw an opportunity to dovetail the two projects. To move his steam-powered dredge from his shop to the waterfront, Evans placed the device on a wheeled frame and connected the crankshaft by another belt to the rear axle. On August 12, 1805, the ponderous 20-ton "Oruktor Amphibolos" chugged through the streets at four miles per hour. But any notion of potential for land use was quickly dispelled; rough cobblestone streets broke the device's iron-rimmed wheels that very day. Potential investors may have been dissuaded from underwriting Evans's experiments by the renowned engineer Benjamin Latrobe, who ridiculed the device. Evans became only a footnote in automotive history. In fact, Europeans had laid similar claims as automotive pioneers in the eighteenth century. Nicholas Cugnot, a military engineer in France, had built a steam-powered carriage in 1769, and several English inventors claimed to have invented comparable vehicles before Evans's device appeared.

Questions of originality aside, practical considerations delayed serious experiments with mechanically propelled automotive devices for nearly a century. Americans associated steam-powered devices with extreme danger. Boiler explosions threatened life and limb. Adverse regulations also prevented their use in densely settled areas. In addition, early steam-powered devices could operate successfully only on smooth surfaces, namely water and iron or steel rails. There were few smooth, durable roads in the United States. Early turnpike operators and public officials overseeing the few good roads connecting cities and towns discouraged automotive experimentation.

Limited advances in automotive technology were centered overseas in the early nineteenth century. In the 1830s, William Hancock, a British entrepreneur, provided daily service between London and Paddington in 20-passenger steam-powered omnibuses with a top speed of 20 miles per hour. However, turnpike operators, fearful of losing horse-powered trade, persuaded Parliament to enact prohibitively large fees for steamers, and Hancock's devices soon disappeared.

Another barrier to automotive development was the rapid advancement in railroad technology, which helped that industry dominate overland travel by the mid-nineteenth century. Railroads also attracted most venture capital that might have assisted automotive experiments. Finally, advances in metallurgy necessary to construct light vehicles were years in the future. Late in the nineteenth century, a number of designers on both sides of the Atlantic built relatively lightweight steamers capable of traveling 30 miles per hour over smooth roads, but they encountered opposition from urbanites who raised safety concerns. In addition, their noise frightened horses and their fumes irritated sensitive nostrils. As automotive historian Clay McShane suggests, by the 1890s the technology to operate economical steamers was available; that they failed was due more to restrictive regulations than to mechanical inefficiency.

In the meantime, other inventors experimented with vehicles powered by electricity. The galvanic battery, invented in the early nineteenth century, was notoriously inefficient; units powerful enough to move vehicles were so heavy as to be utterly impractical, just like steam engines of the period. However, by 1890 William Morrison, of Des Moines, Iowa, had developed a six-passenger wagon, powered by a row of rechargeable storage batteries located underneath the seats. He demonstrated its practicality by operating it continuously for 13 hours at an average speed of 14 miles per hour. Morrison was soon bought out by a promotion-minded entrepreneur who demonstrated the vehicle to tens of thousands of visitors at Chicago's Columbian Exposition in 1893. Viewers were particularly impressed with the vehicle's quiet operation, in sharp contrast to the other buggies with artificial sources of power.

Thus, by the time serious experimentation with internal-combustion vehicles began, automotive technology was fairly

1896 photograph of the first automobile made by Henry Ford.

advanced, and experimental vehicles had been appearing on roads for more than a century. Ultimately, of course, gasoline-powered vehicles swept the field, but both steamers and electrics provided significant competition until the end of World War I. Many Americans date the triumph of the internal-combustion engine to Henry Ford's introduction of the Model T in 1908, but Ford's breakthrough owed a debt to an entire generation of trailblazers.

Given the fact that internal-combustion engines eventually dominated the industry, it is not surprising that many claimed the title of founding father of the invention. According to some sources, Samuel Morey of New Hampshire built a working model of such an engine in 1826. A Belgian, Etienne Lenoir, living in Paris, actually produced the first commercially successful device in 1862, which burned a mixture of air, oil, and gas. This first engine capable of powering an automobile could only move it six kilometers in three hours, but Lenoir improved the machine rapidly. By 1866 he had sold 400 commercial engines in France and another 1,000 in England. Nevertheless, his success was fleeting. Germans Gottlieb Daimler and Karl Benz actually built workable internal combustion–powered vehicles, introduced almost simultaneously in 1885. Scientific magazines published many articles that provided details of their exploits, and many Americans vied for the honor of first producing similar vehicles on this side of the ocean. *The Horseless Age* estimated that by 1895 about 300 Americans had tried to build horseless carriages, many of them gasoline-powered.

Whether or not Frank and Charles Duryea were the first Americans to build an automobile, they were unquestionably the first to go into production, founding their own company and making their first sale in 1896. They were soon joined by many competitors, almost all of whom produced small numbers of handmade automobiles. With small volume, fledgling entrepreneurs had to charge high prices, and early automobiles priced at $4,000 to $6,000 were adult toys for the rich. Early auto-related activities and publications were clearly directed toward high society. Turn-of-the-century Americans admired the ingenuity of bicycle shop tinkerers building automobiles, but few considered the devices practical. They would have to be shown.

Between 1905 and 1913, Boston millionaire Charles J. Glidden set out to do just that, sponsoring annual tours that featured convoys of different brands of automobiles. The tours, each covering hundreds of miles, eventually traversed most of the nation. Manufacturers prized the awards presented annually to models demonstrating durability and ease of handling, rather than speed. As for the latter, automobile racing quickly became a national craze. Again, aristocrats led the way. William K. Vanderbilt sponsored races that attracted tens of thousands of "ordinary" citizens who were dazzled by noise, speed, and perhaps the danger to brave drivers. As early as 1906, a Stanley racer with a running start set a land speed record of 127 miles per hour at a distance of over a mile.

The "masses" were fascinated by speed and power, and young boys dreamed of being race car drivers like Barney Oldfield, but average Americans did not yet see cars in their own futures. Henry Ford, of course, changed all that. Following a decade of experimentation and modest success with several models, Ford unveiled the Model T in 1908. The Model T was a revolutionary vehicle—incredibly durable, easy to operate, reliable, and economical. Produced in volume from the start and originally priced at $850, the Model T attracted middle-class buyers by the tens of thousands. Contrary to popular myth, Ford originally offered the car in six colors, adopting his "black only" policy in 1913. By then, Ford had perfected the assembly-line process at the Highland Park plant in Detroit, and slashing the price to the bone was his obsession. Ford dreamed of putting the entire nation on wheels, and the Model T came close to achieving that goal. By 1925 the renowned "Tin Lizzie" or "flivver" cost only $290, a figure within reach of blue-collar Americans. Between 1908 and 1927, nearly 15.5 million Model T's rolled off the assembly lines.

Ford dominated the automobile industry deep into the 1920s. Over two decades of production, the Model T averaged 42.9 percent of the industry's production! Its durability and flexibility enthralled Americans, particularly farmers. Model T's were routinely hitched to farm equipment, easing backbreaking chores for millions. Simply designed, the Model T was the novice tinkerer's dream. Americans possessing patience and average mechanical skills could repair the cars by themselves with inexpensive parts supplied through Ford's dealer network. Ford clearly "democratized" automobile ownership in America in the first quarter of the century.

Ford's flivvers began transforming the American landscape and creating a loosely integrated system of ancillary enterprises. New gravel and even concrete highways began replacing almost impassable, rutted dirt roads. Roadside businesses and tourist camps dotted the countryside and outskirts of towns and cities. Expanded automobile use revived and invigorated the petroleum industry, and a huge oil strike at Spindletop, near Beaumont, Texas, in 1901 symbolized the beginning of a half-century of domestic energy surpluses and low gasoline prices. Full-service gasoline stations soon made the commodity easily available in all but the most remote parts of the nation.

If Ford democratized automobile ownership, other manufacturers and inventors made critical contributions to the emergence of the car culture. William C. Durant's career rivaled Ford's. "Billy" Durant was an early-century master of the merger. In 1908 he founded General Motors (GM), which included the profitable Buick and Cadillac operations. However, in purchasing numerous shaky enterprises possessing only marginally useful automobile-related products and patents, Durant overextended himself and lost control of GM two years later. Amazingly, the plucky Durant regrouped, and he regained control of GM in 1915. Durant's major contribution was offering models to fit every pocketbook, a strategy that major companies follow even today. Although Durant's volatile managerial style and seemingly reckless financial wheeling and dealing drove some sober-minded, able executives from GM's ranks, he also attracted some brilliant men. Alfred P. Sloan joined the company in 1916 and brought order to the organization's chaotic administrative structure.

A few years later, Sloan introduced the concept of the annual model change. This initiative was essentially a response to the fact that by the mid-1920s industry analysts realized that Ford's functional flivver had essentially saturated the market, at least in terms of providing reliable transportation. Thus, most sales were by then "replacement" sales. Model T's were simply too durable—at least to the Ford Motor Company. When Ford finally replaced them with the Model A in 1927, 70 percent of all Model T's ever produced were still on the road. Industry leaders sensed that they needed to make current automobile owners dissatisfied with mere utility. For years, Ford's philosophy of no-frills economy had dominated car buyers' decision making. By the 1920s, however, rivals were making inroads by offering cars with more comfortable suspension systems, colors that might attract more female buyers, and other features.

For several years, until Charles F. Kettering invented the electric starter in 1911, drivers had to hand-crank their engines, a laborious, even dangerous proposition that sometimes drove operators to tears. Although most automobile producers offered the electric starter as an option as early as 1914, Ford held out until 1919, and the device was not standard in his flivvers until 1926.

Ford's influence peaked in the mid-1920s, even though few models were ever as eagerly anticipated as his Model A, which first rolled off the lines in late 1927. Within two weeks of its unveiling, dealers had orders for 400,000 units. By then, however, comfort and styling dominated discussions among Detroit's decision-makers. By the onset of the Depression in 1929, there were almost 24 million registered automobiles on the road. In hard times, Americans maintained their cars in any manner they could, even holding them together with rope and baling wire. In their classic revisit of Middletown (Muncie, Indiana) in the mid-1930s, sociologists Robert and Helen Lynd discovered that some consumers would forfeit food for gasoline, a demonstration of how deeply entrenched the car culture had become.

The Depression marked hard times for all of the auto companies, including the demise of all but a handful of independent producers. By 1932, total production in the industry was less than a quarter of its 1929 figure. Although World War II brought prosperity to the industry through military contracts, automobile production did not fully revive until after V-J Day in 1945. Surprisingly, the 1930s featured some of the most original and arresting styling advances yet made, Chrysler's Airflow being perhaps the most dramatic. In general, body styles became more rounded, and almost all cars were enclosed. Yet the decade also ended America's romance with Henry Ford, and vicious labor wars shook the entire industry.

Lionized by almost all Americans (except fellow industrialists) when he introduced the $5 daily wage for workers in 1914, Ford had become one of the industrial worker's prime villains by the late 1930s. Although he paid high wages to those still working the assembly lines, management thugs brutally resisted efforts by the United Automobile Workers (UAW) to organize at Ford. The fledgling union decided to attempt to crack GM, the industry giant, first. Workers introduced a new tactic, the "sit-down" strike, in which they physically occupied several GM plants for 44 days early in 1937. Despite scattered violence and dozens of severe beatings, the men held out and gradually won public support. More to the point, neither federal and state officials nor the courts upheld management. GM finally caved in during mid-February. Although Ford and his chief goon, Harry Bennett, blustered that no union men would ever work at their company, the handwriting was on the wall. Ford held out for four more years, but the federal government finally forced a union election in 1941. To Ford's shock and dismay, more than 97 percent of his workers chose the UAW. The aging patriarch was shattered, but by then he was clearly an anachronism.

Wartime restrictions forced suspension of automobile production for more than three years. While workers once again enjoyed fat pay envelopes, they couldn't buy cars—or gasoline or tires. Those fortunate enough to own relatively new models and to gain access to less restrictive rationing kept their vehicles running, but millions of Americans rediscovered public transit during the war.

The two decades following World War II unquestionably marked the heyday of the domestic automobile industry. By 1945, industry analysts anticipated a new age of prosperity, but production records exceeded their wildest expectations. Americans would snap up almost anything on wheels, and a handful of new entrepreneurs vowed to challenge the Big Three producers. Preston Tucker made a small splash in 1948 with prototypes of the Tucker Torpedo, which dazzled some veteran industry observers. However, an SEC investigation into his past business dealings (which some claim was inspired by nervous Big Three kingpins) created negative publicity and scared off potential investors. World War II production hero Henry J. Kaiser and Joseph W. Frazer, an experienced auto executive, made a more determined challenge between 1945 and 1954. For three years, Kaiser-Frazer appeared competitive, capturing nearly 5 percent of domestic sales in 1948. Their products were roomy and comfortable, and they drew praise for advanced safety features. Unfortunately, their models simply were not exciting. Kaiser and Frazer made several strategic errors, the most serious of which was failure to raise sufficient capital when they had the opportunity. By 1950, the last major challenge to the Big Three was on the skids, and the remaining independents were facing elimination by the end of the decade.

At mid-century the Big Three producers appeared impregnable. Detroit had answered the challenge of putting Americans back on the road in the five years following World War II. Most of their models from the late 1940s were uninspired in design, chiefly utilitarian. However, in the 1950s Detroit designers were determined to coax consumers out of their careful buying habits with easy credit and exciting new designs. Ford and Chevrolet introduced several low-to-medium-priced "all new," totally redesigned entries. Higher-priced lines, such as Buick, Lincoln, and particularly Cadillac, featured power and flashy styling. Designers competed to create models with the most chrome and largest tail fins. While some social critics reviled the late 1950s automobiles as obscenely inefficient in terms of fuel use, the fact was that many consumers lusted for flashy status symbols. Gasoline was still cheap, new interstate highways had opened up, and Americans loved the open road. Singer Dinah Shore urged her countrymen to "see the USA in your Chevrolet" in television jingles. Millions of Americans followed her suggestion in all makes and models.

A classic tail fin on a vintage Cadillac in Miami Beach, Florida.

During the 1950s the American autoscape experienced yet another transformation. Before then, with the exception of large petroleum companies, which had built chains of "full-service" stations, most roadside businesses were "mom and pop" lunch stands and modest, low-budget tourist courts. The 1950s marked the beginning of standardized enterprises depending almost wholly upon customers on wheels. Howard Johnson's and McDonald's began offering uniform, predictable table fare from coast to coast. A generation later, some Americans ate a majority of their meals at these and other "fast food" restaurants. Weary travelers could reserve standardized, comfortable rooms at burgeoning chain motels like strategically located Holiday Inns, Motel 6's, Ramada Inns, or similar establishments. It seemed that young people literally lived on wheels. Social life often centered around drive-in hamburger stands and outdoor movie theaters.

In the 1950s these roadside businesses were new and exciting, and only a handful of social critics lambasted the car culture. But voices of dissent grew louder by the 1960s. Ralph Nader's 1965 book *Unsafe at Any Speed* was a withering indictment of the automobile industry's "criminal neglect" of consumer safety. He singled out Chevrolet's economy model, the Corvair, for its tendency to roll over when making sharp turns. By the late 1950s and early 1960s, thoughtful observers realized that never-ending construction of freeways would not resolve mounting urban traffic congestion. New concrete strips were jammed with automobiles as soon as they opened. Millions of Americans awoke to the unpleasant side effects of automobility, some of which were clearly visible. Filthy air, called "smog," most of it caused by tailpipe emissions, made urban dwellers' breathing uncomfortable, and it often irritated their eyes. Later scientific research identified smog as hazardous to the health of virtually all living organisms.

Detroit's response to early criticism was ambivalent, clearly dictated more by market demand than social conscience. Most Americans still wanted "muscle" cars (critics called them "gas-guzzling dinosaurs" and other less flattering names), and "hot" cars still dominated showroom floors in the 1960s and early 1970s. Yet the Big Three also introduced their first "compact" models during those years. In fact, Crosley, Kaiser-Frazer, and a few independents had tried small economy models years earlier, but their timing had been poor. Detroit's sudden, halfhearted attention to economy models was also stimulated by foreign competition, mostly German and Japanese. Initially, American producers chortled at the arrival of Volkswagen's "beetle" and early Datsun and Toyota models. However, by the mid-1970s their ridicule was turning into near panic.

The 1970s marked watershed years for the domestic automobile industry, indeed the entire car culture. The initial Arab oil embargo, which began in October 1973, lasted six months and had a relatively small impact on available fuel supplies. However, the psychological impact upon both consumers and producers was profound. Up to then, few Americans realized that the nation was the world's largest net importer of petroleum, nor how vulnerable they were. For decades, Americans had shown the world not only how to build cars but how and where to drill for oil. Americans arrogantly considered themselves kings of the road, and they were shocked at any challenges to the car culture, particularly from "outside." Generations of Americans had blithely accepted cheap petroleum as a way of life, almost an entitlement. Not only did prices per gallon skyrocket from 35 cents or so per gallon to more than one dollar almost overnight, but there were periodic shortages.

By the late 1970s the car culture was seemingly besieged from all sides. Consumer advocates lambasted Detroit's sluggish response to increasingly urgent demands for greater fuel economy in their products. The same voices compared domestic automobile workmanship and quality unfavorably to that evident in competitive German and Japanese models. Amid reports that domestic petroleum-marketing companies controlled huge inventories, gasoline prices remained suspiciously high, causing some social critics to inveigh against their allegedly rapacious business practices. Federal officials mandated a national speed limit of 55 miles per hour even on highways, arguing that lower average speeds would conserve significant amounts of fuel. American drivers, particularly in the sparsely settled West, perceived such regulation as an assault upon their most sacred freedoms, second only to the right to bear arms. Government officials, pleading a national crisis, also tried to coax drivers onto mass transit. Even fast-food chains came under fire as public health officials scored the poor nutritional value of their most popular offerings.

Yet the American automobile culture proved remarkably resilient. In the 1980s and early 1990s, domestic manufacturers dramatically improved both craftsmanship and average fuel efficiency, more than doubling the latter in the two decades following 1973. American auto makers received a boost from timely tariff hikes against foreign imports, and by the early 1990s their models were becoming more competitive across the board. It was also obvious that Americans stoutly resisted earlier challenges to their automobile addiction. Various public agencies funded the construction of new light rail mass transit systems and the expansion of existing bus lines, but these efforts have affected urban commuting only slightly. In all but the most densely settled American cities, more than 90 percent of all trips are taken by automobile. Despite rising numbers of densely settled apartment and townhouse complexes in most cities, this commuting pattern appears nearly impervious to change, since employment, shopping, entertainment, recreation, and education centers are so widely scattered. Without access to an automobile, the average urbanite feels severely handicapped, while rural dwellers are effectively stranded.

What does the future hold? The twenty-first century will undoubtedly bring nearly universal access to the information superhighway, which may profoundly alter employment and educational commuting patterns. This might alleviate dependence upon the automobile somewhat. The gasoline-powered internal-combustion engine has dominated automobile technology for almost a century, but alternative power sources, both old and new, appear poised to challenge its hegemony. Americans are, collectively, more obese than ever before, but even fast-food chains are beginning to respond to widespread demands for more healthy alternatives to their fat-filled, tasty offerings. The founding fathers of the automobile industry could never have imagined the perva-siveness of the car culture in America a century later. One prediction that appears relatively safe is that humans will still require individualized transportation a century from now. The car culture faces an exciting, if unpredictable, future.

—*Mark S. Foster*

See also
Commuting; Gasoline Stations.

References
Flink, James J. *America Adopts the Automobile, 1870–1910.* Cambridge, MA: MIT Press, 1970.
———. *The Car Culture.* Cambridge, MA: MIT Press, 1975.
McShane, Clay. *Down the Asphalt Path: The Automobile and the American City.* New York: Columbia University Press, 1994.
Rae, John B. *The American Automobile.* Chicago: University of Chicago Press, 1965.
Sears, Stephen W. *The American Heritage History of the Automobile in America.* New York: American Heritage, 1977.
White, Lawrence J. *The American Automobile Industry since 1945.* Cambridge, MA: Harvard University Press, 1970.

Balloon Frame Construction

Balloon frame construction, used to build almost all urban residences in the nineteenth century after its invention in Chicago in 1832 by George Snow, is also the ancestor of modern building practices. The origin of the name is unknown; however, it is certain that by 1837 the term was commonly used in Chicago. Presumably, balloon framing refers to the delicate strengthening webs of lighter-than-air balloons.

Balloon framing is a technique by which walls of buildings are erected using machine-sawed lumber of relatively modest standard dimensions fitted together with butt joints secured by machine-made nails. The width of each piece is generally 2 inches and the depth is in increments of 2 inches, beginning with 4 inches, usually referred to as two-by-fours, two-by-sixes, and so on. The vertical members, called studs, are located every 16 inches, so that, when a building is erected, lengths of lath cut into 48-inch pieces can be secured to every four studs. The studs run the entire height of the wall, and where studs of the required length are not available, they are butted together and secured by a piece of lumber nailed on both sides of the joint.

One of the most important attributes of balloon frame construction is that it requires only ordinary skills to build. Any two persons able to saw and nail can erect a balloon frame. Conversely, to construct the heavy "braced frames" that were previously common in the eastern United States required skilled carpenters to cut the joints that held them together. As a result, balloon framing quickly became preferred wherever skilled labor was scarce.

Balloon framing also proved valuable in the treeless regions west of Chicago where large timbers were not available. Instead, northern white pine from the forests of Wisconsin and Michigan was sawed into dimensioned lumber at Chicago and shipped by rail across the western plains to build balloon frames. Indeed, the rapid settlement of the West may be directly attributed to this new technique.

George Snow used the balloon frame first to build a warehouse on the shore of Lake Michigan in Chicago. Apparently he struck upon the technique out of necessity, for by the winter of 1832 all of the large trees in the immediate vicinity had been cut, and he was facing a wait until spring before he could obtain sizable timbers from distant forests. To solve his problem, he cut small trees into dimensioned lumber and then secured the pieces with machine-made nails, which were plentiful in Chicago.

Although Snow's warehouse has been demolished, later balloon framed buildings in the Chicago area demonstrate that Snow's invention retained several features of braced framing, namely the continued use of large horizontal pieces called sills at the base of each building. The lower end of each stud was mortised into these sills. No doubt, large timbers continued to be used for sills well into the century because buildings in the Midwest were often erected on cedar posts rather than on masonry foundations. As a result, heavy timbers were needed to span between the posts. Mortising the studs into the sills may be attributed to caution, for only where the studs meet the sills in balloon framing is diagonal nailing required.

According to George Woodward, a New York engineer who had worked near Chicago in the 1850s, many buildings there were built this way because of concern about the stability of diagonal nailing. But Woodward would later advise builders that mortising was not necessary because diagonally driven nails held as well as mortises, a belief that time has proved correct. Nonetheless, it was not until the 1880s that dimensioned lumber laid on proper foundations generally superseded the use of heavy timbers for sills, and studs were fixed to these sills by diagonal nailing.

Eventually, this method of framing was replaced by another, said to have been invented in San Francisco. In it, a platform is built on the foundation and then the outside walls are erected on the platform. Unlike balloon framing, the studs of the platform frame are only one story high. On them, another platform is built. This alternation continues until the full height of the building is reached. Platform framing, sometimes called "western framing," had a special advantage over balloon framing in that each wall could be built horizontally on the platform, then tilted up into its vertical position, and secured to the platform with nails. This advantage proved so overwhelming that platform framing completely replaced balloon framing during the first half of the twentieth century. Platform framing remains today the common method for erecting houses and other light structures in cities, suburbs, and the countryside of the United States.

—*Paul E. Sprague*

References

Cavanagh, Ted. "Balloon Houses: The Original Aspects of Conventional Wood-Frame Construction Re-examined." *Journal of Architectural Education* 51 (1997): 1–5.

Sprague, Paul E. "Chicago Balloon Frame." In H. Ward Jandl, ed., *The Technology of Historic American Buildings,* 35–61. Washington, DC: Foundation for Preservation Technology, 1983.

———. "The Origins of Balloon Framing." *Journal of the Society of Architectural Historians* 40 (1981): 311–319.

Woodward, George. "Balloon Frames." *The Country Gentleman* 14 (November 17, 1859): 313–314, (December 15, 1859): 387; 15 (April 5, 1860): 226.

Ballparks

In 1862 William H. Cammeyer built the first baseball park in the United States by converting his Brooklyn ice-skating rink into an enclosed field. Prominent local teams could use the Union Grounds for free, and Cammeyer charged spectators 10 cents for admission. Fencing the fields and building stands facilitated commercialization, offered improved accommodations for fans, and was expected to discourage rowdy lower-class spectators. By 1870, tickets for important games cost 50 cents.

In the nineteenth century, ballparks were inexpensive wooden structures in safe neighborhoods on the urban periphery, near public transportation and cheap land. Because of the instability of sports teams, they were not intended to be permanent, and streetcar lines often subsidized construction in hopes of profiting from increased traffic. Chicago's Lakefront Park, built at a cost of $10,000 in 1883, set the standard, seating 8,000 fans and boasting 18 elegant boxes. Over the next 20 years, the cost of wooden parks averaged about $30,000. These extremely dangerous structures occasionally collapsed and often caught fire; at least 20 fires broke out during the 1890s alone.

By the 1880s the technology to build fire-resistant ballparks was available. In 1894, when Philadelphia's 18,000-seat Huntington Grounds was refurbished after a fire, the park was cantilevered and constructed of steel and brick. High building costs and uncertain profits discouraged further innovation until nearly 1910, when baseball's growing popularity, as well as competition from theaters and amusement parks, rigorous new building codes, declining construction costs, and falling interest rates encouraged team owners to build professionally designed, fire-resistant ballparks. Philadelphia's Shibe Park (later renamed Connie Mack Stadium) was the first of these; built in French Renaissance style at a cost of $300,000 in 1909, it had a seating capacity of about 20,000. Other modern, multilevel, concrete-and-steel edifices cost about $500,000 and seated about 25,000 spectators on average. Innovations in these new parks included inclined ramps and elevators—not to mention higher ticket prices.

By 1914 ten of these "modern" parks had been built, and three are still in use: Detroit's Tiger Stadium (then known as Navin Field and scheduled to close in 1999) and Boston's Fenway Park, both constructed in 1912, and Chicago's Wrigley Field, which opened in 1914 but became the home of the Cubs in 1916. While both Tiger Stadium and Wrigley Field have increased their seating capacities substantially since they opened for business (currently about 52,000 and 39,000 respectively), Fenway Park remains the smallest of all the major league baseball stadiums with a seating capacity of only 34,000. These parks were located in middle-class neighborhoods or underdeveloped areas. The era of classic ballparks culminated in 1923 with construction of Yankee Stadium, a $2.5 million structure that seated 63,000 fans. It was the first ballpark called a stadium rather than a field, park, or grounds, all rural metaphors that emphasized the rustic image of baseball.

The next period of building parks began in the 1950s when classic ballparks were becoming dilapidated and surrounded by deteriorating neighborhoods that frightened away many fans. These new multipurpose parks were all publicly built and financed, except for Dodger Stadium (1962) in Los Angeles, as cities vied for sports franchises that would supposedly bolster their status and their economic future. The most dramatic innovation was the Houston Astrodome (1965), the first roofed ballpark, which was built at a cost of $545 million.

Beginning in the middle of the 1960s, some parks were built in suburbs closer to their fans, while others, like Busch Stadium in St. Louis, were located downtown near major highway interchanges as a means of revitalizing the central business district. Construction costs skyrocketed, none more dramatically than the renovation of Yankee Stadium in 1971 at a cost of $100 million. Thereafter, domed stadiums became popular, and four of the five fields built in North America between 1977 and 1989 were covered. Most recently, however, a new fashion, typified by Baltimore's Camden Yards (1992) and Cleveland's Jacobs Field (1994), is a nostalgic return to the architectural style and idiosyncratic dimensions of an earlier era.

—*Steven A. Riess*

References

Benson, Michael. *Ballparks of North America: A Comprehensive Historical Reference to Baseball Grounds, Yards, and Stadiums, 1845 to the Present.* Jefferson, NC: McFarland, 1989.

Gershman, Michael. *Diamonds: The Evolution of the Ballpark, from Elysian Fields to Camden Yards.* Boston: Houghton Mifflin, 1993.

Kuklick, Bruce. *To Everything a Season: Shibe Park and Urban Philadelphia, 1909–1976.* Princeton, NJ: Princeton University Press, 1991.

Lowry, Philip. *Green Cathedrals.* Reading, MA: Addison-Wesley, 1992.

Riess, Steven A. *Touching Bases: Professional Baseball and American Culture in the Progressive Era.* Westport, CT: Greenwood Press, 1980.

Baltimore, Maryland

The Maryland Colonial Assembly established Baltimore, Maryland, currently the thirteenth largest city in the United States, in 1729 along the banks of the Patapsco River in the northern part of the Chesapeake Bay basin. They named the settlement Baltimore in honor of the English home and the title of Maryland's proprietors, the Calvert family, and it was one of three settlements founded by the Maryland Assembly to be given that name. The other two, one on the Eastern Shore of Maryland and the other along the Bush River further up the Chesapeake, quickly failed. The Baltimore along the Patapsco succeeded and became Maryland's most important city.

The original town consisted of only a few houses in what is now the central business district and inner harbor. Two adjacent settlements just east of Baltimore, Jonestown across the Jones Falls and Fells Point to the southeast, appeared in 1732 and 1733 respectively but were merged with Baltimore in 1745 and 1773. From its beginnings, Baltimore was blessed with a large, easily navigable harbor and was closer to the West than other port cities on the East Coast. Unlike its competitors, Philadelphia, Boston, New York, and Charleston, however, Baltimore grew very slowly during the colonial era and numbered just 6,000 people on the eve of the American Revolution. Despite its strategic location and great harbor, Baltimore did not become a significant center of trade, manufacturing, or government during the colonial period. Annapolis remained Maryland's capital and has retained that position to the present.

Baltimore grew slowly in the colonial period because Maryland's plantation economy based on growing tobacco with slave labor did not require towns for trade and commerce. As in Virginia, the Chesapeake Bay provided deep water inlets where tobacco and other goods could be shipped directly to and from plantations, obviating the need for towns as a place for commerce. As time passed in the 1700s, however, Baltimore and its hinterland began to diverge economically from the rest of Maryland; the city became less and less dependent on tobacco, slaves, and plantations, and more on manufacturing, commerce, and agriculture not based on slaves and plantations.

Baltimore began to grow rapidly during the Revolutionary War. With Philadelphia and New York under British occupation or blockade, Baltimore became a leading entrepot for war materials imported from Europe and the West Indies; in return, it exported corn, wheat, and oats from colonies to the north and cotton and tobacco from colonies to the south. Merchants and landowners such as John Eager Howard, Charles Carroll of Carrollton, Isaac McKim, Robert Oliver, and Charles Ridgely came to the forefront during the Revolutionary Era.

After the war, Baltimore's exponential population and commercial growth continued. It soon became a leader in trade between the infant United States and the Caribbean and Latin America; from those regions, it imported coffee and sugar for shipment to trans-Appalachian America, which was closer to Baltimore than to the city's competitors. Baltimore became the chief port for a hinterland that soon included the upper South and the Midwest, from which it exported cotton, tobacco, and grain.

This commercial activity helped create a small but significant industrial base at the turn of the nineteenth century. The city's location along the Fall Line provided water power for numerous textile and grain mills that appeared in the Jones Falls and Gwynns Falls valleys. These mills provided a demand for imported staples and grains as well as more products to export.

Baltimore's large, protected harbor located close to plentiful forests soon made it a center of shipbuilding. "Baltimore Clippers," sleek and fast sailing ships produced in local shipyards, soon dominated travel and trade with Latin America. Another instance of Baltimore's shipbuilding prowess occurred in 1797 when the U.S. Navy launched its first commissioned ship, the frigate *Constellation,* in the city.

Baltimore's commercial growth generated population growth as well, and it made the transition from town to city between 1780 and 1820. In 1796 Maryland's legislature granted Baltimore a city charter. By 1800, the population had grown to 31,000, doubling its size in 1790, and the population doubled again by 1810, making Baltimore one of the largest cities on the East Coast.

As a major port, Baltimore was an early magnet for immigrants, with Germans and then Irish being the earliest newcomers. Baltimore also attracted free blacks. As slavery diminished in northern Maryland, many freedmen migrated to Baltimore. In fact, by the outbreak of the Civil War, enslaved African Americans were just 1 percent of Baltimore's population, and the city had the largest free black urban population of any city in the country. The early immigrants and free blacks competed with each other for jobs in the growing waterfront and milling industries; most of the skilled jobs went to Germans while the Irish and blacks fought each other for the remainder. Intractable racism soon restricted free blacks to domestic service or the most menial, unpromising day labor and created a dual labor market, one for blacks and one for whites, that has lasted until the present.

Baltimore has always had a large Roman Catholic population, and in 1789 it was designated the primary see of the church in America. John Carroll became the bishop of Baltimore and then, in 1808, the first archbishop in the United States. A cathedral, huge for those days, was constructed in 1821, and it dominated the city's skyline for many years. Baltimore was also home to the first Reform Jewish congregation in the United States, Har Sinai, established in 1842.

The city's free black community, though constantly threatened with reenslavement or deportation and limited to menial economic and social positions, nevertheless established schools, churches, and businesses. Among the earliest black churches were the Sharp Street Methodist, St. James Episcopal, Union Baptist, and Bethel African Methodist Episcopal. These churches, most of which still exist, formed the mainstay of black Baltimore's communal life.

Just as the Revolutionary War accelerated Baltimore's growth, so did the War of 1812. The city became such a center of privateering that the British attempted to conquer it in 1814. Their invasion was a two-pronged affair, with a land incursion up the North Point Road leading northwest from the Patapsco River and a simultaneous attempt to seize Baltimore Harbor from the sea. Both invasions failed. A British army commanded by General Robert Ross was defeated at the Battle of North Point on September 12, 1814, by the militia based in Baltimore. The next day, a British fleet attacked Fort McHenry at the tip of Locust Point. This fort controlled access to Baltimore's harbor, and to take the city, the British had to capture the fort. Fort McHenry successfully withstood a night and a day of bombardment, forcing the British to withdraw. The triumphant defense of Fort McHenry inspired Francis Scott Key, a local lawyer and journalist who witnessed the battle while on a British warship securing the release of an American prisoner, to write the lyrics to the "Star Spangled Banner," which became the U.S. national anthem in 1931.

After the War of 1812, Baltimore continued its social and economic growth. Its trade links with the South, the Caribbean, Latin America, and the Midwest made it a worthy competitor to New York, Philadelphia, and Boston for commercial supremacy on the East Coast. Baltimore's relative closeness to the Midwest and South made up somewhat for its longer distance from Europe compared to its competitors. But Baltimore's economic base came under attack in the 1820s with the opening of the Erie Canal, which put the Great Lakes and Midwest on New York City's doorstep and threatened to minimize the significance of Baltimore's proximity to midwestern markets. In response, the city's merchants and bankers courageously invested in a railroad line west from Baltimore across the Appalachian Mountains. This was the Baltimore and Ohio (B & O) railroad, whose construction started in 1828 with a line 20 miles west to Ellicott Mills. As time passed, the rail line was extended to Wheeling, Virginia (now West Virginia), and then to St. Louis and Chicago, preserving Baltimore's trade with the Midwest. The pioneering use of this new technology, at least partly, neutralized the Erie Canal's negative impact on Baltimore's economy. At about the same time, another vital development in nineteenth-century technology, the telegraph, was pioneered in Baltimore as Samuel F. B. Morse sent the first message over a line strung from Baltimore to Washington, D.C., in 1844.

While never the cultural center that Boston, New York, or Philadelphia became, Baltimore still had its share of noted authors, painters, and musicians. Among the most famous of these was the poet and novelist Edgar Allan Poe, who lived in Baltimore from 1831 to 1835 and died there in 1849.

Unlike earlier wars, the Civil War harmed Baltimore considerably. The city itself was torn between Unionists and Confederates, with southern sympathizers predominant. In April 1861, pro-Confederate Baltimoreans attacked the 6th Massachusetts Infantry as it passed through the city on its way to Washington, D.C. In response to this riot, which left 17 dead, President Lincoln sent a Union army detachment to occupy Federal Hill overlooking the harbor and central business district. With cannon aimed at Baltimore's heart, the Union army occupied the city for the duration of the war.

The Civil War also disrupted Baltimore's trade with the South. Before the war, the city had exported southern cotton, tobacco, and other staples while it supplied the South with manufactured goods, coal, grain, and shellfish from the Chesapeake Bay. The war's disarrangement of this commerce, along with the Union occupation, impoverished the city and allowed its northern competitors to surge ahead in the race for urban primacy. Although Baltimore recovered somewhat after the war, it never again challenged New York or Philadelphia for commercial or industrial ascendance on the East Coast.

Taking initial advantage of resentment about the war and fear of free black Republicans, the Democratic Party took political power in Baltimore after the Civil War and has held it with few interruptions ever since. In the post–Civil War Era, this control belonged to the machine run by Isaac Freeman Rasin. Though Rasin never held an official position higher than Clerk of the Court of Common Pleas, he controlled city contracts, patronage, and elections, and ran Baltimore and Maryland in conjunction with U.S. Senator Arthur Pue Gorman until 1895, when an insurgent Democratic reform faction joined with Republicans to elect the mayor and governor.

By the beginning of the twentieth century, Baltimore had thoroughly industrialized with textiles, brewing and distilling, railroading, shipbuilding, and steelmaking as its leading industries. Unlike other urban-industrial concentrations, Baltimore did not become a headquarters for major corporations. Only the B & O railroad was home-owned and operated, and even that ended during the economic turmoil of the 1890s. As a result, Baltimore became a "branch town" for major corporations. This restricted the city's growth, for without major corporate interests calling it home, the city lost control of its economic future and failed to benefit from the philanthropy and developmental interests that come from being a major headquarters city. Baltimore never generated local banking, mercantile, or industrial infrastructures to match other major cities of the East Coast or Midwest; therefore, while still a significant urban center, it lagged behind New York, Philadelphia, Boston, and Chicago in importance.

During the 1890s, Baltimore did attain prominence in sports as the Baltimore Orioles dominated major league baseball. Sadly, this was short-lived as the Orioles left Baltimore in 1902, not to return until 1954. Still Baltimore could claim baseball distinction as the birthplace of Babe Ruth, who grew up in Baltimore and first played professional baseball with the minor league Orioles before he went on to fame with the Boston Red Sox and New York Yankees.

At the turn of the century, Baltimore was unique among American cities in having a large immigrant population that coexisted with a large African-American one. Cities further north had few blacks, while cities further south had few immigrants. Baltimore's ethnic groups lived mostly on the east and southeast sides of the city while its blacks lived in enclaves adjoining the central business district on its northwest and east sides. Germans, Irish, Italians, Eastern European Jews, Greeks, and Czechs made up the bulk of the immigrants. Baltimore's black community was especially large in relation to other cities. In fact, by 1900, Baltimore had the second largest black population among cities in the country; only that of Washington, D.C., was larger. During the latter half of the nineteenth century, African Americans lived in a racially segregated, oppressive environment. The public schools were segregated, and those allocated to blacks were grossly inferior in facilities and funding. Most public accommodations discriminated against black patrons, and housing opportunities were rigidly limited. Despite these disabilities, Baltimore's blacks developed a significant community infrastructure of churches, businesses, fraternal organizations, and newspapers. One of these newspapers, the *Afro-American,* founded in 1892, is still published and joins the *Sun,* established in 1837, as the longest continuously published local newspapers in the country. The *Afro-American,* owned and operated since 1897 by John H. Murphy and his descendants, soon became the media voice for Baltimore's black community and helped lead the struggle for racial justice in the twentieth century.

The Great Fire of 1904 destroyed most of Baltimore's central business district. The city's establishment quickly responded to this calamity and rebuilt Baltimore's downtown by 1906. This would not, however, be the last occasion on which Baltimore redeveloped its downtown.

World War I brought a new level of prosperity to the city as its proximity to America's industrial heartland made it a major port for exporting war goods to Europe. By this time Baltimore itself had become a major industrial center due to its Bethlehem Steel Company plant and shipyard at Sparrows Point, which produced millions of tons of steel and ships and became the largest such complex on the East Coast.

Although the Great Depression halted Baltimore's economic growth once again, the city rebounded during World War II and entered a boom period during the late 1940s and 1950s. During these years, its population reached almost 1 million, topping off at 950,000 in 1950. It also built a major international airport, a tunnel under the harbor, and a principal expressway paralleling the Jones Falls. Baltimore also became a major league sports town when the Baltimore Colts joined the National Football League in 1953, the Orioles returned major league baseball to Baltimore in 1954, and the Baltimore Bullets joined the National Basketball Association in 1962.

As for its social development, Baltimore was unusually resistant to racial reform in the first half of the twentieth century. The city's blacks elected representatives to the city council with some regularity from 1890 to 1923, but gerrymandering, which merged black wards into majority-white districts, made such representation difficult if not impossible between 1931 and 1955. Furthermore, the city refused to hire black policemen until 1937, workers in the public library until 1944, and firemen until the 1950s. Its public schools remained segregated until the *Brown v. Board of Education* decision in 1954, and public accommodations were still racially discriminatory until the 1960s. Nevertheless, Baltimore's African-American community, led by the National Association for the Advancement of Colored People (NAACP), the *Afro-American,* its churches, and civic groups valiantly struggled against the racist social order. In doing so, it finally, and fatally, undermined Jim Crow in Baltimore.

Since the 1960s, Baltimore has faced the challenges and problems endemic to cities in the Northeast and Midwest. Among these have been urban riots (one of which took place in 1968 after Martin Luther King, Jr.'s assassination), the construction of the interstate highway system, the creation of federally subsidized home mortgages, and the growth of suburban housing developments. All of these eased white flight from Baltimore to surrounding counties. As this took place, the percentage of blacks in Baltimore's population increased to the point where, by the middle of the 1970s, Baltimore's population had a majority of African Americans. Following the white middle class to suburbs were significant segments of Baltimore's industry, business, and retail outlets. To stem this tide, the city government, aided by private and federal funding, rebuilt the central business district and the inner harbor starting in the 1960s. As Baltimore's heavy industry either downsized drastically or disappeared altogether, the city has tried to reposition itself as a service center emphasizing health care (largely due to the presence of the world renowned Johns Hopkins Hospital), tourism, and financial services. To maintain itself as a competitive port, Baltimore constructed facilities for container ships in the 1960s, 1970s, and 1980s, though this did not keep the city from losing a significant part of its shipping to Norfolk and other ports further south. Still, Baltimore in the 1980s, through the efforts of Mayor William Donald Schaefer to attract private and public money to redevelop its inner harbor, became a symbol of "urban renaissance." Among the symbols of this renewal were the National Aquarium, Harborplace, a new convention center, three new hotels, a giant condominium development, gentrified housing adjacent to the downtown, new office buildings, a subway and light rail line, and a new stadium for Baltimore's baseball team, Oriole Park at Camden Yards. As a result Baltimore's physical aspect was irrevocably changed.

Despite these advances, Baltimore faces an uncertain future. The flight of the white and later the black middle class from Baltimore continues unabated, leaving behind an impoverished population less and less able to pay for the social services they require. High crime rates and a chronically underfunded school system along with white discomfort in a majority black city have contributed to this out-migration.

The city's transition from an industrial/commercial economy to a high tech service economy has not been smooth and not enough lucrative service jobs have replaced the high-paying industrial jobs that began to disappear in the 1970s. For example, the Bethlehem Steel Company steel mill and shipyard, Baltimore's largest employer in the 1960s with 38,000 people on its payroll, today employs only about 8,000. This job loss devastated Baltimore's blue-collar communities. Today, Baltimore's two largest employers are Johns Hopkins Hospital and the local government, but their jobs do not pay as well as the industrial jobs they replaced.

Baltimore's African-American community finally elected one of its own—Kurt Schmoke, the local district attorney—as mayor in 1987. That this took place later than in other majority-black cities was due to the presence of William Donald Schaefer, Baltimore's mayor from 1971 to 1986.

Schaefer, one of the last big city machine politicians, skillfully used patronage, contracts, and allocation of federal urban aid to gain biracial support for his efforts to renew Baltimore. His success considerably slowed Baltimore's urban decline and made it better able to deal with its problems.

Baltimore faces daunting challenges. Still, it has successfully faced down challenges in the past in the form of the Erie Canal, the Civil War, and the Great Baltimore Fire, and will continue to do so now and in the future.

—*Hayward Farrar*

References

Argersinger, JoAnn E. *Towards a New Deal in Baltimore: People and Government in the Great Depression.* Chapel Hill: University of North Carolina Press, 1988.

Brugger, Robert J. *Maryland: A Middle Temperament 1634–1980.* Baltimore: Johns Hopkins University Press, 1988.

Crooks, James B. *Politics and Progress: The Rise of Urban Progressivism in Baltimore 1895–1911.* Baton Rouge: Louisiana State University Press, 1968.

Fee, Elizabeth, Linda Shopes, and Linda Zeidman, eds. *The Baltimore Book: New Views of Local History.* Philadelphia: Temple University Press, 1991.

Olson, Sherry. *Baltimore: The Building of an American City.* Baltimore: Johns Hopkins University Press, 1980.

Thomas, Bettye C. "The Baltimore Black Community 1865–1910." Ph.D. dissertation, George Washington University, 1974.

Banks and Banking

The earliest banks in North America appeared in leading commercial centers: Philadelphia (1781), New York (1784), Boston (1784), Baltimore (1790), and Providence (1791). In 1792 banks opened in New London, Hartford, and New Haven, Connecticut; Portsmouth, New Hampshire; Albany, New York; Alexandria, Virginia; and Charleston, South Carolina. By 1800, most towns with at least 5,000 inhabitants had one or more banks. New York, Boston, Philadelphia, New Orleans, Baltimore, Charleston, and Providence, the main banking centers of 1850, were the original "gateway cities" discerned by geographer R. J. Johnston as an urban pattern that developed in the United States

Of the 21 largest cities in the United States, 16 were redemption centers (later called "reserve cities") under the National Bank Act of 1864; a seventeenth, Leavenworth, in eastern Kansas, lost that status in 1872. Banks chartered by the federal government could hold part of their legal reserves as deposits with national banks in these 17 cities.

New York was the sole central reserve city until 1887; its national banks could serve as depositories of legal reserve for national banks in the other 16 cities as well as for "country banks" (national banks in all other locations). In 1887 Chicago and St. Louis also received central reserve city designation. Their national banks hoped thereby to attract deposits from outside banks.

By 1900 there were 30 reserve cities. Of the 14 added after 1864, 9 were west of the Mississippi. Although Newark, Buffalo, Rochester, and Providence were among the largest 21 cities in 1864 and the largest 25 in 1900, they never became reserve cities. Brooklyn became one in 1887 and remained a reserve city even after being consolidated with New York in 1898. Jersey City, among the 25 largest cities in 1900, was never a reserve city under the National Bank Act.

Nineteen additional cities became reserve cities between 1900 and 1910, and all of them were west of the Mississippi River. The minimum population needed to qualify as a reserve city was reduced from 50,000 to 25,000 in 1903, and smaller places vied for deposit growth as correspondent banks.

The Federal Reserve Act of 1913 made the banking system of the United States consonant with the country's dispersed urbanization and harmonized it with emergent metropolitan regionalism. Ten of the 49 reserve cities under the national banking system became headquarters of district Federal Reserve Banks, as did Atlanta and Richmond, although they had not been reserve cities. Ten of the 12 district Federal Reserve Banks (all except Boston and Philadelphia) opened branches in places that had previously been reserve cities, as well as in Buffalo, Charlotte, Chattanooga, El Paso, Helena, Jacksonville, Little Rock, Memphis, Miami, and Nashville.

After 1917, the reserve city designation no longer enabled member banks to attract deposits from correspondent banks to fulfill reserve requirements under the Federal Reserve Act. Nevertheless, in 1918 member banks in nine cities elected to continue as reserve cities rather than have their status (and required reserves) reduced to the rank of country banks: Dubuque, Galveston, Kansas City (Kansas), Peoria, Pueblo, St. Joseph, Toledo, Topeka, and Waco.

A decline in New York City's financial preponderance was one of the objectives of the sponsors of the Federal Reserve Act. New York had 30 of the 100 largest United States commercial banks in 1923, with 49 percent of all deposits in these major institutions; by 1930, it had only 21, with 32 percent of all deposits. More significant than the 1913 law in diminishing the premier status of Wall Street were the forces decentralizing economic activity and population. Even so, New York has remained the nation's leading financial center, and one of very few centers of global finance.

On the eve of the Civil War there were over 1,500 incorporated banks in the United States, and more than 11,400 just 35 years later. Between 1896 and 1908, the total doubled, peaking at 30,456 banks in 1921. Thousands of institutions with less than $25,000 of capital dotted the rural landscape. Of the 6,987 banks that suspended operations between 1921 and 1930, almost 79 percent were in places with a population below 2,500.

Banks were expected to foster local economic growth. Kansas cattlemen opened the Stock Exchange Bank at the south end of Caldwell's business district in October 1881. Within four months, businessmen from the north end organized the Caldwell Savings Bank; the rivalry involved downtown real estate values. Owatonna, 60 miles south of Minneapolis, had 949 residents, but two banks. In 1865 Minnesota granted a city charter in anticipation of the arrival of two railroad lines the following year. Owatonna's National Farmers Bank commissioned a leading architect to design a new headquarters, Louis Sullivan's masterpiece, completed in 1908.

Most banks did business out of a single office until well into the twentieth century. Only 87 had any branches in 1900—119 in all; by 1910, 292 had 548 branches. Downtown traffic volume was a factor encouraging branches in cities (where permitted by state law). They numbered 773 in 1920, and 2,389 a decade later. Depressed business conditions reduced the total to 1,603 in 1940.

At the peak in 1929, 500 banking institutions with branches had almost half of the 5,500 bank offices in cities with more than 25,000 people. The 11 leading branch cities had over 1,700 branches in cities; New York alone had 630, followed by San Francisco, Los Angeles, Detroit, Philadelphia, Cleveland, Baltimore, Boston, Buffalo, Cincinnati, and New Orleans.

The financial district of larger trading centers included insurance and securities firms as well as banks. These districts were compact areas; trade and industrial activities were conducted nearby. Well into the 1830s, the most desirable residential sections were close enough to permit financiers to walk to work, but by the 1860s, growing congestion led the well-to-do to reside farther from their offices. Wall Street emerged around 1805 to 1810 as the first financial district. State Street in Boston developed in the 1830s, and San Francisco's California Street was known as the Wall Street of the West by the 1860s.

Prominent skyscrapers replaced multistory bank buildings in downtown districts of the larger cities. At the junction of Wall, Broad, and Nassau Streets in New York City, Bankers Trust Company sponsored "a monumental building at the vortex of America's financial life." Opened in 1912, the 31-story tower featured a stepped pyramid at the top. The Bank of Manhattan tower at 40 Wall Street in New York (1929) was the fifth-tallest building in the world as late as the early 1960s. The Irving Trust Company completed a 51-story monument at 1 Wall Street in 1931. The first skyscraper in the South was built in 1912 and 1913 for First National Bank of Richmond. Hibernia Bank ordered a building twice the height of any other in Louisiana; its 23-story headquarters (1921) remains a dominant New Orleans landmark.

After World War II, bank skyscrapers were built even in less densely populated cities. The 75-story tower for Houston's Texas Commerce Bank (1981) was said to be the tallest bank building in the world, and the tallest structure west of the Mississippi. Miami's 55-story Southeast Financial Center building (1987) was the tallest in that part of the nation. NCNB (now Nations Bank) in Charlotte, North Carolina, topped this in 1991 with an 871-foot-high corporate center designed by Cesar Pelli, as befits the largest banking company in the South and Southwest. Pelli earlier completed the 57-story Minneapolis headquarters of Norwest Corporation (1988).

In Chicago, long distinguished for its commercial architecture, the 60-story First National Bank's tapered tower in the center of the Loop (1969) was a decisive break with the rectangular box design in great favor for many years after Chase Manhattan Bank opened its 60-story, 813-foot headquarters in 1961. This development served as a powerful stimulus to the revitalization of New York's historic financial district. At the same time, National City Bank chose a new midtown headquarters on Park Avenue. The fast-growing firm inaugurated Citicorp Center due east of this building in 1977. The top 130 feet of the 914-foot structure features a prominent 45-degree angle.

Despite the growing suburbanization of American society and industry in the decades after 1945, major banks continued to be headquartered in the central business district of larger cities. Urban renewal efforts attracted young professionals to reside near their jobs.

Today, banking and other financial services are among the most significant industries whose main task is processing information. Information-intensive industries tend to be concentrated in the central city of large metropolitan areas. So far at least, new communications technologies have not diminished the importance of large cities; they are the hubs of the new systems. However, these technologies have facilitated the shift of back-office functions—routine activities that do not call for direct, face-to-face contact—out of central cities to lower-cost locations.

—Benjamin J. Klebaner

See also
Redlining.
References
Fischer, Gerald C. *American Banking Structure: Its Evolution and Regulation.* New York: Columbia University Press, 1967.
Hammond, Bray. *Banks and Politics in America from the Revolution to the Civil War.* Princeton, NJ: Princeton University Press, 1957.
Klebaner, Benjamin J. *American Commercial Banking: A History.* Boston: Twayne, 1990.
Krooss, Herman E., and Martin Blyn. *History of Financial Intermediaries.* New York: Random House, 1971.
McKelvey, Blake. *The Urbanization of America.* New Brunswick, NJ: Rutgers University Press, 1963.
Robertson, Ross M., with Jesse H. Stiller. *The Comptroller and Bank Supervision. A Historical Approach.* Washington, DC: Office of the Comptroller of the Currency, 1995.
Trescott, Paul B. *Financing American Enterprise.* New York: Harper & Row, 1963.

Barnum, Phineas T. (1810–1891)

Phineas T. (P. T.) Barnum was the leading showman of the nineteenth century. Barnum produced amusements for a United States that, despite the rapid growth of its cities, was still predominately a rural nation. Much of Barnum's success was due to his zealous cultivation of country patrons. But the rural people who read Barnum's autobiographies, listened to Jenny Lind (the Swedish singer who toured the country under Barnum's management in 1850 and 1851), visited his museums (in New York, Philadelphia, and Baltimore), and attended his circus were treated to popular culture with a distinctly urban cast. In two of the century's most popular autobiographies, *The Life of P. T Barnum* (1854) and *Struggles and Triumphs* (first published in 1869, frequently supplemented thereafter), Barnum mythologized himself as a self-made man who rose from rural poverty to urban wealth.

The Barnum of these autobiographies embodies the male virtues of the urban middle class: temperance, self-discipline, relentless industry, and entrepreneurship. *Struggles* documents Barnum's mixed success at enforcing those values as a developer and politician in his adopted hometown of Bridgeport, Connecticut. As a showman, however, Barnum found moral reform easier to sell.

Barnum's American Museum in New York City (actually two museums, the first destroyed by fire in 1865, the second in 1868) framed its attractions in the reformist rhetoric of the urban middle class and their "respectable" working-class allies. In an age when most working-class amusements were male-oriented, Barnum's museum attracted families. Women came for the museum's weekday theatrical matinees, baby shows, and sentimental exhibits; children enjoyed its half-priced tickets and fairy-tale spectacles. The museum circumvented the widespread bias against theater among family patrons by calling its playhouse a "lecture room" and its plays "moral dramas." Since the lecture room's repertoire and personnel were often indistinguishable from those of other New York theaters, its moral pretensions were built less on what happened onstage than off. In 1850, when the lecture room formally dedicated itself to drama, at least one New York theater still included a "third tier" set aside for prostitutes and their clients, and most featured bars; Barnum, however, excluded both. While Barnum's opponents attacked his museum as a "moral humbug," his patrons saw it as a place to participate in the politics, commerce, and the culture of the city while being shielded from its moral taint.

In April 1871, less than three years after the second museum fire, Barnum was back with another major amusement enterprise—P. T. Barnum's Museum, Menagerie, and Circus. Over the next two decades Barnum and his partners—among them, circus veterans William C. Coup and James A. Bailey—helped usher the American railroad tented circus into its Golden Age. The Barnum Circus was as famous for its respectability as its amplitude; boasting the endorsements of noted clergymen, it turned into patrons many Christians who had formerly condemned the circus as immoral. The circus was both the culmination of Barnum's career and a harbinger of twentieth-century popular culture, especially in its assembly of a national audience around the values and cultural styles of the northern business class.

—*Bluford Adams*

See also
Circuses.
References
Adams, Bluford. *E Pluribus Barnum: The Great Showman and the Making of U.S. Popular Culture.* Minneapolis: University of Minnesota Press, 1987.
Harris, Neil. *Humbug: The Art of P. T. Barnum.* Boston: Little, Brown, 1973.
Saxon, A. H. *P. T. Barnum: The Legend and the Man.* New York: Columbia University Press, 1989.

Barrio

As the word is commonly used in the United States, a barrio (literally, quarter or district) is a neighborhood predominantly occupied by residents of Hispanic origin, typically situated in a low-income area of a city or town. Although many middle- and upper-class Hispanics lived beyond the boundaries of barrios in the 1990s, the number and size of these enclaves reflect the continued residential segregation of a substantial part of the nation's second-largest minority.

A barrio typically contains a concentration of a specific ethnic group of Hispanic origin. There are Mexican-American barrios in the Southwest, Puerto Rican barrios in New York and nearby cities in New Jersey, and Cuban barrios in south Florida. Particularly in larger metropolitan areas, however, there is likely to be an admixture of other Hispanics living in conjunction with the primary ethnic group. Sizable numbers of Hispanics have migrated from their original areas of settlement so that Puerto Ricans, for example, live in predominantly Mexican-American barrios in Los Angeles and in Cuban barrios in Miami. In addition, various nationalities from Central and South America, including Nicaraguans, Salvadorans, Guatemalans, Hondurans, and others have entered the United States in large numbers during recent decades. They have tended to migrate to very large cities and take up residence in an already established barrio. This is particularly true for those who enter the United States without legal documentation and are seeking refuge in a predominantly Hispanic milieu.

A barrio will often have an informal name bestowed upon it by nonbarrio residents, such as "Little Mexico" in Dallas, "Little Havana" in Miami, or "Spanish Harlem" in New York City. The residents themselves may identify their community differently; for example, Puerto Ricans speak of their neighborhood as El Barrio rather than "Spanish Harlem." These internally generated names often reveal how the residents view their community. *Sal si Puedes* is a fairly common barrio name, literally meaning "Leave if you can." On the other hand, some names generated by residents reflect a more positive view, such as *La Estrella* (the star), or describe topographical features of the community, including *La Bajada* (the lowland) or *Los Altos* (the heights).

Some barrio settlements date their origins to the nineteenth century, but others have only recently emerged. Many older barrios disappeared through demolition as the cities that contained them instigated new development. "Little Mexico," the oldest barrio in Dallas, was bifurcated by freeways and most of its residents displaced. The barrio known as Chavez Ravine in Los Angeles was destroyed in order to build Dodger Stadium in the 1960s. For several years thereafter, graffiti proclaimed "Remember Chavez Ravine!" and the event was memorialized on part of a large mural painted by local artists. Former residents still feel bitterness and resentment when they see urban renewal programs designed more to benefit Anglos (non-Hispanic whites) in the larger community than Hispanics in the barrios.

The boundaries of barrio communities are typically fluid. When immigration greatly increases population pressure, barrios may expand at the periphery and encompass residues of non-Hispanic residents and institutions. When freeways or other developments destroy Hispanic neighborhoods, whole populations may be transplanted to other locations.

Some researchers have used the concepts of "colony" to describe predominantly ethnic areas, and "frontier" to designate areas with mixed ethnic populations. As barrio residents achieve some economic mobility, they may move away to live in frontier neighborhoods mixed with Anglo residents. In general, there is a close correlation between poverty and the colony, and higher income and the frontier. There is also a slighter correlation between more traditional cultural patterns and colony inhabitants and between acculturated characteristics and frontier residents. Colony barrio residents may identify strongly with their community and view those who leave as *vendidos* (sellouts). In addition, interbarrio rivalry sometimes erupts. This is particularly true when barrio youth gangs clash with gangs from other neighborhoods.

Spanish signs hang in front of a store in Los Angeles, 1993.

East Los Angeles is perhaps the most widely studied area of Mexican settlement in the United States. It was probably the first self-contained barrio in the city and provided a network of related, extended families for longtime residents and a supportive haven for new immigrants. The area around Olvera Street remains a vivid reminder of early Hispanic settlement and still contains many businesses operated by Mexican Americans. Over many decades, the barrio expanded to encompass a larger territory, engulfing and transforming other neighborhoods. In addition, other barrios were established in nearby communities. The 1990 census reported 3.7 million Mexican Americans living in the greater Los Angeles metropolitan area—a number that excludes the illegal and the undocumented.

As the number of undocumented workers escalated, economic competition caused tensions within the barrio between rooted Mexican Americans and new immigrants without legal papers. The strain was heightened during the 1970s when Mexican Americans lost unionized industrial jobs and were replaced by undocumented Mexicans who would work for lower wages. The arrival of large numbers of Central and South Americans into the ethnic mix, as well as the increasing proximity of Asian neighborhoods, created additional rivalries between groups that sometimes led to violence between barrios.

Among the grim realities of many inner-city neighborhoods in the United States during the 1990s was the growing presence of juvenile gangs, some of them engaged in drug dealing and other criminal activities. Rage and frustration engendered by social and economic marginality, families under strain, and alienation from a larger society perceived as unmindful of their predicament contributed to an increase in violent behavior among some barrio youth. In 1992 the Los Angeles District Attorney's office reported up to 150,000 gang members in Los Angeles County, including Hispanic as well as black, Asian, and white gangs. Gang symbols became part of the urban scene, including widespread public graffiti, body tattoos, and distinctive clothing styles using colors to identify gang membership. Drive-by shootings, thefts, assaults, and murders rose as gangs victimized neighborhoods and battled each other to protect territorial boundaries, to gain "respect" as the gang defined it, or to take revenge for real or imagined affronts.

Barrios are often seen in highly negative terms that emphasize widespread poverty, crowded and dilapidated housing, unstable families, juvenile gangs, and high crime rates.

Certainly, census data and sociological research show that "mean streets" and attendant social ills are a grim reality in many large- and small-city barrios in the United States. However, barrios differ considerably in their community structure. The relationship to the larger community in which they are embedded can be relatively open or closed according to the degree of institutionalized discrimination present. Police-minority relations, the responsiveness of schools to the needs of barrio youth, and the representation afforded minorities in the political structure all strongly affect the quality of life in the barrio. Moreover, barrios vary in their socioeconomic mix, accessibility to jobs, ethnic composition, prevailing family structures, extent of church participation, proportion of homeowners to renters, housing and street conditions, and the availability and quality of social services, recreation, shopping, transportation, and other facilities. Barrios with at least some positive environmental features can be socially cohesive, with interrelated families who form tight bonds of kinship and mutual support; here, crime rates are relatively low, juvenile gangs infrequent, and the majority of residents building lives of dignity and stability even in the face of economic hardship. Other barrios, however, with few if any favorable elements, present arduous living conditions that can overwhelm traditional value systems and blight the lives of their residents.

Additionally, these neighborhoods create problems for the larger community, including high crime rates, broken families, welfare dependency, drug addiction, and juvenile delinquency—ills that adversely affect the city as a whole as well as its ethnically distinctive barrios.

—*Shirley Achor*

See also
Chinatown; Ghetto.
References
Achor, Shirley. *Mexican Americans in a Dallas Barrio*. Tucson: University of Arizona Press, 1991.
Bourgeois, Phillipe. *In Search of Respect: Selling Crack in El Barrio*. New York: Cambridge University Press, 1995.
Carlson, Lori Marie. *Barrio Streets, Carnival Dreams: Three Generations of Latino Artistry*. New York: Henry Holt, 1996.
Galarza, Ernesto. *Barrio Boy*. Notre Dame, IN: University of Notre Dame Press, 1971.
Garcia, Maria Cristina. *Havana, USA: Cuban Exiles and Cuban Americans in South Florida*. Austin: University of Texas Press, 1996.
Griswold del Castillo, Richard. *The Los Angeles Barrio, 1850–1890*. Berkeley: University of California Press, 1980.
Heyck, Denis Lynn Daly. *Barrios and Borderlands: Cultures of Latinos and Latinas in the United States*. London: Routledge, 1994.
Horowitz, Ruth. *Honor and the American Dream: Culture and Identity in a Chicano Community*. New Brunswick, NJ: Rutgers University Press, 1983.
Moore, Joan W. *Going Down to the Barrio: Homeboys and Homegirls in Change*. Philadelphia: Temple University Press, 1991.
Moore, Joan W., and Harry Pachon. *Mexican Americans*. 2d ed. Englewood Cliffs, NJ: Prentice-Hall, 1976.
Padilla, Felix M. *The Gang as an American Enterprise*. New Brunswick, NJ: Rutgers University Press, 1992.
Romo, Ricardo. *East Los Angeles: History of a Barrio, 1900–1930*. Austin: University of Texas Press, 1983.
Rubel, Arthur. *Across the Tracks: Mexican Americans in a Texas City*. Austin: University of Texas Press, 1966.
Vigil, James Diego. *Barrio Gangs: Street Life and Identity in Southern California*. Austin: University of Texas Press, 1988.

Barry, Marion S., Jr. (1936–)

Marion S. Barry, Jr., served as mayor of Washington, D.C., from 1979 to 1990 and was reelected to that office in 1994 after a federal conviction for possessing crack cocaine in 1990 preempted an earlier bid for reelection. Associated for most of 20 years in Washington with the drive for black empowerment that first brought him to public office, Barry's growing indiscretions in the 1980s made him a controversial and polarizing figure, even before his conviction. But flaunting his immersion in the church and his identification with so many fellow citizens who were personally familiar with the problems of drug or alcohol abuse, Barry found a responsive following as he campaigned to redeem himself as the city's mayor.

The son of a Mississippi sharecropper, Barry was the first in his family to attend college, where he entered the civil rights movement through involvement in the campus chapter of the National Association for the Advancement of Colored People (NAACP). Subsequently, he took a role sitting in at segregated lunch counters in Nashville, Tennessee, while he was a graduate student at Fisk University. A founder of the Student Nonviolent Coordinating Committee and also its first chairperson, Barry moved to Washington in 1965 to open a branch office as part of SNCC's effort to extend its reach from the rural South to the nation's major cities.

Barry rapidly established a leadership role for himself in Washington, leading a successful boycott of buses in 1966 because of a fare hike that would have harmed the city's black working class. He then launched a "Free DC" movement dedicated to overcoming business opposition to granting the city home rule. As Congress finally allowed local political participation after ruling the city for a century, Barry assumed such power as was available, securing election in quick succession to the school board, a newly elected city council as authorized in home rule legislation in 1973, and finally in 1978 as the city's second elected mayor in the twentieth century.

Barry inherited many residual problems from federal oversight, including an operating budget deficit and an underfunded pension plan. Determined to showcase black talent under the glare of national attention, he assembled a talented staff, many with outstanding civil rights credentials, and set about reducing the deficit, even as he initiated new programs designed to deal with the many social problems besetting the city. With a young city government in place that provided little deference to incumbents, Barry also had to devise a political strategy to get reelected. In 1982, and again in 1986, he overcame primary opposition with a duel strategy of currying favor in the business community he had once challenged and by padding the city payroll that he had been forced to cut when he first gained office.

Barry's political instincts kept him in office, but his reign was troubled by scandal even before the end of his first term, as a succession of his political aides were convicted of misusing public funds. Barry maintained his distance from those convicted, but by the mid-1980s his personal life had became increasingly controversial, not the least through his association with several people being investigated for drug use. Barry insisted he was clean, frequently leading police forays into drug-infested areas in the effort to stem the scourge that was helping make Washington the crime capital of the nation.

On the evening of January 18, 1990, he could no longer claim innocence, however, as the Federal Bureau of Investigation captured on videotape the mayor smoking crack cocaine that he had accepted from a former girlfriend who was now cooperating with the police. Barry denounced the sting operation as a "political lynching," finding many sympathizers among African Americans who remained suspicious of federal efforts to reign in the city's assertive black leadership. Barry's indictment was sufficient to keep him from running again for mayor, however, and his effort to retain public office by running as an independent for a seat on the city council also failed. Sentenced to six months in prison, Barry remained defiant. Shortly after his release he entered the Democratic primary for city council in the city's poorest ward. Utilizing an aggressive registration and get-out-the-vote campaign, Barry overwhelmed a popular incumbent, thereby launching his stunning political comeback. Two years later, he challenged for mayor both the incumbent and a fellow city councilman who was favored in the Democratic primary. Extending the political techniques he had perfected two years earlier, Barry scored an impressive victory, utilizing majorities not just in the poorest areas of the city but also in black middle-class neighborhoods to secure 47 percent of the total vote cast. Despite powerful opposition from the *Washington Post* and an issue-oriented Republican challenger, Barry was elected with 56 percent in the general election. Declaring in his inaugural address, "If Marion Barry can do it, our entire city can get up off its knees and rise up and believe in itself again," the mayor promised he had learned enough from his past mistakes to tackle effectively the social and fiscal problems besetting the city.

The city's dire fiscal condition proved more than the mayor could handle alone, however. The product both of mismanagement and federal restrictions on raising new revenues through such common devices as a commuter tax, the projected deficit for 1995 approached nearly $750 million even before Barry took office. Ascertaining that the city could no longer sustain burdens traditionally assumed by the states, such as Medicare payments and administration of prisons, Barry responded to the crisis by asking for federal assistance in reducing the deficit. Instead, Congress imposed a control board on Washington with instructions to cut costs, largely by a reduction in the city workforce. Together with the assumption through receivership of other key government services, the control board drastically curtailed the mayor's power. While he could take some solace from a December 1996 control board report sustaining his plea for increased federal payments to the city, Barry nonetheless lost the complete dominance he had once had in Washington's affairs.

—*Howard Gillette, Jr.*

References

Gillette, Howard, Jr. *Between Justice and Beauty: Race, Planning, and the Failure of Urban Policy in Washington, D.C.* Baltimore: Johns Hopkins University Press, 1995.

Jaffe, Harry S., and Tom Sherwood. *Dream City: Race, Power, and the Decline of Washington, D.C.* New York: Simon & Schuster, 1994.

Bars and Saloons

Alcohol promotes conviviality, and Americans, like other peoples, have usually consumed strong drink in public places. The colonists commonly imbibed in inns and taverns that also served travelers, but by the mid-1800s wealthy male drinkers in America's large, growing, and prosperous cities increasingly sought out the all-male saloon—a new type of drinking spot whose French name *(salon)* suggested a large room of luxury and exclusivity. In its original version, the typical saloon was dark, ornate, and pompously overdecorated. It often featured a polished marble floor, heavy brass spittoons for tobacco chewers, a richly carved walnut or mahogany bar, a large mirror or oil painting of a beautiful woman behind the bar, impressive rows of bottled liquors, and a well-dressed bartender who expertly mixed such new drinks as the cocktail, the Manhattan, or the mint julep. Gentlemen's saloons were among the first places equipped with shaved ice and carbonated water.

Ordinary taverns tried to improve their image and their revenues by calling themselves saloons, and by the late 1800s almost any place selling alcohol was generally said to be a saloon. Frontier saloons were naturally rough and rowdy (though not all proved as deadly as the one where Wild Bill Hickock was shot in the back), but even urban working-class saloons were boisterous. Brewers owned or controlled many public houses, and after 1880 most saloons sold far more beer than hard liquor. They routinely provided a "free lunch" to anyone who paid his nickel (the going price) for a beer. This midday meal, often important to laborers, usually came from a long table offering ham, pickles, pretzels, potato salad, and other similar fare. Owners of saloons well understood that salty food encouraged their patrons to drink more beer. The saloon often had a back room for gambling, and prostitutes sometimes worked upstairs. Respectable women dared not enter most saloons, lest they be mistaken for merchandise.

The saloonkeeper kept a running tab for regular customers, acted as a pawnbroker, and cashed paychecks. He also helped find work for unemployed patrons and organized votes under political boss rule. For immigrant men, in particular, the saloon's camaraderie contrasted with the loneliness of single life or the drabness of the tenement slums where newcomers usually lived. In the immigrant districts of America's largest cities, saloons flourished on every city block. One could scarcely walk a hundred feet between them.

Immigrants from drinking cultures in Europe, whether Irish, German, or Italian, resisted the temperance campaign of many native-born Americans to give up alcohol voluntarily. After the antiliquor forces turned toward mandatory abstinence by advocating local and state prohibition during the 1880s, they quickly learned that the main obstacle to a dry America came from urban political machines that were organized around immigrants' saloons. The Woman's Christian Temperance Union (WCTU) and, later, the Anti-Saloon League realized that alcohol could only be eradicated by smashing urban saloons and their power, but opponents also saw the destruction of saloons as a precondition of ridding the country of corrupt politics, crime, and vice.

The dry coalition was composed of rural folk suspicious of cities and immigrants, of the urban middle classes who increasingly defined respectability in terms of avoiding saloons, and of women reformers who saw the saloon as a threat to home, family, and motherhood. The most notorious opponent was Carry Nation, who led women in ax-wielding attacks on drinking establishments. After 1900, Progressives worked hard for prohibition as part of their larger goal of reforming society and politics. By 1920, this hatred of saloons had helped produce prohibition, which did destroy old-style drinking halls.

The so-called "speakeasies" of the 1920s replaced saloons, but these illegal watering holes lacked saloons' majesty, power, and male camaraderie. Instead of gleaming bottles of branded liquor behind the bar, alcohol, often of dubious manufacture, was now hidden in a back room and arrived at patrons' tables in teacups. Drinks were often gulped down quickly to hide the evidence in case of a police raid. Women joined men in these drinking places, and owners acquiesced since the female presence tended to camouflage the real business.

With the end of Prohibition in 1933, speakeasies gave way to legal bars that looked bright, spare, and cheery. The

A typical bustling speakeasy during Prohibition.

attempt to be modern was partly designed to cultivate a younger crowd, but this style also was forced on bar owners by the widespread state regulation that followed Prohibition. Although Americans overwhelmingly approved repeal, they opposed saloons, and many states banned liquor by the drink. Americans, however, did not want to drink alone at home, so the demand for licensed premises remained high. Some states sanctioned private clubs and others tolerated bars but precluded saloonlike features. Gone was the free lunch and also, usually, the gambling and prostitution. Bars seldom enjoyed the political power of saloons and, to avoid trouble with the still powerful antiliquor forces, quietly sold alcohol in clean, antiseptic surroundings. After prohibition, bars continued the practice of men and women drinking together. The presence of women appeared to reduce barroom brawling, and music and dancing sometimes seemed to create a more light-hearted atmosphere.

Bars prospered during World War II, but business slumped after the war. The baby boom kept parents at home, and television discouraged people from visiting neighborhood drinking establishments. The rising popularity and low price of canned beer also produced more home drinking. Furthermore, the migration of the middle class to suburbs frequently left city bars with only poor customers, which produced a seedy image, while automobile-oriented suburbs proved inconducive to bars, which had always thrived on neighborhood foot traffic. Drinking places tried to regain customers by installing color television sets and, later, big screens to attract crowds to watch sporting events. To some extent this strategy succeeded, and bars increased their business when the numerous baby boomers became young adults in the late 1960s. As mores changed, both men and women used bars to seek casual sexual partners, and gay and lesbian bars gained notice; the gay rights movement began in 1969 when gay men rioted at the Stone Wall bar in New York City after a police raid.

In the 1970s a reaction against the hedonistic bar culture set in. As liquor consumption peaked and then fell, drinking establishments survived by increasingly selling alcohol alongside food, entertainment, or both. Manufacturers, distributors, and retailers promoted light beer and, somewhat later, nonalcoholic beer and other drinks without liquor. California curdled the atmosphere inside bars by posting signs warning that alcohol caused health problems. One bar waitress refused to serve alcohol to a visibly pregnant woman to protect the baby from fetal alcohol syndrome. Barkeepers grew cautious about serving customers after bars began to face legal liability for their patrons' automobile accidents, and some bars insisted on calling cabs for inebriated patrons. Many Americans adopted a personal policy of never driving after having had a drink, visiting neighborhood watering holes less often. Instead, they traveled to weekend resorts, including casinos and theme parks, where they could drink without driving, or they took nondriving foreign vacations that included sampling exotic liquors. After 1990 bar sales continued to decline as aging baby boomers drank less and the country entered a more sober era.

— *W. J. Rorabaugh*

See also
Drinking, Alcohol Abuse, and Drunkenness; Nation, Carry Amelia Moore; Prohibition; Temperance Movement; Willard, Frances Elizabeth Caroline.

References
Cahalan, Don, and Robin Room. *Problem Drinking among American Men*. New Brunswick, NJ: Rutgers University Press, 1974.
Duis, Perry. *The Saloon: Public Drinking in Chicago and Boston, 1880–1920*. Urbana: University of Illinois Press, 1983.
Kerr, K. Austin. *Organized for Prohibition: A New History of the Anti-Saloon League*. New Haven, CT: Yale University Press, 1985.
Noel, Thomas J. *The City and the Saloon: Denver, 1858–1916*. Lincoln: University of Nebraska Press, 1982.
West, Elliott. *The Saloon on the Rocky Mountain Mining Frontier*. Lincoln: University of Nebraska Press, 1979.

Barthelme, Donald (1931–1989)

Donald Barthelme's greatest contribution to contemporary literature was his radically innovative approach to the short story. *Postmodernist, metafictionist, surrealist, minimalist—*

with these and a host of other terms, critics have attempted to locate Barthelme's chameleon-like genius on the literary map. His fiction demands that readers put aside preconceptions about genre, plot, character, chronology, and situation, thus opening themselves to an active, unmediated engagement with the text and, through the text, with the world.

For Barthelme, despite his technical innovations and linguistic pyrotechnics, the world beyond the written text retains its integrity, and that world is essentially urban. Richard Patteson called Barthelme's "sense of the urban—the sights, sounds, gestures, words, pleasures, and anxieties of city life— unsurpassed among writers of his generation." Whether he is describing a huge balloon hanging over Manhattan ("Balloon") or "strange-looking trees, not trees but something between a tree and a giant shrub" that characterize Los Angeles ("Construction"), Barthelme's cities have immediacy and particularity. "The world reminds us of its power, again and again," proclaims one of Barthelme's narrators ("Aria"). Asked in an interview with Jo Brans to describe "the proper response to the world," Barthelme replied, "embracing it."

Unlike Italo Calvino, whose *Invisible Cities* has been called by William Gass "one of the purer works of the imagination," Barthelme did not render his cities invisible by the preemptive reality of the words that describe them. In the interview with Brans, Barthelme described himself as a realist because his fiction offers "a true account of the activities of the mind." One of his characters reflects that the city is "the most exquisite mysterious muck," but it is "only a part of a much greater muck—the nation-state—which is itself the creation of that muck of mucks, human consciousness" ("City Life"). For Barthelme, according to Alan Wilde, "the horizon of the phenomenal world is not an objective thing or place 'out there,' it is the subjective, but no less real, result of being in the world—the shifting boundary of *human* depth, the pledge of man's necessary interaction with a world of which he is not only part but partner."

Like the balloon in the story mentioned above, Barthelme's fiction is a crucial intersection of art, life, and human consciousness. The titular balloon begins at Fourteenth Street in lower Manhattan and expands until it covers "forty-five blocks north-south and an irregular area east-west, as many as six cross-town blocks on either side of the Avenue in some places." Neither the balloon nor Barthelme's fiction can be viewed in Aristotelian terms—"situations," "resolution," "escape of tension," "meaning." The balloon is simply a "concrete particular" that encourages participation—running, leaping, bouncing, falling—and offers "the possibility, in its randomness, of mislocation of the self, in contradistinction to the grid of precise, rectangular pathways under our feet." The story ends with an autobiographical disclosure by the balloon's creator that seems oddly out of keeping with the claims he has been making for his creation, but incongruity and inconsistency are the essence of Barthelme's irony.

"Cities are erotic," explains one of Barthelme's characters, "in a depressing sort of way" ("City Life"). In cities, "the horrors" wait patiently—"Not even policemen and their ladies are safe, the horrors thought" ("The Policemen's Ball"). New Yorkers take pride in the levels of stress engendered by life in the city. "You can imagine what they'd feel if they were told they weren't under stress" ("Jaws"). Corruption and social injustice characterize urban life in one of Barthelme's most complex stories, where the city's defenders send heroin and hyacinths into the ghetto, torture a captured Comanche, and inadvertently kill children with helicopters and rockets ("The Indian Uprising"). For all its shortcomings, however, and despite the random violence and "lack of angst" that characterize contemporary urban existence, Barthelme's stories reflect the author's life-long love affair with "the complicated city." "Do I want to be loved *in spite of?*" asks one of his characters. "Do you? Does anyone? But aren't we all, to some degree?" ("Rebecca"). Loving *in spite of:* this, perhaps, is what Barthelme meant when he spoke of embracing the world.

—*Lucy Wilson*

References

Barthelme, Donald. *Forty Stories.* New York: Penguin, 1989.
———. *Sixty Stories.* New York: Dutton, 1982.
Brans, Jo. "Embracing the World: An Interview with Donald Barthelme." *Southwest Review* 67 (1982): 121–137.
Patteson, Richard F. "Introduction." In Richard F. Patteson, ed., *Critical Essays on Donald Barthelme.* New York: G. K. Hall, 1992.
Wilde, Alan. *Horizons of Assent: Modernism, Postmodernism, and the Ironic Imagination.* Baltimore: Johns Hopkins University Press, 1981.

Baseball

Baseball originated in the early nineteenth century as an urban sport that evolved from children's versions of the English game of rounders. In 1842 a group of respectable, young, middle-class men began playing a version of baseball in New York City. Three years later, they formed the Knickerbocker Base Ball Club and had formal rules written down for them by Alexander J. Cartwright. The Knickerbockers became the model for future teams, although the first reported game between clubs, played in October 1845, was between the New York Club, already at least two years old, and the Brooklyn Club. One year later, the New York Club defeated the Knickerbockers 23–1 in Hoboken, New Jersey, where the latter team had moved in 1845 because of New York's growth and development.

In the 1850s, baseball surpassed cricket as the leading team sport in the United States because of its youthful base, greater excitement, identification as an "American" sport, and the shorter time required to play its games. Early players were mainly upper-middle- and middle-class men, although one-fourth were artisans. In 1857 the top teams in the New York area organized the National Association of Base Ball Players to define rules, resolve disputes, and control the sport's future. By the 1860s, winning had become increasingly important. Teams recruited top players with cash or sinecures, beginning with pitcher James Creighton in 1860, and a championship system emerged. Commercialization soon followed with the enclosure of playing fields.

The first openly all-salaried nine was the Cincinnati Red Stockings of 1869, organized as a booster venture. Its successful eastern tour (57–0–1) encouraged professionalization, and in 1871 the National Association of Professional Baseball Players (NA) was established. Most of its players were high-level blue-collar workers, and 83 percent of them had been born in cities. The NA lasted only five years because of such problems as players who jumped teams, weak competition, rumors of fixes, inept leadership, and slack admission requirements that admitted teams in small cities.

In 1876 the NA was supplanted by the profit-oriented National League (NL). It hoped to avoid the NA's problems by restricting franchises to cities with at least 75,000 residents, charging 50 cents for admission, and barring gambling, alcohol, and games on Sunday. The NL struggled at first, and several of its franchises folded. There were fixed games and competition from other leagues, particularly the plebeian-oriented American Association (AA), which merged with the NL in 1883.

In 1901 the American League (AL) claimed major league status, which was certified two years later by the National Agreement. The AL's emergence reflected baseball's booming popularity; major league attendance doubled between 1901 and 1909. The minor leagues grew from 13 in 1900 to 46 in 1912, leaving few large cities without professional baseball.

Despite its urban origins, it became conventional wisdom that baseball was a rural game best played by small-town folks and that the sport taught traditional values. Urban reformers recommended that youth play baseball to learn teamwork and respect for authority. It was extremely popular with second-generation urbanites, particularly Irishmen, who comprised as many as one-third of major league ballplayers in the 1890s. Immigrants thought that playing or following baseball symbolized their Americanization. However, there were few Eastern or Southern European men in the major leagues until the 1930s, partly because they lacked the space needed to play the game. African Americans were banned from organized baseball in 1898, and they responded by forming their own teams and leagues, most notably the Negro National League in 1920. Professional baseball remained segregated until 1947, when Jackie Robinson broke the color barrier by playing for the Brooklyn Dodgers.

During professional baseball's first 50 years, most teams were owned by professional politicians or their allies. They used their clout to secure cheap municipal services and protection against government interference or competition. Major league teams, especially in the largest cities, had become very profitable by the early twentieth century. They amassed substantial annual earnings and also enjoyed capital appreciation. For instance, the Chicago Cubs, sold in 1905 for $105,000, earned $1.2 million between 1906 and 1915. In the 1920s, the New York Yankees, featuring Babe Ruth, were the most profitable team. His heroic feats, the emergence of the lively ball, and the stern leadership of Commissioner Kennesaw Mountain Landis enabled baseball to overcome the 1920 Black Sox Scandal in which it was shown that members of the Chicago White Sox had thrown the 1919 World Series.

The best major league teams were mainly situated in large cities that had the greatest potential for profit and could spend the most money. The New York Giants under John McGraw dominated the NL in the first third of the century, with 10 pennants. The Yankees dominated the AL with 15 pennants between 1921 and 1943, and 15 more from 1947 to 1964. The main exception was the St. Louis Cardinals of the National League, who came in first or second 15 times between 1926 and 1946 due to an extensive, well-developed farm system.

Professional baseball has changed in important ways since World War II, beginning with racial integration in 1946 in the minor leagues and 1947 in the majors. Televised broadcasts devastated the minor leagues, whose attendance dropped from 42 million in 1949 to 15 million in 1957. Franchises began moving in 1953 when the Boston Braves migrated to Milwaukee, followed five years later by the move west of the Dodgers to Los Angeles and the Giants to San Francisco. Then, in 1961, the major leagues began expanding, and today there are 30 teams. The most momentous development in recent years has been free agency. This began in 1976 when courts declared that teams could no longer enforce the reserve clause; that is, a club no longer had perpetual rights to a player's services. This produced escalating salaries, and the average annual salary soared from $46,000 in 1975 to nearly $1.3 million at the start of the 1997 season. This largesse has not been spread evenly among all the players, and a few of the most celebrated stars receive more than $5 million a year from their clubs.

—*Steven A. Riess*

See also
Ballparks.
References
Kirsch, George. *The Creation of American Team Sports: Baseball and Cricket, 1838–72.* Urbana: University of Illinois Press, 1989.
Rader, Benjamin G. *Baseball: A History of America's National Game.* Urbana: University of Illinois Press, 1992.
Riess, Steven A. *Touching Bases: Professional Baseball and American Culture in the Progressive Era.* Westport, CT: Greenwood Press, 1980.
Seymour, Harold. *Baseball.* 3 vols. New York: Oxford University Press, 1960–1990.
Voigt, David Q. *American Baseball.* 3 vols. Norman: University of Oklahoma Press, 1966–1970.

Basketball

The origin of basketball is closely connected to the playground movement, a Progressive Era attempt to bring the play of children and adolescents under the control of reform-minded adults. Not surprisingly, this thrust for reform came from people instrumentally involved with urban problems. "Neighborhood lobbies" who, as described by Stephen Hardy, promoted the proposition "that outdoor exercise was wholesome and a deterrent to crime and disease" were joined by "genteel reformers" who considered organized play a vital instrument for shaping the moral and cognitive development of young people. Many of these reformers, such as Luther G. Gulick and G. Stanley Hall, viewed team sports as instrumental in integrating the young into the work rhythms and social demands of a fast emerging, dynamic, and complex urban-industrial civilization.

Gulick, who was thoroughly committed to socialization through team games, challenged one of his students, James Naismith, to invent the game of basketball. Gulick's efforts were directed to Americanizing immigrant youth who, he believed, manifested randomly destructive behaviors. Gulick believed that enthusiasm for team games, such as baseball, basketball, and football, would inculcate the complementary values of individualism and cooperation—antidotes to the gangs that were proliferating in most American cities.

Naismith's new game was born in the early weeks of December 1891. It initially enjoyed immense popularity among a group of YMCA leaders training with Naismith. They had found such indoor winter activities as marching drills, calisthenics, and Indian club and medicine ball routines to be boring, and many of them soon introduced the sport in their home towns.

Since basketball did not require much space or costly equipment, it clearly suited the inner-city environment. This spatial factor allowed many youngsters without access to baseball diamonds to play basketball in schoolyards, settlement houses, and churches, allowing the sport to spread rapidly in eastern and midwestern cities. By 1898, there was already a professional league in Philadelphia. The sport quickly attracted inner-city ethnic groups, and settlement houses became training grounds for future interscholastic, collegiate, and professional stars. Jewish players in New York City at Clark House and University Settlement dominated intersettlement tournaments while Manhattan's Irish youth were served by the Hudson Guild. The Celtics were formed there in 1912 and later became a leading professional team of the 1920s.

Urban basketball's emerging popularity during the 1920s and 1930s facilitated sporting competitions and social events among second-generation immigrants who were unwelcome in prestigious voluntary athletic organizations controlled by more established Americans. Soon, other immigrant organizations were conducting ethnic championship games and drawing more than 10,000 spectators to a game. Although some reformers argued that interethnic basketball competition provided an American socialization experience, it generated as much ethnic hostility as friendship and understanding. Unlike football, which served upper-class

revitalization and the attendant restructuring of college life, basketball became part of the progressive, professional, middle-class effort to channel, guide, and Americanize immigrant youth through elementary and secondary extracurricular activities.

At the professional level, the ethnic factor was very strong. Prior to World War II, professional basketball in major urban areas was predominately an ethnic community entertainment. Teams like the Celtics, which began as an ethnic club and maintained that identity until it fortified its roster with Jewish athletes, was the best team in professional basketball, and its stars earned up to $12,000 a year. Other teams, such as the black barnstorming Harlem Renaissance Five, were important community institutions that instilled pride in their fans and gained respect from other ethnic

A high school basketball game in Baldwin Park, California.

groups. Many games were played in dance halls, where they preceded an evening of dancing in a respectable environment for meeting members of the opposite sex.

By the end of World War II, basketball took a major step toward becoming an important professional sport when businessmen who controlled the 11 best eastern and midwestern arenas organized the Basketball Association of America (BAA). When the BAA merged with the National Basketball League (NBL), which had formed in 1937, the 17-team National Basketball Association (NBA) was established, with clubs in such major urban markets as New York, Chicago, and Philadelphia, as well as smaller markets such as Anderson (Indiana), Waterloo (Iowa), and Sheboygan (Wisconsin). The small-city franchises were weak from the start and soon dropped out of the league; others moved to larger cities, like the Fort Wayne Pistons who moved to Detroit.

The biggest change that basketball experienced during the 1950s was its emergence as the predominant game for inner-city boys without much money or many constructive alternatives for their free time other than sports. Basketball had become the major athletic passion of black ghetto youth, as it had previously been for Jewish, German, and Irish youth. For many black youngsters, the playground became a haven where they practiced diligently for hours a day, all year long, motivated by the immediate gratification of prestige in the neighborhood and the longer-term goals of starring in high school, getting a college scholarship, and ending up in the NBA.

In the era after 1950, high school basketball prospered in towns, smaller cities, and independent suburbs while basketball and other sports declined in the inner city. In terms of attendance as a ratio of population, secondary schools in smaller towns fared better than those in larger cities or independent suburbs. In many Indiana towns, no single activity exceeded the ability of basketball to bind communities together.

In many urban areas today, basketball represents a means of social mobility for many blacks. However, even though only a very small proportion of high school players (4 percent) are good enough to play in college much less the NBA, the idea of escaping the ghetto by means of basketball remains a dream. Black urbanites, who still face severe social, political, and economic restrictions because of class and race discrimination, embrace basketball as a source of self-worth. Many professional and college teams are dominated by black players, and they have used the sport to gain some moderate degree of respect for their broader community.

—*Albert J. Figone*

References

Fox, Larry. *Illustrated History of Basketball.* New York: Grosset and Dunlap, 1974.

Gorn, Elliott J., and Warren Goldstein. *A Brief History of American Sports.* New York: Hill and Wang, 1993.

Hardy, Stephen. *How Boston Played: Sport Recreation, and Community, 1865–1915.* Boston: Northeastern University Press, 1982.

Rader, Benjamin G. *American Sports: From the Age of Folk Games to the Age of Televised Sports.* Englewood Cliffs, NJ: Prentice-Hall, 1990.

Riess, Steven A. *City Games: The Evolution of American Urban Society and the Rise of Sports.* Urbana: University of Illinois Press, 1989.

Bauer, Catherine (1905–1964)

Catherine Bauer (Wurster)—houser, town planner, lobbyist, teacher, and author—played a significant role in shaping American housing policy from 1931 to 1957.

Born in 1905 in Elizabeth, New Jersey, Catherine Bauer was graduated from Vassar College in 1927. Touring Europe in 1928, she became intrigued by the new "functionalist-social" architecture of Le Corbusier and the Bauhaus School. As an advertising manager (1928–1930) for Harcourt, Brace publishers, she met the urbanist-architectural critic Lewis Mumford, who introduced her to the Regional Planning Association of America. In 1932 Bauer joined Mumford on a study tour of housing in Europe. Her extensive research on housing trends there produced *Modern Housing* (1934), a book indicting America for failing to provide good, well-planned, working-class communities and for the lack of a grassroots political movement on behalf of modern housing. By 1934, together with architect Oscar Stonorov and labor leader John Edelman, she led the Labor Housing Conference, an organization responsible for building the "modern" Carl Mackley Homes in Philadelphia. Bauer helped spearhead the 1934 Baltimore Housing Conference, which provided momentum for the 1937 Wagner-Steagall Housing Act. After World War II she vigorously campaigned for the 1949 federal housing and redevelopment legislation. Like Mumford, Bauer accepted the suburban trend, and therefore fought linking public housing projects to slum clearance, and she favored locating them on the urban periphery.

In 1947 Bauer married the prominent architect William Wurster whose low-rise, communitarian designs for public housing epitomized in every way her image of modern housing. However, most postwar urban housing projects defied her vision. As early as 1951 she blasted "Those God-Dammed Skyscrapers." Later she assailed public housing as "Supertenements" and vilified federal policy as a "Dreary Deadlock."

Bauer became a leading "actionist planner," critical of the postwar planning profession's bureaucratic straitjacket and obeisance to zoning. In many writings, she advocated social science research as the foundation for modern community planning and design. As a faculty member in the

1950s and 1960s at Harvard University and then the University of California at Berkeley, where she became dean of the School of Architecture, her interest in town planning broadened to encompass Third World development, especially housing in India. Tragically, Bauer died in November 1964 at age 59, apparently falling to her death while she was hiking alone in the beautiful but rugged hills near Berkeley.

—*John F. Bauman*

See also

Mumford, Lewis; Public Housing; Regional Planning Association of America.

References

Bauman, John F. *Public Housing, Race, and Renewal: Urban Planning in Philadelphia, 1920–1974.* Philadelphia: Temple University Press, 1987.

Cole, Susan Mary. "Catherine Bauer and the Public Housing Movement." Ph.D. dissertation, George Washington University, 1975.

Frieden, Bernard J., and William Nash, eds. *Shaping an Urban Future: Essays in Memory of Catherine Bauer Wurster.* Cambridge, MA: MIT Press, 1969.

Miller, Donald L. *Lewis Mumford: A Life.* Pittsburgh, PA: University of Pittsburgh Press, 1992.

Scott, Mel. *American City Planning since 1890.* Berkeley: University of California Press, 1969.

Bay View, Michigan

Bay View, Michigan, on the west side of the Lower Peninsula overlooking Lake Michigan, was founded in 1876 as a Methodist camp meeting resort on the model of Oak Bluffs, the famed camp meeting on Martha's Vineyard. In 1885 it also became an independent Chautauqua on the model of Fair Point Camp Meeting at Lake Chautauqua, New York, a summer study center and gathering ground for students enrolled in the influential correspondence school for adult college students.

By the early twentieth century, Bay View had some 440 carefully crafted wooden cottages, a panoply of scaled-down rural house types, plus 25 institutional buildings, all set on curving roads on a series of tree-canopied terraces that step down to the lake. Along with such early romantically planned suburbs as Glendale, Ohio; Llewellyn Park, New Jersey; or Park Forest and Riverside, Illinois, Bay View pioneered the subdivision layout of curving and countercurving streets consciously designed to work with topography in creating a sense of dislocation and rural ease as an antithesis to the grid plans of most American cities.

Bay View, with visitors coming to its events from all over the country, may have been more influential than the early suburbs in popularizing a new style of community design. Its plan was derived from that of Oak Bluffs, Massachusetts, a resort designed by a professional designer of cemeteries and suburbs who used the romantic tradition of nineteenth-century cemetery layout to duplicate the "mazy" effect of the Martha's Vineyard Camp Meeting in Bay View. With its excellent design maintained by leasehold land arrangements and board governance, Bay View is now a National Historic Landmark as a monument to the camp meeting and Chautauqua movements as well as an example of ideal Victorian community design.

—*Ellen Weiss*

See also

Llewellyn Park, New Jersey; Riverside, Illinois.

References

Fennimore, Keith J. *The Heritage of Bay View.* Grand Rapids, MI: William B. Eerdmans, 1975.

Weiss, Ellen. "Bay View, Michigan: Camp Meeting and Chautauqua." In John S. Garner, ed., *The Midwest in American Architecture.* Urbana: University of Illinois Press, 1993.

Wheeler, Clark S. *Bay View.* Bay View, MI: Bay View Association, 1950.

Beame, Abraham David (1906–)

Elected in 1973, Abraham D. Beame became the first Jewish mayor of New York City. He inherited a fiscal crisis that he was never able to overcome; nearly continuous financial negotiations with state and federal officials, private banks, and municipal unions dominated his administration. Creation of the Municipal Assistance Corporation and the Emergency Financial Control Board in 1975 severely restricted Beame's ability to exercise the traditional powers of the mayor. To satisfy fiscal requirements, he had to lay off massive numbers of city employees, delay capital expenditures on infrastructure, and abandon any hope of launching major initiatives. Critics, including the Securities and Exchange Commission, charged that Beame used unsound budgeting practices and implied that he misled the city when he reported the condition of its finances. Supporters credited him with averting the city's bankruptcy.

Beame's early career was an immigrant success story. In 1906 his family arrived in New York City from the part of Poland controlled by Russia, via London, where Beame was born and spent the first few months of his life. The family soon settled in the Crown Heights section of Brooklyn. At 24, Beame joined the Madison Democratic Club and became a loyal worker for the Democratic Party. He taught public school, earned an accounting degree from City College, and was appointed deputy budget director of New York City in 1948 and budget director in 1953. In 1961 he was elected comptroller. Two years later, Beame became the first Jew to win the Democratic nomination for mayor, but he lost the general election to John V. Lindsay. Beame was elected comptroller a second time in 1969 and then won the mayoralty in 1973. After serving just one term, he was discredited by the city's fiscal crisis, lost the Democratic primary election for mayor to Edward I. Koch in 1977, and retired from politics.

Beame was the oldest person elected mayor of New York, assuming office at age 67. Throughout his political career he suffered references to his height of five feet, two inches. The family's name was originally Birnbaum but was legally changed about 1912 by Beame's father, Philip.

—*Chris McNickle*

References

Auletta, Ken. *The Streets Were Paved with Gold*. New York: Vintage Books, 1980.

Daly, Robert. "The Realism of Abe Beame." *New York Times*, November 18, 1973.

McNickle, Chris. *To Be Mayor of New York: Ethnic Politics in the City*. New York: Columbia University Press, 1993.

Behrman, Martin (1864–1926)

Martin Behrman, the Louisiana state auditor for a few months in 1904 and mayor of New Orleans from 1904 to 1920 and again for a few months from 1925 to 1926, first entered Louisiana politics in the late 1880s during the divisive 20-year struggle for survival and supremacy between the Democratic and Republican parties following Reconstruction and the restoration of home rule in 1877.

Behrman, said to be the son of Jewish immigrants from Germany who converted to Roman Catholicism, rose from the streets of the New Orleans French Quarter to city boss and five-time mayor of the city. After Behrman's father, Henry, died when the future mayor was only an infant, his mother, Fredrika, opened and operated a small dry goods stand in the French Market; she died when he was 12. Behrman married Julia Collins of Cincinnati, Ohio, and they had eleven children, only two of whom, Stanley and Helen May, survived infancy.

As a political insider, Behrman was an active witness to the violent struggles within the Democratic Party over the Louisiana Lottery Company that climaxed in the 1892 state and municipal elections; the rise and fall of the Populist movement in the state's rural parishes (counties); the death and birth of two New Orleans political machines in 1896 and 1897; and the victory of white supremacy, then synonymous with the supremacy of the Democratic Party, in the state's 1898 constitutional convention.

Behrman rose from the ranks of the Regular Democratic Organization (the Crescent Democratic Club and its successor, the Choctaw Club of Louisiana) in the classical style of most city bosses. The Choctaw Club, also known as the Regular Democratic Organization, the Ring, machine, Regulars, and after 1922 as the Old Regulars, represented all walks of life in New Orleans: laborers, businessmen, lawyers, physicians, gamblers, and professional politicians. Behrman worked hard to bring in the vote for machine candidates and in return was awarded various minor appointed positions. After a few successes at the ballot box, particularly his election to the state constitutional convention in 1898, Behrman became the leader of New Orleans' Fifteenth Ward. This recognition entitled him to sit in the Council of Seventeen, usually referred to as the caucus, with the leaders of the city's other 16 wards.

By 1904, the year he was elected state auditor and then mayor of New Orleans, Behrman had emerged as the central and dominant figure in the organization. At first, he shared decision-making powers with other caucus leaders, but by 1925, the beginning of his fifth term, Martin Behrman was undisputed boss.

Like most city bosses, Behrman faced constant opposition from reform groups. The cry for good government in New Orleans was usually for progressive democracy, that is, abstract and idealistic rather than practical politics. Through the years, Behrman's opposition, under the banner of one reform group or another, was essentially middle class and led primarily by lawyers, businessmen, social uplifters, and newspaper editors and publishers. The machine and reform groups were equally diverse socially, ethnically, and religiously, with as many Catholics as Protestants, and both included Jews.

The first organized assault on the Choctaw Club came from the Home Rulers in the 1904 municipal elections, then the Independents in 1908, and the Good Government League in 1912. It was not until 1920, under the leadership of reform governor John M. Parker and his New Orleans–based Orleans Democratic Association (ODA), that reformers were able to defeat Behrman. The ODA's victory was short-lived. The electorate soon tired of the reformers and reelected Behrman in 1925 for his fifth term as mayor. A year later, he died in office.

Behrman's reign was long and controversial, but his energies and ambition led New Orleans into the twentieth century. His political success was partially due to his affable nature, efficiency, and ability to sense public moods and needs. He was justifiably convinced that the majority of people wanted visible and tangible signs of progress and improved municipal services. In this area, he could boast a long list of achievements: the Public Belt Railroad, extensive street paving, a modern sewerage system, improved public health, schools, playgrounds, and hospitals, and increased police and fire protection. The day after Behrman's death, the *New Orleans Times-Picayune*, the city's largest newspaper and perennial Behrman foe, described the mayor "as a kindly citizen, a forceful leader and a municipal servant who made the most of his opportunities for service to the city he loved."

—*John R. Kemp*

References
Kemp, John R., ed. *Martin Behrman of New Orleans: Memoirs of a City Boss.* Baton Rouge: Louisiana State University Press, 1977.
Reynolds, George M. *Machine Politics in New Orleans, 1897–1926.* New York: Columbia University Press, 1936.

Bellamy, Edward (1850–1898)

Edward Bellamy, American writer and social theorist, was born in Chicopee Falls, Massachusetts, in 1850 and died there 48 years later. As the son of a well-situated Baptist minister, Bellamy enjoyed social and financial security. He attended college and traveled in Europe and the Pacific in his youth. Later, as a husband and father, he enjoyed a peaceful domestic life. Bellamy explored several careers, including the law, journalism, and short-story writing before he undertook his major work, the utopian novel *Looking Backward,* in 1887.

Looking Backward describes the United States as Bellamy imagined it could be in the year 2000, after a century of social and economic change and development. The nation has developed a centrally managed economy in which every citizen receives an identical share of the annual net national product. This utopian society is necessarily urban. People must live in cities to access communal services: central kitchens, laundries, shopping centers that deliver, domestic workers, libraries, cultural entertainment, transportation, and more. The technology supporting these services would be economically efficient only with a high volume of use. The city's services free its citizens from drudgery and inconvenience while providing them with opportunities for physical recreation and intellectual growth.

The novel became an international best-seller following publication of a second edition in 1891. In projecting a classless yet prosperous national community, Bellamy's story had special appeal during the labor unrest of the late nineteenth century. Its popularity endured; in 1935 the *New York Times* ranked *Looking Backward* as the book second only to Marx's *Das Kapital* in social influence during the previous 50 years.

The novel and its author's lesser works continue to draw scholarly attention. In comparison to earlier American utopian fiction, the thoroughness of Bellamy's socioeconomic design sets *Looking Backward* apart. Bellamy himself is the subject of historical studies focusing on the late-nineteenth-century Nationalist movement that his writings fueled.

—*Sylvia P. H. Bowman*

References
Bowman, Sylvia E. *Edward Bellamy.* Boston: Twayne, 1986.
Griffith, Nancy Snell. *Edward Bellamy: A Bibliography.* Metuchen, NJ: Scarecrow Press, 1986.
Patai, Daphne, ed. *Looking Backward, 1988–1888: Essays on Edward Bellamy.* Amherst: University of Massachusetts Press, 1988.

Bellows, George (1882–1925)

George Bellows, one of the greatest American painters of the early twentieth century, was reared in a conservative Methodist household in Columbus, Ohio, but he dropped out of Ohio State University in 1904 to come to New York City with aspirations of becoming an artist. He soon fell under the influence of the artist Robert Henri, one of his teachers, who was gaining a reputation for artistic radicalism. Henri urged his students to avoid the conventional forms and subjects of academic art and to search the streets of the city for motifs closer to "real" life.

Bellows took his mentor's instruction to heart. During the first decade of his career, he produced a stunning series of urban pictures that are related to his explorations of his adopted city and his efforts to comprehend it. Though he also painted portraits and landscapes throughout his career, it was these vigorously brushed early paintings—of life in the tenement districts of New York City, prizefights, and excavations for the new Pennsylvania Station—that established Bellows's reputation and professional identity.

For his urban paintings, Bellows tended to select prominent, often newsworthy subjects that were discussed and pictured in the mass media. As a result, his images evoked particular associations in the minds of his contemporaries. For example, Bellows's depictions of the Lower East Side made use of pictorial conventions widely familiar from reform-minded urban exposé photography. But images of poverty were far from commonplace in exhibitions at the National Academy of Design. Some saw these paintings, which brought the daily activities of New York City's largely foreign-born working classes into the rarefied realm of fine art, as oppositional gestures. To their critics, these subjects implied a deliberate rejection of academic idealism and the tradition of cultural authority associated with it.

Bellows's slashing painting technique and his frank, sometimes gritty urban subject matter cemented his membership in Henri's circle, often labeled in the press as a band of "revolutionaries" who challenged convention and the National Academy of Design. That connection to the Henri circle did Bellows no harm, however, since their challenge to the outworn conventions of the academy was considered overdue by large segments of the art audience. Henri and his protégés attracted both praise and criticism for their stance, and considerable notoriety in either case.

Bellows often garnered more accolades than his colleagues, partly because of his brilliant technical facility and partly because the implicit meaning of his pictures was not revolutionary. The excavation paintings celebrated urbanization; the boxing pictures presented the sport as brutal and its fans as debased; his depictions of the Lower East Side conformed to a moralistic, middle-class view of poverty. When these paintings were first exhibited between 1907 and 1913, they seemed boldly defiant but at the same time reassuringly familiar. By melding the trappings of artistic radicalism with an approach to his subjects that reaffirmed traditional values and priorities, Bellows created a remarkable corpus of paintings exquisitely attuned to their time and to the often conflicting attitudes and preconceptions of many urban Americans.

Bellows's ability to ingratiate himself to both progressives and conservatives fueled his rapid rise to prominence in the art world. Only four years after he arrived in New York City, one of his paintings was purchased by the Pennsylvania Academy of the Fine Arts for its permanent collection, and in the following year, 1909, when he was just 26, Bellows was elected an associate member of the National Academy of Design.

In 1913, the year Bellows became a full member of the academy, the Armory Show reconfigured the contemporary American art scene, and members of the Henri circle fell from the prominent positions they had occupied. Bellows, however, managed to preserve a devoted following during and after the advent of cubism and fauvism in spite of his allegiance to a premodernist, realist idiom. He produced fewer city scenes after 1913 and devoted more attention to landscapes and seascapes, and some of his late portraits of family members must be considered among his finest achievements.

— *Marianne Doezema*

See also
Armory Show.
References

Carmean, E. A., Jr., et al. *Bellows: The Boxing Pictures*, exhibition catalog. Washington, DC: National Gallery of Art, 1982.

Doezema, Marianne. *George Bellows and Urban America*. New Haven, CT: Yale University Press, 1992.

Haywood, Robert. "George Bellows' *Stag at Sharkey's*: Boxing, Violence, and Male Identity." *Smithsonian Studies in American Art* 2 (1988): 3–15.

Mason, Lauris, assisted by Joan Ludman. *The Lithographs of George Bellows: A Catalogue Raisonné*. Millwood, NY: KTO Press, 1977. Rev. ed. San Francisco: Alan Wofsy Fine Arts, 1992.

Morgan, Charles. *George Bellows: Painter of America*. New York: Reynal & Company, 1965. Reprint ed. Millwood, NY: Kraus Reprint, 1979.

Myers, Jane, and Linda Ayres. *George Bellows: The Artist and His Lithographs, 1916–1924*, ex. cat. Fort Worth, TX: Amon Carter Museum, 1988.

Quick, Michael, et al. *The Paintings of George Bellows*, exhibition catalog. Fort Worth, TX: Amon Carter Museum, and Los Angeles: Los Angeles County Museum of Art, 1992.

Zurier, Rebecca. "Hey Kids: Children in the Comics and the Art of George Bellows." *Print Collector's Newsletter* 18 (1988): 196–203.

Benjamin Franklin Parkway

The Benjamin Franklin Parkway is a major thoroughfare connecting the parks along the banks of the Schuylkill River with the center of Philadelphia. A major monument of the City Beautiful movement, the parkway reveals a vision of the modern city that was very different from what reformers in the early twentieth century were accustomed to.

The objective of the City Beautiful movement was usually rooted in the effort to revive the appearance of the drab industrial core that had supported urban growth. Nature was a crucial component of the vision of beauty, but planned areas were also observed with an eye toward utility and functionalism, making many of them into distinctly modern landscapes. Obviously, these changes required a great deal of financing and demolition and therefore generated intense public debate. With construction of the City Beautiful facing these challenges, the achievement of the Benjamin Franklin Parkway in Philadelphia stands out as a monument to inner-city planning.

The plan for the parkway was first submitted in the 1880s, and the original plan closely resembles the project finally completed in 1937. The main function of the plan was simple: to link the parks along the Schuylkill River with buildings of civic prominence, thereby literally creating a parkway leading to the inner city. However, the City Beautiful movement's interest in monumentality was also clearly present in the original plan, which seemed to say: "A convenient approach to the park is necessary. Why not make it something worthy of Philadelphia?"

The debate over uniting style and function combined with politics, zoning, and property acquisition as factors that stalled the project after construction began in 1907. A revised plan by Paul P. Cret, Horace Trumbauer, Charles L. Borie, Jr., and Clarence Zantzinger was accepted in 1917, but problems continued. Finally, Jacques Greber, a French landscape architect, was called in to design a layout that would join the diverse architecture and functions of the 1917 plan.

Using the Champs Élysées in Paris, France, as his model, Greber transformed the parkway from just a boulevard into a wedge of park that reached in toward the city. In addition to incorporating the Art Museum, the Pennsylvania Academy of Fine Arts, and other civic buildings with Logan Square, Greber created a triangular greenspace, Fairmont Park, in the center of the city. Although the architectural styles are classical, the parkway was indeed modern architecture, and much of the debate during its construction was the functionalist discourse of modernity that confronted many City Beautiful projects.

— *Brian Black*

See also
City Beautiful Movement.
References

Boyer, M. Christine. *Dreaming the Rational City: The Myth of American City Planning*. Cambridge, MA: MIT Press, 1983.

Brownlee, David B. *Building the City Beautiful: The Benjamin Franklin Parkway and the Philadelphia Museum of Art.* Philadelphia: University of Pennsylvania Press, 1989.
Ciucci, Giorgio, et al. *The American City: From the Civil War to the New Deal.* Barbara Luigia La Penta, trans. London: Granada, 1979.
Robinson, Charles Mulford. *Modern Civic Art, or the City Made Beautiful.* New York: G. P. Putnam's Sons, 1903.

Benton, Thomas Hart (1889–1975)

Thomas Hart Benton was one of the founding fathers of the artistic movement known as Regionalism. This term came into common usage in December 1934 when Benton appeared on the cover of *Time* magazine as putative leader of a drive to repudiate European innovations in modern art, including abstraction, and to concentrate instead on things American. Because abstraction was closely associated with the artists' enclaves of New York City and because the American artists closest to Benton in pictorial content—John Steuart Curry of Kansas and Grant Wood of Iowa—were already known for a kind of back-to-the-heartland sensibility, Thomas Hart Benton acquired a reputation for being an anti-urban painter.

Although he did make some intemperate remarks about New York museum directors as he prepared to leave Manhattan and go home to Missouri in 1935, Benton was not a foe of the city. Instead, he widened and deepened Americans' appreciation of the urban scene to include not only New York but also places like Memphis, Los Angeles, Pittsburgh, Tulsa, and St. Louis—and Kansas City, where he lived and worked for the rest of his life.

In the years immediately before World War II, as the face of urbanism and industrialism began to assume the configurations of the postwar world, Benton was there, with sketchbook in hand, showing old regional centers in transition and new cities of blast furnaces, cracking towers, and high-tension wires rising out of the cornfields and cotton patches of the nineteenth-century frontier.

In murals that he painted before and after he left New York, Benton probed the character of cities, the terms of their modernity, and how they differed from the rural crossroads of the American past. A brilliant series of mural panels that he painted for the New School for Social Research in 1930 is a case in point. The New York City segments show life as a vast, yowling panorama of chorus girls and movie palaces, Coney Island amusements, skyscrapers, ocean freighters, and lurid neon. Work is subordinate to spectacle. But as the wall unrolls westward and southward, different visions of other kinds of cities appear in vignettes of surveyors laying out factories on empty plains and giant concrete grain silos rising abruptly over farmsteads. Benton shows a nation in a tearing hurry to become one vast, urban agglomerate, from sea to shining sea.

Benton's agent warned that if he drew and painted things exactly as he saw them on his annual tours around the country, he ran the risk of becoming dated. Wouldn't a 1935-vintage blast furnace seem merely quaint to a 1995 viewer? Thomas Hart Benton failed to heed that advice, and his reputation has suffered as a result. Viewers recoil in horror today from his depictions of the lurid industrial infernos that spelled jobs and progress to the cities of the jobless 1930s. Naughty images of glamour girls of easy virtue on the prowl no longer speak sweetly to the excitement and pleasure offered by the city. But Benton's views of America's cities, big and little, depict the infinite promise such places once held, and the reason why young painters from rural Missouri once flocked to them with stars in their eyes.

—*Karal Ann Marling*

References

Adams, Henry. *Thomas Hart Benton: An American Original.* New York: Knopf, 1989.
Baigell, Matthew. *Thomas Hart Benton.* New York: Abrams, 1973.
Marling, Karal Ann. *Tom Benton and His Drawings.* Columbia: University of Missouri Press, 1985.

Birth Control

The term *birth control* is an Americanism, printed for the first time in *The Woman Rebel* (June 1914) by Margaret Sanger, a radical feminist who had been active in New York's socialist labor movement. Sanger had become convinced that reproductive autonomy for women was an issue of primary importance and that women needed an independent voice of their own because, she believed, her radical male comrades shared the patriarchal values of most men. Although she first gained notoriety as a leader of the cultural revolt associated with Greenwich Village, Sanger found broad support among social leaders for her demand that contraceptive literature be removed from the prohibitions of state and federal obscenity laws. The rapid development of the birth control movement coincided with the general rejection of Victorian reticence concerning sexuality and the embrace of modernism by the middle class.

The twentieth-century birth control movement was preceded by a century of demographic and social change that made the prohibition of contraception seem unreasonably oppressive. In the early nineteenth century, large numbers of Americans began to limit their fertility through contraception, induced abortion, and sexual abstinence. While the average native-born white woman gave birth to more than seven children in 1800, by 1900 she had less than four. Thus, the decline in fertility began before any large proportion of the population lived in urban areas or performed nonagricultural work. Throughout the nineteenth century, the declining birthrate of the rural population equaled that of the urban population.

Another prominent feature of the fertility transition in the United States was that it became common for women to give birth less frequently *before* there were widespread declines in infant mortality. Apparently conscious decisions, most often by the married, to limit childbearing despite the risks posed by high infant mortality account for the fertility decline. Although a majority of Americans still lived on farms or in small towns when the fertility decline began, they were increasingly better educated, read more newspapers and books, participated more in the political process, had more faith in material progress, and were more confident than their parents of the individual's ability to control nature. In short, the fertility decline was part of a larger pattern of social change in which new values and behaviors associated with the spread of a market economy preceded industrialization and urbanization and set the stage for those processes.

The decline in fertility was associated with changes in the quality of kinship relations and family functions that were well under way by the early nineteenth century. The rapid

A 1919 cover of Birth Control Review, *one of many publications concerned with this issues over the years.*

expansion of a market economy required geographic mobility that weakened kinship ties and forced the newly married to find alternative sources of advice as they struggled to find personal stability in a rapidly changing world. Marriage manuals, some containing instructions for contraception, were prominent among the mass market self-help books that became a staple of American culture after 1830.

As the home ceased to be a unit of production, and as the manufacture of clothing and other goods moved to factories, children no longer provided necessary labor in the family economies of the emerging middle and white-collar classes. Rather, they became expensive investments who required education, capital, and an abundance of "Christian nurture" from mothers who measured respectability by being able to stay home and efficiently manage the income won by their husbands in a separate, public sphere of work.

The discovery by social leaders of the declining fertility of native-born white women inspired the first self-conscious attempts to influence fertility through legislation. Beginning in the 1840s, prominent physicians led successful campaigns to outlaw induced abortion. The culmination of campaigns against abortion in state legislatures coincided with passage of the Comstock Act (1873), a strengthened national obscenity law, in which no distinctions were made between smut, abortifacients, or contraceptives: all were prohibited. As a result, explicit discussion of contraception disappeared from marriage manuals after 1873, although the subject had previously been included.

The suppression of contraceptive information did not change the pattern of declining birthrates. In 1901 the sociologist Èdward A. Ross coined the phrase "race suicide," and President Theodore Roosevelt declared that America's future as a world power was being undermined by pursuit of the soft life as exemplified by barren marriages. Exhortations to reproduce had limited effect, however, in the emerging consumer economy of the early twentieth century. The emergence of a movement to legitimate and spread contraceptive practice was a logical, if not inevitable, response to a major tension in the personal lives of many Americans. The essential cultural prerequisite for public acceptance of the separation of sex from procreation was the secularization of society, or the celebration of material well-being and pleasure as embodied by the growing advertising industry.

Major events in Margaret Sanger's campaign to win America for birth control cluster around 1920, the historical moment when more Americans first lived in urban rather than rural areas. In 1916 Sanger opened a contraceptive advice center in the Brownsville section of Brooklyn, New York, where nurses provided advice to long lines of foreign-born women. Through litigation following her arrest, Sanger won a judicial decision that allowed physicians to dispense contraceptive advice to preserve a woman's health. In 1921 the American Birth Control League was founded to lobby for changes in the Comstock laws, and in 1923 Sanger opened the Birth Control Clinical Research Bureau in New York, the first birth control clinic in the United States to be staffed by physicians. Under the able leadership of Dr. Hannah Stone, a clinical record was established demonstrating that contraception could be safe and effective. The New York clinic soon became a model and a training ground for a nationwide network of more than 300 urban birth control clinics, supported by local voluntary associations, that were established by the middle of the 1930s. In 1936 Dr. Stone and Sanger won a federal court decision that exempted contraceptive supplies and information from the Comstock laws and prepared the way in 1937 for a resolution by the American Medical Association that accepted contraception as an ethical medical service.

During the Great Depression, the birth rate fell below the level required to maintain the existing population, and many social analysts argued that this trend was an important cause of economic stagnation. Leaders of the birth control movement attempted to broaden their appeal by emphasizing "family planning" rather than "birth control" and by moving away from Sanger's emphasis on autonomy for women. These strategies failed to win broad public support for birth control until the 1960s when increased awareness of rapid population growth in the Third World and the domestic War on Poverty provided a rationale for federal support of contraceptive services both at home and abroad.

In 1965 in the case of *Griswold v. Connecticut,* the U.S. Supreme Court struck down a law prohibiting contraception on the grounds that the law violated a constitutionally protected "right to privacy." The Court continued expanding the rights of an individual to defy restrictions on personal behavior in *Eisenstadt v. Baird* (1972), which decreed that unmarried people had the same right to contraceptives as those married. In 1973 the Court ruled that women and their physicians, rather than legislatures, had the right to decide whether or not to abort a fetus during the first months of pregnancy. Although the *Roe v. Wade* decision evoked a storm of controversy, birth control remained a salient part of private behavior and public policy in the United States, where birth control clinics continue to provoke heated public discussion about the status of women.

— *James W. Reed*

See also
Fertility.
References
Critchlow, Donald T., ed. *The Politics of Abortion and Birth Control in Historical Perspective.* State College: Pennsylvania State University Press, 1996.
Garrow, David J. *Liberty and Sexuality: The Right to Privacy and the Making of Roe v. Wade.* New York: Macmillan, 1994.
Gordon, Linda. *Woman's Body, Woman's Right: Birth Control in America.* Rev. ed. New York: Penguin Books, 1990.
Reed, James. *The Birth Control Movement and American Society: From Private Vice to Public Virtue.* Princeton, NJ: Princeton University Press, 1983.

Blackouts

Occasionally, for various reasons, electric utility companies cannot provide continuous service to all their customers. Typical events that might precipitate downed power lines and a power failure include ice storms, electrical storms, other types of severe storms including hurricanes, and cable failure. At other times, during heat waves, for example, the demand for electricity exceeds generating capacity, and blackouts occur. Thus most, if not all, of the events that might trigger blackouts are unpredictable, and the timing of blackouts is difficult to forecast. It is, therefore, difficult to prepare for them.

Modern society particularly depends on the ability of utility companies to provide continuous, uninterrupted service. Urban areas are especially vulnerable to power failures, and chaotic conditions typically prevail until power is restored. Electrically operated elevators become inoperable, often stranding people between floors. Rooms may become completely dark, even during daylight hours. Refrigeration equipment shuts down without power, and food spoils quickly. Electric pumps that provide water to the upper floors of buildings become inoperable. Traffic signals fail to function, and traffic jams result. Commuter trains are halted, and airline flights are delayed. Conditions are especially chaotic at night when visibility is poor.

Although some people act in brave and even heroic ways during blackouts, others behave less than admirably. One of the most serious consequences of power blackouts is the opportunity for lawbreaking. The ability of law enforcement authorities to enforce the law during blackouts is greatly reduced. Because the police are frequently unable to reach crime scenes during a blackout, potential criminals have relatively free reign for their duration.

Power blackouts sometimes serve as triggers for widespread urban civil disorder, as occurred in New York City in July 1977. On that occasion, many residents, some of whom considered themselves to be victims of circumstance, took to the streets in large numbers. Many broke into stores and stole merchandise that they could not afford to buy but which they considered rightfully theirs. In their view, society had denied them the economic opportunities and relatively high incomes that many Americans take for granted. Because of their low incomes, they had been unable to purchase the consumer goods so heavily advertised and enticingly displayed in store windows. While the city was dark and law enforcement agencies immobilized, looters illegally obtained some of the things that had been denied them legally.

Anger and resentment against the "haves" by the "have nots" is sometimes given free reign during blackouts, and buildings are set on fire. In the looting and rioting that follow some blackouts, millions of dollars in damage are done to structures and their contents, and human life is often lost as well.

— Ernest H. Wohlenberg

References
"Blackout: New Paralysis, New Symptoms: Much Uglier." *New York Times* (July 17, 1977): A15.
Curvin, Robert, and Bruce Porter. *Blackout Looting!* New York: Gardner Press, 1979.
Ireland, Doug. "The Politics of Darkness." *New York Magazine* (August 1, 1977): 8–9.
Llewellyn, J. Bryce, and Adam Walinsky. "Blackout Lessons." *New York Times* (July 31, 1977).
U.S. Congress. House. Committee on Energy and Commerce. *Emergency Energy Responses to Extreme Weather. Hearings before the Subcommittee on Energy and Commerce.* 103d Cong., 2d sess., 1994.
U.S. Federal Energy Regulatory Commission. *The Con Edison Power Failure of July 13 and 14, 1977.* Washington, DC: Government Printing Office, 1978.
White, David F. "Why the Lights Went Out." *Time* (July 25, 1977): 24–25.
Wohlenberg, Ernest H. "The Geography of Civility Revisited: New York Blackout Looting 1977." *Economic Geography* 58 (1982): 29–44.

Blockbusting

The United States Fair Housing Act of 1968 defined blockbusting as the intent "for profit, to induce or attempt to induce any person to sell or rent any dwelling by representations regarding the entry or prospective entry into the neighborhood of a person or persons of a particular race, color, religion, or national origin." The act, which prohibited discrimination and unfair practices in the sale or rental of housing, explicitly banned blockbusting, as did many state and local fair housing statutes.

Historically, blockbusting developed as a tactic in the context of rigid and pervasive patterns of racial residential segregation. Typically, it was ascribed to real estate brokers and agents who settled African-American households in formerly all-white neighborhoods in order to provoke white flight. Their incentive was the excessive profit garnered from buying low from those who fled and selling high to those who sought access to new housing opportunities. Depending upon the refusal of whites to accept the possibility of housing integration, blockbusters "broke" segregated blocks.

Early instances of these practices date to the first decades of the twentieth century. At that time, substantially increased African-American population growth in northeastern and north-central cities was met by rigid segregation, which restricted their settlement to concentrated ghettos. When pressure on housing periodically forced expansion into nearby areas, it was often accomplished by blockbusters. These agents—sometimes called "white blackmailers" or "panic peddlers"—usually operated outside the pale of the mainstream real estate and finance industry, which generally shunned such transactions.

During the 1950s and 1960s, instances of blockbuster-induced racial turnover in urban neighborhoods reached unprecedented proportions in terms of extent and scale, occurring with remarkable consistency and coincidence in numerous cities, including Chicago, New York, Cleveland, Washington, Boston, Philadelphia, and Baltimore. These episodes resulted from several factors: the rapid expansion of new suburban areas (typically on a whites-only basis), the desperate housing needs of African Americans, and the persistence of a segregated housing market. The latter continued to be reinforced not only by individual prejudice, but by discriminatory institutional mechanisms involving the real estate and finance industries and governmental policies, both federal and local. Blockbusters were not solely responsible for creating white flight in this era, but their techniques of panic frequently produced dramatically rapid rates of residential racial change and subsequent resegregation. Moreover, while they helped to increase housing opportunities that had been illegitimately denied African Americans, the high profit margins, exploitative financial mechanisms, and unscrupulous methods often resulted in major obstacles to community well-being and stability.

Since the enactment of fair housing legislation, egregious forms of blockbusting have been less common, though some of the conditions that facilitated it persist.

— W. Edward Orser

See also
Desegregation of Housing; White Flight.
References
Helper, Rose. *Racial Policies and Practices of Real Estate Brokers.* Minneapolis: University of Minnesota Press, 1969.
Hirsch, Arnold. *Making the Second Ghetto: Race and Housing in Chicago, 1940–1960.* New York: Cambridge University Press, 1983.
Levine, Hillel, and Lawrence Harmon. *The Death of an American Jewish Community: A Tragedy of Good Intentions.* New York: Free Press, 1992.
Orser, W. Edward. *Blockbusting in Baltimore: The Edmondson Village Story.* Lexington: University Press of Kentucky, 1994.
Osofsky, Gilbert. *Harlem: The Making of a Ghetto, 1890–1930.* New York: Harper & Row, 1966.
Snow, David A., and Peter J. Leahy. "The Making of a Slum-Ghetto: A Case Study of Neighborhood Transition [Cleveland]." *Journal of Applied Behavioral Science* 16 (1980): 459–481.

Bogart, Humphrey (1899–1957)

Humphrey Bogart's film career, during which he made more than 70 movies, often involved variations on his most famous character type, a tough-guy loner. Among his many notable films were *The Maltese Falcon* (1941), *Casablanca* (1942), *To Have and Have Not* (1943), *The Big Sleep* (1946), and *The African Queen* (1952), for which he won the Academy Award as best actor of the year.

Bogart's screen persona is among the most clearly defined and enduring in all of cinema. Though he played individual roles that varied from this formula, the overall character that he portrayed is tough, cynical, private, sometimes ruthless, but, ultimately, often amiable and even principled. Bogart is most often identified as portraying a gangster or private eye, working either side of the law (or sometimes both, simultaneously) in a series of gritty 1930s and 1940s genre movies.

Indeed, Bogart was a key player in several of the most noted films from two important genres of the era, gangster films and film noir. As such, his characters often inhabit urban landscapes, and, inevitably, these films depict city life as bleak and menacing, set in neon-lit, rain-swept streets and dark, shadowy alleys. While theories abound regarding why these cynical, trust-no-one films achieved popularity in the years surrounding World War II, the consensus is that Bogart embodied the attitude and atmosphere of this genre to a degree that few others could approach.

Of course, *Casablanca* is a special, transcendent case—one of the most famous films of all time—and while the wistful, missed opportunities of its love story evoke sighs at every showing, the film also works on a social and political level in terms of isolation versus intervention, girding its romantic timelessness with an undercurrent that is, in some ways, very specific to the timing of its release. As such, it comments on American society and the pains of urban culture during the 1940s in direct and illustrative ways.

Apart from *Casablanca,* Bogart's key films can be grouped more readily. As both Philip Marlowe and Sam Spade, he portrayed a detective who maneuvered city streets on either end of a chase, running from or seeking out nefarious conspirators in some grand scheme, often at the behest of a mysterious and beautiful woman. On the other side of the law, his personality and behavior weren't really that different, and neither were the cold, impersonal versions of the city he traversed. These stylized treatments of city life were not necessarily meant to be taken literally, but they were never completely removed from reality either, recognizable even then as portraying the dark side of America's urban culture.

—*Robert P. Holtzclaw*

References

Benchley, Nathaniel. *Humphrey Bogart.* Boston: Little, Brown, 1975.

Goodman, Ezra H. *Bogey: The Good-Bad Guy.* New York: L. Stuart, 1965.

McCarty, Clifford. *The Complete Films of Humphrey Bogart.* New York: Carol Publishing Group, 1995.

Ruddy, Jonah. *Bogey: The Man, the Actor, the Legend.* New York: Tower, 1965.

Bohemianism

American journalist Henry Clapp is credited with establishing the first Bohemian enclave in the United States after he visited Paris in the 1850s. He fell in love with its Latin Quarter, inhabited by struggling poets, writers, artists, musicians, and actors who lived in drafty studios and tiny garrets tucked under mansard roofs of urban buildings and who regularly commiserated with one another in sidewalk cafes, cabarets, galleries, and bookshops. Parisians considered the itinerant residents who lived for art to be like carefree Gypsies whom the French called "Bohemian" under the mistaken impression that they originated in Central Europe (Bohemia). The Central European Bohemians had settled in the French capital during the early nineteenth century because they had been marginalized by both the French and Industrial Revolutions. French writers and dramatists romanticized their lives and deaths. Popular stories by Honoré Balzac and Henri Murger impressed Americans, some of whom went to observe the picturesque Bohemian community in Paris.

Clapp vowed to re-create a Latin Quarter back home in New York City. Upon his return, he started to refer to himself as a Bohemian and began to meet regularly with fellow writers at Pfaff's, a subterranean saloon on Broadway near Bleecker Street in Greenwich Village. He founded the first publication about American Bohemianism, and Ada Clare, one of the few women admitted to his intellectual circle, wrote in 1860 what became one of the first definitions of the new way of life: "A Bohemian is . . . by nature, if not by habit, a cosmopolite with a general sympathy for the fine arts, and for all things above and beyond convention." Yet, her interpretation was by no means universally accepted.

Scholars have continued to disagree about an exact definition of Bohemianism. Jerrold Seigel argued that it is "an appropriation of marginal lifestyles by young and not so young bourgeois, for the dramatization of ambivalence toward their own social identities and destinies." Helmut Kreuzer viewed it as part of a Marxist class struggle, "a subculture of nonbourgeois and antibourgeois intellectuals in modern industrial societies." A political scientist, Albert Parry, didn't see it in class terms at all but rather described it as a "temporary, flexible group. . . . Artists' cafes and attics are the meeting ground for many classes," while Cesar and Marigay

Grana characterized Bohemianism as "an attitude of dissent from the prevailing values of middle-class society—artistic, political, utilitarian, sexual—usually expressed in lifestyle and through a medium of the arts; and a cafe." The latter two definitions seem to come closest to the inherent ambiguity of the concept as a cultural practice rooted in a geographic place.

Inexpensive housing and modest restaurants have always been the backdrop for the theaters of Bohemian life acted out by mostly young inhabitants drawn to certain places, according to Emily Hahn by the promise of a "fresh start, cheap living and liberty." Cold-water flats and cavernous lofts with good light have been popular with impoverished artists. In the first decades of the twentieth century, when automobiles began to displace horses in New York City, artists flocked to formerly affluent neighborhoods where mansions had been subdivided with their converted "stables into studios and liveries into libraries." Similar accommodations cropped up in cities around the country as the wealthy moved to outlying areas. Typical Bohemian community activities continued to be poetry readings, plays, art shows, and recitals fueled by the caffeine and alcohol of coffeehouses and bars that became extensions of home. Some would argue that these settings of food and lodging can only occur in an urban setting with its perpetual stimulation by cultural institutions and neighborhoods in transition.

Most American Bohemian communities have formed in cities, and writer Floyd Dell saw the urban setting as a prerequisite when he lived in Chicago and New York City: "It must be in a big city, with a university nearby and a good library. You've got to have an old section of town falling into decay where the rents are low. Paint is what makes Bohemia—bright colors to hide the dingy old brown and cover up the rusty old iron." He worried that the fragile environment could be vulgarized, and indeed his Greenwich Village was transformed with tearooms and tourists during the 1920s. Former first lady Eleanor Roosevelt joined in a fight to save the area's Washington Square from redevelopment a few years later.

Gentrification still threatens urban Bohemias ripe for conversion by real estate developers into expensive condominiums and boutiques. Russell Jacoby argued that Bohemian districts are vulnerable to diffusion. He said they may become ineffectual incubators of creativity when they are relocated to a countryside without the congestion and fast pace of cities. "Fragile urban habitats of busy streets, cheap eateries, reasonable rents, and decent environs nourish bohemia. These can easily be damaged by economic depression, prosperity, urban renewal, expressways, slums, or suburbs."

Yet, Herbert Gold, a Bohemian disciple, noted that while various communities evolved over the century, certain features remained constant and could even be found flourishing in suburbs. "Fellow travelers in the life of art provide the support system, the social context, the economic basis of the bookshops and coffeehouses, maybe even a few of the audience for the other-language and revival movies, street fairs, and performances that the religion of Bohemia requires." The jazz-inspired beatniks of the 1950s and the rock-influenced hippies of the late 1960s and early 1970s are direct descendants of the nineteenth-century Bohemians. Ronald Sukenick contends that the Bohemian tradition endures because of "an unchanging antagonism between the way of life imposed by our pragmatic business society and the humanistic values by which our culture has taught us to experience and judge the quality of our individual and collective lives."

In the United States, certain districts of American cities and suburbs have historically connoted Bohemianism, including New York City's Greenwich Village, SoHo, and East Village; Chicago's Towertown (later Old Town) and south side colony in Hyde Park (on Stony Island and 57th Streets); San Francisco's North Beach and nearby Sausalito, Monterey, and Carmel by the Sea; Los Angeles's Venice West; New Orleans' French Quarter; Provincetown, Massachusetts; Key West, Florida; and Taos and Santa Fe, New Mexico. Bohemian outposts have occurred in many university towns, as well as Boston (Provincetown) and Philadelphia in the East; Red Gap, Austin, Houston, and San Antonio, Texas, Oklahoma City, and Reno, Nevada, in the West; Nashville, Memphis, Atlanta, and Charleston, South Carolina, in the South; and Cleveland, Buffalo, and Detroit in the Great Lakes region.

—*Norma Fay Green*

See also
Greenwich Village.

References
Beard, Rick, and Leslie Cohen Berlowitz, eds. *Greenwich Village: Culture and Counterculture.* New Brunswick, NJ: Rutgers University Press, 1993.

Churchill, Allen. *The Improper Bohemians: A Recreation of Greenwich Village in Its Heyday.* New York: Dutton, 1959.

Clayton, Douglas. *Floyd Dell: The Life and Times of an American Rebel.* Chicago: Ivan R. Dee, 1994.

Easton, Malcolm. *Artists and Writers in Paris: The Bohemian Idea, 1803–1867.* London: E. Arnold, 1964.

Gold, Herbert. *Bohemia: Digging the Roots of Cool.* New York: Touchtone Books, 1993.

Grana, Cesar, and Marigay Grana. *On Bohemia: The Code of the Self-Exiled.* New Brunswick, NJ: Transaction Publishers, 1990.

Hahn, Emily. *Romantic Rebels: An Informal History of Bohemianism in America.* Boston: Houghton Mifflin, 1967.

Jacoby, Russell. *The Last Intellectuals: American Culture in the Age of Academe.* New York: Basic Books, 1987.

Parry, Albert. *Garrets and Pretenders: A History of Bohemianism.* New York: Dover, 1960.

Rigney, Francis, and L. Douglas Smith. *The Real Bohemia.* New York: Basic Books, 1961.

Seigel, Jerrold. *Bohemian Paris: Culture, Politics and the Boundaries of Bourgeois Life, 1830–1930.* New York: Viking, 1986.

Sukenick, Ronald. *Down and In: Life in the Underground.* New York: William Morrow, 1987.

Walljasper, Jay. "From Greenwich Village to Main Street," *Utne Reader* (July/August 1991): 142–143.

Boom Towns

The popular image of the historic "boom town" is often based upon the motion picture industry's depiction of an isolated and violent Wild West settlement. Nineteenth-century mining and cattle towns grew so uncontrollably that they were seen as conflict-ridden settlements with few public amenities and haphazard planning. The local mentality was exploitative: "Get all you can get, get it as fast as you can, and get out." These towns flourished briefly, then died quickly, leaving broken buildings and few people.

While many boom towns across the country fit this characterization, some industrial boom towns were carefully planned and experienced well-managed growth. A great many boom towns fell in between. They grew very suddenly, often because of land speculation or the discovery of natural resources, but they also witnessed a semblance of planning, community, and, most important, persistent, durable growth that prevented them from becoming ghost towns. In the twentieth century, the trend continued, especially after World War II, when private and public authorities sought to build suburban "new towns" as a way to ameliorate urbanization.

The Land Ordinance of 1785 spurred the initial boomtown settlements in eastern Ohio, and speculators in both farm and town lots flooded the Ohio Valley in the 1790s. At the fork of a river or along important roadways, speculators planned cities with attractive street patterns, town squares, and public buildings. They enthusiastically promoted their schemes back east and attracted emigrants. While many of these paper towns were simply means of defrauding settlers, some, like Cincinnati and Zanesville, developed as brisk trading centers and grew rapidly.

The rapid growth of manufacturing after 1815 spurred city development around the cotton mills of New England. One of the best-known examples was Lowell, Massachusetts. Within years, 25 factories sprang up there, and 15,000 inhabitants occupied the town. Developers not only manufactured textiles for profit, but they also engaged in land speculation and sold individual town lots for enormous profits.

The completion of the Erie Canal in 1825 opened the Great Lakes region to settlers. Along the canal route in western New York, raucous and sometimes violent cities sprang up overnight at lock sites that attracted Irish laborers by the thousands and brought many new towns instant prosperity.

The nation's most extensive land boom to date took place in the western Great Lakes when Andrew Jackson destroyed the Bank of the United States and redistributed federal funds to state banks in the early 1830s. Hundreds of speculators bought cheap government land with paper money and laid out future cities in most unlikely places. Maps were carefully printed showing hotels, docks, public buildings, schools, and pleasant homes. While in most places little on-site development actually occurred, some communities grew quickly. Chicago, Saginaw, and Grand Rapids all originated as speculative real estate schemes. Jackson's suspension of the use of paper money to pay for public lands ended the speculative boom in 1837. Overnight, lots in boom towns were worthless.

Early boom towns were often the essential force identified with rapid settlement of the Old Northwest. As the editor of the *Milwaukee Daily Sentinel* wrote on May 26, 1845, "In no other country have towns and villages sprung up so suddenly as in this. Cities grow up here to more importance in ten years than they do in Europe in a century."

Speculators were not only largely responsible for making "every town a boom town," but they also drew upon eastern experience in confronting city problems and planning urban growth. Most Midwest boom towns escaped the violence and lawlessness of Far West communities. These towns repeated patterns set in the development of older cities. Lines of social distinction were established, and urban amenities like schools, churches, newspapers, and theaters developed that reflected eastern culture and political practice.

Natural-resource towns sprang up in the second half of the nineteenth century. Iron- and copper-mining towns in the northern Great Lakes, like Calumet, Michigan, and Hibbing, Minnesota, and lumber towns like Saginaw and Bay City, Michigan, and Hurley, Wisconsin, grew rapidly as thousands of immigrants flocked in to work the mines or sawmills. At the same time, in the gold and silver country of Arizona, California, and the Rocky Mountains, mining camps were the primary form of boom-town settlement. Western settlements were often disposable towns, called "rag cities," because they were mainly tents, a store or two, and several saloons and brothels.

Largely composed of male workers, they had their share of lawlessness, especially in their formative years, but their reputations for rowdiness were often exaggerated. Lumber towns and mining boom towns were frequently company-owned and strictly regulated or governed paternalistically. Miners in the West themselves quickly created ad hoc courts that awarded claims, resolved disputes, and held criminal proceedings. Order was generally maintained (although some "order" resembled lynch law), and schools, churches, and opera houses were built.

Western cattle towns also sprang up overnight along the cattle trade routes leading from Texas to Kansas and Colorado. Towns like Abilene, Wichita, and Dodge City all served

Abandoned storefronts in Dodge City, Kansas, reveal the frequent transformation of boom towns into ghost towns.

as shipping points for cattle being driven north. Cow towns developed a reputation for violence and lawlessness as hundreds of dusty, rowdy cowboys sought recreation in these towns after weeks or months on the trail. City officials often quarantined the vice by keeping the cowboys, saloons, brothels, and gambling halls in a separate area.

Once the cattle trade moved on or natural resources ran out, boom towns frequently became ghost towns. However, many also acquired stability when new industries were brought in, farms and railroads developed nearby, or industrial mining operations sank shafts to mine ore deep beneath the surface of the land.

Company-owned industrial towns began to emerge in the late nineteenth century. The typical town was an isolated community located on the outskirts of a nearby city where land was cheap, taxes low, and managers could exert firm control over the workforce. By 1901, several planned industrial communities like Pullman, Illinois, and Gary, Indiana, blossomed overnight. In the West, company-owned towns sprang up in the lumber industry and in copper and coal mining. All property, commercial services, housing, recreation, and utilities were owned by the company in towns like Morenci and Ajo, Arizona.

Paternalism existed in varying degrees in these towns. Employees who lived in well-regulated, tailor-made communities, like Pullman and Calumet, sometimes precipitated violent strikes to protest rigid management of their daily lives. Still, the grasping, company image in these boom towns has been overstated. Residents frequently cooperated with the company to better the community and took pride in keeping their homes and yards attractive and maintaining city pride.

After natural resources, the next great shaper of boom towns was the automobile. Making and operating cars required steel, glass, rubber, and gasoline. New industries formed, others expanded, and old and new towns grew too quickly for managed growth. Places like Flint, Detroit, Dearborn, Akron, and Gary exploded in the 1920s. Forty-one percent of the new-town residents were foreign-born. Shanty towns, much like the "rag towns" of the Old West, appeared, and water and air pollution became widespread. Homes were strewn helter-skelter along muddy, unpaved streets. Only gradually, after the Depression, did rows of frame houses with porches, lawns, and backyards replace the ugliness of boom towns brought on by the automobile era.

The automobile itself also created a kind of boom town. Some, like Los Angeles, sprang up because the car not only brought people west but essentially enabled the spread-out city to exist. The auto allowed new towns to develop as planned and unplanned suburban communities. Thousands of these communities appeared on the American landscape after World War II. These "packaged suburbs" were often planned by government (like the greenbelt towns of the New Deal); organized by builders (like the Levittowns in Pennsylvania and New York); or built by land developers (like Columbia, Maryland, or Reston, Virginia). Boom towns continue to develop in the Sunbelt and Rocky Mountain states because of recreational opportunities, new technological industries, and casino gambling.

Although the boom-town experience was often short-lived, residents of boom towns characteristically displayed a feeling of optimism and hope for the future. At the outset, boom towns were often chaotic as they experienced rapid, inconvenient growth and development. The people learned to tolerate necessary adjustments as well as a host of different newcomers. Often seeking an escape from the rapid changes of urban society, residents of boom towns brought with them a conservatism that resisted fundamental change. For the most part, boom towns transplanted the traditional cultures and institutional structures of prior experiences. A few survived the boom-town experience, especially when new industries or technology were located there, but most boom towns, if they did not become ghost towns, clung to traditional institutional patterns and very quickly imitated older, established communities.

—Jeremy W. Kilar

References

Allen, James B. *The Company Town in the American West.* Norman: University of Oklahoma Press, 1966.

Clapp, James A. *New Towns and Urban Policy: Planning Metropolitan Growth.* New York: Dunellen, 1971.

Coleman, James S. *Community Conflict.* Glencoe, IL: Free Press, 1957.

Dykstra, Robert R. *The Cattle Towns: A Social History of the Kansas Cattle Trading Centers of Abilene, Ellsworth, Wichita, Dodge City, and Caldwell, 1867–1888.* New York: Knopf, 1968.

Haeger, John Dennis. *The Investment Frontier: New York Businessmen and the Economic Development of the Old Northwest.* Albany: State University of New York Press, 1981.

Smith, Page. *A City upon a Hill.* New York: Knopf, 1966.

Still, Bayrd. *Milwaukee, the History of a City.* Rev. ed. Madison: State Historical Society of Wisconsin, 1967.

Boosterism

Boosterism is a somewhat cynical term referring to the craft and practice of urban public relations. It has served as the ideology of urban rivalry—that is, a set of arguments advantageous to urban real estate and business owners. In the early nineteenth century, boosters were usually individual journalists, land speculators, or commercial entrepreneurs; by the late twentieth century, they were usually professionals within public and private economic development organizations. "Pure" boosterism can be defined as the publication and dissemination of positive comments and evaluations of a city's economic position and prospects. "Applied" boosterism shades imperceptibly into targeted business recruitment, an activity that benefits from a community's positive reputation but which also involves specific inducements and subsidies (whether free land for early railroads or tax abatements for modern manufacturing concerns).

Boosterism in the nineteenth century was especially rife in smaller cities and on the urban frontiers of the Midwest and the Far West. Visitors from the East Coast and Europe frequently commented on the eagerness of Americans to glory in the virtues of their new communities and on the optimism and grandiloquence of their language. James Fennimore Cooper satirized this tendency in the character of land speculator Aristabulus Bragg in *Home as Found* (1835), and in *Martin Chuzzlewit* (1844) Charles Dickens sharply criticized boosterism by telling the story of Eden, a town far grander in word than in fact.

Frontier boosters made energetic use of the local and national press. A primary function of frontier newspapers was to rave about the advantages of their town and to condemn the disadvantages of rivals. Boosters found a new outlet with the emergence of national business periodicals before the Civil War, especially *Hunt's Merchants Magazine* and *DeBow's Review*. Intended audiences for antebellum boosters included potential settlers, investors, and railroad builders. In addition, boosterism was an important tool for deflecting attention away from internal conflicts, unifying communities around economic strategies, and generating enthusiasm for public investment in transportation improvements.

Boosters on the urban frontier often spoke the language of geographic determinism. A mere glance at the map, said the booster, made it obvious why Chicago (or Terre Haute or Denver or Tacoma) was fated for greatness. Several writers, notably Jessup W. Scott and William Gilpin, developed elaborate statistical and geographical theories that claimed to pinpoint the location of the next great world city. In Scott's case that site was on the Great Lakes, in Gilpin's at Kansas City and later Denver. Promoters of individual cities offered their own explanations for their community's obvious natural advantages; typical of the genre was Logan U. Reavis's *St. Louis: The Future Great City of the World* (1870). Boosters were also unabashed in applying the rhetoric of Manifest Destiny and European cultural or racial superiority that were common in the century.

In towns that survived their first decades and achieved a second or third generation of growth, boosters assumed the tasks of inventorying and recording past and present accomplishments as proofs of future success. Boosters such as Cincinnati's Charles Cist produced city histories and statistical compendia that offered the "hard" data of progress and enlisted the past as evidence of imminent greatness. They published sketches of early growth; lists of schools, newspapers, and charitable societies; and tables showing manufacturing output, wheat shipments, street paving, taxes, births, real estate prices, and other quantifiable indicators. As Elias Colbert wrote of Chicago in 1868, "it is scarcely permitted to us to ponder the achievements of today, ere they are swept out of the memory by the still grander conquests of to-morrow."

During the later nineteenth and early twentieth centuries, boosterism became more specialized and organized. Boosters began to offer arguments that unveiled a city's advantages for specific economic functions—Washington, D.C., as a wholesaling center for the South; Colorado Springs as a health resort; Phoenix as the Valley of the Sun (a term coined by an advertising agency in the 1930s) for long winter vacations.

Cities increasingly depended on organizations rather than individuals to sing their praises. The number of local chambers of commerce grew from ten in 1858 to several hundred in 1900. Milwaukee in the late nineteenth century had an Association for the Advancement of Milwaukee, "to advertise to the world the advantages which the city had to manufacturers seeking new locations." Indianapolis had a Manufacturers and Real Estate Exchange and a Board of Trade; Los Angeles had the All-Year Club of Southern California.

Turn-of-the-century cities also resorted to indirect public relations. They built industrial and commercial exhibition halls as standing trade shows. They purchased advertisements in national magazines, a technique especially favored by southern cities. They staged expositions, special events, world's fairs, and festivals such as Pasadena's Tournament of Roses. All these activities were designed to enrich cities both directly by attracting big-spending visitors and indirectly by "putting the city on the map."

In the last decades of the twentieth century, American cities still pursued special events (the 1984 Los Angeles and 1996 Atlanta Olympic Games, for example). They scrambled for recognition and reputation as "major league cities" by subsidizing professional sports teams. Their economic development departments also practiced a modern version of booster writing by circulating glossy brochures that ballyhooed their advantages as places to do business. The comparative statistics, sleek pictures, and carefully oriented maps of this promotional literature are identical in concept to booster publications of the 1850s. The numbers may be more accurate, the pictures are now in radiant color, and the targeted audience is likely to be manufacturing firms rather than land speculators and railroad moguls, but the underlying message and purpose are essentially the same.

—Carl Abbott

See also
Train, George Francis (Citizen); Urban Rivalry and Urban Imperialism.
References
Abbott, Carl. *Boosters and Businessmen: Popular Economic Thought and Urban Growth in the Antebellum Middle West.* Westport, CT: Greenwood Press, 1981.
Glaab, Charles. *Kansas City and the Railroads.* Madison: State Historical Society of Wisconsin, 1962.
Hamer, David. *New Towns in the New World: Images and Perceptions of the Nineteenth-Century Urban Frontier.* New York: Columbia University Press, 1990.
Karnes, Thomas. *William Gilpin: Western Nationalist.* Austin: University of Texas Press, 1970.

Bosses and Machines

The terms *political boss* and *political machine* are not absolutes, and whether a political organization deserved to be labeled a *machine* or a political leader a *boss* was often arguable. Our common definition of these terms is intimately associated with the rise of urban and industrial America at the end of the nineteenth century. And the heyday of machines and bosses was roughly from the 1880s to the 1920s, although such organizations and people existed earlier and later as well.

The question becomes more complicated when one realizes that both terms were pejorative, at least to middle-class groups and interests, which meant the press, the schools, and the leaders of urban society in general. These were the primary foes of the boss system and the forces behind what was generally termed reform. Urban political activities and elections were often seen and portrayed as contests between the malevolent machine and the benevolent reformers, but that interpretation was true only in the eyes of those who opposed the machines, not of those who voted them into power.

The political machine was a new type of urban political organization (there have been state machines as well as city machines) characterized by certain common features that were very much intertwined. First, machines were hierarchically organized; from one or a few people at the top, the machine spread like an inverted "V," with representatives at every level of government, down to the precinct of several thousand voters. The person at the top of the power structure was the boss, although the individual dominance of a single boss varied from one machine to another. Second, the reason for the hierarchical organization was that the machine's strength came from the bottom of the inverted "V," from the mass of voters who made up the urban working class. This distinguished machine organization clearly from alternative urban political groups that drew their strength from societal elites and the general power of the upper-middle and upper classes. Third, machines generally lacked any ideology; the machine sought power for its own sake rather than for reasons of political ideas or policies, whereas its opponents generally had clear policy or issue goals. As it turned out, this did not necessarily result in one form providing better government than the other.

In developing its strength directly from mass support rather than from elites, the machine could survive only by accepting the masses as they were and serving them as they desired. That led to the machine being characterized by what we would now call "ethnic sensitivity"—respecting the languages and customs of new urban immigrants in order to win their political support. Machine representatives spoke the immigrants' languages, attended their ceremonies, and named some of their leaders to public office. The same attitude also led to the characteristic machine roles of welfare organization and employment agent. Both of these services were basic reasons why machines were so popular and frequently successful at the polls.

In contrast, middle-class reformers generally did none of these things. Nativism among the middle and upper classes was rife, the exploitation of workers was common, and government social services were almost nonexistent. But the machine, for its own reasons, succored the poor and the immigrant, and it granted them respect on their own terms. It is difficult to exaggerate the importance of these cultural and socioeconomic factors in understanding the role and the success of political machines.

Two other factors were almost always characteristic of machines. One was partisan politics. The machine succeeded by taking over one of the parties in a city and effectively becoming the city's Republican or, more often, Democratic Party. This permitted building a more enduring base as voters developed loyalty to the party, which was, for a greater or lesser time, the machine. However, it also meant that opposition to a particular machine could come not only from the other party but from factions within its own party who were trying to gain control for themselves. New York is one city where the machine, in this case Tammany Hall, often controlled the Democratic Party but had to fight almost constantly to maintain power against nonmachine Democrats. In Chicago, on the other hand, this situation held into the 1920s, but the machine *became* the Democratic Party by the end of that decade and the two were indivisible for the next 50 years.

Second, patronage was crucial to the machine, the food on which it lived. American cities at the turn of the century were places of tremendous growth and building, with huge demands for labor of all types. Because much of this building, such as subways, was for public agencies, and private building required city permits and licenses, the machine had great influence with contractors and therefore thousands of jobs to dispense to its supporters. Likewise, the expansion of government provided many jobs, from lowly laborers to highly regarded managers, that the machine could dole out. In its own interest, therefore, the machine tended to increase the number of government jobs available, which was one of its characteristics most criticized by opponents.

These jobs were very important to immigrant workers, along with the loans, gifts, and other favors bestowed by the local machine representative. And they also embodied one of the reasons why middle- and upper-class groups in cities detested machines: they empowered the underclass, which, without this empowerment, would be controlled by elites. Beyond that, elite groups saw machines as creating a kind of politics that was both immoral and not recognizing the real needs of burgeoning cities. They wanted centralized power and a strong government geared to those physical, economic, and political changes that they thought necessary for long-term economic growth and general city success, not to mention their own prosperity and power.

This attitude was common by the 1890s when the rate of immigration was rapidly increasing and relations between employers and workers were becoming steadily more contentious. James (later Lord) Bryce's famous study *The American Commonwealth* (1888), based on visits from England to the United States since the 1870s, reflected these beliefs and influenced them. The boss system, he argued, was based on the worst aspects of American society: the "ignorant masses," an amorphous mass of "largely Irish and Germans, together with Poles and Russians, Bohemians, negroes [*sic*], Frenchmen, Italians, and such native Americans as have fallen from their first estate into drink or penury." It was unfortunate, indeed, said Bryce, "that they have been allowed civic power." These sentiments were not uncommon in the supposedly democratic United States in the late nineteenth and early twentieth centuries. Native-born reformers of the Progressive Era, people like Lincoln Steffens and other opponents of machines from the business and professional elites, shared them. The machines had few defenders except among their own.

Of the latter, none is more famous than George Washington Plunkitt (1842–1924), a Tammany Hall district leader, whose ruminations on politics and reform were recorded and made famous by journalist William L. Riordan in *Plunkitt of Tammany Hall*. Plunkitt disdained middle-class reformers and their disregard for the masses. He showed, by describing his own daily efforts, the extent to which the machine served people for whom no one else cared. To Plunkitt, good politics was the kind practiced by the Tammany Hall machine that served the voters and received their votes in return. But Plunkitt also exhibited a self-serving sense of morality; he openly used his positions in the government and the party to enrich himself, thus feeding middle-class generalizations about machine politics being inevitably corrupt.

Part of the traditionally negative view of machines and bosses came about because corruption was not uncommon in machine politics. The first modern political machine, the Tweed Ring of New York City, whose heyday was from the middle of the 1860s to 1871, was exceptionally venal, and Tweed himself ended up in prison. The Ring's Tammany Hall engaged in extensive graft, mounting into the millions of dollars, that played no small role in the rise of a reform, or anti-Tammany, force in the Democratic Party of the city, as well as the disapprobation of any organization labeled a "machine" by the press and the urban elite.

Very different was the reign of Charles Francis Murphy, the boss of Tammany Hall and through it of the New York City Democratic Party for two dozen years starting in 1902. Murphy was personally honest, although, as a practical machine politician, he did not demand the same behavior from others. More to the point, when Murphy's Tammany Hall controlled major offices, it provided the city with government as good as that of the "reformers" when they held power. Murphy himself took great pride in the successful running of his city and in the fact that Alfred E. Smith and Robert F. Wagner, who would become two of the most respected leaders of the Democratic Party, emerged from the Tammany organization. At the same time, Tammany continued serving the urban masses—widows and other deserving poor received support; food baskets, coal, and small loans were available through district and precinct Tammany leaders; picnics, clambakes, and other entertainments were provided for a poor and tenement-dwelling population. Not surprisingly, Murphy's Tammany Hall got their continued support in return.

Machine politics was practical politics, and machine politicians dealt with realities. That is why bosses like Murphy, or like Tony Cermak and Richard J. Daley in Chicago after him, came to terms with some of the more disreputable elements of their cities. Gangsters and numbers racketeers, just like bankers and builders, were forces that had to be reckoned with in order to get votes and maintain power. This also explains why bosses were often effective at governing. While providing welfare services, they were nonetheless often fiscally conservative, and in some cases they provided less profligate government than their harshest critics.

Machines began dying out in the second and third decades of the twentieth century for a variety of reasons. For one, Progressive reformers often succeeded in changing the structure of city government in ways that undercut machines. Primary elections, making many public offices nonpartisan and nonpolitical, civil service laws, open bidding on government contracts, the initiative and referendum—all were structural changes that narrowed the options for machines. One reason machine politics lasted so much longer in Chicago than elsewhere was that patronage remained available; as late as the 1960s Chicago mayors continued to have thousands of jobs to disperse to loyal party workers and supporters.

The changing nature of American government also played a role in machine decline, as Edwin O'Connor's famous novel *The Last Hurrah* (1956) argued. The analysis, which scholars tend to qualify, was that the New Deal killed the remaining machines because the federal government now provided the social services that only machines had previously furnished. Unemployment and old-age insurance, protection of workers' rights, and the general structure of the welfare state, O'Connor claimed, had reoriented the masses from local authority to national, killing the machines by withdrawing their most winning function. In fact, the New Deal worked productively with Democratic city machines and did not try to weaken them, but O'Connor's overall point retains some validity for the long term.

More important was demographic change. As immigrants and their children moved up the socioeconomic ladder, their needs changed and became more varied. Few machines other than that of Chicago could cope well with these more sophisticated needs. And even Chicago's machine ultimately confronted one of the most dynamic factors of mid-twentieth-century cities: race. As Chicago's blacks increased their percentage of the city's population, the machine kept winning, primarily on the basis of poor organization in the African-American community, which continued to support it. By the 1960s, this was changing, and the machine was under real strain when Richard J. Daley died in 1976.

The urban political machine developed because, in the period of extremely rapid urban economic, physical, and demographic growth and change in the late nineteenth and early twentieth centuries, it was needed. The new urban proletariat, largely immigrant and relatively defenseless against the harsh capitalism and bitter nativism of the time, required some agency to serve its economic exigencies and help it in the process of acculturation. Machine politicians were happy to play this role since it provided them (often themselves the children of immigrants, primarily Irish) a basis for their own initial rise to some wealth and status. It was a mutually beneficial, symbiotic relationship. And it was, arguably, good for American society in general, providing a moderately powerful counterweight, at the city level, to the overweening power of the upper-class elite of the time.

More generally, it was part of the overall process of modernization taking place in American life at this time. Urban politics and government, no less than economic organization or social mores, were challenged by the multiple forces of an industrializing society. One political response was the boss and the machine. It had successes and failures, as did other forms of urban political organization. Cities with a strong machine tradition, like New York or Boston or Chicago, experienced neither notably better nor notably worse government in the twentieth century than cities like Toledo or Los Angeles where that tradition was essentially nonexistent. At the very least, the machine provided access to political power for groups that alternative structures generally held in contempt and refused to serve.

—*John M. Allswang*

See also
Coughlin, John Joseph (Bathhouse John); Crump, Edward H.; Kenna, Michael (Hinky Dink); Tammany Hall.

References
Allswang, John M. *Bosses, Machines, and Urban Voters.* Rev. ed. Baltimore: Johns Hopkins University Press, 1986.
———. *A House for All Peoples: Ethnic Politics in Chicago, 1880–1936.* Lexington: University Press of Kentucky, 1971.
Biles, Roger. *Big City Boss in Depression and War: Mayor Edward J. Kelly of Chicago.* DeKalb: Northern Illinois University Press, 1984.
———. *Richard J. Daley: Politics, Race, and the Governing of Chicago.* DeKalb: Northern Illinois University Press, 1995.
Callow, Alexander B., Jr. *The Tweed Ring.* New York: Oxford University Press, 1966.
———, ed. *The City Boss in America: An Interpretive Reader.* New York: Oxford University Press, 1976.
Dorsett, Lyle W. *Franklin D. Roosevelt and the City Bosses.* Port Washington, NY: Kennikat Press, 1977.
Stave, Bruce M., and Sondra Astor Stave, eds. *Urban Bosses, Machines, and Progressive Reformers.* Malabar, FL: Robert E. Krieger Publishing Co., 1984.

Boston, Massachusetts

Boston, the capital city of Massachusetts, is the oldest urban center in the United States established by the English. Bostonians have long considered their city to be the "Athens of America," reflecting its preeminence in democracy, culture, and learning. It is a city that looms large in American consciousness and history. Founded in 1630 as a port city, Boston is today the financial and educational hub of New England and one of the most important cities in the United States despite its relatively small size (46 square miles). Boston now boasts a service-based economy centered on health, education, and government. There are over 30 hospitals and a like number of institutions of higher learning located in the city. Government is an important part of the city's employment base since Boston, in addition to being the capital of Massachusetts, is the regional administrative center of many federal agencies.

Ranked in 1990 as the twentieth largest city in the nation, Boston had a population of just under 575,000 in 1990, a 2 percent increase since 1980. The metropolitan area's population is more than 4 million, the country's sixth largest. The city itself has a population density of 12,484 persons per square mile and is ethnically and racially diverse. Suffolk County, of which Boston is the largest component, is ranked as the twenty-eighth most racially diverse county in the nation (based on Census Bureau studies showing areas where proportions of the population identified by race is nearest to being equal). The city's white population is 62.8 percent of the total, the African-American portion is 25.6 percent of the total, Asians are 5.3 percent, and American Indians are less than 1 percent of Boston's population. Those identified as Hispanics of any race make up 10.8 percent of the city's people, and 6 percent of the city's residents are classified as "other." Boston's population in 1990 was 51.9 percent female and 48.1 percent male. Twenty-eight percent of the people own their own housing while 63 percent of the city's residents are renters.

The city of Boston has a strong mayor form of municipal government. The mayor is elected to a four-year term in a nonpartisan election. A preliminary election in September reduces an unlimited field of candidates to the highest two vote-getters, who face each other in the final election in November. Mayors are not limited in the number of terms they may serve, and Boston has had one recent mayor, Kevin White, who was elected to four terms and served for 16 years (1969–1984).

The mayor proposes the municipal budget and appoints the city's chief officials. Boston's mayor works with a legislative body, the city council, which is, by state charter, weak. The council is required to approve mayoral appointments and the city budget, but most power resides with the chief executive. For example, the council may not increase the budget proposed by the mayor. The council has 13 members who are elected in two ways. Four councilors are elected "at large" by voters throughout the city from a field of eight candidates. The other nine councilors represent single-member geographic districts. This system is the latest in a series of charter plans that, throughout the twentieth century, have attempted to balance the needs of neighborhoods with the need to have a citywide perspective in the council.

The city's police commissioner was appointed by the governor of Massachusetts until a charter revision in the 1960s allowed the mayor to make that appointment. Similarly, the city schools have only recently (1992) come under the mayor's control. Previously, voters elected a school committee based on neighborhoods, but under the current system the mayor appoints a seven-member committee from a list of candidates proposed by a panel of Bostonians. The school committee then selects a superintendent who is responsible for administering the school system.

Boston was settled in 1630 by a group of Puritans led by John Winthrop. The 750-acre peninsula they claimed was named Boston in honor of the English town that provided both people and money for the Puritans' expedition. Boston was dominated by a trio of hills and possessed a great harbor that quickly became the basis for the town's economic prosperity. In the seventeenth century, Boston was England's largest settlement in North America. The city's early economic success was based on shipbuilding and fishing. Commerce became increasingly important, and Boston's merchants ranged up and down the Atlantic coast and prospered by trading with the West Indies. The hinterland of New England provided Boston with lumber to trade, but no staple export crop could fuel the town's continued growth in the eighteenth century. As a result, Boston suffered relative economic decline during the eighteenth century as the competing ports of New York and Philadelphia surpassed it. Taxes, colonial wars, and industrial competition also beset Boston. In part, the economic problems of the town accounted for its leadership in the revolutionary movement of the 1760s and 1770s. That independence movement was also influenced by Boston's founding ideals.

Boston's Puritan founders wanted their settlement to be the center of a "godly commonwealth." As Winthrop originally described it, Boston was to be "a city upon a hill," a model and a spiritual beacon to the world. Puritan ideals have permeated Boston's history, and the city's importance in the American experience is based largely upon the Puritan sense of moral responsibility and its emphasis on education.

This stress on education led the Puritans to create the first free public school in the nation (Boston Latin School) in 1635, a year before Harvard College was chartered. Over time Boston evolved into a national and international mecca for scholars, both young and old. Boston College carries on the Jesuit tradition in education while Boston University, founded by Methodists, also bears witness to the long importance of religion in the old Puritan town. The University of Massachusetts at Boston overlooks Boston Harbor and is a neighbor to the John F. Kennedy Library and Museum, a memorial to the late president and area native. The Massachusetts Institute of Technology (originally located in Boston) and Harvard University are both located across the Charles River in Cambridge and add even more luster to Boston's reputation as an educational center.

Boston's leadership in the realm of intellect and education is matched by its prominence in the social and political development of the United States. While Boston in the eighteenth century was the cradle of liberty and the birthplace of the American Revolution, in the nineteenth century the Puritan traditions of service and idealism contributed to the rise of abolitionism and other reform movements. Massachusetts Bay Colony long possessed a sense of independence. Bostonians' resistance to British taxes and commercial policies led British troops to occupy the city in 1768. Two years later, Sam Adams immortalized the death of five Bostonians

at the hands of British troops as the "Boston Massacre." This tragic event was a key development in the growth of anti-British feeling throughout the colonies and was soon followed by an even more portentous action. The Boston Tea Party of 1773 resulted from Parliament's efforts to create a monopolistic control over tea imports and to exact taxes from Boston and other American ports. The destruction of the tea led directly to England closing the port of Boston and the convocation of the first Continental Congress.

In April 1775 protests over the British blockade of Boston led to "the shot heard 'round the world," armed conflict, and death in nearby Lexington and Concord following Paul Revere's famous ride. Three months later the British attacked a rebel force located in Charlestown, across the river from Boston (and later annexed to the city). Despite a costly victory at the Battle of Bunker Hill, the British continued to be besieged in the rebellious port by a Continental army, soon commanded by George Washington of Virginia. The British were forced to evacuate Boston early in 1776, and although the fight for independence was completed elsewhere, Boston's claim to birthing the American Revolution remains substantial.

Boston suffered great losses while it was occupied by the British army. Its population plummeted, many homes and other buildings were destroyed, and it took years to rebuild and restore the town's economic vitality. Nevertheless, Boston's ships set sail for distant ports at the end of the eighteenth century, bringing new prosperity to the town and region. Yankee entrepreneurs resumed trading with the West Indies under the new American flag and opened new routes to South America, the northwest coast of North America, the Hawaiian Islands, and China. They invested much of their new wealth in transforming the shape and appearance of Boston at the end of the eighteenth century and the beginning of the nineteenth.

Since 1630 Boston's topography has undergone more alterations than that of any other comparably sized city. Boston has been continually reshaped, its hills cut down to fill harbors, mudflats, rivers, and channels, its streets and avenues endlessly redirected. Throughout its history, political and business leaders and ordinary citizens have made decisive choices about the physical growth, shape, and appearance of the city. In the early years of the seventeenth century, the physical community and built environment evolved from the aggregate of decisions made by individuals. Private citizens designed homes and workplaces; private partnerships provided basic services; and private entrepreneurs orchestrated major developments, such as filling in the shoreline and building wharves.

In the eighteenth century, initiative and money continued to come from the private sector, and merchants began to dominate political life. Peter Faneuil, for example, provided the funds to build the hall that bears his name. Faneuil Hall not only provided commercial space for merchants, but also office space and meeting rooms for the local government. In the transformation that occurred at the beginning of the nineteenth century, local architect Charles Bulfinch built a new Boston of brick and granite. Bulfinch's Boston was based on commerce, and he erected temples of business—banks, insurance offices, and wharves—as well as homes for the new commercial princes and a new State House prominently situated atop Beacon Hill. Charles Bulfinch shaped Boston in a way matched by no one else.

The new and revitalized Boston gained additional fame in the nineteenth century as a literary and cultural center. The Boston connections of Ralph Waldo Emerson, Henry David Thoreau, Nathaniel Hawthorne, Margaret Fuller, and others renewed the city's claim to intellectual leadership. The aristocratic "Boston Brahmin" families who dominated the city's financial, social, and political life firmly established Boston's reputation for exclusivity, provincialism, and an attitude of social superiority. Boston earned attention for social reform in the nineteenth century as well. Faneuil Hall and other locations featured abolitionists, pacifists, and temperance advocates as well as women asserting their equality. William Lloyd Garrison's radical call for the abolition of slavery was the most controversial reform effort, but the variety of causes that attracted attention and support in Boston was astounding. During the years before the Civil War, in both literature and social reform, Boston earned its reputation for high ideals.

During the first half of the nineteenth century, the accumulated money of Boston Brahmins and others not only transformed the town's appearance but also financed textile mills along the Charles and Merrimack Rivers, initiating the Industrial Revolution in the United States. The economic shift to manufacturing altered the appearance and thrust of Boston in the nineteenth century. The textile industry required massive construction of new storage facilities and wharves in Boston. Also, in the nineteenth century the Town of Boston incorporated as a city (1822), expanded into the surrounding waters, and annexed adjacent towns. Advances in transportation and building methods altered the city as Boston extended its borders by cutting down hills and filling the surrounding water to create the new districts of Back Bay, the South End, and South Boston. Most of Boston's territorial expansion took place when streetcar lines allowed city dwellers to move to outlying suburbs. Neighboring communities of Boston—Roxbury, Charlestown, and Dorchester— were inundated by Bostonians for whom roads were laid out and paved and water and sewerage facilities provided.

Three of Boston's ablest mayors, all named Josiah Quincy—father, son, and great-grandson—greatly shaped the growth of Boston in the nineteenth century. In the 1820s, "the Great Mayor" (the first Josiah Quincy) energized the municipality to clean the streets, provide for the poor, and develop a grand, new public marketplace to supplement Faneuil Hall. In the 1840s, the second Mayor Quincy led the drive to acquire a reservoir for city residents, and in the 1890s the last Mayor Quincy presided over both the dedication of America's first subway and also the construction of public bathhouses.

In the decades after the Civil War, Bostonians supported a variety of public endeavors, including the regal Public Library at Copley Square, the founding of the Boston Symphony Orchestra, and the park system conceived by Frederick Law Olmsted. Strung together on an "Emerald Necklace" that still runs from central Boston to its neighborhoods, Olmsted's parks brought together disparate elements and sections of the city. Under Olmsted, the park system evolved from 1879 to 1895 to incorporate over 2,000 acres of land throughout the enlarged city. The distinguished landscape architect planned a strand of roadways connecting parks and outlying sections of the city with the original peninsula. These projects helped beautify and unify the city that Boston had become after the annexations of the 1860s and 1870s. Olmsted's plan called for connecting the Back Bay to the proposed West Roxbury Park (now Franklin Park) and labeling the sections along the route as Fenway, Riverway, Jamaicaway, and Arborway. The Fenway was built in the 1880s and the remainder during the next decade. Also during the 1880s, Boston's municipal government created one of the premier water and sewerage systems in the nation as citizens demanded new services from municipal government.

Demographic change also transformed Boston in the last third of the nineteenth century. The city grew from 250,000 people in 1870 to over 560,000 in 1900. This growth reflected not just the annexations but also the immigration of ever-increasing numbers of Irish, Italians, Jews, and other immigrant groups. Boston's African-American population, which predated the American Revolution, also grew during this period.

In the last decades of the nineteenth century and the early years of the twentieth century, Boston's City Hall was taken over by immigrant Irish in the Democratic Party, a political development that had serious consequences for Boston's subsequent history and for its reputation. The conflict between Yankee Protestants and Irish Catholics in the last 20 years of the nineteenth century, when the underlying cultural, religious, and economic conflicts between the two communities first achieved a significant level in political life, defined Boston politics for a century.

In Boston, religious and cultural conflict exacerbated economic competition between members of the working classes and fanned political fires. The manner in which the Irish acquired power in the city long affected them and other ethnic and racial groups in Boston. African-American Bostonians and members of other groups, especially Italians, Hispanics, and Asians, now operate in an arena and environment largely determined by the interactions of Yankees and Irish. In fact, the long Irish control of Boston's mayoralty was broken only in the 1990s when an Italian-American mayor moved into City Hall.

The Irish entered New England in droves in the middle of the nineteenth century, and others felt threatened by their numbers, their religion, and their concentration in construction jobs and unskilled occupations. All these fears were intensified by the growing Irish control of government patronage. The first generation of Irish leaders in Boston, including Patrick Maguire, Hugh O'Brien, and Patrick Collins, worked assiduously to win Yankee support and regarded themselves as Americans first, Irishmen second. It was not so easy, however, for others to accept this distinction, and there was overwhelming and intense opposition to the Irish, a prejudice deeply rooted in ethnic, religious, and economic conflict. That the Irish were not of British origin, were Roman Catholic, and competed economically exacerbated the prejudice that frustrated their entry into local politics.

The mayoral victories of John F. Fitzgerald in 1905 and James Michael Curley in 1914 marked the political ascendancy of the Boston Irish but also coincided with a prolonged period of economic stagnation. Fitzgerald, a North End ward boss (and maternal grandfather of President John F. Kennedy) was elected mayor twice. His administration epitomized for many the corrupt use of City Hall as a means of personal and familial aggrandizement. Fitzgerald was ousted by the even more flamboyant Curley, who served four nonconsecutive terms as mayor of Boston (stretching between 1915 to 1950). Curley gained immediate notoriety for exploiting ethnic conflict for political gain as well as creating public works projects to put his constituents to work.

During the years dominated by the colorful Curley (who also served several terms in Congress and a term as governor of Massachusetts, not to mention two jail sentences), private investment in Boston plummeted and the public sector replaced the private sector as the main stimulant to economic growth. Boston's economic woes of this era stemmed from changing economic conditions. Manufacturing exports increasingly flowed from the ports of New York, Philadelphia, and elsewhere. Boston lost its edge in investment banking to New York. Even fishing activity declined. The Great Depression of the 1930s hit Boston as hard as most American cities, and Boston's, and all of New England's, economic decline continued into the second half of the twentieth century. During the 1950s the dimensions of the disastrous loss of New England's textile industry became apparent in Boston, still the region's financial center.

The grim reality of a deteriorating, nearly moribund city led to desperation, and by the late 1950s the city teetered on the edge of bankruptcy. The resulting "New Boston" campaign, supported by both the private sector and an aggressive local government and bolstered by federal funds, spurred private development under the leadership of Mayor John F. Collins and Edward J. Logue, director of the Boston Redevelopment Authority. Logue and Collins worked strenuously to transform the city physically in an attempt to revitalize its economic base. They wanted to sweep away the poverty at the base of Boston, but too much of the physical change, destruction, and relocation was borne by the poor.

Kevin H. White succeeded Collins as mayor in 1969, and the 16 years of his administration were marked by phenomenal growth in downtown office and hotel space. Boston rebounded as an economic force and center for New England, and its population began to increase. The "New Boston" came to fruition, and by the end of the 1970s, the city possessed a dramatic new skyline. With its unique blend of old and new, Boston became a "world-class city" admired by many as a desirable place to live and work. The oldest sections of the city—the North End, Beacon Hill, and Back Bay—all maintain vitality and charm while accommodating growth and modernity. Historic structures such as Old South Meeting House, the Old State House, and Faneuil Hall are nestled among new office buildings and a centuries-old street pattern.

The social conflicts among Bostonians in the early 1970s, however, did much to detract from Boston's newly rediscovered charm. The bitter and sometimes violent opposition to federal court–ordered integration of the city's public schools through busing brought national media attention and stood in sad contrast to the Puritan ideal of community. Boston became synonymous with northern white fears of the growing African-American population. However, through concerted political effort, many in the city's various minority communities have entered the halls of power and been placed on public and private payrolls. The economic boom and physical expansion of the 1980s made such accomplishments possible, at least for a time.

Massachusetts's prosperity in the 1980s developed largely from the rise and success of the computer industry in and around Boston and Cambridge. Building on the intellectual base of Massachusetts Institute of Technology and the federal dollars invested in the area since World War II, Boston emerged as a center of high tech industries. Hundreds of high tech firms sprouted in the region and fed the economic growth and physical changes in Boston during that remarkable period.

As with other old northeastern cities, Boston seeks to maintain a solid economic base in a rapidly changing world environment. Its long history suggests that this effort will be successful, but the problem of community, which absorbed the Puritans for decades, continues to be a paramount issue. Boston has long been famous for its colorful politics and its tight-knit neighborhoods, but at the end of the twentieth century Bostonians continue to grapple with their heritage of exclusivity, social division, and conflict. Despite its progress, Boston remains divided by race, religion, ethnicity, and class.

—*Lawrence W. Kennedy*

See also

Brookline, Massachusetts; Bulfinch, Charles; Curley, James Michael; Olmsted, Frederick Law.

References

Formisano, Ronald P. *Boston against Busing: Race, Class, and Ethnicity in the 1960s and 1970s.* Chapel Hill: University of North Carolina Press, 1991.

Formisano, Ronald P., and Constance K. Burns, eds. *Boston 1700–1980: The Evolution of Urban Politics.* Westport, CT: Greenwood Press, 1984.

Gans, Herbert. *The Urban Villagers: Group and Class in the Life of Italian Americans.* Rev. ed. New York: Free Press, 1982.

Green, James R., and Hugh Carter Donahue. *Boston's Workers: A Labor History.* Boston: Trustees of the Public Library of the City of Boston, 1979.

Handlin, Oscar. *Boston's Immigrants: A Study in Acculturation.* Rev. ed. New York: Atheneum, 1975.

Jennings, James, and Mel King, eds. *From Access to Power: Black Politics in Boston.* Cambridge, MA: Schenkman Books, 1986.

Kennedy, Lawrence W. *Planning the City upon a Hill: Boston since 1630.* Amherst: University of Massachusetts Press, 1992.

Morison, Samuel Eliot. *Harrison Gray Otis, 1765–1848: The Urbane Federalist.* Boston: Houghton Mifflin, 1969.

O'Connell, Shaun. *Imagining Boston: A Literary Landscape.* Boston: Beacon Press, 1990.

Rutman, Darret. *Winthrop's Boston: Portrait of a Puritan Town.* Chapel Hill: University of North Carolina Press, 1965.

Schultz, Stanley K. *The Culture Factory: Boston Public Schools, 1789–1860.* New York: Oxford University Press, 1973.

Thernstrom, Stephan. *The Other Bostonians: Poverty and Progress in the American Metropolis, 1880–1970.* Cambridge, MA: Harvard University Press, 1973.

Warden, Gerald B. *Boston 1689–1776.* Boston: Little, Brown, 1970.

Warner, Sam Bass, Jr. *Streetcar Suburbs: The Process of Growth in Boston 1870–1900.* Cambridge, MA: Harvard University Press, 1962.

Whitehill, Walter Muir. *Boston: A Topographical History.* 2d ed. Cambridge, MA: Harvard University Press, 1975.

Zaitzevsky, Cynthia. *Frederick Law Olmsted and the Boston Park System.* Cambridge, MA: Harvard University Press, 1982.

Bowery

The Bowery is a street on the Lower East Side of New York City that stretches one mile from Chatham Square to Cooper Union; it is basically the city's skid row.

Beginning in 1626, the Dutch West India Company offered land grants to entice emigration to the New World and, in particular, to Manhattan. Six bouweries (*bouwerij* is Dutch for farm), ranging in size from 50 to 120 acres, were originally leased to settlers. These bouweries, located just north of New Amsterdam, were laid out in large rectangular parcels in the hope of stimulating an agricultural colonial economy. In 1651 Petrus Stuyvesant, the last Dutch governor, purchased 120 acres of Bouwerie No. 1 for $5,000. Bowery, or Stuyvesant Village, grew around the governor's estate and became a place of residence for his employees and slaves. At this time, the Bowery—as conveyance—was simply the bridle path to Stuyvesant's estate.

When the English wrenched control of Manhattan from the Dutch in 1664, Stuyvesant found himself suddenly dethroned. His village took on a life and economy of its own. Its church, St. Mark's-in-the-Bouwerie, and its tavern, general store, blacksmith, wagon shop, and community center were on the whole quite amenable to the enterprising designs of the new English burghers. English rule stimulated growth in and along the boweries. In 1673 Bowery Lane was converted into the first Post Road to Boston. Several boweries had changed hands frequently, and a pattern of parceling took place that steadily diminished the large tracts of farmland.

The Grim Plan of 1742 to 1744 depicted the boweries just before subdivision began to erode the scale of the bucolic setting. By 1750, streets had been laid off adjacent to Bowery Lane. The Ratzer Map of 1767 shows parallel and cross streets on the east and west sides of the southern end of Bowery Lane. The commercial emphasis and capitalistic spirit that promoted expansion also caused the disappearance of the boweries and paved the way for urban planning.

The proclivity for exchange and development was rationalized by the Gridiron Plan for New York City in 1811 (also known as the Commissioner's Plan). The plan imposed on the city a grid structure that reached as far north as 155th Street. Looking ahead to the city's rapid growth, the socioeconomic features of the plan (high land values and intensive building) would have lasting implications for the construction of residential, commercial, and industrial buildings in New York. Not only would the Plan lend itself to a bewildering physical agglomeration, but it would also—when realized and inhabited by a densely concentrated urban populace—encourage the rise of tenements and slums.

In antebellum New York, new urban institutions and associations formed that highlighted the distinctions between village and city forms of social life. After 1830, leisure became more appealing to the residents of the Bowery and they could choose among three popular theaters on the lane. Symbolically evincing a unique cultural identity, the Bowery Boy and Bowery Gal emerged as celebrated American types of working-class origin at this time. A laborer, the Bowery Boy used his hands as tools for his trade

Impoverished men line up for admission to a soup kitchen in New York's Bowery in 1957.

and as weapons in battle. The Boy was closely allied with nativistic Bowery gangs that vied for superiority with less-assimilated immigrant street gangs. The rowdiness that characterized these gangs was epitomized in the riot of 1857 between the Dead Rabbits and the Bowery Boys, in which a thousand men clashed, leaving eight to ten dead and many more injured. As with the bloody Astor Place Riots of 1845, class tensions and turbulent political alliances underlay the gang warfare.

The Bowery's popularity was somewhat diminished after 1850 by the rising prosperity of neighboring Broadway. At this time, the Bowery was host to 27 oyster houses, 52 taverns, and 240 distinct trades. The Bowery, and its residential vicinity of the Lower East Side, soon became a slice of New York hospitable to laborers, immigrant families, thrifty shoppers, and venturesome tourists. Its cheap lodging houses also showed an urbane toleration for transients, tramps, and the homeless. But it was not until the middle of the 1880s that the city's commerce expanded uptown. Up until then, the Bowery was the center of retail trade, housing such department stores as Lord and Taylor and the original Atlantic and Pacific Tea Company. The Bowery was still a lively commercial avenue, with its elevated and surface transportation, glaring storefront lights, and throngs of shoppers milling along the sidewalks.

Soon after the middle of the 1880s, however, respectable businesses began to wane, and places of amusement and entertainment waxed sensational. Saloons, dime museums, con-

cert halls, stale beer dives, eating houses, gin shops, beer gardens, and the like all conspired to shift commerce away from retail to a more broad-based social consumption of pleasure and vice. In 1891, out of 99 known places of leisure, there were 7 theaters, 6 museums, and 4 music halls; the remaining 82 emporiums of joy, an average of 6 per Bowery block, were cheap saloons or similar drinking establishments. Many of these saloons became favorite spots that drew tourists and slumming parties down to the Bowery, where they could sample the netherworld of the city.

During the last decade of the nineteenth century, the Bowery vicinity became the central focus of tenement slum reform, especially after Jacob Riis's exposé, *How the Other Half Lives,* was published in 1890. Ten years later, three wards adjacent to the Bowery—the sixth to the south (Chinatown), the fourteenth to the west (Little Italy), and the tenth to the east (New Israel)—comprised the most dense and overcrowded wards in the entire city. Tenement slums became self-sufficient social entities, worlds of their own, that cut the tissue of urban form, creating a sense of isolation, mystery, and danger. Immigrant enclaves also lent an Old World atmosphere to the area. On the Lower East Side, foreign-born immigrants exceeded native-born citizens, at times by a ratio of two-to-one.

By the turn of the twentieth century, the Bowery was, in Robert Park's terms, a "detached milieu." The denizens of the Bowery were an unassimilated subgroup of the homeless. The extreme results of socioeconomic dislocation, the homeless constituted the entropy of urban-industrial capitalism. Even by the 1890s, the homeless had become conspicuous in the city. At that time, an estimated 60,000 men and women lived on the streets of New York. As many as 116 cheap lodging houses, ranging in price from 7 to 25 cents per night, were located either on the Bowery or within its immediate vicinity. The dormitories on the Bowery itself provided shelter for about 9,000 of the city's homeless population.

The twentieth century bequeathed the Bowery to the homeless, culminating the transition of this street from the center of a heterogeneous urban slum to a more homogeneous skid row. As if to seal the lid on the Bowery's fate, the Third Avenue El was reconstructed in 1916, setting up express and local tracks together in the center of the street (unlike the original design of 1878, which bordered the sidewalks). The material change resulted in an oppressive sense of enclosure underneath the El.

Thereafter, and up until the early 1980s, the Bowery became an ecological base for the homeless of New York. As a skid row, the Bowery was a coordinated network of missions, flophouses, bars, liquor stores, labor agencies, cheap cafeterias and restaurants, used clothing outfits, and pawnshops. Such institutions as the Bowery Chamber of Commerce, *Bow-*

ery News, and the very short-lived Bowery College further cemented the image and setting of skid row as a place of refuge and collective expression for the downtrodden. As a skid row, the Bowery was virtually an all-male community, reflecting the domination of the labor force by men and acting as a barometer of their ebb and flow in times of economic prosperity and depression.

In the early 1900s, close to 25,000 homeless men were lodged nightly along the Bowery. Their numbers increased during 1914 and 1915, a period of widespread unemployment. During the Great Depression of the 1930s, homelessness and joblessness were so closely linked that the extent of occupancy in the Bowery's Men's Shelter provided a reliable index of the unemployment rate in manufacturing.

Improvements in the conditions of labor and the advent of social security under the New Deal, combined with the economic recovery stimulated by wartime industries and recruitment, promoted a broader national affluence. From the 1940s on, skid row responded by becoming less a direct result of capricious labor market forces and an unregulated system of laissez-faire capitalism. Yet the homeless still resided on the Bowery and in other skid rows throughout the country; and though the extent of homelessness diminished in postwar America, the intensity of its condition did not. As Michael Harrington, once a volunteer for the Catholic Worker House just off the Bowery, observed, skid row represented "perhaps the bitterest, most physical and obvious poverty that can be seen in an American city."

The homeless population of the Bowery dwindled from about 14,000 in 1949 to about 3,000 in 1971. By 1980, the number had dropped to perhaps 2,000, and by 1987, it was below 1,000. As of 1995, there were only several flophouses, one mission, one municipal shelter, and no skid row bars along the Bowery. This faded setting exists within an array of restaurant and office equipment supply shops, lighting fixture stores, crockery outlets, banks, and jewelry exchanges. The demise of the Bowery as a skid row and its ascent as a renewed residential and commercial street has been aided by the process of urban renewal. The rapid gentrification of neighboring SoHo in the early 1980s as an arts center and prime living area spilled over into the Bowery, giving rise to experimental theaters, restaurants, rock clubs, art galleries, and enhanced real estate values. In addition, Chinatown has expanded further north, occupying a larger portion of the Bowery than in the past.

The altered demographics and dispersed nature of homelessness in New York City during the 1980s and 1990s released the Bowery from its traditional association with skid row homelessness. However, the decline of the Bowery as an integrated neighborhood—a home to the homeless—has not resulted in the disappearance of the social problem.

Contemporary homelessness—extensive and scattered—has proved to be a disoriented way of life far beyond that of the relatively cohesive skid row subculture. Therefore, the "Bowery" today is neither a reference to rural farmland nor to urban skid row; as a designation, it asserts itself in terms of what it is not.

—*Benedict Giamo*

See also
Skid Row.
References
Bahr, Howard M. *Skid Row: An Introduction to Disaffiliation.* New York: Oxford University Press, 1973.
Cohen, Carl I., and Jay Sokolovsky. *Old Men of the Bowery: Strategies for Survival among the Homeless.* New York: Guilford Press, 1989.
Fields, Armond. *From the Bowery to Broadway: Lew Fields and the Roots of American Popular Theatre.* New York: Oxford University Press, 1993.
Giamo, Benedict. *On the Bowery: Confronting Homelessness in American Society.* Iowa City: University of Iowa Press, 1989.
Harlow, Alvin F. *Old Bowery Days.* New York: D. Appleton, 1931.
Jackson, Kenneth T. "The Bowery: From Residential Street to Skid Row." In Rick Beard, ed., *On Being Homeless: Historical Perspectives,* 68–79. New York: Museum of the City of New York, 1987.
On the Bowery (video). Directed by Lionel Rogosin. New York: Mystic Fire Video, 1956.
Zettler, Michael D. *The Bowery.* New York: Drake Publishers, 1975.

Boxing

Boxing's long reputation as a less than fully respectable sport caused it to be banished from most cities during much of American history. In colonial America, fisticuffs was largely a rural activity where biting and gouging were considered backcountry sport. As early as 1735, "feeling for a feller's eyestrings" was a way of righting wrongs and deciding dominance along the Chesapeake Bay and later in the backwoods of Virginia. North Carolina banned the "barbarous" sport when four men died in 1746, and by 1772, it had become a felony to "gouge, pluck, or put out an eye" in Virginia and to "cut out the tongue" or "bite off the nose" in South Carolina. Calling a man a "buckskin" (implying he was impoverished) or charging he was a "Scotsman" (associating him with low-caste Scots-Irish of the southern highlands) were fighting words likely to lead to the "rough-and-tumble."

The culture of colonial and early Republican brawling was largely confined to gamblers, herders, hunters, roustabouts, and the river men and yeoman farmers who took its techniques down the Ohio River Valley. In 1816 Jacob Hyer proclaimed himself American bare-knuckle champion, ushering in a half-century of bare-knuckled bouts on both sides of the Atlantic to determine the champion of the "fives court" in the English-speaking world. Most self-respecting editors refused to publish news of bare-knuckle fights. But many made an exception when it came to William

Fuller, the sparring master of New York City, who earned the title "professor of pugilism" in 1824 when he retired from the ring to take up fencing and gymnastics.

Throughout much of the nineteenth century, boxing, with its celebration of man's "baser passions," was a hard sell in middle-class urban society. Typical was the Boston paper that argued in 1851 that "we were sent into the world not for sport and amusement, but for labor, not to enjoy ourselves, but to serve others." But the taste for violence and notions of individual and ethnic honor that fueled premodern living continued to fuel challenges that led directly to the squared ring in industrializing America. The city became the place where boxing became rationalized, organized, and commercialized. It became the place where most boxers lived and trained.

While Victorians advocated participatory sports for the sake of moral health and physical well-being, boxing advocates urged the staging of commercial spectacles to test manliness in an age in which rapid industrialization and urbanization seemed to threaten individual autonomy and the efficacy of individual action. The bureaucratized lives of increasing numbers of Americans, combined with the engine of mass media promotion in many major cities, led to the transformation of John L. Sullivan from Boston rowdy to America's foremost man of mettle after he defeated Paddy Ryan in Mississippi City, Mississippi, in February 1882. The Boston Strong Boy's 75-round dispatch of Jake Kilrain seven years later won him a diamond-studded championship belt and established him as the generation's foremost man of muscle.

The end of bare-knuckle brawling and the beginning of gloved fights by Sullivan under Marquis of Queensberry Rules helped sanitize the sport for middle-class spectators. Tom Hyer and Yankee Sullivan (not to be confused with John L. Sullivan) had barely escaped Baltimore authorities before they settled their score outside the city before a few hundred friends. And when Paddy Ryan fought Joe Goss in Colliers, West Virginia, in 1880, it was to allow fightgoers to escape to Ohio or Pennsylvania if the law intervened. But Sullivan and his handlers helped make boxing a business that made him perhaps the first mass cultural hero in American life.

The growing respectability of boxing led New Orleans, San Francisco, Pittsburgh, and various towns in Texas and Nevada to legalize the sport. And after James J. Corbett's scientific dispatch of Sullivan in 1892, contenders increasingly fought in electrically illuminated arenas before thousands of fans from all social classes. The prize ring no longer depended on the saloon-centered, bachelor subculture and was no longer stopped by local laws forbidding the sport. State sanctioning was still a generation away, but a divide had already been crossed. Gloved champions like Corbett were respected figures, even in high society, and could make money promot-

ing themselves on the stage and by gaining sponsorships from athletic clubs. It was only when champions were black, like Jack Johnson during the Progressive Era, that self-promotion prompted public outcry.

The use of boxing as a training device for men in uniform during World War I along with the rise of leisure culture made Jack Dempsey and Gene Tunney among the most celebrated men of their generation, with each representing something quite different to jazz age culture. Dempsey was the frontier fighter, the noble savage, whose blows of "stark ferocity" were played up in the mass media to remind readers of the "pioneering spirit" that had defeated the Indians and subdued the continent. Tunney, on the other hand, was born in Greenwich Village and had worked as a shipping clerk while he embraced the science of a rigorous defense to defeat Dempsey in two widely publicized championship bouts. Tunney's triumph was a victory for the "arrow collar crowd" that was beginning to welcome boxing as a socially sanctioned test of manliness in cities across America.

The urban slum became a training ground for fighters during the Depression and afterward. The *Chicago Tribune* and the *New York Daily News* launched Golden Gloves competitions to pick amateur weight-class winners in their cities. Neighborhood gyms and small boxing clubs flourished in cities across America and produced 8,000 professional fighters during the Depression. One of them was Detroit's Joe Louis, whose defeat of German heavyweight Max Schmeling helped put the lie to Hitler's claims of Aryan superiority. Throughout the 1930s and 1940s, Louis symbolized unequivocal punching power and physical prowess at a time when order seemed threatened by the Depression and war.

For the consumption culture of the fifties, no figures stood larger than Rocky Marciano and Sugar Ray Robinson. Their title defenses won record ratings on infant television, while demonstrating a continuing public appetite for power and grace in its sports heroes. For some cultural commentators, however, the 1950s boxing scene painfully reflected the resurgence of mob activity in urban America.

It was not until the remarkable career of Mohammad Ali (whose birth name was Cassius Clay) that power and grace would be combined so splendidly in a single champion. Ali's unparalleled powers of self-promotion, and the ubiquitous nature of mass media, made his title defenses in the 1960s and 1970s worldwide spectacles. Ali's refusal to fight in the Vietnam War, his being stripped of the title, and then his winning it back in a series of monumental fights with Joe Frazier only made his dramatic story more human.

Few activities in modern, mass-mediated, urban America lend themselves to as wide a series of cultural interpretations as boxing. Whether viewed as a celebration of celebrity, civic spectacle, and rigorous self-promotion, or raised to the level of social significance by spectators searching for manly self-reliance in an increasingly anonymous age, boxing reflects and has helped shape the lived experience of American national character.

— *Bruce J. Evensen*

References
Boyle, Robert H. *Sport—Mirror of American Life.* Boston: Little, Brown, 1963.

Croak, Thomas M. "The Professionalization of Prizefighting: Pittsburgh at the Turn of the Century." *Western Pennsylvania Historical Magazine* 62 (1979): 333–343.

Dawson, James O. "Boxing." In Allison Danzig and Peter Brandwein, eds., *Sport's Golden Decade: A Close-Up of the Fabulous Twenties.* Freeport, NY: Books for Libraries Press, 1948.

Edmonds, Anthony O. "The Second Louis-Schmeling Fight—Sport, Symbol, and Culture." *Journal of Popular Culture* 7 (1973): 42–50.

Evensen, Bruce J. "The Media and the American Character." In James D. Startt and William David Sloan, eds., *The Significance of the Media in American History.* Northport, AL: Vision Press, 1994.

Gorn, Elliott J. *The Manly Art: Bare-Knuckle Prize Fighting in America.* Ithaca, NY: Cornell University Press, 1986.

Hardy, Stephen. "The City and the Rise of American Sport: 1820–1920." *Exercise and Sports Sciences Reviews* 9 (1981): 183–219.

Isenberg, Michael T. *John L. Sullivan and His America.* Urbana: University of Illinois Press, 1988.

Marlow, James E. "Popular Culture, Pugilism, and Pickwick." *Journal of Popular Culture* 15 (1982): 16–30.

Riess, Steven A. *City Games: The Evolution of American Urban Society and the Rise of Sports.* Urbana: University of Illinois Press, 1989.

Roberts, Randy. *Papa Jack: Jack Johnson and the Era of White Hopes.* New York: Free Press, 1983.

Sammons, Jeffrey T. *Beyond the Ring: The Role of Boxing in American Society.* Urbana: University of Illinois Press, 1988.

———. "Boxing as a Reflection of Society: The Southern Reaction to Joe Louis." *Journal of Popular Culture* 16 (1983): 23–33.

Woods, Alan. "James J. Corbett: Theatrical Star." *Journal of Sport History* 3 (1976): 162–175.

Forsaking a regular pulpit to work among the poor of the city, Brace soon became discouraged in his attempts to reform adults, and, like many others, turned his attention to poor children. Inspired by Hamburg's pastoral *Rauhe Haus* in Germany, Brace founded the Children's Aid Society in 1853. Although the society established girls' industrial schools and a newsboys' lodging house, Brace's crowning achievement was to place children from the urban slums in "kind Christian homes in the country."

Widely imitated, his program placed over 100,000 children in rural homes between 1853 and 1929. Until his death in 1890, Brace advocated for children "pure country air, instead of the gases of the sewers . . . trees, and fields, and harvests, in place of the narrow alleys, the drink-cellars, and the thieves' haunts of a poor quarter" and provided the impetus for the system of foster family care that remains in place today.

— *Kristine E. Nelson*

See also
Children in Cities; Olmsted, Frederick Law.

References
Brace, Charles L. *The Dangerous Classes of New York and Twenty Years' Work among Them.* Reprint ed. New York: National Association of Social Workers, 1973.

———. *The Life of Charles Loring Brace Chiefly Told in His Own Letters.* Emma Brace, ed. New York: Scribners, 1894.

Langsam, Miriam Z. *Children West: A History of the Placing-Out System of the New York Children's Aid Society, 1853–90.* Madison: State Historical Society of Wisconsin, 1964.

Nelson, Kristine E. "The Best Asylum: Charles Loring Brace and Foster Family Care." Ph.D. dissertation, University of California, Berkeley, 1980.

Wohl, R. Richard. "The 'Country Boy' Myth and Its Place in American Urban Culture: The Nineteenth Century Contribution." *Perspectives in American History* 3 (1969): 77–156.

Brace, Charles Loring (1826–1890)

Charles Loring Brace, an important figure in social welfare history, founded the foster family care system in the United States. Born in 1826 in Litchfield, Connecticut, to an influential New England family, Brace studied for the ministry at Yale. His first exposure to urban life came in 1848 when he moved to New York City to study at Union Theological Seminary. He found the "flood of humanity" on Broadway overpowering and soon came to see the city as "an immense vat of misery and crime and filth."

Brace often escaped to the Staten Island farm of his friend Frederick Law Olmsted. Brace's friendship with Olmsted, who later designed Central Park in New York City, reinforced his own appreciation of nature. Together, they read the works of Ralph Waldo Emerson that inspired Brace's faith in the transforming power of nature.

Bradley, Tom (1917–1997)

Among African-American politicians Tom Bradley, the longtime mayor of Los Angeles, was a major pioneer. He constructed one of the most powerful biracial coalitions ever to dominate a big city even though Los Angeles has a relatively small black population. He was almost elected governor of California in 1982, and he was mentioned as a possible vice-presidential candidate in the Democratic Party.

Born in Calvert, Texas, in 1917, Bradley was one of seven children of sharecropping parents. A few years later, the Bradleys left the Texas cotton fields and eventually came to Los Angeles in 1924. After he attended the University of California at Los Angeles, Bradley joined the Los Angeles Police Department, where he became the first African American to earn the rank of lieutenant. In 1961 he retired from the police department to pursue a law career. Two years later, in

1963, Bradley defeated an incumbent white city councilman and became the first black elected to a citywide office in Los Angeles.

In 1969 Bradley ran for mayor and nearly defeated the incumbent mayor, Sam Yorty, who won only because of Yorty's race-baiting campaign. Bradley came back to defeat Yorty in 1973 and was reelected four times, in 1977, 1981, 1985, and 1989. Much of his success resulted from the governing coalition Bradley built around a tight alliance between blacks and Jewish liberals, joined by many Latinos and Asian Americans, with strong support from both business and organized labor. In office, his administration challenged the independent power of the police department and finally brought it under full civilian control in 1992.

Bradley's years in power finally ended when widespread riots engulfed the city in 1992 after several policemen were acquitted of beating Rodney King. Bradley chose not to run for a sixth term in 1993, and Republican Richard Riordan defeated Bradley's chosen successor in the mayoral election.

Bradley's conciliatory style, quiet leadership, and symbolic appeal as the city's first black mayor gave him a unique role not only in the history of Los Angeles but also in the evolving history of African-American political power and race relations in the United States.

—*Raphael J. Sonenshein*

References

Halley, Robert M., Alan C. Acock, and Thomas Greene. "Ethnicity and Social Class: Voting in the Los Angeles Municipal Elections." *Western Political Quarterly* 29 (1976): 507.

Patterson, Beeman. "Political Action of Negroes in Los Angeles: A Case Study in the Attainment of Councilmanic Representation." *Phylon* 30 (1969): 170.

Payne, J. Gregory, and Scott C. Ratzan. *Tom Bradley: The Impossible Dream*. Santa Monica, CA: Roundtable Publishing, 1986.

Robinson, James Lee. "Tom Bradley: Los Angeles' First Black Mayor." Ph.D. thesis, University of California at Los Angeles, 1976.

Sonenshein, Raphael J. *Politics in Black and White: Race and Power in Los Angeles*. Princeton, NJ: Princeton University Press, 1993.

Brice, Fanny (1891–1951)

Actress, singer, and comedienne, Fanny Brice won a following in almost every branch of American show business. During her four decades as a performer, she appeared in burlesque and vaudeville, drama and musical revues (including nine Ziegfeld Follies between 1910 and 1936), film and radio. Toward the end of her long career, she became radio personality "Baby Snooks," and that is the role for which she is most often remembered. Yet "Snooks" was only one of many comical creations with which Brice delighted her audiences.

Like many of her contemporaries, Brice was a first-generation American. Born on Manhattan's Lower East Side to Charles and Rose (Stern) Borach, she spent her childhood in Newark, New Jersey, but returned to Brooklyn with her mother and three siblings after her parents separated around 1903. Encouraged by her success in neighborhood amateur night contests, she decided on a career in show business and spent three years in burlesque. Appearing in the "Transatlantic Burlesquers" (1907–1908) as chorus girl Fannie Borach, she became Fanny Brice, the name she would use for the rest of her life, in "The Girls from Happyland" (1908–1909). While performing in "The College Girls" the following year, she attracted the attention of producer Florenz Ziegfeld, Jr., who hired her for his "Follies" of 1910. She starred in six more editions of the "Follies" through 1923, then left Ziegfeld after a contract dispute to join Irving Berlin's "Music Box Revue" (1924).

A popular vaudeville performer, Brice was unsuccessful in dramatic roles in "Why Worry?" (1918) and "Fanny" (1926), as well as in the musical "Fioretta" (1929). Although she made six movies beginning with "My Man" (1928), film stardom eluded her, and she said she never felt comfortable in front of the camera. She appeared in two musical revues created by her third husband, Billy Rose, "Sweet and Low" (1930) and "Crazy Quilt" (1931), and achieved her greatest stage success in two posthumous editions of the Ziegfeld "Follies" (1934 and 1936), produced by the Shuberts. Having moved to Hollywood in 1937, she finally won the national audience she desired with a popular weekly radio show. She continued happily wreaking havoc as "Snooks" until May 24, 1951, when she had a stroke and died five days later at age 59.

In an era when ethnic comedy was the norm, Brice built her career on a Yiddish accent, mobile face, and wonderfully expressive body. All her characters depended on deft parody, broad physical humor, and, with the exception of "Snooks," an accent used for comic effect. Whether spoofing ballerinas, fan dancers, opera singers, silent film stars, evangelists, or nudists, she was a brilliant clown whose flair for zany comedy made her special.

In addition to Billy Rose, whom she married in 1929 and divorced in 1938, Brice had two other husbands. The first, Frank White, was a barber whom she married in 1910, divorced in 1913, and with whom she probably never lived. The second, Jules W. "Nick" Arnstein, whom she married in 1918 and divorced in 1927 because of his flagrant infidelity, was her great love and the father of her two children, Frances (1919–1992) and William (b. 1921). The stage and screen musical *Funny Girl* and its film sequel *Funny Lady* are loosely based on Brice's life.

—*Barbara W. Grossman*

References

Grossman, Barbara. W. *Funny Woman: The Life and Times of Fanny Brice*. Bloomington: Indiana University Press, 1991.

Katkov, Norman. *The Fabulous Fanny: The Story of Fanny Brice*. New York: Knopf, 1953.

Broadacre City

During his last 30 years of life, Frank Lloyd Wright's work was directed by his vision of a new city form in which urban functions would be distributed over a rural setting. *The Disappearing City* (1932) proclaimed that car, telephone, and radio were dissolving the old, concentrated metropolis. In 1935 he displayed a model of a representative section of Broadacre City, where industry spread along motorways and workers of every kind raised some of their own food. He expanded and defended his vision in *When Democracy Builds* (1945) and *The Living City* (1958). Though Wright's city has been labeled utopian, today's exurbias embody many of its features—if not its values.

Wright denied that his city was utopian because it was already taking shape, unnoticed, in the open spaces along America's highways—but haphazardly. In *The Living City*, he asked, "Why not plan it?" For Wright, planning did not mean drawing ground plans and elevations, or writing zoning ordinances. A plan must integrate design with principles of value. In his books and in signboards accompanying the model, Wright proclaimed those values—civilization, individualism, spiritual integrity.

Though the design of Broadacre City afforded every citizen at least an acre of ground, it was neither agrarian nor antitechnological. It retained the city's manifold resources, scattering factories and skyscrapers across the landscape, providing regional markets and local centers of culture, entertainment, and education. Broadacre *was* a city, Wright insisted: telecommunications and sophisticated motorways put each citizen within reach of all the wealth of civilization, previously available only in dense urban centers. There was, however, little social structure in his city. "The true center" of Broadacre, he wrote in *The Living City*, was "the individual in his . . . family home." Wright's essays on the city include polemics against threats to personal selfhood—conformity, class conflict, the subordination of life to labor—all of which he attributed to urban concentration and those economic and political predators who thrived on it.

Wright always paired "decentralize" with "reintegrate." He presented Broadacre as a remedy to America's social disunity and spiritual demoralization. Farmers, machinists, artists, and shop owners all are neighbors on the land, whether they live in self-built houses on single-acre plots, small farms with more complex buildings, luxury homes near country clubs, or apartment buildings. Moreover, he saw the household, on its freehold, as a setting in which each individual could regain spiritual wholeness, reunited with family, nature, and creative work. And for Wright himself, Broadacre became a name for his own inward space, a forum where his ideas all gathered together, a landscape for many of his unrealized buildings.

Like many utopias, Broadacre City is a symbol of harmony and an occasion for polemics against disintegration. But it is not utopian in the sense of "irrelevant." Wright's proposal drew upon other radical architectural and social thinkers of the Depression Era; and the urbanists and planners of today continue to debate its relevance—if not as a specification, then as a conceptual model. For the city is disintegrating, with social and moral consequences unimagined by Wright, and exurbia is spreading without plan or humane value.

—*James Dougherty*

References

Alofsin, Anthony. "Broadacre City: The Reception of a Modernist Vision, 1932–1988." *Center: A Journal for Architecture in America* 5 (1989): 5–43.

Rosenbaum, Alvin. *Usonia: Frank Lloyd Wright's Design for America.* Washington, DC: Preservation Press, 1993.

Wright, Frank Lloyd. *The Living City.* New York: Horizon Press, 1958.

Brookline, Massachusetts

Long renowned as one of Boston's elite suburbs, Brookline is three miles west of the city center. Originally an outlying part of Boston called Muddy River, Brookline was set aside as a town in 1705, and prominent Bostonians began establishing country estates there even before the Revolution. Despite its proximity to Boston, Brookline remained a sparsely populated agricultural community well into the nineteenth century.

Suburbanization came quickly in the 1840s and 1850s, the population growing from 1,682 in 1844 to 5,164 in 1860. The construction of a branch railroad to Brookline Village in 1848 enabled hundreds of commuting businessmen and professionals to move there. Rapid growth also attracted many poor Irish Catholic immigrants seeking work as servants and laborers. Almost nonexistent in 1844, Brookline's Irish-born community made up 24 percent of the town's population by 1850.

In 1873 Brookline became the first suburb of Boston to reject annexation. Although the town had less than 7,000 inhabitants, it already boasted excellent schools, a public library, a paid police force, gas lighting, and playgrounds. Much of Brookline's reputation derived from its gracious estates owned by scions of famous Boston families like the Cabots, Lowells, Lawrences, and Amorys, although upper-middle-class households were much more numerous. At the same time, 48 percent of households were headed by blue-collar workers. Largely absent from Brookline were the lower-middle classes who dominated nearby streetcar suburbs like Dorchester and Somerville. Formal and informal controls segregated most of the Irish working class onto a limited number of streets and kept cheaper construction away from elegant areas.

The reconstruction of Beacon Street into a Parisian-style boulevard in the late 1880s touched off a building boom that rapidly transformed northern Brookline into a built-up suburb of nearly 20,000 persons by 1900. The men who launched the Beacon Street project, developer and subsequent streetcar magnate Henry M. Whitney and landscape architect Frederick Law Olmsted, were only two of the prominent persons who lived in Brookline near the end of the nineteenth century. Among others were financial publisher Henry V. Poor, art collector Isabella Stewart Gardner, industrialist Edward Atkinson, poetess Amy Lowell, and architect Henry H. Richardson. Brookline's excellent schools and efficient town government commanded national attention.

Brookline continued into the twentieth century without losing its elite character. In accordance with its long tradition of guiding growth, Brookline became one of the first municipalities in Massachusetts to adopt bylaws to control zoning and subdivision. After 1915, Brookline also gained a significant middle-class Jewish community. The older working-class neighborhoods once inhabited by Irish immigrants did not expand after 1900, and some of them were destroyed by urban renewal projects after World War II.

Brookline today remains as desirable a suburb as it was a century ago. In 1990 its population was 54,718. While its median family income of $61,799 was lower than that of many newer, more exclusive, and wealthier suburbs, it was still nearly twice that of neighboring Boston. And the median house value reported, $377,800, was exceeded by only four other suburbs, all of them much smaller in population. Unlike the newer suburbs, Brookline has maintained some of its diversity: nearly 9 percent of its population was below the poverty line, 3 percent of the population was black, and 8 percent Asian. In addition to being the birthplace and boyhood home of President John F. Kennedy, it is also the lifelong home of former Massachusetts governor and presidential candidate Michael S. Dukakis.

—*Ronald Dale Karr*

References

Curtis, John Gould. *History of the Town of Brookline, Massachusetts.* Boston: Houghton Mifflin, 1933.

Karr, Ronald Dale. "Brookline and the Making of an Elite Suburb." *Chicago History* 13 (1984): 36–47.

Building Regulations

Building regulations are one of the great, neglected influences on the modern city. They determine what can be built, where, and in what manner. In the process, they shape the urban landscape and the operations of the construction industry. In some countries, their influence is quite widely appreciated. In England, for example, a model regulation of 1877 gave its name to a whole class of "bylaw" housing. In North America, however, the more varied character and impact of building controls has discouraged sustained interest in the subject.

The regulation of construction can be regarded as a distinctively urban practice, for it is largely a response to some of the problems of uncontrolled urban development. Most important of these is the risk of fire, an especially serious issue in North America owing to the early prevalence of wood construction and the rarity of tile roofs. In the nineteenth century, most major cities in North America experienced at least one serious conflagration, the worst being that which destroyed much of Chicago in 1871. By the turn of the century, all major and most minor cities had introduced regulations to prevent, and inhibit, the development of fires. Typically, this took the form of prohibiting wood construction within so-called fire limits, which included the downtown but did not extend to the city limits.

The risks associated with fires depended greatly upon the availability of water. A massive boom in the construction of water systems before World War I reduced the political pressure to extend fire limits farther.

In the late nineteenth century, concern over sanitation and public health inspired other types of regulations, such as those that sought to ensure minimum amounts of space and ventilation in tenements, as well as in factories and offices. Tenement reform attracted a good deal of attention from contemporaries, as it has from later scholars. Tenements, however, were common in only a few cities, and even there they were concentrated in central areas where land costs were highest.

After the turn of the century, most new construction occurred in suburbs where the regulation of construction varied widely and was often completely absent. Some affluent suburbs prohibited frame construction altogether and imposed expensive restrictions on construction in other ways. A large part of their goal was to raise the minimum cost of construction and hence to achieve a measure of social exclusivity. To the same end, in many cases regulations were imposed privately by land subdividers and developers as a way of maximizing the value of their subdivisions. In contrast, industrial suburbs and unincorporated fringe areas often lacked regulations of any kind.

This situation began to change significantly during the 1920s. In 1921 the Department of Commerce introduced a national building code, and other agencies, including the National Board of Fire Underwriters, published influential guidelines. No agency could compel adoption of its code, but many municipalities used one of the standard codes as a guide. Usually they adapted it to local circumstances, often by inserting clauses to placate local suppliers or organized tradesmen. Then, starting in the 1930s, federal housing legislation made it difficult to obtain a mortgage on property that did not conform to new Federal Housing Administration (FHA) standards. This put indirect pressure on laggard municipalities to regulate. Even so, as late as 1949, a survey by the National Bureau of Standards found that among places with a population of at least 2,500, three out of ten had no code whatsoever. A great deal of uncontrolled construction was still taking place, especially in small towns and fringe areas.

Today, building regulations are virtually ubiquitous in metropolitan America, although they vary greatly in their provisions despite the existence of national guidelines. In recent years, aesthetic considerations have become increasingly important, not only in areas designated for historic preservation but also in new subdivisions. As in earlier decades, aesthetic criteria are often used to accomplish social goals, for higher standards almost invariably cost more.

As they have been introduced, revised, and enforced, building controls have had various consequences for city life. Their most visible impact has been to create a more standardized landscape. Unregulated areas typically contain buildings that are diverse in terms of size, construction materials, street setbacks, and architectural style. In fact, given the difficulty of obtaining documentary evidence on the subject, the present landscape provides one of the best clues to the presence or absence of regulation in past times. In contrast, regulated districts often appear homogenous—safe but, depending upon one's point of view, dull.

Less visible, but no less important, has been the effect of regulation upon the construction industry and housing affordability. These effects are poorly understood and in some respects contradictory. When federal housing legislation was enacted in the 1930s, policymakers attempted to modernize the housing industry by encouraging prefabrication and large builder-developers. They soon recognized that diverse and outdated building regulations were one of the main barriers faced by these groups. Despite decades of effort to standardize codes, the same is still true. At the same time, the very existence of regulations has generally discouraged owner-building. Until the early 1950s, it was common for households, and especially blue-collar workers, to build their own homes. Regulations do not make this impossible, but it is nevertheless difficult. In the late 1940s and early 1950s, especially, lumber dealers helped owner-builders meet federal construction guidelines by providing plans, kits, and advice. By meeting these guidelines, owner-builders qualified for FHA loan guarantees, which in turn made their patronage attractive to lenders. But in general, regulations have discouraged owner-building by mandating minimum standards of construction that are too costly for the families in question and by requiring skills that few possess. It seems that the diversity of codes

has generally favored the small contractor at the expense of the owner-builder.

Once instituted, building regulations often mandate materials and methods that become outdated. The task of revising a local code is difficult and politically fraught. For these reasons, the trend in recent decades has been toward "performance" codes that specify what standards (in terms of load-bearing ability, for example) must be met, rather than methods that must be used. Even so, although building regulations have certainly made North American cities safer, they have also added unnecessarily to the cost of housing.

—*Richard Harris*

See also
Height Restrictions; Zoning.

References
Cooke, Patrick, and Robert M. Eisenhard. *A Preliminary Examination of Building Regulations Adopted by the States and Major Cities.* Washington, DC: National Bureau of Standards, 1977.
Gaskell, S. M. *Building Control: National Legislation and the Introduction of Local Bye-Laws in Victorian England.* London: Bedford Square Press, 1983.
Harris, Richard. "The Impact of Building Controls on Residential Development in Toronto, 1900–1940." *Planning Perspectives* 6 (1991): 269–296.
Vitale, Edmund. *Building Regulations: A Self-Help Guide for the Owner-Builder.* New York: Scribners, 1979.

Bulfinch, Charles (1763–1844)

Between 1787 and 1817 Charles Bulfinch had more influence on the physical contours of Boston than any other single person would ever possess. Most famous as the architect of individual buildings such as the Massachusetts State House and many elegant houses on Beacon Hill, Bulfinch was also chairman of Boston's board of selectmen; its chief of police; its designer; and its inspector of schools, prisons, streets, bridges, wharves, and other civic buildings. He beautified its Common, consulted with real estate developers about its design, and envisioned a Federalist city oriented to merchants and their needs. As Harold and James Kirker declared in *Bulfinch's Boston,* Bulfinch "returned from Europe in 1787 to a provincial capital lagging far behind New York and Philadelphia in style and improvement; when he left thirty years later Boston was the most perfect architected city in the nation."

Bulfinch was born in Boston on August 8, 1763, to a distinguished extended family that the Revolution split between Tories who returned to England and moderates who laid low and survived the war with their estates and fortunes intact. In college during the war, Bulfinch received a Master of Arts degree from Harvard in 1784 and then continued his education with travel in England and on the Continent. When he returned home, he found himself comfortably in the midst of a city no longer controlled by revolutionaries.

Back in power once again were pragmatic, Anglophilic merchants who appreciated Bulfinch's orderly, elegant, architectural tastes rooted in the neoclassicism of Robert Adam and William Chambers. *Massachusetts Magazine* reported that "to a good natural genius and a liberal education, having added the advantages of a tour through Europe," Charles Bulfinch "has returned to adorn his native town and country." When a failed real estate venture destroyed Bulfinch's personal finances, his Federalist friends converted him into a salaried public servant. A humble and hardworking man, Bulfinch accepted every office from inspector of sewers to master of ceremonies that subsequently came his way, and from a small office in Faneuil Hall he tried to guide the city's expansion.

Although the mundane work of widening and paving streets and supplying them with lights and sidewalks probably benefited the most people directly, the central work of Bulfinch's career was transforming the Common from a neglected cow pasture into the finest urban park in post-Revolutionary America. He fashioned the boundaries of the Common into "a new social focus" for the city. On the northeast side, he lowered Beacon Hill and built a cluster of houses below the Massachusetts State House for families on the edge of the ruling elite who preferred living in a semirural environment. Bulfinch's plan to gratify their desires was never fully realized, especially his plan to make Mount Vernon Street into the grandest part of the district. Beacon Hill, however, still remains a monument to his influence.

1859 lithograph of Charles Bullfinch, one of the earliest professional architects in the young United States.

On the southeast of the Common, Bulfinch transfigured Park Street after he removed an almshouse, granary, and workhouse. Bulfinch obtained an ordinance restricting the height and style of buildings, then he designed eight houses ascending the hill and meeting another of his houses across from the State House, which he had also designed. Bulfinch defined the southwest boundary of the Common when he laid out Colonnade Row. Bringing newer South Shore money into the Common to balance Beacon Hill and the North Shore money of Park Street, this row of houses united uniform height and similar design with a long colonnade. With three distinct residential boundaries completed by 1812, Bulfinch achieved the conception he had begun in 1803 by creating Charles Street on the northwest border of the Common as "a broad and spacious Street, which would promote the health of the Inhabitants, and the convenience of the invalids."

In 1793 Bulfinch began another great neighborhood design in Franklin Place, a few blocks south of the Common. This was almost certainly the first unified housing development designed in America and was patterned on what Bulfinch had seen in Bath on his travels in England. He originally planned two monumental crescents of row houses to stand opposite each other, but only one of them was built, the Tontine Crescent. Across the street, Bulfinch eventually designed a set of four double houses. In this development, Bulfinch envisioned a cultural center for merchant Boston. He provided rooms for the Boston Library Society and the Massachusetts Historical Society in the central pavilion, and he provided a theater and church at the end of the block.

The Colonnade was destroyed in 1855 and Franklin Place in 1858, but Bulfinch's Common, Beacon Hill, and Park Street did survive. In fact, they more than survived, for they define Boston architecturally and culturally in the mind of most Americans. Thomas Jefferson's embargo and the War of 1812 ended the dynamic city growth that inspired Bulfinch's many projects in Boston.

In 1817 President James Monroe summoned Bulfinch to finish the capitol building in Washington, D.C. Before he died in 1844, Bulfinch retired to Boston. His granddaughter, Susan Ellen Bulfinch, wrote and compiled *The Life and Letters of Charles Bulfinch, Architect* (1896), and Charles A. Place followed with *Charles Bulfinch, Architect and Citizen* (1925). Place correctly emphasized that Bulfinch was both an architect and a citizen who devoted himself to Boston for 30 years. "Few men," wrote Mayor Josiah Quincy in 1844, "deserve to be held by the citizens of Boston in more grateful remembrance."

—*Rick Kennedy*

References
Bulfinch, Charles. *The Life and Letters of Charles Bulfinch, Architect with Other Family Papers.* Susan Ellen Bulfinch, ed. Boston: Houghton Mifflin, 1896.

Kirker, Harold. *The Architecture of Charles Bulfinch.* Cambridge, MA: Harvard University Press, 1969.

Kirker, Harold, and James Kirker. *Bulfinch's Boston.* New York: Oxford University Press, 1964.

Place, Charles A. *Charles Bulfinch, Architect and Citizen.* Boston: Houghton Mifflin, 1925.

Bungalow

Although almost every type or style of house has been called a bungalow at one time or another, it seems best to start with the dictionary definition—"a usually one-storied house . . . characterized by low sweeping lines and a wide veranda" (*Webster's New Collegiate Dictionary*)—and go on from there. The term itself refers to its origins as a typical native dwelling in the Indian province of Bengal, now the independent country of Bangladesh. As is obvious, the house type and the name of the region have the same root in the Bengali language. In the seventeenth century and later, the "bangla" or "ban-ga-la," the Bengali house usually with a thatched roof, was adapted by the British conquerors to their own requirements as a dwelling place for colonial administrators. Bungalows were erected first as summer retreats in the Himalayas and later in compounds near cities. The association with resort living as well as with early suburbs would have consequences for the future history of the bungalow.

The British exported the bungalow, now with a porch or verandah and all the accouterments of the British style of life, to all parts of the Empire. Other imperial powers adopted the house type, and bungalows began appearing all over the world but especially in Western Europe, where they served first as economical second homes near a lake or the seashore and finally, in the late nineteenth century, as a type of dwelling for the burgeoning "streetcar suburbs" near major cities.

The term and the house type both reached the United States sometime in the 1880s, the first reference appearing in a Boston newspaper of a bungalow being built on Cape Cod. Soon, other mentions were made of bungalows on the East Coast and in the Midwest, but the real popularity of the bungalow during the first four decades of the twentieth century was in California, where it satisfied the young, the retiree, the invalid, and the worker of modest means as a place to live that was close to nature, easily affordable, and eminently respectable. Furthermore, it had style, or rather styles, for while a mixture of Asian and Swiss motifs was usually identified as a "California bungalow," the simple house type could be used as a basis for the application of a variety of images, very often Spanish in origin.

Every city in the United States acquired California bungalows, especially during their growth in the 1920s, but by that time bungalows also began to be thought of as quaint, too modest to be considered to possess any "architecture." Nevertheless, while the term was dropped, the type lived after World War II in the vogues of the "Cape Cod cottage" and the ranch house.

—*Robert Winter*

References
King, Anthony D. *The Bungalow: The Production of a Global Culture.* London and Boston: Routledge and Kegan Paul, 1984.

Lancaster, Clay. *The American Bungalow.* New York: Abbeville Press, 1985.

Winter, Robert. *The California Bungalow.* Los Angeles: Hennessey & Ingalls, 1980.

Burgess, Ernest W. (1886–1966)

One of the founding members of the Chicago School of Sociology, Ernest W. Burgess was born in Tilbury, Ontario, in 1886 and died in Chicago, Illinois, in 1966. He was part of the first generation of graduate students trained in sociology at the University of Chicago, and after brief teaching stints at Toledo, the University of Kansas, and Ohio University, he returned to teach at the University of Chicago in 1916 and remained there until he retired in 1952. When he returned to Chicago, he became an active collaborator with Robert E. Park, a scholar some 22 years senior to Burgess. The two men worked together on a number of important undertakings, ranging from the creation and instruction of courses in sociology to the publication of important works on sociology as a science and on the study of urban centers.

The writings of Burgess and Park about the city have greatly influenced research by social scientists on the nature of urban areas and the urbanization process in general. Burgess became most closely identified with an article published in a 1925 collaborative volume on cities with Park and Roderick D. McKenzie. The article provided a portrait of the physical and social characteristics of Chicago, although the authors claimed the portrait could serve as a model for the growth of any city. Consisting of a set of concentric circles, which began with a center called the "Loop," the model provided a map of five key zones that encircled the city. There were, altogether, the "loop"; the "zone in transition"; the "zone of workingmen's homes"; the "zone of better residences"; and the "commuters' zone."

Moreover, Burgess went into greater detail about the social composition of the various zones. Thus, for example, the most central part of the city consisted of the financial district, where the daily movement of people was the greatest and where land values in the city were the highest. Certain ethnic areas were to be found located among the various zones, including an area Burgess identified as Little Sicily. Finally, at the farthest remove from the center of the city were areas of apartments and restricted residential developments, sites where many of those who worked in the central part of the city lived.

This model of the city was intended to convey a kind of social ecology to the nature of cities and how they developed. Burgess claimed that over time cities expanded, and new groups and interests increasingly invaded and provided the momentum for the city's expansion. In addition, he suggested, there was a pattern of succession in the social development of each zone; over time, different groups moved into and came to dominate particular zones.

In general, these patterns of growth and development drew upon an ecological imagery that reflected the ideas of both Park and of Burgess and provided the research agenda for the study of the city at that time at the University of Chicago. The underlying themes to this imagery maintained that there was a continuous process of organization, disorganization, and reorganization as cities grew. Distinctive social groups experienced those processes as did the spatial and social structure of the city itself.

Burgess concluded this famous article by noting that various pieces of research were then under way within the Department of Sociology that went into depth on groups and life at various points in the social space of the city. Here he referred to a variety of works that would later become famous accounts of their own, among them research by Nels Anderson on the hobo and Frederic Thrasher on gangs. Ultimately, a large series of monographs would be published by the University of Chicago that furnished intimate detail on the rich variety of life in the city.

Burgess continued to work in close association with Park until the latter man died in 1944. Park provided much of the intellectual inspiration for the developments of the Chicago School of Sociology, particularly its urban branch, whereas Burgess specialized in administrative and institutional efforts. He became president of the American Sociological Association, chair of the Department of Sociology at Chicago, and editor of the *American Journal of Sociology,* a periodical founded and still published at the University of Chicago. Moreover, he left an important legacy in his influence on the many graduate students who passed through the department, men and women such as Everett Hughes who later would go on to considerable achievement themselves.

—*Anthony M. Orum*

See also

Central Business District; Chicago School of Sociology; Concentric Zone Theory; Park, Robert Ezra; Wirth, Louis; Zone in Transition.

References

Bogue, Donald J., ed. *The Basic Writings of Ernest W. Burgess.* Chicago: Community and Family Study Center, 1974.

Bulmer, Martin W. *The Chicago School of Sociology.* Chicago: University of Chicago Press, 1984.

Park, Robert E., Ernest W. Burgess, and Roderick D. McKenzie. *The City.* Chicago: University of Chicago Press, 1925.

Burlesque

To contemporary Americans, the term *burlesque* is likely to evoke a set of images associated with the landscape of urban, working-class leisure between the two world wars: the emblematic female performer of burlesque, the stripper; gawking male spectators crowded around the runway; baggy-pants male comics; and candy butchers hawking boxes of stale sweets containing saucy French art poses. This historically frozen, nostalgic iconography of burlesque has been solidified in popular memory by such plays and films as *Gypsy, The Night They Raided Minsky's,* and *Sugar Babies* and by periodic resurrection of both the word "burlesque" and its associated icons in Las Vegas and Atlantic City casino revues. What this representation of burlesque belies is a much longer, dynamic, and complex historical association between burlesque and American cities.

As it would have been understood by a New York audience in the 1840s and 1850s, burlesque was a general category of comic theatricality whose principal thrust, as one commentator put it, was to turn serious drama upside down. Between 1839 and 1860, actor/manager/writers such as Thomas Mitchell, William Burton, and John Brougham travestied venerated works of tragedy, opera, and dance; lampooned the famous, notorious, good, and great; and, especially in the case of Brougham, at times infused the inversive and parodic burlesque form with stinging social satire. The formal vehicle for burlesque of this period was the rhyming couplet, its characteristic comic device the outrageous pun, and its rhetorical style an oscillation between enactment and direct address to the audience.

In Britain at the same time, burlesque had absorbed conventions of several other theatrical forms: music and dance from the extravaganza and, from the English tradition of pantomime, the "feminization" of the form through comic cross-dressing, especially the role of the "principal boy," wherein the leading male role was played by the leading female member of the troupe. In the autumn of 1868, a five-person theatrical troupe, headed by Lydia Thompson, brought this brand of burlesque to New York City, and in doing so, changed both the meaning of "burlesque" for American theatergoers and the form's place in American theatrical culture.

Thompson adapted popular English burlesques for middle-class New York audiences by introducing topical and local allusions and reworking the lyrics of popular songs while preserving the form's poetic structure and punning humor. What most startled and, initially at least, delighted audiences of urban middle-class men and women, first at Wood's Theater and then at the city's premiere theatrical venue, Niblo's Garden, was the appropriation of the burlesque form by cross-dressing, slang-spouting, irreverent, revealingly costumed women. Thompson's troupe of "British Blondes"

An 1886 engraving of a burlesque show in Butte City, Montana.

was the most popular attraction on the New York stage during the 1868–1869 theatrical season and drew huge crowds at leading theaters across the country during two subsequent national tours. However, the gender-transgressive, inversive, and spectacular character of Thompsonian burlesque also prompted vehement opposition from ministers, editorialists, and even women's rights activists. Burlesque in this discourse was recast as the "leg show" and the "nude drama," and burlesque performers as but a step removed from prostitutes.

Although Thompson and her imitators continued to perform her brand of burlesque in both Britain and the United States during the next decade, the form was transfigured and socially repositioned in America within a few years of her New York debut. Beginning in 1870, dozens of "female minstrel troupes" combined the parodic humor and feminized spectacle of burlesque with the tripartite formal structure of the blackface minstrel show to produce a new hybrid that increasingly supplanted Thompsonian burlesque in America. As performed by itinerant troupes in cities across the country between 1870 and 1890, burlesque consisted of an ensemble "first part," in which (white) female performers substituted for (white) blackface minstrels in comic repar-

tee; followed by an "olio" of individual variety acts; and concluding with an afterpiece or burlesque—an ensemble sketch comedy that frequently continued the older burlesque tradition of ridiculing high-brow culture. The audience for this new form of burlesque consisted principally of urban working-class white men, although middle-class single and family men, farmers, and even a few intellectuals "went slumming" at burlesque theaters.

Like vaudeville and the "legitimate" theater, burlesque was consolidated as an oligopolistic show business industry by about 1900. Its principal theaters were organized into two competing "wheels" or circuits, around which burlesque troupes moved from city to city. Burlesque's industrial high-water mark occurred around 1910, when 70 touring companies played at more than 100 theaters, and the "industry" employed some 5,000 workers. With the exception of San Francisco, burlesque was largely an East Coast and Midwest phenomenon, and, for the most part, a feature of large cities. Most burlesque theaters by this time were located in "tenderloin" districts, near saloons, arcades, and other venues for working-class male leisure culture, although a few (Chicago's Star and Garter, Brooklyn's New Empire, and Manhattan's

Columbia) rivaled first-class vaudeville theaters in their scale and appointments.

In the 1890s, burlesque's minstrel-show format dropped away, and the form became centered around the spectacle of the eroticized and increasingly revealed female body. Within months of the American debut of the belly dance on the midway of the Chicago World's Fair in 1893, the "cooch" or "hootchy-cooch" dance became a feature of burlesque performances. The "cooch" gave way to the jazz-based shimmy in the 1910s, and in 1917 Morton Minsky introduced the runway as a device to bring performer and spectator into the same space. Burlesque now consisted of female sexual display alternating with male comedy acts. So bifurcated were the appeals of burlesque between the mute gyrations of female dancers and the verbal humor of male comics that a new term had to be invented for a female performer who spoke—she was dubbed the "talking woman."

From the turn of the century until its death as a viable show business form in the 1930s, burlesque's existence depended on an increasingly difficult negotiation of erotic spectacle and civic tolerance. Burlesque had to compete with other theatrical forms that featured the revealed female body, in particular the revue, popularized after 1907 by Florenz Ziegfeld in his annual "Follies," which made the seminude chorus girl an acceptable feature of bourgeois entertainment culture. By the 1920s, movie theaters were drawing away other segments of burlesque's working-class audience, not on the basis of sexual display but entertainment value—for 10 cents one could see a three-hour program of films and live entertainment in an architecturally fantastic picture palace.

The response of one faction of the burlesque industry was to push the limits of erotic display. The striptease was introduced as a part of this strategy around 1917 and became the basis for "stock" burlesque made famous by the Minsky family of New York burlesque entrepreneurs. But the more burlesque theaters touted the erotic appeals of their shows, the more they provoked scrutiny from civic authorities and opposition from property owners' associations and antivice groups. In New York, the industrial hub of burlesque, theater owners fought continual battles with municipal government between 1925 and 1937, when the LaGuardia administration suspended all burlesque theater licenses. Burlesque survived into the 1940s in other cities (particularly those serving large armed-services populations), but with New York theaters barred even from using the word "burlesque," the form was essentially brain-dead after 1937.

The legacy of burlesque can be seen in film, radio, and television comedy from the 1930s to the 1950s, as a generation of male comics (among them Red Buttons, Phil Silvers, Abbott and Costello, and Jackie Gleason) honed their skills in burlesque's rough-and-tumble sketch-comedy tradition.

For female performers, the legacy is more complicated and problematic. With only a few exceptions (Ann Corio and Gypsy Rose Lee), twentieth-century female burlesque performers found it impossible to be recuperated within more mainstream entertainment culture. A large part of Thompsonian burlesque's fascination lay in its showcasing of inversive feminine insubordination. But, as this aspect of burlesque withered with the centering of the form on the objectified female body, the spirit of the "unruly woman" that so infused early burlesque was diverted into other forms. Lydia Thompson is the figurative grandmother of Sophie Tucker and Mae West and the great-grandmother of Madonna and Roseanne.

—*Robert C. Allen*

See also
Brice, Fanny; Vaudeville.

References
Allen, Robert C. *Horrible Prettiness: Burlesque and American Culture.* Chapel Hill: University of North Carolina Press, 1991.
Corio, Ann, with Joseph Dimona. *Burlesque.* New York: Grosset and Dunlap, 1968.
Sobel, Bernard. *A Pictorial History of Burlesque.* New York: Putnam, 1956.
Zeidman, Irving. *The American Burlesque Show.* New York: Hawthorne Books, 1967.

Burnham, Daniel H. (1846–1912)

Between 1880 and his death in 1912, Daniel Burnham was one of the leading architects in the United States, developing the tall office building, reorganizing architectural practice, and giving birth to modern American city planning. The firm of Burnham and his partner, John Wellborn Root (1850–1891), designed three of the most influential office buildings—the Rookery, the Monadnock Building, and the Women's Temple—in effecting the transition from partial to complete metal framing of tall office structures. Their 1890 Masonic Temple was the first of the world's tallest buildings to be highly touted as such.

While Root was principal designer of the firm's rapidly expanding number and variety of commissions, and was responsible for such engineering innovations as the floating raft foundation, Burnham secured and negotiated with clients, planned office space, and engaged in design development and criticism. With this division of labor, Burnham, concurrently with the New York firm of McKim, Mead and White, established the modern practice of architecture by replacing the artist's atelier or studio with the bureaucratically organized architectural firm that relied on a large number of draftsmen, engineers, and secretaries to design a wide range of complex modern building types. These developments accelerated after the untimely death of Root in 1891, the establishment of D. H. Burnham and Company, and Burnham's additional responsibility as construction chief for the 1893 World's Fair in Chicago.

All of the major eastern and midwestern architects, painters, and sculptors who collaborated in the design and decoration of the exposition recognized that Burnham's skills at administration and coordination were crucial components in the extraordinary success of the fair's architecture, particularly the expertly composed Beaux Arts buildings on the Court of Honor. Unfolding and developing the fair precipitated Burnham's pursuit of heroically scaled city planning, even as his firm continued to produce some of the country's most distinctive office buildings, particularly the 1894 Reliance Building and the 1903 Flatiron Building, the second of the world's tallest buildings.

Beginning with his brilliant 1896 plan for Chicago's lakeshore, Burnham directed the preparation of plans for many cities, including downtown Cleveland, San Francisco, and Manila and Baugio in the Philippines. For the 1901 replanning of Washington, D.C., Burnham persuaded the Pennsylvania Railroad to move its terminal and viaduct away from what became the Mall, and he designed the first of the nation's three great neoclassical union stations. His culminating achievement, the 1909 *Plan of Chicago* combined exhaustive research, innovative publicity techniques, unforgettable illustrations, and a vigorous text. All of these elements played key roles in implementing much of what was distinct in Chicago's urbanism, including its comprehensive forest preserve system, the double-decked downtown streets, the Grant Park cultural center, and more than 12 miles of stunning lakeshore park and inlets.

— *Edward W. Wolner*

References

Doumato, Lamia. *Daniel Hudson Burnham*. Monticello, IL: Vance Bibliographies, 1980.

Hines, Thomas S. *Burnham of Chicago: Architect and Planner*. New York: Oxford University Press, 1974.

Moe, Christine. *Daniel Hudson Burnham, Architect and Planner*. Monticello, IL: Vance Bibliographies, 1980.

Buses

As the most ubiquitous part of mass transportation in the United States, the bus hardly needs definition. Some 41,000 transit buses serve almost all of the major cities of the country. The typical bus used for local transit is diesel-powered, about 40 feet long and 8 feet wide, seats 45 to 55 passengers, and accommodates up to 50 more people standing. In most cities, these vehicles furnish the only mass transit, but in a few larger cities they are combined with rail rapid transit and commuter trains. Altogether, buses account for about 52 percent of urban mass transit passenger miles in the United States, with rail transit carrying most of the rest.

Although they figure importantly in parts of larger American cities, urban and suburban buses carried only 1.1 percent of all passenger travel in the United States in 1991, compared to about 90 percent moved by the automobile. Intercity buses carried another 0.65 percent. In an era of school busing and large, centralized schools, school buses are more important than local and intercity buses put together and carry 2.2 percent of total urban travelers.

Buses make their greatest impact in the parts of large metropolitan areas that developed before 1930. Here they operate according to published schedules along designated routes on surface streets. They stop every few blocks to pick up or discharge passengers, many of them less affluent and more often than not female. Routes usually converge on historic central business districts and often provide dense coverage and frequent service. In such areas, urban transit, including both buses and trains, carried 21 percent of all urban travel in 1970. By 1980, however, this number declined to only 16 percent, largely because more women had joined the labor force and purchased automobiles.

Buses (and rapid transit trains) also do relatively well in carrying sometimes affluent commuters from distant suburbs to old central cities. In many larger metropolitan areas, express buses travel along freeways between central business districts and distant suburbs. In a few large urban areas with heavy employment in their central business district, commuter buses operate on special lanes of expressways reserved for buses and car pools. In these markets, bus and rail service attracted 11.6 percent of all travel in 1970 and still moved 11.4 percent of the much larger number of commuters in 1980.

Buses have been less successful in the largest and most rapidly growing type of metropolitan travel: that which is done completely within suburbs. Although bus service that might serve this kind of movement has expanded rapidly since 1970, the transit share of the intrasuburban market fell from 4 percent in 1970 to 2 percent in 1980.

Buses also serve several nontraditional roles. Many transit authorities have operated small buses and vans in dial-a-ride services for elderly or disabled persons for over two decades, and the Americans with Disabilities Act now requires all transit agencies receiving federal funds to do so. About 6,300 small buses and vans now provide this service. Some large employers also charter private buses to bring workers from distant points; and in some of the largest metropolitan areas, groups of commuters charter buses to take them back and forth from jobs in central business districts. Rental car agencies, hotels, and public and private parking bodies also provide specialized van and bus services that connect them with customers in airports. At many larger airports, private

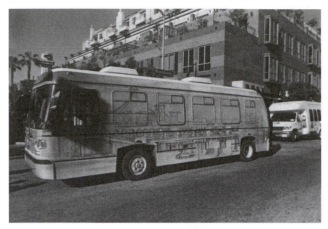

Cities have recently made an effort to beautify public transportation, as shown by this Los Angeles bus.

van and bus companies sell their services to passengers who prefer leaving their cars at home rather than driving and parking at an airport. Finally, one must not overlook the common school bus.

Buses have had little impact on the evolution of American cities or suburbs; their primary importance has been providing a low-cost replacement for the streetcar as trolleys became less significant as a kind of urban transportation. After fighting jitneys and buses from World War I into the 1920s, urban streetcar monopolies began using buses late in the decade to extend service into new suburbs without having to lay track and build electrical power systems. Increasingly, they also began replacing lightly patronized streetcar lines with buses. By the 1930s, the profit margins of trolley systems had so declined that revenue from fares could no longer finance tracks, power systems, and the replacement or renewal of cars. Liquidators, the most notorious being National City Lines, then moved in. National City Lines, a holding company owned partly by General Motors, Firestone, and other automobile-related businesses, bought streetcar companies around the country from the mid-1930s through the late 1940s, scrapped most of the streetcar service, and replaced it with General Motors buses. Many urban critics argue that General Motors used its muscle to jettison America's fine electric streetcar systems in favor of buses. Although there is some truth to this argument, it is also true that streetcar companies not taken over by National City Lines suffered a similar fate, indicating the existence of a more fundamental cause of their disappearance. This was the financial insolvency of streetcar companies at a time that the consensus about the necessity of streetcars to support continued development had disappeared. In some cities, central business district interests favored using public money to rehabilitate old streetcar systems, but powerful suburban developers, who considered such transit irrelevant, blocked their

efforts. As a result, local governments failed to develop a cohesive policy for urban transit and by default allowed streetcar systems to be scrapped.

By the 1960s, large private monopolies continued to operate most transit service in the United States, but they used buses almost exclusively outside of New York, Philadelphia, Chicago, and Boston, which still had extensive rapid transit rail and commuter train systems. Through the previous two decades, private bus companies had barely remained profitable by raising fares and cutting service as traffic fell and costs rose. By the middle of the 1960s, when patronage had fallen 50 percent since 1950, it was clear that the industry could no longer sustain itself. With passage of the Urban Mass Transportation Act of 1964, municipalities and special government districts used federal grants to purchase private bus companies, buy new buses, and build new shops. Cities that still had them also renewed commuter rail and rapid transit lines. After the mid-1970s, some metropolitan areas used newly available state and federal money to build new rail transit lines. A few states, most notably California and New York, also provided substantial funding to subsidize the operation of buses. By the middle of the 1970s, public transit authorities had replaced private monopolies in virtually every city in the country.

Under public control, which saw most of the bus fleet renewed within a few years, fares fell, service reached into suburbs, and the number of riders began to recover in absolute terms, but not as a percentage of the total trips being made. Costs, however, rose dramatically, and by the early 1980s passenger fares covered only about one-third of the operating costs of transit systems, regardless of whether they were composed entirely of buses or had a mix of bus and rail service. Various subsidies, mostly from local taxes, covered the remaining two-thirds.

The future of buses is unclear. On the one hand, future demand remains problematic. Although decentralization of many cities is continuing rapidly and effectively reducing the demand for public transit, migrants are crowding into other cities and creating a new demand. At the same time, the real income of individual Americans has been declining. While one of its consequences, the two-worker household, generally stimulates greater decentralization, declining real incomes may eventually curtail the ownership and use of automobiles. At the same time, some developers, motivated by the Clean Air Act as well as by declining incomes, now believe that they need to create environments where forms of travel other than by private automobile are possible and where housing is supplied for nontraditional families. Such concerns are leading to suburban designs variously called neotraditional development, transit-oriented development, pedestrian-oriented development, and most generally, the new urbanism. At this point it is unclear how these will work out and whether they will influence the demand for transit. Academic planners remain skeptical.

On the other hand, the issue of cost will not disappear. Although transit fares now cover a somewhat greater share of total operating costs than they did in 1980, transit deficits present a significant burden to cities and states with sizable transit systems. For this reason, transit service has not expanded much in recent years and now faces the prospects of either cutbacks, breakups of the traditional public monopolies, or a combination of both. Some policy analysts charge that massive federal grants for rail systems have contributed to this problem, but all-bus systems have experienced runaway costs.

Often heralded as an ideal transit vehicle for sprawling American cities, the bus has rarely found a niche where it makes a significant transportation contribution except in old central cities, airports, and some services from suburbs to central business districts . Unless a solution is found to the high cost of public bus service, and a way is found for buses to serve the suburb-to-suburb market efficiently at the same time that denser suburban forms are introduced, the importance of the bus to American cities and suburbs will continue to decline into the foreseeable future.

—*Gregory L. Thompson*

References

Adler, Sy. "The Transformation of the Pacific Electric Railway: Bradford Snell, Roger Rabbit, and the Politics of Transportation in Los Angeles." *Urban Affairs Quarterly* 27 (1991): 51–86.

Jones, David R. *Urban Transit Policy: An Economic and Political History.* Englewood Cliffs, NJ: Prentice-Hall, 1985.

Busing

The contemporary movement for racial equality in America began in the schools, and during the 1960s and 1970s no word stirred up more explosive feelings than "busing." The transportation of children across school district lines for the explicit purpose of desegregation was the most visible and controversial issue involving race in the United States. Before being limited by court decisions and federal practice, busing was the embodiment of government interference in the local affairs of citizens.

The tradition in education, especially pronounced in the South, to quote W. J. Cash in *The Mind of the South,* was "an intense distrust of, and indeed downright aversion to, any actual exercise of [governmental] authority beyond the barest minimum essential to the existence of a social organism." In the years following passage of the 1964 Civil Rights Act, the Justice Department initiated 500 school desegregation suits, and the Department of Health, Education, and Welfare

(HEW) brought 600 more actions to force nationwide desegregation compliance. The federal government issued strict guidelines governing hiring practices, unequal facilities, educational programs, and special activities for blacks. Many white parents reacted by pulling their students out of public schools and placing them in private academies or educating them at home.

The 1968 presidential election changed the federal approach to desegregation. Richard Nixon's "southern strategy" emphasized the unequal yoke borne by school districts undergoing desegregation. A popular campaign speech cited the fact that only 12 HEW field investigators were assigned to northern cities, while over 50 examined southern school systems. After Nixon took office, southern politicians brought enormous pressure to bear on the president to make good on his promise to ease federal guidelines on school desegregation. Powerful Republicans such as Strom Thurmond and John Tower emerged from the White House saying that the president believed the government had gone too far in pushing school desegregation.

Black leaders countered the Nixon administration "go slow" strategy with statistics showing that the federal government was not doing enough to bring racial justice to the land. They argued that most schools were considered integrated if they accepted any black students, even if they remained overwhelmingly white. Federal officials suggested moving children around within school districts to meet racial standards, but exactly how this strategy would work was unclear and resented by white suburbanites. Shallow enforcement of desegregation standards by the federal government brought civil rights petitioners back into the arena where they had experienced their greatest triumphs, the federal courts.

The petitioners were rewarded by a court decision that mandated integration in public schools and produced a backlash of resentment by both black and white parents. The ruling in *Swann v. Charlotte-Mecklenburg County* in May 1971 established the pattern for busing in school districts across the nation. In a unanimous decision, the Supreme Court upheld the plan of a local district court using mathematical ratios as part of a scheme to end racial separation in the district. The court outlined the elements of an "acceptable" busing plan as: (1) busing outside the neighborhood could be required to achieve "effective desegregation," (2) "pairing" and "gerrymandering" were introduced as alternatives to neighborhood schools, (3) the racial ratio of each school should reflect the racial composition of the entire school district, and (4) state antibusing laws that obstructed desegregation efforts were unconstitutional. Busing grew from the Court's authorization to pair and group schools in noncontiguous parts of the district.

School busing became the most controversial political issue of the time. George Wallace's victory in the 1972 Florida presidential primary shocked political experts and revealed the deep resentment of Democratic voters about the new federal policy. White parents resented the moralizing attitude of the Court's order; for them integration was "forced busing"—the moving of children around at will to satisfy an artificial standard of educational service. Black leaders spoke against the paternalism inherent in a policy that placed their children in the "better" schools of the suburbs.

The firestorm of criticism reached its crescendo in Boston, Massachusetts. The opening of school in the 1974–1975 academic year was marked by the presence of more than 300 state and 100 metropolitan police to help local officers maintain order. Thousands of South Boston residents jeered and threw stones at buses bringing students into predominately white neighborhoods. In September 1975, court-ordered busing in Louisville, Kentucky, resulted in 540 arrests.

The groundswell of public opinion against busing resulted in several landmark Supreme Court cases. Decisions in cases from Richmond and Detroit resulted in limited busing for schools within a school district, denying a proposed merger between city and county schools said to be required to meet acceptable desegregation standards. The decisions had the effect of limiting busing orders to circumscribed areas. During the 1980s busing faded from the public agenda. Other controversial social issues—prayer in the public schools, the content of sex education, and school vouchers among them—seemed more pressing and displaced racial integration, and busing, as the central problem confronting the public education system.

—*J. David Woodard*

See also
Desegregation of Education.
References
Bell, Derrick A., ed. *Civil Rights: Leading Cases.* Boston: Little, Brown, 1980.
Kluger, Richard. *Simple Justice.* New York: Knopf, 1975.

Byrne, Jane N. (1934–)

The first woman to be mayor of Chicago was born in 1934, the daughter of an Inland Steel executive, and spent her childhood in an upper-income, "lace curtain," Irish Catholic family. Educated in Catholic schools, she married young and was soon widowed when her Marine husband's plane crashed. Left with a 15-month-old daughter, she tried teaching school but neither that nor other jobs seemed satisfying.

She turned to politics and worked as a low-level aide in the Chicago office of John F. Kennedy's presidential campaign in 1960. There, she caught the eye of the powerful political boss and mayor of Chicago, Richard J. Daley, who appointed her to a series of city jobs. In 1975, after he felt increasing pressure to open the Democratic Party to women, Daley appointed her cochair of the powerful Cook County Democratic Central Committee. After Daley's death in 1976 Byrne publicly fought with Daley's successor, Michael Bilandic, who fired her as commissioner of consumer affairs.

Without a job, no party backing, and only a shoestring budget, Byrne decided to challenge Bilandic and the machine heavyweights in the Democratic mayoral primary. All the pundits called this move an impossible dream, but in the early evening on January 13, 1979, snow began falling Thirty hours later, more than 20 inches had accumulated. The transit system was a rolling disaster, and stranded cars prevented snowplows from clearing the streets. After a freeze, the unplowed side streets turned into single-lane, rutted sheets of ice. Garbage remained uncollected, and the rat population soared. Meanwhile, the rapid transit system, overflowing with suburban passengers and running behind schedule, began to bypass inner-city stops and inconvenienced thousands of black commuters. The besieged mayor tried to deflect quizzical reporters and angry voters, and he assured them that all was well and that there was no problem. Immobilized Chicagoans were outraged; but they were even more outraged when Jane Byrne revealed that Bilandic had awarded one of his cronies a huge consulting contract to produce a snow removal report that in fact removed no snow.

When the February primary election rolled around, an extraordinarily large number of angry, winter-weary voters waded through snowdrifts to vote against the incumbent. The result was a stunning defeat for the Democratic machine. Jane Byrne, the short, scrappy blonde thereafter tagged with the sobriquet "Snow Queen" had felled Goliath. In the April general election, she handily buried the Republican candidate and garnered an astonishing 82 percent of the vote, the largest majority in the city's history to that time.

Although she had campaigned as a reformer and against the old-boy system, Byrne soon made peace with the machine elements still in the city council, much to the consternation of other reformers. The remaining three years of her administration were turbulent and chaotic. She hired and fired aides so fast that her administration was called a revolving door, and she blamed the city's fiscal problems on her predecessors whom she accused of shoddy bookkeeping practices and cooking the city's books. She recklessly challenged the public employee unions and took on three strikes (of the transit workers, teachers, and firefighters), which caused irreparable political damage with organized labor, the Democratic Party, and thousands of effected voters. Her bombastic and sometimes vindictive ways of handling public conflict soon had newsmen calling her Attila the Hen, Calamity Jane, and a person "who shot from the lip."

To her credit, Byrne faced the new fiscal realities of the cash-short 1980s head-on and stared down powerful unions accustomed to staying ahead of inflation. Yet her never-ending fusillades of verbal pyrotechnics and her constant quarrels with the press and critics obscured her fiscally responsible work as mayor. Byrne's combative governing style and chaotic management methods blurred and nearly erased her achievements, but few politicians in Chicago's colorful history could match her zaniness, madcap, and derring-do acts for the sheer entertainment she provided. Unfortunately, too many Chicagoans mistook her style for her substance. In 1983 she was defeated in her bid for reelection by Harold Washington, who became the city's first black mayor.

—*Melvin G. Holli*

References

Fitzgerald, K. W. *Brass Jane Byrne and the Pursuit of Power.* Chicago: Contemporary Books, 1981.

Grange, B., and L. Grange. *Fighting Jane: Mayor Jane Byrne and the Chicago Machine.* New York: Dial Press, 1980.

Holli, Melvin G. "We Think the Unthinkable and Do the Undoable." In Paul M. Green and Melvin G. Holli, eds., *The Mayors: The Chicago Political Tradition.* Carbondale: Southern Illinois University Press, 1987.

Cable Cars

The cable car had a short and mainly unsatisfactory history during the transition from horsecar to electric streetcar. The incentives in the years after the Civil War to find a replacement for the horsecar were strong, and a purely mechanical solution was in accord with the engineering knowledge of the time. Andrew Smith Hallidie is usually said to have invented the technology for use on his Clay Street Hill Railroad in San Francisco in 1873, but he is more accurately seen only as the entrepreneur of the enterprise. The mechanical detail was the work of his draftsman, William E. Eppelsheimer, but the innovation was highly derivative. Cable assistance of locomotives from termini had been common in early British railway practice, and a cable railway from Fenchurch Street station, London, to Blackwall had operated from 1840 to 1848.

The technology of the cable car was simple and not able to be much improved. The system required a stationary steam engine, an endless steel cable payed out into a conduit, and some device to maintain tension. One of a large number of gripping devices grasped the cable through a slot in the conduit. Initially the technology was thought practical only for cities in warm climates, because the conduit tended to contract in cold weather, trapping the grip shank in the slot. A large installation on the Chicago City Railway in 1882 showed both that the system could be adapted to cities with harsh winters and also that cable traction was economical even in flat terrain. As a consequence, cable traction spread to all of the major cities of the time except Detroit and Boston, and to some secondary ones—Sioux City, Butte, and Spokane— where the technology was used for real estate development on high-lying, undulating land. Cable traction spread to 62 companies in 28 cities. Cable cars had no major impact on the urban pattern because, with the exception of the lines built for real estate promotion, cable traction simply replaced major horsecar lines with a superior technology.

The system had a number of serious drawbacks. Building the conduit strong enough to resist slot closure made it highly capital-intensive. The geographical relation between the line and the powerhouse was very inflexible. Slot closure and fractures of sheaves or pulleys could shut down the operation unexpectedly. Curves had to be traversed at top speed. Worst, if the grip became caught in a loose strand of cable, the car was uncontrollable.

After Frank J. Sprague perfected the electric streetcar between 1887 and 1893, cable traction was suitable only for cities with grades over 10 percent, and for Washington and New York, where local authorities prohibited overhead wires. Development of underground conduit electric pickup in 1895

A cable car passes the St. Francis Hotel in San Francisco, the only city where cable cars still operate.

ended the latter attraction, and the bus and trolley coach eliminated the former in the twentieth century. Cable mileage peaked at 305 in 1893 and declined rapidly after that, being essentially eliminated by 1906, except for special cases in hilly cities. Today, cable traction survives only as an operating museum and tourist attraction in San Francisco.

—*George W. Hilton*

References

Hilton, George W. *The Cable Car in America.* Berkeley, CA: Howell-North Books, 1971.

Smith, J. Bucknall. *A Treatise upon Cable or Rope Traction as Applied to the Working of Street and Other Railways.* 2d ed. George W. Hilton, ed. Philadelphia: Owlswick Press, 1977.

Camp Meetings

Americans invented religious revival camp meetings, with their concomitant physical and spatial forms, during the 1780s and 1790s in Georgia and the Carolinas, using elements from Methodist, Baptist, Scots Presbyterian, Shaker, and African religious practice. By 1820, with approximately 1,000 (mostly Methodist) meetings held each year in all parts of the country, they were a permanent fixture of American life, attracting European observers who interpreted this peculiarly American religious and community event as a sign of the nation's emerging character. Many early meetings, such as the one at Rock Springs, North Carolina, settled on permanent sites purchased by lay associations that built the tabernacles, the great sheds that protected services from the elements, and ordered the land so that thousands of participants could stay for a week, sleeping in tents or simple wooden cabins.

In 1854 the Reverend B. W. Gorham published practical rules for the layout of camp meetings along with their religious justifications in his *Camp Meeting Manual.* His accounts and those of others depicted these places through a variety of biblical allusions: they could be Canaan, Eden, the wilderness of Exodus, a Celestial City, New Jerusalem, Heaven itself, or "Heaven's suburb." Some northern meetings, following Wesleyan Grove on Martha's Vineyard, Massachusetts, developed fanciful campground cottages that merged pictorial references to tents, houses, and churches to create a new building type. Cottages were crowded close together on tent allotments within a grove of trees to form a miniature "city" in the woods. When dense with participants and fellow feeling, they became an expression of an ideal urbanity, offering both immersion in nature and social relief to city and farm dwellers alike.

During the latter part of the nineteenth century and through the twentieth, southern camp meetings retained the simplicity of their pre–Civil War forbears: heavy-timbered tabernacles surrounded by concentric squares of simple wooden cabins. But northern ones took on a Victorian splendor, especially when situated by the ocean or on lakeshores. These became camp meeting resorts modeled on the Martha's Vineyard meeting or its early imitator, Ocean Grove, New Jersey. Some, such as Des Plaines (Illinois), Pitman Grove (New Jersey), or Santa Cruz (California) were laid out on radial concentric plans. At Pitman Grove, the 12 radiating lanes represented the 12 gates to the Heavenly Jerusalem of Revelation. Others, such as Lakeside, Ohio, or Pacific Grove, California, followed the Ocean Grove style with grid plans. Fair Point Camp Meeting at Chautauqua Lake, New York, developed an adult education program, and many others across the country, such as Bay View, Michigan, did likewise, turning into populous but more secular summer "Chautauquas." While some camp meetings specialized for Holiness, temperance, Pentecostal, Spiritualist, women's, or African-American purposes, the physical forms and social structures could also be adapted directly to summer camps, resorts, or in one startling case, in Neshoba County, Mississippi, a state fair.

Camp meetings became, then, a widespread quasi-urban/quasi-rural community type serving particularly American social and psychic needs. They stand someplace between cities, suburbs, resorts, and utopian communities, sharing physical and social qualities with all of them and predicting, to some degree, patterns of anti-urban dispersal to come.

—*Ellen Weiss*

See also

Bay View, Michigan; Wesleyan Grove and Oak Bluffs, Massachusetts.

References

Brown, Kenneth O. *Holy Ground: A Study of the American Camp Meeting.* New York: Garland, 1992.

Cooley, Steven D. "Applying the Vagueness of Language: Poetic Strategies and Camp Meeting Piety in the Mid–Nineteenth Century." *Church History* 63 (1994): 570–586.

Demars, Stanford E. "Worship by-the-Sea: Camp Meetings and Seaside Resorts in 19th Century America." *Focus* 38 (1988): 15–20.

Parnes, Brenda. "Ocean Grove: A Planned Leisure Environment." In Paul A. Stillhorn, ed., *Planned and Utopian Experiments: Four New Jersey Towns,* 48–51. Trenton: New Jersey Historical Commission, 1980.

Weiss, Ellen. *City in the Woods: The Life and Design of an American Camp Meeting on Martha's Vineyard.* New York: Oxford University Press, 1987.

Canadian and U.S. Cities Compared

To visitors, cities in Canada and the United States appear remarkably similar, but Americans and Canadians are often struck by the differences. These reflect the general cultural traditions of each country, as well some more specific differences in the processes of urban development.

All North American cities have been shaped by the capitalist urbanization brought and developed by European settlers. Land is a commodity to be sold to the highest bidder, usually the person (or business) who is able to use it most profitably. By comparison with European cities, restraints on the sale and use of land have been minor. Land use zoning has generally accommodated, rather than constrained, development pressures. Building regulations were introduced late, especially in suburbs. With local exceptions, such as those in Washington, D.C., restrictions on building height have been weak, allowing for the early growth of skyscrapers.

Canadian and U.S. cities are also comparatively new. Many western cities, including Vancouver and Los Angeles, are essentially twentieth-century creations. Even in older eastern cities, such as Montreal, Boston, and Philadelphia, very little survives from the urban fabric before the mid-nineteenth century. By global standards, residents of Canada and the United States are affluent, with rates of automobile ownership among the highest in the world. With abundant and comparatively cheap land they have created cities in which single-family, detached owner-occupied homes are common. By the 1920s, the rate of owner occupancy in both Canadian and American cities had reached almost 50 percent, a far higher proportion than in European countries (although comparable with that in Australia). As a result, urban and residential densities have been low, with the early emergence of a marked segregation of dwellings from other types of land use, including stores.

Social segregation, which in some European cities occurs vertically, from one story to another in multiunit buildings, is organized horizontally in Canada and the United States. Innumerable studies have shown that the degree of social class segregation in Canadian and U.S. cities is similar, and the most segregated groups are those at both ends of the class or income spectrum.

Large numbers of immigrants have made ethnic segregation, and hence the ethnic neighborhood, a common, accepted, and in many cases welcomed element in the cities of both countries. In popular and scholarly discourse, the American "melting pot" is sometimes contrasted with the Canadian multicultural "mosaic." The implication is that immigrants to the United States have been expected to assimilate and integrate, while their Canadian counterparts have been encouraged to remain culturally and geographically distinct. In fact, available evidence suggests that in both countries integration proceeds steadily after the first generation, but that ethnic identities persist. In contrast with the situation in many European countries, then, the immigrant experience in Canada and the United States has been broadly similar.

Within this context, there are national differences in both the patterns and processes of urban development. With a population only about one-tenth the size of its southern neighbor, Canada has not developed cities the size of New York or even Detroit. During the 1970s, Toronto overtook Montreal as Canada's largest metropolitan center, but neither has ever ranked higher than about ninth in all of North America. For this reason, Canadian cities have not experienced the extreme density found in lower Manhattan, the urban congestion of present-day Los Angeles, or the industrial pollution once common in Pittsburgh and Cleveland. With an economy that has always depended more on the extraction and exploitation of natural resources (initially fish, lumber, and minerals, and later wheat and oil), Canada relies more on importing than producing manufactured goods. With the exception of Hamilton, Ontario, none of the major Canadian cities has ever been dominated by manufacturing.

The level of urbanization in Canada lagged about ten percentage points behind that of the United States until World War II. In 1940, 53 percent of Americans lived in urban areas compared with only 43 percent of Canadians. Since then, urbanization has proceeded more rapidly in Canada, and urban proportions are now about the same. This means that, on average, Canadian cities are younger. In general, because they have been shaped by the automobile, younger cities tend to be less densely populated. It is therefore significant that Canadian cities are generally more densely developed than their counterparts of comparable size in the United States. In part, this is because real income and per capita ownership of automobiles have been slightly lower in Canada than in the United States, and the use of public transportation higher. More extensive use of transit reflects, and also helps to maintain, higher urban densities.

Higher densities also reflect stricter land use controls. It has often been said that the Canadian political culture places more emphasis on deference to authority and "good government," and less emphasis on individual freedom, than the political culture of the United States. This contrast helps to explain why the "public interest" has been given more weight in the development of planning and land use control in Canada. Certainly, civic government played an active role in regulating urban life in the larger Canadian cities from an early date, Toronto being a case in point. Political culture cannot explain everything, however, for in the early years of this century fringe development around Canadian cities was no more (and possibly less) regulated than in the United States. Differences in the extent of suburban regulation have emerged most clearly since World War II.

Another reason for higher residential densities in Canadian cities is that inner cities have remained attractive to affluent households. In the United States, affluent, native-born whites have long avoided living in central cities. In the late nineteenth century, they were repelled by the corruption of city government, the rapid growth of immigrant ghettos, and urban congestion. More recently, they have sought to avoid urban crime, the growing number of African Americans, and the deteriorating infrastructure. Corruption has been a less common, and certainly less visible, feature of civic government in Canada.

Until World War II, although Canada received as many immigrants (proportionately) as the United States, a much higher percentage came from northwestern Europe, especially the British Isles. For example, in the 1920s, immigrants were a larger proportion of the population of Toronto than New York. They were far more easily assimilated, however, since three-quarters came from Great Britain and Ireland. In this period, many immigrants to Canada settled in suburbs, probably to a greater extent than those who settled in the United States.

From the late 1950s on, Caribbean and then Asian immigration created new racial minority populations in some Canadian cities, notably Vancouver, Toronto, and Montreal. This has led to the emergence of racial ghettos and social tensions. Although the Canadian census does not gather information on race, it is likely that the level of racial segregation in Canadian cities is about the same as in the United States. Racial minorities, however, are still smaller in Canadian cities. Moreover, race does not have as long and fraught a history as in the United States.

Probably for these reasons, and not (as many Canadians like to believe) because of greater tolerance, race has been much less of a factor in the development of Canadian cities. In cases where minorities lived in Canadian cities before World War II, there is clear evidence of racism. The treatment of the Chinese community in Vancouver is a clear example. Because of small numbers, however, the existence of racial minorities has not led to "white flight" in Canada. Indeed, in recent years, gentrification within cities has displaced many racial and ethnic minorities into (older) suburbs. This process has also affected a number of cities in the United States, but not to the same extent.

Underlying some of the more important differences between cities in Canada and the United States is the organization of local government. In the United States, local government has constitutional rights, but in Canada their powers have been delegated from the provinces. In daily practice, this might seem to make little difference. In Canada, as in the United States, local agencies tax property, regulate land use, support schools, and provide services like water, sewerage, parks, and law enforcement. Because of their dependent status, however, Canadian local governments can be reshaped at the will of the provinces, usually in the name of efficiency and the wider public interest. So, for example, Ontario created a two-tier metropolitan government for Toronto in 1954 while, in 1972, Manitoba established a single metropolitan government for Winnipeg. This type of reorganization has led to

greater efficiency in local government and reduced the need for the types of special service districts that have proliferated in the United States. It has also helped preserve the health of the inner city, which has therefore maintained its attractiveness to affluent, white families. It is significant that all major Canadian central cities—including Montreal's whose economy has not been strong since the 1970s—have experienced a significant amount of gentrification over the past 20 years.

In both countries, regional differences often obscured national ones. Vancouver looks more like Seattle than it does Toronto. Indeed, in a rare comparative analysis, Lionel Frost has argued that western cities in North America have more in common with the newer Australian cities than they do with those on the eastern seaboard and in the Midwest. This indicates that the shape and appearance of cities is determined as much by economic and technological factors as by government at any level. In terms of the experience of city residents, however, the border, and in particular the political culture, makes a significant difference everywhere. Lax gun controls have helped to make parts of many cities in the United States unsafe at any time. Very few neighborhoods in Canadian cities are unsafe by day, only a few more by night. Moreover, the social safety net, including universal health insurance, is stronger in Canada. Homelessness, and the quiet desperation of poverty, is known to many, but social disparities are narrower. The manifestations of urban poverty—crime, drugs, abandoned housing, and a deteriorating infrastructure—are much less extreme; so, too, are the expressions of new wealth, including gated and walled subdivisions. Canadian cities may be more bland but, especially for low- and moderate-income families, they are more livable.

—*Richard Harris*

See also

Building Regulations; Density; Ethnic Neighborhood; Fragmentation of Municipal Government; Height Restrictions; Homeownership; Housing Segregation; Land Developers and Development; Municipal Government; Zoning.

References

Anderson, Kay. *Vancouver's Chinatown. Racial Discourse in Canada, 1875–1980.* Montreal, Quebec, and Kingston, Ontario: McGill-Queen's University Press, 1991.

Cullingworth, J. Barry. *The Political Culture of Planning. American Land Use Planning in Comparative Perspective.* New York: Routledge, 1993.

Frost, Lionel. *The New Urban Frontier: Urbanisation and City-Building in Australasia and the American West.* Kensington, Australia: New South Wales University Press, 1991.

Harris, Richard. *Unplanned Suburbs: Toronto's American Tragedy, 1900–1950.* Baltimore: Johns Hopkins University Press, 1995.

Higgins, Donald J. H. *Local and Urban Politics in Canada.* Toronto: Gage, 1986.

Lemon, James. "Toronto among North American Cities." In Victor Russell, ed., *Forging a Consensus: Historical Essays on Toronto.* Toronto: University of Toronto Press, 1984.

Ley, David. "The Inner City." In Trudi Bunting and Pierre Filion, eds., *Canadian Cities in Transition.* Toronto: Oxford University Press, 1991.

Mercer, John. "The Canadian City in Continental Context: Global and Continental Perspectives on Canadian Urban Development." In Trudi Bunting and Pierre Filion, eds., *Canadian Cities in Transition.* Toronto: Oxford University Press, 1991.

Mercer, John, and Michael Goldberg. *The Myth of the North American City: Continentalism Challenged.* Vancouver: University of British Columbia Press, 1986.

Canals

The impact of canals on American cities is part of the larger relationship between transportation and urban development in which cities have grown due to having access to rivers, roads, canals, railroads, or other transportation technologies. In the canal era, which began in the 1790s and flourished through the 1850s, some 4,000 miles of waterways were built in the United States, mostly in the northeast. They helped to make that section more urban than other parts of the nation.

Chief among the trunk lines linking cities on the Atlantic with the West were the Erie Canal, the Pennsylvania Mainline canal system, the Chesapeake and Ohio Canal, and the James River and Kanawha Canal. Inland, the Ohio and Erie Canal, the Miami and Erie Canal, the Wabash and Erie Canal, and the Illinois and Michigan Canal connected the Great Lakes with the Ohio and Mississippi Rivers. The Louisville and Portland Canal passed the rapids on the Ohio River, and the Sault Canal opened navigation between Lake Michigan and Lake Superior. Some short pioneer canals, such as the Middlesex Canal in Massachusetts, the Dismal Swamp Canal in North Carolina, and the Santee Canal in South Carolina, served seacoast cities well into the nineteenth century.

Cities that were canal termini reflect the impact of canals most strongly. Among them were Albany and Buffalo on the Erie Canal; Easton, Pennsylvania, at the junction of the Lehigh Navigation, the Delaware Division Canal, and the Morris Canal; Richmond on the James River and Kanawha Canal; Cleveland and Portsmouth on the Ohio and Erie Canal; Cincinnati and Toledo on the Miami and Erie Canal; and Philadelphia and Pittsburgh on the Pennsylvania Mainline canal and railroad system. There was intense rivalry for canals in seacoast cities from Boston, New York, and Philadelphia to Baltimore and Charleston. Each of them sought canals to tap the trade of the interior, and most canals profited from urban commercial interests and urban governments who thought them highly desirable.

Along the canal lines it was the basins, ports, towns, and cities that defined the canal routes. Many cities were virtually created by canals, such as Syracuse and Rochester on the Erie Canal and Akron on the Ohio and Erie Canal. Others experienced new growth as canal towns or cities, such as, in Pennsylvania, Reading on the Union Canal and Sunbury and Wilkes-Barre on the upper branches of the Susquehanna River, and, in Ohio, Milan on the Milan Canal. Also in Ohio, Cincinnati, Dayton, and Toledo grew from the trade of the Miami and Erie Canal, and Columbus was on a navigable feeder to the Ohio and Erie Canal. The Wabash and Erie Canal especially illustrates the growth of a long line of interior canal towns and cities in Indiana as its line was marked by Fort Wayne, Huntington, Wabash, Peru, Lagro, Logansport, Delphi, Lafayette, Terre Haute, and finally Evansville on the Ohio River.

Blake McKelvey has described the Erie Canal as the "mother of cities." Charles R. Poinsatte has written a classic urban study of Fort Wayne, Indiana, as it grew from an Indian trading center to a canal port. Stuart Blumin described the way in which Kingston, New York, on the lower Hudson crossed the "urban threshold" as a terminus of the Delaware and Hudson Canal. Hubertis Cummings has described life in a network of more than a dozen canal ports in Pennsylvania. While canal cities drew much of their commerce from the canals that passed through them, they also drew upon the trade of their hinterlands. Diane Lindstrom has studied the growth of Philadelphia in partnership with the growth of its hinterland, which was served by seven canals. John G. Clark's study of the grain trade of the Great Lakes showed that the growth of Cleveland was directly related to hinterland exports by canal from Dresden, Roscoe, Dover, Massilon, and Akron. Harry N. Scheiber has described Cincinnati as "the new West's great urban success story," in which Cincinnati drew trade from the farms of the Miami Valley, and its meatpacking industry helped make it the dominant city in Ohio by 1850. Yet in some places, hinterland growth could be hurt by canals. Roberta B. Miller has used patterns suggested by Eric Lampard to show that the hinterland of Syracuse, at the juncture of the Erie and Oswego Canals in New York, declined in the face of competition from farther west.

Canals changed the life of towns and cities through which they passed. These changes came with rapid growth, as midwestern canal cities were among the most rapidly growing in the canal era. In rural settings, some canal towns had a quiet charm, situated beside a lock or basin where long, narrow canal boats could be loaded, unloaded, or turned around. But canals also brought bustle and excitement to inland villages. Canals provided employment, stimulated business in taverns and country stores, and brought eastern merchandise to western settlements. Canals added cultural leavening as transients passed through, and they brought ethnic diversity as canal laborers often remained where they had come to work on canals. This phenomenon has been traced for the Irish in Worcester, Massachusetts, a terminus of the Blackstone Canal connecting Worcester with Providence, Rhode

An 1825 lithograph of men operating a manual pulley crane to excavate the Erie Canal in Lockport, New York.

Island. In Illinois, the movement of Irish contractors into Chicago business and politics was one consequence of the Illinois and Michigan Canal. Canals were a leading pathway for immigrants heading west, who alternated their travel from canals to schooners or steamboats on the Great Lakes and to steamboats on the western rivers.

Through canal cities came boatmen who were part of a waterborne society in which boat captains were well known and respected, even while canals themselves were the scenes of fighting and violence. Crews raced for precedence at the locks and joined in tavern brawls. Paul E. Johnson has described the efforts of prominent citizens in Rochester, New York, to control the intemperance and violence of boatmen on the Erie Canal. In the cholera epidemics that intermittently plagued cites along the canals, that dread disease was believed to be fostered by unsanitary conditions on canal boats or in canal basins. Canals could also be disruptive to cities as they were being enlarged or rebuilt to accommodate increasing commerce.

Urban manufacturing was also stimulated by canals. The Lehigh Valley navigation system made that valley a birthplace of American industrial development as it brought coal from the anthracite fields to the Delaware River and contributed to Pennsylvania's iron industry. The anthracite canals, including the Delaware and Hudson Canal, the canals of the upper Susquehanna, the Union Canal, and the Morris Canal and the Delaware and Raritan Canal in New Jersey provided a foundation for industries in many Pennsylvania and New Jersey cities. John A. Roebling invented his woven strands of wire for aqueducts in Pittsburgh and on the Delaware and Hudson Canal, as well as for the Allegheny Portage Railroad on the Pennsylvania Mainline system. Roebling moved his factory to Trenton on the Delaware and Raritan Canal.

The life of canal towns has been portrayed in the novels of Samuel Hopkins Adams and Walter D. Edmonds. Greek Revival architecture and the pediments and columns of that style marked canalside buildings while Romanesque arches appeared on canal aqueducts. There were library boats, theater boats, and circus boats that tied up in canal towns and cities. The route of the Erie Canal has been called a pathway of reform, and western New York canal towns became part of the "burned-over district" during the Second Great Awakening.

Canals continued to influence northeastern and midwestern cities long after they became railroad centers. Today, canal towpaths are preserved as recreational areas in urban and suburban areas, and boats run on short sections of still-watered portions of restored canals.

—*Ronald E. Shaw*

See also
Erie Canal.
References
Blumin, Stuart M. *The Urban Threshold: Growth and Change in a Nineteenth-Century American Community.* Chicago: University of Chicago Press, 1976.
Cummings, Hubertis M. "Pennsylvania: Network of Canal Ports." *Pennsylvania History* 21 (1954): 260–273.
Johnson, Paul E. *A Shopkeeper's Millennium: Society and Revivals in Rochester, New York, 1815–1837.* New York: Hill and Wang, 1978.
Lindstrom, Diane. *Economic Development in the Philadelphia Region 1810–1850.* New York: Columbia University Press, 1978.
Maldonado, Edwin. "Urban Growth during the Canal Era: The Case of Indiana." *Indiana Social Studies Quarterly* 31 (1978–1979): 20–39.
McKelvey, Blake. "The Erie Canal, Mother of Cities." *New York Historical Quarterly* 35 (1951): 55–71.
Miller, Roberta B. *City and Hinterland: A Case Study of Urban Growth and Regional Development.* Westport, CT: Greenwood Press, 1979.
Poinsatte, Charles R. *Fort Wayne during the Canal Era 1828–1835.* Indianapolis: Indiana Historical Bureau, 1969.
Rubin, Julius. *Canal or Railroad? Imitation and Innovation in the Response to the Erie Canal in Philadelphia, Baltimore, and Boston.* Philadelphia: American Philosophical Society, 1961.
Scheiber, Harry N. "Ohio's Transportation Revolution—Urban Dimensions, 1803–1870." In John Wunder, ed., *Toward an Urban Ohio.* Columbus: Ohio State University Press, 1977.
Shaw, Ronald E. *Canals for a Nation: The Canal Era in the United States, 1790–1860.* Lexington: University Press of Kentucky, 1990.

Capone, Al (1899–1947)

Born in Brooklyn, New York, of Neapolitan parents in 1899, Al Capone was a run-of-the-mill street tough in his youth who became a notorious gangster. While still a teenager, Capone worked as a bartender and bouncer. Because of trouble caused by his violent nature, Capone was forced to flee New York with his wife and son for Chicago in 1919, where he joined a fellow New Yorker, John Torrio. Torrio had become the principal lieutenant of Chicago's crime boss "Big Jim" Colosimo, who had substantial interests in prostitution and gambling.

After Colosimo's murder in 1920, Torrio took over his illegal empire. He expanded into bootlegging and set up territorial monopolies to keep the various gangs, formed largely along ethnic lines, at peace and in prosperity. Beginning as a pimp and lowly brothel bouncer, Capone rose to be Torrio's trusted subordinate. By the mid-1920s, Chicago's fragile gangland equilibrium was severely strained by the expansionism of several participants. The murder in 1924 of North Side gangster Dion O'Banion, at Torrio's order, sparked nearly five years of uninterrupted and unprecedented gang warfare. It was this disorder that created Chicago's international reputation for violence.

After Torrio himself was nearly killed in 1925, he transferred his interests to Capone, making the 26-year-old youth the leader of Chicago's most powerful gang of racketeers. The elimination of several rivals, including North Side leader Hymie Weiss in 1926, strengthened Capone's position. Finally, in a masterstroke, Capone orchestrated the killing of seven North Side gang affiliates on St. Valentine's Day in 1929. During the next few years, the North Side "Bugs" gang disintegrated, and the remaining gangs were amalgamated into the Capone-led Chicago Crime Syndicate. Capone and his lieutenants also attended several meetings of gangsters from different cities, who established the National Crime Syndicate.

Because he bribed politicians and policemen extensively, Capone was largely immune from local government. However, his publicity-seeking behavior and the more shocking actions of Chicago gangland, such as the St. Valentine's Day Massacre, the murder of a *Chicago Tribune* reporter, and business and labor racketeering, brought him to the attention of federal authorities. Their response was twofold. First, Prohibition agents led by Eliot Ness hindered Capone by raiding his breweries and distilleries. Of much greater importance, Internal Revenue Service agents investigated him for income tax evasion between 1924 and 1929, leading to his conviction in October 1931. Sentenced to 11 years in prison, Capone was paroled from Alcatraz in 1939, by then incapacitated by syphilis. He died in Florida in 1947.

Al Capone left a powerful, though nefarious, legacy. In Chicago he established modern organized crime, extended its activities to business and organized labor, and corrupted public officials on a previously unsurpassed scale, the effects of which can be felt to this day. On a broader level, the formation of the National Crime Syndicate solidified the position of each city's gangsters, fostering expansion into new areas, such as Cuba and Las Vegas.

—John J. Binder

Reference
Schoenberg, Robert J. *Mr. Capone.* New York: William Morrow, 1992.

Carter Administration: Urban Policy

Jimmy Carter took office as president on January 20, 1977, a man publicly committed to giving urban problems high priority. Even before he won the Democratic presidential nomination in July 1976 he had told the U.S. Conference of Mayors that they would have "a friend, an ally, and a partner in the White House." On the day before his inauguration, he sent eight cabinet-level members of his new administration to meet with a group of mayors gathered in Washington to assure them that he was going to give precedence to urban problems.

During the next nine months, the president signed several pieces of legislation recommended by the mayors, including an increase in public service jobs and a $12.5 billion urban aid bill targeted at the nation's most distressed cities. He also established an Urban Regional Policy Group (URPG) headed by Patricia Harris, his Secretary of Housing and Urban Development, whose mandate was developing a national urban policy. To demonstrate his personal concern about the plight of cities, he traveled to the South Bronx in New York City at the beginning of October 1977. With dozens of reporters in tow, he viewed the wreckage of that ravaged area. Obviously moved by what he saw, Carter returned to Washington and instructed the URPG to prepare a plan of action for the South Bronx that would be a prototype for other blighted urban areas.

Despite Carter's stated commitment to a national urban policy, however, he never intended to direct major new resources to cities. A fiscal conservative who had promised to control government spending and produce a balanced budget by fiscal 1981, he always intended that his urban policy and programs would be predicated on what he called "federalism" during the campaign, or shared decision making between Washington, local governments, and public-private partnerships in urban development programs. Instead of seeking costly new urban initiatives, his administration would improve the targeting, coordination, and efficiency of existing programs, supply some (but not much) supplemental funding for economic development, encourage more local and neighborhood planning, eliminate redlining in home purchases, and increase private sector involvement in urban development projects.

Accordingly, the administration rejected the URPG's draft report, which recommended adding $8 billion to $12 billion to the $50 billion in aid that cities and towns were already receiving. Instead, Stuart Eizenstat, the head of Carter's domestic policy staff, recommended to the president a much more restrained and less costly role for Washington. Unlike the Harris task force, which still believed that well-conceived federal programs could produce urban revitalization, Eizenstat argued that Washington could act most responsibly by promoting public-private partnerships at the local level and encouraging greater involvement by neighborhood and citizens' groups. Carter agreed with Eizenstat, and in December 1977 he scolded the URPG for its recommendations on federal spending. The next day, he instructed James McIntyre, the director of the Office of Management and Budget, not to include any urban initiatives in the 1979 budget.

Aside from its price tag, the president had good reason to reject the URPG's report and to send the task force back to the drawing board. Many of its recommendations were conceptually flawed. Its much-touted proposal for an urban development bank, for example, assumed that low-cost credit, which the bank would presumably make available to investors, would spur economic development in distressed areas. But the URPG did not carefully analyze the other critical factors affecting investment, such as operating costs, the availability of land and skilled labor, government regulations, and crime rates.

In deciding not to include any additional funding for cities in his budget, the president also displayed considerable political courage. For, as he had anticipated, his action angered urban interests whose support was essential to his presidency. A spokesman for the U.S. Conference of Mayors stated that if the president failed to provide more aid to cities, his administration would "be viewed as a traitor to urban America." Rather than being intimidated by such warnings, Carter made it clear that his urban policy would stress the role of state and local governments and of neighborhood and voluntary groups, not just spend federal dollars.

The president lost a chance, however, to turn the "urban policy" issue to his advantage. An essential part of his strategy for capturing the presidency, especially before his nomination, had been presenting himself as an alternative to traditional Democrats. He told the American people that more was not necessarily better and that there were limits to what the federal government could do; voters responded by electing him. The issue of aid to cities offered an excellent opportunity to build on these themes and to benefit from the growing suspicion of big government that existed even within his own party. Yet, Carter never seized the moment. Instead of pressing for a "new liberalism" based on a healthy skepticism about Washington and the need for better rather than more government, for citizen participation, and for grassroots activism—all of which had great appeal to the nation's urban residents, according to the polls—he resorted to time-worn conservative arguments about fiscal economy and budgetary frugality. In the process, he failed to articulate strongly enough his own view that cities needed new approaches, not new money.

In 1978 the White House did present what Eizenstat later called "the nation's first comprehensive urban policy," but mostly it provided limited incentives to encourage private investment, and it was largely unsuccessful in achieving even this limited goal. More concerned with other matters, including fighting inflation and foreign policy, Carter allowed urban legislation to fall by the wayside. The president's failure to deliver on his campaign promises had a profound political effect as Carter's lack of action alienated some of the political groups that had helped elect him in 1976. Urban leaders charged the president with doing little for poorer people or areas. The Congressional Black Caucus even accused the administration of providing less federal funding for housing and economic development than there had been under Presidents Richard Nixon and Gerald Ford.

Nevertheless, for the remainder of his administration Carter continued giving relatively little attention to cities. He also rejected any effort to increase significantly the level of federal spending in urban areas. Like other economic programs, assistance to cities took a backseat to Carter's economic conservatism.

—*Burton I. Kaufman*

References
Dumbrell, John. *The Carter Presidency: A Reevaluation.* Manchester, England: Manchester University Press, 1993.

Hargrove, Erwin C. *Jimmy Carter as President: Leadership and the Politics of the Public Good.* Baton Rouge: Louisiana State University Press, 1988.

Jones, Charles O. *The Trusteeship Presidency: Jimmy Carter and the United States Congress.* Baton Rouge: Louisiana State University Press, 1988.

Kaufman, Burton I. *The Presidency of James Earl Carter, Jr.* Lawrence: University Press of Kansas, 1993.

Catholicism

The earliest Roman Catholic urban population in the present United States was in Gulf Coast cities like Mobile (1710) and New Orleans (1718). In these French colonial settlements, Roman Catholics were the founding religious body, "original shareholders" with a sense of belonging and ownership that would not generally be shared by their coreligionists who came as later immigrants to already established colonies. A distinctive culture of African-American Catholicism also developed in the Gulf Coast colonies. In post-Revolutionary times, smaller groups of Catholic merchants, small business people, lawyers, and traders grew up in southeastern coastal cities like Charleston and Savannah, both of which boasted active Irish communities as well as settlements of refugees from turmoil in the French West Indies.

The states of Maryland and Kentucky had substantial Catholic populations in Baltimore, Louisville, and Covington. Maryland was an English colony (1634) where Catholics, although never a majority of the population, initially held political control. Even after they lost political power, many retained elite economic and social status, although they tended to be country gentry rather than city dwellers. The first parish in Baltimore was begun in the 1750s to accommodate Acadian refugees from Canada. Seat of the first Catholic diocese in the United States (1789), Baltimore became an archdiocese in 1808. African-American Catholic communities grew in both Baltimore and Washington, peopled largely by descendants of Catholic slaves from rural southern Maryland. Catholics from Maryland moved west to Kentucky beginning in the 1780s to create a "holy land" centered on Bardstown in Nelson County and dotted with Catholic institutions—several colleges and the motherhouses of three large congregations of religious women. Bardstown, later Louisville, became the seat of the first Catholic diocese in the West in 1808.

Philadelphia's "Dock Ward" was the site of the first urban Catholic parish in the English colonies, St. Joseph's, Willings Alley, organized in 1733. Philadelphia was a busy port with a cosmopolitan population, and the Catholics were no exception. Merchants, ship owners, sailors, tavern keepers—they were English, Irish, Dutch, Spanish, and German. A separate German church was founded in 1788, but ethnic conflicts bedeviled the tiny congregation. During the American Revolution, Congress several times came in a body to the newer Catholic St. Mary's Church, and both George Washington and John Adams paid visits. Most Catholic parishioners were patriots, including Captain John Barry and Thomas Fitzsimons, a signer of the U.S. Constitution. Partially successful efforts were made to recruit a Catholic Tory regiment as well.

Early Catholics often tended to be Federalist in politics, but that changed with the arrival of large numbers of immigrants. Banned from some colonies in colonial times, Catholics streamed into northern port cities like New York and Boston, where they became part of the new urban proletariat. They opened their first church in New York in 1786 and in Boston in 1788. A diverse population resulted from the political and commercial prominence of these cities. Catholic life there was marked by a strong movement toward control of the churches by lay trustees that lasted well into the nineteenth century. Lay people had built the churches and engaged the pastors, and they demanded the right to judge the quality of those pastors and dismiss the ones found wanting. Similar movements occurred in almost every East Coast city, with lay trustees challenging the authority of bishops.

Relative peace came only when a flood of German and Irish immigrants who literally "became" the church arrived. They had their own problems, but by the middle of the nineteenth century the growing apparatus of Catholic bishops established itself in control of Catholic parishes. Germans continued to bemoan a "hibernarchy" that was largely Irish and Irish American. Disputing control by Irish bishops, dissident Poles formed their own Polish National Catholic Church. Hundreds of thousands of Ukrainians and other Eastern Rite Catholics went over to Orthodoxy in reaction to the hostile reception they received from fellow Catholics.

Among the immigrants, the Irish showed little inclination to farm life, and they were discouraged from attempting it by bishops like John Hughes (1797–1864) of New York who urged them to stay together in eastern cities. Beginning in shanty towns and cluttered slums, they worked initially as day laborers, in slaughterhouses, as stevedores, on railroads and canals, and as streetcar drivers. The Irish were unique for the large number of single women among the newcomers, many of whom began lives here "in service" as maids. Many remained single throughout their lives and became generous contributors to church causes. Later generations taught school, and their male counterparts became policemen and firefighters. Irish saloonkeepers found their way into urban politics; and, by the end of the nineteenth century, Irish political machines controlled cities across the country. Catholic institutions absorbed a large number of the immigrants' children as priests and religious sisters and brothers. While most of the Irish were of modest means at best, a few did well in industry and business, and New York City could boast Irish millionaires in the closing years of the nineteenth century. At the same time, their compatriots were disproportionately represented on welfare rolls and police blotters.

The church reacted to its adherents' needs by sponsoring a range of charitable and health-care services—hospitals, protectories, orphanages, and schools. Beginning with parish primary schools, Catholic education soon developed high schools, colleges, and universities. There was no centralized control over these institutions, but the nation's bishops advised them in a series of national councils. Their existence was possible because men and women in religious communities worked for subsistence-level support, contributed chiefly by working people. Among Germans, and then Poles, separate institutions and ethnic congregations of sisters helped preserve cultural and linguistic, as well as religious, inheritances. This was reinforced by the Rhenish Gothic churches and Polish basilicas that dotted cities and the many ethnic societies for both men and women.

Beginning in the 1830s, the urban mood turned ugly. Poor, white, native-born Americans felt threatened by the immigrant Irish, by the Irish affinity for the Democratic Party, by Irish competition for entry-level jobs, and by the apparent consolidation of political power in the hands of Irish bishops. Evangelical Protestant revivalism contributed to the displeasure. Catholic attacks on Protestant-inspired Bible reading and devotional exercises in public schools spilled over into violence in Philadelphia and Boston. Protests against immigrant German voters provoked riots in Louisville on "Bloody Monday," August 6, 1855. This "Know-Nothing" phase of American nativism lasted until the Civil War.

Meanwhile, the nation moved west. New Catholic dioceses were established, with St. Louis as the principal staging area after a bishop was appointed there in 1827. Incorporation of Mexican territory after the Mexican-American War of 1848 saw the Irish and French Catholic church superimposed on a Hispanic and Indian populace, best symbolized by the Gothic cathedral in the center of Santa Fe, New Mexico. California suffered instant Americanization in the wake of the gold rush and Yankee occupation as immigrants from every corner of the world overwhelmed the sparse population of Californios and native Americans. Catholics shared in the prosperity of cities like San Francisco, and a broader spread of ethnic groups moved into the political and financial establishment there than elsewhere. Catholics were in on the ground floor of California statehood, and were not treated as latecomer immigrants.

In the country's midsection, Catholic dioceses continued to multiply. Chicago (which became a diocese in 1843) was paradigmatic of the large urban church. Urban neighborhoods were designated as parishes, and they were identified by the name of their Catholic parish, often an institution serving 8,000 to 10,000 people. Parochial schools catered to upwardly mobile middle-class parishioners and actively participated in building a Catholic subculture.

The Civil War had Irish regiments fighting for both sides, but Germans were more prominent in the Union army. Competition for low-paying jobs on the docks and elsewhere led to the shameful Draft Riots of 1863 when Irish mobs attacked African Americans in the streets of New York. After the war, a new wave of immigrants swept into the United States during the last third of the nineteenth century. Italy and Eastern Europe, relatively small immigrant-providers earlier on, increasingly took the lead. There was a dramatic shift in the pattern of European immigration to the United States; in 1882, 87 percent of immigrants came from

An ultramodern skyscraper forms a backdrop for the tower of St. Augustine's Cathedral in Tucson, Arizona.

Northern and Western Europe, and only 13 percent from Southern and Eastern Europe. By the turn of the century the percentages were reversed. By 1907, slightly more than 19 percent of European newcomers came from Northern and Western Europe, and well over 80 percent came from Southern or Eastern Europe.

One million Roman Catholics arrived in each decade between 1880 and 1920, two million between 1901 and 1910. In 1890 four out of every five people in greater New York City were immigrants or their children. Some Italians became suburban truck farmers, but most helped re-create their native villages in neighborhoods often called "Little Italy." Italians, largely from the southern part of that country, were transplanted from a Catholic cultural setting to the multireligious American city. Some responded to vigorous proselytizing by Protestant groups. Many reacted negatively to what they regarded as a hostile reception by other Catholics, and they found the public schools more attractive than "Irish" or "German" parochial schools. The arrival of Italian sisters (like Mother Francesca Cabrini) and priests reversed this situation. They organized Italian national parishes and Italian health-care institutions, and close-knit Italian Catholic communities flourished. Meanwhile, Slavic and Hungarian Catholics flooded northeastern industrial cities and the coalfields. They brought religious sisters and priests with them, and soon great basilicas and, for Eastern Rite Catholics, onion-domed churches sprouted. Heavy Mexican and French-Canadian immigration began in the 1890s, but the former generally headed for southwestern farms and railroad jobs, and the latter settled in New England mill towns.

Urban Catholics suffered through the Depression with other Americans, just as they had prospered in the early 1920s. Changes in immigration laws had sharply limited the number of Southern and Eastern Europeans who arrived, and this enabled the church to consolidate its gains although it grew more slowly. In the 1930s and 1940s, Catholics were avidly anti-Communist, struggling, for example, to control the docks in ports like New York and Philadelphia. Labor schools trained Catholic workers to contest control of unions. From the right, there came the strong influence of the demagogue Father Charles E. Coughlin, whose Sunday afternoon radio broadcasts mesmerized Catholic city dwellers. The influence of local churches in urban politics was considerable before federal welfare programs helped destroy Irish-Catholic political machines.

The success of labor unions propelled Catholics upward economically, as did the GI Bill of Rights after World War II, which itself was a force for homogenizing the population. In the 1950s and 1960s, Americans raced out of cities and into the suburbs. Catholics, along with others, moved into suburban areas, abandoning ethnic neighborhoods and their huge parish infrastructures of churches, schools, hospitals, and other buildings. New Catholic immigrants crowded in, making new demands on church and community structures. They represented a spectrum of Latin American peoples, creoles from the Caribbean, Filipinos, and Vietnamese and other Southeast Asians, the latest in a long line of immigrant Catholics to come to the United States and crowd its cities.

—*James Hennessey*

See also
Irish Americans in Cities; Italian Americans in Cities; Nativism; Polish Americans in Cities.
References
Dolan, Jay P. *The American Catholic Experience: A History from Colonial Times to the Present.* Garden City, NY: Doubleday, 1985.
Ellis, John Tracy. *American Catholicism.* 2d rev. ed. Chicago: University of Chicago Press, 1969.
Hennessey, James. *American Catholics: A History of the Roman Catholic Community in the United States.* New York: Oxford University Press, 1981.

Cattle Towns

The heyday of cattle towns lasted less than two decades, from 1867 to 1885, but few communities have had a more lasting afterlife, and none has had the romantic appeal of these dusty, end-of-the-trail communities. The cow towns of dime novels, movies, and television have a life and a history of their own, one only tangentially related to the historical cattle towns. Mythical symbols and metaphors of good versus evil, freedom versus restriction, hero versus villain—the fictional image will undoubtedly survive the historical originals and ought not be ignored by anyone interested in the development of the American character.

The historical cattle towns are equally important. In a sense, any place in the 1870s and 1880s that was a shipping point for cattle driven up from Texas could be called a cattle town. At least 16 Kansas towns assumed the label—the most famous being Abilene, Caldwell, Dodge City, and Wichita. Baxter Springs, Brookville, Chetopa, Elgin, Ellis, Ellsworth, Great Bend, Hays City, Newton, Salina, Soloman, and Waterville had briefer careers. Numerous sites, such as Honeywell and Delano and Doan's Store on the Red River, were places on the trail that cowboys remembered, but they lacked the facilities and delights of towns at the end of the trail. Other places such as Tascosa, Texas; Ogallalah, Nebraska; and Trail City, Colorado, also served as cattle towns.

Joseph McCoy originated the true cattle town at Abilene on the Kansas Pacific Railroad line, although Baxter Springs was an earlier (1866) shipping point. Fear of Texas (splenic) fever led the Kansas legislature to draw a line in 1867 that restricted Texas cattle to the southwestern quarter of the state. From time to time, the line was redrawn, forcing the Texas drovers to move their shipping target as the quarantine line and the railroads moved west. McCoy negotiated arrangements with the railroad and sent emissaries to Texas to persuade cattlemen to drive their herds to Abilene. This seasonal trade was profitable, but many in Abilene were hostile from the beginning and eventually drove the trade from town. Other towns followed this pattern. However, the Texas connection was big business while it flourished. In Dodge City, the arriving herds grew to 500,000 head in 1882, and profits for merchants kept pace. For them, the cattle trade was as much a bonanza as was gold for miners.

The false-fronted streets took on a carnival air when the cowboys were in town; bands played to drum up business, con artists hawked their wares, and sidewalk musicians and entertainers added to the noise. Businesses provided all the essentials cowboys needed to unwind after the long drive north: new wardrobes and the delights of barbershops, brothels, dance halls, gambling parlors, and saloons. Lawmen and, more importantly, the legal system maintained a clear line between tolerating macho sin and fun and suppressing serious crimes of robbery, property destruction, and murder. The average number of killings in cattle towns was only 1.5 a year. Still, the towns were rough, rowdy, and no place for a young cowboy trying to save his wages.

As the prosperity of the towns increased and more families moved in, the towns took on the coloring of Victorian America. Churches, schools, opera houses with eastern casts and inoffensive presentations, drug stores, restaurants with oyster bars and ice cream parlors, lodges, concerts, croquet, and private dances flourished. Thus, maturing towns developed two cultures. Occasionally the two met in a general store, the circus, or the roller-skating rink, but the majority of residents never spoke to a prostitute, fired a six-shooter, or lost a dollar playing Keno.

The era ended when new railroads with lower shipping rates were built in Texas, homesteaders crowded the land, and the majority of respectable citizens decided that the flamboyant lifestyle of controlled machismo, gambling, prostitution, and rowdyism was too high a price to pay for the profits of the cattle trade. In 1885 the Kansas legislature closed the entire state to Texas cattle. Dodge City and Caldwell, the last of the cattle towns, became placid, country-market centers.

The fictional cow towns lived on. For novels, television, and theater, the rowdy town was far more exciting than the respectable one; high tea in a Victorian drawing room or the modest rendering of a sentimental ballad at the opera house was no match for high-noon shoot-outs and dance hall girls romping through the cancan. As a genre, the mythical towns have also seen better days, but they still surface occasionally to the applause of the audience.

—*C. Robert Haywood*

References

Dykstra, Robert R. *The Cattle Towns.* New York: Atheneum, 1979.
Haywood, C. Robert. *Victorian West: Class and Culture in Kansas Cattle Towns.* Lawrence: University of Kansas Press, 1991.
Hunter, J. Marvin, ed. *The Trail Drivers of Texas,* 2 vols. Austin: University of Texas Press, 1979.
Young, Fredric R. *Dodge City: Up through a Century in Story and Picture.* Dodge City, KS: Boot Hill Museum, 1972.

Census

The United States has taken a census of its population every ten years, without fail, since 1790. The U.S. Constitution specifies that periodic censuses will be taken for the purpose of levying taxes and, especially, for apportioning membership in the House of Representatives proportionately to the population of each state. Although the federal government has not used the census to determine or allocate taxes, it continues to use the census for reapportioning seats in the House. Although the census was created for these political purposes, it has proved invaluable to social scientists, especially for anyone studying urbanization and urbanism.

Census methodology began quite simply. U.S. marshals traversed their districts, presumably on horseback, enumerating the households of each settlement. Every ten years throughout the nineteenth century, the federal government set up a temporary census office in Washington to tally and publish statistical results. Then, in 1902 the federal government established a permanent census agency. The Bureau of the Census emerged as a modern statistical agency during the 1930s when it began to hire mathematical statisticians who introduced sampling, first into the construction of surveys, and then into the national census itself in 1940.

Until 1970, enumerators going from door to door collected census data and gathered information from each household in face-to-face interviews. The enumerator carried a questionnaire printed in the form of a large matrix; each row represented an individual person and each column represented a variable or question about that person. Research conducted after the 1950 census revealed that enumerators themselves were injecting a certain amount of error into their data collection, and census administrators began to experiment with "self-enumeration" in 1960. In 1970 the majority of households were enumerated with mailout-mailback, self-enumeration questionnaires.

In 1900 for the first time, the census included information about homeownership, and, since 1940, each decennial census has included several questions about the characteristics of housing. Housing statistics are published for small areas, and they have also provided important information about cities and urban places in the second half of the twentieth century.

Over time, census administrators have struggled to decide what actually constitutes an "urban" place. The first definition, one that is still used, is that any settlement whose permanent population exceeds 2,500 is urban. Using that definition, the census of 1920 was the first to show an urban majority for the whole country. In order to deal with cities that had annexed large amounts of undeveloped land, as well as those cities that had annexed contiguous, densely populated suburbs, the Census Bureau introduced a second concept, the urbanized area. An urbanized area is defined as one or more "central places" and the densely settled adjacent territory surrounding it (the "urban fringe") that together have a minimum population of 50,000 people. To qualify for this designation, an urban fringe must be settled at a density of at least 1,000 persons per square mile. The bureau also introduced the concept of a "metropolitan area" to deal with suburbanization that created settlements larger than the cities that nucleated them. The definition of metropolitan area has changed over time, but it still basically represents a county (or group of contiguous counties) that includes a city of 50,000 or more, plus its suburbs.

Census data are frequently used to study urbanization. Because it is gathered regularly, it measures population not only by place but also over time, thereby recording the history of an area and providing one of its greatest strengths. With data in this form, a researcher can choose a particular geographic area, like a state or region, and determine the changing proportion of the population living in cities over time. Likewise, one can choose a particular city and, by using a series of censuses, examine its growth and, in many instances, its decline. One early and notable study of urbanization is *The Growth of Cities in the Nineteenth Century: A Study in Statistics* by Adna F. Weber, published in 1899. While Weber was comparing cities and urbanization internationally, he presented a great deal of information about the United States, including population distribution, urbanization, the growth of particular cities, and conditions in cities. Since publication of Weber's book, historians, sociologists, geographers, and other social scientists have frequently used census data to study urbanization.

City planners and urban researchers have long been interested in statistics about small areas. Since 1950, the census has published information at the level of city blocks and, with increasing coverage of cities and suburbs, of census tracts, the areas by which the data are collected. From time to time, the census generates statistics for other small areas, including Enumeration Districts and Block Numbering Areas, which are aspects of the Census Bureau's mapping and field operations.

Social scientists have made particularly good use of small area statistics to examine racial segregation. Utilizing city block and census tract data by race, they have compiled accurate measures of residential segregation by race in cities and metropolitan areas. Sociologists and demographers Karl Taeuber and Alma Taeuber pioneered this kind of research in their monograph *Negroes in Cities* (1965), which provided segregation indexes for American cities from 1940 to 1960. More recently, Douglas Massey and Nancy Denton continued this type of analysis, reporting on continuing segregation in metropolitan areas until 1990 in their *American Apartheid* (1993). Social scientists have used small area statistics to analyze other spatial patterns as well, examining the distributions of population density, wealth and poverty, ethnic groups, and other characteristics of urban places.

Throughout its history, the census has used a variety of definitions of race and ethnicity. Every census has differentiated whites from African Americans, but the terminology has shifted from time to time. In 1990 the census specified six broad "racial" categories: White; Black; American Indian, Eskimo, or Aleut; Asian, Pacific Islander; and "Other." A separate variable also identified the "Hispanic" population, not treating it as a racial group. The 1980 and 1990 censuses asked individuals to identify their "ancestry," yielding dozens of different subgroups.

Marie Cioffi takes information from New York resident Margaret Napolitana on the first day of the census in 1930.

Since 1950, the Bureau of the Census has computerized many of its operations, beginning with tabulating data and using machine-readable questionnaires. In 1990 it introduced TIGER (Topologically Integrated Geographic Encoding and Referencing System), a comprehensive geographical information system that contained unique identifiers for all addresses in the nation. Also, increasingly, the bureau has converted many of its data products into new technologies. Certain reports that it previously printed in bound books are now distributed on CD-ROM.

The issue of undercounting urban minority populations began to preoccupy census administrators about 1980. Mayors of large cities and leaders of minority organizations complained that decennial censuses failed to count poor, minority populations fully, thus creating inequities in distributing government grants and in apportioning state and federal legislative districts. A number of federal lawsuits considered these complaints. In preparing for the 1990 census, statisticians devised techniques with which to correct these undercounts, but the government continued to rely on raw census numbers in reporting the results of the 1990 census. Plans for the census of 2000 promise a partial solution to the problem of undercounting and adjusting.

—*Harvey M. Choldin*

See also
Metropolitan Area; Urban Fringe; Urbanization.
References
Anderson, Margo. 1987. *The American Census: A Social History.* New Haven, CT: Yale University Press, 1987.

Barrett, Richard E. *Using the 1990 U.S. Census for Research.* Thousand Oaks, CA: Sage Publications, 1994.

Choldin, Harvey M. *Looking for the Last Percent: The Controversy over Census Undercounts.* New Brunswick, NJ: Rutgers University Press, 1994.

Massey, Douglas S., and Nancy A. Denton. *American Apartheid: Segregation and the Making of the Underclass.* Cambridge, MA: Harvard University Press, 1993.

Myers, Dowell. *Analysis with Local Census Data: Portraits of Change.* Boston: Academic Press, 1992.

Taeuber, Karl E., and Alma F. Taeuber. *Negroes in Cities: Residential Segregation and Neighborhood Change.* Chicago: Aldine, 1965.

Weber, Adna Ferrin. *The Growth of Cities in the Nineteenth Century: A Study in Statistics.* New York: Macmillan, 1899.

Centennial Exposition of 1876

Soon after the Civil War, proposals began to emerge for celebrating the upcoming centennial of the nation's independence. While New York, Boston, and Washington, D.C., all put forth claims to host the celebration, Philadelphia, which was then the nation's second most populous city and the one that had played a central role during the Revolution, was chosen by the U.S. government.

The Centennial Exposition was the first major world's fair to be held in the United States and the largest to have been held anywhere to that time. Faced with problems of funding and construction, it officially opened on May 10 rather than a month earlier as originally scheduled to commemorate the battles of Lexington and Concord; it closed exactly six months later. In all, attendance totaled more than 10 million, with 176,000 present the penultimate day to see displays from more than 50 nations. The large number of visitors was partly due to reduced fares by railroads serving Philadelphia as well as to improved local transportation. Some 200 buildings comprised the exposition, whose grounds covered 450 acres of Fairmount Park, which had been planned during the 1850s and which was (and still is) the single largest urban park in the United States.

The Centennial Exposition, for Americans at least, was Janus-faced, looking in two opposite directions at the same time. In part, it nostalgically celebrated the past, the colonies' quest for independence, and the successful venture into nationhood. Art and artifacts, parades, and speeches spoke to a glorious and seemingly simpler past. But the exposition also resonated to the present and picked up sounds of a future that were considerably more complex and uncertain. Technology was rapidly transforming the United States into an industrialized nation, and the single most popular exhibit at the exposition was the 39-foot-high, 680-ton Corliss steam engine that dominated Machinery Hall. When President Ulysses S. Grant and the exposition's most prominent visitor, Emperor Dom Pedro of Brazil, jointly activated this gigantic creation of engineer George H. Corliss, enough power was generated to operate 800 other machines at the celebration. The exposition also featured a host of other newly minted technological marvels, including George Westinghouse's air brake, George Pullman's palace car, Thomas A. Edison's quadruplex telegraph, and Alexander Graham Bell's telephone.

Additionally, the Centennial Exposition broadened the nation's cultural horizons by making it possible for those in attendance to view the largest exhibit of foreign and native paintings and statues hitherto assembled. No art drew as much attention as that of Japan, which had recently opened contact with the West after having isolated itself for more than two centuries. The exotic Japanese wares, housed in two dwellings, apparently ranked second only to the Corliss Engine in inspiring awe, and it set off a rage for things Japanese. Exaggeration or not, Philadelphia, concluded one observer, had proven "as cosmopolitan as Paris and as lively as Chicago." Few, however, questioned that the Centennial Exposition itself had notably expanded public awareness of industrial, commercial, and artistic achievements, just as it had also paid handsome patriotic tribute to the national past.

—*Robert Muccigrosso*

References

Beers, Dorothy Gondos. "The Centennial City, 1865–1876." In Russell F. Weigley, ed., *Philadelphia: A 300-Year History.* New York: W. W. Norton, 1982.

Brown, Dee. *The Year of the Century.* New York: Scribners, 1966.

Rydell, Robert W. *All the World's a Fair: Visions of Empire at American International Expositions.* Chicago: University of Chicago Press, 1984.

Central Business District

In American cities, the emergence of distinct central business districts (CBDs) awaited the arrival of urban industrialization after the Civil War. Previously, even in the center of cities such as Boston, Philadelphia, and New York, residences mixed with businesses, and there were various quarters for marketing commodities or fabricating goods rather than a distinguishable business district.

Compared with this earlier period, in late-nineteenth-century cities the scale of facilities serving as depots for raw materials such as grain or lumber, or of factories turning raw materials into finished products, was immense. Furthermore, the cutting edge of transportation technology in the nineteenth century, the railroad, had a highly centralizing effect on urban business location. Main railroad spurs and depots brought products and people directly into the center of cities. One carryover from the preindustrial era—the face-to-face encounter between buyer and seller, or often more pertinently, potential buyer and commodity sample—also contributed to the centralizing of business activities.

A whole array of operations depended on central places in which merchants, managers, laborers, production sites, warehouses, and commodities were readily at hand. Nor were such centralizing tendencies only evident in the manufacturing economy. The rise of the great department store, which epitomized the emerging consumer economy in the late nineteenth century, resulted from similar centralizing tendencies.

Yet, true CBDs were also the consequence of certain decentralizing tendencies. Photographs of turn-of-the-century central city streets record a visual cacophony of people, vehicles, and products. Central cities were becoming less hospitable living environments, and those who had the means to escape them did so. In New York, elite families moved from lower Manhattan to midtown Fifth Avenue and beyond. In Chicago, the aristocracy of Prairie Avenue escaped to the "North Shore." As mass transit systems evolved around the turn of the century, their terminals within central cities bound together one end of a fanlike system of lines ending at depots spaced around the edge of metropolitan regions. Thus were born commuter suburbs, and a rough hierarchy of residential neighborhoods reaching from near the central city to the metropolitan periphery developed.

The same crowded streets that effected this residential exodus also inhibited movement of products, and by the early twentieth century big industrial combines also began moving their operations to peripheral sites. Land was cheaper there, and rail connections from less centralized points were increasingly possible. In some instances, employers sought to hire a workforce less given to the amusements and union rhetoric found in central cities. At this time, from approximately 1900 until World War II, the CBD achieved its "classic" character. Banks, corporate headquarters, government and professional offices, department stores, and hotels became the mainstays of these CBDs, which also tended to house cities' principal cultural institutions and entertainment establishments. Just as residence was decreasingly associated with this milieu, so was heavy industry. Moreover, the spread of zoning after the 1920s, with its basic designations of commercial, industrial, and residential uses, further formalized the idea of the CBD. Some industry and even housing remained in CBDs, and commercial uses were spread across metropolitan regions, but the CBD stood at the summit of any given city's hierarchy of commercial real estate.

If the character and functions of the classic CBD marked the balance of these centralizing and decentralizing forces, by the middle of the twentieth century the weight of the new decentralizing forces clearly predominated. The rising affluence of the American population helped shift residential preferences toward the suburbs, a trend itself aided mightily by advertising, federal government subsidies of homeownership, and the popularity of the automobile. As a commercial carrier, the railroad gave up business to trucking, a means of moving products that permitted much greater decentralization of production and storage sites. Furthermore, federal financing of interstate highways both accelerated the rise of the trucking industry and also expanded the residential periphery of metropolitan regions.

By the 1940s business and government leaders in many cities contended that their CBDs were in trouble. Downtown department stores were just beginning to experience competition from suburban retailers. In many CBDs, the deterioration of older commercial buildings, typically characterized as "blight," was increasingly evident. Though the topic was sensitive, many urban leaders also worried about the increasing African-American population living in older, run-down residential quarters near CBDs. Throughout the 1940s trade groups such as the National Association of Real Estate Boards, downtown business leaders, and municipal officials lobbied Congress in favor of legislation to support "urban redevelopment." In 1949 a new U.S. Housing Act initiated urban renewal, a controversial program that would reshape CBDs across the United States.

Many supporters of the 1949 Housing Act envisioned this legislation as a mechanism to clear slums for inexpensive, standard-quality housing. Indeed, the 1949 act authorized new spending for the previously mandated public housing program. However, in cities such as Newark, New Jersey, initial efforts to clear slums and attract private housing investment proved difficult; moreover, public officials and business leaders in many cities assumed from the start that the new legislation was fundamentally a tool to preserve CBDs. Thus, in cities such as Baltimore, Boston, and New Haven, downtown rebuilding quickly emerged as a centerpiece of urban renewal. Redevelopment agencies acquired and razed older structures. By substantially writing down the cost of cleared sites (through the federal government's two-for-one subsidy of city expenditures), they offered cheap land to private developers for housing and some commercial development and also to a variety of institutions such as universities and hospitals.

During the 1950s and 1960s, urban renewal refashioned CBDs. Clearance produced thousands of acres of open land, much of which was not quickly redeveloped. Many CBDs did experience expansion of public and nonprofit institutional facilities. With the wave of expressway and parking ramp construction that followed the 1956 Interstate Highway Act, downtown areas became much more oriented to automobiles. Yet at the same time, cities such as Minneapolis experimented with creating pedestrian shopping areas that excluded automobiles.

Contrary to the expectations of its proponents, urban renewal did not rescue sinking CBDs. The broad economic and cultural factors that were undermining CBDs as multipurpose metropolitan centers were not addressed. Moreover, the considerable devastation produced in and around CBDs by urban renewal and expressway construction left them physically isolated, and the population in nearby residential areas was substantially reduced. This "de-densification" of central area population was particularly damaging to downtown retailers.

During the 1970s two innovations in urban design heralded a further redefinition of CBDs. The multipurpose commercial "megastructure," pioneered by architect John Portman's Peachtree Center in Atlanta, and the "festival marketplace" as devised by developer James Rouse at Boston's Faneuil Hall/Quincy Market complex, offered new formats to attract CBD investment and visitors. The commercial megastructure typically includes hotel, meeting, commercial, and office space under a single roof or some network of adjoining roofs. As such, and particularly when combined with eye-opening architectural flourishes such as Portman's signature atriums, the megastructure offers a dizzying variety of activities along with a comforting aura of security. The festival marketplace, which usually glamorizes historic sites within CBDs, offers the "smell of the street" in a tightly composed, well-managed complex. Commentators on megastructures and festival marketplaces often claim that these developments return "fun" to the CBD.

Variations on the megastructure and festival marketplace can be found across the United States; and indeed, newer commercial projects such as Horton Plaza in San Diego and the Cleveland Galleria represent ambitious extensions of these antecedents. In essence, these sorts of downtown complexes recast the CBD as the premier site for special events such as sporting contests, conventions, and trade shows. In fact, even as this new idea of the CBD has emerged, more traditional business operations have continued to leave the central city. Telecommunications innovations, combined with the expense of downtown real estate, have resulted in the movement of routine information storage and management, or "back office" functions, to noncentral locations.

Similarly, the defining feature of CBDs, geographic concentration permitting face-to-face interaction, is no longer so clearly necessary. Again, telecommunications technologies make central places less relevant for transacting business. More mundanely, many contemporary business meetings occur in hotels and conference centers at suburban complexes accessible via highway or airport. Such facilities are an important ingredient of what has come to be called the "edge city." Although it is not yet accurate to characterize the CBD as a vanishing component of the urban environment, the contemporary CBD is much more specialized than it was 50 years ago. Both as a business and entertainment center, the CBD's functions have been greatly reduced. Indeed, the new CBD of megastructures and festival marketplaces promotes an anachronistic image of the central city as a vibrant, exciting focal point of the metropolitan region.

—*Larry Bennett*

See also
Downtown.
References
Cronon, William. *Nature's Metropolis: Chicago and the Great West.* New York: W. W. Norton, 1991.
Frieden, Bernard J., and Lynn B Sagalyn. *Downtown Inc.: How America Rebuilds Cities.* Cambridge, MA: MIT Press, 1989.
Jacobs, Jane. *The Death and Life of Great American Cities.* New York: Vintage Books, 1961.
Warner, Sam Bass, Jr. *The Urban Wilderness: A History of the American City.* New York: Harper & Row, 1972.
Wilson, James Q. *Urban Renewal: The Record and the Controversy.* Cambridge, MA: MIT Press, 1966.

Central Park

In 1853 the New York state legislature authorized New York City to use the power of eminent domain to create Central

Park in the center of Manhattan, the nation's first landscaped public park. Wealthy merchants, bankers, and landowners had led the campaign to create the park, which they argued would make New York a world-class city and provide an attractive, controlled setting for promenades and carriage rides, a new form of recreation among elite families. Newspaper editors also endorsed the proposal for a public park by arguing that it would offer working-class New Yorkers a healthy alternative to the saloon and the tenement.

Although its rough terrain made the site's 843 acres unsuitable for private development, establishing the park required displacing about 1,600 poor people, including Irish pig farmers, German gardeners, and African-American householders who had created a stable settlement known as Seneca Village with three churches and a school. Central Park took five years to build and was one of the city's most massive public works projects, employing as many as 3,500 laborers a year.

In 1857 the Central Park Commission, the administrative body appointed by the New York state legislature to manage the park, held the country's first landscape design contest. The commissioners selected the "Greensward Plan," submitted by Frederick Law Olmsted, the park's superintendent at the time, and Calvert Vaux, an English-born architect and former partner of the popular and highly respected landscape gardener, Andrew Jackson Downing. The designers sought to create a pastoral landscape in the English romantic tradition. Open rolling meadows contrasted with the picturesque effects created by the densely planted Ramble and by the more formal grounds of the Mall (Promenade), where crowds could gather for concerts and public strolls in the out-of-doors. Extensive carriage drives, pedestrian walks, and equestrian paths coaxed visitors through the park's scenery with its views framed (and grades separated) by more than 40 bridges designed by Vaux and Jacob Wrey Mould. In order to reinforce a feeling of uninterrupted expanse and in order to hide crosstown commercial traffic, Olmsted and Vaux also sank four transverse roads eight feet below the park's surface. This design became a model for other urban parks in the United States for the remainder of the nineteenth century.

During the winter of 1859, thousands of New Yorkers inaugurated Central Park by skating on artificial lakes where there had once been swamps. By 1865, Central Park was attracting more than 7 million visitors a year. The largest group to use the park early on (accounting for as many as half of the people who used the park in its first decade) were the city's wealthiest citizens, who assembled for elaborate carriage parades in the late afternoon. Although middle-class New Yorkers also flocked to the park for winter skating and summer concerts on Saturday afternoons, stringent rules governed the use of the park—for example, bans on Sunday concerts and group picnics—and discouraged many working-class German and Irish immigrants from visiting the park in its first years. Over time, however, New Yorkers repeatedly contested rules regulating the park's use, and in the last third of the century it became more democratic. In the 1880s, working-class New Yorkers successfully campaigned to have concerts on Sunday, their only day of rest. Park commissioners gradually permitted other activities on Sunday: visits to the very popular zoo, the carousel, goat rides, tennis on the lawns, and bicycling on the drives.

Throughout the nineteenth century, Central Park, like the Croton Water system and other public works, was caught in the midst of partisan political fights. In 1857 a Republican-dominated state legislature had appointed the first Central Park Commission (1857–1870) with an eye to keeping the park out of the hands of local Democrats. By 1865, the reform-minded lawyer Andrew Green had turned the Central Park Commission into New York City's first nonpartisan planning agency with responsibility for laying out uptown streets in addition to managing the park. In 1870 a new city charter restored Central Park to home rule, with park commissioners appointed by the mayor. With management of the park once more entangled in the thick of city politics, the commissioners became more attentive to the demands of working-class constituents, who were also voters.

In the early twentieth century, residents of immigrant neighborhoods along the park's borders pushed attendance to its all-time high. Progressive reformers joined many working-class New Yorkers in advocating the introduction of facilities for active recreation. When plans were announced to drain the old rectangular reservoir at the park's center, for example, Progressives and working-class supporters urged that it be replaced by a sports arena, swimming pool, and playing fields. Other New Yorkers—imbued with the ideals of the City Beautiful movement—proposed instead a formal civic plaza and promenade linking the two museums at the park's east and west borders. Landscape architects and preservationists campaigned against these design innovations, however, and the site of the reservoir was naturalistically landscaped into the Great Lawn. Such debates over modifications of the Greensward Plan and the proper uses of a public park have continued into the present.

In the 1930s, Robert Moses, who headed a new, centralized, citywide park system after 1934, favored using the park in ways suggested by the Progressives. With the assistance of New Deal money, Moses built 20 playgrounds on the park's periphery, renovated the zoo, realigned the drives to accommodate automobiles, added athletic fields, and expanded recreational programming. In the early 1950s and early 1960s, private benefactors contributed new skating rinks as well as a boathouse, theater, children's zoo, and other facilities. By the time Moses ended his service of 26 years, he had reshaped the face of the park.

The 1960s brought a new style to the park. Mayor John Lindsay's two park commissioners, Thomas Hoving and August Heckscher, welcomed "happenings," rock concerts, and be-ins to the park, making it a symbol of both urban revival and the counterculture. In the 1970s, however, severe budget cuts during a fiscal crisis, a long-term decline in maintenance, and the revival of the preservation movement produced another new approach to managing the park. In 1980 the Central Park Conservancy, a private fund-raising organization, took charge and implemented a preservationist agenda that involved restoring key features of the Greensward Plan, including the Sheep Meadow, Bethesda Terrace, and Belvedere Castle. By 1990, the conservancy was contributing more than 50 percent of the public park's budget and exercising substantial control over its future. Nevertheless, ordinary park users—from joggers, disco roller skaters, and softball leagues to bird watchers and nature lovers—continue to shape the character of what remains one of the nation's most important urban public spaces.

—*Elizabeth Blackmar and Roy Rosenzweig*

See also
Downing, Andrew Jackson; Golden Gate Park; Moses, Robert; Olmsted, Frederick Law.
Reference
Rosenzweig, Roy, and Elizabeth Blackmar. *The Park and the People: A History of Central Park.* Ithaca, NY: Cornell University Press, 1992.

Central Place Theory

Central place theory is a conceptual statement about how the urban places in a region are related in terms of their number, relative size, spatial arrangements, and economic functions. Within the framework of several assumptions concerning the environmental features of a region (for example, that the region is a uniform plain over which movement is possible in all directions) and the rational economic behavior of both the farm population as consumers and the producers of goods and services in urban centers, the theory allows predictions to be made about the character of the urban hierarchy and the spatial patterning of market areas within the region. The most widely reported of these results is the urban pattern that has the regular hexagonal market areas of the more numerous smaller urban places nested within those of the fewer larger centers.

The term *central place* was coined by the geographer Mark Jefferson in 1931 to refer to the fact that "cities do not grow up of themselves; countrysides set them up to do tasks that must be performed in central places." Jefferson's reference to the functional complementarity that exists between urban places and the surrounding rural regions was by no means new and had been the subject of numerous empirical studies by European geographers and American rural sociologists in the early decades of the century. The later emphasis upon theorizing about urban-rural relations flowed from the work of two German scholars. In 1933 Walter Christaller, a geographer, published his dissertation on the central places of southern Germany, in which he inductively derived laws about the "size, number and distribution of central places." When this book was translated into English in 1957, it was seized upon quickly by geographers, who were seeking to move their discipline in the direction of more quantitative and theoretical work. In 1940 August Lösch, an economist, presented a more formal deductive schema to explain the emergence of a system of urban places and market areas within what he called an "economic landscape." The publication of this treatise in English in 1954 provided a major stimulus to the development of the new field of "regional science."

The theory formulated by Christaller and Lösch has fostered many lines of scholarly activity. On the empirical level, it has provided the framework for many studies of urban systems in different parts of the world. Those of the central United States by Brian Berry and of northern China are the most widely cited. Berry also showed how the theory could be used to analyze the hierarchy of retail centers in a large metropolitan area such as Chicago. On the theoretical front, many have sought to formalize the mathematical statements of the theory, to elaborate upon and extend the economic arguments that underpin it, and to demonstrate how it can be integrated with other forms of theoretical spatial analysis.

—*Leslie J. King*

References
Baskin, C. W. "A Critique and Translation of Walter Christaller's 'Die zentralen Orte in Süddeutschland.'" Ph.D. dissertation, University of Virginia, 1957. Published as *Central Places in Southern Germany.* Englewood Cliffs, NJ: Prentice-Hall, 1966.
Berry, Brian J. L. *Geography of Market Centers and Retail Distribution.* Englewood Cliffs, NJ: Prentice-Hall, 1967.
Christaller, Walter. *Die zentralen Orte in Süddeutschland.* Jena, Germany: Fischer, 1933.
Jefferson, Mark. "Distribution of the World's City Folks." *Geographical Review* 21 (1931): 446–465.
King, Leslie J. *Central Place Theory.* Beverly Hills, CA: Sage Publications, 1984.
Lösch, A. *Die räumliche Ordnung der Wirtschaft.* Jena, Germany: Fischer, 1940. W. H. Woglom and W. F. Stolper, trans. *The Economics of Location.* New Haven, CT: Yale University Press, 1954.
Skinner, G. W. "Marketing and Social Structure in Rural China." *Journal of Asian Studies* 24 (1964): 32–43; 25 (1965): 195–228.

Chain Stores

A chain store is one in a retail group that is owned and operated by a single company. However, the term is commonly used to refer to any store that has a number of outlets providing similar goods or services under the same name. Corporate chains fit the more traditional definition and are comprised of more than ten outlets. The greater number of outlets provide chain store organizations the opportunity to employ centralized buying strategies that afford economies of scale (buying more goods at one time for a lower cost per item). Concomitantly, chain stores make use of mass advertising, develop their own storage and distribution channels, can afford to hire specialized personnel, use market forecasting, and rely on computer inventory tracking and control.

What was to become the first chain store organization was the Great Atlantic & Pacific Tea Company, established in New York City in 1859. A decade later the company owned a chain of six stores. Contrary to its name, the first store carried not only tea, but also coffee, spices, and a limited range of foods. This became the A & P Company, and by 1910 the chain was comprised of 370 full-line grocery stores located exclusively in urban areas. A total of 645 chain store companies existed at the end of World War I. Continued development blossomed until the Depression.

Modern development has been toward larger stores, mall developments, and in some instances, international operations. In order to compete with corporate chains, other types of related organizations have evolved. These are cooperative chains, voluntary chains, and franchises. Cooperative chains are marketing organizations formed by independent retailers. Cooperatives have their own purchasing systems and provide integrated promotional programs. An example of the cooperative chain would be True Value Hardware. Voluntary chains are made up of independently owned stores sponsored by wholesalers in order to gain many of the same benefits corporate chains reap because of their large size. Often these stores have contractual arrangements with wholesalers that determine goods sold, promotions offered, and store design. ACE Hardware and IGA food stores are representative examples. Franchise operations offer a somewhat different chain organization, one that may resemble voluntary chains. Whereas voluntary chains may choose to work with existing retail outlets, franchisers prefer to develop their own stores and train personnel from each store's inception. The franchiser develops the goods or services and attendant marketing strategies, leaving implementation to private store owners. Franchisees pay fees or commissions to the franchiser. Risks of business start-up are lessened with this retail method because individual businesses benefit from the reputation, expertise, and marketing experience of the larger fran-

Wal-Mart has become one of the most common stores in suburban America.

chising organization. It has been estimated that first-year business failures for franchise holders are less than 10 percent that of nonfranchisees. By the year 2000 it is estimated that at least half of all retail sales will be through franchise stores. Examples are Arby's Roast Beef restaurants, H & R Block tax preparers, and Howard Johnson motels. Today, franchised outlets blanket city and suburban landscapes from coast to coast.

Chain stores are enlarging their market share in many retail segments, currently accounting for 60 percent of grocery sales and 97 percent of department store sales. The Wal-Mart corporate chain, with nearly 1,400 stores in 32 states, overtook Sears as the nation's largest retailer in 1990, grossing over $32 billion.

However, chain status does not guarantee success, as the demise of W. T. Grant and the shrinking of the chain store founder, A & P, attest. Part of the chain store appeal is attributed to providing familiar shopping options to an increasingly mobile society. Conversely, chains are accused of homogenizing the shopping experience and urban life, contributing to a bland cultural sameness from one end of the nation to the other. Hence, in part due to the proliferation of chain stores of all types, our cities and suburbs seem increasingly alike.

—*Barlow Soper*

References

Berman, Barry, and Joel R. Evans. *Retail Management: A Strategic Approach.* 5th ed. New York: Macmillan, 1992.

Boone, Louis E., and David L Kurtz. *Contemporary Marketing.* 7th ed. Fort Worth, TX: Dryden Press, 1992.

McCarthy, E. Jerome, and William D. Perreault, Jr. *Basic Marketing: A Global Managerial Approach.* 11th ed. Homewood, IL: Irwin, 1993.

Phillips, Charles F., and Delbert J. Duncan. *Marketing Principles and Methods.* 6th ed. Homewood, IL: Irwin, 1968.

Stanton, William J., Michael J. Etzel, and Bruce Walker. *Fundamentals of Marketing.* New York: McGraw-Hill, 1991.

Chaplin, Charlie (1889–1977)

Charles Spencer (Charlie) Chaplin's movie persona, the Little Fellow, was one of the most widely recognized figures in the world in the 1920s and 1930s. A versatile writer/director and gifted actor whom George Bernard Shaw called "the only genius in motion pictures," Chaplin was intimately related to the urban world; he was born and raised in a city, his films often used urban settings, and he first achieved fame when movies were primarily an urban phenomenon.

Chaplin's account of his early years in *My Autobiography* (1964) reads almost like a Dickens novel. Born in London in 1889, his parents were both English music-hall singers. His father, an alcoholic, separated from the family in 1890, providing only minimal and sporadic support for his son before his own death in 1901. Ill health and an ailing voice ended Chaplin's mother's singing career in the middle 1890s. She was in and out of hospitals and asylums with physical and emotional problems for the next five years while Chaplin and his older half brother, Sydney, shuttled between a variety of urban homes and institutions. By late 1898, Chaplin secured his first job as a performer, and he continued working in the theater and in music-hall comedy troupes until he accepted a contract to join Mack Sennett's Keystone Studio in 1913.

Working with three movie companies between 1913 and 1918, Chaplin appeared in 61 films, most of them one- and two-reelers, directing all of them after the middle of 1914. Shortly after arriving at Keystone, he began wearing the costume that became his trademark—a tight-fitting coat, baggy pants, floppy shoes, a derby hat, a narrow mustache, and a cane. The character Chaplin created—known variously as the Little Fellow, the Tramp, or Charlie—served as his comic screen persona in nearly all of his films through *Modern Times* (1936).

This persona became an almost immediate success in urban movie theaters, creating by 1915 what one movie commentator called a national case of "Chaplinitis." Each contract he signed was more lucrative, and in 1918 he decided to build his own movie studio. This ensured him a high degree of financial and creative control that was solidified when in 1919 he joined movie stars Douglas Fairbanks and Mary Pickford, and director D. W. Griffith, to found United Artists, a company that would distribute the films that each of the founders produced independently. All of the movies he made between 1923 and 1951 were distributed through United Artists.

Although Chaplin's movies occasionally satirized rural or small-town life—*Sunnyside* (1919) and *The Pilgrim* (1922) are two examples—they more often had urban settings. Among his shorter films, *Easy Street* (1917), *A Dog's Life* (1918), and *The Kid* (1921) portrayed urban poverty and working-class life in particularly effective ways. His feature films often had urban settings as well, contrasting different classes in urban society or depicting urban versus rural characters. *A Woman of Paris* (1923) poses rural simplicity against urban cosmopolitanism. Chaplin's two greatest films focusing on urban concerns were *City Lights* (1931) and *Modern Times* (1936). The first contrasted the lower-class but humane world of the blind girl with the upper-class luxury and hypocrisy of the millionaire. The second comically portrayed the dislocations engendered by industrialism and the Depression. *The Great Dictator* (1940), Chaplin's satiric attack on Hitler and Nazism, contrasted life in the palace with life in a Jewish urban ghetto. The central setting of *Monsieur Verdoux* (1947) was Paris, *Limelight* (1952) took place in London before World War I, and *A King of New York* (1957) used that city as the setting for a satire on advertising, wide-screen movies, progressive education, and McCarthyism.

Chaplin's progressive political sympathies eroded his popularity in the early Cold War years. After having his reentry permit to the United States revoked while en route to England for the opening of *Limelight* in 1952, Chaplin settled on a Swiss manor, where he lived until his death in 1977. Although the baronial splendor of his final years differed vastly from the urban working-class world in which he was raised, Chaplin will be remembered for the Charlie persona at the center of his best movies. Just as Davy Crockett and Daniel Boone were mythic prototypes of the American frontier in the nineteenth century, Chaplin's Little Fellow was a key mythic representative of the twentieth-century urban American landscape.

—*Charles J. Maland*

See also
Motion Pictures and Cities; Sennett, Mack.

References
Chaplin, Charlie. *My Autobiography.* New York: Simon and Schuster, 1964.
Gehring, Wes. *Charlie Chaplin: A Bio-Bibliography.* Westport, CT: Greenwood Press, 1983.
Lyons, Timothy J. *Charles Chaplin: A Guide to References and Resources.* Boston: G. K. Hall, 1979.
Maland, Charles J. *Chaplin and American Culture: The Evolution of a Star Image.* Princeton, NJ: Princeton University Press, 1989.
Robinson, David. *Chaplin: His Life and Art.* New York: McGraw-Hill, 1985.

Charity

Charity refers simply to acts or habits of kindness and has historically been associated with voluntary material aid given privately by either individuals or institutions. Today, private charity is generally at the margins of voluntarism and is likely to be despised as demeaning by its recipients and inconvenient or unnecessary by public opinion. The historical precedents for the current status of charity are complex, and they originate in preindustrial, preurban cultures.

European settlers of North America in the early seventeenth century had already begun to depart from older ecclesiastical models of charity and poor relief when they arrived in the New World. The image of the role of the church in caring for the infirm or needy or in relieving poverty and want is accurate as long as this picture is understood to be the exception. While the pattern of private, secular, and communal relief rested on deep Christian principles, the church itself was never intended to be the primary agency of relief. From the beginning, care and relief were predicated on a combination of congregational, individual, civic, and local responsibility for the poor and needy, and from the start a distinction was made between those deserving and those not deserving charity.

In the more egalitarian rural communities of New England and the Middle Atlantic colonies during the seventeenth and eighteenth centuries, where poverty was minimal, there was still a need to care for the old, the infirm, the orphaned, and the widowed. The plantation economies of the Chesapeake and tidewater Carolina, based as they were on slaves and indentured servants, created a culture of direct paternalism and dependency from the start. Only in the small farming communities of the southern backcountry did communities collectively provide relief from poverty or need.

The division between the responsibility of the church and that of civil government was ironically foreseen in the holiest of social experiments, the Massachusetts Bay Colony. John Winthrop's "City upon a Hill" blended ecclesiastical and civil authority in such a way that a town and its congregation comprised a single body politic that was simultaneously civil and religious. Winthrop's clear belief that a town must act as moral and material guardian and provider is best illustrated by his observation that while all classes are "knit together . . . as one man" in the ideal Christian community, "God almightie in his . . . providence hath soe disposed of the Condicion of Mankinde, as in all times some must be rich some poore, some highe and eminent in power and dignitie; others meane and in subjeccion." Winthrop then placed responsibility for the care of one's needy "neighbours" on the shoulders of individual Christians acting upon the imperative of Christian "Charitie."

To Winthrop and his contemporaries, the concepts of charity, philanthropy, and alms—meaning affection, love of man, and pity, respectively—had been bound together in the principles of caring and giving. But they did not advocate distributing caring and giving indiscriminately. As a later Puritan divine, Cotton Mather, was quick to make clear, the needy were always to be divided into two distinct types: those needing charity or aid because of misfortune, and those depending on charity because of their own idleness and profligacy, the "able poor" and "sturdy beggars" set against the "undeserving poor."

Slowly, however, the theocratic part of this model eroded in the eighteenth century, while its civil and individual parts remained in place as the public and private guarantors of charitable aid until the New Deal nationalized welfare in the twentieth century. In New England and the Middle Atlantic states, the transformation of charity into public welfare, though always based on Christian ethics, occurred first in the port cities of Boston, New York, and Philadelphia. By the early eighteenth century, America's few cities were managing poverty and need through civic agencies that controlled public relief funds and also managed or administered the bulk of private charity. The public administration of welfare was slower to reach into the more intimate, personalized village and plantation societies of preindustrial America.

Within the first few decades of the eighteenth century, the secular nature of charity was becoming more visible. Indeed, the founding of Georgia in 1733 was designed to relieve epidemic levels of poverty in London and was mostly a secular but genuinely philanthropic venture, at least briefly. Moreover, the populist and emotive Christian revivalism of the Great Awakening in the 1730s and 1740s was accompanied by a practical charitable impulse. George Whitefield's schemes included meshing orphanages with Christian morality, and the ideas that William Tennent, a Presbyterian minister, preached to his students at Log College were equal parts educational philanthropy, indoctrination, and Christian populism.

Perhaps Winthrop's version of the scriptural prediction that "the poor always ye have with you" was not a suitable credo 150 years later when the founding fathers suggested that Republican perfectibility might prevent the poverty and want that characterized Europe. But even before the Revolution, a tension existed between the reality of social inequality and the belief that every citizen had an opportunity and a responsibility to be self-sufficient while simultaneously displaying Christian altruism toward society's failures. The firm establishment of secular authority in America during the Revolution, and the absence of a single state church, resulted in the peculiarly American system of a largely Christian population with no direct, universal role for any single ecclesiastical authority. As a result, Anglicans only helped Anglicans and Baptists other Baptists, and all sects tended to exclude noncommunicants. Just as America had manifested a social and political pluralism, it had also developed a Christian pluralism.

In the early republic, the charitable role of churches remained as it had always been: local, sectarian, and aimed primarily at the deserving poor and needy. In the 50 years after the Revolution, in ways that transcended sectarian Christianity and the moral distinction between the able and the impotent, a three-way system of relief emerged that was firmly in place by the Jacksonian Era. First, the church-based mechanisms of aid remained, mostly for deserving parishioners. This system was augmented and slowly displaced in many urban areas by the phenomenal growth of voluntary associations, each having a special focus, such as educating orphans, feeding widows, or rehabilitating crippled seamen. In the northern states, between the founding of the national government and the 1830s, hundreds of these organizations were formed as republican ideology meshed with notions of virtue, social responsibility, and citizenship. Voluntarism, charity, and social reform became the hallmarks of civic benevolence. But the third strut of the aid structure was the most vital; it was the public one.

Among the distinguishing features of the public or government role in providing welfare was the fact that local and state governments continued to oversee the needy who fell under public responsibility, including all those who were neglected or rejected either by churches or voluntary associations. However, in terms of change, it is important to recognize that public authority was responsible solely for the undeserving poor. Also, while the former colonies had created a national government with significant power, that government had neither the philosophical disposition nor the overt mandate to fund, standardize, or otherwise become involved in providing welfare or relief. Indeed, until the revolutionary changes of the 1930s, all public welfare depended on states and municipalities.

At least until the middle of the nineteenth century, American society remained parochial and predominantly agrarian. As late as 1900, the majority of Americans lived in intimate communities where dispensing aid could still be personalized, and older notions that private charity offered mutual benefits to both donor and recipient prevailed. But even as agrarian America grew and thrived, urban America boomed. As early as the 1840s, older cities like Boston and New York were forced to confront significant changes in their social composition. Foreign immigration and internal migration added complexity to urban populations, including rising levels of poverty and need even in the most affluent times and places. Also, as America moved west, it built new cities that, like older ones in the East, contained substantial populations of dependent poor, infirm, aged, and orphaned. In the South before the Civil War, poverty and need were handled less by the methods of northern cities and seaports and more by older patriarchal networks.

Meanwhile, behavioral theories and rationalism began to replace Providence as the chief explanations for socioeconomic misfortune. Statistical determinism became a byword in treating poverty. It was widely believed that a supported population of poor people would multiply to the point of Malthusian strain, and a shift in thinking emphasized control over care, and punishment and discipline over succor, at least for the undeserving poor. More of the poor were now thought to be undeserving, especially in terms of Manifest Destiny's promise of economic opportunity and mobility for all.

By the middle of the nineteenth century, the majority of poor and dependent Americans who did not qualify for aid from churches or voluntary associations were either left to destitution or were incarcerated. During the eighteenth century in New York, Philadelphia, and Boston, for example, the majority of the needy had been aided out-of-doors (that is, at home), but in those same cities, as well as in newer cities, in the nineteenth century it became the norm to commit all public charges to institutions for rehabilitation or control. The eighteenth century almshouse (a combination of public shelter, hospice, and sanctuary) was complemented first by the workhouse (where the "able" or "idle" poor were put to work), and then both were fused into the generic poorhouse that characterized the popular image of public charity in the nineteenth century, and even today colors our understanding of institutional relief in that era.

The institutionalization of dependency and deviance was mostly complete by the Civil War and included lunatic asylums and separate homes for each kind of the infirm: the old, the orphaned, unmarried mothers, and others increasingly categorized as "deviant." A self-consciously prospering and egalitarian America preferred to sequester its public charges. By the end of the nineteenth century, the diminishing private sources of charity had become so selective and morally conditional that the country's growing lower-class, urban populations during the Gilded Age presented ready subjects for the surge of reform movements that characterized the Progressive Era.

Activists as diverse in outlook, experience, and reputation as Jane Addams, Robert La Follette, and Andrew Carnegie, along with church, social, and professional organizations, came to share a humanitarianism that questioned whether dependents were responsible for their misfortunes. In varying degrees, each came to reflect the great Progressive credo that "the system," rather than individuals, created poverty and deviance. Jane Addams's Settlement House model took middle-class charity into the heart of slums, not only in Chicago but throughout the country and also encouraged delivering aid to the homes of the poor. While it sought to reform individual behavior, the charitable thrust of Addams's humanitarianism also sought to reform the public to help victims of the intensively capitalist urban growth.

Meanwhile, at the level of state governments, the "Wisconsin Idea" and its premise that democratic government itself could be the engine of reform began to affect all aspects of American life. Its legacy, and La Follette's, led indirectly to a more benign and eventually a national reevaluation of the role of elected governments in providing public welfare. Andrew Carnegie's stature as one of America's preeminent capitalists, and the association of his success with his self-proclaimed "Gospel of Wealth," otherwise known as the gospel of self-help, should not obscure his ultimate conversion to an older kind of largesse. If Carnegie had made respectable the ethic of "rugged individualism" and the accumulation of a huge fortune through profit, his later actions suggested that philanthropy was a social obligation that could benefit the giver as well as the recipient in a secularized version of colonial clergymen's view of Christian charity. Thus, the most prominent erstwhile "custodian of the nation's wealth" became a self-proclaimed custodian of the nation's well-being by donating a substantial part of his treasure to improving the lot of the lower classes who now seemed to be a permanent feature of urban life. Carnegie's endowments of libraries and educational institutions sought to attenuate ignorance and help the poor and marginal to compete with the more fortunate members of society. It was really large-scale, permanent philanthropy as a form of old-fashioned charity. While his foundation and those of the Rockefellers, Fords, and other philanthropists would not countenance "handouts" to the poor, the overall effect of their trusts was to acknowledge an obligation to help the less fortunate, and to make larger-scale, even governmental, relief programs acceptable and respectable.

It can be said that Carnegie in fact helped to nationalize a modern form of charity. At the same time, other forces in the early twentieth century helped confirm the need for a radical new approach to what now seemed to be fixed social problems. The net effect of Progressive muckraking and reform was increased awareness of the new conditions of urban, industrial life. For example, the child labor and the tenement conditions revealed in the photographs of Jacob Riis and Lewis Hine would likely not have surprised eighteenth-century realists like Alexander Hamilton, had they seen them, but the images shocked a generation perhaps still assuming that human progress and social equality were yet possible.

For the most part, however, the models for aid established by Progressives lay fallow until the Depression. It is worth noting, too, that the new Christian concern for the poor and needy that began in the Progressive Era seemed to emerge more fully in the 1920s with the appearance of conservative sectarianism, nativism, and normalcy. The social gospel gave way before a sharp-edged revivalism that linked material scarcity with moral weakness. Yet the devastating collapse of the economy, perhaps more than any other factor, reconfirmed the Progressives' belief that the system could create want as well as alleviate it. The New Deal began as a clump of experiments to manage the effects of economic collapse, but

as the Depression seemed to touch all classes and was clearly more than just a grand test of the poor to compete or cope, the federal government eventually rationalized social and welfare programs as national rights. More important, the Depression firmly entrenched the federal government as guarantor of those rights. It elevated Franklin D. Roosevelt to the status of national benefactor and protector, and his image as the charitable head of the charitable government of a charitable nation remains strong.

Even more important, the legacy of the New Deal persists despite some of its conspicuous failures and the politicization of state charity or—more appropriately—welfare. Lyndon Johnson's "War on Poverty" in the 1960s became a lightning rod for discussion of the ends and means of public welfare. Such concepts as "deserving" and "undeserving" were revived in the great public debate that accompanied President Clinton's proposed expansion of Medicare programs for the poor and the Republican Party's 1994 "Contract with America" that explicitly identified separate spheres and responsibilities for public and private welfare and charity. The definition of poverty has changed, too, as political, economic, and social conditions and values have changed. What is meant by "dependence" today would hardly have mattered 300 years ago. Can the charitable cases of the 1690s even be compared with the welfare cases of the 1990s? When it is said that 20 percent of Americans live "below the poverty line," how can that be measured against the rates of poverty in colonial cities?

As the nature and objectives of community and family have changed, so too have American assumptions about rights and obligations. Who today would use the word "alms" (pity) to describe government aid to the poor at home (out-of-doors)? Legislation to put welfare recipients to work, or to ban begging in public, or to relocate the homeless, or to deny material aid to unwed mothers are reminiscent of nineteenth- and even eighteenth-century approaches to people at the margins of security. Yet, how many Americans would tolerate, regardless of their other values, the sequestering or incarceration of the "idle poor" in workhouses? More important, perhaps, is the fact that the means and ends of charity, however we understand that term, have moved away from direct and personal application.

There appears to be no prospect for sufficient private individual or collective sources of charity to meet the needs of the poor. Charities such as the United Way, for example, are financially and strategically limited, as are most privately generated benevolent funds. Together with the great philanthropic trusts, their resources would not scratch the surface of need, and the sheer dimensions of public funding obligations, specifically those of the national government, make any private alternative unfeasible. Several million families receive

It was once common for sidewalk Santa Clauses to collect money for charity during the holiday season.

direct support each year, often complete support, from various levels of government. Until the "welfare reform" of the late 1990s, the federal government spent 20 percent of its budget, or several hundred billion dollars, on various relief and support programs. What does it mean, then, that the richest man in the world, Bill Gates, donates $200 million for computers for the needy? If millionaire entertainment and sports celebrities attach their names to golf tournaments to raise money for specific constituencies of the poor, is that charity? Does that alleviate want? Or are the taxes generated and paid by Bill Gates and Michael Jordan part of what should now be acknowledged as charity?

Today, many inner cities in the United States have become welfare enclaves, and even in areas of full employment there is significant demand for economic assistance. It has become one of the conditions of citizenship, in fact, to expect government, in some way, to attend to want. That is hardly what John Winthrop had in mind when he urged his fellow communicants and citizens to care for the unfortunate collectively, but it may still resemble his insights about the structure of society, even as the Christian imperative to be charitable seems to have become marginalized.

—*Eric G. Nellis*

See also
Philanthropy.
References
Bremner, Robert H. *American Philanthropy.* 2d ed. Chicago: University of Chicago Press, 1988.
Dawley, Alan. *Struggles for Justice: Social Responsibility and the Liberal State.* Cambridge, MA: Harvard University Press, 1991.
Harrington, Michael. *The Other America: Poverty in the United States.* Baltimore: Penguin Books, 1962.
Patterson, James T. *America's Struggle against Poverty, 1900–1994.* 3d ed. Cambridge, MA: Harvard University Press, 1994.
Wright, Conrad E. *The Transformation of Charity in Postrevolutionary New England.* Boston: Northeastern University Press, 1992.

Charleston, South Carolina

Founded in 1670 as Charles Town, the settlers soon moved to a nearby peninsula where the Ashley and Cooper Rivers come together and flow into the Atlantic. By the early 1700s Charles Town was the major port of Carolina and a booming, boisterous frontier town. Approximately 3,500 persons had crowded into the heavily fortified port and its 250 dwellings.

The town was a multiethnic society, a potpourri of nationalities, religions, and racial groups and a Babel of languages and sounds. Even though fires, epidemic diseases, and devastating hurricanes frequently swept through the town, and its inhabitants feared insurrection by black slaves, the economy flourished and grew from the export of low-country rice and the importation of African slaves. Approximately 40 percent of all Africans involuntarily shipped to North America entered across Charles Town's wharves.

Between 1750 and 1770 the population of Charles Town doubled, growing from about 6,000 to 12,000 people, equally divided between black slaves and free whites, and it ranked fourth in population among English colonial cities in North America behind Philadelphia, New York, and Boston. At the same time, power became concentrated in the hands of a tiny elite who had grown wealthy in land and slaves and who were linked by marriage.

The principal city of South Carolina, and its capital, was also becoming the capital of the southern colonies and developing a colorful and varied cultural and intellectual life. The crossroads of Broad and Meeting Streets came to be considered the center of town; and a Customs House was designed and built at the foot of Broad Street. The town's first suburbs were even laid out.

In 1763 the British government, facing a huge war debt, soon declared new colonial policies that ultimately contributed to a revolution in the relationship between Britain and most of its North American colonies. The London government passed a series of acts raising taxes to retire some of the indebtedness, and these measures alarmed Charles Town's well-to-do who considered the measures threats to their own prerogatives. Christopher Gadsden organized Charles Town's "Sons of Liberty" and local opposition to the acts. Prominent South Carolinians met in Charles Town in 1775 in the First Provincial Congress and endorsed the actions of the First Continental Congress. Local Loyalists cheered rumors that slaves in South Carolina had received arms from the British, but the rumors revived old fears of slave insurrections. Several Tories were tarred and feathered, and one African American was hanged. As the threat of revolution approached, Charles Town's elite realized that the revolt against England was also about who should rule at home. A sea and land expedition against Charles Town by British forces in 1776 was unsuccessful, and Charles Town's revolutionaries approved the Declaration of Independence, making South Carolina an independent state. A second British invasion was thwarted, but an invasion by 10,000 British forces in 1780 captured the last open major seaport in the South. The fall of Charles Town was the greatest victory of the war for the British.

At war's end, the legislature incorporated the city of Charleston, which was then divided into 13 wards, each with a warden elected by its free, white, male taxpayers. In turn, the wardens selected the city's chief executive officer, first called the intendant and later the mayor. Much to the dis-

pleasure of Charlestonians, the capital of the state was transferred to Columbia.

In the 1790s, hundreds of French refugees fled to Charleston from the revolutions in Paris and Haiti. These immigrants took various jobs, and the quality of musical performances and the theater improved. The refugees also brought with them an increased fear of black insurrections. In 1800 the city's population was nearly 19,000, and blacks exceeded whites by 2,000. The city had slipped to fifth in size in the United States, but it was on the eve of a boom in rice and cotton prices and enormous profits in the slave trade. Despite this economic prosperity, efforts by the city council to clean up the city did little to stem the outbreak of disease, and 25 epidemics of yellow fever swept through the city between 1800 and 1860.

Charlestonians again plunged into privateering when the United States declared war on Great Britain in 1812. Forts Moultrie and Johnson and Castle Pinckney were garrisoned and armed, and a line of fortifications was again built across the neck of the peninsula. During the years after the war, Charleston's economy once more stagnated due to poor rail connections westward, its shallow harbor, and an insufficient variety of exports. Nevertheless, the city remained the economic, social, and cultural capital of low-country planters. Here they built summer homes to escape the isolation and sickly season on their plantations. From January through March, the planter elite brought their families to Charleston to enjoy the social season, which featured horse races, balls, and the theater. The planters' emphasis on family connections, sociability, and conspicuous leisure influenced the city's character strongly.

William Gilmore Simms was antebellum Charleston's most famous literary figure, but he disliked the local attitude toward intellectual life and the treatment accorded his works. Simms, Henry Timrod, and Paul Hamilton Hayne, who all cared about ideas, met at Russell's Book Store during the 1850s, but the city's physicians and naturalists made the greatest contributions to its intellectual life and helped make Charleston the center of southeastern scientific activity.

During the late antebellum period, local businessmen used their influence to invest municipal money in ways that they hoped would revive the city's economy. By the early 1850s, Charleston had become the manufacturing center of the state. But competing railroads soon siphoned off traffic, and the city remained a "colonial" outpost of the northeastern regional system. Its population of 40,522 made Charleston the twenty-second largest city in the nation in 1859; but its rank of eighty-fifth in manufacturing may be a better indication of the city's declining importance. It was also the most populous South Atlantic port and the major distribution center for the state.

In April 1860 the Democratic National Convention met in Charleston but dissolved into factions. When the nominee of the Republican Party, Abraham Lincoln, was elected president, delegates from across South Carolina convened in Charleston and adopted an Ordinance of Secession from the Union. On December 26, Major Robert Anderson, commanding a federal garrison, moved his troops to Fort Sumter in Charleston harbor, and a few days later, in the first formal military encounter of the war, South Carolina troops seized three local sites occupied by federal troops. Following formation of the Confederate States of America, General Pierre G. T. Beauregard demanded that Fort Sumter surrender. When Major Anderson refused, Beauregard ordered bombardment of the fort on April 12, 1861, and Anderson surrendered the following day. President Lincoln then called for 75,000 volunteers and the blockade of southern ports.

General Robert E. Lee arrived in Charleston on November 6 to take command of the Military Department of South Carolina, Georgia, and Florida. The next day, Hilton Head Island, Port Royal, and Beaufort fell to Union forces, and Charlestonians panicked. Union strategists were determined to seize Charleston, which they considered "the cradle of secession," but two attempts failed. After a third combined attack by the Union army and navy occupied most of Morris Island opposite Charleston in July 1863, costly heroic attacks by black troops failed to seize the last remaining Confederate redoubt. Union forces then began a bombardment of the city that continued for 587 days. Occasional daring military exploits briefly boosted the spirits of Charlestonians, and in early 1864 the CSN *Hunley* became the first submarine to sink an enemy vessel. But in mid-February 1865 Charleston was no longer defensible, and it was evacuated. Union forces immediately seized the city and described it as "a city of ruins, of desolation."

For nearly two centuries Charleston had been the most important city in either the Carolinas or Georgia. Charlestonians had largely controlled South Carolina, and that state had strongly influenced southern policies from about 1837 to 1862. But in the next three years, the city lost forever both its wealth and its influence.

Unlike whites, black Charlestonians and the ex-slaves who poured into the city welcomed Union troops. Well-to-do whites trickled back to the city, angrily complaining about the "utter topsy-turveying" of institutions; but those whose health and fortunes survived the war soon enjoyed again the social life for which the city was famous. The growing bitterness and distance between whites and blacks was reflected in occasional riots and by blacks leaving white churches to establish their own. The city's white voters elected an ex-Confederate colonel mayor along with a white council, and blacks remained disfranchised. Passage of the Reconstruc-

tion Acts in 1867 gave black men the right to vote, and blacks in the city immediately organized a local Republican Party.

The next year, in November 1868, Charleston voters, black and white, elected a northern Republican as mayor and a number of African Americans to the city council. Democrats charged that "intimidation and violence" marred the election, but in the gubernatorial election of 1877, in Charleston as elsewhere in South Carolina, "Hampton's Red Shirts" brandished weapons to keep blacks from voting. Wade Hampton became governor of the state, and white Democrats claimed to have "redeemed" it. No Republicans, either black or white, were elected to Charleston's city council from 1883 to 1967, and local elections were really decided by the all-white Democratic primary, which functioned like a private club and effectively barred black participation in the electoral process. Political control of the city remained in the hands of the "Broad Street Ring," a clique of Charleston's businessmen and lawyers.

The city of 50,000 people remained South Carolina's major port, its rail and trade center, and its largest city. But compared to other urban centers of the New South, the economy of Charleston remained anemic, partly due to the city's aging business leadership. Likewise, the lifestyle that had characterized the city before the war persisted. The city and its economy also suffered in 1885 and 1886 as a hurricane and then an earthquake devastated Charleston; a few years later, another hurricane slammed into Charleston and the nearby sea islands, irreparably damaging the phosphate-mining industry. A new rail axis from southwest to northeast bypassed Charleston completely and made it a commercial backwater by 1900.

For their cultural life, white Charlestonians patronized the local Opera House where they enjoyed musicals and minstrels, and during the summer months they attended open-air concerts on the Battery. They also enjoyed their whiskey in local bars despite a state-owned liquor monopoly that prohibited drinking places. At the end of the nineteenth century, whites blamed rising crime rates on the increased African-American population, which comprised 56 percent of the city's population of 55,000 by 1900, the highest black-to-white ratio of any southern city. The annual homicide rate averaged 20 per 100,000 people, while Boston's was only 6, and homicides were double the national average by 1970. At the end of the century, laws segregated blacks in all public and private facilities, and African Americans who continued to live anywhere in Charleston experienced tightening residential segregation.

By the early 1900s, new money arrived in the Charleston area with the relocation of a federal naval yard that was paying 20 percent of all wages in the area in several years. Charleston progressives touted the city as a trading center, aided secondary education, built playgrounds, and promoted tourism. But the city's anemic economy persisted even though World War I expanded the Charleston Navy Yard tremendously. By 1920 Charleston and its suburbs included a population of about 100,000. The city's health officer continued to advocate the extension of sewer and water lines to black residential districts, where death rates were twice those of whites. This disparity highlighted the racial bias of a political process that unevenly distributed the city's resources for health and sanitation.

Concerned about the threat to the city's historic structures, in 1920 a group of well-to-do Charlestonians founded the Charleston Society for the Preservation of Old Dwellings. Later renamed the Preservation Society of Charleston, the organization pushed a zoning ordinance through the city council to protect the historic district. The law became a model for other cities. About the same time, local writers founded the Poetry Society of South Carolina, called for a southern "poetic renaissance," and invited authors to the city to give readings, which stimulated the growth of similar organizations.

The Depression settled over the land in 1929, and in the early 1930s Charleston could not pay its bonded indebtedness. The Broad Street Ring nominated and elected mayor a member of the low-country elite, Burnet Rhett Maybank, who soon returned the city to a cash basis. His friendships with high officials in Washington funneled $41 million in federal funds from New Deal agencies to Charleston between 1933 and 1939, and these funds saved the local economy from complete collapse. Maybank launched the city's first slum clearance program, and soon health conditions in the city were finally tracking those nationally.

World War II revived Charleston's moribund economy. In 1941 alone, the federal defense program poured $136 million into South Carolina, and 80 percent of that money flowed into the Charleston area. As a result, the Navy Yard supplanted tourism as the low country's largest and most important industry. By the end of the war, Charleston was surrounded by instant suburbs. The influence of First District Congressman Mendel Rivers insured a continuing flood of federal funds into the low country even after the war was long over.

Significant change began to occur after a federal court judge declared South Carolina's all-white primary unconstitutional, a decision upheld by other courts on appeal. In the 1950s, Charleston's mayors—recognizing that African Americans now had become important new voters—began appointing them to city jobs. But in 1955 the number of city aldermen was reduced from 24 to 12 at-large aldermen appointed by the mayor, a change intended to keep the Broad Street establishment in power. The city government also worked closely with the State Ports Authority, and by the early 1970s Charleston ranked twelfth nationally in the value of cargo handled.

At the beginning of the 1960s, Charleston was still a city of thoroughly segregated neighborhoods and public facilities. Early in the decade, the Carolina Student Movement Association launched sit-ins, and within a year the courts had ended segregated facilities in Charleston. Even so, local civil rights leaders recognized that blacks still lacked equal opportunities, and they took their protests into the streets in 1963. As a result, local businessmen promised to meet black demands, and a biracial committee was formed to address problems. For some years afterward, race relations in Charleston remained among the best in the country. In 1967 the first black in 100 years was elected to the city council.

In 1975 the Broad Street establishment tapped a young Democrat and attorney, Joseph P. Riley, Jr., to run for mayor, and Riley became the city's youngest mayor ever. Taking office with him were an equal number of black and white council members, a phenomenon resulting from the existence of new single-member districts that had recently been created as the result of a suit brought by the U.S. Justice Department. Politically, Charleston was an entirely new city. Riley was reelected five times. During his administrations, he revitalized the downtown, attracted more tourists by luring the Spoleto USA Festival to the city, and appointed Reuben Greenberg as chief of police, an African American who was remarkably effective in fighting crime. A vigorous annexation policy increased the size of the city to more than 41 square miles and its population to more than 80,000 by the late 1980s.

Near midnight on September 21, 1989, Hurricane Hugo slammed into Charleston, wreaking devastation. As in the past, the people of the old storm-prone port slowly dug out of the debris and began rebuilding their shattered homes, businesses, and lives. With the end of the Cold War and the federal decision to reduce the size of Charleston's Naval Yard in the early 1990s, the city increasingly depends on commercial port activity and tourism. The city's government is attempting to lure industries to Charleston to compensate for the diminished federal spending on which Charleston depended for so long.

—*Walter J. Fraser, Jr.*

References

Doyle, Don H. *New Men, New Cities, New South: Atlanta, Nashville, Charleston, Mobile, 1860–1910.* Chapel Hill: University of North Carolina Press, 1990.

Fraser, Walter J., Jr. *Charleston! Charleston! The History of a Southern City.* Columbia: University of South Carolina Press, 1989.

Pease, William H., and Jane H. Pease. *The Web of Progress: Private Values and Public Styles in Boston and Charleston, 1827–1843.* New York: Oxford University Press, 1985.

Powers, Bernard E., Jr. *Black Charlestonians: A Social History, 1822–1885.* Fayetteville: University of Arkansas Press, 1994.

Rogers, George C., Jr. *Charleston in the Age of the Pinckneys.* Norman: University of Oklahoma Press, 1970.

Cheever, John (1912–1982)

Through his powerfully imaginative short stories and novels, John Cheever became one of the foremost interpreters of America's mid-twentieth-century migration to the suburbs. He created the ambiguously named Shady Hill and the more sinister Bullet Park, now familiar to generations of readers as the settings for some of the most disturbing yet lyrical stories in American literary history. He has rightly been called an American Chekhov.

Cheever was born in Quincy, Massachusetts, not far from Boston. After establishing himself as a gifted creator of short, realistic narratives in the 1930s and 1940s, he and his young family joined the postwar migration, leaving New York City for suburban Scarborough. His works were routinely accepted by the *New Yorker, Collier's,* and other mainstream magazines, and critics came to regard him as a polished, if artistically conservative, craftsman. A survey of his work, however, shows him to have been a persistent experimenter who used fantastic and poetic forms to illustrate the paradoxes of American life. In "The Enormous Radio" (1947), one of the few urban-centered stories with which he is identified, he interwove realistic detail with surreal effects to uncover the deceptions of apartment dwellers. Their tribulations hint at the reasons behind the population shift to suburbia—anxieties and dreams that Cheever would later treat ironically. His dissections of the ensuing disillusionments would earn him a place among the masters of American storytelling.

A typical Cheever story derives its force from the tension between the poet's love of rustic beauty and the realist's awareness that lovely suburban exteriors often mask the same dark truths that haunt the city. At every Cheever cocktail party, at least one couple is contemplating divorce and several souls are tormented. Earlier suburban tales like "Roseheath" (1947) blended gentle humor with detached observation to mock the pretensions of tunnel-visioned suburbanites. But as American realities became increasingly complex following the Korean War and continuing through the Cold War, Cheever's patience with the foibles of ordinary humanity became increasingly strained, his perspective more bitter and despairing. In "The Five-Forty-Eight" (1954), the cool self-possession of an executive held hostage by the secretary he has casually seduced is stripped away; at the end of the story he grovels at her feet outside a suburban railway station. His soul has been revealed as a hollow shell adorning the netherworld suspended between city office and country home. Like many of Cheever's characters, the antagonist/protagonist is resident in both, but citizen of neither.

Fantastic reshaping of "real" suburban life is both story subject and medium in stories like "O Youth and Beauty!" (1953) and "The Swimmer" (1964). In the former, protagonist Cash Bentley, beset by financial worries, tries to recapture lost youth by hurling furniture at cocktail parties until his wife shoots him accidentally (or perhaps not) with a starter's pistol. In the latter, Neddy Merrill literally swims across a suburban landscape littered with broken dreams. Half-stupefied by alcohol and his own disillusionment, he finishes his race with the devil at the entrance to his abandoned home in Bullet Park. Merrill's empty house might stand as an icon of Cheever's suburbia—lovely homes, empty lives. At the end of another classic story, "The Country Husband" (1954), the narrator sounds a note of wistful sadness; this time his antihero has tried adultery as an antidote for a miserable marriage—a recurring motif in Cheever's work—and predictably failed. Here, Cheever tempers his mockery with lyric compassion. "Then it is dark; it is a night where kings in golden suits ride elephants over the mountains," and the hour when middle America turns to woodworking or mixed drinks to ease its pain.

Starting with *The Wapshot Scandal* and continuing with *Bullet Park, Falconer,* and *Oh What a Paradise It Seems,* Cheever's novels further anatomize the suburban lifestyles sketched in his short stories, but with limited success. The experimental methods that earned him critical praise as a writer of short stories were less effective in longer narratives, although *Falconer* (1977) represented a dramatic return to prominence for him; he was then recovering from his own struggle with alcoholic depression. As in the short stories, his novelistic depictions of suburban discontent appear to scoff at the rootlessness of his characters. "The people of Bullet Park intend not so much to have arrived there as to have been planted and grown there, but this of course was untrue. Disorder, moving vans, bank loans at high interest, tears, and desperation had characterized most of their arrivals and departures." Invariably, despite their upbeat resolutions, the novels leave their readers with a sense of futility.

Cheever's occasional nostalgia, in the novels and stories, for his boyhood village of St. Botolphs proves to be yet another form of fantasy, not an antidote to the evils he complains of. Ironically, his general avoidance of such issues as racism and inner-city decay makes him seem as naive as one of his own characters, hopelessly wedded to the superficiality he despises. There is some truth in this view, but Cheever's revelations of suburban malaise and the personal struggles that define it are nonetheless a major contribution to American letters.

—*James O'Hara*

References

Bosha, Francis J., ed. *The Critical Response to John Cheever.* Westport, CT: Greenwood Press, 1994.

Donaldson, Scott. *John Cheever: A Biography.* New York: Random House, 1988.

Hunt, George. *John Cheever: The Hobgoblin Company of Love.* Grand Rapids, MI: William B. Eerdmans, 1983.

O'Hara, James. *John Cheever.* Boston: Twayne, 1989.

Chestnut Hill, Pennsylvania

The Chestnut Hill section of Philadelphia provides an excellent example of a suburb that evolved inside city limits, rather than outside them. This is not unusual for older suburbs that were often annexed by adjoining municipalities, or that emerged in sparsely populated areas inside city boundaries.

Before 1854, Chestnut Hill was a small farm community and mill village in the far northwestern corner of what was then Philadelphia County, some ten miles from the central portions of Philadelphia City. In 1854 the city and county of Philadelphia were merged, or "consolidated" as it was then called, the largest such annexation to that time in American history. The consolidation swept Chestnut Hill and several dozen other towns and villages into the much enlarged municipality. It was also in 1854 that Chestnut Hill received the first of two commuter rail lines. This earlier route, for many years a part of the Reading system and now known as the "Chestnut Hill-East" line of the local transit authority, allowed wealthy suburban residents of the Hill to commute daily to and from downtown jobs.

Growing up near the terminus of this railroad was a mid-nineteenth-century residential development that has come to be known as North Chestnut Hill. Most of its Victorian villas, rendered in Italianate, Mansard, and Gothic Revival styles, remain more than a century later, along with other original dwellings, which were remodeled in the Colonial Revival style during the early years of the twentieth century. The use of a locally quarried stone, known as Wissahickon schist, links these otherwise contrasting styles in both texture and color.

Far more significant than North Chestnut Hill is the planned suburban development created on the west side of the community between the early 1880s and the late 1920s. Initiated by Henry Howard Houston (1820–1895) and called Wissahickon Heights, it was continued by Houston's son-in-law, George Woodward, MD (1863–1952), who changed the development's name to St. Martin's in 1907. Houston was an executive and later a board member of the Pennsylvania Railroad, as well as a multifaceted entrepreneur, who left a fortune of $14 million at his death. Son-in-law Woodward was a nonpracticing medical doctor who left an important mark as a Pennsylvania state senator and municipal reformer in the Progressive tradition.

Houston began his real estate development by persuading the Pennsylvania Railroad to build a second commuter line into Chestnut Hill, now known as the "Chestnut Hill-West" line. During the next dozen years, he commissioned approximately 100 houses on Wissahickon Heights, most of them in the Queen Anne style. Woodward added about 180 more residences, first in a Colonial Revival design and later in English vernacular motifs, including a spectacular Cotswold Village completed around 1920.

In addition to these houses, Houston had provided his development with several institutional structures: the Wissahickon Inn, the Philadelphia Cricket Club, and St. Martin-in-the Fields Episcopal Church, the latter lending its name to the neighborhood and the local train station after 1907. Members of the Houston and Woodward families also came forward with generous subsidies for private schools in Wissahickon Heights/St. Martin's, namely Chestnut Hill Academy and the Wissahickon Heights School (later absorbed by the Springside School). Nearly all these structures, as well as the residential properties commissioned or supported by the Houston and Woodward families, were constructed of Wissahickon schist, thus harmonizing them with the suburban properties in North Chestnut Hill.

Unlike most suburban developers, Houston and Woodward rented rather than sold their houses in order to maintain control over who lived in the neighborhood. Their descendants (several of whom continue to reside in the area at the time of this writing) have continued this rental policy with the 200 or so dwellings that remain in their possession.

During the last century, residents of Wissahickon Heights/St. Martin's, as well as of other parts of Chestnut Hill, have often been frustrated by being part of Philadelphia, especially because they have wanted public services and improvements that the city has been unwilling or unable to provide. Wealthy and resourceful "Hillers" have met this challenge by evolving a unique system of quasi-government, an unofficial and extralegal system of local coordination, planning, and sometimes providing and maintaining public works. This practice had its roots in several improvement associations during the late nineteenth and early twentieth centuries. After World War II, these earlier organizations were replaced by the Chestnut Hill Community Association and a number of affiliated civic groups. Thus, in many ways, Chestnut Hill is an interesting and instructive example of the suburb in the city.

—*David R. Contosta*

References

Contosta, David R. *A Philadelphia Family: The Houstons and Woodwards of Chestnut Hill.* Philadelphia: University of Pennsylvania Press, 1988.

———. *Suburb in the City: Chestnut Hill, Philadelphia, 1850–1990.* Columbus: Ohio State University Press, 1992.

Hotchkin, Samuel Fitch. *Ancient and Modern Germantown, Mount Airy, and Chestnut Hill.* Philadelphia: P. W. Ziegler, 1899.

Macfarlane, John J. *History of Early Chestnut Hill.* Philadelphia: The Society, 1927.

Chevy Chase Village, Maryland

Chevy Chase Village, Maryland, exemplifies a planned suburban community of the late nineteenth century whose physical and sociological character has, perhaps, had unrivaled continuity. This achievement was possible because the founding owner-planner and his land companies had sufficient wealth to sustain his coherent vision for as long as necessary. Chevy Chase was further assured political autonomy by its incorporation in Maryland.

Washington, D.C., came of age as a city in the last third of the nineteenth century. In 1871 the old city designed by L'Enfant annexed the surrounding Washington County and multiplied its area sixfold. This newly expanded Washington, D.C., had the sixth largest number of new housing starts in the country in 1889. By 1890, its 23,000 government employees contributed the economic stability of a large federal payroll. Laws passed by Congress assured aesthetic harmony between any new developments and the downtown capital city.

Throughout this period, downtown Washington, unlike the industrial and tenement nightmares of other cities, remained, in most of its neighborhoods, an attractive and interesting place in which to live. Suburbanites were not driven out by hostility toward the city but seduced outward by the charms and promises of the rural ideal. The one dark shadow over this happy civic picture and its romantic environs was racial division and strife. Every suburban subdivision created by a Washington developer in the late nineteenth century was segregated by a formal covenant or an implicit understanding.

Striding onto this stage as if from central casting was Senator Francis Griffith Newlands (1848–1917), a man of wealth, vision, and strength of purpose. As early as 1887, he had advocated a program of improvements for San Francisco, which he said would turn that frontier city into "the Paris of America." He was a personal friend of Frederick Law Olmsted and later became the most ardent supporter of the McMillan Plan for the City of Washington.

Once a law student at George Washington University, he returned to the capital in 1893 as a congressman from Nevada and the trustee and an heir of the fabulous estate of Senator William Sharon. He soon became an inspired developer on a scale rarely matched in his generation. He engaged agents to buy all of the available land contiguous to a then unbuilt Connecticut Avenue that he envisioned running all the way into Maryland. These straw man purchases of some 1,700 largely undeveloped acres were assembled as holdings of the Chevy Chase Land Company, a maneuver saluted by the *Washington Star* as the "most notable transaction that has ever been known in the history of suburban property." His colleagues in Congress helped by "taking 2,000 acres out of the market" to create Rock Creek Park and appropriating funds for a National Zoo as an amenity. Newlands became principal stockholder in the Rock Creek Railway and built the power plants and bridges necessary to run his electrified trolleys along Connecticut Avenue from downtown to suburban Maryland in 35 minutes.

Newlands deeded the finished Connecticut Avenue to the governments of the District of Columbia and Maryland in order to concentrate on the point of it all: a 250-acre subdivision just across the district boundary bearing a name with just the right slightly foreign tone for a better-quality suburb. Newlands was a model of the enlightened progressive entrepreneur. He engaged the New York landscape architect, Nathan F. Barrett, who specified all the plantings. The architect Lindley Johnson, known for designing large country houses, was asked to develop designs for a number of homes that would establish an appropriate style and scale. Newlands also had model water and sewerage systems installed.

No home built on Connecticut Avenue could cost less than $5,000, none on the side streets less than $3,000. Homes on the avenues had to be set back from the street 35 feet, those on the side streets, 25 feet. No lots could be less than 60 feet wide. Restrictive covenants allowed only single-family dwellings to be constructed, and alleys were proscribed. All of this was enough to achieve an impressive but restrained character that did not require either large pieces of land or conformity to a single style of architecture.

All but a few minor commercial services were banned from the village. This forced the development of convenient but geographically segregated businesses on upper Connecticut Avenue just inside the District of Columbia boundary.

Newlands's comprehensive planning vision included social institutions. A troubled hunt club was subsidized to relocate and rename itself the Chevy Chase Club. Newlands himself was elected president of what subsequently became one of America's most exclusive country clubs, emphasizing golf rather than riding to the hounds. He also provided land for a school and paid the teacher's salary. Two of his daughters began a library for the community, and the Episcopal Church was given land to build a parish church on the circle (now named as a memorial to Newlands) that marks the entrance to the village. Later would come a town hall, post office, and fire engine.

The power of Chevy Chase Village to maintain its character for a century in the face of dynamic metropolitan population movement has several sources. Not only totally planned and tightly controlled from the start, it also was completed—unlike most twentieth-century social experiments—while the controls of the original plan were still in effect. More importantly, because the village was located well ahead of the frontier of suburban expansion and because the Chevy Chase Land Company controlled so much of the intervening real estate, the adjacent areas were much more compatible with the village than would have been the case if dozens of private land speculators were involved. Finally, over the years, the social authority, as it were, of the village has tended to influence the quality of surrounding neighborhoods rather than the reverse.

There are ironies embedded in this narrative of success. This exemplary environment of individualism was itself the product of corporate paternalism. The necessary condition of domestic individuality for some 2,000 residents in 700 homes was "a big comprehensive plan" with uncompromising standards both explicit and communal. Moreover, like subdivisions in other cities differentiated along ethnic and class lines, the strength of the subcommunities contributes to the weakness of the entire metropolitan community.

—*Roderick S. French*

References
Atwood, Albert W. *Francis G. Newlands, a Builder of the Nation.* Washington, DC: Newlands, 1969.

French, Roderick S. "Chevy Chase Village in the Context of the National Suburban Movement, 1870–1900." *Records of the Columbia Historical Society* 49 (1976): 300–329.

Lilley, William. "The Early Career of Francis G. Newlands 1848–1897." Ph.D. dissertation, Yale University, 1965.

Robinson, Judith H. "Chevy Chase," In K. S. Smith, ed., *Washington at Home,* 191–201. Northridge, CA: Windsor Publications, 1988.

Chicago, Illinois

The city of Chicago is located on the banks of the Chicago River at the southwest corner of Lake Michigan. The city owes its existence to its relationship with both the river and the lake. From its first "discovery" by the French explorers, Father Jacques Marquette, a Jesuit missionary, and Louis Jolliet, in 1673, the location has provided a vital link between the East Coast and the West. Chicago developed as a connection between the natural resources of the interior of North America and the vast Atlantic market.

Originally the fur trade encouraged the integration of the Chicago region into the expanding European economy, but involvement in Europe's economy also meant involvement in its politics and wars. In 1756 war broke out in Europe and created an offshoot in North America, the French and Indian War. At the end of that war in 1763, France lost its vast North American holdings to England and Spain, and 20 years later political control of the region around Chicago passed to the new United States.

The American Revolution had an important impact on the Chicago region almost immediately. Although Native Americans and French fur trappers had passed through and camped in the area regularly, Jean Baptiste Pointe DuSable, the son of a French fur trader and a black Haitian, came to Chicago in 1781 as its first permanent resident. He had previously lived in St. Joseph, Indiana, but settled in Chicago after being imprisoned for anti-British activities. After his release, DuSable chose the mouth of the Chicago River at Lake Michigan for his new home, and his cabin provided a focus for the local fur trade.

But it took the military campaign of General "Mad" Anthony Wayne to bring American rule to the area; in 1791, Wayne's victories resulted in the Treaty of Greenville, which called for Native Americans to cede their land at the mouth of the Chicago River to the federal government. Wayne suggested erecting a fort at the location, and the U.S. Army built Fort Dearborn in 1803. By that time, DuSable had sold his cabin to Jean La Lime, who in turn sold it to John Kinzie. Fort Dearborn provided an American military presence in the West and a place for trade. The War of 1812 brought about the destruction of the fort by Native Americans; but the new Fort Dearborn, rebuilt by the U.S. government in 1816, marked the permanent establishment of federal power in the area. A lively society of fur traders evolved alongside the military post at the same time that Chicago was becoming a gateway for Yankee migration from New England to the West.

Yankee control over the district meant the quick end of French and Indian cultures, and Chicago grew quickly as a white settlement. Chartered as a town in 1833, Chicago was a city of roughly 5,000 inhabitants only four years later. That same year, 1837, the last Native Americans and many of their French-Indian relations crossed the Mississippi and went west, forced to move by the Blackhawk War and aggressive federal policies.

The opening of the Erie Canal (1825) in New York dramatically changed and improved the geographic connection between Chicago and the East. The new canal joined the Great Lakes directly with New York City and its harbor via the Hudson River. This alliance guaranteed the victory of New York over other Atlantic ports and of Chicago over its rivals. It also reinforced the link between Chicago and the East. In the 1830s Chicago began shipping grain east for the first time and inaugurated a second phase in the area's economic history as farmers replaced fur traders. Chicago soon emerged as a broker between the prosperous eastern seaboard and the agricultural Midwest.

Chicago grew faster than any other American city in the nineteenth century. In 1836 Chicagoans began building their own canal, the Illinois-Michigan Canal, which allowed the city to tap into the Mississippi Valley and compete with St. Louis for western trade. The depression of the 1830s slowed construction, but the canal opened in 1848. This era proved crucial for the city in various ways. In 1847 the McCormick Reaper Works opened in Chicago and helped begin a third phase of the city's economic development. Chicago became an industrial center providing manufactured goods for midwestern farmers. By 1848 the city already contained about 20,000 inhabitants and looked forward to continued growth.

That same year Chicago entrepreneurs embraced another new transportation technology, the railroad, and the Galena-Chicago Union Railroad ushered in a new age. Within six years Chicago emerged as an important railroad hub. The trade routes that had developed as a result of the canals were strengthened and expanded with railroad connections between eastern cities and Chicago. In turn, Chicago's railroads pushed west and crossed the Mississippi.

Chicago's position as a rail center enhanced its position in the national economy during and after the Civil War. The city's population and industrial base increased dramatically between 1850 and 1900. In 1861 Chicago surpassed Cincinnati in the slaughter of hogs, and four years later Chicago investors opened the Union Stock Yard. The stockyard, after the development of refrigeration and refrigerated railroad cars, became the center of the nation's meat industry. Chicago firms also began producing steel because of the city's location near iron ore ranges and coalfields. These factors combined with excellent access to water and rail transportation proved crucial for the industry. With the emergence of meatpacking and the steel industry, the city moved into its fourth economic phase, the production of goods for national and international distribution. After the Civil War, Chicago rose as a major force in the international economy, both as a broker of natural resources and as an industrial giant.

While Chicago grew quickly, it also grew haphazardly. The city was basically wooden; it contained the world's largest lumber yards, shipping lumber from Michigan and Wisconsin throughout the Midwest and West. The balloon frame accounted for much of the city's residential construction, and sidewalks, plank roads, and many city streets were all built of wood. In 1869 the city created a professional fire department to replace volunteer fire brigades, yet still the threat of fire hung over the city. On the night of October 8, 1871, fire broke out in a barn owned by the O'Leary family on the west side of the city. The result was the tragic and legendary Chicago Fire. Twenty-one hundred acres and nearly 17,000 buildings were destroyed in the conflagration. Though the fire had a terrible impact on the city's infrastructure, it did not destroy Chicago's economic base. By 1871 Chicago was too good an investment to ignore, and within 18 months Chicago rebuilt the fire district.

The disaster actually provided an opportunity for the young city. In its aftermath Chicago modernized laws, stimulated a building boom, and attracted many new residents. Among these were a group of young architects led by William Le Baron Jenney, Louis H. Sullivan, and John Wellborn

Root who reworked the meaning of American architecture. The so-called Chicago School of Architecture, a direct result of the fire, evoked the American experience. Chicago's quick recovery from the fire brought increased investment, and it became a world-class city when its population passed the 1 million mark in 1890 and three years later the World's Columbian Exposition, designed by Daniel H. Burnham and Frederick Law Olmsted, was held on the city's South Side. The "White City," as the exposition came to be known, placed Chicago in the first rank of the world's cities. Chicago's population marked it as the second largest city in the United States, a position it held until the 1990 census. To a degree, this rapid population growth resulted from Chicago's annexing most of its immediate suburbs in 1889.

Along with an extensive industrial base, the city developed a large and diverse workforce, and Chicago became a center of labor strife in the years after the Civil War. In 1877 Chicago's workers joined the bloody nationwide railroad strikes. In 1886 Chicago's Haymarket tragedy shook the nation, and eight years after that the Pullman Strike brought federal troops into the city to break the strike. Meatpacking strikes in 1904 and 1921 helped define the role of unskilled workers in American industry, and the 1919 steel strike, fought largely in Chicago and nearby Gary, Indiana, once again made the city a center of labor agitation. Despite all of these clashes, Chicago's economy continued to grow.

While Chicago developed important ties to the Atlantic economy, it attracted waves of both American migration and international immigration. Northern and Western Europeans dominated the early waves of immigration. Many Irish laborers arrived to build the Illinois and Michigan Canal, but Germans quickly surpassed them in numbers; from 1850 to 1930, they were the largest ethnic group in the city. Scandinavians, Welsh, English, Scottish, and Scots-Irish immigrants also flooded into Chicago. From its beginning the city contained a diverse population; also from the beginning, native Protestants, primarily from New England, dominated its economic, cultural, and political life. Quickly, however, the Yankee elite lost demographic, and therefore political, dominance. Many moved to the original railroad suburbs just outside the city, particularly Oak Park, Evanston, Hyde Park, and Kenwood. Commuters followed railroads to the edges of urban settlement, and as native-born whites fled to the fringes of the city, newer groups, particularly from Eastern and Southern Europe, entered Chicago. By 1930 Poles surpassed Germans as the largest ethnic group in the city. In 1910 the foreign-born and their children made up nearly 80 percent of the city's population.

The outbreak of World War I in 1914 had a direct effect on Chicago's immigrant population. Its most important immediate impact was stopping European immigration just as wartime production increased. The number of jobs increased, and wages rose as immigration almost came to a halt. In turn, a new native migration took place. From 1915 to 1920, Chicago's African-American population doubled. African Americans tended to settle on Chicago's South Side, where a large ghetto emerged as a result of residential racial segregation. In July 1919 a major race riot shook the city and resulted in 38 deaths (23 blacks and 15 whites) and over 500 injuries. This single racial clash shaped race relations between Chicago's white ethnic groups and the African-American community for the rest of the century: with some notable exceptions, intense racial segregation has marked the city's residential patterns since then. During the 1920s African Americans built a black city-within-a-city along the boulevards of the South Side. The Black Metropolis contained an almost self-sufficient institutional base.

During the 1920s, a strong sense of neighborhood identity emerged. This intense local attachment had appeared in the late nineteenth century, but the mass transit system as well as ethnicity, race, and social class reinforced and increased a sense of separate neighborhoods. Also, the emergence of a large Roman Catholic parish and parochial school system based largely on ethnicity and rooted in local economies contributed to this pattern. The Poles alone organized almost 60 parishes and parochial schools in the Chicago Catholic Archdiocese. Lutherans, other Protestants, and Jews also created solid institutional bases for their communities.

As the neighborhood system emerged in the 1920s, so did the automobile. The car transformed the city for the rest of the twentieth century. The traditional pattern of locating settlements near railroad stations or mass transit lines broke down as the automobile increased residential mobility and opened new tracts of land for development. Still the full impact of the automobile would not be felt for 40 years, when the highway system, beginning with construction of the Congress (Eisenhower) Expressway, is built.

Chicago's political machine developed late in the history of urban machines. The election of William Hale Thompson in 1915 marked the emergence of an attempt to create a citywide Republican machine. Thompson's crude use of patronage, favors, and public works construction failed to create a truly citywide and Cook County–wide organization. Thompson included the growing African-American community in his coalition, and his years in office also marked creation of the organized-crime machine, headed by Al Capone and often allied with the local Republican Party. In 1931 the Democratic Party challenged Thompson under the leadership of Czech-born Anton Cermak, the only immigrant mayor in the city's history. Cermak, who was assassinated in 1933 by a gunman trying to kill Franklin D. Roosevelt, created his own powerful machine based on the city's white ethnic neigh-

borhoods. Blacks did not leave the Republican Party until the mid-1930s, when they joined the Democratic machine. Cermak's victory marked the end of a vital Republican Party in the city, and no Republican has been elected mayor since Thompson's defeat in 1931.

After Cermak's death the Democrats, under the leadership of Chairman Patrick Nash, placed Edward J. Kelly as mayor from 1933 to 1947, and the Kelly-Nash machine increased its power over the next decade. After the two terms of Martin H. Kennelly (1947–1955), Richard J. Daley surfaced in 1955 as Chicago's most powerful politician, winning six elections for mayor before he died in 1976.

Daley forged a powerful coalition that ran the city with an iron hand. He must be credited with Chicago's development, after 20 years of depression and war, as still being a vital city at the center of an expanding metropolitan area. Early in Daley's administration, Chicago's Loop began to show signs of revitalization. The construction of the Prudential Building (1955) signaled the return of development, after more than 20 years, in the Loop. Daley's Chicago saw the rise of the Hancock Building (1969) and the Sears Tower (1974), as well as the McCormick Place Convention Center (1960–1967, rebuilt 1971–1974 after a destructive fire) on the lakefront. At the same time, Chicago's industrial base shifted. After two decades of decline, the Union Stock Yard closed in 1971. The next 20 years witnessed the erosion of the city's traditional manufacturing base as the city entered the postindustrial era.

The city's African-American population continued to grow during Daley's years. Increased economic opportunity within Chicago and the mechanization of southern agriculture resulted in the migration of large numbers of southern blacks. After World War II, the South Side ghetto expanded well beyond its traditional boundaries, and by 1960, Chicago's African-American population numbered more than 1 million. At the same time, as in other American cities, Chicago's white population began moving to the suburbs. In 1940 Chicago contained 73 percent of northeastern Illinois's population, but by 1990 that figure slipped under 40 percent. That same year, whites provided only about one-third of Chicago's population as demographic change reshaped the city. African Americans, and a quickly growing Hispanic population, provided two-thirds of the city's residents. This demographic change, in motion since 1950 when the city's population peaked at 3,620,962, changed the Democratic machine and gave blacks a larger and increasingly more important role.

In the mid-1960s, Chicago's African-American community began to demand more economic and political rights. In 1966 Dr. Martin Luther King, Jr., arrived to assist the Chicago Freedom Movement. King led open housing marches into white ethnic neighborhoods that resulted in rioting, particularly on the city's southwest side. When King was assassinated in April 1968, Chicago's West Side African-American community responded with renewed rioting, and for the next 15 years black activists labored to bring about black empowerment.

In the summer of 1968, Chicago hosted the Democratic Party's national convention. Still recovering from April's riots, the city braced for anti–Vietnam War demonstrations as Democrats gathered at the International Amphitheater. The resulting conflict between the police and the demonstrators marred Chicago's reputation once again. Daley's last years in office were marked not so much by his reputation as a great builder, but as a reactionary facing an increasingly hostile national press and a restless black population. When Daley died in 1976, his machine began to split apart along racial and ethnic lines.

Daley's immediate successor, his alderman and neighbor Michael J. Bilandic, kept the machine together for a short period. But after he mishandled what most Chicagoans considered an emergency during the blizzard of 1979, he lost the mayor's office to Jane Byrne, an independent Democrat and the first woman to become mayor of Chicago. Byrne allied herself with regular Democrats and seemed invincible, but she lost to Harold Washington in a three-way race in 1983. Washington served as the city's first African-American mayor, winning a second term in 1987. His first administration was bogged down in a power fight with white ethnic aldermen. Washington died in office on November 25, 1987, just after his reelection. A struggle for power occurred immediately and resulted in the brief mayoralty of another African American, Eugene Sawyer (1987–1989). After a special election in 1989, Richard M. Daley, the son of the man who had forged the most powerful machine in the city's history, came to power. The era of the mighty Democratic machine had, however, passed.

As the twentieth century ground to an end, Chicago was a very different city from the city that had held the Columbian Exposition in 1893. During the 1980s, not a single white or black community area grew in population. Yet, demographic shifts transformed Chicago once again as Hispanic and Asian immigrants arrived in the city. Also, Chicagoans witnessed gentrification and new investment along the lakefront and in some outlying neighborhoods such as Beverly, Austin, and Wicker Park. The city's economy maintained a large industrial base, but the service economy experienced the greatest growth. New sports complexes were built in the late 1980s to mid-1990s to house the White Sox (baseball), Bulls (basketball), and Blackhawks (hockey). The downtown Loop remained vital, but it also changed as speculators converted many commercial and industrial buildings to apartments, and many upscale retail stores moved from State Street to North Michigan Avenue.

Chicago remains a vital center for northern Illinois, but its relationship to outlying areas such as Du Page County has been greatly transformed. The city is no longer the population center or economic and political powerhouse that it had once been. Political, economic, and perhaps even cultural power has shifted to suburbs as the metropolis spreads across portions of Illinois, Indiana, Wisconsin, and Michigan.

—*Dominic A. Pacyga*

See also
Armour, Philip Danforth; Burnham, Daniel H.; Byrne, Jane N.; Chicago School of Architecture; Chicago School of Sociology; Chicago World's Fair of 1893 (World's Columbian Exposition); Coughlin, John Joseph (Bathhouse John); Daley, Richard J.; Hammond, George Henry; Jenney, William Le Baron; Kenna, Michael (Hinky Dink); The Loop; Pullman, Illinois; Richardson, Henry Hobson; Skokie, Illinois; South Side of Chicago; Sullivan, Louis H.; Swift, Gustavus Franklin; Thompson, William Hale (Big Bill); Union Stock Yard.

References
Biles, Roger. *Richard J. Daley: Politics, Race, and the Governing of Chicago*. DeKalb: Northern Illinois University Press, 1995.
Bluestone, Daniel. *Constructing Chicago*. New Haven, CT: Yale University Press, 1991.
Cronon, William. *Nature's Metropolis: Chicago and the Great West*. New York: W. W. Norton, 1991.
Green, Paul M., and Melvin G. Holli, eds. *The Mayors: The Chicago Political Tradition*. Carbondale and Edwardsville: Southern Illinois University Press, 1987.
Mayer, Harold M., and Richard C. Wade. *Chicago: Growth of a Metropolis*. Chicago: University of Chicago Press, 1969.
Pacyga, Dominic A., and Ellen Skerrett. *Chicago: City of Neighborhoods*. Chicago: Loyola University Press, 1986.
Pierce, Bessie L. *A History of Chicago*. 3 vols. New York: Knopf, 1937–1957.

Chicago School of Architecture

A group of twentieth-century architects, historians, and critics brought the term *Chicago School* into common usage in their effort to characterize Chicago architecture of the late nineteenth and early twentieth centuries. More specifically, the term referred to the commercial skyscrapers of Louis H. Sullivan, William Le Baron Jenney, Burnham & Root, and Holabird & Roche. The leading enthusiasts of this work portrayed it as a bold effort to let modern building technology— elevators, steel-frame construction, fireproof cladding, concrete foundations, and curtain wall systems—shape modern architectural expression. In the eyes of twentieth-century architects and critics, such structural and technological expressionism served as the foundation for modernism's eclipse of traditional architectural forms.

Recent historians have seriously challenged the critical and historiographical concept of a Chicago School. There is little evidence that the architects of late-nineteenth-century Chicago skyscrapers conceived of themselves or worked as a school who were self-consciously attempting to create a modern, structurally expressive style. One of the earliest chroniclers of their work, the anonymous editors of *Industrial Chicago,* argued in 1891 that the "commercial style" was "largely technic." They wrote, "a gigantic skeleton or box structure of steel is ornamented with columns, pilasters, piers, capitals, bandcourses, arches, paneling, gables, moldings, etc., gathered from every nation of the earth and from every chronological cycle." In the 1890s, observers considered the style eclectic. Skeleton construction and predominant height characterized the early skyscrapers of Chicago more than a shared architectural style.

The term *Chicago School* first appeared around 1900 in reference to literature. People who applied the term to architecture used it with imprecision, often referring to domestic architecture. What became the dominant canonical concept of the Chicago School gained particular power in the 1920s and 1930s in the wake of an emerging American and European interest in modernism. The development appeared in many venues—from university lectures to critical and scholarly writing to museum exhibitions.

The display of 33 photographs in a 1933 exhibition titled "Early Modern Architecture, Chicago 1870–1910" at the Museum of Modern Art, for example, clearly contributed to the canonization of the Chicago School in the 1930s. The museum's typescript catalog and the text accompanying each photograph narrowed the interpretation of significant Chicago architecture to focus primarily on skyscrapers. The catalog included biographies of Jenney, Richardson, Adler & Sullivan, Wright, Burnham & Root, and Holabird & Roche. The two central sections surveyed the technical and aesthetic development of the skyscraper and then presented what soon became the standard historical trajectory: they linked Henry H. Richardson to Louis H. Sullivan to Frank Lloyd Wright and used 1910 as an ending date. Richardson's Marshall Field Wholesale Store provided for the young Chicago architects an aesthetic discipline of regularity and simplicity from which Sullivan rapidly created a new personal style. The influence of Sullivan's style was so great that it attracted a group of young architects who formed the Chicago School under his leadership. The free, nontraditional architecture of the Chicago School retained its vigor until about 1910 when the stylistic revivalism (which had made its first striking appearance in Chicago with the World's Fair of 1893) vitiated its force.

The exhibition at the Museum of Modern Art asserted not only the existence of a Chicago School but also a "Chicago formula of skyscraper design." To reinforce this judgment, the exhibition included a photograph of George B. Post's domed Pulitzer skyscraper in New York (1889) and called it "progressive neither in structure or design." In contrasting Chicago with the East and in setting out an architectural genealogy, the exhibition considerably distorted the form and meaning of Chicago skyscrapers. In the late nineteenth century, Chicago architects did not share a consensus on style or ornament or a design formula except within single firms. In fact, their buildings were filled with ornament and historical architectural elements, most notably in the base of the building, its lobbies, and its upper cornice, the points where people visually engage a building most readily. The critical enthusiasts of the Chicago School notion tended to focus more exclusively on the gridded middle level of skyscrapers, the part least noted by the general public. In the view of many contemporaries, these buildings represented highly ornate monuments of refined middle-class, white-collar work, separated from the unpleasant sites of blue-collar industrial production. Chicagoans at the turn of the century knew the technological basis of their world intimately; in the skyscraper, they relied on technology and design to insulate themselves from the rawer, bleaker aspects of industrial urbanism.

Even at the center of curatorial and scholarly study of the Chicago School, considerable tentativeness persisted through the 1930s. The 1936 revision of Thomas Tallmadge's book *The Story of Architecture in America* (first published in 1927) suggests the ferment surrounding the construction of the history of the Chicago School. Tallmadge had used the term *Chicago School* in 1908; however, he was referring primarily to residential design. The same use appears in his 1927 book. However, Tallmadge rethought the importance of Chicago architecture in the 1930s and broadly gestured toward commercial skyscrapers as a distinct contribution of Chicago architects. In 1927 Tallmadge titled his chapter on Sullivan "Louis Sullivan and the Lost Cause." Under the sway of contemporary architectural and critical thinking in the 1930s, Tallmadge retitled the Sullivan chapter "Louis Sullivan, Parent and Prophet" in the 1936 edition. Tallmadge's genealogy had Sullivan parenting the "functionalist movement." He also asserted that the skyscraper was indeed "far and away the most important architectural achievement of America, her great gift to the art of building. In its train has come the most brilliant era of structural engineering that the world has ever known."

Hugh Morrison's 1935 biography, *Louis Sullivan, Prophet of Modern Architecture,* also insisted that, "Until the work of the Chicago School is better known than it is at present . . . it will be impossible to estimate correctly the real force and character of Sullivan's direct practical influence in this country." The hedging disappeared in Siegfried Giedion's *Space, Time and Architecture: The Growth of a New Tradition* (1941) and Carl Condit's *The Rise of the Skyscraper* (1952) and *The Chicago School of Architecture: A History of Commercial and Public Buildings in the City Area, 1875–1925* (1964). These books, strongly sympathetic with stylistic modernism and enthusiastic about it, gave depth and foundation to the myth of Chicago School modernism that had been presented in the exhibition at the Museum of Modern Art.

Work by museum curators, historians, and critics of modern architecture in the 1930s and 1940s established the terms and configuration of the Chicago School. This work undoubtedly won some popular adherence from the museum-going and journal-reading public. However, to appreciate the tenacity and pervasiveness of the Chicago School construct, it is important to focus less on academic discourse and more on Chicago itself in the 1950s and 1960s—the time when the canonical view gained its greatest currency in popular culture.

In the context of urbanism after World War II, the Chicago School construct operated as a polemic concerning style and, perhaps more importantly, as an ideology promoting the definition and redevelopment of the city. Strong civic boosterism promoted widespread, popular diffusion of the Chicago School construct. Postwar enthusiasm for the Chicago School must be understood in the context of the economic and social condition of Chicago—and other American cities—after the war. Building interests confronted a socially and economically troubled city in those years. Aging buildings occupied a landscape that had stagnated through a decade of depression and almost a decade of war. Despite the full employment and prosperity of the war years, Chicago's economy seemed threatened by decentralization, suburbanization, and urbanization in the southern and western United States. In the face of these challenges, history and an invented tradition of the Chicago School seemed especially reassuring; by looking back, many builders in Chicago discovered hope for a more promising future. Chicago's nineteenth-century skyscrapers had testified to the city's commercial vitality and growing economic prominence. Boosterism pervaded their development and promotion. In the mid-1950s, as the city's business and political leaders organized a Central Area Committee to promote massive downtown redevelopment, they invoked a "Chicago School" to give them a sense of historic mission, and even destiny.

Similarly, in 1957, history and boosterism pervaded the introduction of a new journal published by the Chicago chapter of the American Institute of Architects. Titled *Inland Architect,* the journal adopted the name of a nineteenth-century Chicago periodical that had chronicled the early development of skyscrapers. The journal helped explore the instrumental utility of invoking a Chicago School in the architectural and planning discourse of the 1950s. The illustration on the cover of the first issue showed an etching of the entry to Sullivan's Transportation Building at the Columbian Exposition and a photograph of Harry Weese's apartment building at 227 Walton Street with its Chicago windows. The caption read "Chicago Builds 1893 and Today." The journal's introduction

recalled the "strength and stature," the "pioneering" work, and the "bold brash builders" of the Chicago School.

Architects were not alone in having much to gain from a historically inspired effort to generate a postwar building boom. Nor did they stand alone in their enthusiasm to use the myth of the Chicago School as boosterism for a building campaign. One important crystallizing point for this effort occurred during Chicago Dynamic Week in 1957, an event sponsored by U.S. Steel and other business groups. Mayor Richard J. Daley proclaimed Chicago Dynamic Week in August 1957, only a few weeks after blacks and whites had clashed in Calumet Park, sparking one of the city's worst race riots in years. The mayor's proclamation rang with boosterism and local pride.

> WHEREAS, Chicago is the birthplace of American architecture, the curtain wall building, which ushered in the age of the skyscraper; and
>
> WHEREAS, Chicago today is concerned with the continued use of the newest building forms, materials and techniques to make Chicago a better place in which to live and work; and
>
> WHEREAS, the Chicago Dynamic Committee comprising our community's business and civic leaders has been organized to honor the sound building and far-sighted planning of Chicago, the world's most dynamic city . . . I, Richard J. Daley, Mayor of the City of Chicago, do hereby proclaim the week of October 27 through November 2, as "Chicago Dynamic Week."

Edward C. Logelin, vice president of U.S. Steel Corporation and chair of the Chicago Dynamic Committee, insisted that the week would attract people capable of recognizing the "possibilities" of the city, leaders who might give direction and form to the city's "billion-dollar rebuilding." Calling attention to Chicago's "great architectural and building tradition," Logelin forged a continuum between past and present, "We have enormous talent, unused power, and we must begin to use it now. We must think about our city building problems, about our creative, life-enriching, unknown art known as architecture, and keep doing something about it. For, as Sullivan said, 'Chicago can pull itself down and rebuild itself in a generation.'" Participants in Chicago Dynamic Week held symposia on redevelopment, took part in workshops on curtain wall construction, laid the cornerstone of a new, modern-style bank building, and held a conference on the question, Can Good Architecture "Pay Off"?

For Chicago's architects of modern curtain wall buildings, the Chicago Dynamic emphasis on local architectural heritage could steer new commissions to a circle of select, local firms, effectively barring competition from firms in other cities. In Chicago, architects jockeyed for the mantle of the Chicago School. Historians and critics proved quite willing to assert the existence of a connection between local architects and the origins of modern architecture. They established a clear lineage between a First and a Second Chicago School; and they set the mantle of successor to the Chicago School upon the shoulders of the German immigrant modern architect Mies van der Rohe. In 1963 George Danforth reported in the *Inland Architect,* "It seems natural that Mies should be asked to come here, because in his every work is the essence of the spirit of the Chicago School of architecture so long gone unrealized." Mies worked alongside other local modernists, including Skidmore, Owings & Merrill; I. M. Pei; C. F. Murphy; and Perkins & Will.

The Chicago School construct also derived part of its narrative power from an extraordinary coalition of modernists and preservationists in Chicago. Since the middle of the nineteenth century, American preservationists have tended to assume oppositional stances to the most palpable forms of modern capitalist development. There was, of course, no small irony in the preservationist interest in nineteenth-century skyscrapers, the icons of an earlier, quite unfettered age of capitalist development. Nevertheless, because of the peculiarities of the Chicago School, preservationists and modernists worked as allies. Both camps shared allegiance to, and complete agreement about, the terms of the Chicago School's constructed heritage. Modernists were interested in the mantle and in boosterism. Preservationists strived to define and buttress a sense of place. In the context of preservation, the supposed history of the Chicago School actually doomed many more buildings than it saved. The canon established both relevance and irrelevance. An architectural heritage defined as buildings primarily standing on commercial downtown land effectively rendered much of the city unimportant and beneath the preservation interest. This modest conception of Chicago's architectural history reigned during the years of urban renewal in Chicago—the most destructive period in the city since the Great Fire of 1871.

In the end, many of Chicago's troubles persisted and even deepened. But the city did start to rebuild. The influence of the Chicago School rhetoric is of course hard to assess. Nevertheless, by 1962 *Life* magazine reported that "the city is giving itself the most dramatic change of profile since the fire. . . . Though the modern shape and pell-mell expansion worry some conservative, old Chicagoans, they delight boosters who have always maintained that with enough push their city could surpass all others. Chicago was due for a renaissance." The idea of the Chicago School provided some of that push and gave it a staying power beyond its life in the academy.

In the 1980s and 1990s, the critical and historiographic challenge to architectural modernism has substantially weakened the idea that the work of a few architects, narrowly interpreted, can in any way represent the architectural production or heritage of an entire city. Postmodernism's interest in history, diversity of forms and perspectives, and even in ornament has supported fundamental reconceptions of buildings both inside and outside of the Chicago School canon. It has generated substantial skepticism concerning the historical reality and importance of the concept itself.

—*Daniel Bluestone*

See also
Burnham, Daniel H.; Jenney, William Le Baron; Richardson, Henry Hobson; Skyscraper; Sullivan, Louis H.
References
Bluestone, Daniel. *Constructing Chicago.* New Haven, CT: Yale University Press, 1991.
———. "Preservation and Renewal in Post–World War II Chicago." *JAE: Journal of Architectural Education* 47 (1994): 210–223.
Brooks, H. Allen. "Chicago School: Metamorphosis of a Term." *Journal of the Society of Architectural Historians* 25 (1966): 115–118.
Bruegmann, Robert. "The Marquette Building and the Myth of the Chicago School." *Threshold* 5/6 (1991): 7–18.
Condit, Carl. *The Chicago School of Architecture: A History of Commercial and Public Buildings in the City Area, 1875–1925.* Chicago: University of Chicago Press, 1964.
———. *The Rise of the Skyscraper.* Chicago: University of Chicago Press, 1952.
Giedion, Sigfried. *Space, Time and Architecture: The Growth of a New Tradition.* Cambridge, MA: Harvard University Press, 1941.
Museum of Modern Art. *Early Modern Architecture. Chicago 1870–1910* [catalog]. New York: Museum of Modern Art, 1933.

Chicago School of Sociology

In the early part of the twentieth century, a group of scholars in the Department of Sociology at the University of Chicago came to exercise a great deal of influence over the way research was done in the field of sociology. The height of the group's influence came in the period from roughly the late teens through the early forties. The key members of this group were W. I. Thomas, Robert E. Park, Ernest Burgess, and Louis Wirth. Among them, they managed to train a large number of graduate students and helped set the field of sociology on the path toward becoming a strong, empirically oriented academic discipline. The general perspective of this group has come to be embraced by the term *Chicago School of Sociology,* although there probably were as many differences among some of the key figures as there were identifiable common points of view.

There were, however, several distinguishing features among this group of scholars. The first was a major emphasis on the actual empirical study of social phenomena. They viewed themselves as moving beyond European sociologists, particularly those who were given over to broad speculative philosophy, such as Auguste Comte. Their task, they felt, was to collect and assemble as much empirical observable data on human societies and communities as possible.

This effort to assemble a wide range of empirical data led to a number of important innovations in the work of sociologists. Thomas, for example, along with Florian Znaniecki, put together a massive work, *The Polish Peasant in Europe and America,* based upon a variety of personal documents, such as diaries. These sources, together with lengthy personal histories of representative figures, were intended to reveal in detail the experiences of immigrants in the process of their moving and later settling in America. Life histories, as such materials would become known, became the second distinguishing feature of the way that graduate students working with members of the Chicago school would carry out their research.

A third central feature of the work done under the auspices of the Chicago school was that most of it was actually done in the city of Chicago. Chicago at the time was a rapidly growing metropolis, flooded with immigrants from many different lands and filled with the tensions produced through the experiences of industrial expansion. It was these realities that would shape the contents and form of the work of the Chicago school, providing grist for insights into the process of immigration, into how particular social types, such as hoboes or call girls, were formed, and into how cities themselves would develop and expand over time. The general assumption of the Chicago school of sociologists was that the experiences within Chicago were representative of the experiences to be found in other American cities. Moreover, it was also commonly assumed that once Chicago had been thoroughly mapped, in terms of its social structure, then comparisons could be pursued with other cities to reveal differences, if they existed.

Finally, there was a theoretical paradigm that seemed to embrace and to inspire much of the work of these scholars. Park was the one most responsible for articulating the view that the human community shared many parallels with the natural community, in general, and that, therefore, the essence of sociology was that of human ecology. By this, Park came to mean that human beings had to be seen in their relationship to their larger natural environment and that they exhibited certain traits in common with other forms of life. Park was particularly impressed by the fact that both human communities and animal life were fraught with conflict, a struggle for survival of the fittest as Charles Darwin had put it. Among humans, he maintained, such conflict was evident and worked through in the economic sphere of the community. But Park further argued that the human community was distinct from those of other forms of life in that there existed a realm of culture in which the forces of consensus operated. This realm, Park believed, deserved the special attention of sociologists.

Not all members of the Chicago school embraced the theoretical paradigm that came to be known as human ecology. W. I. Thomas, for example, developed a social psychological theory of the human personality, arguing that there were four central wishes that motivated people. But Park's influence was decisive, and he came to exercise his powers over a number of colleagues, including Burgess, with whom he collaborated for several decades. A host of dissertations were written under the supervision of both Park and Burgess, and they served to refine and to further develop the special kind of empirical research done by the Chicago sociologists. Works by Nels Anderson on hoboes and by Frederic Thrasher on gangs helped define the nature of case studies by sociologists, studies that went into great depth on particular social types or particular forms of social phenomena, using a battery of personal documents and observational techniques.

Today, the ideas of the Chicago school are still found in research done within the ecological paradigm as well as in studies that focus on specific types of social phenomena. Human ecology has been updated and made more sophisticated, particularly through the writings of figures such as Amos Hawley, who helped to make the insights of Park and Roderick McKenzie, another sociologist, more systematic. Case studies of particular social groups, using observational techniques, remain a very important way for sociologists to do research. And personal documents, such as diaries, figure prominently in the research not only of sociologists but also of historians and political scientists, among others.

But the Chicago school of sociology, particularly that which focused so heavily on the city of Chicago and the manner of its growth, has come in for considerable criticism as well. Manuel Castells, for example, argued in a famous work, *The Urban Question,* that the Chicago school of sociologists, particularly Park and Burgess, had misconstrued the nature of the city. The city, he maintained, was not the site of ecological struggles, but rather of class struggles. Classes struggled among themselves to dominate the city; moreover, there had been an important historical change and the main function of the city had shifted from production, as in the industrial era, to consumption. The city today, therefore, should be viewed as the site of collective consumption units or, in other words, as the site of struggles over housing. David Harvey also took up a neo-Marxist argument, maintaining that the underlying dynamic of the city lay in the tension between land as a commodity, or exchange-value, and land as a use-value. The net result of these kinds of criticisms is that the ecological paradigm is no longer as popular as it once was; in fact, among sociologists and other social scientists, various kinds of political and economic paradigms are today far more popular as filters through which to refract life in the city.

—*Anthony M. Orum*

See also
Burgess, Ernest W.; Park, Robert Ezra; Urban Ecology; Wirth, Louis.
References
Bulmer, Martin W. *The Chicago School of Sociology.* Chicago: University of Chicago Press, 1984.
Castells, Manuel. *The Urban Question: A Marxist Approach.* Cambridge, MA: MIT Press, 1977.
Harvey, David. *Social Justice and the City.* Baltimore: Johns Hopkins University Press, 1973.
Park, Robert E. *Human Communities: The City and Human Ecology.* Glencoe, IL: Free Press, 1952.
Park, Robert E., Ernest W. Burgess, and Roderick D. McKenzie. *The City.* Chicago: University of Chicago Press, 1925.
Reiss, Albert J., Jr., ed. *Louis Wirth: On Cities and Social Life.* Chicago: University of Chicago Press, 1964.

Chicago World's Fair of 1893
(World's Columbian Exposition)

As the nation had been determined to celebrate the centenary of its independence, so too, a few years later, was it bent upon marking the quadricentennial of Christopher Columbus's encounter with the New World. The choice of Philadelphia as the site of the Centennial Exposition of 1876 seemed highly appropriate, but the choice for commemorating the first encounter of the Old World and the New World was more difficult. Ultimately, the selection narrowed to two cities: New York, the nation's largest, wealthiest, and most renowned city, staked impressive claims to hosting this world's fair, but it was Chicago that Congress and President Benjamin Harrison chose in 1890.

Devastated by the Great Fire of 1871, Chicago had risen phoenixlike from the ashes during the next two decades to become the nation's second largest city and, in some respects, its most important. With its brisk port trade, the most active in the nation, its burgeoning commerce, highlighted by the Union Stock Yard, the Pullman Palace Car Company, and the McCormick Harvesting Machine Company, Chicago had become internationally renowned. The city had also taken lengthy cultural strides. By the time of the Columbian Exposition, the Art Institute, the Newberry Library, and the Auditorium had been completed, while the University of Chicago and Crerar Library were at various stages of their development. Moreover, Chicago was generally acknowledged to be the home of the recently developed skyscraper and the center of progressive American architecture. In a decidedly different vein, the midwestern metropolis could also boast a monument of another sort: Jane Addams's Hull House. Small

wonder a visiting reporter predicted that Chicago itself would serve as the chief exhibit of the forthcoming celebration.

Building the exposition entailed an enormous undertaking. First, the partners Daniel Burnham and John Wellborn Root were selected as chief architects for the event. (Root died soon thereafter.) In turn, they invited other prominent firms, both local and national, to participate. Frederick Law Olmsted, creator of New York's Central Park and the nation's most eminent landscape architect, agreed to design the sprawling fairgrounds, which were erected on a dreary, undeveloped site fronting Lake Michigan. The Herculean labors began in early 1891 and consumed two full years before the fair, originally scheduled to begin in 1892, opened on May 1, 1893, to a paid crowd of more than 100,000. Before the exposition closed six months later total attendance exceeded 27 million.

While offering a wide variety of engaging attractions, the fair provided two distinctly different featured attractions, the Court of Honor and the Midway Pleasance. Better known as the White City because of its color, the court consisted of five major buildings picturesquely grouped around a basin with two large sculptured fountains. Widely praised by architects and the general public alike, their neoclassical design exerted an enormous impact on American architecture for several decades. In the opinion of some, like Louis H. Sullivan, who designed the fair's Transportation Building, the endorsement of this academic historical style inflicted immense harm by short-circuiting the acceptance of progressive modern design. Whatever the validity of this heated argument, the huge crowds—exceeding 700,000 on one day alone—reportedly thrilled to the national and international representations of manufacturing, commerce, and the arts; they appreciated the splendors of the past and present and anticipated progress in the future.

The Midway Pleasance, more familiarly called the Midway, stood in marked contrast to the formal elegance and spirit of the Court of Honor. Filled with exotic exhibits of indigenous cultures from around the world, the Midway educated, but above all it entertained. It also titillated and scandalized many who witnessed the Syrian-born "Little Egypt" gyrate and perform what the French called the *danse du ventre,* but which Americans quickly called the "hootchykootchy." More than Little Egypt, however, it was George Washington Gale Ferris's wheel that attracted the most attention and ultimately served as the exposition's chief icon. With a diameter of 264 feet and the ability to carry more than 2,100 people at one time, the Ferris wheel became a staple of later fairs and amusement parks throughout the world. At the Chicago World's Fair of 1893, it afforded passengers excitement and a unique panorama of the surrounding city.

The elegance and monumentality of the Chicago World's Fair of 1893 influenced American architecture and planning for many decades.

The 1893 World's Fair may or may not have been "the grandest Exposition this planet has ever witnessed," as one guidebook boasted, but it assuredly produced powerful effects on American culture and life, not least of all the urban experience. The fair solidified the position of the host city as an important international as well as national city and led to remarkable civic transformations. Chicago's transportation system was significantly enlarged and upgraded to meet the needs of the fair and its anticipated throngs of visitors. The city's lakefront, hitherto a wasteland, subsequently became prime real estate for developers. The abandoned structures of the fair itself, however, were largely destroyed by fire during the Pullman Strike of 1894. Among the most notable buildings, only the Palace of Fine Arts survived to become the Field Museum of Natural History (presently the Museum of Science and Industry). But the example of the White City lived on for decades to come by providing an example of— and for—urban aesthetics. It is possible that it did not, as widely credited, launch the City Beautiful movement; but it did help propel it. In the two decades following the World's Fair, countless architects, artists, art leagues, city planners,

and city commissions battled to beautify the nation's urban scene. Fittingly, Daniel Burnham played a major role. The chief architect of the World's Fair of 1893 went on to plan the complex revitalization of Washington, D.C., Cleveland, San Francisco, and even far-off Manila. Moreover, it was Burnham's ambitious Plan of Chicago that helped preserve more than 100 blocks of lakefront property in the city whose architecture he had done so much to promote.

—*Robert Muccigrosso*

See also

Burnham, Daniel H.; Centennial Exposition of 1876; City Beautiful Movement; Olmsted, Frederick Law.

References

Badger, Reid. *The Great American Fair: The World's Columbian Exposition and American Culture.* Chicago: Nelson Hall, 1979.

Burg, David F. *Chicago's White City of 1893.* Lexington: University of Kentucky Press, 1976.

Gilbert, James. *Perfect Cities: Chicago's Utopias of 1893.* Chicago: University of Chicago Press, 1991.

Hines, Thomas S. *Burnham of Chicago: Architect and Planner.* New York: Oxford University Press, 1974.

Muccigrosso, Robert. *Celebrating the New World: Chicago's Columbian Exposition of 1893.* Chicago: Ivan R. Dee, 1993.

Child Labor

Industrialization and urbanization created the social issue of child labor. In agricultural societies, children traditionally contributed their work to help support the household. When the Industrial Revolution removed the tasks of production from the home, children went to work in mines, shops, and factories, away from the protection of parents or guardians. In response, reformers of the nineteenth and twentieth centuries defined child labor as work that endangered children's physical, moral, or mental development, almost always done outside the home.

With the advance of industrial capitalism, children became sources not of household help, but of added income. When the wages of adult men failed to suffice, families often sent children to work. In American towns and cities, boys commonly worked as shoe shiners, messengers, shop assistants, and newspaper hawkers. Both boys and girls, but most commonly girls, found jobs in the woolen, silk, and cotton mills of New England, the Middle Atlantic states, and the South. In Pennsylvania's hard coal region, young boys worked in the breakers and picked slate out of the coal. Twelve-hour shifts and sixty-hour weeks were common, and some children worked nights. Conditions in mills and mines were often grim, unsanitary, and dangerous. Working children typically brought their wages home to help support parents and younger siblings.

Some people believed that work was good for children. In the 1880s, boosters in Scranton, Pennsylvania, welcomed the arrival of new silk mills, which would provide jobs for girls and young women, who might otherwise drift into prostitution. Working-class parents often favored, or at least accepted, child labor. In southern textile mills, whole families often found jobs, and many adults depended on the wages of their children to help support their households. In the 1890s, John Gunckel founded the Toledo (Ohio) Newsboys' Association, or Boyville, to shelter young newspaper vendors, who assaulted the eardrums and tugged at the heartstrings of pedestrians on city streets. This nationally famous organization supposedly encouraged entrepreneurial spirit while teaching the boys middle-class virtues of sobriety, self-discipline, and respect for the law. Dime novelist Horatio Alger popularized the image of hardworking lads who reaped the benefits of capitalism through a combination of luck, pluck, and virtue.

Others felt only sympathy for toiling children. Reformers like Jane Addams of Hull House and Florence Kelley of the National Consumers League denounced child labor on humanitarian grounds and portrayed child workers as stunted in body and spirit. Mother Jones, eloquent spokeswoman for the United Mine Workers, described child workers as slaves of capitalistic greed. In 1903 she aroused public indignation by leading a pathetic band of young mill workers from Philadelphia to the New York retreat of President Theodore Roosevelt. *The Bitter Cry of the Children,* a 1909 exposé by socialist John Spargo, condemned the physical and moral atmosphere of industrial plants as poisonous to young souls. Industrial work, he argued, did not train young people for future success but rather condemned them to grim and hopeless lives. In 1914 Edwin Markham, author of *Children in Bondage,* wrote that factory work stole children's youth and blighted their future.

Some reformers feared that young workers would become radicalized. Most advocates of prohibiting child labor insisted that young people belonged in schools, not factories. Idealists held out the hope that public education might help working-class children escape the drudgery of the mills and achieve middle-class dreams of success. Pessimists envisioned young industrial laborers blossoming into full-blown revolutionaries. Describing Pennsylvania's coal towns, Markham presented an alarming image of abandoned schools turned into union halls where young girls and boys learned about strikes, picket lines, and scabs. Schools, on the other hand, indoctrinated children in middle-class values and steered them away from labor militancy.

Union leaders regarded child workers as competitors for jobs. The American Federation of Labor, founded by craft unionists in 1886, opposed child labor not only as a social evil but as an economic force that increased competition for jobs and put downward pressure on wages. Part of the conflict resulted from child labor being cheap labor. With increasing mechanization, employers often chose to hire unskilled children and adolescents instead of skilled adult men. Moreover, children were unlikely to belong to unions, although some children did engage in strikes and demonstrations.

Reformers fought to increase adult wages in order to eliminate the need for child labor. Many Catholic clergymen, union leaders, and middle-class reformers endorsed the concept of the family wage, insisting that employers had a moral obligation to pay working people enough to maintain themselves and their families. Mother Jones used the spectacle of thin, exhausted children reporting for work as an argument for raising coal miners' pay. Underlying the demands for a family wage was the assumption that male breadwinners should support and protect women and children, who would remain sequestered at home. Many reformers blurred or ignored any distinction between adult female labor and child labor.

Several organizations lobbied for state laws against employing children. The Society for the Prevention of Cruelty to Children (SPCC), founded in 1875, attacked vagrancy, homelessness, and child labor. Beginning in 1904, the National Child Labor Committee (NCLC) hired Lewis Hine and others to gather information about children and work. Traveling thousands of miles with his camera, Hine shocked the public with images of boys harnessed to wagons in coal mines, exhausted young girls tending machines in textile mills, and newsboys sleeping in subway stations. The NCLC used public awareness of the problem to win legislative battles. Basing its recommendations on existing laws in Massachusetts, New York, and Illinois, the committee urged a minimum age of 14 for employment in manufacturing, 16 in mining. By 1916, nearly every state had passed legislation setting a minimum age for working, varying from 12 to 16, and regulating hours and working conditions for child workers.

The federal government also took halting steps to restrict child labor. In 1903 President Theodore Roosevelt demonstrated the government's reluctance to confront the issue by refusing to speak with Mother Jones and her marching mill children. Senator Albert J. Beveridge, a Republican from Indiana, tried and failed to enact federal legislation in 1906. In 1912 President William Howard Taft signed a bill creating the Children's Bureau, a research agency charged with studying child welfare. Under the leadership of Julia Lathrop, the small, poorly funded agency investigated infant mortality, poverty, and child health and labor. In 1916 Congress passed the Keating-Owen Act, restricting child labor, but the U.S. Supreme Court overturned it, ruling that the law limited freedom of contract.

Efforts to end child labor continued to meet strong resistance. Employers continued to disregard state laws and hire young workers. Families who needed the wages of secondary breadwinners filed false affidavits and lied about their children's ages. Many people who opposed child labor in principle refused to support federal legislation against it. Even the members of the American Federation of Labor and the NCLC did not unanimously favor federal restrictions. The Catholic Church, which took strong positions in favor of childhood and the family, opposed federal restrictions on child labor as a possible threat to family autonomy.

The Depression and the New Deal of the 1930s inspired new federal regulations about child labor. In response to high unemployment and economic chaos, Congress passed the National Industrial Recovery Act (NIRA) of 1933, which established a minimum age of 16 for employment in most industries, 18 in mining and logging, but despite President Franklin Roosevelt's optimism, the NIRA did not end child labor. Employers resisted its provisions, and children continued reporting to work. In 1935 the U.S. Supreme Court declared the law unconstitutional and its provisions null and void.

In 1938 Congress passed the Fair Labor Standards Act (FLSA), which did not prohibit, but did restrict, child labor. The law allowed children of 14 or 15 to work if their jobs did not interfere with their schooling, but children under 18 could not have dangerous occupations such as mining and logging. The law limited the number of hours children could work, but it did not apply to children who worked on farms, in restaurants, retail stores, or beauty shops, or who sold newspapers.

After World War II, growing numbers of adult women but fewer children went to work. By 1960, 30 percent of married women worked outside their homes, and by the 1980s a majority of wives worked for wages. The two-income family, with two working parents, had become common. For the most part, children remained at home, in school, or in day care. The Occupational Safety and Health Act of 1970 extended federal protection to workplaces omitted from the FLSA. Although the worst abuses of child labor diminished, teenagers and children continued to work legally or illegally in many different work places.

—Bonnie Stepenoff

See also
Alger, Horatio, Jr.; Apprenticeship; Children in Cities.
References
Ashby, Le Roy. *Saving the Waifs: Reformers and Dependent Children: 1890–1917*. Philadelphia: Temple University Press, 1984.
Greene, Laura. *Child Labor: Then and Now*. New York: Franklin Watts, 1992.
Markham, Edwin. *Children in Bondage*. New York: Hearst's International Library, 1914.
Nardinelli, Clark. *Child Labor and the Industrial Revolution*. Bloomington: Indiana University Press, 1990.
Spargo, John. *The Bitter Cry of the Children*. New York: Macmillan, 1909.
Trattner, Walter I. *Crusade for the Children*. Chicago: Quadrangle, 1970.

Children in Cities

One of the defining characteristics of cities has been the visible presence of children. Not only have they often been seen in cities, they have also been heard as they have played games and pursued other activities typically found on city streets. Many people drawn by the opportunities available in cities brought large families with them, and as early as colonial times the streets teemed with children. Although many more children lived in rural areas, rural children were less visible to society as a whole. Children outside the city were often working, generally supervised, and more spread out. On city streets, children and young people who were less controlled and less organized frequently seemed like a menace to society, which responded with a variety of efforts to master and restrain them.

Colonial cities were few in number—Boston, New York, Philadelphia, and Charleston were the leading ones—but they grew steadily in the seventeenth and eighteenth centuries. As their populations expanded, the number of children also increased and so did the number of perceived problems. In the colonial world, there were few impersonal public services, including ones for children. Destitute children would most likely have been placed as servants in a family. Colonial laws admonished children to obey their parents, and colonial authorities supervised families and threatened to remove children from improper parents. As cities grew and as it became more difficult to place poor, unprotected, or improperly supervised children in families, institutions grew in importance, notably orphanages and workhouses. Workhouses, sometimes called Bridewells after a notorious English example, were places where the destitute were kept alive by public funds and forced to labor to earn their keep. Children were no exception and were expected to labor as soon as they could. The Ursuline Convent in New Orleans established the first orphanage in what was to be the United States in 1729; George Whitefield's better-known institution, Bethesda, was established near Savannah, Georgia, in 1739.

Cities continued to increase in size and number in the nineteenth century, and as they grew, problems involving children were also heightened. The growth of poverty especially distressed early city leaders; they believed that poverty resulted from failed resolve and that curing it required the inculcation of the value of hard work and the importance of a moral character. Bridewells, workhouses, prisons, and houses of correction included both adults and children, and some students of pauperism, the condition of perpetual poverty, believed that children learned the culture of poverty by being incarcerated with adults. The creation of the New York House of Refuge in 1825 flowed directly from these perceptions, which also shaped the construction and administration of early orphanages and houses of refuge throughout the country. Americans in the early nineteenth century made little distinction between orphanages and juvenile penal institutions. Both were designed to offer destitute or delinquent youth a fresh start, and the instruments for reformation were a vigorous moral education and on-the-job training in a craft.

Children and young people, whether destitute or delinquent, could be placed in these institutions, and they could remain until they reached the age of 21 or were indentured to a family. While in the institution, the children attended school and worked at contract labor, performing such tasks as shoemaking or sewing.

As cities grew the nature of work also changed. Urban work increasingly demanded new and different skills. The old master-apprenticeship system whereby craft skills were passed on declined, while wage work and the demand for higher-order skills involving mathematics and literacy increased. A corresponding expansion of schooling followed

these demands, and in 1852 the state of Massachusetts passed the first compulsory school attendance law, followed by New York in 1874.

By the middle of the nineteenth century, the sheer number of children roaming the streets of major American cities came to be considered a major social problem. The lack of social order these children represented moved reformers and philanthropists to devise new programs. These included larger numbers of public (or charity) schools, more orphanages with greater capacities, and modified forms of penal institutions for children. Reformer Charles Loring Brace founded the New York Children's Aid Society in 1853. Its programs included the Newsboys' Lodging House (rent was charged) and the New York placing-out system, which sent city children to live with rural families. In many cases the children so placed were not orphans, and families were sometimes coerced into sending their children away. Brace claimed that he had found a way to rid cities of juvenile delinquents, but western states complained that this system filled their juvenile penal institutions and passed laws regulating the arrival of "orphan trains."

Placing-out systems sought to remove potentially threatening children from the city streets, but reformers recognized that children could be victims, too. The creation of the Society for the Prevention of Cruelty to Children in New York in 1875 was a milestone in the development of child-helping agencies in American cities. Other agencies, such as the Florence Crittenton homes, tried to rescue prostitutes (many of them children) from the streets and to care for unwed mothers and their children. By the end of the nineteenth century, most major cities had an agency to protect children from abuse, as well as other charities that cared for dependent children. Most states also had some sort of juvenile reform school that sometimes took in dependent children, too. The rapid increase in immigration after 1880 meant that many of these agencies were overwhelmed with demands for their services.

The Progressive period in U.S. history was a time of major urban reforms, including a concentrated effort to help children, and some reformers hailed the new age as the "Century of the Child." The most notable reforms involving children in this period were the creation of the Juvenile Court in Illinois in 1899, the development of a campaign against child labor, and the development of compulsory school attendance laws. In Denver the probate court judge, Ben Lindsey, used a truancy statute as the basis of his juvenile court. As these new institutions appeared, a new conception of American childhood was emerging, a view that saw children as valuable in their own right and therefore deserving of protection from such evils as child labor and dangerous urban environments. In 1912 Congress created the Federal Children's Bureau, which worked with the National Child Labor Committee to pass the Keating-Owen Act of 1916 regulating child labor; but this law was declared unconstitutional in 1918. Not until passage of the Fair Labor Standards Act in 1938 did a federal law prohibit child labor.

During the early twentieth century, children spent a great deal of their time on city streets. Unlike the "Street Arabs" of the nineteenth century, these children were not orphans, and they went to school. But they worked and played on the streets, selling newspapers, candy, and gum and playing games that sometimes found them dodging traffic in the streets. Reformers considered this behavior pathological and sought to remove the children from streets by passing truancy laws, imposing curfews, and creating well-equipped playgrounds away from the streets. Reformers often sought to give structure and instruction to children on the playgrounds, an approach that limited the interest of children in being there.

After World War I, the Federal Children's Bureau helped sponsor legislation that would try to bring down the high rate of infant mortality in the United States, a rate that was regarded as overly high in the crowded neighborhoods of poor immigrants. The resulting legislation, the Sheppard-Towner Act of 1921, established a cooperative program between states and the federal government that funded prenatal care and helped to bring down infant mortality rates. The program ended in 1929 because of strong opposition from the American Medical Association.

Urban social agencies also expanded their services in the twentieth century. The Young Men's Christian Association and the Young Women's Christian Association saw their mission as bringing physical and mental culture to the urban masses. Scouts and other youth organizations saw themselves preserving some sense of the natural world for city children. The well-known Fresh Air Fund of New York City, which had existed since the nineteenth century, continued to collect funds to send city children to rural settings during the summer.

During World War II, millions of Americans migrated to large cities, following the lure of jobs in defense industries or the many newly inducted members of the military. Huge displacements in services resulted. Schools were overcrowded, housing was stretched to the breaking point, and many experts worried about the impact on children as young mothers answered the call to work in defense plants. Day care, which had been funded by the government during the 1930s to preserve the skills of teachers, became common in most cities. Defense plants discovered that they had to establish

Children playing with the water from an opened fire hydrant, a common sight on the streets of New York City during the summer.

day care facilities if they wished to attract young mothers to their labor forces. Some communities were able to use the provisions of the Lanham Act to set up day care centers. In 1942 the Children's Bureau set up an Emergency Maternal and Infant Care Program for the families of enlisted men, a program it justified in terms of soldier morale rather than the needs of children.

During the war, authorities worried that the absence of parents would cause an outbreak of juvenile misbehavior, a worry that seemed justified when a wave of violence involving soldiers and young men of Hispanic descent broke out in Los Angeles in 1943. These so-called "Zoot Suit Riots" (named after the elaborate outfits worn by the young men) convinced many Americans that the nation's youth were in serious trouble, a perception that continued after the war when Senator Estes Kefauver, a Democrat from Tennessee, held hearings to investigate threats (such as comic books) to the morals of the nation's youth.

After World War II, the character of cities underwent another major change. Urban neighborhoods, characterized by diversity in the early twentieth century, became identified as havens for racial and ethnic minorities, and most inner-city neighborhoods housed people at the bottom of the socioeconomic ladder. Migrants had come to the cities seeking higher wages, but they found that the better jobs demanded skills many of them did not possess. Since migrants often lacked the resources to obtain these skills, their situation frequently became desperate. The streets were now far less diverse than they had been at the beginning of the century, and children had to be "street smart" and learn their ways quickly in order to survive. Playgrounds now attracted older young men, who hoped to develop their athletic prowess, and younger children were crowded off the playgrounds that were supposedly designed for them.

Of those families who had prospered in the city, many moved out of downtown neighborhoods into suburbs where tree-lined streets and newer homes beckoned. Children no longer worked on the streets in large numbers; while they may have played on suburban streets, so much of their time was occupied and organized by schools and other activities that there was little time to create a world of their own on suburban streets. Instead, children were attracted to suburban shopping malls, which ironically sought to re-create the atmosphere and life of early-twentieth-century urban neighborhoods. Games, playgrounds, and even amusement parks occupied central places in the new malls and drew thousands of children, all eager to spend money on amusement.

As the number of urban poor expanded and as the housing stock of cities, both public and private, declined in quality after World War II, the rolls of people on Aid to Families with Dependent Children (AFDC) expanded dramatically.

AFDC had originated during the Depression as a part of Social Security to shield children from the rigors of economic hard times. The sheer size of the welfare rolls generated sharp opposition among the middle classes in American suburbs; in the late twentieth century, Congress limited the time on welfare to two years. Gone was the idea that government would provide support to the poorest of the nation's children. Thus ended the "Century of the Child" in American history.

—*Joseph Hawes*

See also

Apprenticeship; Brace, Charles Loring; Child Labor; Children in Suburbs; Juvenile Delinquency and the Juvenile Justice System; Playgrounds.

References

Berol, Selma Cantor. *Growing Up American: Immigrant Children in America, Then and Now*. New York: Twayne, 1995.

Elder, Glen H., Jr., John Modell, and Ross D. Parke, eds. *Children in Time and Place: Developmental and Historical Insights*. New York: Cambridge University Press, 1993.

Hawes, Joseph M., and N. Ray Hiner, eds. *American Childhood: A Research Guide and Historical Handbook*. Westport, CT: Greenwood Press, 1985.

Nasaw, David. *Children of the City, at Work and at Play*. Garden City, NY: Anchor Books, 1985.

West, Elliott. *Growing Up in Twentieth-Century America: A History and Reference Guide*. Westport, CT: Greenwood Press, 1996.

Children in Suburbs

Children have historically been the first citizens of suburbia. Since the early nineteenth century, they have comprised a significant segment of its population, shaped its distinctive culture, and constituted a main reason for its existence. Indeed, the health, education, and perceived well-being of children have provided a primary impetus for the 150 years of migration by upwardly mobile families away from American cities toward their outskirts.

Migrants to suburbia have also been motivated by a desire to distance themselves from the crime and poverty of cities, to own their own homes, and to better commune with nature, but the underlying interests of children have made these reasons all the more compelling. As early as 1807, the English physician Thomas Trotter wrote that city children, denied sufficient space for sport, became dwarves who lacked firmness of muscle and energy of nerve. His prescription—suburban living—was heartily endorsed by Americans.

So profound has children's influence on suburbia been that in the 1950s and 1960s sociologists coined terms such as "child-centered," "familism," and "filiarchy" to describe its way of life. Supposedly, the typical middle-class suburban family of this period was headed by a commuting father, maintained by a stay-at-home housewife mother, and oriented around 2.3 children. This family lived in a detached single-family ranch house set off by a front lawn, backyard, and "good neighbor" fences. Its scrapes and antics were the subject of sitcoms and comics like "Leave It to Beaver" and "Dennis the Menace."

These images cannot be trusted, however, and they do not reflect the complexity and diversity of suburban communities. Suburbs are politically separate, economically dependent residential areas located within commuting range of a central city. Their inhabitants tend to be socially homogeneous families in their child-rearing years. But there is no single experience of childhood in America and no uniform place called suburbia. Hence, the lives of children in these places cannot be summed up with a few statistics or stereotypes. Suburban children, like suburbs themselves, have come in every class, color, and condition. They have been rich and poor, Anglo and ethnic, thriving and depressed, coddled and abused. Moreover, they have changed over time.

Both childhood and suburbs can be understood as physical stages of life, the borders of which are constantly changing. Their intersecting histories are best charted through four periods that roughly correspond to the first and second halves of the nineteenth and twentieth centuries. Each period is characterized by a unique blend of demographic, intellectual, economic, political, architectural, and technological traits, the sum of which has continually changed America's social landscape.

The first suburbs in America were rural townships and industrial satellites on the fringe of major eastern cities between 1815 and 1850. They were populated by farmers, merchants, laborers, and their families, most of whom worked close by. Only a small minority of elite men used the new roads, bridges, omnibuses, and steam-powered ferries to commute to work in the city. Nevertheless, this emerging middle class wielded great influence. It embraced a suburban ideal in reaction to the noise, squalor, and contagion associated with rapid industrialization, urbanization, and immigration. This ideal was propelled by an evangelical fervor that valorized families and family life. Catherine Beecher, author of many books on housekeeping, vigorously promoted the idea that women's moral superiority fitted them to preside over a domestic sphere best located in a bucolic setting.

This emphasis on domesticity coincided with a trend toward smaller families and a more nurturing approach to child rearing. Notions of child depravity and practices such as will-breaking were largely consigned to a Puritan past. Yet corporal punishment and productive labor remained integral to children's moral and practical education. "The sooner children are taught to turn their faculties to some account," advised Lydia Maria Child in her 1829 manual for frugal housewives, "the better for them and for their parents." She claimed that even six-year-olds could knit stockings, make patchwork, and pick cranberries. Model suburban cottages of the period featured yards, gardens, and such innovations as playrooms. More and more young families settled in these areas and established churches, schools, and parks.

In the 1850s, railroads accelerated the movement of city folk and the transformation of peripheral towns. A comic sketch in *Frank Leslie's Illustrated Newspaper* in 1857 satirized the flight of a salaried New Yorker and his family to the Brooklyn suburbs, where overly friendly neighbors continually asked to borrow things, including the couple's baby. Kindergartens and common schools, despite their urban origins, flourished in many suburbs. As Ralph Waldo Emerson said of Concord, Massachusetts: "We will make our school such that no family which has a new home to choose can fail to be attracted hither as to the one town in which the best education can be secured." Books and magazines written especially for children flooded the market in the 1860s and 1870s, as did dolls, trains, and other toys. Birthday parties and family holidays and vacations also became fashionable.

By the 1890s, a large number of ethnic, working-class families had moved to new streetcar suburbs. Their boys hopped rides and peddled papers on the electrified trolleys that rattled to and from the city center. They and their sisters went to school more and worked less than their counterparts on farms and in cities, but theirs was not a bourgeois upbringing. Studies of the Boston area have found that working-class families who owned their own houses gave their children less education, relying on their income to help defray the cost of a mortgage. As a result, these children enjoyed less upward mobility than others.

Children's welfare and the environment in which they lived were major concerns during the Progressive Era. Reformers established playgrounds, curtailed child labor, certified milk supplies, and formed child-study circles. They focused mainly on urban and rural areas, but lauded the moral order of suburbia. The Children's Aid Society, which had long placed poor city children on farms, began in the 1920s to find them homes in suburbs. Their stated ideal was a "comfortable, unpretentious middle-class detached house with a yard or garden where the children may play." Boys generally enjoyed greater freedom than girls, but Progressive ideas of masculinity and femininity spurred more fathers to share in child rearing and more mothers to enter the workforce, a trend reinforced by World War I.

The construction of bungalows in suburban areas sped up after the war. Automobiles made commuting easier and revolutionized high school dating. Half of all teenagers attended secondary schools by 1930, up from 11 percent in 1900. Child mortality rates dropped as once fatal diseases like scarlet fever, meningitis, and polio were overcome. Young people became central to the new consumer economy, a trend dampened only by the Depression. President Roosevelt's New

Deal policies revived suburbanization by making home-ownership easier and foreclosure more difficult, except in declining or black neighborhoods. Still, the largest migration in the 1930s was from rural to urban areas.

During World War II, thousands of fathers went to war and mothers went to work, creating worries about "latchkey" children and juvenile delinquents and leading to demands for state subsidized child-care centers. As in the previous war, home-front children in cities and suburbs collected scrap and sold war bonds. They joined scout troops, went to matinees, played war games, and pledged allegiance to the flag.

The baby boom after World War II precipitated a stampede to the suburbs, aided by unprecedented prosperity, government money for highways and sewers, and low-interest home loans for veterans and others. Also important were the assembly-line methods of home construction pioneered by the family firm of Levitt and Sons. In 1947 the company broke ground on Levittown, a Long Island community of 17,500 nearly identical homes that sold for $8,000 each, often with no down payment. New houses went up at a rate of 1.5 million per year after the war, 85 percent of them built in suburbs. By 1960, 62 percent of American families owned their own house, up 19 percent from 1940.

Patterns of child labor and leisure also changed. Aside from mowing lawns, delivering newspapers, and baby-sitting, suburban children rarely worked. They played more at home, using backyard swing sets and basketball hoops at the end of driveways. Even television came directly into the house. The best-selling book of the period, Dr. Benjamin Spock's *Baby and Child Care,* encouraged parents to "trust themselves" and eschew harsh discipline. Conservatives of the 1960s and 1970s blamed this "permissive" formula for hippie culture and the antiwar movement.

All was not paradise in suburbia. Restrictive "covenants" excluded nonwhites from many areas. Fathers were expected to be the sole providers for their family and also to coach Little League. Mothers suffered the isolation of long days with toddlers. And children felt pressure to conform, achieve, and, in some cases, keep up appearances despite their parents' marital or drinking problems. Youths also suffered from a dramatic rise in divorce rates, which ended a third of all marriages contracted in the 1950s. Actor James Dean personified the angst of suburban teens in the 1955 film *Rebel without a Cause.*

By 1970, more Americans (38 percent) lived in suburbs than in cities or rural areas. The proportion reached 45 percent in 1980 and topped 50 percent in 1990. There was a simultaneous decline in the birthrate of suburban women due to later marriages, easier access to birth control, and abortions. Consequently, children younger than 19 were no longer the dominant age group in suburban households. In Nassau County, New York, that group declined from 40 percent in 1960 to 29 percent in 1980.

Suburban children in the 1970s and 1980s grew up in neighborhoods different from those their parents knew. Some suburbs had deteriorated into slums and were occupied by renters. Many households were headed by single mothers or older people raising their grandchildren. Affluent suburbs now featured walls, gates, and guards. Fearful parents increasingly opted to place their children in recreational programs rather than let them romp with friends. Shopping malls became the hangout of choice for adolescents. Eric Bogosian's 1994 play, *Suburbia,* sought to explore the stultifying environment that produced a generation of dispirited youths. Set in the parking lot of a 7-Eleven convenience store, the play follows a pack of terminally bored "mall rats" who seek escape via drugs, sex, drinking, driving, and suicide. "The suburbs," observed Bogosian, "can be a dangerous place at a certain age."

Suburbanites still extol their communities as being safer and more wholesome than cities. Stories about inner-city youth gangs, drug wars, and schoolyard shootings are common news. But the dichotomy between safe, white, affluent suburbs and dangerous, black, poor cities is a media fiction. Violence on streets, in schools, and at home is a problem in both places. Poverty is more common outside large cities than inside them. In 1980, 30 percent of the nation's poor lived in small towns and rural districts, 20 percent in suburbs, and 20 percent in small metropolitan areas. Fewer than 7 percent of the remainder lived in urban ghettos—neighborhoods where one in five residents are poor. Furthermore, cities and suburbs are inextricably linked to the drug trade; Representative Walter Fauntroy claims that 80 percent of those buying drugs on the streets of Washington, D.C., are suburbanites. Cities do not hold a monopoly on commercial sex either, as massage parlors have recently sprung up in suburban strip malls.

Some of the drawbacks of suburbia are currently being addressed by a new generation of developers, many of whom grew up in Levittowns after World War II. They are designing suburbs patterned after an idealized vision of small-town life. These planned communities are smaller, denser, more diverse tracts built near offices or industrial parks and mass transit links. They feature smaller yards, cozier tree-shaded streets, neighborly porches, and a range of housing types—including row houses, granny flats, and shopkeeper apartments—intended to attract a variety of ages and incomes. One such project, Celebration, Florida, is being built on 5,000 acres by the Disney Corporation near its Orlando amusement parks. It remains to be seen if these retrovillages are indeed the wave of the future, and how extensively they might affect, and be affected by, the youth of America.

—*Vincent DiGirolamo*

See also
Levittown; Middle Class in Suburbs; Playgrounds; Streetcar Suburbs; Suburban Ideal; Suburbanization; Working Class in Suburbs.

References
Baldassare, Mark. *Trouble in Paradise: The Suburban Transformation in America.* New York: Columbia University Press, 1986.

Gaines, Donna. *Teenage Wasteland: Suburbia's Dead End Kids.* New York: Pantheon, 1991.

Marsh, Margaret. *Suburban Lives.* New Brunswick, NJ: Rutgers University Press, 1990.

Mintz, Stephen, and Susan Kellogg. *Domestic Revolutions: A Social History of American Family Life.* New York: Free Press, 1988.

Stilgoe, John R. *Borderland: Origins of the American Suburb, 1820–1939.* New Haven, CT: Yale University Press, 1988.

Strickland, Charles E., and Andrew M. Ambrose. "The Baby Boom, Prosperity, and the Changing Worlds of Children, 1945–1963." In Joseph Hawes and N. Ray Hiner, eds., *American Childhood: A Research Guide.* Westport, CT: Greenwood Press, 1985.

Wilson, Hugh A. "The Family in Suburbia: From Tradition to Pluralism." In Barbara M. Kelly, ed., *Suburbia Re-examined.* Westport, CT: Greenwood Press, 1988.

Chinatown

Substantial immigration to the United States from China began about 1850, but Chinatowns as urban concentrations of Chinese residents in U.S. cities originated roughly a generation later. Early Chinatowns included mining villages like Chinatown, Nevada (renamed from Hall's Station in the 1850s), and small towns like Locke, California, established in the 1910s. Some early Chinatowns disappeared in the face of gradual attrition through death, migration, or sudden evacuation before angry mobs.

San Francisco held the first urban Chinese community of consequence in the United States in the 1850s. Honolulu's Chinese district developed at about the same time and, after the United States annexed Hawaii in 1898, remained the largest or second largest (after San Francisco) Chinatown in the nation well into the twentieth century. Honolulu reflected the urbanization of Chinese residents: between 1900 and 1950, while the total number of people of Chinese ancestry living in Hawaii showed little change, the percentage living in Honolulu jumped from 35 to 83. Compared with mainland American cities, the Honolulu Chinatown was less exclusively Chinese, and fewer Chinese in Honolulu resided in Chinatown.

Reflecting political developments and settlement patterns, Chinatowns changed over the years in their size, composition, and functions. The East Coast (notably New York), the West Coast (especially San Francisco), and Hawaii (chiefly Honolulu) displayed varying patterns as well. For many years, Chinese immigrants, more than any European migrant group, were men who intended only a temporary stay. Then, as a result of the Chinese Exclusion Act (1882), which cut off further Chinese immigration, Chinatowns remained small and mostly male through World War II. In 1943, with China nomi-

The construction of artificial entrances, such as this one in Los Angeles, illustrates the extent to which Chinatowns have become tourist attractions.

nally an ally of the United States against Japan, American policy began to change. Congress repealed the Chinese Exclusion Act, assigned a small annual quota for immigrants of Chinese ancestry, and repealed the ban on naturalization of Chinese immigrants. After 1945, Chinese war brides were permitted, and the sex ratio edged toward parity.

In the second half of the twentieth century, the number of U.S. residents of Chinese ancestry rose through both immigration and natural increase. Following establishment of the People's Republic of China, immigration legislation in 1952 permitted roughly 30,000 refugees from China. Beginning in 1965, the rules governing legal immigration were greatly eased. The Immigration Act of 1965 assigned annual quotas of 20,000 to each Asian nation, including China (meaning, at that time, Taiwan). Then came actions permitting immigration, much of it Chinese, from Vietnam. Finally, following formal recognition of the People's Republic of China in 1979, that nation also received an annual quota of 20,000. Illegal immigration from China, too, has been great in recent years.

Given the substantial immigration, whether legal or illegal, by people of Chinese ancestry in the 1970s, 1980s, and 1990s, many Chinatowns—from New York and Washington, D.C., to Houston and Los Angeles—grew rapidly in population, and satellite Chinatowns developed. New York City's Chinatown emerged as the largest of all, and youthful lawyers and social workers added to the vibrant mix of old and new immigrants and old and new industries. Meantime, Chinatowns in various cities—among them Chicago, Boston, Philadelphia, and Pittsburgh—lost much of their original territory to expressways and other development schemes.

In some respects, Chinatowns have functioned much as have other ethnic communities in American cities. They have served as temporary havens for new immigrants, sanctuaries with familiar food, customs, and language as well as opportunities for housing and employment, during a time of transition to fuller assimilation. Such communities have also generated, sustained, and prospered a middle class—restaurant owners, garment contractors, newspaper publishers—with a captive community clientele.

Yet the differences have been notable. Until after World War II, Chinatowns contained mostly men, not families, and thus the community displayed populations with few women or children and served less as places to nurture new generations. Significant numbers of longtime Chinatown residents, particularly in New York City, have continued to speak and read no English, and they have grown old never having sought and gained citizenship, never, for that matter, having sought or obtained residence or employment outside Chinatown. Chinatowns have supplied little in the way of a power base in electoral politics. Until after World War II, relatively few Chinese were citizens, and, into the 1980s, their numbers typically remained relatively small. Hiram Fong, a Hawaiian native of Chinese descent, began serving in the Hawaii territorial legislature as early as 1938 and was elected U.S. senator when Hawaii became a state in 1959. Through the 1994 elections, however, no Chinese-American candidate had yet been elected to Congress from any mainland constituency.

—*Peter Wallenstein*

See also
Asian Americans in Cities; Barrio; Ghetto.
References
Chan, Sucheng. *Asian Americans: An Interpretive History*. Boston: Twayne, 1991.
Gillenkirk, Jeff, and James Motlo. *Bitter Melon: Inside America's Last Rural Chinese Town*. Berkeley, CA: Heyday Books, 1987.
Glick, Clarence E. *Sojourners and Settlers: Chinese Migrants in Hawaii*. Honolulu: University Press of Hawaii, 1980.
Hing, Bill Ong. *Making and Remaking Asian America through Immigration Policy, 1850–1990*. Stanford, CA: Stanford University Press, 1993.
Kinkead, Gwen. *Chinatown: A Portrait of a Closed Society*. New York: HarperCollins, 1992.
Kwong, Peter. *The New Chinatown*. New York: Hill and Wang, 1987.

Chrysler Building

The formal and symbolic flamboyance of the Chrysler Building in New York City was occasionally witty, often elegant, and resolutely unorthodox. Designed by the architect William Van Alen for the automobile magnate Walter P. Chrysler and constructed between 1928 and 1930, the building had its origins in a real estate scheme by William H. Reynolds to erect the tallest structure in the world. Its novel forms of corporate advertising, its several phases of design under the successive ownership of Reynolds and Chrysler, and its participation in the race for supreme height that characterized skyscraper development in the late 1920s have exercised an irresistible appeal for the many historians who have recounted these events.

With a craftman's skill and an executive's canniness, Chrysler selected materials of unprecedented luxury for the building's interiors and approved a skyscraper iconography that expressed the 1920s version of the American myth of the self-made man. On the building's Expressionist-inspired observation deck, Chrysler installed a glass case displaying the first set of machine tools he had fashioned as a boy of 18. In the main lobby, Edward Turnball's enormous (97 feet by 110 feet) ceiling mural on the progress of mankind culminated in a huge painted image of the Chrysler Building itself. These and other exhibits more pointedly expressed the highlights of Walter Chrysler's self-begotten career than did the better-known hubcap freize or the eagle-head and radiator-cap gargoyles high on the building's exterior. Examples of Van Alen's architectural wit, these latter two icons exemplified business boosterism in the twenties and expressed the decade's militant patriotism.

—*Edward W. Wolner*

See also
Skyscraper.
References
Hampson, Carol Anthony. *Architecture of Celebration: A Companion to the Chrysler Building*. Los Angeles: n.p., 1994.
N.Y. Landmarks Preservation Commission. *Chrysler Building, 405 Lexington Avenue, Borough of Manhattan . . . Built 1928–1930, Architect William Van Alen*. New York: Landmarks Preservation Commission, 1978.
Reynolds, John B. *Chrysler Building, 42nd to 43rd Streets, Lexington Avenue, New York City: The World's Tallest Building*. New York: n.p., 1930.

Circuses

The history of the circus in the United States has been fundamentally shaped by the growth and spread of the nation's cities. While urban expansion in the nineteenth century sparked such innovations as the railroad tented circus and enabled circuses to tour extensively, urban sprawl in the twentieth century killed such institutions as the circus parade.

John Bill Ricketts introduced Americans to the circus in the 1790s by touring with a company of riders, clowns, and acrobats. Ricketts was the first of many impresarios who attempted to establish permanent indoor circuses in American cities, but by the early nineteenth century, the circus was largely an itinerant form. Crisscrossing the country by steamboat and wagon, antebellum tented circuses often met violence from local rowdies and attacks from clergymen who blamed them for corrupting the morals and emptying the pockets of their predominantly white male audiences. After the Civil War, however, the circus shed its disreputable image to emerge as one of the nation's most popular family-oriented entertainments.

The United States boasted over 20 large companies in the early 1880s (the beginning of the circus's golden age in the United States), and many of them traveled by railroad. The largest circuses employed hundreds of laborers and performers who routinely paraded, performed (often twice), loaded up, and traveled to the next stand—all in one day. Railroads enabled the big shows to bypass smaller towns in favor of population centers capable of filling tents whose capacity could exceed 10,000. Rural patrons rode excursion trains as far as 75 miles to reach large towns and cities where

the big shows performed. They could also take in the second tier of smaller, overland "mud shows" that served towns bypassed by the railroad circuses.

By 1900 both tiers of circuses enticed patrons with a glimpse of the urban-industrial future. For many Americans the railroad circus stood as a paragon of modern capitalist enterprise, with its huge payroll, innovative and enormously expensive marketing methods, rationalized labor, and international scope. The circus heralded modernism by incorporating cultural and technological innovations; while bands played the latest tunes, patrons marveled at displays of electric lights and automobiles. Under the leadership of the Ringlings, the circus extended its golden age into the first decades of the twentieth century. With celebrity performers like equestrienne May Wirth, aerialists Lillian Leitzel and Alfredo Codona, and the high-wire Wallenda troupe, the Ringling show was a force in popular culture during the 1920s and the undisputed ruler of the circus world.

By the 1930s, however, the circus spoke less to its patrons' dreams of the future than their nostalgia for a simpler past. The railroad tented circus looked increasingly anachronistic as street traffic and suburban sprawl spelled the end of the urban circus parade; by mid-century, most circuses

Circus elephants parading through the streets of Ephrata, Pennsylvania.

had abandoned railroads to travel by truck. The circus survived by accommodating itself to demographic and cultural change. Numerous shows folded their tents to exhibit in urban indoor arenas, and the circus sought alliances with younger cultural forms—especially television and the movies—that had it had previously viewed as dangerous rivals. As the century closes, however, the circus is in the midst of a resurgence led by companies—most notably the one-ring Cirque du Soleil—that have returned to the form's roots in small-scale, tented performances focused on acrobatics, aerialists, and clowns.

—*Bluford Adams*

See also
Barnum, Phineas T.
References
Fox, Charles Philip, and Tom Parkinson. *The Circus in America.* Waukesha, WI: Country Beautiful, 1969.
Thayer, Stuart. *Annals of the American Circus, 1793–1829.* Seattle, WA: Dauven & Thayer, 1976.
———. *Annals of the American Circus, 1830–1847.* Seattle, WA: Peanut Butter Publishing, 1986.
———. *Annals of the American Circus, 1848–1860.* Seattle, WA: Dauven & Thayer, 1992.

City Beautiful Movement

The phrase "City Beautiful" first entered popular use in the United States in 1899 among New York City artists and reformers who wanted to adorn their city with civic sculpture, public fountains, waterfront parks, indoor murals and statuary, artistic street fixtures, and much more. They had borrowed the term from the arts and crafts movement in England, where it had evoked the rarefied ideal of the city as a work of art. In the United States, it quickly became a catchphrase used throughout the nation for all manner of efforts to upgrade the appearance of towns and cities.

The movement flourished for nearly a decade and then faded slowly. Its activists were drawn mainly from native-born, well-educated Protestant families who were prominent in local businesses and the professions. Many women became deeply involved. In major cities—New York, Baltimore, Chicago, Cincinnati, Hartford, Philadelphia—beautifiers championed "municipal art," which initially meant placing artworks in government buildings and parks but soon embraced the design of such places as well as of the city itself. Elsewhere, advocates favored "civic improvement," another catch-all phrase that licensed almost any impulse to combat ugliness and raise civic environmental standards.

Two national organizations, the American Park and Outdoor Art Association, begun in 1897, and the National League of Improvement Associations, founded in 1900 and renamed the American League for Civic Improvement in 1901, mixed concepts of naturalistic, small-town beauty with municipal art. They campaigned against outdoor advertising, such as fence placards and the then-novel billboards and gaudy street signs, smoke pollution, and the prevalent male spitting habit. By 1904, the two groups merged as the American Civic Association. A year later, near the peak of the movement, the association reported 2,426 improvement societies in the nation.

Art and architectural interpreters of the City Beautiful movement have portrayed it too exclusively as an architectural and planning movement wedded to showy monumentalism. Unquestionably, public enthusiasm for classical architecture and Baroque civic design, kindled by the Chicago World's Fair of 1893, strongly influenced the McMillan Plan for Washington, D.C. (1902); the civic center design of Cleveland, Ohio (1903); Daniel H. Burnham's celebrated Plan of Chicago (1909); and many other grand schemes. But Charles Mulford Robinson, whose two books, *The Improvement of Towns and Cities* (1901) and *Modern Civic Art* (1903), made him the chief popularizer of the movement, emphasized naturalistic beauty and idealized the shade-dappled residential street. More significantly, the local groups that energized the movement favored small projects achievable on a piecemeal basis—cleanup campaigns, flower beds, a tasteful public library, a new park, street trees, and tidy yards and vacant lots. Sanitary concerns permeated local efforts.

The City Beautiful movement may best be understood as a cultural movement that sought to give outward and visible expression to Progressive Era reform impulses to revitalize public life and instill civic awareness. As a movement, it declined after the 1907 financial panic undercut turn-of-the-century optimism, and the genteel idealism that infused the cause lost its hold among the educated middle classes in America. In city planning, the City Beautiful yielded to the City Efficient.

—*Jon A. Peterson*

See also
Benjamin Franklin Parkway; Burnham, Daniel H.; Central Park; Chicago World's Fair of 1893 (World's Columbian Exposition); Progressivism; Urban Beautification.
References
Bogart, Michelle H. *Public Sculpture and the Civic Ideal in New York City, 1890–1930.* Chicago: University of Chicago Press, 1989.
Peterson, Jon A. "The City Beautiful Movement: Forgotten Origins and Lost Meanings." *Journal of Urban History* 2 (1976): 415–434.
Wilson, Richard Guy. "The Great Civilization" and "Architecture, Landscape, and City Planning." In Brooklyn Museum, *The American Renaissance, 1876–1917,* 9–109. Brooklyn, NY: Brooklyn Museum, 1979.
Wilson, William H. *The City Beautiful Movement.* Baltimore: Johns Hopkins University Press, 1989.

City Charter

City charters are the legal device by which state governments give municipalities the authority to govern. Originally, city charters derived from the English institution of the municipal corporation. In the English town system, a select few of the town's leading men incorporated the town under a town charter. This corporate charter gave the municipal corporation power to regulate and promote the town's commercial affairs and to protect the rights of private property. English settlers brought this system to the colonies, where they organized colonial towns and cities as private, chartered municipal corporations.

In the early nineteenth century, urban residents sought to end the control of the private urban corporation and turned to state legislatures to formulate legal arrangements that would transform municipalities into public corporations. States had this power because the constitutional provisions concerning legal and political powers do not apply to municipalities. Thereafter, state legislatures incorporated towns and cities, and city charters became the means by which states conferred some of their own authority to govern upon cities and towns, a practice that continued for much of the nineteenth century.

A state's first intent when granting a corporate charter was to protect and foster the financial needs of the community. City charters thus contained various provisions that allowed the town or city to borrow money, issue bonds for public improvements, and levy taxes. Charters strictly defined and limited all these financial powers, and cities could not wield any fiscal jurisdiction beyond that granted in its charter. By these means, charters enabled cities to act as a legal person, encouraged financial investment in cities, and protected those investments by clearly limiting the scope of a city's borrowing and spending power.

As to political needs, a city charter generally dictated the type of governing structure and the specific political offices that would govern a city. The charter sometimes enumerated the precise powers the city government could assume and clearly defined the extent of its political powers. State legislatures invariably and explicitly reserved certain powers to itself.

As cities and towns developed and multiplied across the United States, the process of writing, granting, and amending city charters became so cumbersome and time-consuming that state legislatures and municipal residents both sought relief from the process. One method that states adopted was to enact a general incorporation law that would apply to all incorporated cities and towns in the state. Large cities increasingly found this procedure detrimental to their growth in the late nineteenth century because it required them to regulate their fiscal affairs and govern themselves under laws that applied equally to much smaller towns that had very different financial and political needs. As a result, large cities began to seek municipal home rule charters that applied explicitly to that city alone and gave the city certain discretionary powers to manage its own financial and political affairs without the involvement of the legislature. This essentially political process has been more or less successful in different cities depending on their size, their state of location, and how much home rule their state legislature was willing to give.

—*Maureen A. Flanagan*

References

Dillon, John F. *Commentaries on the Law of Municipal Corporations.* 2 vols. Boston: Little, Brown, 1881.

Flanagan, Maureen A. *Charter Reform in Chicago.* Carbondale: Southern Illinois University Press, 1987.

Monkkonen, Eric H. *America Becomes Urban: The Development of U.S. Cities and Towns, 1780–1980.* Berkeley: University of California Press, 1988.

Teaford, Jon C. *The Municipal Revolution in America: Origins of Modern Urban Government, 1650–1825.* Chicago: University of Chicago Press, 1975.

City Directory

City directories were, and are, books that list the names and addresses of city residents; their primary purpose is enabling commercial or business users to locate suppliers and customers easily and to advertise the resources and opportunities of a community. The first specialized directories appeared in Philadelphia in 1785. Until about 1860, the directories were often an ancillary activity of a local printer or newspaper editor. Their content varied, and their publication was irregular.

The earliest directories simply listed the name, occupation, and address of heads of households and businesses. In a few cases other information such as homeownership status, marital status, or number of persons in the household was provided. Information was obtained by surveyors who went from door to door. Lower-income groups and persons other than the head of a household were seldom included, although the scope of coverage expanded during the nineteenth century.

In the 1840s, the separate classified business directory came into vogue. The classified section also contained lists of public officials; officers of fraternal, civic, or charitable societies; members of local militia units; the staff of educational institutions and hospitals; as well as executives of banks or corporations and illustrations of products ranging from stoves and plows to clothing and household furnishings. Community histories, maps, and illustrations of important buildings were also a common feature. Directories often contained listings for suburbs or nearby towns, and a few regional directories offered information about major business centers in several states.

Late in the nineteenth century, street directories became more common, and by the turn of the century, several companies specialized in the production of city directories. Directories for cities in many parts of the country continued to identify African Americans in the early twentieth century. In recent decades a telephone directory section has been added. City directories are a rich resource for understanding aspects of urban development: the emergence of the central business district; population growth and turnover; occupational and residential mobility; the transformation of a city's economy over time; the nature and extent of social services, especially in the nineteenth century; ethnic and sometimes racial residential and occupational patterns; occupational patterns of women; and advertising techniques. Because of the additional information they frequently provide—such as race and occupation—city directories are an unusually rich source of information for anyone studying cities.

—*Jo Ann Rayfield*

References
Knights, Peter R. "City Directories as Aids to Ante-Bellum Urban Studies: A Research Note." *Historical Methods Newsletter* 2 (1969): 1–10.
Rayfield, Jo Ann. "Using City Directories to Teach History and Historical Research Methods." *Teaching History: A Journal of Methods* 16 (1991): 14–26.
Spear, Dorothea N., comp. *Bibliography of American Directories through 1860*. Worcester, MA: American Antiquarian Society, 1961.

City Efficient Movement

From the 1870s to the 1920s, urban reformers in the United States developed a nationwide campaign to curb machine politics, boss rule, and the spoils system of appointments in local government, often in the name of efficiency. Cities, they argued, should not be run by men whose futures depended more on party loyalty than job performance. Efficiency stood above all for ending waste, corruption, and incompetence.

Before the 1890s, most urban reform was short-lived and nationally uncoordinated. Local mercantile and professional elites waged one-shot campaigns against the Tweed Ring in New York, the Gas Ring in Philadelphia, and similar regimes elsewhere. State legislators in New York and Massachusetts authorized civil service appointments, and strong mayor charters were devised for Philadelphia, Boston, Brooklyn, and Los Angeles.

In the 1890s, a new generation of reformers took hold and made city governance a national issue. In city after city, they founded reform clubs and civic leagues and, in 1894, began the National Municipal League. Within five years, they had crafted a national agenda that defined the efficiency ideal for the Progressive Era. Home rule, nonpartisan elections, merit-based appointments, centralized administration, and reliance on trained experts were key components. Progress ensued. For example, the federal Bureau of the Census introduced standard statistical measures of civic performance in 1903, and many cities adopted uniform cost accounting procedures.

An efficiency craze swept the nation beginning in 1911, adding an engineering dimension to the efficiency ideal. That year, Louis Brandeis captured public attention by arguing, in the Eastern Freight Rate case before the Interstate Commerce Commission, that railroads could save $1 million a day by implementing the scientific management ideas of Frederick W. Taylor. A steel industry consultant, Taylor had systematically studied factory work routines, which, he claimed, could be redesigned to save money and boost output. Middle-class Americans, fearful of price inflation and railroad rate increases, embraced efficiency as never before. Henry Ford's mass production assembly line, also pioneered about this time, added more glamour to the term.

The craze lasted about five years. Although it yielded few direct results for cities, it imparted new sanction to bureaus of municipal research, the council-manager form of government, and city planning along "practical" lines, all of which made significant headway before World War I.

—*Jon A. Peterson*

References
Fox, Kenneth. *Better City Government: Innovation in American Urban Politics, 1850–1937*. Philadelphia: Temple University Press, 1977.
Haber, Samuel. *Efficiency and Uplift: Scientific Management in the Progressive Era, 1890–1920*. Chicago: University of Chicago Press, 1964.
Schiesl, Martin J. *The Politics of Efficiency: Municipal Administration and Reform in America, 1880–1920*. Berkeley: University of California Press, 1977.

City Hall

City Hall, the principal municipal building found in every city and town in America, is often thought prosaic. Often located in the decayed heart of a city's old downtown and in a physical condition less than perfect, the building is easy to dismiss as unimportant within the context of a city's total architectural infrastructure and unglamorous compared to newer centers of commercial and cultural life.

But the city hall as a building type has a distinguished history. More importantly, in each individual community, despite its careworn appearance, the city hall renders in concrete form the ongoing experience of local governance, with its accumulated memories of colorful leaders, political controversies, crises, scandals, and, above all, endless changes. Thus, the city hall is a significant part of the urban landscape whose meaning extends far beyond the physical structure itself.

The city hall as an architectural concept originated in the late Middle Ages. In antiquity urban places existed, of course, but no single building was devoted exclusively and comprehensively to local governance. In the Greek city state, a number of civic buildings were clustered around the agora, such as the temple, bouleterion (council house), academy, and treasury. Similarly, the important urban centers of the Roman Empire had several public structures lining the forum, such as the curia, the basilica, a counting house, temples to Apollo and Jupiter, a bazaar, voting area, and banquet room.

The unification of all urban governance under a single roof had to await two developments: the emergence of civil government as a discrete function of society and the establishment of independent local authority. Beginning around the thirteenth century, these began to happen. Urban places attained significant size as trade and commerce joined agriculture as the basis of economic life. Towns grew in wealth and produced new elites that chafed under external control by the church, crown, or nearby manor lord. Because of the influence of craft guilds, banking houses, and local ruling families, cities became increasingly autonomous from outside forces. The Hansa, or German trading towns of the North and Baltic Seas, formed their own Hanseatic League. In England, municipal incorporation laws established a legal concept of local autonomy.

The locus of power in this new kind of polity was displayed architecturally. Town towers were built that could be used to store bullion and records in case of attack. A belfry was built into the tower so that residents could be summoned in case of emergency or to hear proclamations. Also, these towers could be seen at a distance, marking the town's presence to the countryside.

Also, an accompanying or attached building was often constructed, usually on the market square, to provide a place for town bodies to meet and to furnish offices and reception rooms for officials. In northern Europe and England this structure often contained a public assembly room and hence was known as a hall. An open market surrounded by arcades usually occupied the ground floor, and other public buildings were attached or located nearby, such as law courts, prisons, guildhalls, and cloth halls. In Italy the principal civic structure was the palace of the ruling prince, with members of his family and court in residence.

During the Renaissance, the municipal building as the seat of centralized local government took shape. It was erected not on the market square but placed on a square of its own, creating a focal point for the city. The guildhalls and cloth halls were no longer part of the municipal complex; the structure's ground floor was enclosed and used for municipal purposes rather than as an open market. Whenever possible, all governmental functions were brought into the structure, which now typically contained the mayor's office, ceremonial reception rooms, a public assembly hall, council chambers, courtrooms, administrative offices, strong rooms, and sometimes the jail.

As a city's wealth and pride grew, these buildings began to become massive. Their design displayed, sometimes lavishly, currently fashionable architectural styles—Gothic in Louvain and Bruge, Baroque in Paris and Rome, Greek Revival in Birmingham and Liverpool, and Neoclassical in Brussels. The Hanseatic towns built two distinct kinds of edifice, of massive brick in the maritime regions and of ornamented stone elsewhere. Interiors as well as exteriors were grand, with many great Victorian town halls in England fitted out with fine auditorium organs to which Handel's *Messiah* could be sung.

In America, the municipal building is called "city hall," rather than "town hall" as in England, Australia, and other English-speaking countries. This usage probably stems from Americans' use of the word "city" for any large urban place rather than a crown-designated borough or financial center, as in London. The term *hall* has been retained despite the absence of public assembly rooms in American city halls since about 1800.

As in Europe and Great Britain, the city hall was an ornate and costly structure in large American cities during the nineteenth century. Like the underlying concept itself, the building's architectural style was taken from Europe, with Romanesque buildings in the style made popular by Henry H. Richardson in some small cities, particularly in the Northeast. The New York City Hall, the oldest American city hall in continuous use, is French Renaissance in style, while the gigantic Philadelphia City Hall, the world's tallest masonry-bearing structure, is Second Empire.

Other splendid early city halls are found in Baltimore, Providence, Louisville, Milwaukee, and St. Louis. In the early twentieth century, another generation of great city halls was built, many of which are Beaux Arts in style and, as inspired by the City Beautiful movement, integral to large civic plazas. Prime examples are in San Francisco, Cleveland, Duluth, Minnesota, and Springfield, Massachusetts. All have lavish interiors, which for the most part have been restored.

The city hall of Pasadena, California, with its central dome, typifies such buildings across the United States.

As the twentieth century unfolded, several changes occurred in the use of the American city hall. Following the Progressive movement, big city bosses receded in importance, lessening the motivation to build costly city halls to enlarge the opportunities for graft. At the same time, however, progressive and professionalized city governments took on increasing regulatory and social functions, creating the need for greatly expanded office space. This pressure for space gradually pushed law enforcement, courtrooms, reception rooms, and eventually council chambers out of the building. More and more, the city hall became the municipality's central office building rather than an edifice of ceremony and display; citizens came to them to pay their taxes and protest rezoning decisions, not to hear the *Messiah*.

During the latter half of the twentieth century, the American city itself changed with important consequences for city hall. As population moved to the suburbs, governance in the metropolitan area took place in many newer city halls, not just the old one downtown. In cities where the inner city remained vital, the old city hall was often overshadowed by glamorous skyscrapers. In decayed inner cities, the building too decayed, or it was perhaps

replaced by a "partnership" urban renewal complex that put commercial and governmental structures cheek-by-jowl. Another development was the performance of various public services by community organizations, nonprofit enterprises, and private contractors, whose offices are scattered all through the urban fabric. The blending of private and public use of civic architecture and the physical decentralization of governance found in antiquity and the Middle Ages was, in a way, now being revisited.

—*Charles T. Goodsell*

See also

Richardson, Henry Hobson.

References

Cunningham, Colin. *Victorian and Edwardian Town Halls*. London: Routledge & Kegan Paul, 1981.

Goodsell, Charles T. *The Social Meaning of Civic Space*. Lawrence: University Press of Kansas, 1988.

Kump, Earnest J. "Town and City Halls." In Talbot Hamlin, ed., *Forms and Functions of Twentieth-Century Architecture*. New York: Columbia University Press, 1952.

Lebovich, William L. *America's City Halls*. Washington, DC: Preservation Press, 1984.

Pevsner, Nikolaus. *A History of Building Types*. Princeton, NJ: Princeton University Press, 1976.

City in Literature

The land that became the United States was founded as a colonial culture. Its first major cities, Boston and Philadelphia, like the colonists themselves, were transplants of then-current English models and values, not the slow products of an indigenous culture. These colonial cities were physically new and raw, but their psychological and architectural models were the embodiment of an old, foreign culture and their mores remained largely English until late in the nineteenth century. American cities were vital to the development of commerce in the new country, and they afforded all the urban opportunities for the growth of culture and personal and social advancement. But, in terms of the national American myth, cities were relegated to the background as a necessary, but evil and pernicious, influence.

The paradigm of this myth was formed by two dominant images—that of the Pilgrim fathers confronting the wilderness and that of the pioneers confronting the West. As Janis P. Stout has put it, "the view of America as a vast wilderness ready to be transformed into a garden supporting widely separated, independent, virtuous farmers persisted well after the Civil War, reflecting, as Henry Nash Smith has demonstrated, the force of fantasy rather than geographic fact."

Even though this myth had no room for cities, there had been from the beginning the Puritan esteem for the ideal of the new world as a "Citty upon a Hill," and in everyday life, the colonial city was a magnet for commerce, trade, wealth, and social mobility. There was a schism, for example, between L'Enfant's grandiose plan for the city of Washington and Thomas Jefferson's philippic against the city in his *Notes on the State of Virginia,* which portrayed the countryside and its settlers as ideal and good, the city and its denizens as evil and corrupt. Paradoxically (and typically), Jefferson's attitude was the product of an urbane and cosmopolitan intellect. In arguing against cities, Jefferson was essentially objecting to the Old World values they represented, as opposed to what he saw as America's mission to remake society on a different model—to "make it new," to borrow Ezra Pound's phrase.

American cities therefore embodied from the start a conflict of values that has dogged the United States to the present day, a conflict reflected in its literature. As opposed to the more nuanced European urban experience and its representation in literature, America has shown a profound and often brutal ambivalence in its attitude toward cities, understanding on the one hand that culture and civilization are urban phenomena, but on the other regarding cities as "Sodoms in Eden" as Stout has put it. This ambivalence reflects not only the opposition between country or wilderness values and city values, but also the perceived discontinuity between transplanted Old World city paradigms and a new vision of human society.

Cities have been portrayed in literature since there has been literature. Literature itself is an urban phenomenon that addresses a primarily urban audience. Cities as depicted in literature have, as organizing images and ideas, fulfilled many complex functions—mythic, symbolic, emblematic, and hieroglyphic—at various times in Western history. Early cities were founded in accordance with elaborate mythic rituals, not the dictates of common sense. As the largest man-made artifacts in the natural world, and an imposition on nature, cities have from the beginning aroused ambivalence: pride in the achievement mixed with doubts about interfering with the powers in or behind nature. The Tower of Babel, that archetypal symbol of human presumption, was a city within a city (Babylon). Cities were also centers of worldly (royal, military, economic) and otherworldly (priestly) power. The fall of Troy, the plague in Thebes, the Earthly and the Heavenly Jerusalem, Sodom and Gomorra, Rome, Babylon and, in more recent times, the Paris of Honoré de Balzac and Victor Hugo, the London of Charles Dickens and T. S. Eliot, Albert Camus's Oran, and William Carlos Williams's Paterson have served both to crystallize cultural attitudes and give expression to them.

The city both is and symbolizes the notion of society and community—the word "citizen" is derived from "city." Its centrality as an expressive literary figure is a natural extension of both its social and mythic aspects. In Nathaniel Hawthorne's shadowy allegorical schemes, the town is the bearer of the unitary collective values of the community. And most fundamentally, cities are collective images. Novelists work with the relations of individual characters to the social world of the city; in poetry it is more likely to be the poetic consciousness rather than a defined character that may be said to constitute this "individual," as in the poems of Walt Whitman and William Carlos Williams. In city novels, such as William Dean Howells's *The Rise of Silas Lapham,* and in stories such as Hawthorne's "My Kinsman, Major Molineux," the characters relate to the city as actors, agents, perceiving consciousnesses, and/or spectators.

The topos of city versus country that looms so starkly in American culture was formalized by Theocritus (270 B.C.E.) and in Vergil's *Eclogues* (43 B.C.E.), and it has had a long history. But it is worth remembering that the *Eclogues* and most subsequent writings that praise country over city, including those of Jean-Jacques Rousseau, were written by urban authors for an educated urban audience. Stout points out that both Vergilian pastoral and Juvenalian satire are genres that, in differing ways, put rural and urban values in opposition. It might be argued that this apparent duality of vision has changed in the twentieth century, as life in American society, even small-town life, has become increasingly and overwhelmingly urban and suburban in its habits and values. It can be argued that as a literary resource a rural counterpole to these ubiquitous urban values no longer exists. There is still a great deal of nostalgic "re-creation" of the old rural myth (as in Western novels and movies), but it is fantasy. The reality of carving out a settlement in the American wilderness was brutal (as described, for example, in Ole Edvart Rølvaag's *Giants in the Earth*). There is, on the other hand, a large body of literature concerned with immigrants from abroad in American cities, of which Henry Roth's *Call It Sleep* is a leading example.

At various times, a few cities—New York, Chicago, Boston, Los Angeles—have achieved mythic status in literature, as well as in cinema and television, even beyond our shores. Walter Benjamin called Paris the capital of the nineteenth century, and New York can lay claim to being the capital of the twentieth. But the uses to which cities have been put in American literature have been so many and so varied that it is better to be circumspect with generalizations.

In distinction to European cities, which are for the most part independent political entities, cities in the United States are politically the creatures of the state legislatures that charter them. They have limited local powers, and they must compete for resources with rural and suburban interests. This political dependence, while not often overt in literature (as opposed to film), still bears important witness to the negative attitude toward cities that has been part of the American political heritage from the beginning.

Cities in the United States also differ physically from their European counterparts as well as in the cultural and literary niches they occupy. The centers of European cities are residential, and factories and workers have relocated to the outskirts, sometimes voluntarily, sometimes not. In American cities during the nineteenth century, factories, businesses, and the poor came to occupy the city center, while the more affluent classes gradually migrated to the newly developing suburbs. (Suburbs, now a growing phenomenon in Europe, were essentially a nineteenth-century Anglo-American invention.) Los Angeles—Alison Lurie's *The Nowhere City*—is a nomadic city as opposed to a centered city, and was a creation of the automobile age and might be considered the essential home-grown American city, a role it plays in fiction and film. Its major characteristic is an absence of structural definition.

In addition, the values that frame the functions of the city in American literature have changed over time, partly as the result of changes in historical and social conditions (especially as prose fiction became the dominant genre and more realistic), partly in response to changes in valuations of the American foundation myth. Through the eighteenth and early nineteenth centuries, city and large town (size is relative; until well into the nineteenth century very few cities were large in our current terms) were opposed to the task of settling the wilderness. Nostalgic echoes of this are found in Henry David

Thoreau's *Walden* and Mark Twain's *Huckleberry Finn*. In the nineteenth century, increasingly complex urbanization and industrialization, and the consequences of the growth of railroads and better transport, began to affect writers' conceptualization of the city in their work. Throughout the twentieth century, the inescapable diffusion of city culture and urban values (suburbs, transportation, television) has essentially displaced the once rural ideal, which survives in the form of green suburbs and increasingly artificial national and theme parks. Nature as a countervailing concept has disappeared, along with a farm-based population of any size, and indigenous small-town life. Thanks to travel, TV satellite dishes, and shopping malls, small-town and suburban life have become thoroughly urbanized, a phenomenon to which the novels of John Updike bear rueful witness. The old confrontation between the city and nature—nature redefined in mostly suburban terms, with split-level houses and white picket fences—lives on only as a fantasy for some moviemakers and politicians. The city is everywhere in contemporary literature.

Aside from cultural, historical, social, and archetypal factors, as a purely literary device, the city offers writers an incredibly rich field of operations: interactions, collisions, and games of power among myriad characters, types, occupations, and social classes, colliding in an architecturally defined place whose functioning is determined by complicated and subtle social and political codes. (Someone once called the corner of an urban street an "angle of surprise.") For a writer facing an increasingly complex world, the city in the twentieth century has become more than ever a metaphor for the tangled skein of existence, a spatial plane on which life takes place. The city in literature acts as a spatializing device, providing a grid that orders actions and values, either explicitly, as in the novels of Theodore Dreiser, or implicitly, as in those of Henry James. With postmodernist writers such as Thomas Pynchon and William Burroughs, the city also provides a grid, whose laid-out squares spatialize even the hallucinatory timelines of the narrative.

It would be easier to list those contemporary American literary works, especially novels, that do *not* depend in some important way on the urban environment and urban values than to list those that do, and on close examination the same might be said of American theater and poetry. The problem in pursuing the topic is how to characterize or categorize the role of the city in these works. One quickly realizes that the presence of cities in literary works is so varied and multiform that trying to sort them into types or groups does not contribute meaningfully either to an understanding of the individual work or to an understanding of the city as a thematic element. There are, in even a quick and partial descriptive scan, urban novels of social realism (the works of Dreiser,

James T. Farrell, or Frank Norris's *McTeague,* in which an urban setting summarizes the dehumanization of the individual by the forces of rampant industrialization, and at the other end of the urban social scale Edith Wharton's *House of Mirth* and *The Age of Innocence*), of magic social realism (John Dos Passos's *USA*), and of social satire (Henry James's *The Bostonians*). F. Scott Fitzgerald's *The Great Gatsby* might be called the quintessential suburban novel, while in Herman Melville's *Moby-Dick,* Ishmael and the *Pequod* leave cities, and the *Pequod* has been seen as a floating city. In Howells's *A Hazard of New Fortunes,* one of the most interesting American urban novels, the social instability of the characters is measured against the instability of a New York in flux, with a somewhat more stable Boston as a counterweight in the background. In Saul Bellow's novels, Chicago and New York function as trampolines on which the characters bounce higher and higher; Thomas Pynchon abstracts his cities in pseudo-allegorical fashion, much in the manner of a latter-day Hawthorne. Donald Barthelme's "City Life" apotheosizes the inescapable twentieth-century metropolis. For Barthelme, as for William Burroughs, the city as a way of thinking has swallowed up everything, to the point that there is no standpoint outside the city from which to comprehend it.

The richness of the city in literature is also evident in the American short story, from Hawthorne and Edgar Allan Poe to O. Henry, Ring Lardner, and many moderns. Detective and science fiction have also been major urban genres in American literature.

In poetry, Dickinson and Frost would seem to be major exceptions, poets for whom the city is not an important thematic or organizing element. But to list just Whitman, Ezra Pound, Eliot, Wallace Stevens, Marianne Moore, Hart Crane, William Carlos Williams, Robert Lowell, and John Ashbery gives some indication of the scope and variety of the city topos in poetry. In drama, especially that of the twentieth century, the city has also become ubiquitous: Arthur Miller, Tennessee Williams, and almost all contemporary playwrights concentrate on urban settings, values, and problems. Many of Eugene O'Neill's plays would seem to form an exception, but—a typical case of the subtle complexity of the literary thematics of urban life—this can be more apparent than real; for instance, the country setting of *Long Day's Journey into Night* is the summer home of the thoroughly urban Tyrone family, none of whose standards, values, or literary references are "country."

In searching for some method by which to organize the ways the city is used in a literary work, one is confronted with a bewildering variety of critical approaches. There is, in addition, often a fuzzy line between what interests the literary critic on the one hand and the social critic and historian on the other; the literary city seems to demand a broader approach. For instance, the city can be regarded historically, sociologically, politically, anthropologically, psychoanalytically, phenomenologically, statistically, existentially, as structuralist or deconstructionist, and archetypally or mythically (as suggested at the beginning of this essay). However, no single approach imposes itself; everything depends on the critic's approach and angle of attack. Earlier attempts by critics to classify cities in literature according to fixed types and categories have fallen out of fashion since the 1970s in favor of an *ad hoc,* often multidisciplinary approach that, while it may be confusing, at least has the merit of respecting the complexity of this subject.

If classifying generalizations are to be avoided, the question remains of how the city can be understood and analyzed as an organizing metaphor in individual literary works. The basic problem is that the city in literature is an image and not a concept, an "unreadable rebus" (Paul Ricoeur), and thus not readily accessible to purely analytic approaches, of whatever kind. As has been indicated, the use of the city can be described fairly well in prose narratives that are nominally realistic and that present an internally coherent image of the city, one that at least resembles or feigns a social reality. But even here, the better the writer, the more difficult it is to isolate the city from its literary context as a freestanding thematic device. Lesser writers tend to rely on stock or stereotypical ideas, attitudes, and language in conjuring the image of the urban environment, techniques that are more historically timebound and more loosely connected to the work's imaginative structure. This makes it difficult for a modern reader to connect the motives and actions of the characters with the assumed values of the urban setting, which would have been clear to readers at the time without having to be part of the text. The Horatio Alger stories are one example of this, and J. D. Salinger's *The Catcher in the Rye* may be becoming a more modern one. On the other hand, the novels of Dreiser, Howells, and Dos Passos provide the reader with the necessary internal compass points to connect the city as image to plot, characters, and action in a way that has remained meaningful over time.

In modernist and postmodernist writing, and in poetry and drama generally, the presence of the city is harder to analyze; the city or urban environment tends to be more abstract and more diffused. There is Hart Crane's strenuous attempt at an epic poem, *The Bridge,* in which the Brooklyn Bridge, as a central symbol of the nation's premier city, is meant to anchor a poem about the entire United States; there is Robert Lowell's requiem "For the Union Dead," in which, captured in a historical urban monument in the historical Boston, an age of past national unity, purpose, and heroism is opposed to Boston's venal present; there is William Carlos Williams's *Paterson,* in which the city spins out, on and on, the continuing dream of its founder and of its poet, unraveling in the process into a thousand kaleidoscopic threads. In Arthur Miller's *Death of a Salesman,* the city represents home and rootedness to the Loman family. But in the works of William Burroughs, Donald Barthelme, and many other contemporary writers, the city functions not as a place but as a buzz, a gaseous, semitransparent cloud that envelops the characters from beginning to end, an environment that seems to have largely detached itself from a specific sense of place.

—*Burton Pike*

See also

Alger, Horatio, Jr.; Barthelme, Donald; Bellamy, Edward; Cheever, John; Dreiser, Theodore; Fitzgerald, F. Scott; Howells, William Dean; Irving, John Winslow; Kerouac, Jack; Whitman, Walt; Williams, William Carlos.

References

Hurm, Gerd. *Fragmented Urban Images: The American City in Modern Fiction from Stephen Crane to Thomas Pynchon.* New York: Peter Lang, 1991.

Machor, James L. *Pastoral Cities: Urban Ideals and the Symbolic Landscapes of America.* Madison: University of Wisconsin Press, 1987.

Mumford, Lewis. *The City in History.* New York: Harcourt, Brace and World, 1961.

Pike, Burton. *The Image of the City in Modern Literature.* Princeton, NJ: Princeton University Press, 1981.

Smith, Carl S. *Chicago and the American Literary Imagination, 1880–1920.* Chicago: University of Chicago Press, 1984.

Squier, Susan Merrill. *Women Writers and the City: Essays in Feminist Literary Criticism.* Knoxville: University of Tennessee Press, 1984.

Stout, Janis P. *Sodoms in Eden: The City in American Fiction before 1860.* Westport, CT: Greenwood Press, 1976.

White, Morton, and Lucia White. *The Intellectual versus the City: From Thomas Jefferson to Frank Lloyd Wright.* Cambridge, MA: Harvard University Press, 1962.

City Planning

The term *city planning* originated in the United States during the Progressive Era, in 1907 or 1908, about the same time that *town planning* emerged in Great Britain and 17 years after *Stadtebau* had been introduced in Germany. In each country, these words expressed new hopes to achieve greater public control over the growth and development of the physical city. By 1917, when the United States entered World War I, city planning had taken root as a novel field of public endeavor. In the 1920s, it gained wide acceptance but produced a spotty record. Seemingly eclipsed by the Depression and World War II, the planning ideal as conceived by reformers earlier in the century survived into the postwar era, only to be eroded by the decentralizing forces that recast twentieth-century urbanism and by disenchantment with the original vision. The city planning era, thus, extended from the first to sixth decades of the twentieth century. By the 1970s, it had effectively ended.

What perished was faith in the workability and centrality of the era's core concept: the comprehensive city planning ideal. This principle held that the physical development of an existing city should be controlled by a single, overall scheme—or comprehensive city plan, usually called a Master Plan from the 1920s on. Its advocates argued that an expert or team of experts—architects, landscape designers, civil engineers, lawyers, and the like—should formulate a citywide, integrated, multipurpose scheme to guide all subsequent development of a city. Based on exhaustive study, it would be published as a report replete with diagrams, maps, and statistics. In principle, its recommendations would touch virtually every aspect of city making: everything from traffic and transit systems to replacing public buildings, from construction of parks and community facilities to the management of utilities and harbor works, as well as zoning and subdivision regulations.

City planning, thus conceived, presumed the capacity of specialists to identify and give specific form to the public interest and the willingness of the public to accept the proffered advice. Implicitly, it valued rationality, centralization, and the city as a unitary entity. With few exceptions, no one during the nineteenth century had sought to shape entire cities in this fashion.

The impetus for city planning came from the buildup and proliferation of large cities that had begun in the nineteenth century. By the start of the twentieth century, Germany and England had already become predominantly urban; and the United States, despite its vast farmlands, was moving in the same direction. Big city growth had overwhelmed older forms of urbanism rooted in maritime trade. New means of energy production and of transport and communication—coal-fired steam engines, railroads, the telegraph—had concentrated people and economic activities more than ever before, yielding enormous, densely built cities with disorderly commercial and civic cores; crowded, smoky factory districts; and congested, unsanitary housing, all of which provoked new ideas about how such places might be better built to meet human needs.

City planning also reflected trends in western thought toward the interventionist state, expressed through Progressive Era reform in the United States and both reform liberalism and socialism in Europe. Wherever the change to industrial urbanism occurred, new forms of public guidance had seemed necessary. In all, then, city planning is best understood as a historical phenomenon—it was the American version of the interventionist state with respect to the big city environment that was first conceived during the Progressive Era.

Prior to the twentieth century, other forms of urban planning had flourished in America. To better understand the distinctive thrust of city planning, a brief overview of this earlier activity is necessary. From the first European settlements along the eastern seaboard of North America in the seventeenth century until the final conquest of the trans-Mississippi West after the Civil War, the primary task of city builders had been creating new townsites. On land never before colonized or only lightly developed, speculators, land companies, railroads, reformers, religious groups, and public officials had projected thousands of townsites in the seventeenth, eighteenth, and nineteenth centuries. This activity can be called townsite planning. Unlike city planning, it focused on *de novo* settings.

Initially, no single formula dominated townsite planning. Seventeenth-century New England towns, which were based on huge land grants given by colonial authorities, included both a village or town center and also outlying farm lots and considerable land reserved for later distribution. Town centers followed no set pattern. Only that of New Haven, designed in 1638 as a nine-square grid, took precise geometric form. In the Middle Atlantic area, New York City grew along irregular lines after 1624, despite contrary instructions from the Dutch West India Company. Philadelphia, projected in 1682–1683 as a grid of immense size for its day (two square miles), featured two wide cross streets (Broad and Market) and five symmetrically placed public squares. These traits mirrored Renaissance town design and won favor among European travelers accustomed to the more erratic layouts common in the towns they know best.

Two southern colonies introduced Baroque civic design, with its penchant for closed street vistas and geometric spaces. Annapolis, Maryland, begun in 1695, combined two circles and a great square with radial and grid streets, and Williamsburg, Virginia, dating from 1699, featured a street closed at each end by public buildings as the spine of a "miniature grand plan." Savannah, Georgia, begun in 1633, though not Baroque, became famous for its regularly spaced public squares. Finally, and most spectacularly, Washington, D.C., designed by Peter Charles L'Enfant in 1791, pushed Baroque grandeur to a scale and complexity beyond anything seen before or since in the American experience, laying out a capital city of world significance.

By then, however, gridiron design dominated townsite planning. Almost from the outset of American history, land speculation became commonplace, and the grid, an arrangement in which all intersecting streets and lot lines meet at right angles, offered the easiest method for platting and selling town lots. Much used in the seventeenth century, it became all but universal by the late 1700s, just in time for the westward movement to carry it beyond the Appalachians. Cheap to design, easy to stake out, and adaptable to varied usage, it required only a surveyor to produce it. As the nineteenth century progressed, it gained supremacy over Manhattan by way of the 1811 extension plan, began its conquest of the lakefront site of Chicago in 1830, and was imposed on

San Francisco, despite its hills, between 1847 and 1849. Mormons in Utah, miners in Colorado, and railroad companies throughout the West all used the grid. Had nineteenth-century townsite planning required more knowledge and skill, as did the layouts of New England mill towns of the 1820s, 1830s, and 1840s, and Pullman, Illinois, in 1880, where the physical demands of mills and factories imposed a different form, then it might have become more than a nameless convention and sometime art.

The antecedents of twentieth-century city planning lie elsewhere. From the 1820s onward, urban growth began to outpace rural growth. From 1710 to 1820, cities of 8,000 or more had simply kept pace with the rest of society, never exceeding 4.9 percent of total population; by 1900, they comprised almost 33 percent. Before the 1820 census, no American city had exceeded 100,000 in size, the threshold for what European demographers called great cities. In 1820 New York achieved this status. By 1840 there were 3 such places; by 1860, 9; by 1880, 20; by 1900, 38; and by 1910, 68. By the latter date, three cities—New York, Chicago, and Philadelphia—exceeded 1 million residents. All this happened because cities took on new functions and embroidered old ones.

Great city urbanism, as this phenomenon will be called, overwhelmed inherited arrangements for laying out cities and satisfying human needs. Epidemics, crowding, riots, lost access to nature, vulnerability to fire, confusion over standards of public behavior, visual disorder, and shoddy building practices all seemed to worsen and require correction. Many solutions involved the urban environment. Prominent among them from the 1840s on were public water supply, systematic sewerage, parks and park systems, planned institutional sites, transit systems, picturesque suburbs, and massive urban landfills.

Such undertakings had limited objectives and may thus be called special purpose planning. Wherever such planning emerged, it supplanted less coherent and more piecemeal forms of growth. Its physical reach might be citywide, as in water supply, sewerage, or park systems; or it might address very large sites, such as university settings, suburban tracts, or exposition grounds. All this planning involved heavy capital outlays and entailed novel degrees of expertise and forethought, well beyond that required by most townsite planning.

Progressive Era urban reformers built on the experience accumulated with special purpose undertakings by seeking to plan the great city environment as if it were the unitary realm they believed it to be and wanted it to be. Two events set the stage for their generalist approach. In 1893 the Chicago World's Fair, or World's Columbian Exposition, featured classical buildings arrayed around an immense lakeside lagoon. It was a stunning scene. Dubbed the White City, it reintroduced the nation to Baroque design and suggested an ideal city fulfilling middle-class dreams of a better-ordered public life. But how to reach this vision of the future remained unclear. Not until the McMillan Plan for Washington, D.C., did a path become apparent.

Issued early in 1902, the McMillan Plan marks the beginning of American city planning. The elite architects who pressed hardest for the scheme had wanted to resurrect L'Enfant's plan as the basis for locating new buildings and monuments in the nation's capital. Theirs was an architectural vision. But local politics forced them to do more: design a citywide park system—a form of special purpose planning popularized in the United States after the Civil War—and address still more issues such as slum clearance, railroad station placement, and playgrounds. The upshot was a plan touted as unique for being comprehensive.

Before 1902 many civic groups had begun urging city beautification along piecemeal lines—cleaner streets, a civic monument, artistic street fixtures, a public fountain, a riverfront park, or a government center. The McMillan Plan, however, suggested that experts might be summoned to focus and coordinate local energies.

In 1904 a national movement for city planning emerged, exploiting this idea as its paradigm. By 1909 Charles Mulford Robinson, the nation's most prolific City Beautiful writer, had produced at least 17 reports or city plans. Architect Daniel H. Burnham, famous as the master builder of the Chicago World's Fair and the dominant force on the McMillan Commission, devised city plans for Manila and Baguio in the Philippine Islands (1904–1905) and for San Francisco (1904–1905) and Chicago (1907–1909). The Plan of Chicago remains the best known and most consequential of the comprehensive city plans issued in the United States before World War I. Frederick Law Olmsted, Jr., and a younger landscape architect, John Nolen, also emerged as city planning consultants.

A turning point came in 1909. By then, planning reports, some quite modest, others elaborate, had been devised for at least 37 towns and cities, and "city planning" had come into public usage. Meanwhile, certain New York social reformers had attacked American planning as preoccupied with beauty and callous toward the masses of city laborers trapped in congested tenement districts, especially in New York. Foreign practice suggested alternatives: zoning limits on population density as in Germany and factory villages in the countryside as in Britain. In 1909 the social progressives, working through Benjamin Marsh of the Committee on Congestion of Population in New York, staged the first National Conference on City Planning in Washington, D.C., hoping to seize the initiative.

They failed. But what emerged from their challenge was city planning itself—a movement wedded to controlling urban growth and development on the basis of comprehensive city planning. Neither beauty nor social welfare alone would fix the agenda. In the years from 1909 to 1917, under the leadership of Frederick Law Olmsted, Jr., the major features of this new field of public endeavor were worked out. Previously concerned with public improvements, planning now included private property as well, chiefly through zoning and subdivision regulations. In 1916 New York City adopted the first comprehensive zoning act in the nation, establishing the legal standard by which all subsequent zoning in the United States was measured. A planning literature—books, articles, and special publications—began to appear. In 1916 John Nolen edited *City Planning: A Series of Papers Presenting the Essential Elements of a City Plan;* and Nelson P. Lewis, the first engineer to figure prominently in the movement, published *The Planning of the Modern City.* Finally, those most deeply engaged in the new field organized the American City Planning Institute in 1917, a quasi-professional body established to foster discussion of technical issues.

At this time the city planing commission became the accepted institutional device for local planning. Customarily, state and local governments had set up commissions to fulfill special objectives, such as park oversight. But commissions for planning, if empowered to shape the entire city, might usurp the functions of elected officials. State and local governments thus granted them only advisory authority, except for the power to approve new subdivisions. And once created, they often put them on starvation budgets, killing all possibilities for serious plan making.

The gap between aspirations and achievement loomed large from the outset of city planning. Could comprehensive city planning be made to work? The meager tools available to control city growth suggested not. In response, most early advocates concentrated on winning public favor. The "city practical" and "city efficient" themes, prominent within the movement from 1909 to World War I and beyond, represented a recasting of planning rhetoric to enhance its appeal, especially to local chambers of commerce. Support from almost any business quarter was welcomed. Thus, in 1915–1917, when Kansas City realtor J. C. Nichols and other developers of upper-class residential areas expressed interest in drawing up plans for their new subdivisions, planners embraced them forthwith and awarded them strong political support.

The problem of workability—the key issue never solved by the city planning movement—forced planning advocates into an opportunistic stance. Presenting themselves as expressing the public interest but lacking real power to attain their full program, they seized whatever opportunities appeared, even at the price of advancing one aspect of their field at the expense of another.

Zoning offers a clear example. This idea arose outside the planning movement, chiefly as a device for protecting residential property from intrusive, nonresidential use. Early efforts along this line emerged in California (1909) and in Wisconsin and Minnesota (1913) without the benefit of planning expertise. But once planning advocates in New York City seized the issue and marshaled top-flight legal and technical talent, even they ignored a key planning principle—that zoning be based on a prior, comprehensive city plan. As zoning spread like wildfire in the 1920s, planners helped to frame the Department of Commerce Standard State Zoning Enabling Act, issued in 1923, and to argue the *Euclid Village* decision of the U.S. Supreme Court, which upheld zoning in principle in 1926. But locally they often crafted ordinances without benefit of a comprehensive plan. As one investigator discovered in 1929, over 754 places had adopted zoning since 1916, but since 1904 only about 200 cities had produced about 300 comprehensive plans.

American planning in the 1920s progressed institutionally but could not move much beyond opportunistic action. Thus, in 1927 the Department of Commerce encouraged states to authorize city planning commissions by publishing its *Standard City Planning Enabling Act;* by 1929 over 650 communities had established these bodies. But it was booming growth, combined with phenomenal increases in automobile use, that dictated action, not the abstract claims of comprehensive planning. Traffic jams and parking woes translated into urgent studies of street openings and widenings, thoroughfare plans, and traffic management proposals, sometimes by means of a comprehensive plan, but often not. Not surprisingly, engineers, most notably Harland Bartholomew, began to play more critical roles in the planning movement as independent experts. Significantly, only one city in the 1920s fulfilled the city planning ideal of legally adopting and enforcing a comprehensive plan. That was Cincinnati in 1925.

Ironically, planning in the 1920s is best remembered for two developments that forecast the end of great city urbanism. Radburn, New Jersey (1928–1929), a brilliant but isolated experiment in suburban townsite planning inspired by English garden city ideas, was a response to the auto-based urbanism then emerging. And the high profile Regional Plan of New York, prepared from 1921 to 1929, pushed comprehensive planning to a multistate regional scale (5,528 square miles), indicating the staggering sweep that auto-based urbanism would attain while outstripping the capacities of local government to exert general control.

In the few places where regional planning showed any success in the 1920s, it usually focused on highways, parks, or some other special purpose goal, thus reverting to noncomprehensive intervention. During the Depression, federal initiatives began to determine planning opportunities, a pattern that would persist until the presidency of Richard Nixon but virtually die out with that of Ronald Reagan. The Depression crippled locally funded city planning. Many dislodged planners moved to state government planning boards then being founded at the prompting of the federal government. Public housing emerged as a novel issue for most Americans after the National Industrial Recovery Act of 1933 authorized slum clearance and federal construction of public housing and the Housing Act of 1937 made government-financed public housing a national goal. Neither of these New Deal measures, however, made city planning a prerequisite to action.

On another front, the Resettlement Administration built three garden suburbs between 1935 and 1938: Greenbelt, Maryland, near Washington, D.C.; Greenhills, Ohio, near Cincinnati; and Greendale, Wisconsin, near Milwaukee. Each generated jobs and, like Radburn, essayed higher standards of townsite design. Finally, the National Resources Committee in 1937 outlined what might have become a national urban policy had political leaders wanted it, but they didn't. Despite such fragmentation and agenda setting, the pre–New Deal planning ethos remained alive. During World War II, for example, as allied victory came into sight, cities such as Pittsburgh geared themselves for postwar reconstruction along comprehensive lines, partly seeking to counteract the anticipated return of economic depression.

During the quarter-century after World War II, the nation's economy surged, and its cities exploded far beyond their old boundaries, evolving into vast metropolitan regions. Activities previously found at or near the urban core now spread far and wide: retail shopping, light industry, warehousing, office buildings, and the like. Two federal policies, neither rooted in city planning, subsidized much of this explosion. Federally insured mortgages, originated by the 1934 National Housing Act and extended to war veterans in 1944, underwrote much postwar suburbanization, while the Interstate Highway Act of 1956 projected 41,000 miles of limited-access highways that opened once remote countryside to development. Unable and unwilling to create governmental authorities commensurate with this new scale, metropolitan regions became fragmented realms, defying hopes for comprehensive, integrated control of growth just as had happened in the 1920s.

City planning, although historically rooted in great city urbanism, regained considerable prominence, especially after the 1949 National Housing Act and, more forcefully, the 1954 National Housing Act required cities to produce comprehensive plans before proceeding with federally financed slum clearance and urban renewal. But this was an illusory gain. In practice, most core city rebuilding in the late 1950s and the 1960s occurred on a project-by-project basis by setting up federally subsidized local agencies that were empowered to hire a technical staff, assemble land by purchase or eminent domain, demolish all structures, and sell the cleared site to a private developer for rebuilding. Comprehensive planning, under these circumstances, survived more as a program requirement than as a springboard for action.

From the 1950s onward, it became apparent both in older cities and in the metropolitan regions beyond that effective planning concentrated of necessity on programmatic strategies backed by aggressive politicians and business interests. Well-defined if complex goals, such as downtown renewal or the creation of regional industrial parks, stood some chance. When critics of American planning in the 1960s faulted the emphasis on physical development, they succeeded in broadening its agenda to include social issues. But this "new comprehensiveness" proved no more workable. Thus, when the "Great Society" Model Cities program (1966–1973) begun during Lyndon Johnson's administration sought to develop a social approach, little of lasting value was achieved. Finally, when Richard Nixon commenced withdrawing federal funding for housing, urban renewal, and local planning about 1973, neither the nation's urban areas themselves nor the array of techniques available to shape their future bore much resemblance to the great cities of an earlier era or to the city planning field that had been framed in response to their needs. Even theorists within the movement declared comprehensive planning dead as a foundation ideal and as a workable procedure.

Urban planning today is perceived to inhere in diverse activities: public-private partnerships aimed at core city growth, historic preservation, antigrowth policies, transportation design, open space and environmental preservation, neighborhood revitalization, and economic development. Some of these conflict with one another. Thus, like the late-twentieth-century urbanism it mirrors, planning today is diffuse, multifaceted, and subject to continuous change. Portions of its agenda may utilize a comprehensive approach, but the field as a whole has passed beyond coherent, unitary definition.

—*Jon A. Peterson*

See also
Burnham, Daniel H.; Chicago World's Fair of 1893 (World's Columbian Exposition); Greenbelt Towns; L'Enfant, Peter Charles; Master Plan; Nicholson, Francis; Nolen, John; Olmsted, Frederick Law; Olmsted, Frederick Law, Jr.; Perry, Clarence Arthur; Planned Community; Regional Plan Association; Regional Plan of New York and Its Environs; Regional Planning; Resettlement Administration; Stein, Clarence S.; Tugwell, Rexford Guy; Zoning.

References
Krueckeberg, Donald A., ed. *Introduction to Planning History in the United States.* New Brunswick, NJ: Rutgers University Press, 1983.
Peterson, Jon A. "The Mall, the McMillan Plan, and the Origins of American City Planning." In Richard Longstreth, ed., *The Mall in Washington, 1791–1991,* 101–115. Washington, DC: National Gallery of Art, 1991.
Reps, John W. *The Making of Urban America: A History of City Planning in the United States.* Princeton, NJ: Princeton University Press, 1965.
Schaffer, Daniel, ed. *Two Centuries of American Planning.* Baltimore: Johns Hopkins University Press, 1988.
Schuyler, David. *The New Urban Landscape: The Redefinition of City Form in Nineteenth-Century America.* Baltimore: Johns Hopkins University Press, 1986.
Scott, Mel. *American City Planning since 1980.* Berkeley: University of California Press, 1969.
Sies, Mary Corbin, and Christopher Silver, eds. *Planning the Twentieth-Century American City.* Baltimore: Johns Hopkins University Press, 1996.
Sutcliffe, Anthony. *Towards the Planned City: Germany, Britain, the United States and France, 1780–1914.* New York: St. Martin's Press, 1981.

City-Size Distribution

Research on population distribution among cities or urban areas within an urban hierarchy dates back to 1913 when Auerbach discovered that the city-size distribution of several countries follows a well-defined pattern. Since then, scholars from different disciplines have studied the pattern closely, especially focusing their interest on three topics: the empirical verification of the shape of the distribution, the analysis of theories and mechanisms capable of generating alleged distributions, and the empirical study of factors shaping the distribution.

Much of the literature concerning the shape of the distribution has focused on investigating the conformity of city-size distribution to the so-called "Pareto distribution." This is a skewed distribution, represented by a parameter called the Pareto exponent, in which the upper tail is much longer than the lower tail. This line of research was stimulated when systematic investigation revealed that the city-size distribution of several countries follows this distribution remarkably well, and the Pareto exponent can serve as a concise measure of population concentration.

Associated with study of the Pareto distribution, and following Zipf's work of 1949, scholars discovered the "rank-size rule," which seems applicable to almost all countries around the world. According to this rule, when cities are ranked from the largest to the smallest, the products of a city's rank and population are approximately constant. According to this rule, the second-largest city is half the size of the largest, the third-largest city is one-third the size of the largest, and so on. If this rule is correct, the remarkable regularity warrants an explanation.

In fact, the rank-size rule is a special case of Pareto distribution where the Pareto exponent equals one. For many years, this observation was used to design statistical procedures for testing the validity of the rank-size rule. Many empirical studies employing this line of investigation confirmed the validity of the rank-size rule for many countries.

Numerous theories explain the rank-size distribution. The justifications are based on diverse principles from different social sciences, primarily economics, geography, sociology, and statistics, each emphasizing its own distinct point of view. Two explanations that influenced the literature are by Beckmann and Simon. Beckmann's explanation is rooted in the Central Place Theory, and it relies on two simple but powerful assumptions to reach its conclusions. First, each city specializes in producing goods that are locally consumed and exported to smaller cities. The quantity exported depends on the level of production, which, in turn, depends on city population. Second, a city of a given size can serve a fixed number of cities of the next smallest size. According to Beckmann, the sizes of cities that will emerge under these assumptions form a hierarchy that conforms to the rank-size distribution. Unfortunately, objections to this model challenge its ability to provide a sound explanation for the rank-size rule.

The explanation by Simon hinges on the Central Limit Theorem in statistics. Accordingly, if city size is determined by a large number of well-behaved, independent, random variables, its distribution will be approximately normal. Suppose that the population of each city depends on a large number of interacting random factors, whose effects are proportionate in nature. Such factors might include birth and death rates, rural-to-urban migration, employment opportunities, and urban amenities. The Central Limit Theorem suggests that the distribution of the logarithm of city size is approximately normal and the distribution of city size is lognormal. Whereas the lognormal distribution differs from the rank-size distribution, a truncated lognormal distribution where the lower side of the distribution is discarded—as is done in empirical studies—has a shape similar to the rank-size distribution.

Recently scholars have challenged the conventional procedure used to validate the rank-size rule. Employing more appropriate, alternative test procedures, Alperovich and others have found that the rank-size rule is unsound for most countries. At the same time, scholars have also challenged the more general Pareto distribution. It has also been proposed that conventional procedures used to infer the relevancy of Pareto distribution are also inadequate. Instead, a satisfactory test can be conducted using the Box-Cox general transformation function appropriate for this purpose. Using this approach, it was found that the Pareto distribution is not warranted by data from a wide range of countries.

Another line of investigation has focused on the systematic study of factors that shape city-size distributions. Theoretically, the distribution of people among cities of different size depends on economic and noneconomic factors falling into two broad categories. One category comprises all factors that enhance the desirability of producing and consuming goods in a concentrated, rather than dispersed, manner. These are mainly economies of scale, agglomeration economies, and consumers' preferences for consuming goods and services that are available only in large cities. The second category includes factors that bring about spatial dispersion, such as the cost of distributing goods and high land rents in large cities. Empirical investigations reveal that scale and agglomeration economies are most important in promoting urban concentration.

City-size distribution is often used to investigate the relationship between economic development and economic concentration. A leading view argues that at an initial phase of development economic growth leads to population concentration in a few core cities where growth can best be realized. A second phase follows in which economic growth causes population dispersal. Studies that have used international cross-sectional data in conjunction with Pareto distribution have failed to confirm this relationship. In contrast, studies that have utilized time-series data from a few countries have succeeded in demonstrating the relationship between economic development and population concentration.

—*Gershon Alperovich*

References

Alperovich, G. "A New Testing Procedure of the Rank Size Distribution." *Journal of Urban Economics* 23 (1988): 251–259.

Auerbach, F. "Das Gesetz der Vevolkerungskoncnetration." *Petermanns Geogrphische Mitteilungen* 59 (1913): 74–76.

Beckmann, M. J. "City Hierarchies and the Distribution of City Size." *Economic Development and Cultural Change* 4 (1958): 243–248.

Simon, H. "On a Class of Skew Distribution Functions." *Biometrika* 42 (1955): 425–440.

Zipf, G. K. *Human Behavior and the Principle of Least Effort.* Cambridge, MA: Addison-Wesley, 1949.

Civil Defense

Civil defense was the name given the effort to protect civilians from the ravages of nuclear war. Concern for civil defense, however, predated the Atomic Age. An Office of Civilian Defense helped Americans prepare for an attack that never came during World War II. The British did even more to protect themselves from German bombs in the same war, and their successful air-raid precautions provided a model for later campaigns for survival.

The United States began exploring the possibilities of civil defense soon after World War II. Although the Office of Civilian Defense disappeared, government officials considered new alternatives in an era of atomic weapons. A board appointed by the War Department in 1946 declared that "the fundamental principle of civil defense is self help," and it recommended that civilian agencies teach rescue skills. In 1948 Secretary of Defense James Forrestal established an Office of Civil Defense Planning. The next year, the National Security Resources Board assumed responsibility for protecting the civilian population, and in early 1951 President Harry S. Truman established a new Federal Civil Defense Administration.

At first, the civil defense effort stressed decentralization. Cities seemed likely targets, and policymakers believed it important to disperse industrial and governmental centers. Physicist Ralph Lapp argued that "dispersion is the only really effective answer to the atomic bomb." In September 1951, the *Bulletin of the Atomic Scientists* devoted an entire issue to the question. That same year, a National Industrial Dispersion Policy encouraged new defense plants to locate in less-congested areas but failed to disperse government offices and buildings.

The Truman administration also began a shelter program. Americans assumed that they could protect the civilian population in cities and suburbs in hiding places if nuclear attack took place. Proposed shelters should be blast-proof structures that could withstand a nuclear attack. The major problem turned out to be cost—such shelters were prohibitively expensive. The first estimate for a national program ran to $32 billion. Even a scaled-down figure of $16 billion was more than the government could manage.

Instead, government officials began cajoling Americans to protect themselves in other ways. The "Duck and Cover" campaign aimed at schoolchildren in the early 1950s told them to drop down on their knees and cover their heads with their arms if an atomic attack occurred. Bert the Turtle told young readers, "Bert ducks and covers. He's smart, but he has his shelter on his back. You must learn to find shelter."

With the development of the hydrogen bomb, the problem of civil defense became more serious. New weapons were far more powerful than the bombs dropped on Hiroshima and Nagasaki. In 1954 Lewis Strauss, chairman of the Atomic Energy Commission, shocked a press conference when he admitted that "an H-bomb can be made . . . large enough to take out a city," even New York. Dispersion was no longer the answer. And blast shelters, which had never seemed an effective means of protection, were even less useful now.

Instead, the administration of Dwight D. Eisenhower began to consider evacuation. "The advent of the H-bomb has necessitated a modification in earlier civil defense planning," one official wrote in 1955. "The only 100 percent defense against it is not to be there when it goes off." The focus now changed, according to the *Bulletin of the Atomic Scientists,* "from 'Duck and Cover' to 'Run Like Hell.'"

Evacuation of American cities and suburbs required an adequate road system. To that end, the administration pushed for an act creating an interstate highway system. Passed in

1956, it provided access to the burgeoning suburbs as well as an expeditious means of fleeing America's cities in case of nuclear war. It also had a tremendous effect on subsequent urban development.

Then scientists discovered the consequences of radioactive fallout. The creeping cloud that accompanied any nuclear blast minimized the value of running away. Following contamination from tests in the Pacific Ocean in 1954, scientists in the United States and around the world began to focus on the dangers of radiation. Now Americans began to reconsider shelters, not to withstand the shock of a nuclear blast but rather to provide a shield from the fallout.

Americans debated different kinds of shelters. Edward Teller, the physicist most responsible for the hydrogen bomb, advocated a chain of deep underground shelters, each able to hold 1,000 persons. Others proposed more modest structures. The Office of Civil and Defense Mobilization, created in 1958, distributed free copies of "Family Fallout Shelter," a booklet that told readers how to protect themselves. The Boy Scouts of America delivered 42 million copies of another civil defense publication—an emergency manual—to homes throughout America.

Building shelters boomed in the Eisenhower years. In cities and suburbs, Americans constructed rooms for their own protection. Some were expensive; others were dirt cheap. At the end of the 1950s, the government asked the American Institute of Decorators to design a shelter that looked inviting enough for everyday living. Properly built, it could double as a den or playroom.

The preoccupation with shelters continued into the early 1960s. John F. Kennedy, who became president in 1961, was intent on providing more fully for American defense, and civil defense was part of his plan. In his first year in office, he found himself tangling with Soviet leader Nikita Khrushchev over Berlin. In the midst of this crisis, Kennedy called on Congress to increase defense appropriations, double the number of draft calls, activate reserve units, and expand the fallout shelter program. He asked for—and received—$207.6 million for shelters, with most of the money allocated for marking and stocking existing community shelter spaces in subways, tunnels, corridors, and basements that could temporarily house 50 million Americans. "At cocktail parties and PTA meetings and family dinners, on buses and commuter trains and around office watercoolers," *Time* magazine noted, "talk turns to shelters."

Then the crisis passed. The Limited Test Ban Treaty of 1963, which prohibited testing nuclear devices in the atmosphere, minimized the danger of fallout and neutralized the proponents of protection. Civil defense, which had always had critics, fell victim to the process of arms control. Despite a brief resurgence of interest during the presidency of Ronald

Reagan, most Americans acknowledged that real protection from nuclear attack was impossible. Civil defense might serve as a signal of national resolve, but it was hardly worth additional effort or expense.

—*Allan M. Winkler*

References

Wigner, Eugene P., ed. *Who Speaks for Civil Defense?* New York: Charles Scribner's Sons, 1968.

Winkler, Allan M. "A 40-Year History of Civil Defense." *Bulletin of the Atomic Scientists* 40 (June–July 1984): 16–23.

———. *Life under a Cloud: American Anxiety about the Atom.* New York: Oxford University Press, 1993.

Civil Rights

Cities and civil rights have been intimately related in twentieth-century America. The major issues emerged even before the modern civil rights movement. In the pre–Civil War North, black or biracial organizations—from churches to antislavery associations, located in such cities as Boston and Philadelphia—pressed for an expanded understanding of black freedom. After the Civil War and Reconstruction, efforts to resist the development of Jim Crow often centered in cities, as when black southerners resisted the segregation of urban transit—in Norfolk, Savannah, and other cities—through boycotts in the years around 1900.

The modern pattern, in which civil rights and cities were even more closely connected and substantial change was often achieved, emerged by the 1930s. Black auto workers pressed for social improvement in Detroit. In New York, Chicago, and other northern cities, a major movement during the Depression called for a new type of direct economic action. With the slogan of "don't buy where you can't work," the effort during the 1930s focused on obtaining jobs for black workers in shops owned by whites in black communities. The March on Washington Movement, led by A. Philip Randolph and beginning in 1941, organized principally in New York, Chicago, and other northern cities. Randolph's partial victory, securing President Franklin D. Roosevelt's executive order to open jobs in defense plants, benefited black workers in many industrial cities.

A litigation campaign against racist policies by the National Association for the Advancement of Colored People (NAACP), headquartered in New York and closely associated with Howard University Law School in Washington, D.C., often found itself concentrating on southern cities. In Norfolk, Virginia, in 1940, for example, the NAACP secured the major legal precedent for equalizing teachers' salaries across racial lines, and the organization found it far easier to gain compliance in Richmond and other southern cities than in rural areas.

Cities shaped the emergence of civil rights in a broad cultural way in twentieth-century America. Washington, D.C., for example, produced significant black leadership through the M Street (later Dunbar) High School and Howard University. Black urban communities could depend on separate black institutions—churches and schools, music clubs and baseball teams, newspapers and a range of businesses—to provide rich cultural experiences as well as the financial underpinnings of civil rights efforts. Jazz music in cities was important in various ways—as a significant expression of the African-American experience and as an opportunity for black and white musicians to work together and for black artists to perform for integrated audiences. The Harlem Renaissance in New York during the 1920s produced an outpouring of literature and other arts, vital to bridging the chasm between black and white America. Marian Anderson's famous concert at the Lincoln Memorial in 1939 and the great March on Washington in 1963 also took place in cities.

The world of sports offers any number of examples of the connection between civil rights and cities. Joe Louis defeated boxer Max Schmeling in New York in 1938. Jackie Robinson desegregated major league baseball when he joined the Brooklyn Dodgers in 1947 and played before huge multiracial audiences in such cities as Philadelphia, Cincinnati, St. Louis, Chicago, and New York. During preseason the next two years, the Dodgers played in southern cities ranging in size and geography from Macon, Georgia, to Dallas, Texas. Within a few years, biracial teams played ball in cities of every size and in every part of the country. Great changes occurred in racial attitudes as well as interracial behavior.

The modern civil rights movement in the South, as a grassroots, direct-action phenomenon, originated in the 1950s in such cities as Baton Rouge, Louisiana, and Tallahassee, Florida. Best known of these episodes is the boycott of segregated buses in Montgomery, Alabama, after Rosa Parks was arrested for declining to give her seat to a white man. As the movement escalated in 1960, sit-ins—characteristically in cities, among them Greensboro, North Carolina; Richmond, Virginia; and Nashville, Tennessee—became another tool to chip away at Jim Crow laws and customs. The cities proved promising venues for achieving change in the Jim Crow South. In 1960, when black students at Atlanta University conducted sit-ins and other demonstrations, white residents marveled that there were so many black college students at all, let alone that they were directly challenging racial segregation.

African Americans could organize more easily in cities, even in the Deep South, than on isolated Mississippi plantations. Terror could not so easily be directed toward them, nor could economic retaliation. When violence erupted, as it did in Birmingham, Alabama, in 1963 and on "Bloody Sunday" in Selma, Alabama, in 1965, it attracted national attention and forced federal intervention. The confrontation in Birmingham led directly to passage of the Civil Rights Bill of 1963, harbinger of the Civil Rights Act of 1964, and the violence in Selma led directly to the Voting Rights Act of 1965. Moreover, white southerners who were sympathetic to the aspirations of black southerners—for whatever reason and to whatever degree—found that they might give support more readily in cities. Smaller towns and rural parts of the Deep South proved far more intractable.

These indigenous southern efforts found allies outside the region. Those outside supporters tended to be—or to be responding to—black southerners who had migrated to northern cities. As early as the 1880s, tens of thousands of black Virginians left their native state and migrated to Washington, Baltimore, Philadelphia, and New York. From the Deep South, for the half-century beginning in the 1910s, millions of African Americans moved to cities in the North and West—from Georgia to New York, from Alabama to Chicago, from Texas to Los Angeles. Those migrants could exercise their right to vote once they moved from farms in the South to cities in the North or West. And that fact, combined with their numbers, began to transform the way northern politicians won office and acted as officeholders.

As early as 1928 transplanted southerners living in northern ghettos began to elect African Americans to Congress. The first was an Alabama native, Oscar De Priest, elected in 1928 as a Republican from Chicago. He was unseated after three terms by another native of Alabama, Arthur W. Mitchell, a Democrat who served four terms. Following Mitchell was William L. Dawson, a native of Georgia and former Republican, who won election to fourteen successive terms beginning in 1942. Beginning in 1944, Adam Clayton Powell, Jr., won election from New York City's Harlem in every election until another black Democrat narrowly defeated him in the 1970 primary. Increasingly, there were others as well. For year after year, Powell insisted on proposing the "Powell amendment" to appropriations and other bills.

The March on Washington in August 1963 was one of the most significant events leading to social and political gains for African Americans during the era.

He hoped to obtain greater employment and educational opportunities for African Americans by making federal programs contingent on including and implementing antidiscrimination requirements.

At the same time as black political leaders were emerging in northern cities, white politicians in the North were becoming increasingly attuned to the needs and demands of black voters. Presidents and presidential candidates, as early as Franklin D. Roosevelt in 1936 and 1940 and especially Harry S. Truman in 1948, adapted their promises and their performance to black voters in large cities in populous northern states. In 1940, for example, President Roosevelt promoted Col. Benjamin O. Davis, Sr., as the army's first black general, and in 1948 President Truman issued an executive order to desegregate the military. In 1957 and 1960, Congress passed the first civil rights bills since 1875, and in 1964 Congress enacted an aggressive bill that addressed civil rights in employment, education, and public accommodations. In 1965 another act addressed voting rights in the South. Living in northern cities, those hundreds of thousands of transplanted black southerners (together with their children and grandchildren) had a tremendous impact in reconfiguring the policy context of developments in their native region.

Urban areas sometimes experienced a transition between segregated and desegregated facilities during which public services were simply suspended. During Virginia's era of resistance against implementing the Supreme Court's decision in *Brown v. Board of Education,* Norfolk closed its white schools for many weeks during the 1958–1959 school year rather than allow desegregation. Urban areas responded similarly to the assault on Jim Crow at municipal swimming pools. Town after town in Louisiana, from Monroe to Thibodeaux, drained and chained their swimming pools for a time in the wake of the 1964 Civil Rights Act. "Equal protection of the laws," as the Fourteenth Amendment required, or equal access to public facilities, as the new federal civil rights act dictated, could demand racially integrated access to public facilities only if there were, in fact, public facilities. Shut them down—deny everyone access—and no law was violated. Nonetheless, no one group could any longer be directly privileged by public policy. And the transition generally proved brief, as schools and pools alike soon reopened under the new regime as desegregated facilities.

Much had changed. The most blatant aspects of Jim Crow had fallen. Laws could no longer mandate segregated schools or parks or transit in America's cities. The presence of African-American officeholders in southern cities—from the mayor of Tuskegee, Alabama, to the mayor of Atlanta, Georgia—testified to the fruits of the modern civil rights movement. So did vast improvements in many public services for blacks—from municipal services in a small Florida city to the presence of black students at historically white southern state universities from Charlottesville, Virginia, and Athens, Georgia, to Fayetteville, Arkansas, and Austin, Texas.

And yet the nation's major cities also revealed the existence of sharp limits to the movement's accomplishments. Though commentators continued to distinguish between *de facto* and *de jure* segregation, the white suburbs surrounding black central cities reflected federal housing policies that, in the 1930s and 1940s, facilitated the movement of white, middle-class families to suburbia while impeding the exit of black families regardless of their finances. The political organization of urban areas often militated against school desegregation. Charlotte, North Carolina, successfully integrated its schools by busing children within a metropolitan area that included both the city and surrounding Mecklenburg County. By contrast, after desegregation first occurred in Richmond, Virginia, its public schools soon became overwhelmingly black, as white families (and significant numbers of middle-class black families, too) moved into Henrico and Chesterfield Counties, beyond the city's jurisdiction.

Events as well as structural legacies intruded. Beginning in Los Angeles in 1965, rioting in black ghettos left death and destruction in dozens of cities. As these episodes captured headlines, they demonstrated that ills were not confined to the South and not all had been satisfactorily addressed. White residents of Boston fiercely resisted busing to achieve more racially balanced public schools. With little success, Dr. Martin Luther King, Jr., sought to achieve breakthroughs in housing and employment equality in Chicago, and he died seeking to support black workers in Memphis, Tennessee.

Thus it might be said that the civil rights movement died, or at least metamorphosed, in cities, much as it had been born there.

—*Peter Wallenstein*

See also
African Americans in Cities; African Americans in Suburbs; Blockbusting; Busing; Desegregation of Education; Desegregation of Housing.

References
Broussard, Albert S. *Black San Francisco: The Struggle for Racial Equality in the West, 1900–1954.* Lawrence: University Press of Kansas, 1993.
Button, James W. *Blacks and Social Change: Impact of the Civil Rights Movement in Southern Communities.* Princeton, NJ: Princeton University Press, 1989.
Douglas, Davison M. *Reading, Writing, and Race: The Desegregation of the Charlotte Schools.* Chapel Hill: University of North Carolina Press, 1995.
Formisano, Ronald P. *Boston against Busing: Race, Class, and Ethnicity in the 1960s and 1970s.* Chapel Hill: University of North Carolina Press, 1991.

Franklin, Jimmie Lewis. *Back to Birmingham: Richard Arrington, Jr., and His Times.* Tuscaloosa: University of Alabama Press, 1989.

Goldfield, David R. *Black, White, and Southern: Race Relations and Southern Culture: 1940 to the Present.* Baton Rouge: Louisiana State University Press, 1990.

Greenberg, Cheryl. *"Or Does It Explode?" Black Harlem in the Great Depression.* New York: Oxford University Press, 1991.

Honey, Michael K. *Southern Labor and Black Civil Rights: Organizing Memphis Workers.* Urbana: University of Illinois Press, 1993.

Jackson, Kenneth T. *Crabgrass Frontier: The Suburbanization of the United States.* New York: Oxford University Press, 1985.

Lemann, Nicholas. *The Promised Land: The Great Black Migration and How It Changed America.* New York: Knopf, 1991.

Meier, August, and Elliott Rudwick. *Black Detroit and the Rise of the UAW.* New York: Oxford University Press, 1979.

Morris, Aldon D. *The Origins of the Civil Rights Movement: Black Communities Organizing for Change.* New York: Free Press, 1984.

Norrell, Robert J. *Reaping the Whirlwind: The Civil Rights Movement in Tuskegee.* New York: Knopf, 1985.

Pratt, Robert A. *The Color of Their Skin: Education and Race in Richmond, Virginia, 1954–89.* Charlottesville: University Press of Virginia, 1992.

Ralph, James R., Jr. *Northern Protest: Martin Luther King, Jr., Chicago, and the Civil Rights Movement.* Cambridge, MA: Harvard University Press, 1993.

Rogers, Kim Lacy. *Righteous Lives: Narratives of the New Orleans Civil Rights Movement.* New York: New York University Press, 1994.

Tygiel, Jules. *Baseball's Great Experiment: Jackie Robinson and His Legacy.* New York: Oxford University Press, 1983.

Vose, Clement E. *Caucasians Only: The Supreme Court, the NAACP, and the Restrictive Covenant Cases.* Berkeley: University of California Press, 1959.

Civil Service

A civil service system is one in which hiring and promoting government employees depend on examination scores or other objective criteria related to the work being performed. Except for relatively high-level policymaking positions, promotion is usually from within an agency. This fosters the division of labor, increases expertise, and ideally assures that hiring and promotion are not based on partisan or personal connections.

Civil service systems differ from spoils systems, in which government employment requires support from political party officials. Spoils systems force bureaucrats to be accountable to politicians, but they also take time away from work and allow some to win jobs because of partisan connections rather than merit. Spoils can also allow a political party to hold power through patronage and to "assess" government employees a percentage of their wages.

In 1881 municipal reform leagues began agitating for civil service on the local, state, and national levels, many after a "disappointed office seeker" assassinated President James A. Garfield. In 1883 the Pendleton Act established a civil service covering 10 percent of federal jobs. This was gradually extended.

On the state and local levels in the late 1800s, urbanization made the delivery of services more important than ever, and it was thought that merit would be less corrupt and more efficient than spoils. As a result, America could be as modern as Britain, France, and Prussia. Since native-born Americans usually performed better than immigrants on examinations, civil service could also favor educated Protestants at the expense of (usually Irish) Catholics. These effects were mitigated in many cities by good public schools and because tests were designed for particular jobs rather than general academic training.

In 1883 New York established the first merit system at the state level, and Massachusetts followed a year later. In 1884 Albany, New York, became the first city with a merit system, and in 1895 Cook County, Illinois, became the first county to do so. Ironically these were among the last places to adopt merit systems fully.

By World War II, federal statutes required cities to use merit systems in local agencies that received federal funds. Recent U.S. Supreme Court decisions mandate the use of merit systems for all positions that do not determine policy on the grounds that spoils systems violate the free speech and free association rights of government employees.

The percentage of employees in civil service systems varies among localities and across agencies. Smaller incorporated areas are less likely to use formal merit systems, though informal practices often have the same intent, and for some professions (e.g., police) statewide examinations are used to screen applicants.

Today, civil service is still defended on the grounds of efficiency and honesty. Surveys and case studies suggest that local bureaucrats appointed on the basis of merit are more likely than political appointees to allocate services according to professional norms and standards rather than partisan or constituency demands. At the same time, merit bureaucracies are criticized as limiting the control of elected officials over government. Conservatives see them as inflexible, unaccountable, and inefficient; therefore, some governments use consultants and contract out work previously done by civil servants. Liberals complain that merit systems are elitist and underrepresent minorities and women. Affirmative action and comparable worth programs are often seen as contradicting merit systems.

—*Robert Maranto*

References

Abney, Glenn, and Thomas P. Lauth. *The Politics of State and City Administration.* Albany: State University of New York Press, 1986.

Bowman, Ann O., and Richard C. Kearney. *State and Local Government.* Boston: Houghton Mifflin, 1990.

Gottfried, Frances. *The Merit System and Municipal Civil Service.* Westport, CT: Greenwood Press, 1991.

Lowi, Theodore. *The End of Liberalism.* 2d ed. New York: W. W. Norton, 1979.

Maranto, Robert, and David Schultz. *A Short History of the United States Civil Service.* Lanham, MD: University Press of America, 1991.

Schiesl, Martin J. *The Politics of Efficiency: Municipal Administration and Reform in America, 1800–1920.* Berkeley: University of California Press, 1985.

Schultz, David. "Supreme Court Articulation of the Politics/ Administration Dichotomy." In Ali Farazmand, ed., *Handbook of Bureaucracy.* New York: Marcel Dekker (forthcoming).

Stein, Lana. *Holding Bureaucrats Accountable.* Tuscaloosa: University of Alabama Press, 1991.

Clifton, Ohio

Clifton, Ohio, was America's second designed suburb, after Robert Phillips's Glendale (1851), a few miles north, and before either Llewellyn Park, New Jersey (1853), or Riverside, Illinois (1869), the famed Olmsted and Vaux project near Chicago. Clifton's proprietors, founders, and designer, Adolph Strauch, developed lofty goals central to greening the Cincinnati metropolitan area by blending naturalism with urban design.

In the early 1840s, some of Cincinnati's "merchant princes" built hilltop estates north of the city in an area rising 600 feet above the Ohio River and having dramatic views. They hoped to escape the recurring epidemics that ravaged the city, and an outbreak of cholera in 1849 hastened their move to a place beyond urban problems but close enough to maintain their involvement in the city.

In the 1840s, Cincinnati became the sixth largest and the fastest-growing city in the country. Its population skyrocketed from 46,000 to 115,000, but it remained jammed along the riverfront in an area contained by a semicircle of high hills. As the city grew, noxious packing plants also began moving north into the sylvan Millcreek Valley, threatening the luxuriant natural setting valued so highly by the elite.

Clifton's founders ran a curving avenue along a ridge and down to a valley road, providing access to the city by carriage. Only the wealthy could afford carriages, and for decades they feared no incursions from the unsavory. At first, they used Clifton for summer cottages, but many soon built primary residences there. In 1850 they incorporated the village of Clifton and passed regulations to prohibit fast riding, pollution, and selling alcoholic beverages, especially as smaller lots and middle-class homes were built along an access road.

To keep encroaching industry from destroying the views and fresh air, early residents established the "rural" cemetery of Spring Grove just northwest of their villas in 1845. They hired Howard Daniels, a local architect, to design it, launching a career that quickly carried him away to plan a dozen other cemeteries, to become a finalist in the 1858 design competition for New York's Central Park, and to plan Baltimore's Druid Hill Park. Daniels left horticulturists Robert Buchanan and Henry Probasco to finish developing the picturesque cemetery and the landscapes of Clifton estates.

By a stroke of luck, the Prussian landscape gardener Adolph Strauch (1822–1883) arrived in 1852. The year before, Strauch had met Robert Bowler, a rich Cincinnati merchant and gentleman horticulturist, and liked his easygoing demeanor, "free from the pompous ostentations of the European aristocracy." Strauch declined a position as director of an estate near Florence and set out to see America's "sublime" wonders. Unable to visit the Rockies, Strauch headed for Niagara Falls on his way to seek work designing a model village being planned near Cambridge, Massachusetts. Strauch missed his train in Cincinnati, retrieved Bowler's calling card, and received a warm welcome from him.

Bowler persuaded Strauch to stay and design the grounds of his and other grand baronial houses in Clifton. Strauch gave Bowler's large estate, Mount Storm, a lake, waterfall, orchards, irrigation, gardens, greenhouses, and a hilltop Temple of Love. (The estate later became a public park.) Strauch extended this landscape through neighboring properties to form a unified "open lawn system." The residents wanted to turn their properties into a unified picturesque landscape resembling eighteenth-century English gardens.

Strauch's sweeping lawns or "greenswards" across property lines created the look of a single, large estate. Bosks of trees framed palatial homes, fountains, statues, and distant vistas, especially over the Millcreek Valley. Strauch's sinuous drives wound through the undulating terrain, creating "a sequence of carefully designed, gradually unfolding views" for those in carriages. Rambling paths formed an internal network on and between properties. This "rural" system of drives and paths contrasted with the urban grid, and Clifton was a "village park."

Inevitably, Strauch's clients took him to Spring Grove cemetery, seeking advice on how to "improve" its landscape. Strauch became the cemetery's landscape gardener in 1854 and promised to implement his "landscape lawn plan" to produce "the pictorial union of architecture, sculpture, and landscape gardening," blending the "well-regulated precision of human design with apparently wild irregularities of divine creation." There, as in Clifton, Strauch created a sense of landscape unity. His careful placement of vegetation created an illusion of spaciousness.

In 1867 park advocates suggested that the city turn the Millcreek bottom into a "pleasure ground" by enlarging the narrow, green avenue that linked Cincinnati to the cemetery and Clifton. Reclamation would have turned a strip of bottomland into a linear park, an unprecedented green corridor, and a model of urban design. (Not until 1876 did Boston propose the parks and parkways system that Olmsted later designed as the Emerald Necklace, and even that preceded the City Beautiful movement.) The new corridor would "prevent hog-pens, distilleries, starch factories, slaughterhouses, bone-boiling establishments, or stink factories of any kind" from destroying the valley's pastoralism. But even though the Cincinnati Academy of Medicine endorsed the plan in 1872, the project never materialized. Opponents termed it "a fraud" and called it "a most flagrant humbug" and "puerile."

Despite the opposition, Cincinnati's public parks movement had successes. Two years later Strauch designed Eden Park (1870) on the heights above the city, and he created a second pastoral park, Burnet Woods, on the Clifton heights, using the only woodland within city limits. He converted ravines into "graceful slopes and rounded hillocks" and created a pond; it later became part of Clifton. Strauch himself served as superintendent on the Cincinnati Board of Park Commissioners from 1871 to 1875.

Strauch worked with Andrew Erkenbrecher, founder of the Society for the Acclimatization of Birds, to create a Zoological Garden (1873–1875) in Cincinnati's new suburb of Avondale next to Clifton—the nation's second major zoo. Theodore Findeisin, an engineer experienced in such work in Europe, laid out the grounds around a central lake, smaller ponds, and streams with Strauch's advice on plantings; architect James McLaughlin designed the buildings, including an Italianate restaurant that served as a "country club." It, too, became part of Clifton.

One observer noted in 1880 that the entire area—Clifton, Spring Grove, the newer villages of College Hill, Winton Place, St. Bernard, Avondale, as well as the Zoo and Burnet Woods Park—formed an extensive preserve. Its 4,000 acres, protected by state laws and village ordinances, formed "in effect one grand park, each bounding . . . the other." Concerted efforts beautified the metropolitan area and created a naturalistic preserve as an antidote to the crowded, polluted central city.

The original residents of Clifton had resisted building roads to improve access from surrounding suburbs, but they could not counter the commuter railroads and streetcars that brought Cincinnati to their doors. In the 1870s, the middle class suburbanized, just when many early residents of Clifton met financial failure and their estates were divided into multiple plots. Linear streets obliterated Strauch's landscape, and the exclusive suburb became first a true "village" and finally just a neighborhood as the city annexed Clifton, Avondale, and the Zoo in 1896. The automobile further eased accessibility and increased traffic.

Subdivision left little of Strauch's work in Clifton intact; but as late as the 1930s Clara Longworth, a privileged local daughter, proclaimed Clifton "the most fabulously beautiful paradise of a suburb in America." Even in the 1950s an observer called the place "the most imperatorial" of suburbs with lawns "measured by acres and rooms by the dozens in pinnacled chateaux," like "Castles on the Rhine." Clifton remains a treasury of historic architecture. But fine Tudor Revival and then modernist homes have chewed away parts of old estates. Modern apartment houses have arisen as have hospitals. Clifton itself succumbed to the University of Cincinnati and others who wanted something of what remained from an older version of suburban life, albeit one with a distinctive urban character.

—*Blanche M. G. Linden*

References

Clubbe, John. *Cincinnati Observed: Architecture and History.* Columbus: Ohio State University Press, 1992.

Ehrlinger, David. *The Cincinnati Zoo and Botanical Garden: From Past to Present.* Cincinnati: Cincinnati Zoo and Botanical Garden, 1993.

Linden, Blanche M. G. *Spring Grove: Celebrating 150 Years.* Cincinnati: Cincinnati Historical Society, 1995.

Shapiro, Henry D., and Zane L. Miller. *Clifton: Neighborhood and Community in an Urban Setting: A Brief History.* 2d ed. Cincinnati: Laboratory in American Civilization, 1981.

Coal Towns

During the latter half of the nineteenth and first half of the twentieth centuries, coal towns, although not an integral part of the actual production process, were an important component of the bituminous coal and coke industry of the United States. These towns were financed, built, and operated by coal companies for the sole purpose of housing a labor force to extract coal or produce coke at nearby mines. From the perspective of coal companies, the practical purpose of constructing company housing was to increase productivity and profits for the coal company by attracting labor, reducing labor turnover, and establishing control over the labor force.

Mines were rapidly opening in unsettled rural and often remote townships with little housing available for the influx of workers and their families. As a result, the coal town was an almost instant creation that developed adjacent to mines in order to minimize the miners' walking distance. Their location was determined by geological considerations rather than transportation or other factors.

Housing, like mining buildings and structures, was simply part of the general investment in the mining enterprise. Because of the relatively short life expectancy of a mine and the high cost of housing, coal operators were reluctant to spend large sums of money on costly construction. They generally laid out these towns in accordance with a number of factors—geographic location and physical setting (whether the site was a narrow valley or an open, flat plateau), location with respect to other towns, size and probable life of the mine, class and nationalities of employees, and the conscientiousness of the company in community planning. Depending on the size and location of the mine, some coal operators constructed workers' housing and also provided such services and facilities as water, a retail store, a medical facility, a school, a church, and sometimes a social center.

Construction varied throughout the different coalfields. Mine engineers, rather than architects or town planners, laid out the entire complex including the buildings and structures needed to extract coal or manufacture coke as well as housing and other facilities for the labor force. Some mining villages were extremely primitive and consisted of minimal accommodations necessary to attract and house an increasingly immigrant labor force. They were constructed from simple designs with minimal attention to the aesthetic qualities or town planning that foster a sense of community. Streets were usually unpaved with no sidewalks, although cinders and waste from the nearby slag heaps, called "red dog" or "boney," were used to keep the dust down.

Mixtures of single-family, duplex, and semidetached houses were often found in the same town. Single-family houses consisted of three, four, or five rooms. Duplex houses were eight, ten, or twelve rooms and were rented to two families. Multiple housing, including six or more units, was also constructed by some companies. Boarding houses and hotels rented rooms and provided meals, laundry, and other services for single or transient workers.

The exteriors of frame houses were whitewashed or painted with cheap barn board paint—lead gray, dull brown, or drab red. Flooring was a single layer of knotted or split board, permitting cold air to rise through the holes, and generally lacked carpets. Few houses had cellars, and most of them sat directly on the ground or were propped on stilts. Housing was generally constructed without electricity, running water, or indoor plumbing. Light was usually provided by candles or kerosene lanterns, and the coal stove in the kitchen was used both for cooking and providing heat. Most houses lacked running water; water for both cooking and washing had to be hauled from outdoor pumps or hydrants nearby. A variety of outbuildings— privies, coal bins, animal cages, baking ovens—were located behind the houses. There were usually no sewers, and every house had an outdoor privy—one for single houses and a double for duplexes. Near each privy was an outdoor bin for storing coal.

Miners' wives purchased food, sold surplus food from their gardens, and took in boarders to stretch their family's limited income. Bread was a principal food consumed by miners and their families in these towns. Common ovens were located in backyards for baking the bread, pies, rolls, and specialty foods made by the various immigrant groups. Some mining companies allowed workers to enclose their yards with fences so they might keep a cow, chickens, or pigs. Common land in coal towns was sectioned into garden plots varying in size and the type of crops grown. Here, mining families could supplement their diets by raising vegetables and owning livestock without having to make costly purchases at the company store.

Churches were built in most of the communities controlled by companies. The buildings often served more than one denomination, and services were often segregated. Mine workers raised most of the money to build churches in some villages, while the company contributed the land and some of the funds for construction. Larger coal companies provided a doctor and dentist in bigger coal towns while smaller communities had no medical services at all. Professional facilities, including hospitals, were only available in neighboring towns. The companies trained first-aid teams to treat victims of mining accidents. Some large coal companies helped subsidize wards for their workers at the local hospital. Minor medical services in the smaller towns—including obstetrical care—was provided by skilled midwives.

Virtually all company-owned coal towns had a company store. Like housing, it was constructed by coal companies as a convenience for their workers and families, and a source of profit for themselves. Great variety typified the physical size and architectural style of company stores. Each was custom-built of brick or wood, except for a few prefabricated stores. Because many of these towns were isolated, and only dirt roads connected them to neighboring towns, the company store (called a commissary in the southern coalfields) was the real commercial and social center of the coal town, serving as a gathering place, post office, bill-collection center, and shopping center. It provided all the daily material necessities of life in the isolated village.

These stores stocked and sold a variety of mining equipment as well as foodstuffs. Coal miners, unlike most industrial workers, provided and maintained their own tools and mining supplies. Miners paid for these necessities themselves and usually bought them at the company store, which stocked such tools and supplies as black powder or dynamite, caps, miners' lamps and fuel, carbide and oil-wick lamps, squibs (fuses), electric exploders, picks, shovels, flints, and machine oil.

—*Carmen P. DiCiccio*

See also
Company Towns; Mining Towns.
References
Dix, Keith. *What's a Coal Miner to Do? The Mechanization of Coal Mining*. Pittsburgh, PA: University of Pittsburgh Press, 1988.
Gates, John K. *The Beehive Coke Years: A Pictorial History of Those Years*. Uniontown, PA: privately printed, 1990.
Long, Priscilla. *Where the Sun Never Shines: A History of America's Bloody Coal Industry*. New York: Paragon House, 1989.

Miller, Donald L., and Richard E. Sharpless. *The Kingdom of Coal: Work, Enterprise, and Ethnic Communities.* Philadelphia: University of Pennsylvania Press, 1985.

Roy, Andrew. *A History of the Coal Miners of the United States.* Westport, CT: Greenwood Press, 1905.

Sheppard, Muriel E. *Cloud by Day: The Story of Coal and Coke and People.* Pittsburgh, PA: University of Pittsburgh Press, 1991.

College Towns

As the term suggests, a college town is a town where a college or university plays a central role in the economic, physical, cultural, and often political features of the town. Most often, a large portion of the town's population is comprised of college students, professors, administrators, and college-affiliated workers. College towns are distinct from other settings of higher education, like urban universities, because they are communities in themselves, shaped by the design, culture, and policies of the educational institution.

Much of the cohesive feeling associated with college towns results from planning decisions early Americans made when building colleges. When they established colleges during the colonial era, they frequently eschewed the European tradition of locating them in cities, choosing instead rural settings, where the urban evils they perceived would not be present. This was partially a result of the mission of many early colleges to train future ministers. The isolation of the college supposedly replicated the cloistered environment of monastic education at the same time that it created a new design ideal for American towns and villages. Some of the oldest colleges in the nation, including the College of William and Mary at Williamsburg, Virginia (1693), incorporated the layout of the surrounding town into the plan for the college campus. Building the town around the college helped foster the collegial spirit sought by educators. The University of North Carolina at Chapel Hill, North Carolina (1789), the first state university in the nation, followed a similar plan, seeking land away from urban areas and laying out plans to create a village adjacent to the university that would be incorporated as part of a comprehensive design scheme.

The development of the earliest women's colleges also reflected this desire for isolation from the cities. Founders highlighted the need for a protective environment for young women leaving home to pursue higher education, and they too adopted the model of the seminary for campus design. Unlike the academic villages common to college campuses for men, the seminary model left little room for the development of collegiate subcultures. At Mount Holyoke (1837) in Massachusetts and Vassar (1861) in New York, all activities took place in a single building erected on a picturesque hillside. This seclusion allowed teachers and supervisors to monitor all the activities of the students, thereby creating an insular college experience. Later women's colleges, including Smith (1871) in Massachusetts and Bryn Mawr (1885) in Pennsylvania, sought to distance themselves from the sphere of domesticity symbolized by the earlier seminary-like campuses and created Gothic-style campuses. This change in design reflected the desire to found institutions of higher learning for women equal in stature to those of men. The Gothic quadrangle, symbolic of "male" colleges, became the favored style for new women's colleges.

The Morrill Land Grant Act of 1862, which provided federal lands to create colleges to promote the study of agriculture and mechanics, further helped democratize higher education by making it available to farming families. It also encouraged the selection of nonurban settings for colleges. Many schools, including the Iowa State Agricultural College and State Farm in Ames (1858; name later changed to Iowa State University), bought land for experimental farms that served as laboratories for students. This agricultural focus mandated the selection of remote areas where this farmland acreage could be purchased. Moreover, the popularity of naturalism in the mid-nineteenth century, which linked morality and spirituality with appreciation of nature, further encouraged the development of isolated college towns. The noted landscape architect Frederick Law Olmsted designed many campuses, including the College of California (1864; name later changed to University of California at Berkeley) and Cornell University (1866) in Ithaca, New York, to reflect his belief in the role natural landscapes could play in shaping civic virtue and aesthetic refinement.

The advent of research-oriented institutions based on the German model of graduate education brought a change in design ideals for turn-of-the-century universities. Institutions like Johns Hopkins University (1876) in Baltimore, Maryland, and Clark University (1887) in Worcester, Massachusetts, symbolized a utilitarian design aesthetic reflective of scientific and professional educational goals. Their founders located these institutions in cities since they were less concerned with creating a collegial atmosphere than with fostering research and applied science. Similarly, the rapid growth and changing demographics of many American cities contributed to an increase in college attendance. This urban shift coincided with the rise of Beaux Arts ideals in urban planning and led to the integration of many universities, including Columbia University (1892) in New York City and the University of California at Los Angeles (1892), into large-scale urban planning models.

This trend toward creating urban universities instead of college towns continued into the 1920s. Yet, within these urban settings, many educators sought to reestablish the collegiate setting reminiscent of earlier college towns by adopting new design schemes. Plans for the University of Chicago (1892) included dormitories built around a "house system"

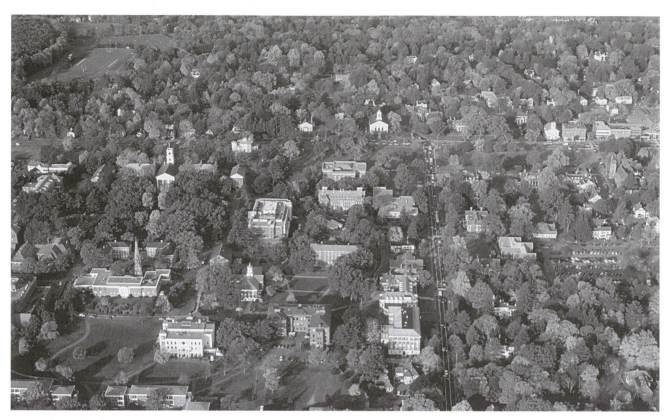

An aerial view of Amherst College bordering the town commons near the business district of Amherst, Massachusetts.

to promote the feeling of a scholarly community. Similarly, both Harvard and Yale, in 1928 and 1930 respectively, established "house systems" to provide homelike living quarters and social settings for students.

The post–World War II boom in college attendance also contributed to the decline in the development of traditional college towns. In 1890 only 3 percent of Americans between the ages of 18 and 21 attended college; by 1920 the figure was 8 percent; in 1940, 16 percent; and in 1970, 48 percent. Planners of college campuses responded to this vast increase in students by moving away from the fixed, comprehensive designs reminiscent of early college towns. Instead, the new plans stressed the function of particular buildings and provided room for future growth without needing to adhere to a strict plan. Similarly, the growth of community colleges, the most rapidly increasing type of college since the 1970s, fostered building facilities easily accessible to nonresident students. The insular, remote college campus could not meet the requirements of commuting students and educators whose primary goal often was access to education rather than the promotion of collegiate culture.

Since the time of their founding, college towns have continued to grow and become more connected to surrounding urban and suburban environments as a result of expanding transportation systems. Yet, college towns were able to maintain much of their character because of their separation from large industrial and manufacturing areas. While surveys found many urban and suburban areas suffering from poor air and water quality, failing school systems, rising crime rates, and overcrowding in the 1980s and 1990s, many college towns rated among the most desirable places in the country to live. Burlington, Vermont (University of Vermont), Madison, Wisconsin (University of Wisconsin), Ann Arbor, Michigan (University of Michigan), and Boulder, Colorado (University of Colorado), were ranked among the best places in the nation to live and raise a family in the early 1990s. As a result, many college towns attract not only students and educators but also new workers in technological fields and the service economy who have helped promote economically and culturally vibrant communities.

—*Robin F. Bachin*

References

Bender, Thomas, ed. *The University and the City: From Medieval Origins to the Present.* New York: Oxford University Press, 1992.

Dober, Richard P. *Campus Design.* New York: Wiley, 1992.

Gaines, Thomas A. *The Campus as a Work of Art.* New York: Praeger, 1991.

Horowitz, Helen Lefkowitz. *Alma Mater: Design and Experience in the Women's Colleges from Their Nineteenth-Century Beginnings to the 1930s.* New York: Knopf, 1984.

Turner, Paul Venable. *Campus: An American Planning Tradition.* Cambridge, MA: MIT Press, 1984.

Columbus, Ohio

Columbus is the capital of Ohio and, according to the 1990 census, the largest city in the state. It was laid out in 1812 specifically to serve as the seat of state government. Until then, Ohio's legislature had met at either Chillicothe or Zanesville, but lawmakers sought a central location within the state to serve as the permanent seat of government. Recognizing this, a syndicate of land promoters offered to lay out a new capital in central Ohio on the east bank of the Scioto River. To make their offer more attractive, they promised to give the state ten acres as a site for a state house as well as an additional ten acres for a penitentiary. The townsite promoters also agreed to expend up to $50,000 on the construction of buildings to house the state government. Ohio's legislature accepted the offer, and in 1816 state officials moved to the new capital of Columbus.

As early as 1815, the town had 700 inhabitants, but by 1830 its population had risen to only 2,400, about one-tenth the size of the state's largest city, Cincinnati. During the 1830s, however, Columbus's prospects as a center of trade and transportation improved. In 1831 the small capital celebrated the opening of a feeder canal that linked Columbus with the Ohio Canal and provided water access to the Ohio River and Lake Erie. Two years later, in 1833, the National Road reached Columbus, giving the capital overland access to the East. With both canal transportation and the National Road, Columbus seemed destined to be something more than a seat of government. By 1850, its population had risen to almost 18,000, though the western metropolis of Cincinnati continued to dwarf the state capital.

During these same years, Columbus strengthened its position as the center of state government, becoming the site of all the major state institutions. Unlike many states that distributed their various institutions among a number of communities, Ohio concentrated on Columbus. From its founding, it was the site of the penitentiary, and in 1829 the state "deaf and dumb asylum" opened there, followed in the 1830s by a school for the blind, a "lunatic asylum," and an "asylum for idiots" in 1857. In the 1870s, Columbus would also become the permanent site for the state fair and the location of the state's land-grant university. Columbus was not simply the place where the legislature met; it was the hub of all state government activities.

In 1850 the first railroad reached Columbus, and it was soon followed by others. Especially important were the rail lines linking the city to the coalfields of southeastern Ohio. After the Civil War, Ohio's capital emerged as a major coal shipping center and served as the headquarters for a number of coal companies. With a cheap supply of fuel as well as access to the iron, timber, and natural gas of southeastern Ohio, Columbus became the home of an increasing number of industries. Foundries and machine shops flourished, as did factories specializing in mining equipment. Among the most prominent manufacturing plants were buggy works. By the late 1880s, 18 establishments, employing 2,800 persons, produced 20,000 buggies and carriages annually. The city claimed to outrank all others in the manufacture of high-class buggies. Yet Columbus was a highly diverse manufacturing center, producing cigars, beer, shoes, and watches, as well as buggies and iron goods. Moreover, it boasted the world's largest manufacturer of regalia for fraternal lodges.

Many of the workers in these burgeoning industries were Germans who migrated to the city in the mid– and late nineteenth century. From the 1840s through the 1930s, Germans constituted the principal foreign-born group in Columbus. As early as 1875, the first German-born mayor took office, testifying to the growing influence of the immigrant population on city politics. German singing societies, German Lutheran and Catholic churches, and German-language newspapers all were evidence of the Teutonic influence in Columbus during the second half of the nineteenth century. Yet by 1900 Columbus had acquired a reputation as an unusually American community. Other than Germans, relatively few newcomers from Europe found their way to Ohio's capital. In 1900 more than 90 percent of the city's residents were native-born, whereas the figure for cosmopolitan Cleveland was only 67 percent.

Columbus did, however, attract thousands of migrants from rural Ohio, and its population continued to rise rapidly. In 1900 the population exceeded 125,000, and in 1930 it was just short of 291,000. In the latter year, the capital city still had less than one-third the population of Cleveland, was only about 60 percent the size of Cincinnati, and even ranked slightly behind Toledo in population. Though the center of government and politics in Ohio, it stood fourth in the state in population. Like many other state capitals, Columbus was surpassed in size by cities that had more vibrant economies.

During the early twentieth century, the growth of the city spawned a number of suburban municipalities that became home to many wealthy Columbus business leaders. In 1906 the suburb of Grandview Heights incorporated as a separate municipality, and a decade later real estate entrepreneur King Thompson began to lay out the elite suburban retreat of Upper Arlington. Meanwhile, on the east side of Columbus, Bexley was emerging as a posh community of lush lawns and large Tudor or neocolonial manses.

Columbus, however, was not surrounded by independent suburban municipalities, and after World War II it overcame the threat of suburban strangulation through a vigorous annexation program. During the 1950s and 1960s, under the leadership of Mayor M. E. Sensenbrenner, the city more than tripled its size. Because of this success in acquiring additional land, Columbus's population continued to rise, unlike the populations of Cleveland and Cincinnati, cities that were unable to extend their boundaries. By 1970, Columbus had 540,000 residents, surpassing Cincinnati for the first time, and in 1990 it reached 633,000, displacing Cleveland as the largest city in the state.

This population growth was not wholly due to annexation. Throughout the half-century from 1940 to 1990, central Ohio's buoyant economy attracted newcomers and discouraged existing residents from leaving. During the 1940s and early 1950s, manufacturing employment soared as North American Aviation, General Motors, and Westinghouse all established plants in the city. Drawn by thousands of new factory jobs, migrants from the rural South converged on Columbus. Many were black, but even more were white, refugees from the impoverished coal-mining regions of West Virginia and Kentucky. The African-American share of the city's population rose from 12.4 percent in 1950 to 22.1 percent in 1980, but by 1970 southern-born whites in Columbus actually outnumbered southern-born blacks by a ratio of about two-to-one. A "hillbilly ghetto" developed on the city's near north side while African Americans dominated the east side.

As in most midwestern cities, manufacturing no longer generated growth after the 1960s, but a diverse economic base kept Columbus relatively prosperous. Most notably, state government employment and higher education aided the city's economy. As the state capital and the site of Ohio State University, the city enjoyed the benefits of increased public-sector spending, and in 1980 the state was by far the largest employer in the metropolitan area, with 50,000 people working in government offices or at the state university. The insurance and banking industries and local hospitals also buoyed central Ohio's fortunes, permitting Columbus to avoid the worst effects of rust belt decline. During the last decades of the twentieth century, Columbus remained what it was founded to be, the center of Ohio's public sector, and in part because of this, it was one of the few bright spots in the economy of the industrial Midwest.

—*Jon C. Teaford*

References

Garrett, Betty, with Edward R. Lenz. *Columbus: America's Crossroads.* Tulsa, OK: Continental Heritage Press, 1980.

Hunker, Henry L. *Industrial Evolution of Columbus, Ohio.* Columbus: Ohio State University Press, 1958.

Lee, Alfred E. *History of the City of Columbus, Capital of Ohio.* 2 vols. New York: Munsell, 1892.

Studer, Jacob H. *Columbus, Ohio: Its History, Resources, and Progress.* Columbus, OH: Jacob H. Studer, 1873.

Commercial Strips

Commercial strips dominate American land use patterns. Consisting of independent stores and services stretching along arterial roads, they are found in or near almost every community. Strips attract convenience-oriented businesses that need easy highway access such as fast-food restaurants, banks, and copy centers. Businesses that need extensive space also locate on strips, including auto dealerships, recreational vehicle sales centers, lumberyards, and garden nurseries. Additionally, many strips include shopping centers with a cluster of retail establishments and services.

The evolution of commercial strips is essentially a post–World War II phenomenon that can be attributed in large part to the movement of people from cities to suburbs and the widespread availability of personal automobiles. Another impetus was the changing nature of retail practices, specifically the demand for large, single-floor buildings with free parking, neither of which could be readily accommodated in cities' central or neighborhood business districts. Small parcels of land, fragmented ownership patterns, and existing buildings made redeveloping these districts extremely expensive even if it was feasible. Consequently, central business districts and neighborhood retail districts experienced a long period of disinvestment as businesses relocated to commercial strips and were not replaced. Ironically, however, from a historical perspective, strips may have been the salvation of these districts for the greatest pressure to develop came at a time when historic resources were not valued. Had redevelopment occurred then, it almost certainly would have resulted in the loss of the historical context that is today the driving force behind the successful revitalization of Main Streets and neighborhood business districts in many older cities.

Commercial strips have received a lot of bad press. They are perceived as ugly, functionally inferior, and hosts of blight. They are often typified by large signs and gaudy building designs meant to attract the attention of drivers. Large expanses of asphalt separate buildings from streets. Uncontrolled vehicular access is common, contributing to complex traffic maneuvers, slower travel speed, and a high potential for accidents. It is not surprising, therefore, that transportation engineers refer to commercial strips as "marginal friction."

Local governments have used zoning regulations and development standards to tame these excesses. Signs are limited in size and number, landscaping is required, traffic is channeled with cut curbs, and, in some cases, separate access roads parallel the arterial in order to restrict turns and thereby maintain traffic flow.

With the growing recognition that American land use practices foster overdependence on automobiles, planners are beginning to rethink the design of strips in order to encourage walking and the use of public transit. Clues are being taken from development patterns of older Main Streets and the neighborhood business districts of inner cities, which are, in essence, preautomobile commercial strips. Their pedestrian orientation stems from the location of buildings on the front property line, smaller signs on a more human scale, and mixed uses including apartments in upper stories. Traffic is typically slower as a result of on-street parking and fewer lanes.

Developers on the strips, however, resist the idea of locating parking behind buildings because they believe that a business will be viable only if parking is readily visible from the street. And efforts to develop linkages between adjacent parcels of land are often difficult to implement because of liability concerns. Nevertheless, federal mandates such as the accessibility requirements of the 1990 Americans with Disabilities Act and state mandates such as Oregon's Transportation Rule, which requires a reduction in per capita vehicle miles traveled, may force these and other design changes.

In any event, the strip continues to evolve. An increasing amount of "big box" retailing such as Toys R Us and Costco means that developers are seeking larger parcels. Freestanding banks and restaurants are being constructed in the parking lots of existing developments and in so doing breaking up the asphalt with smaller buildings and much-needed landscaping. The mix of land uses is changing as empty stores are converted to office space or other uses, such as branch libraries and veterinary offices. High-density housing is being explored in conjunction with the redevelopment of obsolete shopping centers.

As strips expand, diversify, and strengthen, they are blurring the distinction between nucleated and linear commercial development patterns. Even large, regional shopping centers are becoming part of a "grand strip" as commercial uses fill nearby arterials.

It is difficult to predict what strips will look like 20 to 30 years from now. Technology such as home-based computer shopping, local land use controls, financing policies, and the overall state of the economy will be important determinants. It is evident, however, that commercial strips are here to stay and that they will continue to play a major role in shaping American cities and suburbs.

—Deborah A. Howe

References

Berry, Brian J. L. *Commercial Structure and Commercial Blight.* Chicago: University of Chicago Press, 1963.

Bishop, Kirk R. *Designing Urban Corridors. Planning Advisory Service Report Number 418.* Chicago: American Planning Association, 1989.

Howe, Deborah A., and William A. Rabiega. "Beyond Strips and Centers: The Ideal Commercial Form." *Journal of the American Planning Association* 58 (1992): 213–219.

Commission Government

The commission form of municipal government was an early-twentieth-century invention—born of necessity, promoted with vigor, and, at least briefly, promising better things to come. But it proved less durable than many of its initial backers had hoped, and today the plan's significance lies principally in what it reveals about the history of municipal reform in the United States and about the nation's long-standing commitment to institutional engineering.

In theory, the commission system vests all municipal authority, executive as well as legislative, in a single, multimember governing body, thus unifying power. In practice, commissions legislate collectively and administer individually. While policy theoretically concerns the entire commission, day-to-day management falls to individual commissioners, each responsible for a different city department.

Combining executive and legislative powers in a single body was a distinctive feature of the plan and departed from the country's more familiar separation of powers. In the latter half of the nineteenth century, state governments often created boards and commissions to handle major policy areas like public works, public safety, and public health, all of which required more expertise than city councils possessed, but these bodies exercised limited jurisdiction. By contrast, a commission charter assigned overall municipal authority to a single multimember board of commissioners and made this board responsible both for deciding and administering policy.

The immediate impetus for the commission form was the tropical storm that devastated Galveston, Texas, in September 1900. The storm and accompanying tidal surges swept off the Gulf of Mexico during the early morning hours of September 8, crippling the city of 33,000. Death and destruction were extensive, so widespread that the *New York Times* speculated that "the city may be wiped out." Martial law was declared, and troops were deployed to prevent looting. "Armed men compel[led] idlers to help dispose of the dead at the point of a bayonet." The toll was so great, however, that eventually "all attempts at burying the dead [were] utterly abandoned." Even efforts to dump the bodies at sea proved futile since the bodies washed back on shore, thus increasing the threat of epidemic and disease.

Martial law ended on September 20, and in its aftermath, Texas Governor J. D. Sayers appointed five prominent citizens to run Galveston's affairs. This temporary arrangement was later formalized by statute with the establishment of a five-member commission, three appointed by the governor and two elected by the city's voters. The Supreme Court of Texas later invalidated the statute on the grounds that gubernatorial appointment violated the state constitution's guarantee of home rule. The law was revised and reenacted, this time with all five commissioners elected at large.

What began as an ad hoc response to a local crisis was quickly rationalized and promoted across the country as an innovative and effective way to govern cities. Within a decade, an estimated 300 cities had adopted the plan. Writing in 1913, Professor Charles A. Beard reported that: "the growth of the [commission] movement during 1912 was fully as vigorous as in the previous years." And, he added, "it has not been confined to any particular section of the country or class of cities."

What accounts for the transformation of an ad hoc emergency arrangement into a reform ideal? One factor was the Englishman James Bryce's oft-repeated criticism that the "government of cities [was] the one conspicuous failure of the United States." This critique is central to understanding the early enthusiasm for the commission plan. Cities had expanded rapidly during the latter half of the nineteenth century, but, according to many, city governments had been slow to adapt. There was disarray, with public authority scattered among many independent and often competing governing units. Moreover, city officials all too often lacked the managerial and technical skills to cope with the new challenges and, equally important, the integrity to prevent the wholesale plunder of the city treasury.

The commission plan offered hope in the face of this "failure," promising more efficiently managed, cost-effective, and ethical city government. This hope rested on reports of its success in Galveston and other cities that had followed its example, notably Des Moines, Kansas City, Houston, and Dallas. These reports circulated widely in reform networks—networks that are an additional key to understanding the plan's early popularity.

The networks in question had their roots in the early years after the Civil War. The success of New York City's Committee of Seventy, which was instrumental in ousting the city's infamous Tweed Ring in 1871, and of Philadelphia's Committee of One Hundred, which successfully challenged the "Gas Ring" a decade later, spurred similar efforts elsewhere. In the early 1890s, local organizations like these federated nationally to form the Council of Confederated Good Government Clubs, and later, in 1894, the National Municipal League.

These organizations spearheaded a broad array of municipal reform initiatives, spreading the word about such innovations as Galveston's commission plan. Galveston's story was widely celebrated, as were the achievements in other commission cities. The story, in brief, was that these cities had introduced businesslike practices into city government and as a result had been able to "reduce taxation," "abolish annual deficits," "provide intelligent and efficient accounting," "substitute efficiency for red tape," and "create a new and better civic spirit." Moreover, and this was an additional selling point, the plan was linked to a number of other important reforms. Early commission charters typically included the direct primary, the initiative, the recall, the referendum, the short ballot, and nonpartisan, at-large elections, all of which, reformers insisted, were essential to a well-crafted charter and hence to a well-governed city.

Despite its early appeal, the commission plan's popularity was short-lived. By 1915, the *National Municipal Review* was no longer citing the "vigorous progress" it had two years earlier. Instead, the *Review* noted that "the last few months have presented a period of incubation rather than actual accomplishments in the adoption of new city charters." And while the *Review* continued to publish supportive comments, there was growing skepticism about the plan's effectiveness.

One concern was whether Galveston's success had been due to the extraordinary nature of the city' crisis. "As can well be imagined," one observer noted, "the men selected at such a crisis would be of the very best obtainable," but crises were no sure guide for ordinary times. Moreover, the political task in times of crisis was simplified, since crises heightened a community's common interests and common resolve rather than its differences and disagreements.

Other cities faced lesser crises, namely the "failure" of their municipal governments, but still serious enough to persuade citizens to "revolutionize their whole form of government." But whether the reform itself produced the positive results its backers claimed was often questioned. Some skeptics insisted that "much of the improvement [in city government was] due not so much to the new [commission] system as to an aroused public spirit." Others suggested that "the plan [would] prove beneficial as long as the novelty lasts," but that it offered no assurances beyond that.

Novelty notwithstanding, there was another major problem—that commissioners were elected officials. It was difficult enough, remarked one reformer, to "get good men to run when they were obliged to abandon their private careers," the more so when they faced grueling campaigns and possible repudiation at the polls. Worse yet, one commentator complained, "the Commission form is still far from perfect [since] unskilled men" were being elected to head city departments.

The challenge of recruiting qualified commissioners was all the greater because of the collective nature of the institution. Legally, power and authority were shared within the commission, which made the office less attractive to a forceful individual inclined to exercise strong leadership. This was often mitigated in practice, since there was a "tendency on the part of each individual commissioner to regard himself as supreme in his own department and to resent control by the commission as a whole." As a consequence, however, the community ended up with "five little mayors," instead of a strong, central governing body, a reason frequently cited for the commission system's declining popularity.

Troubling as they were, these shortcomings contributed less to the decline of the commission plan than did the growing popularity of the other new alternative, the council-manager plan. Originally billed as a variant of the commission form, the council-manager charter called for appointing professional managers to oversee municipal administration. The commission, and later the city council, would set broad policy, and the manager would ensure that the council's wishes were fulfilled. By thus "removing all attempts to choose administrators by popular election," the manager plan would, claimed its advocates, help "rid the community of amateur and transient executives," ensure the availability of "experienced experts," and provide the community with stability in administrative leadership. "The city manager feature is a valuable addition to the commission plan," the National Municipal League's Committee on Commission Government noted in its famous 1914 Report, "and we recommend to charter makers serious inclusion of this feature in new commission government charters."

The manager feature proved more valuable yet, and within the decade this addition to the commission plan had supplanted the plan itself as the premiere charter reform. The manager plan's principal appeal was its stress on professionalism. The manager was to be a full-time, salaried official, appointed by the council, with full authority over the municipality's departments and their affairs. And since the charter insulated the manager from the distracting, sometimes compromising, and always changing demands of city politics, he would provide a steadier hand and more stability than would the "transient amateurs." And even if a manager resigned or retired, there would still be a degree of continuity since those who followed would share the same professional norms and possess the same professional skills as the previous manager.

Indications reveal that there has been a long-term decline in the number of communities governed under commission plan charters. The evidence is not conclusive, since there are no systematic, continuous data on forms of local government in the United States. But the data that are available suggest that relatively few communities are any longer governed under commission charters. In 1992, for example, only 111 cities, or 2 percent of all cities over 5,000 in population, were listed in the International City Management Association's survey as commission cities. Fifty years earlier, in 1940, there had been some 300, or 17 percent of the cities over 5,000. And today, cities seldom adopt the commission plan; communities are more likely to abandon this kind of government and instead adopt the council-manager plan in small and medium-sized cities, or the mayor-council form in larger ones.

Brief though its moment was, the commission plan is important to understanding the history of municipal government in the United States. It emerged during those turbulent, transitional years between the close of the Civil War and the beginning of World War I when the nation was struggling to adapt to being an urbanized and industrialized society. The commission plan was part of this struggle, and it served as an early rallying point for municipal reformers. As such, it gave new hope and new courage to citizens. And it provided a focal point for organizing into an effective civic force like-minded citizens whose efforts have had an enduring impact on the way the nation both thinks and goes about the business of local government.

—*Russell D. Murphy*

See also
Council-Manager Government; Mayor-Council Government; Municipal Government.

References

Beard, Charles Austin. "News and Events." *The National Municipal League* 1 (1913): 116.

Bruere, Henry. *The New City Government: A Discussion of Municipal Administration Based on a Survey of Ten Commission Governed Cities.* New York: D. Appleton, 1912.

Bryce, James. *The American Commonwealth.* 2d rev. ed. 2 vols. London: Macmillan, 1891.

Fassett, Charles. "The Weakness of Commission Government." *National Municipal Review* 9 (1920): 642–647.

Foulke, William Dudley. "Evolution in City Charter Making." *National Municipal Review* 4 (1914): 13–25.

Gemunder, Martin. "Commission Government: Its Strengths and Its Weaknesses." *National Municipal Review* 1 (1912): 170–181.

Griffith, Ernest S. *The Modern Development of City Government in the United States.* London: Oxford University Press, 1927. Reprint ed. College Park, MD: McGrath, 1969.

Grumm, John G., and Russell D. Murphy. *Governing States and Communities: Organizing for Popular Rule.* Englewood Cliffs, NJ: Prentice-Hall, 1991.

National Municipal League. "The Coming of the City Manager Plan: A Report of the National Municipal League's Committee on the Commission Form of Government." *National Municipal Review* 3 (1914): 44–48.

New York Times (September 1911).

Community

Community is one of the most important units of historical and sociological analysis, as well as one of the most diffuse: a scholar once counted 94 different definitions of it. In academic and popular discourse, community usually implies a common sense of bonding, a deeper sense of belonging that carried the harmonious values of family outward to the broader society. Although community, as a collectivity, can refer either to a social unit or a social relationship, it is most widely used to describe a combination of the two in which territoriality shapes social interaction and organization.

In 1887 the German sociologist Ferdinand Tonnies traced the evolution of community from traditional village-like society built upon interlocking bonds of family, friends, and neighbors to a modern impersonal world where each social role was segmented between different individuals. Although Tonnies felt that aspects of the traditional community could coexist with those of modern society as typified by the modern city, the transition from *Gemeinschaft* (society characterized by strong reciprocal bonds of sentiment and kinship) to *Gesellschaft* (society characterized by impersonal relationships) that he first proposed served to describe the process of community decline and the depersonalization of urbanization for several generations of sociologists. Tonnies's theory culminated in Louis Wirth's classic article "Urbanism as a Way of Life," which appeared in 1937.

The idea of community decline began to come under attack in the early 1960s when Herbert Gans uncovered the persistence of strong communal ties within urban ethnic village communities. Most scholars now agree that community did survive urbanization, although many still debate the extent to which social interaction was limited by territory. Increasingly, sociologists have come to view community in terms of its constituent interpersonal ties. Social network analysis is widely used to study the whole constellation of primary social ties that extend beyond the household to encompass neighbors, the workplace, relatives, and even the distant linkages among telephone contacts.

Historical studies of community reflect sociological debates. Towns and cities have long served as territorial units of analysis in historical community studies, as scholars sought places through which to study social processes in microcosm. But not until the 1970s did historians like Thomas Bender and Gary Nash begin to challenge a wide range of historical studies that traced the decline of community in numerous locales over various periods. Subsequent historical studies of Italian, German, Canadian, and Eastern European immigrants have shown how city dwellers preserved strong family and communal bonds despite increased crowding and the ordeal of immigration. Labor historians have likewise shown how displaced artisans and factory workers clung to institutions of mutual support and cooperation in the midst of industrial upheaval.

The debate between proponents of the community lost, whose scholarship mirrors the writings of Tonnies and Wirth, and those who argue for the survival of community continues to be of central importance for historians. And many criti-

Residents of Harlem express their sense of community during a monthly block party held at 7th Avenue and 125th Street.

cal questions remain to be answered: How did Americans reconcile communal values with social change? Did institutions of *Gesellschaft* like charitable associations, unions, and voluntary associations make it easier for city people to preserve elements of *Gemeinschaft* in the nineteenth century? How disruptive of community were historically high levels of transience? And to what extent were urban communities structured in terms of gender, ethnicity, and class? Indeed, historians have only recently begun to study the historical dimensions of aspatial community, the widely dispersed network of friends and relations first described by sociologists. The interrelationships between this unbounded community and local attachments rooted in work, church, business ties, homeownership, and politics promise to be a rich sphere for historical study for some time to come.

—*Kenneth A. Scherzer*

References
Bender, Thomas. *Community and Social Change in America.* New Brunswick, NJ: Rutgers University Press, 1978.
———. *The Urban Villagers: Group and Class in the Life of Italian Americans.* New York: Free Press, 1962. Rev. ed., 1982.
Nash, Gary. "The Social Evolution of Preindustrial American Cities, 1700–1820." In Raymond Mohl, ed., *The Making of Urban America*, 24–44. Wilmington, DE: Scholarly Resources, 1988.
Slayton, Robert. *Back of the Yards: The Making of a Local Democracy.* Chicago: University of Chicago Press, 1986.
Wellman, Barry. "The Community Question Re-evaluated." In Michael Peter Smith, ed., *Power and the City*, 81–107. New Brunswick, NJ: Rutgers University Press, 1988.

Community Action Program

The Community Action Program (CAP), or Title IIa of the Economic Opportunity Act of 1964, was a cornerstone of President Lyndon Johnson's War on Poverty. CAP, modeled after two concurrent programs inaugurated during the administration of John F. Kennedy (Ford Foundation Gray Areas and the President's Committee on Juvenile Delinquency), offered an innovative departure from past efforts by the government to redress income inequality. CAP was a policy aimed principally at community development—an approach not thought to be of much significance in federal policy before 1964. While the notion of community development has survived to present-day discussions of urban social life, federal funding for CAP was relatively short-lived, having ended in 1967.

CAP was premised on the assumption that the poor themselves should play a central role in economic, social, and political development of local communities. Hence, the notion of "participatory democracy" or—in a key phrase that would be repeated in local community debates as well as in discussions among federal policy officials—"with the maximum feasible participation of the poor" became the central

axiom on which to build, develop, and evaluate community action programs. CAP's clear articulation of a client-based, or community-based, vision of antipoverty programs and corresponding rejection of supply-side orientations to poverty centrally located the philosophy of "participation of the poor" as the guiding quintessence of all federal antipoverty initiatives during the 1960s. Indeed, the legacy of the participatory element of the War on Poverty continues to thrive in contemporary community development organizations, programs, and policy.

Federal guidelines for local communities tended toward the general, leaving much of the specifics to city councils, mayoral offices, and local economic opportunity offices. As local communities began to create new community institutions, neighborhood groups, and grassroots organizations, two major types of conflict emerged. One conflict, for control of local policy and programs, occurred between newly formed community organizations and older established institutions, for example, political regimes in city governments. A second conflict, for control and power within the newly formed CAPs, occurred over "who" was poor, "how" the poor should be included, and "what" kinds of programs and organizations might best serve the interests of the poor.

—*Dana Y. Takagi*

References
Greenstone, David J., and Paul E. Petersen. *Race and Authority in Urban Politics.* Chicago: University of Chicago Press, 1973.
Haveman, Robert. *A Decade of Federal Antipoverty Programs.* New York: Academic Press, 1977.
Kramer, Ralph M. *Participation of the Poor.* Englewood Cliffs, NJ: Prentice-Hall, 1969.
Moynihan, Daniel. *Maximum Feasible Misunderstanding.* New York: Free Press, 1969.

Community-Based Corrections

Community-based corrections includes a wide range of programs aimed at avoiding incarcerating criminals in county penitentiaries, prisons, juvenile reformatories, and reformatory-prisons. Probation, parole, halfway houses (for adults), group homes (for children), work release, study release, and furloughs are the traditional forms of community-based corrections, although some criminologists and penologists employ a wider definition and also include community service, fines (paid to the state), restitution (paid to the victim), shock incarceration (incarceration followed by probation), and the American correctional system's latest innovation, house arrest and electronic monitoring.

Even though research on the history of American corrections and social control has increased in recent years, the development of community-based corrections has received relatively little attention. It is known, however, that fines and restitution are not American innovations and have been used in Asia and Europe for thousands of years. John Augustus, a shoemaker, is credited with introducing probation to Massachusetts in 1841, and Zebulon Brockway, the superintendent of New York's famed Elmira Reformatory, introduced parole in 1877. Halfway houses and group homes developed in the United States in the late nineteenth century, and work release was started in Wisconsin in 1913. Historians generally trace furloughs and study release to the 1960s, shock incarceration to the 1970s, and electronic monitoring to the 1980s.

Community-based corrections was not, however, a central component of the American criminal justice system in the nineteenth century. Penologists generally believed that adult prisons, juvenile reformatories, and reformatory-prisons for young adults were effective ways of taming, training, and disciplining America's "dangerous classes" (i.e., poor, urban immigrants and their children). The wide use of parole was, to be sure, rapid during the last two decades of the nineteenth century, but the spread of other forms of community corrections—including probation—was slow until the Progressive Era.

Community-based corrections did not become a key element of the American penal system until the late 1960s and early 1970s. Publication of the *Task Force Report: Corrections* (1967) by the President's Commission on Law Enforcement and the Administration of Justice was pivotal in the history of American penology. The authors of this report concluded that a wide disparity existed between the goals and the results of prisons and reformatories—in fact, these places were "factories of crime." The *Task Force Report: Corrections* called upon penologists and legislators to drastically reduce the use of prisons and reformatories and, instead, divert offenders into programs designed to reintegrate them into the community.

Its proponents argued that community-based corrections would benefit offenders, the criminal justice system, and the public. First, the expanded use of community corrections would divert delinquents and criminals from prisons and reformatories, thereby avoiding the dangers of incarceration—violence, sexual attacks, moral contagion—and the stigmatization that results from it. Second, offenders would receive better rehabilitative services in the community. Third, the removal of offenders would reduce overcrowding in correctional institutions and save the government money. Finally, it was argued that community-based corrections would reform inmates and, therefore, reduce recidivism and crime.

Thus, in the late 1960s and early 1970s, some analysts were hailing community-based corrections as a reform panacea, and legislators and penologists were making a concerted effort to implement these programs. However, researchers quickly uncovered a wide range of unanticipated consequences. Most significantly, they discovered that community-based programs did not divert less-serious offenders from prisons and reformatories; in fact, community supervision was being extended over less-serious offenders. These programs, then, were expanding—not reducing—the state's network of social control. Researchers also uncovered other serious problems: prison and reformatory overcrowding was not reduced; the state did not save money; negative labels were attached to more, not fewer, offenders; the community did not provide superior rehabilitative services; and these programs did not reduce rates of recidivism.

The proliferation of community-based corrections in the 1960s and 1970s has had a profound influence on America's "criminal class." In particular, the spread of community corrections, coupled with the Reagan administration's "get tough on crime" strategy, has greatly expanded the state's social-control network over the urban black community. Recent studies by Jerome Miller, for example, reveal that 30 percent of African-American men between the ages of 18 and 35 who lived in Baltimore, Maryland, in 1991 were on probation or parole; and 21 percent of the African-American men of the same age who lived in Washington, D.C., were also on probation or parole. The urban African-American community is, quite simply, under state surveillance and state coercion.

Community-based corrections is, then, one of the most controversial components of the American criminal justice system. Fears of increasing urban crime, concerns about the costs of prisons and reformatories, and the general fiscal crisis of the federal and state governments, together with "advances" in technology (electronic monitoring), do not bode well for the future. America's cities are becoming community prisons for urban, black males and other minorities—a disconcerting trend and a troubling commentary on our society.

—*Alexander W. Pisciotta*

References

Carter, Robert M., and Leslie T. Wilkins. *Probation, Parole, and Community Corrections.* 2d ed. New York: Wiley, 1976.

Cromwell, Paul F., and George G. Killinger. *Community-Based Corrections: Probation, Parole, and Intermediate Sanctions.* 3d ed. St. Paul, MN: West Publishing, 1994.

Fox, Vernon. *Community-Based Corrections.* Englewood Cliffs, NJ: Prentice-Hall, 1977.

Miller, Jerome G. *Hobbling a Generation: Young African-American Males in the Criminal Justice System of America's Cities: Baltimore, Maryland.* Alexandria, VA: National Center on Institutions and Alternatives, 1992.

———. *Hobbling a Generation: Young African-American Males in Washington, D.C.'s Criminal Justice System.* Alexandria, VA: National Center on Institutions and Alternatives, 1992.

Perlstein, Gary R., and Thomas R. Phelps, eds. *Alternatives to Prison: Community-Based Corrections, A Reader.* Santa Monica, CA: Goodyear Publishing, 1975.

President's Commission on Law Enforcement and the Administration of Justice. *Task Force Report: Corrections.* Washington, DC: Government Printing Office, 1967.

Smykla, John Ortiz. *Community-Based Corrections: Principles and Practices.* New York: Macmillan, 1981.

Community Development Block Grants

The Community Development Block Grant (CDBG) program is a major source of federal aid to state and local governments. CDBG funds are to be used for community development, a broad term that refers to using the many resources of a community toward its improvement. As specified in the enabling legislation, the 1974 Housing and Community Development Act, all activities must meet one of three national objectives:

1. Principally benefit low- and moderate-income persons.
2. Aid in the elimination or prevention of slums and blight.
3. Meet an urgent need that threatens the health and safety of the community.

A wide range of activities may be undertaken within the parameters of the three national objectives. They include:

- acquisition and rehabilitation of real property
- historic preservation
- energy conservation
- acquisition, construction, reconstruction, or installation of public works, public facilities, neighborhood facilities, senior centers, centers for the handicapped, recreation facilities, and streetlights
- code enforcement in deteriorated areas
- clearance and demolition of privately and publicly owned buildings
- removal of architectural barriers to the handicapped
- relocation assistance
- public services
- payment of the nonfederal share of other federal grant programs
- payment of the cost of completing urban renewal projects
- comprehensive planning
- administrative costs
- assistance to nonprofit entities in acquiring real property, or acquiring or rehabilitating public facilities, site improvements, utilities, and commercial and industrial facilities and improvements
- assistance to nonprofit entities for economic development or energy conservation or neighborhood revitalization activities
- assistance to for-profit entities undertaking economic development that helps achieve community development objectives
- provision of technical assistance to public or nonprofit entities
- housing services
- housing construction
- assistance to facilitate homeownership among low- and moderate-income persons
- lead-based paint abatement

Funds for the CDBG program are allocated by formulae that may be computed on the basis of population, poverty, overcrowded housing, and other factors. The block grant funding format grants states and localities wide discretion, with only a few specific strings attached.

The CDBG program addresses problems that are national in scope, such as affordable housing, neighborhood revitalization, and declining business districts. It awards funds to cities and counties designated as entitlement communities. By statute, 70 percent of the funds appropriated for CDBG activities are designated for use by entitlement communities and 30 percent to states for distribution to nonentitlement communities and other ancillary activities. Also, the statute requires that communities and states spend 70 percent of the funding on activities that principally benefit low- and moderate-income persons. As intended by Congress, block grant funding gives the recipient broad discretion to use the money to solve problems in a broad area.

The CDBG program has had a major impact on housing and economic development policy in the United States. Traditionally, CDBG funding has been a barometer of the national government's commitment to central cities. However, several initiatives designed to give states more control over the distribution of CDBG funds have disadvantaged central cities. Urban areas usually do not fare very well when federal grant money is channeled through states.

Also, as the connection between urban and suburban areas continues to weaken, central cities find that they can no longer rely on suburbs as an ally. In the past, suburbs maintained a connection with central cities because of employment. Now, suburbs are becoming employment centers in their own right. Accordingly, the central city is no longer the obvious beneficiary of CDBG funds in a metropolitan area. As more and more suburban areas are designated as entitlement communities, funding to central cities is thus impacted.

As national demographics change and the number of entitlement communities increases, central city politicians have revised their strategies for obtaining CDBG funds. Mayors of major metropolitan areas now argue that cities are essential for healthy regional economies and international competitiveness. Also, they assert, it is the central cities that can support cultural amenities such as opera houses, art museums, and ballparks, and funding should be available for these activities.

The political climate portends a major revamping of the Community Development Block Grant program. As this restructuring evolves, a reordering of CDBG priorities is certain.

—*Elsie M. Barnes*

References
Boyd, Eugene, and Sandra Osbourn. *Block Grants: An Overview.* Congressional Research Service Report for Congress No. 95–264. Washington, DC: U.S. Government Printing Office, 1995.
Dumouchel, J. Robert. *Dictionary of Development Terminology.* New York: McGraw-Hill, 1975.
U.S. Congress. "Housing and Community Development Act of 1974," P.L. 93–383, as amended.

Commuting

Commuting is the daily travel of workers from residential areas to their places of employment. Commuting patterns involve significant policy issues (planning for housing, highways, and transit systems, controlling traffic congestion, etc.), and scholars have developed numerous urban transportation models to assist in urban and regional planning. Commuting patterns are closely related to the dynamics of both housing and labor markets, and the daily journey to work is one of the most closely scrutinized facets of the American city. In the last half-century, scholars have undertaken literally thousands of studies to describe the geographical patterning of commuter flows within urban areas and to document the travel behavior of various social groups.

Four main features distinguish commuting patterns in the contemporary American city. First, the vast majority of workers commute by private automobile. Reliance on the automobile is both a cause and an effect of the spatial structure of American cities and is one legacy of the massive suburbanization of population and jobs since World War II. In 1990 more than 85 percent of all workers drove to work alone; only 5 percent used public transit. However, these figures mask wide geographic variations that reflect differences in urban structure and historical development. First, fewer than 1 percent of workers use transit in some southern and western states, for example, compared to 27 percent of those living in the New York metropolitan region. Second, commuting patterns have pulled extensive rural and fringe areas into the orbit of metropolitan economies; the construction of high-speed freeways since the late 1950s has permitted longer trips to work, often without corresponding increases in travel time. Third, changes in the labor force have created more in-

tricate and dynamic patterns of commuting than are often recognized. Under the simplifying assumptions of conventional urban theory, each worker undertakes a single "journey to work," departing in the morning for the office or factory and returning home in the evening. But since the late 1960s, the rising participation of women in the labor force, along with increased part-time employment and multiple job holding, have added to the complexity of commuter flows. Multiple-purpose and multiple-destination work trips are common, and planners have responded to the increased congestion caused by suburban employment by encouraging "off-peak" travel, staggered work hours, and other ways to increase the carrying capacity of already existing roads. Finally, the spatial dimensions of commuter flows have become more complex. Until the middle of the twentieth century, employment remained concentrated in the central areas of most American cities, and the predominant flow of commuters brought workers from low-density residential neighborhoods into the urban core. In the last two generations, however, accelerated job growth in suburban areas has attracted much more of the total urban commuting and has created a complex mosaic of daily traffic patterns. By the middle of the 1970s, the number of workers who both lived and worked in suburbs was twice the number who commuted from suburbs to central cities. Between 1954 and 1990, the share of workers crossing a county boundary on their way to work increased from 12 percent to 24 percent.

—*Elvin Wyly*

See also
Automobiles; Journey to Work; Multicentered Metropolis; Multiple Nuclei Theory.
References
Cervero, Robert. *Suburban Gridlock.* New Brunswick, NJ: Center for Urban Policy Research, 1986.
———. "Suburban Traffic Congestion: Is There a Way Out?" *Built Environment* 17 (1991): 205–217.
Giuliano, G., and K. A. Small. "Is the Journey to Work Explained by Urban Structure?" *Urban Studies* 30 (1993): 1485–1500.
Hanson, Susan, ed. *The Geography of Urban Transportation.* 2d ed. New York: Guilford Press, 1995.
Nelson, A. C., and K. J. Dueker. "The Exurbanization of America and Its Planning Policy Implications." *Journal of Planning Education and Research* 9 (1990): 91–100.
Plane, D. A. "The Geography of Urban Commuting Fields: Some Empirical Evidence from New England." *Professional Geographer* 33 (1981): 182–188.

Company Towns

A company town is a settlement founded or sustained by a single enterprise that is also its chief employer. In the United States, as elsewhere, most company towns were founded between 1830 and 1930 by firms engaged in manufacturing, mining, and lumber milling. Company towns were usually small, and their populations rarely exceeded several thousand, although there were exceptions. Many were not incorporated or did not have a government charter. Although the Depression and organized labor forced many companies to liquidate their holdings and terminate unfair employment practices, a few manufacturing and mining towns continued to operate as company towns until the 1960s. And one lumber town, Gilchrist, Oregon, survived until 1990.

The term *company town* came to be used at the turn of the century and may have had its origin in Appalachia and western Pennsylvania. Industrial villages, mill towns, and mining towns are the descriptive terms most often used when reading about these settlements. When the term *company town* does appear, it usually carries a negative connotation.

The United States was not the only country in which single enterprises founded towns. Some of the earliest were built in Scandinavia, France, Germany, and Great Britain, but by far the greater number appeared in the United States. Hundreds of towns were established in conjunction with mining anthracite and bituminous coal, copper- and iron-bearing ores; drilling for and refining petroleum; and logging and lumber milling.

Fewer in number, although less dispersed by region, were towns founded to produce textiles and textile machinery. America's best-known company town, Pullman, Illinois, established in 1880, manufactured railroad coaches, diners, and sleepers. Urban America largely developed during the nineteenth and early twentieth centuries, and the company town was one aspect of this national pattern.

In terms of planning and architecture, those company towns involved in manufacturing were among the more interesting because of the money invested in them and the provisions they made for workers and their families. The better of these have been labeled "model company towns." North Easton, Massachusetts, for example, was transformed from an industrial village to a model company town by Oliver Ames and Sons, who founded a tool and shovel company there in 1844. The family became the principal property owner and employer during the middle decades of the nineteenth century, and in the late 1870s they hired the noted architect, Henry H. Richardson, and the landscape architect, Frederick Law Olmsted, to design a library, town hall, railroad station, and two private residences, and also to landscape the public grounds of the town as well as their private estates. Their intent was to make North Easton an attractive place in which to work and live.

Hopedale, Massachusetts, was similarly transformed between 1886 and 1916 from a small utopian village to a thriving model company town by the Draper family, who employed the landscape architects Warren Henry Manning and Arthur A. Shurcliff to plan a cemetery, park, school grounds, and housing estates for their employees. Both Manning and Shurcliff would become founding members of the American Town Planning Association, and in later commissions they used the knowledge they had gained in designing Hopedale. Among their other work, Manning later planned Goodyear Heights (1913) and Firestone Park (1916) near Akron, Ohio, while Shurcliff laid out Hyde Park Village (1910–1915) for the American Felt Company.

Paternalism cast a shadow over many company towns, and it almost always caused resentment among workers and their families. Because the company was both employer and landlord, it could dictate many different kinds of policies. A worker who failed to obey company rules could lose his job, and the loss of a job meant expulsion from the community because a company town had only one employer. Workers were expected to be punctual, abstemious, and loyal and to remain independent or nonunion.

Paternalism rarely stopped at the workbench or mine shaft. It could follow the worker into his home and during times of leisure. Renting a company house meant maintaining the premises, and rents and repairs could be subtracted from wages. To encourage compliance with their rules, the company sometimes offered prizes for well-maintained yards and gardens. A "field day" or holiday sponsored by the company assumed participation by an employee and his family. Even when an employer donated a library to the town, this act was more than just philanthropic. Because the company purchased the books and thus determined what could be read, it was also paternalistic.

The real conditions of life and work in company towns could easily be concealed from outsiders, and companies often withheld information from county or state officials. The Massachusetts Bureau of Labor, established in 1869 as one of the first state labor departments, had limited power to improve working conditions, but it compiled statistics and published reports annually that illuminated labor conditions among men, women, and children regarding hours, compensation, and hazards to health. The bureau's commissioner, Carroll D. Wright, was the first person to be appointed director of the United States Bureau of Labor in 1883, and he commissioned several studies that examined company towns and company housing.

Advances in technology that permitted the development of company towns also brought about their demise. During the nineteenth century, resource sites were often isolated. Towns built around factories and mines grew rapidly and often haphazardly. Traditional market forces that would have led to building houses, stores, and schools did not exist at the outset, and the company had little alternative but to provide everything; the subsistence earnings of miners and textile workers did not provide sufficient income or savings to build homes. The absence of merchants, except for those employed by the company, eliminated competition in purchasing staples. But improved roads, canals, and especially railroads, necessary for shipping the company's products, facilitated mobility among the employees. Those unhappy with their job or wages could leave, and many did. Moreover, the advent of the steam engine and the abundance of cheap coal permitted companies to abandon sites dependent on water power and to relocate nearer to large cities with improved markets and better shipping. Mining and lumber milling towns were often victims of their own success, abandoning sites as their minerals were exhausted or their timber harvested. The more successful they were, the more rapidly they depleted their resources and lost their reason for existing.

The company town that had benefited from its relative isolation and exclusivity during the nineteenth century was eventually ensnared by the network of twentieth-century transportation, hydroelectric transmission, and communications. The Depression and the rise of big labor, following earlier recessions in mining and textile manufacturing, administered the final blow. In the Far West, only a few survived, but their days were numbered. To dismiss the company town as mere welfare capitalism would overlook its contributions to resource planning, low-cost housing, and the urban design of America's industrial suburbs and new towns.

—*John S. Garner*

See also
Coal Towns; Mill Towns; Mining Towns; Pullman, Illinois.
References
Allen, James B. *The Company Town in the American West.* Norman: University of Oklahoma Press, 1966.
Buder, Stanley. *Pullman: An Experiment in Industrial Order and Community Planning, 1880–1930.* New York: Oxford University Press, 1967.
Coolidge, John P. *Mill and Mansion: A Study of Architecture and Society in Lowell, Massachusetts, 1820–1865.* New York: Columbia University Press, 1942.
Garner, John S. *The Model Company Town: Urban Design through Private Enterprise in Nineteenth-Century New England.* Amherst: University of Massachusetts Press, 1984.
Garner, John S., ed. *The Company Town: Architecture and Society in the Early Industrial Age.* New York: Oxford University Press, 1992.
Hall, Jacquelyn Dowd, et al., eds. *Like a Family: The Making of a Southern Cotton Mill World.* Chapel Hill: University of North Carolina Press, 1987.
Reps, John W. *Cities of the American West.* Princeton, NJ: Princeton University Press, 1979.

Concentric Zone Theory

The concentric zone theory is an idealized model of urban spatial structure developed by Ernest W. Burgess in 1925 to describe neighborhood variation in Chicago in the early 1920s. As one of the central contributions of the Chicago School of Sociology, Burgess's theory influenced urban sociology and urban geography through the 1960s and 1970s.

Observing that socioeconomic status tended to increase with distance from the city center, Burgess divided the city into five concentric zones. At the center was the central business district (Chicago's "Loop"), encircled by warehouses and light manufacturing plants that were gradually encroaching on the deteriorating homes of a "zone in transition." Beyond were three residential rings differentiated by workers' relative ability to afford commuting costs: a "zone of workingmen's homes" inhabited by second-generation immigrants leaving the zone in transition; a "zone of better residences" with high-class apartment buildings and exclusive upper-middle-class districts; and finally a "commuters' zone" of suburban neighborhoods and satellite cities. New immigrants sustained the growth of the city, settling first in the low-rent districts of the zone in transition and working their way to better neighborhoods in outer zones. Over time, each inner zone gradually expanded into the next outer zone, a process that Burgess explained in terms of the ecological concepts of invasion and succession.

Burgess's theory accurately described the effects of rapid growth and industrialization on Chicago's neighborhoods in the early twentieth century, but it has been criticized as an oversimplification. More fundamentally, Burgess's theory accepted racial, economic, and ethnic segregation as the natural equilibrium resulting from spatial competition among different social groups—thus ignoring the roles of inequality, racism, and conflict in urban society.

—*Elvin Wyly*

See also
Burgess, Ernest W.; Central Business District; Chicago School of Sociology; Multiple Nuclei Theory; Sector Theory; Zone in Transition.
References
Berry, Brian J. L., and J. D. Kasarda. *Contemporary Urban Ecology.* London: Macmillan, 1977.
Burgess, Ernest W. "The Growth of the City: An Introduction to a Research Project." In Robert E. Park, Ernest W. Burgess, and R. D. McKenzie, *The City.* Chicago: University of Chicago Press, 1925.
Harvey, David. *Social Justice and the City.* Baltimore: Johns Hopkins University Press, 1973.
Hawley, Amos H. *Human Ecology: A Theory of Community Structure.* New York: Ronald Press, 1950.

Condominiums

Condominiums are a housing option that gives the buyer sole claim to a particular dwelling unit in a multiunit building and also partial ownership of the common facilities, built structure, and land on which the building sits. Condominiums differ from cooperatives by assigning ownership of a specific dwelling unit, i.e., the space between the walls, to the buyer while coops assign a share of the entire building to all owners. The owners of all the units in a building of condominiums form a corporation that is managed by an elected council or board.

Condominiums are a relatively new, but rapidly growing, tenure option in North America, although they have had a long history in Europe. Roman law coined the term *condominium* over 2,000 years ago. The Code Napoleon of 1804 advanced the concept of joint ownership of property, but not until 1938 did France introduce comprehensive legislation that made this tenure option viable. In 1951 Puerto Rico enacted legislation that became the model for both the United States and Canada.

Perhaps the single most important legislation in the United States itself was the 1977 Uniform Condominium Act. The legislation evolved to reduce serious problems in the transfer of ownership from the developer of a project to a condominium's board. Problems had also arisen in managing an asset that was owned jointly by people who had notions of freehold ownership. Legislation introduced throughout the 1970s sought to reduce these problems by:

- regulating the behavior of developers, especially during the marketing phase
- establishing the rights and responsibilities of condominium owners and occupants and the board or council that manages the affairs of the corporation
- regulating the responsibilities of owners and the condominium board or council
- determining the status of the mortgage in terms of the priority of the mortgage relative to the other claims against the property

Condominium tenure makes homeownership possible in high-density projects and enables people to move back to the inner city or to high-density vacation resorts while maintaining their status as homeowners. Condominium tenure is not necessarily defined by the building type, and in some cases subdivisions of single-family homes have been sold as condominiums; the condominium corporation owns and maintains the common spaces between houses and, at times, manages the residents' golf course or marina. The condominium board or council maintains the facilities, and owners pay monthly fees for operation, maintenance, repair, taxes, and other expenses. The board enforces the rules and regulations of the condominium corporation to assure the furtherance of communal goals.

The nature of the condominium sector has changed since the option first developed in North America. Early studies showed condominiums attracting primarily young households who could not afford single-family houses. Units in condominiums were 30 percent smaller than single-family homes on average and considerably less expensive. The market evolved and diversified during the 1970s to include a larger proportion of older people. In 1988 Andrejs Skaburskis showed that the Canadian market had developed two distinct submarkets—one formed by young families buying more affordable condominiums as a step on their way to single-family homeownership, the other formed by empty nesters buying condominiums to maintain their position as homeowners while gaining the amenities and physical security of large, supervised buildings without having to worry about maintenance.

By the late 1980s, developers were diversifying the condominium market even further by offering "lifestyle" condominiums aimed at the tennis crowd, fans of country and western music, and so on. In the Province of Ontario, Canada, human rights legislation prohibited condominium corporations from discriminating against families with children regardless of the "adult" orientation of their project.

The condominium sector is still relatively new, and difficulties emerge when condominium corporations, as collectives, make rules governing the behavior of individual owners who, regardless of having agreed to abide by those rules, maintain deep-rooted notions about the freedom that is an integral aspect of their sense of homeownership.

Today, condominiums have replaced traditional rental developments in many cities. Condominium syndicates are formed to develop and manage buildings occupied entirely by renters. Investors in condominium units can physically identify and see their property, and they find that condominiums are more liquid than the alternatives available through partnerships or shares in real estate companies. Investors can develop condominium portfolios that diversify their real estate holdings by project location and type. The expansion of the rental stock by building condominiums preempts future problems with "condominium conversion" should market conditions, or increasingly stringent rent controls, make owner occupancy more attractive.

—*Andrejs Skaburskis*

References

Barton, Stephen E. *Management and Governance in Common Interest Community Associations.* Berkeley, CA: Institute of Regional and Urban Development, 1987.

Barton, Stephen E., and Carol Silverman. *Common Interest Homeowners' Associations Management Study.* Sacramento: California Department of Real Estate, 1987.

Blankstein, Murray, et al. *National Surveys of Condominium Owners.* Toronto, Ontario: Condominium Research Associates, 1970.

Dinkelspiel, A. *Condominiums—The Effects of Conversion on a Community.* Boston: Auburn House, 1981.

Hamilton, S. W., and R. Roberts. *Condominium Development and Ownership.* Vancouver, British Columbia: Real Estate Board of Greater Vancouver, 1973.

Hamilton, S. W., et al. *Condominiums—A Decade of Experience in British Columbia.* Vancouver, British Columbia: British Columbia Real Estate Association, 1978.

Skaburskis, A. "A Comparison of Suburban and Inner-City Condominium Markets." *Canadian Journal of Regional Science* 10 (1988): 259–285.

———. "The Nature of the Canadian Condominium Submarkets and Their Effect on the Evolving Urban Spatial Structure." *Urban Studies* 25 (1988): 109–123.

Coney Island

Coney Island, a five-mile stretch of beach on the Atlantic Ocean once separated from the main body of Brooklyn by a creek, was discovered by Henry Hudson in 1609 and was part of the land sold to the English in 1643 by the Dutch West India Company. The island, inhabited by "conies," or rabbits, and consisting mainly of marshes and sand dunes, remained an isolated settlement until the early nineteenth century. Development as a seaside resort began in 1824 with the construction of a causeway across the creek and the first hotel, the Coney Island House. Visitors were attracted to the island's combination of seclusion and surf; a small steamboat service linked it to lower Manhattan, and restaurants, bathhouses, barrooms, and sanitoria were built along the beach. In the 1870s and 1880s, with improvements in rail and water transportation and the erection of several large hotels, Coney began to lose its rustic character.

By the turn of the century, the island developed into four distinct areas, the characters of which still remain. The eastern tip, Manhattan Beach, with its fashionable hotels and spacious homes, was decidedly well-to-do. Next to it was middle-class Brighton Beach, and to the west again was working-class West Brighton Beach, often referred to as "Coney Island" because of its mass amusement section. At West Brighton, Italian and Jewish immigrant families settled in districts adjacent to the amusements, rides, and sideshows. The west end, formerly known as Norton's Point (a hangout for criminals, gamblers, and prostitutes), became Sea Gate, a fenced-in residential community determined to remain isolated from West Brighton's crowds, noise, and day-trippers.

Turn-of-the-century Coney Island became world famous because of its great amusement parks. Three different ideas or park formulas originated here, styles of outdoor entertainment extant today. Sea Lion Park (1895–1902), with water rides and aquatic exhibitions, is the forerunner of today's Marinelands, Sea Worlds, and local water parks from Maine to California. At Steeplechase (1897–1964), the prototype of the modern amusement park, technology was utilized extensively, novel mechanical rides were continually introduced, and audience participation in carnival-like activities was encouraged. By contrast, Luna Park (1903–1944) structured its attractions around historical, geographical, or cultural themes and impressed audiences with its building design, illusions, spectacular live shows, and park ambiance. Dreamland (1904–1911), a second theme park, sought not just fantasy but architectural grandeur and aesthetic appeal as well with its pure white buildings, broad promenades, massive arches, 375-foot-tall Beacon Tower, and 1 million lightbulbs. An updated and more sophisticated Luna Park or Dreamland lives on in contemporary Disney attractions around the globe.

The twentieth century's second decade was a time of great change for Coney Island. Dreamland burned down and was never rebuilt. All the large hotels on the eastern half of the island were razed as the "money crowd" went to cleaner and less congested resorts on Long Island. Thrill rides, freak shows, and wax museums replaced mechanical wonders and awe-inspiring sights. Luna Park passed into the hands of its creditors and lost much of its creative spirit. The extension of the New York subway in 1920 permitted millions of tenement dwellers to reach Coney Island for only 5 cents, and the prices on everything from hot dogs to roller coasters quickly dropped to a nickel. The building boom of the 1920s dramatically increased the year-round residential population of all four areas. West Brighton's large bungalow colony enabled New Yorkers of modest means to take extended summer vacations there. In the 1930s, the island's reputation further worsened due to its widespread use of ballyhoo, girlie shows, and crooked skill games. Robert Moses, the new parks commissioner and an open critic of Coney's "cheap commercialism," gained control of the beaches and sought to reduce overcrowding, improve transportation, eliminate amusements and ballyhoo, and enlarge the beach.

Throughout the 1940s and 1950s, western Coney Island contained both a thriving amusement section, the largest collection of rides and games in the world, and also stable residential communities of second- and third-generation Italians and Jews. All that changed suddenly in the 1960s. Young families moved to the suburbs, older residents relocated to the new middle-income high-rise cooperatives near Brighton Beach, large numbers of blacks and Puerto Ricans moved in, the city designated West Brighton as an urban renewal zone, and low-income high-rise apartments replaced bungalows and multistory houses. In addition, the crime rate soared, businesses along the main avenues closed, Steeplechase failed to open for the 1965 season, and the amusement section deteriorated severely. While white flight accelerated in the 1970s and West Brighton turned almost totally minority, Sea Gate retained its exclusivity, immune from the crime and poverty just beyond its fence. Meanwhile, Brighton Beach remained middle class, absorbing many immigrant Russian

A crowded beach with fairgrounds in the background shows why Coney Island remains one of New York's most popular tourist attractions.

Jews, and Manhattan Beach continued to attract luxury apartment owners.

Today, a walk through Coney Island's dilapidated amusement section brings tears to the eyes of those New Yorkers who remember it only a generation ago. Nostalgia for the "old Coney Island" is apparently quite strong, not to mention potentially profitable, judging from current efforts to redevelop and revitalize the entire area. Chief among them is an ambitious plan for a $350 million state-of-the-art amusement park, designed by former Disney employees, to be called Steeplechase and built on the original site. The scale model and artist's drawings for the new park, including rides and attractions with themes taken from the four turn-of-the-century parks, conform to and sentimentalize Coney's historic past. Perhaps the coming turn of a new century, as it did before, will change for the better the face of Coney Island.

—*Raymond M. Weinstein*

See also
Amusement Parks; Disneyland.

References
Kasson, John F. *Amusing the Millions: Coney Island at the Turn of the Century.* New York: Hill and Wang, 1978.
Onorato, Michael F. "Another Time, Another World: Coney Island Memories." Oral History Program. California State University at Fullerton. No. 930046–09–9.
Weinstein, Raymond M. "Disneyland and Coney Island: Reflections on the Evolution of the Modern Amusement Park." *Journal of Popular Culture* 26 (1992): 131–164.
Weinstein, Stephan F. "The Nickel Empire: Coney Island and the Creation of Urban Seaside Resorts in the United States." Ph.D. dissertation, Columbia University, 1984.

Congestion

Traffic congestion is the reduction in the speed of travel because of crowding. It was recently estimated that traffic congestion in large (a population of more than 1 million) American metropolitan areas (which together contain about 75 million licensed drivers) results in 6 billion vehicle-hours of delay annually. Assuming that the average vehicle-hour of delay is valued at $8 this translates into a congestion cost of $640 per driver per year!

Transportation is the lifeblood of cities. Goods have to be moved and people have to travel. Since transportation capacity is finite, congestion is inevitable. Thus, the appropriate questions are, "what is the optimal level of congestion? and how can it be achieved?" Urban economics textbooks say that economic agents make efficient choices if they understand the true social costs of their actions. Since one traveler slows others, he or she should pay the cost of the increased delay s/he causes over and above the costs s/he directly incurs. This can be achieved by congestion pricing. As well, the capacity of traffic should be fixed so that the cost of an extra unit of capacity equals the resulting reduction in travel costs.

Except on a few freeways, congestion pricing of urban automobile travel is not employed in American cities. This means that urban automobile travel is underpriced. As a result, people take too many auto trips and road congestion is excessive.

There is no simple remedy. Transportation planners have a variety of other policy instruments at their disposal, but none is as effective as congestion pricing. The benefits of road expansion may be neutralized by an increase in the number of auto trips taken. High-occupancy lanes do encourage car pools but typically cause increased congestion for other drivers. Gasoline taxes reduce the number of urban automobile trips but have the unwanted side effect of also discouraging rural travel. And so on.

A significant minority ardently believe in public transit. Unfortunately, the underpricing of urban automobile travel for the past 50 years has resulted in sprawling, low-density cities for which mass transit is not cost effective. The situation is worsened by a vicious cycle. A smaller number of riders causes transit authorities to eliminate routes, to operate them less frequently, and to provide less reliable and comfortable service. The result is further reductions in the number of riders.

It is predicted that traffic congestion will become significantly worse during the next two decades. Transportation planners will continue to use the same policies with limited effectiveness. Eventually, congestion will become so severe that urban residents will accept the need for some form of congestion pricing. This is already happening in some of the most congested cities in Western Europe and East Asia—which are considerably more congested than American cities of comparable size—where a variety of congestion pricing schemes are in place.

—*Richard Arnott*

See also
Traffic.
References
Small, K. A. *Urban Transportation Economics.* Chur, Switzerland: Harwood Academic Publishers, 1992.
Vickrey, W. S. "Pricing in Urban and Suburban Transportation." *American Economic Review, Papers and Proceedings* 53 (May 1963): 452–465.

Consolidation

Ways of dealing with problems of governance and service delivery in metropolitan areas include annexation, special districts, interjurisdictional agreements, empowering counties, councils of government, and city-county consolidation.

The most radical of these approaches is city-county consolidation. In its purest form, consolidating a county with one or more cities unifies the governments of one or more municipalities with their surrounding county governments, thus making the boundaries of the jurisdictions involved coterminous. It is a structure that intrigues metropolitan reformers because it reduces structural fragmentation and produces functional consolidation. Simply put, advocates of consolidation contend that it has the potential to eliminate duplication and waste as well as ensure economies of scale and improve service quality and professionalism.

In spite of these attractive features and benefits, city-county consolidation has been relatively rare. To date, there have been 29 successful city-county consolidations, with 20 of these occurring after World War II. Only 2 city-county consolidations have occurred since 1980. All 9 successful consolidations occurring prior to World War II were the products of state legislative action. The Indianapolis/Marion County consolidation in Indiana is the only other one to have been brought about by state legislative action. Most consolidation proposals, however, have been submitted to local voters, and they have failed. In fact, only about one-fourth of the consolidation proposals that come to a vote are approved. Most have been in medium-size or smaller metropolitan areas with populations ranging from 150,000 to 800,000. All consolidation adoptions have occurred in the South or West, and furthermore, successful consolidations have always been characterized by a unique array of political factors. Frequently, it has been necessary to permit the independent existence of small municipalities, special districts, and some offices in order to obtain political support for consolidation (e.g., retaining a separate sheriff's office and city police department).

Although city-county consolidation makes sense from an administrative standpoint, several critical political obstacles are difficult for pro-consolidation forces to overcome. At the core of these barriers is the allocation of influence over policymaking. Suburbanites frequently fear that consolidation will give city residents a dominant voice in county affairs. Conversely, minority city residents are reluctant to surrender the political control that they have recently gained in the central city. Suburbanites also typically fear that city-county consolidation may result in larger taxes to support the higher costs of running the city. In addition, suburbanites are not likely to support uniform, countywide policies in taxation and zoning or help pay for costly municipal services they may neither want nor will receive. For instance, suburbanites who are content with their own wells and septic tanks and volunteer fire departments are not likely to welcome the opportunity to help pay for city water and sewerage services or a full-time city fire department. Suburbanites with well-established, high-quality public schools may be unenthusiastic about integrating their schools with city schools into a countywide system.

Other political realities have frequently overwhelmed the "logic" of city-county consolidation. For example, consolidation entails considerable disruption of public officials—redesigning governmental structure, reordering the authority of various offices, combining offices and agencies, and enlarging the magnitude of government operations. Moreover, suburban fears of being "submerged" into a large, impersonal, unresponsive government works against consolidation referenda. As a result, there is little chance that consolidation efforts will be successful unless a significant majority of influential community residents are very dissatisfied with the current state of affairs and are motivated to support consolidation actively.

A final obstacle to city-county consolidation can be the type of vote that state law requires to approve a proposed charter. A "double majority" requirement means that a majority "yes" vote must be secured within the city and within the area outside the city; a "double-count majority" vote requirement means that the vote of city residents is counted twice—once for the city and again for the county because they are also county residents. As expected, it is more difficult for consolidation to win under the "double majority" requirement and not certain even under the "double-count majority" if there is a high turnout.

—*J. Edwin Benton*

See also
Annexation.
References
Benton, J. Edwin. "Voter Attitudinal Factors and Metropolitan Consolidation: A Re-evaluation." *Midwest Review of Public Administration* 13 (1979): 207–224.

Benton, J. Edwin, and Darwin Gamble. "City/County Consolidation and Economies of Scale: Evidence from a Time-Series Analysis in Jacksonville, Florida." *Social Science Quarterly* 65 (1985): 190–198.

Hawkins, Brett W. *Nashville Metro: The Politics of City-County Consolidation.* Nashville, TN: Vanderbilt University Press, 1966.

Marando, Vincent. "City-County Consolidation: Reform, Regionalism, Referenda, and Requiem." *Western Political Quarterly* 32 (1979): 409–421.

Cooley, Charles Horton (1864–1929)

Charles Horton Cooley, who spent his career at the University of Michigan contributing to the developing field of sociology, is primarily known for his trilogy of books, *Human Nature and the Social Order* (1902), *Social Organization* (1909), and *Social Process* (1918). Greatly influenced by his reading of both Darwin and William Spencer, Cooley was equally captivated by the idealism of Thoreau and Goethe. His approach to social structure, while influ-

enced by concern about the ill effects of modern urban industrialism, was optimistic in asserting confidently that democratic principles would spread with advances in communication and technological innovation, especially in transportation. He believed, for instance, that street railway lines could reconcile the conflicting demands of industry and humanity by enabling workers to live close to nature in suburban enclaves set apart from the degrading influence of their worksites.

For urbanists, Cooley's most influential ideas lay in the importance of primary associations, notably the family, the play group, and the community group of elders. Noting in *Social Organization* that "In our own time the crowded tenements and the general economic and social confusion have severely wounded the family and the neighborhood," he nonetheless emphasized their basic vitality and stressed the importance of "restoring them to health." He saw the neighborhood as the nursery for what he called primary ideals, such as loyalty, truth, service, and kindness.

By his own account, Cooley was hardly a radical. Like his reformist colleagues concentrated at the University of Chicago, he spent some time at social settlements. But he left it to others to find practical applications for his social philosophy, those like the Russell Sage Foundation's Clarence Arthur Perry, who attempted to enhance the primacy of the face-to-face contacts Cooley valued through a strategy of neighborhood planning.

Although Cooley provided a groundbreaking discussion of class relations in *Social Organization,* he remained confident that the organic nature of society that bound all people together through common experiences in family and neighborhood groups was sufficient to overcome class conflict. Individuals might be tempted to be greedy, he noted, but such instincts ultimately would be harmonized by the positive influences of family and friends.

—*Howard Gillette, Jr.*

See also
Perry, Clarence Arthur.
Reference
Angell, Robert Cooley. "Charles H. Cooley." In David L. Sills, ed., *International Encyclopedia of the Social Sciences*, vol. 3, 378–383. New York: Free Press, 1968.

Correctional Institutions

Correctional institutions have played a central role in the development of American cities and suburbs. A historical overview of the origin, aims, and development of penal institutions—jails, county penitentiaries, adult prisons, juvenile reformatories, and adult reformatories—reveals that they have served, first and foremost, as dumping grounds for America's urban "criminal class."

During the colonial period, correctional institutions were not primary forms of social control, and crime was rare. Small villages could not afford to build and maintain costly penal structures, and while jails and county penitentiaries were opened in some colonies, these institutions were small and served a limited function. They were used to hold criminals serving short sentences, debtors, material witnesses, and defendants who could not post bail. Corporal punishment, the stocks, banishment, and the death penalty were the foundations of the disciplinary system.

The rise of cities in the late eighteenth and early nineteenth centuries changed America's approach to treating criminals. New waves of "inferior" immigrants, rising population density, and poverty laid the foundation for increases, or at least perceived increases, in a wide range of urban social ills: alcoholism, moral decay, crime, and delinquency. Fear of crime and criminals prompted native-born Americans to seek more effective kinds of social control. Their efforts laid the basis for the birth of America's first penal system, the prison.

Cell block C in Attica Prison in New York is typical of cell blocks in maximum security prisons across the United States.

The opening of the Walnut Street Prison in Philadelphia in 1790 marks the birth of the American prison movement. A simple approach to "reform" was introduced to transform criminals into law-abiding citizens. Offenders were placed in solitary confinement in stark cells, each containing a Bible. They were deprived of labor, education, and contact with fellow inmates. It was supposed that inmates would turn to the Bible for penance and salvation. This innovative approach to incarceration, which became known as the "Pennsylvania" or "separate system" of penal reform, was developed in Philadelphia's Walnut Street Prison along with the Western Penitentiary, which opened in Pittsburgh in 1826, and the Eastern Penitentiary, which opened in Philadelphia in 1829.

The opening of the Auburn Prison in Auburn, New York, in 1817 and the Sing Sing Prison in Ossining, New York, in 1826 introduced a competing approach known as the "congregate" or "silent" system. This system, like the Pennsylvania system, was designed to instill lower-class offenders with habits of order, discipline, self-control, and cheerful submission to authority. Under this system, inmates wore striped uniforms and marched in lockstep. During the day, prisoners worked together in shops, where they made chairs, whips, and other items that were sold for profit. But at night they were locked in solitary confinement, and strict silence was maintained at all times under threat of severe corporal punishment.

Claims of "miraculous success" by advocates of both systems captured the attention of penologists, social reformers, and legislators and sparked an intense debate: which system was more effective at taming and training adult criminals? Prison inspectors from across the United States and around the world traveled to New York and Pennsylvania in the first half of the nineteenth century to determine which system was more effective. Opinion was divided as prison inspectors from Europe generally favored the Pennsylvania system; inspectors from across the United States generally favored the more profitable New York system. Prisons opened in the United States through the end of the nineteenth century were, then, generally modeled after New York's system.

Nineteenth-century Americans were also concerned about the increasing amount of urban delinquency. In 1825 reformers opened the nation's first correctional institution for juveniles, the New York House of Refuge. This asylum, which marked the birth of America's "second penal system," was designed to remove juveniles from adult correctional facilities and introduce a new regimen, at least in theory, aimed at treatment and reform. New York's fallen children—largely the progeny of lower-class immigrants living in urban areas—were exposed to academic and vocational education, labor, religious instruction, an elaborate mark-and-classification system, indenture, and later parole. New York's congregate system of juvenile reform was designed and intended to transform juvenile delinquents into respectable, productive lower-class citizens.

The New York House of Refuge served as the nation's model juvenile reformatory for three decades. The opening of the Lancaster Industrial School for Girls in Lancaster, Massachusetts, in 1856 and the Ohio Reform School for Boys in Lancaster, Ohio, in 1858 introduced an alternative approach to reforming juveniles, the cottage or family system. This system rested on the belief that placing a large number of juveniles together in urban settings (as at the New York House of Refuge) caused moral decay. The Lancaster Industrial School for Girls and the Ohio Reform School for Boys consisted of cottages located in the country. Each cottage, which housed 15 to 30 children, was controlled by house parents who served as role models. Academic and vocational education aimed at preparing boys to work as farmers and girls as domestics was the foundation of the family system.

The opening of the Lancaster Industrial School for Girls and the Ohio Reform School for Boys sparked another intense debate. Which system—New York's congregate system or Massachusetts's and Ohio's family system—was more successful at reforming juvenile offenders? Visitors and prison inspectors toured these institutions, just as they had traveled to New York and Pennsylvania earlier in the century to study adult prisons. With isolated exceptions, the choice was clear: the family system was thought superior. Juvenile reformatories opened in the United States through the end of the nineteenth century were, then, generally modeled on the cottage system.

The opening in 1876 of the Elmira Reformatory in Elmira, New York, marked the birth of America's third penal system, the reformatory-prison movement. Penologists after the Civil War were alarmed by their discovery of a new criminal class, the dangerous youthful offender, and so they introduced a new penal experiment to reform first-time male offenders between the ages of 16 and 30. Under the direction of Superintendent Zebulon Brockway, America's most respected penologist, youthful offenders were, in theory, subjected to a new regimen of reform based on individualized treatment and prison science. The "new penology" extended the notion of rehabilitation from juveniles to young adults. Brockway's "Elmira system" used academic education, vocational education, indeterminate sentencing, recreation, religion, military drill, and parole to transform youthful offenders into productive citizens.

There was, however, a wide disparity between the promise and the practice of nineteenth-century correctional institutions. Treatment programs rarely achieved their stated goals and objectives. Punishments were severe, including whipping, solitary confinement, and the ball and chain. Inmate resistance—escape, violence, revolt, smuggling, drugs, arson, sexual attacks, suicide—was common. Female and "colored" offenders were exposed to racist and sexist versions of "treatment" and "reform" that were designed to fit them into their "proper place" in the social, economic, and political order as domestics and obedient laborers.

Adult prisons, juvenile reformatories, and adult reformatory-prisons, along with jails and county penitentiaries, have continued as the foundation of the American correctional system in the twentieth century. Twentieth-century reformers have eliminated some of the harsher elements of earlier correctional institutions, such as lockstep, striped uniforms, and whippings. Unfortunately, there are many disturbing similarities between past and present correctional institutions.

Modern institutions, much like their predecessors, are overcrowded, underfunded, understaffed, and plagued by "inmate resistance." Contemporary institutions continue trying to instill the dangerous classes—now poor, unskilled, city-raised blacks, Hispanics, and lower-class whites—with the Protestant ethic and fit them into a subordinate place in the social, economic, and political order. Modern correctional institutions are, quite simply, dumping grounds for the "human refuse" of urban America.

—*Alexander W. Pisciotta*

See also
Community-Based Corrections.

References

Clear, Todd R., and George F. Cole. *American Corrections*. 2d ed. Pacific Grove, CA: Brooks/Cole Publishing, 1990.

McKelvey, Blake. *American Prisons: A History of Good Intentions*. Montclair, NJ: Patterson Smith, 1977.

Pisciotta, Alexander W. *Benevolent Repression: Social Control and the American Reformatory-Prison Movement*. New York: New York University Press, 1994.

Rafter, Nicole H. *Partial Justice: Women, Prisons and Social Control*. 2d ed. New Brunswick, NJ: Transaction Publishers, 1990.

Rothman, David J. *The Discovery of the Asylum: Social Order and Disorder in the New Republic*. Boston: Little, Brown, 1971.

———. *Conscience and Convenience: The Asylum and Its Alternatives in Progressive America*. Boston: Little, Brown, 1980.

Schlossman, Steven L. *Love and the American Delinquent: The Theory and Practice of "Progressive" Juvenile Justice, 1825–1920*. Chicago: University of Chicago Press, 1977.

Coughlin, John Joseph (Bathhouse John) (1860–1938)

John Coughlin, one of Chicago's most well known and flamboyant political bosses, was born in "Connelly's Patch," the Irish district on Chicago's West Side, on August 15, 1860. His father, Michael, owned a grocery store, and his mother, Johanna, was a housewife who died in childbirth when John was six years old. John attended school with the future Republican Party boss Billy Lorimer, but both dropped out as teens. John went to work in a neighborhood Turkish bath where he became a "rubber." Eventually, he went to work in the baths at the Palmer House Hotel (the most prestigious in the city), where he saved enough tip money to buy his own bathhouse in 1882. Within five years Bathhouse John, as he became known, owned a string of bathhouses throughout the Loop. Here he came to know the gamblers, saloonkeepers, and politicians who ran the city's notorious Levee District, a vice area segregated from the rest of the Loop that became world famous during the World's Fair and Colombian Exposition of 1893.

Bathhouse John entered politics as a precinct captain for the First Ward Democratic organization and soon gained a reputation for being a man who could deliver votes. He perfected the method of having roving bands of drifters and unemployed workers move quickly through several precincts on election day, voting as often as necessary to ensure victory in return for 50 cents a vote. In 1892 Coughlin became an alderman, a position he held for the next 46 years. In the city council, he became a leader of the Gray Wolves, as reformers called them, those aldermen who supported horse racing, wide-open gambling, and prostitution. They also sanctioned "boodling," another term used by good government types to refer to the bribes, payoffs, and graft that had to be offered before businesses could be opened, contracts could be let, and police and fire protection could be received.

Coughlin kept his bathhouses and opened a saloon, the Silver Dollar, in the Levee, where he formed a lucrative alliance with a fellow alderman from the First Ward, Michael (Hinky Dink) Kenna. Bathhouse John liked fancy clothes and diamond rings, and the First Ward balls that he and Hinky Dink sponsored received wide notoriety for their vulgarity and decadence. Prohibition came as a major blow to the Levee; when it ended in 1933 Al Capone had seized control of the liquor and gambling interests. Coughlin continued to sit on the city council until he died on November 8, 1938, heavily in debt because of his gambling losses.

—*Leslie Tischauer*

See also
Kenna, Michael (Hinky Dink).

References
Gosnell, Harold F. *Machine Politics: Chicago Style*. Chicago: University of Chicago Press, 1968.
Wendt, Lloyd, and Herman Kogan. *Bosses in Lusty Chicago: The Story of Bathhouse John and Hinky Dink*. Bloomington: Indiana University Press, 1974.

Council-Manager Government

The council-manager plan of government, with the mayor-council and commission forms, is a principal structure for organizing a municipality. Counties and special districts are often organized according to similar plans. The essence of the council-manager plan is a professionally trained executive who operates the local government on a daily basis while always being responsible to the popularly elected (political) governing board. "Professional" refers to education and to progressively more responsible experience that covers such practices as strategic leadership, democratic responsiveness, service delivery, budgeting, and personnel. It also refers to a keen sense of democratic and personal values that have been embodied in a strong code of ethics.

Through the early years of the United States, the local council was very powerful, while the executive—the mayor—had limited political power. In the 1880s Brooklyn and Boston introduced the strong mayor form of government to provide greater executive leadership. Coupled with active local political parties and a lingering belief in the Jacksonian idea of frequent rotation of officeholders, the strong mayor form led to a heavy emphasis on the spoils system. By the early part of the twentieth century, local governments began to look for an alternate arrangement that would feature both a strong executive and some separation of politics and administration.

This search for a different local government structure was part of the reform movement in American politics. Unreformed government is characterized by such features as partisanship, district elections, patronage, a strong mayor, and a long ballot. Reformed government is characterized by such features as nonpartisanship, at-large elections, a short ballot, a merit system, and professional management. Council-manager government is widely considered the epitome of reform government.

The first recognized use of the council-manager plan occurred in Staunton, Virginia, in 1908. The hope of the plan's proponents was that the new structure would overcome governance problems created by a large, unwieldy, bicameral council and provide expertise to improve the city's infrastructure. The city manager was perceived as a "business director" and the city council as a "corporate board of directors." Efficiency and a dichotomy between politics and administration were thus implicit goals of the plan.

The major characteristics of the classic council-manager plan include:

1. A small council that is elected at large on a non-partisan ballot to serve as the legislative and policymaking body.

2. A professionally trained manager appointed by the council who appoints and removes department heads, prepares the budget, and oversees municipal operations. The council can dismiss the manager at any time.

3. A mayor, who plays a largely ceremonial role, is selected by the council or, occasionally, is the member of the council who received the greatest number of votes in the election.

In addition, the mayor and council are paid only expenses or a very low honorarium and generally serve no more than two to three terms.

City managers were seen to play three essential roles: management (administrative activities), policy (council relations, agenda development), and political (community relations and leadership). Initially, heavy emphasis was placed on the management role, a role that most clearly demonstrates the quest for efficiency and a desire to separate administration and politics. However, the actual practice of local government made it clear that politics and government could not be separated and that different municipal councils often expected the manager to work with the council in developing public policy and in articulating the city's stance to the public. During the 1950s and 1960s both scholars and local government practitioners hotly debated the extent to which the manager should be politically oriented.

Another debate began in the 1970s over whether large cities, especially those whose population exceeded 250,000, should abandon the council-manager model in favor of a strong mayor–council model. In larger cities, this issue was important because someone needed to provide policy and political leadership that citizens could understand easily and that met the needs of a diverse constituency. A companion argument ensued over whether managers should be the spokesperson when major policies were in the offing and whether they should be involved at all in shaping fundamental public policy.

At the heart of these controversies were the demographic and economic changes taking place in the nation's cities, especially in major metropolitan areas. Because of its historic identification as a businesslike plan and its traditional support by the business community, council-manager government was inherently suspect as a device for resolving emerging inner-city conflicts and problems. Moreover, its critics had long suggested that council-manager government, with its emphasis on efficiency, suppressed conflict, thereby leaving cities vulnerable to the rage that has often accompanied unresolved public policy questions. The plan's detractors were quick to add that

council-manager government has always enjoyed its greatest success in middle-sized, homogeneous, suburban communities. Indeed, the plan flourishes in cities between 10,000 and 250,000 in population but is often too expensive for smaller cities and too lacking in overt political leadership for larger ones.

Because of concerns over the plan's ability to foster solutions to political conflict, some cities changed governmental forms entirely. However, most responded pragmatically and adjusted their city charters in an effort to keep professional management while still having strong elected leaders. Two of the most significant changes, now enacted in almost all council-manager cities over 50,000 in population, are that the mayor is usually elected at large and some or all of the council members are elected by districts.

These changes were designed to produce political leadership, greater representation, and effective service delivery. In turn, they have caused a major shift in managerial attention to the areas of policy and council relations because heterogeneous councils have greatly increased the manager's need to help the council build a governing consensus.

Other changes in local government have represented a compromise between those who prefer an unreformed, openly political model such as a strong mayor–council, and those who think that council-manager government still has much to offer, especially in an era of scarce resources and a constant quest for efficiency and productivity. For example, council-manager government and strong mayor–council government have been combined to produce a hybrid in which the manager reports only to the mayor. Such changes reflect the political realities of the moment and acknowledge that many mayors, particularly in larger cities, want to play a more significant role than classic council-manager government allows. Traditional strong mayor cities also have adopted this hybrid form when the mayor acknowledged a need for managerial expertise.

Modifications in local government structure have followed national political developments. In the 1990s, for example, the trends included greater productivity through better-managed performance, frequent changes in legislative body membership, and more attention to constituent demands. These changes in council-manager government not only afforded the plan the flexibility to survive but also allowed cities to continue to benefit from trained experts.

—*Charldean Newell*

See also

Commission Government; Mayor-Council Government; Municipal Government.

References

Frederickson, George W., ed. *Ideal and Practice in Council-Manager Government.* Washington, DC: International City Management Association, 1989.

Nalbandian, John. *Professionalism in Local Government: Transformation in the Roles, Responsibilities, and Values of City Managers.* San Francisco: Jossey-Bass, 1991.

Stillman, Richard J., II. *The Rise of the City Manager: A Public Professional in Local Government.* Albuquerque: University of New Mexico Press, 1974.

Svara, James H. *Official Leadership in the City: Patterns of Conflict and Cooperation.* New York: Oxford University Press, 1990.

Councils of Governments

A council of governments is a voluntary association of local governments, either in a metropolitan or rural area, established to facilitate intergovernmental cooperation between nearby member governments. These members are usually represented in council deliberations by their chief elected officials. Since it lacks taxation and policymaking powers, a council of governments is not a government per se.

The Supervisors Inter-County Committee (SICC), situated in the Detroit metropolitan area and established in 1954, was the first council of governments. Eventually, this body was succeeded by the Southeastern Michigan Council of Governments (SEMCOG), a much more inclusive body. Since 1954, hundreds of these councils have been established throughout the United States, a development that was strongly stimulated by various federal and state area-wide review policies.

Although the primary responsibility of a council of governments is to promote dialogue and cooperation between member local governments, most councils of governments have also been involved in regional land use, economic development, and transportation planning. Commencing in the 1980s councils of governments began to provide an array of technical and planning services to their member governments, a trend that continues to increase.

—*Nelson Wikstrom*

References

Scarborough, George, "A Council of Governments Approach." *National Civic Review* 71 (1982): 358–361.

Wikstrom, Nelson. *Councils of Governments: A Study of Political Incrementalism.* Chicago: Nelson-Hall, 1977.

Counties and Cities

Counties and cities have two things in common. First, they are both creatures of state governments. While counties are political and administrative subdivisions of states, cities come into existence (that is, incorporate) when they are granted a charter (sometimes called the city's "birth certificate") by states. As such, counties and cities exist in a unitary relationship to their state governments. Second, cities and counties are both general-purpose governments. That is, they provide a larger number and assortment of services than do other types of local governments (i.e., townships, special districts, and school districts).

Cities and counties also differ in several ways. On the one hand, cities have always possessed home rule, which has allowed them to respond more readily to the demands of their residents for a higher level and wider menu of services. On the other hand, until recently many states have been reluctant to grant home rule to counties, thus making it more difficult for county governments to provide a number of services that historically have been associated with cities (e.g., fire protection, garbage collection, utilities, libraries, and protective inspections and regulations). Moreover, county governments have been less inclined to provide services to residents of both the unincorporated and incorporated areas of counties, such as airports, parks and recreational programs and facilities, solid waste and sewage disposal, housing and urban renewal, economic development, and mass transit. Furthermore, counties have greater responsibility for the traditional services of local governments, including highway and bridge construction and maintenance, health and hospitals, public welfare, law enforcement, courts and corrections, public buildings, and financial and other forms of record keeping and administration, due both to resident expectations and state mandates.

Over the years, these similarities and differences have had a significant effect on the relations between cities and counties. Specifically, these similarities and differences, along with state requirements that counties and cities work together in many areas and the frequent instance of overlapping jurisdiction, has meant that city-county relations have been characterized by both cooperation and conflict.

In the last several decades, cities and counties have been reexamining the "go it alone" approach to solving problems. More and more, many of the problems associated with providing services or the regulatory responsibilities of local governments transcend geographic or jurisdictional lines. In many instances, this has meant that cities and counties have found it preferable—if not absolutely necessary from the standpoint of efficiency, economics, and effectiveness—to join together to fashion area-wide solutions to problems. Moreover, some of these city-county efforts have involved cooperation with the private sector and nonprofit entities. This is not to say that concerns over turf or interjurisdictional jealousies are no longer present, but there does appear to be a new appreciation for common problems.

City-county cooperation can usually be found in three principal areas: coproduction of services, contracting for services with another jurisdiction, and planning and training. Many of the efforts at coproducing services are fairly modest in application. For instance, a county and the cities in its boundaries may agree to operate a sanitary landfill jointly, use the same jail facility, house emergency vehicles and personnel in the same facility, send out consolidated tax or fee notices and operate a joint collection facility for their payment, jointly provide a mosquito abatement program or library services, or form a countywide police and investigative squad to respond to serious crimes. In addition, counties and cities usually have both written and informal agreements (mutual aid pacts) for fire and police protection and assistance in disasters. Although these attempts may hardly be noticeable to the public, they illustrate service delivery alternatives that were rarely considered a few decades ago.

City-county cooperation can also be found in the myriad of agreements whereby one or more jurisdictions contract with another government to provide services. For example, it is not unusual for governments to contract out to other governments for the provision of water, treatment of sewage, police services, solid waste disposal, fire protection, tax and utility billing, housing and transportation of prisoners, code enforcement, and emergency medical services. At this time, contracting out appears to be the fastest-growing area of cooperation between cities and counties, and the explanation is largely financial. The opportunity for smaller jurisdictions to realize economies of scale and for larger jurisdictions to enhance their revenue is quite appealing. In addition, there appears to be a growing awareness that contracting with another government may be a more effective way to provide services.

Cooperation among cities and counties can also be found in the area of planning. Although the federal government prodded cities and counties into cooperation in this area by initiating a new review process in the 1960s, it was only a matter of time before they would have recognized the necessity of planning in a number of areas of joint concern. Indeed, counties and cities have increasingly been confronted with issues—particularly those related to growth management—that defy a city or county solution. Environmental quality, educational instruction and facilities, housing availability, crime and public safety, water supply, recreational and cultural needs, treatment of sewage, and disposal of solid waste have been some of the major areas in which counties and cities have recognized the need to plan jointly for the future. Therefore, planning among counties and cities (sometimes encompassing several counties in one metropolitan area) has been one of the fastest-growing areas of cooperation.

In spite of the increased cooperation between counties and cities, several areas of conflict remain. The issue that seems to surface most often involves the incidence of double taxation. Historically, counties and cities have provided different classes of services and have only infrequently offered the same service to individuals who, while residing in municipalities, are also county residents. For instance, whereas many county services are mandated by state constitutions (e.g., health and hospitals, public welfare, transportation, police protection, legal and judicial), cities were typically created to provide a number of optional services for large concentrations of people (e.g., water and sewerage, solid waste collection and disposal, parks and recreation, fire protection, libraries, sidewalks, streetlights, parking, planning and zoning). More and more frequently, however, counties find themselves providing services that duplicate those already being provided by cities within the county. Therefore, the controversy over double taxation revolves around the concern of municipal residents who believe that they are being taxed by their county for services currently provided to them by their municipality, or that they are helping to subsidize the provision of services to county residents who live in densely populated unincorporated areas. The problem of double taxation is most readily apparent whenever an area is annexed into a city but county property taxes do not decrease, although the county's service responsibility for the area has lessened.

Consequently, the issue of double taxation has led to two opposing points of view. On the one hand, municipal governments, while seeking tax relief for their residents, also see the potential for added revenue to either ease the pain of fiscal stress on the city or to pay for new or expanded services. On the other hand, counties, while arguing that municipal citizens are also county residents and should pay their fair share in taxes, are not willing to surrender what usually has been a bountiful source of revenue regardless of the apparent unfairness of the situation.

Another related potential source of conflict can be found in the long-seated battles that have accompanied efforts by cities to either expand their boundaries through annexation or enlarge their service area beyond the city limits in the unincorporated portion of counties. Strained relations between county and city officials are much more apt to surface when the area to be annexed or served is already developed and the county has made substantial investments to provide services such as water and sewerage, street lighting, sidewalks, fire protection, parks and recreation, libraries, drainage, and so on. Furthermore, resentment among county officials could result from the fact that they stand to lose potential revenue generated from providing services to residents in the area to be served. If the territory in question is rural or undeveloped, the possibility for conflict between the county and the city may be less likely because the county probably has not invested in infrastructure or increased the size of its workforce to serve the area. Nevertheless, conflict still can arise if there are pending plans to develop the area and county officials feel that the city—and not the county—will reap the tax benefits as a consequence of appreciating property values.

Opportunities for conflict between counties and cities can also emerge when uncontrolled development by one jurisdiction causes problems for the other. Several scenarios illustrate the potential for such confrontations. Unbridled growth by one or more cities in a county, for instance, could mean that the demand for water rises dramatically, thus lowering the water table for the entire county, area, or even region. Consequently, it is more difficult and costly for the county to supply water to the residents that it serves in its unincorporated sections. In a similar fashion, a city's uncontrolled growth could strain the capacity of a county-operated solid waste facility, thereby making it necessary to either expand the present facility or construct a new one. Unrestricted growth in the city could also impose a hardship on the county's ability to provide a number of other staple services to residents of unincorporated areas, particularly if most newcomers choose to reside outside the city. Other examples can be found in the areas of natural resource conservation and environmental protection. Problems in these areas know no political boundaries. Therefore, threats to the environment caused by uncontrolled growth by either cities or counties pose serious and often costly problems for the other. Although the increased incidence of cooperation between counties and cities in the area of planning has reduced the potential for these kinds of situations to develop, conflicts still result from rapid, unrestricted growth.

Counties' legal authority to supersede cities in certain service and policy domains that cities find objectionable provide still another occasion for conflict. In the area of planning and zoning, for example, many states require that city development plans, zoning ordinances, and subdivision regulations conform to county plans and ordinances whenever the county has acted first. Consequently, city plans for growth and development can be stymied. A gross example of this occurred in Sarasota, Florida, in 1989. There, the county government considered a three-year moratorium on new construction in the county, including the county's three municipalities. As expected, this proposal produced a great deal of resentment toward and criticism of the county by the three cities, which cited, among other things, the grave potential for a reduction in city revenues, high unemployment, a decrease in property values, and a blatant disregard for the feelings of city residents. (The referendum was defeated overwhelmingly by the voters.) More common is the incidence of conflict whenever counties supersede their cities in matters relating to law enforcement by virtue of the sheriff having state constitutional authority as the chief law enforcement officer in the county. In some instances where county officials have "pulled rank" on their city counterparts in highly visible and sensitive investigations, the results have been devastating to the potential for cooperation in other areas of mutual interest.

In addition, conflict can result from long-standing inequitable situations whereby residents of unincorporated areas enjoy the benefits of city services and facilities without paying for them. For instance, it has not been uncommon for residents of unincorporated parts of counties to use services provided by a nearby city to its residents when county governments fail to provide these services to all residents of the county or to those who live outside cities. In short, gross episodes of this sort have been the result of a pattern whereby cities have tended to be the providers of a larger menu and higher level of services than county governments. That is, cities usually have been the first to construct and maintain such things as libraries, hospitals, airports, parks, and cultural and recreational facilities and programs.

Finally, conflict between cities and counties has stemmed from political, ideological, and personality clashes between elected and appointed public officials of these governments. In fact, every community, to some degree, encounters this problem. Of course, this source of conflict has the potential to create a problem where one did not exist before, or to exacerbate strains on relations that were caused by the other factors mentioned previously.

Events of the last several decades, while suggesting that relations between cities and counties will be marred sometimes by conflict, also indicate that cooperation between these two units of local government will be far more common in the years ahead. This prediction is predicated on the fact that states are encouraging and facilitating—and when necessary, mandating—joint or cooperative efforts. Nevertheless, the greatest incentive to increased cooperation may be rooted in the recognition by cities and counties that they frequently confront similar and related problems and challenges that require a concerted, area-wide response or solution.

—*J. Edwin Benton*

See also

Annexation; Consolidation.

References

Benton, J. Edwin. *Counties as Service Delivery Agents: Changes, Expectations and Roles.* University: University of Alabama Press, 1997.

Benton, J. Edwin, and Donald C. Menzel. "Contracting and Franchising County Services in Florida." *Urban Affairs Quarterly* 27 (1992): 436–456.

Benton, J. Edwin, and Platon N. Rigos. "Patterns of Metropolitan Service Dominance: Central City and Central County Roles Compared." *Urban Affairs Quarterly* 20 (1986): 285–302.

Hawkins, Brett W., and Rebecca M. Hendrick. "County Governments and City-Suburban Inequality." *Social Science Quarterly* 75 (1994): 755–771.

Schneider, Mark, and Kee Ok Park. "Metropolitan Counties as Service Delivery Agents: The Still Forgotten Governments." *Public Administration Review* 49 (1989): 345–352.

Country Clubs

The American country club has evolved in complex ways during the last century. The process began in 1882 when a group of Boston Brahmins founded the Country Club in Brookline, Massachusetts (just west of Boston), and others soon followed. St. Andrews Golf Club (1888) in Yonkers, New York, and Shinnecock Hills Golf Club (1891) on Long Island are important examples of early clubs.

These three clubs differed in important ways. Shinnecock, for example, was a seasonal club that catered to an upper-class clientele in Southampton only for the summer months. Shinnecock also allowed fuller participation by women than either Brookline or St. Andrews. But while they differed, each of the clubs grew and prospered because of golfing's popularity in the late nineteenth and early twentieth centuries. In fact, country clubs, led by Brookline, St. Andrews, Shinnecock, and a few others, became the controlling influence in the development of the sport when they formed the United States Golf Association in 1894.

The number of country clubs grew rapidly until 1930. These clubs, with their golf courses, swimming pools, and tennis courts, became an important aspect of middle-class life. Golf and tennis were easily accessible to anyone regardless of age or gender. Thus, the country club became an important cultural site where family members sought leisure together. In the 1920s, American businessmen also found the country club useful for conducting business. The growth in the number of clubs was especially rapid after World War I, and by 1930 there were approximately 5,000 country clubs in the United States.

Country clubs were also related to urban and suburban growth after 1890. Many of the early clubs developed as part of attempts to escape deteriorating cities and establish exclusive rural enclaves for Anglo-Saxon Americans who were frightened by unhealthy cities and increasing ethnic pluralism. The clubs were also closely connected to suburbanization. In order to lure middle-class buyers into suburbs, developers often built clubs as the social center of a development. They meant these clubs to replace the taverns, restaurants, and city clubs that Americans left behind when they moved to suburbs.

The growth of country clubs slowed, or even declined, during the Depression and World War II. Since about 1950,

Golfers putting on a practice green near the clubhouse at the Olympia Fields Country Club in Illinois.

the country clubs have evolved in a number of ways. They have become an important feature of real estate developments aimed at retirees and the wealthy. These clubs often make ample provision for golfers who pay daily fees, but at the same time they offer memberships to homeowners in a surrounding development.

The country club was also an important element in the leisure revolution that has taken place during the last century. As a voluntary association devoted to providing sport, leisure, and social life to elite and middle classes, it has assumed and been granted considerable symbolic meaning. Membership in a prestigious club is evidence of having "made it" in America. Clubs also serve as important markers that delineate the social structure of towns. Memberships in a few clubs (Augusta National, for example) are ardently sought as evidence of prestige on the national stage. To a great degree, the country club and golf have become emblematic of the privileges and the lifestyle of middle- and upper-class white Americans.

—*Richard Moss*

References

Curtiss, Fredric H., and John Heard. *The Country Club: 1882–1932.* Brookline, MA: n.p., 1932.

Moss, Richard. "Sport and Social Status: Golf and the Making of the Country Club in the United States, 1882–1920." *International Journal of the History of Sport* 10 (1993): 93–100.

Rader, Benjamin G. "The Quest for Subcommunities and the Rise of American Sport." *American Quarterly* 29 (1977): 355–369.

Crime and Criminals

A consistent feature of American urban life has been a preoccupation with crime. Since the nineteenth century, both formal study and public opinion have marked the urban environment as uniquely criminal and dangerous. Although the social problems of the city have long been a staple of social scientific research, historians have begun studying crime only comparatively recently. These historical investigations, however, have yielded insights into the development of urban crime and crime control with value for historians and for contemporary policymakers.

The study of crime emerged during the 1970s as an important historical specialty. Influenced by social history and its methods, historians of crime sought to re-create the worlds of the dangerous and delinquent classes. Historians also began to link patterns of crime to broader historical trends, including the growth and development of cities. Indeed, the history of urban crime and punishment is a mirror that reflects the changing social, political, and economic organization of American cities.

The value of studying the history of crime and criminals becomes even more apparent in light of the tremendous quantity of time and resources devoted to combating urban crime problems in the 1990s. Indeed, crime control is regarded today as a central function of urban administrations, and it may be that urban history can inform the contemporary analysis of crime problems. At the very least, a better appreciation for historical developments destroys the old adage, "the more things change, the more they stay the same." Instead, the history of crime counters that sense of inevitability that leads some to dismiss prospects for positive change. Historical analysis can also reemphasize the role of human action, rather than impersonal and uncontrollable forces, in shaping the quality of life in the city.

Those who lived in or wrote about the city in nineteenth-century America frequently observed that urban life was distinctly different than it had been in smaller, more homogeneous, colonial era communities. The organization of the nineteenth-century city was widely regarded as fertile ground for numerous social problems, from poverty and disease to crime and delinquency. Whether observers referred to the problem of crime specifically or not, the city was considered to be a dangerous place. During the first half of the nineteenth century, the perception of danger within the rapidly growing urban environment grew, with the links to crime, vice, and delinquency becoming more specific. The dramatic changes in cities included a growing proportion of wage laborers, many of whom were transient residents of the city; a population increasing in size, density, and diversity; and an urban spatial organization in which all of the city's residents lived close to each other. Then and now, those who sought to explain the accompanying increase in crime have explained the change in terms of loss—of traditional colonial community organization or of face-to-face social controls.

But were these new cities in fact more disorderly, more violent, and more crime prone? The cities of the mid-nineteenth century did feature distinctive crime problems. The most visible were the riots and mob violence that plagued most cities through the Civil War. The rapid pace of urbanization, combined with tensions between native-born Protestants and Catholic immigrants, contributed to periodic outbreaks of mass disorder. In northern cities, competition for scarce resources and city space also involved the small black population. In everyday life, the organization of criminal activity also reflected the organization of growing cities: youth gangs populated poor immigrant neighborhoods, and pickpockets and con men preyed on new arrivals on crowded streets. Organized vice, including prostitution and gambling, flourished in the nineteenth-century city, with illicit trades growing side by side with legal commerce. Cities also led the way in shifting criminal concerns from older patterns that emphasized moral conduct to a new concern for protecting personal property.

These new patterns of criminal behavior seemed to confirm that an expansion of criminal activity was an inevitable part of city growth. The nature of the relationship, however, was the subject of debate. For some, the loss of community created a degrading environment capable of turning good men into bad. The living conditions of the city, therefore, spread crime and delinquency in the same way they assisted the spread of contagious disease. For others, the city was not merely a degrading environment but actually attracted a class of people inclined toward bad behavior. This concept was well developed by the 1840s, and best expressed through the identification of such persons as part of the "dangerous classes."

For elites at mid-century, the idea that the growth of the dangerous classes was part of urbanization seemed so obvious as to hardly merit debate. Indeed, though the language has changed, the basic premise has remained a staple of American social thought through the twentieth century. Recent historical studies of crime, however, offer two important qualifications to this traditional conception of the relationship between urbanization and crime.

First, historians have sought to re-create the lives of the "disorderly" and the "dangerous" in ways that give meaning to their actions. Actions once regarded as mindless behaviors caused by disorganization and rapid change are now fraught with meaning. The urban riots of the pre–Civil War decades, for example, have been studied within the framework of the competition for urban space or as expressions of ethnic or class solidarity. Likewise, historians have reconsidered prostitution. Where antebellum reformers saw young women as morally degraded and ruined by their environment, historians have redefined prostitution as a choice made by some women within the limited range of social and economic opportunities available to them. Without romanticizing their lives, all of these images of nineteenth-century criminals defy the stereotypical image of the helpless or ignorant poor floundering in an urban wilderness.

The second qualification is the evidence that the rate of crime in the nineteenth century did not rise and fall with city growth. Although crime and disorder surely increased before the Civil War, rates of crime leveled off by the 1870s. Measuring the decline in crime rates is easier than explaining them, however, and there are various theories as to why cities apparently became more orderly. The decline in serious crime may have reflected the capacity of the institutions of an industrial society, such as the school and the factory, to organize and control behavior. Newly organized criminal justice institutions may have improved the ability to control serious crime. It may be that the increasing separation of urban space after the 1870s, made possible by new technologies such as the streetcar, allowed much of the population to avoid contact with increasingly isolated dangerous neighborhoods. Whatever the explanation, the evidence strongly challenges the assumption that an increase in crime was a constant, "natural" companion of urban growth.

The cities of the early twentieth century had become giants in America. More than ever, their densely populated immigrant neighborhoods were regarded as breeding grounds for delinquency, vice, and crime. Sociologist Ernest Burgess, whose work helped define what came to be known as the Chicago School of Sociology, identified the conditions of the urban slums as the outcome of urbanization. The result of life in the slums—on the social and economic margins of modern American life—was what Burgess and others referred to as social disorganization, a condition of which crime and delinquency were but one symptom. Other symptoms included poverty, intemperance, and disease, but all (including crime) were interrelated. The result of this belief in the interdependency of crime and the conditions of urban life was to make every urban policy—whether designed to deal with housing, public health, or recreation—a crime-prevention measure. The connection of urban policy and crime problems became a hallmark of urban administration for the remainder of the century.

As in the nineteenth century, cities suffered periodic outbreaks of mob violence and rioting, which reinforced the identification of urban areas as uniquely dangerous and crime-ridden. "Race riots" such as those experienced in East St. Louis in 1917 or Chicago in 1919 were violent conflicts between black and white residents. The rioting stemmed in part from competition over the control of urban territory. Race riots were characterized by brutal assaults by whites on black residents in contested areas of the city, violence that the police and city governments did little to prevent. By the 1960s, however, a new wave of rioting was largely confined within the urban ghettos, whose residents bore the brunt of the destruction. As the Los Angeles riots of 1992 illustrate, cities are still vulnerable to violence born of racial and ethnic tensions, poverty, and inequality.

The great problem of the late-twentieth-century city is not periodic rioting, however, but the daily experience of violent death and serious crime. In such times, Americans again relied on traditional ideas about the relationship of the city to crime. The President's Commission on Law Enforcement and the Administration of Justice (established by Lyndon Johnson in 1966) said that "the social institutions generally relied upon to guide and control people in their individual and mutual existence simply are not operating effectively in the inner city." Rising levels of violence during the 1980s seemed to confirm the validity of old truisms about cities as crime-breeders, or as receptacles for the inherently violent and deviant. The source of the danger, personified by the "dangerous classes" in the nineteenth century, was reconceptualized as the urban "underclass" of the 1980s.

The recent history of American cities suggests, though, that the problems of crime and violence are not simply natural products of urban life. One example is illegal enterprise, including prostitution, gambling, and drug dealing, which has been a constant part of urban life. In the early twentieth century, cities from New York to San Francisco could boast of famous "red-light" districts, where illegitimate trades of all sorts were carried on. Although most of the red-light districts were broken up by the 1920s, immigrants carved out niches of illegal enterprise during Prohibition and beyond. The explosion of drug distribution and drug-related crime in cities since the 1960s has, as much an any single development, isolated the city as a place of danger. Yet even growth of this illicit economic activity becomes more understandable when drug dealing is placed in the context of urban history—specifically, the collapse of the legal economy and the disappearance of industry and economic opportunity.

However the origins of crime are understood, there is no question that the fear of crime has continued to influence the organization of cities and suburbs. Fear of crime was one factor in the exodus of city residents to suburban developments, as developers appealed to future suburbanites by advertising the freedom from crime that escape from the city could bring. For those who would not, or could not, escape the perceived danger from crime, there was the option of adapting their communities to defend against the threat. Like a medieval walled city, some areas in the twentieth-century city have tried to insulate themselves from danger: gated communities surrounded by walls, the use of private police forces, and barricaded streets all testify to the power of fear to shape the urban environment.

The institutions of criminal justice, perhaps more than formal law, define the boundaries of crime in society, and their records provide the most important clues to discerning historical trends in crime. Historical patterns of crime are not so much objective measures of actual criminal behavior as they are measures of criminal justice behavior. Consequently, the evolution of crime control is a critical element in the history of crime.

Institutions of crime control also reflect the social and political order of the day and mirror the development of urban institutions more generally. Cities of the United States in the 1830s struggled to govern with administrative structures largely inherited from the colonial era. Crime control was no exception; city governments faced rising levels of disorder with wholly inadequate mechanisms for maintaining order. Policing the city was still largely the task of night watchmen. Their forces, composed entirely of civilians, were the subject of constant criticism for their failure to keep the peace. A parallel, informal, and less bureaucratic type of policing was the reliance on private prosecution, a system by which the wronged party, rather than the state, acted as the initiator and controller of criminal cases. Finally, methods of punishment still reflected the needs of smaller, colonial cities. Most punishments were designed either to rid communities of nonresident troublemakers or to dish out public humiliation on residents who broke the law.

From the 1830s through the Civil War Era, city governments led the way in transforming criminal justice. Professional uniformed police forces had emerged in many major American cities at mid-century as impersonal and bureaucratic forces for controlling an increasingly impersonal urban landscape. At the same time, cities constructed enormous institutions dedicated to crime control: expanded criminal court systems, houses of correction and jails, and houses of refuge for young delinquents. The expanding crime-control bureaucracy paralleled the expansion of city government more generally; indeed, the emergence of the new criminal justice system cannot be understood outside the larger context of urban political history. Moreover, like many other branches of urban government, the criminal justice system bureaucracies accommodated the demands of political leaders in ways that modified the original vision of the reformers who inspired the system.

Progressive reform movements in the early part of the twentieth century focused on strengthening the professional identity of those in the criminal justice system and wresting control of the system from established political figures. At the same time, reformers also expanded their view of crime control to include crime prevention. Many of the innovations of the Progressive Era combined both goals. The creation of the first juvenile court in Chicago in 1889, for example, was intended to deal with delinquents—not merely to punish, but to prevent, what reformers regarded as the inevitable slide from delinquency into adult criminal careers. The juvenile court also furthered the causes of professionalization and depoliticization by taking the judging of youth out of criminal courtrooms widely regarded as corrupt and inefficient, and placing young delinquents in the hand of a professionally trained juvenile court judge. The setting for the juvenile court innovation, Chicago, is an indication that the city was the stage for much Progressive experimentation and innovation.

As urban criminal justice systems grew more complex in the first half of the twentieth century, they inevitably grew larger. As a result, more people than ever found themselves in contact with the formal institutions of criminal justice. Yet even the enthusiastic advocates of crime control in this era could not have foreseen the enormous increase in the size of the criminal justice system since the 1980s. Indeed, it has already been noted that a key component to crime-control philosophies was crime prevention. As late as the 1960s, advocates of crime-prevention programs envisioned a time when crime would be successfully controlled, perhaps even eliminated. Recent decades have seen a return to pessimism and retributive justice. The battleground is the inner city, whose isolation has encouraged popular support for a punitive approach. At the close of the twentieth century, it is therefore important to recognize that change, for better or for worse, is in our own hands. Responsibility for violence and crime in our cities cannot be shifted away from the conditions and human actions that have helped to create them.

—*Joseph F. Spillane*

See also

Community-Based Corrections; Correctional Institutions; Crime Mobility; Criminal Justice System; Crowds and Riots; Drinking, Alcohol Abuse, and Drunkenness; Drugs, Drug Abuse, and Drug Addiction; Gambling; Gangsters; Juvenile Delinquency and the Juvenile Justice System; Organized Crime; Police and Police Departments; Prostitution; Public Disorderliness; Race Riots; Red-Light District; Violence.

References

Ayers, Edward L. *Vengeance and Justice: Crime and Punishment in the Nineteenth Century American South.* New York: Oxford University Press, 1984.

Currie, Elliott. *Reckoning: Drugs, the Cities, and the American Future.* New York: Hill and Wang, 1993.

Inciardi, James A., and Charles E. Faupel, eds. *History and Crime: Implications for Criminal Justice Policy.* London: Sage Publications, 1980.

Johnson, David R. *Policing the Urban Underworld: The Impact of Crime on the Development of the American Police, 1800–1887.* Philadelphia: Temple University Press, 1979.

Lane, Roger. *Violent Death in the City: Suicide, Accident, and Murder in Nineteenth Century Philadelphia.* Cambridge, MA: Harvard University Press, 1979.

Monkkonen, Eric H. *Police in Urban America, 1860–1920.* New York: Cambridge University Press, 1981.

Steinberg, Allen. *The Transformation of Criminal Justice: Philadelphia, 1800–1880.* Chapel Hill: University of North Carolina Press, 1989.

Crime Mobility

While crime has generally been understood as a city phenomenon, in recent years its impact on other places has been more severe. The ability of crime to infiltrate areas surrounding cities and spread into suburbs is an indication of what is termed *crime mobility.* It has been most visible in suburbs, but it has also affected transition areas surrounding cities and even rural areas. Criminals do commute to commit crimes. The distance criminals commute often depends upon the type of crime. Property crimes are still less prevalent in nonurban areas than in cities, but the constant threat of legal transgressions still persists. Although suburbs were once considered a haven from crime-infested cities, they no longer are.

Nevertheless, cities are still the center of criminal activity, and statistical data continue to indicate that crime is more heavily concentrated, per person and in terms of damage inflicted, in urban settings. Moreover, not all property crimes committed in large cities are reported because of a lack of insurance coverage against such crimes. The resilience of the criminal element to diversify and branch out into surrounding locales merits the study of crime mobility. One of the first studies of crime mobility surveyed over 600 cases of personal and property felonies, calculating the mean distance from a criminal's home to the site of the crime. It was found that a criminal would generally travel farther to commit a property crime than an act of violence against another person. The average distances were 3.43 miles for auto theft, 2.14 for robbery, 1.76 for burglary, 1.53 for grand larceny, 1.52 for rape, 0.91 for assault, and 0.11 for manslaughter. Several subsequent studies related the proximity of a criminal's residence to the target and explained why certain areas are subject to higher rates of crime.

The tendency of crime to move to suburbs was observed in a landmark study by Shaw and McKay (1942), who studied crime in and around Chicago. They divided the city into equal statistical regions and discovered an inverse relationship between the occurrence of a crime and its distance from the central city. Moreover, the gradient did not change over time, even if the socioeconomic characteristics of a population did. This finding points to the conclusion that central cities "export" crime to outlying neighborhoods. Even with changing demography, there was still a constant supply of crime.

More recent studies have found that the average distance juvenile delinquents travel to commit assault and vandalism is less than half a mile and that 75 percent of these crimes occur within one mile of a juvenile's residence. Another study discovered that 72 percent of rapes occur within five blocks of a rapist's residence, while a third study showed that the mean distance traveled to commit a robbery is about half a mile and that 90 percent of robberies occur within a mile and a half of the criminal's residence.

In a landmark study of 1966, Boggs examined variations in the availability and profitability of targets for a wide variety of crimes, including anything from homicide to joyriding auto theft. Boggs found that different neighborhoods are exploited for different kinds of crime. She identified two widespread components of crime occurrence. One is the familiarity of offenders with their targets, which leads to the specific kinds of crimes that occur in high-offender neighborhoods. The other general element of crime occurrence is the expected profitability of a crime. This notion suggests that crime is more likely to occur in elite neighborhoods where its targets are probably of greater value than targets closer to an offender's own residence.

Hakim and Weinblatt's theoretical paradigm shows the adverse effect of criminal mobility on land values, how the composition of property crimes varies among different urban zones, and how crime rates diminish at different rates in different regions. Each zone is characterized by the prevalence of one particular type of property crime. The innermost zone, or central city, comprises a large share of burglaries, the next zone sustains mainly auto theft, and the third zone comprises primarily robberies. The outer zone experiences a large share of larcenies in shopping centers and department stores. Not only does crime move outward, it adapts to locales as it progresses. Since crime rates vary in different places, the result is a mosaic of crime that affects property values.

The spread of criminal activity out from the city has several profound effects on suburban life. Investors use information about crime to make decisions on investment projects. Insurance companies use crime statistics to determine the premiums for home and automobile policies, and local government officials consider the implications for the allocation of resources, including police. And of course, homeowners always want to live in "safe" neighborhoods. In short, the fact that crime moves has affected suburban life both directly and indirectly.

Most models of criminal mobility assume that central cities generate crime. The widely discussed "flight" of central city residents to other parts of the metropolitan area has produced increased poverty in central cities while creating greater heterogeneity of income and wealth in suburbs. The persistence of crime in different sections of the metropolitan area challenges many long-held assumptions about the causes of crime, which are based mainly upon the setting of the city. Central cities have the highest rates of crime because they have the highest concentrations of social and physical conditions associated with crimes. The decline of traditional social norms is also associated with the disproportionate rise of crime in cities. Yet, studies have shown that the criminal is not uniquely urban, shaped only by the central city.

What, then, brings the crime wave so prevalent in central cities out to the suburbs? All theories of suburban crime suggest that crime "spills over" city boundaries. The traditional wisdom is that crime rates are high close to city boundaries and diminish with distance. The level of property crime is high along the boundary roads between a city and its suburbs. The rate of breaking and entering in suburbs close to the boundaries is very high because such neighborhoods are closer to the criminal's residence, their ability to hit their targets and flee is greater, and those suburbs are affluent and provide a higher return per burglary than a site within the city limits.

Suburbs themselves are not noted for generating large amounts of criminal activity, so it follows that the primary motivator for mobility must still be the city. Furthermore, crime diminishes less rapidly along the major arterial roads that lead between city and suburb. The probability of property crime occurring is higher at homes and businesses more accessible to the central city. Adding distance to our understanding of crime helps explain if and where crime is committed.

This extended economic model explains the mosaic of property crime over the entire metropolitan area. Increasing penalties for criminal offenses and spending more on central city police would probably cause increasing crime levels in surrounding suburbs. This stems from potential criminals trying to avoid the higher costs of committing crime by commuting to areas where lower expected costs more than offset the added costs of transportation and becoming acquainted with a new area. In turn, this implies that an increase in police expenditure itself does not prevent crime and must be taken into account when policymakers decide how to combat crime. Seemingly then, the only hope of combating the spread of crime is through better coordination among central city and suburban law enforcement.

In conclusion, the mobility of crime refers specifically to the tendency of property criminals to seek targets that yield the highest net return on their activity. The attractiveness of suburbs compared to cities for criminals is due to the fact that cities have had a long history of combating the criminal element, suburbs offer more attractive opportunities and have fewer police patrols, and suburban homes are easier to enter and provide more concealed access relative to property in the central city.

—*Simon Hakim and Yochanan Shachmurove*

See also
Crime and Criminals; Juvenile Delinquency and the Juvenile Justice System; Suburban Crime.
References
Boggs, Sarah. "Urban Crime Patterns." *American Sociological Review* 30 (1966): 899–908.
Brown, Marilyn A. "Modeling the Spatial Distribution of Suburban Crime." *Economic Geography* 58 (1982): 247–261.
Deutsch, Joseph, Simon Hakim, and J. Weinblatt. "Interjurisdictional Criminal Mobility: A Theoretical Perspective." *Urban Studies* 21 (1984): 451–458.
Hakim, Simon. "The Attraction of Property Crimes to Suburban Localities: A Revised Economic Model." *Urban Studies* 17 (1980): 265–276.
McIver, John P. "Criminal Mobility: A Review of Empirical Studies." In Simon Hakim and G. F. Rengert, eds., *Crime Spillover*. Beverly Hills, CA: Sage Publications, 1981.
Reppetto Thomas A. "Crime Prevention and the Displacement Phenomenon." *Crime and Delinquency* 22 (1976): 166–177.
Shaw, Clifford R., and Henry D. McKay. *Juvenile Delinquency and Urban Areas*. Rev. ed. Chicago: University of Chicago Press, 1969.

Criminal Justice System

Like most of the American legal system, the criminal justice system emerged from traditions and customs of English common law. In towns of the seventeenth and eighteenth centuries, this meant a system rooted in courts of law. The most important figures in urban courts were private citizens and the justices of the peace to whom aggrieved people typically brought their complaints. The justice decided whether to set the wheels of criminal justice in motion; many times, the justice settled the case on the spot, informally or through dispensing legal "summary" justice. Only rare, serious crimes went on to a grand jury hearing, and perhaps a jury trial.

There were few important exceptions to this state of affairs. Even though watchmen patrolled cities at night, their job was a temporary, unpaid duty for which all adult men were eligible. Watchmen had no legal authority beyond that of ordinary citizens, and when serious disorder occurred, cities called out the militia. About the only aspect of urban criminal justice that had a distinctly "public" character was punishment. People convicted of crimes were not shut away in prisons but physically punished in public spectacles that were the most visible way of demonstrating the power of the criminal law.

The institutions that dominate modern criminal justice developed piecemeal over two centuries, the way paved by two fundamental changes in Americans' perception of the relationship between crime and society. First, the Enlightenment, the great intellectual movement that transformed Western thought at the beginning of the Modern Era, encouraged people to believe that concerted human action could solve social problems. The initial fruit of the new ideas in criminal justice was the emergence of the rehabilitative ideal and the spread of imprisonment as an alternative to public corporal punishment. Philadelphia's Walnut Street Prison became America's first penitentiary in 1790, dedicated to the notion that criminals could be reformed into law-abiding citizens.

The second change was viewing crime as a social problem during the first half of the nineteenth century, the result of social conflict over religion, race, ethnicity, and politics in the rapidly changing antebellum city. By the 1840s, cities were dangerously violent and urban riots a national embarrassment. Watchmen and private prosecutors could neither pacify city streets nor check the popular culture based on alcohol that many people believed was the source of disorder. After London established its Metropolitan Police in 1829, many (mostly elite) Americans demanded something similar, and beginning in the late 1830s Americans began constructing military-style, "preventative" police forces. By the Civil War, policemen were fixtures in most cities, but the general public received them neither happily nor easily.

Almost overnight, in most places, the police force became primarily responsible for enforcing the criminal law and initiating criminal prosecutions. At first, they used the same system of lower courts as private citizens, and they quickly became enmeshed in the web of informal relations central to private prosecution. But policemen were also expected to quell disorder on city streets. There they encountered overt resistance and developed their own, often violent, means of dispensing informal justice. Policemen also depended on local politicians for their positions and actively participated in local politics. As a result, police brutality, corruption, interference in elections, and lax enforcement of vice laws became routine. In only a few years, urban policing became as scandalous as the disorder that had inspired it.

Still, the police force was a major step in the development of public, institutional control of the criminal law. This tendency was evident in other ways as well, notably the establishment of Houses of Refuge, publicly supported reformative institutions for children. But the creation of a genuine, public, criminal justice "system" would not be accomplished for another half-century.

By 1900, the police were the most conspicuous failure of urban public administration. Local control of the force meant that powerful and sometimes conflicting interests, both in and out of government, held considerable sway over the administration of justice. Serving many masters, the police could please none of them. Their great visibility on city streets provoked repeated violent confrontations for the control of public space. One New York policeman aptly summarized the relationship between the people and law enforcement when he observed that there was "more justice" at the end of his nightstick than in all the city's courts.

Hostility toward the police sprang from all quarters, and the passage of liquor and vice laws in many cities at the end of the century only intensified it. When the police failed to enforce these laws according to their advocates' wishes, reformers began enforcing the laws themselves, in much the same manner as the old private prosecutors. From time to time, they took control of a district attorney's office and made it virtually their private arm of the state. In places like New York and Chicago, bitter rivalries developed between the police and private vice reformers.

Though this battle raged on for years, it produced a major change in the criminal justice system. The office of district attorney rose to unprecedented prominence. Beginning with William T. Jerome in New York at the turn of the century, the district attorney's office became an independent force to investigate and prosecute crime, and sometimes to use law enforcement for political purposes.

Even before this, the district attorney had a major influence on the conduct of criminal justice. The great number of arrests by the police forced public prosecutors to develop the practice of plea bargaining, or resolving cases rapidly through a negotiated plea settlement rather than a jury trial. Well before 1900, plea bargaining was the typical way of resolving criminal cases in urban courts, but a new form of nontrial adjudication had replaced the older form of private prosecution, overseen by a new staff of public prosecutors. The size of the district attorney's office grew rapidly during the early twentieth century, becoming the central agent of law enforcement it remains today.

The reform enthusiasm of the late nineteenth century generated other innovations in urban criminal justice. Reformers devised nonincarcerative alternatives to imprisonment, both as an extension of the rehabilitative ideal and a response to inhumane prison conditions. Parole, probation, and the indeterminate sentence became commonplace, putting many convicted criminals back on city streets and creating yet another level of public supervisory officials. Beginning in Chicago in 1889, cities developed special juvenile courts to serve the needs of child offenders while sacrificing some elements of due process to the educational and quasi-parental ends of a public system of "juvenile justice." And beginning with the Lexow Committee in New York in 1895, reformers began conducting hearings into police corruption and brutality, setting the stage for the great wave of police professionalization of the early twentieth century.

For all their faults, urban police departments developed sophisticated methods of investigation, forensic technique, and detective squads. Then, during the first quarter of the twentieth century, police departments across the country became meaningfully disconnected from local politics. Under the auspices of organizations like the International Association of Chiefs of Police, prodded by crime commissions, and influenced by a new generation of highly educated reformers like August Vollmer in California and Arthur Woods in New York, police departments adopted new standards for recruitment and promotion, an ethic of efficient crime control, and improved techniques of officer training and public relations. By 1920, urban criminal justice had become an effective tool for pursuing criminals and prosecuting vice. On the one hand, this development was positive because crime was becoming increasingly organized and would become markedly more so after 1920. But on the other hand, it gave policemen an even freer hand in dealing with suspected criminals and encouraged the use of criminal justice as a solution to urban social ills.

During the 1920s, the police perfected the means of surveillance and raiding begun by private vice reformers and developed their own brutal method of interrogation known as the "third degree." Law enforcement became strikingly more national and pervasive, thanks to federal laws like Prohibition, the rise of the automobile, and, especially, the advent of the Federal Bureau of Investigation (FBI). Started by Theodore Roosevelt in 1908 and modeled after vice law enforcers, by 1930 the FBI was making major contributions to

the crime-fighting efficiency of urban police and prosecutors. That year, they began the first system of national crime records. Two years later the FBI opened a national crime laboratory, and in 1935, the National Police Academy. The Bureau also accelerated the process of heavily arming urban policemen during the 1930s, which, with the adoption of automobile patrol and two-way radio communication, increased the effectiveness and power of the police, as well as their social distance from city residents. Under J. Edgar Hoover, the Bureau accomplished all of this by cultivating national hysteria—first over vice, then organized crime, and finally political radicals—and then by glorifying the police and the FBI as national saviors. The crisis mentality, modern technology, and a cult of crime fighting made urban police forces a formidable force for order—and potential abuse—by the middle of the century. The best example during the 1950s was, perhaps, Los Angeles under chief William Parker, whose authoritarian style ran roughshod over civil liberties, severely strained relations between the police and other groups (especially nonwhites) whom Parker targeted in his "war on crime," and substituted law enforcement for social policy.

Though the police had many champions, their excesses created many critics. Protests about police violations of constitutional rights by organizations like the American Civil Liberties Union led courts to apply restraints. First, some state courts invoked the exclusionary rule, which discarded all evidence that the police gathered in illegal searches. In the 1960s, under Chief Justice Earl Warren, the U.S. Supreme Court issued a series of decisions that, when taken together, comprised a "due process revolution." They extended the exclusionary rule to all states, required that everyone in police custody be offered an attorney, and forced the police to advise all suspects of their constitutional rights before beginning to interrogate them. These decisions helped curb police abuse but came too late to prevent the utter collapse of relations between the police and urban racial minorities during the 1960s. Chafing under years of unrestrained police harassment and inspired by the civil rights movement, urban blacks lashed out in fear at the police, producing riots in many cities. As a result, federal involvement in urban criminal justice reached new heights, including improved research on crime and training of police and the development of new techniques ranging from elaborate police armaments and hardware to community-based correctional and treatment programs.

The upheavals of the 1960s provoked a backlash, however, and it proved impossible to reverse the tendency to use criminal justice to solve urban social problems. The politics of "law and order" began to shape criminal justice, and crime became a surrogate word that often meant race. Guns, drugs, and the increasing segregation of urban areas according to class and race during the 1970s and 1980s neutralized many of the gains made in police and community relations. Enthusiasm for lengthy incarceration and capital punishment grew. In the 1990s, urban criminal justice remains disturbingly prominent and discriminatory. American cities spend more on prisons than they do on education. The United States has the highest per capita imprisonment rate in the Western world, and young black men are much more likely to be incarcerated than in college. Though recent innovations like "community" policing offer some hope for improvement, the criminal justice system remains both a major and troubling feature of urban life.

—*Allen Steinberg*

See also

Community-Based Corrections; Correctional Institutions; Crime and Criminals; Police and Police Departments.

References

Bodenhamer, David J. *Fair Trial: Rights of the Accused in American History.* New York: Oxford University Press, 1992.

Fogelson, Robert M. *Big-City Police.* Cambridge, MA: Harvard University Press, 1977.

Friedman, Lawrence M. *Crime and Punishment in American History.* New York: Basic Books, 1993.

Johnson, David R. *American Law Enforcement: A History.* St. Louis, MO: Forum Press, 1991.

Monkkonen, Eric H., *Police in Urban America, 1860–1920.* New York: Cambridge University Press, 1981.

Ungar, Sanford J. *FBI.* Boston: Little, Brown, 1976.

Walker, Samuel. *Popular Justice: A History of American Criminal Justice.* New York: Oxford University Press, 1980.

Crowds and Riots

If *riot* is defined as any crowd action taken by 12 or more people to enforce their collective will by using violence or the threat of violence outside of normal legal channels, then rioting has been part of the American urban scene almost from the beginnings of English colonization. However, the nature of that rioting has changed over time.

The small cities of the colonial period experienced periodic rioting. In the seventeenth century this rioting sometimes toppled colonial governments, as occurred in 1689 with Leisler's Rebellion in New York City and the overthrow of Governor Andros in Boston. Riotous crowds typically had more limited goals in both the seventeenth and eighteenth centuries. Bread riots occurred in Boston in 1710, 1713, and 1729, and a New York mob protested the valuation of pennies in 1754. Every colonial city experienced some rioting against customs collection, and many saw crowds battle British navy press gangs. These riots tended to be limited affairs, with 100 to 200 participants, and the action ordinarily focused on property and did not include physical violence against persons. This mode of rioting continued in the disturbances against imperial regulation that broke out during the 1760s and 1770s.

By the opening decade of the nineteenth century the character of rioting had begun to change. Mobs now struck out at opponents with brutality as cities divided into competing elements of neighborhood, ethnicity, class, and race. In 1844 two riots leading to fatalities broke out in Philadelphia over ethnic and religious tension. During the 1850s, nativist Know-Nothings and Democratic Irish and Germans battled in Baltimore, St. Louis, Louisville, Cincinnati, and other cities. These conflicts involved hundreds, and sometimes thousands, of participants and left scores dead. In 1849 the working class of New York City took umbrage at the aristocratic pretensions and patronage of English actors by the city's elite and rioted outside the Astor Place theater. The military rushed to the theater's defense and 22 died in the melee.

Race, too, became a major source of conflict. Before the Civil War, whites developed the technique of race rioting that would continue for over a century: invading black neighborhoods, destroying black institutions like schools and churches, and murdering blacks who came their way. This type of rioting occurred in many cities, including Providence, Rhode Island, in 1824 and 1831; Cincinnati, Ohio, in 1829 and 1841; New York City in 1834; and Philadelphia in 1834 and 1849. The most violent of these disturbances took place in New York City during the Civil War. The draft riot of July 1863 lasted four days. Rioters expressed their hatred of blacks, opposition to the draft, resentment against wealth, and animosity toward the police. Between attacks on blacks and pitched battles with the forces of law and order over 120 were killed.

The draft riots left an indelible mark on urban America. Throughout the nineteenth century there developed a middle-class suspicion of the urban lower orders. The middle class viewed members of the underclass as volatile and dangerous people who somehow needed to be controlled. The draft riots testified to the potential explosions of unrest that plagued cities as populations reached into the hundreds of thousands and millions.

The spread of the Industrial Revolution did little to alter this view. Labor violence, such as that which gripped cities like Baltimore, Pittsburgh, and Chicago during the 1877 railroad strike, reminded the middle class of the dangers they faced. Not content with the development of police forces, state governments expanded their militias into the national guard, built armories in cities that looked like and could be defended as medieval castles, and in the early twentieth century created state police to help guard capital and property from the underclass.

These fears may have been misplaced because the underclass seemed as bent upon fighting each other as they were upon attacking the property of the more affluent. Repeatedly, as in the Protestant and Irish clashes on July 12, 1870,

PROVOST GUARD · ATTACKING THE RIOTER'S

Undated woodcut of the Provost Guard attacking the crowd during the Draft Riots in New York, July 13 to 16, 1863.

and in 1871, working-class people fought against each other. A striking worker was far more likely to beat and kill a scab than to assault the wealthy.

Race remained an important category of conflict. In the late nineteenth and early twentieth centuries, African Americans flocked to cities in search of new opportunities. Competition for jobs and housing exacerbated existing tensions and led to many race riots, including ones in Atlanta in 1906; East St. Louis, Illinois, in 1917; Chicago in 1919; Tulsa, Oklahoma, in 1921; and Detroit in 1943. These disturbances left scores dead as thousands of whites and blacks fought each other in a brutal and gruesome manner.

However, by the middle of the twentieth century rioting had changed again. With some government support, labor's right to organize was accepted during the 1930s. No longer did strikes lead to the extremes of violence. Some jostling on the picket line and even the occupation of property through sit-down strikes occurred. But the days of armed men shooting each other over labor issues had ended. Ethnicity could still bring crowds into the streets, as in the 1943 zoot suit riots in Los Angeles, but the violent intensity was absent. Whites also no longer invaded black neighborhoods. Confrontations broke out

at demonstrations and sit-ins instead. Although some cracked heads and deaths occurred in cities during the civil rights movement, the violence had declined compared to the murder and mayhem of previous generations.

A new type of race riot confined to the ghetto emerged, as can be seen in Harlem in New York City in 1935, 1943, and 1965; Watts in Los Angeles in 1964 and 1992; Newark in 1967; and Detroit in 1967. The thousands and tens of thousands who participated in these riots destroyed property, looted, and occasionally assaulted whites. While these disturbances spread like wildfire during the 1960s, and have continued intermittently since then, they included less physical violence against people than earlier. Usually those who were killed in these riots died at the hands of the forces of law and order.

—*Paul A. Gilje*

See also
Race Riots; Violence.
References
Bernstein, Iver. *The New York City Draft Riots: Their Significance for American Society and Politics in the Age of the Civil War.* New York: Oxford University Press, 1990.
Feldberg, Michael. *The Turbulent Era: Riot and Disorder in Jacksonian America.* New York: Oxford University Press, 1980.

Fogelson, Robert M. *Violence as Protest: A Study of Riots and Ghettos.* Garden City, NY: Doubleday, 1971.

Gilje, Paul A. *Rioting in America.* Bloomington: Indiana University Press, 1996.

———. *The Road to Mobocracy: Popular Disorder in New York City, 1764–1834.* Chapel Hill: University of North Carolina Press, 1987.

Graham, Hugh Davis, and Ted Robert Gurr, eds. *Violence in America: Historical and Comparative Perspectives.* Washington, DC: Government Printing Office, 1969.

Hofstadter, Richard, and Michael Wallace, eds. *American Violence: A Documentary History.* New York: Vintage Books, 1970.

References

Biles, Roger. "Ed Crump versus the Unions: The Labor Movement in Memphis during the 1930s." *Labor History* 25 (1984): 533–552.

———. *Memphis in the Great Depression.* Knoxville: University of Tennessee Press, 1986.

Dorsett, Lyle W. *Franklin D. Roosevelt and the City Bosses.* Port Washington, NY: Kennikat Press, 1977.

Miller, William D. *Memphis during the Progressive Era.* Memphis, TN: Memphis State University Press, 1957.

———. *Mr. Crump of Memphis.* Baton Rouge: Louisiana State University Press, 1964.

Tucker, David M. *Memphis since Crump: Bossism, Blacks, and Civic Reformers, 1948–1968.* Knoxville: University of Tennessee Press, 1980.

Crump, Edward H. (1874–1954)

Edward H. Crump, a mayor of Memphis, Tennessee, and one of the most visible city bosses in the urban South, was a native of Holly Springs, Mississippi, who came to the Tennessee city at the age of 19. There he launched a series of successful business enterprises that eventually made him a millionaire, and he became active in local Democratic politics. Elected mayor in 1909, 1911, and 1915, Crump became the subject of a recall petition for failing to enforce the state's prohibition statutes, and he resigned from office in 1916. With the exception of a brief stint as county trustee and two terms in the U.S. House of Representatives (1931–1935), he eschewed elective office thereafter. Controlling the local Democratic Party until his death, he dominated city hall through a series of surrogate mayors who owed their election to the boss's endorsement.

A successful entrepreneur himself, Crump enjoyed the support of Memphis's business community. Under his watchful eye, city officials provided reliable public services, and Memphis won a number of national awards for public safety and city beautification. While ignoring the city's flourishing vice trade (an important source of funds for the political machine), Crump's police harassed labor unions, civil libertarians, and any other dissenters who dared criticize the local leadership.

For most of his reign, Crump relied on the city's sizable black vote. At a time when few blacks voted in the Jim Crow South, the machine's operatives trucked Memphis blacks to the polls by the thousands, paid their poll taxes for them, told them how to vote, and gave them food, liquor, and cash. An ardent segregationist and white supremacist, Crump nevertheless granted blacks a limited franchise, opposed the Ku Klux Klan, and doled out a modicum of patronage to black leaders. Unlike many urban bosses who preferred to exercise power behind closed doors, Crump was a colorful, quotable showman who kept a high profile. As a result, he was the South's most visible big city boss.

—*Roger Biles*

Cultural Tourism

During the eighteenth and nineteenth centuries, members of the upper class traditionally completed their education with a Grand Tour of Europe's cultural heritage. Today, cultural tourism no longer belongs only to the wealthy, nor is this kind of travel restricted to great cities like Rome, Paris, Tokyo, or Cairo. A General Agreement on Tariffs and Trade white paper concluded that travel and tourism is now the world's largest single industry; tourism has become the third largest retail segment of the American economy and the largest segment of export. Not surprisingly, cities and towns across the United States now compete for a coveted place on today's tourist agenda, using their cultural heritage as the main attraction.

Cultural (or heritage) tourism, according to the National Trust for Historic Preservation, is the practice of traveling to experience historic and cultural attractions in order to learn about a community's, region's, or state's past in an enjoyable and informative way. It can involve a broad spectrum of a community's heritage, including art museums, historic sites, botanical gardens, and ethnic neighborhoods, or it can focus entirely on a single aspect of a town's character and history, but it essentially involves experiencing what environmental psychologists call a "sense of place."

At its best, cultural tourism offers a community several important benefits. It can help a locality preserve and enhance its cultural heritage and built environment, bring badly needed revenue into a place, and offer jobs in a clean, growing industry that, at least in theory, can continue indefinitely. However, while cultural tourism offers significant benefits to towns and cities, it can also pose serious challenges to social equity and cultural integrity if it is not carefully planned and monitored.

Cultural tourism stems from several key factors. Its material base reflects the trend toward less leisure time and shorter vacations near one's residence. At a different level, it reflects the desire by growing numbers of tourists to encounter and observe a different culture or way of life, including its past. Cultural tourism provides sightseers a much-needed sense of depth in a highly transient society. For example, the National Park Service reports that visitors to its historical and archaeological sites now outnumber by far those going to national parks. Many analysts of tourism believe that cultural tourism represents the rejection of contemporary mass culture, a search for better or different ways of life. For many people, this kind of travel has become a form of therapy and self-fulfillment. Like medieval pilgrims, contemporary tourists seek out extraordinary places and experiences that they hope will change their lives.

However, in their rush to capitalize quickly on the economic opportunities that cultural tourism offers, many communities ignore or fail to recognize the inherent problems and disadvantages of cultural tourism. They are unwilling to acknowledge finite limits to the number of visitors that these special places can accommodate without damaging themselves, or that the quality of the experience is the key attraction. Misuse and exploitation have the potential to destroy the very community resources that

attract visitors to begin with. In the words of noted tourism expert Arthur Frommer: "If preservation is to be effective, if the warp of our civilization is to be maintained, if even the goals of increased tourism are to be achieved, then we as a nation must step back from extreme marketplace theories." Mass marketing, for example, can lead to overcrowding historic Main Streets, threatening the unique sense of place that visitors came to experience. Ever-present vendors and shops constantly remind tourists that they have not escaped from the present. And community residents often develop antagonistic attitudes toward the hordes of visitors whose overwhelming presence complicates their daily lives.

Another problematic approach that communities often adopt toward cultural tourism involves developing theme parks in which every aspect of a place relates to a general theme. Small towns become Paul Bunyanland or New Olde Country with a special ethnic character. Events and attractions are sometimes created with little or no basis in historical reality. Very often, these theme parks and ancillary facilities like hotels and restaurants depend

A class picture being taken in front of the U.S. Capitol building during a school trip to Washington, D.C., in 1995.

on local residents who work at low-paying service jobs or execute traditional arts and crafts disconnected from their cultural contexts. In another related vein, some communities like Colonial Williamsburg have become living museums in which everyone reenacts community life at a given historic time, as if its culture had frozen at that instant. Many communities that have become dependent upon these approaches to cultural tourism are now rethinking their strategy.

The key to successful cultural tourism, then, is balancing short-term profits with other public needs. Cultural tourism requires a thorough understanding of a community's special character and resources and its role in the surrounding area, as well as the particular needs and interests of visitors. For example, the World Council of Churches has recommended that the tourism industry acknowledge its social responsibility to host communities by arranging informal meetings between local residents and visitors to educate tourists about local customs and issues.

Since cultural tourism treats a community and its public goods as commodities, it is vitally important that the entire community be involved in planning and implementing tourism. Some scholars even portray cultural tourism as a drama in which everyone must get into the act. Planning for cultural tourism must acknowledge a broader context, so that its relative importance and contribution to a community can be properly evaluated. Such a planning process also helps to ensure that the products of cultural tourism accurately reflect a community's heritage and create broad support for the industry. Finally, communities need to consider multiple uses for their heritage resources to spread out costs, reduce the competition for scarce resources, and allow all groups, not just visitors, to enjoy and benefit from them.

In an address to the Czech Federal Assembly, Premier Ladislave Adamec stated that his government regarded tourism "as the citizen's important right to get to know the world, gain experience, and establish personal contacts." Although not without serious difficulties, community-based cultural tourism offers cities and towns an ideal opportunity for sustainable development and the creation of a more democratic Grand Tour of the new global village.

—*W. Arthur Mehrhoff*

References

Lynch, Kevin. *What Time Is This Place?* Cambridge, MA: MIT Press, 1972.

MacCannell, Dean. *The Tourist: A New Theory of the Leisure Class.* New York: Schocken Books, 1976.

Murphy, Peter. *Tourism: A Community Approach.* New York: Methuen Press, 1985.

Curley, James Michael (1874–1958)

James Michael Curley, the most colorful, memorable, and talented mayor Boston ever had, was born on November 20, 1874, in the Irish working-class neighborhood of Roxbury. The son of humble Irish-Catholic immigrants, Michael and Sarah (Clancy) Curley from Galway, he left public school at the age of 16. The tall, handsome Curley worked in local shops and as a traveling salesman before he attached himself to the ward boss of Roxbury, P. J. Maguire. He failed in his first campaign for office in 1899, but he won seats on the Boston Common Council (1900–1901), in the state legislature (1902–1903), and on the city's Board of Alderman (1904–1909).

After serving a year on Boston's new city council (1910–1911), Curley was elected to the U.S. House of Representatives on the Democratic ticket in 1911, but he resigned when he was elected mayor, an office he sought in ten campaigns, winning four of them in 1914, 1922, 1930, and 1947 and losing on six other occasions. Defeated in his first bid for reelection in 1918, he was returned to office in 1922, defeated in 1926, and again elected in 1930 and, for a last term in 1946.

By 1915, Curley had built a powerful, personal, citywide machine, but he was never a ward boss or Democratic Party boss in the traditional sense. He boasted that he was not a ward politician, and strangely this was true. Ward bosses neither trusted nor supported Curley. His machine was a multiethnic, biracial network of personal allies, admirers, and friends, and his genius for building coalitions was as legendary as it was unprecedented in Massachusetts government. His considerable oratorical skills and his genteel but dangerous style made him a formidable opponent in debate or on the campaign trail. Denied a seat at the 1932 Democratic National Convention, the irrepressible Curley appeared on the convention floor as a delegate from Puerto Rico and cast his votes for Franklin D. Roosevelt.

When Roosevelt defeated Al Smith and received the Democratic nomination, Curley returned to Boston in triumph. He had supported Roosevelt very early and campaigned for him nationally, but when Roosevelt denied Curley the cabinet seat (and public recognition) he craved, the two became enemies. Curley's revenge was winning the governorship in 1934 and undertaking large public works that foreshadowed Roosevelt's New Deal programs.

Defeated for the Senate in 1936 by Henry Cabot Lodge, Jr., and losing campaigns for the mayoralty of Boston in 1938 and 1942, Curley was again elected to the House of Representative in 1942 and 1944 and then returned for a fourth term as mayor of Boston in 1946. He spent five months of that term in federal prison after being convicted of mail fraud, but President Truman paroled and then pardoned him, and he returned to city hall. He ran again for mayor in 1950 and

1954, but these were largely symbolic efforts to replenish his war chest. His personal fortune was never large, and he spent money liberally. Accused of wholesale graft, charges he denied and relished, Curley was like a flowing river to his impoverished supporters. The long lines of favor-seekers outside his posh Jamaicaway home and at his city hall office were almost never disappointed; "James Michael" lavishly distributed jobs, favors, recommendations, and cash to them. It was said that businessmen and contractors who sought public contracts paid for Curley's largesse.

Edwin O'Connor's best-selling novel *The Last Hurrah* (1956) is a fictional but useful account of bosses like Curley, as was John Ford's sentimental 1958 movie with the same title. Although he threatened to sue O'Connor's publisher and the film company, Curley delighted in the portrayal of a kind-hearted rogue, and it inspired his autobiography, *I'd Do It Again* (1957). James Michael Curley died on November 12, 1958, in the Boston City Hospital he had built for his needy constituents.

When he left office, the city was in sad disrepair, its population declining as postwar suburbs attracted the young and its future dim. Recent critics blame much of this on Curley, but this interpretation overlooks his role as a hero to the poor and the friendless. The self-proclaimed "Mayor of the Poor" was a larger-than-life figure of a type now obsolete, but one whose career symbolized both public service and showmanship.

—*Peter C. Holloran*

References

Beatty, Jack. *The Rascal King: The Life and Times of James Michael Curley.* Reading, MA: Addison-Wesley, 1992.

Curley, James Michael. *I'd Do It Again: A Record of All My Uproarious Years.* Englewood Cliffs, NJ: Prentice-Hall, 1957.

Dinneen, Joseph Francis. *The Purple Shamrock.* New York: W. W. Norton, 1949.

O'Connor, Edwin F. *The Last Hurrah.* Boston: Atlantic, 1956.

Daley, Richard J. (1902–1976)

Richard J. Daley was the most powerful mayor in Chicago's history and the most influential mayor of his time nationally. He was born in an ethnic neighborhood of Chicago, the son of a of an Irish Catholic blue-collar worker. Educated in local Catholic schools, he became a lawyer and won his first public office as a state legislator in 1936. He fathered four sons including one, Richard M., who was elected mayor of Chicago in 1989, and three daughters.

The key that opened the mayor's office to Daley was his appointment as chairman of the Cook County Democratic Central Committee in 1953. From that position, he mounted a primary election campaign against the incumbent mayor, Martin H. Kennedy, whom he defeated in 1955, and he then defeated the Republican candidate. During the next two decades, Daley was reelected five times against nominally nonpartisan, but generally Republican, candidates. The source of Daley's great power was his dual role as mayor and Democratic Party chairman. He ran a tightly organized party structure with control over 35,000 city workers and patronage employees, and he paid close personal attention to the delivery of municipal services in the "city that works." He first attracted national attention in 1960 for his key role in helping John F. Kennedy win the Democratic Party presidential nomination and then the presidential election.

A "builder" mayor, Daley was committed to the physical development of Chicago and encouraged the construction of downtown skyscrapers, including the Sears Tower, then the world's tallest building; stimulated expressway expansion and mass transit; and enlarged the world's "busiest" airport, O'Hare (which he always mispronounced "O'Hara"). His "Midas touch" in Washington brought Chicago extensive federal funding to demolish blighted areas, build public housing, and set a rapid pace for urban renewal. As with all of his enterprises, he mixed politics and business, and when he was criticized, he repeated again and again, "Good politics makes for good government." When taunted about the evils of his machine, Daley snapped back at reporters, "Organization, not machine. Get that, organization, not machine." Although evidence of wrongdoing occasionally tainted Daley's cronies, the mayor himself appeared to remain clean. Not a single, solid charge of corruption ever stuck to Daley, despite numerous investigations by federal, state, and local agencies and by newspapers.

The shooting and death of Dr. Martin Luther King, Jr., in April 1968 triggered a firestorm of arson, looting, and rioting on Chicago's black West Side, which provoked the mayor to issue an order that the media broadcast across the nation, "shoot to kill any arsonist . . . with a Molotov cocktail in his hand." Daley's command enraged the liberal news media and aroused resounding denunciation of the mayor. But those events foreshadowed an even more bitter experience that August when Daley and the city attempted to host the 1968 Democratic national convention. Peace activists opposed to the war in Vietnam and Chicago's tough-minded police department turned the convention into a week of antiwar turmoil, street violence by demonstrators, and a police "riot," which made a shambles of the event, not to mention Daley's reputation. The media predicted the end of Daley's political career, and the refusal of the 1972 Democratic national convention to seat Daley's delegation seemed to confirm that view. But the naysayers were wrong. Daley won his largest victory ever in 1975, being elected mayor for an unprecedented sixth four-year term. Early in that new term, on December 20, 1976, he died.

During his 21 years in office, Daley was one of the best and most effective mayors of the twentieth century. He used his position to rescue Chicago's downtown from impending blight; he made use of his superior ability as a money manager to steer Chicago away from the rocky shoals that had thrown New York City and Cleveland into bankruptcy; and he had few peers as a political broker and organizer. He earned lower marks for his unwillingness to reach out to the suburbs, for his slow accommodation of blacks and Latinos into the Democratic Party, and for his frequently stormy relations with the press and reformers. On the other hand, the city's bankers, its real estate interests, and organized labor were happy with the solid financial base he helped to build in Chicago and the city's consistently high bond ratings.

—*Melvin G. Holli*

References

Biles, Roger. *Richard J. Daley: Politics, Race, and the Governing of Chicago.* DeKalb: Northern Illinois University Press, 1995.

Green, Paul M. "Richard J. Daley and the Politics of Good Government." In Paul M. Green and Melvin J. Holli, eds. *The Mayors: The Chicago Political Tradition,* 144–159. Carbondale: Southern Illinois University Press, 1995.

Kennedy, Eugene. *Himself: The Life and Times of Richard J. Daley.* New York: Viking Press, 1978.

O'Connor, Len. *Clout: Mayor Daley and His City.* Chicago: Contemporary Books, 1978.

Rakove, Milton. *Don't Make No Waves, Don't Back No Losers: An Insider's Analysis of the Daley Machine.* Bloomington: Indiana University Press, 1975.

Royko, Mike. *Boss Richard J. Daley of Chicago.* New York: New American Library, 1971.

Dallas, Texas

Dallas, Texas, grew up in the period when the passive, regulatory cities of the nineteenth century developed into locally financed, service-oriented cities, and then into metropolises dependent on federal largesse and no longer able to rely solely on continuing growth to ensure their fiscal stability. Like other Sunbelt cities, however, the population of Dallas continued to increase well into the 1980s, a circumstance that allowed the city to maintain conservative patterns of taxation and more extended prosperity than urban areas in the North and East. Throughout the entire history of the city, the rhetoric of loosely regulated capitalism and laissez-faire individualism has prevailed.

Between 1880 and 1920, Dallas resembled its rivals of similar size and age on the developing prairies. Few residents of early Dallas or other "new" nineteenth-century towns preferred standing still or advocated returning to a simpler time. Within a broad, general consensus favoring growth—virtually all of the city's residents supported growth and were convinced that the destiny of Dallas was becoming a "great" city—competing interests presented different visions of exactly how urban expansion should occur. In formal statements of purpose, or through giving priority to one project rather than another, the commercial-civic elite, club women, populists, socialists, trade unionists, and municipal reformers articulated their visions of the ideal city. Competing groups formed short-lived coalitions when elements of their respective visions of growth and the future overlapped. Significantly, racism severely hampered the efforts of those who tried to unite the city's working classes.

A series of bitter conflicts in the years after World War I convinced a new generation of businessmen that the unruly nature of urban affairs was threatening continued growth. The elite that matured in the 1920s and consolidated power by forming the Dallas Citizens Council in 1937 abruptly ended the internecine feuding characteristic of relationships among the city's early leaders; instead, they aired intraclass disputes behind closed doors and presented a united front in public.

Political scientist Stephen Elkin considers Dallas after World War II an extreme example of the entrepreneurial political economies characteristic of Sunbelt cities in which strong alliances developed between businessmen and public officials. What distinguished Dallas was not that business leaders dominated the city but the extent and duration of their dominance in the postwar decades or, to use Elkin's words, "the range of actors who become active bargainers being more restricted in Dallas."

The city originated in 1840, when John Neely Bryan left Van Buren, Arkansas, to establish a trading post on the upper Trinity River in north-central Texas. The Republic of Texas had already provided funds for a military highway from Austin to the Red River to cross the Trinity near the convergence of its three forks.

Like Dallas County (organized in 1846), the town might have been named for George Mifflin Dallas, a Pennsylvanian who was elected vice president in 1844 partly on the issue of annexing Texas. But the town was called Dallas before the election campaign, and the future vice president had a brother who, as a naval commander, also had a well-known name. To further complicate the question, John Neely Bryan had a friend named Joseph Dallas who moved to the region and settled three miles north of Bryan's settlement. The uncertainty surrounding the origins of the town's name suggests both the ambivalence of Dallas's residents toward the past and the recent nature of local interest in the city's historical identity. Regardless of whichever Dallas gave his name to the city, the townsite had been surveyed and platted by 1846.

From its origin as a river crossing located strategically along a military highway, early Dallas benefited from the rapid settlement of much of its hinterland. Between 1842 and 1854, when Dallas emerged as a county seat, most migrants to Texas had to purchase their land, usually from speculators. The only areas in which land remained free were the established *empresario* reserves—land reserves owned by the Republic of Texas that stemmed from Austin's original contract with Mexico and the State Colonization Law of 1825. In 1841, just as the settlements of east Texas began expanding onto the blackland prairies, Texas granted William S. Peters and his associates from Louisville, Kentucky, approximately 16,000 square miles in the region of the upper Trinity. Texas law prohibited an *empresario* from settling a colony with migrants from other parts of the state so the Peters Colony attracted

A cattle drive crossing the Texas plains with Dallas looming clearly in the background reveals the cultural conflicts and ambiguities inherent in many young cities.

small farmers from areas to the north and east—many from northern or border states and mostly without slaves.

This migration of relatively homogeneous settlers to the Peters Colony so close to early Dallas had a tremendous impact on the entire region. Committed to family farming, the majority of the Peters colonists grew grains and vegetables. Those growing cotton did so on a smaller scale than the plantation owners of south Texas. Many farm families received 640 acres of free land near Dallas and, because they possessed cash reserves, developed a lively interest in trade.

Another impetus for the rapid rise of Dallas as the region's dominant town was the arrival of the first French, Swiss, and Belgian settlers of La Reunion in 1854. Eventually numbering almost 350 persons, the La Reunion colony contained highly educated professionals, scientists, writers, musicians, artisans, and naturalists. This colony, however, lacked the agricultural expertise to ensure success under strange and somewhat primitive conditions. After a three-year struggle, the immigrants disbanded La Reunion and the colony's leaders returned to France. Most of the European settlers remained, however, and 160 colonists originally from La Reunion lived in Dallas by 1860. The infusion of so many skilled Europeans

into a commercial crossroads serving relatively prosperous farmers further distinguished Dallas, a town of not quite 2,000 in 1860, from other county seats in north Texas.

Although it served as a supply center for the Confederate army west of the Mississippi River, its location shielded Dallas during the Civil War. After the war, as southern migrants poured into Texas, Dallas County's thriving wheat lands and the city that served them became, for many, the destination of choice. The decades following the Civil War transformed Dallas from a crossroads marketplace to the largest city in north Texas, second only to Houston in the state.

Dallas was somewhat insulated from the panics that followed the Civil War because of its mixed economy and the acquisition of two railroads, the Houston & Texas Central in 1872 and the Texas & Pacific the following year. Aside from processing wheat and cotton, the town possessed important publishing, lumber planing, and saddling operations.

After Texas awarded Dallas its charter in 1856 (the original town charter was exchanged for a city charter in 1871), the city's independent and often unruly citizens elected a mayor and aldermen who served on a single council, but in 1907 a new charter established a commission form of government. Then, in 1930, the city adopted the council-manager form of government, which it still retains.

Perhaps not surprising in a commercial center catering to a vast agricultural hinterland, merchants and landowners figured disproportionately among the city's early leaders. Male members of the commercial-civic elite established a series of local organizations dedicated to economic growth (including the Board of Trade, the Commercial Club, the Chamber of Commerce, and the Open Shop Association) and ran for political office as Democrats in what was essentially a one-party state. Disputes among businessmen typically enlisted their allies from among groups favoring increased municipal spending against fiscal conservatives.

"Organized womanhood"—often the wives, mothers, and daughters of prominent businessmen—sought to refine ostensibly laissez-faire capitalism through environmental reform and increased spending on cultural institutions and social services. Through the Dallas Federation of Women's Clubs, female members of the elite influenced civic affairs decades before the passage of the suffrage amendment to the U.S. Constitution.

Between 1886 and 1917, Dallas populists and socialists organized and maintained local chapters of national political parties. The city's political radicals functioned as local interest groups that moderated the choice of candidates by the elite rather than by achieving their own consistent electoral victories. Despite ultimate political failure, local radicals established significant urban institutions, including a cooperative cotton exchange, a night school for adults, and an employment service. Dallas radicals also joined local trade unionists to form the city's first liberal coalitions. Although several champions of organized labor including painter Patrick H. Golden, butcher Max Hahn, and musician John W. (Bill) Parks won state and local elections or were appointed to important municipal offices, Dallas unionists, like their radical allies, were unable to mount consistent political challenges to candidates of the elite. Key strikes included a successful work stoppage by street railway workers in 1898 and a protest by electrical linemen in 1919 that was accompanied by sympathy strikes involving thousands of building tradesmen.

The militancy of local trade unionists, the division of the city's middle and upper classes into camps that favored or opposed various reforms and city planning measures, and the reemergence of the Ku Klux Klan made the years after World War I an especially unsettling time. Middle-class professionals and their allies among the elite who challenged the prevailing view that growth depended on fiscal restraint and minimal taxation soon discovered that their relatively late attempts to institutionalize social reform would be overshadowed by businessmen who sought changes in the structure of city government as a means of thwarting the Klan's political ambitions.

During the 1930s, continued feuding among members of the elite, renewed demands for fairness by local factory workers, and Dallas's financial obligations to the state's Centennial Exposition motivated the city's most powerful bankers, merchants, and utility heads to establish the Dallas Citizens Council, the forum through which they dominated civic affairs for the next 40 years. The hegemony of this group—its self-discipline, control of the local media, and repression or co-optation of challengers—and the lack of inquiry into the city's past have resulted in the view among both scholars and Dallas residents that the city has always been an "empire of consensus." Indeed, the notion that apolitical officials guarded the interests of the entire city proved especially appealing to Dallas voters well into the 1970s. Modern Dallas differs from other Sunbelt cities primarily because of the remarkable duration of the influence of the Citizens Council and the relative weakness of coalitions that challenged the business community's rule in the 1960s and 1970s.

In the decade after the assassination in Dallas of President John F. Kennedy in 1963, the Citizens Council feared that racial violence would harm the city's reputation irreparably. Motivated businessmen therefore included moderate leaders of minority groups in forums like Goals for Dallas and supported the election of several African Americans to the city council. The pace of change quickened after federal courts mandated single-member school board elections in 1974 and city council districts a year later. By the 1980s, African-American and Hispanic candidates with few ties to prominent business leaders had built political bases in particular neighborhoods. An influx of immigrants from the Midwest and from northern states invigorated white neighborhood groups and contributed to the growing complexity of municipal government.

The political atmosphere of contemporary Dallas corresponds closely to that of the city prior to the 1920s—when the commercial-civic elite spoke with multiple voices and the politics of competition and cooperation characterized urban life. Residents of Dallas can only benefit from an awareness that they share an urban legacy in which calls for fairness, cooperation, and greater attention to human services accompanied rapid growth.

—*Patricia Evridge Hill*

References

Acheson, Sam. *Dallas Yesterday.* Dallas, TX: Southern Methodist University Press, 1977.

Elkin, Stephen L. *City and Regime in the American Republic.* Chicago: University of Chicago Press, 1996.

Hill, Patricia Evridge. *Dallas, the Making of a Modern City.* Austin: University of Texas Press, 1996.

————. "Real Women and True Womanhood: Grassroots Organizing among Dallas Dressmakers in 1935." *Labor's Heritage* 5 (1994): 4–17.

————. "Women's Groups and the Extension of City Services in Early Twentieth-Century Dallas." *East Texas Historical Journal* 30 (1992): 3–10.

Leslie, Warren. *Dallas, Public and Private: Aspects of an American City.* Reprint ed. Dallas, TX: Southern Methodist University Press, 1998.

Payne, Darwin. *Dallas: An Illustrated History.* Woodland Hills, CA: Dallas Historic Preservation League and Windsor Publications, 1982.

Santerre, George H. *Dallas's First Hundred Years, 1856–1956.* Dallas, TX: Book Craft, 1956.

Wheeler, Kenneth W. *To Wear a City's Crown: The Beginnings of Urban Growth in Texas, 1836–1865.* Cambridge, MA: Harvard University Press, 1968.

Davis, Alexander Jackson (1803–1892)

Alexander Jackson Davis was an architect who began his career by depicting the cityscape; he subsequently designed monumental civic buildings as well as country houses, reflecting his appreciation of both naturalistic and picturesque values. Born in New York, the son of an unsuccessful bookseller and publisher, Davis initially trained to be a printer with his brother in Alexandria, Virginia, before studying at the American Academy of the Fine Arts, the New York Drawing Association, and the Antique School at the National Academy of Design. His facility for drawing buildings and their environs brought him employment as an illustrator of the urban scene for the *New-York Mirror,* a series being published in 1827 as *Views of the Public Buildings in the City of New York.*

A year before, he had begun to work as an architectural draftsman, soon being hired by Ithiel Town, whose partner he became from 1829 to 1835 and 1842 to 1843. Town's extensive architectural library enabled Davis to acquire a broad vocabulary of European architectural historical motifs that fostered an associational, pictorial attitude to design. Under Town's tutelage he developed a crisply stylish rendering technique that was matched by his adept selection of appropriate antiquarian sources. Especially in the Greek Revival style, they created impressive yet quite modestly scaled churches such as those for the West Presbyterian (1831–1832) and French Saint Esprit (1831–1835) congregations in New York City that added architectural dignity to the more conventional surrounding structures.

Similarly, their neat combination of a restricted number of major classical features resulted in powerful freestanding structures of a size and substance previously absent from American urban design. Of these, the most notable are the U.S. Customs House in New York City (1833–1842, completed by others) and state capitol buildings for Indianapolis, Indiana (1831–1835), and Raleigh, North Carolina (1833–1841, completed by David Paton). Davis thereby reflected the contemporary view of the civilizing potential of architecture, with major public buildings representing the cultural aspirations of the community as well as reflecting the processes of settlement and urbanization in the West and South. Moreover, antiquarian study accentuated Davis's sense of architectural imagery, which yielded schemes exhibiting intriguing abstract geometrics, exemplified by the hexagonal and circular projects for Brooklyn City Hall (1834) and the neo-Gothic plan for the University of Michigan (1838).

Those characteristics were to be augmented in Davis's late, abortive, civic schemes, of which the grandest were for the New York City Post Office (1867) and a Museum of Geography, History, Art, Science and Literature (ca. 1872), itself reflecting Davis's eclectic and synthetic thought. If such buildings were conceived as dominant visual incidents in the urban topography, he also demonstrated a keen appreciation for the relation of building to site. An outstanding example is the design of the Virginia Military Institute (conceived in 1848, erected 1850–1861), set strategically on an eminence and equipped in the Gothic style as more appropriate to the distant Blue Ridge.

That Romantic sensibility had already been realized in his handsome book, *Rural Residences,* published in 1836. Influenced by British Picturesque literature and inspired by the Hudson River Valley, Davis advocated using both the cottage and villa types (and Gothic-derived styles between 1840 and 1850), on the grounds of their aesthetic, functional, and contextual suitability.

Davis collaborated with Andrew Jackson Downing toward the completion of his important works on landscape architecture, contributing designs for villa and cottage. This confirmed Davis's preeminence as a country house architect—although he completed fine, generally Neoclassical, city houses, outstanding among which is the John Stevens house in New York City (1845–1848)—signified by such inventive adaptations of the English Gothic tradition as Blithewood in Annandale-on-Hudson, New York (1836–1851), Knoll (later Lyndhurst) in Tarrytown, New York (1838–1841), and Walant Wood in Bridgeport, Connecticut (1845–1848). Smaller gabled houses, typified by the elegantly articulated William Rotch House in New Bedford, Massachusetts (1845–1847), became canonic models in North America, much as his version of the Italianate villa established a popular genus before the Civil War (which had an adverse effect on Davis's career).

However, Davis's most important contribution to the urban landscape was the development, in collaboration with the pharmaceutical entrepreneur Llewellyn S. Haskell and the landscape gardener Eugene Baumann, of the picturesque, hillside, residential suburb of Llewllellyn Park in West Orange, New Jersey, in which he was responsible for a large proportion of the villas, cottages, and houses, most notably Eyrie

(1853–1854), Wildmont (1856–1857), and Castlewood (1857–1866). These buildings were designed to enjoy the view while contributing to the scenery and creating a sylvan domestic enclave. Thus, although the majority of Davis's work continued the traditional idea of individual, variably monumental buildings dominating the urban context, or of symbolically evocative edifices, at Llewellyn Park Davis anticipated a major theme in late-nineteenth- and early-twentieth-century international and American design—the landscaped garden suburb.

—*R. Windsor Liscombe*

See also
Downing, Andrew Jackson; Llewellyn Park, New Jersey.
References
Davies, Jane B. "Alexander Jackson Davis." In A. K. Placzek, ed., *Macmillan Encyclopedia of Architects*. 4 vols. New York: Free Press, 1982.
Peck, Amelia, ed. *Alexander Jackson Davis, American Architect, 1803–1894*. New York: Rizzoli, 1992.

Default

Municipal default—the inability of a city's government to repay its long- and short-term general obligations—is symptomatic of failure in city administration. As municipal corporations, cities are empowered to gather revenue from taxation to meet expenses and provide services. Cities can also borrow funds for capital improvements or, through short-term anticipatory notes, keep finances afloat pending future revenue from taxes or state aid. A widening gap between expenditures and revenues, problems such as economic panics or depressions, and long-term fiscal mismanagement can leave governments unable to pay the interest and principal on its loans or notes.

Since the first failure of Mobile, Alabama, in the wake of the panic of 1837 more than 6,600 state and local bond issues have resulted in default. Even the rapidly growing city of Chicago was forced into temporary default following the panic of 1857. The economic downturn of 1873, the shaky financial position of southern state and local governments during Reconstruction, and the failure of railroad aid bonds to produce their promised returns led to 159 defaults during the 1870s. Likewise, the use of public funds for private speculation, particularly in land bonds, led to a succession of municipal failures during the 1890s. But the most spectacular outbreak of defaults occurred during the Depression when 4,770 governmental units failed. Of these, 191 were cities whose populations exceeded 50,000, including Fall River, Massachusetts; Asheville, North Carolina; Fort Lee and Asbury Park, New Jersey; Akron, Ohio; Grand Rapids, Michigan; and, most notably, Detroit.

In the majority of cases, defaults have resulted from heavy borrowing in regions experiencing rapid and optimistic expansion that subsequently experience economic downturns. Industrial development bonds, which use public debt to finance private economic activity (Private-Purpose Revenue Bonds or Notes) and municipal improvement districts (Government-Purpose Revenue Bonds), have been particularly prone to default in recent years, culminating in the spectacular 1983 collapse of the Washington Public Power Commission System; at a loss of $2.25 billion, this fiasco equaled all the defaults during the Depression combined.

The recession of the early 1990s, coupled with tax protest initiatives and the continuing decline of per capita income in the largest cities relative to their suburbs (from 89 percent in 1980 to 58.5 percent in 1990) has led more than one city in four to experience severe budget gaps. In 1991, Chelsea, Massachusetts, and Bridgeport, Connecticut, both defaulted with the latter taking the additional step of seeking Chapter 9 bankruptcy protection. The most notable recent crisis, the 1994 bankruptcy and subsequent chain of defaults of Orange County, California, hit one of America's most affluent counties. Bad investments in an uncertain financial market produced losses exceeding $2 billion for the county and many of its municipalities.

More important, the municipal crisis of the 1970s, which pushed cities such as Cleveland and New York to the brink of financial receivership, underscored how default is usually the culmination of historical political processes and conflicts that underlie budgetary decision making.

Initially, struggling frontier communities undertook creative financing for capital expenditures related to civic boosterism despite the inability of taxpayers to fund these debts. One such city was Duluth, Minnesota, where a small coterie of elite speculators hoped to capitalize on a pledge by Jay Cooke to build the eastern terminus of the Northern Pacific Railroad in the city. In anticipation, voters authorized a bond issue of $30,000 to fund a blast furnace company. Cooke's collapse in the panic of 1873 ended the project, leading Duluth to default on its bonds. The state legislature subsequently dissolved the debt, easing the burden on local taxpayers and forcing creditors to settle for payments of 25 cents on the dollar.

Even in the nineteenth century, fiscal emergencies could also provide opportunities for wide-reaching reforms not possible under the normal operation of politics. Memphis, Tennessee, offers a classic example. Plagued by a rise in municipal debt from $4 million to $6 million between 1872 and 1876, devastated by a yellow fever epidemic in 1878 that killed one-eighth of the city's population and also depressed tax collections by 50 percent, and suffering a decline in income from cotton factoring throughout much of the 1870s, Memphis defaulted in 1879. The response to Memphis's fiscal woes was little more than a thinly disguised power grab by the mercantile elites—members of the Memphis Cotton Exchange, the Chamber of Commerce, and a People's Protective Association—culminating a six-year effort to remove voters without property from political power. The dissolution of the city government by the Tennessee state legislation in 1879 and its replacement by the Taxing District of Shelby County became a model for other top-down reform in southern cities like Selma and Mobile, Alabama.

The roots of indebtedness in the twentieth century have shifted from capital expenditures to operating costs, over which the tax-paying population exerted relatively little control. But the process of default has remained essentially political. The Depression imposed genuine burdens on a host of American cities. Detroit's municipal default was precipitated by a statewide banking crisis over which it had no control and left the city financially strapped. Detroit had been a boom city in the 1920s and followed an aggressive policy of annexing surrounding areas. However, the Depression and the decline that it caused in the automobile industry undercut tax revenues while increasing welfare needs. Mayor Frank Murphy's effort to prevent starvation, even if it meant feeding unemployed Ford workers from outside the city, enjoyed widespread support from business, labor, and political leaders. Home rule survived intact despite attempts by the Association for Tax Reduction, a grassroots coalition of homeowners and real estate speculators unable to pay their property taxes, to pass a budget limitation initiative.

Such was not the case in the first major city to succumb to hard times in the 1930s. Like that of Detroit, the default of Fall River, Massachusetts, in November 1930 was ostensibly triggered by the Depression. In this case, however, default gave old commercial leaders an opportunity to regain the political power they had lost to political organizations of both parties that catered to ethnic voters. The decline of Fall River's cotton textile industry during the 1920s and the strain placed upon finances by political leaders who sought to continue welfare services despite the falling tax base prompted an unsuccessful elite-led taxpayers revolt. After failing to change the city charter, former members of the Fall River Taxpayer's Association convinced bondholders and the Boston bankers who underwrote Fall River's securities of the necessity of default, thus initiating a financial emergency. Using the unassailable imperative of "fiscal necessity," the same leadership drafted and successfully lobbied for a reorganization plan under state receivership. With the Fall River Finance Board, the state legislature effectively removed fiscal self-government until 1942.

After the Depression, bouts with insolvency like New York City's near default in 1975 confirmed that financial disputes were not aberrations but integral to urban politics. Fiscal crises were usually part of a process in which business leaders attacked machine control over City Hall for its failure to fulfill its obligations to manage municipal finances responsibly and to promote economic growth. Imminent municipal bankruptcy had precipitated political reform in New York City in 1871, 1933, and 1971, as well as when new subway construction threatened to increase indebtedness in the periods of 1894 to 1901 and 1907 to 1913. From 1969 to 1975, the administrations of Mayors John Lindsay and Abraham Beame held together broad coalitions of consumers of city services and municipal employees by spending more than the city collected from taxes and state and federal aid. Until a downturn in New York's economic growth brought a change, major commercial banks continued to underwrite ever-larger purchases of city securities, which were used to finance day-to-day city operations in exchange for healthy fees and commissions. When these banks finally refused any further refinancing, state political leaders intervened to forestall the disastrous consequences of default or bankruptcy. The Financial Emergency Act passed by the legislature established a Municipal Assistance Corporation (MAC), which issued securities on behalf of the city, provided short-term loans, and converted existing notes into long-term bonds, thereby making debt payments more manageable. When investors continued to avoid MAC-issued securities, the state established an Emergency Financial Control board that froze city spending, instituted sound accounting practices, ended generous subsidies for subways and tuition at the City University, and compelled a balanced budget. After investors once again balked, the federal government (after some resistance) finally intervened to offer short-term loans and loan guarantees for MAC-issued securities.

Cleveland's default mirrored that of New York City. Having narrowly escaped insolvency in 1971, Cleveland finally defaulted on bond anticipatory notes in 1978 following years of poor accounting practices and overspending. As the city's accounts payable deficit reached $36 million and its cash deficit skyrocketed to $32 million by the end of 1979, Ohio passed a law that allowed the state to declare "Local Fiscal Emergencies." Even before state auditors invoked the statute for Cleveland in early 1980, community business leaders were able to elect a reform administration under Mayor George Voinovich. The new government reduced municipal spending and persuaded voters to approve a 2 percent increase in the income tax to retire Cleveland's debt and support improvements in the city's sagging infrastructure. In response, Ohio lent the city money to pay its overdue debts and helped refloat defaulted securities through a new issue of bonds that was underwritten by eight Cleveland banks.

The outlook for increasing local indebtedness suggests that strapped cities will continue to flirt with insolvency and that urban finances will remain highly politicized. As with many nineteenth-century failures, areas experiencing rapid growth followed by cyclical economic downturns will remain at the highest risk of default. For several years during the 1980s and 1990s, the tax rebellion symbolized by California's Proposition 13, Massachusetts's Proposition 2½, the Reagan administration, and the prospect of tightened funding posed by public demands to cut spending and balance budgets threatened future fiscal crises resembling those already felt by Chelsea and Bridgeport. The threat was averted because of the robust economy of the 1990s, but should the economy enter another period of stagnation, many city governments will discover the difficulty of remaining solvent in a changed political environment where less is more.

—*Kenneth A. Scherzer*

References

Monkkonen, Eric H. *The Local State: Public Money and American Cities.* Stanford, CA: Stanford University Press, 1995.

———. "The Politics of Municipal Indebtedness and Default, 1850–1936." In Terrence J. McDonald and Sally K. Ward, eds., *The Politics of Urban Fiscal Policy.* Beverly Hills, CA: Sage Publications, 1984.

Scherzer, Kenneth. "The Politics of Default: Financial Restructure and Reform in Depression Era Fall River, Massachusetts." *Urban Studies* 26 (1989): 164–176.

Shefter, Martin. *Political Crisis/ Fiscal Crisis.* New York: Basic Books, 1985.

Deindustrialization

The term *deindustrialization* was first popularized in the United States in 1982 by Barry Bluestone and Bennett Harrison in their book, *The Deindustrialization of America.* They defined it as widespread disinvestment in industrial capacity, caused mainly by the transfer of productive industrial investment into unproductive and speculative acquisitions, mergers, and foreign investments. Bluestone and Harrison believed that deindustrialization, as they defined it, occurred primarily after 1970, but if one defines it more broadly, as a loss in industrial capacity and even more critically a loss in manufacturing jobs, the phenomenon has a much longer history in American cities.

Even in the late nineteenth century, after only a few decades of industrialism, many smaller cities experienced declining industrial output and employment. Larger cities garnered an increasing share of manufacturing output and employment at the expense of their smaller counterparts. In the railroad age, transportation rates and services favored larger cities. As the extent of mass production increased, larger cities provided economies of scale, larger and more specialized labor markets, and better access to financial resources. And in an age of more rudimentary communications, bigger cities provided superior access to technological innovations and new industrial methods.

In the first half of the twentieth century, urban deindustrialization took new forms. During the 1920s, a number of specialized industrial centers, particularly those in coal mining and textiles, saw the beginnings of long-term loss of jobs and industrial capacity. The textile industry, foreshadowing later developments in other kinds of manufacturing, moved south to areas of lower wages and less urbanization. Some textile cities, such as New Bedford and Fall River, Massachusetts, never recovered from the economic decline that began during the 1920s.

While deindustrialization in the late nineteenth century had occurred mainly in smaller cities, in the twentieth century the most important manifestation of the phenomenon was the movement of industry from larger central cities to suburbs. As early as 1915, Graham R. Taylor in *Satellite Cities: A Study of Industrial Suburbs* described the shift of factories to fringe areas that was already well under way in many American metropolises. In the 1920s, the proportion of manufacturing employment located in central cities declined in every American city with more than 100,000 residents. During World War II, factories built under the auspices of the Defense Plant Corporation were rarely located in central cities, furthering the trend toward dispersed manufacturing. Still, industry remained the largest employer in central cities until the 1950s, but in that decade the race away from core areas accelerated. The 16 largest and oldest central cities lost an average of 34,000 factory jobs between 1947 and 1967, while the suburbs of those metropolises gained an average of 87,000. By 1963, more than 50 percent of industrial employment was located in suburbs, and by 1981 almost two-thirds of manufacturing was found there.

A number of factors contributed to the suburbanization of industry during the twentieth century. The growing use of trucks, particularly since the 1920s, ended the absolute necessity of railroad connections and allowed manufacturing to move out of central cities into suburbs where land was cheaper and taxes were lower. Cheaper land was particularly important as assembly-line production, which preferred large-area, one-story factories, became common. The dominance of electric power in factories after World War I also freed them from the constraints of central coal transfer facilities required to generate steam. The widespread ownership of automobiles and the mass movement of Americans to suburbs meant that industry no longer relied on a labor force who walked or rode streetcars to work.

Many central cities tried to reverse the trend of deindustrialization in the 1950s and 1960s by clearing land for light industrial development, using funds made available by the federal urban renewal program. In cities such as St. Louis, Milwaukee, Cincinnati, and Boston, these projects failed to revitalize industry with the result that the municipalities had to sell the land for warehouses and service activities (the latter of which were increasingly dominating urban employment).

After 1970, urban industrial decline, particularly the loss of factory jobs, became more pronounced and even spread to suburban areas as well as newer cities in the Sunbelt. A significant part of the job loss resulted from foreign competition. Economies such as those of Japan and Germany had rebuilt their industrial sectors after World War II and possessed advanced technological bases because of this retooling. The United States had accepted much of the cost and responsibility for defending these nations, thus freeing their capital and expertise for sophisticated civilian industrial activities. In addition, as American industrial technology and methods spread around the world, American industry found it increasingly difficult to compete with mass-produced goods made in countries where labor received lower wages.

Also contributing to the manufacturing crisis of the 1970s and 1980s was the "paper entrepreneurialism" of the period. Leveraged buyouts, hostile takeovers, "greenmail" defenses, and an overall preoccupation with short-term profits diverted capital and talent from more productive activities. When real investment was made in industry, it often paid for new technologies such as robots that reduced the need for workers in the already shrinking industrial job base.

The 1970s was a particularly devastating decade for the industrial base of America's largest cities. The loss of manufacturing jobs ranged from 25 percent in Minneapolis, to 38 percent in Youngstown, Ohio, and 40 percent in Philadelphia. These trends continued in the 1980s, and even Chicago's relatively healthy economy lost 33 percent of its factory jobs.

By the middle of the 1990s, American industrialism had recovered some of these losses. Some metropolises such as Pittsburgh, Buffalo, Cincinnati, Phoenix, Boston, and San Francisco had shifted to a high technology manufacturing base. And some writers described advanced industrial cities, such as Cleveland and Pittsburgh, where "knowledge workers" in cities with advanced service bases provided command-and-control administration to worldwide industries.

As promising as these developments might be for the economy as a whole, they did little to stem the national slide of manufacturing employment that dropped from 35 percent of the workforce in 1947 to 16 percent in 1993. And the metropolises and central cities suffered even heavier losses. New factories, such as those built by foreign investors in industries like automobiles, were almost always built outside of central cities and were usually located outside of metropolitan areas as well. Meanwhile, the drive toward automation continued unabated.

In the late nineteenth century, the industry of the United States was overwhelmingly urban. One hundred years later, few factories could be found in America's central cities, and the suburbs were also losing manufacturing employment. The loss of relatively well paying manufacturing jobs, particularly in central cities, had become one of the most serious economic and social problems of urban America.

—*Thomas A. McMullin*

References
Bernstein, Michael A., and David E. Adler, eds. *Understanding American Economic Decline.* New York: Cambridge University Press, 1994.

Bluestone, Barry, and Bennett Harrison. *The Deindustrialization of America: Plant Closings, Community Abandonment, and the Dismantling of Basic Industry.* New York: Basic Books, 1982.

Jackson, Kenneth T. *Crabgrass Frontier: The Suburbanization of the United States.* New York: Oxford University Press, 1985.

Kinsella, Timothy K. "Traditional Manufacturing Cities in Transition to Human-Centered Cities." *Journal of Urban History* 13 (1986): 31–53.

Pred, Allan R. *City-Systems in Advanced Economies: Past Growth, Present Processes and Future Development Options.* New York: Wiley, 1977.

Reich, Robert B. *The Next American Frontier: A Provocative Program for Economic Renewal.* New York: Times Books, 1983.

Teaford, Jon C. *Cities of the Heartland: The Rise and Fall of the Industrial Midwest.* Bloomington: Indiana University Press, 1993.

Density

The density of an economic activity is defined as the ratio of a measure of its size to the land area it occupies. Accordingly, population density is the ratio of the total population residing in a given location to the land area in that location, and employment density is the total employment in a given location divided by its total land area. The spatial distribution of population, depicted by the density of population, that emerges in urban areas is a crucial economic and social feature affecting the efficient functioning of these places. Population density, therefore, is the most widely used notion of urban density.

Urban economics originated as a distinct branch of economic theory with the observation that population and employment densities are not uniform across space. Rather, they vary enormously. The study of the factors and processes operating to produce this variability is at the heart of modern urban economic analysis. This explains why the generic economic definition of an urban area hinges on the notion of population density. Accordingly, an urban area is defined as a place with a much higher population density than elsewhere in a country, where total population exceeds a minimum threshold size.

The study of the factors and processes that create areas with dramatically high population and employment densities seeks to explain the hierarchical system of urban areas in all countries. This study focuses on four major topics—the existence of urban areas, the prevalence of areas of different sizes, the interrelation among areas of different sizes, and the growth and decline of areas. A comprehensive account of the factors and processes at work yields an understanding of the structure of the urban system, its functioning, and changes that occur over time.

Urban population and employment densities are also key variables in economic and social analysis of the internal structure of urban areas. The decline of population densities as one moves away from the center and toward the periphery is of major concern to economists and geographers who are well aware of the tendency of population to disperse between an urban center and its suburbs. The term *urban population density function* is given to any mathematical formulation describing population density at each distance from the center.

The notion that population and employment densities both decline with distance from the center of cities is one of the outstanding features of economic models of the internal structure of urban areas. This is a theoretical conclusion derived from the fundamental assumption that urban activities benefit from proximity to the center. When located further away from the center, benefits can be acquired through interactions with the center, but these entail transportation costs that increase with distance. The desire to economize on transportation costs places a premium on land values close to the center. This produces a land-rent configuration in which rent declines with distance from the center. Population density, which mirrors land-rent, also declines with distance. This relation has been confirmed empirically.

Population density functions have proved extremely useful in measuring the exact degree of the tendency of population to spread out toward suburbs. Of two density functions, the flatter one represents the more suburbanized area and the steeper one represents the less suburbanized area. The exact degree of suburbanization can be measured by the curvature of the functions. A recent contribution (Alperovich and Deutsch) extended the usefulness of density functions by demonstrating their effectiveness in identifying locations of unknown urban centers.

In the late 1960s and early 1970s research (Muth and Mills) revealed that suburbanization has been a massive and pervasive characteristic of metropolitan areas in the United States since 1880. Contrary to the widespread belief that suburbanization is a post–World War II phenomenon, studies show conclusively that suburbanization started long before then. Population and employment density functions have flattened throughout the twentieth century and probably even before.

This tendency toward greater suburbanization is explained as adjustments made by households and firms in response to declining transport costs, rising income, and declining importance of the urban center resulting from the emergence of many competing secondary centers in suburbs. Specifically, declining transport costs throughout the period increased the relative attractiveness of outlying areas. Likewise, the enormous rise in income that took place reinforced this trend through its impact on rising demand for suburban housing. As more and more people moved to suburbs, their buying power supported many more subcenters for social and economic activities, which in turn reinforced the attractiveness of the suburbs.

—*Gershon Alperovich*

See also
Congestion.
References
Alperovich, G., and J. Deutsch. "Joint Estimation of Population Density Functions and the Location of the Central Business District." *Journal of Urban Economics* 36 (1994): 239–248.
Christaller, Walter. *Central Places of Southern Germany.* C. Baskin, trans. Englewood Cliffs, NJ: Prentice-Hall, 1966.
Losch, A. *The Economics of Location,* W. H. Woglom and W. F. Stolper, trans. New Haven, CT: Yale University Press, 1954.
Mills, E. S., *Studies in the Structure of the Urban Economy.* Baltimore: Johns Hopkins University Press, 1972.
Muth, R. F. *Cities and Housing.* Chicago: University of Chicago Press, 1969.

Denver, Colorado

Native Americans frequented the site of Denver along the South Platte River for at least 11,000 years before gold discoveries in 1858 led to the demise of the Cheyenne and Arapaho, the last natives to occupy the area. In July 1858 a party led by William Green Russell found a promising gold placer deposit on the South Platte, and by early November Russell's group had established Auraria, a hamlet on the southwest bank of Cherry Creek near its junction with the South Platte. On November 22, William H. Larimer, Jr., a real estate promoter, and his associates organized the Denver City Town Company and claimed land across from Auraria on the northeast bank of Cherry Creek. Within 18 months, the two towns had consolidated, and Auraria became a memory. Denver, named for James W. Denver, a governor of the Kansas Territory, endured.

Tens of thousands of prospectors, mainly young men from Ohio, Illinois, New York, Missouri, and other midwestern and northern states, streamed into the region in the spring and summer of 1859 hoping to get rich. Finding prospects dim and prices high, many gold seekers quickly returned to the East. Others went west into the mountains, where some found substantial placer and lode deposits. Denver, not much of a gold producer itself, survived as a jumping-off point for the mountains.

During the 1860s, the town's population increased by only 10 people to reach 4,759 in 1870. The Civil War and a mining slump partly accounted for the slow growth. A fire in

1863 destroyed much of the business district, and a flood the next year swept away buildings constructed in the sandy bed of Cherry Creek. After the Union Pacific decided in the mid-1860s to bypass Colorado and lay track for the first transcontinental railroad through southern Wyoming, a Cheyenne newspaper declared, "Denver is too near Cheyenne to ever amount to much."

Denver entrepreneurs quickly turned their town's proximity to Cheyenne into an advantage by building the 106-mile Denver Pacific Railroad north to join the Union Pacific. Its completion in the summer of 1870, along with a connection east provided by the Kansas Pacific Railroad, assured Denver's survival. A frenzy of railroad building gave Colorado nearly 4,300 miles of track by 1890, putting Denver at the hub of what historian Thomas J. Noel has called "a spider web of steel."

Feeding on Colorado's prosperity between 1870 and 1890, Denver grew as a trade, transportation, service, and processing center. Its reputation as a healthful place attracted legions of tuberculosis sufferers. Less than a dozen miles from the base of the Rocky Mountains, it also became a jumping-off point for tourists. With a population of 35,629 in 1880, it was Colorado's largest city, a distinction that helped it win designation as the state's capital in 1881. By 1890, its 106,713 residents made it the nation's twenty-sixth largest city.

Growth brought opportunity. In 1867, private investors completed the 24-mile-long City Ditch, a forerunner of many massive projects to water-parched land that often got less than 16 inches of precipitation a year. In the early 1870s, capitalists began manufacturing gas to light the town's streets and homes, and a telephone exchange with 200 subscribers opened in 1879. A year later, some Denverites switched on electric lights in their homes, and by the mid-1880s they were lighting streets with electricity. An extensive street rail network made it easy for many middle-class citizens to reside in suburbs where they could escape the core city's political corruption, saloons, and brothels.

Despite its problems, the central city made many advances during these boom years. Its schools gained national attention, and its firefighters became a professional force in the 1880s. Its merchants established a free lending library in the same decade, and its business district, of modest size and structure in the early 1870s, boasted grand edifices such as the ten-story Brown Palace Hotel by the early 1890s. East of downtown, the elite constructed showy mansions on Capitol Hill, where the granite-faced state capitol rose during the 1890s. A few miles north, great smelters extracted thousands of ounces of gold and silver from thousands of tons of ore.

Smelter owners secured cheap labor by employing Poles and other Eastern and Central Europeans who lived in industrial suburbs such as Globeville and Argo. As early as the

1860s, Germans, Irish, and English had given Denver something of a cosmopolitan air. By 1880 the city tallied a substantial Swedish community as well as several hundred Chinese, whose presence so rankled some Denverites that in October 1880 a mob destroyed Chinese businesses and killed one Chinese man. Nevertheless, the number of Chinese kept growing and reached a nineteenth-century peak of 1,002 in 1890. By then, the city's foreign-born population of 25,464 included 5,373 Germans, 4,216 Irish, 3,622 Swedish, and 3,338 English.

The magnet of economic opportunity that drew more than 100,000 people to Denver between 1870 and 1890 temporarily lost strength in the early 1890s. Heavily dependent upon Colorado's extractive economy, the city plunged into depression as drought destroyed farms and overproduction drove down the price of silver. Census takers in 1900 found 133,859 Denverites, many of them added by the annexation of South Denver and Highlands.

The economic chaos of the 1890s fostered political change. Women waged a drive to win the right to vote, and their victory in November 1893 made Denver the largest city in the United States to have equal suffrage. On the state level, voters rejected both Republicans and Democrats in 1892 and elected a Populist, Davis H. Waite, as Colorado's governor. His battles with city officials, which once caused him to oust Denver's police and fire commissioners, helped deepen the desire for home rule and freedom from state interference. In 1902, the city achieved some independence when a state constitutional amendment made the city of Denver coterminous with the county and increased its size to nearly 60 square miles. In the process of expanding, the city swallowed nearby suburbs including Argo, Berkeley, and Globeville.

Home rule coincided with economic improvement and the election of Robert W. Speer as mayor under a city charter that gave him substantial power. He used his power to beautify and expand parks, build parkways, construct a city auditorium, initiate mountain parks, dig storm sewers, pave streets, purchase land for a civic center, and plant more than 100,000 trees. Denver, which prided itself on being the queen city of the plains, began living up to its boast.

In 1910, Benjamin Barr Lindsey, a local judge famed for his crusade to create a humane juvenile justice system, published *The Beast,* an exposé of nefarious connections between businessmen and politicians in Denver. Reformers accused Speer of conniving with the wealthy and consorting with the underworld. Mauled by muckrakers, Speer declined to seek a third term in 1912. In 1916, after experimenting with commission government for several years, voters again elected Speer mayor, an office he retained until his death in 1918.

The influenza epidemic of 1918 and 1919 killed more than 1,500 Denverites and foreshadowed troubled times. Between 1920 and 1940, residents turned on one another, the economy faltered, and the growth rate slowed. Anti-German sentiment during World War I gave way to anti-Bolshevism after it. Six people died in 1920 as streetcar drivers struck the powerful Denver Tramway Company. Then the city suffered a hate wave engineered by the Ku Klux Klan. Targeting African Americans, Jews, and Roman Catholics, the local Klan membership grew to more than 10,000. Splits within the hooded empire caused its decline, but bigotry persisted. When African Americans tried to swim at Washington Park's Smith Lake in August 1932, a white mob attacked and drove them back to the predominantly black district northeast of downtown.

The stock market crash in October 1929 jolted Colorado's economy, which had already faltered in the 1920s. By 1934 an estimated 60,000 Denverites, more than 20 percent of the population of 287,861 in 1930, were on relief. To revive the economy, the city, the state, and especially the federal government poured money into projects such as constructing the Red Rocks amphitheater west of the city and diverting water through the Moffat Tunnel. Lavish federal spending on arms production and military installations such as Lowry Air Base helped Denver overcome the Depression by the early 1940s.

Denver grew slowly between 1920, when it numbered 256,491 people, and 1940 when it reckoned 322,412. After World War II, it boomed. Ex-servicemen, remembering the city's pleasant climate and proximity to the mountains, made Denver their home. Cold War defense spending, including multimillion dollar annual expenditures to manufacture plutonium at Rocky Flats, chemical weapons at the Rocky Mountain Arsenal, and missiles at Martin-Marietta, provided thousands of high-paying jobs. Peaceful governmental pursuits also benefited Denver, which, as the largest city in a region embracing several hundred thousand square miles, served as district headquarters for various federal agencies. In 1950 the core city claimed 415,786 people; in 1960, 493,889; and in 1970, 514,678.

Far more impressive than Denver's growth in the years since World War II has been the growth of its suburbs. In 1950 more than 70 percent of the people in the Denver metropolitan area lived in Denver itself. By 1990, of the nearly 2 million people residing in the Denver-Boulder-Greeley Consolidated Metropolitan Statistical Area, more than 70 percent lived outside of Denver. Between 1980 and 1990 Denver's population fell from 492,694 to 467,610, a decline of slightly more than 5 percent.

In the same period Aurora, Denver's largest suburb, grew from 158,588 to 222,103, an increase of slightly more than 40 percent, which placed it among the nation's fastest growing cities; in 1940 Aurora had counted only 3,347 people. Lakewood, Denver's principal western suburb, had a population of nearly 100,000 when it incorporated in 1969; 30 years earlier it had been a kingdom of farmers and ranchers.

Suburban growth reflected Denver's postwar failure to annex large amounts of territory. In the 1950s, the city hesitated to add land because it did not want to supply city services to the suburbs. By the early 1970s, many suburbanites did not want to join Denver because they feared that their children would be bused to achieve school integration.

Before World War II, the city's African-American population, which totaled 7,836 in 1940, was, by custom, coercion, and restrictive real estate covenants, concentrated in the Five Points neighborhood northeast of the central business district. After the war, the black population, which exceeded 46,000 in 1970, expanded east of Five Points. School segregation mirrored residential segregation. Moreover, the city's school board gerrymandered school boundary lines and made other arrangements to accommodate whites who did not wish to attend school with blacks. In 1968, reformers on the school board proposed measures, including busing, to reverse segregation. Voters objected and in 1969 elected opponents of busing to the board. African Americans and others then sued in federal court, which ordered Denver in 1974 to integrate its schools. Fearful that their children might be bused, suburbanites backed a 1974 amendment to Colorado's constitution, which made it extremely difficult for Denver to annex territory.

Blacks were not alone in demanding rights and demonstrating their power. The city's Hispanic population, which reached 86,345 in 1970, was generally politically quiet until the late 1960s when Rodolfo (Corky) Gonzales founded the Crusade for Justice. The Crusade's forceful rhetoric, coupled with its confrontations with other Hispanic groups and the police, led to its demise. Hispanic political activism, however, continued. In 1983, voters elected Federico Peña mayor, in the process rejecting such longtime political figures as the city's previous mayor William McNichols, Jr., and district attorney Dale Tooley. When Peña left office in 1991, he was succeeded by Wellington Webb, the first African American to serve as Denver's mayor.

Women also became a political force during the 1970s. From 1930 to 1968 voters tended to elect conservative Democrats to the U.S. House of Representatives. Patricia Schroeder's victory in 1972 gave Denver and Colorado its first woman representative in Congress. In 1975 Cathy Donohue and Cathy Reynolds became the first women elected to the city council, and by 1990 women held more than half the council seats.

Dramatic physical changes paralleled Denver's political changes. Beginning in the early 1950s, increasing numbers of automobiles, improved highways, suburban sprawl, shopping centers, and office parks threatened the central business district. Private entrepreneurs decided to get out of public transportation, so the city bought the anemic Denver Tramway Company. Air travel made Stapleton Airport one of the nation's busiest hubs, so busy that citizens decided in the late 1980s to build a new airport. But Union Station, once a bustling railroad depot, turned into a quiet barn as it and much of lower downtown decayed. By clearing more than 100 acres of lower downtown, a process it started in the 1960s, the Denver Urban Renewal Authority (DURA) created land suitable for new skyscrapers. DURA also razed homes and businesses south of the business district to make room for Metropolitan State College of Denver, the University of Colorado at Denver, and the Community College of Denver. The expansion of an old baseball stadium for the Denver Broncos, the city's professional football team, the construction of a baseball stadium in the mid-1990s to house the Colorado Rockies, and the relocation in 1995 of Elitch Gardens Amusement Park to a South Platte site helped assure the central business district's future. Philanthropists and foundations supported the core city by pouring millions of dollars into the Denver Center for the Performing Arts, a concert hall and theater complex. In the 1970s the state erected a new home for the Colorado Historical Society, and Denver built a new art museum. Voters backed construction of a convention center in the 1980s, and in 1995 the city completed its new public library, one of the country's largest.

Fearful that the city would bulldoze its past, some citizens formed Historic Denver in 1970. That group worked to preserve historic districts such as Larimer Square in lower downtown and to save individual structures such as the Molly Brown house, a monument to the city's most famous social climber. Some residents hoped that by reviving a light rail streetcar system in 1994 they might control some of the pollution created by the more than 1 million automobiles in the metropolitan area. Citizens also worried about the financial health of the city's new airport, a $5.3 billion endeavor, and about disposition of tons of deadly plutonium stored at the Rocky Flats nuclear weapons plant.

Location, leadership, luck, climate, and natural resources produced the city. Whether those factors would continue sustaining it was a question left unanswered as Denver neared the end of the twentieth century.

—*Stephen J. Leonard*

References

Dorsett, Lyle, and Michael McCarthy. *The Queen City: A History of Denver.* Boulder, CO: Pruett, 1986.

Goodstein, Phil. *The Seamy Side of Denver.* Denver, CO: New Social Publications, 1993.

———. *South Denver Saga.* Denver, CO: New Social Publications, 1991.

Leonard, Stephen J., and Thomas J. Noel. *Denver: Mining Camp to Metropolis.* Niwot: University Press of Colorado, 1990.

Noel, Thomas J. *The City and the Saloon: Denver, 1858–1916.* Lincoln: University of Nebraska Press, 1982.

Noel, Thomas J., and Barbara Norgren. *Denver: The City Beautiful and Its Architects, 1891–1941.* Denver, CO: Historic Denver, 1987.

Department Stores

The new Lord and Taylor store looks "more like an Italian palace than a place for the sale of broadcloth," observed the *New York Times* in 1869. From the middle of the nineteenth century, elegant and imposing department stores graced emerging downtowns in American cities and towns, including Lord and Taylor (founded in 1826), A. T. Stewart (1846), and R. H. Macy and Company (1858) in New York; Jordan Marsh (1841) and Filene's (1881) in Boston; John Wanamaker (1861) in Philadelphia; and Field, Leiter and Company (1865, later Marshall Field) in Chicago. These luxurious bazaars sold a wide variety of goods in separate departments under central management, which supervised and coordinated store operations and personnel.

By the 1890s, department stores had proliferated, becoming influential economic, social, and cultural institutions. They systematized the distribution of consumer goods, profoundly transformed American behavior and attitudes toward consumption, and created a new downtown public institution for women that was staffed primarily by women. The historian William Leach recently argued that department stores (as well as theaters, hotels, restaurants, dance halls, and amusement parks) sparked Americans' passionate devotion to consumer capitalism, fascination with the "new," and vision of the United States as the "land of desire," to use the words of the merchant John Wanamaker.

Department stores evolved from two earlier agents of distribution, the wholesale merchant and the small businessman who sold dry goods. Throughout most of the nineteenth century, wholesalers controlled the marketing and distribution of consumer goods by purchasing merchandise in lots and employing traveling salesmen to resell the wares to small merchants. A few wholesalers, most notably Stewart in New York, and Field, Leiter and Company in Chicago, grafted successful retail branches onto these operations. Stewart's retail store, the Marble Palace, attracted several thousand people to its grand opening in 1846. By the 1880s, mass retailers, department stores, mail-order houses, and chain stores were all challenging wholesalers by buying consumer goods from manufacturers and selling them directly to consumers. As retailing became more profitable, some merchants began to disengage from wholesaling altogether. Although Marshall Field's is still a prominent store, it discontinued its wholesale operations in 1935.

Other department stores grew out of much smaller retail businesses. Macy's opened in 1858 as a small, fancy dry goods shop on Sixth Avenue in New York and regularly expanded for nearly 40 years. First, the firm moved to 14th Street, and by 1874 it had bought space from ten neighboring shopkeepers. It expanded again in 1892 and 1894, and it finally moved to Herald Square in 1902, where the store occupies an entire city block today. John Wanamaker first sold boys' and men's clothing and furnishings in a 30-foot by 80-foot shop in 1861. By 1876, he had renovated an old railroad depot and moved into its three acres of selling space. The remarkable growth of these stores reflects the imagination and ambition of their founders as well as new business practices and the rapid growth in the population of American cities in this era.

Two of the most important business innovations of department stores were the one-price policy and the low markup. Early merchants often displayed their goods without marked prices and bargained with their customers, but the owners of department stores insisted that prices be marked on goods and be unchangeable. Similarly, proprietors of small stores and shops bought goods in limited quantities and profited from high markups. In contrast, owners of department stores demonstrated that selling larger quantities of merchandise at lower prices and turning their stock over rapidly yielded more profit than higher markups. R. H. Macy and Company sold low-priced merchandise for cash only; "goods suitable for the millionaire at prices in reach of the millions," boasted one of its advertisements in 1887.

To entice "the millions," store owners built ornate, luxurious structures and advertised "bargains" aggressively. A. T. Stewart's Marble Palace, designed in Anglo-Italianate style, featured a marble facade with columns, pillars, and corniced windows; a large central rotunda rising the full height of the interior; curly maple and mahogany shelves and counters; and specially designed chandeliers. At the center of John Wanamaker's Grand Depot stood a circular counter 90 feet in diameter for the sale of silks and an "elegantly carpeted dark room" lighted only by gas to "display silk for evening dresses," according to the *Philadelphia Ledger* in May 1876. The newspaper also remarked that the store's entrance was "handsomely ornamented, and the arcade . . . tiled with marble . . . lighted by day by . . . stained glass skylights, and by night by elaborate chandeliers." A Chicago newspaper described Field and Leiter's 1868 emporium as "a Dazzling Assemblage of Wealth, Beauty and Fashion."

Store architects took advantage of the latest building technologies that used steel and plate glass while merchants furnished their grand emporiums with the latest, most modern conveniences. In 1872, Lord and Taylor installed the recently invented steam elevator, and Macy's introduced electric lights in 1879. By the 1880s, Macy's contained a branch of Western Union, a Bell telephone, and a special ventilation system. The 1902 Macy's in Herald Square was 9 stories high and housed 26 acres of selling space; its 33 hydraulic elevators, 4 escalators, conveyor belt for moving merchandise, pneumatic tube system for routing cash and sales slips, early air-conditioning, and built-in vacuum cleaning system made the store more than comfortable and convenient for shoppers. It was an urban marvel.

Department stores' massive buildings, sumptuous interiors, elegant exteriors, and splashy, copious advertising invested shopping and material accumulation with a new cultural meaning for Americans. "Department store grandeur," claims historian Daniel Boorstin, "gave dignity, importance, and publicity to the acts of shopping and buying. Store advertising promised shoppers that purchasing newly available consumer goods would improve the quality of their lives." Macy's, for example, told readers of the *New York Herald* in 1895 that if they would "ride our bicycles, read our books, cook in our saucepans, dine off our china, wear our silks, get under our blankets, smoke our cigars, drink our wines . . . life will cost you less and yield you more than you dreamed possible." John Wanamaker believed that department stores had a social mission. "We help people to shop wisely . . . inspire and influence them to wear good things and to have the right things in their homes, and that leads to higher thinking and to higher living."

The founders of early department stores believed that innovative merchandising, clever advertising, and low prices would ensure retail profits, but intensified competition in the 1880s and 1890s forced them to find new strategies for success. They introduced extensive customer services and developed courses to teach their clerks how to sell. Stores liberalized their return policies, instituted delivery service and charge accounts, built restaurants, and provided ladies' lounges. In 1902, Marshall Field's customers could leave their children in a fully equipped nursery and spend a leisurely afternoon reading in the store's wood-paneled library. Some stores built auditoriums and art galleries where they held concerts, art exhibitions, and other public events, encouraging shoppers to regard the department store as a civic center or, as the *New York Times* called the new Siegel-Cooper store in 1896, a "shopping resort."

Managers also sought to improve sales by cultivating employee loyalty through "welfare work" and with systematic training courses. Like other industrial employers at the turn of the century, department store owners tried to reduce employee turnover and improve workplace performance by building locker rooms, lunchrooms, resting rooms, hospitals, libraries, and recreational facilities on the store premises. In addition, they organized mutual benefit associations, clubs, and schools, and they planned picnics and purchased vacation homes and campgrounds for their employees' use.

Both the employees and the customers of department stores were almost entirely women. The great emporiums became downtown "clubs" where middle-class women could socialize and learn about the latest fashions. Noting the growing presence of women shoppers in the late 1860s, New Yorkers called the shopping district from Union Square to Madison Square and from Broadway to Sixth Avenue the "Ladies Mile." At its height, "Ladies Mile," with its department stores, specialty shops, and showrooms, was a Mecca of style and commerce. Here, noted one commentator, American women learned to worship the "new" and disdain the "old."

Most of the white, working-class women who served the middle class from behind the counters preferred store employment to the jobs available in factories or as domestic servants. Department stores offered a clean, stimulating work environment and an education in middle-class manners, consumer culture, and fashion. Though working conditions could be harsh—with low wages, long hours, sexual harassment, and managers' insistence that saleswomen stand for hours on end—young store employees usually found a congenial peer group and the chance for a long-term career in retailing. Most female employees held positions as saleswomen, but some became department heads, buyers, or personnel officials with considerable responsibility and respectable salaries.

The key features of the modern department store—a large, elegant building staffed primarily by women clerks serving women customers, innovative merchandising, skilled selling, elaborate customer service, and imaginative advertising that portrayed the store as the arbiter of fashion—were all in place by 1910. Between 1910 and 1940, store officials refined their operations and established personnel offices to select, train, and monitor employees more efficiently. Yet, though they prospered, retailers worried that their formula for success saddled them with high fixed costs while their profits depended on external economic conditions and on unpredictable saleswomen and customers. A few stores opened suburban branches as more of the middle class moved to suburbs in the 1930s. Marshall Field's opened three suburban stores in the Chicago area, and B. Altman opened a branch in White Plains, New York, in 1930.

During World War II, labor shortages gave store managers a chance to lower costs by eliminating some customer services and introducing self-service. Mass movement of the urban population into suburbs after the war impelled retailers to open branches in shopping centers and malls. These suburban stores were usually smaller, more austere, and less service-oriented than the original stores downtown. Owners of department stores also began to rely more heavily on part-time employees. By 1980, nearly 75 percent of all retail employees worked only part-time. Because downtown stores usually suffered as their more affluent customers moved away, store officials either abandoned them altogether

One of the most famous department stores in the world, Macy's, has its headquarters in New York City's Herald Square.

or restructured them on the suburban model. Self-service helped department stores remain competitive in the face of new discount retailers like K-Mart, which came to dominate general merchandising in the 1960s and 1970s.

Department stores still capture the imagination of American consumers and hold a preeminent place in contemporary retailing. Their future seemed uncertain in the 1980s as discount department stores (e.g., K-Mart and Wal-Mart), specialty shops (e.g., The Limited, The Gap, and Talbot's), and "category killers" or discounted specialty superstores (e.g., Bed, Bath and Beyond; Sports Authority; and Home Depot) grabbed an increasingly large share of the retail market. Today, traditional department stores have remained profitable through corporate reorganization and consolidation. Most independently owned department stores have not survived, but national chain stores (e.g., Dillard's) and those owned by holding companies (e.g., May Department Stores and Federated Department Stores) are making dramatic comebacks. Corporate ownership enables stores to benefit from economies of scale in merchandising and planning. As cities renovate their downtowns, stores like Marshall Field's and Macy's have refurbished and modernized their older buildings. They price their merchandise to be competitive with discount stores, and they have begun to emphasize, once again, skilled selling and customer service. Nordstrom's attracted considerable attention in the late 1980s when it announced that its distinctive feature would be customer service.

Finally, as the leading advertisers in daily newspapers, department stores still set fashion trends. Though commentators have predicted that Internetmall, the Home Shopping Network, and QVC will make the department store obsolete, a former CEO of Macy's noted in 1995 that other types of stores do not know how to "do" fashion, while department stores are fashion experts. The *New York Times Magazine* of April 6, 1997, confirmed this view in a special series of articles entitled "The Store Strikes Back: The Store as Theater, Taste Machine, Billboard." Department stores will flourish into the twenty-first century, the series suggests, because many Americans who work alone, perhaps at a computer, and watch movies at home on their VCRs are eager for a public event or entertainment "experience." A visit to the mall, the redesigned glitzy department store, or the upscale specialty shop satisfies their needs for fantasy and pleasure just as the splendor and novelty of grand emporiums fascinated their great-grandparents a century ago.

—*Sarah S. Malino*

References

Abelson, Elaine S. *When Ladies Go A Thieving: Middle Class Shoplifters in the Victorian Department Store.* New York: Oxford University Press, 1989.

Benson, Susan Porter. *Counter Cultures: Saleswomen, Managers, and Customers in American Department Stores, 1890–1940.* Urbana: University of Illinois Press, 1986.

Bluestone, Barry, Patricia Hanna, Sarah Kuhn, and Laura Moore. *The Retail Revolution: Market Transformation, Investment and Labor in the Modern Department Store.* Boston: Auburn House, 1981.

Hendrikson, Robert. *The Grand Emporiums: The Illustrated History of the Great Department Stores.* New York: Stein and Day, 1979.

Leach, William. *Land of Desire: Merchants, Power and the Rise of a New American Culture.* New York: Pantheon, 1993.

The Depression and Cities

During the 1920s, America's largest cities experienced strong growth. With the end of large-scale immigration early in the decade, populations stabilized, and the plentiful jobs in cities provided social mobility to many families and individuals. Investment in office buildings, stores, factories, utilities, streets, and, especially, apartments and single-family houses added greatly to the urban infrastructure, supported a strong construction industry, and bolstered confidence in the future. After 1929, this optimism ebbed away, overwhelmed by a growing pessimism that discouraged long-term private investment.

The Depression's damage to large cities, suburbs, and towns varied according to their economic base. Most serious, in larger cities, was the collapse of the construction industry; new building starts fell to less than 10 percent of the annual average of the late 1920s. Although much necessary work was deferred, maintenance and repair of existing structures comprised over one-third of spending for construction by the private sector in the 1930s. Devastating was the disappearance of 2 million high-paying jobs in construction trades, along with the loss of profits and rents that abashed countless landlords and real estate investors.

Second came the general downturn in industry, especially heavy manufacturing. Steel and automobile production took the heaviest hits, along with railroads and coal mining. In these industries, the largest cities suffered somewhat less than smaller mill towns, mining camps, and railroad centers. Unemployment was a problem everywhere, but it was less severe among women, workers in industries that produced nondurable goods (such as food and clothing), services and sales, and government jobs. A sharp educational gradient meant that less-skilled men in inner cities had much higher rates of unemployment than those with high school and college educations who lived in the outer zones of cities and suburbs. Although suburbia stopped growing as rapidly, it suffered much less than central cities. While some of the jobless (especially African Americans) came to cities looking for relief, it appears that even more returned to family farms. For the first time ever recorded, the movement of the native-born population was away from cities and toward rural America.

The fiscal soundness of local governments was challenged by rising expenditures for relief and sharply declining tax collections. The Hoover administration encouraged state and local governments to expand public works projects as a way of providing jobs, and they complied in 1930 and 1931. While this expansion may have slowed the rise in unemployment, it was an expenditure that cities had to discontinue as they confronted falling tax revenues and the unwillingness of investors to buy municipal bonds. After 1933, new sales taxes and infusions of federal money helped relieve their fiscal distress to a degree.

While local relief focused on providing small amounts of cash or baskets of food and coal to the neediest, the federal programs launched during Hoover's administration and greatly expanded during the Roosevelt years tried to use massive construction projects to jump-start the economy and solve the unemployment crisis. The New Deal's alphabet agencies built and repaired public infrastructure dramatically, but they did little to further the recovery of the private sector. In sharp contrast to England, where the construction of private housing pulled the country out of its depression, American cities had little private construction or investment, and they languished in the economic doldrums even as their parks, sewers, airports, and municipal buildings were improved. In retrospect, the New Deal's investment in public infrastructure had only a small "multiplier" effect, in contrast to the high multiplier for jobs that private investment might have created. In other words, reconstructing the public infrastructure provided no economic benefits once the projects were completed.

Roosevelt himself had a magnetic appeal to city dwellers, especially poorer members of ethnic groups who received recognition, unions, relief jobs, and beer thanks to the president. Taxpayers, small business people, and the middle class voted for Roosevelt in 1936, but they turned against him sharply after the new recession of 1937–1938 seemed to belie his promises of recovery. As a result, Roosevelt found an entirely new use for city machines in his subsequent reelection campaigns. Traditionally, local bosses had minimized the voting turnout in order to guarantee reliable control of their wards and legislative districts. To carry the electoral college, however, Roosevelt needed massive majorities in large cities to overcome the hostility of suburbs and towns.

With Harry Hopkins as his majordomo, Roosevelt used the Works Progress Administration (WPA) as a national political machine from 1935 to 1942. Men on relief could get WPA jobs regardless of their politics, but local Democratic machines tightly controlled hundreds of thousands of well-paying supervisory jobs. The 3.5 million voters on relief payrolls during the 1936 election cast an overwhelming 82 percent of their ballots for Roosevelt. The vibrant labor unions, heavily based in cities, likewise did the utmost for their benefactor, voting 80 percent for him, as did Irish, Italian, and Jewish voters. In all, 70 percent of voters in the nation's 106 cities with populations greater than 100,000 voted for FDR in 1936, compared to his 59 percent elsewhere. In 1940, Roosevelt again won reelection thanks to the cities. In the North, cities larger than 100,000 gave Roosevelt 60 percent of their votes, while the rest of the North favored Wendell Willkie by a margin of 52 percent to 48 percent. The urban vote was just large enough to provide the critical margin in the electoral college.

With the beginning of full-scale mobilization for war during the summer of 1940, the cities revived. The new wartime economy pumped massive amounts of money into new factories and funded round-the-clock munitions production, guaranteeing a job to anyone who showed up at the factory gate.

—*Richard Jensen*

See also
New Deal: Urban Policy.
References
Argersinger, JoAnn E. *Toward a New Deal in Baltimore: People and Government in the Great Depression.* Chapel Hill: University of North Carolina Press, 1988.
Biles, Roger. *Big City Boss in Depression and War: Mayor Edward J. Kelly of Chicago.* DeKalb: Northern Illinois University Press, 1984.
Smith, Douglas L. *The New Deal in the Urban South.* Baton Rouge: Louisiana State University Press, 1988.
Trout, Charles H. *Boston, The Great Depression, and the New Deal.* New York: Oxford University Press, 1977.

Desegregation of Education

The paradox of the United States has always been the conflict between its general creed and the reality of its race relations. The Declaration of Independence and the U.S. Constitution set forth principles of human rights that have been contradicted by slavery, segregation, racial prejudice, and discrimination. After World War II, the federal government began to correct some of these injustices, and a crucial venue for these changes has been the public school.

Schools have been one focus of the movement for racial equality, and long after other issues of discrimination had been settled, courts continued to act frequently and forcefully with regard to education. Schools were touted as bridges across the separation between races, and the original goal of desegregation was to bring blacks and whites together. The "table of brotherhood," to quote Dr. Martin Luther King, Jr., was to be found in public school classrooms, lunchrooms, and athletic fields throughout the land.

At the heart of the transformation of the legal basis of race relations, and the status of black Americans, was the

Supreme Court's *Brown v. Board of Education* decision of 1954. *Brown* abolished the status of black Americans as legal pariahs and established the goal of eliminating discrimination and segregation nationwide. Northern cities and suburbs began to desegregate first by political, rather than legal, measures because no northern state had established segregation with law.

But in southern school districts, local educators slowed integration by implementing pupil-placement laws, freedom-of-choice plans, and "incremental desegregation" plans, such as desegregating one grade a year. Between 1954 and 1958, 11 southern states enacted 145 statutes to thwart the *Brown* ruling. At first, the delaying tactics had the desired effect as southern schools remained segregated. White parents in Alabama, Mississippi, and Georgia formally complied with the federal desegregation order but quickly applied to have their children reassigned under relevant new state laws. The state's "freedom of choice" laws allowed children to be transferred because of various "nonracial" factors such as the "psychological trauma" associated with attending a certain school, the possibility of disruption within the school, and the likelihood that whites would take economic retaliation by firing blacks, not hiring them, or not patronizing their businesses or services. By 1964, barely 12 percent of schools in the 11

southern states were integrated, and in Georgia, Alabama, and Mississippi the figure was closer to 2 percent.

The administration of President John F. Kennedy stimulated desegregation efforts and pressured the Justice Department to speed it up in the South. State institutions of higher education witnessed especially strong opposition by whites to federally enforced integration. A gun battle accompanied James Meredith's enrollment at the University of Mississippi in 1962, and the next summer, Governor George Wallace stood in the front door at the University of Alabama to prohibit even token integration there. After the murder of President Kennedy in 1963, the new president, Lyndon Johnson, told a joint session of Congress, "We have talked long enough in this country about equal rights. . . . It is now time to write the next chapter, and to write it in the books of law." In the decade following passage of the 1964 Civil Rights Act, the Justice Department initiated 500 school desegregation suits, and the Department of Health, Education and Welfare brought 600 more actions. Countless school districts were desegregated even though many parents reacted to federal orders by pulling their children out of public schools and enrolling them in private academies.

U.S. Supreme Court decisions continued to dismantle desegregation. In 1965, its decision in *Bradley v. Richmond*

Boys talking at a desegregated school in Berkeley, California, in 1971.

School Board outlawed plans that called for desegregating one grade a year, and its *Green v. Board of New Kent County* ruling prohibited "freedom of choice" plans in 1968. Throughout the 1960s, Congress continued to supply HEW officials with large federal education grants to entice reluctant school districts into compliance. The Civil Rights Division of the Justice Department updated its standards for integration, and school districts nationally dismantled dual school systems.

Richard Nixon's election to the presidency in 1968 changed the focus of desegregation efforts. Southerners resented the attention they were receiving from federal investigators, and Nixon sympathized by pointing his finger at the lack of school desegregation in northern cities (which had mostly voted Democratic on election day). Nixon's "Southern Strategy" nationalized desegregation with the goal of eliminating racial discrimination and establishing unitary school systems in every district of the country.

The Supreme Court handed down one of its most important decisions in 1971 in the case of *Swann v. Charlotte-Mecklenburg Board of Education.* In it, the Court upheld the plan of a local district court that used mathematical ratios as part of a plan to end racial separation in a school district. The Court ruled that a school board that had established school district boundaries on the basis of race (such as locating black schools in the middle of black neighborhoods and creating segregated feeder patterns) was guilty of *de facto* segregation. This finding foreshadowed the decision to declare the segregation of northern school districts unconstitutional. "Busing"—the transportation of students who lived in one part of a district to a school in another part to achieve racial balance—was an acceptable tool to remedy racial isolation.

The Court's decisions, coupled with the "go-slow" approach of the Nixon administration, made education, public schools, and busing the hottest issues of the 1972 presidential election. A groundswell of opposition in cities like Boston and Louisville led to many lawsuits and a rethinking of the federal role in desegregation. Parents resented the moralizing attitude of court orders that dictated pupil assignment, and busing was labeled "forced busing" for the way it moved children around, ignoring the wishes of parents in local communities. "White flight," defined as the withdrawal of white students from public schools to enroll in private schools, dramatically changed public school enrollments and finances.

Throughout the 1970s, national polls showed that the majority of Americans believed "integration should be brought about gradually" and that black groups and the federal government were "pushing too hard" for integration. By 1975, court rulings had limited busing to transportation within county boundaries and limited the time and distance children could travel to create integrated schools.

School systems shifted to magnet plans to attract students to bring about desegregation. In such plans, the targeted school population had freedom to choose among a wide range of educational alternatives as if they were operating in a marketplace, making decisions consistent with the goal of desegregation.

By the 1980s, the cry of the civil rights movement had changed from "We Shall Overcome" to "We Shall Hold Our Own." The Reagan administration's conservative policies on welfare and civil rights, coupled with falling test scores and safety disruptions in public schools, led to new thoughts about the federal government's role in school desegregation. The protest against rules enforced by the government and the escalating social costs in the 1980s meant that remedies of the past were insufficient for the problems ahead. The discussion of educational policy shifted from racial balance to academic achievement.

In 1982 a popular song with lyrics about racial harmony was recorded by Paul McCartney and Stevie Wonder. "Ebony and ivory," they sang, "live together in perfect harmony, side by side on my piano keyboard, Oh Lord, why don't we?" Cultural assimilation in the form of desegregation was begun in the public schools, but after 40 years of struggle, protest, and achievement, no chorus of racial harmony has issued from school systems across the nation.

—*J. David Woodard*

See also
Busing; Desegregation of Housing; White Flight.

References
Allport, Gordon. *The Nature of Prejudice.* Garden City, NY: Doubleday, 1958.
Coleman, James S., Sara D. Kelley, and John Moore. *Trends in School Desegregation, 1968–1973.* Washington, DC: Urban Institute, 1975.
Kluger, Richard. *Simple Justice.* New York: Knopf, 1975.
Orfield, Gary. *The Reconstruction of Southern Education.* New York: Wiley, 1969.
Pride, Richard A., and J. David Woodard. *The Burden of Busing.* Knoxville: University of Tennessee Press, 1985.

Desegregation of Housing

Racial desegregation of housing is the process whereby two or more racial groups are moving into and out of neighborhoods at a rate that maintains approximately proportional representation among the racial groups. Unlike segregation, the desegregation process is rare in most U.S. metropolitan areas. Desegregation implies that proportional numbers of each race reside in a neighborhood for an extended period of time. In practice, long-term desegregation seems elusive in the United States. Few neighborhoods in cities and suburbs that were once desegregated by the in-migration of blacks have remained desegregated over time.

America has achieved very little progress in housing desegregation despite passage of the Fair Housing Act of 1968. In fact, racially desegregated neighborhoods are the exception. It is estimated that in 1990 only 20 percent of Americans lived in desegregated neighborhoods.

Some progress toward the racial desegregation of neighborhoods has occurred in the last several years because the black middle class, to some degree, has moved to suburbs. But racial discrimination has continued to prevent a large percentage of the black middle class from participating in this movement, even when income is not a barrier.

If housing desegregation is to occur, there must be both strong antidiscrimination efforts and also strong economic incentives to encourage it. Antidiscrimination efforts must primarily be in the form of legal changes that affirm and expand the role of organizations and governments as collective vehicles to enforce the Fair Housing Act. Although individuals can be targets of discrimination in housing without realizing it, organizations and governments have a proven legal means of detecting discrimination that is not available to individuals. Effective detection of housing discrimination requires that an ongoing program of comprehensive and random fair housing audits be conducted throughout a metropolitan area. Given the subtle nature of housing discrimination, the audit is the only effective means of uncovering it.

The fair housing audit is a field survey to determine the extent of minority access to housing within a metropolitan area. It also assesses the impact of the federal Fair Housing Act. In the United States, the audit has been widely used since the act was passed in 1968. Originally, the audit was conducted by private, nonprofit fair housing agencies, but in 1978 the Department of Housing and Urban Development sponsored a nationwide audit that discovered widespread discrimination.

In a fair housing audit, two families, one black and one white, are matched in terms of social and economic characteristics and trained to pose as home seekers. Both families separately contact a real estate agent or landlord and attempt to purchase a home or rent an apartment. The treatment received by both families is compared to detect any differences. The extent of differential treatment indicates whether racial discrimination has occurred.

Discrimination exists if the black family is given less or different information than the white family. The most specific way of preventing racial integration is to deny blacks or other racial minorities access to information about the availability of housing. A carefully designed and managed fair housing audit controls for other factors so that any difference in treatment between the minority and white families must result from discrimination. The audit also controls for

characteristics of a housing agency by sending families to the same agency at about the same time.

Most analysts agree that for desegregation of housing to occur there must be incentives beyond simply a desire to live in a racially integrated neighborhood. Among the key incentives for desegregated housing by a minority population has been the desire for quality homes and a safe, quality environment, including good public schools, low crime rates, responsive police and fire departments, and regular garbage collection. These amenities are more often found in predominantly white neighborhoods in newer suburbs. Evidence suggests that a higher percentage of residents who live in mostly white suburban neighborhoods think that municipal services are excellent than is the case for residents who live in mostly black neighborhoods in central cities. Thus, quality housing and quality municipal services are strong incentives for blacks to move toward desegregated suburban housing.

A second group of incentives is associated with employment opportunities. Since many jobs are relocating from central cities to suburbs, blacks who seek work or desire to reduce commuting time between home and job can maximize their opportunities by moving to mostly white suburbs. Thus, the incentives for desegregation are not racial composition per se but social and economic byproducts of racial composition.

Among the key incentives to desegregate housing for a white or majority population has been an opportunity to purchase low-cost homes in declining inner-city neighborhoods. This process, often called gentrification, involves the movement of whites with higher incomes into predominantly black inner-city neighborhoods. In sum, the incentives for both blacks and whites are social and economic, and desegregated housing is their side effect.

Advocates of fair housing have recognized the importance of these incentives and have incorporated them into integration programs. In the affirmative integration incentive method, for example, economic incentives are used as a primary tool to counteract racial steering and to encourage home seekers to choose housing without being constrained by the effects of previous housing discrimination. One of the key economic incentives is low interest rates.

An affirmative incentive loan program is designed to serve both black and white home buyers. This program does not set aside a quota of loans for particular racial groups, and participation in the program is voluntary. The program merely gives people with enough resources to buy a house an incentive to purchase in an area where their own race is underrepresented. Home buyers possess the freedom to participate or not, and they are not restricted as to where they can live if they choose not to participate. These incentives may include low-interest loans to cover part of the down payment or any needed maintenance. Unfortunately, affirmative incentive loan programs have been adopted in only a few cities in the United States, such as Southville, Michigan, and Shaker Heights, outside of Cleveland, Ohio, so they have not really had the opportunity to accomplish what they might.

—*Joe T. Darden*

See also
Housing Segregation; Racism and Discrimination.
References
Darden, Joe T. "Residential Segregation of Blacks in Metropolitan Areas of Michigan, 1960–1990." In *The State of Black Michigan: 1992,* 13–24. East Lansing: Urban Affairs Programs, Michigan State University, 1992.
Darden, Joe T., Harriet Duleep, and George Galster. "Civil Rights in Metropolitan America." *Journal of Urban Affairs* 14 (1992): 469–496.
Leigh, Wilhelmina, and James McGhee. "A Minority Perspective on Residential Racial Integration." In John Goering, ed., *Housing Desegregation and Federal Policy,* 31–42. Chapel Hill: University of North Carolina Press, 1986.
Saltman, Juliet. *A Fragile Movement: The Struggle for Neighborhood Stabilization.* New York: Greenwood Press, 1990.
U.S. Department of Housing and Urban Development. *1978 Survey of the Quality of Community Life: A Data Book.* Washington, DC: Government Printing Office, 1978.

Deviance

Deviance is a subarea of sociology that incorporates all violations of norms, from improper dress and jaywalking to rape and murder. Criminology and penology, in turn, are subareas of deviance. Deviance, with its intellectual twin, social control, lies at the heart of sociology, for no human group can exist without norms. Norms make social life possible by making behavior predictable. Without norms, social chaos would exist. Norms lay out the basic guidelines for everyday life, for how people play their roles and how they interact with others. In short, norms allow for social order, a group's customary social arrangements. Because social life is based on those arrangements, deviance is often seen as threatening because it undermines predictability, one of the foundations of social life.

A central proposition of deviance theorists is that deviance itself is not an act; it is the reactions to some act that make the act deviant. In other words, people's behaviors must be viewed from within the framework of the culture in which they take place. Because different groups have different norms, what is deviant to some groups is not deviant to others. This principle of relativity holds within societies as well as across cultures. Thus, acts acceptable in one culture—or in one group within a society—may be considered deviant in another culture, or by another group within the same society.

Unlike most of the general public, sociologists use the term *deviance* nonjudgmentally to refer to acts that receive a generally negative response. Their use of the term is not an evaluation, either negative or positive, about the behavior being examined. To sociologists, deviance is not some rare, exotic behavior. Rather, everyone is a deviant of one kind or another, for everyone violates norms from time to time.

To be considered deviant, a person does not even have to do anything overtly. People may be considered deviant because they possess attributes such as blindness, deafness, mental retardation, physical deformity, and obesity. These characteristics violate norms of appearance and ability. Membership in some groups, even though it is involuntary, can also bring stigma, such as having AIDS or being the brother of a rapist. This stigma can become a person's master status, defining him or her as deviant, a status that cuts across all other statuses that the person occupies.

Reacting to deviance is vital to group welfare, for groups need boundaries in order to continue claiming a unique identity. Disapproval of deviance, called negative sanctions, ranges from frowns and gossip for breaking folkways (minor norms) to imprisonment and capital punishment for breaking mores or laws (major norms). In contrast, positive sanctions—from smiles to formal prizes—are used to reward people for conforming to norms.

While psychologists and sociobiologists explain deviance by seeking reasons within individual makeup and think that characteristics such as genetic predispositions or personality disorders lead individuals to become deviant, sociologists look for answers in factors outside the individual, assuming that something in the environment influences people to become deviant. Sociologists look for social influences that recruit some people rather than others to break norms. To account for why people commit crimes, for example, sociologists examine such external influences as socialization, subcultural membership, and social class.

Certainly no single factor causes deviance. Causes differ according to people's background experiences and internal predilections that arise from either biology, social experiences, or a combination of the two. Sometimes, even deviance causes deviance.

Three sociological perspectives have been developed to account for deviance—symbolic interactionism, functionalism, and conflict theory. A basic principle of symbolic interactionism is that people interpret social life through the symbols they have learned. From their associates, people learn to deviate or conform to society's norms. There is nothing mysterious about the process; learning deviance is like learning anything else, which contradicts the theory that deviance is biological or due to pathological personalities. Consequently, in the subtheory called differential association, family, friends, schools, churches, and neighborhoods are highly significant, and it comes as no surprise that delinquents tend to come from neighborhoods in which their peers are involved in crime. Thus, in a neighborhood where an insult is defined as a threat to manliness and honor requires a man to stand up to an insult, an adolescent boy is more likely to fight than an adolescent who grows up in a group that considers fighting unmanly.

Some sociologists do acknowledge that internal states can influence behavior. In one form of symbolic interaction theory, control theory, everyone is thought to be propelled toward deviance—by temptations, inner drives, hostilities, resentments, pressures from peers, and so on. But two control systems—inner control and outer control—work against the motivations to deviate. The inner control system is a person's ability to withstand external pressure. Inner controls include internalized morality—conscience, ideas of right and wrong, and reluctance to violate religious principles. Inner controls also include fear of punishment, feelings of integrity, and desires to be a "good" person. The more people feel attached to society, the more effective are their inner controls. The outer control system consists of groups and individuals—such as family, friends, and the police—who influence people to stay away from deviant behavior. The likelihood that anyone will deviate from social norms depends on the strength of these two control systems relative to the strength of the pushes and pulls toward deviant behavior. If control systems are weak, deviance results. If they are strong enough, however, individuals do not commit deviant acts. The key to learning strong inner controls is socialization, especially during childhood.

Symbolic interactionists have also developed a labeling perspective, which focuses on the significance of the labels (tags, names, reputations) given to people. Labels tend to become internalized, to become a part of people's self-concept, which helps to set them on paths that propel them to, or divert them from, deviance. Most people resist being labeled deviant, and they develop various strategies to prevent being tagged with a deviant label. A few people, however, revel in a deviant identity. Motorcycle outlaws and many teenagers, for example, make certain by their appearance that no one misses their deliberate status outside the dominant norms. Their status among fellow members of a subculture, within which they are inveterate conformists, is vastly more important than any status outside it.

Functionalists examine the functions and dysfunctions of deviance. While most people are upset by deviance, especially crime, and assume that society would be better off without it, functionalists note that deviance, including crime, is functional for society. Deviance clarifies moral boundaries, promotes social unity (as people react to a deviance that is seen as threatening to the group), and promotes social change (when people who push beyond the acceptable ways of doing things gain enough support for the behavior to become acceptable).

Functionalists also examine how social values produce deviance. The industrialized world needs to locate and train the most talented people of every generation—whether born in wealth or in poverty—so that they can perform the key technical jobs of modern society. When children are born, no one knows who will have the ability to become dentists, nuclear physicists, or engineers. To get the most talented people to compete with one another, society tries to motivate everyone to strive for success. It does this by arousing discontent—making people dissatisfied with what they have so that they will try to "better" themselves. Although everyone is socialized into desiring cultural goals (the legitimate objectives held out to everyone, such as owning material possessions), many are denied access to the institutionalized means (socially acceptable ways) of achieving those goals, such as gaining an education or acquiring a good job. With paths blocked, they often turn to deviant avenues to pursue the goals.

Conflict theorists see power and social inequality as the primary characteristics of society. To them, the most fundamental division in industrial society is between the few who own the means of production and the many who do not, those who sell their labor and the privileged few who buy it. Those who buy labor, and thereby control workers, make up the capitalist class; those who sell their labor form the working class. Toward the most depressed end of the working class is the marginal working class, people with few skills, who are subject to unexpected layoffs and whose jobs are low paying, part-time, or seasonal. Unemployment and poverty mark this class, and from its ranks come most of the prisoners in the United States. Desperate, these people commit street crimes, and because their crimes threaten the social order, they are severely punished.

According to conflict theorists, the idea that law is a social institution that operates impartially and objectively administers a code shared by everyone is a cultural myth maintained and promoted by the upper classes. To conflict theorists, the law is an instrument of repression, a tool designed to maintain the powerful in their privileged positions. Because the working class holds the potential to rebel and overthrow the existing social order, they must be carefully controlled. When its members get out of line, they are arrested, tried, and imprisoned.

From the perspective of conflict theory, then, the criminal justice system does not focus on the owners of corporations and the harm they cause with billowing pollution, unsafe products, and price manipulations but, instead, directs its energies against violations by lower classes. The small penalties imposed for crimes committed by the powerful are typical of a legal system designed to mask injustice, control workers, and ultimately stabilize the social order. From this perspective, law enforcement is simply a cultural device through which the capitalist class carries out self-protective and repressive policies.

—*James M. Henslin*

See also
Bohemianism; Greenwich Village.
References
Becker, Howard S. *Outsiders: Studies in the Sociology of Deviance.* New York: Free Press, 1966.
Durkheim, Emile. *The Division of Labor in Society.* George Simpson, trans. New York: Free Press, 1993.
Goffman, Erving. *Asylums: Essays on the Social Situation of Mental Patients and Other Inmates.* Chicago: Aldine, 1961.
Henslin, James M. "Deviance and Social Control." In *Sociology: A Down-to-Earth Approach,* 193–221. 2d ed. Boston: Allyn & Bacon, 1995.
Hirschi, Travis. *Causes of Delinquency.* Berkeley: University of California Press, 1969.
Merton, Robert K. *Social Theory and Social Structure.* Enlarged ed. New York: Free Press, 1968.
Miller, Walter B. "Lower Class Culture as a Generating Milieu of Gang Delinquency." *Journal of Social Issues* 14 (1958): 5–19.
Reckless, Walter C. *The Crime Problem.* 5th ed. New York: D. Appleton, 1973.
Sutherland, Edwin H. *Criminology.* Philadelphia: J. B. Lippincott, 1924.
Sutherland, Edwin H., Donald R. Cressey, and David F. Luckenbill. *Principles of Criminology.* 11th ed. Dix Hills, NY: General Hall, 1992.

Dinkins, David N. (1925–)

David N. Dinkins was elected mayor of New York City in 1989, becoming the first African American to win the city's highest elective office. He was born in Trenton, New Jersey, where his father owned a barber shop and a successful real estate business. After serving briefly in the Marines at the age of 17, Dinkins attended Howard University and graduated in 1950 with an honors degree in mathematics. He then moved to Harlem where he married Joyce Burrows, the daughter of a New York State assemblyman, and became a member of the Carver Democratic Club. In 1956 he earned a law degree from Brooklyn Law School and began the practice of law.

In 1965 Dinkins was elected to the New York State Assembly and served one year before reapportionment eliminated his district. He was elected Democratic district leader in 1967, a position he held for 20 years. In 1970 he became counsel to the Board of Elections, and in 1972 he was appointed to the board itself. One year later, in 1973, he was forced to withdraw his name as nominee for deputy mayor because he had failed to file federal, state, and city income taxes for four years. In 1975, after paying his back taxes, Dinkins was appointed city clerk, an office he held for 10 years.

Dinkins ran unsuccessfully for Manhattan borough president in 1977 and 1981, but he won the office on his third attempt in 1985. In 1989, he declared his candidacy for mayor against the three-term incumbent, Edward I. Koch, declaring his desire to restore racial harmony to the city. He defeated Koch in the Democratic primary and won the general election against Republican-Liberal Rudolph Giuliani by a narrow margin of 917,544 (50 percent) to 870,464 (48 percent). In 1993, Giuliani defeated Dinkins in a rematch by a similarly slim margin of 903,114 (51 percent) to 858,868 (48 percent). A coalition of African Americans, Hispanics, and a small but crucial segment of liberal white voters, mostly Jewish, provided Dinkins's electoral support.

Supporters praised Dinkins's commitment to minority causes and the dignity he provided his office with courteous demeanor and elegant attire. Critics expressed disappointment that race riots occurred in Crown Heights, Brooklyn, during his administration, and they accused him of applying a double standard that favored minorities and of a general lack of leadership.

—*Chris McNickle*

Reference
McNickle, Chris. *To Be Mayor of New York: Ethnic Politics in the City.* New York: Columbia University Press, 1993.

Disneyland

In the late 1930s, Walt Disney wanted to build a kiddieland park structured around his cartoon characters adjacent to his movie studio north of Los Angeles. The idea grew from unsatisfying visits to local amusement parks with his young daughters and especially from his intense dislike for Coney Island and its disorganized, garish, honky-tonk atmosphere. Disney envisioned a new kind of park—a clean, safe, friendly place where children and adults could have fun together. During World War II, when the studio moved to Burbank, he wanted to include an amusement area, but the heavy new investments coupled with the loss of overseas film markets ruled that out. In 1948, Disney's longtime fascination for miniature trains provided some planning and direction as he wanted an actual railroad to define the perimeter of the park. That same year, he wrote down his initial ideas.

What Disney had in mind for his unnamed amusement park was an extremely sentimental and nostalgic place where children could experience the material culture of past generations and where adults could relive their own or their parents' childhood. The park was to have a Main Village, a Western Village, an Indian Village, an Old Farm, and a Carnival section, and people would be able to travel from one theme area to another via a horsecar, stagecoach, surrey, or buckboard.

Sleeping Beauty's Castle, the central landmark at Disneyland, in Anaheim, California.

corporations to finance exhibits at Disneyland and sold licenses to merchandising companies for products pertaining to the park's themes or Disney films. Built on a 160-acre orange grove in Anaheim, California, the population center of southern California, the park opened on July 17, 1955.

Disneyland was the embodiment of one man's prepossession toward America's most important beliefs, values, ideals, and symbols. In the creation of a new type of amusement park, Disney essentially combined three different elements—his boyhood experiences in the rural Midwest, his famous cartoon and feature film characters, and his vision of the future. In the Main Street theme area he sought to re-create the look and sense of a small town in middle America at the turn of the century. Fantasyland brought to life children's stories and cartoon characters from his animated movies. In Adventureland and Frontierland, entertainment was structured around favorite people, places, or motifs from Disney's feature films. Futuristic rides and attractions presented in Tomorrowland, based on state-of-the-art technology, underscored Disney's optimistic view of the world and Americans' basic belief in progress, pragmatism, applied science, and materialism.

During Disneyland's first fiscal year, 4 million people passed through its gates, and the park became a premier tourist attraction for both Americans and foreigners. One of the most important representations of America, its characters and attractions were recognized around the globe. In the wake of Disneyland's impressive commercial success, a plethora of other corporate theme parks (Six Flags, Great Adventure, Great America) appeared all around the country. Kings Dominion near Richmond, with its cartoon characters from the Hanna-Barbera television shows, imitated Disney's formula more directly. Virtually every theme park today has re-created some kind of "old time" American urban or rural scene, and numerous towns and cities have poured large sums of money into downtown areas to restore a nineteenth-century look to buildings and shops, to "Disney-fy" their own main streets.

The viability of these other theme parks, although none was as well-off financially as Disneyland, breathed new life into America's outdoor amusement industry and actually increased the demand for Disney-built parks. In 1971, Walt Disney World opened in Florida, followed by Epcot Center in 1982, and Tokyo Disneyland a year later. The 5,000-acre Euro-Disneyland outside Paris, the first phase of which opened in 1992, was supposed to become the capstone to the Disney corporation's commercial empire. Plans to build Disney's America, an ambitious park committed to the 1951 concept, in rural Virginia were scrapped in the face of strong opposition by environmentalists, and corporate officials are now looking at a new site. Walt Disney's view of America and techniques of entertainment—a unique blend of ideas, values,

In 1951, Disney decided to call his park "Walt Disney's America" and focus on highlights of American history. At the same time, he was working on another project for a traveling exhibit called "Disneylandia," miniature stage sets with cartoon characters depicting American folklore. Later that year, Disney met with network executives in New York to discuss entering television. He had no visual material with him but discussed his ideas for a new kind of amusement park at length. No agreement for a television series was reached since none of the executives would commit themselves to help finance the park. Nevertheless, by 1952 a master plan for "Walt Disneyland" had evolved, and Disney formed WED Enterprises, a personal corporation with the initials of his own name, to design the park and keep its activities separate from the studio. In 1953, the park was called "Disneyland," and an artist's sketch and written materials reveal various theme areas encircled by a one-third scale railroad. Once again, Disney turned to television for financing and made a deal with ABC for cash, guaranteed loans, and a weekly series in which he would be free to promote the park. To meet the $11 million construction costs, Disney contracted with major norms, symbols, and technology—can be termed "Americana Disneylandia" and may very well be the foundation of a cross-national culture of outdoor amusement in the twenty-first century.

—*Raymond M. Weinstein*

References

Bright, Randy. *Disneyland: Inside Story.* New York: Henry N. Abrams, 1987.

Miller, Diane Disney. *The Story of Walt Disney.* New York: Henry Holt, 1957.

Schickel, Richard. *The Disney Version: The Life, Times, Art, and Commerce of Walt Disney.* New York: Simon and Schuster, 1968.

Thomas, Bob. *Walt Disney: An American Original.* New York: Simon and Schuster, 1976.

Weinstein, Raymond M. "Disneyland and Coney Island: Reflections on the Evolution of the Modern Amusement Park." *Journal of Popular Culture* 26 (1992): 131–164.

Distribution of Wealth

Distribution of wealth refers to the allocation of property in a given place at a particular time. It measures the concentration of wealth at any one moment and can also indicate if the ownership of wealth is becoming more concentrated or egalitarian (that is, widely distributed) over time. The distribution of wealth is often defined as the amount of property owned by each individual (or family or household) relative to the total wealth in a society. Since the distribution of wealth summarizes differences in wealth owning among individuals, it is often used synonymously with the term *wealth inequality.*

The most common method economists use to measure the inequality, or distribution, of wealth is to calculate the percentages of the total wealth owned by selected percentages of a sample population. To do this, they rank individuals according to their wealth and report the shares of the total wealth that are owned by given proportions of the population—for example, the top 1, 5, and 10 percent of wealth holders own what percentage of the total wealth.

Studies of the inequality of wealth often analyze the demographic and economic correlates of individual wealth holding and how these correlates affect inequality. These studies agree that the most important demographic characteristic in determining wealth holding is age; typically, wealth increases with age. For example, in 1953, men older than 50 were more than twice as likely as younger men to have more than $60,000 of total assets. Income generally increases with age, and people tend to save while they are employed and then consume their savings after retirement.

In addition to age, occupation and nativity also affect the ownership of wealth. Professionals and merchants generally have higher incomes than manual and unskilled laborers, and they tend to be overrepresented among the wealthy. Historically, immigrants to the United States arrived with little or no wealth. Some recent studies have found, however, that the income of immigrants increases more rapidly than that of the native-born, controlling for other factors, and perhaps mitigating immigrants' initial disadvantage in wealth holding.

In addition to characteristics of individuals, characteristics of the economy affect both the degree of wealth inequality at any particular time and its trend over time. For example, wealth is generally more concentrated in large cities than in rural areas. One possible explanation is related to Adam Smith's notion that the division of labor is limited by the extent of the market. The economies of large cities are generally more developed than those of smaller areas, and the potential gains from specializing in certain economic activities are greater. As a result, large cities usually have a more diverse occupational structure with more specialized professionals and large merchants. The share of the total wealth owned by the largest wealth holders is therefore usually higher in large cities than in less densely populated areas.

Economic historians have long known that the distribution of wealth has been highly unequal throughout American history; a small percentage of the population has always owned a disproportionately large share of the wealth. Yet it is nearly impossible to determine long-term trends in the inequality of wealth because there are no consistent, representative data for extended periods of time. It is possible, however, to survey a number of studies to understand wealth inequality in different periods.

Estimates of wealth before 1850 most often come from inventories of probated estates. Evidence from these inventories for the American colonies in 1774 indicates that the wealthiest 1 percent of people who owned any wealth at all possessed 13 percent of the total, and the wealthiest 10 percent of individuals owned roughly half of the total wealth. Although figures calculated from records of taxes on real estate in 1798 are not directly comparable, they present similar estimates of wealth inequality in the late eighteenth century.

Ratios of the concentration of wealth derived from probate inventories in Boston between 1650 and 1861 suggest that wealth was more concentrated in Boston than it was in the nation as a whole. These data also suggest that the distribution of wealth in Boston remained fairly stable from 1650 until about 1800, but that inequality in Boston increased dramatically in the first half of the nineteenth century. In other words, a smaller part of the population owned a greater share of the wealth. Though the evidence suggests that wealth inequality increased in Boston during the first half of the nineteenth century, it is not clear whether this increase mirrored a national trend; most of the available evidence suggests that if any increase in wealth inequality occurred in the country as a whole, it was probably slight.

The federal censuses of 1850, 1860, and 1870 are the only ones ever taken in the entire United States that asked questions about individual wealth and property. Concentration ratios constructed from samples of the 1860 census show that the wealthiest 1 percent of adult men in the United States owned 29 percent of the nation's aggregate wealth that year, and the poorest 50 percent of the population owned less than 1 percent of the nation's wealth. The data also indicate that wealth was significantly more concentrated in urban America than in the rural North. For example, the wealthiest 1 percent of men in urban areas owned fully half of the urban wealth, while the wealthiest 1 percent of men in rural areas owned only 12 percent of the wealth in the rural North. Moreover, the wealthiest 10 percent of men in cities owned 90 percent of the total wealth, whereas the wealthiest tenth of men in the rural North owned less than half of the rural wealth.

In several large American cities in 1860, wealth was extremely highly concentrated. The richest 1 percent of men in these cities owned at least 45 percent, and perhaps as much as 65 percent, of the total wealth in those cities. This is about twice as large a proportion as the wealthiest 1 percent owned nationally.

Since the federal census has not collected information about individual wealth and property since 1870, reliable evidence about wealth holding and wealth inequality during the late nineteenth and early twentieth centuries is scarce. Estimates of wealth inequality in the twentieth century have, however, been constructed from estate tax returns. The concentration ratios suggest that wealth inequality decreased markedly during the twentieth century. For example, the wealth possessed by the richest 1 percent of individuals declined from 38 percent of the aggregate wealth in 1922 to 27 percent in 1958, and 19 percent in 1976. When the present value of pension benefits is included in the calculation of wealth holding, the share of wealth owned by the richest 1 percent of individuals declines even further, from 38 percent of the total in 1922 to 21 percent by 1958 and 14 percent in 1976.

Several recent analyses have suggested that this trend reversed during the 1980s and that the distribution of wealth has become somewhat more unequal since then. This recent increase appears to result from demographic changes in the population as well as from increasing inequality in the distribution of incomes during this period. It remains to be seen whether these changes in the distribution of wealth are temporary or are the beginning of a trend toward increasing wealth inequality.

—*Steven Herscovici*

References

Feldstein, Martin S. "Social Security and the Distribution of Wealth." *Journal of the American Statistical Association* 71 (1976): 800–807.

Gallman, Robert E. "Trends in the Size Distribution of Wealth in the Nineteenth Century: Some Speculations." In Lee Soltow, ed., *Six Papers on the Size Distribution of Wealth and Income Studies in Income and Wealth,* 1–30. New York: Columbia University Press, 1969.
Herscovici, Steven. "The Distribution of Wealth in Nineteenth Century Boston: Inequality among Natives and Immigrants, 1860." *Explorations in Economic History* 30 (1993): 321–335.
Kuznets, Simon. "Economic Growth and Income Inequality." *American Economic Review* 45 (1955): 1–28.
———. *Shares of Upper Income Groups in Income and Savings.* New York: Columbia University Press, 1953.
Lampman, Robert J. *The Share of Top Wealth-Holders in National Wealth, 1922–1956.* Princeton, NJ: Princeton University Press, 1962.
Main, Gloria L. "Inequality in Early America: The Evidence from Probate Records of Massachusetts and Maryland." *Journal of Interdisciplinary History* 7 (1977): 558–581.
Miller, Herman P. *Income Distribution in the United States.* Washington, DC: Government Printing Office, 1966.
Pope, Clayne L. "Households on the American Frontier: The Distribution of Income and Wealth in Utah, 1850–1900." In David W. Galenson, ed., *Markets in History: Economic Studies of the Past,* 148–189. New York: Cambridge University Press, 1989.
Shorrocks, Anthony F. "Inequality between Persons." In John Eatwell, Murray Milgane, and Peter Newman, eds., *The New Palgrave Dictionary of Economics,* vol. 2, 821–824. London: Macmillan , 1987.
Soltow, Lee. "Distribution of Income and Wealth." In Glenn Porter, ed., *Encyclopedia of American Economic History,* 1087–1119. New York: Scribners, 1980.
———. *Men and Wealth in the United States, 1850–1870.* New Haven, CT: Yale University Press, 1975.
———. "The Wealth, Income, and Social Class of Men in Large Northern Cities of the United States in 1860." In James D. Smith, ed., *The Personal Distribution of Income and Wealth, Studies in Income and Wealth,* 233–276. New York: Columbia University Press, 1975.
———. "Wealth Inequality in the United States in 1798 and 1860." *Review of Economics and Statistics* 66 (1984): 444–451.
Weicher, John C. *The Distribution of Wealth: Increasing Inequality?* Washington, DC: AEI Press, 1996.
Wilcox, Nathaniel T. "Understanding the Distribution of Urban Wealth: The United States in 1860." In Robert W. Fogel, Ralph A. Galantine, and Richard L. Manning, eds., *Without Consent or Contract: The Rise and Fall of American Slavery: Evidence and Methods,* 419–458. New York, W. W. Norton, 1992.
Wolff, Edward N. "Changing Inequality of Wealth." *American Economic Review* 82 (1992): 552–558.

Division of Labor

A key concept in theories of urban development and change, the division of labor is central to understanding the structure and function of cities. As a principle element of ecological theory, it has been employed both to explain the internal structure of individual cities and the national and international urban hierarchy. As an empirical fact of city life, the division of labor—in all of its dimensions—has evolved significantly with time. And in recent years, dramatic new developments may call for its place in metropolitan society to be reconceptualized.

At its base, the concept itself is quite simple: the labor necessary to perform any complex task is broken into smaller assignments that can be performed better or with greater efficiency. Classic examples are drawn from manufacturing, where a wide variety of products once made by individual craftsmen were reorganized so that individual components were produced separately by less-skilled workers. The specialization that resulted allowed for the application of new technologies and the achievement of higher productivity. This, according to mainstream urban theory, is directly analogous to what occurs on a somewhat larger scale in cities.

Certain prerequisites exist for the development of a highly complex division of labor. Perhaps the most imperative is a market large enough to warrant the higher levels of production typically necessary to realize efficiencies, and to sustain the unusual activities that often accompany the division of complex tasks into component parts. It is an axiom of ecological theory, in that case, that the division of labor is most highly developed in large cities, where local markets can support a wide variety of specialized products and services. It also follows that large cities, with highly developed and specialized productive enterprises, can often furnish goods and services more efficiently than smaller communities. Thus a relatively stable "urban hierarchy" has evolved over time, dictated by city size and command of regional hinterlands, and defined by an array of specialized functions emanating from the larger metropolitan areas.

Historically, technology has played a critical role in the evolution of the division of labor and the urban hierarchy, particularly for centers of manufacturing. Pittsburgh rose to national prominence as an urban center because of the steel industry (as did such smaller places as Gary, Indiana, and Birmingham, Alabama), and Detroit grew with the automobile industry. With industrialization, cities themselves began to specialize in certain productive activities, and an interurban division of labor developed. While most cities today sustain a wide variety of economic activities, many also specialize in certain products and services—traded to regional, national, or even international markets—which support the local economy.

The division of labor also has figured significantly in the internal structure of cities and the evolution of a distinctively urban cultural milieu. Classical models of urban spatial organization, such as Ernest Burgess's theory of concentric zones, held that residential areas of the industrial city were built around productive activities. Working-class neighborhoods, in that case, were clustered around factory districts, while more affluent groups lived in close proximity to the central business district or in more remote areas, arrayed along transportation lines leading into the city. Burgess and other observers of the urban scene noted that these

patterns of settlement were closely linked to social status distinctions, which themselves grew more complex as the division of labor in large cities became more refined. Eventually, Louis Wirth—in his famous article "Urbanism as a Way of Life"—noted that the constantly evolving division of labor undermined traditional status indicators, making status itself something subject to constant redefinition in the urban environment.

Other commentators have noted that status distinctions may be related to the division of labor in yet other ways. Members of such low status groups as racial or linguistic minorities and women have been relegated historically to low skill or poorly compensated jobs, a tendency aggravated by the fact of residential segregation along lines of race and ethnicity in American cities. In these and similar instances, the division of labor is often seen as less a function of productive efficiency than the maintenance of prevailing patterns of authority and privilege.

In contemporary metropolitan systems, such questions of prerogative are frequently associated with distinctions between central cities and their surrounding suburbs. New transportation and communications technologies have made central locations less critical to many productive activities. As industry has moved away from central cities, business districts have specialized in a new assortment of service functions, many of them revolving around financial affairs. At the same time, suburban communities have benefited from rapid growth, shifting the balance of power in many metropolitan communities away from core cities. The result is a newly evolving metropolitan division of labor, with particularly critical implications for larger cities.

Today, many cities struggle with the challenge of adapting their workforces and institutional infrastructures to meet the demands of these rapidly changing conditions. In this regard, the constantly evolving division of labor continues to play a fundamental role in the evolution of American cities and suburbs.

—*John L. Rury*

References
Blau, Peter M. *Inequality and Heterogeneity: A Primitive Theory of Social Structure.* New York: Free Press, 1977.
Gottdiener, Mark. *The Social Production of Urban Space.* Austin: University of Texas Press, 1985.
Hawley, Amos H. *Human Ecology: A Theory of Community Structure.* New York: Ronald Press, 1950.

Downing, Andrew Jackson (1815–1852)

Andrew Jackson Downing was the father of American "landscape architecture," a term he himself coined. Downing greatly influenced the spread of picturesque landscape design and earned a national reputation as the "apostle of taste."

As early as 1832, he advocated "landscape gardening," then in its infancy in the United States; and through his prolific writings and many disciples he bequeathed the profession and the discipline as his legacy.

Downing had as much academic preparation as then existed, having studied classical antiquities and "Drawing, Landscape, and Perspective" at an academy. He developed horticultural expertise in his father's nurseries in Newburgh, New York, which he would later inherit and manage with his brother. His book, *The Fruits and Fruit Trees of America* (1845), won wide acclaim, but his attention soon turned from arboriculture to landscape aesthetics.

Downing captivated the country's cultural elite, who drafted him to design their estates along the Hudson River, then a Mecca for artists and writers like Thomas Cole and William Cullen Bryant who sought picturesque and pastoral nature, scenic views associated with national values. Art and nature balanced, they believed, had spiritual powers; and Downing preached the gospel of naturalism, moral philosophy set in place through architectural "embellishments" in "harmony of expression with the landscape." He rejected formalism in favor of "highly graceful" sinuous lines to preserve and augment the "genius of place."

In 1848, Downing declared his mission was to "teach men the beauty and value of rural life." He did this by writing four widely read books that went through multiple editions: *A Treatise on the Theory and Practice of Landscape Gardening Adapted to North America* (1841), *Cottage Residences; or a Series of Designs for Rural Cottages, and Cottage Villas and Their Gardens and Grounds* (1842), *The Architecture of Country Houses* (1850), and *Rural Essays* (1853). As editor of *The Horticulturist: A Journal of Rural Art and Rural Taste* (1846–1852), he won further acclaim.

Downing's collaboration with the architect Alexander Jackson Davis (1803–1892) sparked the Romantic revival—Gothic, Italianate, Swiss, and Flemish—for domestic structures from simple cottages to elaborate villas. His "passion," wrote one contemporary, was "improving" the "homes of The Many." He crusaded to democratize taste and spread gentility to everyone in the name of "social progress" and "civilization." Although he thought that taste would prevent replicating the hierarchical class structure of the Old World, Downing drew inspiration from eighteenth-century English aesthetic philosophers and their successors as he sought to stabilize the young and restless society of the United States.

By 1842, he was advertising "professional" design services in periodicals, and his fee was $20 a day plus travel expenses. His work extended beyond domestic properties, however, and he incorporated the "influence of the beautiful" into his designs for the grounds of the New York and New Jersey Lunatic Asylums. Although he was disappointed when the Massachusetts Horticultural Society could not implement the plans he had prepared in 1847 for the Boston Public Garden, he recruited the English architect Calvert Vaux to be his partner in 1850 as his commissions expanded.

In championing the "rural," Downing was anything but anti-urban. At that time, the term *rural* referred to what Leo Marx has called "middle landscapes." Downing believed that bringing nature into and around dense, burgeoning cities would be a civilizing force. He lavishly praised the designs of the "rural" cemeteries that were founded in city after city following the example of Boston's Mount Auburn Cemetery (1831), and Downing noted how these cemetery landscapes were the "rage" as "pleasure grounds" for salutary, passive recreation. The "rural," the "natural," or the "modern" style of landscape gardening, he argued, could refine "coarse" cities and "improve" new neighborhoods surrounding them—the origin of suburban aesthetics.

The Horticulturist served as a pulpit from which Downing advocated public libraries, lyceums, galleries, museums, and schools. In an 1851 article titled "The New-York Park," he pleaded for "spacious" parks and gardens accessible to residents of the city. His efforts produced state legislation to fund an unprecedented public works project, Central Park. Had Downing not met an untimely death at the age of 36 in a steamboat accident on the Hudson River, he almost certainly would have collaborated with his partner Vaux as the landscape gardener–architect team for its design. At his death, he left uncompleted an urban design project for Washington, D.C., commissioned by President Millard Fillmore, that would have unified the grounds of the Capitol, White House, Mall, and Smithsonian Institution in a naturalistic setting quite unlike their present formality.

Downing deserves credit for launching the public parks movement that improved so many American cities during the nineteenth century. If most of Downing's papers had not been lost, if he had lived to practice what he so effectively preached, perhaps Frederick Law Olmsted would be known only for travel writing, since Vaux would not have asked him to collaborate in the design competition for Central Park, launching him on a new career.

—*Blanche M. G. Linden*

References

Schuyler, David. *Apostle of Taste: Andrew Jackson Downing, 1815–1852*. Baltimore: Johns Hopkins University Press, 1996.

Tatum, George Bishop. "Andrew Jackson Downing: Arbiter of American Taste, 1815–1852." Ph.D. dissertation, Princeton University, 1950.

Tatum, George Bishop, and Elisabeth Blair MacDougall, eds. *Prophet with Honor: The Career of Andrew Jackson Downing, 1815–1852*. Philadelphia: Athenaeum of Philadelphia; Washington, DC: Dumbarton Oaks Research Library and Collection, 1989.

Downtown

In the United States, *downtown* is probably the most characteristic expression designating the city's geographic core as well as the array of institutions found in the center of the city. As such, the term is a near synonym for *central business district,* although the latter usage has tended to take on a technical connotation. In contrast, downtown is a pervasively used expression and in its typical application emphasizes the central city's cultural and entertainment functions more than its economic purposes. In the mid-1960s, pop singer Petula Clark's hit song, "Downtown," described this part of the city as the place where a lonely person could escape personal cares and find amusement. This is exactly the sense of downtown that most Americans would find familiar.

In fact, the downtown's function as the geographic focus of a city's, or metropolitan region's, cultural and entertainment activities has had a checkered history. In many nineteenth-century American cities, the downtown area was the place where those with a taste for vice—gambling, drinking, or prostitution—sought their pleasures. In certain parts of the downtown with particularly large transient populations, vice districts developed in waterfront areas or, later, in the vicinity of train depots. As a rule, the main services offered in these districts skirted (or sometimes quite explicitly violated) local statutes. Thus, their orderly provision required collaboration between vice-brokering businesses and the local police. The efforts of these vice entrepreneurs to influence local politicians was a major source of urban corruption during the nineteenth century, as well as one of the principal targets of urban reformers.

By the early twentieth century, American downtowns had entered a new and more respectable phase in their evolution as cultural and entertainment centers. On the one hand, urban business and civic elites endowed museums, symphony orchestras, opera companies, and auditoriums, which were typically located in downtown areas. Moreover, with the rise of the City Beautiful movement at the turn of the century, local civic and municipal leaders were provided with a physical model for dignifying such institutions, and, more generally, their downtown surroundings. For urban designers such as Daniel Burnham, whose civic vision shaped municipal and arts complexes in central Chicago, Cleveland, and San Francisco, the downtown of grand city halls, municipal offices, museums, and auditoriums was intended to enhance the public's aesthetic sensibility and municipal pride—even before entering these facilities.

Whether or not Burnham or any of the other City Beautiful practitioners achieved their objectives is arguable, but other developments of the era were also contributing to the legitimization of downtown amusements. By the end of the nineteenth century, an emergent mass entertainment culture required new types of physical facilities to accommodate the crowds attending sporting events, vaudeville shows, and other theatrical presentations. After the turn of the century, cinema joined this list of popular culture enticements, and by the 1920s the experience of attending movies was magnified by the grandiose architecture of the era's newly built movie palaces. The concentration of auditoriums, movie palaces, and sports arenas in downtowns followed from precisely the same factors that concentrated business activities. There was a large population living in the vicinity of downtowns, and for residents of outlying neighborhoods the mass transit system focusing on downtown meant that the most economical sites for theaters and arenas were also the most centralized. These new forms of entertainment catered to numbers far in excess of the vice-seeking population, and in so doing redefined the moral tenor of downtowns.

However, just as the high tide of the classic central business district can be demarcated between the late nineteenth century and the early post–World War II period, the notion of the safe, respectable downtown can be defined by the same time frame. Moreover, in the view of many municipal leaders who were vexed by the decline of central business districts, the reemergence of the vice-ridden downtown was one of the factors producing decay of the central business district. Suburban population movement, the rise of the automobile and the decline of mass transit use, and the development of suburban entertainment complexes—most notably, cinemas—were at the heart of declining downtown entertainment in the 1950s. As a consequence, the owners of the old movie palaces and other entertainment venues sought to reach less-affluent customers with racier forms of entertainment and, rather like the landlords of impoverished residential tenants, reduced expenditures on the physical maintenance of their properties.

This process produced two anxieties for municipal leaders: (1) the sense that downtowns were increasingly the venue of unruly, unsophisticated, and threatening publics, and (2) that physical blight was fast overwhelming central cities. For instance, by the 1950s downtown Scollay Square in Boston had become the city's premier low-brow entertainment district and, as such, an embarrassment for Boston's leadership. As a result, with the coming of urban renewal, Scollay Square was cleared by the city, its site redeveloped as the architecturally modernist, forward-looking Government Center complex.

The redevelopment of downtown entertainment areas has exasperated municipal leaders across the country since World War II. The tortuous efforts to upgrade Manhattan's Times Square during the 1980s illuminate various pitfalls associated with such ventures. In the first place, and quite like the Boston Brahmin attitude toward old Scollay Square, New York City municipal and civic leaders sought to reshape Times

Square not so much because this district had lost its popularity, but rather because they objected to the kind of popularity that Times Square retained. On the one hand, presumably uplifting forms of entertainment, such as dramatic theater presentations, had fallen into decline. On the other hand, intellectually objectionable sex and action movies and other forms of low-grade entertainment such as video arcades had taken over the district's commercial frontage, which served a street clientele widely perceived to include disproportionate numbers of drifters, homeless people, and hucksters. Armed with this perception of popular squalor, and interpreting Times Square as a blemish on Manhattan's reputation, from the mid-1970s the city initiated redevelopment planning. However, identifying a new image for Times Square and winning the approval of neighborhood interests proved difficult. As is characteristic of most major downtown redevelopment efforts, technical problems growing out of the land acquisition process were extremely complicated. However, even more interesting were the city's difficulties in drafting design guidelines that would steer a safe course between Times Square's contemporary rakishness and an oversanitized "entertainment center" that would repel the crowds. In effect, Times Square's redevelopers were caught between contradictory impulses: the recognition that Times Square's attraction was, in part, based on a hint of danger, and the long-standing reformer's inclination to rid the city of its vices.

In fact, during the 1970s and 1980s, a stylized renaissance of the downtown vice district emerged in lower Manhattan and "loft areas" in other major cities. Visual artists, galleries, and musicians occupied old factory and warehouse spaces, which were turned to the production and display of art/entertainment with a self-consciously demimonde character. The names of the musical genres associated with this setting—punk, new wave, thrash, speed metal, and techno—indicate the orientation of the performers, who contributed to what in New York was termed the "downtown style." The hint of corruption in downtown settings was further popularized by films such as *After Hours* and *Desperately Seeking Susan*. Both of these movies loosely reworked the plotting of Joseph Conrad's *Heart of Darkness* as an understimulated middle-class individual falls into the clutches of the downtown scene, comes very close to personal breakdown, but in the end emerges more or less unscathed.

The irony of this recent, morally ambiguous redefinition of the downtown image is its final domestication in various development plans. During the 1980s, James Rouse cleaned

An aerial view of downtown San Francisco as seen in 1995.

up and repackaged the old South Street Seaport fish market in lower Manhattan. On the West Coast, preservationists fought a long battle to preserve Seattle's Pike Place Market, an old-style outdoor wholesale market. In Atlanta, the municipal government financed a $140 million redevelopment of the Atlanta Underground, a subterranean entertainment district whose marginal businesses and questionable clientele had led to its closing in the previous decade. In each of these cases, cities were marketing a safe representation of downtown seediness. In the United States of the late twentieth century—with its depopulated central city areas, decentralized residential populations increasingly dependent on home-based entertainment, and urban economic development models emphasizing convention and tourist attraction—any self-respecting big city must include a district featuring a modicum of traditional urban rakishness. Otherwise, their downtowns would only be central business districts.

—Larry Bennett

See also

Central Business District; Downtown Redevelopment Strategies.

References

Barth, Gunther. *City People: The Rise of Modern City Culture in Nineteenth-Century America.* New York: Oxford University Press, 1982.

Bennett, Larry. *Fragments of Cities: The New American Downtowns and Neighborhoods.* Columbus: Ohio State University Press, 1990.

Hines, Thomas S. *Burnham of Chicago: Architect and Planner.* Chicago: University of Chicago Press, 1979.

Levine, Lawrence. *Highbrow/Lowbrow: The Emergence of Cultural Hierarchy in America.* Cambridge, MA: Harvard University Press, 1990.

Nasaw, David. *Going Out: The Rise and Fall of Public Amusements.* New York: Basic Books, 1993.

Downtown Redevelopment Strategies

The suburbanization of residents, retailing, and business in the decades following World War II led to significant changes in the form and function of downtowns throughout the United States. No longer the economic and cultural centers of their metropolitan areas, downtowns large and small have utilized a well-established set of redevelopment strategies to compete with suburban centers. The seven strategies described here are all related to urban design and land use, although in most applications they are implemented in conjunction with financial and promotional tactics.

The first strategy is making downtown attractive to pedestrians. While many pedestrian planning tactics have been used in American downtowns, ranging from wider sidewalks to improved lighting, the most visible and acclaimed tactics involve the physical separation of pedestrians from vehicular traffic—grade-level pedestrian malls and above-grade skywalk systems. Most downtown planners agree that making downtown more pedestrian-friendly will yield positive results in terms of traffic management, economic revitalization, and environmental quality, and will create an image of a vital and active downtown district.

Borrowing from the popularity of suburban indoor shopping malls, a second strategy is constructing an indoor shopping center downtown. Such downtown shopping centers share some key characteristics with their suburban counterparts: centralized management, a carefully planned retail mix, and a clean, secure, climate-controlled environment. Key differences are the vertical construction of downtown centers and the lack of free parking. One problem associated with this strategy is the "fortress effect," wherein many of these centers tend to be self-contained structures that integrate poorly with the remainder of the downtown, thereby minimizing potential spillover benefits.

The third strategy for redeveloping downtowns, historic preservation, takes advantage of the large stock of older buildings usually found downtown, an attribute rarely found in suburbia. One preservation approach is to convert a historic yet underused building (e.g., a railroad terminal) into a festival marketplace. Success stories include Union Station in St. Louis and Ghirardelli Square in San Francisco, although there have also been numerous failures. In smaller cities, the Main Street approach, sponsored by the National Trust for Historic Preservation, is more likely to be implemented. The Main Street approach is guided by four key principles: (1) organization of downtown interests, (2) promotion, (3) design that enhances heritage and visual qualities, and (4) economic restructuring and diversification.

Waterfront development, the fourth strategy, takes advantage of another amenity found more frequently in downtowns than in suburbs. Many downtowns have worked to make their waterfronts accessible to the public and to encourage residential, retail, and tourist-oriented waterfront developments. A highly acclaimed waterfront project is Baltimore's Inner Harbor, which includes a festival marketplace, a historic tall ship, an aquarium, and ample open space that encourages complete public access to the water's edge.

A fifth strategy to redevelop downtowns is encouraging or sponsoring office building development. This is very important to most downtowns because offices serve as feeders to other activities (e.g., retailing, restaurants), and they form the building blocks of the downtown skyline, which helps to project an image of a modern corporate city. The office sector is the cornerstone to the "corporate center approach" to the redevelopment of downtowns, wherein the goal is to transform downtowns into financial, administrative, and professional service centers. The construction boom of the 1980s resulted in overbuilding downtown office space, which has reduced the use of this strategy in many cities in the 1990s.

Special activity generators such as convention centers, stadiums, or arenas constitute the sixth strategy. These large assembly facilities can draw large numbers of visitors into the downtown. It is anticipated that many of these visitors will spend money at nearby hotels, restaurants, stores, and tourist attractions, and that the influx of people will increase pedestrian volume. Examples of downtown convention centers are Minneapolis, Ft. Worth, Philadelphia, and Denver, to name but a few, while sports facilities have been built in the downtowns of Buffalo, Indianapolis, Cleveland, Minneapolis, and Baltimore.

The final strategy—transportation—is crucial to the success of the other six. Without easy access to the downtown, and without easy movement within the downtown, people will tend to stay away from the attractions located there. Some downtowns have strived to improve mass transit access by constructing transit malls (Minneapolis and Madison, Wisconsin), by implementing downtown shuttle services (Denver), or by integrating with a light rail system (Buffalo; Portland, Oregon; San Diego). To accommodate automobiles, many downtowns are implementing parking systems, creating high occupancy vehicle lanes, and utilizing traffic engineering techniques to improve traffic flow.

These downtown redevelopment strategies are not exhaustive (housing, open space, and entertainment are others) nor are they meant to be utilized in isolation. Oftentimes, particularly in larger cities, all seven strategies are used, ideally as part of a comprehensive downtown plan. The success of these strategies is mixed and often tied to their timing and the extent to which they are integrated with other features and attributes of the downtown.

—*Kent A. Robertson*

See also
Downtown; Pedestrian Malls; Skywalks for Pedestrians.
References
Frieden, Bernard J., and Lynne Sagalyn. *Downtown Inc.: How America Rebuilds Cities.* Cambridge, MA: MIT Press, 1989.
Krohe, James. "Is Downtown Worth Saving?" *Planning* 58 (1992): 9–13.
McBee, Susanna. *Downtown Development Handbook.* 2d ed. Washington, DC: Urban Land Institute, 1992.
Robertson, Kent A. "Downtown Redevelopment Strategies in the United States: An End-of-the-Century Assessment." *Journal of the American Planning Association* 61 (1995): 429–437.

Drake, Daniel (1785–1852)

Pioneer physician, educator, naturalist, and citizen of Cincinnati, Daniel Drake announced to the world that the frontier settlement of Cincinnati was emerging as an important focus for agricultural, mercantile, and cultural developments in the American West. Drake's *Picture of Cincinnati,* published in 1810, attracted immigrants from the East and Europe, and

by 1819 the city's early population had tripled. Cincinnati was no longer a village; it was now a city.

To Drake, education was the key, and science—through the study of nature—was the pathway to understanding. Cincinnati would be the laboratory in which he labored. Henry Shapiro writes of Drake: "the scientific and educational institutions which he helped establish . . . [were] to function as a sensorium commune—a common receptor, collator, and distributor of the data of science."

After 1807, not content with medical activities alone, Drake became involved in the civic, commercial, and cultural life of Cincinnati. He founded the Cincinnati Lyceum, First District Medical Society, School of Literature and Arts, Cincinnati Lancasterian Seminary, the Medical College of Ohio, Cincinnati College (which became the University of Cincinnati), two additional medical schools, the Commercial Hospital, a circulating library, a historical society, and the Western Museum Society, the forerunner of the Cincinnati Museum of Natural History.

Drake also had commercial interests. His family operated a drugstore and brought the first soda fountain to the city. Some of his other concerns included the development of the Erie Canal and a railroad to link Cincinnati with Louisville, Kentucky, and Charleston, South Carolina. He was also a director of the Cincinnati branch of the United States Bank.

Drake, the farm-boy physician, used his tremendous energy and abilities to better the city he loved, Cincinnati. Drake's determination to help shape the city's destiny during the early nineteenth century led to the establishment of many educational, cultural, commercial, and civic institutions that still remain in place.

—*Billie Broaddus*

References
Drake, Daniel. *Daniel Drake, M.D. Frontiersman of the Mind.* Charles D. Aring, M.D., and Cory Oysler, eds. Cincinnati, Ohio: Crossroad Books, 1985.
Horine, Emmet Field. *Daniel Drake (1785–1852): Pioneer Physician of the Midwest.* Philadelphia: University of Pennsylvania Press, 1961.
Juettner, Otto. *Daniel Drake and His Followers.* Cincinnati, Ohio: Harvey Publishing, 1909.
King, Arthur G. "Drake, the Many-Sided Physician." *Journal of the American Medical Association* 254 (October 18, 1985): 2117–2119.
Shapiro, Henry D., and Zane Miller. *Physician to the West.* Lexington: University of Kentucky Press, 1970.

Dreiser, Theodore (1871–1945)

Although born and raised in small-town Indiana, Theodore Dreiser, more than any novelist of his time, concerned himself with the American urban landscape. So impressed was Dreiser with his first boyhood stay in Chicago, the great industrial magnet of the Midwest, that he determined to return on his own as soon as he completed high school. From Chicago, he went on to St. Louis, Cleveland, Pittsburgh, and New York, and his progress as a young man became a practical education in the impact of industrialism on every aspect of American city life.

From Dreiser's experiences emerged the most pervasive theme of his fiction: the (often unsuccessful) struggle of the individual to survive and even triumph in contention with the great social forces unleashed by the machine age. Dreiser's first novel, *Sister Carrie* (1900), concerns the difficult necessity of individual adjustment to urban-industrial life. Carrie Meeber, 18, impressionable and fresh from a Wisconsin village, observes and learns as she pounds the teeming sidewalks of Chicago hunting work. What Carrie learns is that within America's new economic order the individual is a commodity. Wholly dispensable as units, people exist largely as cogs in factory processes (Carrie runs an assembly-line machine that punches shoelace holes).

Money having emerged as the chief measure of worth, in Dreiser's world human lives are quantified, their value measured by the rising or falling contents of weekly pay envelopes. Thus, *Sister Carrie* has an obsessive emphasis upon the itemization of wages and the corresponding specifics concerning costs of shelter, food, clothing, and entertainment, when the basics are satisfied. Eventually Carrie Meeber triumphs over economic necessity by finding her place in the entertainment industry where individual personality still counts for something and whose close examination by Dreiser is one important mark of his modernity.

In *The Financier* (1912) and *The Titan* (1914) Dreiser deals with the exceptional career of Frank Cowperwood who, unlike Carrie, is born into a family knowledgeable about the power of money. Cowperwood grows up learning and experimenting with ingenious ways of manipulating money. His exploitation of the streetcar systems of Philadelphia and Chicago make him a multimillionaire, providing Dreiser with an opportunity to dissect the emerging system of socioeconomic castes then rapidly dividing urban society along lines of wealth and its consequent power. The struggle pitting rich against poor, strong against weak, continues to dominate Dreiser's attention and engage his sympathy, especially, in *Jennie Gerhardt* (1911) and *An American Tragedy* (1925), for those victimized by the system.

Dreiser spent a large part of his life in New York and his later years in Los Angeles, but in his fiction it is Chicago (and quite rightly so, considering that city's flamboyant history) that continues to epitomize industrialism and its many problems. To this day no other writer has been more closely identified with Chicago than Dreiser. Even in works to which the city is not central, *The "Genius"* (1915) and *The Bulwark* (1946) being cases in point, Dreiser arranges for his heroes

to visit or spend part of their lives in what he admiringly called "The Florence of the West."

That concentration of wealth, power, and population that describes the urban centers established by the American turn from agrarianism to manufacturing somewhat ironically also produced the greater chance for an individual to pop out of the anonymous mass, almost by accident, and take the public fancy by storm—to become a "celebrity," with the adulation and financial rewards that the term implies. In one way or another, celebrity describes the lives of Carrie Meeber, Frank Cowperwood, and Eugene Witla, the artist-hero of *The "Genius."* In an inverted sense, celebrity is what happens to Jennie Gerhardt after newspaper headlines exploit the irregularity of her marital life with Lester Kane. In the same manner, but more extravagantly, Clyde Griffiths is tossed up by the press onto the roiling surface of life for his Warhol-like quarter-hour of fame. In modern America a murderer, as well as an actress or a millionaire, could be celebrated.

Incongruous as it might otherwise be considering Dreiser's humble beginnings, it was somehow fitting that in death he should lie in Los Angeles's Forest Lawn, a metropolitan cemetery whose name had become synonymous with the celebration of personalities from the entertainment industry.

—*Philip Gerber*

References

Elias, Robert H. *Letters of Theodore Dreiser.* 2 vols. Philadelphia: University of Pennsylvania Press, 1959.

———. *Theodore Dreiser: Apostle of Nature.* Ithaca, NY: Cornell University Press, 1970.

Gerber, Philip. *Theodore Dreiser Revisited.* New York: Twayne, 1992.

Lingeman, Richard. *Theodore Dreiser: An American Journey, 1908–1945.* New York: Putnam, 1990.

———. *Theodore Dreiser: At the Gates of the City, 1871–1907.* New York: Putnam, 1986.

Moers, Ellen. *Two Dreisers.* New York: Viking Press, 1969.

Swanberg, W. A. *Dreiser.* New York: Scribners, 1965.

Drinking, Alcohol Abuse, and Drunkenness

For thousands of years, people in many parts of the world have used mildly alcoholic fermented beverages such as beer and wine, and for the last several hundred years Europeans, European migrants to North America, and their descendants have consumed vast quantities of much more potent distilled beverages such as gin, rum, and whiskey. This long history has meant that alcohol has become integrated into American culture. The substance has been widely used to bond friendship, pursue sexual desires, seal political or business bargains, and signify manhood. In American culture, drinking has frequently been associated with masculinity and violence. Technically, alcohol reduces inhibitions, and its use enables people to engage in behavior that might otherwise be socially or legally proscribed or discouraged. Thus, alcohol has frequently been introduced to relieve anxiety in stressful situations or to break down social or psychological barriers. Alcohol has thus functioned as society's principal recreational drug.

Alcohol, however, poses significant social problems. First, a small but significant percentage of drinkers become addicted to alcohol in such a way that they consume increasing quantities over time, and this heavy drinking threatens family life, jobs, and health. Second, other drinkers, while not addicted, neglect home and work through too great a devotion to drink. Third, alcohol's reduction of inhibitions leads some drinkers to engage in acts that are not socially sanctioned. Some become violent, and prisons hold many people who committed crimes while under the influence of alcohol. These criminals often have no memory of their drunken behavior.

Throughout American history, alcohol has been recognized as dangerous, and cities have banned or regulated its sale and use. Colonial towns, following English precedent, licensed taverns. Boston sellers had to prove respectability by belonging to the established church. Furthermore, visits to drinking houses were monitored. One preacher watched those who entered from his study window, and if anyone stayed more than an hour, he would escort the drinker home. Reputable women did not drink in public houses unless they were staying overnight at the inn as a traveler.

In the nineteenth century, antiliquor forces often tried to restrict either the number of licenses or the hours of operation. By 1850, most American cities had banned alcohol sales on Sunday. Some cities limited saloons to certain locations, and in the twentieth century many wet cities were surrounded by legally dry suburbs. Indeed, many towns were incorporated specifically to keep out alcohol. As city zoning became common in the twentieth century, restrictions on outlets grew. Most cities did not allow the sale of alcohol near schools or churches. After 1933, most states restricted the number of licenses available, controlled locations and hours, and set a legal drinking age of 21.

Despite attempts at prohibition and restriction, alcohol has continued to appeal to Americans. Consumption was heavy in the colonial period, and drinking increased during the generation following the American Revolution. The settlement of the Midwest corn belt produced much cheap whiskey, as little as 5 cents a fifth, and by 1820 consumption of hard liquor was about five gallons per person per year. Women, children, and slaves consumed little, while the typical adult white male drank about half a pint of whiskey a day. They seldom got drunk, however, but sipped whiskey continually throughout the day.

After 1830, consumption fell, and patterns of use changed. Because factory machinery was expensive and dangerous, owners banned alcohol both from the workplace, where it had been traditional, and from workers' private lives after hours. A drunken stagecoach driver's horses could find their way home, but a drunken steamboat captain risked sinking the ship. As drinking shifted away from the workplace, alcohol became associated with recreation or unemployment. For the first time, binge drinking became common in America.

The nineteenth-century temperance movement made intoxicating beverages less respectable. About half of all Americans gave up alcohol, which lessened the role of drinking as a way of building community. Drinkers, however, continued to enjoy each other's company, especially in the family-oriented beer gardens that German immigrants built on the edge of major cities. After the Civil War, urban immigrants who had recently arrived from hard-drinking countries in Europe contributed to rising consumption, which increasingly consisted of lightly taxed beer.

Alcohol use declined by half or more again between 1920 and 1933 when the Eighteenth Amendment to the U.S. Constitution mandated Prohibition and forbade the manufacture, distribution, and sale of alcoholic beverages in the United States. Many Americans who reached adulthood during the dry years never drank at all, but young people in the 1930s were drawn to beer and mixed drinks. Liquor was glamorized in magazines such as *Time*, which broke the taboo against respectable publications advertising liquor, and in popular movies such as *The Thin Man* (1934). Consumption rose during the 1930s and increased more rapidly during World War II, although the use of alcohol for military purposes led to shortages of hard liquor.

Since 1933 alcohol abuse has been increasingly considered a disease. This disease model has replaced the older moral view that prohibitionists stressed, and as a result much money has been spent on research and treatment. By the 1980s, treatment programs often combined psychosocial therapies with a drug regime in order to take into account the whole person. Alcoholics Anonymous, while founded on other bases, has adopted a similar outlook.

Consumption of alcohol slowly increased after World War II. Alcohol consumption often rises during prosperity, just as use is heaviest among the wealthiest segments of the population (doctors and lawyers drink heavily, as reducing stress is a major concern in both professions). In the postwar years beer sales continued strong with growing home consumption in bottles and, later, aluminum cans. Brewers shrewdly took advantage of television to identify their product with athletic success. Wine consumption also rose due to vigorous marketing and a growing sophistication about wine. Hard liquor, in contrast, enjoyed little growth, as drinkers switched from whiskey to the so-called white beverages of vodka, gin, and light rum. In the 1970s, many states lowered the legal drinking age, allowed more liquor advertising, and otherwise reduced controls. By 1975, per capita alcohol consumption had reached levels not seen since before Prohibition, although the rate of use was only one-third that of its peak in the early 1800s.

Since 1975, alcohol consumption has declined. The most important reason is demographic. Use is always heaviest among persons in their twenties, and the numerous baby boomers have now aged. Changing attitudes about alcohol, however, have also played a role. Concerns about fetal alcohol syndrome have led many women to abstain, while the high percentage of fatal automobile accidents that involve alcohol (ranging up to half) has produced a public campaign against driving after drinking. Mothers against Drunk Driving (MADD) was largely responsible for a federal law that pressured states to adopt a legal drinking age of 21 in the mid-eighties.

In recent years neoprohibitionists have tried to reduce consumption by restricting advertising, raising liquor taxes, and reducing the number of licensed outlets. They have also sought to make sellers liable for damages caused by drunken patrons, to include alcohol in antidrug programs in schools, to use police roadblocks for random alcohol checks, to lower the amount of alcohol in the legal definition of drunkenness, and to link alcohol abuse by men with concerns about women's and children's rights and safety. Despite these attempts at restriction, alcohol continues to play a prominent role in American culture.

—*W. J. Rorabaugh*

See also
Bars and Saloons; Nation, Carry Amelia Moore; Prohibition; Temperance Movement; Willard, Frances Elizabeth Caroline.
References
Barrows, Susanna, and Robin Room, eds. *Drinking: Behavior and Belief in Modern History.* Berkeley: University of California Press, 1991.
Blocker, Jack S., Jr. *American Temperance Movements: Cycles of Reform.* Boston: Twayne, 1989.
Kurtz, Ernest. *Not-God: A History of Alcoholics Anonymous.* Center City, MN: Hazelden Educational Services, 1979.
Rorabaugh, W. J. *The Alcoholic Republic: An American Tradition.* New York: Oxford University Press, 1979.

Drugs, Drug Abuse, and Drug Addiction

Drug use is as old as mankind, beginning in the need for relief from pain and distress, expanding in modern times into a demand for heightened experience, pleasure, or escape from personal problems that may be rooted in social ills. Western societies have tended to divide drugs and the experiences they produce into several categories of tolerance. A narcotic, for instance, is acceptable when it alleviates pain and helps restore normal body and social function. It is illicit when used to sustain an addiction or to withdraw from reality. Until about the middle of the nineteenth century, derivatives of the opium poppy, whether prepared as a laudanum tonic or concentrated as morphine, were the chief painkillers and tranquilizers available to doctors in treating a wide variety of ailments, from enteric fevers to heavy pain associated with injury to psychic distress known as nervousness. The twentieth century has seen a rapid expansion of chemical substances that alter mood or behavior in ways societies have disapproved because these transformations allegedly threaten individual values such as liberty and free will (as opposed to "habit" or "addiction") and social values such as cooperation, work, and mental alertness.

Drug use, or "abuse," to create an altered state of consciousness, historically knows few boundaries of class, place, or circumstance. Nineteenth-century users included men with some kind of persistent pain, children with indefinable or chronic distress (or whose guardians desired to tranquilize them), and the intellectual or experimenter who sought intensified experiences. But most habitual drug users in America in the nineteenth century were white, middle-class women for whose varied complaints doctors prescribed opiates and new chemical compounds such as chloral hydrate, chiefly to produce calm or even torpor. The concept and

A morphine addict on a city street in the late nineteenth century.

understanding of addiction developed only slowly and from experience. By the middle of the twentieth century, various experts saw addiction as a medical or psychological disease. As often as not, treatment was ineffective, which intensified public fear of the enslavement of will and the ruin of talent that drug use came to represent.

While many early users lived in small towns or the rural countryside, drug use was quickly identified in the public mind with urban life. By the late nineteenth century, medical, social, and political commentators saw it as another aspect of the crowding, impersonality, danger, and disorderly individualism of life in industrial cities. There were few laws and little regulation against drug use prior to about 1914; anyone who could pay could buy almost any drug in any quantity. By the end of the nineteenth century, social workers and reformers were well aware that every major city, and many towns, had areas where various forbidden activities such as drug and alcohol use, prostitution, and gambling flourished, usually under police surveillance.

The era of Progressive reform at the beginning of the twentieth century saw concerted efforts on both local and federal levels to control and then forbid the use of drugs. This movement paralleled wars against alcohol, prostitution, white slavery, and many other ills associated with city life. The ultimate result was a web of laws at all levels that drove drug use underground after the early 1920s. The three decades that followed were the high point, especially at the federal level, of police regulation of drug use. This coincided with a popular consensus that drug use destroyed the personality and cohesive social values. The problem continued but seemed confined to marginal elements of society such as criminals, suspect but controllable ethnic groups, and some persons in the intellectual and artistic community.

This consensus and the police power to sustain it broke down rapidly after World War II. New interpretations of constitutional rights eroded police authority. A large cohort of young people came of age in the 1960s and combined curiosity, a strong sense of personal freedom to experiment, and protest over social ills in a fresh wave of drug use. Chemistry produced a cornucopia of substances for experimentation, and both these and the number of users further thwarted efforts at police or consensual control.

By the last generation in the twentieth century, drug use had crossed almost all lines of division in society. Persons in every profession, social group, and age cohort were involved. The period of rapid economic growth and diversification that followed World War II had created a fresh sense of both the possibilities of urban life and of the comforts of suburban living. Some kind of drug use became acceptable to many people. City, suburb, small town, and countryside all witnessed it in some form and degree. The consensus against use, in the name of protecting either social values or individual personality, had lapsed in many groups.

Drug use was also associated with the glamour of life in the world of sports, popular music, and the chic upper class. Politicians promised, and sometimes produced, wars against drugs, focused on interdicting supply, chiefly because attacking demand involved dangerous political decisions to regulate the conduct of influential constituents in suburbs, for example, or using unconstitutional methods. The public in general still opposed drug use, especially among minors. But any war on drugs was confused, given the nature of user populations. It was one thing to assault crack cocaine or heroin addicts in decrepit inner cities, but quite another to prosecute users in expensive apartment houses and manicured suburbs.

As the twentieth century closed, there was a growing public sense that a wave of uncritical belief in individual freedom to experiment had ignored or denied the real dangers in some kinds of drug use. No war against drugs came anywhere near victory. This failure in turn produced demands for even harsher penalties against sellers of drugs, treatment for users, and interdiction of supplies. Drug use was identified with crime against persons and property that now reached into every aspect of national life, rather than being confined to identifiable people or areas, as formerly. It also seemed part of life among criminal and ethnic elements that society found more threatening than ever. And the deaths from drug use of many celebrities symbolized its perils to many who once saw drug use as an aspect of personal liberty. Public opinion generally supported antidrug efforts that combined police control, education, and a range of therapies. The complexity and breadth of this response may indicate the formation of another self-enforcing consensus against drug use, similar to what has happened with the assaults on tobacco use and drunk driving.

The city has played an important role in the nation's long effort to control, forbid, or tolerate drug use. It first appeared to offer areas of anonymity where users did not seem to threaten society. It then became an example of the alleged corrosive effects of drug use on both individuals and the polity. It finally symbolized the need for controls to protect both potential users and society. The suburb passed through a similar experience. It first seemed to be a place where drug use was unlikely, given the affluence and authority of its population, their social aspirations and educational level. But those very attributes seemed somehow to foster or tolerate some drug use after the wave of experimentation in the 1960s. And the suburb, like the city, then became an example and laboratory of the ways in which drug use could appeal to almost anyone inclined to ignore social controls or apparent majority values. The historical associations of drug use with crime, deviance, and social disengagement returned. The fear that drug use had no limits, and threatened all elements of society, like the crime with which it was identified, underlays new demands for control through reasonable education and therapy rather than police methods, which were expensive and often ineffective.

—*H. Wayne Morgan*

References

Courtwright, David. *Addicts Who Survived: An Oral History of Narcotic Use in America, 1923–1965.* Knoxville: University of Tennessee Press, 1989.

———. *Dark Paradise: Opiate Addiction in America before 1940.* Cambridge: MA: Harvard University Press, 1982.

Morgan, H. Wayne. *Drugs in America: A Social History since 1800.* Syracuse, NY: Syracuse University Press, 1981.

———. *Yesterday's Addicts: American Society and Drug Abuse, 1865–1920.* Norman: University of Oklahoma Press, 1974.

Musto, David. *The American Disease: Origins of Narcotic Control.* New Haven, CT: Yale University Press, 1973.

Walker, William O. *Drug Control in the Americas.* Albuquerque: University of New Mexico Press, 1981.

Dumbbell Tenement

In one of the great ironies in the history of American cities, the dumbbell tenement emerged in the late nineteenth century as a reform alternative to the slum tenements that multiplied as New York City's population exploded. Builders had been covering every available inch of the city's standard lots—25 feet wide by 100 feet deep—with tenements of every description. In 1878, *Plumber and Sanitary Engineer,* a trade publication, sponsored an architectural competition for the tenement design that would most effectively and affordably house low-income workers with the greatest safety and sanitation. When the awards committee examined the submissions, it despairingly declared that its mission was impossible; safe, sanitary, affordable, low-income housing could not be built on a lot 25 feet wide and 100 feet deep. Nevertheless, the judges awarded first prize to James E. Ware, whose design was the prototype for what came to be called the dumbbell tenement.

The dumbbell essentially was a building with a front and rear apartment on each floor that were attached by a narrow hall. The indentation of the hall, which was not as wide as the apartments, created an enclosed air shaft approximately 28 inches wide, which provided a source—the sole source—of light and air for the interior rooms on each floor of the five- or six-story building. The shaft was far from adequate; rather it served as a fire conductor, a dumping ground for garbage, a collection point for cast-off items of every description, and a home for rats and other vermin. Instead of ventilating the tenement, it facilitated the transmission of odors from each apartment to the others. The dumbbell usually covered 75 to 90 percent of the lot instead of the 65 percent required by New York's Tenement House Act of 1879.

Despite its limitations, some variation of the dumbbell became the most common type of tenement in New York City until 1901. Opponents proposed different designs for model tenements, but in 1900 most of the city's 80,000 tenements were in buildings shaped like dumbbells that had been erected since 1880. During those two decades, New York's population ballooned from 1,844,785 to 3,369,898.

In 1900, Lawrence Veiller, the young secretary of the Tenement House Committee of the New York Charity Organization Society, put together an exhibition about tenement houses that attracted 10,000 viewers; among them was Theodore Roosevelt, then governor of New York. The exhibition included photographs, maps, charts, and cardboard models; the most sensational of these portrayed an actual city block of tenements housing 2,781 inhabitants living in 39 tenements (at a density of 1,515 persons per acre). Taking advantage of the exhibition's publicity, Roosevelt helped Veiller shepherd a bill to create a Tenement House Commission through the state legislature. Veiller became the commission's secretary, and he and its chairman, Robert DeForest, published a two-volume report, *The Tenement House Problem,* which recommended remedial legislation. The Tenement House Act of 1901 resulted.

The law of 1901 effectively proscribed the future construction of dumbbell tenements in New York City. Its requirements for greater open space precluded the air shaft, led to the creation of open courtyards, and made it impossible to build tenements on the city's narrow lots. Every apartment had to contain its own toilet and running water, and each room had to have a window. Monthly inspections by the newly created Tenement House Department were to enforce this law, which marked the zenith of enthusiasm for restrictive housing legislation.

Because dumbbells could no longer be constructed as formerly, the law raised construction costs and thus rents. Builders responded by moving into the market for middle-class apartments, and immigrants crowded even more tightly into the thousands of remaining "old law" (pre-1901) tenements. Thus, the proscription of the dumbbell tenement in 1901 did nothing to resolve the problem of low-income housing in New York City.

—*John F. Sutherland*

See also

Tenement; Veiller, Lawrence Turnure.

References

Jackson, Anthony. *A Place Called Home: A History of Low-Cost Housing in Manhattan.* Cambridge, MA: MIT Press, 1976.

Lubove, Roy. *The Progressives and the Slums: Tenement House Reform in New York City, 1890–1917.* Pittsburgh, PA: University of Pittsburgh Press, 1962.

Plunz, Richard. *A History of Housing in New York City: Dwelling Type and Social Change in the American Metropolis.* New York: Columbia University Press, 1990.

Dummy Lines (Steam Street Railways)

In the middle of the nineteenth century, suburban communities beyond the range of horsecar lines were sometimes served by lightly built steam railways, called dummy lines. These railways were named for their peculiar locomotives, called "dummys," in which the engine was surrounded and hidden by a body much like that of a passenger car. In theory, horses were less frightened by these strangely designed engines, and street traffic could proceed in a more orderly fashion.

Dummy lines were introduced in the 1860s. A few ran on city streets but most operated beyond the edge of town where horsecars terminated a few miles from the city center. Most of these railways were small operations with one or two dummy engines and only half a dozen cars. A few cities did, however, develop fairly sizable dummy systems. Birmingham, Alabama, had about a dozen lines, and one line in Minneapolis had 26 miles of track, 15 locomotives, and 56 cars. Brooklyn and San Francisco also had sizable dummy operations.

Passengers did not ride inside the body of the dummy engine—they rode in small cars pulled behind it. Many lines used ordinary horsecars for coaches, although some used diminutive, eight-wheel passenger cars. Speeds rarely exceeded 15 miles per hour, but even so, the light tracks offered less than a smooth ride. The smoke and oily smell of the engine added little to passenger comfort. Patrons of one line near Chicago contemptuously referred to their local dummy as the Dingle Dangle—yet all of its patrons understood that it was either take the Dingle or walk.

Steam dummy operations peaked in 1890 when about 80 lines operated around 600 miles of track in the United States. None were very profitable because of high operating costs—some were as much as 300 percent greater than a horsecar line. However, greater speed and passenger capacity partially offset the higher operating costs. In almost all ways, the dummy lines were a make-do compromise until something better came along, and come along it did. When the electric streetcar became a commercial reality in the late 1880s, it began to replace all other forms of city transportation, be it horse, cable, or steam-propelled car. By 1900, the smoky, wheezing dummy was a relic of urban transit's past.

—*John H. White, Jr.*

See also
Interurban Transit.
References
Haupt, Herman. *Street Railway Motors.* Philadelphia: H. C. Baird, 1893.
Hilton, George W. *American Narrow Gauge Railroads.* Stanford, CA: Stanford University Press, 1990.
Poor, Henry V., and H. W. Poor, eds. *Poor's Manual of the Railroads of the United States.* New York: 1878, 1888.

Dutch Colonial Towns

During the 1620s, New Netherland's first communities housed Dutch West India Company soldiers and Walloon farmers at Fort Orange on the Hudson River and on the upper reaches of the Connecticut and Delaware Rivers. After 1625, New Amsterdam on Manhattan Island emerged as the colony's administrative and commercial center. Until the English conquered it in 1664, Manhattan, adjacent to Long Island and the Hudson Valley, remained the primary focus of Dutch settlement and community development.

New Netherland attracted only a fraction of the Dutch West India Company's colonizing resources, and it expected greater profits from the sugar-producing regions of Brazil and the salt pans at Curaçao in the West Indies. The 1629 Charter of Freedoms and Exemptions—the Company's first plan for settlement—enabled private individuals (patroons) to receive land as well as political and legal privileges in return for transporting at least 50 people to the colony. Only one patroonship survived, that founded during the 1630s by an Amsterdam merchant and official of the Dutch West India Company, Kiliaen van Rensselaer. Located along the Hudson River, Rensselaerswyck was only a modest success, although it had 4 farms under cultivation in 1640 and 18 by 1651.

For the colony as a whole, however, the 1640s and 1650s marked a significant period of population growth and community development. By 1664, New Netherland's population had grown to about 8,000, both white and black. Increasing numbers of wives and children joined employees and single men bound for agricultural service. Moreover, after Holland lost Brazil in 1654, the colony became a market for the Dutch slave trade.

A revision of the Charter of Freedoms and Exemptions in 1640 established a town form of government for both Dutch and English inhabitants. New Englanders on Long Island had agitated for local political rights, and the Dutch chartered communities at Flushing, Hempstead, and Gravesend. The New Netherland government sought to establish agricultural villages, but only after additional ordinances did the Dutch also charter Brooklyn, Flatbush, and Flatlands.

Population growth and community creation was a colony-wide phenomena. Dutch farmers founded Esopus on the Hudson River and Schenectady on the Mohawk River west of Fort Orange. Director-General Petrus Stuyvesant also granted independent status, including a court and magistrates, to the settlement of traders and artisans at Beverwyck near Fort Orange.

Dutch town charters made no provision for the kind of popular political participation that was common in New England. Court members such as those at Beverwyck were chosen from a list of candidates submitted to the director-general. However, Dutch courts acted on petitions from inhabitants and, at times, called the residents together to obtain their opinion on important issues.

Local officials included the *schepen* and *schout.* The former had jurisdiction over minor criminal offenses while the *schout* corresponded to a modern-day prosecuting attorney. Notaries recorded land transactions, marriage contracts, and wills. Other local officials cared for orphans, operated schools, or were responsible for almshouses. Churches were built at New Amsterdam and Beverwyck, but only a few Dutch Reformed Church ministers ever settled in the colony.

The arrival of Petrus Stuyvesant as director-general in 1647 brought a much-needed infusion of leadership and military ability. An expedition against a Swedish colony on the Delaware River was followed by the creation of New Amstel, a community sponsored by the city of Amsterdam. At New Amsterdam (whose population grew to 2,000 by 1664), civic improvements sponsored by Stuyvesant included building the city's first pier, creating a police force, enforcing the fire laws, and improving defenses such as repairing the fort at the island's southern tip.

By 1664, New Netherland had achieved a sustained level of population growth and community development, although historians disagree about the nature of the Dutch colony. Donna Merwick emphasizes urban, bourgeois values that the colonial Dutch derived from Holland. David Cohen argues for a broader view of the geographic and social background of New Netherland settlers. Up to half the people who came to the colony were not Dutch; they came from various localities elsewhere in Northern Europe. Rather than merchant traders, according to Cohen, most were farmers, craftsmen, soldiers, or petty traders. In the New World, they settled on isolated farms, as tenants of patroons, or in agricultural communities such as Flatbush or Schenectady.

—*Thomas E. Burke, Jr.*

References

Burke, Thomas E., Jr. *Mohawk Frontier: The Dutch Community of Schenectady, New York, 1661–1710.* Ithaca, NY: Cornell University Press, 1991.

Cohen, David Steven. *The Dutch-American Farm.* New York: New York University Press, 1992.

Elting, Irving. *Dutch Village Communities on the Hudson River.* Baltimore: Johns Hopkins University Press, 1886.

Kammen, Michael. *Colonial New York: A History.* New York: KTO Press, 1975.

Kross, Jessica. *The Evolution of an American Town: Newtown, New York, 1642–1775.* Philadelphia: Temple University Press, 1983.

Merwick, Donna. *Possessing Albany, 1630–1710: The Dutch and English Experiences.* New York: Cambridge University Press, 1990.

Rink, Oliver. *Holland on the Hudson: An Economic and Social History of Dutch New York.* Ithaca, NY: Cornell University Press, 1986.

Smith, George. *Religion and Trade in New Netherland.* Ithaca, NY: Cornell University Press, 1973.

Wright, Langdon G. "In Search of Peace and Harmony: New York Communities in the Seventeenth Century." *New York History* 61 (1980): 5–21.

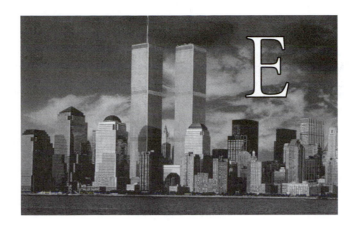

Earthworks

Earthworks are modern sculptures, usually in large geometric configurations, made from the environment itself, that have a random quality that seems to question the impact of urbanism on the individual locale. In the United States, the Abstract Expressionist movement, mostly in the 1960s and 1970s, led artists to create forceful, eccentric, and nonmetaphoric art. Earthworks artists add to these qualities a purpose, to bridge the technology of the urban environment and the rawness of pure nature, using materials new to art, such as rock, dirt, flotsam, and water. In this art, the sculpture is not only the object created but also the very process of creation. While creating pieces that were deliberately ephemeral in some cases and purposely durable in others, these artists kept meticulous records of their efforts and included those records as part of the art.

One example of an outdoor earthwork is Robert Smithson's *Spiral Jetty*. The sculpture itself, 1,500 feet long and 15 feet wide, was built in 1970 near Ogden, Utah, in the Great Salt Lake. It is made of black rock, salt crystals, earth, and water red with algae. As part of the total piece, Smithson made a film of the process, telling about locating the site, ruminating about the history of the site, and detailing construction of the jetty and the resulting displacement of water.

Other earthworks and their artists show a similar concern for locale and history. Among them are Christo's *Running Fence* (1972–1976) outside of San Francisco, California, for which a giant fabric fence was strung across miles of land, and Michael Heizer's *Compression Line* (1968), a ditch 192 feet long and lined with plywood at El Mirage Dry Lake in California's Mojave Desert. In 1971–1972, Dennis Oppenheim built *Polarities*. He took two drawings, one by his young daughter and the other by his recently deceased father, enlarged both on a map to a 500-foot scale, and then plotted the result with magnesium flares on Long Island. Aerial photographs accompanied the original drawings at the gallery showing.

Smaller versions of earthworks are suitable for gallery installation and use many of the same techniques but on a smaller scale. Smithson's 1968 *Non-Site: Franklin, N.J.* is an aerial map of a suburb of New York City. The sculpture consists of a grid system laid out on an inclined plane that is overlaid with a map of Franklin, New Jersey. In five bins behind the photographs are ore rocks placed in layers that replicate the ore layers at Franklin.

—*William Klink*

References
"Earthworks: Past and Present." *Art Journal* 42 (1982): 191–233.
Gabriel, Bertram. "Works of Earth." *Horizon* 25 (1982): 42–48.
Rosenblum, Robert. "A Postscript: Some Recent Neo-Romantic Mutations." *Art Journal* 52 (1993): 74–84.

Economy of Cities

The economy (or political economy) of cities in the United States constitutes the network of urban markets within which local political communities compete to promote their economic well-being through the allocation of public and private resources. The position of cities in a market economy differs from that of higher governmental units. Unlike the national government, cities cannot impose much control over the movement of people and wealth across their borders. Cities lack the ability to regulate capital movement, to control immigration by issuing passports and visas, to print currency or regulate its supply, to impose trade laws that control the import and export of commodities, or to influence other economies with military and foreign policy. Consequently, cities generally face a more competitive market environment than do the national and, to a lesser degree, state governments. Economic rivalry among cities within the domestic and sometimes even the global market disciplines urban communities to compete for capital investment and labor to a degree not usually found at the national level, where economic development is subject to relatively greater political control. Local governments are therefore economically dependent on market pressures to a degree that is not shared by higher-level governments within the American federal system.

The permeability of urban economies is best illustrated by the relatively large proportion of externally produced goods and services consumed by city residents as compared to the much smaller proportion of foreign goods and services bought by American citizens. This economic vulnerability means that the general prosperity of citizens within a city is ultimately tied to the city's market position vis-à-vis other cities that produce and export goods to other communities. A city's wealth depends upon its capacity to produce goods and services for external markets. When goods are sold in markets outside of the city, labor and capital move in to increase the production of those goods. This continues until no more goods can be sold because the marginal cost of producing them exceeds their marginal value in external markets.

This export process causes urban growth. As city exports increase, those who produce them utilize their profits to consume other goods and services. Furthermore, ancillary businesses locate in the city to provide export industries with goods and services or because they can benefit from the exporter's presence or its by-products. This chain of economic activity has a multiplier effect on city incomes, producing perhaps a four- or fivefold increase in economic activities for each increment in export earnings. Likewise, a decrease in these activities precipitates city economic decline. As a community exports less, the multiplier works in reverse and produces shrinking economic activity.

Since urban growth and decline have great political importance, the economies of American cities are rarely managed entirely by market forces. Local governments have a major stake in promoting and developing their economies. Indeed, they are disciplined to undertake management activities by pressures of economic competition, which encourages them to avoid policies that undermine economic development. Local governments are also pressured by political competition to promote the economic well-being of their constituents and to deal with the political consequences of growth. Similarly, urban economies are shaped by the activities of higher-level governments. State and national governments tax, spend, and regulate economies in ways that can influence the fortunes of particular cities and regions. Hence, the economy of cities is more properly described as a political economy of cities. In this kind of urban system, there is a division between market and governmental institutions, but they work interdependently to shape the economic well-being of urban areas.

Three major urban political economies have developed during the history of the United States: the mercantile (1787–1860), industrial (1860–1930), and postindustrial (1930 to the present). In each of these periods, the American urban system possessed distinctive market structures, political relationships, and patterns of policy intervention. Consequently, great changes in the degree and scope of intercity economic competition and the role of political authorities in managing this competition have occurred.

The mercantile political economy (1787–1860) was characterized by precapitalist market relations and active political management by fledgling local and state governments. Land, labor, and capital were yet to be organized into a system of well-integrated urban and regional markets. Nevertheless, the destruction of the British colonial system by the American Revolution precipitated increasing regional economic competition among cities and states. In the new American federal system, local and state governments competed for trade, something that had not occurred when they had protected status in the imperial commonwealth of the colonial period.

At the beginning of this era, the economy was largely self-sufficient and rural in which the business of most Americans was on the land, not in the city, in work undertaken on farms or in households, rather than in factories, warehouses, or offices located in urban areas. During this preindustrial era, the majority of the population lived in rural areas; in 1790 only 5 percent of the American people lived in cities, and even by 1860 only 20 percent of Americans lived in places with a population of 2,500 or more. Cities had yet to become important population or economic centers. Yet, they had begun to assume an important strategic economic function; they were emerging from their agricultural surroundings to convert an essentially self-sufficient agrarian economy into a more commercialized system by organizing markets for domestic agricultural products.

The dominant economic function of cities was trading. Farmers would come into the cities from rural areas and exchange their agricultural surplus for goods shipped from abroad or produced by urban craftsmen. Because of these activities, cities developed important commercial functions: they housed the discounting, lending, wholesaling, retailing, and other entrepreneurial functions important for marketing products of the hinterland and supplying rural populations with finished goods.

The primary means by which mercantile cities expanded their export market was to increase the supply of goods from rural areas. The major obstacles to economic growth were physical barriers that impeded the exchange of goods between rural and urban areas and among commercial centers themselves. Consequently, city growth and prosperity was linked with transportation improvements that permitted easier, faster, and cheaper commercial penetration of the new nation. Since the resources for fueling urban growth lay mainly outside of the city in the nation's vast hinterland, public officials focused on enhancing the city's position as a marketplace. The dominant public policies were those that promoted access to urban markets, that effectively opened the hinterland and its resources to cities by creating cheap and fast transportation. The most important development programs for cities were the construction of canals, railroads, and turnpikes.

The public sector led in the development of these early transportation improvements. Due to the risks of these enormous undertakings, the scarcity of private capital, and the lack of experience with corporate organization, the private sector was incapable of assuming a dominant role in developing transportation systems. City and state governments, rather than the federal government, emerged as the dominant policymakers. Early attempts at federal assistance in building canals were dashed because of intense sectional rivalries between the rural, slave-owning South and the commercial, industrializing North. Due to states' ability to raise large sums of money through their bonding authority, states emerged as important early actors in constructing canals. New York State's building of the Erie Canal in 1825 precipitated intense urban and regional competition. The completion of the Erie Canal enabled western farmers to ship agricultural commodities to New York's ports, rather than to southern ports via the Mississippi River. The canal also threatened the positions of other eastern ports, such as Baltimore and Boston, as trading centers. Consequently, New York City's rapid commercial growth after 1825 precipitated a canal-building boom throughout the United States, as state governments and cities struggled to win regional economic dominion as centers of commerce and trade.

The promotion of railroads became an even more important development policy that, in turn, had important ramifications for the next political economy based on industrial capitalism. Because railroads could be built anywhere, cities and other places not located on major waterways saw railroads as the avenue for economic growth; railroads would provide links to the canal systems and thus to other commercial sites. In promoting railroads, cities themselves provided the major impetus. Private capital was more readily available than it had been for canals, but it was used in conjunction with assistance from cities, and sometimes states, in the form of land grants, charters, and financing. Cities that were best able to capture trade by sponsoring and supporting transportation improvements set themselves up to occupy prominent positions in the new industrial political economy.

A fundamental reorganization of the urban economy occurred during the industrial era (1860–1930). Once entrepreneurs broke out of their local trading hinterlands to serve a larger market, land values began to be determined by market forces arising far beyond local borders. The labor market underwent a profound transformation as the industrial economy required a larger pool of wage labor for its factories and mills. In 1849, the number of "gainful workers" totaled 7.7 million, but by 1889 the workforce had grown to 48 million.

The wage-labor market imposed a new discipline on workers. The old labor organization of small craft enterprises and family shops was shattered in order to organize large-scale production. Capital was also transformed. A national market for capital emerged as growing national wealth created financial and banking institutions that provided credit for businesses throughout the country, ending the days when merchant entrepreneurs depended on foreign and limited local sources of capital.

The transformation of land, labor, and capital profoundly affected both the role of cities in the new economy and also public policies that dominated their political agenda. Unlike the previous era when cities had only a peripheral role in the economy, cities emerged as the focus of the Industrial Revolution by becoming central places where the factors of production could be efficiently organized for large-scale manufacturing. Large cities were best able to meet the requirements of industrial production: assembling and housing large numbers of skilled and unskilled workers; providing a transportation infrastructure to promote efficient, reliable movement of freight and labor; providing access to power, water, and other services. Cities housed allied services including legal services, banking and credit, repair facilities, raw materials processors, medical facilities, and other goods and services directly related to undertaking large-scale business activity.

Railroad building by cities during the mercantile era proved critical to the development of industrial capitalism. The railroad directly stimulated economies of agglomeration to such a degree that businesses were essentially tied to the terminals, docks, wharves, and central business districts of large cities. Cities that had attained prominence in the mercantile era because their transportation networks had given them access to hinterlands became "core" cities while others developed "peripheral" or symbiotic relationships to them.

This core and periphery system of cities reduced competition among cities to such a degree that a hierarchical urban political economy emerged that was dominated by a small number of large metropolitan areas. Core cities were mainly the large urban centers that had become prominent during the commercial period, and with few exceptions they were concentrated in the Northeast, Midwest, and Middle Atlantic states, a region that became the nation's industrial heartland. After 1870, manufacturing generally concentrated in fewer large cities. By 1910, New England and the Middle Atlantic region had about 40 percent of their labor force concentrated in manufacturing, followed by the Great Lakes states with over one-third; in contrast, other sections fell below the national average of about 29 percent. By the same year, cities of the Northeast had won absolute ascendancy. They housed 70 percent of the nation's urban population and had 14 of the country's 19 largest cities.

As the large core cities became focal points of the urban industrial system, opportunities for building additional large cities disappeared. By 1890, most of the cities that achieved even moderate size during the industrial period had been founded. This left vast areas of urban America in a peripheral economic position. Although populations and businesses tended to decentralize around central cities during the entire industrial period, this trend did not begin to threaten the economic dominance of large cities until after the 1920s. Even then, the suburban challenge lay in the future. Outside of the industrial heartland, cities grew in different regions of the country, most often in symbiotic relationships with core metropolises. They consistently trailed other regions of the country in urbanization; only in the Far West did some urban centers emerge with greater economic independence from the great cities of the industrial belt.

Due to the important economic functions of cities, Americans began to live in different places, and the United States changed from being overwhelmingly rural to having a substantial urban population. Between 1860 and 1910, as total population grew from 31 million to nearly 92 million, the number of people living in incorporated municipalities (of 2,500 or more) grew from 6 million to nearly 45 million—a growth in the urban population from almost 20 percent to nearly 45 percent of the population. By the early 1920s, the United States had become a predominantly urban nation.

Coupled with this population growth were changes in the internal structure of cities. Because of their central role in the industrial economy and their tremendous population growth, the physical structure of cities changed. The use of land in cities became much more specialized than in the mercantile era. Cities not only had to meet the physical requirements of the new economic system but also the needs of the constantly growing number of residents. There were also pressures for residential segregation according to class, ethnicity, and religion as increasing numbers of immigrants arrived and became the industrial labor force.

Economic constraints on city development in the industrial era differed from those of the mercantile period. Regional wars of city imperialism dissipated as industrialization gave birth to the less competitive core and periphery system of cities in which central cities were the prime locale for economic activity. The internal physical development of the city itself, rather than that of the hinterland, became the primary determinant of city growth. Yet, beyond tightly bound commercial districts lay an essentially underdeveloped city pro-

viding only rudimentary, hodgepodge patterns of land use, poor roads, rickety bridges, and scarce housing. All of these were barriers to community prosperity. Industrial development demanded an urban setting that fostered the efficient organization of land, labor, and capital to succeed.

The thrust of public policy was to use government resources and regulatory powers to organize the physical urban infrastructure needed for large-scale industrial production. However, the character of these programs did not diminish the importance of private market decisions in city building. Because these ventures were less risky than canal and railroad projects, cities found a private sector eager to be involved and invest. Furthermore, city governments usually led in promoting their local economies. The dominance of a laissez-faire attitude in the federal government limited its role in economic regulation until after the turn of the century, and there was little political support for national intervention in local affairs. At the same time, state intervention in urban development remained limited.

City governments used three major policy strategies to guide their development: (1) policies to build the physical infrastructure, (2) policies to reorganize land use, and (3) policies to expand political and economic boundaries. Cities undertook programs to encourage investment in public infrastructure: roadways, bridges, tunnels, public buildings, wharves, port and transit facilities, sewerage systems, water systems, and other public services. Cities invested on an unprecedented scale for these purposes and usually financed them with long-term capital borrowing. The private sector also played a role not before seen. During the first half of this period, political leaders generally allowed the private sector to dominate the development of the infrastructure. Cities generally granted franchises for enterprises such as utilities and transportation to private companies that constructed, operated, and provided services. However, as abuses in these franchises grew, the reactions of citizens and business communities caused many cities to expand public control over the city's physical plant. By the turn of the century, many cities had constructed and were operating public transportation systems and ports or were relying on greater state regulation of private facilities.

Land use policies constituted the second major component of city development policy. Apart from land, there is virtually no economic resource over which city governments have such direct control; and because it is scarce, highly valued, and determinative of location in the production process, its allocation among competing uses provides city authorities with influence over economic development. However, most city governments adopted a laissez-faire attitude about regulating land use. City commissioners typically permitted the decisions of private builders, developers, and businesses to control the allocation of urban open space. After the turn of the century, reform groups began to demand city planning and zoning to enlarge the role of local government in shaping the use of land. This movement failed to rival the private regulation of urban space significantly.

The third type of policy to promote the central city's economic position was annexing areas outside of their political boundaries. Businesses in unincorporated areas outside the city proper were generally unable to obtain many important public services that they needed to function or expand, creating a major obstacle to city growth. Also, when economic growth spilled beyond the city's political jurisdiction, tax revenues were beyond the city's grasp. Consequently, the industrial era witnessed ambitious territorial expansion by cities all over the country. Because of the strategic economic importance of large cities, state legislatures surrendered much of their control over annexation to cities to facilitate their expansion. Between 1870 and 1900, the nation's 20 largest cities (as of 1940) made their greatest territorial conquests, expanding their combined legal area about 18 percent every decade. Although the total area of the 20 major cities expanded less rapidly after 1900, the trend continued until the 1920s but had virtually ceased by 1930.

The postindustrial era since 1930 has posed very different challenges for cities than did previous political economies. American cities now found themselves in a highly competitive environment not only with each other but also, for the first time, with suburbs and with international cities. Since about 1930, there has been a restructuring of the urban economy because of the development of multilocational corporations as the dominant form of economic organization. Due to this restructuring, the dominant economic function of cities and the kinds of public policies that city governments pursue to manage their economies have changed dramatically. Perhaps most important, the scope and intensity of urban and regional economic competition have grown enormously because of the dramatic dispersal of jobs and people. Consequently, suburbs, towns, cities, and sometimes even rural enclaves have become part of a new political economy in which they all depend on private-sector decisions about capital location.

Multilocational corporations are distinguished from ordinary businesses by their size, their multiple administrative and operational units, and their location in scattered business sites. After World War II, huge corporations were able to take advantage of dramatic technological advances. Almost countless innovations revolutionized manufacturing, including automation, the computerized assembly line, and the development of synthetics. Greater efficiency in production and distribution processes occurred as a result of communications and information innovations, and advances such as the computer and electronic data processing enabled managers to know more about the flow of goods within their firm and in the market. Today, multilocational corporations control the movement of most goods, services, and capital in the United States and have decisively shaped the economic fortunes of communities ranging from the largest American cities to rural outposts in Third World countries.

The changes in land, labor, and capital wrought by multilocational corporations have undermined the once dominant position of central cities in the United States. Urban land use and land values in urban areas have shifted in ways that do not favor central cities. Production and distribution have become highly dispersed to multiple geographic locations, where component parts of finished products are increasingly produced in separate factories and then shipped to assembly locations that are usually near the point of consumption. These decentralizing tendencies have altered urban land values. Cities in the Northeast and Midwest contained the most valuable land during the industrial era because they were the key business and manufacturing centers. But, as firms have dispersed their facilities, land values have declined in the older cities compared to other areas of the country. Similarly, advances in communications technology have permitted the dispersion of services to scattered locations of sometimes global scope. Capital has also been reorganized as corporate headquarters have split off from the multiple operating units of large enterprises, all of which can function in different locations.

As opportunities to decentralize production and distribution increased after World War II, most large corporations reorganized internally to cope with expansion and decentralization. The new corporate structure generally provided for a central headquarters staff and separate divisions for each important product line of the company. The central office became responsible for guiding the growth and operation of the entire enterprise, and its functions include allocating funds and resources within the organization, resolving conflicts among the various units, and developing new products and facilities for the company. Divisional staff headed the operating level and were responsible for producing, distributing, and marketing products and accountable for earning profits.

This reorganization of the corporation has decisively influenced capital investment patterns. The large corporation has achieved unprecedented centralized control over the distribution of capital to cities and regions across the nation and the world. Located in cities that are usually removed from production sites, the investment decisions of corporate staff determine production, distribution, and marketing systems and develop raw material sites in Western Europe, the United States, and the Third World.

The labor market has also been transformed. The service sector of the economy has mushroomed at a rate far surpassing manufacturing employment, the key labor market during the industrial period. Corporate service jobs have mainly expanded from enlarging the managerial component and the propensity of these giants to employ more office workers. By reorganizing labor and using new labor-saving technologies, American corporations have caused a greater division between blue-collar and white-collar workforces. Low-skill, low-wage jobs have become more separated from higher-skilled occupations and are increasingly located in less-developed areas of the nation and world. The work of assemblers in automated industries and of office clerical workers often takes place in different geographic settings from that of managers, professionals, and technicians.

This territorial emancipation of business and people from central cities has not only diminished the traditional market position of central cities, but it has also thrust all cities, towns, and suburbs into a new competitive environment. Furthermore, the traditional relationship between cities and business that was forged during the industrial age has for the most part been reversed. This decline of cities' economic position is dramatically seen in the reversal of historic patterns of urbanization. Population growth has shifted dramatically away from central cities to the outlying areas of cities. In 1950, three-fifths of the population in metropolitan areas lived in central cities; by 1980, three-fifths lived in suburbs. This suburban growth reflects the movement of blue-collar and white-collar jobs to the fringes of cities. Multilocational firms have built new manufacturing plants on the edge of metropolitan areas, and they have increasingly located their administrative units in suburban locations. The result is that central cities are becoming smaller, poorer, and nonwhite. Former core cities have become "converting" and "declining" cities. Some central cities—New York, Chicago, Philadelphia, Cleveland, Boston—have become a primary location for the national headquarters of large corporations. Declining cities—Buffalo, Youngstown, Gary, Newark, Toledo, Harrisburg—have emerged in far greater numbers, however.

The physical structure of former core cities has also changed because of their new economic function. In declining cities, downtown shopping and entertainment districts have been abandoned and are now primarily used by poor minorities; thrift shops have replaced once fashionable stores. In converting cities, other physical features stand out—skyscrapers for corporate offices and related services; high-rise, upper-income residences; and a network of expensive shops, restaurants, hotels, and thriving cultural institutions. In contrast, decentralization and deconcentration of social and economic activities characterize the physical and social structures of newer cities and suburbs, reflecting their essentially postindustrial origins.

The federal government has also decisively shaped the postindustrial economy of cities and suburbs. Postwar federal urban programs did little to limit the growing economic rivalries faced by local governments; in fact, they generally exacerbated these pressures. Sometimes, federal programs did so by expanding the scope of economic competition among cities. Postwar Congresses passed an array of transportation, housing, and finance programs that stimulated the development of new towns and suburbs, effectively subsidizing the flight of business and population from central cities. For example, federal transportation money was overwhelmingly directed at highway construction, rather than to support mass transit; FHA mortgage guarantees mainly assisted suburbs and discriminated against minorities.

In turn, these programs were part of a larger national policy matrix that indirectly stimulated disinvestment in older urban areas. The huge growth of federal spending on defense, public works, and research and development, together with the national government's vast tax, regulatory, and spending policies, stimulated the development of the urban periphery, especially in Sunbelt states. At the same time, the net effect of federal grant-in-aid programs on state fiscal capabilities did little to equalize the provision of public services among states and localities, leaving local governments dependent on their own local and state revenues.

Even when the federal government has sought to direct the economic development of older central cities, the effect of policy has usually been to encourage competition between cities and newer communities that other federal policies have nurtured. Beginning with urban renewal, federal programs designed to revitalize cities have promoted projects contingent on support from private capital markets and developers rather than assisting community improvements that have depended only on government financing. Consequently, policy helped tilt local capital budgets in favor of projects designed to stimulate private business development. In effect, federal urban programs have done relatively little to offset the impact of postindustrial change on city economies. Federal policy has essentially stimulated, rather than offset, competition among local governments for jobs and people.

Public intervention in the marketplace has become dramatically open-ended because few urban governments expect that any single program or series of one-time initiatives can assure a community's economic future. Local governments now frequently compete to attract capital and labor by using public policy to assume many of the risks of private enterprise on a more or less continuous basis. Such programs include tax abatements, free land, loans, worker training, and other subsidies; some large cities and state governments have attempted to create new markets via venture capital and development bank funds. They have entered fierce bidding wars with other localities by routinely "selling" public authority and resources to the private sector in hopes of attracting and keeping business investment in the locality.

The postindustrial urban system is increasingly influenced by the globalization of capital and labor. Although globalization began about 100 years ago with direct investment by industrial corporations and the establishment of production operations outside their own countries, the creation of one-world markets and world products is more recent and is gaining momentum rapidly. In a sense, the emerging globalization of business activity parallels on an international scale what has been happening since the 1930s in the United States. It is driven by the natural progression of technological advances and the emergence of multinational corporations that have been important in transforming the postindustrial urban system of the United States. The growing multinational character of large corporations has increasingly caused the dispersion of production in order to obtain cost advantages for labor and economies of scale, management organization, sales, transportation, and so on. This trend favoring the decentralization of jobs and business has also generated a greater need to coordinate business operations, resulting in international patterns of centralization with respect to strategic business functions, especially support services and financing. Consequently, international patterns of decentralization and centralization of business activities are influencing the American urban political economy.

Key trends include the growth of international financial markets, the expansion of international trade in services, and the repatterning of direct foreign investment. This internationalization is characterized by a global network of factories, service outlets, and financial markets, along with continued economic concentration. Yet only a limited number of countries and major cities account for most of the international transactions. A few cities, especially New York, London, and Tokyo, have emerged as the leading financial centers. In certain respects, a global hierarchy of cities is developing, with New York, London, and Tokyo not only the leading cities, but also the ones fulfilling coordinating roles and functioning as international marketplaces for buying and selling capital and expertise. These three cities not only compete with each other for the same business, but they also fulfill distinct roles and function as a triad. Most other cities in the global network have been unable to capture such a strategic role.

What economic globalization may mean for American cities and suburbs is that economic competition will extend further. Even American cities and suburbs that have been successful in "converting" to the postindustrial political economy will not be immune from this competition, and they may find themselves once again challenged to ensure their own economic well-being—but this time with world cities as well as American.

How American cities and suburbs will attain roles in the international urban marketplace will not be determined primarily by locational or geopolitical considerations but, rather, by their capacity to accommodate change and provide continuity and order in a turbulent environment. In all likelihood, the market position of cities will be linked to new forms of power derived from forging global relationships. There are probably no grand overarching developmental policies that city governments can pursue to attain this position. Rather, to find a niche in this emerging economy, cities and suburbs must learn how to manage development by upgrading institutions and infrastructure, conserving human and cultural resources, and improving the quality of life in order to provide the people and urban environment upon which such an economy depends. The assistance of higher-level governments in achieving these goals may be necessary, renewing interest in a national urban policy in the United States. Such aid will be forthcoming from the federal government if the viability of the nation's economy becomes identified with the role of its cities in the global economy.

—*Paul Kantor and Dorothy Krynicki*

See also

Apprenticeship; Artisans; Banks and Banking; Canals; Deindustrialization; Factory System; Factory Workers; Hinterland; Land Developers and Development; Office Work; Retail Workers; Retailing; Service Labor; Trade and Commerce; Unemployment; Unions; Women's Work.

References

Blumberg, Phillip. *The Megacorporation in American Society: The Scope of Corporate Power.* Englewood Cliffs, NJ: Prentice-Hall, 1975.

Chandler, Alfred D., Jr. *The Visible Hand: The Managerial Revolution in American Business.* Cambridge, MA: MIT Press, 1975.

Dielman, Frans M., and Chris Hamnet. "Globalization, Regulation and the Urban System: Editors' Introduction to the Special Issue." *Urban Studies* 31 (1994): 357–364. See also other articles in this issue of *Urban Studies.*

Eisinger, Peter. *The Rise of the Entrepreneurial State.* Madison: University of Wisconsin Press, 1988.

Fainstein, Norman I., and Susan S. Fainstein. *Restructuring the City: The Political Economy of Urban Redevelopment.* 2d ed. New York: Longman, 1986.

Gelfand, Mark I. *A Nation of Cities: The Federal Government and Urban America, 1933–1965.* New York: Oxford University Press, 1975.

Goodrich, Carter, ed. *Government Promotion of American Canals and Railroads, 1800–1890.* New York: Columbia University Press, 1960.

Kantor, Paul. *The Dependent City Revisited.* Boulder, CO: Westview Press, 1995.

Kirkland, Edward. *Industry Comes of Age: Business, Labor and Public Policy, 1860–1897.* New York: Holt, Rinehart and Winston, 1961.

Knight, Richard V., and Gary Gappart, eds. *Cities in a Global Society.* Newbury Park, CA: Sage Publications, 1989.

Noyelle, Thierry, and Thomas M. Stanback, Jr. *Economic Transformation in American Cities.* New York: Columbia University Press, 1989.

Pred, Allan R. *Urban Growth and City Systems in the United States, 1840–1860.* Cambridge, MA: Harvard University Press, 1980.

Sassen, Saskia. *The Global City.* Princeton, NJ: Princeton University Press, 1991.

Savitch, H. V. *Postindustrial Cities: Planning and Politics in New York, Paris, and London.* Princeton, NJ: Princeton University Press, 1988.

Savitch, H. V., and Ronald K. Vogel, eds. *Regional Politics: America in a Post-City Age.* Thousand Oaks, CA: Sage Publications, 1996.

Taylor, George Rogers. *The Transportation Revolution, 1815–1860.* New York: Holt, Rinehart and Winston, 1951.

Teaford, Jon C. *City and Suburb: The Political Fragmentation of Metropolitan America, 1850–1970.* Baltimore: Johns Hopkins University Press, 1979.

Education in Cities

Education has long been an integral part of city life in the United States, and cities have been the setting for much educational innovation and development during the past several hundred years. Schools of various sorts have existed to transmit knowledge and skills, but they have also played a key role in the socialization of youth and as guardians of acceptable standards of behavior.

It was in the nation's cities that modern school systems assumed the highly bureaucratic form characteristic of contemporary public educational systems. Because of the diverse range of students they served and the successes they experienced, these schools were often regarded quite highly in the past. Today, however, urban public schools often struggle to teach large numbers of children from backgrounds of poverty and from cultural or linguistic minority groups. As a result, education has become a significant problem in many of the nation's largest cities.

The earliest schools in North American cities appear to have been church-sponsored or conducted by private masters who taught for a fee. Only in New England were schools established by community authority, and these were predominantly religious in purpose. By the end of the eighteenth century, the largest American cities had acquired loosely structured systems of private, church-sponsored, and government-supported schools serving different classes of the population. The vast majority of these schools served only white males. Special schools did exist for blacks and for women, but they were few in number. In the eighteenth century formal education was largely a patriarchal preserve, and the best schooling was reserved for boys. This changed somewhat in the years to come.

As cities grew larger and more diverse in the nineteenth century, dramatic new developments occurred in education. With the appearance of more poor and unskilled working-class residents in the larger cities, civic leaders looked to schooling for the inculcation of bourgeois mores and standards of behavior. Whether maintained by private groups (such as the New York Public School Society) or public agencies (like the public schools in Boston) these "free" (no tuition) primary schools were initially designed to serve indigent children. Eventually they developed into fully articulated public educational systems, intended for all groups. This process occurred roughly between 1790 and 1850 and overlapped substantially with the Common School movement, which advocated greater public support for public schools and new professional standards for educators.

As city school systems grew they became differentiated, with schools representing various levels of education and specialized purposes. By the latter part of the nineteenth century, most large urban school systems had both grammar and high schools, serving graduates of the primary schools, along with schools for manual training and other vocational objectives.

While only a minority of students ever attended high school at this time, less than 25 percent in most cities, these institutions became important repositories of learning and culture. In determining entrance requirements, usually by examination, the high schools also helped set high academic standards for other institutions in urban school systems. Eventually, many big city school districts established normal schools (teacher's colleges) to meet their growing need for teachers.

The late nineteenth and early twentieth centuries were a time of rapid growth for most American cities, particularly those in the industrial Northeast, and the major challenge facing urban school districts was immediate expansion. There were also controversies over matters of curriculum and local control of schools, which led to the establishment of parochial (religious) school systems parallel to the public schools. Although they rarely educated more than one-fourth of the school population, these schools represented an important alternative to state-sponsored schools in certain cities, particularly in the industrial Northeast.

In most cities, public schools were originally decentralized, with control often located at the local (usually ward) level. This—combined with frenetic building campaigns to keep abreast of growing demand for schooling—contributed to an atmosphere rife with corruption. Reform efforts focused on taking the schools "out of politics" by instituting highly centralized bureaucratic administrative systems. This "progressive" model of school administration continues to exist in most city school systems today.

Urban schools served a diverse clientele of immigrant and native-born children, and some of these institutions became famous for the accomplishments of their students. In a number of areas, but especially in high schools and municipal colleges, many city school systems were noted for academic excellence. There were major problems as well, as cities struggled with overcrowded schools and large numbers of poor immigrant students. Most city schools were coeducational (except for some in the Northeast and South), and women outnumbered men in high schools and teacher's colleges through the 1920s, providing local schools with a steady supply of teachers. Schools also provided the necessary skills for thousands of youth, men and women alike, to take jobs in the burgeoning office economy of most cities. As formal schooling became more important in employment, education contributed to the division of labor in urban society.

Following a period of retrenchment during the Depression of the 1930s and wartime dislocations in the 1940s, urban schools underwent another period of expansion and diversification in the 1950s and 1960s. This was partly due to the baby boom of the postwar years, a rapid increase in the birthrate that caused school systems to resume building to meet rising demands for education. Schools, however, were also profoundly affected by the continuing growth patterns of North American metropolitan areas, particularly differences between central cities and their suburban surroundings. When the former president of Harvard University, James Conant, authored a report on the problems of urban education in 1961, he titled it "Slums and Suburbs."

During the 1950s and 1960s, schooling became even more critical to employment and social status, and the urban high school became an increasingly universal institution. As larger proportions of youth entered the high school, it came to represent a distinctive youth culture, which became more important in urban areas as the baby boom generation moved into adolescence. Eventually, postsecondary school enrollments increased as well, as larger numbers of these students entered colleges and universities.

The most important aspect of education in metropolitan areas, however, was the growing distinction between schools in large cities and suburban communities. The suburbs expanded quickly in the postwar years, fueled by highway construction and federally backed mortgages. At about the same time, the massive migration of rural southern blacks to cities changed the racial character of most urban areas, particularly in the North. The exodus of largely white, middle-class city residents from central cities and the arrival of poor African Americans marked a new era in urban education.

Because of nearly ubiquitous housing segregation along racial lines in American cities, the spatial organization of metropolitan schools quickly came to reflect racial differences in the larger social order. These patterns were often abetted by school authorities, who conspired to maintain segregated schools in order to pacify white

Detainees study in a classroom on Ellis Island in 1947.

parents and local real estate interests. The question of racial segregation in education became a volatile political issue in the 1950s and 1960s, both on the national level and as a local matter in cities across the country.

Following the historic *Brown v. Board of Education* U.S. Supreme Court decision in 1954, the question of desegregating urban schools became a focal point of public attention. Although concerned initially with *de jure* systems of school desegregation (mainly in the South), by the early 1960s the attention of civil rights advocates had turned to large northern city school districts, where segregated schools existed as a result of discriminatory housing practices. It was in these cases of *de facto* segregation that the fiercest battles were waged over school integration in the late 1960s and 1970s.

Buoyed by early court decisions, civil rights organizations protested school segregation in the 1960s and launched legal challenges to existing metropolitan patterns of racially separate school systems. Literally hundreds of cities undertook desegregation plans. In the early phase of this process, children were often bused between schools to achieve racial balance, a practice that engendered sometimes violent opposition from whites. Later incentive programs such as the use of "magnet" schools were employed to foster higher levels of integration.

Experts on desegregation maintain that the battle against segregation generally was more successful in the South, where formal segregationist policies could be abolished. The 1974 decision of the Supreme Court in the case of *Milliken v. Bradley,* which rejected a plan to desegregate schools throughout metropolitan Detroit, ended most efforts to desegregate across city lines.

As central cities have continued to lose white, middle-class residents to suburbs in the past 15 years, many have come to see the desegregation effort as a failure. Most big city school systems today enroll a large majority of their students from poor families or from racial or linguistic minorities. As cities have lost both industry and affluent residents, the tax base for urban school districts has declined. Federal and state dollars augment local revenues to some extent, but they are often earmarked for particular programs; and this hardly compensates for the adversities that big city schools endure. Once proud vehicles of social mobility for thousands of urban youth, city schools today are known more for dismal academic performance and a host of social problems associated with the inner-city neighborhoods they serve.

Meanwhile, many suburban schools have become centers of excellence in American education, highlighting the deterioration of urban institutions even more. While there is great variety in both contexts, the difference between central city schools and their suburban counterparts has never been greater. Overcoming this difference, and everything it represents, remains the biggest challenge to urban education for the future.

—*John L. Rury*

See also
Desegregation of Education.
References
Kaestle, Carl F. *Pillars of the Republic: Common Schools and American Society.* New York: Hill and Wang, 1983.
Rury, John L., and Frank A. Cassell, eds. *Seeds of Crisis: Public Schooling in Milwaukee since 1920.* Madison: University of Wisconsin Press, 1993.
Tyack, David C. *The One Best System: A History of Urban Education in the United States.* Cambridge, MA: Harvard University Press, 1974.

Electrification

The electrification of cities was a piecemeal affair that began with laying telegraph lines in the 1840s. These bestowed commercial advantages on cities (as opposed to the countryside) by focusing news and information on them. Likewise, the telegraph facilitated the expansion of large enterprises, notably railroads and stock markets. At the same time, a series of technologies based on the telegraph, such as burglar alarms, stable calls, and doorbells, familiarized people with the idea that a current carried over wires could be instantaneously transmitted virtually anywhere.

However, practical applications of this notion were few because most electricity still came from batteries, and the use of electricity to provide light, heat, or power was limited until the availability of large, efficient generators in the 1870s. Until then, "impractical" electric lighting was confined to special effects in theaters.

Both in Europe and the United States, regular public electric lighting first appeared in the late 1870s as a spectacular display in city centers and at expositions and fairs. In each setting, electric lighting had to compete with existing gas systems. Department stores and clothiers quickly adopted arc lights because they were cleaner, brighter, and safer than gas, and because they proved popular with customers.

For similar reasons of cleanliness, brightness, and safety, Thomas Edison's enclosed incandescent light (whose distribution system and pricing were designed with competing gas systems in mind) was rapidly adopted where convenience and fashion were most important. First displayed in 1879, his system spread rapidly during the following decade into the wealthiest homes, the best theaters, and the most exclusive clubs in New York, Chicago, and other large cities. In many cases, isolated plants were installed (in skyscrapers, for example) obviating the need to secure permission to deliver current through public streets via overhead wires (which soon became a public nuisance because of their number) or conduits (which were costly to lay under streets). As a result, a patchwork of competing and incongruent services developed in the 1880s. These were later integrated into unified, mostly privately owned, utility companies, though Progressives did create some public systems, notably in Seattle and Cleveland. Nevertheless, because of the high cost of producing electrical current, as well as the high cost of changing systems, gas supplied the vast majority of private homes with light and heat until 1910. The major shift to electricity did not occur until the years between 1918 and 1929.

In contrast, electric lighting dominated public spaces quickly and by 1900 had already reached an intensity well beyond the purely functional. American cities became the most intensively lighted in the world, not least because of the speed of electric advertising. Spurred by the "white way" campaigns of General Electric and the utility companies, even smaller cities aspired to have a "great white way" in imitation of New York, where millions of bulbs flashed in Times Square, creating a new, artificial environment.

During these same years, electric traction, often powered by its own generating plants, rapidly displaced horsecar lines and steam transit systems because of its aesthetic and technological advantages. Electric trolleys were faster and cleaner than horsecars; they could stop more precisely and climb steeper grades than cars powered with steam. Electric cars could also be lighted at night and heated in winter. Real estate promoters often invested in or owned traction companies, whose spreading lines defined much suburban and regional development, as in Los Angeles, Boston, and Minneapolis. By 1902, residents of large cities averaged between 230 and 265 trips a year, and Americans as a group took 4.8 billion journeys a year on streetcars.

In addition, on evenings and weekends electric companies used their superfluous generating capacity to power amusement parks. The technology of electric traction was the basis of the roller coaster, the subterranean tour, and many other rides. Trolley parks—so called because trolley companies constructed them to attract more riders—spread rapidly after 1888, and by 1901 more than half of all traction companies operated at least one amusement park, and frequently more. These diversions typically generated as much as 30 percent of a line's overall traffic, as well as providing a market for electricity. Thus, the trolley established the city as the center of an easily accessible network, from the downtown shopping district to streetcar suburbs to the amusement park and on out to rural hamlets on interurban lines.

Factory and industrial electrification also began with lighting and traction. Flour and cotton mills quickly adopted electric light because of its safety and ease of handling; printers, artists, and others whose work required accuracy and true color values found incandescent light preferable to gas;

and factory owners soon discovered that artificial light allowed large interior spaces without regard for windows.

Electric traction proved especially useful in moving materials, particularly in mines and other closed environments. Traction was adapted to overhead hoists and cranes, which began to move their loads more freely overhead when electric motors replaced drive shafts. In short, electricity revolutionized factory design by brightening and opening up work space; it also made new work flows possible, most notably on assembly lines where machines powered by electricity could be arranged in combinations that were impossible with older systems of delivering power.

This is not to say that electrification necessarily caused a particular form of mass production. Rather, it facilitated experiments and new designs. At the same time, electrification changed the location requirements of factories that no longer needed access to rushing water or to coal. Because power lines could reach virtually anywhere, factories could move to the edge of cities or out along main highways. Thus, electrification transformed factory layouts and the location of industry, and it contributed to the gradual disaggregation of walking cities into postindustrial cities that sprawled beyond suburbs into the hinterland. While the automobile has received more attention as an explanation for this development, full deployment of the electrical grid was a precondition for decentralization away from railway lines and the older urban core.

The electrification of homes spread from the wealthy to the middle class only after factory electrification was well under way. The domestic market became attractive to utilities once the overall load curve peaked during the day, creating a need for compensating nighttime demand from homes and apartments. At first, only lighting was installed, but a series of domestic electric appliances soon appeared, in roughly the order of irons, fans, vacuum cleaners, and washing machines by the 1920s, followed by radios, stoves, phonographs with loud speakers, and refrigerators in the 1930s. Thereafter came a host of other technologies, the most important being air conditioning. It began in public buildings such as movie theaters well before World War II but only became widespread after the war, gradually assuming central importance in climate control, particularly in the warmer parts of the United States. Since electricity also makes possible the creation of artificial daylight, precise delivery of ventilation, and rapid vertical movement on escalators and elevators, it clearly played a central role in creating new urban environments, ranging from the skyscraper, giant department store, amusement park, assembly-line factory, and subway of the early twentieth century to the malls and domed stadiums of later decades. In short, the modern city is unimaginable without electricity, a technology that underlies many changes in design and function at every level of society. Its importance becomes starkly apparent when power fails, and a city is plunged into darkness and many of its functions are paralyzed, most obviously communications, work, law enforcement, entertainment, and transportation.

—David Nye

See also
Blackouts; Cable Cars; Street Lighting; Streetcars.
References
Hughes, Thomas P. *Networks of Power: Electrification in Western Society, 1880–1930.* Baltimore: Johns Hopkins University Press, 1983.
Nye, David E. *Electrifying America: Social Meanings of a New Technology.* Cambridge, MA: MIT Press, 1990.
Platt, Harold L. *The Electric City: Energy and the Growth of the Chicago Area, 1880–1930.* Chicago: University of Chicago Press, 1991.

Elevated Railways

Elevated railways, usually called els or elevateds, are electric railroads that run on tracks raised above the ground. The tracks are supported by strong steel beams or rest on embankments. Elevated trains help make traffic less crowded on the ground.

The elevated car gets its power from a third rail that runs along the track. A powerhouse sends electric current along the third rail, and the elevated train picks it up from a metal plate that slides along the rail. The plate is connected to the monitor, which turns the car wheels. The engineer who runs the train has a lever on his platform that controls the amount of current the motor receives. With this lever the engineer starts and stops the train and controls its speed.

The elevated railroad was a partial solution to congestion that had reached critically high levels in densely populated areas by the mid-nineteenth century and had begun to prohibit fast, high-volume traffic. Elevated railways are expensive to build, and, therefore, despite their advantages, they developed more slowly than less capital-intensive alternatives such as streetcars.

New York was the first city to construct an elevated railway in 1868, and Chicago followed in 1892. Chicago's system was connected together in 1900 to form the downtown Loop that still operates today. An extensive network of both elevated and subway lines was built in New York City, with the elevateds on Manhattan Island ultimately being eliminated because of their unsightly features.

Elevated railways usually connected the more developed residential and business areas of cities to the central business district, following the pattern of previous transportation routes. This provided already heavily populated areas with an alternate means of transportation, which helped to decrease traffic congestion.

When el systems were expanded, new feeder lines were constructed and new routes developed. As these new lines extended farther outside the downtown area, growth appeared to follow Homer Hoyt's theory of sectoral growth. Due to the speed of elevated trains, el stations were spaced farther apart. This enabled new business and residential activities to develop around outlying stations, creating many new independent suburbs along the radial transportation nodes.

Many people have criticized the elevated structure itself for its unsightliness and the excessive noise caused by passing trains. Other criticisms have been leveled at el structures located in streets instead of alleys. This latter condition shut out light and adversely affected abutting property unless it was industrial. Some individuals defended elevated structures by emphasizing their lower cost in comparison to subways.

The high cost of building elevateds and subways could be justified only in large cities that generated extremely high volumes of traffic. Elevateds and subways built in the United States during the latter part of the nineteenth and early part of the twentieth century were restricted to New York, Chicago, Boston, and Philadelphia. In recent years Miami, Florida, has added an elevated system, which is referred to as heavy rail.

The most comprehensive study of the impact of an elevated railway on an urban area was made in Chicago. Construction of Chicago's elevated railway system began in 1892 and was completed in 1908. This system followed the previous transportation routes of horse railways, early railroads, and cable cars. The el was first built on Chicago's South Side, then the West Side, and later the North Side. Prior to the construction of this system, Chicago's North Side was minimally developed due to its lack of accessibility to the rest of the city. Construction of the el changed that, as the system provided the North Side with the fast, convenient, low-cost transportation required to serve and promote public convenience and necessity. On the North Side of Chicago, the greatest amount of new construction after the el first operated occurred in areas farthest from the central business district that had previously been ineffectively served by transportation. Settlement tended to occur as close to the el stations as the availability of land permitted, with a consistent pattern of decreasing new settlement away from the el stations.

The greatest increase in land values also took place in the areas farthest from the central business district. More than 80 percent of the northernmost stations had their highest land values in the first block around the el stations, while more than 40 percent of those stations had a pattern of decreasing land values away from the stations.

Chicago's elevated railway system turned out to be one of the country's largest public works. A decline in ridership later occurred due to the automobile, but the el still benefits the city by providing a congested metropolitan area with another source of fast, efficient, high-capacity transportation.

—*James L. Davis*

References

Davis, James Leslie. *The Elevated System and the Growth of Northern Chicago.* Northwestern University Studies in Geography, no. 10. Evanston, IL: Northwestern University Press, 1965.

Fellman, Jerome D. "Pre-Building Growth Patterns of Chicago." *Annals of the Association of American Geographers* 47 (1957): 58–82.

Hanson, Susan, ed. *The Geography of Urban Transportation.* 2d ed. New York: Guilford Press, 1995.

Pickrell, Don H. "A Desire Named Street Car: Fantasy and Fact in Rail Transit Planning." *Journal of the American Planning Association* 58 (1992): 158–176.

Spengler, Edwin H. *Land Values in New York in Relation to Transit Facilities.* New York: Columbia University Press, 1930.

Elevators

The vertical movement of people and goods has always been a challenge. For centuries, lifting machinery consisted of contrivances of ropes and pulleys powered by animals or humans themselves. Only in nineteenth century England was the technology rationalized and mechanized, and by the 1830s the teagle, a type of open-platform elevator, was in use. The teagle was a simple, slow-moving machine adequate for hoisting and lowering mill workers and goods to the floors of multistory factory buildings. Power to operate it came from the same steam engine that drove a factory's other machinery.

The general acceptance and widespread use of passenger elevators came about only after the machinery had been improved enough to be considered safe. Prior to that time, riders faced possible injury or even death from uncontrolled descent resulting from broken lifting ropes. When Elisha Graves Otis introduced a reliable safety catch designed to stop a falling platform automatically, the use of elevators in public places became a reality. The first successful installation took place in 1857 in the five-story building of New York china merchant E. V. Haughnout.

A steam-powered winch raised and lowered passenger cars equipped with the Otis safety catch by reeling in or paying out cable. Not only did the elevator enable customers to reach all floors of a building, it demonstrated the viability of multistoried commercial structures. The number of flights of stairs people were willing or able to climb had been a major factor in determining building height; floors difficult to reach were an economic liability but no longer.

Rather than being hoisted from above, the cars of direct-acting or plunger-type hydraulic elevators were pushed up from below. Hydraulic pressure acting against a piston encased in a cylinder provided the necessary force. Introduced in the late 1860s, this type of elevator was used in private residences as well as in larger and taller public buildings. Analogous in operation, using water pressure to raise and gravity to lower cars, rope-geared hydraulic elevator machinery appeared in the 1870s. Functioning as a giant tackle, its cable-and-sheave construction multiplied force and distance, enabling it to raise a car to the top of the era's tallest structures.

Despite the success of these lifting systems, they were suitable only for buildings of limited height. In those of 15 or more stories, the machinery was so large and cumbersome that it was itself an economic liability. Despite its importance to the utilization of the facility, space dedicated to hoisting machinery produced no direct revenue.

Of no less significance in determining building height were construction techniques. With traditional methods employing load-bearing walls, multistory buildings had a practical height limitation. Although some stood as high as 10 or even 16 stories, 6 or so was the norm. As height increased, lower walls had to be increasingly thick in order to support the weight of the mass above. As a result, usable interior space on bottom floors diminished, a critical matter in commercial structures.

In 1885, a watershed was reached with the construction of William Le Baron Jenney's Home Insurance Building in Chicago. Not only was it 10 stories high, it was the first building with a metal-frame skeleton structure, and although not particularly tall, it demonstrated that construction techniques need not limit the height of buildings. Metal columns extending its full height supported the entire weight of the metal framework on which it was built. Walls no longer critical to structural integrity now functioned merely as curtains providing protection from the elements. But, although a building might rise to any height in theory, steam and hydraulic elevating equipment was being designed and operated at its physical and practical limits. The means for overcoming these bounds were at hand in 1889 when the first electrically driven elevator was installed in New York City's Demarest Building.

Finally, the innovation came to fruition with the introduction of electric gearless traction. It was both a simplification of the machinery and also a breakthrough. The basic equipment was reduced to nothing more than an electric motor and sheave. An elevator could reach the top of any structure regardless of its height, but the machinery was compact and mounted above the car at the top of the shaft. The installation in 1903 of a gearless elevator in the Beaver Building in New York ushered in the era of the tall building, opening the way for 40, 60, 100, or even more stories.

An entire structure could be economically viable regardless of its height. Space previously set aside for hoisting machinery could be used profitably. While the lower floors had been more desirable previously because they could be reached easily, upper floors were now sought for their views and their isolation from street-level noise. The means of getting people to upper floors no longer determined a building's height. Construction technology and the elevator complemented each other, and what resulted was the ability to construct "skyscrapers"—buildings of seemingly unlimited height. Speeds steadily increased to the point where an elevator might travel 700 feet or more per minute. So satisfactory has this mechanism been that later improvements in elevators have been mostly refinements in the basic mechanical design.

A recent innovation, brought about by economic considerations as well as aesthetics and one found primarily in hotels, is the exterior observation elevator. Truly space savers, they travel on either interior or exterior exposed walls or columns. Cars, some quite ornate, consist primarily of windows and offer dramatic panoramic views. And interior building space formerly lost to elevator shafts can be used more profitably.

—*William Worthington*

References

Baxter, William. *Hydraulic Elevators, Their Design, Construction, Operation, Care and Management.* New York: McGraw-Hill, 1910.

Elliott, Cecil D. *Technics and Architecture.* Cambridge, MA: MIT Press, 1992.

Gavois, Jean. *Going Up: An Informal History of the Elevator from the Pyramids to the Present.* New York: Otis Elevator Co., 1982.

Goldberger, Paul. *The Skyscraper.* New York: Knopf, 1981.

Jallings, John H. *A Practical Treatise on the Development and Design of Hand, Belt, Steam, Hydraulic, and Electric Elevators.* Chicago: American Technical Society, 1915.

Eliot, Charles (1859–1897)

Charles Eliot was born and educated in Cambridge, Massachusetts, and he practiced landscape architecture from 1887 until his death from spinal meningitis in the spring of 1897. His reputation rests on two key accomplishments. In 1891, he led the fight to establish Massachusetts's Trustees of Public Reservations, the first private sector, statewide organization for the conservation of natural areas and the preservation of historic sites, which became a model for subsequent efforts in the United States and abroad. Second, Eliot was the landscape architect for the Boston Metropolitan Park System, the first regional landscape authority in the United States.

Eliot was the son of Charles W. Eliot, the influential president of Harvard University for four decades and the author of the modern American university system. The younger Eliot developed an intimate love of nature by hiking throughout the Boston area as a boy and sailing along the coast of Maine during summers. At Harvard, he formed the Champlain Society, a group of undergraduates who spent two summers camping and recording the natural history of Mount Desert Island in Maine. After graduation from Harvard, young Eliot attended courses at the Bussey Institute and spent two years as an apprentice in the Brookline office of Frederick Law Olmsted. There he worked on a wide range of projects, including the Boston Metropolitan Park System and the Arnold Arboretum. From the fall of 1885 through the end of 1886, Eliot traveled and studied independently in Europe, where he read the literature of landscape architecture and gardening and visited private estates, public parks, and the offices of landscape architects from England to Italy to Russia.

When he returned to the United States, he began a career writing on landscape issues for the professional and the popular press and as a landscape architect. His important early commissions included the Longfellow Memorial Park (1887) in Cambridge, Massachusetts, and the White Park (1890) in Concord, New Hampshire, where he began to develop a philosophy of landscape design and landscape conservation. In frequent contributions to *Garden and Forest,* he began devising schemes to preserve and manage landscapes of natural, scenic, or historic significance.

Early in 1893, he formed a partnership with Frederick Law Olmsted and John Charles Olmsted. Until his death in 1897 he was consumed with the rapid development of the Boston Metropolitan Park System and the Cambridge Municipal Park System. His ideal of a regional plan that would include diverse types of landscape—ocean beach, harbor islands, tidal estuaries, woodland reservations, and public playgrounds—led to the emergence of city planning as an extension of landscape architecture.

—*Keith Morgan*

See also

Landscape Architecture and Urban Design; Olmsted, Frederick Law.

References

Eliot, Charles. *Vegetation and Scenery in the Metropolitan Reservations of Boston. A Forestry Report Written by Charles Eliot and Presented to the Metropolitan Park Commission, February 15, 1897 by Olmsted, Olmsted and Eliot.* Boston, New York, and London: Lamson, Wolffe, 1898.

———. "The Waverley Oaks." *Garden and Forest* 3 (March 5, 1890): 117–118.

Eliot, Charles W. *Charles Eliot, Landscape Architect.* Boston and New York: Houghton Mifflin; Cambridge, MA: Riverside Press, 1902.

Morgan, Keith N. "Held in Trust: Charles Eliot's Vision for the New England Landscape." *National Association for Olmsted Parks Workbook* 1 (1991): 1–12.

Newton, Norman. *Design on the Land: The Development of Landscape Architecture,* 318–336. Cambridge, MA: Harvard University Press, 1971.

Empire State Building

For many years, the Empire State Building was the most famous of New York's many skyscrapers, eclipsed perhaps only since 1972 when the World Trade Center exceeded its height. The building was renowned not only for its height (1,454 feet with 102 stories) and its appearance but also for its construction. That 3,500 laborers were able to erect an average of five and a half stories a week and that not more than a year elapsed between groundbreaking ceremonies and the arrival of the first tenants in 1931 depended on the exceptional efficiencies of the architects and developers. Skillful designers of office buildings in Manhattan, the architectural firm of Shreve, Lamb and Harmon were familiar with the imperatives of design and construction that meant to maximize returns to investors by filling the building with tenants as quickly as possible. For more than a decade, contractor William Starrett had been refining a construction process that grew out of his leadership during World War I in the rapid construction of domestic military training facilities, a process that maximized the number of building operations carried out simultaneously or in overlapping sequences.

Due to the city's setback requirements, the limestone-clad building appeared to be a sculpted masonry mass, giving to business imagery the substantial character that businessmen demanded. The uninterrupted metal mullions gleaming in the sunlight emphasized the building's radical height and served to set off the handsome proportions of its upper and lower setbacks in relation to the soaring tower. Pulled out in front of the rest of the building, the first five stories put the skyscraper's enormity at a comfortable remove from passersby. Inside, the stylistically transitional lobby sported modernistic chevrons on the floor, while the metal bridge and other rounded features were inspired by modern motifs in recent transport design. In marble and aluminum inlay, a huge elevation of the Empire State Building dominated a large wall mosaic, whose radiating beams celebrated the building's thoroughly rationalized and improbable elegance.

—*Edward W. Wolner*

References
Goldman, Jonathan. *The Empire State Building Book.* New York: St. Martin's Press, 1980.
James, Theodore. *The Empire State Building.* New York: Harper & Row, 1975.
Tauranac, John. *The Empire State Building: The Making of a Landmark.* New York: Scribners, 1995.

Erie Canal

Blake McKelvey, an early urban historian, called the Erie Canal the "mother of cities." Cutting across New York State from Albany to Buffalo, this first canal to connect East and West was especially notable for the cities it created. Along the Mohawk River, the canal passed Schenectady, Little Falls, and Utica. But the decision for a canal to strike out parallel to the shore of Lake Ontario, north of the older stage route through Batavia, made it inevitable that the canal would create new towns and cities.

Syracuse grew at the junction of the Erie Canal and the Oswego Canal to Lake Ontario; Rochester grew where the Erie Canal crossed the Genesee River; at Lockport the canal surmounted the "mountain ridge" using a five-lock combine; and Buffalo became the terminus of the canal on Lake Erie. Syracuse was noted for its salt industry, and Rochester became a flour and milling center for wheat from the shores of the Great Lakes and western New York. In Buffalo, elevators rose to hold grain to be shipped east on the canal. Other towns added the suffix "port" to their names, such as Weedsport and Brockport. While some city hinterlands grew, one study has shown that the hinterland of Syracuse declined because of competition from places further west.

Among older Mohawk Valley cities, Schenectady was a passenger terminus for the Erie Canal as most passengers took the short stage route to Albany, saving a day's travel by canal; after 1831 they rode the Mohawk and Hudson Railroad. At Rome, the Erie Canal connected to the Black River Canal, which led into the foothills of the Adirondacks. Cities such as Utica, Seneca Falls, and Rochester connected to branch canals, reaching south toward the Susquehanna and Allegheny Rivers. Canal traffic at the Hudson River reached both Albany and Troy. The canal ran five miles along the Hudson to Albany, but boats could lock into the river opposite Troy, which received about a third of the canal commerce. At the mouth of the Hudson, New York City grew dramatically, in part because of the canal, although its growth was largely due to its position in world trade.

The Erie Canal had a social and cultural impact on towns and cities through which it passed. It brought thousands of immigrants west, and canal laborers added to the ethnic diversity of canal settlements. Whitney R. Cross has found the Erie Canal to have been a primary influence on the "burned-over district" when western New York was caught up in revivalism and social reforms. Rochester was the location of the Millerite movement in the 1840s, the spiritualism of the Fox sisters, and the establishment of the North Star by the former slave, Frederick Douglass. Paul E. Johnson has described the efforts of Rochester's gentry to control the intemperance and violence associated with canal boatmen, and at Palmyra, near Rochester, Joseph Smith founded Mormonism.

The Erie Canal became part of the New York Barge Canal in 1905, and though its commerce has declined, it is increasingly used for recreational purposes.

—*Ronald E. Shaw*

References
Cross, Whitney R. *The Burned-Over District: The Social and Intellectual History of Enthusiastic Religion in Western New York, 1800–1850.* Ithaca, NY: Cornell University Press, 1950.
Johnson, Paul E. *A Shopkeeper's Millennium: Society and Revivals in Rochester, New York, 1815–1837.* New York: Hill and Wang, 1978.

Maddox, Vivian Dawn. "The Effect of the Erie Canal on Building and Planning in Syracuse, Palmyra, Rochester, and Lockport, New York." Ph.D. dissertation, Cornell University, 1976.

McKelvey, Blake. "The Erie Canal, Mother of Cities." *New York Historical Quarterly* 35 (1951): 55–71.

Miller, Roberta B. *City and Hinterland: A Case Study of Urban Growth and Regional Development*. Westport, CT: Greenwood Press, 1979.

Shaw, Ronald E. *Erie Water West: A History of the Erie Canal, 1792–1854*. Lexington: University of Kentucky Press, 1966.

Sherriff, Carol. *The Artificial River: The Erie Canal and the Paradox of Progress, 1817–1862*. New York: Hill and Wang, 1976.

Ethnic Neighborhood

The ethnic neighborhood is a complex entity. The concept itself, compound in nature, embraces a wide range of cultural, historical, political, and geographical ideas, debates, and theories. The simplest definition of ethnicity is that it is a collective identity supported by social institutions like language, family, and religion. Ethnicity can be further reinforced by residential proximity, hence ethnic neighborhoods are often seen to be a highly tangible arena for the construction and maintenance of collective identity. It is important to point out, however, that these descriptions leave out much of the history and the differing theoretical explanations of a fairly ubiquitous aspect of American urban social and cultural geography.

The history of ethnic residential segregation in the United States appears very much to parallel the related processes of industrialization and urbanization. The evidence from censuses of population, maps, city plans, and so on indicates that the physical or population growth of urban areas fosters the internal differentiation of land uses, including the separation of population largely by class and ethnicity. Residential division is further aided and reinforced by technological innovation, especially the transformations of communication and transportation.

American cities first experienced significant ethnic residential segregation at the beginning of the nineteenth century as the national economy changed from a preindustrial to an industrial base. Residential segregation based on class had been a prominent feature of most preindustrial urban settlements, with wealthy and politically prominent residents occupying central locations, the poor at the urban fringes, and craft and tradespeople in between.

Early urban industrialization in the United States was accompanied by substantial immigration from Ireland, Germany, and Scandinavia. These immigrations transformed preindustrial residential patterns and created a new layer of differentiation based on an emerging "ethnic" identity that was constructed as much from within the immigrant group as from outside it. As urban scholars have shown, walking distance to important functional areas of preindustrial cit-

ies was the attraction of residential locations in the central city. As immigration accelerated and the intensified economic activity of the central city was accompanied by noise, pollution, and other sorts of hazard and unpleasantness, the affluent (eventually encouraged by transportation innovations) began moving outward, to locations adjacent to the still fairly compact cities but where they could enjoy a more "healthy" and spacious lifestyle and yet have the city within easy reach.

As wealthy residents began abandoning the central areas of American cities in the early nineteenth century, they left behind a housing stock that could be subdivided and rented cheaply to the new immigrant populations. For example, in Lowell, Massachusetts, one of the first industrial cities in the United States, Irish immigrants were a large part of the labor force responsible for constructing factories, housing, roads, bridges, and administrative buildings. In the 1830s, as the village of Chelmsford was developing into the mill town of Lowell, its social geography duplicated the classic model of the "walking city." A small group of mill owners and managers and other social elites lived in the city center; small business owners, commercial agents, and factory operatives resided in boarding houses just beyond the elite; and the immigrant Irish occupied "shanty towns" on the fringe of the city. Within several decades, transportation innovations enabled the wealthy, and later the emerging middle class, to move away from deteriorating conditions in the city center to peripheral locations.

This migration to outlying areas left even more housing stock available for immigrants, and while "the Acre," Lowell's shanty town, continued to house poor, Irish laborers, other more central locations became available for Irish residence. By 1860, there were Irish neighborhoods in several parts of the city, as well as French-Canadian neighborhoods. In the 1880s and 1890s, Greek, Polish, and Italian neighborhoods began appearing. One hundred years later, Dominicans, Cambodians, and Laotians, along with other "new immigrant" groups, occupy Lowell neighborhoods as the "suburbanization" of the middle- and upper-income classes continues.

It is generally accepted that ethnic residential patterning has become a permanent feature of American cities as international, national, and regional migration impulses continue drawing new and different immigrant groups to cities. Intellectual approaches to understanding and conceptualizing the American ethnic neighborhood are closely coincident with the unfolding phenomenon itself. As David Ward has demonstrated, social reformers in the mid-nineteenth century used words like "slum" and "ghetto" to describe ethnic residential districts in American cities and conceived them as sites of deprivation, dissolution, and despair. Whereas the word "slum" was originally invoked to describe the negative consequences of industrialization on the residential areas of poor, sometimes immigrant, populations, the word "ghetto" was (and continues to be) used as a way of describing the segregation of immigrants in slum areas.

Throughout the nineteenth century, these concepts represented ethnic residential and social space as environmentally bankrupt and its occupants as morally pathological. The outsiders who deployed these concepts, mostly social reformers and clergy, addressed the supposed pathologies by attempting to change the environment, individuals, and families affected by them. Amelioration came in the form of missions and asylums operating within the very environment that the missionaries sought to change. By the end of the nineteenth century, a professional cadre of social reformers was tackling (what they perceived as) the environmental and social problems of slums and ghettos by advocating public policies to improve sanitation and water systems, as well as other large-scale environmental improvements.

As the American population became predominantly urban by 1920, a new group of scholars began to advance theories and models that explained ethnic neighborhoods in terms of both the institutional and moral orders operating there, as well as the potential for assimilating immigrants into mainstream society. Conceptualizing ethnic neighborhoods as living, changing organisms, this approach modeled the occupancy dynamics of neighborhoods themselves. This scholarly outlook tended, through ethnographic methods, to emphasize both the positive and the negative forces at work in ethnic neighborhoods where "communities" became a way of coping with urban industrial pressures and constraints.

In the newly created Department of Sociology at the University of Chicago, Robert E. Park, Ernest W. Burgess, Louis Wirth, and others developed and refined an inductive model of the changing social geography of Chicago at mid-century. They then generalized their model in order to understand the dynamics of neighborhoods in other American cities. Urban ecology (or *human ecology,* as this approach came to be known) is a dynamic model of the city that seeks to explain how various subgroups of the population organize spatially as a response to changes in the urban environment. Ecologists regard urban social geography as the ever-changing outcome of competition among groups for particular urban spaces; for example, ones with locational advantages to jobs or with stocks of cheap housing. The ecological approach views the residents of ethnic neighborhoods not so much as victims or carriers of moral contagion but as active participants in the changing urban landscape.

The Chicago school has continued to influence research and conceptualizations about American ethnic neighborhoods. Yet, while numerous adherents have refined the early model, there are major detractors as well. One criticism of urban ecology has come from social history and argues that the accounts of the Chicago school have misrepresented the multiethnic complexity of American urban neighborhoods. Based on quantitative, historical census data, these analyses have demonstrated that ethnic neighborhoods in the nineteenth century were not homogeneous and that ethnic groups mixed a great deal geographically. In fact, specific measures of segregation, such as the index of dissimilarity, were developed to assess just how segregated particular ethnic groups were. When applied to a range of American cities, the index demonstrates that ethnic residential concentrations in nineteenth- and twentieth-century cities were not as pronounced as has been assumed, and arguments about the problematic relationship between urban space and different ethnic groups lost a great deal of their cogency.

In the late 1960s and early 1970s a more comprehensive criticism of urban ecology emerged. This critique argues that urban ecology seriously undervalued broader structural forces shaping the choices and constraints of immigrants and others seeking to construct new lives in American cities. These critics see ethnic neighborhoods as one product of the structural inequalities of a capitalist political economy. As such, they conclude that previous interpretations of ethnic neighborhoods, slums, and ghettos are misdirected in attempting to alter individual behavior or reform the spaces of ethnic neighborhoods rather than the political economy that produces them.

David Harvey, in *Social Justice and the City,* elaborates this structural approach to urban residential spaces and the limitations of human ecology and the Neoclassical economic approach. Arguing that capitalist urban development emphasizes the market value of land over its practical and sentimental value, Harvey shows how ethnic neighborhoods result from capitalist market functions; from federal, regional, and local planning; and from administrative decisions and practices. While accepting the position that the capitalist political economy is a pervasive force in shaping cities, John Logan and Harvey Molotch also assert that ethnic neighborhoods are sites of cultural production and sentimental attachments and that a comprehensive assessment of them must consider both the relationships that constitute neighborhoods as communities as well as the capitalist market value of ethnic neighborhoods.

Most recently, feminist scholars and other social theorists have addressed ethnic neighborhoods and other spatial groups by critically reevaluating the concept of community. The predominant question for theorists of contemporary culture, particularly urban culture, has been what constitutes a community? By extension, how do the powerful forces of difference and diversity within a group undermine traditional notions about social groups with a territorial base that are apparently (ethnically or otherwise) homogeneous? So far, the most interesting attempts to address these questions have looked not at numerical measures, such as geographical propinquity, but at self-defining measures, such as participation in a common enterprise. The existence of an ethnic neighborhood can be confirmed by analyzing block-level census data, but whether the inhabitants constitute themselves as a cultural, political, economic, or social community with respect to their common residence is a more complex and subjective issue that has yet to be resolved.

The history of American ethnic neighborhoods is long, and the phenomenon has been the object of much intellectual debate and theorizing, as well as social reform and policy attention. Social reformers, journalistic observers, policymakers, and academics have all contributed to understanding the multifaceted meaning of the ethnic neighborhood in cities. Unfortunately, this meaning is the construction of outsiders who have observed the routines and practices of the residents of ethnic neighborhoods but who have rarely experienced the neighborhoods themselves as residents. Even rich and evocative portraits of ethnic neighborhood life, such as Herbert Gans's classic *The Urban Villagers,* construct their meaning from the perspective of a sympathetic outsider looking in. The meanings of ethnic neighborhoods generated by residents themselves are often fragmentary and somewhat idiosyncratic renderings of festivals, pageants, or other forms of street life that outsiders see as merging political, cultural, and recreational expressions of ethnicity. More recently, the emergence of rap music can certainly be regarded as a commercialized commentary on the meaning of ghetto life by (mostly young male) African-American and Hispanic residents.

—*Sallie Marston*

See also

Barrio; Burgess, Ernest W.; Chicago School of Sociology; Chinatown; Community; Ghetto; Neighborhood; Park, Robert Ezra; Walking City; Wirth, Louis.

References

Gans, Herbert. *The Urban Villagers: Group and Class in the Life of Italian Americans.* New York: Free Press, 1962. Rev. ed., 1982.

Harvey, David. *Social Justice and the City.* Baltimore: Johns Hopkins University Press, 1975.

Logan, John, and Harvey Molotch. *Urban Fortunes: The Political Economy of Place.* Berkeley: University of California Press, 1987.

Pratt, M. B. "Identity: Skin Blood Heart." In E. Burkin, M. B. Pratt, and B. Smith, eds., *Yours in Struggle: Three Feminist Perspectives on Anti-Semitism and Racism.* New York: Long Haul Press, 1984.

Ward, David. *Poverty, Ethnicity, and the American City, 1840–1925.* Cambridge, England: Cambridge University Press, 1989.

Factory System

The factory system was at the core of the Industrial Revolution. This system brought human labor, technology, and managerial strategies together to produce goods faster and more cheaply. Factories encompassed a growing population of workers and subjected those laborers to a work regimen that was divided into a series of discrete tasks, subjected to specific rules and regulations, measured in precise blocks of time, and paid by the piece or the hour. It is also important to note, however, that not all factories were mechanized—the introduction of power-driven machinery added another dimension of technical control and constraints to the lives of factory operatives.

Factories, or manufactories as they were sometimes called, first appeared in colonial America, often in association with workhouses for poor women and children. Their goal was to develop a regimented system of work for the indigent and produce goods (usually textiles) at a low price.

The first factory to introduce water-powered machinery was Samuel Slater's mill in Pawtucket, Rhode Island, in 1790. By 1814, a group of investors called the Boston Associates had built the first fully mechanized cotton mill in Waltham, Massachusetts, on the outskirts of Boston. Raw cotton entered the mill, and woven cloth came out at the end of the production process. In the 1820s, many of these same capitalists underwrote construction of massive mills at Lowell, Massachusetts, and Manchester, New Hampshire, which hired thousands of young women to tend the spinning frames and power looms. (It is also important to note that although some of these early factories provided the physical and economic foundations for new industrial cities, many antebellum manufacturing sites were located in rural areas where water power was readily available from swiftly moving streams and did not subsequently become cities.)

During the decades preceding the Civil War, the mechanized factory system spread to other industries such as paper, clocks, rope, armaments, woodworking and furniture manufacturing, metalworking, and even some machine building itself. At the same time, major industries such as shoemaking and garment manufacturing continued not to be mechanized. At all of these work sites, an increasing number of workers were drawn together in large industrial buildings, their labor was increasingly divided into a series of discrete steps that undermined the remaining craft skills, their workday was usually measured by a factory clock and bells, and their wages were frequently paid according to a piecework arrangement. In addition, work rules became increasingly elaborate and specific in their regulation of behavior both on and off the job, and management was increasingly remote and formal in its relationship with the growing industrial workforce

Operatives in mechanized factories faced the additional challenge of tending machines whose speed they could not control. Also, primitive machinery that had few safeguards and frequent breakdowns posed distinct physical risks. Over time, many workers were subjected to both the stretch-out, which increased the number of machines each worker watched, and the speedup, in which management increased the pace of mechanized production processes.

In the late nineteenth century, enormous factory complexes—especially steel and ironworks and slaughterhouses—started to be built, taking advantage of technological developments in plant design, power systems, metallurgy, and machinery that allowed larger enterprises to run at faster speeds. Thousands of workers—many of them recent immigrants from Eastern and Southern Europe—filled these new industrial complexes; this was the period when the linkages between industrial development, urban growth, and the burgeoning immigrant population were strongest. Many of the great cities, especially in the Northeast and Midwest—places like Pittsburgh, Cleveland, Chicago, Detroit—grew in large part because they housed these tremendous industrial operations. Industrial growth also contributed, to a lesser extent, to the emergence of cities in the South and Far West—such as Birmingham and Denver.

The assembly line at a Michigan automobile plant, one of the many ways in which factories can be organized.

In 1914, Henry Ford introduced the moving assembly line at his Highland Park automobile factory in Detroit. Ford did not invent this production technology, which some scholars have called the cornerstone of the second American Industrial Revolution; he actually took the idea from the meatpacking industry, which used a moving "disassembly" line to slaughter and process carcasses. What he did do was combine the continuous moving production system with specialized machine tools to remove much of the skill from automobile manufacturing.

He also incorporated some of Frederick Winslow Taylor's ideas about scientific management to develop elaborate classification and compensation schemes for thousands of his employees. Ford's Sociological Department investigated workers' home lives in great detail to see if they had the proper "character" to participate in the company's profit-sharing programs. This department also became the locus for spies and goon squads aimed at destroying any efforts to organize Ford workers. More than most capitalists and companies, Ford understood that the factory system was more than a combination of labor and machines; it was a system of social relations and social control on the shop floor.

The decades following World War II have seen new breakthroughs in manufacturing technology, such as the use of numerically controlled machine tools starting in defense production plants during the 1950s, the emergence of robotics in the 1970s, and the development of computer-assisted manufacturing in the 1980s and 1990s. All of these changes add up to what some have called the third Industrial Revolution. Designers and managers continue to insist that these new forms of manufacturing are socially neutral and are driven merely by the forces of technological change themselves. But organized labor and industrial sociologists have been quick to point out that many of these new technologies on the shop floor have led to further deskilling and loss of control by workers, as well as significant technological displacement of employees in certain industries.

Even today, however, the dreams of some managers for a completely automated factory without workers—and therefore without labor costs and labor unions—is far from reality. Many companies have learned that workers who are deliberately excluded from decision making about introducing new technology, and who believe that new inventions threaten job satisfaction, safety, and security, do not get maximum productivity from new equipment because their alienation and resentment undermines whatever mechanical efficiencies may exist. Often, workers quickly discover ways to make new machines work faster or slower, and ways to repair machines that (like their historical ancestors) may still be subject to bugs and breakdowns. These workers may also be more reluctant to share on-the-job knowledge and skill with a managerial hierarchy who seem ever more distant and condescending. Attempts to bridge these gaps through quality circles and work life councils, unless accompanied by a real effort by management to listen and share decision-making authority, are likely to be viewed with deep suspicion by workers on the line.

Today, the United States is often seen as a service-based economy. However, the factory system is still alive and well—especially in industries such as automobiles, specialty steel products, and computer hardware. And factories are once again moving outside of major cities to more rural locales, particularly in the Midwest, where a large pool of underemployed industrial workers remains. Thus, the factory remains the site for fundamental questions and conflicts over power, control, and authority between American capital and labor.

—*David Zonderman*

See also
Division of Labor; Factory Workers.

References
Faler, Paul. *Mechanics and Manufacturers in the Early Industrial Revolution: Lynn, Massachusetts, 1780–1860.* Albany: State University of New York Press, 1981.
Grenier, Guillermo. *Inhuman Relations: Quality Circles and Anti-Unionism in American Industry.* Philadelphia: Temple University Press, 1988.
Hounshell, David. *From the American System to Mass Production, 1800–1932: The Development of Manufacturing Technology in the United States.* Baltimore: Johns Hopkins University Press, 1984.
McGaw, Judith. *Most Wonderful Machine: Mechanization and Social Change in Berkshire Paper Making, 1801–1885.* Princeton, NJ: Princeton University Press, 1987.
Meyer, Stephen. *The Five Dollar Day: Labor Management and Social Control in the Ford Motor Company, 1908–1921.* Albany: State University of New York Press, 1981.
Montgomery, David. *The Fall of the House of Labor: The Workplace, the State, and American Labor Activism, 1865–1925.* Cambridge, England: Cambridge University Press, 1987.
Nelson, Daniel. *Managers and Workers: Origins of the New Factory System in the United States, 1880–1920.* Madison: University of Wisconsin Press, 1975.
Noble, David F. *Forces of Production: A Social History of Industrial Automation.* New York: Oxford University Press, 1984.
Shaiken, Harley. *Work Transformed: Automation and Labor in the Computer Age.* Lexington, MA: Lexington Books, 1984.
Smith, Merritt Roe. *Harpers Ferry Armory and the New Technology: The Challenge of Change.* Ithaca, NY: Cornell University Press, 1977.
Tucker, Barbara. *Samuel Slater and the Origins of the American Textile Industry, 1790–1860.* Ithaca, NY: Cornell University Press, 1984.

Factory Workers

Throughout U.S. history, factory workers have defied easy categorization. Men and women, whites and blacks, skilled and unskilled, immigrants and native-born have all found employment in factories. Over the course of the nineteenth and twentieth centuries, the total number of manufacturing workers swelled from a mere 75,000 in 1810 to nearly 6 million in 1900 to over 18 million in 1995.

The first factory workers were usually children of poor families placed into the textile mills of southern New England in the 1790s. By the 1820s, young women were being recruited to spin and weave cotton in the factories of Lowell, Massachusetts, and other sites in New England. In the decades preceding the Civil War, factories flourished around Philadelphia, as well as westward in Pittsburgh, Cincinnati, and St. Louis, and southward into Virginia and the Carolinas. As new industries operated under a factory system—such as armaments, clocks, paper, and rope—a growing number of men were also employed in these manufacturing sites.

In the latter half of the nineteenth century, more immigrants took jobs as semiskilled machine tenders and operatives in the expanding industrial sector. Fathers, sons, and daughters might toil under the same factory roof or at nearby industrial sites. Mothers were more likely to stay home caring for younger children and taking in boarders or homework to make extra money.

Giant industrial complexes emerged at the turn of the century—such as the steel mills surrounding Pittsburgh or the McCormick agricultural works in Chicago. These work sites might encompass literally thousands of workers. Managers often went to great lengths to deliberately recruit a wide variety of immigrant groups into their factories in order to fracture along ethnic lines any emerging sense of working-class solidarity. Industrialists also sometimes hired African Americans for particularly onerous or dangerous occupations, stirring up racial animosity in the process.

As working conditions in factories were often unsafe and insecure, workers increasingly struggled to organize unions to protect themselves and their jobs. However, until the 1930s, the skilled craft unions of the American Federation of Labor (AFL) found industrial workers especially difficult to unionize. AFL organizers argued that factory operatives' heterogeneous backgrounds weakened their solidarity, and their lack of essential skills undermined their bargaining power. In the midst of this hostile climate within the labor movement, several industrial unions developed before World War I—most notably among mine workers and garment workers.

During the Depression, prodded by desperate conditions that demanded amelioration, changes in labor law that protected workers' rights to organize and bargain collectively, and charismatic leaders like John L. Lewis of the United Mine

Workers of America, factory workers surged into industry-wide unions that broke down parochial jurisdictional disputes between narrowly based craft unions. Autoworkers, steelworkers, rubber workers, packinghouse workers, and others formed organizations based on the principle of strength in the number of employees in an entire industry, as opposed to the craft union notion of strength in monopolizing skills and controlling access to the trade itself. These industrial unions formed the core of a new national labor confederation, the Congress of Industrial Organizations (CIO), which broke away from the AFL in 1937.

When the United States entered World War II, factories were pushed to retool for military production and operate at more than 100 percent capacity while millions of men were drafted into the armed forces. There was an immense demand for new workers in the defense plants. More than 1 million African Americans moved to defense production centers such as Oakland, Chicago, Detroit, Pittsburgh, and Philadelphia; and 4 million women who had not planned on working outside their homes entered the workforce from 1940 to 1944, many of them in defense plants. (A similar process, though smaller in magnitude, had occurred during World War I as nearly 500,000 blacks went to industrial cities and 1 million women joined the labor force for the first time.) At the war's end, most of the women were pushed out of their factory jobs (many quite unwillingly) so that a man who "really" needed the work could reclaim his previous position. Some African-American men retained their spots on the factory floor, and they used their achievements as reliable and productive workers (as well as their service records) to make renewed arguments for civil rights and opportunities within the labor movement.

The second half of the twentieth century experienced a decline in the strength of the industrial sector relative to the nation's burgeoning service economy. However, the United States continues to be a world leader in the production of automobiles, computers, and other consumer durable goods. And these industries—many of them with state-of-the-art factories using the latest in computer-assisted production and robotics—continue to employ more than 18 million workers, though under conditions far different from what past employees labored under, for better and worse.

—*David Zonderman*

See also

Division of Labor; Unions.

References

Barrett, James R. *Work and Community in the Jungle: Chicago's Packinghouse Workers, 1894–1922.* Urbana: University of Illinois Press, 1987.

Bodnar, John. *Immigration and Industrialization: Ethnicity in an American Mill Town, 1870–1940.* Pittsburgh, PA: University of Pittsburgh Press, 1977.

Dublin, Thomas. *Women at Work: The Transformation of Work and Community in Lowell, Massachusetts, 1826–1860.* New York: Columbia University Press, 1979.

Hirsch, Susan. *Roots of the American Working Class: The Industrialization of the Crafts in Newark, 1800–1860.* Philadelphia: University of Pennsylvania Press, 1978.

Korman, Gerd. *Industrialization, Immigrants, and Americanizers: The View from Milwaukee, 1866–1921.* Madison: State Historical Society of Wisconsin, 1967.

Milkman, Ruth. *Gender at Work: The Dynamics of Job Segregation by Sex during World War II.* Urbana: University of Illinois Press, 1987.

Shelton, Cynthia. *The Mills of Manayunk: Industrialization and Social Conflict in the Philadelphia Region, 1787–1837.* Baltimore: Johns Hopkins University Press, 1986.

Zonderman, David. *Aspirations and Anxieties: New England Workers and the Mechanized Factory System, 1815–1850.* New York: Oxford University Press, 1992.

Families in Cities

Family norms and patterns have never been uniform among the groups that comprise U.S. society, and they have evolved as the nation's society changed from rural/agrarian to urban/industrial to suburban/postindustrial. As society changed, city life highlighted some of the varieties among American families and muted others.

Colonial America was overwhelmingly rural, and urban families shared many characteristics with their rural counterparts. Norms dictated that everyone live as part of a household, referred to as a "family," under patriarchal supervision. Especially in wealthy families, such as the Drinkers of Philadelphia, members of an extended family, who were characteristically not present in a household, often lived nearby. Extended kin typically involved themselves in related families by frequent visiting, caring for the elderly, pooling resources for business, and providing apprenticeships and other opportunities for youth.

But urban families were not identical to rural ones. Lower rates of population stability meant that early American cities were much less likely than rural communities to consist of a few interrelated families. For example, in the mid-eighteenth century, the 155 families in the rural Massachusetts town of Chatham had 34 surnames; in Germantown, a manufacturing village near Philadelphia of a similar size and longevity, the 211 households had 143 different surnames. Furthermore, some issues that particularly affected the urban family subsequently—ethnic diversity within the population, poverty, and structural change in response to new economic conditions—appeared in American cities before 1815.

The fate of Dutch family practices after the British conquered New Netherland in 1664 anticipated the future of non-British immigrant groups. Although they did not remain as distinct in cities as they did in rural places, Dutch families did not quickly adopt British patterns. Well into the eighteenth century, marriage among the Dutch in New York City remained highly endogamous. Families maintained Dutch customs, including the preparation of mutual wills by husband and wife and the practice of a wife generally receiving half of their deceased husband's estate. During the middle third of the eighteenth century, however, Dutch families began to adopt characteristic British behaviors.

Families of all nationalities felt the effects of social and economic change in eighteenth-century cities, especially poverty and increased social stratification. Casualties from the wars with France left many broken families. In 1751, for example, Boston's tax assessors identified 1,153 widows (perhaps a quarter of the city's adult white women) "of which at least half are very poor." Relative to the country, cities had always had more unmarried adults and single parents, and their numbers were now swelled both by widowhood and the increasing propensity of youth to migrate from overpopulated rural areas to cities, especially in New England. As wage labor gradually replaced term labor, such as apprenticeship and indentured servitude, by the end of the eighteenth century these single people were no longer considered part of their employer's "family." Laborers secured independence from supervision of their private lives by their employer and could form their own households, but they could no longer rely on a master who owed them the personal obligation of an economic safety net.

In 1800, 1 in 20 residents of the United States lived in a city; in 1920, most did. The total fertility rate for the white population exceeded 7.0 in 1800; it had fallen by half in 1900. Cross-sectional analysis shows that urban families were usually smaller than rural ones. However, it does not appear accurate to conclude that urbanization caused fertility to decline. The decline actually began late in the eighteenth century, a quarter-century before urbanization began to occur. In addition, fertility was declining in all parts of the country; in Michigan between 1850 and 1880, for example, it decreased more in rural than in urban areas. Furthermore, parents were not having smaller families simply because children were less of an economic asset in urban as opposed to rural environments. In fact, the contribution of secondary workers such as children remained vital to the "family economy" of urban working-class families in the nineteenth century. Smaller families and relocating to secure the advantages of urban life may both have been expressions of a basic desire among nineteenth-century Americans to gain greater control over their lives.

Values of privacy, child-centeredness, and strict gender roles defined American families in the nineteenth century. Emotional ties rather than obligations of mechanical reciprocity now bound family members together. Responsibilities such as education and health care that had previously been shouldered by individual families began to be borne by institutions. Work became separated from home. While in the eyes of many contemporaries, and in the opinion of some subsequent scholars, urban life was incompatible with these values and practices, in many ways urbanization encouraged family patterns along normative lines.

It is true that the increased crowding that characterized large cities in the nineteenth century restricted privacy, especially in working-class families, and reformers lamented conditions in which families shared small tenement apartments. A mid-nineteenth century report on Boston's slums by the Committee on Internal Health pointed out with alarm that people were "huddled together like brutes without regard to sex, age or a sense of decency, grown men and women sleeping together in the same apartment, and sometimes wife, husband, brothers and sisters in the same bed." But the *goal* of most families was a separate residence, especially a single-family house, which would shelter just a nuclear family. Outside of New York City, this was feasible—two-thirds of working-class men who remained in Newburyport, Massachusetts, for 20 years did acquire their own homes. Middle-class families rejected other alternatives. There was little support for visionary proposals by architects and feminists in the late nineteenth century, such as those of the Cooperative Housekeeping movement to build large apartment buildings with communal facilities for cooking and child care.

In many ways, the normative characteristics of nineteenth-century families were more pronounced in the city than in the country. Since urban families were smaller, they could be more child-centered. The network of female charitable, reform, and religious organizations that developed in antebellum cities, especially in the Northeast, helped to define separate spheres for men and women. Hospitals and public school systems first developed in urban America, where they took on some responsibilities previously assumed by families. And urbanization may have encouraged development of the family as an emotional support agent as the intensified pace of city life led middle-class men in particular to see their home as a refuge.

In the eyes of these men, however, an alarming degree of instability characterized urban working-class families. The rapidly growing rural-to-urban migration brought more single people to cities; within cities, a growing percentage of the labor force worked at unskilled jobs with declining real wages; and urban mortality continued to be higher than in rural areas. Together, these developments created more orphans and abandoned children and required intact families to move frequently since unskilled workers needed to live within walking distance of their low-paying, insecure jobs. Many contemporary observers interpreted these patterns as evidence of the weakness of urban families, and they feared that the increasing number of individuals living outside of families in cities threatened the social order. Some scholars have argued that the efforts to correct this weakness—creating institutions like orphanages and programs like the juvenile court system for children and adolescents—introduced outside influences that further weakened the urban family.

These fears appear to have been exaggerated. Migrants to cities were not rejecting family life. For example, the adolescent girls who moved from the New England countryside to staff textile mills in places like Lowell, Massachusetts, during the first wave of industrialization worked primarily to save money to start their own families; most eventually married and settled in rural areas. Furthermore, nineteenth-century city life did not erase many existing family patterns, such as the maintenance of ties with extended kin. For example, the responsibility for care of the elderly remained within the family; indeed this function of families became more important as growing numbers of older workers could not support themselves. At the end of the nineteenth century, most older Americans in cities lived with kin (although most urban households did not include extended kin).

Additionally, in some ways the creation of special institutions and programs to address perceived family problems reflected the continued strength and importance of individual families. For example, boarding and lodging in private households furnished housing and socialization for new migrants to the city, and about one in six urban households included at least one boarder in the late nineteenth century. Furthermore, child-welfare institutions, at least when they opened in the late nineteenth century, sought to reinforce and not replace individual families. From the time of its establishment in 1860, the goal of the Chicago Nursery and Half-Orphan Asylum was to provide short-term care for children from working-class families who had lost a parent; most of the residents stayed less than six months.

Conditions in cities on the western frontier in the nineteenth century, which were affected by boom-and-bust spurts, hindered but did not prevent the development of families with normative characteristics. Cities on the mining frontier, like Helena, Montana, initially had unbalanced sex ratios, a relatively low percentage of residents living in families, high divorce rates, and an above-average percentage of women in the workforce, especially as prostitutes. But by the end of the nineteenth century, as mining cities sought respectability in order to encourage economic diversification and growth, strictly separated gender spheres developed, most residents lived in families, and prostitution was proscribed.

Although industrialization diminished their importance as units of production, families remained central to economic practices in nineteenth-century cities. The family residence itself was an important economic resource—income from boarders might supply as much as one-quarter of a working-class family's budget. Furthermore, by performing unpaid household tasks like washing and cooking in the crowded and dirty conditions of nineteenth-century cities, women and children allowed working-class men to assume 12-hour shifts at strenuous factory jobs.

Working-class families also frequently depended upon the earnings of multiple family members, especially as the industrialized economy became more cyclical and employment more insecure for factory workers. It was unusual for married women to work regularly in the paid labor force, but many earned cash from "outwork" they performed at home. Children's work was even more significant; in 1900 one-fifth of the children under 16 were in the paid labor force. In Massachusetts, a survey of working-class families in 1875 found that money earned by children under 15 constituted almost 20 percent of their family's income. Whether children worked depended on their family's situation. They were less likely to have a job if their father was present, if their father earned higher wages, if there were other adult kin (e.g., uncles or cousins) living in the household, or if they had older siblings (who could work while younger children stayed in school). Except for small sums, the money earned by women and children was not spent on personal consumption but was pooled as part of a "family economy."

The norms of the family economy could even affect marriage practices. Adult wage-earning children, especially women, often postponed marriage until a dependent parent died or a younger sibling matured. As the unmarried daughter of a Jewish family in Providence, Rhode Island, explained, "I would have liked to have had a husband . . . but when you're married and have children, you cannot as much as you want to, devote your life to your mother and father."

In the century after 1820, over 30 million people immigrated to the United States; compared to native-born Americans, they overwhelmingly chose to live in cities. By distancing themselves geographically from kin, encountering vastly different social customs, and usually working in economically inadequate jobs, immigrants seemingly were most vulnerable to the supposed family-weakening pressures of urban America. Evidence suggests, however, that while immigrant families did change in the United States, they remained important as ways of *engaging* American society while *preserving* what immigrants and their children valued most from their ethnic heritage. Similar to the situation among the native-born, the changes that gradually occurred in immigrant family patterns showed the continued strength rather than the growing irrelevance of the urban family.

Family was central to how immigrants settled in the United States. While some immigrants were single males who typically stayed in the United States for only a few years, "chain migration" was common among Jews and eventually among Italians, the largest groups of the post-1880 "new" immigrants. Recent arrivals went to communities in the United States where they had kin, often settling together in urban neighborhoods that took on the character of their ethnic group. For example, in the heavily Italian neighborhood of Federal Hill in Providence, Rhode Island, 69 percent of the Italian immigrant families in 1915 had at least one parent or sibling in Providence, as did 42 percent of the Jewish immigrant families in the Smith Hill neighborhood. It is true that the urban industrial economy did not allow adult immigrants to pass useful craft skills along to their children, as might have happened in Europe, but securing employment was still often linked to family connections. Before the era of scientific managers and personnel offices, industrial employment practices were casual, and foremen often preferred hiring relatives of workers already in their shops who could train and interpret for the new employees.

In general, work patterns illustrate the familial focus of urban immigrants. Generally poorer and larger than families of the native-born, immigrant families in particular needed secondary workers. Patterns varied among different nationalities, but if anything patriarchal norms were stronger among immigrant than native-born Americans, and wives therefore tended not to work for wages. In Buffalo, New York, for instance, fewer than 2 percent of the wives of Italian immigrants worked outside the home in 1905. Maintaining the family economy, therefore, depended on the labor of children. In New York City in 1905, almost half of all unmarried Italian-born women over the age of 16 were wage earners, double the rate for all single women in that age group in the United States. Consequently, among most immigrant groups other than Jews, children were less likely to be in school.

Immigrant families did not remain unchanged in the United States. By earning wages and learning English, the children of immigrants gained confidence to challenge patriarchy in their families. In general, immigrant families gradually came to resemble those of native-born Americans. Children of immigrants moved toward the American norm by marrying at younger ages than their European-born parents while having smaller families, consistent with the growing American practice of family limitation. Subsequently, as first- and second-generation immigrant males began finding better-paying jobs and having responsibility for feeding fewer children, and as legal restrictions increasingly limited work by adolescents and the growing service segment of the economy demanded more trained workers, the children of immigrants began to remain in school longer. In the New York SMSA (Standard Metropolitan Statistical Area) in 1950, Italian immigrants aged 25–44 had completed a median of 8.3

years of school; the median for second-generation Italian Americans of the same age was 9.9.

These changes altered, but did not necessarily weaken, immigrant family patterns. In some instances, it was easier for immigrant families to follow traditional norms in America than in their homelands. For instance, immigrant Italian women in Rochester, New York, in the early twentieth century were less likely to become pregnant before marriage than women in the Italian villages from which they migrated. A younger age at marriage meant fewer years to repress sexual urges, and self-confidence gained from work experience enabled Italian girls to resist unwanted seductions. Furthermore, while most second-generation immigrants shook off direct parental control over marriage, they usually choose a partner with a similar ethnic background. In early-twentieth-century Cleveland, two-thirds of second-generation Italians still practiced endogamous marriage.

The urbanization of the Southwest after its incorporation into the United States in 1848 affected the family life of the Chicanos already living there and those who subsequently migrated to the United States from Mexico. Growing manufacturing sectors and rising populations particularly characterized Los Angeles and San Antonio, where Mexican-American wage earners increasingly found themselves in low-paying jobs. Extended-family households became less common, while the proportion of single, unattached individuals increased. Existing family norms, which emphasized patriarchal control to maintain family honor and communal regulation of sexual behavior through public shame, weakened among Chicanos. There was public concern about the supposed consequent weakening of Mexican-American families; the dangerous individuality of adolescent male Chicanos was said to explain the "zoot suit riots" directed against them in Los Angeles in the early 1940s. But like the families of European immigrants, in reality Mexican-American families did not completely lose their distinctiveness or cohesiveness. At the beginning of the twentieth century, an extended structure was still more common among Chicano families in the urban Southwest than among other groups, and exogamous marriage was rare. Migration from Mexico continued after 1924, when it was sharply curtailed from the rest of the world, and it worked to maintain traditional family practices in the Mexican-American community. Intermarriage with non-Chicanos did increase after World War II, and family structure came to resemble closely that of other Americans. But survey research in the late twentieth century reported an unusually strong ideology of family solidarity and patterns of familistic behavior among Chicanos.

Urban life has also had complex effects on the families of American Indians. Centuries before Europeans came to America, some Native Americans had built "cities," which were complexes of large earthen mounds, such as that at Cahokia in what is now Illinois. By the time of European contact, Native Americans characteristically lived in small villages and often followed family practices radically different from those of Europeans such as matrilineal structure and marriage rules determined by clan membership. The significance of these practices lessened by the nineteenth century as whites imposed their own family norms on Native Americans, and some Indians themselves encouraged the adoption of European practices to revitalize their culture and resist extermination. In the twentieth century, especially after World War II, American Indians rapidly moved to cities, impelled by poverty on the reservations to which they had been located and by the assimilationist policies of government agencies. This migration affected families in many ways. Urban Indians were now distant from their kin who remained on reservations; they began to intermarry with Indians of other tribes and non-Indians at increasing rates; and they received less support for their families from the educational and health programs provided by the government for Native Americans.

The federal government played an increasingly significant role in the twentieth century and has directly and indirectly affected both families and cities. At the same time, at first gradually and then more rapidly after 1973, the economic base of older manufacturing cities declined, white, middle-class populations fled, and poverty and attendant social problems increased (partly as a result of government programs that favored suburbs). These changes especially resonated in complex ways in African-American families.

As African Americans migrated out of the South in the twentieth century, they shifted from being disproportionately rural to being disproportionately urban. At the same time, their family structure increasingly distinguished them from other Americans. A smaller percentage of blacks lived in biologically complete families, and these families were increasingly headed by an unmarried woman. Between 1970 and 1990 alone, the percentage of black children living with both parents fell from about 60 percent to about 30 percent. To be sure, these changes exaggerated parallel developments in the families of white Americans, especially at similar socioeconomic levels. But alarmist critics saw them as *causes* of the poverty, crime, low educational achievement, and high mortality that plagued African-American society at the end of the century. One public policy response in the late 1990s was to eliminate the federal Aid to Families with Dependent Children program in the belief that it was weakening the black family.

But there are other explanations for these family patterns among black Americans. Their African heritage and the legacy of slavery, both of which encouraged the frequent use of foster parents, were significant. But the patterns became pronounced as these historical experiences became more distant and as African Americans increasingly experienced urban life, suggesting that urbanization had a significant impact on the black family. In cities, racism prevented black males from obtaining the kind of manufacturing jobs available to immigrants and left them unable to place their children informally in good-paying jobs. Consequently, black adolescents left home at a younger age than other adolescents, making the functioning of the family economy more difficult for blacks and more dependent on kin other than children living in the household. Furthermore, in the period of their greatest urban influx just after World War II, blacks tended to move to cities that had begun to lose manufacturing jobs, that were more racially and economically segregated, and that provided poorer public services. From this perspective, it was urban America that *caused* change in the African-American family.

—Robert Gough

See also
Children in Cities; Children in Suburbs; Fertility; Women in Cities.
References
Berrol, Selma. "Immigrant Working Class Families." In Joseph M. Hawes and Elizabeth I. Nybakken, eds., *American Families: A Research Guide and Historical Handbook.* New York: Greenwood Press, 1991.
Degler, Carl N. *At Odds: Women and the Family from the Revolution to the Present.* New York: Oxford University Press, 1980.
Hareven, Tamara K. *Family and Kin in Urban Communities, 1700–1930.* New York: New Viewpoints, 1977.
———. *Family Time and Industrial Time: The Relationship between the Family and Work in a New England Industrial Community.* Cambridge, England: Cambridge University Press, 1982.
Hershberg, Theodore, ed. *Philadelphia: Work, Space, Family and Group Experience in the 19th Century.* New York: Oxford University Press, 1981.
Katz, Michael B., ed. *The "Underclass" Debate: Views from History.* Princeton, NJ: Princeton University Press, 1993.
Mintz, Steven, and Susan Kellogg. *Domestic Revolutions: A Social History of American Family Life.* New York: Free Press, 1988.

Federal Government and Cities

Historically, there has been little interaction between the federal government and cities in the United States. Two reasons seem to account for this. First, citizen expectations—and hence, the policy responsibilities—of the federal government and cities have varied greatly. For instance, the federal government has been concerned with national policies (e.g., defense, international affairs, foreign and interstate commerce, etc.). Cities, on the other hand, have concentrated on the direct provision of local services (e.g., police and fire protection, streets and sidewalks, garbage collection and disposal, water and sewerage, parks and recreation, zoning, etc.).

Second, there has been no legal connection between the federal government and cities. The federal government and the states are the only governments recognized by the U.S. Constitution. Legally, cities—like other units of local government—are creatures of states. Hence, until fairly recently, cities were more likely to interact with their states or other local governments than with the federal government.

This depiction of federal-city relations is perhaps best understood within the context of the notion of *dual federalism*. According to this description of American federalism, the national government and the states are supreme in their spheres, and these two spheres of action should be and are kept separate. Given the unitary relationship between local units of government and states, their activities, including those of cities, have been circumscribed by what has been permitted under their state constitutions. Cities, therefore, only interacted directly with, and subsequently were subservient to, their states. Interaction between cities and the federal government—to the extent that it occurred—was indirect (that is, it was permitted or happened only through the auspices of their states).

This description of the relations between the federal government and cities, however, changed radically in the second half of the twentieth century. Contact between the federal government and cities—but particularly between officials of these governments—has increased markedly because of the expansion and contraction of the federal grant-in-aid system and because of the proliferation of federal mandates. The political science/public administration literature abounds with studies that have described and analyzed the growth of federal aid and mandates as well as the subsequent interaction and relationships that have been forged. Of particular interest has been the widespread observation that federal-city relations have been characterized by both cooperation and conflict.

The growth of federal grants-in-aid to cities has been dramatic. In 1952, federal aid amounted to around $122 million, or about 2 percent of the total revenue of cities. The amount of federal aid to cities, although increasing to $330 million in 1962, still comprised only about 2.5 percent of city revenues. As a result of the massive expansion of the federal grant-in-aid system during the Johnson administration's Great Society and its aftermath, federal aid to cities climbed to almost $3.1 billion by 1972; more importantly, federal fiscal assistance constituted nearly 9 percent of the total revenue of cities. Federal aid to cities continued to grow almost unabated during the next ten years. By 1982, it topped $13.5 billion and accounted for approximately 12 percent of the money spent by cities.

The conservative fiscal policies of the Reagan and Bush administrations, however, meant a downsizing of the federal grant-in-aid system. With a phasing out of general revenue sharing, a reduction in the amount of money allocated to traditional grants-in-aid, and an increase in block grants to states, the amount of federal money flowing directly to cities had actually decreased to around $7.6 billion by 1992, or 4.6 percent of their budgets.

The provision of federal aid to cities has had a variety of effects. Viewed positively, the infusion of "outside" money into city budgets has allowed local city officials to provide new or expanded services and programs (e.g., road and bridge construction, police protection, low-income housing, mass transit, urban renewal, water and sewerage projects, parks and recreational facilities) to their residents that would not have been feasible given most cities' limited fiscal resources. This role played by the federal government has been supported on two main grounds. First, the federal government has superior revenue-raising capacity than any other government and, therefore, has an obligation to "share" some of its resources with cities (or, as the case may be, counties, townships, school or special districts, or states). In addition, the federal government should use its power to "provide for the general welfare" to assist or encourage state and local governments, including cities, to provide a number of services that otherwise would not be available.

Federal fiscal assistance, which escalated enormously during the 1960s and 1970s, could not have occurred at a more opportune time. State legislatures had become increasingly unresponsive to the plight of cities, particularly those located in large metropolitan areas. Decaying infrastructure, rising crime rates, growing unionization and militancy of city employees, and, perhaps most importantly, an increasingly poor and dependent population meant a rapid rise in the cost of providing city services at a time when the revenue-raising capacity of many cities was declining for both economic and political reasons. Cities seemed to suffer more from the recessions and inflationary periods of the 1960s, 1970s, and 1980s. Moreover, city officials were increasingly confronting an antitax sentiment among their residents and having to deal with state constitutions that limited taxation and hampered borrowing. At the same time, cities were experiencing a mass exodus of their most lucrative and reliable taxpayers—businesses, industries, and white-collar and professional workers—who were moving to suburbs. Therefore, the coincidental timing of a decline in the fiscal fortunes of cities with a rapid increase in federal fiscal assistance produced, for the most part, a cooperative spirit within the context of federal-city relations.

In spite of this positive perspective, federal aid also has produced negative consequences. Critics of the federal grant-in-aid system complain that it distorts local government-spending priorities. In short, federal grants—but particularly those with matching requirements—entice cities to divert funds away from programs given high priority by city officials but for which there is no federal funding. Federal grants also have the potential to create greater (and sometimes unrealistic) citizen expectations. That is, city residents grow accustomed to having services that would not have been possible except for federal fiscal assistance. Third, the provision of an expanding menu of local services made possible by federal grants-in-aid retards fiscal and political accountability. City officials always find it easier to spend money that they did not have to raise, while members of Congress are usually too distant to be held accountable. In addition, cities have become increasingly dependent on outside funding. This has become especially alarming since 1982, given the erosion of city tax bases and the willingness of Congress to curtail the amount of federal funds available to state and local governments. Finally, conditions or "strings" attached to the receipt of federal aid frequently have been perceived as a form of political blackmail.

Because federal grants-in-aid have both positive and negative effects, city officials have developed an ambivalent attitude toward federal aid and have been confronted with several interesting challenges. Mainly, city officials seek to maximize the positive results of receiving federal aid, while they endeavor to minimize or even avoid the negative outcomes associated with receiving federal funds.

Increasing interaction between the federal government and cities resulting from the expansion of the federal grant-in-aid system can be traced back to the 1950s and 1960s. This is not the case for federal mandates. The federal mandate issue did not emerge nationally until the 1970s. In its 1984 report, "Regulatory Federalism: Policy, Process, Impact and Reform," the United States Advisory Commission on Intergovernmental Relations (ACIR) identified 36 federal mandates affecting state and local governments, including cities, as of 1980. Applying the same definition of mandates used in the 1984 ACIR report, Timothy Conlan and David Beam count an additional 24 mandates legislated by Congress between 1981 and 1990.

The imposition of federal mandates has engendered much more harsh criticism from city officials than have the requirements that traditionally accompany federal grants-in-aid. While city or other local government officials have usually conceded that the federal government has the right to impose certain conditions (referred to as "strings" attached to the receipt of federal aid) on jurisdictions receiving fiscal

Federal aid to cities funds programs such as this curbside recycling effort.

assistance, they have adamantly opposed unilateral mandates that force them to perform certain functions or provide a variety of services and receive nothing in return. More specifically, mandates are viewed as an intrusion into local home rule and as a callous lack of respect for local self-governance. In its quest to impose Washington's will or perception about what is in the best interest of cities, the federal government, according to many city officials, has violated one of the basic assumptions of federalism—the right of local communities to tailor programs and policies to their own needs and peculiar culture. In fact, organizations representing city interests, such as the League of Cities, have frequently pointed to the imposition of mandates as a classic example of "coercive federalism."

In addition, federal mandates have been associated with the spiraling cost of city government operations and the inability of city officials to spend dwindling revenues effectively and efficiently. City officials constantly complain that the cost of implementing mandates has meant less money for programs deemed "high priorities" by local citizens and their policymakers. This has come at a time when city officials have been confronted with eroding tax bases and an antitax climate as well as revenue forecasts that have been clouded by recessionary and inflationary forces. In sum, federal mandates have become the principal irritant in federal-city relations.

In spite of the criticism leveled at the federal government for its willingness to impose mandates on cities as well as states and other local governments, mandates can be defended. The argument can be made that state and local governments have been reluctant—and at times, even hostile—to the suggestion that they provide basic safeguards or services to their citizens. Practicing equal opportunity and affirmative action in government hiring or providing easy access for the handicapped to public facilities are good examples. Therefore, it is incumbent upon the federal government to secure compliance from state and local governments, since it is constitutionally responsible for "providing for the public welfare."

On balance, however, the imposition of costly and intricate federal mandates has probably been responsible for curtailing intergovernmental cooperation while increasing conflict in the federal-city arena. As a consequence, a number of organizations representing state and local governments have joined forces in recent years in an effort to prevent Congress from enacting unfunded mandates. By early 1995, these efforts appear to have been partially successful as Congress passed legislation that requires careful scrutiny of future proposed mandates.

Federal grants-in-aid and mandates, although responsible for an increasing level of contact between the federal government and cities over the last 40 years, do not represent the only opportunities for interaction between these levels of government. Numerous other actions and events—perhaps not generating the same level of public attention and concern—also bring the federal government and cities into contact with one another. In fact, the implications of some of these other contacts have been significant and at times more important than the impact of federal aid and mandates.

On the positive side, certain actions and decisions of the federal government historically have spurred economic development in cities. The decision to locate or expand military bases and other federal government operations—whether within city limits or close by—has almost always been "a shot in the arm" to the local and city economy. Minimally, these actions provide jobs for people who buy homes, pay taxes, and become customers in new businesses that pay taxes. A good example would be the 1994 decision of the federal government to build a new federal courthouse complex in Tampa, Florida. In addition to pumping $50 million of construction money into the local economy, the federal government's decision to build in a decaying part of the downtown is expected to rejuvenate this area and trigger a new wave of construction downtown.

Over the years, the federal government also has contributed to the decline and undesirability of cities as places to live, work, and recreate. The availability of low-cost VA and FHA mortgages has made it possible for people and families to leave the city with its growing crime rates, declining schools, and decaying infrastructure and move to the suburbs. Moreover, water and sewerage as well as other city-type services increasingly have been made available at an affordable cost for these new suburban residents—and usually in the unincorporated part of counties—as a result of federal grants or loans. Additionally, the massive expansion of the highway system that permits individuals to live further away from their place of work has been made possible by federal funds.

The bitter experience of declining federal aid and the imposition of federal mandates, as well as remembrance of the negative effects of other federal decisions, are certain to leave their imprint on federal-city relations for some time. Nonetheless, a shift to more positive relations between cities and the federal government may be on the horizon. It appears that the Clinton administration and the Republican majority in Congress may have gotten the message that local officials and their citizens are tired of the intrusive and overbearing role played by the federal government in local affairs. Indeed, there is even some evidence coming from both the White House and Capitol Hill to suggest that remedial action is already under way and that more cooperation and less conflict is likely to characterize federal-city relations as we move into the third century since the nation's founding.

—*J. Edwin Benton*

References

Benton, J. Edwin. "The Effects of Federal Aid on State-Local Expenditures." *Publius: The Journal of Federalism* 22 (1992): 71–82.

Burchall, Robert W., James H. Carr, Richard L. Florida, and James Nemeth. *The New Reality of Municipal Finance: The Rise and Fall of the Intergovernmental City.* New Brunswick, NJ: Center for Urban Policy Research at Rutgers University, 1984.

Conlan, Timothy J., and David R. Beam. "Federal Mandates: Record of Reform and Future Prospect." *Intergovernmental Perspective* 18 (1992): 7–15.

MacManus, Susan A. " 'Mad' about Mandates: The Issue of Who Should Pay for What Resurfaces in the 1990s." *Publius: The Journal of Federalism* 21 (1991): 59–75.

MacManus, Susan A., J. Edwin Benton, and Donald C. Menzel. *Personnel Cost Study: Florida Municipalities, A Survey.* Tampa, FL: Center for Public Affairs and Policy Management, 1993.

Federal Housing Administration

The Federal Housing Administration (FHA), established by Franklin Roosevelt's New Deal, offers government insurance for private residential mortgages and is credited with popularizing the long-term, self-amortizing, low–down payment mortgage loan.

During the Depression, the high rate of unemployment and the collapse of the financial system brought the building industry to a halt and pushed huge numbers of homeowners into default on their mortgages. The Federal Housing Administration, which was created by the national Housing Act of 1934, was one of several measures taken by the Roosevelt administration to solve the crisis in the housing industry, which at the time was generally believed to be the largest sector of the economy.

The purpose of the FHA was to assist and encourage private lenders by restoring liquidity to the mortgage business—and thereby help revive the housing industry. It was meant to eliminate the risk in lending money for mortgages by insuring and guaranteeing mortgage loans. Before the FHA, most mortgage loans were short-term "balloon" notes due in ten years or less with down payments frequently over half the value of the property. The FHA loosened the standard requirements for mortgages, making them accessible to middle-class home buyers. Originally the FHA required 20-year mortgages with a 20 percent down payment, but over time it eased these requirements. Today, the typical FHA-insured loan runs for 30 years and requires a down payment

of only 10 percent, or even less. In addition, the FHA has insisted that the properties of its insured mortgages meet minimum standards for construction that eventually were accepted throughout the building industry.

The FHA had a widespread impact upon the home-buying public. According to historian Kenneth Jackson, between 1934 and 1972 FHA insurance helped 11 million families purchase houses, 22 million to improve their properties, and financed 1.8 million apartments in multiunit buildings. During this period, the rates of owner occupancy in the United States rose from 44 percent to 63 percent.

For most of this time, however, the FHA sought to limit its risk by following a very conservative underwriting policy. The FHA guidelines specifically warned against loans on property in older, industrial, or mixed-use neighborhoods or in areas that might become home to low-income people or racial minorities. Only in 1949, after the National Association for the Advancement of Colored People (NAACP) led a sustained campaign against FHA policies, did the agency finally agree to delete references to race in its manual, and not until 1950 did the agency cease insuring mortgages on deeds with racial restrictions. Even so, the FHA's policies encouraged metropolitan dispersion and racial segregation by insuring far more suburban single-family homes than it did apartment buildings and inner-city properties.

In the era after World War II, the mission of the FHA broadened beyond serving the middle-class homeownership market. From the 1940s through the 1960s, Congress charged the FHA with insuring mortgages for specialized categories of housing such as war workers' housing, veterans' housing, urban renewal housing, cooperatives, and condominiums.

During the 1960s, the FHA was charged with helping to house low-income Americans. The chief means of advancing the agency's new social agenda were programs that combined subsidies—achieved by extremely low interest rates on mortgages—with lenient underwriting criteria. Although the subsidized programs had many successes, the Section 235 homeownership program and the Section 236 multifamily rental program, both enacted in 1968, were marred by scandals.

An effort to reorganize the FHA in the early 1970s scattered its operations within the Department of Housing and Urban Development (HUD) and greatly reduced efficiency. During the 1980s, the Reagan administration brought greater problems to the FHA: corruption in the subsidized housing programs, poor management of assets, and slovenly accounting methods. The funds established for the subsidized programs suffered great losses, and in the mid-1980s the records were in such chaos that neither the General Accounting Office nor the accounting firm of Price Waterhouse could conduct an audit of the agency.

Meanwhile, the FHA increasingly focused on mortgages for the lower end of the housing market. While standards for its conventional home mortgage insurance were lowered to reach low-income home buyers, private mortgage insurers entered the field and competed successfully for the high end of the mortgage market. By the late 1980s, even the FHA's original mortgage insurance fund was in danger of insolvency.

During the Bush and Clinton administrations, matters improved considerably. Recent reforms such as stricter loan oversight and higher fees have restored soundness to the FHA insurance funds and improved the agency's management problems. Nevertheless, many questions about the future of the FHA remain. The agency's overall mission and its operations in both single- and multifamily housing areas are, and will continue to be, the subject of much debate.

—*Alexander von Hoffman*

See also
Housing Act of 1934.
References
Jackson, Kenneth T. *Crabgrass Frontier: The Suburbanization of the United States.* New York: Oxford University Press, 1985.
Jacobs, Barry G., Kenneth R. Harney, Charles L. Edson, and Bruce S. Lane. *Guide to Federal Housing Programs.* Washington, DC: Government Printing Office, 1982.
Vandell, Kerry D. "FHA Restructuring Proposals: Alternatives and Implications." *Housing Policy Debate* 6 (1995): 299–393.
Wheaton, William L. C. "The Evolution of Federal Housing Programs." Ph.D. dissertation, University of Chicago, 1953.

Fertility

Fertility in the United States, with the single exception of the baby boom just after World War II, has been declining since at least 1800, when the typical white woman in the United States bore seven living children. In a predominantly rural society such as the early Republic, large families served several functions that added to the family economy and also provided company and comfort. Boys worked on the farm, or in the family sawmill, or at the father's craft. Girls wove and spun, and sometimes took over enough of the housekeeping to allow their mothers to perform other kinds of labor. As the nation urbanized, and as commerce and industry increased their importance, the birthrate slipped. By 1850, the average number of children born per family was 5.42. Although the decline in the birthrate occurred in the more settled rural areas of the nation as well as in cities, urban dwellers led the way. Not only did they have smaller families, but they also experienced increasing levels of childlessness. In mid-nineteenth-century Boston, for example, nearly 20 percent of marriages among the urban poor were childless, as were some 13 percent of marriages among the city's well-to-do couples.

During the latter half of the nineteenth century, family size dipped further, to an average of 3.56 children per family in 1900. However that figure masked, in the words of one demographic historian, "extremes of differential fertility" between 1890 and 1915. Middle-class, native-born, urban whites living in the East and Midwest produced the fewest children, while couples in rural and frontier societies had larger families. Immigrants and rural African Americans had more children than did the native-born. Among rural whites, the fertility rate (number of births per 1,000 women between the ages of 15 and 44) in 1875 was approximately 175; for urban whites it was approximately 92; for immigrant whites, approximately 197 births; and for blacks, 208. By 1925, the numbers had fallen to approximately 140, 75, 120, and 125, respectively.

In addition to smaller families, childlessness was also rising. Among white women born in 1835 who ever married, approximately 7 percent never had children. Among African Americans, the figure was approximately 5 percent. (These women would have reached childbearing age around 1855.) Within the next 20 years, there was first a slow increase and then a sharp jump in these figures. Among white women born in 1870 who ever married, nearly 16 percent, or about one-sixth, remained childless; among their African-American counterparts, the figure was 13 percent. After 1870, though, the rate of childlessness among blacks outpaced that of whites, rising first to 18 percent (almost one-fifth) among women born in 1880, then to a peak of 28 percent (more than one-fourth) for women born between 1910 and 1915.

Although the rise of childlessness among African Americans evoked no call among policymakers or in the press to reverse the trend, the fact that native-born white Protestants were having smaller families generated cries of "race suicide," a term originated by sociologist Edward A. Ross and popularized by Theodore Roosevelt. However, in spite of the alarm, family size continued to decline—in 1910 fully one-quarter of all completed urban families had only two children. In the middle-Atlantic and Great Lakes regions, the proportion of two-child families rose to 40 percent. The rate of white childlessness grew as well, although it remained lower than among blacks. About 20 percent of white women born between 1910 and 1915 who ever married remained childless. Such high levels of childlessness coincided with, and are generally considered to be a product of, the Depression.

During the first four decades of the twentieth century, differential fertility rates declined, and by 1940 the fertility gap, both geographically and ethnically, had narrowed considerably. The Depression impelled all but the wealthiest Americans to decrease the size of their families. The fertility rate in 1940 had dipped to approximately 80. (If we calculate the birthrate per 1,000 of total population, rather than the fertility rate, the 1940 figure stood at 19.4.)

The decline, however, was about to reverse itself, if only for a few years. After World War II, the United States experienced a baby boom of unprecedented proportions. By the time it ended in 1960, the cohort of baby boomers numbered some 63.5 million children. This was the largest generation in this country's history and was much larger than the 41.5 million children born during the previous 15 years. Fueled both by prosperity and a resurgence of traditional gender role expectations, the fertility rate rose among all segments of the American population, but particularly among the well educated. Men and women married earlier and quickly became parents. In the middle of the 1950s, the average white woman bore her first child before she turned 22. Her African-American counterpart became a mother for the first time, on average, shortly after she turned 20. In contrast, the women of their mothers' generation would have been about 24 and 21, respectively. Couples planned large families, and most young Americans claimed that they wanted to have four children. Birth control had become much more acceptable as it transformed itself into "planned parenthood," a means of spacing births rather than avoiding childbearing altogether. In 1957, the year in which the baby boom peaked, the fertility rate stood at 123. A gradual decline followed until 1965 as the cultural imperative for large, planned families continued to reign. But then the birthrate began to plummet again, as young people began to marry later and have fewer children.

The fertility pattern of late marriages and smaller families that emerged in the mid-1960s has continued until the present day. By 1972, the fertility rate had slipped to levels of the Depression Era (73.1), and its descent continued until 1984, when it stood at 65.4. After that came a steady but very gradual rise to 69.2 at the end of the 1980s. Once again, differential fertility patterns emerged as more highly educated women had the fewest children, and new immigrants and African Americans had more.

Despite this decline in the fertility rate, Americans have abandoned neither marriage nor parenthood. More than 90 percent of women born during the baby boom have now married, and the overwhelming majority of them have produced offspring, although they often waited until their thirties to have their first child. Of the cohort of women born between 1948 and 1952 (who have presumably ended their childbearing years), only 16 percent, including both married and single, remained childless. This figure is lower than the 22 percent recorded for women (married and single) born in the 1880s. Women born in the later years of the baby boom have not yet ended their childbearing years. Since statistics about fertility into the 1990s have shown a continued increase in childbearing among women in their thirties, it is impossible to know what their rates of childlessness might be, although the estimate is 16 or 17 percent.

In analyzing the reasons for the fertility decline, the greatest weight should be given to urbanization and economic change, including levels of relative prosperity and privation as well as changes in the work patterns of women. At the moment, there appears to be no prospect of a return to the baby-boom fertility patterns. The immediate prospect is for a continuation of the contemporary pattern of late marriages and small families.

—*Margaret Marsh*

See also
Birth Control.
References
Cutright, Phillips, and Edward Shorter. "The Effects of Health on the Completed Fertility of Nonwhite and White U.S. Women Born from 1867 through 1935." *Journal of Social History* 13 (1979): 191–217.
Goldin, Claudia. *Understanding the Gender Gap: An Economic History of American Women.* New York: Oxford University Press, 1990.
Leavitt, Judith Walzer. *Brought to Bed: Childbearing in America, 1750–1850.* New York: Oxford University Press, 1986.
Marsh, Margaret, and Wanda Ronner. *The Empty Cradle: Infertility in America from Colonial Times to the Present.* Baltimore: Johns Hopkins University Press, 1996.
National Center for Health Statistics. *Vital Statistics of the United States, 1989.* Vol. 1, Natality. Department of Health and Human Services Pub. No. (PHS) 93–1100. Washington, DC: Government Printing Office, 1993.
Ross, Edward A. "Slow Suicide." *Century Magazine* 107 (1924): 509.
Van Horn, Susan Householder. *Women, Work, and Fertility.* New York: New York University Press, 1988.

Fire Departments

Early municipal governments took an active interest in providing protection against fire. New Amsterdam taxed its citizens in 1646 to pay chimney inspectors after several small fires broke out as the result of careless chimney cleaning. The city also ordered tanned leather water buckets from Holland and introduced an official fire watch. Several cities also required homeowners to keep a bucket free at all times to transport water to fires. Technological innovations and increasing urban density helped replace these early bucket brigades with more organized and effective ways of fighting fires. In 1718, Boston citizens organized the first volunteer fire company in America, complete with a small hand-operated fire engine and uniforms for its members. In 1736, Benjamin Franklin established and publicized a Philadelphia fire company in which he actively participated.

By the early nineteenth century, every American city was protected by at least one fire company organized around a hand-pump fire engine voluntarily manned by citizens at the alarm of fire. Members could be fined for being absent at fires, for attending a fire while drunk, or for disobeying the orders of the company president or engineer. Fire companies quickly multiplied, and by the mid-nineteenth century between 15 and 30 companies protected a city from fire. Together these companies formed a volunteer fire department, under the loose control of a municipal overseeing organization.

Nineteenth-century cities were extremely flammable, and nearly all experienced extensive conflagrations that burned much of them to the ground. Between 1849 and 1851, San Francisco suffered six extensive fires that provided the impetus for forming a volunteer fire department in that newly settled city. In the intensely flammable environments of these early cities, firemen were the only reliable guardians of life and property. Fire companies also provided early social services. Firehouses contained rooms for public use, and several early-nineteenth-century fire companies in Baltimore contained libraries for firemen and others. As early as 1792, fire departments set up widow and orphan funds to support dependents of injured or killed firemen.

While volunteer firemen were not actually paid salaries, they did receive other kinds of payment. They were absolved from jury and militia duty, and they obtained many less tangible benefits for participating in these prestigious and crucial organizations. Cities helped purchase elegantly appointed firehouses for companies, and held balls and benefits in their honor. Poems, songs, and plays were written for them, and newspapers regularly published elaborate tributes to their valor and ability. Firemen marched in parades, received gifts from thankful citizens and insurance companies, and generally enjoyed increased status and respect as a result of their activities. The symbolic payment that firemen received for their invaluable service was as significant to the public as to the firemen, providing citizens with the faith and confidence to rebuild, despite overwhelming evidence of their city's perishability.

Early fire companies were selective in their membership and combined social activities with firefighting. They entertained companies from other cities and held elaborate balls and parties. In short, fire departments provided as many as

Chicago firefighters battling a blaze at Our Lady of Angels parochial school in 1958.

1,000 men with a tightly knit community, with status, and with an outlet for competition, which sometimes turned into elaborate brawls between companies. These fights, which in some cities interfered with firefighting, were the source of extensive criticism of volunteer firefighting by the mid-nineteenth century and transformed both the reputation and composition of companies. Everywhere but in a few East Coast cities, fire company membership retained its original heterogeneous character, joining wealthy and working men together. Merchants, however, increasingly left the once-exclusive companies, and working-class members took their places.

Volunteer fire departments also participated in constructing the political culture of nineteenth-century cities. A visible and significant portion of urban politicians were volunteer firemen, including Boss Tweed of New York. In antebellum St. Louis, all but three mayors were members of that city's volunteer fire department. Machine politics was widely regarded as having an unnatural affinity for ward-based volunteer fire departments, producing public condemnation of political fire departments that sometimes bordered on hysteria. Yet it appears that volunteer fire departments were not particularly corrupt—or even particularly powerful—in most cities. They were often too disorganized and divided to mobilize politically in the interests of the organization as a whole. The general condemnation of these departments, which helped precipitate their demise, was more reflective of the public's definition of good politics and good firefighting than it was of the political power of firemen as a group. In this view, firefighting was increasingly considered by proponents of professionalization as being "above" politics, and good politics, i.e., noncorrupt politics, as being above firemen. Although politicians today are often members of local fire departments in towns and rural areas, the taboo against political firemen in cities has held.

Volunteer fire departments were almost impossible for cities to control. Fire companies built houses where they pleased, which provided some parts of a city with too many companies while generally providing inadequate protection for early suburbs. Because of increasing involvement in both politics and violence, and because of the increasing financial demands that these companies placed on insurance companies, citizens, and city governments, volunteer fire departments were being widely denounced by the 1850s. Reformers, aided by fire insurance companies, worked to develop alternatives. Technological innovations, including the fire-alarm telegraph and steam engine, paved the way for changes. In 1853 Cincinnati took the lead in replacing volunteer forces with a paid department manned by a small band of professional firefighters and equipped with horse-drawn steam engines built locally. Volunteer firemen vainly rallied against this threat to their organizations. They opposed steam engines through political means and with violence, while they belittled the abilities of paid firemen. But cities across the United States followed the well-publicized example of Cincinnati, and by the 1860s almost every city had a professional fire department, steam fire engines, and a fire-alarm telegraph.

Technological innovations, improved water supply, and tightly controlled membership improved the efficiency and order of the new departments. Into the late nineteenth century, however, most firemen were not full-time municipal employees. The majority of them worked on call, were paid small salaries, and were expected to leave their usual employment at the alarm of fire. Firemen actively protested shortsighted funding policies by cities, as well as the tendency to appoint firemen for political reasons rather than merit, even though the increasingly complex equipment was demanding better-trained firefighters.

In 1865, New York introduced the first full-time, paid fire department in the country, and by the end of the century most large cities agreed that a full-time department was worth the cost. Early-twentieth-century developments, including civil service exams and training programs for firemen, helped to produce firefighting forces that were well trained and competent. In the late twentieth century, efforts to diversify fire departments along racial and gender lines and to increase firefighters' salaries to the same level as other municipal employees have overshadowed the almost universally applauded performance of these groups. Firefighters consistently rank among the most trusted and appreciated municipal employees by the public. Although there are still ten times as many volunteer as paid fire departments in the United States, paid departments have effectively protected American cities from fire for over 100 years.

—*Amy S. Greenberg*

References
Burger, Jim. *In Service: A Documentary History of the Baltimore City Fire Department.* Baltimore: Paradigm Books, 1976.
Dana, David D. *The Fireman: The Fire Departments of the United States, with a Full Account of All Large Fires, Statistics of Losses and Expenses, Theaters Destroyed by Fire, and Accidents, Anecdotes, and Incidents.* Boston: James French, 1858.
Greenberg, Amy S. *Cause for Alarm: The Volunteer Fire Department in the Nineteenth Century City.* Princeton, NJ: Princeton University Press, 1997.
Hazen, Margaret Hindle, and Robert M. Hazen. *Keepers of the Flame: The Role of Fire in American Culture, 1775–1925.* Princeton, NJ: Princeton University Press, 1992.
Lyons, Paul Robert. *Fire in America!* Boston: National Fire Protection Association, 1976.

Fitzgerald, F. Scott (1896–1940)

This chronicler of the Jazz Age, the decade between the end of World War I and the onset of the Great Depression, was largely an urban writer. Born in St. Paul, Minnesota, he moved east as a young man, attending the Newman Academy in New Jersey and Princeton University. While at these institutions, he made his first acquaintance with New York City, which was to become a major setting for his fiction.

In his novel *The Beautiful and Damned* (1922), Fitzgerald ties the fall of his central characters (Anthony Patch and Gloria Gilbert) from a state of careless merriment and idleness to one of poverty, marital discord, and in Patch's case alcoholism to New York. The great gaudy and exciting city is evoked in its fashionable streets, bars, hotels, restaurants, nightlife, and theaters both as a source of the Patches' frenetic enjoyment and an instrument in their fall. Fitzgerald uses New York, as well, as a backdrop for one of the novel's most notable ironies. As their dwindling assets force the Patches from their comfortable apartment into less and less fashionable flats and neighborhoods, they never realize that their current dwelling places them in contact with a vitality and a proximity to life and children that they have never experienced.

In *The Great Gatsby* (1925) Fitzgerald again evokes New York as a place of meretricious beauty and pleasure, emphasizing also its sordid underside. But much of the action takes place away from the city, in the nearby Long Island communities of East Egg and West Egg, a fictional rendering of suburban Great Neck where Fitzgerald lived with his wife, Zelda, and daughter, Scottie, between the fall of 1922 and the spring of 1924. In this novel, the juxtaposition of East Egg and West Egg reflects one of its major themes and subjects: Jay Gatsby's aspiration to be part of the American upper class in the face of his current status as just a nouveau riche.

In the last decade of his life, Fitzgerald moved to Los Angeles, first working as a scriptwriter for films and then on a novel, *The Last Tycoon,* in which he intended to provide a realistic picture of the Hollywood film industry. The novel was unfinished when Fitzgerald died in 1940, but it was published in 1941.

—*Joseph Griffin*

References
Fitzgerald, F. Scott. *The Beautiful and Damned*. New York: Scribners, 1922.
———. *The Great Gatsby*. New York: Scribners, 1925.
———. *The Last Tycoon*. New York: Scribners, 1941.
———. "May Day." In F. Scott Fitzgerald, *Tales of the Jazz Age*. New York: Scribners, 1922.
———. "The Rich Boy." In F. Scott Fitzgerald, *All the Sad Young Men*. New York: Scribners, 1926.
Mizener, Arthur. *Fitzgerald and His World*. London: Thames and Hudson, 1972.

Flophouses

Flophouse is a generic term, referring to any large residential structure designed to house substantial numbers of single men in small rooms or spaces. In more recent times, flop-houses are frequently called single room occupancy hotels (SROs).

Flophouses were usually located in the skid row section of a city. The first of these was in Seattle, and the term denoted the street down which logs were skidded to be sent to the lumber mills. This "Skid Road" was lined with the kinds of facilities needed or desired by temporary residents: cheap housing and restaurants, bars, and brothels. Later, all such districts, usually located near the downtown railroad hub of a city, were called skid row. Residents here were unable or unwilling to be part of the standard, family-style social economy and thus needed alternative means to provide necessities.

Flophouses, the most essential feature of any skid row, spanned a wide range of housing. At the apex of this system was the workingman's hotel, which provided a small, pleasantly furnished, single-room apartment; these were relatively expensive and thus patronized by skilled or clerical workers who commanded superior wages but preferred a bachelor lifestyle.

Far more common, however, were cage hotels and dormitories. The former referred to large industrial buildings, including lofts and warehouses, where the main floors were divided into rows by wooden walls or by unrolling sheets of corrugated iron. These would then be sealed off, creating a warren of tiny individual rooms, usually about 5 feet x 7 feet. They were called "cage hotels" because the walls never met the floor or ceiling; in order to prevent theft, the gaps were closed with chicken wire. As many as 200 rooms could be crammed into a single floor, and at the turn of the century in Chicago approximately 100,000 men lived in these facilities during the winter.

Dormitories, on the other hand, left the entire floor wide open, and beds were lined up next to each other, similar to a modern shelter. Bunk beds could also be used, sometimes constructed simply by nailing two poles into place across from a wall, then tacking boards or even canvas to the wall and then to the posts. Many states passed health laws dictating how much space had to be provided for each resident (Illinois, for example, mandated two feet on either side of every bed), but these were rarely, if ever, obeyed.

Below dormitories were true flophouses. In these facilities, the worker paid merely to have a place to lie down—that is, the right to flop down on the floor. Conditions were uniformly horrible, with disease and vermin constantly present. Even here, however, residents made distinctions, preferring places that had significant molding around the base of the wall, as this helped provide some semblance of a pillow.

The typical customers of a flophouse also varied. Many of them were itinerant workers, often skilled, whom Kenneth

Allsop referred to as "the shock-trooper of the American expansion." Others were men on pensions or who had been crippled by industrial accidents. Some were alcoholics, although their presence on skid row, particularly at the turn of the century, was usually exaggerated. All of these individuals, however, shared the common condition of poverty, which is why they sought inexpensive housing.

—*Robert A. Slayton*

See also
Homelessness; Skid Row.
References
Allsop, Kenneth. *Hard Travellin'*. New York: New American Press, 1967.
Anderson, Nels. *The Hobo: The Sociology of the Homeless Man*. Chicago: University of Chicago Press, 1923.
Hoch, Charles, and Robert A. Slayton. *New Homeless and Old: Community and the Skid Row Hotel*. Philadelphia: Temple University Press, 1989.
Solenberger, Alice. *One Thousand Homeless Men*. New York: Russell Sage, 1911.

Fragmentation of Municipal Government

Local government in the United States is highly fragmented, with authority widely dispersed. This fragmentation, along with its diversity, is one of the principal hallmarks of the system. It is also, however, a source of consternation to those who insist that there are more orderly and efficient ways to go about the business of local government. But the situation has endured, in large part because there is far more to political rationality than simply a well-ordered system of government.

The sheer number of local governments indicates how fragmented they are. According to the Bureau of the Census, there were approximately 85,000 units of local government in 1992. This count includes only those entities that have some form of corporate existence, such as the right to perpetual succession, and are accountable to the public. To qualify as a government, moreover, such entities must possess a high degree of fiscal independence, with their own revenue sources and the authority to spend without detailed review by other local governments. Not included, then, are the innumerable but largely administrative or advisory entities such as election districts, volunteer associations, or statistical areas.

In addition to being numerous, local governments are also ubiquitous. Every state relies on a system of local governments, although some do so more extensively than others. In 1992, for example, there were 6,723 local governments in Illinois, 5,159 in Pennsylvania, and 4,792 in Texas. Hawaii, by contrast, had only 21, the fewest in the nation, followed by Alaska with 175 and Nevada with 208.

Impressive as they are, these numbers alone indicate the full extent of the system's fragmentation imperfectly. Fragmentation occurs whenever public responsibilities are allocated among different governments within the same or overlapping geographic areas, and this is common in the United States. Relatively few governments have exclusive jurisdiction over all local functions within their boundaries. More often, they are but one of several governments in the area, each independent and each with its own responsibilities.

The largest kind of local government, geographically, is the county—or the borough in Alaska and the parish in Louisiana. All the other states have counties, and in most the entire state is served by organized county governments. There are exceptions, such as San Francisco and Denver, where city and county government are consolidated, and New York City, where smaller counties (or boroughs) are consolidated into the greater City of New York. In Connecticut and Rhode Island, on the other hand, there are no county governments. In those states, the county exists merely as an administrative convenience, as a geographic area for organizing judicial districts, and for collecting and aggregating social and economic data.

Though important, few county governments have exclusive jurisdiction over all local functions within their boundaries. Within each county, there are typically other local governments—on average, some 27 for every county in the nation. Like all averages, these conceal important variations among states. In Jefferson County, Kentucky, for example, there are 126 units of local government; in Jefferson County, Illinois, 51; in Jefferson County, Georgia, 9; and in Jefferson County, Mississippi, 3.

Some of these are general-purpose governments—municipalities, independent cities, and in some states, towns and townships. Like counties, these governments have broad responsibilities, and in New England, where counties are of minor significance, they are the principal forms of local government. Elsewhere, they are generally more limited, most obviously with respect to their territorial reach but also with respect to their public responsibilities.

Far more numerous than general-purpose governments, however, are so-called special districts (35,555), which, along with independent school districts (14,422), constitute more than one-half of the local governments in the United States. Despite their names, these districts are distinct, independent units of government. As their names imply, however, their responsibilities are typically limited, in over 90 percent of the cases to a single public function. Their specific functions can, and do, vary. Many of these governments (6,228) are responsible for programs that fall under the general heading of natural resources—drainage and flood control, for example, or irrigation and soil conservation. Others are responsible for basic municipal services such as water supply and sewerage (4,646) or fire protection (5,620). Still others administer public housing (3,470), libraries (1,043), or cemeteries (1,628).

The districts also differ in terms of significance. They include governments of lesser import and minor impact, including those responsible for parking, pest control, highway rights of way, and convention facilities. But they also include such major governments as the Port Authority of New York and New Jersey, the Chicago Transit Authority, the Metropolitan Water District of Southern California, and the Omaha Public Power District.

What accounts for these differences, and, more generally, for the fragmentation and decentralization that characterize the system? One factor is state government. In formal, legal terms, the state is the single most important actor in determining the overall structure of local governance. Even in home rule states, where localities are assured a degree of autonomy, the state government ultimately decides how many local governments there will be and which governments will have what responsibilities.

Deciding these questions includes, to begin with, determining how much the state government does itself and how much it delegates. States differ in this respect, and the differences are evident, albeit imperfectly, in the ratio of direct state spending to total state and local spending. On average, states accounted for approximately 45 percent of these expenditures in 1989. But the ratio varies, ranging from a high of 77 percent in Hawaii to a low of 30 percent in New York, with 38 states in the range of 30 to 50 percent.

Second, states determine what responsibilities they will delegate to local governments. Public welfare, for example, is principally a state function, although in a few states, California and New York among them, city and county governments play a major role. Schools, on the other hand, are generally run locally, although in Hawaii the state directly controls and operates them. Responsibility for other public functions—public safety, including fire, police, public health, and code enforcement; libraries; parks and recreation; hospitals; roads and public transportation—varies more across states. What one state assigns principally to local governments, another may handle itself. Moreover, states may shift administrative and fiscal control from, or to, a local government, as states have done recently with respect to public welfare.

States determine, finally, how responsibilities are allocated among local governments—how many governments there will be in a given area and who will be responsible for doing what. Again, there are substantial variations both among and within states in this regard. And, since states do not treat all local governments equally, governments that are nominally the same may operate radically differently.

This is especially true of what the Bureau of the Census terms "General Purpose Governments," counties, for example, or municipalities or towns. Functions assigned to a municipality in one state may be handled elsewhere by special dis-

tricts, independent school districts, or the state itself, all of which helps account for striking differences in what municipalities spend. In 1990, New York City, which has major budgetary responsibilities for education, welfare, and hospitals, spent roughly $4,256 per capita. This far exceeded the $962 per capita spent by Chicago, where these functions are controlled by other local governments. Los Angeles, like Chicago, is responsible for a limited number of functions and spends roughly the equivalent of Chicago. On the other hand, San Francisco spends almost three times as much per capita ($2,577) as either Los Angeles or Chicago, largely because of its programs in public welfare, health, and hospitals.

In turn, state policy concerning the number and kind of local governments is influenced by several factors. One of these is population. Simply because they have more people to govern, the most populous states are more likely to rely on elaborate and extensive systems of local government. As noted, Alaska and Hawaii have relatively few local governments, California and Illinois, substantially more. Indeed, the seven largest states account for approximately one-third of all local governments in the United States.

Though important, population is not the only important factor. States with roughly the same number of people often have substantially different numbers of local governments. Florida and Illinois are examples, as are Tennessee and Wisconsin. In 1990 Florida's population was about 12.3 million and Illinois's was 11.4 million; however, Illinois had more than six times as many local governments as Florida, 6,772 to 1,013. Both Tennessee and Wisconsin had populations of about 4.9 million, but Wisconsin had 2,739 local governments while Tennessee had only 923. Nor does geographic size, or size in combination with population, explain much. In statistical terms, the correlation between population and territory, on the one hand, and the number of local governments, on the other, is quite low.

Of greater significance than population are intergovernmental and political considerations. Among the former are federal programs that, though not requiring the creation of distinct units of local government, encourage and support such arrangements. The nation's many soil conservation districts are one example. These districts owe their existence largely to efforts during the New Deal to develop grassroots support for national programs. In 1937, for example, President Franklin Roosevelt distributed a "Model State Law" to governors recommending the creation of special local governments to facilitate cooperation among local farmers, landowners, and the recently created U.S. Soil Conservation Service.

State policies with respect to the structure of local governance are also determined by more localized factors, not the least of them finances. Specialized local governments are often created to circumvent constitutional limits on the revenue and spending authority of general-purpose governments. This is especially true when large capital expenditures are required, as in the case of transit systems, bridges, and water works. It is often simpler for a state legislature to create an entirely new governmental entity, with its own revenue and spending powers, than to eliminate restrictions on an existing government by amending the state constitution.

Additionally, it is sometimes simpler to create a new government as a way of minimizing conflicts. Special districts are commonly used to lessen tensions between older, settled parts of a community and newer, expanding ones. Extending facilities, such as sewer and water lines, or services, such as fire protection, to newer neighborhoods is often costly and frequently opposed by those who already receive, and have already paid for, those services. A special district for the newly settled areas is one way to handle the issue.

Finally, there is the matter of limiting access to the process of making policy. Many local governments are designed to deal with a limited range of issues, and this in turn reduces the number of interested political actors. In some instances, the goal is to distance government process from politics, especially from the vagaries and uncertainties of party and electoral politics. This goal has been foremost in creating independent school districts and forming public housing authorities. Many housing authorities, for example, were made independent to shield them from unsympathetic voter reaction or because a particular general-purpose government was out of favor or was ethically suspect.

Limiting the range of issues not only reduces the number of interested political actors, it also increases the access and influence of those who remain. It also ensures that an issue receives the attention it "deserves," something not likely if it must compete for attention with all the other issues handled by a general-purpose government. Within the setting of a special district, with limited policy concerns, officials may develop greater understanding and sympathy for the views of citizens who have a stake in the district's affairs.

There are, then, powerful political reasons for the existence of so many, and so many different kinds, of local governments in the United States, and why the nation's system of local government is so fragmented. And since there are, and since so many individuals and interests benefit from the status quo, there seems little prospect of a dramatic change in the foreseeable future. Nor have past efforts at change been notably successful. The school consolidation movement, it is true, substantially reduced the number of independent school districts—from 50,000 in 1942 to 14,400 in 1992. This was done principally by eliminating school districts that had only the legendary one-room schoolhouse. But efforts to reduce the number of other local governments—for example, by

consolidating smaller governments into a single metropolitan unit—have met little success. Indeed the number of other governments, and special districts in particular, has grown steadily in recent years. This suggests that there is not a critical mass of citizens who believe they would be better off under a new and reordered system of local government than they are under the long-standing system that remains so much a part of the nation's heritage of self-government.

—*Russell D. Murphy*

See also
Commission Government; Consolidation; Municipal Government.
References
Bollens, John. *Special District Governments in the United States.* Berkeley: University of California Press, 1957.
Campbell, Alan K., and Seymour Sacks. *Metropolitan America: Fiscal Patterns and Governmental Systems.* New York: Free Press, 1967.
Grumm, John G., and Russell D. Murphy. *Governing States and Communities: Organizing for Popular Rule.* Englewood Cliffs, NJ: Prentice-Hall, 1991.
Kaufman, Herbert. *Politics and Policies in State and Local Governments.* Englewood Cliffs, NJ: Prentice-Hall, 1963.
Ostrom, Vincent, Charles Tiebout, and Robert Warren. "The Organization of Government in Metropolitan Areas: A Theoretical Inquiry." *The American Political Science Review* 55 (1961): 831–842.
Wood, Robert. *1400 Governments.* Cambridge, MA: Harvard University Press, 1961.

Franchises and Franchising

Franchising is a form of business organization in which one firm, often called the parent company, grants another company the right to make or sell its products and use its name. There are two general types of franchise arrangements: product format and business format. Both originated in the United States.

Product-format franchises began to evolve in the 1840s when improved production techniques and transportation systems allowed manufacturers to escape the local market and sell their goods over large parts of the country. Makers of complex goods like sewing machines discovered that to succeed in a national market they needed their own dealers closely tied to the company to sell and service expensive and unfamiliar machines. Over time the relationship between a manufacturer and its agents became so close that the latter, although legally independent, were effectively incorporated into the organization of the parent company.

Business-format franchising began in the 1920s when gasoline retailers and fast-food pioneers like Howard Johnson developed techniques to mass-produce uniform outlets that sold uniform products. Under this arrangement, the parent company typically locates, designs, builds, and equips an outlet, trains its owner, and provides close, continuing support once the owner opens the new store. Business-format franchising developed into a distinct industry when perceptive entrepreneurial franchisers discovered that more money could be made by selling hamburger stands than by selling hamburgers, although they actually do both, by supplying hamburgers to the hamburger stand.

For most of the twentieth century, franchising has been closely connected to the rise and development of American cities. In the first part of the century, product franchising fueled the rapid expansion of automobile ownership. Just as the automobile was central in determining the shape of the modern city, the franchise system was vital to the rapid spread of the automobile. In 1920, there were more than 9 million cars on American roads; ten years later there were more than 26 million. They all needed gasoline, routine maintenance, and repairs. Because cars were complex and the products needed to service them, such as gasoline and oil, were dangerous, franchising was the preferred method of establishing outlets to provide these services. Nearly all auto, tire, and battery manufacturers and gasoline and oil refiners have sold their goods either predominantly or exclusively through franchises.

In the second half of the twentieth century, business-format franchising has contributed significantly to a growing sameness in the layout and the look of American cities. The essence of business-format franchising is to find or develop a successful small business and then develop techniques to reproduce and market large numbers of nearly identical units as efficiently as possible. Most are not only indistinguishable from the other outlets established by the same company, but their locations are also based on similar criteria. One result has been a nearly identical mix of uniform outlets located in the same general types of places within and across American cities. By 1990, there were well over 500,000 franchised outlets in the country. Most are located in cities and along transportation arteries, the natural place to offer strangers a known commodity in otherwise unfamiliar surroundings.

—*Thomas S. Dicke*

References
Dicke, Thomas S. *Franchising in America*. Chapel Hill: University of North Carolina Press, 1991.
Langdon, Philip. *Orange Roofs, Golden Arches: The Architecture of American Chain Restaurants*. New York: Knopf, 1986.
Luxenberg, Stan. *Roadside Empires: How the Chains Franchised America*. New York: Viking, 1985.
Preston, Howard. *Automobile Age Atlanta: The Making of a Southern Metropolis, 1900–1935*. Athens: University of Georgia Press, 1994.
Ritzer, George. *The McDonaldization of Society*. Thousand Oaks, CA: Pine Forge Press, 1996.

French Colonial Towns

French colonial towns in North America were founded by either private or public institutions, and this marked their character. Without traditions of urban self-government, the French crown easily took over civic administration from the founding body, if it were not already the monarchy itself.

Because the administration of New France was entrusted to chartered trading companies until 1663, Quebec and Montreal resulted from private enterprise. Quebec was established in 1608 by the de Monts fur-trading company to command the St. Lawrence River at a point where it narrows to a cannon's range and also to be a gateway to the continent's interior. Quebec became the capital of New France and, after the imposition of royal government in 1663, its dominance over the rest of the colony increased. Despite a population of less than 8,000 during the French regime, Quebec had those functions that distinguished cities in France. In addition to housing the highest royal officials, it was a bishop's seat and a center of higher education with a Jesuit college dating from 1635 and a seminary for training priests. Quebec was then the farthest point upriver that seagoing vessels could reach, and so wholesale merchants made it the mainland colony's principal port. Those engaged in commerce tended to live in the Lower Town, close to the river, while government officials and religious houses were mostly in the Upper Town, along with the cathedral and governor's palace.

Montreal (1642) was established for purely religious purposes. Devout members of the Society of Our Lady of Montreal for the Conversion of Indians intended to make the island community in the upper St. Lawrence a base for Christian missions. This was the most western French settlement in the seventeenth century, and Montrealers were repeatedly attacked by the nearby Mohawks of the Five Nations Confederacy. Montreal Island was near the junction of the St. Lawrence River with the Ottawa River, a route used by fur traders going inland to the Huron country and to Lakes Huron and Superior, where they harvested the best pelts. The commercial advantages of Montreal's location were quickly recognized, and the town's religious vocation was eclipsed by its role as a fur-trading center.

Trois-Rivieres (1634), too, was a trading post at a river junction, but the poorly drained, sandy terrain surrounding it deprived the settlement of the rich agricultural hinterland that made Montreal the fastest-growing French colonial city in the eighteenth century. Trois-Rivieres remained a village with no more than a thousand inhabitants. Rural villages were rare in the St. Lawrence Valley, and farming people obtained what they could not produce themselves from merchants and craftsmen in the three towns.

The fortress city of Louisbourg and New Orleans were eighteenth-century creations. Under the 1713 Treaty of Utrecht, France surrendered its territorial claim to Newfoundland, and residents of the fishing settlement of Plaisance (Placentia) removed themselves to Cape Breton, a French possession close to the cod-fishing banks. The government

Bilingual signs are the norm in parts of Canada where the law mandates that all street signage be in both English and French.

of France decided in 1717 to make the migrants' settlement, renamed Louisbourg, a fortified haven for the seasonal fishing fleet from Europe as well as for resident fishermen. It was also to be the administrative capital for the remaining French territories along the Atlantic coast.

The public money spent for defenses and the military garrison provided revenue for those not engaged in fishing. Louisbourg, like Montreal, acquired an unexpected commercial role as a point for the transshipment of cargoes carried between "Canada" (the St. Lawrence Valley and Great Lakes), New England, France, and the French West Indies. Because of its barren location, this great port depended on imported food delivered by French-speaking Acadians from Nova Scotia and by New Englanders.

New Orleans was founded in 1718 to control the mouth of the Mississippi River, which was highly valued as an all-weather route into North America's interior. This was especially important since the St. Lawrence River was ice-bound for nearly half the year and therefore not navigable. The government of French Louisiana had been located at Biloxi and Mobile before it was transferred to New Orleans in 1722. While

the population of New France numbered in the tens of thousands, Louisiana had only 8,830 residents in 1746, half of them slaves. Louisiana produced little, apart from animal hides, tobacco, and pitch, that was not already available from the French West Indies. Although New Orleans was Louisiana's capital and had governmental and religious institutions similar to those at Quebec, the impoverished French crown had stunted the city's commercial development by granting trade monopolies and had allowed the colony to revert to company rule in 1712 to save itself the costs of defending and administering Louisiana. Direct royal government, in the fashion of New France, resumed in 1731 and lasted until the Spanish took possession of New Orleans in 1766. The rest of New France was ceded to Britain in 1763 as part of the settlement of the Seven Years' War.

The civic administration of Quebec, New Orleans, and Louisbourg was provided by the king's *lieutenants-généraux civil et criminel,* who acted as magistrates and lawgivers. Before 1663, townsfolk in the St. Lawrence Valley elected spokesmen or *syndics* to an advisory council at Quebec, and, in the early 1670s, Quebec had a short-lived municipal government of a mayor and two aldermen. The king's ministers disapproved of representative institutions, and Quebec's elected civic officials soon were replaced by royal magistrates. Montreal followed the same route in 1693 when the Sulpician Fathers, successors of the Society of Our Lady as the island's seigneurs, surrendered their judicial powers. Occasionally, leading residents at "public order assemblies" advised the local magistrate before he set the official prices for bread and beef. Although residents described themselves as *bourgeois de cette ditte ville,* their communal spirit was weak.

Townsfolk paid seigneurial dues to religious orders, which provided hospitals and schools and cared for the old and the poor. The towns lacked piped water, street lights, and public garbage removal, and public order regulations punished those who left filth and debris on public thoroughfares. The royal magistrates were concerned primarily with regulating twice-a-week markets, bakers and butchers, and taverns, and with reducing fire hazards. Despite fire-prevention regulations, every town but Louisbourg suffered devastating conflagrations. Government road surveyors watched for private encroachments on the streets, and court officers and soldiers acted as policemen to maintain public order.

The Sulpician Fathers defined the width and alignment of streets in Montreal, but other towns in the seventeenth century developed haphazardly. Grandiose schemes to make Quebec worthy of being a capital were proposed, and under royal government, military engineers tried to impose some order on urban development. Their ideal was a rectilinear grid with the principal governmental and religious institutions at the town's center. Quebec's suburb of St. Roch followed the grid pattern, and an extension of the Lower Town was to do the same. Montreal had two main thoroughfares parallel to the river with an erratic pattern of cross-streets. Only Louisbourg, Fort Detroit, and New Orleans conformed to the engineers' orderly plans.

Louisiana's capital expressed the ideals of order, symmetry, and hierarchy. The parochial church faced a central parade square (the Place d'Armes, now Jackson Square) from which perfectly square blocks spread out on either side and to the rear. Religious houses and government offices, as well as the prison and barracks, were located close to Place d'Armes. The governor's residence was on one side of the square whereas the home of the *lieutenant-général,* a subordinate official, was farther away from the Place. The town's leading families tried to locate their homes close to these representatives of earthly and heavenly power. One's proximity to the central square tended to correspond with one's social rank.

Two-story structures made the most of lots within colonial towns. Not only were town houses higher than rural homes, they were more likely to be built of stone or brick rather than of wood or half-timbering with a rubble or clay infill. Building facades lined the streets. However, French colonial towns did retain a rural aspect with kitchen gardens, stables, paddocks, and orchards. Pigs wandered in the streets.

The *ville* was geographically defined by its defenses. Wooden palisades enclosed seventeenth-century towns; they were superseded, in Montreal, Quebec, and Louisbourg, by stone walls with bastions. New Orleans was a defenseless town until expanding farms around Fort Rosalie provoked the Natchez tribe to kill some 240 French settlers in 1729. The massacre caused panic in New Orleans, which was then provided with a ditch and a wall for protection against the natives.

The *fauxbourgs* (or *faubourgs*), or suburbs, were those parts of the community outside the city's walls. The very name, which means false or sham towns, gave them an air of illegitimacy. Suburbs spread outward along the principal roads from the towns. Tanneries, because of their foul smell, and lime kilns were banished to suburbs. Some *faubourg* residents were farmers, but at Louisbourg they were fishermen who wanted space for their drying platforms. The humble folk who lived just outside the city walls risked having their homes leveled if an enemy attack was imminent; demolition deprived attackers of cover and gave the town's defenders a clear field of fire. Life in an unprotected suburb was precarious and not to be envied.

—*Peter N. Moogk*

See also
New Orleans, Louisiana.
References
Charbonneau, André, Yvon Desloges, and Marc Lafrance. *Quebec, the Fortified City from the 17th to the 19th Century.* Ottawa, Ontario: Parks Canada, 1982.
Chénier, Rémi. *Quebec: A French Colonial Town in America, 1660 to 1690.* Ottawa, Ontario: National Historic Sites Parks Service, 1991.
Crowley, Terry. *Louisbourg: Atlantic Fortress and Seaport.* Ottawa, Ontario: Canadian Historical Association, 1990.
de Charlevoix, Pierre F. X. *Histoire et description générale de la Nouvelle-France.* 6 vols. Paris: Pierre-François Giffart, 1744.
Desloges, Yvon. *A Tenant's Town: Quebec in the 18th Century.* Ottawa, Ontario: National Historic Sites Parks Service, 1991.
Lachance, André. *La vie urbaine en Nouvelle-France.* Montreal, Quebec: Les Éditions du Boréal Express, 1987.
Moogk, Peter. *Building a House in New France.* Toronto, Ontario: McClelland and Steward, 1978.
Reid, Allana G. "The Nature of Quebec Society during the French Regime." *Canadian Historical Association Annual Report* (1951): 26–35.
Wilson, Samuel. *The Vieux Carré, New Orleans—Its Plan, Its Growth, Its Architecture.* New Orleans, LA: Historic District Demonstration Study, Bureau of Governmental Research, 1969.

Gambling

Gambling has always been a part of American culture, especially in urban areas. As early as 1610, lotteries held by the Virginia Company of London helped finance the building of Jamestown and the settlement of Virginia. Whether games of chance, betting on sporting or racing competitions, or speculating on financial markets, gambling has pervaded urban society and proved impossible to eradicate. Because cities contain large numbers of people and represent the location of concentrated wealth, they became the focal points for gambling. Gambling has been an egalitarian recreation and has attracted people from all walks of urban life.

While Puritan New England restricted gambling, it flourished in other sections of the colonies, especially in cities like Charleston, New York, Savannah, and Baltimore. Inhabitants of America's new cities enjoyed card games, dice, backgammon, pitching pennies, horse racing, billiards, cockfighting, ninepins for money, and buying lottery tickets. Local taverns served as the venues for many of these forms of gambling.

The lottery was a particularly popular form of gambling in colonial towns. Although Boston ministers in 1699 branded lottery agents as "pillagers of the people," by 1762 its city officials were using lotteries to raise money to rebuild Faneuil Hall. Other cities used lotteries to finance city streets, city buildings, wharves, defense installations, halfway houses for immigrants, new industries, and jail construction. Lotteries also provided funding to build entire cities, like Federal City in the District of Columbia in 1793.

Townspeople also enjoyed horse racing. In the late seventeenth century, racetracks appeared in lower Manhattan, and throughout the eighteenth and nineteenth centuries, horse racing remained a staple urban recreation. Taverns and gambling establishments in New York and other urban centers provided games like faro, E. O., Old Sledge, cockfights, dice, checkers, backgammon, roulette, and horseshoes, as well as a place to buy lottery tickets. In the 1790s gambling in government script and company stocks gained popularity. Gambling fever was especially high in southern cities like Charleston, because gambling was associated with aristocracy in many minds—and in Charleston, the lower classes wanted to emulate the aristocracy, the upper classes wanted to become "aristocratic," and Charleston fancied itself an aristocratic place and therefore had to have races. In 1735 residents of Charleston organized the world's first Jockey Club to arrange races and determine prizes.

Washington, D.C., exemplifies the pervasive influence of gambling in American cities from 1800 to 1860. Congress often lacked a quorum because so many of its members were at the racetrack. Betting on congressional and presidential elections became a favorite pastime in the gaming establishments along Pennsylvania Avenue. In the 1830s new forms of wagering began to appear in New York—speculating in the Wall Street stock market, betting on the arrival times of oceangoing ships, gambling on Hudson River steamboat races, and playing policy games, a forerunner of the twentieth-century "numbers" game.

From the 1820s to the 1860s, antivice associations formed in many cities to combat gambling, as well as prostitution and alcohol abuse. Reform efforts centered on the belief that gambling affected the working class negatively and that they needed protection from the questionable activities of professional gamblers, known as "sharpers." But reform groups like the New York Association for the Suppression of Gambling received "frigid indifference" when they asked city officials to curb the vice.

New towns in the Old Southwest offered many forms of gambling entertainment. Dens, gambling houses, and entire neighborhoods with names like "Pinch Gut" in Memphis and "Natchez Under-the-Hill" in Natchez became recognized for their vices and their gambling establishments. Professional gamblers attracted to these haunts turned many kinds of gambling into dishonest activities, and the increasingly negative reputation of professional gamblers provided another impetus for reform movements. In 1835, citizens of Vicksburg, convinced that professional gamblers were impeding the city's commercial growth, violently expelled professional gamblers from town. The reform movement in Vicksburg encouraged antigambling movements in New Orleans, Chicago, Mobile, and New York.

After the Civil War, crusades against gambling subsided, and betting enjoyed a resurgence. In fact, casinos from New York to San Francisco played an important role in the economy of growing urban centers. Policy games became a favorite of the urban working class, and by the 1880s a cartel controlled more than 7,000 policy shops nationally. Western towns remained a hotbed of gambling, especially cattle towns like Topeka, Abilene, and Dodge City that were traversed by the great cattle drives in the 1870s and 1880s. Dens, saloons, houses, palaces, halls, and parlors offered all forms of gambling for western society.

Horse racing regained its popularity in the late nineteenth century. As towns and cities grew, many townspeople, especially those of the lower classes, were unable to attend the races, but poolrooms provided a place to bet on the ponies as well as play billiards. And when they were unable to get to a poolroom, urban gamblers placed bets through the "handbook," or bookmakers. In the twentieth century, bookies expanded their field of operations; they no longer limited their services to horse racing and offered odds on all kinds of sports, including professional, collegiate, and even high school football, basketball, soccer, and baseball.

Although antivice organizations in cities renewed their attacks on gambling in the late nineteenth century, poolrooms, policy shops, and saloons remained open by buying protection from city bosses and policemen. Where reforms did banish gambling from open view, professional gamblers became more discreet or moved outside the city. Demands for reform in New Orleans ended not with the abolition of gambling or prostitution but with the confinement of them to an area that became known as Storyville. In the late nineteenth century, George Canfield, faced by a strong reform movement in New York City, opened a lavish gambling parlor in Saratoga Springs, New York. Spas became popular sporting locations in the early part of the twentieth century with locations like Saratoga Springs and Hot Springs, Arkansas, serving as gathering places for gambling enthusiasts. Progressive reformers failed to eradicate gambling, but they succeeded in passing laws that outlawed most forms of gambling. Casinos in Detroit, Pittsburgh, Chicago, Denver, San Francisco, New Orleans, and Hot Springs all shut down in the early twentieth century.

During the 1920s and 1930s, urban gambling revived. Numbers games became the dominant form in lower-class and ethnic neighborhoods like Harlem and similar sections of Chicago, Philadelphia, and Detroit. Bingo and church lotteries provided another form of gambling while still retaining the appearance of legal and moral activities. Horse racing, banned in most areas of the country during the Progressive period, experienced a renewal, supervised by state and local governments and assisted by the introduction of parimutuel betting.

Casino gambling also recovered during the 1920s and 1930s. In New York, Boston, and Atlantic City, casinos attracted a large number of urban residents, but with the development of the transportation infrastructure and the growth of the urban population nationally, Nevada became the nation's Mecca for commercial gambling. Las Vegas, with the support of organized crime, slowly grew as the center of casino gambling. In 1940 the city had six casinos; by 1955 the Vegas "strip" was attracting countless gamblers. In 1978, Atlantic City reopened for business as the center of casino gambling in the East. From the 1960s to the 1990s, many cities and states legalized gambling or instituted lotteries as a strategy to increase their revenues. Gambling in the twentieth century has been turned into a product of mass consumption, and the urban areas of America, with their concentrations of inhabitants and wealth, serve as the premier location for this traditional American recreation.

—*Craig Pascoe*

References

Asbury, Herbert. *Sucker's Progress: An Informal History of Gambling in America from the Colonies to Canfield.* Reprint ed. Montclair, NJ: Patterson Smith, 1969.

Boyer, Paul. *Urban Masses and Moral Order in America, 1820–1920.* Cambridge, MA: Harvard University Press, 1978.

Chafetz, Henry. *Play the Devil: A History of Gambling in the United States from 1492–1955.* New York: Clarkson N. Potter, 1960.

Fabian, Ann. *Card Sharps, Dream Books, and Bucket Shops: Gambling in Nineteenth-Century America.* Ithaca, NY: Cornell University Press, 1990.

Findlay, John M. *People of Chance: Gambling in American Society from Jamestown to Las Vegas.* New York: Oxford University Press, 1986.

Longstreet, Stephen. *Win or Lose: A Social History of Gambling in America.* Indianapolis, IN: Bobbs-Merrill, 1977.

Gangs

Gangs have been a significant phenomenon of American cities for more than a century. Beginning with the large flow of immigrants who came in the last decades of the nineteenth century and continuing with later groups of immigrants in the twentieth century who continued to live in impoverished areas, gangs have persisted in low-income neighborhoods. The phenomenon of gangs represented, and continues to represent, an organizational response to a particular economic condition—poverty. However, the exact nature of this organizational response has not always been consistently or precisely defined, nor has it been fully understood sociologically.

Throughout most of the nineteenth and twentieth centuries, the term *gang* has been used interchangeably with the terms *band* and *organized crime syndicate.* The problem with having used gang interchangeably with band is the looseness of the concept. As a result, both gangs and bands were labeled gangs, confusing two separate concepts describing collective behavior and clouding the understanding of just what could be attributed to the organizational behavior of a gang and what behavior was better understood by the concept of *ganging.* Likewise, associating the concept of the gang only with organized crime was much too stringent, suggesting that gang members were equivalent to members of the Mafia rather than being part of the intricate network into which crime is organized.

What then have gangs been? And what are they today? In the past, gangs have been associated primarily with adolescent males who came together for purposes of fraternity, entertainment, and material possession. Of course, the same can be said of gangs today. The difference is simply that a greater proportion of gang members today join primarily to acquire material possessions. That is to say, in the past the primary reason for joining gangs was friendship and fun, but as the structure of low-income neighborhoods has changed, so too have the reasons for joining gangs, and those reasons have centered around accumulating material possessions.

Furthermore, as the motives for joining a gang have changed, so too has the organizational structure of gangs. In the past, many commentators described a gang as a band of individuals with a loose association. However, as a matter of sociological distinction, gangs are not bands; they are organizations. As such, as Martìn Jankowski has written, a gang is rightly "an organized social system that is both quasi-private (not fully open to the public) and quasi-secretive (much of the information concerning its business remains confined to the group) and whose size and goals have necessitated that social interaction be governed by a leadership structure with defined roles; where the authority associated with these roles has been legitimized to the extent that social codes regulate the behavior of both the leadership and the rank and file; that plans and provides not only social and economic services for its members, but also for its own maintenance as an organization; that pursues such goals irrespective of legality; and that lacks a bureaucracy (i.e., a hierarchically organized administrative staff that is separate from the leadership)."

As the reasons for joining gangs have changed over the years, the structure of gang organization has also changed. Gangs during the first half of the twentieth century, whose members joined for fraternity and entertainment, had no need to develop complicated organizational structures. Thus, the typical structure resembled that of fraternities and sororities; there was a leadership structure, but fewer rules were associated with that leadership, fewer rules governed the rank and file, and less emphasis was placed on discipline.

Since the 1950s, however, the structure of the low-income community has been changing. Before the 1960s adolescent males from poor neighborhoods understood their probable life trajectory well. They would be allowed to have fun during their teenage years and then be forced (by social expectations and the negative sanctions of stigmatization) to assume working-class factory jobs that were part of their community and supported it. The gang provided young men having these life expectations with a brief window of opportunity to have fun before they assumed adult responsibilities. In essence, for low-income male adolescents the gang was part of a normal life passage, an organization associated with the transition from adolescence to adulthood in much the same way that fraternities and sororities have acted for middle- and upper-income youth.

However, since the 1960s, the factory jobs that low-income youth once grudgingly anticipated are no longer a realistic occupational option because of economic changes that have either driven factories out of central cities (perhaps even out of the country) or caused their total disappearance. This economic change has caused ensuing changes in adolescents and the organizations they create—like the gang. For example, the gang has ceased to be primarily associated with social life and recreation and has become more important as a source of income, material possessions, and for some, a niche in the occupational structure associated with the underground economy. As gangs have increasingly become economic institutions, and the need to become more disciplined and durable has increased, it has necessitated changes in their organizational structure, especially the development of more formal leadership.

The increasing participation of gangs in the drug economy has also produced increasing violence. This is because the drug economy does not have the advantage of being regulated by government, so the various participants are subject to power as the primary means of gaining economic advantage. Thus, as the number of gang members competing in the drug market increases and violence becomes the primary instrument used to gain power, the number of violent confrontations increases rapidly.

As the number of violent confrontations has increased, so too has the number of gang members who have been incarcerated. While in prison, urban gang members have had to associate with the main prison gangs in their particular facility. And because gang members spend a good part of their lives in prison, the prison gangs have gradually acquired greater control over a variety of street gangs that had previously resisted efforts to control them. This has caused gangs to become more persistent and increasingly resilient to efforts at eradication.

Gangs have created a nightmare for those who form both criminological and urban social policy. There can be no better evidence than the fact that gangs have been part of the low-income urban community for more than a century despite the inordinate resources that have been used to destroy them. In fact, the government's present policy of "Weed and Seed" recognizes that a holistic approach is necessary in order to be effective. Many years after the policy was drawn up, it has bogged down. The government has developed a number of programs around the concept of "weeding out" gang members involved in criminal behavior. However, it has not been able to implement programs to rebuild poor neighborhoods economically and provide greater opportunities to the young men who live in them—that is, they have not been able to "seed" these neighborhoods with opportunities that would make participation in a gang less attractive.

Government at all levels has found it easier to "weed" than "seed" for two reasons. First, "weeding" primarily involves law enforcement, something familiar to all levels of government, and they have a great deal of experience at it. Second, where "weeding" involves a single government agency, "seeding" involves a number of agencies such as the departments of Labor, Commerce, Health and Human Services, Education, and Housing and Urban Development at the federal level. The problems of developing, implementing, and coordinating among these various departments a broad policy to revitalize poor neighborhoods where many gangs operate has, to this point, proved insoluble. The result has been the persistence of gangs as an important social institution in low-income urban neighborhoods and they are likely to remain so for the foreseeable future.

—*Martín Sánchez Jankowski*

References

Huff, R. Ronald, ed. *Gangs in America*. Newbury Park, CA: Sage Publications, 1990.

Jankowski, Martín Sánchez. *Islands in the Street: Gangs and American Urban Society*. Berkeley: University of California Press, 1991.

Padilla, Felix M. *The Gang as an American Enterprise*. New Brunswick, NJ: Rutgers University Press, 1993.

Thrasher, Frederic. *The Gang*. Chicago: University of Chicago Press, 1928.

Gangster Films

Films about gangsters are almost as old as the movie industry itself, and some of the earliest silent films concerned the activity of gangsters (D. W. Griffith's *The Musketeers of Pig Alley* in 1912, for example). The real beginning of a distinct gangster genre, however, occurred in the early 1930s when three hard-hitting films, released in consecutive years, generated controversy and received great public attention. This trio—*Little Caesar* with Edward G. Robinson (1930), *The Public Enemy* with James Cagney (1931), and *Scarface* with Paul Muni (released in 1932 although filmed a year earlier)—launched a type of film that expands every decade, falling in and out of favor but never disappearing for long. Among the most important films in this genre made since the early 1930s are *Key Largo* (1948); *White Heat* (1949); *Bonnie and Clyde* (1967); *The Godfather*, Parts I & II (1972 and 1974); and *Goodfellas* (1990).

The genre's heyday lasted through the 1930s and 1940s. Most subsequent gangster films have been period pieces, while the films made in those two decades were more "ripped from today's headlines" than nostalgic evocations of an earlier (albeit dangerous) time. With very few exceptions, the gangster's world in these films was the "modern" city of the 1920s or 1930s, often a city seen only at night, in shadowy, rain-soaked back alleys or at shootouts on a deserted street. Audiences of the time who were used to reading about gangsters in their daily newspapers were taken on a vicarious tour of the underworld, given glimpses into a way of life that went on in the big cities that some of them had fled or, for that part of the audience who had stayed in the city, a life that went on as they slept.

The city functions as more than just a setting, however, in gangster films. With their complexity, sense of impersonalization, and rapid growth and change, urban areas are often depicted both as catalysts for the development of gangsters themselves and also as reflections of gangsters' motivations and ultimate goals. In his essay "The Gangster as Tragic Hero," Robert Warshow writes that, "the gangster is the man of the city. He must inhabit it in order to personify it." Thus, the urban setting is significant both as a backdrop and as an integral element of character development, as Warshow and others have explained.

While early gangster films were often criticized for (and sometimes prohibited from) "glorifying" the gangster as a tragic hero, this construction can be inherently built into the gangster-genre narrative. Often, it is the civilizing force of the city and its representatives who are the gangster's enemies. In a sense, he is a lone wolf fighting to stay alive beneath the crushing forces of social order that created the city. Sometimes mythic in presentation, many gangster films incorporate urban settings in ways that run far deeper than as mere settings for action.

—*Robert P. Holtzclaw*

See also

Bogart, Humphrey; Robinson, Edward G.

References

Raeburn, John. "The Gangster Film." In Wes D. Gehring, ed., *Handbook of American Film Genres*, 47–63. New York: Greenwood Press, 1988.

Sacks, A. "An Analysis of the Gangster Movies of the Early Thirties." *Velvet Light Trap* 1 (1971).

Shadoian, Jack. *Dreams and Dead Ends: The American Gangster/Crime Film.* Cambridge, MA: MIT Press, 1977.

Thomson, David. *America in the Dark: Hollywood and the Gift of Unreality,* ch. 7. New York: William Morrow, 1977.

Warshow, Robert. *The Immediate Experience: Movies, Comics, Theatre, and Other Aspects of American Culture.* Garden City, NY: Anchor Books, 1970.

Gangsters

A gangster is a member of a criminal gang, an enduring, organized group formed for the purpose of achieving its ends by illegal means. The outlaws and desperadoes of the Old West, the river rats and pirates of the country's waterways, the social bandits and public enemies of the nation's heartland, the bootleggers and rumrunners of the Prohibition era, the ethnic mobsters and wise guys of the organized crime syndicates, the violent youth in inner-city posses and crack crews all are gangsters who have played a major role in American social history. Their sometimes noble and oftentimes infamous deeds are ingrained deeply in American folklore and the national consciousness, reflecting a dynamic image that blends facts with romanticized myth. Even astute observers have trouble deciphering the truth.

American gangsters flourished both in rural, small-town areas and in cosmopolitan, urban environments. The relatively brief "golden age" of the rural gangster extended from the 1870s to the 1930s, a mere interlude between the country's agricultural and industrial phases when the cultural, social, political, and demographic reference points shifted to the cities. The reign of urban gangsters begins in the 1830s and continues to the present, gathering steam in the early decades of this century and mirroring the growing dominance of cities in American life.

In the nineteenth century, rural gangs flourished. Those operating before the Civil War have been largely forgotten, consigned to the dustbin of history. The historical record of those gangs that operated after the war is more abundant, particularly for those operating in the new territories (such as Oklahoma, Arizona, and so on) and in the border states of the former Confederacy (Missouri, Kansas, Kentucky, and so on) where wartime guerrilla tactics and resistance to legal authority were common. Relatively small, these gangs rarely exceeded 15 members who are commonly referred to as outlaws, desperadoes, bandits, and renegades. Some were known as gangsters, but eventually this term was reserved for urban criminal gang members rather than their rural counterparts. Some of the better-known gangs included those headed by Jesse James, Billy the Kid (William Bonney), the Dalton Brothers, and the Younger Brothers. These gangs exhibited minimal hierarchy and social organization, and they were based primarily on family ties and the charisma of their leader. These rural gangsters identified closely with the "common people" of their regions and embodied the small-town Protestant ethos with its distrust of authority, its fierce individualism, its strong allegiance to family, and its uncompromising espousal of Anglo-Saxon values. In their crimes, these outlaws expressed the social consciousness of the have nots—the poor, the downtrodden, the sharecropper, the tenant farmer—those swept aside by the growing urbanization and industrialization of American society. The enemies of the common ordinary folk became the victims of the outlaw, whether they were bankers, railroad owners, businessmen, or others from the East, groups and people perceived as usurping an established way of life.

By the 1930s, these rural outlaws had gradually disappeared, but not without the violence and spectacular exploits of the last of their kind—Pretty Boy Floyd, John Dillinger, Baby Face Nelson, Bonnie Parker and Clyde Barrow, Ma Barker and her sons. What remained became memorialized in ballads and Hollywood film, enshrined in myth and folklore.

The differences between these rural gangsters and their urban counterparts are striking. Urban gangs developed in the expanding cities in the early 1800s and became large, formidable criminal units by the 1840s. Originally nativist and Protestant in origin, they soon became overwhelmingly Irish and Catholic. By the 1850s, dozens of gangs thrived in Irish slums, some attaining membership of 500 or more. New York City hosted the largest and most violent of these groups, gangs such as the Dead Rabbits, the Plug Uglies, the Bowery Boys, the Gophers, and the O'Connell Guards. Similar organizations existed in Boston, Philadelphia, New Orleans, Baltimore, and San Francisco. The power of these gangs became apparent in the 1863 Draft Riots in New York City when gangs controlled the city for four days and created havoc. This insurrection became so destructive and so uncontrolled that it was quelled only after President Lincoln ordered Union regiments to be force marched from Gettysburg. When they arrived, they discharged cannons loaded with grapeshot, subduing the rioters.

The urban gangs engaged in a variety of criminal activities, including gambling, extortion, murder, prostitution, political intimidation, street violence, theft, and robbery. The more successful gangsters allied themselves with local political machines, making payments to the ward boss and providing services such as ballot stuffing, repeat voting, and intimidating the opposition on election day, in return for protection from the police.

By the late 1800s, the power of the Irish gangs began to wane as new immigrant groups created their own criminal structures. Chinese tongs in San Francisco and New York continued to grow, and Polish gangs appeared on Chicago's South

Side. But the most important of new gangsters came to dominance in New York, in Jewish gangs such as the Eastmans led by Monk Eastman, and in Italian gangs such as the Five Points Gang under Paolo Vaccarelli (Paul Kelly) and the Black Hand gangs such as the one headed by Ignacio Lupo (Lupo the Wolf). Many of the more famous gangsters of this century (Meyer Lansky, Little Augie Orgen, Big Jack Zelig, Bugsy Siegel, Johnny Torrio, Al Capone, Lucky Luciano, and Frank Costello) began their careers in the internecine warfare among these groups. Prohibition fueled the rise of these Jewish and Italian gangsters, who eventually eliminated their Irish and Polish rivals. Al Capone spearheaded this transition in Chicago by eliminating the Irish, including Dion O'Banion and the O'Donnells, and Poles such as Hymie Weiss and Bugs Moran. In New York, a similar scenario resulted in the elimination of such Irish mobsters as Legs Diamond, Mad Dog Call, and Peg Leg Lonegan. In turn, most of the important Jewish gangsters were neutralized in the 1930s and 1940s, including Arthur Flegenheimer (Dutch Schultz), Louis (Lepke) Buchalter, Jacob (Gurrah) Shapiro, and Bugsy Siegel.

By the late 1950s, Italian gangsters dominated the world of organized crime, moving beyond regional bases by creating a national web that they still control. The true extent of this dominance is debated by experts. Some argue that there is a hierarchical structure ruthlessly dictated by the Mafia or the Cosa Nostra. Others see a loose federation of numerous local and regional criminal gangs and families composed mainly, but not exclusively, of those of Italian background who periodically assist each other when it is in their interest. By the 1990s these gangs (or crime families) were in serious disarray as a result of numerous factors, foremost of which were enforcement of the RICO (Racketeer Influenced and Corrupt Organization) Act and the changing ethnic and racial composition of areas historically dominated by Italian criminal factions, such as the Gambino, Genovese, Colombo, Accardo, Patriarca, Bonanno, Lucchese, and Trafficante crime families. Waiting in the wings to succeed Italian mobs are the new ethnic gangsters—the African Americans, Hispanics, and Asians who have taken over many of the criminal rackets and drug enterprises in inner cities and are poised to move into the organized crime mainstream. If they do so, these gangsters will have continued the long tradition of ethnic succession in American organized crime.

—*James M. O'Kane*

See also
Capone, Al.
References
Asbury, Herbert. *The Gangs of New York: An Informal History of the Underworld.* New York: Knopf, 1929.
Bell, Daniel. "Crime as an American Way of Life." *Antioch Review* 13 (1953): 131–154.
Fried, Albert. *The Rise and Fall of the Jewish Gangster in America.* New York: Holt, Rinehart and Winston, 1980.
Hobsbawm, Eric. *Bandits.* Rev. ed. New York: Pantheon, 1981.
O'Kane, James. *The Crooked Ladder: Gangsters, Ethnicity, and the American Dream.* New Brunswick, NJ: Transaction Publishers, 1992.

Garbage and Garbage Collection

Solid waste disposal became a serious issue in American cities during the Industrial Revolution as crowded cities produced mounds of garbage and coal mines left hills of slag. Even earlier, pigs or turkeys had roamed streets and alleys looking for scraps; horses dumped tons of manure into thoroughfares; and rivers, lakes, and the oceans became sinks for tons of urban discards. Today, the United States produces more than 180 million tons of municipal solid waste each year, representing about four pounds per person per day.

While the discards of the nineteenth century were largely food wastes, wood and coal ash, rubbish, and horse manure, our current waste stream includes a complex mix of hard-to-replace as well as recyclable materials, and a variety of toxic substances. Of all current discards, paper, plastics and aluminum have increased the most.

Collection of solid wastes has been made difficult by the growing volumes and kinds of materials discarded, the larger populations to be served, and the greater territory that sanitation workers are required to cover. There is no best method of collection. Before the turn of the century, some cities chose to collect unseparated discards while others experimented with source separation. Historically, collections were most frequent in business districts, less frequent in outlying areas or poorer neighborhoods. As more affluent suburbs grew, cities diverted collection teams from inner-city routes to upper- and middle-class neighborhoods.

After World War II, some technical advances helped ease the problems of collection, especially the introduction of compaction vehicles and the use of transfer stations. But over the years, collection has remained heavily dependent on hand labor. No matter the method, collection is costly and does not serve every citizen equally well. Surveys estimate that from 70 to 90 percent of the cost of solid waste service in the United States goes for collection.

Of all the problems associated with waste disposal, none raises the cry of "garbage crisis" louder than recent concern over the shrinking amount of space available for landfills. The lack of landfill sites, especially in the East, has forced states such as New Jersey, Pennsylvania, and New York to export their garbage to locations in the Midwest. It is estimated that 28,000 tons of garbage are hauled on the nation's highways each day.

Finding adequate landfill sites has remained a goal for most cities, although dumping on land has been losing appeal. Modern sanitary landfills originated in Great Britain in the 1920s, and American versions were first attempted in the 1930s in New York City and Fresno, California. Through the 1950s and 1960s, engineers and waste managers believed that this was the most economical method of disposal. By the 1970s, however, experts began to doubt that landfills could serve the future needs of cities. Part of the reason was citizen resistance and increasingly rigid environmental standards. The NIMBY syndrome—Not in My Back Yard—spread across the country as some neighborhoods refused to act as dumping grounds for the whole community. Many times, sanitary landfills did not live up to their name, becoming a haven for insects and rodents, threatening groundwater, producing methane gas linked to ozone depletion, and containing various hazardous materials.

Of the available alternatives, incineration has had the strongest following. The first *cremators,* as they were called, were built in the United States in 1885, but incineration never achieved the status of the sanitary landfill. In the 1930s, incineration made a brief comeback, but it was no match for the enthusiasm for landfills. In 1991, only 18 percent of municipal solid waste was incinerated, while 64 percent entered landfills. Despite the fact that incineration drastically reduces the volume of waste, it has been plagued by high costs and by chronic problems of air pollution.

Questioning the use of incinerators as well as landfills has resulted in a major dilemma over what alternatives are acceptable for waste disposal. More recently, recycling has emerged as an alternative strategy. Once regarded simply as a grassroots method of source reduction and a protest against overconsumption, recycling grew in the 1980s as an alternative—or a complement—to more traditional disposal methods. By the 1990s over 1,000 communities in the United States had curbside recycling collection service. It has become a major goal for most communities to increase the recycling rate, which stood at 10 percent in the late 1980s. The Environmental Protection Agency (EPA) has called for a national recycling goal of 25 percent by the early 1990s, a goal that has not been updated since, perhaps because so few places have even met it.

A former mayor of Lincoln, Nebraska, stated that "garbage is an issue that can unseat an incumbent mayor." This observation suggests that the way solid waste is managed—or mismanaged—is crucial to the success of collection and disposal practices. Beginning in the late nineteenth century, a major concern of city government was to determine responsibility for delivering needed services such as refuse collection and disposal; for many years, the question was whether public or private service was better. Between the 1890s and the 1960s, publicly managed systems dominated, but today we have a mixed system of service providers in the solid waste

field, with a trend toward increased privatization. The recent interest in integrated waste management systems—systems that use some or all disposal options—requires strong cooperation between public and private parties. The EPA's promotion of integrated waste management also suggests a significant role for the federal government in setting a national agenda for dealing with solid waste, as well as its playing an expanded regulatory function.

Since the 1960s the federal government has broadened the attention given to the waste disposal problem and stressed that it is an environmental issue with national ramifications. The 1965 Solid Waste Disposal Act was the first major federal law to recognize solid waste as a national problem. Since that time several new laws have been added, shifting attention among issues of recycling, resource recovery, conversion of waste to energy, hazardous wastes, and more traditional concerns over municipal solid wastes.

Solid waste is no longer perceived as merely a nuisance, as it was in the early nineteenth century. It now has standing as a "third pollution" behind only air and water pollution.

—*Martin V. Melosi*

See also
Air Pollution; Land Pollution; Water Pollution.
References
Melosi, Martin V. "Down in the Dumps: Is There a Garbage Crisis in America?" In Martin V. Melosi, ed., *Urban Public Policy: Historical Modes and Methods,* 100–127. University Park: Pennsylvania State University Press, 1993.
———. *Garbage in the Cities: Refuse, Reform, and the Environment, 1880–1980.* College Station: Texas A & M University Press, 1981.
Rathje, William, and Cullen Murphy. *Rubbish! The Archeology of Garbage.* New York: HarperCollins, 1992.

Gasoline Stations

Cities' dependence on complex technologies, especially for transportation, helped create the gasoline station in the first decade of the twentieth century. Long familiar as a drive-in facility retailing chiefly petroleum products to gasoline-powered vehicles, the gasoline station in fact evolved from several previous forms to satisfy both producer and consumer. Garages, general stores, and hardware stores were the first retail outlets to add gasoline to their primary goods and services for the convenience of the consumer. But because gasoline supplies were vulnerable to impurities in open containers and because service was slow from retailers who focused on other sales, consumer demand for a place dedicated primarily to petroleum sales developed. Furthermore, automobile owners storing gasoline at home often struggled with a sloppy, smelly task as well as a serious fire hazard.

A St. Louis jobber is generally credited with opening the first gasoline station in 1905. However, petroleum producers'

A typical gas station with customers' automobiles being serviced in Minnesota, circa 1960.

desire to maximize their profits from costly exploring, refining, and supplying soon led to "downstream" integration in which company-owned outlets more fully controlled sales. In Seattle, Standard Oil of California opened the first series of producers' drive-in stations in 1907. Special gasoline pumps that drew gas from underground storage tanks to minimize the incendiary potential and the amount of land needed for a station completed the common drive-in gasoline station ensemble by the 1910s.

Gasoline stations have had different names reflecting their changing functions. "Filling stations," as they were first called, reflected their exclusive dedication to resupplying customers with the bare essentials, gasoline and oil. "Service stations," as gas stations began to be called in the late 1920s, represented a new commitment to repair as well as resupply. Considered a threat to gasoline stations, "convenience stores" began to subsume the original resupply function in addition to selling small foodstuffs in the 1970s. Gasoline stations declined from their high of 226,459 in 1972 to 114,784 by 1987.

Gasoline stations have been principal redefiners of urban boundaries. As automobile highways radiated out

from cities, gasoline stations were often among the first services located alongside highways. And, as associated services—motels, restaurants, and garages—developed automobile conveniences adjacent to gasoline stations, central business districts declined and "strips" developed at the cities' edges.

Urban and suburban imagery emerged as critical strategies in the fierce competition among corporate gasoline station networks starting in the 1920s, when the number of gasoline stations skyrocketed to roughly 155,400 by 1933. Corporations were able to expand rapidly when they overcame popular impressions of the gas station as grimy, noisy, and dangerous. This changed image also modified residential zoning rules against gas stations by softening familiar stereotypes and reassuring urban and suburban residents about their acceptability and harmlessness. Some corporations, notably Texaco, which standardized its stations between 1936 and 1938 by basing them on prototypes designed by Walter Dorwin Teague in the international style, pursued an urban appeal, but most, including Texaco by 1964, relied on suburban residential architecture with its conservative links to gentry aspirations and the nuclear family. Of this suburban style, the "English cottage" designed for the Pure Oil Company by C. A. Petersen in 1927 was the most memorable early expression. Embodiments mostly of suburban imagery, gasoline stations are both a cause and a consequence of the hegemonic American vision not only about the suburban look but also the suburban location of the "good life."

—Keith A. Sculle

References

Jakle, John A., and Keith A. Sculle. *The Gas Station in America*. Baltimore: Johns Hopkins University Press, 1994.

Liebs, Chester H. "Gas Stations." In *Main Street to Miracle Mile: American Roadside Architecture*. Boston: Little, Brown, 1985.

Vieyra, Daniel I. *"Fill'er Up": An Architectural History of America's Gas Stations*. New York: Collier Books, 1979.

Gateway Cities

Geographers originally invented the term *gateway city* to describe cities that were essentially wholesaling and commercial centers. The gateway city was emphatically not a political capital, although it might develop a manufacturing sector. During the middle and latter years of the nineteenth century, when the interior of North America was being settled, the distribution of goods by waterway was the essential factor in the location and development of gateway cities. Characteristically, they were located at strategic points on great rivers that were the first centers of commerce. Usually, the earliest European settlers were Frenchmen or Spaniards, intrepid spirits who traded with the Native Americans. They were displaced by English and then American merchants whose grasp of the distribution function was more sophisticated. By the early nineteenth century, these men were positioned to take advantage of the coming of the railroad. The importance of this event in the history of gateway cities cannot be stressed too strongly. It meant that a place was connected with the outside world and could achieve its destiny as a wholesaling center.

Basically, the wholesaler supervised the distribution of trade. In a period when overland transportation was limited to railroads and horse-drawn vehicles, he performed a vital service for farmers and small-town storekeepers. His expertise was knowing who produced the goods they required and how to bring supplier and customer together. Thus, he had to be familiar with freight rates, forwarding agents, and storage facilities. In combination, jobbers could constitute a force capable of bargaining effectively with the railroads, the greatest industrial corporations of the age. The jobbing function was essential to an economy that remained largely agrarian throughout the nineteenth century.

In order to house his stock of goods, the wholesaler needed buildings. These structures were concentrated in one section of the city, the warehouse district. This area became one of the most distinctive parts of gateway cities. It was located close to the old steamboat landings and adjacent to railroad freight yards; at the same time, it was not far from the business district where attorneys, accountants, insurance agents, and other similar types had offices. Nor was it far from the theatrical district and hotels, as traveling salesmen were a vital part of the distribution system. On their visits to the city, these individuals required shelter and entertainment. So the warehouse district was an important generator of jobs, both blue collar and clerical.

Architecturally the warehouse district could be distinguished. Its cobblestone or brick-paved streets were lined with five- and six-story structures that were usually among the best-designed buildings in the city. The single most important prototype for the gateway city warehouse was Henry H. Richardson's great wholesale store for Marshall Field (Chicago, 1885), but a number of provincial architects contributed distinguished designs. Among the most significant were Eckel and Mann (St. Joseph, Missouri), Thomas Kimball (Omaha, Nebraska), Clarence Johnston (St. Paul, Minnesota), and J. H. Collins (Winnipeg, Canada). Their solutions to the problems of warehousing were original, bold, and forceful. Perhaps because of the nature of their commissions, they hardly ever indulged in historicism. And the architect had the advantage of simple instructions from men who knew what they wanted and were ready to spend a certain sum of money for a building that would be both an emblem of their success and also an ornament to the city. To a great extent, they achieved these objectives.

The presence of a fully developed warehouse district may thus be taken as the distinguishing feature of the North American gateway city. The heyday of the district (and of the city) was, in most cases, from about 1880 to around 1910. This period coincided with the dominance of the railroad and the opening of the vast, enormously rich interior of the continent. In order to exploit the fertile soil of the plains, farmers needed a variety of industrial products, most notably farm machinery. Thus, the warehouses of such firms as Deere & Company, International Harvester, and J. I. Case became prominent features of the gateway city scene. Warehouses for hardware, pharmaceutical products, and groceries were almost equally important.

As the twentieth century wore on, methods of transportation for goods handled in warehouses changed. More and more freight traveled by truck rather than rail. And other technologies, such as freezing food, also affected the jobbing trade profoundly. By 1950 or so, the multistory warehouse, which had been so fundamental in gateway cities, was seen by many as outmoded. And agriculture, which had been a key element in the development of the West, became much less labor intensive. Thus, the original gateway cities had to find new economic bases in various kinds of manufacturing or white-collar work. The warehouses remain as evocative reminders of an important phase in the history of midcontinent North America.

—*Leonard Eaton*

References

Eaton, Leonard K. *Gateway Cities and Other Essays.* Ames: Iowa State University Press, 1989.

Porter, Glenn, and Harold C. Livesay. *Merchants and Manufacturers: Studies in the Changing Structure of Nineteenth Century Marketing.* Baltimore: Johns Hopkins University Press, 1971.

Vane, James E., Jr. *The Merchants World: The Geography of Wholesaling.* Englewood Cliffs, NJ: Prentice-Hall, 1970.

Gentrification

Gentrification refers to the process that occurs when a professional and managerial population moves into a neighborhood, frequently run-down, that has primarily been inhabited by people of a lower socioeconomic class. The newcomers then rehabilitate and improve their new properties, driving up housing costs and displacing the earlier residents. Although gentrification has occurred in many cities, it has generally been confined to a small number of neighborhoods in each of them and encompasses only a small part of their housing stock.

Gentrification often occurs in stages. Initially, many new arrivals are attracted by the relatively low housing prices in these sections of the city, as well as by the demographic diversity, historical character, or architectural quality of an area. Over time, as housing units are renovated and their prices increase, later arrivals in these neighborhoods are likely to be more affluent than the earlier "pioneers" and are often attracted to the area largely as an investment. Some neighborhoods become almost completely gentrified, and the existing population becomes displaced by newcomers. Other neighborhoods begin the gentrification process but retain much of their earlier population as gentrification slows or comes to an early halt.

Those who have studied gentrification have offered several explanations for its occurrence in the 1970s and 1980s. One focus has been the characteristics of gentrifiers, especially those in the early years of a neighborhood's gentrification. They were likely to remain unmarried and childless longer than the norm; therefore, they were not as interested in a relatively homogeneous suburban environment and more willing to live in diverse urban neighborhoods. Compatible

with this interpretation is one that interprets gentrification primarily as a "market" phenomenon. As housing prices decrease in these neighborhoods, potential residents see an economic bargain. The decision to move can also bring gentrifiers nearer their places of employment because these neighborhoods are often close to central business districts or other job centers.

Other analyses have emphasized the role of institutions in creating conditions under which gentrification can occur. For example, banking institutions often contributed to the decline of these neighborhoods by redlining them and making loans difficult to obtain for either rehabilitation or purchase. Now these financial institutions saw a chance to profit and "greenlined" these areas, making capital more readily available. Other institutions whose policies contributed to decline and then gentrification included the real estate industry and national and local governments.

Although there are benefits to gentrification, such as improving the housing stock within a city and perhaps enhancing a city's tax base, there are also costs. The most significant has been the involuntary displacement of many residents. Displacement has primarily acted upon renters whose buildings were purchased by gentrifiers who turned them back into single-family homes, or whose buildings were bought by investors who converted them into condominiums or increased rents significantly. Some homeowners also faced dislodging as property taxes on their houses increased to reflect higher values. In many communities, there have been conflicts over whether to provide some kind of protection to those subject to displacement. Examples of policies advocated by those concerned about displacement are guaranteeing tenure for certain classes of renters, such as the elderly, and placing restrictions on condominium conversions.

—*Robert Kerstein*

References

Nelson, Kathryn P. *Gentrification and Distressed Cities.* Madison: University of Wisconsin Press, 1988.

Palen, John J., and Bruce London, eds. *Gentrification, Displacement and Neighborhood Revitalization.* Albany: State University of New York Press, 1984.

Smith, Neil, and Peter Williams, eds. *Gentrification of the City.* Boston: Allen & Unwin, 1986.

German Colonial Towns

There were no German cities in colonial America. While Philadelphia, and to a lesser extent New York and Charles Town, each had significant German populations and served many of the cultural and political functions of an *Oberamt* (high city or capital), none can be described as a German city. There were German towns, though. German speakers made up approximately 9 percent of the white population in Britain's mainland colonies in 1776, and every province south of New England contained regions in which German speakers were a majority or large minority. In these areas were a number of towns in which most of the residents were German, in which the language of commerce, religion, and education was German, and in which the chief social institution was a German church—Lutheran, Reform, or one of several Pietist groups. Among the better known of these German settlements are Germantown, Pennsylvania (1683); New Bern, North Carolina (1710); Hebron, Virginia (ca. 1729); Purrysburg, South Carolina (1730); New Ebenezer, Georgia (1736); Bethlehem, Pennsylvania (1741); and Salem, North Carolina (1766).

These and other German-American towns were almost always farm towns. Most American colonists, whatever their ethnicity, chose to establish farms; so where Germans did settle in an urban environment it was usually in smaller, looser settlements that included or were surrounded by farmland. The only exceptions occurred when some organizing authority was able to overcome the centrifugal effects of cheap farmland. Both Bethlehem and Salem, for example, were established by the Moravian Church, which specifically intended them to be trade and administrative centers and which had the institutional power to realize that intention.

The most common street plans in German-American towns were linear, various types of which were common in Medieval and Early Modern Germany. Some of the towns built in America resembled traditional German *Strassendörfer* (street villages). This was one of the most common settlement forms in the southwestern region from which many German speakers emigrated during the eighteenth century, in which small town lots fronting on a single road were surrounded by common fields or individual holdings. Germantown, Pennsylvania, for example, stretched over a mile on either side of the Great Road, north of Philadelphia. Its founder, Francis Daniel Pastorius, laid out 44 town lots, each of approximately 25 acres, along the road to Philadelphia and corresponding "side lots" beyond the village center but often still on the Great Road. In the years that followed, population growth and the division of lots made Germantown both longer and denser, bringing it even closer to the *Strassendörfer* model.

German speakers in America also established *Angerdörfer* (villages with central greens), street villages in which the central thoroughfare was widened to form a green or square in the middle of the village. Bethania, a farming village outside of Salem, North Carolina, followed this plan. At its center were a small square and 24 house lots, 6 of them fronting on the square; around its perimeter lay gardens and

fields for each of the house lots. Still other settlements were linear but less compact than Germantown or Bethania, more like *Waldhufendörfer* (forest villages). The latter were found in areas of forest clearance throughout the German states and usually consisted of two rows of farmhouses along a road and stream in the bottom of a valley with attached farmland running back from the road, up the sides of the valley. Hebron developed this way on either side of Robinson Run. In Hebron's case, however, most of the holdings straddled the creek; so there was only a single row of houses, and it was less orderly than a *Waldhufendorf* in Silesia or Saxony.

Not every German-American town was linear, though, or based on a German model. German speakers also used the gridiron form that was so common in new or expanded communities in Europe and America after the Renaissance. Both New Ebenezer and Salem were arranged in grid plans. The former, an exact square subdivided into four identical quadrants with a market place and public buildings in the center of each, was probably modeled on James Oglethorpe's plan for Savannah and thus owes its form to British experiences in America and Ireland rather than to German examples of rectilinear town planning.

Salem, on the other hand, was explicitly based on a German precedent. Leaders of the Moravian Church told Salem's founders to build a town like Nisky, which the church had established in Silesia 20 years earlier. Both Nisky and Salem contained a central square around which the public buildings stood and a modest network of streets forming rectangular blocks on which family homes and shops were erected.

The two most interesting German-American town plans of the colonial period, however, were never built. In the original design for New Bern, Christopher de Graffenreid laid out streets perpendicular to one another but placed the entire town on a diagonal in order to accommodate the riverain geography of eastern North Carolina. The result would have been a sort of diamond-shaped town at the junction of the Trent and Neuse rivers. The town was barely started before the Tuscarora Indians destroyed it (1711), and Graffenreid's design was forgotten (or ignored) when the town was later rebuilt. Equally spectacular was Nicholas von Zinzendorf's octagonal plan for what later became Salem. Zinzendorf wanted eight grand avenues to radiate out from a central plaza surrounded by public buildings, but the plan was utterly unsuited to the site's geography and was ultimately replaced by the gridiron mentioned above.

—*Daniel B. Thorp*

References
Murtaugh, William J. *Moravian Architecture and Town Planning: Bethlehem, Pennsylvania, and Other Eighteenth-Century Settlements.* Chapel Hill: University of North Carolina Press, 1967.

Pillsbury, Richard. "The Urban Street Pattern as a Culture Indicator: Pennsylvania, 1682–1815." *Annals of the Association of American Geographers* 60 (1970): 428–446.

Reps, John W. *Town Planning in Frontier America.* Princeton, NJ: Princeton University Press, 1969.

Roeber, A. G. " 'The Origin of Whatever Is Not English among Us': The Dutch-Speaking and the German-Speaking Peoples of Colonial British America." In Bernard Bailyn and Philip D. Morgan, *Strangers within the Realm: Cultural Margins of the First British Empire.* Chapel Hill: University of North Carolina Press, 1991.

———. *Palatines, Liberty, and Property: German Lutherans in Colonial British America.* Baltimore: Johns Hopkins University Press, 1993.

Thorp, Daniel B. "Assimilation in North Carolina's Moravian Community." *Journal of Southern History* 52 (1986): 19–42.

———. "The City That Never Was: Count von Zinzendorf's Original Plan for Salem." *North Carolina Historical Review* 61 (1984): 36–58.

Wolf, Stephanie Grauman. *Urban Village: Population, Community, and Family Structure in Germantown, Pennsylvania, 1683–1800.* Princeton, NJ: Princeton University Press, 1976.

Ghetto

A ghetto is a section of a city, often part of the inner city, where one particular ethnic or racial group predominates, frequently because of social and/or economic restrictions imposed by the majority population. Initially a European institution that established and required segregated Jewish residential areas, scholars in the United States have applied the term *ghetto* to inner-city residential areas of racial minorities and white ethnic groups. However, while African, Asian, and Hispanic Americans have experienced compulsory ghettoization (either *de facto* or *de jure*), European immigrants were more likely to live in ghettos voluntarily. Not only have the origins, forms, and conditions of ghetto life varied from city to city and region to region, scholars have disagreed about the impact of the ghetto on minorities in the United States.

The word *ghetto* developed in the Jewish section of Venice, Italy. While many Jewish residents of medieval European cities clustered in voluntary ghettos as much for internal benefits as in response to growing legal restrictions upon where they could live, the compulsory ghetto—the place where all urban Jews were required to live—emerged in the sixteenth century. In many cities, gates and stone walls set the ghetto apart physically, and extensive economic and social restrictions further limited the opportunities available to ghetto residents. As a result, conditions were often bleak, and many residents (but not all of them) were poor. However, occupants developed a rich array of customs and institutions, including synagogues, which gave shape and form to ghetto life.

Based on these origins, sociologists and historians initially applied the word *ghetto* to urban settlements of immigrants from Central, Southern and Eastern Europe who came to the United States between 1880 and 1920. These ethnic clusters, especially in eastern and midwestern industrial cities, were generally located near industrial jobs in older urban areas. These enclaves resulted largely from unforced factors such as proximity to employment; chain migration of family, friends, and neighbors; and the presence of ethnic and religious institutions. Nativist hostility provided an element of compulsion as well. Although they were seldom public policies, employment and housing discrimination, and occasional violence, helped restrict immigrants' access to housing elsewhere. By 1910, new immigrants in large cities were more segregated residentially than African Americans. But unlike the Jewish ghettos of Europe, no physical walls or gates locked residents in or restricted their movements about the city.

While contemporary observers usually focused on the overcrowding, abysmal living conditions, rampant social disorganization, and crime in ghettos, some sociologists tempered these views by noting the extent of order and organization. Louis Wirth (*The Ghetto,* 1928) reported that the "ties of family, of village-community . . . bind the ghetto inhabitants" while families survived "crises that would tear an ordinary family asunder." Nevertheless, historians initially concluded that immigrants' inability to adapt Old World ways to New World cities produced periods of disorder and chaos until newcomers eventually adjusted to city culture. Since about 1960, historians have generally emphasized the ethnic enclave as a place where immigrants maintained and adjusted their cultures to American urban life while city institutions, such as the boss and machine politics, assimilated them into the political system.

In recent years, scholars have questioned the appropriateness of using the word *ghetto* to refer to these immigrant enclaves. Few immigrant enclaves had homogeneous populations; most housed a variety of ethnic and religious groups, although one group often made up a significant proportion of a neighborhood's population. Ethnic groups often produced a number of residential clusters rather than a single, large concentration, and some immigrants never lived in a ghetto. By 1930, only 37 percent of Chicago's Jews lived in a ghetto area while 50 and 61 percent of Italians and Poles did, respectively. Although these enclaves survived for many years, the second generation increasingly moved away, demonstrating that these neighborhoods were less compulsory than the ghettos of racial minorities.

African Americans have lived in American cities from their founding, although as late as 1900 the vast majority lived in the rural South. Before 1900, black residents of northern cities lived in small clusters and in close proximity to whites. However, from 1870 to 1915, African Americans encountered increasing racism and overt discrimination; at the same time, northern cities experienced enormous changes with the development of mass transit, the growth of large-scale industry, and massive European immigration. After 1900, black ghettos began to emerge in some northern cities; by 1915, New York's and Chicago's were already identifiable. The Great Migration in the years around World War I dramatically increased black populations in northern and western cities; in Cleveland and Los Angeles, ghettos emerged between 1915 and 1930, while Milwaukee's did not fully form until after World War II. African Americans confronted much greater hostility than had European immigrants, as well as institutional racism, and black ghettos continued to grow for several generations.

Since the end of Reconstruction and the South's reversion to white supremacy, southern blacks increasingly migrated to improve their lives. While some of the middle-class "talented tenth" moved north before World War I, the war's demand for labor and the removal of racial restrictions from unskilled industrial jobs in northern cities encouraged working-class African Americans to migrate to the North. During the war, more than 500,000 moved to northern and western industrial cities; the next decade witnessed the migration of nearly a million more. From 1910 to 1930, Chicago's black population increased by nearly 190,000, a more than fivefold increase. Migrants and longtime residents alike found themselves increasingly limited to housing in older, run-down, congested neighborhoods near the downtown.

These migrations dramatically increased white hostility. The wave of race riots that swept through American cities from 1917 to 1919, in which white mobs attacked African Americans, represented the most extreme forms of malice. Neighborhood protective associations, developers, banks, and real estate agents severely restricted black access to white areas. The practice of attaching racially restrictive covenants to property deeds furthered this process; by 1940, five square miles of St. Louis had such covenants. Other institutions, private and public, furthered the growing segregation of African Americans in public accommodations. While no physical walls surrounded these emerging ghettos, the forces, both legal and illegal, were no less powerful. By 1930, Chicago's black residents were much more ghettoized (93 percent) than recent immigrants. As black migrants sought housing in an artificially restricted market, costs within the ghetto skyrocketed.

While the timing of ghetto emergence depended on circumstances unique to each city, northern black ghettos, unlike immigrant enclaves, continued to grow and expand. The forces of racism, the changing urban structure, and public policy all contrived to make the invisible walls even more powerful in the years following World War II. The war and the prosperity that followed it produced even greater migra-tions north and west; between 1940 and 1960, Chicago's black population almost tripled. White violence checked, but did not always stop, the ghetto's advance into white working-class neighborhoods.

While local forces continued to restrict where African Americans could live, the federal government played a major role in the formation of a second ghetto. Discriminatory policies of the Federal Housing Administration denied blacks access to new suburban developments at the same time that they allowed the construction of public housing to be restricted to the inner city. Finally, urban renewal disrupted established black business districts and devastated neighborhoods while the construction of interstate highways isolated black communities even further. These conditions set the stage for the civil disorders and riots that erupted in African-American ghettos after 1964.

Ghettos housed the vast majority of most cities' black population, although different social classes did not necessarily share exactly the same areas. Middle- and upper-class residents tended toward the outer edges of ghettos while working-class African Americans lived in older, more congested sections nearer the downtown. By 1970, structural economic changes were beginning to erode the position of blue-collar African Americans, while open housing laws and improved opportunities in white-collar employment permitted middle- and upper-class blacks to move to suburbs. These changes led sociologists to conclude that an "underclass" remained trapped in inner-city ghettos who, lacking traditional support networks and resources, increasingly turned to crime and drugs. These underclass theories, however, fit the traditional pattern of labeling the poor (from the "undeserving poor" to the "culture of poverty") in ways that distort more than they reveal.

Border and southern cities experienced different patterns of ghetto formation. As late as 1910, border cities like Washington and Baltimore had the largest black populations in the United States; from at least 1870 until the present, Washington has had a higher percentage of African Americans than any other major city in the country. As in many older southern cities, black residents lived scattered throughout the city, although often in clusters found in alleys, or on minor streets adjacent to white residential areas, or as live-in servants. At the same time, African Americans established a number of discrete residential neighborhoods, and some of them combined with expansion to produce several smaller ghettolike areas. Washington, Baltimore, Cincinnati, and Philadelphia produced several concentrations, each of which emerged as ghettos based on their own specific conditions. As early as 1880, Washington had four districts with populations at least 60 percent black; Cincinnati's basin area began to emerge as a ghetto after 1920.

Because of their slower growth and smaller size, southern cities tended not to develop large ghettos until after World War II. Traditional black residential patterns included both clusters in cities and suburban development; after the end of Reconstruction, segregated housing increasingly became the rule. Unlike in the North, this policy did have legal standing; between 1910 and 1917, border and southern cities enacted segregation ordinances requiring separate residential areas for blacks and whites. When the U.S. Supreme Court declared these ordinances unconstitutional in *Buchanan v. Warley* (1917), southern cities used restrictive covenants and discriminatory practices by the real estate and banking industries to maintain segregation. Violence also played a major role in southern cities. By 1980, Houston claimed the South's largest black urban population; typical of southern cities, African Americans lived in three separate sectors, each beginning in the inner city and radiating out to the suburbs.

Other racial and ethnic minorities have also experienced compulsory ghettoization. Even before black ghettos formed, some Asian Americans had this experience. By 1910, San Francisco's Chinese immigrants found themselves confined to Chinatown, as did Chinese Americans in other cities. Japanese Americans were restricted to Japantowns (or J-towns), and Hispanic Americans to barrios. Anglos used both laws and violence to establish and maintain these areas; extensive economic and social discrimination reinforced the invisible walls and impoverished the residents. Escape from these ghettos was not easy; they housed rich and poor alike, and multiple generations.

While scholars initially interpreted ghetto life as a series of pathologies that resulted from the inability of migrants' institutions and traditions to maintain order in an urban environment, more recent studies emphasize the central importance of traditional institutions in helping residents survive and adapt. Rather than passive victims, migrants used the chain migration of relatives and friends to build neighborhoods. They brought a wide range of institutions with them and modified their traditions to fit the new environment. Save for Chinese immigrants, who were almost exclusively male in the first generation, family was the most important institution. Extended families housed and cared for multiple generations and helped others migrate, while informal friendship networks and neighborhood groupings linked residents together and provided them with aid and support. Religious organizations provided a range of services to assist the needy and rendered spiritual continuity at the same time that they introduced change. Similarly, social, cultural, civic, political, and recreational organizations, as well as ethnic businesses, eased adjustment and helped bond residents together despite growing differences in social class. White racism and nativism also encouraged these bonds. For the most part, outside agencies such as the police, social service workers, and social settlements failed to reach most ghetto dwellers, and many residents avoided them whenever possible.

Migrants, then, adapted their cultures and institutions to the urban environment while they incorporated host institutions and cultural elements into their lives. The product of extensive battles between older and newer residents, such as those between German and Eastern European Jews or between African Americans born in the North and those born in the South, these new cultures demonstrated migrants' ability to shape their own lives and futures despite the considerable hostility they confronted. As cities within cities, ghettos presented opportunities for empowerment and self-realization. For African Americans, the great migrations produced critical masses that supported efforts to challenge discrimination directly, sustained black businesses and institutions, and provided entry into mainstream politics.

The word *ghetto* covers a variety of forms, and easy generalizations are dangerous. This extends to the notion that all ghettos are slums. While many ghettos emerged in older residential districts close to downtown, not all did so. Harlem formed as a newly constructed community intended for middle- and upper-income whites; the Great Depression helped turn it into a slum. Nevertheless, wealthy neighborhoods have continued to persist within the ghetto.

Finally, not all ghettos are alike. Black ghettos have drawn residents from different parts of the South and the Caribbean to environments that already possessed their own discrete black and urban histories; these new additions produced equally diverse patterns and experiences. In Detroit, southern-born and northern-born African Americans clashed, but Philadelphia's ghettos did not experience these problems. Ghettos present very different landscapes; in densely packed Harlem, continuous rows of six-story brick apartment buildings hug the streets, in contrast to the Watts section of Los Angeles where single-family, detached homes with grassy front and back yards predominate. In 1930, few residents of Harlem owned their own homes; in Los Angeles, one-third of African Americans did.

—*James Borchert*

See also
Barrio; Chinatown; Housing Segregation; Neighborhood Protective Association; Restrictive Deed Covenants.

References
Borchert, James. *Alley Life in Washington: Family, Community, Religion and Folklife in the City, 1850–1970.* Urbana: University of Illinois Press, 1980.
Hirsch, Arnold. *Making the Second Ghetto: Race and Housing in Chicago, 1940–1960.* New York: Cambridge University Press, 1983.
Kusmer, Kenneth L. *A Ghetto Takes Shape: Black Cleveland, 1870–1930.* Urbana: University of Illinois Press, 1976.
———, ed. *Black Communities and Urban Development in America: 1720–1990.* 9 vols., vols. 4–9. New York: Garland, 1991.

Vergara, Camilo José. *The New American Ghetto.* New Brunswick, NJ: Rutgers University Press, 1995.

Wirth, Louis. *The Ghetto.* Chicago: University of Chicago Press, 1928.

Ghost Towns

Despite a century of attempts by various authors, the ghost town has managed to elude definition. Some insist that a town must be completely uninhabited to qualify, while others believe a ghost town to be any settlement that is only a shadow of its former self; some include only sites where buildings and their remains are still readily visible, and others include those sites with virtually no tangible remains. In fact, this lack of a single definition is an essential part of the place of ghost towns in American culture—one never knows quite what one will find.

Ghost towns are widely considered to be a "western" phenomenon (the West itself having variable boundaries). Although a few ghost towns do exist in other regions, in popular culture ghost towns are thoroughly embedded in ideas of the mythic West and the nation's frontier heritage. Most ghost towns result from a late-nineteenth or early-twentieth-century mining boom and subsequent bust, and hence they lend themselves to identification with the gold rush and the nation's perceived frontier spirit.

Ghost towns are increasingly popular tourist destinations, and brochures published by various states prominently feature ghost towns as tourist attractions. States that claim them publish books on the locations, histories, and myth-histories (ghost stories, legends, etc.) of these town sites. This literature often emphasizes rowdy reputations during boom years, usually highlighted by descriptions of saloons, red-light districts, gunfighters, and ruffians.

Now, however, these towns survive in varying states of decay or reconstruction, and most contain only sparse remnants of a century of neglect. Some, like Aurora, Nevada, survive mainly in books—on the landscape, hardly a trace of their former prominence remains. Many ghost towns, like Mogollon, New Mexico, however, still boast a collection of ruins and partial buildings. Only a few, like Bodie, California, can boast of more than 100 original buildings. While some ghost towns, like Bodie, are maintained in a state of arrested decay, others are restored to their former condition (or beyond), like Cripple Creek, Colorado. Still other "ghost towns," such as Knott's Berry Farm in Buena Park, California, exist where nothing existed before, as

A rusty car in Bodie, California, a typical ghost town. This former high desert mining town was declared a state historic park in 1961 and is preserved in a condition of "arrested decay."

tourist recreations, or contain many buildings that are replicas or were moved from other locations, as is the case of Hell Roaring Gulch, Montana.

Protection of ghost town sites varies as much as the towns themselves; some are preserved by state or federal agencies or private concerns, others by the town's remaining residents (if there are any), still others by their relative isolation. Many ghost towns receive little or no maintenance and are generally thought to be threatened by the elements and the ravages of time.

Just as ghost towns differ in their definition, condition, and protection, so does their popularity vary. Some of their sites are virtually inaccessible, either by road or in literature; as a result, they see virtually no visitors and hear nothing but the hollow echo of memory's tread. Others, like Deadwood, South Dakota, are heavily advertised and inundated by tourists. While some ghost towns provide no services of any kind, others are highly commercialized and offer meals, lodging, souvenirs, and any number of other attractions (like Tombstone, Arizona). One California ghost town is even said to have enticed more tourists than the gold rush lured miners.

In popular perception, ghost towns offer glimpses into the past and are often seen as visible reminders of the Wild West. In fact, all ghost towns, whatever their condition or state of disrepair, represent the history of a specific place only selectively. This selectivity itself (sometimes due to the vagaries of weather, fire, and neglect; at other times to careful reconstruction or replication) increases their appeal as visitors' imaginations readily fill the gaps. The mythic West has been an escape from the dolorous present for several generations of Americans, and in ghost towns tangible history offers an additional patina of reality. The lines between original, restored, and reproduced sometimes become blurred because the past itself is malleable, molded partly by present values and desires. The allure of the past lies partly in its intimation of hidden mystery. The very variability among ghost towns (in their definition, popularity, state of repair, etc.) contributes to this mystery and to their popularity and place in American imaginations.

—Dydia DeLyser

References

Florin, Lambert. *Ghost Towns of the West.* New York: Promontory Press, 1993.

Francaviglia, Richard V. *Hard Places: Reading the Landscape of America's Historic Mining Districts.* Iowa City: University of Iowa Press, 1991.

Lowenthal, David. *The Past Is a Foreign Country.* Cambridge, England: Cambridge University Press, 1985.

Toll, David W. "In the Matter of Certain Ghost Towns." *Westways* 64 (1972): 18–74.

Gilman, Charlotte Perkins (1860–1935)

Charlotte Perkins Gilman was born in Hartford, Connecticut, to Frederick Beecher Perkins, a nephew of Harriet Beecher Stowe, and Mary Westcott Perkins. She attended the Rhode Island School of Design in 1878–1879, and in 1884 she married the artist Charles Walter Stetson. After the birth of her daughter Katharine in 1885, she suffered severe postpartum depression and was eventually treated by a nerve specialist, S. Weir Mitchell, an experience that inspired her story "The Yellow Wallpaper" (1892). She separated from Stetson in 1888, whereupon she joined the Nationalist movement in California. In 1894, with her divorce from Stetson final, she moved to San Francisco to edit the magazine of the Pacific Coast Women's Press Association. Her best-known book, *Women and Economics,* a treatise on "the economic factor between men and women as a factor in social evolution," appeared in 1898. In 1900, she married her cousin George Houghton Gilman and settled in New York.

Early in the twentieth century, Charlotte Gilman was the most prominent intellectual in the American women's movement. While living in New York, she repeatedly addressed questions of city design in her writings. She modeled the town in her utopian romance *Herland* (1915), for example, on the White City of the World's Columbian Exposition, a baroque assemblage of parks, monumental buildings, and boulevards in ersatz-Renaissance style near the Chicago Loop. As Gilman wrote in 1903, "the White City by the lake was an inspiration to myriad lives, and wrought a lovely change in architecture." She reiterated the point in a 1915 piece: "since the World's Fair at Chicago in 1893, we have had our dream cities. Soon we can have them real."

As early as 1904, Gilman proposed a solution to the ills of urban congestion, the apartment hotel. By centralizing heating plants, kitchens, and laundries and organizing all residential blocks into self-contained communities of unified construction with an inner court—that is, by rationalizing the delivery of urban services—she believed that every family might enjoy "a more reliable food supply at less cost; better heat and light at less cost; better air, more sun, a roof space for their own children, and far more beauty."

Over the years, however, Gilman became more xenophobic and grew increasingly disillusioned with New York, which epitomized for her "our acromegous citys, breeders of disease and crime, degraders of humanity, impeders of progress," as she wrote in 1916. She was especially disturbed by the "swarming human forms" of recent immigrants. She abandoned the city in 1922 and retired to Norwichtown, Connecticut. "I increasingly hated New York and its swarms of jostling aliens," she wrote her friend Alice Stone Blackwell in 1923. Her faith in the efficacy of social planning did not wane, however, although she shifted her attention from the overcrowded

Nekropolis (a word meaning city of death that she used to refer to New York) to the self-sufficient "new town" set in the country.

Her ideas on this subject distinctly echo those of the English city planner Ebenezer Howard, who had designed and advocated garden cities on the outskirts of major urban centers. With improved modes of transportation, she thought, "the swollen city" might be replaced by "loose-linked, wide-lying chain-cities, radiating like snow crystals, connected by rings and spokes of traffic lines." In her essay "Applepieville" (1920) she described a planned community of about a hundred homes and farms organized around a social nucleus. Similarly, in "Making Towns Fit to Live In" (1921), she propounded the advantages of planned industrial communities of perhaps a thousand persons—socialized company towns where specialists would supply basic domestic services.

Like the women in her putative Applepieville, Gilman spent much of the next decade working in her garden. Suffering from terminal cancer, she moved to Pasadena, California, to be near her daughter in May 1934, and she died, a suicide, 15 months later.

—*Gary Scharnhorst*

See also
Chicago World's Fair of 1893 (World's Columbian Exposition).
References
Hayden, Dolores. "Charlotte Perkins Gilman and the Kitchenless House." *Radical History Review* 21 (1979): 225–247.
Knight, Denise D. *The Diaries of Charlotte Perkins Gilman.* Charlottesville: University Press of Virginia, 1994.
Scharnhorst, Gary. *Charlotte Perkins Gilman.* Boston: Twayne, 1985.

Gladden, Washington (1836–1918)

Washington Gladden, a Congregational minister and Christian reformer, was one of the earliest spokesmen for a "social gospel" in American Protestantism as an antidote to the serious social unrest that characterized urban, industrial life in the late-nineteenth-century United States. His *Applied Christianity* (1886), which advocated the application of Christ's teachings as a solution to social problems, served as a spark for other Christians to reconsider the place of religious institutions and beliefs in an urban, industrial setting. Their writings and their programs of reform, which formed the foundation of the social gospel, represented a major reorientation of Protestant belief and practice in the United States.

Born in 1836 in Pottsgrove, Pennsylvania, Gladden studied to become a minister in the 1850s before the worst effects of industrial expansion attracted the attention of American social observers. After the Civil War, he accepted a call to a congregation in North Adams, Massachusetts, where he witnessed a labor conflict between local striking shoemak-

ers and Chinese strikebreakers in 1870. Over the next decade, he divided his time between magazine work and the ministry, and he became increasingly conscious of social problems portended by his experience in North Adams. After he arrived in Columbus, Ohio, in 1882, Gladden focused more attention on social problems, and he began to formulate a Christian response to them in a number of influential books. Books such as *Tools and the Man* (1893) and *The Labor Question* (1911) addressed work and social justice in industrial life, and *Social Salvation* (1902) and *The Church and Modern Life* (1908) explored the implications of social change for religious experience.

In his written work, Gladden called for social consciousness, cooperation, and reform as ideals for modern Christians. By urging Protestants to obey the laws of service, sacrifice, and love, Gladden effectively counterbalanced traditional American Protestant individualism with a social ethos.

Like other ministers confronting the social effects of urban and industrial development in the late nineteenth century, Gladden did not believe that traditional sermonizing—either from the pulpit or the printed page—offered an appropriate solution to the monumental problems. Gladden urged Christians to become involved in reform movements and to take an active approach to Christian commitment. Near the end of his career, Gladden himself served on the Columbus city council in hopes of applying his social gospel ideals to the problems that beset his community. Moreover, he supported the Social Creed of the Churches adopted in 1908 by the Federal Council of Churches. He also spent much of his career fighting the pernicious effects of racism in the United States. He supported the educational efforts of the American Missionary Association in southern black communities, and he served as its president in the early twentieth century.

Gladden's books and ministry contributed to the reorientation of Protestant thought at the end of the nineteenth century. Though he never completely stopped supporting individual effort, his social gospel sought to balance individual striving with social consciousness and collective action. Gladden must be considered one of the early architects of modern social thought in the United States.

—*Susan Curtis*

References
Curtis, Susan. *A Consuming Faith: The Social Gospel and Modern American Culture.* Baltimore: Johns Hopkins University Press, 1991.
Dorn, Jacob H. *Washington Gladden: Prophet of the Social Gospel.* Columbus: Ohio State University Press, 1968.
Gladden, Washington. *Applied Christianity: Moral Aspects of Social Questions.* Boston: Houghton Mifflin, 1886.
———. *Recollections.* Boston: Houghton Mifflin, 1909.
White, Ronald C., Jr., and C. Howard Hopkins. *The Social Gospel: Religion and Reform in Changing America.* Philadelphia: Temple University Press, 1976.

Golden Gate Park

Located in San Francisco, California, Golden Gate Park was created in 1870 during the widespread, nineteenth-century movement that led to the creation of large urban parks in such cities as New York, Brooklyn, Buffalo, Chicago, St. Louis, and Los Angeles. Approximately one-half mile wide and four miles long, the rectangular park covers 1,019 acres and stretches from the Pacific Ocean to Stanyan Street near the middle of San Francisco's peninsula with a thinner stretch, known as "the Panhandle," reaching another three-quarters of a mile east. In the beginning, the site was sparsely populated, and blowing sand dunes covered its western two-thirds. The site that was selected for the park provided an opportunity to end two public controversies: the demand that a large park be created and competing land claims over where such a park should be created.

Park advocates can best be described as reform-minded environmental determinists. They believed that the major social problems of San Francisco—poverty, sickness, crime, and undemocratic actions—occurred because the populace as a whole was unable to come into direct contact with nature. These park advocates imagined that "uplifting" nature looked like an eastern woodland with trees, grassy meadows, and reflecting waters. Here, a person could quietly contemplate the scenery and be improved, that is, become more likely to be healthy, wealthy, law-abiding, and democratic. Nothing of the sort existed in San Francisco so it had to be created.

Although America's premier park designer, Frederick Law Olmsted, had prepared plans for a large park, his scheme was never executed. Instead, the task went to William Hammond Hall, the civil engineer who surveyed the site shortly after the city created the park. He had privately suggested a tentative plan for the park that explained how to control the shifting sand dunes inexpensively and had incorporated landscape design features used in New York's Central Park, Brooklyn's Prospect Park, and Philadelphia's Fairmont Park. In 1871, Hall was appointed engineer and superintendent. He immediately began creating walks and roadways and started planting grass, shrubs, and trees. His plan became the basic framework for contemporary and successive work. The park was an immediate success and attracted over 250,000 visitors during 1873. The number of annual visitors soon grew into the millions and has remained so ever since.

Progress on the park proceeded rapidly until the middle of the 1870s, when financial difficulties and shifting political winds buffeted Hall and the park. Frustrated and second-guessed, Hall resigned in 1876 and for the next decade the park had a series of unremarkable superintendents. Then, in 1887, John McLaren joined the management of Golden Gate Park. Unlike Hall, McLaren was an experienced horticulturist. He had emigrated from Scotland to the San Francisco area in 1873 to landscape and maintain the estate of a local magnate. McLaren gave up that post to be the park's assistant superintendent, and in 1890 he became superintendent. The park was financially and politically supported during his tenure, and McLaren remained in this post until he died in 1943.

An indefatigable defender and modernizer of Golden Gate Park, McLaren transformed what had been a scenic landscape of trees, shrubs, and grass into a colorful, recreation-oriented place with flowers, ball fields, tennis courts, swimming pools, and more. Unlike Hall, McLaren and his supporters saw the park as a place for uplifting activities rather than as a contemplative landscape. While they were reformers like Hall and other park supporters of his era, natural scenery alone, in these park supporters' opinion, was insufficient to promote a better social order. They wanted therapeutic activities *in* nature rather than quiet contemplation *of* nature to lead them to wealth, health, and so on.

In recent decades, Golden Gate Park has taken on another dimension in urban life. Not only is it a quiet setting for contemplation and a stage for athletics, it has become a part of the local ecology. For example, drought-tolerant plantings have been laid out in the arboretum to encourage the consumption of less water by local gardeners. Elsewhere, the California Native Plant Society is studying and trying to understand the original vegetation of the area. This new view of nature is concerned with the ability of our society to be improved as a result of a scientific understanding of nature. Unfortunately, recent financial support for the park has been inconstant, leading to its deterioration, but it is currently undergoing restoration.

—*Terence Young*

See also
Central Park.

References

Aikman, T. G. *Boss Gardener: The Life and Times of John McLaren.* San Francisco: Don't Call It Frisco Press, 1988.

Clary, R. H. *The Making of Golden Gate Park: The Early Years, 1865–1906.* San Francisco: Don't Call It Frisco Press, 1984.

———. *The Making of Golden Gate Park: The Growing Years, 1906–1950.* San Francisco: Don't Call It Frisco Press, 1987.

Cranz, Galen. *The Politics of Park Design: A History of Urban Parks in America.* Cambridge, MA: MIT Press, 1982.

Olmsted, Frederick Law. *The Papers of Frederick Law Olmsted. Vol. V.* V. P. Ranney, G. J. Rauluk, and C. F. Hoffman, eds. Baltimore: Johns Hopkins University Press, 1990.

Young, Terence. "Modern Urban Parks." *Geographical Review* 85 (1995): 544–560.

———. "San Francisco's Golden Gate Park and the Search for a Good Society, 1865–1880." *Forest and Conservation History* 37 (1993): 4–13.

Goodman, Paul (1911–1972)

Paul Goodman was born in New York and spent most of his life there. Psychotherapist, novelist, poet, and social thinker, he can best be described as a man of urban letters. In the preface to *Utopian Essays and Practical Proposals* (1962) he pointed out that he had only one subject, "the human beings I know in their man-made scene." His writings on architecture and city planning, often influenced by his brother Percival, an architect, began with "A Romantic Architecture" (*Symposium,* 1931) and "A Rationalistic Architecture" (*Symposium,* 1932), and matured with the eloquent manual for city planning, *Communitas,* which he wrote during the early 1940s with Percival, published in 1947, and revised in 1960. Moreover, writing fiction allowed Goodman to explore how deeply intertwined were urban and community life with pedagogy, myth, and character formation, as he did in *The Empire City* (1959) and *Making Do* (1963).

Goodman's sense of the city was influenced by classical thinkers, as well as by regionalism, anarchism, and gestalt therapy. *Gestalt Therapy* (1951; coauthored with Frederick Perls and Ralph Hefferline) is a necessary companion to his urban thought. Goodman believed that the metropolis is that environment that ought to make possible a good figure/field relationship and "organismic self-regulation." Urban planning had to consider the engagement of people with their environment so that individuals could understand, select, and control the means and ends of life. Regional self-sufficiency would express decentralization, inventiveness, cooperation, and community. Central to this idea of the city is neofunctionalism, in which urban planning and technologies are brought under moral control.

—*Lewis Fried*

References

Fried, Lewis. *Makers of the City.* Amherst: University of Massachusetts Press, 1990.

Goodman, Paul. *The Empire City.* Indianapolis, IN: Bobbs-Merrill, 1959.

———. *Making Do.* New York: Macmillan, 1963.

———. *Utopian Essays and Practical Proposals.* New York: Random House, 1962.

Goodman, Paul, and Percival Goodman. *Communitas.* Chicago: University of Chicago Press, 1947.

Goodman, Percival. *The Double E.* Garden City, NY: Doubleday, 1977.

Nicely, Tom. *Adam and His Work: A Bibliography of Sources by and about Paul Goodman.* Metuchen, NJ: Scarecrow Press, 1979.

Parisi, Peter, ed. *Artist of the Actual: Essays on Paul Goodman.* Metuchen, NJ: Scarecrow Press, 1986.

Perls, Frederick, Ralph Hefferline, and Paul Goodman. *Gestalt Therapy.* New York: Julian Press, 1951.

Stoehr, Taylor. *Here Now Next: Paul Goodman and the Origins of Gestalt Therapy.* San Francisco: Jossey-Bass, 1994.

Widmer, Kingsley. *Paul Goodman.* Boston: Twayne, 1980.

Great Migration

On the eve of World War I, black America was rural and southern. Only one-fourth of all African Americans lived in cities, a proportion even lower in the South where 90 percent of all black Americans lived. Moreover, even southern black city dwellers lived in neighborhoods that often lacked standard amenities of urban life: running water, electricity, and sewerage; even police and fire services were meager at best. A half-century later, black Americans had become overwhelmingly urban and equally divided between the South and the rest of the nation. Most had left the South between the 1940s and 1960s, but the initial wave of this Great Migration, as this exodus is called, began in 1916 and ebbed and flowed through the 1920s. This movement of nearly 7 million black Americans from the rural South to cities in the Northeast, Midwest, and West transformed African-American culture and American urban life.

Although African Americans had been moving to southern cities—and to a lesser extent northern cities—ever since emancipation, 1916 denotes a significant turning point because of a dramatic shift both in the direction and the magnitude of African-American migration. Until then, most black southerners contemplating long-distance moves had looked to new opportunities for cotton cultivation in the Gulf States and Oklahoma. Urbanization was more of a local migration strategy, as black southerners made their way from the countryside to the growing cities of the New South. Women could always find work cooking or cleaning for white southerners, but the burgeoning industries of the New South offered few opportunities to their husbands and sons. For most black southerners, urban work was servile; for men, it was often itinerant as well.

Moreover, the grip of white supremacy and Jim Crow transcended the boundaries between the rural and urban South. Although thousands of black southerners were attracted to urban life between 1890 and 1910, partly because of the institutional vitality of black urban communities, separate was anything but equal.

The appeal of the southern city might well have been even thinner had there been options outside the region. With European immigrants pouring into northern cities, employers could choose their workforce according to conventional assumptions about the aptitudes of different "races" for different types of work. These stereotypes limited immigrants' choices, but they virtually excluded African Americans, whom few employers considered capable of any but the most menial chores. Referring to employment patterns in northern cities, the *New Republic* observed in the middle of 1916 that "the Negro gets a chance to work only when there is no one else."

By 1916, however, World War I had left northern employers with "no one else." Exports to European combatants and a revitalized domestic market that was stimulated by President Woodrow Wilson's preparedness initiatives inflated the demand for labor. At the same time, there was no possibility of the influx of European immigrants that employers had come to expect during tight labor markets.

Many employers first reconsidered whether white man's work was necessarily only man's work. Thousands of white women moved into jobs previously reserved for their husbands, fathers, and brothers. But powerful stereotypes about gender undermined consideration of jobs for women, and they were generally deemed unsuitable for most types of industrial work. To keep the production lines running, industrialists were forced to experiment with black men. The experiment even spread to smaller numbers of black women when improved opportunities for white women left places open at the bottom of the hierarchy of female jobs. For the first time in American history, the nation's basic industries offered industrial production jobs to African Americans. From New York, Boston, and Philadelphia to Pittsburgh, Chicago, Detroit, and to a lesser extent Los Angeles, factory gates opened to the black population.

Jobs in railroad yards, shipyards, steel mills, food processing plants, garment shops, and other industries paid wages far beyond what was available in either the rural or urban South. But it was more than money that attracted black southerners to the North. These jobs also represented gates into an aspect of American life that promised a new basis for claims to full citizenship, claims that had once seemed possible only through the attainment of agricultural independence. With schools, voting booths, legal rights, and no formal laws mandating segregation, northern cities seemed to offer black southerners the prospect of what one woman leaving New Orleans called "all the privilege that the whites have."

So they moved, approximately 500,000 black southerners between 1916 and 1919, with twice that many following during the 1920s. Migration slowed to approximately 300,000 during the Depression years, accelerating only when employment opportunities emerged once again after employers ran out of other alternatives a year after the United States formally entered World War II. By 1950, this second stage of migration had led to the consolidation of the urban ghettos that had emerged from the "First Great Migration." It had also produced virtually new, or dramatically expanded, black communities on the West Coast, with nearly 350,000 African Americans moving to California alone between 1942 and 1945. Both in the North and in the West, black communities built economies and institutional matrices atop the foundation of industrial, working-class families, generally charac-

terized by two wage earners (black women had higher rates of labor force participation than white women and were more likely to earn wages nearly equal to what their husbands could bring home). Within these communities, tensions between newcomers and established residents ran along lines of both class and regional origins.

The movement of African Americans to the North and West surged even more in the 1950s. By then, however, the Great Migration was beginning to show more of the characteristics of a refugee migration, caused in this case by the impact of the mechanization of cotton cultivation and picking. Unlike their predecessors during and immediately after the two world wars, black southerners heading north or west during the final two decades of the Great Migration had no choice other than to leave, as they no longer had places in the southern agricultural economy. And southern cities still offered only limited opportunities to African Americans. Moreover, by the 1950s the process of chain migration—the movement of people along routes established by kin and community connections—had created vast networks connecting southern communities with northern cities. Unlike their predecessors, who had moved toward jobs and opportunity, the final wave of black migrants entered northern cities that were experiencing industrial decline, with midwestern cities alone losing 1.3 million jobs in industry, retail, and wholesaling between 1947 and 1972. The Promised Land had become the rust belt.

—*James Grossman*

See also
African Americans in Cities; Ghetto.
References
Gottlieb, Peter. *Making Their Own Way: Southern Blacks' Migration to Pittsburgh, 1916–1930.* Urbana: University of Illinois Press, 1987.
Grossman, James R. *Land of Hope: Chicago, Black Southerners, and the Great Migration.* Chicago: University of Chicago Press, 1989.
Trotter, Joe William, Jr., ed. *The Great Migration in Historical Perspective: New Dimensions of Race, Class and Gender.* Bloomington: Indiana University Press, 1991.

Greenbelt Towns

The greenbelt town program originated as part of the New Deal, aiding the poor by hiring the unemployed to build the towns and then by providing housing for low-income families. Placed within the Resettlement Administration headed by Rexford Tugwell, the Suburban Division, administered by John Lansill, constructed three towns: Greenbelt, Maryland, outside of Washington, D.C.; Greendale, Wisconsin, outside of Milwaukee; and Greenhills, Ohio, outside of Cincinnati. Economist Tugwell yearned for a collectivized society and included his desires in the town plans, emphasizing economic and social "cooperatives" to serve the town residents.

Tugwell left design of the towns to planners, who relied heavily on Clarence Perry's concept of the Neighborhood Unit in which neighborhood boundaries consisted of major streets, but neighborhood roads carried only local traffic. A central area containing shops and a park, as well as an elementary school that also served as a community center, provided a focus for the neighborhood and was within walking distance of neighborhood residents. The planners for Greenbelt and Greenhills were also influenced heavily by Clarence Stein's design of Radburn, New Jersey, which utilized superblocks with central greens, separation of automobile and pedestrian traffic, cul-de-sacs, and homes facing the garden side with their backs facing the street.

Frederick Bigger functioned as chief planner for all three towns, and Hale Walker was town planner for Greenbelt. Tenants began moving into the 885 row houses and apartment units in Greenbelt in September 1937. Justin Hartzog and William Strong were the town planners for Greenhills' 676 units, which looked much like Greenbelt with row houses and apartments built in "contemporary" or "international" style. Residents first moved into Greenhills in April 1938 and into Greendale in May 1938. Jacob Crane and Elbert Peets, town planners for Greendale, used recently opened Colonial Williamsburg, Virginia, as a model for their work, which contained 572 units, including 274 single-family detached homes, with the remainder row houses.

The greenbelt town program in general, and Tugwell in particular, received much negative press coverage. Congressional critics of the New Deal focused on the expense of the towns, and businessmen clamored against "communistic" and "socialistic" aspects. As a result, Tugwell resigned and Roosevelt dismantled the Resettlement Administration at the end of 1936. The Farm Security Administration oversaw completion of the towns that, after World War II, the government resolved to sell. In response, town residents who wished to maintain their communities as planned cooperatives formed groups to purchase the government housing.

In 1952, Greenbelt Homes Inc. purchased 1,580 dwelling units and 709 acres of vacant land from the government. (An increase from the original 885 units occurred during World War II when the government built housing for war workers.) In May 1955, Greenbelt Homes sold almost all the remaining vacant land to a private developer, thus losing control of planning and development in the area. Throughout the 1960s, 1970s, and 1980s developers built on much of the greenbelt, and the town of Greenbelt itself grew into a city of over 20,000. The cooperative businesses and social institutions still flourish.

At Greenhills, the Greenhills Home Owners Corporation purchased their homes and town center from the government in 1950. The government sold an additional 3,500 acres of land to a company intending to build low-cost housing; however, this venture was not realized and the expensive homes of Forest Park emerged instead. Greenhills currently has 1,690 homes and the shopping center contains 55 stores and businesses. Unique among the three towns, Greenhills preserved its greenbelt.

In Greendale, efforts by cooperative groups to purchase the homes failed, but residents were allowed to buy their own houses throughout 1952. The federal government gave the town its central public space, but the remaining 2,300 acres, most of the open space and greenbelt area, were purchased by the Milwaukee Community Development Corporation. Elbert Peets created the plan for its development, leading to a smooth growth process consistent with the original planning concepts. Greendale is now a city of 17,000 with mainly residential development, but it also houses the largest enclosed shopping center in Wisconsin.

In spite of changes over the last 50 years, the original government buildings still exist in all three towns, demonstrating their original plans for interested visitors. However, a primary goal of the Suburban Division planners remains unfulfilled. They hoped that their plans for community design would be an important influence on future development in the United States. But other than being examined by those who formed the New Towns of the 1960s and 1970s, the greenbelt towns have largely been ignored. Now, in an era of community breakdown, the greenbelt towns deserve study for their demonstration that residents can successfully cooperate to create the communities they desire for themselves and their families.

—*Cathy D. Knepper*

See also
Perry, Clarence Arthur; Stein, Clarence S.; Tugwell, Rexford Guy.
References
Alanen, Arnold R., and Joseph A. Eden. *Main Street Readymade: The New Deal Community of Greendale, Wisconsin.* Madison: State Historical Society of Wisconsin, 1987.
Arnold, Joseph L. *The New Deal in the Suburbs: A History of the Greenbelt Town Program, 1935–1954.* Columbus: Ohio State University Press, 1971.
Knepper, Cathy D. "The Gospel According to Greenbelt: Community Life in Greenbelt, Maryland, 1935–1990." Ph.D. dissertation, University of Maryland, 1993.
Mayer, Albert. *Greenbelt Towns Revisited.* Washington, DC: Department of Housing and Urban Development, 1968.

Greenwich Village

For more than a century, New York's Greenwich Village has been an internationally recognized center of cultural innovation. Lacking definitive geographical boundaries, the neighborhood lies two miles north of the southern tip of Manhattan Island on its west side. Called Sapokanican by the Indians who hunted and fished there, seventeenth-century Dutch and English settlers transformed the marshy terrain into farmland. The area's remoteness from urban settlement survived the American Revolution but quickly eroded when New Yorkers fled north to escape a series of epidemic fevers and swelled the area's population fourfold between 1825 and 1840.

Historically, in the nineteenth century the Village was actually three communities. The oldest, the West Village, was home to middle-class merchants and artisans who capitalized on the trading advantages of the nearby Hudson River. Beginning in 1820, the uniform blocks laid out near Broadway to the east, and the ensemble rows planned along Lafayette and Bleecker Streets, emerged as residential enclaves for the affluent. Simultaneously, Washington Square—"The American Ward"—became home to patrician New York. Institutions essential to serving the spiritual, educational, and entertainment needs of this expanding community quickly materialized. Prestigious church congregations sprang up, and the arrival of New York University in the 1830s lent an intellectual tone to Washington Square. By 1850, the neighborhood sheltered a disproportionate share of the city's writers, editors, and publishers, whose presence was bolstered by an infrastructure of local salons, libraries, clubs, booksellers, and presses both large and small. From the middle of the nineteenth century on, the Village also nurtured a vigorous art colony whose legacy has endured in the form of private picture galleries, schools of art, and studio workshops.

Entering its Victorian heyday, Greenwich Village stood secure in its identity as a prospering domestic stronghold. By the 1890s, however, a combination of economic and demographic changes stripped the Village of its dignified image. The housing stock deteriorated, and slums, manufactories, and brothels filled the side streets to the south and east of Washington Square. Plummeting per capita income led nervous property owners and businesses to abandon the area to newly arrived waves of Irish, German, and Italian immigrants. As it entered the twentieth century, Greenwich Village boasted a surfeit of cheap lodgings in the homes being vacated by affluent Victorian society in a setting of small-town intimacy; the "village-like" qualities provided an ideal refuge for artists, writers, actors, and social radicals of all varieties.

Pockets of Bohemian activity had flourished in the Village intermittently before 1900, but it was the dawn of the twentieth century that ushered in a permanent colony of rebels. The radicals who colonized Greenwich Village before World War I subscribed to a principled creed that spurned all traditions of structured socialization. Their array of progressive causes ranged from the modern suffrage, birth control, and left-wing labor movements to radical feminism, psychoanalysis, and free love. Village intellectuals also experimented incessantly with new educational methods, new domestic arrangements, and new ways to oppose American militarism. The list of those who lived in or passed through the Village in this era reads like a veritable who's who of American literati, artists, and radical reformers: Max Eastman, Edmund Wilson, Edna St. Vincent Millay, Willa Cather, Eugene O'Neill, Mabel Dodge Luhan, "Big" Bill Heyward, Emma Goldman, John Reed, Theodore Dreiser, John Sloan, and Alexander Berkman lived in the Village at one time or another during the first two decades of the twentieth century.

Although revolution was an end in itself for many Village radicals, their spirit of dilettantism prompted critics to note that Village activists were often unable to sustain their enthusiasm once an immediate crisis passed; accordingly, their impact often proved negligible. Despite the ephemeral nature of much that transpired in the Greenwich Village of the early twentieth century, the era was not without lasting contributions. The seminal Armory Show of 1913 and the founding of the Whitney Studio Club (forerunner of the Whitney Museum of American Art) as a showcase for the cutting-edge work of contemporary artists both helped propel the cause of progressive art forward and firmly established the Village's reputation for artistic innovation and creativity. The "little theater" movement inaugurated in the 1910s matured into innovative repertory companies whose production theories helped free American drama from the stranglehold of Broadway's commercial influence.

By the middle of the 1910s, a new breed of Villager, the self-invented "character" who exploited the district's reputation for eccentricity by acting accordingly, often for a price, began to appear. In conduct and concerns, this group contrasted sharply with the issue-oriented generation that had preceded them. After 1917, the cult of unconventionality for its own sake steadily gained converts who catered to the ever swelling influx of tourists armed with maps and guidebooks and versed in the lore that now clung to the district. The modern discovery of the Village as a popular tourist destination led local realtors and restaurateurs, merchants and movie makers, bus lines and theater companies to capitalize on the notion of nonconformity that distinguished Village culture.

In the 30 years after World War I, rising housing costs and the growing presence of institutions like New York University combined with the passing of the radical generation that had lived here between 1900 and 1920 to change the character of the neighborhood. The Village increasingly became as much a state of mind as a physical place. Its historic boundaries expanded to encompass areas to the east and south that still contained the sort of affordable housing that had previously typified the immediate environs of Washington Square. The artistic community, once centered in the Village, scattered to areas south of Houston Street (Soho) and in midtown Manhattan.

Despite its changing nature, the Village continued to attract the socially disaffected and culturally innovative. It was home for many of the abstract painters collectively known as the New York School, and it nourished the Beat Generation talents of Jack Kerouac, Allen Ginsberg, William Burroughs, and others. The Village reinforced its reputation as a haven for political and social dissent during the 1960s protests against American involvement in Vietnam, and it continues to serve as a headquarters for the nationwide movement for gay and lesbian rights. Greenwich Village has simultaneously endured the crime, drug use, homelessness, and other problems that characterize many American urban neighborhoods in the late twentieth century. Despite their intrusion, the Village remains a compelling physical location for political, social, and cultural differences. In the words of an early-twentieth-century habitué, the Village is a "spiritual zone of mind . . . [and] the city which hasn't a Greenwich Village is to be pitied. It has no life, no illusion, no art."

—*Rick Beard and Jan Seidler Ramirez*

See also
Armory Show; Bohemianism.
References
Beard, Rick, and Leslie Cohen Berlowitz, eds. *Greenwich Village: Culture and Counterculture.* New Brunswick, NJ: Rutgers University Press, 1993.

Delaney, Edmund T., and Charles Lockwood. *Greenwich Village: A Photographic Guide.* New York: Dover, 1976.

Miller, Terry. *Greenwich Village and How It Got That Way.* New York: Crown, 1990.

Ware, Caroline. *Greenwich Village: 1920–1930.* Boston: Houghton Mifflin, 1935.

Hague, Frank (1876–1956)

Frank Hague was born in Jersey City, New Jersey, the son of poor Irish immigrants, John and Margaret (Fagen) Hague. When he left school at age 14 in the sixth grade, this tall, tough, self-confessed juvenile delinquent worked as a blacksmith's helper in the Erie Railroad yards, and he was later a boxing manager. His political career began in 1899 when he was elected constable with help from the Second Ward Democratic Party boss, and he moved up the ladder to become city commissioner in 1913 and mayor from 1917 to 1947. Hague married Jennie W. Warner in 1903, and they had two biological children and an adopted son.

Hague dominated Jersey City and Hudson County politics. He was the Democratic boss of New Jersey from 1917 to 1947, and his power base was unrivaled on the East Coast and impervious to the New Deal. From 1924 to 1952, Hague was also a vice-chairman of the national Democratic Party. Often compared to Alfred E. Smith, Hague supported Smith's presidential aspirations in 1924, 1928, and 1932, but he threw his support to Franklin D. Roosevelt in time to swing New Jersey behind FDR's coalition. With Roosevelt's support, and controlling the city and county Democratic parties, Hague constructed a model political machine. His major defeat occurred in 1939, when a suit in federal court decided that a local ordinance violated civil rights by limiting free speech and free assembly. Hague was also investigated in 1938 for political corruption that occurred when he was mayor.

During the course of his regime, Hague reorganized the police and fire departments of Jersey City, provided efficient public services for loyal voters, built a modern medical center, and stressed humane child welfare programs. However, the election of Republican governors of New Jersey in 1943 and 1946 indicated that Hague's power was waning. At the same time, welfare programs of the New Deal and the growing power of Italian-American and Polish-American candidates undercut his power base. In 1947 Hague resigned as mayor in favor of his nephew, Frank Hague Eggers, a man so inept that younger Democrats and even some Republicans won postwar elections. Hague resigned as county party leader in 1949 and as Democratic national committeeman and national vice-chairman in 1952. An attempted comeback in 1953 was futile, and the death of Eggers in 1954 ended his long career. He died in New York City in 1956, largely forgotten as a Democratic Party leader and masterful political boss.

—*Peter C. Holloran*

References
Connors, Richard J. *A Cycle of Power: The Career of Jersey City Mayor Frank Hague.* Metuchen, NJ: Scarecrow Press, 1971.
Rapport, George. *The Statesman and the Boss: A Study of American Political Leadership Exemplified by Woodrow Wilson and Frank Hague.* New York: Vantage Press, 1961.
Smith, Thomas F. X. *The Powerticians.* Secaucus, NJ: L. Stuart, 1982.

Hammond, George Henry (1838–1886)

George Henry Hammond, American meat merchant and industrialist, is known for developing the first successful refrigerated railway car and for the first shipments of fresh dressed beef from the Midwest to the eastern seaboard. Hammond also founded a fully integrated meat company that was an early member of the famous "Big Four" meatpacking oligopoly.

Hammond entered the industry as the operator of a butcher shop and slaughterhouse in Detroit, and he adapted a refrigerated railway car designed to ship fish and fruit to the shipment of beef. In 1869 Hammond made the first refrigerated rail shipment of fresh beef, from Detroit to Boston. Fresh western dressed beef was a novelty, especially in the warmer months of the year, and commanded high prices, making the venture quite successful. Hammond established a new plant, which became the industrial nucleus of present-day Hammond, Indiana (part of the Gary-Hammond Metropolitan Statistical Area). Situated just across the state line from Chicago's Union Stock Yard, Hammond was attractive due to the availability of unpolluted ice from the Calumet River. The new business made the most of its early monopoly, reaching $1 million in sales by 1873. However, Gustavus Swift developed a superior refrigerator car design in 1878. Hammond brought suit against Swift but without success. Thus, the monopoly rents of Hammond's innovation dissipated within ten years, and by 1886 George Hammond and Company was the smallest of the "Big Four" meatpackers.

Hammond went on to be the first to export chilled dressed beef from the United States to Great Britain in 1879. But here, too, Swift soon imitated him. In the 1880s the meatpacking industry had already begun to decentralize and shift westward from Chicago's South Side. In 1885, Hammond was the first of the full-line national meatpackers to establish a large-scale plant in Omaha, Nebraska, just outside the South Omaha Stock Yards at the eastern terminus of the Union Pacific Railroad. Long after the meatpacking industry abandoned Chicago's "Packingtown," Omaha has maintained its critical price-setting role as North America's preeminent livestock market.

Soon after Hammond died in 1886 at the age of 48, George Hammond and Company was sold and eventually came under the control of Armour and Company. In the 1890s, the company's Indiana plant was among the first in the industry to be unionized by the American Federation of Labor. And, when the union struck in 1893, the firm was among the first industrial enterprises to demonstrate the flexibility of the multiplant firm by shifting production into other packinghouses in the company chain.

As the first to ship Chicago beef to New York in 1869, Hammond was one of the pioneers of Chicago's infant meatpacking industry. He was also important as an innovator who lost control of his invention and lived to see it used against him. His Indiana and Nebraska packinghouses were the industrial nucleus so vital to the late-nineteenth-century growth and development of manufacturing belt cities such as Hammond, Indiana, and Great Plains entrepots such as Omaha.

—Ian MacLachlan

References

Brody, David. *The Butcher Workmen: A Study of Unionization.* Cambridge, MA: Harvard University Press, 1964.

Clemen, Rudolph A. *George H. Hammond: Pioneer in Refrigerator Transportation.* New York: Newcomen Society of England, 1946.

Cronon, William. *Nature's Metropolis: Chicago and the Great West.* New York: W. W. Norton, 1991.

Skaggs, Jimmy M. *Prime Cut: Livestock Raising and Meatpacking in the United States, 1607–1983.* College Station: Texas A & M University Press, 1986.

Harlem

Harlem, in northern Manhattan, originated as a pastoral Dutch community in colonial times, but in the early twentieth century it became the most famous and influential black American ghetto. Its informal boundaries, stretched steadily by the influx of African Americans and, more recently, Hispanics, now range from 178th Street in the north to 96th Street in the south, and from the East and Harlem Rivers in the east to the Hudson River in the west. Harlem's checkered history reveals how industrialization and urbanization transformed the area's sparsely settled agricultural land, led it through speculative boom and bust, afforded unprecedented opportunity to African Americans, yet ultimately stunted that opportunity through racist barriers and social decay.

The Dutch settlement of New Haarlem, founded in 1658 or 1659, was known for its fertile lands a short remove from the village of New Amsterdam. Through the early nineteenth century most residents were prosperous descendants of Dutch, English, or French settlers, but in the 1840s exhaustion of the soil at last drained Harlem's productivity. Working-class newcomers, often immigrants, were soon buying much of the depreciated property or squatting on nearby marshlands. Harlem became a village of shanties and huts interspersed with an occasional farmhouse.

In the late nineteenth century, Harlem revived as a quasi-suburban refuge from New York City, which was drawing waves of poor immigrants and rural migrants to work in its burgeoning factories. As elevated railroads linked Harlem residents with New York's downtown commercial center, a real estate boom in the 1880s displaced Harlem's shanties with spacious brownstones and apartment buildings. The new residents of this exclusive area were mainly older Americans, disproportionately native-born, plus immigrants from Great Britain, Ireland, and Germany, including German Jews.

Harlem changed during the first decades of the twentieth century from a white enclave into the first black ghetto in the history of New York City. Until the late nineteenth century, black residences had been scattered in small groups of blocks throughout poor white working-class neighborhoods. Then a surge of rural black migrants seeking jobs in New York's expanding economy created pressures for new housing. A plunge in Harlem's real estate market in 1904 let well-to-do, longer-settled blacks slip past the racial barriers typical of elite neighborhoods; soon "panic selling" by white tenants further depressed property values and enabled poorer blacks to join the influx. By the early 1920s, most black institutions in downtown Manhattan had relocated to Harlem, while black migration to the region from the rural South continued to intensify.

The concentration of blacks in Harlem stimulated a proliferation of churches, sects, and cults; increased political involvement, as many southern black migrants could now vote; spurred organizations for racial uplift, exemplified by Marcus Garvey's Universal Negro Improvement Association; and encouraged cultural creativity, culminating in the "Harlem Re-

Harlem as it appeared in the early twentieth century. At the center of the picture is the entrance to the Cotton Club, an important cultural site.

naissance" that flourished in the 1920s. Musicians pioneered in jazz, blues, and ragtime, while writers such as Zora Neal Hurston and Alain Locke and poets such as Langston Hughes probed black life and identity. These and other artists gained national renown, patronized (in every sense) by whites alienated from mainstream Puritan values and romanticizing black life as exotic, sensual, and uninhibited. Hughes observed of this rush both to glorify and stereotype blacks, "Harlem was in vogue."

During the 1920s Harlem's cultural flowering coincided with a less publicized but momentous change: its deterioration into a giant slum, plagued by overcrowding, poverty, and high rents. Unsuitable housing structures, originally intended for large wealthy families rather than young migrants with low incomes, added to the congestion and weakened social cohesion by inducing poor tenants to rent space to lodgers who were often strangers of widely varying respectability. All these problems bred a multitude of other ills, including disease, high mortality rates, family instability, crime, delin-

quency, truancy, and vice. The peasant backgrounds of most migrants further impeded their adjustment, for they were ignorant of basic principles of health and sanitation and they faced a daunting transition from extensive rural kinship networks to urban anomie.

In some respects, Harlem's woes echoed the experiences of other ethnic arrivals seeking opportunity in New York City, who also weathered poverty, prejudice, congestion, and social dislocation. But white racism vastly compounded and perpetuated these problems, shutting blacks off from union membership and decent jobs, and denying them exit from the ghetto slums no matter their level of income or education.

Riots, often sparked by perceptions of police mistreatment and directed at white-owned businesses, periodically gave vent and voice to Harlem's ongoing social and economic frustrations. The best known occurred in 1935, spurred by soaring unemployment during the Depression; in 1943, when blacks sharply lagged in benefits from the wartime economic boom; and in 1964, when the ghetto's continued decline appeared in stark relief against the widely publicized civil rights gains of southern blacks.

In recent decades, community renovation projects have enjoyed isolated successes, yet Harlem's basic character as a ghetto slum has persisted. In recent years, however, the influx of black migrants to Harlem has been outweighed by an exodus to other black neighborhoods, including some in the South. The black population of Harlem, which had numbered about 300,000 in 1970, declined to just over 200,000 by 1990; there were nearly as many Hispanics (189,000), plus some 70,000 whites and 14,000 Asian Americans.

Despite its tenacious social problems, Harlem has remained a center of black culture and consciousness. A small sampling of eminent African Americans who have either grown up or lived in Harlem at some point in their lives includes the musicians Duke Ellington, Cab Calloway, Lena Horne, and Harry Belafonte; the writers Richard Wright, Ralph Ellison, and James Baldwin; the civil rights leaders W. E. B. DuBois, Roy Wilkins, and Thurgood Marshall; and the black nationalist Malcolm X. Their achievements stand against the wreckage of inner-city life that stamps Harlem as emblematic of so much of black urban history.

—*Robert Weisbrot*

References

Anderson, Jervis. *This Was Harlem: A Cultural Portrait, 1900–1950.* New York: Farrar, Straus and Giroux, 1981.

Capeci, Dominic J., Jr. *The Harlem Riot of 1943.* Philadelphia: Temple University Press, 1977.

Greenberg, Cheryl Lynn. *"Or Does It Explode?" Black Harlem in the Great Depression.* New York: Oxford University Press, 1991.

Lewis, David Levering. *When Harlem Was in Vogue.* New York: Oxford University Press, 1979.

Osofsky, Gilbert. *Harlem, the Making of a Ghetto: Negro New York, 1890–1930.* 2d ed. New York: Harper & Row, 1971.

Scheiner, Seth M. *Negro Mecca: A History of the Negro in New York City, 1865–1920.* New York: New York University Press, 1965.

Hearst, William Randolph (1863–1951)

The most reviled figure in the annals of American journalism, William Randolph Hearst was a man of many parts. The son of a U.S. senator, he never relied on his inherited millions; instead he threw himself into building a media empire. A willful, opinionated man, he elicited equally strong reactions from both contemporaries and historians.

After rejuvenating a failing San Francisco daily, he bought another moribund daily, the *New York Journal,* in 1896. Following a bruising five-year battle with Joseph Pulitzer's *New York World,* his paper became the largest circulation publication in the nation. Hearst's saber-rattling editorials and screaming headlines were widely blamed for instigating the Spanish-American War, but many other factors were involved. America was pugnacious, and it is clear there would have been a war even without Hearst. Nonetheless, the stigma clung to him and intensified when a copy of the paper with an editorial denouncing William McKinley was found in possession of the president's assassin.

Hearst served one term in the U.S. House of Representatives, barely lost a race for the governorship of New York, and seriously contended for the Democratic nomination for president. As he turned his attention to enlarging his newspaper chain and other publishing ventures, his politics moved steadily to the right. By the 1930s, he bitterly opposed the New Deal and organized labor. After visiting Europe, he praised some accomplishments of Mussolini and Hitler, and his newspapers were stridently isolationist.

With Marion Davies, his movie actress mistress, he entertained the cream of the political and entertainment worlds at San Simeon, his 100-room estate, midway between San Francisco and Los Angeles. He tirelessly collected works of art, many plundered from European castles. The 1941 movie *Citizen Kane,* based on his life, was a *roman à clef* that helped seal his reputation.

Although Hearst was forced to reduce his media holdings during the Depression, his corporation still operated 18 dailies in 12 cities, a news service, a feature and photo service, nine magazines, and a book publishing concern when he died in 1951. His personal estate at the time totaled nearly $60 million, and his sons continued the multimedia empire he had built.

—*John D. Stevens*

References

Lundberg, Ferdinand. *Imperial Hearst.* New York: Equinox, 1936.

Swanberg, W. A. *Citizen Hearst.* New York: Scribners, 1961.

Height Restrictions

Restrictions on building heights have been a part of property law since time immemorial. Blackstone describes as an actionable nuisance "To erect a building so close to mine that it obstructs my ancient windows." This English doctrine of ancient lights protected the first building from later encroachments by neighboring buildings that would eliminate a long-enjoyed benefit. However, the doctrine proved inappropriate in the undeveloped and fast-growing New World, and it was universally rejected by American courts.

Not until the late nineteenth century, when skyscrapers emerged as an urban building form, did American cities begin to limit building heights legislatively. The first laws imposed a blanket restriction ranging from 100 to 200 feet. By the early 1900s, however, some major cities (Boston, Washington, and Baltimore) had introduced differential height restrictions that varied from district to district.

These laws faced three levels of constitutional challenge. First, they were said to be aesthetically motivated and, therefore, not reasonably related to public health and safety; consequently, they were not within the state's police power. Second, they were said to be a taking of property without compensation. Third, they were said to deny equal protection of the law.

State courts generally upheld these laws on the grounds that they were reasonably calculated to limit fire hazards, promote building safety, and permit the free passage of light and air. The arguments against taking land were rejected because of the importance of health and safety concerns and because landowners could do things with their property other than construct tall buildings. The inequality of treatment that resulted from districting was justified as being related to the ability to fight fires (i.e., more equipment and higher water pressure was located downtown where taller buildings were permitted). The U.S. Supreme Court agreed with state courts in the 1909 case, *Welch v. Swasey.* Overlooked in all these opinions were background facts that suggested that height limitations were sometimes an instrument to protect upper-class neighborhoods from the arrival of underclass newcomers.

In 1916, New York City adopted the first comprehensive zoning ordinance. The "use controls" it contained were constitutionally suspect, but the building height and bulk regulations were soon accepted. Taken together, they conceptualized a "sky exposure plane" calculated as an angle from the center of the street to permit light and air to reach the lower floors of buildings and the street. The setbacks mandated by these restrictions resulted in the development of a whole new style, sometimes referred to as "wedding cake" architecture, with upper floors smaller than lower floors and receding back from them.

After the use restrictions found in zoning ordinances were constitutionally legitimized by the Supreme Court in 1926, the "taking issue" lay dormant for a half-century. It came back to life, however, in the case of *Penn Central Transportation Co. v. City of New York* (1978). New York City's Landmarks Preservation Commission had denied the Penn Central Railroad permission to construct a multistory office tower above Grand Central Station. Denial of the proposed use, which was otherwise consistent with zoning laws, cost Penn Central more than $50 million. Although the Court denied Penn Central relief, it admitted that it had been "unable to develop any 'set formula' for determining when 'justice and fairness' require that economic injuries caused by public action be compensated by the government."

One reason the Court did give for denying relief was that Penn Central's preexisting air rights had been made transferable to other building sites. New York, and many other cities, have developed "transferable development rights" policies that sever development from other rights in land. In essence, Penn Central was permitted to exceed zoning height restrictions at a nearby site as a payback in return for the loss of its air rights over Grand Central Station. The idea behind this policy is to ease the burden of lower-density development at one building site by allowing higher-density development at another. The legitimacy of such leveraging of the police power remains an open constitutional issue.

—*Garrett Power*

See also
Skyscraper.
References
Costonis, John J. " 'Fair' Compensation and the Accommodation Power." *Columbia Law Review* 75 (1975): 1021–1022.
Cribbet, John Edward. "Concepts in Transition: The Search for a New Definition of Property." *University of Illinois Law Review* 1 (1986): 1–26.
Penn Central Transportation Co. v. City of New York, 438 U.S. 104 (1978).
Power, Garrett. "High Society: The Building Height Limitation on Baltimore's Mt. Vernon Place." *Maryland Historical Magazine* 79 (1982): 197–219.
Toll, Seymour I. *Zoned American.* New York: Grossman, 1969.
Weiss, Marc A. "Skyscraper Zoning: New York's Pioneer Effort." *Journal of the American Planning Association* 58 (1992): 201–212.
Welch v. Swasey, 214 U.S. 91 (1909).

Hempstead, New York

Hempstead Village, with a population of approximately 50,000, is the fourth largest municipality in Nassau County on New York's Long Island. Sitting astride Long Island's major transportation arteries, it has historically played an important role as the commercial "hub" of western Long Island. In more recent times, it has suffered economic decline due to the development of neighboring shopping malls and has figured among the first suburbs to experience substantial growth in its minority population. Over the past three decades, Hempstead has served as a veritable laboratory for policy experimentation in economic revitalization.

Founded in 1644, Hempstead is the oldest settled community on Long Island. Its strategic location made it an important commercial location throughout the 1700s and 1800s. During World War I, Hempstead became an army boom town providing services to 300,000 soldiers at nearby Camp Mills. The war left the lasting legacy of an upgraded infrastructure and the establishment of the army's Mitchell Field as a center for aviation experiment and development; Roosevelt Field, abandoned by the army, flourished as a commercial airport. Hempstead served as the regional shopping center for the burgeoning aviation industry and also attracted academic institutions like Hofstra University and services like New York Telephone.

World War II fueled the local defense-based economy, inflating demand for Hempstead's vast offerings of consumer goods. Ironically, however, the postwar growth of Long Island planted the seeds of Hempstead's economic decline. With new tract houses replacing vast acres of farmland, mounting concern for public health and safety brought aviation activities to a halt. Roosevelt Field was sold to developers, opening the way for construction of a major shopping mall and office complex beyond the borders and tax coffers of Hempstead Village.

When Hempstead sought federally funded urban renewal money as a way out of its economic difficulties in the 1960s, it was not without previous experience in the politics of redevelopment. In 1951, Hempstead opened Nassau County's first state-funded low-income housing project in a blighted section of its black neighborhood. This pioneering initiative in public housing created a progressive social image that contrasted sharply with the exclusionary practices of neighboring municipalities. From 1950 to 1960 the black population grew from 9 percent to 22 percent, as poor blacks came to occupy the now-abandoned stores and rooming houses in the central business district.

In 1960 Hempstead embarked on its first comprehensive redevelopment program. Spanning a decade, it used federal funds for extensive commercial and residential construction. Other remedial initiatives followed, including the relocation of state, county, and town offices to Hempstead. By the mid-1970s Hempstead had acquired a high-rise profile, but its economy continued along a downward course.

In the late 1970s a second major planning effort was launched. Drawing on a mix of public and private funds, it promoted development on three fronts: commercial revitalization, the development of Hempstead as a cultural and arts center, and the building of a solar energy pavilion. The pavilion failed to acquire the necessary funding, while the other projects achieved only limited success.

By the 1990s Hempstead's population was younger, had lower incomes, and was more ethnically mixed than Nassau County as a whole. A ten-year plan adopted in 1993 abandoned the long-standing goal of making Hempstead into a regional shopping center to focus on the residential and commercial needs of its population. Future development focuses on building a discount shopping mall, a smaller retail market of ethnic specialty shops and restaurants, and creating a mixed-use "Village-within-the-Village" designed to link with Hempstead's upgraded transportation facilities.

—*Susan Tenenbaum*

References
Barron, James. "In Nassau, an Inner Suburb Plans Revival." *New York Times* (April 4, 1982).
Comprehensive Development Plan, Village of Hempstead, New York. Prepared by the Community Development Agency and Saccardi & Schiff, 1993.
Faron, Adelaide. "The Birth of Hempstead." *Community Club Magazine* 1 (1934): 11–16.

Henry Street Settlement

Next to Hull House, the Henry Street Settlement is the most significant settlement house in the United States. Visiting nurse Lillian Wald established it on New York's Lower East Side in 1893. Besides housing a charitable nursing service, Henry Street offered social clubs, English and citizenship classes, and strong programs in the visual and performing arts. Henry Street Settlement volunteers developed a prominent little theater, and in 1927 added a Music School.

Henry Street's neighborhood was originally known as an area of Jewish immigrants, but in reality many nationalities lived there. By 1990, Latinos and Asians constituted over half the neighborhood. Henry Street became a place where a variety of people could come together and have their lives culturally enriched.

Henry Street was also a setting for social reform. Under Wald, the settlement worked for neighborhood betterment. Partly as a result of its efforts, Seward and Corlears Hook Parks were created. Henry Street also worked to improve public education. In addition, the settlement was a pioneer in developing a vocational counseling service for the unemployed. Finally, Henry Street established a branch settlement for blacks on West 60th Street called Lincoln House at a time when few services were available to African Americans.

The second director, Helen Hall, took over Henry Street in 1933 and remained until her retirement in 1967. Hall continued the settlement's traditional mix of social action and strong arts programs. While Henry Street provided meeting space for the Socialist Party–sponsored Workers Committee on Unemployment, Hall served on Franklin Roosevelt's Advisory Council on Economic Security, which made recommendations for the Social Security Act that laid the foundations for our federal welfare system. Hall, along with Henry Street's club for the elderly, worked energetically for national health insurance. She also worked for the construction of public housing and strongly advocated including community space in the projects. Finally, under her leadership, Henry Street initiated Mobilization for Youth, the prototype program for the War on Poverty.

The third director, Bertram Beck, served from 1967 to 1977. He brought Henry Street into the modern age of government grants and project partnerships with various government agencies. Under Beck, Henry Street became one of the early pioneers of transitional housing. That program assisted the homeless with intensive social services to improve their living skills so they could obtain housing on their own. In 1977, the settlement also opened one of the early battered women's shelters.

Following Beck, Henry Street went rapidly through three directors before settling on Daniel Kronenfeld in 1985. Kronenfeld has continued to expand Henry Street's social service and arts programs while also launching the settlement's successful centennial renovation of its three original row houses and historic theater buildings. By 1994, Henry Street's facilities included an adjacent playground, a modern building for clubs and classes, the theater building and adjacent arts center, and use of community space in nearby public housing projects. More so than any other settlement, including Hull House, Henry Street has maintained a vital, healthy, and socially significant program.

—*Judith Ann Trolander*

See also
Settlement House Movement; Wald, Lillian D.
References
Hall, Helen. *Unfinished Business in Neighborhood and Nation.* New York: Macmillan, 1971.
Trolander, Judith Ann. "A Historical Glance." In *Voices of Henry Street: Portrait of a Community.* New York: Henry Street Settlement, 1993.
———. *Professionalism and Social Change: From the Settlement House Movement to Neighborhood Centers, 1886 to the Present.* New York: Columbia University Press, 1987.

Hinterland

The term *hinterland* conjures up several images, for it is a concept that can be interpreted at various scales and in different ways. At the local and national levels, the hinterland has traditionally been viewed as the tributary area of any settlement from which raw materials are collected and to which finished products are distributed.

Earlier in the twentieth century, the term *umland* was used to describe the hinterland of an urban settlement, but urban field is the concept employed at present. The urban field represents an extension of the city into the countryside and a merging of metropolitan and rural spaces. Within this urban field is the rural-urban fringe, a discontinuous zone between city and country in which urban and rural land uses are intermixed. Urban uses dominate closer to the city while rural uses are dominant but declining in the outer fringe. Beyond the rural-urban fringe is the so-called urban shadow, in which visible metropolitan influences are minimal but present in terms of nonfarm ownership and commuting patterns.

All of these concepts convey the increasing control of the city over its surrounding countryside. In this fashion, hinterland has become almost synonymous with rural and is juxtaposed with metropolis, both comprising parts of a single socioeconomic space that centers on the latter. *Rural* ceases to exist as a place as both it and *urban* are transformed into *hinterland* and *metropolis* as part of the unifying process known interchangeably in the historical literature as urbanization, modernization, or the Great Transformation. On an international scale, modernization theory views the developed world as the metropolis and the Third World as the hinterland, with the latter again being integrated into a world system directed by the former.

Ideology plays a major role in how scholars view the process. Those who see modernization favorably view it as a progressive process that serves development even though it results in the decline of rural population (out-migration), functions (loss of services), ways of life (the penetration of urban values facilitated by technological developments in transportation and communications), and other places (towns and villages). These scholars make the assumption, at least at the global level and arguably at the national scale also, that the more backward should mimic the more advanced.

Those who view modernization more critically portray it as a process whereby hinterlands are subjected to international and internal processes of imperialism and colonialism. The integration of metropolis and hinterland ensures a dependency relationship in which the hinterland provides a pool of labor, raw materials, and capital exploited and controlled by the metropolitan core. The political, economic, and cultural hegemony of the metropolis is ensured by the mechanism of unequal exchange that effectively subjugates the hinterland.

Although these views differ, particularly with regard to the benefits of industrial capitalism, both assume that social change in rural areas parallels urban and industrial trends, a process eventually leading to the complete disappearance of rural places. Yet, there are those who believe that modernization and core-periphery interpretations are spatially "overgeneralized." While rural communities and small towns in European colonies (in both the Americas and the rest of the world) were integrated into larger regional, national, and international systems of production, the specifics of history, place, and human agency play a major role in molding and determining the local impact of these forces. Not every rural place was an incipient metropolis or even an embryonic hinterland for that matter. There have existed rural-designed and rural-oriented alternatives that promoted local control in spite of the macroeconomic and macrosocial climate. Even today, when the development of hinterlands is almost entirely dictated by decisions and tastes imposed according to metropolitan standards, there survive distinct rural values, places, and environments, even though many exist as alternatives to urban-industrial life, at least in the context of the developed world.

—*Randy William Widdis*

References

Barron, Hal. *Those Who Stayed Behind: Rural Society in Nineteenth Century New England.* Cambridge, England: Cambridge University Press, 1984.

Christaller, Walter. *Central Places in Southern Germany.* C. W. Baskin, trans. Englewood Cliffs, NJ: Prentice-Hall, 1970.

Conzen, Michael. "The Progress of American Urbanism, 1860–1930." In Robert Mitchell and Paul Groves, eds., *North America: The Historical Geography of a Changing Continent,* 347–370. Totawa, NJ: Rowman and Littlefield, 1987.

Hahn, Steven, and Jonathan Prude, eds. *The Countryside in the Age of Capitalist Transformation.* Chapel Hill: University of North Carolina Press, 1985.

Widdis, Randy William. "Belleville and Environs: Continuity, Change and the Integration of Town and Country during the Nineteenth Century." *Urban History Review* 19 (1991): 181–208.

Hispanic Americans

The term *Hispanic American* refers broadly to persons of Spanish descent living in the United States. It is not in itself an ethnic designation as it encompasses peoples of diverse national backgrounds, histories, and cultural traditions. Nor is it a racial category—Hispanic peoples may trace their forebears to Caucasian antecedents or to a blend of Caucasian, Indian, and black populations. *Latinos* is also used to designate this general population, and several terms refer to a specific Hispanic ethnic group; for example, people of Mexican descent may speak of themselves as *Chicanos* or *La Raza* (the race), while Puerto Ricans may use the Arawak Indian word *boricuas* (brave lords).

In 1990, the United States Bureau of the Census enumerated persons of Spanish or Hispanic origin as those who classified themselves in one of four predetermined categories: Mexican, Puerto Rican, Cuban, or Other Spanish/Hispanic origin. Those choosing the Other category were additionally asked to provide their country of origin; the most frequent responses indicated Central and South America nationalities.

People of Mexican derivation make up by far the largest segment of Hispanic Americans. In the mid-1990s, they accounted for almost two-thirds (64.3 percent) of this population, followed by Central and South Americans (13.4 percent), Puerto Ricans (10.6 percent), "Other Hispanic" (7.0 percent), and Cubans (4.7 percent).

Hispanic Americans comprise one of the nation's largest minority groups, second only to African Americans. In 1995, Latinos numbered 27 million while African Americans totaled 32 million. Hispanics are also among the fastest-growing parts of the population. They experienced a 53 percent growth rate between 1980 and 1990, a decade when the national population grew by only 9.8 percent. The Census Bureau projects that the population of Hispanic origin will increase to 31 million by the year 2000 and will be larger than the black population by 2005. If the present projections are correct, Hispanics will double their 1990 population by 2015,

and quadruple it by 2050. By that date, they will number 88 million. Almost one of every four Americans will be of Hispanic origin.

The dramatic increase in the Hispanic population is partially explained by a higher fertility (birth) rate compared to non-Hispanics. Sixty-two percent of the Mexican-American population were native-born Americans in 1995, and sizable numbers of Hispanic peoples have lived in America for several generations. Net immigration, however, is a powerful driving force, accounting for about one-third of the current population growth rate. It is estimated that 3,000 persons enter the United States daily, either legally or illegally, with the majority coming from Mexico and other Hispanic countries.

Early Spanish colonists founded several *pueblos* (towns) in the seventeenth and eighteenth centuries that are now major cities, including Santa Fe and Albuquerque, New Mexico; San Antonio, Texas; Tucson, Arizona; and San Diego, Los Angeles, Santa Barbara, Monterey, San Jose, San Francisco, and Sonoma, California.

Hispanics who arrived later have tended to settle near their point of entry into the United States. The majority of Mexican Americans today live in the southwestern states of Texas, California, Arizona, New Mexico, and Colorado. Cubans are largely concentrated in south Florida, where about 62 percent lived in the early 1990s. Roughly two-thirds of the Puerto Rican population on the mainland reside in New York, although there are sizable communities in other states, including New Jersey, Illinois, Florida, California, Pennsylvania, and Connecticut. South and Central Americans have increased their immigration in recent years, among them those fleeing unrest at home and entering the United States without legal documentation. These are a widely dispersed population, but they typically choose to settle in large metropolitan areas, especially greater New York, Los Angeles, Chicago, Miami, and Washington, D.C.

In fact, the increasing urbanization of all Hispanic Americans has been notable during recent decades. By the late 1990s, approximately 92 percent of them lived in or near cities. Among large cities, Los Angeles, California, ranks behind only Mexico City in the Western Hemisphere. Miami, Florida, has been called "the capital of Latin America" and ranks third in the nation in its percentage of Hispanic population. New York City's Puerto Ricans have been joined by other Hispanic peoples, including Central and South Americans, giving it a population with more different Hispanic origins than any city in the country.

The case of Mexican Americans resembles that of Native Americans in that they originally became minorities in the United States by losing their homeland rather than by immigrating voluntarily. Under terms of the treaty ending the war with Mexico in 1848, Mexico relinquished almost half of its territory, including most of present-day Texas, New Mexico, Colorado, Arizona, Utah, Nevada, and California. Former Mexican nationals who remained north of the Rio Grande River thus became the first Mexican Americans. These early settlers and later immigrants in the late nineteenth and early twentieth centuries were rural people. While a few were wealthy landowners, the majority were farm laborers, ranch hands, or members of remote mining or railroad crews that were largely isolated from non-Hispanic populations. This early occupational isolation slowed their assimilation and helped preserve the Spanish language. So, too, did the proximity to Mexico, which allowed frequent visits to the homeland and a continuing influx of new immigrants.

During the last half of the twentieth century, however, the rapid economic development and increasing urbanization of the Southwest provided impetus for Mexican Americans to leave their rural occupations and move to cities. By the 1980s, about 90 percent of Mexican Americans lived in urban places and engaged in nonfarm occupations. Many remained in the Southwest in such metropolitan areas as Los Angeles, Houston, San Antonio, Denver, Albuquerque, and El Paso. In addition, sizable numbers of former migrant farm laborers dropped out of the migrant stream permanently to live in large cities of the Midwest and Northeast, especially Chicago and New York.

The shift from rural to urban residence and the accompanying change from a simpler agrarian to a more complex modern economy created strong pressures for cultural change and greater assimilation into American life. Some Mexican Americans have left the barrios, or predominantly Hispanic neighborhoods. They speak English exclusively, and have relinquished many other elements of their traditional culture. Counterbalances to assimilation pressures also operate, however. Many low-income Mexican Americans remain isolated in ethnically segregated neighborhoods and have menial, poor-paying jobs. The flow of new immigrants from Mexico also continues almost unabated. Finally, barriers of prejudice and discrimination still impede assimilation in many areas of American life. The reluctance of the dominant society to share economic, political, and social power has been matched by mistrust of the Anglo world by many Latinos. Census figures in March 1994 showed that 86.6 percent of the Mexican foreign-born were not citizens, even though about one-third have been residents long enough to qualify for naturalization.

Puerto Rico became a colony of the United States at the end of the Spanish-American War and achieved commonwealth status in 1948. Anyone born on the island is a citizen of the United States and may travel to and from the mainland without legal restrictions. However, the citizenship of Puerto Ricans is ambiguous in its privileges and duties. They are subject to military service and federal laws, yet they may not vote in presidential elections, nor do they have voting representation in Congress.

The per capita income in Puerto Rico is less than half—and unemployment rates usually double and sometimes triple—that of the United States. Therefore, the economic pull of the mainland is strong. During the 1950s and 1960s, as airfares between San Juan and New York City declined, the section of Manhattan known variously as East Harlem, El Barrio, or Spanish Harlem became a densely populated center of Puerto Rican settlement.

However, Puerto Rican migrants are often disadvantaged by poor English-language skills, low educational status, lack of employment opportunities for unskilled labor, and racial prejudice toward anyone with darker skin. Thus, the discouraged return to the island even as hopeful newcomers arrive. In the 1970s more Puerto Ricans departed than entered the United States, but this trend reversed during the 1980s.

By 1990, census figures showed 2.7 million Puerto Ricans in the United States and 3.5 million in Puerto Rico. New York housed 1.7 million Latinos, of whom 49.5 percent were Puerto Ricans. Spanish Harlem was less important as a center for Puerto Rican settlement; instead, growing concentrations were found in the economically deprived areas of Brooklyn, the South Bronx, and nearby cities in New Jersey.

In addition, sizable Puerto Rican communities emerged in widely separated mainland cities, including Los Angeles, Miami, Cleveland, Philadelphia, and Hartford. In the locales outside the Northeast, many migrants are professionals or educated business entrepreneurs. Most migrated directly to their mainland destination from Puerto Rico, a departure from the previous pattern of New York providing a hub from which migrants dispersed.

Nevertheless, Puerto Ricans as a group remain the least economically successful of any of the major Latino populations in the United States. They are also poorer than African Americans. In 1990, the poverty rate for all Puerto Ricans was 40.6 percent, compared to 31.9 percent for blacks, 28.1 percent for all Latinos, and 10.7 percent for whites.

Small Cuban settlements have existed in Florida since the early nineteenth century, when workers were imported to communities organized around cigar manufacturing and other enterprises related to Cuba. But the presence of Cubans on a pronounced scale in the United States did not begin until 1959 when Castro's successful revolution caused many middle- and upper-class Cubans to flee. Because this first wave was generally drawn from educated, well-to-do, business or professional classes, Cubans have generally prospered in the United States. As a group, they have been the most economically successful of all Hispanic Americans, enjoying considerably higher median incomes, higher educational attainment, and lower poverty rates.

About 62 percent of Cuban Americans live in south Florida, with the heaviest concentration in Miami and its environs. Joining the Cubans in the 1980s were 300,000 other Hispanics, including Puerto Ricans, Nicaraguans, Salvadorans, Colombians, Guatemalans, and Hondurans. By the mid-1990s, half the population of Miami's Dade County was foreign-born and nearly 60 percent of its more than 1 million residents spoke a language other than English at home.

The Latinization of Miami stimulated the city's growth as a hub of international trade and transportation. In the 1990s, international trade through the city exceeded $26 billion. Miami's port district regularly reported multibillion dollar surpluses, and Miami International Airport was the nation's second busiest. About one-third of the country's 50 largest Hispanic-owned firms were located in the area. Cuban Americans, traditionally conservative in their political views, gained in political power, electing representatives not only to local posts but also to state and federal offices.

In the late 1990s Miami faced serious problems. Charges of corruption were leveled at high-ranking local officials, and the city's budgetary deficit created a financial crisis. There were severely depressed areas of the city, many with concentrations of illegal immigrants from Central America or the Caribbean. In addition, the city's ethnic diversity at times produced heightened interethnic and interracial tensions. Four major and several minor racial disturbances took place in Miami during the 1990s. Crime rates rose, gang violence became more frequent, and organized drug cartels were reputed to operate distribution networks into and out of the city.

It can be seen that adjustment to city life has been uneven. Recent decades have witnessed a growing number of upwardly mobile Latinos. By 1994 more than one-quarter of employed Hispanic males and more than one-half of employed Hispanic females had professional or managerial positions. At the same time, poverty and its attendant problems remained the lot of many urban Hispanics. In 1995, the overall rate of poverty among Hispanics reached 30.3 percent, for the first time exceeding black Americans whose poverty rate, although still excessive, had declined to 29.3.

Ethnically segregated, low-income Latino neighborhoods exist in numerous American cities, many experiencing severe social problems. The educational attainment of Hispanics remains lower than that of blacks and non-Hispanics, despite progress in recent years. The proportion of Hispanics with less than a fifth-grade education in the mid-1990s was 11.8 percent—more than 14 times greater than that of non-Hispanic whites (0.8 percent). Retention of the Spanish language, impoverished living conditions, and school districts sometimes unresponsive to Hispanic needs have led to poor school performance and exorbitant dropout rates, especially among Puerto Rican and Mexican-American youth. School districts in large central city districts face formidable problems in meeting the needs of students who lack English-speaking skills, dealing with high student turnover, and coping with discipline problems caused by the growing presence of juvenile gangs.

The radical Brown Power political movements of the 1960s and 1970s have largely subsided as the growing Latino electorate has been more successful working through established political processes. During the late 1980s and throughout the 1990s, Latinos elected city officials, state representatives, governors, and members of the U.S. Congress. Their growing presence augurs increasing political power at all levels of government. Despite these gains, leaders charge that government is often not responsive to Hispanic needs and that prejudice and discrimination have accelerated due to rising anti-immigrant sentiment at the close of the twentieth century.

The term *Hispanic American* clearly conceals enormous diversity. Many nationalities are included—each with distinct histories in their relationship to the United States. Furthermore, within each ethnic group salient differences are associated with such variables as socioeconomic class, educational attainment, length of residence, and the number of generations who have lived in America.

Latinos have contributed much to American life. Their music, art, and colorful celebrations have added zest to the urban scene. Many Hispanics have reached prominence in education, law, medicine, literature, science, government, the arts, and business. But it remains clear that large segments of this rapidly expanding population continue to confront significant and persistent problems that will require thoughtful and enlightened social policy in the years ahead.

—*Shirley Achor*

See also

Barrio.

References

Boswell, T. D., and J. R. Curtis. *The Cuban-American Experience.* Totowa, NJ: Rowman and Littlefield, 1984.

Browning, Harley L. *Mexican Immigrants and Mexican Americans.* Austin: University of Texas Press, 1986.

Chavez, Leo. R. *Shadowed Lives: Undocumented Immigrants in American Society.* Troy, MO: Harcourt Brace Jovanovich, 1992.

Falcón, Angelo. *Latino Voices: Mexican, Puerto Rican and Cuban Perspectives on American Politics.* Boulder, CO: Westview Press, 1992.

Fitzpatrick, Joseph P. *Puerto Rican Americans.* Englewood Cliffs, NJ: Prentice-Hall, 1987.

Garcia, Maria Cristina. *Havana, USA: Cuban Exiles and Cuban Americans in South Florida.* Berkeley: University of California Press, 1996.

Grebler, Leo, Joan W. Moore, and Ralph C. Guzman. *The Mexican American People: The Nation's Second Largest Minority.* New York: Free Press, 1970.

Jennings, James, and Monte Rivera, eds. *Puerto Rican Politics in Urban America.* Westport, CT: Greenwood Press, 1984.

Llanes, Jose. *Cuban Americans: Masters of Survival.* Springfield, NJ: Enslow, 1984.

Meltzer, Milton. *The Hispanic Americans.* New York: Thomas Y. Crowell, 1982.

Moore, Joan, and Harry Pachon. *Hispanics in the United States.* New York: Prentice-Hall, 1985.

Padilla, Felix M. *Latino Ethnic Consciousness.* Notre Dame, IN: University of Notre Dame Press, 1985.

Portes, Alejandro, and Robert Bach. *Latin Journey: Cuban and Mexican Immigrants in the United States.* Berkeley: University of California Press, 1985.

Torres, Andres. *Between Melting Pot and Mosaic: African Americans and Puerto Ricans in the New York Political Economy.* Philadelphia: Temple University Press, 1995.

U.S. Bureau of the Census. *The Hispanic Population in the United States: March 1993.* Current Population Reports, Series P20–475. Washington, DC: Government Printing Office, 1993.

———. *Population Profile of the United States, 1995.* Current Population Reports, Series P23–159. Washington, DC: Government Printing Office, 1995.

Home Insurance Building

The Home Insurance Building (1883–1885), located at the corner of La Salle and Adams Streets in Chicago, remains the most well known and the most influential building designed by William Le Baron Jenney (1832–1907). The significance of the building rests on its place in the history of the skyscraper. Although the building is often cited as the first skyscraper, this is still debated. Iron frames had been used in earlier buildings such as the St. Ouen warehouse in Paris, and George B. Post's New York Produce Exchange (1882–1884) provides a rival in the United States.

Whether considered the first skyscraper or an embryo- or a proto-skyscraper, most critics agree that the Home Insurance Building brought together technical achievements that set the standard for future tall buildings.

Originally nine stories tall (two more were added in 1891), the building rested on a concrete base over hardpan clay; each pier and column had its own separate footing. The first floor, sometimes called a superterrene foundation, consisted of granite blocks battered from four feet to two feet, ten inches. This granite base was surmounted by a metal frame of cast-iron columns and wrought-iron girders that reached the sixth floor. From the sixth floor to the roof, steel girders replaced the wrought iron. The bolted metal members created a frame whose stability remained unconstrained by the masonry walls. (In order to fireproof the building, Jenney encapsulated the iron columns in masonry.) The presence of this metal skeleton construction thus mitigated the need for thick masonry bearing walls to support the building. The structure had no interior masonry walls, and superimposed columns supported the floor loads. Carried by the outside girder of each floor, the exterior walls, made of unvitrified red pressed brick, simply sheathed the building and separated inside from outside. However, brick party walls

on the north and east sides of the building (included by order of the building commissioner) carried a portion of the building's weight, as did the granite first story.

While acknowledging the technical merits of the building, many historians criticize Jenney's formal articulation of the elevations. Although he professed to use ornament only as a complement to structure, the elevations of the Home Insurance Building reveal a plethora of historical ornamentation in its brick and terra cotta spandrels and pilasters, its iron lintels and mullions, and its cornices and parapet. In addition, the cornices at the third, sixth, and eighth stories encourage awkward proportions, and balconies over the entrances add distracting detail. According to Elmer Jensen, a member of Jenney's office, Jenney's deeper interests seem to have rested in the development of efficient and economic structures.

Trained in civil engineering at the École Centrale in Paris, Jenney developed the building's structural design with another engineer, George B. Whitney. The metal frame they created allowed him to meet the functional demands of a commercial building more easily, to increase the amount of usable floor space, to admit more natural light, and to decrease the use of costly masonry. The Home Insurance Building was demolished in 1931.

—*Marie Frank*

See also
Jenney, William Le Baron.
References
Condit, Carl. *The Chicago School of Architects and Their Critics: A History of Commercial and Public Building in the Chicago Area, 1875–1925.* Chicago: University of Chicago Press, 1964.

Randall, Frank. *History of the Development of Building Construction in Chicago.* Urbana: University of Illinois Press, 1949.

[Tallmadge, T.] "Was the Home Insurance Building in Chicago the First Skyscraper of Skeleton Construction?" *Architectural Record* 76 (1934): 113–118.

Turak, Theodore. *William Le Baron Jenney: A Pioneer of Modern Architecture.* Ann Arbor, MI: UMI Research Press, 1986.

Home Rule

Home rule is the power granted municipalities and counties to draft their own charters and control purely local matters without intervention from the state legislature. It may be authorized by the state constitution or by an act of the state legislature, but in either case the goal is to ensure the locality greater flexibility in structuring its own government. Moreover, home rule is intended to relieve the legislature of the burden of handling local legislation and to exempt the local unit from state interference in matters best dealt with at the local level.

Such state interference was rampant during the nineteenth century. Courts viewed municipal corporations as creatures of state legislatures that had the power to establish, alter, or destroy city governments at will. Though municipal charters were generally formulated by city leaders, they had to be submitted to state legislatures for approval. Any group favored by a majority of state lawmakers could revise the charter or secure special legislation to further its economic interests or political ends.

To stop special interests from appealing to the state legislature, St. Louis leaders secured the nation's first home rule provision in the Missouri Constitution of 1875. California's Constitution of 1879 embodied a similar provision, and Washington became a home rule state in 1889, with Minnesota following seven years later. Home rule became one of the chief planks in the Progressive reform platform of the early twentieth century, for state legislative interference was deemed conducive to corruption. Responding to reform demands, Maryland, Ohio, Michigan, Nebraska, Oklahoma, Texas, Colorado, Arizona, and Oregon all adopted constitutional provisions for home rule during the first two decades of the twentieth century. According to these and later home rule provisions, local commissions were to draft municipal charters and then submit them to the city's voters for approval. Moreover, municipalities were authorized to exercise control over all municipal matters but could not legislate on subjects of statewide concern.

In the ensuing decades, courts struggled to differentiate municipal affairs from state concerns. For example, in the mid-1920s Ohio courts decided that home rule did not allow a city to require a building permit for a school, to create a municipal court, or to license automobiles owned by city residents. Schools, courts, and auto licensing were not municipal matters and thus not within the control of cities. Defining the line of authority between home rule cities and states remained a troublesome task for courts throughout the twentieth century.

Despite the problem of defining home rule powers, the idea remained popular among devotees of good-government reform and was also applied to counties, especially heavily populated metropolitan counties that needed a form of government better suited to urbanization. In 1911, California adopted the first constitutional provision for county home rule, and one year later Los Angeles County voters approved the nation's first home rule county charter. By the late 1980s, 23 states offered counties the option of adopting a home rule charter. During the late twentieth century, the states were moving, then, toward greater local control over the governmental structure of both cities and metropolitan counties.

—*Jon C. Teaford*

See also
Fragmentation of Municipal Government; States and Cities.

References
McBain, Howard Lee. *The Law and the Practice of Municipal Home Rule.* New York: Columbia University Press, 1916.
McGoldrick, Joseph D. *Law and Practice of Municipal Home Rule 1916–1930.* New York: Columbia University Press, 1933.
Mott, Rodney L. *Home Rule for America's Cities.* Chicago: American Municipal Association, 1949.

Homelessness

In the 1980s the homeless became a familiar presence in many communities across the United States. A *New York Times*/CBS News poll taken in January 1992 asked Americans to respond to the question, "Do you think that when most people see the homeless they feel upset, or do you think that most people have gotten so used to seeing the homeless that they don't feel upset by them?" Of the respondents, 42 percent felt that people were upset by the sight of the homeless; 44 percent felt that people were not upset. By age group, 45 percent of people 65 and older responded that people felt upset by the sight of the homeless, compared to only 35 percent of people 18 to 29 years old. Of those 18 to 29 years old, 55 percent felt that "people have gotten so used to seeing the homeless that they don't feel upset by them." In other words, people who came of age in the 1980s were considerably more likely to accept the existence of homelessness as a normal part of the social landscape than those who reached adulthood in preceding decades.

If the homeless have become a familiar sight, they have nonetheless remained a poorly understood phenomenon. Estimates of the number of homeless persons in the United States seem to vary with every academic study, every interest group, and every presidential administration that has addressed the question. In the 1980s, under conservative Republican administrations, official federal studies estimated the total homeless population at between 250,000 and 600,000. When the Democrats returned to the White House in 1993, a federal task force on homelessness concluded that as many as 7 million Americans had been homeless at some point in the late 1980s. These widely differing estimates reflect differences in definitions. Are only those who are found in shelters on any given night part of the homeless population? Should the definition of homelessness be broadened from the "chronically homeless" to include the "episodically homeless" and the "precariously housed"? Varying definitions embody different sets of values and policy prescriptions.

The Steward B. McKinney Homeless Assistance Act of 1987, the first federal legislation designed as a comprehensive response to the homeless problem, offered a broad but still rather vague definition of a homeless person: "1) An individual who lacks a fixed, regular and adequate nighttime residence; and 2) an individual who has a primary nighttime residence that is A) a supervised publicly or privately operated shelter designed to provide temporary living accommodations (including welfare hotels, congregate shelters, and transitional housing for the mentally ill); B) an institution that provides a temporary residence for individuals intended to be institutionalized; or C) a public or private place not designated for, or ordinarily used as, a regular sleeping accommodation for human beings." No consensus, however, existed as to what constituted a "fixed, regular, and adequate nighttime residence."

Like the question of numbers, the demographic characteristics of the homeless remain hotly contested. Some see a homeless population that consists largely of the mentally ill and those who abuse drugs and alcohol, that is, people whose personal inadequacies accounted for their homelessness. President Ronald Reagan told a television interviewer in December 1988 that he believed that a "large percentage" of the homeless were "retarded" people who had voluntarily left the institutions in which they had earlier been housed. Others regard the homeless as part of a large and shifting population of inadequately housed poor people, whose vulnerability to homelessness was primarily due to economic and social forces beyond their control. The Reverend Thomas J. Harvey, president of Catholic Charities, USA, told a reporter in 1991 that the current economic recession was a good reminder "that there are capricious forces at work" increasing homelessness and poverty, and "explodes the myths that the poor are poor out of choice."

Complicating the debate over homelessness is the fact that the most visible portion of the homeless population tends to be made up of those least likely to evoke sympathy from casual observers: mostly male, mostly minorities, some obviously engaging in substance abuse or suffering from mental illness. The average citizen is much more likely to have encountered an aggressive, homeless, male panhandler than a homeless mother and her children. In 1988, the U.S. Department of Housing and Urban Development (HUD) produced a "National Survey of Shelters for the Homeless," which found that, indeed, 45 percent of the homeless population consisted of single men and that 34 percent of the homeless population suffered from mental illness. On the other hand, in contradiction to popular stereotypes, HUD also found that 40 percent of the homeless population consisted of families, 26 percent consisted of children under the age of 18, and 14 percent consisted of single women.

The current crisis of homelessness dates to the late 1970s and early 1980s; some point to media coverage of homeless people in the vicinity of the 1980 Democratic National Convention, held in New York City's Madison Square Garden, as the moment when homelessness first entered public consciousness as a social problem. There have, however, been persons without permanent shelter in America since colonial times. Attitudes toward homeless people have varied over the years, but there are some common themes. One recurrent motif, as historian Michael Katz has noted, is the attempt to divide the homeless population, and the poor in general, into favored and despised categories. In the colonial era, treatment of the poor tended to mirror laws in England, which divided the poor into "neighbors" or "strangers." Communities were obligated to assist those who were permanent residents but were free to deport impoverished strangers to their place of origin. As agriculture gave way to industry, migrants in search of employment became more common and, in an increasingly mobile society, membership in a particular community became more difficult to determine. In place of neighbors and strangers, the poor now began to be thought of as "deserving" or "undeserving." The deserving poor—widows, orphans, those too old or crippled to work—were considered to have some claim on public conscience and private charity, but able-bodied adults without employment or shelter were believed to have brought about their own troubles through some flaw in their own character, such as intemperance, improvidence, or the like.

In the years after the Civil War, hundreds of thousands of men wandered from town to town seeking employment, public relief, or a handout. Though scorned for their alleged unwillingness to work, these "tramps" actually played a vital economic role as a mobile reserve labor force. Some were skilled artisans, such as carpenters, while the unskilled provided labor for seasonal industries, such as agriculture, and extractive industries, such as lumbering and mining. Some of these wandering men found permanent jobs and homes, but hundreds of thousands of others remained migratory laborers. Neighborhoods sprang up in many cities devoted to housing and servicing these men, characterized by flophouses, saloons, pawnshops, cheap restaurants, used clothing stores, and religious missions. These areas became known collectively as "skid row"—the name deriving from the nineteenth-century waterfront district of Seattle, where timber was "skidded" along greased log roads until it reached the water where it could be floated to sawmills.

In the twentieth century, skid rows shrank in size and changed in character. Increasing mechanization of agriculture and extractive industries reduced the demand for migratory labor (the remaining demand in agriculture was satisfied by a workforce that was largely minority, often foreign-born, and thus largely "invisible" to the general population). By the early decades of the twentieth century, skid rows came to be associated in the public mind with a more or less permanent "home guard" of alcoholics and other "derelicts," overwhelmingly white, male, and aging. In the Depression of the 1930s, the skid row population expanded as did the ramshackle communities of scrap-wood shacks that grew up on the edge of many cities and towns, known as "Hoovervilles." But with the coming of World War II and full employment, homelessness ceased to be a major social concern.

Skid row neighborhoods shrank dramatically in size and population in the prosperous decades that followed the war. So it came as a surprise in the late 1970s and early 1980s when homeless people once again could be found sleeping on park benches and subway grates. Unlike the skid row homeless, the new homeless population was younger and more mixed sexually and racially than the stereotypical "Bowery bum." And, unlike their predecessors, the new homeless were not concentrated in skid rows. Instead, they could be found throughout the urban community.

Grasping for a historical analogy, in the early 1980s the media revived memories and images of the Depression. In the "Reagan Recession" of 1981–1982, newspapers and news broadcasts carried many stories about unemployed "rust belt" workers, sleeping in their cars or on the streets as they searched for employment in the "Sunbelt" communities of the Southwest. Parallels were drawn between the experience of these homeless workers and the "Okies" of the 1930s. "Homeless Crisscross US, Until Their Cars and Their Dreams Break Down," a headline in the *New York Times* reported in December 1982, noting in the story that followed that the House Subcommittee on Housing and Economic Development had scheduled "the first Congressional hearing on homelessness in America since the Depression."

Within a few years, however, the media was no longer portraying the homeless as a reincarnation of displaced "Okies" during the Depression. If the 1980s were the 1930s reborn, then it followed that the federal government had a responsibility to return to the philosophy and programs of the New Deal. But that was not a message that many Americans were prepared to hear, especially since the Democratic opposition to the Reagan administration was stressing its own willingness to discard the unpopular liberal policies of bygone years. The conventional wisdom became that "you can't solve problems by throwing money at them." Distinctions between the "deserving" and "undeserving" poor once again came into vogue. Soup kitchens and shelters, not expensive government entitlement or public housing programs, were the order of the day.

The reasons for the resurgence of homelessness in the 1980s are complicated and controversial. Among the causes most frequently cited are the deinstitutionalization of mental patients, the deindustrialization of the urban economy, and the gentrification of urban neighborhoods.

The deinstitutionalization of mental patients resulted from public outcry against the often squalid or brutal conditions in American mental hospitals, whose population peaked at over 550,000 in the 1950s. Responding to demands for reform, in 1963 President John F. Kennedy proposed phasing out custodial care of the mentally ill, and Congress passed the Mental Retardation Facilities and Community Mental Health Centers Construction Act later that year, providing federal funding for outpatient and emergency treatment centers for the mentally ill. State mental hospitals began to discharge large numbers of patients. As a result, the mental hospital patient population declined to less than 138,000 by 1980. But the federal government reneged on its commitment to provide new forms of treatment for the former state hospital patients. Only 700 of the originally planned 2,500 community mental health centers were opened in the 1960s and 1970s, and these often wound up serving a more affluent and less severely disturbed clientele than the population previously confined to state mental hospitals.

The importance of "deinstitutionalization" can, however, easily be exaggerated as a cause of homelessness. Throughout most of the 1960s and 1970s, the recently discharged mentally ill (and those who were never admitted to mental hospitals due to more stringent entry requirements) were not, in fact, reduced to homelessness. Only a small percentage of the homeless population went directly from institutions to living on the street. Many found shelter in halfway houses or single room occupancy hotels (SROs). But changes in urban neighborhoods, and cutbacks in federal social spending, reduced those opportunities. When the Reagan administration slashed federal spending in the early 1980s, nearly 500,000 recipients were cut from the rolls of the Social Security Disability Insurance program. Nearly one-third of these were people suffering from psychiatric disabilities, and many of them wound up living on the street.

The deindustrialization of the country and the gentrification of urban neighborhoods have also led to increased homelessness. With the decline of the manufacturing industries that had once provided reasonably stable and well-paid employment for working-class Americans, urban economies have become service-oriented and increasingly polarized. Low-paying clerical, sales, restaurant, and health-care occupations have become the main sources of employment at one end; and the high-paying financial, legal, medical, and management professions have expanded at the other. The coexistence of two economic populations, one characterized by low income and uncertain employment and the other by high social status and considerable disposable income, has not proven easy. This economic polarization has been manifested in spatial terms at the neighborhood level, by enclaves of urban "gentry" (or middle-class professionals) forming in inner-city working-class neighborhoods.

When a neighborhood begins to change in this way, housing costs rise, local homeowners sell their properties for windfall profits, and low-income tenants (particularly the elderly and others living on fixed incomes) are displaced from rental housing. Powerful pressures were brought to bear on city officials to encourage such changes. A declining urban tax base and cuts in federal funding for local programs forced city officials to develop ways of attracting residents who pay higher taxes and who do not use underfunded social service programs. As the manufacturing sector has declined, other sources of investment have been the redevelopment of urban waterfronts for recreational and commercial functions, the growth of the tourist industry and construction of urban hotel and convention complexes, corporate office-space development, and the growth of "trendy" retail and restaurant districts. Inexpensive forms of housing like SROs have been demolished through downtown redevelopment projects, while tens of thousands of other low-rent housing units have been allowed to deteriorate, or have been abandoned, or have been destroyed by arson.

In a 1986 study of displacement in New York City, sociologist Peter Marcuse estimated that from 1970 to 1980, between 10,000 and 40,000 households were displaced annually by gentrification alone. Personal vulnerability to homelessness (because of mental illness, substance abuse, or other causes) is exacerbated by changes in the urban economy and housing market. Sociologist James Wright has argued, "An inadequate low-income housing supply is probably not the proximate cause of homelessness in most cases, but it is the ultimate cause of homelessness in all cases."

By the 1990s, homelessness seemed an insoluble problem to many Americans, and public opinion polls recorded a marked drop in sympathy for the homeless. In San Francisco and New York, voters turned out of office mayors perceived to be too soft on the homeless. A number of private agencies and religious and advocacy groups have experimented with strategies to provide transitional housing and programs for the homeless and to encourage the construction of low-income housing. While these initiatives have often enjoyed modest local success, there have been no comparable efforts by federal, state, or local governments to end homelessness.

—*Maurice Isserman*

See also
Flophouses; Hoovervilles; Skid Row.
References
Blau, Joel. *The Visible Poor: Homelessness in the United States.* New York: Oxford University Press, 1992.
Fantasia, Rick, and Maurice Isserman. *Homelessness: A Sourcebook.* New York: Facts on File, 1994.
Jencks, Christopher. *The Homeless.* Cambridge, MA: Harvard University Press, 1994.
Wolch, Jennifer R. *Malign Neglect: Homelessness in an American City.* San Francisco: Jossey-Bass, 1993.

Homeownership

Although varying by location, age of household, race, and ethnicity, high levels of homeownership have characterized the American urban and suburban experience. Studies of social mobility and immigrants in nineteenth- and early-twentieth-century communities, for example, indicate high rates of homeownership not only among the middle class but also among unskilled workers. Moreover, immigrant rates of homeownership frequently surpassed those of the native-born population. In 1900, immigrant rates in cities of 100,000 or more ranged from 11 to 58 percent, compared to 15 to 40 percent for the native-born population. By 1920, overall homeownership reached 45 percent and hovered around that mark until the suburban boom after World War II, which saw the rate surpass 60 percent in 1960. Since then, rates have increased only slightly. The best estimates suggest that historical rates of owning homes have far exceeded those of European nations and that contemporary rates are about double those of Western European nations.

Several factors account for these high rates of ownership. Since at least the publication of the song *Home Sweet Home* in 1823, the desire for homeownership has been deeply embedded in the American value system. Writers, publicists, and business and political leaders have all advocated homeownership as symbolizing success, fostering self-fulfillment, and promoting civic virtue, thrift, conservative social and political values, and social stability. Consistent with the Old World emphasis on property accumulation, these admonitions also found ready acceptance among the foreign-born population who viewed homeownership as a means of enhancing their social status and providing security against the uncertainties of urban-industrial life.

Affluence, the relative affordability of housing, and access to credit have made the aspiration for homeownership a reality. From the inception of the United States as a nation until at least the 1970s, Americans have had a higher per capita income than Europeans. Concomitantly, relatively low population density and historically low transportation costs resulted in housing lots that cost only one-fourth to one-half the price of comparable land in Europe. Similarly, balloon frame construction has kept building costs below those of other industrialized nations. Last, access to credit has enabled large numbers of Americans to become homeowners; as early as 1890, an array of financial institutions provided mortgages for over 25 percent of all homes. Public policy has further encouraged homeownership, particularly on the fringes of urban areas. In the second half of the nineteenth century, cities spent substantial portions of their budgets to extend transportation lines and city services to outlying areas.

By further reducing the cost of housing and increasing access to credit, homeownership has been stimulated by federal policies even more in the twentieth century. The establishment of the Federal Housing Administration in 1934 and the Veterans Administration in 1944 provided programs of national mortgage insurance that increased access to credit, reduced the cost of mortgages, increased the amount that could be borrowed, and extended the length of mortgages. These programs spawned a sharp increase in the level of homeownership, particularly in the suburbs, after World War II. Subsequent federal policies, such as Fannie Mae (FNMA, Federal National Mortgage Association) and Ginnie Mae (GNMA, Guaranteed National Mortgage Association), not only increased accessibility but also encouraged the flow of mortgage money to the fast-growing areas of the South and West.

Unequal access to credit under these programs, however, has accounted for differences in homeownership between black and white Americans and between central cities and suburbs. The Highway Acts of 1916 and 1921 and the Interstate Highway Act of 1956 also helped contain housing costs by opening vast tracts of land on the periphery of cities. Likewise, tax codes, beginning with rising income tax rates during World War II, have subsidized homeownership (estimated at $53 *billion* in 1984) by allowing homeowners to deduct the cost of mortgage interest and property taxes from the income reported to the Internal Revenue Service.

Historically high rates of homeownership and the factors accounting for them have profoundly affected American life. Together, these conditions have fostered increasingly low-density cities and rapid suburban growth. Given the importance of the property tax for financing urban government, widespread ownership has directly tied a broad spectrum of citizens to local politics. The identification of property accumulation with social advancement and middle-class status has also reinforced Americans' conception of themselves as middle class. For working-class Americans, and particularly European immigrants, homeownership not only symbolized "making it" but also provided a modicum of control over their social and economic environment and an improved standard of living. In short, widespread homeownership has been intimately related to the physical structure and political nature of cities, the middle-class view of American society, and the assimilation of immigrants.

—*Gordon W. Kirk, Jr.*

See also
Balloon Frame Construction; Single-Family Detached House.
References
Barrows, Robert G. "Beyond the Tenement: Patterns of American Urban Housing, 1870–1930." *Journal of Urban History* 9 (1983): 395–420.
Jackson, Kenneth. *Crabgrass Frontier: The Suburbanization of the United States.* New York: Oxford University Press, 1985.
Kirk, Carolyn Tyirin, and Gordon W. Kirk, Jr. "The Impact of the City on Home Ownership: A Comparison of Immigrants and Native Whites at the Turn of the Century." *Journal of Urban History* 7 (1981): 471–498.
Kirk, Gordon W., Jr., and Carolyn Tyirin Kirk. "Home Is Where the Heart Is: Immigrant Mobility and Home Ownership." In Timothy Walch, ed., *Immigrant America: European Ethnicity in the United States,* 67–88. New York: Garland, 1994.
Monkkonen, Eric H. *America Becomes Urban: The Development of U.S. Cities and Towns, 1780–1880.* Berkeley: University of California Press, 1988.

Hoovervilles

Hoovervilles were squatter settlements during the Depression of the 1930s. They acquired their descriptive name in an effort to blame President Herbert Hoover for his reluctance to initiate radical measures to combat the dislocation caused by the Depression. Despite the association of squatting with the Hoover presidency, Hoovervilles thrived during the Roosevelt administration and continued their presence in many cities until America became involved in World War II.

Located on the edges of cities and in rural regions throughout the United States, Hoovervilles occupied previously vacant land and provided the homeless with a cost-free and sometimes stable, although miserable, living arrangement. Ideally, a Hooverville had convenient access to a water source and was located near employment and transportation. Many temporary squatter homes were constructed from burlap sacks, corrugated steel, cardboard, scrap wood, and other scavenged materials. Personal resources, including tents and rickety automobiles, also were used to build the makeshift shacks. The squatting men, women, and children settled in groups that varied in size from a few families to hundreds of people. The larger settlements tended to be relatively permanent, occasionally surviving the Depression, while smaller Hoovervilles were often routinely demolished by local police who used vagrancy laws and health ordinances to oust squatters.

Hooverville squatters usually lived in tension with their neighbors. In some places, especially in rural regions, squatters provided a necessary cheap labor supply, and their presence was tolerated for the duration of the employment season. In other places, squatters had neither work nor a means of "moving on" and encountered intense hostility from local residents who feared that squatters would drain relief budgets and overburden social services.

Federal, state, and local governments all hesitated to assume responsibility for the care of transients and squatters. State and local residency requirements ensured that aid was dispersed only to the local resident poor, not to "wanderers." Since most squatters kept moving, they were unable to establish the residency required to receive assistance. With the establishment of the Federal Transient Bureau (FTB) in 1933, the federal government temporarily acknowledged that it was the only governing body with sufficient scope to care for this mobile population. However, the FTB was disbanded after only two years. For the duration of the Depression, New Deal assistance programs failed to ameliorate squatters' living conditions.

California encountered a particularly severe squatting problem as migrants flocked to the state from the impoverished dust bowl region. These southwesterners, or "Okies" as they were derogatorily dubbed, were lured to California by tales of abundant crops and jobs. Unable to find steady employment or obtain relief, many of these migrants found themselves trapped in Hoovervilles, unable to improve their condition. The plight of California's squatters gained national attention late in the Depression. John Steinbeck sympathetically portrayed their situation in his immensely popular and controversial novel, *The Grapes of Wrath*.

—*Christina Sheehan Gold*

References

Crouse, Joan. *The Homeless Transient in the Great Depression: New York State, 1929–1941*. Albany: State University of New York Press, 1986.

———. "The Remembered Men: Transient Camps in New York State, 1933–1935." *New York History* 71 (1990): 68–94.

Gregory, James N. *American Exodus: The Dust Bowl Migration and Okie Culture in California*. New York: Oxford University Press, 1989.

Simon, Harry. "Towns without Pity: A Constitutional and Historical Analysis of Official Efforts to Drive Homeless Persons from American Cities." *Tulane Law Review* 66 (1992): 631–676.

Hopper, Edward (1882–1967)

Painter Edward Hopper is America's Michelangelo of the urban scene. His pictures of tired old buildings and their lonely denizens are all the more poignant in that nature—the world outside the city—is always present tacitly, in the form of morning light or evening shadow. In the man-made, hard-edged city, Hopper seems to be saying, the normal God-given rhythm of the day has been subverted.

There is one place that amounts to a signature in Hopper's work—a two-story row of red brick storefronts, a commercial block of the Garfield era with dingy flats upstairs and awnings and faded gilt letters on the downstairs windows. The artist began using this trademark motif in the mid-1920s, after he had returned from Paris and immersed himself in a lifelong meditation on American urban geography. Over time, in a powerful series of canvases that now seem essentially Hopperesque, he explored the meaning of this single diagnostic structure.

In *Early Sunday Morning* (1930), the dark, ominous shadow of a rising skyscraper looms over it. The building slumbers wearily in the path of utopian progress—but not, one senses, for much longer. In *1 A. M.* (1948), it stands on the edge of a small city, near a patch of forest; already, long before the advent of the golden arches, any anonymous street corner in the nation looks just like any other. In *Drug Store* (1927), the red brick structure forms the background for a garish window display as, in fact, such humble buildings once made up the unexamined fabric of the American city. Glimpsed through the spare interior of the diner in *Nighthawks* (1942), each separate window comments on the isolation and loneliness of the nocturnal coffee drinkers quarantined in their plateglass cage on New York's Greenwich Avenue. Hopper's old brick building houses every ill the city ever spawned, every anxious question ever asked about its building up and tearing down. Yet, because the row of storefronts was cheap and mass-produced to start with, Hopper's work defies the viewer to sugarcoat such places with nostalgia.

Before his name became a household word, Hopper earned his living doing illustrations for magazines aimed at the restaurant trade and businessmen. The themes carried over into his paintings, works that explore how the urbanite must perform essentially private functions in public. Thus, he examines the etiquette of dining out in restaurants and Automats, conversing in hotel lobbies, managing an office romance, or peering in on intimate scenes enacted in lighted nighttime windows. The city, he submits, makes performers and voyeurs of us all. His buildings are the sets on which the poignant drama of American life is enacted.

Hopper's views of the landscape outside the city read the countryside according to the sensibilities of a person accustomed to peering in at store windows and looking at pictures of tourist sites in magazines. His is a nature framed and processed; a Hopper landscape is what lies just beyond the lights over the gas pumps, just across the railroad track. It is the postcard vista on the other side of the motel's picture window, vaguely unreal, infinitely sad.

—*Karal Ann Marling*

References

Hobbs, Robert. *Edward Hopper*. New York: Harry W. Abrams, 1983.

Levin, Gail. *Edward Hopper: The Art and the Artist*. New York: W. W. Norton, 1980.

Marling, Karal Ann. *Edward Hopper*. New York: Rizzoli, 1992.

Horsecars

Horsecar lines, in which horses pulled passenger cars over lightweight rails in city streets, were the principal form of public transportation in American cities for much of the second half of the nineteenth century. They began supplanting horse-drawn omnibuses (in which the cars were not pulled on rails) around 1850 because of their smoother ride and larger passenger capacity. The New York and Harlem Railroad began passenger service in 1852 in lower Manhattan and served as a model for horsecar operations elsewhere. Boston copied New York's system in 1856, and by the end of the decade horsecar lines were running in Philadelphia, Cincinnati, Chicago, and elsewhere. By the early 1880s, every major city and many minor ones had well-developed horsecar systems. Some 3,000 miles of track, 18,000 cars, 100,000 horses, and 35,000 employees moved more than 1.2 billion passengers annually. The success of horsecar lines in the United States prompted cities in Europe and South America to copy this American city railway. Parisians called their premier street railway simply *L'Américain.*

Most horsecar lines operated within city limits. Individual lines tended to be short, not more than five miles, because horses were unable to handle long distances without frequent changes. Travelers living beyond the end of the line were obliged to walk home. In some cases, a stage or omnibus might provide service into more distant suburbs. A few outlying communities might be served by a steam dummy or light suburban railway that ran a few miles farther out.

Those living in the city enjoyed convenient, cheap service. The cars might move slowly, perhaps at a rate of five to six miles per hour, but fares were low, generally 5 cents, and the cars ran only minutes apart during normal hours on heavily traveled routes. Nighttime service was much more limited and did not exist on poorly patronized routes. Some lines charged double fares for night service, but thrifty travelers could buy daytime tickets for only 4 cents apiece in booklets of 25. Even these low fares were too high for many working-class people, where the dollar-a-day wage prevailed. Poor folks tended to walk while the middle class rode the cars.

The typical horsecar was 24 feet long overall, 7 feet wide, and had open platforms at each end with exit/entrance doors. Benches along the sides provided seating for 22 passengers, but during rush hour or at other busy times, a fully loaded car might carry as many as 90 passengers, which was an amazing load for a vehicle weighing only 4,800 pounds. With few exceptions, no heating was provided in cold weather, and lighting was generally limited to two small oil lamps at either end of the car.

Two men operated the car. The driver stood on the front platform to manage the horses and manual brake. The conductor worked the rear platform to collect fares, deal with passenger questions, and generally supervise operation of the car. While these cars were built for hard service, and got it, they were far from drab. In fact, they were painted bright colors and highlighted in gilt or silver-leaf lettering, scrolls, and strips. Varnished wooden interiors and polished brass hardware added to their luster. Color sometimes designated destinations; for example, route 1, the Elm Street line, might also be known as the Red Line because its cars were painted predominantly red. Route 4, the Navy Yard line, might have yellow cars, and so on. In a large metropolis, the downtown streets were a rainbow of red, blue, green, yellow, and white horsecars. Illiterate folks unable to decipher words or numbers found this color code helpful in getting around town; just take a red car, and it would get you home.

These early animal-powered urban railways carried millions of passengers annually and performed a vital transportation service, but their profits were meager. The problems were easy to identify—high operating costs mostly attributable to the means of power. Horses could surely do the job but not very economically. They were costly, could only work a few hours a day, and required careful feeding and fairly elaborate health care. Horses were retired from street railway service after about four years, when they could be sold for about three-quarters of their initial cost. The process of stocking fresh horses was never ending. So was sweeping up the city streets: city railway horses dropped tons of manure and countless gallons of urine onto the pavement every day. Surely, people thought, there must be more economical and sanitary ways to propel the cars.

Almost from the inception of street railways, inventors attempted to harness steam power plants to city cars. None of these vehicles proved very successful except in suburban service. Steam power succeeded notably on main line railways and elsewhere, but it failed miserably on city streets. Compressed air, ammonia, and spring-powered cars fared no better. Cable railways worked well in many cities, but they were very expensive to build and costly to maintain.

The answer was found in electric traction. After a decade or so of experimentation, practical electric cars were available by the late 1880s. These vehicles were faster and larger than the cars pulled by animals. They were much cheaper to operate, and their installation costs were not excessive. The transit industry responded to the new technology with enthusiasm. By 1890 one-sixth of American street railways had been electrified, and by the beginning of the twentieth century the conversion was complete except for a few minor lines. The gaily painted little horsecars vanished from the urban scene in a single decade. The clip-clop of the double teams and the tinkle of the harness bells was gone as well.

—*John White*

See also
Dummy Lines (Steam Street Railways); Omnibuses; Streetcars.

References
Middleton, William D. *Time of the Trolley.* Rev. 2d ed. San Marino, CA: Golden West Books, 1987.
Miller, John A. *Fares Please: From Horsecars to Streamliners.* New York: D. Appleton-Century, 1941.
Rowsome, Frank. *Trolley Car Treasury.* New York: McGraw-Hill, 1957.
White, John H. "Horse Power." *American Heritage of Invention & Technology* 8 (1992): 40–57.

Hospitals

For most of American history, life has revolved around small communities and narrow personal contacts. The wide variety of groups that made up cities, while close to each other physically, lived in highly structured communities separated from each other by culture, ethnicity, and language. Until after the Civil War, the vast majority of health services were provided by informal networks of caretakers, families, and friends whose construction of health care reflected local customs, social practices, and religious beliefs. Care for society's dependents was provided in the home, the community, or not at all.

Before the Civil War, only a handful of hospitals existed. New York Hospital, Massachusetts General Hospital, and Pennsylvania General Hospital were the oldest nongovernmental institutions in the nation and were generally administered by lay trustees, many of them descendants of early Dutch and English settlers. The few large pre–Civil War institutions often served as long-term care institutions for the city's dependent poor, travelers, or the mentally ill. Others, such as Bellevue and Kings County in New York and Brooklyn, were municipal institutions, sometimes appendages to public penitentiaries or almshouses.

After the 1870s, however, hospitals began to be built throughout the growing cities of the Northeast and Midwest. Generally, these diverse institutions served a wide variety of social and medical needs. Very often the elite of a community, generally its merchants, businessmen, and clergy, would initiate and sponsor "charity hospitals" to serve the working class and dependent poor. Hospitals generally differed from each other in their religious and ethnic orientation, source of financial support, size, medical orientation, and the types of services they provided.

Most of these hospitals reflected the idiosyncratic qualities of their community. Specific hospitals catered specifically to Jews, Catholics, Italians, Germans, or blacks. Children's hospitals cared for orphans, and maternity hospitals, often located in working-class neighborhoods, were as much a shelter for unwed mothers as a maternity medical service. In communities with a significant number of elderly and dependent persons, local merchants often organized a home or hospital for "incurables" or the chronically ill.

Most of the institutions that developed were small, local facilities sponsored by local charities to serve working-class and poor patients almost exclusively. Because they reflected the social diversity of their ethnic and religious sponsors and their working-class patients, there was no "typical" hospital. Many looked and functioned like homes or churches and could not be readily distinguished from other structures and organizations in the community.

The hospitals that developed during the years of early growth before 1920 were organized around different ideas of purpose and function. First, there was little interest or concern with establishing "standardized" institutions. In fact, most hospitals were tiny in comparison to even the smallest of today's institutions and were seemingly established haphazardly. Many institutions showed a degree of spontaneous organization characteristic of the fluidity of nineteenth-century social organization. Small hospitals (those with 50 beds or less) had an average life span of barely five years, often being organized and disbanded with a frequency that would shock modern observers.

Not only were these small hospitals liable to close at any moment, but they were also in danger of immediate eviction. During the late nineteenth century, the economic and social organization of East Coast cities changed fundamentally, and those changes placed tremendous pressure on charitable institutions, not only forcing them to adjust to new demands for services but also forcing them to relocate and adjust to changing uses of land and space. As older walking cities gave way to new industrial and commercial centers, the land occupied by many institutions often increased in value. Streets were widened, electric trolley tracks were laid in many cities, elevated train lines were introduced, and new means of personal transportation such as the bicycle and automobile forced city governments to pave streets and keep them clean. Sleepy commercial shopping districts that served a local clientele suddenly emerged as busy, bustling downtowns with large department stores, massive traffic jams, and crowded streets. Stores, warehouses, and government offices all demanded space in growing downtowns. Older communities were destroyed as people moved out to new "streetcar suburbs" that began to develop on the periphery of central cities. As a new, economically segregated city emerged, institutions developed identities specific to particular classes that tended to undermine the older identities based on ethnicity.

The relative fluidity of hospitals in the nineteenth century might seem to have been a sign of weakness or instability, but this is only partially accurate. While individual institutions were subject to tremendous social, demographic, and economic pressures that often forced them to move or go out of existence, the system as a whole flourished. The number of charity hospitals increased throughout the period, and the system continuously experimented with form and function. The tremendous variety of institutions that served the dependent poor in nineteenth-century American cities gave remarkable dynamism and stability to the system as a whole.

Institutions at the start of the twentieth century were not solely medical facilities. Rather, they provided shelter, food, and care to the needy. Because the upper and middle classes generally received care in their homes, hospitals treated members of the working class who were forced to become dependent on the larger society during hard times. This hardship took various forms for different segments of working-class communities. Illness created some dependence, but social circumstances often caused the growing dependence of part of the population. In fact, the modern urban hospital originated in the variety of forms that dependence, not illness, took in the late nineteenth century.

Within this context, the nineteenth-century institution played a varied and ambiguous role. It functioned simultaneously as a health-care facility, a social service, and an agent of social control. Admission to one of the many hospitals depended less on a patient's medical condition than on a determination by wealthy patrons that a patient's physical and social circumstances made him or her an appropriate candidate for admission.

In many ways, hospitals reflected the diversity of the communities that sponsored, organized, and populated them. The values of trustees, patients, and workers were often incorporated into the very nature of the institution. Assumptions regarding the meaning of dependence and disease, their moral context, and their relationship to poverty or occupation actively helped shape the institutions that addressed the special needs of particular neighborhoods, religious groups, occupations, and races. Institutions differed from each other in much the same way that the diverse communities that founded them differed.

The moral and political objectives of these diverse nineteenth-century institutions had a profound impact on their internal order and organization. In general, the use of large, undifferentiated wards with many beds, the usual form of housing in nineteenth-century hospitals, met the needs of institutions trying to supervise and control patients hospitalized for long periods. The ward, with beds lined up along its walls, allowed nurses or attendants to watch many patients simultaneously and guaranteed strict supervision of potentially disruptive or untrustworthy poorer "inmates." Moreover, the ward arrangement allowed patients to socialize in an institution that in practice substituted for the home. Also, ambulatory patients could learn good work habits by serving as orderlies and nurses and by helping other patients incapable of helping themselves. By performing assigned and necessary tasks, patients made hospital administration less complex and also "paid" for their stay. At the same time, they learned the "value of work" by performing vital tasks for their fellow patients. The only social characteristics used to separate patients in wards were sex, age, and medical condition.

Although specific religious or sectarian orders often managed these institutions, most trustees believed there was a moral obligation to admit poor patients regardless of race or religion. In fact, given their strong missionary zeal, many trustees understood that including a wide range of religious, racial, and ethnic groups was an important indication of an institution's usefulness. Furthermore, the missionary function of some facilities dictated that hospitals not only accept poor patients who presented themselves but also seek out and welcome such people. Every year, the annual reports of various hospitals emphasized the wide variety of races, religions, and nationalities of their patients. Even the architectural details of many institutions reflected the paramount awareness of social and moral objectives, with many institutions built to resemble churches, mansions, and homes rather than prisons, schools, or factories.

The organizational changes that overwhelmed hospitals during the early years of the twentieth century profoundly affected the relationship between trustees and medical staffs. In part, the new relationship was forced on trustees and physicians by the changing social conditions under which medical and hospital care functioned. A new internal economy altered the traditional paternal control that trustees had exerted over hospitals. While it is sometimes said that the voluntary hospital has become a workshop for physicians, closer examination of the history of relationships between trustees and physicians shows that the modern professional and administrative structures of hospitals were created by a series of profound compromises and adjustments in the running of the facility.

To understand the changing relationships between trustees and the medical and administrative staffs, it is necessary to briefly review some of the central elements of a crisis in financing faced by American hospitals late in the nineteenth century. For many years, charity hospitals were inexpensive institutions that operated on relatively small budgets. In New York in the 1890s, for example, nearly all of the voluntary institutions in the city spent less than $30,000 a year to provide care. Partly because they were small, rarely having more than 150 beds, partly because patients provided much of the labor, and partly because medical care was a decidedly low-tech enterprise, these institutions generally cost less than $1.50 per patient day. Funded by an institution's benefactors, a variety of state and local governments, and minimal payments from patients, hospitals ran modest deficits every year, deficits that were generally covered by contributions from trustees.

By the end of the century, however, the cost of patient care began to increase substantially as advances in medical technology and changing standards of cleanliness began to affect the provision of care. Also, as philanthropists faced competing demands from other agencies and as the number of poor increased substantially, hospitals found themselves strapped for funds. Increasingly, hospital trustees had to make hard choices about the future of charitable enterprises and began turning to a new and untested source of income— private, middle-class patients. In order to attract paying patients into charity hospitals, however, trustees needed to change the types of services that hospitals provided and the administrative structure of those facilities. First, they needed to bring into the facility private practitioners from the community. Without these practitioners, there was no mechanism to attract patients who could afford to pay for their care. Second, hospitals had to underplay their traditional image as facilities for the poor. Finally, they had to introduce new services and amenities that a wealthier clientele would expect. During the decades before the Depression, many hospital trustees faced wrenching decisions about whether or not to restructure their facilities fundamentally.

In many institutions, the introduction of private practitioners was the most troubling aspect of restructuring. Previously, trustees had run closely controlled institutions in which most workers, patients, administrators, and even "staff" physicians lived together in a closed environment. In fact, within the older closed "house," in which the limited number of physicians were younger "house staff" dependent on the paternal authority of trustees, the hospital superintendents generally didn't hesitate to reprimand, limit, and even dismiss rebellious doctors. In Brooklyn, New York, for example, as late as the 1890s, protests by physicians about living and working conditions resulted in dismissal of the entire staff. In another facility, doctors who protested their treatment by the head nurse and demanded her dismissal were themselves dismissed by indignant trustees. As late as 1900, trustees believed that the efficient functioning of a hospital depended more on the nursing staff than on the medical staff. But in the early years of the twentieth century, in institution after institution, trustees reluctantly and slowly opened their facilities to private community practitioners.

Many trustees facing the challenge of private practice in previously closed houses responded by organizing two different but parallel structures of health service. Trustees sought to protect the traditional charitable institution from entrepreneurial private practitioners by offering local doctors visiting privileges rather than staff appointments at their institutions. By excluding local practitioners from the formal structure of the facility, trustees believed that they could shield charitable hospitals for the deserving poor from the commercial aspects of private care. Trustees organized private wings, wards, and rooms in the institution to shield the charity patient from the commercialization of medical care that paying patients, private practitioners, and private services implied. As part of this process, care became structured around social class, with the poor or uninsured treated in wards by "ward staff" and paying patients treated by "attending" or "visiting" physicians in private or semiprivate rooms.

The tensions that plagued hospital administrators reflected larger pressures that were affecting the very leadership of the institution. After World War II, trustees lost sight of that earlier commitment to charity and community, as traditionally defined. The growing involvement of the federal government in financing research, construction, and medical education altered the relationships between institutions and local communities. Furthermore, the long, historical movement of private medical practice into hospitals and out of private offices significantly changed the internal culture of hospitals as trustees lost their role and legitimacy as guardians of the poor, the dependent, and the sick. Slowly, along with the changing social class makeup of the hospital went the commitment to traditional religious, ethnic, or economic constituencies. In their place, a newer commitment to communities of professionals—most notably doctors—developed. With this new community came the abandonment of older, traditional rationales of social service and their replacement by new, if vaguer, definitions of success. Medical definitions of disease now replaced older social definitions of dependence as the reason for the institution, and less specific community needs became less important than medically defined priorities. The institution relied less and less on the decisions of trustees who understood little about new technology and medical decision making. The trustees became concerned solely with finances.

The very idea of community was significantly altered in the aftermath of World War II. While earlier generations of trustees and patients often shared certain religious or moral assumptions, the development of highly stratified communities divided along class or racial lines made the very concept of community much vaguer. As affluent suburbs grew and inner cities declined economically, trustees found themselves even more removed socially and physically from the communities they ostensibly served. The social origins of a patient became a mere abstraction in the larger efforts of trustees and administrators to maintain the economic integrity of an institution dedicated to medical care rather than social service. By the mid-1960s, as hospitals responded to calls for unionization, the notion of an institution closely connected to its community seemed like a romantic remnant of the "prescientific" era.

Health planners and activists alike began to trumpet calls for community-based services even as institutions that had once appeared central to community life now seemed more remote. Federal programs run through the Office of Economic Opportunity were organized under the belief that health was "a community affair" that demanded the creation of Neighborhood Health Centers to respond to needs defined locally. At the very time that an interest in locally based health services was reborn, hospital leaders seemed increasingly distant and even antagonistic to those concerns. In some communities, such as the South Bronx and Bedford-Stuyvesant in New York City, and elsewhere, hospitals, once the cornerstone of community social service, were perceived as an enemy and even occupied. The growing distance between community leaders and hospital trustees spoke to the tremendous odyssey taken by community hospitals during the twentieth century.

—David Rosner

See also
Almshouses.
References
Rosenberg, Charles. *The Care of Strangers: The Rise of the American Hospital.* New York: Basic Books, 1987.
Rosner, David. *A Once Charitable Enterprise: Hospitals and Health Care in Brooklyn and New York.* New York: Cambridge University Press, 1982.
Stevens, Rosemary. *In Sickness and in Wealth.* New York: Basic Books, 1990.

Hotels

During the eighteenth century, inns and taverns were usually small-scale, family-run enterprises. Located in large houses, they provided simple meals and scant toilet facilities in keeping with ordinary domestic practices. All of the guests usually slept in a single room and often shared beds with strangers. In the 1790s, a few hotels serving the elite in eastern cities began to expand and take on the trappings of mansions. At the same time, Americans began to use the word *hotel,* borrowing it from the French term for a nobleman's city house.

The "modern" hotel emerged in the first three decades of the nineteenth century. It was distinguished by eight major innovations: some form of collective or corporate financing; the development of management separate from ownership; a purpose-built edifice with commercial rather than residential architectural style; cutting-edge plumbing, heating, lighting, and other technologies; location on a major thoroughfare near the business district; lavish interior decor and personal service; a generous table and sophisticated cuisine; and a growing spatial specialization, including the provision of separate public rooms for women and children.

Contemporaries labeled these great urban landmarks "palaces of the people," identifying the commercial appropriation of royal grandeur as a major achievement of a republican society. No European hostelry offered such luxury. Hotels provided a stage to display and to flaunt middle-class and elite wealth at the same time that they created genteel enclaves within cities that were often dirty and contentious. By using the "American plan," in which the guest paid a single fee for room and meals, hotel keepers fostered a sense of community among their patrons as they dined collectively under the kindly eye of the landlord. Often, hotels housed a large number of semipermanent guests in family suites.

The model of the hotel established in the 1820s and 1830s persisted through the 1870s, albeit greatly enlarged and brought up-to-date technologically. New cities like Chicago in the 1850s and San Francisco in the 1860s were eager to have first-class hotels as symbols of their metropolitan status and gathering places for the "best" people. In the 1870s, however, urban hotel keepers began to change the organization of their service. The gradual adoption of the "European plan" involved the commercialization of hotel services and the erosion of efforts to foster community among the guests.

The European plan required guests to pay only for their rooms, and hotel dining rooms became public restaurants offering à la carte service. This rationalization of food service highlighted the hotel's status as a profit-making business and downplayed its role as a place of public hospitality, and by the 1890s most first-class city hotels used the European plan. They also frequently hosted elite social events and large conventions and rented out their ground floors. Celebrity events and small retail shops attracted large numbers of guests and sightseers. Hotels such as New York's Waldorf-Astoria (opened in 1892–1897) represented the culmination of the nineteenth-century tradition of "palace" hotels.

The construction of the Waldorf-Astoria touched off a major hotel building boom that continued, with a few delays induced by recession and war, through the 1920s. These hotels adopted the skyscraper style typical of new office buildings. They also grew increasingly standardized in their construction and management while incorporating as much labor-saving technology as possible. Ellsworth Statler's hotels in Buffalo (1908) and Cleveland (1912) represented a new trend toward midpriced, comfortable but not luxurious hotel accommodations. They also heralded the rise of corporately owned hotel chains.

Throughout the nineteenth and early twentieth centuries, first- and second-class hotels had a significant proportion of resident guests. The line between the hotel and the boardinghouse was one of size and management rather than clientele; boardinghouses were usually conducted by women in private homes. "Family" hotels, serving mostly long-term patrons, and apartment hotels, catering to single men and young couples, emerged in the 1870s. From the 1880s on, rental apartments siphoned off a growing number of hotels' long-term patrons. The standardized hotels that Statler pioneered eliminated family suites and relied upon short-term transients.

During the nineteenth century, hotel management became increasingly sophisticated and hierarchical. Landlord, bartender, cook, and maid gave way to a hotel manager supervising a legion of clerks, stewards, waiters, bellboys, porters, housekeepers, chambermaids, laundresses, and others. The white-collar staff began forming city, state, and regional professional organizations in the late nineteenth century. At the national level, they began with broad-based groups like the Hotel Men's Mutual Benefit Association (1879). In 1910, clerks created the Hotel Greeters of America out of many local groups. Managers and owners formed the American Hotel Association in that same year to lobby against state and federal hotel regulation and to found a hotel management school at Cornell University (1922). Waiters and other hotel workers struggled from the late nineteenth century to form unions, without much success until the 1930s.

Prosperous and glamorous throughout the 1920s despite the negative effects of Prohibition, the great urban hotels were hard hit by the Depression and the demands of war. Following World War II, suburbanization undermined the ability of urban hotels to survive. Hotel chains came to dominate the business, springing up at highway interchanges, airports, and in some downtown business centers. In the 1970s and 1980s, tax incentives encouraged the restoration of some older, inner-city hotels.

—*Catherine Cocks*

See also
Lodging, Boarding, and Rooming Houses; Motels.

References
Berger, Molly. "The Modern Hotel in America, 1829–1929." Ph.D. dissertation, Case Western Reserve University, 1997.
Brucken, Carolyn. "Palaces for the People: Luxury Hotels and the Building of a New Public in Antebellum America." Ph.D. dissertation, George Washington University, 1997.
Cocks, Catherine. "At Home in the City: Urban Hotels, 1850–1915." In "'A City Excellent to Behold': Urban Tourism and the Commodification of Public Life in the United States, 1850–1915." Ph.D. dissertation, University of California, Davis, 1997.
Josephson, Matthew. *Union House, Union Bar: The History of the Hotel and Restaurant Employees and Bartenders International Union, AFL-CIO.* New York: Random House, 1956.
King, Doris. "Early Hotel Entrepreneurs and Promoters." *Explorations in Entrepreneurial History* 8 (1956): 148–160.
———. "The First-Class Hotel and the Age of the Common Man." *Journal of Southern History* 23 (1957): 173–188.
Raitz, Karl, and John Paul Jones III. "The City Hotel as Landscape Artifact and Community Symbol." *Journal of Cultural Geography* 9 (1988): 17–36.
Williamson, Jefferson. *The American Hotel: An Anecdotal History.* Reprint ed. New York: Arno Press, 1975.

Housing

Before the late nineteenth century, lower-, middle-, and upper-class residents of most American cities lived relatively close to each other. Workers lived in former homes of the upper classes that had been subdivided or in shacks and shanties. The middle and upper classes tended to live in single-family row houses, because population growth and rising land values had made detached houses financially unaffordable for all but the most affluent residents of cities. New York City's brownstones and Philadelphia's and Baltimore's neat, brick row houses are the best-known of these residences. Until the last two decades of the nineteenth century, the middle and upper classes, imbued with the belief in private ownership, avoided apartment buildings. However, as urban land values rose early in the twentieth century, renting became a necessity for poorer urban residents.

Suburbs also existed in the eighteenth and early nineteenth centuries, but not in the same form as in the late twentieth century. In the colonial and early national periods, the well-off lived in the center of town; so, too, did many workers and less fortunate people. Indeed, a good deal of integration, both by class and function, existed, and the poor frequently found homes in alleys adjacent to residences of the affluent and near their own places of business and work. In the absence of mass transit, "walking cities" allowed residents to travel to work, shop, and participate in civic life. Suburbs were disdained as places where society's lower orders lived. But fires, diseases, and the fear of both, combined with rapid population growth and the transportation revolution, caused a change in attitudes toward urban and suburban life.

With industrialization in the nineteenth century, America's cities grew at spectacular rates. On the eve of the Revolution, for example, Philadelphia, with approximately 25,000 residents, was the second largest city in the British Empire. By 1870 ten American cities housed more than 50,000 people, and New York was the largest with a population of 942,000. Although the country was still predominantly rural, its industrial cities nevertheless faced serious housing problems. As in so many aspects of urban life, New York City set precedents in attempting to deal with them.

In the middle of the nineteenth century, three events took place in New York that foreshadowed much of this country's future housing policies. Gotham Court, a housing project of six tenement buildings for the poor that was meant to produce a profit, was built on Cherry Street in 1863. Two decades later, it contained 240 families instead of the 140 for which it had been planned. At about the same time, the New York Association for Improving the Condition of the Poor (AICP) built a nonprofit, philanthropic tenement, called the Workingmen's Home. Originally planned for blacks, it was ultimately purchased by a private investor, attracted European immigrants, and became known as the notoriously overcrowded Big Flat. In the 1880s, the AICP itself condemned the building as hopeless. Finally, in 1853, the architect Andrew Jackson Davis designed Llewellyn Park in Orange, New Jersey. Llewellyn Park was intended as a suburb for affluent New Yorkers who commuted to the city in the morning but returned in the evening to homes set in open spaces near streams that were reached by curvilinear roads. The commuter suburb was made possible, of course, by the transportation revolution. Thus, the mid-nineteenth century experienced the first attempts to provide adequate housing for the urban poor by keeping them in the city while the well-to-do began to flee.

In 1867, New York made another attempt to solve the problem of low-cost housing; the city began to regulate it. The Tenement House Act of 1867 provided the first legal definition of a tenement—a building that housed more than three families who cooked for themselves in separate quarters. The law mandated fire escapes and a minimum number of toilet facilities and required that no tenement cover more than 65 percent of a standard New York lot, which was 25 feet wide and 100 feet deep.

This restrictive legislation set the pattern for urban housing reform until the 1930s. The provision of low-income housing was left to private builders, occasionally supplemented by model tenements, such as those built by Alfred T. White in Brooklyn or Theodore Starr in Philadelphia. These tenements and many parks and playgrounds appeared after the demolition of buildings that had been regarded as slums but which nevertheless had provided housing for poor people, who were now displaced by their destruction. The role of government was restricted to that of the night watchman—enforcing minimum building code requirements. But these regulations had little or no impact on the substandard housing that already existed. Moreover, to the extent that these regulations were enforced (by understaffed or corrupt bureaucracies), they caused building costs, and hence rents, to increase, often making housing too expensive for low-income residents.

New York City's dumbbell tenement provides a graphic example of how efforts to improve low-income housing sometimes produced precisely the opposite effect. In 1878, the *Plumber and Sanitary Engineer,* a trade journal, sponsored an architectural competition for the best design of a safe, sanitary tenement that could be built on a 25-foot by 100-foot lot. Significantly, the judges declared that none of the entries was satisfactory; nevertheless, they awarded first prize to the entry that became known as the dumbbell because of its shape. Each of the five or six stories of the building contained a front and rear set of rooms connected to each other by a narrow corridor; when two buildings were constructed side-by-side, the space between the corridors formed an air shaft approximately 28 inches wide that was the primary source of light and air for the inner rooms. By 1900, most of the tenements built after 1880 in New York were overcrowded and unsanitary dumbbells. Reformers increasingly called for their abolition, and the reformers' outrage ultimately led to New York's Tenement House Act of 1901, which became a model followed by other cities.

Housing reformers in the early twentieth century were of several types. They included settlement workers such as Chicago's Jane Addams and Boston's Robert Woods, philan-thropic "friendly visiting" landlords such as Hannah Fox and Helen Parrish of Philadelphia's Octavia Hill Association, newspaper reporters such as Jacob Riis of New York, and technician-reformers such as New York's Lawrence Veiller, Philadelphia's Bernard Newman, and Chicago's Charles Ball. Often paternalistic and imbued with contemporary stereotypes of immigrants and the poor, they nevertheless were the vanguard of housing reform in the early twentieth century. Their leader, at least in terms of national stature and influence, was Veiller.

As secretary of the Tenement House Committee of New York's Charity Organization Society, in 1900 Veiller organized an exhibition about tenement houses. Portraying the shockingly overcrowded and unsanitary poor neighborhoods of the city at their worst, the exhibition generated support for restrictive tenement legislation. With the backing of then-Governor Theodore Roosevelt, the state legislature went on to pass the Tenement House Act of 1901. Its requirements for adequate light and ventilation effectively replaced air shafts with courtyards in new tenements; it also mandated running water and water closets in every apartment. The law was to be enforced by a Tenement House Department. Veiller became the department's deputy commissioner, and in 1910 he spearheaded creation of the National Housing Association to help other cities establish minimum requirements for low-income housing. The 1901 law and the books that Veiller wrote became texts for urban housing reformers throughout the country.

Restrictive housing legislation set the limits for housing reform in the Progressive Era. In most cases, legislation dealt only with new tenements and left the "old law" tenements that had been built earlier unregulated. Proponents of restrictive legislation assumed that well-regulated private builders could provide enough decent housing for the poor. Little support existed for the government to build and manage any housing, and Veiller opposed public housing for the remainder of his career.

Equally important, restrictive legislation often drove up construction costs, thereby sending builders into the middle-class housing market and decreasing the supply of low-income housing. The fearful example of New York's dreaded dumbbell tenements sometimes caused reformers in other cities to overlook local conditions. For example, Philadelphia passed legislation that effectively prohibited dumbbells but which had little impact on the thousands of small, unregulated rear tenements that were that city's primary problem. By the end of World I, several reformers were calling attention to the limitations of restrictive legislation and calling for more positive government action.

During World War I, America's industrial cities experienced enormous population growth, particularly those cities with shipyards and defense industries. Two federal agencies, the Emergency Fleet Corporation of the U.S. Shipping Board and the U.S. Housing Corporation, assumed responsibility for housing workers in shipyards and defense plants, respectively. Together, the two agencies started constructing fewer than 25,000 houses and apartment units, and most of them were not completed by the war's end. The construction included some planned communities such as Yorkship Village in Camden, New Jersey, but the real purpose of federal construction was providing housing for (mostly) skilled workers so that they could effectively produce the weapons necessary for successful prosecution of the war. Therefore, America's first venture into public housing was not, in the words of one writer, an effort to solve "the old conundrum of how to house common labor." Nor was federal intervention intended to be permanent. At the conclusion of the war, the government sold the houses and quit the housing business altogether.

Meanwhile, conditions peculiar to the United States had encouraged Americans of modest means to move to the urban periphery or to suburbs in the late nineteenth and early twentieth centuries. The trolley with its low fares, balloon frame house construction that radically reduced the cost and effort of building houses, and the low price of suburban land all encouraged middle-class urbanites to dream of homeownership. The lower prices of Henry Ford's cars made it possible for people who worked in cities to live away from their jobs and greatly accelerated the growth of suburbia in the 1920s.

Historian Kenneth T. Jackson notes that the suburbs of America's 96 largest cities grew twice as fast as the urban core between 1920 and 1930. High labor and material costs and the diversion of building materials to war needs during World War I had produced an acute housing shortage; in 1920, the editor of the American Building Association *News* estimated that 2,139,000 units needed to be built by 1926 to meet the shortage. One estimate placed the deficiency of apartments in New York City at 40,000 in 1920. The Chicago Department of Health reported the increased use of tents, shacks, and even houseboats. The low cost of suburban land and the increased availability of automobiles caused most of the new building to occur in suburbs. Many of the new communities possessed little or no public transit and relied entirely on automobiles for movement. The Depression ended the housing boom and would propel the federal government to set policies that encouraged and renewed suburban growth.

These residential buildings in Brooklyn, New York, use all available land in an attempt to meet the demand for housing in the city.

By 1933, half of the nation's home mortgages were in default, and victims of the disaster often belonged to the middle class. However, they no longer had the money to make payments on mortgages that usually called for repayment in a short time, often only 5 to 10 years. The Roosevelt administration believed that the federal government could no longer continue the laissez-faire attitude toward housing that it had maintained since World War I. Therefore, the New Deal instituted three new policies in regard to housing: the Home Owners Loan Corporation (HOLC), the Federal Housing Administration (FHA), and public housing. Through the HOLC homeowners could refinance their mortgages and repay them over 20 years. The FHA, and after World War II the Veterans Administration (VA), guaranteed mortgage loans made by private banks for 25 or 30 years.

These measures had a phenomenal impact on urban housing as the long-term, low-interest mortgage became an American institution. Private lenders could grant mortgages and be confident that the FHA would reimburse them if borrowers defaulted. And the long-term, low-interest-rate loans often made homeownership cheaper than renting. Thus, between 1934 and 1972, the percentage of American families who owned their houses rose from 44 to 63 percent.

But the policies of the two agencies also ensured that most new construction would occur in suburbs. In evaluating property, both the HOLC and the FHA developed rating systems that favored neighborhoods outside the urban core and that conformed to contemporary ethnic and racial biases. The emphasis on new, single-family homes and the consideration given to the presence of "inharmonious racial or nationality groups" in a neighborhood hastened white flight to the suburbs.

Public housing became a permanent aspect of America's housing landscape during the Depression, and it too furthered the social distance between white, middle-class, suburban residents and the poor of inner cities. In 1933 Congress authorized the Public Works Administration to acquire land and build low-income housing. Only 21,709 units were built, most of them too expensive for poor families. In 1937, the Wagner-Steagall Act (the Housing Act of 1937) authorized the U.S. Housing Authority to lend money to local housing authorities to construct low-income housing. But one provision of that law determined the future location of low-income housing in metropolitan areas: local communities had the option to create housing authorities and apply for federal funds or not at their will. There was no compulsion to request federal funds to build housing for the poor. This voluntary aspect of the legislation empowered suburbs not to have public housing in their midst, thereby excluding the poor from them. Moreover, the primary purposes of New Deal housing programs were reviving the construction industry and reducing unemployment, not making desirable public housing available. Thus, as in World War I, the major motivation behind public housing was something other than resolving the shortage of low-income housing.

During World War II, the government constructed approximately 2 million housing units, either apartments or houses. Once again, the major purpose was housing war workers. The Housing Act of 1949 continued the commitment made to public housing during the Depression; but decision making still remained in the hands of local authorities, and Congress never authorized enough units to meet the need. As an example, by 1984 New York City had a waiting list of 175,000 people for public housing. Public housing construction in the years after World War II was inadequate in scope, concentrated in the urban core, and increasingly associated in the public mind with a permanent underclass, an image that reinforced the desire of suburbs to exclude it.

If government policy promoted the concentration of the poor and minorities (the two were often the same) in inner cities, it also encouraged the white middle class to settle in suburbs after the war. The Depression and the war had both hampered home building, and the postwar years experienced a rising birthrate. The FHA and the VA met the new housing crisis by continuing to insure long-term mortgages with minimal down payments. Then, 11 years after the war, the Interstate Highway Act of 1956 produced a highway system financed by the federal government, further encouraging the spread of middle-class suburbs by making commuting easier. The continued attractiveness of federally guaranteed mortgages almost ensured the entry of large-scale entrepreneurs into the home-building industry; and no one is more associated with this phenomenon than Abraham Levitt and his sons.

The Levitts purchased and cleared enormous plots of land, used prefabricated parts, and applied assembly-line techniques to house construction. Their methods of building lowered prices and placed homes in the several mass-produced Levittowns and their imitators well within reach of the middle class. Social critics derided these low-density communities of detached single-family Cape Cods and brick ranch-style houses as homogeneous, dreary tracts of stultifying sameness; but to the young families who moved into them, many of them second- or third-generation immigrants, these houses were the stuff of upwardly mobile dreams. Nevertheless, suburban growth also contributed to the increased social and geographic distance between white, middle-class suburbanites and the poor and minority citizens who remained in central cities.

By 1970 more people in the United States lived in suburbs than cities, and in 1980 two-thirds of the country's dwelling units were single-family detached houses. Forty percent of all Americans lived in suburbs. Meanwhile, the departure of the middle class decreased the tax base of most cities at the very time that poorer urban residents required more social services. And there still were not enough adequate homes in the United States. Most Americans, the middle and upper classes, were generally well housed in the suburban nation. But the problem of providing adequate housing for people with low incomes persisted. In 1994, sociologist Christopher Jencks estimated that 325,000 Americans were homeless.

The 1980s and 1990s revealed that adequate housing was no longer a problem that affected only the poor. The dream of middle-class homeownership began to disintegrate. Rising energy and land costs, declining reserves of savings to finance low-interest-rate mortgages, and increasing construction costs have awakened many middle-class Americans from the dream of owning a single-family detached house. Innovations such as the condominium have only partially relieved the problem. Housing continues to be a major domestic policy issue as the United States enters the new millennium.

—*John F. Sutherland*

See also

Apartment Buildings; Balloon Frame Construction; Condominiums; Dumbbell Tenement; Federal Housing Administration; Gentrification; Homeownership; Levittown; Llewellyn Park, New Jersey; Lodging, Boarding, and Rooming Houses; Public Housing; Residential Construction; Residential Differentiation; Residential Mobility; Row House; Single-Family Detached House; Tenement; Veiller, Lawrence Turnure; White Flight.

References

Abrams, Charles. *The City Is the Frontier.* New York: Harper & Row, 1965.

Friedman, Lawrence M. *Government and Slum Housing: A Century of Frustration.* Chicago: Rand McNally, 1968.

Jackson, Anthony. *A Place Called Home: A History of Low-Cost Housing in Manhattan.* Cambridge, MA: MIT Press, 1976.

Jackson, Kenneth T. *Crabgrass Frontier: The Suburbanization of the United States.* New York: Oxford University Press, 1985.

Lubove, Roy. *The Progressives and the Slums: Tenement House Reform in New York City, 1890–1917.* Pittsburgh, PA: University of Pittsburgh Press, 1962.

Philpott, Thomas Lee. *The Slum and the Ghetto: Neighborhood Deterioration and Middle-Class Reform, Chicago, 1880–1930.* New York: Oxford University Press, 1978.

Plunz, Richard. *A History of Housing in New York City: Dwelling Type and Social Change in the American Metropolis.* New York: Columbia University Press, 1990.

Sutherland, John F. "A City of Homes: Philadelphia Slums and Reformers, 1880–1918." Ph.D. dissertation, Temple University, 1973.

Housing Act of 1934

In the depths of the Depression, one of the many crises facing President Franklin D. Roosevelt was an epidemic of home mortgage foreclosures as Americans were losing their houses at the rate of 1,000 a day in 1933. That year, Congress created the Home Owners Loan Corporation (HOLC), a temporary agency empowered to refinance home mortgages by establishing the federal government as a second source of credit. On June 27, 1934, President Roosevelt signed the most significant piece of legislation in the history of American homeownership, the Housing Act of 1934. This law created the Federal Housing Administration (FHA), which made the federal government the guarantor of home mortgage loans by banks and savings-and-loan institutions. With adoption of the self-amortizing mortgage, the FHA extended the length of home mortgage loans from 8 or 10 years to 20 or 30 years while reducing both the size of down payments from approximately 50 percent to 10 to 20 percent and the resultant amount of monthly payments. The Federal Savings and Loan Insurance Corporation (FSLIC), which was also chartered by the Housing Act of 1934, insured savings of up to $5,000 in savings-and-loan and building-and-loan associations.

By generally eliminating the need for second mortgages, and by making first mortgages more accessible to potential home buyers, the FHA extended the possibility of homeownership to many more people. In the three decades following the law's adoption, the percentage of homeowners increased from 44 to 63 owing to the availability of FHA and Veterans' Administration funds. While the FHA provided only limited guarantees for the repair and expansion of existing dwellings, the agency primarily subsidized the construction of low-density, single-family housing units. As a consequence, the Housing Act of 1934 encouraged new housing construction on the urban periphery, suburbanization, and population deconcentration. It thus fundamentally changed the morphology of American cities.

—*Roger Biles*

References

Arnold, Joseph L. "Housing and Resettlement." In Otis L. Graham, Jr., and Meghan Robinson Wander, eds., *Franklin D. Roosevelt, His Life and Times: An Encyclopedic View.* Boston: G. K. Hall, 1985.

Gelfand, Mark I. *A Nation of Cities: The Federal Government and Urban America, 1933–1965.* New York: Oxford University Press, 1975.

Jackson, Kenneth T. *Crabgrass Frontier: The Suburbanization of the United States.* New York: Oxford University Press, 1985.

———. "Race, Ethnicity, and Real Estate Appraisal: The Home Owners Loan Corporation and the Federal Housing Administration." *Journal of Urban History* 6 (1980): 419–452.

Housing Act of 1937

A product of the New Deal reform movement, the Housing Act of 1937 established a foundation for federal support of low-income Americans unable to obtain safe, sanitary housing in the private real estate market. Title II of the National Industrial Recovery Act (1933) had authorized the Public Works Administration (PWA) to subsidize the construction of low-cost housing, and the PWA's Housing Division had stimulated 31 states to adopt housing legislation. But by 1937 it had launched construction of just 21,800 dwellings in 51 public housing projects. Disappointed with the slow pace of construction, housing reformers worked closely with New York Senator Robert F. Wagner and his aide, Leon F. Keyserling, to draft a new housing bill. In 1935 and 1936 Wagner introduced housing legislation that Congress failed to pass, largely due to lack of support from the White House. In 1937 another Wagner bill, which was simultaneously introduced into the House by Alabama Representative Henry B. Steagall and which received Roosevelt's tepid endorsement, was passed by Congress and signed into law on September 1, 1937.

The Housing Act of 1937, often referred to as the Wagner-Steagall Act, created the U.S. Housing Authority (USHA) in the Department of the Interior to augment the construction of federally funded, locally administered housing projects. The law authorized the USHA to extend 60-year loans at 3 percent interest (for up to 90 percent of the total cost) to public housing agencies to acquire, develop, and administer low-rent housing or for slum-clearance projects. The authority could also make capital grants (for up to 25 percent of development or acquisition cost) to local public housing agencies.

Such generous conditions quickened the tempo of activity, and within a year 221 communities had established housing authorities. In subsequent years, local agencies used federal largess under the auspices of the Housing Act of 1937 to erect hundreds of thousands of public housing units.

—*Roger Biles*

References

Arnold, Joseph L. "Housing and Resettlement." In Otis L. Graham, Jr., and Meghan Robinson Wander, eds., *Franklin D. Roosevelt, His Life and Times: An Encyclopedic View.* Boston: G. K. Hall, 1985.

Biles, Roger. "Nathan Straus and the Failure of Public Housing, 1937–1942." *The Historian* 53 (1990): 33–46.

Huthmacher, J. Joseph. *Senator Robert F. Wagner and the Rise of Urban Liberalism.* New York: Atheneum, 1968.

McDonnell, Timothy. *The Wagner Housing Act: A Case Study of the Legislative Process.* Chicago: Loyola University Press, 1957.

Housing Segregation

Segregated housing exists whenever the residential distribution of population groups in a single district differs from the groups' distribution within the total population in a larger area. Segregated housing leads to segregation in other areas of life—schooling, religion, recreation, and employment, for example. Housing segregation is related to inequality and subordination; it limits the options for social mobility by consigning a segregated group to inferior schools and low-paying jobs.

The standard measure of segregation is the index of dissimilarity that assesses the degree to which two groups are unevenly distributed in neighborhoods. Unevenness is determined by the percentage composition of an area as a whole. For example, if an area is 30 percent black and 70 percent white, to have a residential distribution with no segregation, every neighborhood would also have to be 30 percent black and 70 percent white. As the racial composition of each neighborhood deviates from the racial composition of the entire area, the segregation index increases. The index values range from "0," reflecting no segregation (i.e., complete evenness of racial groups across neighborhoods), to "100," indicating complete racial segregation. The higher the index, the greater the amount of segregation.

In most places, the extent of housing segregation between Hispanics and whites and Asians and whites increased between 1980 and 1990. On the other hand, the extent of segregation between blacks and whites decreased. Hispanic segregation occurred most notably in large metropolitan areas with growing immigrant populations, primarily in the West and Southwest. This trend conforms to the expected pattern of assimilation of immigrant groups; as new immigrant groups move into an area, housing in that area becomes more segregated.

Census reports reveal that the Asian population of the United States doubled between 1980 and 1990. Because of the large Asian immigration, slight increases in housing segregation occurred as recent immigrants located in specific metropolitan neighborhoods. Despite these small increases in segregation during the decade, the level of Asian segregation remains below the level for Hispanics and far below the level for blacks.

The decline in black segregation was first observed between 1970 and 1980. The decline during the 1980s was most pronounced in newer metropolitan areas where the percentage of blacks was smaller, many of them located in the South and West. Some reasons given for the decrease in black segregation are changing white attitudes toward open housing and increasing black suburbanization.

Despite the recent decline in black-white housing segregation, blacks are the most residentially segregated of all minority groups. They are also the least suburbanized. According to one study, the differential levels of minority-group residential segregation and suburbanization can be explained by the process of racial and ethnic integration in America since World War II, a process that links residential segregation with suburbanization. To the extent that suburban residence is precluded for a minority group by discriminatory housing practices, an important avenue of residential integration is closed off.

This situation applies to blacks, but much less to Asians and Hispanics. Several studies have indicated that the underrepresentation of blacks in suburbs is not due to black socioeconomic status. On the other hand, both Asian and Hispanic residential segregation, and the degree of their suburbanization, are highly related to socioeconomic status. As the socioeconomic status of these groups rises, residential segregation decreases and suburbanization increases. For Asians and Hispanics, suburbanization, a process largely closed to blacks, is a key step in the larger process of spatial assimilation. Since the level of black segregation is not strongly related to socioeconomic status, and the socioeconomic status of blacks is not strongly related to black suburbanization, then regardless of socioeconomic status most blacks remain highly segregated in the central cities of metropolitan areas.

The white majority population appears to use different criteria to evaluate blacks, Hispanics, and Asians. Evidence suggests that Asians and white Hispanics are characterized and evaluated according to the criteria of ethnicity. This circumstance leads to greater spatial assimilation for Asians and white Hispanics. As social and economic mobility increases, a reduction in residential segregation occurs and a corresponding increase in suburbanization takes place. In this sense, the position of Asians and white Hispanics resembles that of white ethnic groups from Eastern, Central, and Southern Europe. On the other hand, blacks (including black Hispanics) are evaluated according to a racial criterion, a situation in which spatial assimilation is not strongly related to socioeconomic status.

The fact that more than two-thirds of the black population of the nation's SMSAs (Standard Metropolitan Statistical Areas) reside in central cities (a level higher than that of any other racial or ethnic group) has serious social and economic consequences. Many blue-collar jobs that once constituted the economic backbone of cities and provided employment for poorly educated residents have either vanished or moved to suburbs. Thus, newer and better job opportunities are locating farther away from areas of black residence, forcing black families to spend more time and money commuting to work or looking for work. In addition, employers tend to hire workers who reflect the racial character of the area in which they are located, so there may also be an indirect effect of housing segregation on employment opportunities.

The problems of black residents of central cities are intensified by the fact that employment opportunities in blue-collar, semiskilled, and low-skilled jobs are moving to suburbs so rapidly that a surplus of labor in these categories has developed in central cities. In other words, there has been a substantial shift in the occupational mix of jobs in central cities. The number of jobs for craftsmen, operatives, and laborers has declined, while professional, sales, clerical, and service employment have increased proportionally.

Despite recent trends, however, because of persistent discrimination in the housing market based on color, blacks are the most residentially segregated race and remain largely excluded from suburbs, regardless of their education, income, or occupation. Thus, future improvements in the social and economic status of blacks will not necessarily produce residential integration and greater suburbanization. This pattern differs from that of any other minority group and reinforces the significance of color—i.e., blackness—in explaining the unequal status of African Americans compared to other minority groups. Color, unlike ethnicity, is a perceived difference based on kind rather than degree. As a result, blacks continue to experience more discrimination and segregation, and they have less opportunity for suburbanization than other groups.

—*Joe T. Darden*

See also
Desegregation of Housing; Racism and Discrimination.
References
Clark, Thomas. "The Suburbanization Process and Residential Segregation." In Gary Tobin, ed., *Divided Neighborhoods: Changing Patterns of Racial Segregation,* 115–137. Beverly Hills, CA: Sage Publications, 1987.
Darden, Joe T. "Accessibility to Housing: Differential Residential Segregation for Blacks, Hispanics, American Indians, and Asians." In Jamshid Momeni, ed., *Race, Ethnicity and Minority Housing in the United States,* ch. 7. Westport, CT: Greenwood Press, 1986.
———. "Blacks and Other Racial Minorities: The Significance of Color in Inequality." *Urban Geography* 10 (1989): 562–577.
Frey, William, and Reynolds Farley. "Latino, Asian, and Black Segregation in Multi-Ethnic Metro Areas: Findings from the 1990 Census." Research Reports, Population Studies Center, University of Michigan, April 1993.
Kasarda, John D. "Urban Industrial Transition and the Underclass." In William J. Wilson, ed., *The Ghetto Underclass,* ch. 2. Beverly Hills, CA: Sage Publications, 1989.
Massey, Douglas S., and Nancy A. Denton. *American Apartheid: Segregation and the Making of the Underclass.* Cambridge, MA: Harvard University Press, 1993.
———. "Trends in the Residential Segregation of Blacks, Hispanics, and Asians: 1970–1980." *American Sociological Review* 52 (1987): 802–825.

Housing and Urban Development, Department of

The U.S. Department of Housing and Urban Development (HUD) is one of the newest cabinet-level departments of the federal government. Created in 1965 during the Johnson administration, its mandate is to

achieve the best administration of the principal programs of the Federal Government which provide assistance for housing and for the development of the Nation's communities; to assist the President in achieving maximum coordination of the various Federal activities which have a major effect upon urban community, suburban or metropolitan development; to encourage the solution of problems of housing, urban development, and mass transportation through state, county, town, village, or other local and private action, including promotion of interstate, regional, and metropolitan cooperation; to encourage the maximum contributions that may be made by vigorous private home-building and mortgage lending industries to housing, urban development and the national economy; and to provide for full and appropriate consideration at the national level, of the needs and interests of the Nation's communities and of the people who live and work in them.

HUD's goals are lofty, and its mission is broad, but in general it has been thought that it has not met its objectives successfully. From the outset, HUD had a broad mandate but limited power to address the myriad housing and urban problems facing the nation. Many key activities affecting urban areas (such as transportation and economic development) were administered by other entities. Also, several key agencies involved with housing, notably the Federal Home Loan Bank Board, the Veterans Administration, and the Farmers Home Administration—with authority, respectively, over the thrift-housing financing system and housing programs for veterans and farmers—have continued to function independently of HUD. Also important is that the array of subsidies for housing that operate through the federal income tax system are under jurisdiction of the Internal Revenue Service (IRS), not HUD. Furthermore, the housing portion of welfare payments has constituted another large pool of money going into housing over which HUD has no control.

Although some of HUD's difficulties can be blamed on mismanagement and corruption, many of its problems have been beyond its control. For example, HUD has been charged with implementing programs that have often had conflicting components and that have frequently depended on the private construction industry and financial institutions; their profit-oriented goals have often been at odds with the goal of providing housing and community development resources for low-income people and neighborhoods.

Another source of HUD's problems lies in the very nature of the issues in its concern. HUD has been asked to address a host of serious and complex problems, the origins of which generally lie outside the locale in which the problems manifest themselves. For example, poverty and unemployment largely result from international, national, and regional economic decisions rather than local actions or inactions. Also, the very complexity of the problems makes it difficult, if not impossible, to "get it right the first time." Instead, even at best, one might expect a process of trial and error. However, the very visibility of many of HUD's blunders makes the agency susceptible to criticism, rather than fostering a sense that mistakes are inherently part of a learning process.

HUD has also been saddled with inconsistent support from the president and Congress. By the time President Clinton took office in early 1993, HUD was widely perceived to be teetering on the brink of collapse. A major evaluation of HUD, authorized by Congress in 1992 to be carried out by the National Academy of Public Administration, opened its final report with the message, "The Clinton administration and the secretary of HUD offer what may be the last best chance to create an accountable, effective department." The lofty goals of this message may well have been compromised by the indictment of HUD Secretary Henry Cisneros in 1997 on charges of conspiracy to defraud, making false statements and representations, and obstruction of justice.

Although it appears that HUD, having weathered various attacks, will be preserved as an agency, it is likely to emerge in an even weaker and more marginalized state. It seems likely that various HUD programs will be incorporated into a small number of block grants as a way of making their implementation more manageable. Whatever administrative structure is chosen, the problems facing HUD will continue to present enormous challenges for whichever federal agency or agencies receive the task of addressing the housing and urban ills facing the nation.

—*Rachel G. Bratt*

References

Bratt, Rachel G., and W. Dennis Keating. "Federal Housing Policy and HUD: Past Problems and Future Prospects of a Beleaguered Bureaucracy." *Urban Affairs Quarterly* 29 (1993): 3–27.

Gelfand, Mark. *A Nation of Cities: The Federal Government and Urban America, 1933–1965.* New York: Oxford University Press, 1975.

McFarland, M. Carter. *Federal Government and Urban Problems; HUD: Successes, Failures, and the Fate of Our Cities.* Boulder, CO: Westview Press, 1978.

National Academy of Public Administration. *Renewing HUD: A Long-Term Agenda for Effective Performance.* Washington, DC: National Academy of Public Administration, 1994.

Weaver, Robert C. "The First Twenty Years of HUD." *Journal of the American Planning Association* 51 (1985): 463–474.

Wood, Robert, and Beverly M. Klimkowsky. "HUD in the Nineties: Doubt-ability and Do-ability." In Marshall Kaplan and Franklin James, eds., *The Future of National Urban Policy.* Durham, NC: Duke University Press, 1990.

Houston, Texas

In 1990 Houston, Texas, covered 540 square miles, possessed a population of 1,631,000, and ranked as the fourth largest city in the United States behind New York, Los Angeles, and Chicago. The Houston Consolidated Metropolitan Area of Houston-Galveston-Brazoria ranked tenth in the nation with a population of 3,711,000. Over 100 ethnic groups composed the population of the city, but government statistics in 1990 classified 56 percent as white, 18 percent as black, 21 percent as Hispanic, and 4 percent as Asian. The impressive growth of Houston into a major city with international linkages resulted historically from the construction of transportation systems, the nearby location of natural resources, and an entrepreneurial spirit.

The city began on August 30, 1836, when Augustus Chapman Allen and his brother John Kirby Allen ran an advertisement in the leading Texas newspaper, *Telegraph and Texas Register,* for the "Town of Houston." The site was a level plain of timber and grassland on the banks of a moderate, spring-fed river, Buffalo Bayou, in south-central Texas 50 miles inland from the Gulf of Mexico. The Allens claimed that the town site enjoyed a cool, healthy sea breeze and that Houston would become a "great interior commercial emporium" for ships from New York and New Orleans. Their advertisement mentioned plans for a sawmill and lots for sale at modest prices. As was so often the case with town promoters, the Allens exaggerated. The 43 inches of annual rainfall and temperatures that averaged 93 degrees during a long summer created a steamy climate that inspired later Houstonians to create one of the most air-conditioned cites in the world. Moreover, the town site could hardly be found by Francis R. Lubbock when he arrived after a difficult passage across an entangled bayou on the first steamship, the *Laura,* in January 1837.

The Allens, who had come from New York and participated in the Texas Revolution as supply agents, named their town after the hero of the moment, Sam Houston, and persuaded the Texas Congress to designate their site as the temporary capital of the new republic. In return, they promised land and buildings for government use. At the start of 1837, there were only a dozen people and one log cabin at Houston, but within four months there were about 1,500 people and 100 houses. Gail and Thomas H. Borden surveyed and platted the town in typical gridiron fashion with broad streets running parallel and perpendicular to the bayou. The Texas Congress met there on May 1, 1837, and despite the efforts of Masons, Presbyterians, and Episcopalians, the town became notorious for drunkenness, dueling, brawling, prostitution, and profanity.

The Congress of the Republic of Texas granted incorporation on June 5, 1837, and James S. Holman became the first mayor. Houston also became the seat of government of Harrisburg County (Harris County in 1839) the same year, but lost the capital to the village of Austin in 1839. During the nineteenth century, aldermen elected by ward directed a city government that worked mainly to create a favorable climate for enterprise. Early settlers used lumber to build frame houses, ditches for drainage, and pigs as scavengers on the streets. Yellow fever struck periodically from 1839 to 1867, after which it was controlled by a quarantine of the coastline.

Since many of the town's citizens were from the South, they endorsed the cotton plantation–slavery system and used urban slaves for menial tasks. Thus, Houston followed the same bifurcated path of other southern towns where a black minority developed a submerged and separate social culture. Slaves lived scattered through the neighborhoods, were subject to an 8:00 P.M. curfew, and could not take outside employment without their owner's permission. There were few free blacks in the city.

Following the Civil War, the customary separation of the races continued with different schools, churches, clubs, bands, businesses, and sports teams. Segregation by law began to be put in place with separation on streetcars in 1903 and continued throughout the first half of the twentieth century with racial rules for parks, depots, schools, drinking fountains, buses, rest rooms, theaters, and restaurants. Separate residential areas developed for whites, blacks, and Hispanics by the end of the nineteenth century, although residential segregation never became part of the legal code.

In 1904, a change to elections of officials at-large rather then by ward ensured continuation of white majority rule. Despite occasional outbursts, such as the one that occurred in 1917 when a northern black army unit shot up the town and left 19 people dead, the legacy of slavery remained basically unaltered until the civil rights movement of the 1950s and 1960s.

Even though Houston began as a boomtown in the nineteenth century, its livelihood depended upon cotton and commerce. Merchants such as William Marsh Rice, Thomas M. Bagby, Charles Shearn, William J. Hutchins, Paul Bremond, and A. S. Ruthven developed trade connections between south Texas planters and markets in New Orleans, New York, and England. Oceangoing ships brought cargoes of cloth, whiskey, gunpowder, iron castings, lead, coffee, nails, books, and hundreds of small items to the deep-water port at Galveston Island. Small steamboats moved the goods from Galveston, through Galveston Bay, and up Buffalo Bayou to Houston, where merchants sent them on to backcountry farmers by ox-team. In the reverse direction came cotton, corn, and hides that the merchants sent on to Galveston for transfer to eastern markets.

Although Buffalo Bayou was one of the more reliable rivers in Texas, it was difficult to navigate due to sharp bends, sandbars, and snags. Following the Civil War Houston merchants mounted various unsuccessful efforts to dredge a better channel. Charles Morgan, a Gulf Coast shipper operating out of New Orleans, eventually took over, and in 1876 he dug a 12-foot-deep outlet across Galveston Bay to Clinton, a port town on Buffalo Bayou well below Houston. The federal government assumed Morgan's work in 1892 and after long delays dredged a cut 25 feet deep down Buffalo Bayou and through Galveston Bay to the Gulf of Mexico. The Houston Ship Channel opened in 1914 with a turning basin just above Harrisburg, a small town that has since become part of Houston. Since that time, the Houston Ship Channel has been widened and deepened to over 400 feet wide and 40 feet deep. It provided Houston with a deepwater port that eventually ranked third in tonnage in the United States and gave the city access to the world.

Previously, Houstonians had worked to build rail lines into the countryside to replace the rutted and often impassable dirt roads. In 1853, Paul Bremond, a Houston merchant, began the slow construction northwest of the Houston and Texas Central Railroad. The line started as the Galveston and Red River Railroad Company, changed its name in 1856, and reached Hempstead, 50 miles away, in 1858. The citizens of Houston, meanwhile, financed the 7-mile Houston Tap and Brazoria Railway, which joined the nearby Buffalo Bayou, Brazos, and Colorado Railway in 1858. Other rail enterprises started, and by 1861 Houston was the center of railroads in Texas, with five major lines radiating 50 to 100 miles to the south, southeast, west, east, and northwest. The Civil War interrupted further construction, but building revived afterward. When the Houston and Texas Central reached the Missouri, Kansas, and Texas Railroad at Denison on the Red River border between Texas and the Indian Territory of Oklahoma in 1873, Houston joined the national rail network.

These railways efficiently reached into the cotton hinterland of Houston. Although roadways and trails existed from the earliest years of settlement in Texas, overland travel was often slow and rough. Road improvement was costly and remained the responsibility of counties or cities until the state assumed it in 1917. The first all-weather highways appeared in the 1920s. In 1952 Houston's first expressway, the Gulf Freeway, which later became part of the interstate highway system, linked Houston and Galveston. Houston opened its first municipal airport in 1928, followed by Houston International Airport in 1954 (renamed William P. Hobby Airport in 1967) and Houston Intercontinental Airport in 1969.

The various transportation systems and the communications systems of mail, telegraph (1853–1854), and telephone (1878) supported Houston's development as a cotton and lumber market in the nineteenth century. The discovery of oil at Spindletop at nearby Beaumont in 1901, however, dramatically changed the Houston economy. As the oil market developed, companies chose to locate their refineries and shipping facilities along the Houston Ship Channel where they were safe from Gulf Coast hurricanes. The city also had helpful rail connections and financial institutions. By 1929, 40 oil companies had located in Houston, including the Texas Company (Texaco), Humble Oil and Refining Company (Exxon), and Gulf Oil Corporation (Chevron).

By 1930 Houston had a population of 292,000 and was the largest city in Texas. At this point, the city possessed three newspapers—*Houston Post* (founded 1880), *Houston Chronicle* (1901), and *Houston Press* (1911–1964)—and four radio stations. The Depression struck Houston only a glancing blow. There were no bank failures, but in 1935–1936, at the peak of its enrollment, the Works Progress Administration employed 12,000 people in Harris County. Federal resources were used to improve roads, parks, and buildings. The new City Hall as well as the San Jacinto Monument were Depression projects.

World War II boosted Houston's economy significantly. The ship channel became the site for the construction of steel merchant vessels, concrete barges, and midsized warships. Houston Shipbuilding Corporation, a Todd Shipyard Corporation subsidiary, for example, built Liberty Ships and employed 20,000 workers by July 1942. Brown Shipbuilding Company, a local business, pioneered broadside launching and produced over 300 vessels by the end of the war. Nearby deposits of salt, sulfur, natural gas, and petroleum supplied the ingredients for petrochemicals, and the U.S. government provided wartime contracts for synthetic rubber, gasoline, and explosives.

Following the war, the Houston area developed one of the two largest petrochemical concentrations in the United States. In 1990 a complex of some 250 interrelated chemical refineries extended along the Texas coast from Corpus Christi to the Louisiana border. The main exports and imports of the Port of Houston, consequently, involved petroleum products. Houston, thus, became a world energy capital in the 1970s, expanded with the rise in global oil prices, and fell with the decline in prices during the 1980s. During the mid-1980s, for the first time in its history, Houston lost population.

The infrastructure needed for urban life kept pace with the economic growth. Efforts to defeat the mud and dust of city streets featured experiments with cypress blocks, gravel, planks, shell, limestone blocks, and finally cement and asphalt. By 1915 Houston possessed almost 196 miles of paved streets, and in 1922 the city began to replace its wooden bridges with ones made of steel and concrete. Electric street lights appeared in 1884 and electric streetcars in 1891. Automobiles began to show up on the streets in the early twentieth century, and by 1911 there were more than 1,000 cars in Harris County. By 1930 there were 98,000 motor vehicles in the county, and this produced a need for speed limits in 1907, one-way streets in 1920, and traffic signals in 1921. The popularity of automobile transportation eventually led to more than 200 miles of expressways in 1990—along with air pollution, urban sprawl, and traffic jams.

The most essential urban utility, a safe water supply, improved in the late 1880s after several citizens discovered water by drilling shallow wells. Subsurface water thus replaced the contaminated bayou water provided by the Houston Water Works Company, a private water distribution business started in 1878. The city bought the company in 1906. Continual pumping from the aquifer, however, resulted in serious land subsidence in southeastern Houston in the 1960s. To avoid further sinking and to keep up with industrial demands, most of the water supply for the city was then brought from the Trinity and San Jacinto Rivers.

Extensive paving of land resulted in a significant flooding problem due to the quick runoff of rainwater. Severe floods in 1929 and 1935 inspired formation of the Harris County Flood Control District, but storm flooding in parts of metropolitan Houston has continued. Surges of storm water into the bayou, moreover, flushed contaminants from the ship channel into Galveston Bay and caused massive fish kills. Water pollution has thus been a long-standing problem. When contemplating construction of the ship channel, the Army Corps of Engineers insisted upon an efficient sewerage system. After its completion in 1902 the system was among the best in the nation, but urban growth and neglect shortly overcame the advance. Since that time there has been a continuing struggle to stop water pollution in the ship channel.

Land developers encouraged the spread of the city when they built suburbs such as Pasadena (1891), Houston Heights (1891), Deer Park (1893), Bellaire (1911), and West University Place (1919). The most famous subdivision, because of its wealth, was River Oaks (1923–1924), built by Hugh Potter, Will Hogg, and Mike Hogg. Architect John F. Staub designed sedate mansions on curved streets with large green lawns undivided by walls or fences. An important recent suburban development is The Woodlands, a new town built by oilman George T. Mitchell north of Houston. With minimal environmental disturbance, Mitchell blended homes, businesses, and recreation facilities into the thick pine woods of the area.

To avoid encirclement by other incorporated towns, the Houston City Council under Mayor Oscar Holcombe used its annexation power in 1948–1949 to envelop the older suburbs. As a result, the city doubled in size. In 1956, the council voted more annexation, and in 1960, while arguing with neighboring towns, the council threatened to annex all of the unclaimed land in Harris County. Part of the dispute involved the rich and prestigious land around Clear Lake to the south where the National Aeronautics and Space Administration built the Lyndon B. Johnson Manned Spacecraft Center in 1961. Compromises ended the annexation war of the 1960s,

The skyline of Houston, Texas, in 1993.

but aggressive policies since then have prevented the encirclement of the central city.

For the ordering of urban space, interestingly, Houston voters, embracing conservative business arguments, rejected master zoning ordinances in 1938, 1948, 1962, and 1993. The lack of zoning has not affected development to any great extent, however, since heavy industry has concentrated near the ship channel and subdivisions have controlled land use with deed restrictions. Houston, nonetheless, remains the largest unzoned city in the United States.

For its government after 1905, the city used a modified commission form with at-large elections to replace the earlier aldermanic structure. Houston briefly tried a city manager from 1942 to 1947, and then changed to a strong mayor with council. A ruling by the Justice Department in 1979 concerning fair representation, however, forced a change to nine city council members elected from districts, with five elected at-large. Voters selected the first African American for the council in 1971 and the first Mexican American in 1979. Kathy Whitmire, Houston's first woman mayor, led the city from 1981 to 1991.

An easy attitude toward land use combined with low taxation encouraged business expansion. The greatest city builder in the first half of the twentieth century was banker Jesse H. Jones. By the middle of the 1920s, he had erected about 30 commercial structures, and in 1956 he controlled 50 buildings. Jones brought the 1928 Democratic Convention to Houston and later served as Franklin D. Roosevelt's secretary of commerce. Prosperity after World War II made the city a showcase for modern architecture: the Astrodome (1965), the first enclosed, air-conditioned sports stadium; the world-famous Galleria (1970), a shopping mall with an interior ice-skating rink; and Pennzoil Place (1976), a startling black-glass downtown building that challenged the flat-roof tradition of international style offices.

Houston, meanwhile, evolved culturally and socially. The Texas Medical Center, which started in 1942, eventually attracted 14 large hospitals as well as various supporting institutions. The center, famous for the treatment of cancer and heart disease, was the largest employer in Houston in 1990. John and Dominique de Menil built the Rothko Chapel in 1971 and a museum for the de Menil collection in 1987. This augmented the art collections of the city that began with the building of the Museum of Fine Arts in 1924. A free secondary school system began in 1877, became the Houston Independent School District in 1924, and is now one of the largest in the nation. Rice University started in 1912, supported by the endowment of William Marsh Rice, who made his fortune in Houston during the nineteenth century. The University of Houston began as a junior college in 1927, found

financial support from oilman Hugh Roy Cullen in its early years, and became a part of the state system in 1963. Texas Southern University began in 1934 as a school for black students, the Roman Catholic University of St. Thomas opened in 1945, and Houston Baptist University was founded in 1963.

The Houston Symphony Orchestra started in 1913; the Houston Grand Opera in 1956; the Alley Theater, a repertory company, in 1947; and the Houston Ballet in 1969. The Houston Public Library opened in 1904 with the aid of Andrew Carnegie, and television began in 1949 with broadcasts from KLEE-TV (which became KPRC-TV in 1950). Seven other stations followed, with the first color broadcasts in 1954. Professional sports teams formed—the Houston Oilers football team in 1959 (although it moved to Tennessee in 1997); the Houston Astros (Colt .45s until 1964) baseball team in 1962; and the Houston Rockets basketball team in 1971. All of these accomplishments designated the growing maturation of the city and its people.

—David G. McComb

References

Bullard, Robert D. *Invisible Houston: The Black Experience in Boom and Bust.* College Station: Texas A & M University Press, 1987.

Feagin, Joe R. *Free Enterprise City: Houston in Political-Economic Perspective.* New Brunswick, NJ: Rutgers University Press, 1988.

Houghton, Dorothy Knox Howe, et al. *Houston's Forgotten Heritage: Landscapes, Houses, Interiors, 1824–1914.* Houston, TX: Rice University Press, 1991.

McComb, David G. *Houston, a History.* Austin: University of Texas Press, 1981.

Shelton, Beth Anne, et al. *Houston: Growth and Decline in a Sunbelt Boomtown.* Philadelphia: Temple University Press, 1989.

Sibley, Marilyn McAdams. *The Port of Houston: A History.* Austin: University of Texas Press, 1968.

Howells, William Dean (1837–1920)

William Dean Howells, one of the great American novelists of the nineteenth century, was born in Martin's Ferry, Ohio, and raised in Jefferson, where his father edited the local newspaper. Howells worked in Columbus, Ohio, from 1857 to 1860, and in 1861 he was rewarded with a consular appointment to Venice, Italy, for writing a campaign biography of Abraham Lincoln. His first important book, *Venetian Life,* based on his newspaper columns about that city, appeared in 1866, the same year he moved to Boston to join the staff of the *Atlantic Monthly.*

As editor of this magazine for a decade (1871–1881), Howells publicized the tenets and promoted the practice of literary realism, becoming the patron to a cadre of young American writers including Mark Twain, Henry James, and Bret Harte and the champion of such European realists as Tolstoy, Zola, and Turgenev.

Widely regarded by his contemporaries as the most important American writer of fiction of the generation, Howells practiced what he preached in such novels as *A Modern Instance* (1882) and *The Rise of Silas Lapham* (1885), set largely in Boston, and *A Hazard of New Fortunes* (1890), set almost entirely in New York. In the first novel, however, Howells used the urban setting largely as backdrop for a story of marital discord, and in the second he evaded the darker implications of his urban material, as Kenneth S. Lynn notes, with "intellectual irony, anesthetizing wit, and comic perspective."

Particularly in the "frantic panorama" of *A Hazard of New Fortunes,* however, Howells wrote an urban novel that foreshadowed the urban naturalism of Theodore Dreiser's *Sister Carrie.* From the street life of the slums to the salons of the upper crust, Howells explored the class divisions endemic to the modern industrial city through the eyes of his protagonists, Basil and Isabel March. Much as the March family moves from Boston to New York in the novel, the Howells family had recently moved to New York to exploit its increasing importance as a publishing center—an experience Howells later described as his "ugly exile." Moreover, as Amy Kaplan remarks, "Howells's narrative strategies for representing the city parallel the Marches' strategies for settling it." In effect, Howells represents the city as a series of fluid borders or boundaries to be negotiated by the reader even as the characters in the text encounter different camps, classes, and neighborhoods in New York. The novel "both fulfills and exhausts the project of realism: to embrace social diversity within the outlines of a broader community and to assimilate a plethora of facts and details into a unified narrative form," according to Kaplan.

Howells's later novels, such as *The Quality of Mercy* (1892), *A Traveller from Altruria* (1894), and *The Landlord at Lion's Head* (1896), largely eschew urban representation to consider utopian ideas and more conventional domestic themes. Still, Howells praised without stint Stephen Crane's naturalistic treatment of the Bowery in *Maggie; A Girl of the Streets,* and he enthusiastically reviewed Henry Blake Fuller's Chicago novel *The Cliff-Dwellers* when it appeared in 1893.

Though he feared he had been relegated to the status of a "dead cult" with changes in literary fashion after the turn of the century, at his death Howells was the author of well over 100 books, including 35 novels.

—*Gary Scharnhorst*

References

Arms, George. "Howells' New York Novel: Comedy and Belief." *New England Quarterly* 21 (1948): 313–325.

Kaplan, Amy. " 'The Knowledge of the Line': Realism and the City in Howells's *A Hazard of New Fortunes*." *PMLA* 101 (1986): 69–81.

Lynn, Kenneth S. *William Dean Howells: An American Life.* New York: Harcourt, Brace and World, 1971.

Hull House

Hull House is the best-known settlement house in the United States, perhaps in the world. Jane Addams began the settlement in a large house originally belonging to the Charles Hull family in a deteriorated slum neighborhood near Chicago's loop. By 1910, a complex of a dozen buildings, all part of the settlement, surrounded the original house. In addition, Addams persuaded the son of a neighborhood landlord to donate nearby land for what became Hull House's first playground. That playground served as a demonstration project, helping to convince the Chicago city government to add publicly financed playgrounds to its existing park system. Daily programming at Hull House emphasized education and recreation for the predominantly Italian immigrants in the neighborhood. Besides a nursery, the settlement offered English and citizenship classes, social clubs, and large group activities, such as a neighborhood orchestra.

Addams attracted many well-to-do, college-educated residents who lived in dormitory rooms and ate in a common dining room. At its peak, this group numbered around 60. Living at Hull House were some of the most famous reformers of the early twentieth century, such as Julia Lathrop and Grace Abbott, who served respectively as the first and second heads of the Children's Bureau; and Alice Hamilton, who pioneered the field of industrial medicine. These people used Hull House as a base to support their individual reform operations. Others, such as Frances Perkins, the first woman cabinet officer, and Robert Weaver, the first African-American cabinet officer, were also Hull House residents, although not prominent in settlement house activities. Following Addams's death in 1935, Hull House had more difficulty attracting talented residents. Increasingly, professional social workers, especially men with families like Hull House head Russell Ballard, objected to the requirement that they live at the settlement. Hull House dropped the practice of requiring residence in the house in 1962.

Since Jane Addams's death, Hull House has never had a director approaching her stature. Adena Miller Rich (1935–1937) served as acting director. Subsequent directors were Charlotte Carr (1937–1943) and Russell Ballard (1943–1962). Stability evaporated when the University of Illinois decided to build its Chicago campus on the Hull House site. The original house plus the dining room building were reconstructed on the campus as a museum. Meanwhile, the settlement reconstituted itself as Hull House Association and began operating at various locations around Chicago. These included the Jane Addams Center on Chicago's North Side, Henry Booth House in a large public housing project on Chicago's South Side, and the Senior Centers of Metropolitan Chicago. By 1994, the settlement was operating six community-based centers and 26 satellites throughout Chicago. Some sites only worked with seniors or day care. Others had a mixed program of the arts, recreation, and social services. Paul Jans, who served as director from 1963 to 1969, oversaw this conversion to a multicenter operation. Robert T. Adams (1969–1980) expanded the organization. Patricia Sharpe (1980–1992) succeeded him, and then turned over the directorship to Gordon Johnson, the first African American to lead Hull House.

—*Judith Ann Trolander*

See also
Addams, Jane; Kelley, Florence; Settlement House Movement.
References
Bryan, Mary Linn McCree, and Allen F. Davis. *One Hundred Years at Hull-House.* Indianapolis: Indiana University Press, 1990.
Lissak, Rivka Shpak. *Pluralism and Progressives: Hull-House and the New Immigrants, 1890–1919.* Chicago: University of Chicago Press, 1989.
Polachek, Hilda Satt. *I Came A Stranger: The Story of a Hull-House Girl.* Dana J. Polachek, ed. Urbana: University of Illinois Press, 1989.

Immigration in the Late Twentieth Century

The mosaic of the United States has been changed by the significant increase of international migration since 1970. At the beginning of the twentieth century, the destinations of most immigrants were the growing industrializing cities of the Northeast and Midwest. At the close of the century, the patterns of urban migration have new implications for economic development and the labor market; social, cultural, and geographic concentration; political mobilization and agenda setting; and community organizations and cleavages. All in all, the increase of international migration has had a mixture of positive and disconcerting effects on urban communities and local governments.

A recent development is the transformation of many major American cities by the increasing flow of immigrants since 1970. *Current Population Reports* (1995) reveals that in 1994, the foreign-born population of the United States was 8.5 percent. This was nearly double the percentage of foreign-born residents in 1970 (4.8 percent). Although the 1994 level is the highest since World War II, greater proportions of the population were born abroad during the early part of the century (14.7 percent in 1910). Yet, during each period, the destinations of immigrants were not randomly distributed throughout the country; in both eras, they were primarily large urban communities.

Early in the century, the East Coast was the destination of most immigrants, but the primary recipient of recent immigrants has been the West Coast. More specifically, California is home to 11.7 million foreign-born persons, more than one-third of all immigrants to the United States and nearly one-fourth of all Californians. New York ranks second with 2.9 million foreign-born residents and Florida stands third with 2.1 million. In fact, only six states (those three along with Texas, Illinois, and New Jersey) are home to 64.7 percent of all the foreign-born living in the country. In addition to their destinations, the origins of these immigrants are important. The largest immigrant group is from Mexico (6.2 million), and the next largest group is from the Philippine

Islands (1.033 million). In fact, about 60 percent of immigrants to the United States between 1994 and 1996 came from either Asia or the Americas south of the United States.

The demographics of these newcomers are also significant. Twenty percent of the foreign-born population have come to the United States in the past five years. The most recent of these immigrants are younger, on the average, than the native-born population, and they have a bifurcated educational pattern (that is, the foreign-born are both more educated and less educated than their native counterparts). They have a higher unemployment rate than the native-born (9.1 vs. 6.8 percent), and they have a lower median income than native-born Americans ($12,179 vs. $15,816). Finally, the foreign-born are much more likely (1.6 times) to live in poverty than the native-born, and the more recent immigrants are *twice* as likely to be experiencing poverty. When using these numbers, it is important always to remember that figures concerning the foreign-born population include some undocumented immigrants, refugees, and temporary residents such as students and guest workers as well as legally admitted permanent immigrants. In fact, some figures about foreign-born immigrants are heavily weighted to count undocumented immigrants.

As indicated earlier, California was the "welcoming harbor" for waves of immigrants during the mid-1990s, and New York was their second choice. Between 1994 and 1996 nearly 2.5 million immigrants were admitted to the United States, and nearly 40 percent of them intended to live in either New York State or California. The leading metropolitan destinations were New York (about 15 percent) and Los Angeles–Long Beach (about 8 percent), followed by Chicago (about 5 percent), Miami-Hialeah (just under 5 percent), and the area including Washington, D.C., and the surrounding parts of Maryland and Virginia (about 3.5 percent).

Most immigrants from certain countries have primary destinations and concentrate in specific areas. For example, more than seven of every ten Mexican immigrants live in either California, Texas, or Illinois. New Jersey and New York were the leading destinations for immigrants from the Dominican Republic. Cubans, Haitians, and Jamaicans headed for Florida, and immigrants from the Philippines, Vietnam, China, India, Korea, and Taiwan had California as their primary residential destination. As a result, the international migration of the past 25 years has not only been substantial, but the receiving communities are not randomly distributed.

As in the early years of the century, contemporary immigrants head for urban communities, although they are in the West and Southwest rather than the East and Midwest. As a result, the urban cultural milieu has become more multicultural than ever. Traditional ethnic/immigrant enclaves such as Chinatowns and barrios have expanded, but other immigrant subcommunities have also been established. "Little Havana" and "Little Haiti" in Miami are examples of enclaves created since the 1960s. But the new ethnic regions are not just composed of Asians and Latins. In Brooklyn, the influx of Russian émigrés has altered that community's composition as well as entrepreneurial activities there.

The infusion of sizable numbers of immigrants in the neighborhoods of many major cities has contributed to housing problems of overcrowding, high rents, competition among groups for the limited amount of lower-cost housing, and neighborhood succession (i.e., the conversion of a residential area from predominance by one group to another). In several cases, immigrants have helped to reinvigorate declining neighborhoods by reducing vacancy rates, upgrading housing stock, and starting small businesses.

Another social and cultural impact of the new urban immigrants has been the development of organizations and societies defined by the cultural or national origins of their members. Mutual aid societies, rotating credit associations, and immigrant social clubs are all found in urban areas, just as they were early in the century. These organizations ease the adaptation and survival of newcomers by providing networks of information and, potentially, economic resources. Simultaneously, when immigrants maintain their native cultures, they place some demands on local social, political, and educational systems. The multiplicity of languages among school populations has produced programs such as English as a second language or mulitcultural/multilingual emphases and awareness in primary and secondary schools. While, on the one hand, school districts may be experiencing increased student populations because of immigration and therefore receive increased state funding allocations, on the other hand, they might have to develop different or additional curricula, or both, and might have greater staffing needs.

The provision of social services, including education, has been another aspect of cities that has required service providers to make bureaucratic adjustments and modify language and cultural mores and values. Recent federal policies regarding immigrants' (both legal and illegal) access to and participation in social services have raised volatile issues such as equity, immigrants as contributing members of society, fairness versus self-sufficiency, Americanization, and the cost-benefit ratio. That is, a public discourse focuses on the relative worth and contribution of immigrants compared to the economic "drain" and cultural balkanization they supposedly cause. The debate especially manifests itself in cities with the expression of concerns about the social and economic effects of excluding immigrants from social welfare services that they had previously received.

Finally, in the cultural and social realms, recent immigrants have magnified the urban possibilities regarding food, traditions, festivals, and other activities in which immigrant and nonimmigrant populations both participate. Many cities have seen the establishment of cultural centers, restaurants, and other businesses in areas like Little Tokyo, Little Korea, or Olvera Street in Los Angeles. The net result has been additional contributions to tourism and the formation of small businesses.

It is not insignificant that many of these cultural and economic centers have developed in older, declining parts of cities. The Brighton Beach section of Brooklyn is only one example of this dynamic as increasing Russian immigration to the area has brought new shops, coffeehouses, restaurants, and small retail businesses. The residential and economic resurgence has not only changed the cultural milieu but has also stimulated the local economy.

Both the magnitude of immigration and its urban destination have had important consequences for American cities and raised significant questions. Among the critical issues that they have evoked are (1) the human capital skills of immigrants relative to the needs of local labor markets; (2) the competition for jobs between immigrants and native-born workers; (3) the establishment of businesses, capital formation, and expansion of the urban economic base; and (4) the impact of immigrants on costs of housing and other local amenities, goods, and services.

In terms of its participation in the labor force, the foreign-born population has a higher unemployment rate than the native-born, 9.1 percent compared to 6.8 percent. Also, these immigrants are among both the least and the most educated parts of the urban population. Recent immigrants 25 years and older are more likely to have a college degree than either natives or immigrants who came earlier. That is to say, 11.5 percent of the recent immigrants have a graduate or professional degree, but only about 7.5 percent of the native-born and earlier immigrants have such degrees. At the same time, a recent immigrant is less likely to have graduated from high school. Only 17.1 percent of the native-born over the age of

25 did not graduate from high school, but 36.0 percent of immigrants do not have a high school degree.

These characteristics present a labor force bifurcated in such a way that some new immigrants are doctors, engineers, scientists, and so on, while others have entry-level, low-paid positions in the service sector. Most large cities have experienced the economic transformation from manufacturing and industrially related businesses to service, financial, and high tech industries based on information and knowledge. As a result, immigrant workers have participated at both "ends" of the job spectrum because of their differential educational attainments. Some of these labor market developments have been influenced by the immigration policy reforms of 1990, which provide more "slots" for individuals possessing "employment needed skills and training" rather than for those who would come to reunify their families. In addition, an allotment of places for foreign entrepreneurs with liquid capital (more than $1 million) has been incorporated into the current immigration admission policy.

Thus, the labor market participation by urban immigrants is determined by their competitiveness for jobs and their location in specific labor markets. Lesser-educated immigrants are more likely to be found in the service and light-industry sectors of the economy. In communities like Los Angeles or San Diego, Hispanic immigrants work as laborers and domestics; in construction, hotels, and restaurants; or in the garment industry. Similar patterns exist for cities like New York, Miami, Chicago, Houston, and San Francisco. In some areas, these workers are Mexican or Central American; in other communities, they are Haitians, Vietnamese, Dominicans, or Filipinos. It is in these segments of local labor markets that some direct competition does exist between immigrant and native-born workers.

For example, in 1995 Alejandro Portes and Guillermo Grenier examined the impact of immigration on the Miami–Dade County metropolitan area. They found that the influx of Cubans, Nicaraguans, Panamanians, and Haitians created some labor tensions between the immigrants and African-American workers. Immigrant workers penetrated service and unskilled jobs at the expense of native-born minorities. One consequence has been tension between groups as immigrants competed not only for lower-end jobs but also for the limited supply of lower-cost housing. Economists have determined that increasing numbers of immigrants in residential areas are accompanied by increasing rents and land values and that competition for restricted segments of the

Immigrants take the citizenship oath at the Flag Pavilion in Seattle Center, Seattle, on July 4, 1993.

housing market usually results in a succession of ethnic neighborhoods or fierce contention for "neighborhood turf." For example, south central Los Angeles had been a primary area of African-American concentration until the 1980s. Then the influx of Central American and Mexican immigrants into the district resulted in a declining number of African Americans and higher rents for all.

Immigrants do much more than participate in the urban labor force. In particular, the emergence of immigrant entrepreneurs has also accompanied increased immigration to cities, and the nature of capital formation has been particularly important. Sometimes immigrants bring investment capital with them to start new ventures. This has been the case among some Korean and Chinese immigrants. At the same time, some immigrants have arrived with substantial human capital and skills (i.e., educational levels, professional status, and previous work experience) and received returns on their human capital in a few years, following some initial downward job mobility. Thus, one important aspect of ethnic enclaves is the residential concentration of immigrants, which serves as a resource base or market for new immigrant enterprises. The presence of immigrants creates both consumer demands and also preferences for "cultural" goods and services at the same time it provides a labor supply.

A conducive environment exists for such entrepreneurial activities as ethnic/immigrant succession enterprises (i.e., newer waves of immigrant group members buying existing businesses) and/or new businesses that rely heavily on immigrant clientele and workers. Another aspect of ethnic urban enclaves is the economic activity generated by increases in the immigrant population. For some groups, rotating credit associations have accumulated capital and provided access to funds to start small businesses. Korean and Chinese immigrants have been especially quick to use these organizations to help start small family businesses. This process allows them to enter certain niches of the local economy. They might open small grocery stores, retail outlets, bakeries, flower shops, dry cleaners, and so on, in which immigrants establish entrepreneurial activities in their own neighborhoods or other minority sections of the city. The latter has been another source of conflict between newer immigrants and native-born residents, particularly African Americans, as was evident in the Los Angeles riots of the 1990s.

Still another aspect of ethnic enclaves and enterprises is their economic effect on the local economy and housing market. Studies of housing markets indicate that greater numbers of immigrants exert positive effects on local economies, partly by increasing the price of housing and land. This pattern is most discernible in rents in concentrated immigrant neighborhoods. Economists have called this the "cost of culture" in which the preference to reside and work inside the enclave raises the demand for limited housing. At the same time, the growing number of immigrant enterprises has benefited the small business sector, either by reviving local retail or service operations or by introducing new small businesses. Although not as readily identifiable, increasing immigrant populations have also produced foreign capital investments or access to foreign markets. One example is the growth of trade with Latin American countries brought about by the increased number of Cubans and other Latin American immigrants in Miami.

Another economic dimension of immigration to American cities is the participation of immigrants in public assistance programs. Recent immigrants are more likely to receive public assistance than natives (5.7 percent vs. 2.9 percent), but the rates drop dramatically for immigrants who have been here for five years or more. Aid for Families with Dependent Children (AFDC) is the primary source of public assistance income. Nevertheless, analysis of the economic impact of immigrants on cities reveals both costs and revenues (retail sales, tax revenues, gains in property value, etc.) but shows that the balance generally favors the positive side.

The changing composition of urban populations, with sizable numbers of immigrants from specific ethnic groups heading for particular cities, has also brought about some important political developments. Most immediate has been the political definition of newer immigrant groups. For some of them, especially Hispanics and Asians, the reformulation of group boundaries has been part of the assimilation process. That is, the coming together of Dominicans, Colombians, and Salvadorans or of Chinese, Filipinos, and Vietnamese into single groups, to varying degrees, has been part of the American pattern. At the turn of the century, Italians who immigrated to the United States identified themselves within specific regions in Italy. After they had spent some time in America, the idea of being Italian rather than Venetian or Roman became a new ethnic identity. Thus, local politics in cities with high rates of immigration are often characterized as Asian-American, Hispanic-American, or Eastern European politics. Some have used terms like "the newer ethnic politics of contemporary cities" to identify this trend.

With the formation of these new conglomerate groups come new group interests and activities. Residential concentration and the expansion of immigrant enclaves in accord with the new identities create new, common interests regarding such issues as neighborhood enhancement, access to policymakers, city services (e.g., social services, public safety, infrastructure maintenance), and representation. Moreover, the development of organizations based on these newly defined immigrant communities has allowed the communities to use perceived cultural linkages to define their group interests, including economic advancement, access to capital, cultural maintenance, and adequate housing. At the same time, the process has contributed to tensions between one group and others that are not considered part of the larger conglomerate. One notable example is the friction that exists between Korean-American merchants and African Americans, particularly in Los Angeles. Issues of hiring local residents, cultural and linguistic differences, perceptions that immigrants dominate the local economy, and a sense of unbalanced and unfair competition (from the perspective of native-born residents) have all become sources of tension between groups.

Competition for jobs, especially in the service sector, has created an anti-immigrant stance among native-born and older ethnic communities (or both). This competition can also manifest itself between newer and older immigrant groups. Since World War II, Puerto Ricans have largely migrated to the Northeast, and among Latinos, they have been the most influential in New York metropolitan region politics. But the growth of Dominican and Colombian communities in New York City has presented challenges within the larger Latino community for political positioning with City Hall, local political elites, and civic organizations.

The character of the relationship between immigrant communities and local politics is almost always shaped, at least in part, by the degree of intergroup competition or concord in the distribution of limited resources and services. Their ability (or inability) to unite, organize, and mobilize for political action are key determinants of local politics. For immigrants, political, organizational, and economic development are a crucial part of the arrival on the urban scene.

The nature of future relations between immigrants and cities will be determined by whether or not immigrant groups receive greater empowerment (politically and economically) and the degree to which their political interests and agenda are recognized and acknowledged in the next millennium. Competition between immigrant groups and native-born Americans, especially minority communities, will almost certainly continue to increase in intensity. This heightened competition can lead to greater social, political, and economic hostility and strife, but it can also produce opportunities for coalitions across immigrant and native-born lines. It all depends on whether American society recognizes the legitimacy of the new diversity and if its cities serve as social, economic, and political venues for a new dynamic.

—*John A. Garcia*

References

Bouvier, Leon. *Peaceful Invasions: Immigration and Changing America.* Washington, DC: Center for Immigration Studies, 1991.

Browning, R., D. Marshall, and D. Tabb. *Racial Politics in American Cities.* New York: Longman, 1990.

Foner, Nancy, ed. *New Immigrants in New York.* New York: Columbia University Press, 1987.

Horton, John. *The Politics of Diversity: Immigration, Resistance and Change in Monterey Park, California.* Philadelphia: Temple University Press, 1995.

Jennings, James, ed. *Blacks, Latinos, and Asians in Urban America.* Westport, CT: Praeger Publishers, 1994.

Muller, Thomas. *Immigrants and the American City.* New York: New York University Press, 1993.

Muller, Thomas, and Thomas J. Espenshade. *The Fourth Wave: California's Newest Immigrants.* Washington, DC: Urban Institute Press, 1985.

Ong, Paul, Edna Bonacich, and Lucie Cheng, eds. *The New Asian Immigration in Los Angeles and Global Restructuring.* Philadelphia: Temple University Press, 1994.

Portes, Alejandro, and Alex Stepick. *City on the Edge: The Transformation of Miami.* Berkeley: University of California Press, 1993.

Portes, Alejandro, and Ruben Rumbaut. *Immigrant America.* Berkeley: University of California Press, 1990.

Waldinger, Roger, and Mehdi Bozorgmehr, eds. *Ethnic Los Angeles.* New York: Russell Sage Foundation, 1996.

Incorporation

The right of local self-government has been highly valued throughout American history, and nowhere is this more evident than in the municipal incorporation process. Incorporation is the procedure for vesting a locality with the powers of a municipal corporation. Through incorporation, thousands of crossroads communities have become governmental units with the authority to levy taxes, make ordinances, and generally determine the policies guiding their future. While incorporation has permitted localities to exercise governing authority, it has also contributed to the fragmentation of metropolitan America. One suburban tract after another has become a governing unit under permissive incorporation laws, ensuring that the typical American metropolis is a mosaic of independent municipalities.

During the colonial era, municipal incorporation was not such an easily obtained privilege. A locality became a municipal corporation through grant of a royal charter, and generally only the larger communities received such charters. After the Revolution, state legislatures assumed responsibility for municipal incorporation, and during the nineteenth century state lawmakers handed out charters to virtually every community with any aspirations of being a city. In the course of the next century, to relieve legislatures of the burden of incorporating each municipality separately, most states adopted general incorporation laws that defined a standard procedure for incorporating municipalities. Typically, these general laws provided that residents seeking municipal incorporation had to petition county officials, and then the county officers authorized a referendum on the question of incorporation in the petitioning community. If a majority of the community's voters favored incorporation, then the community became a municipality. Some states imposed a minimum population requirement for incorporation, but it was usually low. For example, California fixed the minimum at 200 inhabitants, whereas in Illinois the figure was only 150. The barriers to incorporation, then, were minimal. State law facilitated the creation of municipal corporations and did nothing to limit the proliferation of these local government units.

Consequently, by the early twentieth century, thousands of municipalities dotted the map of America. In 1910, there were 1,066 municipalities in Illinois, 880 in Pennsylvania, and 784 in Ohio. Some localities incorporated to provide such municipal services as water, sewerage, and fire and police protection. But other municipalities were created as tax havens where manufacturing concerns were assured of low tax rates. Still other communities incorporated to protect local morals, for as municipalities they could enact ordinances outlawing saloons. Yet others were created as refuges for saloons and sinners who faced prosecution in surrounding communities. Municipal incorporation could serve many purposes, and Americans readily exploited the permissive incorporation laws.

During the twentieth century, the increasing number of municipal corporations in suburban areas was especially noteworthy. Because the statutory requirements for absorbing incorporated territory was generally stiffer than for annexing land that was not incorporated, suburbanites often used incorporation as a defense against annexation. For example, municipalities in Missouri could annex land that was not incorporated without the consent of the residents of the area to be annexed. Yet consolidation of incorporated municipalities required majority approval of the voters in each community. Consequently, between 1945 and 1950, 54 new municipal corporations were created in suburban St. Louis County, in large measure to escape annexation by adjacent communities. Builders also sponsored incorporation to avoid the county's zoning and building restrictions, which were effective only in unincorporated territory. Through incorporation, a region could thus avoid annexation and the regulations and taxes imposed by neighboring municipalities, as well as the requirements mandated by county government. Permissive incorporation, in effect, allowed the creation of government units dedicated to avoiding government.

In any case, by the middle of the twentieth century a myriad of municipal corporations surrounded some of the nation's largest cities. By 1960 there were 98 municipalities in St. Louis County and 68 in Los Angeles County. Good-government reformers and political scientists strongly criticized this governmental fragmentation, writing of the balkanization of suburbia and referring to suburban America as a crazy quilt of cities and villages.

Responding to this criticism, state lawmakers attempted to tighten the requirements for incorporation. Beginning with Minnesota in 1959, some states created local government

agencies to review petitions for incorporation and to deny such petitions if they were deemed detrimental to the good of the metropolitan area as a whole. Other states adopted what became known as anti-incorporation statutes. For example, in 1967 Ohio provided that no new community could incorporate within three miles of the boundary of an existing municipal corporation unless it, in effect, had the consent of the existing municipality. This clearly was an attempt to stop the use of incorporation as a defense against annexation.

Yet not every state adopted review commissions or anti-incorporation laws, and in some parts of the nation scores of new municipalities continued to appear. During the 1970s and 1980s, 1,014 new municipalities were created in the United States, but 236 of these were in the single state of Texas. In fact, during the 1970s the South alone accounted for 430 of the nation's incorporations, or 60 percent of the total, whereas in the Northeast only 14 municipalities were created, or 2 percent of the national figure. Incorporation of municipalities thus continued, but it was most significant in the South and of minor importance in the Northeast.

—*Jon C. Teaford*

See also
Fragmentation of Municipal Government; Home Rule; States and Cities.

References
Bigger, Richard, and James D. Kitchen. *How the Cities Grew: A Century of Municipal Independence and Expansionism in Metropolitan Los Angeles.* Los Angeles: Haynes Foundation, 1952.
Teaford, Jon C. *City and Suburb: The Political Fragmentation of Metropolitan America, 1850–1970.* Baltimore: Johns Hopkins University Press, 1979.

Indianapolis, Indiana

When Indiana became a state in 1816, Congress donated four sections of public land for a state capital. Four years later, a commission recommended, and the legislature approved, a wilderness site near the geographic center of the state. Surveyors platted a one-square-mile area in the middle of the congressional donation, and the downtown of Indianapolis is still known as the "Mile Square." One of the surveyors had assisted Pierre L'Enfant in laying out the nation's capital, and the Washington influence is obvious in the 1821 plat: broad streets, diagonal avenues, and a circle (intended as the location of the governor's residence) at the center of the city. Centrality in the state was the town's only natural advantage; the adjacent White River proved unsuitable for navigation, and early land routes were poor. Well into the 1840s, the capital remained a barely accessible village.

Railroad connections secured during the late 1840s and early 1850s (and completion of the nation's first "union" depot in 1853), followed by growth during the 1860s that the Civil War induced, transformed the town into Indiana's principal urban center. By 1870, its population was more than double that of its closest intrastate rival, and the state's capital had also become its manufacturing and commercial leader. Continued growth was fueled (literally) during the 1890s by exploiting nearby natural gas fields that had been discovered a few years earlier; both the population and the number of manufacturing establishments in the city increased by 60 percent during the decade. The 1890s also witnessed construction of the capital's most recognizable edifice, the Indiana Soldiers and Sailors Monument located on (the renamed) Monument Circle in the center of the Mile Square.

As was generally true of American cities, the city's population growth largely resulted from immigration. During the middle of the nineteenth century, Ireland and, especially, the German states supplied most of the city's foreign-born residents. In 1870, when 22 percent of the capital's residents were foreign-born, almost half of the immigrant population was German and almost one-third was Irish. Compared to many other urban areas, however, the "new" immigration from Southern and Eastern Europe during the late nineteenth and early twentieth centuries touched Indiana's largest city only slightly. By 1920, the Board of Trade could, with some justification, proclaim Indianapolis the "most American section of the country" and a "100 percent American town." While these assertions were exaggerated, they did reflect the reality that only 5 percent of the city's population was foreign-born in that year—one of the lowest rates among large northern cities. The African-American population, on the other hand, grew steadily during the decades after the Civil War. Comprising only 6 percent of Indianapolis residents in 1870, blacks accounted for 11 percent of its population in 1920; by 1990, the figure stood at 21 percent.

The years of the late nineteenth and early twentieth centuries are often considered the city's Golden Age. In addition to the benefits of the gas boom (which did not last much beyond 1900), Indianapolis became the hub of the nation's most extensive interurban railway network. Throngs of shoppers, businessmen, conventioneers, and sightseers arrived and departed daily through the Traction Terminal, reputedly the country's largest, which opened in 1904 within blocks of major department stores and hotels. Interurban connections could be made for most of the state's major cities, and 400 cars were soon entering the city daily on the various lines.

The capital also benefited from development of the automobile industry. Of negligible importance in 1900, by 1920 the industry ranked second in the city both in the number of persons employed and the value of its product. While Detroit assumed command of the mass production market, the Hoosier capital was home to such high-performance, elegant, and costly makes as Cole, Marmon, and Stutz. Even after automobile production had ceased, fabricating automobile parts continued as a mainstay of the city's economy until the early 1980s. Completion in 1909 of the Indianapolis Motor Speedway as an automobile testing facility led to the inauguration two years later of the Indianapolis 500-Mile Race. This "Greatest Spectacle in Racing" is said to attract the largest one-day crowd of any sporting event in the world.

The city also attained some national prominence in politics and publishing. Local lawyers Thomas A. Hendricks and Charles Warren Fairbanks were elected vice president of the United States in 1884 and 1904, respectively. Another Indianapolis attorney, Benjamin Harrison, served as president from 1889 to 1893. And a former mayor, Thomas Taggart, chaired the Democratic National Committee in the early twentieth century. The Bobbs-Merrill publishing house issued books that won both popular and critical acclaim, and the city's literary reputation was secured by the presence of such well-known authors as James Whitcomb Riley, Meredith Nicholson, and Booth Tarkington. Several of Tarkington's novels (including *The Magnificent Ambersons,* which won a Pulitzer Prize in 1919) were set in a thinly disguised "Midland city" based on his hometown of Indianapolis.

Indianapolis was not immune to the national xenophobia of the years after World War I. The Ku Klux Klan was powerful throughout Indiana during the first half of the 1920s, and state and municipal politics in the capital were both influenced for several years by the hooded order. The twenties also saw construction of a new, segregated high school that all the city's African-American youth were required to attend, as well as passage of a residential zoning ordinance (invalidated by the courts) that would legally have restricted the housing options of black residents.

The Depression of the 1930s affected Indianapolis much as it affected other urban areas across the country. The city's economy, increasingly reliant on the production and sale of consumer goods, was sensitive to deferred household purchases. Interurbans had been in perilous financial shape even before 1929, and the closure of one line after another during the Depression further weakened the local economy. Starting in 1940, however, defense dollars and defense workers began to trickle, and then pour, into the capital. The city's metalworking industries rapidly converted to wartime production, and the transition to "Toolmaker to the Nation" was accompanied by full employment and burgeoning payrolls.

The demographic history of Indianapolis after World War II has mirrored the national pattern of suburban growth and central city decline. During the 1950s, the city's population grew 11.5 percent, but the suburban ring within Marion County leaped ahead by 78 percent growth. That trend has continued, and population loss has been especially severe in Center Township, the core of the city, in spite of various efforts to stanch the flow.

This residential deconcentration was greatly facilitated by the construction of multiple interstate highways around and through the metropolitan area. As it was for the railroads and interurban railways, Indianapolis remains a "crossroads" for much of the automotive traffic crossing the Midwest. Its strategic location and highway connections have led an increasing number of warehouses, distribution centers, and motor and air freight firms to locate in or near the capital. The I-465 beltway, in particular, has been a magnet for development.

The most important governmental and political innovation in the city's recent history was the implementation, on January 1, 1970, of a consolidated city-county government dubbed "Unigov." State legislation permitting the merger had passed the previous year after relatively little public debate and no popular referendum. This unusual circumstance is partially explained by the fact that Republicans controlled both the executive and legislative branches of government at the city, county, and state levels and pushed the measure through in order to incorporate thousands of suburban, mostly Republican, voters into the city's electorate. Democrats then and since have considered the consolidation a Republican power play ("Unigrab") that had a particularly pernicious effect on the political influence of the capital's African-American community. Since Unigov's enactment, Republicans have won every mayoral contest and have controlled the City-County Council, although during the early 1990s this one-party domination was showing signs of perhaps weakening.

In spite of its name, Unigov is by no means a complete consolidation of all governmental functions in Marion County. School systems, police forces, and fire departments, for example, all remain decentralized. But a single executive and a central legislative body have brought increased coherence to the formation of countywide policies. Indeed, some observers credit the reorganization, especially the creation of a Department of Metropolitan Development, with making a number of downtown revitalization initiatives possible during the 1970s and 1980s.

Mayors Richard G. Lugar (1968–1976) and William H. Hudnut III (1976–1992) were highly successful in energizing what they described as a "public-private partnership" on behalf of the city. Lugar generally receives substantial credit for Unigov, for strengthening ties with the business and philanthropic communities, and for aggressively seeking federal aid. Hudnut and his administration get most of the plaudits for orchestrating and overseeing the revitalization of downtown Indianapolis and for using amateur and professional sports as a path to civic visibility and economic development. Hudnut's successor, Stephen Goldsmith, has focused on "privatizing" many governmental functions.

The Unigov consolidation expanded the city's boundaries to the Marion County lines (for an area of 402 square miles) and increased the city's population from 476,258 (in 1960) to 744,624 (1970). It stood at 741,952 in 1990.

—*Robert G. Barrows*

References

Bodenhamer, David J., and Robert G. Barrows, eds. *The Encyclopedia of Indianapolis.* Bloomington and Indianapolis: Indiana University Press, 1994.

Dunn, Jacob Piatt. *Greater Indianapolis.* 2 vols. Chicago: Lewis Publishing, 1910.

Leary, Edward A. *Indianapolis: The Story of a City.* Indianapolis, IN: Bobbs-Merrill, 1971.

Owen, C. James, and York Willbern. *Governing Metropolitan Indianapolis: The Politics of Unigov.* Berkeley: University of California Press, 1985.

Industrial Suburbs

Suburbs are independently incorporated municipalities or districts on the fringes or outskirts of cities, and industrial or manufacturing suburbs are a special type. Historically, industrial suburbs were classified separately from manufacturing suburbs. According to Victor Jones, communities were classified as industrial rather than manufacturing if more than 30 percent of local jobs are in retail trades—making industrial communities more diversified than manufacturing communities. The terms are now used interchangeably as industrial suburbs have evolved and changed since World War II.

Today, industrial suburbs are specialized places of employment that feature manufacturing or industrial jobs. Thus, all suburbs in which 50 percent or more of the local jobs are in manufacturing or industry are classified as either industrial or manufacturing suburbs. This is so even if the percentage of workers employed in retail trade exceeds 30 percent of all local employment. In whatever combination, manufacturing institutions must provide the majority of the employment opportunities. Additionally, the value added to the local economy from adjusted manufacturing value of product sales must exceed that of total retail sales and banking and finance.

Industrial suburbs share the definitive characteristics of functional specialization in manufacturing. They are not residential or bedroom communities. Their very existence is based on the production of goods and commodities for wholesale distribution. These suburbs provide jobs for local and neighboring community residents—including nearby central cities. They are part of the metropolitan structure as a whole but are functionally differentiated and semi-independent of the larger central cities. Harlan Paul Douglass called them suburbs of production rather than suburbs of consumption or residential suburbs. Today, we simply call them manufacturing or industrial suburbs.

Although industrial suburbs are generally larger than residential suburbs, the size of industrial manufacturing enterprises is unimportant. There can be a mix of many small, medium, and large enterprises, or several large manufacturers and no medium or small enterprises, or only small enterprises. Traditionally, the basic enterprises in industrial suburbs have been auto assembly, petroleum refining and related industries, rubber and plastics, transportation equipment, chemicals and allied products, metals fabrication, and appliance and machinery manufacturing.

The quality of residential life in traditional industrial suburbs is secondary to manufacturing. Local government, education, and service industries are all focused on supporting the manufacturing interests. Residents tend to have comparable socioeconomic status to blue-collar, inner-city workers. The nature of traditional production creates an environment of pollution, foul air, acid rain, carcinogens, and other industrial wastes. Hence, fewer professionals, technical and kindred workers, managers, and proprietors reside in these communities. This results in a higher proportion of residents who rent rather than own their dwellings when industrial suburbs are compared to residential suburbs. Further, major shopping centers, with all of the attendant retail services, are usually located in cleaner, neighboring, more white-collar, middle-class communities.

In the past few decades, new, nontraditional, high tech communications and microchip manufacturing are changing the quality of life in industrial suburbs. A combination of suburban middle-class amenities and new technologies has resulted in the development of the novel high tech industrial parks that now typify the newer, cleaner industrial suburbs.

The new trend is toward specialization of industrial suburbs and regional clustering of economic competitors. Vanguard industries include those in advanced aerospace, electronics, and communications—all low-pollution high technology fields. This is supported by the movement of central offices and even corporate headquarters to suburbs. The new industrial suburbs are thus becoming professional, technical, and managerial havens of employment and residence.

These changes have resulted in a reversal of the trend in the late 1970s toward declining industrial suburbs and have led to further decentralization of industrial manufacturing both nationally and internationally. According to the 1986 Municipal Year Book, the 1980 census lists 267 industrial suburbs for which data are available and recorded. They are concentrated in the West (79 suburbs) and the North-Central (76 suburbs) portions of the United States. Historically, they were concentrated in the Northeast and North-Central regions.

The future suggests continuing evolution of the industrial suburbs. This includes greater numbers, greater product specialization, greater decentralization, and greater regional and international specialization. There will be improved quality of life in these communities coupled with better life chances and employment opportunities. These changes may well also lead to a change in the very definition of these communities. The term industrial or manufacturing suburbs may no longer be applicable in the foreseeable future.

—*Bruce B. Williams*

References

Douglass, Harlan Paul. "Suburbs." In *The Encyclopedia of the Social Sciences.* New York: Macmillan, 1934.

Jones, Victor. "Economic Classification of Cities and Metropolitan Areas." In *The Municipal Year Book, 1953.* Chicago: International City Managers' Association, 1953.

Muller, Peter O. *Contemporary Suburban America.* New York: Prentice-Hall, 1981.

Noyelle, Thierry J., and Thomas M. Stanback, Jr. *The Economic Transformation of American Cities.* New York: Rowman and Allanheld, 1983.

Schnore, Leo F. "The Functions of Metropolitan Suburbs." *American Journal of Sociology* 61 (1956): 453–458.

Inner City

During the 1960s, urban experts and lay citizens alike used the expression *inner city* to refer to the deteriorating core of American cities. The term subsequently fell out of fashion as urban problems lost their leading place among major national issues. During the 1990s, as domestic problems have reemerged as an important subject of public debate, inner cities have also received renewed attention. The rise and fall of the term *inner city* is thus a suggestive marker of American society's ambivalent attitude toward cities and their problems.

In the 1960s, academicians, policy experts, political figures, and ordinary citizens meant approximately the same place when they discussed the inner city. However, this consensus on the location of the inner city was not matched by any agreement about the causes of neighborhood decline in the urban core. One common view of the inner city associated neighborhood decline with racial transition from white to black. In many cities, political and business leaders assumed that the expansion of inner-city slum neighborhoods threatened nearby areas, particularly downtown business districts. As a result, early urban renewal projects routinely sought to raze inner-city minority neighborhoods.

A contrasting perspective, one favored by many social workers, policy analysts, and neighborhood activists, sought to explain neighborhood deterioration by referring to a "culture of poverty," which sapped inner-city residents of initiative, produced poor school performance by inner-city youth, resulted in adult social problems, and reproduced itself in successive generations. This general argument, which had many variants, provided the intellectual justification for many of the urban policy initiatives of the administrations of John

When people hear the term inner city, *they usually think only about the slums, not about the glass and concrete skyscrapers so close by.*

F. Kennedy and Lyndon Johnson. If one thinks of urban renewal as having sought to rebuild inner cities in the 1950s, programs such as Community Action and Head Start in the 1960s sought to rebuild inner-city residents.

With the passing of the 1960s, the federal government withdrew its support for such urban social policy measures. For example, the Nixon administration's principal urban program, Community Development Block Grants (CDBGs), was nominally targeted at inner-city areas, but many municipalities distributed federal funds much more broadly. Moreover, most CDBG spending underwrote physical development projects. As such, the previous decade's programmatic emphasis on the social or economic origins of inner-city problems was transformed. In effect, the Nixon, Ford, Carter, and Reagan presidencies represented a consistent movement away from federal government engagement with inner cities, with the Reagan administration crowning the transition by claiming that there were few if any inner-city problems appropriately within the purview of the federal government.

In fact, during the 1970s and 1980s conditions in inner-city neighborhoods deteriorated catastrophically. Physical decline continued as before, but in most inner-city areas, far more ominous were trends in social indicators such as male unemployment, incidence of serious crimes, and pregnancy out of wedlock. In the mid-1980s, the sociologist William Julius Wilson contended that these tendencies signaled the emergence of a ghetto "underclass" whose members were irreparably separated from mainstream American society. Wilson's analysis and its policy implications have occasioned much debate. One result of the controversy about the nature and existence of an urban underclass has been the reemergence of inner-city problems as a public policy issue. One of the principal tests of the Democratic Clinton administration has been its resoluteness and creativity in seeking to define new policies to address the problems of inner cities, and many have been disappointed by the administration's adoption of traditionally more Republican policies of noninvolvement.

—*Larry Bennett*

See also
Community Development Block Grants.

References
Clark, Kenneth B. *Dark Ghetto: Dilemmas of Social Power.* New York: Harper & Row, 1965.
Jencks, Christopher, and Paul Peterson, eds. *The Urban Underclass.* Washington, DC: Brookings Institution, 1991.
Lemann, Nicholas. *The Promised Land: The Great Black Migration and How It Changed America.* New York: Knopf, 1991.
Marris, Peter, and Martin Rein. *Dilemmas of Social Reform: Poverty and Community Action in the United States.* New York: Atherton Press, 1969.
Wilson, William Julius. *The Truly Disadvantaged: The Inner City, The Underclass, and Public Policy.* Chicago: University of Chicago Press, 1987.

Interurban Transit

The term *interurban* derives from the Latin, meaning "between cities," and refers to electric railways that operated in the United States primarily between the 1890s and the 1930s. Scholars generally agree that interurbans can be differentiated from other railroad operations because they usually have four distinguishing characteristics: electrical power (usually overhead), emphasis on passenger service, vehicles heavier and faster than city streetcars, and operation on streets in cities but beside roadways or in separate rights-of-way in rural areas.

Interurban railways grew logically out of the electrified street rail systems that expanded rapidly after Frank J. Sprague successfully developed and installed electric streetcars in Richmond, Virginia, in 1888. The first true interurban line that proved successful was the East Side Railway in Oregon, a 15-mile line connecting Portland and Oregon City, which began revenue service in February 1893. Later the same year, the 20-mile Sandusky, Milan & Norwalk line opened in Ohio. However, it was not until the technological problems of long-distance electrical distribution were solved in 1896 that interurban lines began to proliferate. Thereafter, interurban lines spread because they filled a market niche between electric street railways in cities and local steam railroad passenger service, which was typically sooty, infrequent, and slow.

Interurban lines expanded most rapidly between 1901 and 1908. By 1903, for example, Toledo, Cleveland, and Akron were linked by interurban lines, as were Cincinnati, Dayton, Columbus, and Springfield, also in Ohio. In most of New England, there was little difference between street railway and interurban operations, but elsewhere interurban lines were more clearly distinct. The Midwest, with its relatively flat terrain and multiple cities not too far apart, proved most amenable to interurban construction. Indeed, 40 percent of all American interurban mileage was found in just five states: Indiana, Ohio, Michigan, Illinois, and Wisconsin. By 1908 the Midwest network was largely in place; thereafter, most new construction took place west of the Mississippi River. Interurban mileage peaked in 1917 when approximately 18,100 miles of line were operating in the United States.

Interurban lines offered service that was fast, frequent, inexpensive, quiet, and clean. Companies typically aimed for hourly single-car service on most lines so that patrons did not need to consult timetables as was necessary for steam railroad travel. In cities, where the lines ran in city streets, interurban operations were slow as traffic and pedestrians impeded the cars, but in the country speeds increased. Although cars might reach speeds of 60 miles per hour or more, operating speeds were slower; with frequent stops and running on city streets, average speeds were typically 20 miles per hour for an entire line (but this was considered rapid at the time). The Houston-Galveston Electric Railway, which opened in 1911, was built to high standards and routinely traveled from Houston to Galveston in 75 minutes, achieving an average speed of 40 mph, among the fastest in the industry.

Although no full-scale study of the influence of interurban transit on city form has yet appeared, it is possible to make some preliminary observations. In the Northeast, the suburban pattern had been established by steam commuter railroads, but in the Midwest and West, interurban lines could shape urban development. Interurban lines developed in a "hub and spokes" pattern around major cities such as Indianapolis, Chicago, Toledo, Rochester, Dayton, Kansas City, Los Angeles, Seattle, Portland, and Atlanta. Indianapolis was the center of the largest network, with 13 different lines converging on the city, but Los Angeles, with the 1,000-mile Pacific Electric Railway system, was probably the best example of population growth following interurban extensions. Growth in the Los Angeles area eventually transformed Pacific Electric from its initial interurban operation into something more like a contemporary urban rail transit system.

Interurban lines were generally built inexpensively. Because interurbans were not expected to carry heavy cars or freight, their track and roadbed were built to standards significantly below those for steam railroads. Along the lines, only the simplest of shelters were built and frequently there were none at all. In cities, major terminals were rarely constructed; those in Salt Lake City, Sacramento, and Los Angeles were notable exceptions. The Union Traction Terminal in Indianapolis, designed by D. H. Burnham & Company and completed in 1904, was the largest ever built.

This interurban network disappeared almost as rapidly as it had been created. After World War I, automobiles began drawing passengers away from the interurban lines. Most lines were poorly financed and could not sustain the competition from automobiles on tax-supported roads and highways. Some interurban lines attempted to move into mail and freight transport to replace declining passenger revenues, but such operations remained peripheral. In 1927, the Houston North Shore became the last new line to enter service, but it was an exception. Throughout the 1920s, service was reduced, and track was abandoned. The Depression required further cutbacks. By 1933, only 10,000 miles of interurban line remained in operation; by 1941, mileage had been reduced to 2,700. By the 1970s, no interurban lines survived.

—*Jeffrey Karl Ochsner*

See also
Dummy Lines (Steam Street Railways); Streetcars.
References
Bullard, Thomas R. *Street, Interurban and Rapid Transit Railways of the United States: A Selective Historical Bibliography.* Forty Fort, PA: Harold R. Cox, 1984.

Cavin, Ruth. *Trolleys: Riding and Remembering the Electric Interurban Railways*. New York: Hawthorne Books, 1976.

Hilton, George W., and John F. Due. *Electric Interurban Railways in America*. Stanford, CA: Stanford University Press, 1950.

Middleton, William D. "Good-Bye to the Interurban." *American Heritage* 17 (1966): 30–41, 66–71.

———. *The Interurban Era*. Milwaukee, WI: Kalmbach, 1961.

Rowsome, Frank, Jr., and Stephen D. Maguire, eds. *Trolley Car Treasury: A Century of American Streetcars, Horsecars, Cablecars, Interurbans, and Trolleys*. New York: McGraw-Hill, 1956.

Irish Americans in Cities

While it would be oversimplifying—almost verging on stereotyping—to connect the American Irish and cities too tightly, no ethnic minority in the United States has drawn more identity from its association with cities. As home to an overwhelmingly large proportion of Irish immigrants and their children, cities made most of the distinctive features of Irish-American life possible: the institutionalized Roman Catholic Church, politics as a group defense and means of social mobility, associations, fraternal organizations, chain migration and employment, and even an informal, face-to-face oral culture. Ironically, for most of the history of Irish immigration to the United States, Ireland itself was anything but urban.

The unsettled conditions caused by the English Civil War and Oliver Cromwell's "reconquest" of Ireland impelled more than 10,000 Irish men and women to the West Indies between the 1640s and 1660s, with some spillover into the English colonies in North America. As landholding by the "native" Irish shrank to less than one-seventh of Ireland's acreage because of population pressures and English policies, departures to the colonies on the North American mainland accelerated. During the hard times of the 1720s and between 1740 and 1780, many Irish took advantage of contractual servitude to pay for passage across the Atlantic. By 1790, roughly 400,000 people of Irish birth or descent populated the new United States, three-quarters of them Roman Catholics.

Between 1820 and about 1925, some 4,750,000 Irish migrated to the United States. Among non-English immigrants, only Germans were more numerous. The number of residents of the United States who had been born in Ireland peaked at about 1,750,000 in 1890, but the number of immigrants and their children together reached its all-time high a decade later, almost 3,500,000 in 1900. The peak years of Irish immigration occurred between 1847 and 1851, when more than 100,000 Irish arrived in the United States annually as they fled the potato famine. Some 220,000 Irish newcomers disembarked in the United States in 1851 alone. These are the only years in all of American history when the number of Irish immigrants exceeded 100,000, and arrivals from Ireland accounted for about one-half of all the immigrants to the country during the 1840s. Although Irish immigration

never again constituted as large a proportion of the immigrant flow as before the Civil War, and although it experienced brief, but diminishing, surges after each world war of the twentieth century, Irish immigration remained sizable as recently as the 1970s and 1980s. By 1970, Irish Americans of the second and third generation outnumbered actual immigrants tenfold.

Until a few decades into the twentieth century, it was not really significant whether the American Irish were born in Ireland or the United States. A social and cultural Irish—actually Irish-Catholic—America existed both by choice and also (for much of the period) by necessity, The Irish-American community that developed in the United States before the Civil War owed much to the nature of Irish immigration itself. It was a calculated movement—even in the most desperate famine years—of men and women seeking better opportunities than those that were circumscribed by law, custom, or economic conditions at home. Moreover, it was characteristically a chain migration, with relatives, neighbors, and coworkers paving the way for later arrivals who followed them. Irish immigration, then, tended to reassemble families, parishes, and even villages in the United States.

For much of the nineteenth century, Irish Americans of the first and second generations found their social and economic mobility hampered by a lack of capital, insufficient skills appropriate to professional and managerial jobs in a modernizing society, and outright Anglo-American prejudice. Upward mobility—whether through politics, the Roman Catholic Church, or trade—generally built upon the patronage of Irish communities and held the most ambitious sons and daughters within the group rather than propelling them out.

Spatial concentration in cities was both a cause and an effect of Irish-American community building. Although a fair proportion of emigrants from Ireland to the English colonies before the middle of the eighteenth century—particularly the Scots-Irish of Ulster—found their way to the far frontier, concentrations of Irish were beginning to appear in places like Boston, New York, and Baltimore by the 1740s. These concentrations were small enough but nevertheless an omen of things to come. Often arriving as indentured servants or redemptioners looking for work to pay for their ocean passage, and as rural people possessing rural skills but without land or capital, many Irish remained in or near their port of arrival. Culturally marginalized by their poverty, religion (the majority being Catholic), and even their accent, the Irish looked to one another for support, and this reinforced residential proximity for the group.

Generally tolerated before the Revolution when their numbers were small, the Catholic Irish began to encounter more Protestant, Anglo-American prejudice during the 50 years that followed as their numbers increased and they developed more formal institutions, usually through the church. Chains of migration added people to places where concentration was already most pronounced. When the steadily increasing flow of Irish immigrants in the 1820s and 1830s gave way to an explosive rush in the 1840s and 1850s, the weight of the newcomers would be felt first in New York City, Philadelphia, Boston, and Baltimore, and secondarily in minor ports like New Orleans, Galveston, and Mobile. The emergence of jobs for factory operatives and semiskilled hand workers in regional manufacturing centers took the Irish into smaller cities like New Haven, Lowell, Providence, and Jersey City before the Civil War. And the labor-intensive construction of canals, and then railroads, between the Atlantic seaboard and the Great Lakes and Ohio Valley took immigrants and their children to cities like Buffalo, Cleveland, Cincinnati, Pittsburgh, Chicago, and Detroit. In consequence, while the "urban" population of the United States increased by some 70 percent between 1830 and 1860, and about 20 percent of Americans lived in cities on the eve of the Civil War, by 1850 about 80 percent of Irish immigrants could be found in the urbanizing Northeast. The 1860 census revealed that fully one-third lived in just a dozen cities.

This concentration could be dramatic. Between 1847 and 1861, 1,100,000 Irish immigrants landed at the port of New York, with 163,000 arriving in the peak year of 1851. So many remained in the city that by 1855 the Irish-born constituted more than one-third of the residents in 10 of New York City's 22 wards, and in 3 wards their number was closer to half. In 1860, the city was home to over 204,000 people born in Ireland, compared to 430,000 born in the United States and 180,000 born in other foreign countries. Of the native-born, besides, many were the children or grandchildren of Irish immigrants. In 1830, only 4,179 Philadelphians were foreign-born, about 2 percent of the population. Just 20 years later, more than 121,000 were foreign-born, almost one-third of the city's residents. Of these, about 60 percent were Irish.

The proximity of Irish Americans to each other promoted the formation of aid societies, fraternal organizations, small businesses, informal community gathering places (typically the "grocery," a place to obtain food, drink, and information), and Catholic parishes. The Roman Catholic Church was a particular source of strength in Irish neighborhoods and provided a significant path of social mobility through the clergy. Estimates indicate that more than 35 percent of all priests were Irish by the time of the Civil War. The church was particularly useful as a rallying point for cultural defense against periodic assaults by native-born Anglo-American Protestants upon the alleged unreliability of a people putatively loyal, on account of their religion, to a "foreign prince." In fact, some of the most dramatic demonstra-

tions of Anglo-American hostility accompanied the formation of new Irish urban institutions—such as an effort to establish an Irish-American militia company in Boston in the late 1830s—or the defense of existing ones—such as Irish-Catholic protests against reading the Bible in public schools. The latter touched off the most violent anti-Irish and anti-Catholic incidents in the United States before the Civil War, the Philadelphia "Bible Riots" of May and July 1844. Ultimately, in the 1860s the urban church would establish parochial schools in most cities of any size. Episodes of "nativist" hostility—sometimes political, sometimes physical, and sometimes an amorphous but hurtful and disabling prejudice—reinforced the ability of Irish Americans to create an identity as a people dispossessed—first by the English and subsequently by the Anglo-Americans.

Politics, like the church, served urban Irish communities at the same time that it served individuals. In the middle decades of the nineteenth century (both before and after the Civil War), thousands of Irish Americans earned their wages as policemen, firemen, and clerks, while the politicians who secured places for them built impressive urban vote-getting machines. Initially wooed by both major parties, Irish Americans solidified their relationship with the Democratic Party during the tumultuous 1850s. With naturalized voters—heavily Irish—a majority in fully nine of New York City's wards by 1860, the Irish were a political force to be reckoned with.

Not until 1880 could as many as one-third of the Irish and their children be found outside of New England and the Middle Atlantic states. And while some of them penetrated the hinterlands, the principal destinations were to central, and even western, cities located on the major water and rail routes of trade. As early as 1870, the Irish were the largest European ethnic minority in California but were heavily concentrated in San Francisco. In fact, the period after the Civil War experienced an even more dramatic wave of building Irish-American institutions in cities than had the antebellum years. Some of these new institutions looked back to Ireland, such as the Fenian order of the 1860s, which sought to mobilize Irish civil war veterans to liberate British Canada from bases in Cleveland, Buffalo, and Chicago and the support enlisted among Irish Americans for the Irish home rule movement of Charles Stewart Parnell in the 1880s.

But most new institutions focused on the needs of the Irish in American cities. Repeated battles with Protestants over the curriculum in public schools launched a new wave of building Catholic school systems that extended even to the erection of colleges like Catholic University in Washington, D.C., Loyola University in Chicago, and Boston College.

The Irish-dominated urban political machines of the 1860s and 1870s, as notorious as they were effective, adapted to "reform" in the last years of the century and some sur-vived—like the Pendergast organization in Kansas City or the Curley machine in Boston, still trading jobs, welfare, and cultural recognition for votes. Irish Americans staked out early leadership positions in the urban, industrial unions of the second half of the nineteenth century, contributing such important figures as Terence Powderly of the Knights of Labor.

Nothing demonstrates the strength and fragility of the urban Irish better than the Knights of Columbus, a frater-nal organization for young Catholic men founded in New Haven, Connecticut, in 1881. An outgrowth of the institu-tional muscularity of the Roman Catholic Church, it graphi-cally illustrated the leading position of the Irish in American Catholicism. Yet it was not an ethnic organization per se but a "pan-Catholic" one. By the time the Knights gained na-tional attention after 1892 because of their visibility at public celebrations of the five hundredth anniversary of the "dis-covery" of the New World, it was already apparent that pat-terns of endogamy were breaking down in Irish America, and the Irish were beginning to meld into a more general-ized urban, Catholic machine.

Irish immigrants continued to settle disproportionately in cities until well into the twentieth century. As late as 1920, approximately 90 percent of first-generation Irish Americans resided in urban areas. But by this date, second- and third-generation Irish Americans had come to outnumber actual immigrants by a margin of about three-to-one. In the de-cade following World War I, significant erosion of Irish ur-ban neighborhoods began to occur. This trend accompanied a more general geographic dispersion across the United States as the children and grandchildren of immigrants experienced greater economic and social mobility. In the 1930s, New Deal policies undercut many of the services previously provided by ethnic politicians, and the erosion of Irish-American ur-ban neighborhoods weakened the pressures for political con-formity that had been a source of ethnic cohesion.

Although Irish Americans might continue to identify with Catholic institutions, these were no longer specifically Irish institutions. With the growing secularization of Ameri-can culture, religious identity proved to be a less effective cultural glue by the middle of the twentieth century. At the same time, a more superficial Irishness was embraced as part of American national culture and particularly urban culture. In the twentieth century, St. Patrick's Day, shorn of its reli-gious meaning, became a national festival day marked by parades in big cities. By the census of 1980, it was as much evidence of fashionability as of assimilation that Ireland was claimed as an ancestral home by more Americans than any other part of the world save England and Germany.

—*Dale T. Knobel*

References

Bayor, Ronald H., and Timothy J. Meagher, eds. *The New York Irish.* Baltimore: Johns Hopkins University Press, 1996.

Clark, Dennis. *The Irish Relations: Trials of an Immigrant Tradition.* Rutherford, NJ: Fairleigh Dickinson University Press, 1982.

Handlin, Oscar. *Boston's Immigrants: A Study in Acculturation.* Rev. and enlarged ed. New York: Atheneum, 1977.

Meagher, Timothy J., ed. *From Paddy to Studs: Irish-American Com-munities in the Turn of the Century Era, 1880–1920.* Westport, CT: Greenwood Press, 1986.

Mitchell, Brian C. *The Paddy Camps: The Irish of Lowell, 1821–61.* Urbana: University of Illinois Press, 1988.

O'Connor, Thomas H. *The Boston Irish: A Political History.* Boston: Northeastern University Press, 1995.

Irving, John Winslow (1942–)

John Winslow Irving was born on March 12, 1942, in Exeter, New Hampshire. His father was a World War II airman who was shot down over Burma and survived the war, but Irving never knew his father nor knows if he is still alive. When he was six, his mother married a Russian history teacher at New Hampshire's Phillips Exeter Academy with whom Irving is still close. Irving had a happy childhood but an "uninterest-ing" life. At Phillips Exeter Academy, he made mainly "C"s and "B"s, learned to wrestle, and decided to become a writer. After attending the University of Pittsburgh between 1961 and 1962, he enrolled in the Institute of European Studies at the University of Vienna. In 1964, he married Shyla Leary, whom he met at Harvard University, where he studied Ger-man before going to Vienna. He earned his B.A. degree at the University of New Hampshire in 1965, the year his son Colin was born. Irving received the M.F.A. degree at the University of Iowa in 1967, returned to Vienna in 1969 to work on a screen version of *Setting Free the Bears,* but eventually moved his family—his son Brendan was born in 1970—back to Putney, Vermont, in 1972. The Irvings were divorced in 1981, and in 1987 Irving married Janet Turnbull, a literary agent he met in Toronto, Canada. He is the author of *The World Ac-cording to Garp* (1978), *The Hotel New Hampshire* (1981), and *A Son of the Circus* (1994), among others.

Irving emphasizes that although his life has been happy and generally uninteresting, he uses his own experiences as grist for his fiction; biographical details are not only trans-lated into his fiction, but they also color his literary vision. Irving's prep school days become, for example, the basis for prep schools in *The World According to Garp* and *A Prayer for Owen Meany;* his college years are the basis for settings in *The Water-Method Man, The 158-Pound Marriage,* and *Owen Meany;* his interests in sports and especially wrestling pro-vide the sports metaphors in *Setting Free the Bears, The 158-Pound Marriage, Garp, The Hotel New Hampshire,* and *Owen Meany.* According to Irving, his most recent novel, *A Son of the Circus,* a tale about the westernized Dr. Farrokh Daruwala, originated when, on a snowy Toronto morning, Irving saw a "well dressed and dignified man who newspapers would call an 'immigrant of color.' "More important, Irving's experiences in Vienna made him aware of the *Anschluss* (Austria's violent union with Nazi Germany) that contributed to the outbreak of World War II. For Irving, the violence, terror, and bloodshed that preceded and followed the *Anschluss*—a theme in his first five novels—not only established the precedent for World War II's brutal, chaotic fury, but also for the sudden violence and bizarre deaths that Irving sees lurking in the postmodern world and its cities.

Whether in Vienna, Toronto, or American cities and towns, sudden violence and death stalk Irving's characters. In *Setting Free the Bears,* Siggy Javotnik is stung to death when he crashes his motorcycle into some beehives, Gottlub Wut is stuffed head-first down an outhouse stall, and severed Serbian heads are stacked in a pyramid on a raft; in *Garp,* T. S. Garp's younger son dies in the car crash that blinds his older son in one eye, and Garp and his mother are assassinated; in *The Hotel New Hampshire,* Franny is gang-raped, Mother and Egg die in a plane crash at sea, Father is blinded by a bomb blast, and Lilly commits suicide; in *Owen Meany,* protagonist John Wheelwright's mother is killed by a foul ball, and Owen Meany is killed by a hand grenade as he protects some Vietnamese refugees. In refuting critics who fault his plots for excessive violence, Irving told Richard West in *New York Magazine* (August 17, 1981): "How could anyone who reads newspapers think it excessive? I think events in American social and political life have borne me out. There have been more assassinations than exist in the novel [*Garp*], certainly more radical and terrorist groups." Moreover, in justifying the forces plaguing his fictional families, Irving explained to Richard West that, out of a hypothetical family of eight, "someone is going to hit the wall. . . . In a car crash, a plane crash, a wipeout, a premature tragedy, of course it will happen!" While Irving's plots underscore the violence at the core of all life, they also emphasize the comedy, or, as the narrator in *Garp* says, "In the world according to Garp, an evening could be hilarious and the next morning murderous."

Yet, despite life's violence, pain, and tragedy, Irving's novels end affirmatively with his characters establishing purpose and meaning within the confines of their lives, whether they live in small towns like St. Cloud's and Heart's Rock *(The Cider House Rules)* or cities like Vienna, Toronto, or New York. In fact, Irving wryly says that *Garp* is a "life-affirming novel in which everybody dies." How his characters have happy, meaningful lives varies from novel to novel, but the bases for happiness remain constant: men and women accept responsibility for their own actions ("We're doing the wrong thing. . . . It's time to do everything right," affirm Homer Wells and Candy Worthington in *The Cider House Rules*); they

refuse to be intimidated by life's forces ("You've got to get obsessed and stay obsessed" is the Berry family maxim in *The Hotel New Hampshire*); they appreciate life's beauties and graces ("be grateful for small favors" Garp learns); and, more important, they nurture family ties and relationships ("A good hotel is always there. . . . If you come to a great hotel in *parts,* in broken pieces . . . when you leave . . . you'll leave it whole" metaphorically suggests family values in *The Hotel New Hampshire*).

In imitating the nineteenth-century novelists he admires, especially Charles Dickens, Irving's novels are expansive, with a great deal of narrative interest; the writer's first task, he says, is to tell a good story. At the same time, Irving examines contemporary issues ranging from homosexuality, lesbianism, and women's rights to rape, incest, abortion, murder, and an absence of God in the modern world. Irving's analyses of the these issues are not only interesting, but above all, they emphasize what lies at the heart of life in American towns and cities.

—*Edward C. Reilly*

References
Harter, Carol C., and James R. Thompson. *John Irving.* Boston: Twayne, 1986.
Miller, Gabriel. *John Irving.* New York: Frederick Ungar, 1982.
Reilly, Edward C. *Understanding John Irving.* Columbia: University of South Carolina, 1991.

Italian Americans in Cities

Between 1880 and 1930, almost 5 million Italians came to the United States as immigrants. Although the vast majority had worked in agriculture or rural handicrafts in Italy, 90 percent settled in cities, especially in the Northeast and most notably in New York, where 97 percent of Italy's immigrants disembarked. Immigrants from Southern and Eastern Europe fueled urban economic growth in the United States. Both as workers and as urban dwellers, immigrants transformed small "walking" cities into sprawling agglomerations of industrial workplaces and overlapping but distinctive working-class enclaves, connected by new transport systems to the emerging suburbs. The new immigration thus greatly sharpened the regional distinctions in the United States between a predominantly rural, Protestant, and "native" South and West and an urban, ethnic, Catholic, and Jewish Northeast.

Today, almost two-thirds of the 11 million Americans of Italian descent still live in and around the large cities of New England and the Middle Atlantic states, where they have been joined by half a million new Italian immigrants since 1960. Italian-American lives reflect the fundamental spatial and ethnic changes that have occurred in these cities in the last 50 years. Slight majorities now live in suburbs of large metropolitan regions, but the persistence of Italians and Italian Americans in older working-class neighborhoods also remains the object of public awareness—and of controversy.

The men and women who left Italy for the United States worked in agriculture or the rural trades, but few had lived on the land they worked. Instead—whether in northwestern Italy or in the southern provinces where three-quarters of all immigrants headed for the United States originated—Italian peasants returned nightly or fortnightly to homes in urban villages, sometimes called agrotowns. There, 1,000 to 50,000 peasants and artisans lived densely packed together, alongside churches, city halls, shops, and a small middle class of professionals and shopkeepers. Dense settlement encouraged intense sociability—the central piazza, cafe, and tavern functioned as labor market and gathering place for peasant men; women more often worked and socialized together in the streets and courtyards outside their houses. Although agricultural work required Italian peasants to house small animals in their humble one- and two-room homes, urban life defined the social ideals of rural Italians.

The separation of fields and homes was particularly sharp in parts of the Italian south, where it limited women's participation in agriculture and encouraged a peasant way of life that assumed that men would be absent in order to support their families. Beginning in the 1870s, increasing numbers of these men followed *padrone* labor recruiters to seasonal construction, harvesting, and mining jobs abroad. For them, the large cities of the northeastern United States served as way stations en route to railroad construction camps; the majority of these "sojourners" returned to Italy. By 1900, however, men experienced in locating and obtaining more stable positions as unskilled laborers could offer help to their relatives and friends at home, creating the migration chains that soon linked particular Italian villages to particular urban neighborhoods in the United States. Italian women began to join the men who lived in urban clusters of *paesani* (fellow villagers) on "Second Avenue" or "Halstead Street."

Italian immigrants soon became an important element of American urban life. In 1870, New York already had the largest group of Italian residents (2,800), but both New Orleans and San Francisco claimed over 1,500 Italian residents each. By 1910, more than two-thirds of the 500,000 Italians in America's largest cities lived in New York, while Philadelphia, Chicago, and Boston had all surpassed New Orleans and San Francisco as centers of Italian work and residence. In each of these cities, and in smaller cities like Scranton, Pittsburgh, and Buffalo, distinctive neighborhoods called "Little Italy" developed, and American urban institutions—from public schools and charity visitors to labor unions and Catholic parishes—began responding to the arrival of new, and often quite poor, immigrants.

Urban labor markets generating work for more than one family member proved the most attractive to Italians hoping to settle more permanently. In New York, dynamic physical expansion accompanied the city's political consolidation and provided jobs for newly arrived, unskilled male immigrants in the construction of streets, sewers, subways, bridges, tunnels, and skyscrapers. Italians soon dominated New York street sweeping as well, and Italian women flocked to the burgeoning garment industry. The children of immigrants worked in the garment industry and in the many other light industries of the city (shoes, candy, furniture, boxes); others entered the skilled trades, especially in construction, garment making, and food retailing. With over 340,000 Italian-born residents in 1910, Italian-born doctors, importers, lawyers, piano teachers, and journalists formed a small immigrant middle class of *prominenti*.

In New York and Chicago (where over 45,000 Italians had settled in 1910), immigrant workers lived in tenement buildings close to their places of work. Tenements housed six to twenty families, usually in small three- or four-room apartments. Although American observers were undoubtedly justified in their negative views of aging tenements, newly arrived Italians assessed them more favorably, for immigrants found intense sociability in tenement neighborhoods. By housing a family of ten in a three-room apartment or by sharing their homes with boarders or a family of kinsmen, the poorest immigrants also reduced the high tenement rents typical of central city districts to about one-quarter of their yearly incomes. The installation of water and toilets in the oldest tenement housing in the twentieth century earned immigrant praise. Nearby urban services heightened the appeal of tenement life; for example, vendors hawked produce and fish from pushcarts, which competed with children seeking play space in the streets below their families' tenement homes.

New York's Italian population dwarfed that of other American cities; it was so large that by 1900 New Yorkers could identify many Little Italies, rather than just one. The best known and oldest of them developed in the adjacent Sixth and Fourteenth Wards, surrounding Mulberry and Mott Streets, just west of the Bowery. Other Little Italies grew in Greenwich Village, East Harlem, Staten Island, and in the Williamsburg and Red Hook sections of Brooklyn. As New York's outer boroughs developed with improving subway connections over the next 30 years, Little Italies also appeared in south Brooklyn, in Queens, and in the Bronx.

The history and social life of Manhattan's Little Italy on Mulberry Street exemplifies ethnic communities throughout urban America. First occupied by political émigrés, artisans, and petty merchants from Italy's north, the Mulberry Street district by 1870 included ragpickers, organ-grinders, and representatives of Italy's many "wandering trades." In the 1880s and 1890s, the community revolved around institutions organized by *padroni* to serve and exploit male labor migrants—boarding houses, cafes, employment bureaus, steamship agents, and small banks handling the return of remittances to families in Italy. After 1890, Neapolitans and Sicilians settled in particularly large numbers in the Mulberry Street district, as women and children arrived to join the migratory male sojourners. *Paesani* from particular regions and hometowns concentrated in particular tenements and streets, using their own dialects in grocery stores, cafes, bars, and street corner and stoop gatherings.

The formal institutions of New York's Little Italies at best supplemented kinship and friendship as organizers of community. Newspapers ranging from the mainstream *Il Progresso* to the syndicalist *Il Proletario* published for the literate minority. More widespread in their influence were mutual benefit societies or fraternals organized by men from small towns and villages in Sicily and southern Italy—most offered death benefits or health insurance to poor immigrant workers or sponsored festivals honoring hometown patron saints. Italian ethnic parishes like the Madonna di Loreto also emerged, and both Catholic and Protestant missionaries worked in the neighborhood. Public schools, an industrial school for Italian children, and city health clinics offered services aimed at easing immigrants' transition from Old to New World; outside of the Mulberry district several of New York's most famous settlement houses, notably Greenwich House, served other Little Italies.

With time, too, Little Italies supported labor and political initiatives organized by Italian Americans to improve the conditions of urban life. After 1910, New York's Italians rose to prominence in both the Industrial Workers of the World and in their own ethnic locals in the International Ladies Garment Workers' Union and the Amalgamated Clothing Workers of America. Irish political leaders in Tammany Hall maintained dominance over New York's Little Italies until the 1920s, when rates of naturalization began to rise. By the 1930s, New York claimed both a mayor and a congressional representative of Italian descent in the persons of Fiorello La Guardia and Vito Marcantonio.

Outside the Northeast, Little Italies differed mainly in the occupations and backgrounds of their immigrant settlers. San Francisco's North Beach community employed proportionately more sailors and workers in local food industries, especially canning; since the days of the gold rush, San Francisco had remained a more attractive destination for northern Italians than most American cities. Similarly, Sicilians dominated the Little Italy in New Orleans called Little Palermo; the fruit trade and dock work employed many Italians there. In San Francisco and New Orleans,

Undated photograph of the owner of an Italian grocery store on Mulberry Street in New York.

however, the range of ethnic institutions—from mutual aid societies to Italian-language newspapers and ethnic parishes—closely resembled those developing in New York, Chicago, or Philadelphia.

Although Little Italies offered many social and economic advantages to their immigrant residents, few people settled there permanently. A new job, the birth of a child, or the arrival of relatives sparked frequent moves, both within and among Little Italies. American observers claimed astonishment at the constant moving they observed. With time, the earnings and opinions of the second generation encouraged moves outward along transport lines to newer, yet still urban, residential districts within the boundaries of physically expanding cities.

The suburbanization of Italian Americans began early, even as new immigrants poured into the central city Little Italies. Already in 1900, some immigrants from Italy traveled directly to the suburban fringes. Small ethnic enclaves—the suburban equivalents of Little Italy, complete with ethnic parishes and self-help societies—appeared in Long Island suburban counties as early as the 1920s. On Long Island and in New York's northern Westchester County suburbs, employment drew Italians—work in nurseries and as gardeners and groundsmen on upper-class estates attracted some new arrivals, while light industries relocating to the suburbs and the construction of commuter railroads and suburban water works employed others. Early suburbanites were neither upwardly mobile nor Americanized. Few commuted back to jobs in the central city until after World War II. Suburban life did, however, facilitate homeownership, and many suburban immigrant families enjoyed the opportunity to raise some of their own food.

In the immediate postwar years, a combination of a large, better-educated second generation, the GI Bill, and inexpensive housing loans supported a massive move of Italian Americans—alongside other upwardly mobile, white ethnics—into the suburban middle class. Considerable numbers also found themselves pushed toward suburbs by postwar urban renewal projects that targeted older working-class neighborhoods. The suburban-bound found better housing but still mourned the homes and neighborhood social networks they had been forced to leave.

In 1980, Americans of Italian descent remained almost evenly divided between suburbs and older working-class urban settlements in the large metropolitan regions of the North and East. One of five residents of suburban Westchester County (New York) was of Italian descent, as was one of six residents of suburban Bergen County (New Jersey) and Nassau and Suffolk Counties (both on Long Island). The residential segregation of Italian Americans, which had been very high as late as 1930, remained moderately high in 1970, but only for the second generation. Third-generation Italian Americans, whether in suburbs or central cities, largely resemble other white, urban Americans in their education, incomes, and employment.

Still, distinctive residential choices among Italian Americans hint at the persistent cultural legacy of Italian urbanity. Survey data suggests that Italian Americans are less likely to change residence than other Americans and more likely to reside where they grew up. As urban villagers, and steadfast small property owners, Italian Americans have also frequently, and sometimes violently, sought to defend their neighborhood "turf" from new arrivals, notably African-American or Hispanic neighbors in Chicago's and New York's neighborhoods in transition. Conflicts like these symbolize racial and class tensions in aging, postindustrial cities. Still, more than one observer has noted the irony of Italian Americans becoming such visible symbols of racial conflict—for unlike many other white Americans, they have proved less willing to flee either city life or the new immigrants pouring into them.

—*Donna Gabaccia*

References

Cinel, Dino. *From Italy to San Francisco: The Immigrant Experience.* Stanford, CA: Stanford University Press, 1982.

Gabaccia, Donna R. *From Sicily to Elizabeth Street: Housing and Social Change among Italian Immigrants.* Albany: State University of New York Press, 1984.

LaGumina, Salvatore John. *From Steerage to Suburb: Long Island Italians.* New York: Center for Migration Studies, 1988.

Mormino, Gary R., and George E. Pozzetta. *The Immigrant World of Ybor City: Italians and Their Latin American Neighbors in Tampa, 1885–1985.* Urbana: University of Illinois Press, 1987.

Jackson, Maynard (1938–)

Maynard Jackson became the first black mayor of a major southern city in 1973, serving three terms as mayor of Atlanta, Georgia. Jackson had run unsuccessfully against U.S. Senator Herman Talmadge in 1968 but was elected vice-mayor in 1969. In 1973, black residents constituted a slight majority of Atlanta's population, and in that year's election, Jackson garnered most of their support and enough white votes to receive 59.8 percent of the total cast.

Jackson's first term as mayor solidified black influence in Atlanta city government. Minority participation in city contracts was required, and blacks were appointed to more visible positions in city government. Jackson also enhanced his support among neighborhood groups by actively supporting neighborhood planning. Yet this first term was not without controversy. While Jackson was supported by some business leaders, his electoral base was largely among black residents concerned about crime, housing, and neighborhood preservation. Jackson's rhetoric often appeared inconsistent with the economic development and traffic concerns of business leaders and suburban residents.

After easily winning reelection in 1977 and overseeing the completion of Hartsfield International Airport in 1980, Jackson developed a working relationship with business and suburban interests, albeit less friendly than that of previous city administrations.

Atlanta's city charter limits mayors to two consecutive terms, and Jackson left office in 1982. Andrew Young succeeded him and also served two consecutive terms. In the election of 1989, Jackson was returned to the mayor's office in a landslide victory. During his third term as mayor, Atlanta was selected to host the 1996 Olympic Games. Yet this administration, too, was marked by controversies surrounding the availability of low-income housing, the deterioration of the city's infrastructure, and an airport corruption scandal.

Although Jackson underwent bypass surgery in 1992, he remained an articulate spokesman nationally and helped shape proposals for an urban policy agenda. Nonetheless, he declined to run for a fourth term in 1993 and, in 1994, left public office to lead a financial securities business.

—*John D. Hutcheson, Jr., and Carol Pierannunzi*

References

Pierannunzi, Carol, and John D. Hutcheson, Jr. "Electoral Change and Regime Maintenance: Maynard Jackson's Second Time Around." *PS: Political Science and Politics* 23 (1990): 151–153.

Pomerantz, Gary M. *Where Peachtree Meets Sweet Auburn: The Saga of Two Families and the Making of Atlanta*. New York: Scribners, 1996.

Stone, Clarence N. *Regime Politics: Governing Atlanta, 1946–1988*. Lawrence: University of Kansas Press, 1989.

Jacksonville, Florida

Before the city there was the river, flowing north and then east toward the Atlantic Ocean. Timucuan Indians established villages at the bend in the river, and French Huguenot explorers came later, building Fort Caroline in 1562. Spanish troops from St. Augustine defeated them in 1565, and the Spanish ruled until 1763, although they did not settle the city site. Following The Seven Years' War, the British took control, building a road from their Georgia colony south and crossing the river, which they named the St. Johns, at the bend. They called the hamlet there Cowford. British rule lasted 20 years followed by the Second Spanish period. The United States purchased Florida from the Spanish in 1819, and two years later, at the same river bend, American settlers platted Jacksonville, naming it after the hero of the War of 1812 and military governor of Florida, Andrew Jackson.

Jacksonville grew slowly before the Civil War. Its main asset was the St. Johns River, flowing deep into the state, and the city became the trading center for the river hinterland. It also shipped timber and naval stores. The first tourists, often wealthy or sickly, arrived before the war.

Although Florida was strongly secessionist, Jacksonville residents were divided during the Civil War, and Union troops occupied the city on four different occasions. The end of the war brought the Freedman's Bureau and the first schools for African Americans. Many black Union soldiers stayed in the city, and freedmen arrived from the countryside seeking jobs. Between Reconstruction and World War I, approximately half the population of Jacksonville was African American.

Economic development after the Civil War once again focused on timber, naval stores, and tourism. By the 1880s, Jacksonville businessmen had organized a board of trade. The leading tourist hotel, the St. James, had installed electric lights and telephones, and Henry Flagler built the first bridge across the St. Johns River, pointing his railroad south to St. Augustine and beyond.

Like other southern cities, Jacksonville had its epidemics; yellow fever killed 474 city residents in 1887. Fires, too, took their toll; the great fire of 1901 destroyed most of the downtown, leaving two-fifths of the city's residents homeless. Yet the fire gave Jacksonville the opportunity to become a modern city. Newcomers like architect Henry Klutho, a disciple of Frank Lloyd Wright, joined local entrepreneurs to build Jacksonville's first skyscrapers, modern department stores, hotels, theaters, a train station, and an automobile bridge across the St. Johns River. The Army Corps of Engineers dredged the river channel, opening the port to world trade. Following J. P. Morgan's consolidation of southern rail systems, Jacksonville became the gateway to Florida, by land as well as by sea. Bank services, transportation, wholesaling, and retail trade expanded exponentially. By the eve of World War I, Jacksonville was Florida's largest city in both population and economic importance. Urban popular culture reached Jacksonville in the print media and in the forms of vaudeville, amusement parks, and silent movies. Film producers came from New York during the winter months, taking advantage of the milder climate and varied terrain, to make motion pictures. Meanwhile, local residents took themselves to the beaches on hot summer weekends by train and later by car.

Accompanying Jacksonville's development as a city of the New South in the early twentieth century were hardening racial attitudes. The civil rights leader, diplomat, poet, and playwright James Weldon Johnson grew up here during the 1880s and remembered it as a "good town for Negroes." After attending college in Atlanta, he returned to his native city as principal of the Stanton Graded School, but he left in 1903 and never returned permanently. He later wrote that by then, Jacksonville had become "a cracker town," not good for blacks.

A. Philip Randolph, the founder of the Brotherhood of Sleeping Car Porters and a national civil rights leader, also grew up in Jacksonville. After he graduated in 1910 from Cookman Institute, the city's best private high school, he could find only menial jobs so he too headed north, anticipating the Great Migration that began on the eve of World War I.

The Great War brought increased growth and prosperity for Jacksonville that continued into the 1920s. The city contributed capital and goods to the Florida boom, but the sensational, speculative growth of Miami and its environs overshadowed the slower, steadier development of the Gateway City. Tourists routinely only passed through Jacksonville on their way south. The collapse of the boom had ripple effects in Jacksonville that were eased by the arrival of Alfred I. Du Pont, the Delaware industrialist, who helped stabilize the city and the state's banking structure. But even Du Pont money could not withstand the Depression following the stock market crash of 1929. Jacksonville, like other American cities, benefited from the New Deal and was the location of three public housing projects, Civilian Conservation Corps camps, and Works Progress Administration jobs, but it took the arrival of the U.S. Navy before the outbreak of World War II for the economy to move forward once more. The war and subsequent Cold War kept federal dollars flowing into Jacksonville's three major naval facilities. In the 1950s, state legislation afforded tax breaks to the regional home offices of insurance companies, attracting Prudential, State Farm, and other national firms to the city. Insurance joined the navy, banking, transportation, and wholesale and retail trade in strengthening the city's economy.

During the 1960s, the civil rights movement and rioting in Jacksonville made national headlines or network news only infrequently, but both took place as African Americans sought to enter the mainstream. More serious to many local residents during these years, however, were the suburban exodus and governmental corruption. White flight followed by the construction of regional shopping malls threatened downtown hotels, restaurants, and stores. In addition, the public schools lost accreditation because of inadequate funding; moreover, environmental pollution was despoiling the St. Johns River and its tributaries. A declining city, whose rapidly expanding countryside had inadequate public services, prompted civic, business, and professional leaders to act. In 1965, they secured legislative authorization and began planning to consolidate the city and county, a process that took three years. The indictment of seven city officials by a local grand jury helped influence a successful referendum campaign, and voters in both city and county, black and white, endorsed consolidated government in August 1967.

Although consolidation worked, it was no panacea for larger racial, environmental, and social problems, and the national "stagflation" of the 1970s did not assist economic development. Conditions improved only with the national economy in the mid-1980s. The arrival of a Mayo Clinic satellite and major expansion of medical services provided one strong boost; another was the coming of national firms, including AT&T Universal Card. The Rouse Company built an entertainment center downtown on the river, and cultural institutions including the Jacksonville Symphony, the city's three major museums, the zoo, and local colleges and universities improved. The surprise acquisition of a National Football League franchise was perhaps the most popular achievement as indicated by the rapid sale of season tickets to its games.

As the twentieth century neared its end, Jacksonville, like other American cities, faced a panoply of problems. Despite considerable progress in race relations, racial conflicts still occurred. Inner-city homelessness, drugs, crime, and poverty beleaguered the city. The rates of homicide, divorce, teenage pregnancy, school dropout, alcoholism, and family abuse ranked high in national statistics. Meanwhile, funding for parks, police, and education ranked below national norms.

Still, the city had its beautiful river and attractive beaches. Golf, sailing, and tennis were almost year-round recreational diversions. Many suburban and magnet schools were outstanding. The cost of living was not high by national standards. Private citizen groups, including the NAACP and Jacksonville Community Council, kept pressuring for enlightened governmental policies. But limited resources (resulting from federal budget deficits), combined with restricted state funding (in the absence of a state income tax) and caps on already low local property taxes, remained barriers to improving the quality of life for all Jacksonville residents.

—*James B. Crooks*

References

Crooks, James B. *Jacksonville after the Fire, 1901–1919: A New South City.* Gainesville: University Presses of Florida, 1991.

Davis, T. Frederick. *History of Jacksonville, Florida and Vicinity, 1513–1924.* Facsimile ed. Gainesville: University of Florida Press, 1925.

Martin, Richard A. *The City Makers.* Jacksonville, FL: Richard A. Martin, 1975.

———. *Consolidation, Jacksonville, Duval County: The Dynamics of Urban Political Reform.* Jacksonville, FL: Crawford Publishing, 1969.

Ward, James Robertson. *Old Hickory's Town: An Illustrated History of Jacksonville.* Jacksonville, FL: Miller Press, 1985.

Jazz

Rooted in the African-American experience, jazz pioneers drew freely on black and white and rural and urban elements to create a new music that took on a distinctive form only in cities. Following the Civil War, free and recently freed Americans of African origin mingled with each other and with whites; as Reconstruction failed, they found racial lines reestablished through a system of legal and cultural segregation.

African in origin, the rhythmic propulsion of jazz melded with European melodies and instruments constructed to play the Western ("well tempered") seven-note scale. Musicolo-gists argue that if the common African five-note system is played on instruments designed for the seven-note scale, an ambiguity is created around the third and fifth intervals, thus producing the "blue notes" characteristic of African-American music. Other musical elements were also playfully synergized. Improvisation—experimentation with harmony and melody—combined with a complex yet "relaxed" African rhythmic sensibility. Playful improvisation on a "bluesy" harmonic structure, the embellishment and reconstruction of melody together with an open sense of percussion, produced a musical feeling that jazz listeners and players call "swing."

One place swung like no other—New Orleans, often referred to as "The Cradle of Jazz." New Orleans was America's leading seaport in terms of tonnage until 1841, when New York surpassed it, and a city long under Spanish and French control. It was a place of cross-cultural confluence, conflict, and paradox. The richness of European (French, Spanish, Moorish, Italian, Jewish, Irish, Anglo-Saxon), African (primarily West African but also southern U.S. Protestant and Spanish-influenced Catholic culture), Caribbean, and other exotic musical elements met and mixed in New Orleans to produce an altogether new music—American jazz.

By the early 1900s, this jazz music, usually played by small ensembles, spread rapidly to other cities where additional musical traditions continued to shape and redefine it. As this new music spread out from New Orleans, it encountered and appropriated elements of African-American musical culture such as blues song and instrumental approaches (often in twelve bar formats); piano traditions developing in northern cities ("stride" piano techniques, for example); and popular ethnic dance rhythms from a variety of sources, both black and white. Branching into black, white, and crossbred forms, jazz became identified with other cities as restless jazz players moved about and established reputations in places such as Kansas City, Chicago, New York, and, eventually, Los Angeles and other cities on the West Coast.

As America underwent the transformation from an agricultural to an industrial society, its population—black and white—began pouring into cities looking for jobs. Immigrants from abroad joined internal migrants in this movement. As they migrated, entertainment became a mass "industry." Theater and show circuits, traveling bands, and other forms of entertainment attracted performers of all types to centers of population where they hoped to find an audience. The demand for entertainment "products" for a large, diverse, and growing audience became voracious.

Kansas City was an early "hot spot" for entertainers of all sorts. Musicians from New Orleans came by riverboat; country blues players from dusty Texas towns and the Southwest were also drawn to the city and influenced the music of

"Boss" Tom Pendergast's wide-open town during Prohibition. The best-known Kansas City black band of the 1920s was led by Bennie Moten. His band incorporated ragtime and vaudeville glisses as well as a rock-solid, swinging, and danceable beat. By the late 1930s, William (Count) Basie from Red Bank, New Jersey, had taken over Moten's band and created the "riff" style—a repeated short theme alternated with instrumental improvisation that excited listeners and dancers to a, sometimes, veritable frenzy. Along with many others, Basie took his band "on the road" and recorded their music. As a network of roads began to lace America's urban areas together, there were indeed routes for bands' buses to roll on, through endless nights and into endless one-night stands, in towns and cities across the country.

Along with local musicians, road bands, and others, key New Orleans players such as Joe (King) Oliver and Louis (Satchmo) Armstrong were drawn to the bright lights of Chicago. Night life in Chicago personified the rapid and often dizzying pace of urban expansion, and an "anything goes" ethos developed in the city. Dance crazes hit Chicago (and the rest of the country) as hot bands and hot night spots popped up like mushrooms after a rainstorm. White bands that were influenced by jazz, such as the Paul Whiteman Or-

Noted American jazz pianist Count Basie performs for a London audience in 1957.

chestra, became immensely popular. And, of course, popular bands, musicians, and singers recorded phonograph records and were heard throughout the land on radio.

If one key to the diffusion of jazz and its growing popularity (often in anemic and watered-down versions) from the turn of the century through the 1920s and 1930s was the combination of rapid and diverse population growth, the development of rail and highway transportation, and the concentration of people in cities, the other key was the revolution in mass communication that was occurring. It is impossible to overemphasize the impact of the phonograph and radio on the diffusion and development of jazz. Rooted in novelty of construction (an emphasis on individual sound, invention, and phrasing) and both individual and collective improvisation, jazz obliterates traditional distinctions among composer, player, and singer. The skilled improviser, within broad and often sketchy musical parameters, continuously creates renewed expressions. Jazz is more like a vision than a blueprint. As a consequence, jazz defies conventional musical notation and must be heard—over and over—to be learned. Phonographs and radios, mass-produced and affordable to most people, became "textbooks" for the jazz study hall.

New York, America's largest and most diverse city and the center of broadcasting and recording, became the Mecca for jazz musicians. To really make it, one had to make it in New York. From small groups playing in clubs and recording in studios to the big bands of giants such as Duke Ellington, New York became, and remains, the world center of jazz. With World War II, however, jazz (and popular music itself) experienced a transformation. A new and more intimate form of jazz, based primarily in New York, emerged in the 1940s and 1950s. Called "bebop," this new manifestation was complex and demanding, and it carried the art of improvisation to new levels by using unusual and ever-changing harmonic variations and duple rhythms. Musicians such as Dizzy Gillespie, Charlie Parker, and, later, John Coltrane took jazz in a new direction. Often race conscious, the black creators of bebop were harbingers of the coming civil rights revolution.

Jazz music is vital and there are many well-known players and composers who use its forms. Wynton Marsalis and others extend and explore its connections to other musical forms and traditions. It is unlikely, however, that jazz will ever again become music for a mass audience or a rallying point for rebels. Rock and roll, hip hop, and the visual fixations of the MTV generation will continue to carry popular music away from serious jazz listening. Jazz now thrives as an art music, as a foundation for popular and other forms of music, as a deep and abiding source of pleasure for avid fans, and as a music taught in music departments in schools and universities.

—Charles Nanry

See also
Armstrong, Louis.
References
Nanry, Charles. *The Jazz Text.* New York: Van Nostrand Reinhold, 1979.
Sales, Grover. *Jazz: America's Classical Music.* Englewood Cliffs, NJ: Prentice-Hall, 1984.
Schuller, Gunther. *The History of Jazz.* Vol. I, *Early Jazz* (1968). Vol. II, *The Swing Era* (1989). New York: Oxford University Press.

Jenney, William Le Baron (1832–1907)

The contributions of William Le Baron Jenney to American architecture and urbanism in the post–Civil War period were substantial. These included work on the site engineering and architecture of Riverside, Illinois, one of the nation's most important suburban designs, and the plan for Chicago's West Park System, a fresh synthesis of nineteenth-century French and American urban park theory. Jenney also earned an international reputation for refining the technology of the steel skeleton frame, which facilitated the construction of high-rise buildings. During his 38-year career, he designed, mostly in Chicago and a few other midwestern cities, many residences, churches, and commercial buildings noted for their restrained use of ornament, structural innovations, and straightforward functional plans. He was also an influential teacher who helped train many of the more distinguished members of the Chicago School of Architecture. Louis Sullivan, Daniel Burnham, William Holabird, and Martin Roche all served apprenticeships in his office, as did Ossian Simonds, founder of the Prairie School of landscape architecture.

Jenney was born on September 25, 1832, in Fairhaven, Massachusetts, into the family of a wealthy shipowner. After traveling in South America and the Philippines, Jenney studied engineering at the Ecole Centrale des Arts et Manufactures in Paris, graduating in 1856 with a degree in civil engineering. At the Ecole he was deeply influenced by the teachings of Louis Charles Mary, who stressed the derivation of a building's form from its function and the subordination of ornament to structure. These remained basic principles of Jenney's architecture throughout his professional career. He also observed the construction of the Parisian park system during the reign of Napoleon III and put this experience to good use in his design of Chicago's West Park System.

In 1861, Jenney enlisted in the Union army. As a member of the engineering corps, first under General Ulysses S. Grant and later General William T. Sherman, Jenney honed his practical experience designing bridges and fortifications. After the war, he moved to Chicago, America's fastest growing major city, and began his architectural practice at the relatively late age of 35.

One of Jenney's first projects was a collaboration in 1868 with Frederick Law Olmsted and Calvert Vaux on the design of the Riverside suburb. Jenney designed Riverside's large hotel, water tower, and several residences. He also consulted on the site engineering of the project's parks and curvilinear road system, which set precedents for later nineteenth-century suburban designs. In 1869 Jenney designed Chicago's West Park System, comprising eight miles of boulevards and three parks of about 175 acres each. Jenney shared Olmsted's belief that urban parks were necessary to relieve urban stress through the healing power of carefully designed landscapes of large turf areas, trees, and lakes. Jenney's parks were characterized by strong axial geometries and subtropical plantings reminiscent of the Parisian parks he had observed as a student. Later designers substantially modified his initial plans.

From 1870 until he retired in 1905, Jenney concentrated his professional practice on designing private residences, churches, and commercial buildings. His office was one of the first to be organized according to the division of tasks among specialists, which enabled it to undertake several large projects at the same time. In 1869, Jenney coauthored with his partner Loring Sanford *Principles and Practice of Architecture,* a work on architectural theory that espoused an eclecticism based on strict adherence to a building's function and structure as the main determinants of its form.

Jenney's most famous building, and the one that earned him an international reputation, was the Home Insurance Building of 1885, in Chicago. This work was an astute and original synthesis of existing skeleton frame technology. It stimulated the further development of the structural system employed in all subsequent high-rise commercial architecture throughout the United States and Europe. Jenney's other important buildings, which were also noted for their structural sophistication, included the second Leiter Building (1889), the Manhattan Building (1889), the Ludington Building (1891), the Horticultural Building at the World's Columbian Exposition (1893), and the Fair Store (1905).

After a distinguished career, Jenney died on June 15, 1907. The context of his practice had been the rapidly growing industrial city, and his contributions to American architecture and urbanism had helped to make that highly volatile and complex city, especially Chicago, a more ordered and humane environment.

—*Reuben M. Rainey*

See also
Olmsted, Frederick Law; Riverside, Illinois.
References
Giedion, Siegfried. *Space, Time, and Architecture.* Cambridge, MA: Harvard University Press, 1954.
Jenney, William Le Baron. "Autobiography." *Western Architect* 10 (1907): 59–66.
Jenney, William Le Baron, and Loring Sanford. *Principles and Practice of Architecture.* Cleveland and Chicago: Cobb, Pritchard, 1869.
Turak, Theodore. *William Le Baron Jenney: A Pioneer of Modern Architecture.* Ann Arbor, MI: UMI Research Press, 1986.

Jitneys

The jitney, a form of paratransit, is a small motor vehicle that operates as a common carrier on a regular route, but without fixed stops or schedule, picking up passengers wherever they hail it. Its name, California slang for a 5-cent coin, is reportedly of Creole slave origin, from the French *jeton* (token). In the United States, jitneys date from 1910 or earlier but became remarkable only in the middle of 1914 when they competed against trolleys in Los Angeles. A year later, they were a national fad.

Jitney riders were attracted by their speed, flexibility, novelty, social status, and intimacy. They offered an alternative to local traction monopolies and to segregated public transit in the South. Many communities received their first public transportation from a jitney. Drivers came from the unemployed (there was a severe recession from 1913 to 1915, especially in the West) and from families seeking extra income to maintain a car. Hence, hundreds of women drove the family car as a jitney.

At the peak of their popularity in 1915, there were at least 62,000 jitneys driving the streets of more than 250 American municipalities. Typically, jitneys captured about 5 percent of all transit patrons, but occasionally as much as half (as, for example, in Bridgeport, Connecticut; Paterson, New Jersey; and Detroit, Michigan), and route associations organized the trade on a cooperative basis. About half of the jitneys were Model T Fords, some with an extra seat attached to one of the rear doors. Others were constructed from the chassis of a Model T, onto which a customized, buslike body seating 12 to 16 was fastened. Larger jitneys tended to operate as motor buses with fixed, scheduled stops, but Americans called any motor vehicle a jitney in 1915 if it charged a low fare, including "cut rate" cabs.

Electric railroads demanded suppression of jitneys and said that they threatened the survival of a transit system they could not replace. That system included the citywide coordination of routes and uniform fares that subsidized suburbanization at the expense of inner-city residents. It also included taxes on earnings and special assessments for paving streets and removing snow that helped finance municipal government. What would happen to property values in central cities and suburbs, railroads asked, if the cost of traveling between them were doubled, either by zone fares or dependence on high-cost jitney buses? Jitneys also congested traffic and menaced jobs on electric railroads. In addition, moralists fretted about misbehavior in the backseat.

These concerns produced hostile municipal or state regulations calculated to make jitneys unprofitable by reducing their load capacity, expelling them from trolley routes, or requiring an onerous indemnity bond. Public Service Commissions usually denied them a certificate of "convenience and necessity." By 1918, jitneys had disappeared from most trolley routes.

Still, they fought a tenacious rearguard action in several cities, using the courts and referenda, and survived until the middle of the 1920s in Detroit, Atlanta, Birmingham, and some other cities, and until 1965 in St. Louis. Tourist cities like San Francisco, Miami Beach, and Atlantic City never entirely proscribed jitneys, and they have been tolerated, though illegal, in Chicago, Pittsburgh, Chattanooga, and New York. Many suburban jitney operations metamorphosed in the 1920s into independent bus companies or coops.

By 1965, the jitney was remembered only as a nuisance. However, dissatisfaction with motor buses and cars renewed interest in paratransit. Some scholars contended that suppression of jitney buses had curtailed innovation and investment in public transit after 1920. After 1980, jitneys were reintroduced to Los Angeles, San Diego, and Indianapolis with modest results.

—*Donald F. Davis*

References

Brownell, Blaine. "The Notorious Jitney and the Urban Transportation Crisis in Birmingham in the 1920's." *Alabama Review* 25 (1972): 105–118.

Davis, Donald F. "The North American Response to the Jitney Bus." *Canadian Review of American Studies* 21 (1990): 333–357.

Eckert, Ross, and George W. Hilton. "The Jitneys." *Journal of Law and Economics* 15 (1972): 293–325.

Salzman, Arthur, and Richard J. Solomon. "Jitney Operations in the United States." *Highway Research Record* 449 (1973): 63–70.

Schwantes, Carlos. "The West Adapts the Automobile: Technology, Unemployment, and the Jitney Phenomenon of 1914–1917." *Western Historical Quarterly* 16 (1985): 307–326.

Johnson Administration: Urban Policy

Shortly after he succeeded John F. Kennedy in the White House, Lyndon Johnson appointed a Task Force on Metropolitan and Urban Problems to come up with ideas for legislation. This body duly provided a long list of initiatives for the president's consideration shortly after he won reelection in 1964. The ideas of the task force—urban revitalization, anticrime programs, aid to education, more public recreation facilities—sought to give substance to the vision of a Great Society, which Johnson had announced as the theme of his presidency. The goal, he had said, paraphrasing Aristotle, was "to make the city a place where people come, not only to live, but to live the good life."

In the next several years, an extraordinary legislative whirlwind followed. As Johnson embarked on the legislative agenda for his Great Society, there were approximately 115 federal grant programs available to state and local governments. By the end of his presidency, the number had swelled to nearly 400. Great Society legislation touched nearly every aspect of urban life. The Economic Opportunity Act of 1964 was the centerpiece of the War on Poverty, a complex bill that established the Job Corps (job training for young people), VISTA (Volunteers in Service to America, a domestic Peace Corps), and most important, the Community Action Program. This last initiative provided federal subsidies directly to neighborhood community organizations, often bypassing city governments. The law provided that these organizations be administered with the "maximum feasible participation" of the people in the areas served, a clause that was taken to mean that poor people themselves had to have a role in the governance of programs. Community action agencies had the freedom to develop their own array of programs, and these ranged from teen recreation and pregnancy counseling to consumer education and political organizing.

A host of other Great Society programs were deployed on other fronts in the War on Poverty: Head Start for early childhood education and preventive health care; food stamps for the hungry; Medicaid and Medicare, health insurance for the poor on welfare and the elderly; the 1965 Elementary and Secondary Education Act providing funds to school districts for programs to assist economically disadvantaged students; and the Housing Act of 1968 calling for the construction of 6 million units of publicly subsidized housing during the subsequent decade. To bolster urban police forces, Congress passed the Safe Streets Act in 1968. To provide help in building urban mass transit systems, Congress provided construction and capital equipment subsidies in the Urban Mass Transportation Act of 1964 (one of its first projects was the Washington, D.C., metro system).

Some programs of the Johnson era had no special urban content, but they affected cities nonetheless. One example is the Public Works and Economic Development Act of 1965, which was originally designed to combat structural unemployment by helping poor rural areas attract industry with federally subsidized public works and industrial parks. Very quickly, however, urban congressmen moved to broaden the eligibility criteria, thus enabling cities to apply for grants from the new Economic Development Administration.

The two major civil rights acts were also federal initiatives with no specifically urban objectives but whose effect on cities has been profound. The Civil Rights Act of 1964 opened public accommodations, including hotels, restaurants, parks, and public transportation, to people of all races and barred the use of federal aid by institutions or programs that did discriminate. The Voting Rights Act of 1965 (President Johnson had invoked the civil rights anthem *We Shall Overcome* in calling for its passage) laid the basis for the electoral mobilization of African Americans who lived in cities. Among the other impacts of mass registration among black citizens was the achievement of controlling city halls across the country, beginning with mayoral victories in Gary, Indiana, and Cleveland, Ohio, in 1967.

To manage the Great Society, President Johnson created a host of new federal institutions, including the Office of Economic Opportunity to oversee the War on Poverty, the Economic Development Administration in the Department of Commerce, and two cabinet-level departments, Housing and Urban Development (whose establishment had eluded President Kennedy) and Transportation. And in an attempt to pull together this bewildering myriad of programs and grants, Congress enacted the Model Cities program (formally called the Demonstration Cities and Metropolitan Development Act of 1966), which provided support to establish local model city agencies to develop plans for the coordinated use of Great Society programs.

By the end of the Johnson administration, federal aid in constant dollars to state and local governments had nearly doubled, the swiftest expansion of intergovernmental fiscal transfers since the emergency programs of the Great Depression. Big cities enjoyed a particular advantage for they received twice as much federal aid per capita as smaller communities around the nation. When Johnson's presidency ended in 1969, the Vietnam War was absorbing most federal dollars and political energies, but poverty rates had nevertheless fallen substantially (from 19 percent of the population in 1964 to 12.1 percent in 1969), and the safety net programs that became the subject of vigorous political debate three decades later were in place.

—*Peter Eisinger*

See also
Community Action Program; Housing and Urban Development, Department of; War on Poverty.

References
Blum, John Morton. *Years of Discord: American Politics and Society, 1961–1974*. New York: W. W. Norton, 1991.
Peterson, Paul. *The Price of Federalism*. Washington, DC: Brookings Institution, 1995.
Schwarz, John. *America's Hidden Success*. New York: W. W. Norton, 1988.

Joplin, Scott (1868–1917)

Scott Joplin composed and performed ragtime music, which became a popular musical form in American cities around 1900. Born in 1868 near Texarkana, Texas, Joplin grew up in a region deeply influenced by African-American culture. As a teenager, he began blending elements of black church and work music with white waltzes, marches, and schottisches and setting this music to a lively syncopated rhythm. He spent much of his youth as an itinerant musician, visited the World's Fair in Chicago in 1893, and eventually landed in Sedalia, Missouri, where he enrolled for advanced music theory and composition courses at the George R. Smith College for Negroes. He then began writing the syncopated music that Americans, since the Chicago fair, had come to love. When *Maple Leaf Rag* appeared in 1899, Joplin achieved national fame as a ragtime composer and quickly became known as the King of Ragtime.

The popularity of *Maple Leaf Rag* prompted John Stark, its white publisher, and Joplin to move to St. Louis, where they generated new ragtime compositions. Thanks to inexpensive pianos, piano rolls and player pianos, recording processes, and mass production of sheet music, Joplin's music reached millions of Americans.

By the time Joplin moved from St. Louis to New York, he had written such popular rags as *The Entertainer* (1902), *Elite Syncopations* (1902), *Cascades* (1904), and *Heliotrope Bouquet* (1907). He continued to write short pieces but became obsessed with more serious work. A ragtime ballet, *Ragtime Dance* (1902), and an opera, *A Guest of Honor* (1903), had already failed, but undeterred, Joplin devoted his last years to another opera, *Treemonisha*. It was performed only once, without props or costumes, in one of Harlem's less reputable theaters. After this failure, Joplin, broken in spirit and suffering from an advanced case of syphilis, wrote little music and died in 1917.

—*Susan Curtis*

See also
Ragtime.
References
Blesh, Rudi, and Harriet Janis. *They All Played Ragtime: The True Story of an American Music.* New York: Knopf, 1950.
Curtis, Susan. *Dancing to a Black Man's Tune: A Life of Scott Joplin.* Columbia: University of Missouri Press, 1994.
Gammond, Peter. *Scott Joplin and the Ragtime Era.* New York: St. Martin's Press, 1975.
Haskins, James, and Kathleen Benson. *Scott Joplin.* Garden City, NY: Doubleday, 1978.

Journey to Work

The journey to work is one of the most important patterns of movement in American cities. It involves numerous policy issues and contains several theoretical implications about how the daily flow of workers binds together distinct land uses in the metropolis. Yet in fact the work journey is historically specific and reflects the spatial separation of residence and workplace that occurred during the development of industrial capitalism in the middle of the nineteenth century.

From the perspective of an individual worker, the journey to work has several distinguishing features. It is nondiscretionary, since it is a condition of virtually all types of employment; it should be predictable, since it is a daily routine; and it involves recurrent costs in both time and money. Thus, a particular work trip results from a multiplicity of time

and space trade-offs by individuals and families, and travel patterns provide insight into important social and economic patterns. The journey to work has attracted considerable attention from scholars and policymakers during the past several decades, and commuting patterns have become important variables in a wide range of theories and models in urban geography, economics, and planning.

The ways in which people get to work in the American city have undergone sweeping changes in the last 150 years, and these trends have both reflected and contributed to changes in urban form. By the turn of the twentieth century, the steam locomotive and the streetcar had made it possible to develop residential areas that had increasingly lower densities and were at greater distances from centralized employment nodes. These transportation innovations stimulated the growth of suburbs on the outskirts of cities and greatly expanded the area occupied by urban regions. The increasing use of the automobile accelerated the processes of decentralization and deconcentration after World War II, further stretching the distance between home and work and altering the spatial structure of housing and labor markets in American cities.

While new modes of transport have allowed dramatic increases in workshop distance, the amount of time that workers spend everyday journeying to work has remained relatively constant during much of the twentieth century. Travel surveys conducted in American cities since the late 1940s revealed that the vast majority of workers spent between 15 and 30 minutes getting to work, and subsequent census surveys have yielded similar figures. In 1990, the average one-way trip to work by all workers in the United States was 22.4 minutes, compared with 21.7 minutes in 1980. Several studies suggest that the time spent in the work journey has remained remarkably stable in recent years.

Yet the work trip varies in important ways within and among American metropolitan regions. In many cities, the distance of the average work trip has increased, even without corresponding increases in travel time. Moreover, the time and distance spent in work-related travel vary directly with the density of housing and employment opportunities across different parts of the urban fabric. Widely scattered residential suburbs that have few commercial or industrial districts nearby necessitate longer trips (for shopping and other needs as well as for work), effectively isolating suburban residents without reliable access to an automobile.

The journey to work also diverges among different groups of workers, and commuting patterns mirror social divisions in the American city. Workers with higher status and higher incomes typically live farther from their place of work, and they are less likely to use public transit than other workers. Minority workers spend more time in the work journey than whites, and more often rely on public transportation. A growing body of research also shows that women work closer to home than men, although this finding does not apply in all settings or among minority workers.

While there is no simple or necessary relationship between individuals' socioeconomic characteristics and their travel behavior, these persistent differences have prompted scores of studies of commuting patterns among various social groups. Given the nondiscretionary and recurrent costs associated with the work trip, workers must balance the time and expense of commuting against other locational choices, such as where to live and where to work. The journey to work is thus a uniquely observable spatial outcome of a variety of choices and constraints, and scholars seek to interpret the length of the journey to work in terms of broad, underlying social relations in the city.

In so doing, however, scholars have highlighted two contradictory interpretations of the link between home and work. The first (and most influential) interpretation of commuting distance portrays the spatial separation of home and work as a sign of affluence or prestige. Overcoming the distance between home and work requires variable expenditures (commuting costs and travel time) and, for the vast majority of Americans, a substantial capital investment (purchasing an automobile). In order to minimize these costs, workers of modest means seek homes close to their work, thus crowding into more congested working-class neighborhoods and bidding up the per-unit price of land. In contrast, more affluent workers overcome the daily "friction of distance" more easily, and they can often spend more time getting to work. Thus, higher-status workers may search for more spacious housing at sites distant from job concentrations, essentially trading commuting time for the space and amenities available at the urban fringe. If employment in an urban area remains centralized, a social patterning emerges in which socioeconomic status rises with distance from the city center. These relations create an apparent paradox, since affluent workers end up living on sites that are comparatively inexpensive (when adjusting for the size of the lot), while poorer workers occupy relatively expensive land.

A second interpretation of commuting distance was formalized in the late 1960s and became an important point of departure for researchers interested in how transportation and housing policies affected social equity. The spatial distribution of suitable employment opportunities constrains each worker's available options, and any changes in this pattern necessarily entail corresponding limits on workers' evaluation of alternatives. To adjust to a plant relocation, for example, workers have three alternatives: they may move their place of residence accordingly, search for a job closer to their current home, or shoulder the increased travel costs required to reach their employer's new location. Each of these alternatives represents an increased burden on workers that results directly from a firm's locational decision. The first coherent synthesis of these relationships was John Kain's celebrated "spatial mismatch" hypothesis, an enormously influential work that served as the catalyst for hundreds of studies in academic and public policy outlets over the next three decades. Kain argued that pervasive racial discrimination in the housing market effectively barred African-American workers from using residential relocation to cope with structural changes in urban labor markets. When transportation costs, increased congestion, and other factors caused the widespread decentralization of manufacturing away from the cores of metropolitan regions, African Americans were left spatially isolated from jobs, many of which had provided comparatively high wages and required little formal education. These workers were either left with poorly paying, temporary local jobs or faced additional travel costs to reach suburban jobs. A study of Chicago in the early 1970s concluded that "the typical work trip for white suburbanites is a 20-mile ride in an air-conditioned train to a downtown desk job paying $17,000 a year. A typical work trip for a black reverse commuter is a 30-mile ride in a car pool to an $8,000 factory job."

A growing body of literature on gender differences in the journey to work exemplifies both interpretations of commuting distance and illustrates the complexity of the links between socioeconomic factors and spatial behavior. Many studies find that women tend to work closer to home than men, whether proximity is measured in terms of travel time, straight-line distance, or road distance. This "gender gap" typically ranges between 15 and 25 percent, although in some suburban settings men's work trips exceed women's by 40 percent or more. This gap results from women's greater reliance on poorly paid and part-time employment, and also from the constrained time-budgets of married women and mothers who have to balance paid employment with housework and child rearing. In turn, these factors perpetuate occupational sex segregation—differences in the kinds of work men and women do.

Most studies of gender differences in commuting have focused on middle-class white women in North American cities, and so many analysts have incorporated the empirical finding of women's shorter work trips into a "spatial entrapment" thesis. According to this theory, married women's domestic responsibilities force them to narrow the spatial range of their daily routines and job-search networks. Poor transit systems prevent suburban women from reaching well-paying jobs across town. Thus, suburban women find themselves spatially trapped and reliant on locally available jobs, many of which offer poor earnings and few advancement opportunities. These constraints then become an attractive locational factor for suburbanizing firms that require large numbers of workers for jobs typically filled by women (e.g., typists or data-entry clerks). Suburban women's restricted commuting patterns thus help to reinforce gender divisions in the workforce, limiting women's employment opportunities to poorly paid clerical and service work.

The spatial entrapment thesis has been hotly contested, and studies have revealed contradictory findings about the relation between women's employment opportunities and the length of the work journey. Some studies show that many women endure commutes that do not seem justified by economic considerations; in contrast to men, women are often unable to obtain higher wages by lengthening the work journey. Moreover, the finding of women's shorter work trips does not apply in all settings, and several studies show that minority women commute farther than do white women.

By itself, the length of the work journey bears no inherent relation to the socioeconomic characteristics of workers, and commuting patterns reflect the outcome of varied and often contradictory choices and constraints. Thus, journey to work patterns must be evaluated in relation to job quality and housing circumstances, as well as to gender, racial, and class divisions in the urban economy.

—*Elvin Wyly*

See also

Automobiles; Commuting; Horsecars; Omnibuses; Streetcar Suburbs; Walking City.

References

Blumen, O. "Gender Differences in the Journey to Work." *Urban Geography* 15 (1994): 223–245.

England, K. V. L. "Suburban Pink-Collar Ghettos: The Spatial Entrapment of Women?" *Annals of the Association of American Geographers* 83 (1993): 225–242.

Fernandez, R. M. "Race, Space, and Job Accessibility: Evidence from a Plant Relocation." *Economic Geography* 70 (1994): 390–416.

Hanson, S., and G. Pratt. *Gender, Work, and Space.* New York: Routledge, 1995.

Kain, John F. "Housing Segregation, Negro Employment, and Metropolitan Decentralization." *Quarterly Journal of Economics* 82 (1968): 175–197.

Muth, R. F. *Cities and Housing.* Chicago: University of Chicago Press, 1969.

Vance, James E., Jr. "Human Mobility and the Shaping of Cities." In J. F. Hart, ed., *Our Changing Cities,* 67–85. Baltimore: Johns Hopkins University Press, 1991.

Wachs, M., B. D. Taylor, N. Levine, and P. Ong. "The Changing Commute: A Study of the Jobs-Housing Relationship over Time." *Urban Studies* 30 (1993): 1711–1729.

Wheeler, J. O. "Occupational Status and Work-Trips: A Minimum Distance Approach." *Social Forces* 45 (1966): 508–515.

Judaism

Until the middle of the nineteenth century, Jews in the German kingdoms and the Russian Empire lived in villages rather than cities. But as political barriers to trade were eased, commerce and petty industry became concentrated in expanding cities. Jews, slowly emancipated first in France, Holland, and some of the German states, migrated to the cities also.

Those who came to America likewise spread themselves along trade routes to the cities of the expanding nation. Because American Jews in the nineteenth century made themselves urban in a land that afforded them religious liberty, their religious expression became strongly influenced by the people whom they most admired—the Protestant upper-middle class.

In Europe, Jewish communities (*gemunde* in German or *kehillah* in Hebrew) had been legally incorporated. The *kehillah,* a body elected by male heads of households, collected taxes and enforced the biblical laws under which all Jews were required to live. Rabbis were considered divinely inspired legal scholars who presided over law courts, not religious services. As states like France and the German principalities emancipated Jews and ended most of their support for Jewish communities, individual Jews felt freer to define Judaism and the meaning of being Jewish. In cities like Hamburg and Berlin in the middle of the nineteenth century, and in Vienna, Warsaw, Vilna, and Lodz by the end of the century, secular Jews defied communal authority by creating new religious rituals, hiring rabbis who considered Judaism a creedal religion rather than a religious civilization, or even professing atheism as they joined the Jewish Workers "Bund." Rebels, like those Jews who wished to follow the mystic teachings of a *wunder rebbe* in a Hasidic court, defied communal leadership.

In America, Jews were never recognized as a corporate entity by any colony or state. Instead, they organized religious communities as voluntary associations. No ordained rabbis came to America until the mid-1840s, so laymen not only raised money to support Jewish religious and welfare work but also made decisions about religious ritual and ceremonies such as marriage. Congregations considered themselves traditional, although the Hebrew ritual was incomprehensible to most of their children, and complex decisions concerning dietary and family law had to be referred to the chief rabbi in London. Synagogue boards required members of their congregations to close shops on the Jewish Sabbath, supervised kosher slaughtering procedures, and governed marriage, divorce, and burial. In the cities of largest Jewish settlement after 1840, such as New York, Philadelphia, and Cincinnati, congregations proliferated as new people arrived and felt uncomfortable with the rituals already worked out in older synagogues. Without a *kehillah* to define norms and dispense funds, groups of Jews were free to organize new congregations and perform rituals as they chose.

When German rabbis did arrive in the middle of the nineteenth century, they had usually received their training in seminaries like the one at Breslau that were redefining Judaism as a creedal religion. Though many immigrant rabbis deplored the lack of ritual observance, they came to see themselves as religious teachers more than as legal scholars. They also accepted the authority of laymen to make major decisions for the religious congregation. Their own projects, by an educated layman like Isaac Leeser in Philadelphia or by ordained Reform rabbis like Isaac Mayer Wise in Cincinnati, David Einhorn in Baltimore and then New York, and Leo Merzbacher in New York, were to translate the Bible into English, to prepare prayer books that their congregants could read and religious ceremonies that inspired them, and to start seminaries to train rabbis. Wise, who was well supported by local Jewish merchants, opened the first seminary, Hebrew Union College, in Cincinnati in 1875. He also organized 28 Reform temples in the Midwest and South into a loose "synod" called the Union of American Hebrew Congregations and whose rabbis organized the Central Conference of American Rabbis.

As urban residents, American Jews and their rabbis carved their niche in the mercantile, Republican sector of local societies. As individuals, they became accustomed to America's personal freedom and civic activism, but they retained a sense of Jewish familial identity. Individual Jewish men and women, emulating Protestant merchant families, expected to belong to a religious body led by an inspirational preacher, to practice a religion that had clear ethical precepts, and to take responsibility for communal charity. Judaism has rarely attempted to formulate or decree a defining set of beliefs, or a dogma, but Jewish leaders in urban America saw their congregants attracted to the religious styles of Protestant merchant families whose moral beliefs were set down in creeds. Felix Adler, the son of a renowned rabbi and a young professor at Cornell University, left for New York in 1876 where he founded the Society for Ethical Culture. Adler rejected Judaism's ancient rituals and idea of God, accepted scientific methods for explaining natural phenomenon, and sought to discover universal ethical guidelines for human conduct.

When Ethical Culture attracted many liberal intellectuals, including young Jews, Reform rabbis, led by Kaufman Kohler, called a conference for Pittsburgh in 1885, where they drafted an unofficial creed for Reform Jews. The Pittsburgh Platform rejected the European view that Jews were a minority "nation" among other nations, and defined Jews as a "religious community" within the United States. While the Ten Commandments were still considered divinely inspired, Reform Judaism rejected the view that decisions reached by rabbinical courts carried divine approval and found many rituals like animal sacrifice and *kashrut* (the Jewish dietary laws) archaic. The Pittsburgh Platform also enjoined Jews to engage in a "mission of Israel" to bring ethical monotheism to other people and to advance social justice through political activism.

To celebrate and demonstrate their high social status and standing, Reform Jews built elaborate temples in major cities like New York, Cincinnati, and Philadelphia. Temple Emanu-el on Sutter Street in San Francisco was a civic landmark until it was badly damaged in the earthquake and fire of 1906. Emanu-el in New York, Isaac M Wise's Plum Street Temple in Cincinnati, Rodeph Shalom in Philadelphia, and even smaller structures like Beth Israel in Portland, Oregon, and Beth Elohim in Charleston, South Carolina, were architectural gems. Young rabbis who had graduated from Hebrew Union College, such as William Friedman in Denver, Colorado, Henry Cohen in Galveston, Texas, or Judah Magnes in New York, became leaders of civic reform as well as organized charity.

As large numbers of Jewish immigrants from Eastern Europe began arriving in the United States in the latter half of the 1880s, the "mission of Israel," now refocused on social justice, was directed toward them. American cities became a locale where different kinds of Judaism met and have remained in conflict ever since.

The relatively open real estate market allowed Jewish merchant families to move along streetcar lines to new suburban residential neighborhoods, while immigrant Jews settled miles away in older housing near the city's core. Women from suburban Jewish families who belonged to Reform temples organized themselves into Ladies Aid societies to assist the local Jewish poor, and between 1893 and 1900 these women also started local sections of the National Council of Jewish Women to educate themselves on Jewish ritual, history, and literature. By 1900 they had started settlement houses in immigrant districts, in part to counter the Protestant "missions" located there, but also to bring health care and social services to immigrant women, and knowledge of Jewish ritual to children. Settlement houses allowed immigrants to conduct their own educational classes, but the religion dispensed by settlement volunteers to immigrant children was only the ritual veneer of Reform. A holiday like Purim that allowed children to wear costumes, or like Hanukkah where presents were dispensed, suggested that Judaism—like Christianity—could be fun. The struggle for Jewish freedom that both festivals celebrated reinforced the democratic political creed that Americanization promoted.

By 1900, Jewish immigrant districts contained conflicting philosophies of Judaism and images of the Jewish future. New York's Lower East Side, by far the most densely settled district of any American city, had dozens of storefront *shuls* that sponsored mutual benefit societies organized by poor men from the same town or province in Russia or Rumania. Within a few blocks, one could find the Beth Hamidrash

Hagadol, which projected the vision of a unified, orthodox Jewry, and the Isaac Elchanan Yeshiva, which trained rabbis for the emerging Orthodox middle class of clothing manufacturers. A block away was the building of the *Jewish Daily Forward,* which sponsored Marxist trade unionism; the Educational Alliance, which brought liberal democracy to the immigrant masses; and the Henry Street Settlement, which brought modern medicine and social science.

By the 1890s, Jewish philanthropists in New York and Philadelphia like Jacob Schiff, himself the descendant of Orthodox rabbis, Judge Mayer Sulzberger, and Cyrus Adler feared that the children of immigrant Jews would not be attracted to Reform, whose creed and ritual might seem alien, and would drift into atheism. As a counterweight, they sponsored a new Jewish Theological Seminary to train rabbis who would adhere more closely to traditional ritual than the graduates of Hebrew Union College. The new head of the seminary, Solomon Schecter, had been brought from Cambridge University, where he was trained in biblical archaeology. Though Orthodox in his own religious practices, he interpreted Judaism not as a set of divinely ordained commandments or of timeless ethical precepts but as an evolving civilization. Judaism, for Schecter, was not a religious community but a people with branches in many lands. To bring focus to the scattered people, Schecter believed that Jews should restore their homeland in Zion, where they could construct a modern society inspired by the historic relics of their past. Schecter's Zionism, however, did not require a Jewish state or even that most Jews migrate to Palestine. Instead, he saw a spiritual link between a revitalized cultural center in Palestine and the religiously revitalized Jewries of the Diaspora.

This vision of Judaism as evolutionary, and yet respectful of tradition, became the core of Conservative Judaism, a uniquely American philosophical and ritual compromise. Its rabbis were also required to earn college degrees, and they studied modern philosophy as well as Bible, Talmud, and homiletics. By the 1950s, as the children of East European immigrants started families of their own, the Conservative movement became the largest branch of Judaism in the United States. It was estimated that Jews in the United States had spent almost $1 billion in the 1950s alone to construct hundreds of new suburban synagogues, with most of them belonging to the Conservative movement.

However, since Jews who practiced traditional Judaism continued to come to America, even after World War II, and these newcomers, too, settled in large cities, Jewish communities included the most traditional forms of religious expression alongside congregations that prided themselves on ritual innovation. By 1900, the Orthodox had created several small *yeshivas* in New York and elsewhere. In 1915 the largest, the Rabbi Isaac Elchanon Theological Seminary, merged with a smaller one and took as its head Bernard Revel, who was then only 30 years old. He had been a Talmudic scholar in Kovno, and he moved to America in 1906, where he earned a Ph.D. in biblical studies from Dropsy College in Philadelphia. Revel wanted his students to earn a secular college degree and be able to preach in English to American-born youth so that they could hold the next generation for what came to be called "Neo-Orthodoxy." Revel's "yeshiva," unlike those in Eastern Europe, required the study of Greek, Latin, and modern philosophy, as well as the Talmudic knowledge required of all Orthodox rabbis. From this seminary developed Yeshiva University in New York, which graduated well over 1,000 Orthodox rabbis between 1906 and the early 1970s.

By the 1980s Orthodoxy held about 10 percent of America's Jews, scattered all over the country. Orthodoxy, however, became more prominent than it had been since World War I, as its middle-class members built dozens of all-day schools to educate their children. These schools combined instruction in secular subjects with the study of Hebrew, Bible, and Talmud. Especially in western cities like Denver, Los Angeles, and Portland, Oregon, where Orthodoxy seemed to have faded, young families from the East brought new life to synagogues and schools, importing rabbis and teachers whose beliefs coincided with their own. By the late 1980s, even Lubavitcher Hasidim (a group of very Orthodox Jews) were sending rabbis and establishing teaching centers.

New York remained the center for the Hasidic sects, whose members had fled from the Nazis to the United States just before World War II. The Satmar Hasidim in the Williamsburg section of Brooklyn created a "court" in which their rabbi functioned much as he had in Hungary. The Lubavitcher Hasidim in Brooklyn's Crown Heights, however, developed an evangelical calling to bring the Jews of the world back to the divinely inspired word of their *rebbe,* the remarkable Menachim Mendel Schneerson, who died in his nineties in 1994. The Lubavitchers number in the tens of thousands, with *yeshivas* in Australia, Canada, and Israel, as well as in Brooklyn. Their young rabbis have started teaching centers all over the United States, where they especially try to attract young Jews. Reform and Conservative rabbis have supported liberal social reforms and advocate the separation of church and state, but Lubavitchers, when they speak politically, oppose abortion and favor state-supported parochial education.

The most dynamic changes in Judaism since the 1960s, however, have occurred through the rapid migration of college-educated Jews from older, industrial cities like Cleveland, Detroit, Philadelphia, and Chicago to the cities of the South and West, typified by Miami and Los Angeles. In the late 1940s, Miami attracted many retired people, and later builders and professional families. Soon, new Conservative and Reform synagogues were constructed while the hotels in Miami Beach featured kosher food and elaborate religious rituals for the Jewish New Year (Rosh Hashanah) and the Day of Atonement (Yom Kippur). Miami Jews also slowly became involved in court cases challenging Christian "fundamentalist" influence in the public schools.

Los Angeles, the most dynamically expanding city in the country, attracted hundreds of thousands of Jews. With 500,000 Jews by 1980, it had become the second largest center of Jewish settlement in the world. To educate these people in things Jewish, in 1946 Rabbi Edgar Magnin of Wilshire Boulevard Temple had started a large adult education project, which grew into its own huge synagogue. To recruit young men for the rabbinate, Hebrew Union College started a branch of its seminary in Los Angeles. The Conservative movement, inspired by Rabbi Mordecai Kaplan, started its own adult education program in 1949, which developed into a small undergraduate college called the University of Judaism. Year-round camps promoting Zionism, or Jewish cultural life, as well as synagogues trying to win young people away from southern California hedonism, gave vitality to the city's west side. While Jewish communal leaders deplored the high rate of Jewish "intermarriage" starting in the 1960s, Reform and then Conservative rabbis used conversion ceremonies to bring young people into the community who would have been rejected as ethnically inappropriate a generation before.

—*William Toll*

References

Cohen, Arthur. *The Natural and the Supernatural Jew: An Historical and Theological Introduction.* New York: Pantheon, 1962.

Cohen, Steven M. *American Modernity and Jewish Identity.* New York: Tavistock Publications, 1983.

Diner, Hasia. *A Time for Gathering: The Second Migration, 1820–1880.* Baltimore: Johns Hopkins University Press, 1992.

Jick, Leon. *The Americanization of the Synagogue, 1820–1870.* Hanover, NH: University Press of New England, 1976.

Moore, Deborah Dash. *To the Golden Cities: Pursuing the American Jewish Dream in Miami and Los Angeles.* New York: Free Press, 1994.

Raphael, Marc Lee. *Profiles in American Judaism: The Reform, Conservative, Orthodox, and Reconstructionist Traditions in Historical Perspective.* San Francisco: Harper & Row, 1984.

Rosenbaum, Fred. *Architects of Reform: Congregational and Community Leadership, Emanu-el of San Francisco, 1849–1980.* Berkeley, CA: Western Jewish History Center, 1980.

Rosenthal, Gilbert S. *Contemporary Judaism: Patterns of Survival.* New York: Human Sciences Press, 1986.

Sklare, Marshall. *Conservative Judaism: An American Religious Movement.* New York: Schocken Books, 1972.

Juvenile Delinquency and the Juvenile Justice System

During the first half of the nineteenth century, middle-class reformers who lived in America's most populous cities created the concept of juvenile delinquency to distinguish the rowdy and defiant behavior of poor, immigrant youngsters from the misconduct of their own (the reformers') offspring. The term reflected a growing class-consciousness in the cities, and also a relatively new belief that the misbehavior, misconduct, and lawlessness of young people differed from the criminal behavior of adults and required a special age-appropriate institutional response.

It was not happenstance that public concern about juvenile delinquency and the impetus to build special institutions for juvenile offenders came from America's largest and most populous urban areas. As cities filled with immigrants during the nineteenth century, reform-minded citizens (who by the 1890s called themselves "child savers") observed that urban children of the lower classes seemed particularly at risk of being drawn into criminal pranks and antisocial behavior. The behavior of the young was seen as further evidence of the social decay caused by the larger and more varied urban population.

Public concern about juvenile delinquency also reflected new ideas about childhood becoming prominent in nineteenth-century urban settings. Middle-class family values challenged the older Puritan belief in infant damnation and showed little sympathy for the farm family's economic need to use child labor. Instead, childhood in middle-class culture came to be seen as an age of innocence, a time that required careful nurturing of character. Humanitarian reformers usually believed the urban poor—especially the expanding population of immigrants in cities such as Boston, New York, Philadelphia, and Chicago—did not measure up to new standards for child welfare.

Evidence of delinquency among urban youths led some reformers to look to age-segregated institutional training as a substitute for the children's faulty families. Activists in many cities created separate detention facilities for miscreants and special provisions to hear charges against young people in separate court sessions. Boston reformers led the way, opening the House of Reformation in 1826. In Chicago, a much younger city, child advocates established a reform school in 1855, and during the 1880s created "industrial schools" for troublesome youths not actually convicted of criminal behavior. Throughout the century reformers relied on the British common law doctrine of *parens patriae* (the right of courts to make decisions freely for people unable to care for themselves) for authority to institutionalize these youngsters. In 1838 the Pennsylvania Supreme Court, in the case of *Ex parte Crouse*, first used the doctrine to legitimize state supervision of troublesome children. By the end of the century an apparent increase in urban delinquency and the seeming failure of the institutions to rehabilitate young offenders generated interest in separate "juvenile" courts.

In 1899, Illinois legislators responded to pressure from Chicago activists and passed the nation's first juvenile court act to try boys no older than 16 and girls no older than 17 in separate court proceedings. Other states quickly followed suit. The juvenile court thus culminated almost a century of discussion about the separate and special needs of children, about the malleable nature of childhood, and about the obligation of reformers to construct institutions to protect and police the urban young.

In 1909 Chicago reformers once again led the way by establishing a psychological clinic—the Juvenile Psychopathic Institute—to assist the juvenile court judge with the task of diagnosing the causes of individual acts of delinquency. The success of the court-clinic relationship in Chicago prompted the creation of similar "child guidance" clinics in other urban centers during the first half of the twentieth century. Child guidance practitioners laid the groundwork for a psychological explanation of delinquency that focused on personality maladjustment, rather than poverty or mental ability, as the source of misconduct. At present, every state requires the psychological evaluation of delinquents before they are sentenced.

But regardless of how child advocates in the late nineteenth and early twentieth centuries explained juvenile delinquency—as hereditary weakness, mental incapacity, faulty upbringing, or some other psychological disorder—they all agreed that young people deserved separate treatment and age-specialized facilities. The special care provided by age-specific trial and detention facilities was expected to forestall a lifetime of criminality or public dependency, social problems often associated with the urban poor. Judgment in a separate juvenile court, where rules were flexible and judges had great latitude when probing the causes of misbehavior and devising solutions for them, fit with new concepts about the uniqueness of childhood. The juvenile court was also predicated on new ideals in criminology that replaced the notion of punishment with the concept of treatment.

By the 1960s advocates of children's rights had begun to criticize the separate court proceedings intended to protect children from criminal judgments and punishments meant for adult offenders. The wide latitude accorded the courts because of the perceived need to treat a juvenile delinquent in a special way often meant that juvenile justice superseded a youngster's constitutional rights. A series of Supreme Court cases between 1966 and 1971 opened juvenile court procedures to public scrutiny and questioned juvenile courts' disregard of guarantees in the Bill of Rights. The most far

reaching of the cases, *In re Gault* (1967), upheld the right of minors to be given counsel, to confront and cross-examine witnesses, and to refuse to incriminate themselves.

Throughout the nineteenth and twentieth centuries, interest in the problem of juvenile delinquency has reflected public concern about social change and the costs of urbanization. During the nineteenth century poor immigrant boys described as idle, unschooled, and unsupervised by their parents caused great anxiety because they symbolized the transformation of a rural, agricultural economy into one both urban and industrial, and charging young urban girls with "sex delinquencies" reflected apprehension about looser standards of morality in cities. These conditions helped create the juvenile court movement in the nineteenth century. Today, the juvenile delinquent conjures up a more vicious, violent youngster, an urban monster molded by drugs and guns who makes the city a dangerous living environment. The new delinquent has prompted modern critics of juvenile justice to question the special treatment of young offenders, and to raise questions, once again, about the age at which a young person can and should be held responsible for his or her behavior and actions.

—*Kathleen W. Jones*

See also

Children in Cities; Correctional Institutions; Crime and Criminals; Criminal Justice System.

References

Bernard, Thomas J. *The Cycle of Juvenile Justice.* New York: Oxford University Press, 1992.

Gilbert, James. *A Cycle of Outrage: America's Reaction to the Juvenile Delinquent in the 1950s.* New York: Oxford University Press, 1986.

Hawes, Joseph M. *Children in Urban Society: Juvenile Delinquency in Nineteenth-Century America.* New York: Oxford University Press, 1971.

Mennel, Robert M. *Thorns and Thistles: Juvenile Delinquents in the United States, 1825–1940.* Hanover, NH: University Press of New England, 1973.

Odem, Mary. *Delinquent Daughters: Protecting and Policing Adolescent Female Sexuality in the United States, 1885–1920.* Chapel Hill: University of North Carolina Press, 1995.

Platt, Anthony M. *The Child Savers: The Invention of Delinquency.* 2d enlarged ed. Chicago: University of Chicago Press, 1970.

Schlossman, Steven L. *Love and the American Delinquent: The Theory and Practice of "Progressive" Juvenile Justice, 1825–1920.* Chicago: University of Chicago Press, 1977.

Schneider, Eric C. *In the Web of Class: Delinquents and Reformers in Boston, 1810s–1930s.* New York: New York University Press, 1992.

Sutton, John R. *Stubborn Children: Controlling Delinquency in the United States, 1640–1981.* Berkeley: University of California Press, 1988.

Kahn, Louis I. (1901–1974)

The international reputation and influence of the American architect Louis I. Kahn was established late in life. His masterwork, done from 1951 to 1974, harmoniously synthesizes preindustrial urban traditions with the American automobile culture that developed after World War II. Kahn's criteria for choosing which aspects from each source to integrate was based on its pragmatic service to human nature. The essence of this collective client, he perceived, was unchanging and witnessed across time in the persistence of "tradition." An exact self-portrait of this ancient nature and its programmatic needs is found in the physiognomies of classical and medieval pedestrian cities. Kahn allied "tradition" with the changed circumstances of modern life rooted in the social and industrial revolutions that occurred after the Enlightenment. Kahn's critical reevaluation of the revolutionary mission of orthodox modern urban design and architecture makes him a pivotal figure in all later assessments of the built environment for a secular, industrialized world civilization.

The objectivity of Kahn's critique was based upon the breadth of his urban and architectural culture. Educated at the University of Pennsylvania from 1920 to 1924 in a design curriculum adapted from the Ecole des Beaux-Arts in Paris, he studied and mastered a nineteenth-century patrimony derived from pagan antiquity and medieval Christianity. During the Depression, Kahn initiated an autodidactic study of twentieth-century modern architecture and urban design where he focused especially on the writing and work of Le Corbusier. From 1931 to 1934, he led and directed the Architecture Research Group (ARG), a group of unemployed architects and engineers that he founded with the French architect Dominique Berninger. The ARG won praise for its modern urban designs and established Kahn's national prominence and his working associations with Alfred Kastner, Oscar Stonorov, and George Howe. In 1951, after visits to Italy, Greece, and Egypt while serving as resident architect at the American Academy in Rome, he came under the influence of a Neo-Palladianism,

sparked by Rudolf Wittkower's influential book, *Architecture Principles in the Age of Humanism.*

Like the ancients, Kahn always viewed the architect as a designer of cities and buildings, both analogous human dwellings. The city, a big house, and the house, a small city, were each, in his words, "a world within a world." By expressing humankind's timeless existential need for physical and spiritual sanctuary, the citadel—a protecting, fortified castle within a walled city—typified the microcosmic nature of house and city. The defensive towered walls of the castle were conceived by Kahn as "hollow servant spaces" and "viaducts," providing a guarded threshold between the dispersed culture of the automobile—with its high-speed movement and massive parking requirements—and the density of the traditional pedestrian city—with its forum, or City Center—where communal life in matters sacred, civic, institutional, and commercial gathered.

Kahn's visionary designs for Philadelphia (1951–1962) first proposed these urban solutions and included his City Tower Project, 1952–1957, done in association with Anne G. Tyng. His twentieth-century citadels are symbolic sanctuaries, heavenly fortresses, which provide a covert spiritual dimension to a secular epoch. They recall the ritual monumentality that served the democratic myths of the Progressive Era, the period of Kahn's formal aesthetic training. Named after the reform-minded Progressive movement, the time, approximately 1893–1918, marked America's shift from a rural, agrarian-based economy to an urban, industrialized one. The civic ideals of the Progressives were manifested in the City Beautiful movement. Largely led by white Anglo-Saxon Protestants professing a social gospel, they envisioned a secular heaven on earth, a "New Jerusalem" projected into material form. As chief designer of Philadelphia's Sesquicentennial Exposition, 1925–1926, Kahn created such a millennial utopia—polychromed in pink, yellow, and salmon and illuminated at night with a wash of colored lights and beacons blazing from giant crystals perched atop towers like ziggurats and decorated with Neoclassical solar ornaments. Called "the

Rainbow City," the Sesqui's scintillating imagery was reflected in large lagoons and followed symbolism already established by earlier national expositions in Buffalo (1901) and San Francisco (1915). These polychromed Progressive fairs, unlike the "White City" of Chicago's 1893 Columbian Exposition, celebrated the American skyscraper, a building type understood to be original to the new industrialized world.

Kahn's Sesqui consciously emulated the fashionable "setback" style of New York City skyscrapers in the 1920s. This style, stimulated by a zoning ordinance of 1916 to allow sunlight to reach the city's streets, was led by Harvey Wiley Corbett and typified by the Expressionist renderings of Hugh Ferris. In the early designs for the Sesqui, a symbolic citadel featuring a reconstruction of Solomon's Temple that looked like a ziggurat was planned to serve as the fair's City Crown. Corbett, a coauthor of this heavenly fortress and primordial high-rise, apparently saw it bestowing a quasi-divine authority upon the setback style. The monumental aspect and luminous symbolism of Kahn's mature urban visions, such as the capitol complex at Dhaka, Bangladesh, and the unrealized 1976 Bicentennial Exposition schemes for Philadelphia, may all be traced back to the utopianism of the Progressive Era.

—*Joseph A. Burton*

References
Brownlee, David B., and David G. DeLong. *Louis I. Kahn: In the Realm of Architecture.* New York: Rizzoli International, 1991.
Burton, Joseph A. "Notes from Volume Zero, Louis Kahn and the Language of God." *Perspecta, the Yale School of Architecture Journal* 20 (1983): 69–90.
Wurman, Richard Saul, ed. *What Will Be Has Always Been, the Words of Louis I. Kahn.* New York: Access Press and Rizzoli, 1986.

Keaton, Buster (1895–1966)

Buster Keaton (born Joseph Francis Keaton) is most remembered for more than 30 silent films that he made primarily in the 1920s, including *Our Hospitality* (1923), *Sherlock, Jr.* (1924), *The Navigator* (1924), *The General* (1927), and other classics. With only minor variations in his character from film to film, he became known as "the Great Stoneface" because of his sometimes comic, sometimes poignant lack of facial expression or reaction; his reputation was equally developed by the risky, complicated physical stunts he performed in many of his films.

While some of Keaton's films have rural settings, he made many films set in contemporary cities. In these films, Keaton's comments on urban life—either directly or indirectly—often include depictions of snarled traffic and malfunctioning transportation systems, as in *Sherlock, Jr., Our Hospitality* (with its famous train-trip sequence), and even *The General,* although that film is set in the 1860s. Keaton also focused on the technological and architectural advances of "modern"

A dashing Buster Keaton poses with a cigarette in Hollywood, ca. 1928.

homes, presenting them alternately as solid, appreciable improvements and as ghastly, inefficient disasters.

One of Keaton's most famous (and dangerous) individual sequences occurs in *Steamboat Bill, Jr.* (1928), when a cyclone tears through town destroying everything in its wake that has been made by people. The forces of nature are a frequent concern in Keaton's films, and they never let people forget exactly who has control. In *Steamboat Bill,* Keaton's character runs through a deserted town as winds destroy buildings and level entire city blocks. Its most celebrated sequence has a housefront fall on Keaton, and he avoids being crushed only because he happens to be standing precisely where a small window in the building's frame misses him by just a few inches on all sides. *One Week* and *The Scarecrow* (both 1920) are other Keaton films that revolve partly around the perils and virtues of the modern home, and *Sherlock, Jr.* produces a few laughs by having Sherlock's front door open directly onto a busy stretch of highway. Keaton's character, befuddled yet resourceful in almost all of his films, is often challenged by the intricacies of urban life.

—*Robert P. Holtzclaw*

References
Blesh, Rudi. *Keaton.* New York: Macmillan, 1966.
Dardis, Tom. *Keaton: The Man Who Wouldn't Lie Down.* London: Deutsch, 1979.

Keaton, Buster. *My Wonderful World of Slapstick.* New York: Doubleday, 1960.

Kerr, Walter. *The Silent Clowns.* New York: Knopf, 1975.

Robinson, David. *Buster Keaton.* London: Secker and Warburg, 1969.

Wead, George. *Buster Keaton and the Dynamics of Visual Wit.* Reprint ed. New York: Arno Press, 1976.

Harmon, Sandra D. "Florence Kelley in Illinois." *Journal of the Illinois State Historical Society* 74 (1981): 19–22.

Sklar, Kathryn Kish. *Florence Kelley and the Nation's Work.* New Haven, CT: Yale University Press, 1995.

Kelley, Florence (1859–1932)

Florence Kelley, the settlement house worker and social reformer, was born in Philadelphia. She graduated from Cornell University in 1882 and continued her studies at the University of Zurich in Switzerland. There she became a socialist in response to her growing concerns about the human costs of urbanization and industrialization. Her translation into English of Friedrich Engels's *The Condition of the Working Class in England in 1844* was published in 1887. In 1883 she married Lazare Wischnewetzky, whom she divorced in 1891, retaining custody of their three children.

Moving to Chicago in 1891, she became a resident at Hull House and conducted the investigations that laid the groundwork for passage of a factory act by the Illinois legislature in 1893. Appointed chief factory inspector by Governor John Peter Altgeld, she and her staff monitored compliance with the law. During these years, she also earned a law degree from Northwestern University (1894).

Dismissed from her position by Altgeld's successor in 1897, she accepted in 1899 the position of general secretary of the National Consumers' League (NCL), founded that same year by prominent women reformers in New York City. The NCL marshaled the power of consumers to promote good working conditions in factories and stores, and she lobbied effectively for labor laws and social welfare legislation at both the state and federal levels. Kelley oversaw the work of the NCL, and by 1910 it included more than 60 local leagues. She outlined her goals in a book, *Some Ethical Gains through Legislation,* which she published in 1905.

Kelley's social activism led her to join others in founding the National Child Labor Committee in 1904, the National Association for the Advancement of Colored People in 1909, and the Women's International League for Peace and Freedom in 1919. She joined Eugene V. Debs's Socialist Party of America in 1912. A suffragist, she was for many years a vice-president of the National American Woman Suffrage Association, but she opposed a proposed Equal Rights Amendment to the Constitution, fearing that it would endanger the protective labor laws for women that she and the NCL had championed. She died in Philadelphia at the age of 72 in 1932.

—*Sandra D. Harmon*

References

Goldmark, Josephine Clara. *Impatient Crusader: Florence Kelley's Life Story.* Urbana: University of Illinois Press, 1953.

Kenna, Michael (Hinky Dink) (1856–1946)

Michael Kenna was born on the South Side of Chicago in 1856 to Irish-Catholic parents. At the age of ten, he quit school and started selling newspapers. His friends called him Hinky Dink because of his small size. Kenna left the city in 1880 after accepting a job in Colorado as a newspaper circulation manager, but he returned two years later with enough money to buy a saloon in the Levee, Chicago's downtown vice district. Kenna soon became involved with the First Ward Democratic Party organization headed by the flamboyant Bathhouse John Coughlin.

Kenna raised money for the organization's "defense fund," set up to provide lawyers for prostitutes, gamblers, and saloonkeepers who got into legal trouble. One survey found that more than 7,000 bars, 100 gambling casinos, and 700 "opium dens" in the First Ward all paid between $100 and $1,000 a month to the ward organization for protection.

Kenna's political career began during the Depression of 1893 when he provided weekly meals at his saloon for over 8,000 unemployed workers. A few years later, these men remembered the Hink's assistance and helped elect him to the city council in 1896. Until 1923 each Chicago ward had two aldermen, so the Hink and Bathhouse John sat together in the council and promoted a wide-open city. In council meetings, the Hink rarely said a word and always voted with Coughlin in opposition to any reform. He earned the title "Prince of Grafters," and he and Coughlin both became wealthy. Their gangs of thugs and enforcers ruled the Levee until Prohibition closed the saloons in 1920, and three years later redistricting forced Kenna out of office. Coughlin remained alderman while Hink ran a cigar store and served as ward committeeman; but when the Bathhouse died in 1938, Hinky briefly reappeared at City Hall and served out the remainder of Coughlin's term. By now he was 82 years old, pale and listless, and soon stopped attending meetings. He died in 1946, leaving behind a legacy of corruption, bribery, and payoffs.

—*Leslie Tischauer*

See also

Coughlin, John Joseph (Bathhouse John).

References

Gosnell, Harold F. *Machine Politics: Chicago Model.* Chicago: University of Chicago Press, 1937.

Wendt, Lloyd, and Herman Kogan. *Bosses in Lusty Chicago: The Story of Bathhouse John and Hinky Dink.* Bloomington: Indiana University Press, 1974.

Kennedy Administration: Urban Policy

The problems of the cities, declared John F. Kennedy as a presidential candidate, constitute "the great unspoken issue in the 1960 election." That pronouncement distinguished this Boston-bred politician from his opponent, Richard Nixon of Yorba Linda, California, whose Republican Party increasingly relied on support from the burgeoning suburbs. The Democratic Party platform, aiming for victory in the heavily urbanized Northeast, advocated vigorous federal action to eliminate slums, assist mass transit, build public housing, encourage metropolitan planning, and expand public parks.

Yet for all its early promise, the Kennedy administration did not produce substantial aid for the nation's cities. The only important legislation that bore directly on urban well-being was the Housing Act of 1961, which provided more funds for public housing and urban renewal, but essentially this law only expanded the Housing Act of 1949. Its one major new element was a small pilot program of grants for demonstration projects in urban mass transit, the first such federal funding.

The only other legislative initiative worth noting was the failed attempt to create a cabinet-level Department of Urban Affairs and Housing. The effort foundered when southern congressmen resisted in the expectation that Kennedy would appoint Robert Weaver, the black head of the Housing and Home Finance Agency, as the department's secretary. Kennedy did take one significant step on the racial front, however, when he signed an executive order in 1962 banning discrimination in public housing and Federal Housing Administration lending programs.

Kennedy's meager legislative record is not the full measure of his urban policy legacy, however. Several months before his assassination in November 1963, the president, apparently inspired by reading Michael Harrington's book *The Other America* (some say Kennedy simply read a lengthy review of the book), asked Walter Heller, head of the Council of Economic Advisors, to begin developing a program to attack poverty. Planning was well under way when Lyndon Johnson succeeded to the presidency, and he seized the idea of a War on Poverty both as a signal of continuity with the Kennedy administration and also as the core of his own agenda for urban revitalization.

—*Peter Eisinger*

References

Gelfand, Mark. *A Nation of Cities: The Federal Government and Urban America, 1933–1965.* New York: Oxford University Press, 1975.

Judd, Dennis, and Todd Swanstrom. *City Politics.* New York: HarperCollins, 1994.

Kerouac, Jack (1922–1969)

Jack Kerouac is best known for his second novel, *On the Road* (1957). The story of two young men's cross-country dashes in pursuit of jazz, sex, drugs, and conversation, it spawned the beat generation. *Road,* however, was just one small part of Kerouac's life's work: the chronicling of a literary Everyman, Jack Dulouz, and his exploration of the United States at the middle of the twentieth century. At the heart of what Dulouz finds is the tension between city and road, between pause and motion. In a dozen novels, Dulouz witnesses the changes wrought in the American landscape and psyche as the country moves from the euphoria after World War II into optimistic trust in technology, roads, and marketing. Kerouac's characters suffer and comment upon suburban sprawl, interstate sameness, the oppressive nature of the split between life and work based on commuting, and a variety of other dichotomies in, and failures of, the American dream, including, foremost, the breakdown of the family. Along the way, they have a lot of fun, too, as they generally thumb their noses at 1950s conformity and the generation that has sold them a bankrupt dream.

At the crucial center of Kerouac's personal and literary aesthetics is his exploration of the loss suffered by America's soul as it moved from towns to cities. According to Kerouac, the differences between them are simple and distinct: in towns, people live with their families, and their children grow up, marry, and settle there to raise *their* families. Cities—where cheaper labor and materials force family businesses to close—lure the young away from home to a place where they run amuck in the night. Given the option, they will spend their time and money exploring New York, San Francisco, New Orleans, Denver, Chicago, and the roads that connect them. For Kerouac, this wandering exploration is a natural step in individual maturity, one that leads, eventually, to introspection and an appreciation of "home." But when the young of America after World War II finally want to go home, there is no home they can return to—or, if it is there, someone else is living in it. The result is a rootless, soul-less, commercialized, consuming society based on products and profits.

Kerouac's first novel, *The Town and the City* (1948), most directly addresses these concerns. A family much like his own, but with more siblings, grows up in the idyllic Galloway, a thinly disguised Lowell, Massachusetts, where Kerouac grew up. The patriarch loses his business, and the family must move to New York City. The move, coupled with the outbreak of World War II, disintegrates the family. Increasingly abundant roads make it possible for them to maintain contact, but their original closeness can never be recaptured.

On the Road is a logical outgrowth of that world, where the road systems have made it easy to connect the cities of

America. But the young men in *Road* prefer to see themselves passing the American commuters en route to boring, self-destroying jobs; as they pass in their speeding (sometimes stolen) cars, the heroes turn up the music. This theme—the search for meaningful ways to fill our time—haunts all of Kerouac's work.

The same search occupied much of Kerouac's personal life. Lowell and the French-Canadian world in which he grew up was a city divided by ethnicity, like many of America's early industrial cities, suffused with immigrant laborers who brought with them strong family values. Kerouac himself experienced relative security in his own early life, which was dominated by the printing shop his family operated. His father's loss of that shop, and then World War II, significantly interrupted and changed that life.

Kerouac himself seemed groomed for proper fame, but he ended a promising academic and athletic career at Columbia University by dramatically quitting the football team and school to hitchhike south. His first novel, traditionally written and heavily influenced by Thomas Wolfe, was followed by years of rejection as he worked on various versions of what would become *On the Road*. Its publication, which brought Kerouac the fame he so desperately sought, also brought a public scrutiny that changed his life irrevocably. In the end, both in his work and his personal life, he became a conservative pessimist, a reclusive victim of America's great anesthetizers, booze and television.

Kerouac's complete work—the chronicles of Dulouz—is a modern blending of Emerson's romantic philosophy of self-reliance with Whitman's passion for the great, democratic American road, yet tempered with the pessimism of Melville's "Bartleby the Scrivener." He wrote in these traditions, even as he claimed to be breaking new grounds with his "spontaneous prose" theories. But his work also fits easily with the study and enjoyment of bebop jazz and abstract expressionism in their respective artistic explorations of America's post–atomic bomb culture.

—*Alex Albright*

References

Albright, Alex. "Before He Went West, He Had to Go South: Kerouac's Southern Aesthetics." *North Carolina Humanities* 1 (1993): 53–70.

French, Warren. *Jack Kerouac*. Boston: Twayne, 1986.

Hunt, Tim. *Kerouac's Crooked Road: Development of a Fiction*. Hamden, CT: Archon, 1981.

Nicosia, Gerald. *Memory Babe: A Critical Biography of Jack Kerouac*. New York: Grove, 1983.

Stephenson, Gregory. *The Daybreak Boys: Essays on the Literature of the Beat Generation*. Carbondale: Southern Illinois University Press, 1990.

Weinreich, Regina. *The Spontaneous Poetics of Jack Kerouac: A Study of the Fiction*. Carbondale: Southern Illinois University Press, 1987.

Koch, Edward Irving (1924–)

Edward I. Koch was elected mayor of New York City in 1977 and reelected in 1981 and 1985, becoming one of only three mayors to serve three terms since the consolidation of New York City's five boroughs in 1898.

Koch was born in the Bronx, the son of Jewish immigrants from Eastern Europe. He fought in the U.S. Army in World War II, attended the City College of New York, graduated from New York University Law School, and established a law practice in Greenwich Village. By the early 1960s, he had become a leader of the reform wing of the Democratic Party. In 1963 and 1965, he was elected Democratic district leader, thus preventing a comeback by the Tammany Hall leader Carmine DeSapio. Koch won election to the city council in 1966 and to the U.S. House of Representatives in 1968. He ran unsuccessfully for mayor in 1973 before he succeeded in 1977.

Koch assumed office during a severe financial crisis. He restored budget discipline by demanding concessions from municipal unions, and he secured federal loan guarantees. He termed himself a "liberal with sanity" who was committed to government programs but also to fiscal responsibility. With his forceful personality, he restored confidence to a city shaken by its near-bankruptcy. He received both the Democratic and Republican nominations for mayor in 1981, the only candidate ever to do so, and he won reelection with a landslide majority. He ran for governor of New York State in 1982, losing to Mario Cuomo in the Democratic primary.

Koch's second term coincided with a strong local economy that allowed him to restore city government services and to expand city employment. In 1984, he published a best-selling autobiography, *Mayor*. Reelected in another landslide in 1985, Koch's popular support diminished during his third term due to corruption scandals involving close political allies, accusations that his rhetoric was racially divisive, and economic recession. In 1989, Koch failed to win a fourth term when David Dinkins, an African American, defeated him in a racially polarized Democratic primary. After leaving office, Koch maintained a high profile career as a radio talk-show host, newspaper columnist, television judge on *The People's Court,* and public speaker while serving as a partner in a Manhattan law firm.

—*Chris McNickle*

References

McNickle, Chris. *To Be Mayor of New York: Ethnic Politics in the City*. New York: Columbia University Press, 1993.

Mollenkopf, John H. *A Phoenix in the Ashes: The Rise and Fall of the Koch Coalition in New York City Politics*. Princeton, NJ: Princeton University Press, 1992.

Ku Klux Klan

No social movement in the United States has organized popular sentiments of racial hatred, religious bigotry, and xenophobia more effectively than the Ku Klux Klan (KKK). From the post–Civil War Reconstruction Era to the present, the KKK has used lynching, bombing, and gang terrorism to promote its agenda of white Protestant supremacy. African Americans and Jews have been the particular targets of Klan violence over time, but Catholics, immigrants, labor organizers, gays and lesbians, and political progressives have also faced repeated attacks by the Klan. The first, third, and fourth waves of Klan activity were concentrated in rural areas and small towns, especially in the South, but the largest Klan chapters were those of the second Klan in the 1920s, which was based in northern cities and their surrounding suburbs.

The first Klan was organized by a group of defeated Confederate soldiers immediately after the Civil War in Pulaski, Tennessee, a small city on the border of Alabama. The Klan grew quickly, taking root primarily in the rural and predominantly white piedmont and upland areas of the South. Large cities and areas with significant African-American populations, like the rural Delta, experienced

The cover for sheet music for the song "Here's to the Klan," written in the 1920s in Indiana.

little Klan activity in this postbellum period. A combination of factors fueled this first Klan, including widespread fear among whites that the region's former slaves would retaliate against them and virulent opposition to the potential influence of African Americans and northern politicians on southern politics. A loosely knit vigilante network, this Klan terrorized African Americans, election officials, schoolteachers, and others whose actions they saw as jeopardizing the legal structures of white supremacy. Within several years, federal attacks and internal chaos caused the Klan to disintegrate, and it dissolved in 1870.

After lying dormant for several decades, the Klan reemerged in 1915 at a ceremony staged at Stone Mountain, near Atlanta. By the mid-1920s, approximately 4 million women, men, and even children had joined the Klan's crusade for white Protestant supremacy. Unlike its predecessor, this second Klan had an urban and northern base. It was strong in the Midwest, East, and Far West, constituting a substantial presence in small towns as well as in some of the nation's largest cities, including Indianapolis, Memphis, Chicago, Knoxville, Little Rock, Portland (Oregon), Detroit, Dallas, Tulsa, and Denver. The agenda of the Klan broadened along with its geographic base—this Klan targeted Catholics, Jews, and immigrants along with African Americans. Because local Klans were given substantial autonomy to fashion scapegoats, other groups too fell victim to local Klan violence. Utah Klan members targeted Mormons. Labor radicals were terrorized by East Coast Klans.

The success of the Klan in urban and suburban areas was partly due to its use of family and neighborhood networks to recruit new members. In many areas, the Klan positioned itself as a focal point of local white Protestant culture, staging elaborate parades, fairs, picnics, and sporting events and commemorating births, weddings, and deaths with klannish ritual and ceremony. Moreover, Klan chapters in some heavily white and Protestant cities and towns enlisted a substantial proportion of the local population and controlled municipal officials, judges, and police. The few Jews or Catholics in such places faced violence and threats as well as rumor, boycott, and law enforcement campaigns meant to drive them from their jobs, undermine their businesses, and force them from their homes. At the height of its power in the late 1920s, however, the Klan began to crumble. Conflict among Klan leaders and a number of highly publicized scandals eroded the Klan from within while newly imposed quotas greatly reduced the number of non-Protestant and nonwhite immigrants arriving in American cities, thereby costing the Klan one of its major issues.

After 1930, the Klan never regained a substantial foothold in America's cities or suburbs. The subsequent waves of the Klan—in the mid-1960s and the 1980s—were centered in rural areas and small towns, primarily in the South. States' rights, white privileges, and racial segregation were again the main agenda of the Klan, which evoked rhetoric from the Reconstruction Era to rally whites against what it perceived as the growing political strength of African Americans and a liberal federal government that favored integration.

—*Kathleen M. Blee*

See also
Nativism.

References
Bennett, David H. *The Party of Fear: From Nativist Movements to the New Right in American History.* Chapel Hill: University of North Carolina Press, 1988.
Blee, Kathleen M. *Woman of the Klan: Racism and Gender in the 1920s.* Berkeley: University of California Press, 1991.
Chalmers, David H. *Hooded Americanism: The History of the Ku Klux Klan.* Durham, NC: Duke University Press, 1987.

La Guardia, Fiorello (1882–1947)

Fiorello La Guardia was mayor of New York City from 1934 through 1945. A seven-term member of Congress (1917–1921, 1923–1933), LaGuardia helped lay the groundwork for the New Deal but, a Republican, lost a bid for reelection in the Democratic sweep of 1932. He then ran for the mayoralty of the nation's largest city, won election, and served three four-year terms. He embodied the rise to power of the "new immigrants," particularly Italians, and the displacement of the Irish from major-city dominance. Campaigning in half a dozen languages and then looking after his constituents, he displayed a passionate commitment to the needs of urban, working-class, ethnic Americans. Resembling reform mayors of the Progressive Era who displayed a commitment both to honest government and to social reform, he, unlike they, benefited from the availability of New Deal programs to help propel his vision, and thus was better able to employ the tools of government to attack social ills.

As mayor from the Depression and New Deal through World War II, he proved to be a central figure in the transformation of his city's physical and institutional environment. He did much to forge a new relationship between American cities and the federal government, obtaining greater federal funding of municipal programs to create jobs and provide relief to the poor. From 1936 through 1945, he presided over the U.S. Conference of Mayors, which had been organized in 1933 to lobby Congress about the acute needs of big cities. Under his leadership La Guardia Airport, a new airfield within the city limits, opened in 1939. Other public works projects, too, addressed urgent needs to generate jobs and revamp the city's transportation system. Teaming up with Robert Moses, his parks commissioner, La Guardia produced the Triborough Bridge, the Henry Hudson Parkway, and the Brooklyn-Battery Tunnel. Working to improve health and education, his administration also promoted hospital and school construction.

La Guardia took on Tammany Hall, the Democratic machine that, as he saw it, had long misruled New York City, and

he pushed it out of power. He announced when taking office that his mayoralty would comprise an "experiment" as to whether honest, efficient, nonpartisan government was possible in an American city. He proceeded to demonstrate that a reform mayor could get power, keep power, and use that power effectively. When La Guardia is called the best mayor New York City has ever had, his admirers have in mind not only his energy, leadership, and public works but his determination that public service should not be primarily a means to private gain.

—*Peter Wallenstein*

See also
Moses, Robert.
References
Kessner, Thomas. *Fiorello H. La Guardia and the Making of Modern New York.* New York: McGraw-Hill, 1989.
Mann, Arthur. *La Guardia Comes to Power: 1933.* Philadelphia: J. B. Lippincott, 1965.

Land Developers and Development

Cities are made by developing land for urban use. Typically, this process begins with the subdivision of fields or woods into building lots. A survey of the subdivision and lot boundaries is undertaken and recorded for legal purposes in a local registry office. Depending upon the building and zoning regulations then in force, these lots are serviced and built upon. In some countries, the development process is closely constrained and shaped powerfully by local and national governments. In North America, however, it has typically depended upon the initiative of private entrepreneurs.

The way in which the land is developed has an enduring impact upon the shape and appearance of the city. This is obviously true of the built environment for, even in North America, most structures are built to last decades. In recent years, more people have become interested in preserving and renewing such structures, thereby extending their life and hence the evidence of past city-building. Just as important, and even more enduring, are the size and shape of the original building lots. Occasionally these have been obliterated through the resubdivision of land, but owing to the difficulties of acquiring numerous adjacent parcels from many owners, resubdivision has usually required the intervention of the state under the auspices of a program such as urban renewal. The present city, then, presents abundant evidence of the past processes of land development.

Over the past century or so, these processes have changed greatly, with manifold consequences for the urban landscape. In the nineteenth century, different people or companies were involved at each stage of the process. Investors surveyed and registered subdivisions, intending to sell the resulting building lots, often at auction, for several times the original price. These lots were typically bought by speculators who hoped to resell for a profit within a few months, at most a year or so. Many lots changed hands several times before being "developed" by builders of one sort or another. At first, development simply meant erecting a structure, but in time it came to include the provision of services such as running water, sewers, street lighting, paved roads, and sidewalks. These services had become the norm in new subdivisions for the affluent by the late nineteenth century. Their installation preceded, or coincided with, home building. Especially in suburbs and unincorporated fringe areas, however, many working-class districts grew up without basic services as late as the 1940s.

Because lots were sold and developed piecemeal, the result was often a rather anarchic pattern of development, with dwellings of various sizes and styles juxtaposed and with businesses and homes intermingled. Many subdivisions were small and, for ease of surveying, were laid out in a rectangular pattern of streets. This usually extended the existing city grid, although subdividers paid little attention to adjacent tracts of land. The resulting juxtaposition of dissimilar grids created inconvenient "jogs" that irritate motorists to this day.

Over the course of the past century, the process of land development has been consolidated. The first step, begun in earnest in the late nineteenth century, was for subdividers of land to exert more control over the building process. Recognizing that lots in controlled subdivisions commanded a higher price, they began to impose building, deed, and land use restrictions. These defined minimum standards of construction (a dollar figure was common) and, until struck down by courts after World War II, might prevent the sale of property to members of specified ethnic or racial groups. The second step was for entrepreneurs to combine land subdivision with construction. In practice, this was often accomplished by speculative builders who acquired extensive landholdings as a means of ensuring an adequate supply of serviced lots. This required much more capital and a larger scale of operation. It was encouraged by changes in federal housing policies and mortgage markets during the Depression.

In the years after World War II, the land developer—combining the functions of land subdivision and construction—has become the norm in larger cities. Operating on a large scale, developers are able to impose distinctive street layouts on their subdivisions. These typically involve limited access points from arterial boundary roads, with curvilinear streets and culs-de-sac on the interior. Such patterns have the stamp of approval of urban planners for they minimize servicing costs and reduce through traffic and attendant accidents. They also maximize salable front-footage while enhancing the distinctiveness, and hence the marketability, of each subdivision. Controlled by the developer, as well as by the local planning department, recently developed areas are usually homogenous in terms of land use (commercial, industrial, or residential) while residential areas usually contain only a limited range of housing types.

In recent years, some variations have been introduced into this general pattern. Flexible zoning arrangements have permitted the selective recombination of residential and certain commercial land uses as well as the creation of residential areas (planned unit developments) where high densities (by American standards) are counterbalanced by the creation of more open space. Probably the most significant trend has been the growth of private common-interest developments in which private property has deed restrictions enforced by homeowners' associations that also manage common areas. The latter have increased in numbers from about 500 in 1964 to approximately 150,000 in 1992. These are changing the appearance of newer suburban developments, and in principle they can create more diversity both within and between subdivisions.

These recent innovations do not entail any significant change in the process by which land is developed. Into the foreseeable future, this will be driven by the developer's perception of what new home buyers want. It will be constrained only incidentally by planners who articulate a wider public interest.

—*Richard Harris*

See also

Building Regulations; Levittown; Planned Community; Real Estate Developers and Development; Restrictive Deed Covenants; Rouse, James; Subdivision.

References

Clawson, Marion. *Suburban Land Conversion in the United States.* Baltimore: Johns Hopkins University Press, 1971.

Cullingworth, J. Barry. *The Political Culture of Planning: American Land Use Planning in Comparative Perspective.* New York: Routledge, 1993.

Doucet, Michael, and John Weaver. *Housing the North American City.* Montreal, Quebec, and Kingston, Ontario: McGill-Queen's University Press, 1991.

Keating, Ann Durkin. *Building Chicago: Suburban Developers and the Creation of a Divided Metropolis.* Columbus: Ohio State University Press, 1988.

McKenzie, Evan. *Privatopia: Homeowner Associations and the Rise of Residential Private Government.* New Haven, CT: Yale University Press, 1994.

Weiss, Marc. *The Rise of the Community Builders: The American Real Estate Industry and Urban Land Planning.* New York: Columbia University Press, 1987.

Land Pollution

As Americans pondered new solutions to air and water pollution during the 1970s and 1980s, they also began to seriously consider the impact of land pollution, also known as third-wave pollution. In a literal sense, *land pollution* encompassed the negative consequences caused by all forms of waste disposal on land, including urban landfills. By the 1970s, however, the term increasingly became identified with the disposal of hazardous substances.

The catalyst for the new awareness of land pollution was the rapid proliferation of synthetic chemicals and other toxic substances after World War II, such as asbestos, formaldehyde, benzene, radiation, and dioxin. Before the 1970s, regulating the use and disposal of these substances and their residues was generally the responsibility of state and local governments. Some of the most popular disposal sites were landfills, waterways, vacant land, and open pits. The flaws in this system included not only weak enforcement of existing rules but also a tendency to allow hazardous dumps to be located near large centers of population. One of the most common procedures was for potential dumpers to obtain a permit from the county health department. This usually required only that the dump not attract flies and other vermin that posed a danger to public health. This rule, of course, had little relevance for the new problem of chemical wastes.

The revelations in 1978 about conditions near Love Canal dramatically changed public attitudes and government policies. The Hooker Chemical Company had routinely used the canal, located in Niagara Falls, New York, as a disposal site from 1942 to 1952. Its dumping site was filled with synthetic resins, caustic substances, chlorinated hydrocarbons, and other hazardous chemicals. In 1953, the company had conveyed the property to the local school board, and the deed included a disclaimer from the Hooker Chemical Company warning about the hazardous wastes buried at the location. Despite this information, the school board authorized construction of an elementary school on the site. Eventually, the storage drums ruptured, and waste seeped into the basements of nearby homes. The residents filed suit and obtained a settlement of $20 million from Hooker in 1984. This episode inspired similar litigation in Times Beach, Missouri; Woburn, Massachusetts; and many other municipalities.

Congress soon reacted by passing the Comprehensive Environmental Response, Compensation and Liability Act of 1980 (CERCLA). Its provisions included establishing a trust fund of $1.2 billion, later dubbed Superfund, to clean up hazardous waste sites. Money for the fund was raised by combining special taxes on chemicals and general appropriations. Amendments passed in 1984 completely banned the land disposal of specified chemicals. Although the federal government spent billions of dollars under Superfund, by 1992 only 84 dumps had been cleaned. Thousands of other sites remained on the waiting list, and some estimates projected future costs at more than $200 billion.

—*David T. Beito*

References

Anderson, Richard F. "Solid Waste and Public Health." In Michael R. Greenberg, ed., *Public Health and the Environment: The United States Experience,* 173–204. New York: Guilford Press, 1987.

Hays, Samuel P. *Beauty, Health and Permanence: Environmental Politics in the United States, 1955–1985.* New York: Cambridge University Press, 1987.

Huber, Peter. "Environmental Hazards and Liability Law." In Robert E. Litan and Clifford Winston, eds., *Liability: Perspectives and Policy,* 128–154. Washington, DC: Brookings Institution, 1988.

Levine, Adeline Gordon. *Love Canal: Science, Politics, and People.* Lexington, MA: Lexington Books, 1982.

Melosi, Martin V. *Garbage in the Cities: Refuse, Reform, and the Environment, 1880–1980.* College Station: Texas A & M University Press, 1981.

Landlord Organizations

In the nineteenth and early twentieth centuries, landlords in large cities began to form permanent, protective associations in response to the growing activism of tenants. Accustomed to noninterference by state authorities and not used to associational activities, landlords often found collective action difficult to sustain except in times of extreme crisis. However, as conflict between landlords and tenants increased in the 1910s and 1920s in New York, Chicago, and other large cities, landlord organizations successfully mobilized formidable opposition, and their confrontational tactics often proved effective in breaking rent strikes.

Many early leaders of landlord associations, such as Stewart Browne and Isador Berger in New York, tried to promote professional and ethical standards and to articulate a long-term vision of urban development distinct from the views of homeowners, builders, and realtors. Most of their organizations, however, failed to resolve the tension between the espoused professionalism of some leaders and the entrenched hostility of most landlords toward housing laws, tenant empowerment, and state intervention of any kind.

Between 1880 and 1905, real estate organizations first emerged in large urban centers such as New York, Chicago, and Los Angeles. Local real estate interests banded together primarily to guide regional development but also to standardize certain business practices and influence housing legislation. Landlords and property managers often joined local real estate associations, but realtors, builders, and brokers normally controlled their policies and programs.

These early real estate organizations rarely catered to the specific needs of urban landlords. While tenement landlords routinely pressed for stronger leases and tenant liability for damages, real estate leaders were usually interested only in promoting growth in new urban areas. For example, the Washington Heights Taxpayers Association, formed in 1891 in New York, pursued local public works projects and supported other stimulants to regional development. According to a study conducted in 1901, most of New York's tenement districts lacked real estate organizations altogether, whereas these associations proliferated in midtown and on the urban periphery.

At times, mainstream or elite real estate interests pushed landlords out of organizations they had previously controlled. In 1883, the Chicago Real Estate and Renting Agents Association was formed to standardize landlord practices and impose more controls on Chicago tenants. The association's early efforts clearly reflected landlord issues and concerns. However, realtors and brokers quickly took over the organization. Under its new name, the Chicago Real Estate Board, the association established a real estate exchange in 1887, and its agenda quickly shifted away from the concerns of landlords.

In many large cities at the beginning of the twentieth century, greater tenant activism pushed landlords to take collective action by establishing more permanent lobbies and protective associations. As working-class immigrants began to demand better housing, lower rents, and more political influence, conflict between landlords and tenants proliferated. Rent strikes, evictions, resistance, assaults on landlords and their families, and public vilification in the press forced many landlords to develop new responses. On New York's Lower East Side, tenant agitation in 1904 and 1907–1908 led to the formation of the Greater New York Taxpayers Association (GNYTA). With its emphasis on serving its members and actively confronting rent strikers, GNYTA policies contrasted significantly with other real estate organizations. It offered its members liability insurance, legal aid, discounts on fuel and skilled labor, assistance negotiating mortgage payments with banks, and other services. By 1920, GNYTA had become the largest landlord association in the United States; it claimed more than 7,000 members and controlled more than 18,000 tenements in New York's older tenement districts. GNYTA and similar associations routinely focused on the immediate needs of urban landlords: keeping tenants pliant, stopping legislation that increased maintenance costs, and providing services that gave landlords greater financial security.

Landlord organizations differed from other real estate groups in several important respects. First, their visceral an-
tipathy toward state intervention in landlord-tenant affairs usually exceeded even the virulent rhetoric of most real estate lobbyists. Mainstream and elite organizations, such as the New York Real Estate Board and the Allied Council of Real Estate Interests, often compromised with elected officials, and in the process they crafted key roles for themselves in municipal policymaking. These leaders saw many ways that regulations would promote stability in the professional buying and selling of real estate. In contrast, landlord organizers usually resisted compromise because of their rigid antigovernment beliefs, and for the most part they remained on the political margins.

Unlike other real estate lobbies, landlord groups often adopted divisive, confrontational, and sometimes even violent tactics to intimidate tenants either in the courts or on the streets. During New York's citywide rent strikes after World War I, groups such as the Brownsville Landlords League hired thugs to break up demonstrations and forcibly evict leaders of the strikes from their apartments. During the summer of 1919, these assaults became so common that tenant leaders referred to the landlords' "reign of terror" in the city's tenement districts. During the national housing crisis of 1919–1920, similar episodes of conflict between tenants and landlord organizations occurred in large cities across the country.

For a number of reasons, these early landlord organizations often dissolved. As rent strikes subsided, many of the most confrontational associations drifted apart, and member landlords returned to traditional political isolation and individual problem solving. Other organizations specialized in certain aspects of tenement management. For example, GNYTA became an insurance company, specializing in landlord liability insurance. Most important, many of these organizations foundered on their inability to create a role for themselves in urban policymaking.

Not until the creation of rent control in 1943 and the resurgence of tenant organizations in the post–World War II era did a new generation of landlord associations develop, including the Metropolitan Fair Rent Committee. However, their efforts, largely defensive in nature, only moderated the housing programs that transformed New York (and many other cities) in the postwar period. Only with the establishment of the Rent Stabilization System in 1968 and the establishment of the Rent Stabilization Association did landlord lobbyists create an important place for themselves and their constituents at the policymaking table.

—Jared N. Day

References
Day, Jared N. "Urban Castles: Tenement Housing and Landlord Activism in New York City, 1901–1943." Ph.D. dissertation, Carnegie Mellon University, 1994.

Hughes, Everrett C. *The Growth of an Institution: The Chicago Real Estate Board.* Chicago: University of Chicago Society for Social Research Series II, Research Monograph No. 1, 1931.

Lawson, Ronald. "The Political Face of New York's Real Estate Industry." *New York Affairs* 6 (1980): 88–109.

Landscape Architecture and Urban Design

During the nineteenth century, before the term *landscape architecture* gained currency, landscape gardening described the practice of design in urban and suburban areas by horticulturists, engineers, surveyors, and architects. Many of them received their formal training abroad, and many worked through committees for nonprofit corporations. Most of the design took place on private estates or for quasi-public institutions until the idea of creating public parks slowly gained acceptance in the 1860s. During the last century, professionalized landscape architecture has expanded in multidisciplinary, collaborative ways to encompass urban, and even regional, planning and design, as public and private projects have become larger and more complex.

American landscape architecture began with urban plans. John Brockett arranged New Haven (1638) around a public green, and Francis Nicholson created a garden setting for Virginia's capital at Williamsburg (1682). Both William Penn's Philadelphia (1683) and James Oglethorpe's Savannah (1729) interspersed park squares among city blocks. Nevertheless, most colonial design took place informally on private plantations and estates where gentlemen with little training or advice beyond reading English theory laid out their properties. Thus, William Byrd II designed his plantation "Westover" on the James River in the 1730s, and Lawrence Washington erected Mount Vernon's first buildings in 1743. The governor of Massachusetts, Christopher Gore, took advice from a French architect about his "mansion" when he began building a country seat in 1804, but he landscaped his grounds according to Humphry Repton's gardening idiom. Of them all, the most adept was Thomas Jefferson. Better read and more widely traveled than most others, he brought his combined architectural and landscape skills not only to his home at Monticello (1771–1809) but also to the University of Virginia at Charlottesville (1817–1826) and the new state capitol building in Richmond (1780). Although Jefferson and his generation rejected linear French formalism, which to them represented authoritarianism, he helped adopt Major Pierre L'Enfant's plan for the new federal city of Washington (1791).

Despite these clear precedents, the formal beginnings of urban landscape architecture can perhaps be traced back to the "rural" cemetery movement. Launched with the establishment of Mount Auburn (1831) in Boston by the Massachusetts Horticultural Society, this cemetery provided laboratories for picturesque design and whetted the Americans' appetite for it. Initiated by a generation interested in horticulture, landscape gardening, and improving civic institutions, these cemeteries simultaneously became experimental gardens, arboretums, historic repositories, "museums without walls," even schools for landscape and architectural taste, not simply places for burying the dead. General Henry A. S. Dearborn, the president of the horticultural society and a man adept at engineering, laid out Mount Auburn, aided by a committee of colleagues and a surveyor. Dr. Jacob Bigelow, the physician-horticulturist who coined the word *technology,* guided Mount Auburn's design for a half-century, and it became a model followed in city after city. Dearborn also designed the Forest Hills Cemetery (1847) in Roxbury near his Brimley Place gardens with surveying help from the Scottish landscape gardener Daniel Brims.

A major new period of design had begun, honing the expertise of horticulturists, surveyors, architects, engineers, and landscape gardeners through their collaborations with each other. James Barnes, an engineer, laid out the Worcester Rural Cemetery (1838). Horticulturist John Jay Smith called on Scottish architect John Notman to design Philadelphia's Laurel Hill (1836), albeit in a more geometric "gardenesque" fashion, but Notman later applied the "picturesque" (slightly wild) at Richmond's Holly-Wood (1848). Major David B. Douglass, an engineer, designed Greenwood in Brooklyn (1838) with six lakes, 22 miles of roads, and 30 miles of paths before he was hired to plan the Albany Rural Cemetery (1841–1844). Other important rural cemeteries were laid out in Baltimore, Cincinnati, Washington, New York, and New Orleans.

The list of examples grew longer as rural cemeteries proliferated, even in smaller towns; and most of these nonprofit corporations, only a few municipal, expanded their grounds over the next decades. They provided prototypes for the first national cemeteries after the Civil War. The town of Gettysburg, Pennsylvania, had a small rural cemetery adjacent to which President Lincoln dedicated the Soldier's National Cemetery (1863), the occasion on which he delivered his Gettysburg Address. The original section of Arlington National Cemetery (1864), across the Potomac River from Washington, D.C., was laid out in rural fashion on the hilltop estate seized from Confederate General Robert E. Lee.

Andrew Jackson Downing, the most influential antebellum landscape designer, particularly praised the "rage" for "rural" cemeteries as "pleasure grounds" for cities. Throughout the 1840s, he preached the gospel of "rural art and rural taste" through four widely read books and his journal *The Horticulturist.* He created tableaux of "picturesque" and "beautiful" (groomed) nature around domestic and institutional structures, and he urged the creation of public institutions and landscapes to "civilize" the republic. Advertising his "professional" services, Downing earned a national reputation and invited collaboration with architects such as Calvert Vaux, whom he recruited from England in 1850.

Largely due to Downing's crusade for a "country park" with free access for city dwellers, New York's legislature funded the first Park Act in 1851 to create a Central Park in New York City. Vaux persuaded the park commissioners that their initial plan was defective, and they sponsored a design competition in 1858. Vaux knew that as an outsider he would have only a slim chance of winning, but Frederick Law Olmsted, a well-connected literary man, had been hired to superintend the project. Collaborating on a design entry with Olmsted gave Vaux a foot in the door; they joined forces on their "Greensward" plan and won.

Olmsted and Vaux accepted the title of landscape architects for the project in 1863, although Olmsted—not happy about the term for himself—often threatened to resign and did so periodically. In 1863, he went off to work for the Mariposa Mining Company in California. By chance, he arrived just as President Lincoln presented Yosemite Valley and the Mariposa Grove of Big Trees to California to become the first state park and first public scenic area reserved in perpetuity. Olmsted managed the ceded lands for a time. Then, a few years later, in 1865, being the only person with any semblance of design authority in the West, Olmsted provided plans for "a village and grounds for the College of California," now the University of California, Berkeley, across the Bay from San Francisco.

The parks movement gathered momentum and swept across city after city, producing the first large public projects and providing work for professionalizing designers. Philadelphia laid out Fairmount and Huntington Parks (1858). Boston held a competition for its Public Garden (1859–1860) and chose the plan drawn by architect George F. Meacham and modified by the city engineer James Slade. To design Druid Hills Park (1860–1863), Baltimore recruited Howard Daniels, the only finalist in the Central Park competition without ties to the park commissioners. When Vaux won the commission for Brooklyn's Prospect Park (1865), he summoned Olmsted east to help him. Until then, Olmsted had vacillated, unable to decide whether to follow the new career Vaux had mapped out for him, but the firm of Olmsted, Vaux and Company endured until 1872. Later, Vaux alone served as landscape architect to the city of New York, from 1881 to 1883 and from 1888 untile his death in 1895.

By the middle of the 1850s, landscape architecture was developing as a distinct field. A disciple of Downing and Ralph Waldo Emerson, Horace William Shaler Cleveland advertised "landscape and ornamental gardening" in 1854 with architect Robert Morris Copeland in New England; he sought to plan not only cemeteries but also "public squares, pleasure gardens, farms," as well as "every species of building and gen-

eral rural improvement." Taking advantage of their Transcendentalist connections, they designed Sleepy Hollow Cemetery (1855) in Concord, Massachusetts; Cleveland then left for Chicago where he worked with architect William Le Baron Jenney on Graceland Cemetery (1860). Although Cleveland and Copeland had not received the Central Park commission, Cleveland returned to Brooklyn in 1867 to work on Prospect Park with Vaux and Olmsted.

Going back to Chicago again in 1869, Cleveland opened an office and published a pamphlet on how to improve Chicago's flatlands for parks. Aided by two engineers, he won projects throughout the Midwest, on the prairies, and as far afield as Georgia and Nova Scotia. Moving to Minneapolis in 1886, he completed the Twin Cities metropolitan park system (1872–1895), with his son Ralph as his partner. Cleveland's book *Landscape Architecture as Applied to the Wants of the West* (1873) became a classic, writes Norman Newton, "brimming with concern over the probable visual fate" of the area between the Mississippi River and the Pacific Ocean, a clarion call for urban planning and design.

Many early landscape designers like Vaux, immigrants who had the kind of extensive training that was unavailable in America, found a great demand for commissions other than cemeteries. Their significance has been largely overlooked as the profession later wrote its own history and overemphasized the role played by Frederick Law Olmsted. Many of these early landscape designers had education and experience in landscape gardening, horticulture, architecture, and engineering that surpassed anything Americans could find at home. Perhaps the most highly skilled was Adolph Strauch, a Prussian protégé of Prince Herman von Pückler-Muskau, the "great European parks reformer," who arrived in Cincinnati in 1852. While designing a unified picturesque landscape among the estates in suburban Clifton, Strauch became superintendent and landscape gardener of the Spring Grove Cemetery (1855). His innovative "landscape lawn plan" prescribed maintenance and zoning to create the "beautiful" there and at many other cemeteries nationally. The model he used to reform or design cemeteries became so influential that it was dubbed the "American system." In 1877, Strauch redesigned the grounds of Oak Ridge Cemetery after Abraham Lincoln's burial there, and he planned cemeteries in Buffalo, Detroit, and Cleveland, among other places. His projects also included an asylum for the insane in Cincinnati, Amherst College in Massachusetts, and commissions in Nashville, New York, Washington, Philadelphia, and Chicago. Strauch brought the public parks movement to Cincinnati with designs for Eden Park (1870) and Burnet Woods (1872) despite opposition to "municipal ruralizing."

Maximillian G. Kern's career paralleled that of Strauch. Born and trained in Tübingen, Germany, especially in botany,

Kern worked at the royal gardens in Stuttgart and on the Tuileries in Paris before he, too, moved to Cincinnati and published his acclaimed *Practical Landscape Gardening*. In St. Louis in the 1870s, Kern planned several parks and designed the residential developments of Portland Place and Westmoreland Place before he received a commission for the large Forest Park (1876). Kern later oversaw the park system in Toledo, Ohio (1892–1895).

Strauch and Kern were only two of the prominent landscapers who came to the United States from abroad. Jacob Weidenmann immigrated from Switzerland, for example, and William Salway came from England. But there were also native-born Americans interested in, and concerned about, the appearance of American cities and the presence (or lack) of open space in them. As superintendent of Brooklyn's Greenwood Cemetery, Almerin Hotchkiss expanded it from 178 to 478 acres in the 1840s when he worked with horticulturist Zebedee Cook, one of the founders of Mount Auburn, and the architects Richard Upjohn and Son. Henry and Joseph Earnshaw of Cincinnati advertised themselves nationally as "landscape engineers." Drawing on their experience at Spring Grove Cemetery where their surveyor-father Thomas had trained them, these brothers earned commissions for parks, zoos, and corporate buildings from the 1870s on. In their own era, the Earnshaws were in the vanguard of "engineering of the beautiful," transforming older landscapes from the picturesque to the "beautiful" with high standards of maintenance through new technologies—running water, sewers, and paving.

Even before the parks movement had developed fully, picturesque suburbs followed cemeteries to the front of popular favor. Perhaps the first was Glendale (1851), north of Cincinnati, laid out by a civil engineer, Robert C. Phillips. Other early designed suburbs include Evergreen Hamlet (1851) near Pittsburgh; Cincinnati's Clifton (1850), designed by Strauch; and Lake Forest (1857), north of Chicago and designed by Hotchkiss. Inspired by Downing, Eugene A. Baumann designed Llewellyn Park, New Jersey (1853), in collaboration with architect Alexander Jackson Davis, a colleague of Downing's. All of these suburbs used picturesque aesthetics with curvilinear streets, topographical irregularities, and other "rural" features.

After the Civil War, Olmsted recognized a growing demand for landscape design, and he threw himself into this work until he retired in 1895. His busy firm planned individual parks, or whole park systems, in Buffalo, Chicago, Montreal, Detroit, Louisville, and Rochester. It also designed new grounds for the U.S. Capitol building among about 600 projects completed by his firm throughout the United States.

Olmsted's firm served as a training ground for an entire generation of professionalizing landscape architects. Olmsted and Company settled in Brookline, Massachusetts, because

Aerial view of Central Park in New York City, ca. 1960.

of its extensive work in the Boston area—the Fens (1883), Franklin Park (1884), and the Arnold Arboretum (1885), which it designed in conjunction with the academic horticulturist Charles Sprague Sargent. These parks were all part of the Emerald Necklace system (1878–1895), which the firm expanded on with the Charlesbank parks along the river (1892).

Olmsted primed his son Frederick, Jr., and his nephew John Charles, whom he adopted as a son, to carry on this work as Olmsted Brothers (1898). John had developed practical experience working on the 40th Parallel survey in Nevada and Utah in 1869 and 1871, graduated from Yale's Sheffield Scientific School (1875), apprenticed in his adopted father's firm, and became a dual partner in 1884. Frederick, Jr., trained primarily as an apprentice to his father and stepbrother.

Olmsted also took Charles Eliot as an apprentice in 1875, thus launching another important career. For a time, Eliot's own office had projects including a park in Concord, New Hampshire, a plan for a new town in Salt Lake City, and Mill Creek Park in Youngstown Gorge, Ohio. The reconfigured firm of Olmsted, Olmsted, and Eliot redesigned the Grand Army Plaza (1893), an architectonic entry to Prospect Park in Brooklyn. Eliot's influential voice championed nature reserves and an awareness of "nature systems" in design. His work in 1891 promoting open space along the estuaries and rivers of Massachusetts led to formation of Boston's Metropolitan Park Commission (1893), the first in the nation. Eliot helped win preservation of Revere Beach (1895–1896), just north of Boston, as the nation's first public seashore with easy access for residents of the city.

Zoological gardens also developed after the Civil War and combined the functions and characteristics of all the new landscape designs. Displays of animal collections appeared at New York's Central Park (1864), Chicago's Lincoln Park (1868), and Boston's Franklin Park (1884)—vanguards of such exhibits in park settings. Following German models of displaying animals in a parklike landscape, Cincinnatians launched their zoo, designed by a local engineer, an architect, and Strauch, as a "permanent ornament" to the city in 1873. Philadelphia quickly followed suit.

The era of great fairs also extended urban park systems. Philadelphia's Fairmount Park expanded with the grand Centennial Exposition of 1876. The rage for large exhibitions led to other world's fairs that left parks behind after the temporary structures had been demolished. The greatest of these fairs was Chicago's World's Columbian Exposition (1888–1893), the work of architects Daniel H. Burnham and John Wellborn Root, engineer Abram Gottlieb, landscape architects Frederick Law Olmsted and Henry Sargent Codman, and others who drew inspiration from the Universal Exposition at Paris in 1889. Epitomizing the new influence of Paris's Ecole des Beaux-Arts, the "White City" left a legacy of urbanism—the City Beautiful movement—that transformed cities with a wave of Neoclassical grandeur for the next two decades, moving away from the picturesque tradition toward architectonic formalism, yet blending naturalistic and classical forms with a focus on civic centers rather than the periphery.

The ideals of the City Beautiful movement spread as Progressives demanded governmental acquisition of, and accountability for, "public" space as well as new agencies of normative "moral control" in the chaotic urban environment. They wanted design by "experts." Burnham's 1909 plans for Chicago and San Francisco demanded monumentality. John Olmsted brought the City Beautiful to Seattle, and it touched Denver, Seattle, Dallas, Kansas City, and Harrisburg, Pennsylvania. Although he was untrained in design, Charles M. Robinson spread the City Beautiful vogue in all its dimensions through his influential writings, including *The Improvement of Towns and Cities; or, the Practical Basis of Civic Aesthetics* (1901) and *Modern Civic Art, or the City Made Beautiful* (1903). He particularly demanded art in public places, centralized commerce, sanitation of every sort, and social environmentalism, optimistic new prescriptions for urban planning and design. The University of Illinois offered him its first chair of civic design in 1913, just as the City Beautiful movement waned after encountering opposition that ranged from real estate interests to voters unwilling to approve bond issues.

In that spirit, the McMillan Commission's plan for Washington, D.C. (1902), called for rehabilitating L'Enfant's Neoclassical design. Led by Senator James McMillan, its membership included architects Burnham and Charles F. Mecum, landscape architect Frederick Law Olmsted, Jr., and sculptor Augustus Saint-Gaudens. Supervised by the Commission of Fine Arts (1910), landscape architect George E. Burlap designed the Tidal Basin's parks (1912), long famed for their cherry trees. Later developments extended new axes to the Lincoln (1914–1922) and Jefferson (1938–1943) Memorials. The commission later controlled design and development to make the national capital both beautiful and monumental.

Long before the City Beautiful movement, efforts to improve the appearance of towns and cities had roots in the volunteerism of the Village Improvement tradition, led by female city dwellers who summered in New England from the 1850s on and who wanted to renovate old towns. Many towns in the Midwest and South replicated such local societies by the 1890s. The movement spread to cities like Springfield, Massachusetts, and resulted in the formation of the National League of Improvement Associations (1900; renamed the American League for Civic Improvement in 1902) and the American Civic Association (1904). Headed until 1924 by the businessman and activist J. Hoarse McFarland, the American Civic Association's national Crusade against Ugliness mustered support from Progressives like Jane Addams. The short-lived American Park and Outdoor Art Association (1897–1904) also aimed to be a general organization for anyone concerned with landscape design, while the National Municipal League (1894) united diverse urbanists. The American Society for Municipal Improvements (1894) addressed civil engineers, and practitioners and citizen activists alike shared ideas through publications like *Garden and Forest,* a weekly that Sargent, Olmsted, Sr., and others founded in 1888.

Not to be ignored or overlooked is the impact of women on urban and suburban beautification after the 1890s through the garden club movement. Local and regional groups united in 1913 in the Garden Club of America and in 1929 in the National Council of State Garden Clubs. As "municipal housekeepers," members planted street trees, lobbied for parks, maintained public spaces, fought billboards' commercial clutter, and joined the playground movement to improve tenement neighborhoods as well as their own yards—creating new standards for design and maintenance.

Peripheral to public work, a generation of privileged estate designers shaped early professionalization into the 1930s. Charles A. Platt planned neo-Renaissance gardens, sometimes drawing on ties from the artists' colony at Cornish, New Hampshire, and sometimes working with the Olmsted Brothers. James L. Greenleaf, Percival Gallagher, Bryant Fleming, Fletcher Steele, and Edward C. Whiting all forged their careers by designing the estates of wealthy exurbanites, many of them later succumbing to subdivision. The work of these landscape architects epitomized the supposed gentility of the mannered elite trying to escape urban turmoil, but it also defined the early direction of the profession of landscape architecture as elitist.

Early definitions of professionalism proved contentious, often pitting the eastern establishment against midwestern practitioners. The American Association of Cemetery Superintendents (AACS), founded at Spring Grove in 1887, staked an early claim for designers involved in long-term "scientific" maintenance in the Strauch tradition. *Modern Cemetery* (the AACS journal) was renamed *Park and Cemetery and Landscape Gardening* by its editor, F. J. Haight, in 1895 to reflect the scope of its members' work. The founding of the American Society of Landscape Architecture (ASLA) in 1895 marked another important step. Olmsted's sons joined a host of others in launching the ASLA as its first "Fellows." Only Simonds bridged the gap between members of the AACS and the ASLA, later becoming the ASLA's first president not from the East.

None of the ASLA's founders had followed a formal course of study because none existed in the United States. Some horticultural societies had put developing such a pro-gram on their agenda much earlier. In Boston, Dearborn had wanted to make Mount Auburn an "Institution for the Education of Scientific and Practical Gardeners." Cincinnati's horticulturists had the same unfulfilled aim for the naturalistic complex created by Spring Grove, Clifton, the Zoo, and nearby suburbs by the 1870s. From the 1880s on, some aspiring landscape architects like Charles Eliot found preliminary training at Harvard's Bussey Scientific Institute; others relied on related course work and then apprenticeships with the likes of Olmsted.

But it was Olmsted, Jr., and Arthur A. Shurcliff who put together the first four-year landscape architecture program at Harvard's Lawrence Scientific School in 1899. Following Harvard in 1900, the Massachusetts Institute of Technology allowed architectural students to declare a concentration in landscape. Liberty Hyde Bailey, Bryant Fleming, and their student Albert Davis Taylor developed a degree at Cornell University in the College of Agriculture, and many other programs developed in the next few years.

John Olmsted codified standards and principles of practice for the ASLA. Dominated by Olmsted affiliates with Harvard connections, the early ASLA screened its membership and rejected some important designers like George Edward Kessler for membership. Kessler had immigrated from Germany as a child but returned to Weimar to study landscape gardening. After he returned to New York, he consulted with Cleveland and Weidenmann, and inquiries made through Olmsted sent him off to study real estate developments across the country. His designs for Merriam Park and Hyde Park in 1887 enticed residents to Kansas City. Work for developers Jarvis and Conklin along with Olmsted Brothers produced Roland Park, a suburb of Baltimore, Euclid Heights in Cleveland, and a subdivision of Ogden, Utah. Oklahoma City called on Kessler to design its cemetery, and his plan for Kansas City embodied the City Beautiful through a system of parks, boulevards, and suburbs.

With national renown for his ideal of "the city in a park," Kessler began a decade of work in Memphis on Riverside Park, and his St. Louis office tackled long-term projects in New York, Nebraska, and South Dakota. The park and boulevard systems he designed for Indianapolis, Syracuse, Fort Worth, Pensacola, Denver, and Dallas blended the "City Practical" with the "City Beautiful." From 1911 to 1913, Kessler provided master plans for Fort Wayne, South Bend, and Terre Haute, Indiana, and St. Joseph, Missouri. His plan for uniting 18 parks, 17 public squares, and 35 parkways and connectors in Cincinnati enraged "purists" and special interests; work stalled in the 1920s as opponents of "master plans" under public auspices mustered their forces.

During World War I, the U.S. Housing Corporation and the War Department hired Kessler's firm to design emergency towns and housing in Oklahoma, Texas, Arkansas, New Mexico, and Washington, D.C. After he was admitted to the ASLA in 1919, Kessler's practice boomed with projects for city plans in Wichita Falls, El Paso, Salt Lake City, and elsewhere. Working with a Kansas City firm, Kessler received commissions for the new town of Longview, Washington, the Butler University campus in Indianapolis, and a residential subdivision of Mexico City. His motto was "Get It Done," and he died from overwork in 1923.

In this favorable climate, the firm of Olmsted Brothers blossomed with over 3,500 commissions, including asylums, hospitals, and state capitols. They planned new park systems in Dayton; Seattle; Spokane; Portland, Maine; and Portland, Oregon. The firm expanded the park work of Olmsted, Sr., in Boston, Hartford, Brooklyn, Rochester, Buffalo, Louisville, and Atlanta, and it designed new parks in Charleston and New Orleans. The firm expanded college campuses—Smith, Mount Holyoke, Amherst, Chicago, Iowa State, Ohio State, and Washington—and took on exposition grounds in Portland, Seattle, and Winnipeg. After John died in 1920, Frederick, Jr., carried on until 1950.

The profession of landscape architecture expanded rapidly during the first half of the twentieth century, and the career of Henry V. Hubbard exemplifies its development as clearly as any. He received the first degree ever given in landscape architecture at Harvard in 1901, after he had studied architecture at MIT and before he had an apprenticeship with Olmsted Brothers. His firm of Pray, Hubbard and White designed wartime housing before he returned to Olmsted Brothers as a partner in 1920. He served the National Park Service, Federal Housing Administration, Tennessee Valley Authority, National Capital Park and Planning Commission, and the cities of Boston, Providence, and Baltimore. A professor of landscape architecture at Harvard from 1906 to 1941, Hubbard was first chairman of the School of City Planning, then of the department of regional planning. With Charles D. Lay and Robert Wheelwright, Hubbard founded the ASLA journal *Landscape Architecture* in 1910 and served as its editor until his death. He collaborated with Theodora Kimball, the librarian of landscape architecture and city planning at Harvard (and later his wife), in writing *An Introduction to the Study of Landscape Design,* the standard book on the subject for decades. Hubbard and Kimball also founded and edited the journal *City Planning* and coauthored *Our Cities To-day and To-morrow: A Survey of Planning and Zoning Progress in the United States.*

Hubbard also worked with John Nolen. With "civic improvement" as his mission, Nolen, too, earned a degree in landscape architecture at Harvard. The first person to identify himself as a city and regional planner, Nolen developed the first planning degrees at Harvard and MIT. The work of his Cambridge, Massachusetts, firm spanned the years from the Progressive Era through the New Deal (1904 to 1937) and prepared plans for more than 50 new towns and suburbs, over 50 metropolitan areas, and about 18 regions and states, including Madison, Wisconsin; San Diego, California; and Kingsport, Tennessee, just to name a few.

Many of Hubbard's contemporaries expanded landscape practice, as did Nolen's associates. Phillip Foster, Justin Hartzog, and Hale Walker developed the planning fields. Elbert Peets used his Harvard degree in landscape architecture as the basis for a career in town planning and urban design. But other developments were also broadening the interests and involvement of landscape architects. Arthur A. Shurcliff played a major role in restoring Colonial Williamsburg, even though his interpretation of the historic landscape was more nostalgic than accurate. Later, he planned Old Sturbridge Village, Massachusetts, an outdoor museum complex replicating town life in 1800. There, one of his goals was avoiding the "hodge-podge" that Henry Ford had produced at Greenfield Village in Dearborn, Michigan, where the auto magnate had had no professional advice. These historic park landscapes or outdoor museums fostered tourism, popularized the past, and proliferated widely. By 1949, in Massachusetts, private enterprise was restoring a Deerfield Village and constructing Plymouth Plantation to resemble the town of 1627; work also began on Mystic Seaport in Connecticut and the Shelburne Museum in Vermont. A landscape architect supervised the Colonial National Historical Park in Yorktown, Virginia.

Suburban country clubs with facilities for active recreation—golf, tennis, swimming, boating, and horseback riding—provided another new focus for urban landscape architecture. By 1902, the nation had over 1,000 of these designed landscapes; by 1948, there were over 6,000. After 1910, concerted efforts by the U.S. Golf Association and the Department of Agriculture, urged on by the renowned efficiency expert Frederick Winslow Taylor and the Garden Club of America, developed turf grasses that transformed public and private American landscapes. After World War II, many landscape architects developed projects that combined residential developments with these country club settings.

The automobile also created new opportunities for landscape architects in urban settings. Many cities built "parkways" with the goal of providing a beautiful setting for long drives. The Arroyo Seco Parkway connecting Los Angeles with Pasadena and the Benjamin Franklin Parkway in Philadelphia exemplify this phenomenon. One of the most accomplished parkway planners, Gilmore D. Clarke, designed the Westchester Park System as a counterpoint to Manhattan's grid system of metropolitan planning with its parallel and perpendicular streets. His innovative parkways were divided, limited-access roads for automobiles within a strip park. Unlike classical boulevards, they banned commercial vehicles and eliminated cross streets while uniting about a dozen separate park areas, including Clarke's Playland in Rye, a well-regulated alternative to the perceived chaos of Coney Island. His Bronx River, Hutchinson River, Sawmill River, and Cross County parkways preserved natural settings around the burgeoning metropolis.

In 1937, Michael Rapuano, another experienced park and parkway designer, joined Clarke. Together, they designed the Palisades Interstate Parkway in New York and parts of the Garden State Parkway system in New Jersey. They also designed landscapes for the 1939 and 1964 World's Fairs in Flushing Meadows, New York, near New York City. They used a modernist idiom for designing the United Nations headquarters in New York City but redesigned Montreal parks to preserve their historic significance.

Landscape design for workers' housing provided even more work and another setting for landscape architects. The experimental company town of Pullman, on the south side of Chicago, was briefly a model of industrial village planning. Designed by Nathan F. Barrett, it failed because of the authoritarian behavioral controls its founder imposed. Still, planning industrial towns continued the precedents set by towns designed by the Olmsteds and other landscape designers. Housing developments during World War I provided other projects under federal auspices, and the migration of textile mills south during the 1920s brought additional work at mill villages like Chicopee, Georgia.

During the late 1920s and into the 1930s, Clarence Stein and a group of other architects, planners, and landscape architects in the Regional Planning Association of America (RPAA) advocated building housing for low- and moderate-income people in "new towns." After experimenting at Sunnyside in Queens (a borough of New York City) with private funds, Stein and his colleagues planned Radburn, New Jersey, in 1927. Radburn was a new sort of suburb that segregated cars from human activities with "closes," collective gardens, and other shared open spaces. Radburn became a model for New Deal "greenbelt towns"—experiments near Washington, Milwaukee, and Cincinnati—as well as the workers' town of Norris for the Tennessee Valley Authority (TVA). Similarly, private enterprise built Baldwin Hills Village in Los Angeles, where Reginald D. Johnson worked with the firm of Wilson, Merrell & Alexander to cluster housing around a village common.

Through the Resettlement Administration (later the Works Progress Administration), the New Deal took on landscape projects ranging from large-scale regional planning to recreational parks and local playgrounds although some prominent practitioners believed that the latter should be created by educational boards. Between 1933 and 1943, the TVA hired many landscape architects for its massive plans involving hydroelectric power, flood control, navigation, reforestation, public recreation, agriculture, and industry in an area extending 650 miles along the Tennessee River and serving 4.5 million people. The Civilian Conservation Corps also employed many landscape architects. However, World War II did not provide as many design possibilities as World War I.

Despite all of these precedents, developers overlooked or deliberately bypassed landscape architects and urban designers when they built most suburbs after World War II. William Levitt's formula for mass-producing suburbs on former farmland required such haste that he ignored Stein's ideals when he built his Levittowns on Long Island (1947) and near Philadelphia in New Jersey and Pennsylvania. Change came with the 1962 utopian plan of developer Robert E. Simon, Jr., for Reston, Virginia, as well as with the new towns of Columbia, Maryland; Irvine, California; Maumelle, Arkansas; The Woodlands, Texas; and the "new towns-in-town" of Cedar-Riverside in Minneapolis and Roosevelt Island in New York.

But many major private development projects totally ignored landscape architects—Disneyland in Anaheim, California; Disney World in Orlando, Florida; and other similar formulaic, fantasy landscapes. So widespread had commercial vernacular become in the automobile landscape that Robert Venturi, Denise Scott Brown, and Steven Izenour developed a following through their book *Learning from Las Vegas* in 1972; it quickly became the bible of pragmatic designers who tried to win commissions by catering to popular tastes as "high" style trends changed from "modern" to "contemporary" to "postmodern."

Large design firms grew after World War II along with the large, multiuse, public and private projects that required multidisciplinary expertise. For instance, Dan Kiley provided a dramatic, modernist context for the architecture of Eero Saarinen at the Dulles Airport outside of Washington, D.C., in Virginia. Most notably, Hideo Sasaki, who had been a principal in several design firms, formed Sasaki Associates. Its staff of interdisciplinary planning and design professionals numbered into the hundreds in several offices that would provide planning, architecture, landscape architecture, civil engineering, and environmental services for projects anywhere in the world. Style became increasingly pragmatic, responsive to trends abroad, and no longer distinctively American. In their work on college campuses, or revitalizing waterfronts, or renovating downtowns, civic centers, "vest-pocket" parks, plazas, malls, resorts, golf courses, corporate complexes, and other large projects, the identities of primary landscape designers are often lost in these megafirms and are subsumed by the "team." Prominent firms like Eckbo,

Dean Austin and William; Kallman, McKinnel and Knowles; and M. Paul Friedburg and Partners illustrate the trend toward large, multidisciplinary design firms. Some of these firms have actually adopted minimalist names that obscure the identity of even the founding principals, e.g., RTKL in Baltimore; HOK; HMFH Architects, Inc.; MGB + A in Salt Lake City; The 606 Studio; EDAW in Alexandria; and the SWA Group.

Revitalizing rather than razing old central city buildings has provided great opportunities for creative urban design. Successful models were the adaptive reuse of Ghirardelli Square from a factory into a congeries of boutiques and restaurants in San Francisco, and the Paseo del Rio, a Riverwalk designed for San Antonio's Hemisfair Exposition. Boston's Quincy Marketplace provided a model for the "festival marketplace" concept that was later applied at New York's South Street Seaport and Baltimore's Harborplace. This idea of the open-air urban shopping center provided classic projects and was really an adaptation of Herbert Hare's Country Club Plaza shopping center in Kansas City, Lawrence Halprin's Nicollet Mall in Minneapolis, and M. Paul Friedburg's State Street Mall in Madison, Wisconsin. But in smaller cities like Providence, Rhode Island, and Battle Creek, Michigan, in the 1970s, simplistic attempts to convert main streets into pedestrian malls by forbidding automobiles became failed experiments at revitalization that only hastened the drain of commercial life to suburban malls.

Despite the existence of the so-called "urban renewal" of the 1950s and 1960s, a renewed urban sensibility emerged among the better landscape architects. Carol R. Johnson's Cambridge, Massachusetts, firm with its large staff of women brought "clarity" and "simplicity" to parks and housing projects around Boston and Washington, D.C. Her designs for the John F. Kennedy Park and Lechmere Canal Park in Boston in the 1980s and her John Marshall Park on Pennsylvania Avenue in Washington are exemplary, as is her dramatic resurrection of old public housing at Columbia Point in Boston. Johnson now terms her humane version of modernism "traditionalist" in light of the postmodern stylistic experiments of the 1980s.

Another important recent trend has been to bring landscape *inside* of buildings, into very large structures as Dan Kiley did in the atrium of the Ford Foundation Building in New York City. The collaboration of César Pelli and Diana Balmori is flawless—pocket parks encased in large glass spaces where plants can flourish year-round. Such also was Balmori's Winter Garden in the World Financial Center in Battery Park City and M. Paul Friedburg's Winter Garden at Niagara Falls, where a park and playground surround an extensive garden inside a "glass mountain."

Since the 1970s, centrifugal movement away from city centers has multiplied demands for suburban office "parks" to house major business headquarters, particularly for new high tech companies. Equidon Investment Builders told its architect that "good landscape is good business." Developers commissioned a dramatic design for a parcel of once "dreary" land, a triangular glass office building set in a circular lagoon in order to attract 25 other corporations to the Wateridge Corporate Business Park in San Diego. Recent developments in Reston, Virginia, illustrate this trend. Many recent "greenways" projects have reclaimed old railroad beds, utilities corridors, and landfills in and around cities for recreational purposes and have extended city park systems. Reclamation of wetlands and waterfronts has opened other opportunities for design. Hargreaves Associates provided plans for a green solution to flood control in San Jose, California, rather than adopting standard Army Corps of Engineers culverts; that firm also prepared a master plan for parks along the banks of the Ohio River in Louisville, Kentucky.

Some landscape architects have recently branched into the arts. Large reclamation projects under the auspices of public arts commissions have provided opportunities for sculptural earthworks like those of artists Robert Smithson, Robert Morris, Nancy Holt, Herbert Bayer, and Michael Heizer. Although these are often located in remote areas, some of them have become new parks. In a more urban context, landscape architect Marsha Schwartz produced both permanent and temporary postmodern installations on rooftops, in urban front yards, and on campuses. Under programs for art in public places, other sculptors have made careers working with landscape architects.

Notable examples of landscape as sculpture appeared with Lawrence Halprin's Lovejoy Fountain and Auditorium Forecourt in Portland, Oregon, a composition of falls and monoliths designed for water play, and Cincinnati's Serpentine by Zion and Breen, curvilinear steps along the Ohio River that double as a recreational park and flood control to revitalize the downtown waterfront. It inspired similar renewal of the Tennessee River waterfront in Chattanooga, an architectonic composition designed by at least four separate firms.

Urban design projects have become so complex during the last few decades that it is hard to consider—perhaps even to contemplate—all of them. In 1990, Peter Walker assessed the situation: "Much of the recent history of our profession is largely unknown . . . individuals may be tremendously influential in shaping a particular place yet remain unknown." Because so much of the work "is fundamentally collaborative, the vast majority of our projects result in ensemble compositions to which many have made contributions." Increasingly, "authorship" is "being credited to specific individuals within a firm," given principals' demands. Walker feels that historians rather than landscape architects should identify designers, but landscape architects have been notorious in not leaving full documentation of their working procedures. But this is not so different from the attribution to Olmsted, Sr., of work done by Vaux, Weidenmann, Eliot, or his sons, not to mention the talented others who passed through various incarnations of the Olmsteds' firms. In large part, the problem arises because many landscape architects leave a project after it has been accepted on paper and do not oversee its construction, let alone its ongoing maintenance. Especially on public projects, this threatens quality and longevity.

In this context, an increasing amount of attention is now being given to preserving historic landscapes, both designed and vernacular. Early efforts were focused on the work of Olmsted and Sons by the National Association for Olmsted Parks, and in 1972 the Olmsted-Vaux suburb of Riverside, Illinois, won recognition as a National Historical Landscape Architecture District. New York State allotted millions of dollars in grants under its 1986 Environmental Quality Bond Act to undo decades of neglect and vandalism in parks, and by the 1980s the Society for the Preservation of New England Antiquities and the National Trust for Historic Preservation had expanded their focus beyond buildings. Over the years, the Trustees of the Reservations in Massachusetts has been a model, preserving many designed and natural landscapes, especially near Boston. The Massachusetts Heritage Parks have continued these efforts, providing work for new urban plans and even new art in the context of the old. Senator Paul Tsongas of Massachusetts mustered collaboration between state parks and the National Park Service for the creative restoration of Lowell, Massachusetts, as the first National Urban Heritage Park (1984). The design, which acknowledges the Victorian city as well as the mill town of 1822, has revitalized the city through creative reuse and tourism, put housing for the elderly and offices into historic mills, and created vibrant streetscapes.

Plans to preserve Central Park and other landscapes attributed to Olmsted have led to the recognition of other historic landscapes. Susan Child and Associates restored and preserved the Stan Hywet estate in Akron, Ohio, in model fashion, and the Walker-Kluesing Design Group wrote a plan to rescue Boston Common from overuse. The Mount Auburn Cemetery master plan by Halvorson Company promises to be an exemplar for restoring historic integrity to areas developed over 150 years during different stylistic eras while permitting ongoing use. A new spirit has arisen with renewed respect for historic design.

—*Blanche M. G. Linden*

References
Birnbaum, Charles A., and Julie K. Fix, eds. *Pioneers of American Landscape Design II: An Annotated Bibliography.* Washington, DC: U.S. Department of the Interior, National Parks Service, Historic Landscape Initiative, 1995.
Birnbaum, Charles A., and Lisa E. Crowder, eds. *Pioneers of American Landscape Design: An Annotated Bibliography.* Washington, DC: U.S. Department of the Interior, National Parks Service, Historic Landscape Initiative, 1993.
Burg, David F. *Chicago's White City of 1893.* Lexington: University of Kentucky Press, 1976.
Costonis, John J. *Icons and Aliens: Law, Aesthetics, and Environmental Change.* Urbana: University of Illinois Press, 1989.
Creese, Walter L. *The Crowning of the American Landscape: Eight Great Spaces and Their Buildings.* Princeton, NJ: Princeton University Press, 1985.
Frankel, Felice, and Jory Johnson. *Modern Landscape Architecture: Redefining the Garden.* New York: Abbeville Press, 1990.
Fromm, Dorit. *Collaborative Communities: Cohousing, Central Living, and Other New Forms of Housing with Shared Facilities.* New York: Van Nostrand Reinhold, 1991.
Garner, John S. *The Model Company Town: Urban Design through Private Enterprise in Nineteenth-Century New England.* Amherst: University of Massachusetts Press, 1982.
Jenkins, Virginia Scott. *The Lawn: A History of an American Obsession.* Washington, DC: Smithsonian Institution Press, 1994.
Little, Charles E. *Greenways for America.* Baltimore: Johns Hopkins University Press, 1990.
Manning, Warren H. *Thomas Jefferson as an Architect and a Designer of Landscapes.* Boston: Houghton Mifflin, 1913.
Newton, Norman T. *Design on the Land: The Development of Landscape Architecture.* Cambridge, MA: Harvard University Press, 1971.
Nichols, Frederick Doveton, and Ralph E. Griswold. *Thomas Jefferson, Landscape Architect.* Charlottesville: University Press of Virginia, 1978.
Reps, John W. *Town Planning in Frontier America.* Princeton, NJ: Princeton University Press, 1969.
Tishler, William H., ed. *American Landscape Architecture: Designers and Places.* Washington, DC: Preservation Press, 1989.
Wilson, William H. *The City Beautiful Movement.* Baltimore: Johns Hopkins University Press, 1989.

Lawn

The word *lawn* has a dual etymology; one possibly from Laon, a town in France, and the other, from *launde,* a glade, both now obsolete. In modern usage, lawn means a surface planted with grass kept closely mowed. The spelling is not old, and the older version *launde* was used until the eighteenth century; the meaning of a mowed grassy ground is first recorded in 1733.

Late medieval French illustrations of castle gardens show patches of green ground used for such activities as dancing, embroidering, courting, and social gathering. This green carpet of grasses was mixed with other vegetation such as wild flowering plants that could withstand these heavy uses. Such green patches were known as flowery meades or, as they are called in tapestry, *mille fleurs* (a thousand flowers). The diversity of these medieval greenswards curiously accords with our current ecological recognition of the importance of a biologically diversified and self-sustaining landscape. The castle meade more nearly approximates the ideal landscape of modern ecological theory than does the American industrialized lawn, species-poor and sustained by fertilizers and chemicals to control pests.

The lawn made its next appearance as the *parterre* in formal gardens in France during the seventeenth century. These were usually raised beds of grass ornately patterned with low groundcovers or crushed colored stones inlaid between them. The grass was not to be trod upon but only viewed from paths laid out among them geometrically.

Although the lawn in its present industrialized form has become identified with a particularly American way of life, its origins are actually British and relatively recent, dating only from the eighteenth century. Indeed, it is not a garden element common to all cultures, not even to all European cultures. Its specifically British origin can be attributed to the British Isles' mild, moist climate, which is ideal for cultivating a lawn. With the invention of the lawn mower by Edward Budding in 1830, the industrial lawn announced its common, established presence in the English garden of the nineteenth century. The coincidental development of the suburb, precipitated by the appearance of new urban transportation systems, further extended the spread of this new garden feature.

The industrial revolution of eighteenth-century England, which transformed the economic, social, agricultural, and cultural life of the nation, prepared the way for creating landscapes organized around the lawn as we know it and arranged informally to create an idealized image of nature. This kind of garden accompanied the emergence of a new moneyed class who sought to vest their commercially acquired wealth in the status and prestige identified with the large estates and gardens of the landed gentry.

The new garden design also embodied a change in the way of perceiving nature. Domestic gardens and surrounding nature were seen as a continuum; the extension of lawns across the newly invented sunk fence, or ha-ha, helped create the perception that an estate's domain stretched to the farthest horizon. William Kent, an eighteenth-century gardener, was credited with having "leapt the fence" and seen "that all nature was a garden." This new aesthetic of an ideal nature that provides no evidence of any human labor in the landscape contrived to simulate a garden created by nature alone without human assistance. This aesthetic was translated intact to urban parks in the United States during the nineteenth century, many designed by Frederick Law Olmsted. With them came the lawn as we know it today.

In the United States the lawn made its first civic appearance during the nineteenth century on town greens and around courthouses as an early herald of the park movement. Until the 1830s, town "greens" had usually been open, muddy spaces for fairs and other town activities such as making rope, military maneuvers, crop production (the sale of which fed town coffers), blacksmithing, graveyards, or pasturing livestock. With the advent and progress of the park movement, these civic spaces were transformed into green oases planted with lawn and trees and removed from economic life.

The earliest American suburbs, Llewellyn Park, New Jersey, 12 miles west of New York City and designed by Andrew Jackson Davis in the early 1850s, and Riverside, Illinois, outside of Chicago and designed by Frederick Law Olmsted in 1860, established the lawn as the connecting fabric of an entire residential development. With the emergence of both the lawn mower and the suburb, the lawn was enshrined as a symbol of domestic American life.

Thus, a lawn may be understood as a specialized use of grass to form a continuous, uniform, green carpet that can tolerate being walked upon. The suitability of grass to lawn making derives from this plant's peculiar habit of growing from its crown. The crown, near the surface of the soil, produces a stem composed of leaf bases and blades. A lawn mower or grazing animal crops the blades but leaves the plant's crowns intact so that it can generate new blades. If mowing or grazing ceases, the stems flower and produce seed.

In this present form, the lawn represents the industrialization of the landscape comparable to single-crop food production in modern agriculture. Like industrialized agriculture, the lawn industry seeks a uniform product dependent upon a few species of grass, which, in the United States, usually include Kentucky bluegrass, red fescue, and seeded bent grass. The modern lawn has generated an enormous industry to support its production, from the cultivation and marketing of select seeds to the manufacture and sale of irrigation and cutting devices to the preparation of chemical aides for fertilizing grass and controlling pests. Except for its use in sports and parks, the lawn remains primarily a small-scale domestic commodity.

—*Diana Balmori*

Lawrence, David L. (1889–1966)

David L. Lawrence, the third child of unskilled Irish laboring parents, Charles B. and Mary Conwell, grew up in the rough-and-tumble Gaelic Irish neighborhood of Pittsburgh's Point district. The revitalization of this same neighborhood would later give Lawrence much of his renown as the architect of the Pittsburgh Renaissance.

Young Lawrence, schooled in the principles of Democratic, labor, and liberal politics by a local ward alderman and county Democratic chairman, William Brennen, became committed to a political career after he attended the Democratic National Convention in 1912. Although Woodrow Wilson defeated Lawrence's own candidate, Champ Clark, Lawrence returned to Pittsburgh thoroughly "devoted to politics."

In 1920, Lawrence succeeded his mentor, Brennen, as chairman of the Allegheny County Democratic organization. What Lawrence inherited was a loose group of individuals who considered politics an interesting hobby. They had not elected a Democrat to any major office in 60 years and willingly yielded to the powerful Republican opposition headed by William L. Mellon. Lawrence's efforts at molding an efficiently run organization were hardly successful. After 9 years of his leadership, only 5,200 residents of the county had registered as Democrats, while the Republicans had registered 169,000. The absence of a willing successor spared Lawrence from being replaced as the leader of his own party.

The Depression, a corrupt Republican organization, Franklin D. Roosevelt's coattails, and a massive reorganization of the Democratic Party in Pittsburgh by Lawrence accomplished a political revolution in Pittsburgh. The city elected its first Democratic mayor in 1933, and the following year the party swept the county and has never been successfully challenged since. In 1995, the party had four times as many voters registered Democratic as Republican in both the city and the county.

In 1945, Lawrence surprised many by transforming himself from a behind-the-scenes political boss into a nationally known and admired urban statesman when he ran for mayor of Pittsburgh. Following his narrow victory in the election of 1945, Lawrence recruited a talented team of urban policy experts and city planners to team with Richard King Mellon, a nephew of Andrew W. Mellon, and the city's corporate elite to rebuild the city's deteriorating, flood-prone, smoke-filled central business district. During the next 13 years, this public-private partnership effected a revitalization that is still admired and imitated by urban leaders across the nation. Although Lawrence left Pittsburgh to become governor of Pennsylvania in 1959, his dominance over Democratic politics in both the city and the county enabled him to continue presiding over the city's redevelopment until his death in 1966.

Lawrence's single term as governor of Pennsylvania from 1959 to 1962 produced a massive highway construction program, a campaign for strict highway safety, and significant social legislation mandating fair housing, creating a statewide human relations commission, expanding minimum wage and workers' compensation laws, and new child labor laws, including protection for the children of migratory workers.

Lawrence served as the nation's first and only chairman of the President's Council on Equal Opportunity in Housing, under Presidents John F. Kennedy and Lyndon Johnson, until he died in 1966. Much of the council's work was later incorporated in the Civil Rights Act of 1968.

—*Michael P. Weber*

References
Lubove, Roy. *Twentieth Century Pittsburgh: Government, Business and Environmental Change*. New York: Wiley, 1969.
Teaford, Jon C. *The Rough Road to Renaissance: Urban Revitalization in America, 1940–1985*. Baltimore: Johns Hopkins University Press, 1990.
Weber, Michael P. *Don't Call Me Boss: David L. Lawrence, Pittsburgh's Renaissance Mayor*. Pittsburgh, PA: University of Pittsburgh Press, 1988.

The Laws of the Indies

Shortly after Christopher Columbus reached America in 1492, Spain began to develop a complex set of laws and regulations to govern the American continent. The need for coordinating these laws became evident, and by 1552, Luis de Velazco, viceroy of Nueva España (Mexico), was assigned the task of compiling and organizing all of the legislation related to the Indies, a work he published in 1563. Seven years later, in 1570, Phillip II ordered an update and review, a task that continued for 110 years. On May 18, 1680, Charles II signed a *Real Cedula* adopting the Compendium of the Laws as the official guide of Hispanic America. The Laws of the Indies, as they are commonly called, included 6,400 laws organized into four volumes of nine books and dealt with almost every activity regulated by the Spanish government in the New World. The seventh title of the fourth book specifically concerned the settlement of cities, towns, and villages.

The legislation concerning the policies and procedures for settling the new continent continued expanding from 1492 to 1563. The first indication of any centralized guidance was the set of orders that Phillip II gave Nicolás de Ovando in 1501 to create "the number of towns you consider appropriate in places that you select." In 1509, Diego Colón received orders from the king "to report to us your decisions, based on your opinion, on the abandonment of some settlements and the establishment of new ones." This reliance on the judgment of officials in the new continent started to change, and in 1512 the king ordered Pedrarias Dávila, governor of the Province of Castilla de Oro (Panama's region), "to design the new settlements, giving order at the beginning." He was directed to locate a plaza and church, design the streets with a clear order, and assign residential lots to future householders according "to the quality of persons."

These guidelines were reiterated to other colonial officials and finally issued to Hernán Cortez in 1523 to direct the urbanization of Mexico. The first Compendium in 1563 established specific rules, regulations, and procedures for establishing new settlements and modifying older ones. The final Compendium of 1680 resembled the previous work in regard to cities and urban matters.

The Laws of the Indies provided guidelines to plan and create cities, but they also established a very precise and complex legal context for the urbanization of Hispanic America. The legislation of Charles II remained in force for more than 100 years.

—*Felipe J. Prestamo*

References

Stanislawski, Dan. "Early Spanish Town Planning in the New World." *Geographical Review* 37 (1947): 94–105.

Violich, Francis. "Evolution of the Spanish City." *Journal of the American Institute of Planners* 28 (1962): 170–179.

The Legal Basis of Municipal Government

"The village or township," wrote Alexis de Tocqueville in his 1836 classic *Democracy in America*, "is the only association which is so perfectly natural that, whenever a number of men are collected, its seems to constitute itself." And, he added by way of emphasis, while "man . . . makes monarchies and establishes republics . . . the township seems to come directly from the hand of God."

Whatever the historical or theological merits of Tocqueville's views, juridically it is otherwise. In American law, local governments are not sovereign entities, and neither the federal nor the state constitutions recognize any unqualified right to local self-government. In general, local governments are subordinate to states, and their powers depend largely on what the state gives them. This is so despite long-standing efforts to empower and protect local governments, among other ways by granting them constitutional standing and by limiting state intervention in their affairs.

The legal status of local governments did not become a major public issue until the late nineteenth century. Previously, state supremacy was widely accepted and generally not contested. Amendments to the Massachusetts Constitution in 1821, for example, granted the legislature, or General Court as it is officially known, "full power to erect and constitute [municipal or city governments] and to grant such powers, privileges, and immunities as [it] shall deem necessary and expedient." Admittedly, Massachusetts was somewhat unusual in this regard; most state constitutions were largely silent about the issue. Local governments were simply presumed to exist, and states were presumed to have plenary powers over them. Citing numerous state court precedents, the New Hampshire Supreme Court noted in *Berlin v. Gorham* in 1856: "The legislature has entire control over municipal corporations, to create, change, or destroy them at pleasure, and they are ab-solutely created by the act of incorporation, [with or] without the acceptance of the people."

That state supremacy was generally accepted and not contested was due partly to the limited role of government in society. Although by no means inconsequential, the official acts of local government were confined and without far-reaching consequences for citizens, either inside or outside the community. Given this, the issue seldom arose, and there was little need for constitution makers or legal commentators to confront either the philosophical foundations or the practical implications of the doctrine. As Chief Justice Thomas Cooley of the Michigan Supreme Court noted in *People ex rel LeRoy v. Hurblut* in 1871: "We seldom have [had] occasion to inquire whether this amplitude of legislative authority is or is not too strongly expressed."

By the time Cooley was writing, the issue of state supremacy and local autonomy was very much on the judicial agenda. The context was the extraordinary growth in the size and scope of local government after the Civil War, especially in the nation's larger cities. The growth was evident in much larger municipal budgets, expanded regulatory activity, the creation of new city departments, and greatly increased local capital investments in bridges, waterworks, streets, sewerage, and public buildings.

The growth was evident, additionally, in the struggle to control the fiscal resources and regulatory powers of local government. These were now a matter of high-stakes politics, and as such the occasion of a more self-conscious and systematic debate about the philosophical foundations and practical implications of the traditional doctrine of state supremacy. At issue, according to Cooley, was "Whether local self government . . . is or is not a mere privilege, conceded by the legislature in its discretion, and which may be withdrawn at any time at pleasure."

Cooley's own view, radical for the time, was that local self-government was a right, not a privilege. He acknowledged that constitutionally "the . . . verbal restrictions . . . upon legislative authority" over localities were "few and simple," and that local government lacked the same kinds of constitutional guarantees afforded "life, liberty and property." He nonetheless insisted that certain fundamental principles, among them the right to local self-government, were "equally imperative in character . . . [even] though their limits [were] not so plainly defined as express provisions might have made them." The right existed, he argued, because of local government's historical and political primacy. According to Cooley:

> First, the constitution has been adopted in view of a system of local government, well understood and tolerably uniform in character, existing from the very earliest settlement of the country, never for a mo-

ment suspended or displaced, and the continued existence of which is assumed; and second . . . the liberties of the people have generally been supposed to spring from, and be dependent upon, that system.

Though engaging, Cooley's challenge failed to carry the day; indeed the traditional doctrine of state supremacy emerged from the early debates even more robust and elaborate than before. This elaboration is best illustrated in what has come to be known as Dillon's Rule, named after Chief Justice John Forrest Dillon of the Iowa State Supreme Court. Dillon first enunciated his Rule in 1868 in the case of the *City of Clinton v. the Cedar Rapids and Missouri River Railroad,* and he later expanded it in his widely cited and classic *Treatise on the Law of Municipal Corporations,* first published in 1872.

According to Dillon, there was no inherent right to local self-government, and without constitutional provisions to the contrary, localities were mere administrative conveniences of the state. As such, the state could create or destroy them entirely at its discretion and could grant or withhold powers as it deemed appropriate and expedient. The authority of local government was restricted to that which the state expressly granted, and courts were responsible, as they were when dealing with delegated powers, for scrutinizing such authority closely and construing it narrowly. Such was the judicial orthodoxy of the day.

Dillon's Rule helped legitimate extensive state intervention in local affairs after the Civil War. Intervention took various forms—the imposition of charters and charter amendments, for example, or the creation of new agencies and new staff positions, paid for locally and often designed to accommodate recently defeated local officials. There were frequent mandates, on occasion obligating local governments to enter into contracts with specified individuals or firms, and numerous occasions when local governments were forced to petition states for authority to embark on some new initiative. The last were especially troublesome, not only for the delays they entailed but for the political price localities often paid to gain state approval.

With state intervention thus legitimated, proponents of local self-government turned to another arena, that of constitutional politics. As Professor Frank Goodnow of Columbia University noted in 1895:

The continual legislative interference in purely local matters has caused us to resort to the remedy to which we had resorted before, in order to protect the sphere of freedom of private individuals. We have incorporated into most of our later state constitutions provisions which limit very largely the power of legislatures to interfere with the affairs of municipal corporations.

The goal of what became known as the home rule movement was twofold—first, to limit state intervention in local affairs and, second, to ensure some degree of local autonomy. The former included, most notably, prohibitions on so-called special legislation aimed at individual communities. These were often coupled with requirements that all local legislation be enacted under general law, on the assumption that legislatures would be more responsible if they had to deal with localities collectively rather than individually. In some instances, special legislation would be allowed, but only if requested and/or approved by the locality itself.

The initiatives were also intended to empower local communities. The most common of these gave citizens broad, though not always unconditional, discretion over local charters and the organization of local government. Less common, but no less crucial, were efforts to go beyond organization and procedure and to assign substantive powers to local governments. In some cases, municipalities received jurisdiction over "local" matters, a term otherwise left unspecified; in others, control over matters enumerated in the Constitution. Left unanswered was the question of whether the enumerated powers were the limit of local government's jurisdiction—or whether the legislature could add new ones as needs arose.

The initiatives also included, more recently, efforts to reverse the so-called expressed powers doctrine. The goal has been to create a constitutional presumption that local governments can act whether or not the legislature has expressly authorized them to do so. The formula varies. The constitutions of both Missouri and Massachusetts, for example, declare that local governments "shall have all powers which the general assembly has the authority to confer on any city." The Michigan Constitution, on the other hand, stipulates that the power of local government "shall include those fairly implied and not prohibited by the constitution," and Michigan, along with a number of other states, requires that "a liberal construction . . . be given the powers of local government."

The home rule movement helped politicize the issue of state supremacy and popularize the goal of constitutional guarantees for local self-government. In terms of actual constitutional change, however, the record has been uneven. For one thing, while most state constitutions include some kind of home rule provision, several do not, including some that make the subordinate status of localities explicit. Second, most home rule provisions concern charter-making authority, not substantive powers. Finally, even in states with strong home rule traditions, liberal home rule constitutions, and, consequently, sympathetic judges, state government remains a commanding legal presence.

This presence is evident in constitutions themselves and the qualified way in which home rule provisions are written. They do not, for example, preclude the state from creating new units of local government or from shifting program responsibilities among existing units or even to the state itself. Nor do they preclude the imposition of statewide policies with respect to local government employment (collective bargaining, workers' compensation, civil service, pension and health plans), local health and safety regulations, or land use planning. Nor, finally, have traditional home rule provisions prevented states from increasing the number of unfunded mandates, though in some states, among them New Hampshire and New Mexico, such mandates are now expressly prohibited constitutionally.

Fiscal constraints are even more pervasive. Home rule never implied fiscal autonomy, and constitutions typically limit the taxing and borrowing powers of localities. In some instances, most commonly in the case of debt, constitutions are explicit and often quite detailed. Among other things, they usually specify the purposes for which debt can be incurred, the procedures that must be followed when borrowing money, and the overall amount—often expressed as a percentage of the tax base—that can be outstanding at any given time.

Absent specific constitutional constraints, local taxing and borrowing powers are subject to the general laws of the state. Article 8 of the Nevada Constitution, for example, instructs the legislature to "restrict the taxing, assessment and borrowing" power of municipal corporations. Most other state constitutions, including those with otherwise liberal home rule provisions, contain similar restrictions. The Massachusetts Constitution, after affirming in majestic language the "customary and traditional liberties of the people with respect to the conduct of their local government, and granting and confirming the right of self-government in local affairs," quickly adds that "Nothing in this Article shall be deemed to grant any city or town the power to: . . . (2) levy, assess or collect taxes; (3) to borrow money or pledge the credit of the city or town."

Whatever the specific provisions, the debate over the constitutional status of local government has been profoundly shaped by history and politics, as has the actual impact of home rule. One factor is the widespread recognition, except, perhaps, among the most unrelenting home rule advocates, that some matters require uniform, statewide policies—criminal codes, for example; or codes governing commercial and real estate transactions, banking, and insurance; or laws chartering corporations. These are ancient responsibilities, and as such are taken for granted, although in earlier times they were far less elaborate than they are today.

Second, state government often functions as an appellate arena for those who lose, or expect to lose, locally. It is also the arena in which special interests can use limited resources most efficiently. For groups whose interests transcend local boundaries—environmentalists, for example, or developers, contractors, labor unions, and business associations—it is more economical to concentrate their resources on one state government than on hundreds of local ones. Moreover, organized groups are less likely to encounter citizen opposition at the state level, even from those directly affected, since such opposition is generally unorganized and not easily mobilized.

There are, finally, the superior resources of state government, most especially in fiscal matters. As a general rule, the more extensive a government in terms of people and place, the more productive are its sources of revenues. Thus, for example, the state is better situated than the locality to exploit such important revenue sources as income, capital gains, sales, or inheritance taxes. These revenue sources are highly mobile, far more than property, and thus it is not surprising that, independent of legal constraints, local governments traditionally have relied more on property taxes than on any other revenue source. Nor is it surprising that, as governments have grown, so, too, has the state's share of overall state and local revenues and expenditures. It is no longer the case, as it once was, that localities outspend and outtax the states.

Though a commanding fiscal as well as constitutional presence, states have not entirely overshadowed local governments. It is true that states are now far more active than at any time in the past, but the unmistakable growth in the level and range of state activity has not always and everywhere been at the expense of local governments.

Finances are a case in point. As state revenues and expenditures have increased, so too have those at the local level. This includes revenues and expenditures from local sources, as well as support from the state (and federal) government. The latter, of course, have increased substantially. State aid now accounts for roughly 34 percent of all local revenues, compared to less than 10 percent in 1932.

Since few grants-in-aid are entirely unconditional, state aid has traditionally been a way to enhance, albeit indirectly, state control over local affairs. This is especially true in the case of education, which historically, and today, accounts for most of the state aid to local governments. But the fact that states rely on grants, rather than doing the job themselves, testifies to the staying power of local governments. Moreover, with state funds, localities can undertake programs they otherwise could not afford, thus expanding local government's own role in the community.

All this, one suspects, helps reinforce the popular presumption that local self-government is part of the "natural" order of things and the expectation, legal discourse aside, that localities are entitled to a degree of political and programmatic autonomy. This includes the right to elect local public officials, a right frequently set forth in the earliest state constitutions. These ancient liberties and privileges are not only a way to make local officials accountable to their communities but, equally important, a way to make these officials independent of the state. And given this independent electoral base, local officials have a powerful claim to speak on behalf of the locality in state (and national) councils. These are important resources in a democratic society and essential to the continued viability of local self-government.

—*Russell D. Murphy*

See also
Home Rule.
References
Berlin v. Gorham, 34 New Hampshire 266 (1856).
Columbia University Legislative Research Drafting Fund. *Constitutions of the United States: National and States.* Dobbs Ferry, NY: Oceana Publications, 1994.
de Tocqueville, Alexis. *Democracy in America,* ch. 5. New York: Vintage Books, 1945.
Dillon, John Forrest. *Treatise on the Law of Municipal Corporations.* New York: James Cockcroft, 1872.
Goodnow, Frank. *Municipal Home Rule: A Study in Administration.* New York: Columbia University Press, 1895.
Grumm, John G., and Russell D. Murphy. "Dillon's Rule Revisited." *Annals of the American Academy of Social and Political Science* 416 (1974): 120–132.
People ex rel Le Roy v. Hurblut, 24 Michigan 44 (1871).
Sandalow, Terrence. "The Limits of Municipal Power under Home Rule: A Role for the Courts." *48 Minnesota Law Review* 643 (1964).
Sharpe, L. J. "Theories and Values of Local Government." *Political Studies* 18 (1970): 153–174.
Syed, Anwar. *The Political Theory of American Local Government.* New York: Random House, 1966.
Thorpe, Francis Newton. *The Federal and State Constitutions, Colonial Charters, and Other Organic Laws of the States, Territories and Colonies.* Washington, DC: Government Printing Office, 1909.

L'Enfant, Peter Charles (1755–1825)

Peter Charles L'Enfant is remembered as the temperamental designer of the city of Washington, D.C. Born in Paris as Pierre (but always going by Peter in the United States), L'Enfant was educated by his father, a painter of military scenes, and was among a group of French engineers who fought in the American Revolution. George Washington initially used him as a courier, a position of trust that offered L'Enfant opportunities to travel extensively. In 1779, he was wounded during the Battle of Savannah and the following year taken prisoner in the Battle of Charleston. Thus, when L'Enfant settled in New York in 1784, he had already experienced the country's geography, varied population, and Revolutionary War history.

Three projects with national implications secured L'Enfant's reputation as an innovative designer during the 1780s. In 1787, he incorporated emblems of the Franco-American alliance into a dancing pavilion he designed for the grounds of the French minister's residence in Philadelphia. The following year, he designed a huge dining pavilion that seated several thousand participants celebrating ratification of the Constitution in New York's Grand Federal Procession. Ten long tables ending in pavilions decorated with insignia of the ratifying states radiated from the central table where Washington, congressmen, and foreign ministers were seated. L'Enfant's most influential early design was Federal Hall in New York, where the first federal Congress convened and Washington was inaugurated in 1789. Sculpture decorating its marble Neoclassical facade announced its national purpose, including the Great Seal of the United States in the pediment, 13 stars in the entablature, and reliefs of arrows and olive branches on the third level. Both legislative chambers were ornamented with symbols of the new nation that L'Enfant either invented or adapted.

The new political order expressed so vividly in these early projects explains why Washington chose L'Enfant in 1791 to design the new federal city and all of its public buildings on the Potomac River. L'Enfant intended the city's immense scale—6,111 acres—to be a microcosm of what he called "this vast empire." He distributed public buildings, monuments, and squares throughout the city, locating them on or near prominent topographical features. He connected these widely separated places with an infrastructure of diagonal avenues, which are named for states. (Thomas Jefferson, James Madison, and the city commissioners determined that the underlying grid of streets would be denominated by letters and numbers.) L'Enfant's third design decision was to interlock an irregular grid of neighborhood streets to the public spaces and connective avenues.

The internal logic of the street names suggests that L'Enfant intended the city's plan to symbolize national union like the flag, the union chain (used on the federal government's first money), and the Great Seal of the United States. The avenues named for New England states were located in the northern part of the city, for central states in the center of the scheme, and for southern states on Capitol Hill, the southernmost part of the city. The three most populous states (also the only commonwealths)—Massachusetts, Pennsylvania, and Virginia—gave their names to avenues that traversed the entire city. The streets fell geographically within the city as the states did in the country. The avenues may also have been grouped to reflect the political history of the nation's founding; except for Delaware, those radiating from the Capitol were states where the Continental and Confederation Congresses had met (and Delaware was the first state to ratify the Constitution). New York Avenue may be bisected by the White House grounds because Washington was inaugurated at New York's Federal Hall.

French precedents in Paris for symbolically representing an entire nation include Claude Chastillon's design of 1610, which had eight streets named for the major provinces of France radiating from the semicircular Place de France. The L-shaped configuration in central Paris formed by the Louvre, Tuilleries Gardens, Place Louis XV (the Place de la Concorde after the French Revolution), and the Church of the Madeleine probably inspired L'Enfant's arrangement of the Capitol, Mall, equestrian statue of Washington, and President's House. In 1784, when L'Enfant returned briefly to France, Victor Louis designed for Bordeaux, France's second city, the Place Ludovise to celebrate the return of victorious French forces from America. Had it been built, 13 streets converging on a semicircular *place* were to have been named for the 13 states.

L'Enfant addressed many pragmatic and aesthetic issues when he set about designing the new federal city: competing rivalries among local landowners; a full complement of common urban structures as well as buildings to house (and express) the country's new governing system; and preserving, even enhancing, a site of great natural beauty that one congressman considered the most picturesque spot in America. L'Enfant was also concerned with creating a great national symbol that expressed the contributions of the states and America's French allies to the creation of the federal government.

—*Pamela Scott*

References

Caemmerer, H. Paul. *The Life of Pierre Charles L'Enfant.* Washington, DC: National Republic Publishing Company, 1950.

Jusserand, J. J. *With Americans of Past and Present Days,* 137–198. New York: Scribners, 1916.

Kite, Elizabeth S. *L'Enfant and Washington, 1791–1792.* Baltimore: Johns Hopkins University Press, 1929.

Reiff, Daniel D. *Washington Architecture . . . 1791–1861,* 1–18. Washington, DC: Commission of Fine Arts, 1971.

Reps, John W. *Monumental Washington.* Princeton, NJ: Princeton University Press, 1967.

Scott, Pamela. " 'This Vast Empire': The Iconography of the Mall, 1791–1848." In Richard Longstreth, ed., *The Mall in Washington, 1791–1991,* 37–60. Washington, DC: National Gallery of Art, 1991.

Levittown

Levittown is a particular housing development that has come to represent all of the suburbs built in the United States after World War II. In the popular imagination, Levittown is where thousands of families differing from each other only in the gender distribution of their children and the color of their station wagon live in endlessly replicated houses on endlessly winding streets. The word is used as shorthand for white flight, separate spheres of family and economic life, cultural wastelands, and the feminine mystique.

The real Levittown is a distinct community of 17,447 houses built between 1947 and 1951 by the construction and development firm of Levitt and Sons on about seven square miles of farmland on Long Island about thirty miles east of New York City. It is the product of a happy confluence of circumstances: an infestation of golden nematodes that rendered acres of flatland useless for farming; an eager market of young veterans returning home from war to find a housing shortage; wide-ranging federal initiatives like the National Housing Acts and the GI Bill of Rights; a good local network of roads thanks to Robert Moses; the growth of Long Island's aerospace industry; and the genius of William Levitt, one of the sons of a firm that had been building developments for the upper-middle class on Long Island's northern coast since the early 1930s.

In the spring of 1947, Levitt and Sons began applying its wartime experiences building emergency housing and its expertise in marketing the suburban dream to some land it had recently acquired on Long Island. They hired an army of carpenters, roofers, electricians, plumbers, and landscapers, and put together the first of the four-room houses that would become Levittown. Levitt's innovative construction methods—using standardized components, buying directly from manufacturers (or sometimes becoming manufacturers themselves), and turning the entire tract into an enormous assembly line where workers moved from house to house—allowed the firm to construct 150 houses a week by the summer of 1948. Levitt and Sons soon acquired a national reputation as builders who were solving the housing crisis.

But the Levitts were not only building houses. The veterans and young families who lined up to rent (and later to buy) the two-bedroom, one-bath, expandable Cape Cods and ranch houses before the paint was even dry were also buying a community. A thousand sidewalks and lanes lit with street lights defined and enclosed different neighborhoods, which clustered around school yards and "Village Greens," landscaped complexes of shops, playgrounds, and swimming pools. The Levitts built a community center, Levittown Hall, to provide space for civic organizations, clubs, and recitals by dancing schools. To ensure the maintenance and preservation of this fledgling community, the Levitts required their customers to sign covenants prohibiting them from building fences, hanging the wash outside on Sundays, and selling to people of color.

None of this was particularly revolutionary. The Levitts were following formulas to build economical houses worked out by the federal government and blueprints for community design that had been debated and drafted by architects in the nineteenth century and urban planners in the twentieth. Even the covenants had antecedents in the nineteenth century. Levittown was essentially a "knock-off" of traditional upper-class suburbs, and as such it appalled many architects and critics who predicted that it would soon become a slum.

But they were using the wrong context to interpret all those little houses on the Long Island prairie. Levittown became neither a slum nor a suburb. The people who lived there did not see themselves as tiny particles orbiting New York but as constituting a town in its own right. The modest price of a Levitt house had let them join the home-owning middle class, and they protected their new status by investing heavily in their homes and neighborhoods. They added on to their houses, and they joined PTAs and political parties almost as soon as they moved in. Their sheer numbers provided the critical mass necessary for the development of increasingly diversified local jobs, shopping, recreation, education, and even the arts outside the central city. The people who lived in the first Levittown on Long Island, and later in those in Pennsylvania and New Jersey, thus helped transform the single-centered city into the multicentered metropolis that characterizes so much of the United States today.

—*Mollie Keller*

References
Fishman, Robert. *Bourgeois Utopias: The Rise and Fall of Suburbia.* New York: Basic Books, 1987.
Gans, Herbert. *The Levittowners: Ways of Life and Politics in a New Suburban Community.* New York: Random House, 1967.
Jackson, Kenneth T. *Crabgrass Frontier: The Suburbanization of the United States.* New York: Oxford University Press, 1985.
Keller, Mollie. "Levittown and the Transformation of the Metropolis." Ph.D. dissertation, New York University, 1991.
Kelly, Barbara M. *Expanding the American Dream: Building and Rebuilding Levittown.* Albany: State University of New York Press, 1993.

Lewis, Sinclair (1885–1951)

The novels of Sinclair Lewis reveal an ambivalence toward the cities and towns of the Midwest. Lewis was born in Sauk Centre, Minnesota, in 1885. Although he admired the atmosphere of small towns where people worried about the welfare of others, these same towns depressed him because, too often, the inhabitants perpetuated the social hierarchies, prejudices, and intolerance prevalent in cities of the eastern seaboard and Europe. It frustrated Lewis that midwestern citizens had had a chance to create a new and better society but spoiled their opportunity.

Like William Faulkner and his Yoknapatawpha County, Lewis created a fictional area that serves as a vehicle for his critical comments on society. Between 1920 and 1947, Lewis created three distinct midwestern towns: Gopher Prairie, a town of fewer than 5,000; Zenith, a bustling metropolis of more than 360,000; and Grand Republic, an established city of 90,000. He drew maps, relied on architecture and real es-

tate magazines, and created an urban infrastructure to make these places seem real.

Lewis belonged to the "Revolt from the Village" literary movement that debunked the idea that small towns were perfect places in which to live. This is evident in his depiction of Gopher Prairie, Minnesota, which first appeared briefly in the 1919 novel *Free Air.* In his next novel, *Main Street,* Gopher Prairie represents both the dreams of a growing nation and the nightmares of an impossibly rigid society. In one of *Main Street*'s most famous passages, Lewis sums up his accusations against towns such as Gopher Prairie by calling them "dullness made God."

Zenith, the setting of *Babbitt, Arrowsmith,* and *Elmer Gantry,* is located in the fictional state of Winnemac and represents the prosperity of the 1920s. In these novels, Lewis criticizes the business mind-set in which all values are sacrificed to making money. Everything is done to maintain the status quo, even if it means subverting democracy.

Lewis's final fictional city, Grand Republic, which appears in his two best novels of the 1940s, *Cass Timberlane* and *Kingsblood Royal,* presents his darkest view of America. Neither as young as Gopher Prairie nor as striving as Zenith, Grand Republic is a deceptively pleasant, self-satisfied city. In Lewis's earlier novels, communities' vices grew from their virtues, but the possibility for goodness existed. In Grand Republic, however, the virtues are completely superficial. The vices, especially racial hatred and sexual hypocrisy, are much more powerful. The midwestern ideal of a place where equality and democracy can exist is exposed as meaningless. The towns of Lewis's fiction reflect the anger and confusion over the American dream in the twentieth century.

—*Sally E. Parry*

References
Batchelor, Helen. "A Sinclair Lewis Portfolio of Maps: Zenith to Winnemac." *Modern Language Quarterly* 32 (1971): 401–408.
Hutchisson, James M. *The Rise of Sinclair Lewis, 1920–1930.* University Park: Pennsylvania State University Press, 1996.
Parry, Sally E. "Gopher Prairie, Zenith, and Grand Republic: Nice Places to Visit, but Would Even Sinclair Lewis Want to Live There?" *Midwestern Miscellany* 20 (1992): 15–27.
Schorer, Mark. *Sinclair Lewis: An American Life.* New York: McGraw-Hill, 1961.

Lincoln Center for the Performing Arts

In the early 1950s, eager entrepreneurs slated Carnegie Hall and the Metropolitan Opera House in New York City for demolition and replacement by office buildings. Thus, the New York Philharmonic Orchestra and the Metropolitan Opera Company expected to be homeless. Lincoln Center not only rescued them but was the first in a giant wave of arts centers that appeared in and affected every major American city.

A model for a performing arts hub existed in the New York City Center, which Mayor Fiorello H. La Guardia had created to make low ticket prices possible for ballet, opera, theater, and symphony orchestra performances. But from its inception in 1943 through the 1950s, almost no City Center season ended without dire predictions of a financial collapse.

To create a visible, tangible symbol of an American awakening in the performing arts, to replace Carnegie Hall and the Metropolitan Opera House, and not least to enhance his family's real estate interests in the Lincoln Square section of Manhattan, John D. Rockefeller III agreed, in September 1954, to chair a fund-raising campaign for an arts center on New York City's West Side.

The effort to build Lincoln Center proved far more difficult than anticipated, even with a Rockefeller as chairman. Construction, estimated to cost $55 million, actually cost $184 million. One consequence became apparent when the center's first building, Philharmonic Hall, opened in September 1962; ticket prices immediately soared beyond the means of thousands of prospective patrons. Today, high ticket prices remain a prominent feature of center operations. Another problem has been that constituent organizations, desperate to remain solvent, offer safe and sure programming, presenting "artists" whose reputations are sometimes greater than their current ability. Nonetheless, the center remains a bellwether of the performing arts in America. Clearly, public subsidies for the arts are essential if tickets are to be reasonably priced and high standards of quality maintained.

—*Milton Goldin*

References

Gastner, John. "Center for the Uncommon Man." *New York Times Magazine* (November 8, 1953).

Goldin, Milton. "'Why the Square?' John D. Rockefeller 3 and the Creation of Lincoln Center for the Performing Arts." *Journal of Popular Culture* 21 (1987): 17–30.

Muschamp, Herbert. "Lincoln Center's Enduring Vision." *New York Times* (July 19, 1996): C:1.

Llewellyn Park, New Jersey

In 1853 Llewellyn Haskell, a New York City pharmaceutical merchant, chose the site for his new country residence in the Orange Mountains near West Orange, New Jersey. Suffering from severe rheumatism, Haskell thought that the site, immediately adjacent to two mineral springs that had been popular resorts in the 1820s, would be healthful for him. Over the next three years, Alexander Jackson Davis carried out residential improvements for Haskell and also built a summer house for himself on an adjacent site.

Haskell soon transformed the site into an entrepreneurial venture; by 1857 he had acquired 350 acres, which grew to 500 by 1860 and 750 by 1870. He slated much of the site for subdivision into house lots—for which Davis, Andrew Jackson Downing, and Calvert Vaux, among others, provided designs—but substantial pieces as large as 50 acres were retained as landscaped natural preserves for the common enjoyment of all residents. An 1856 map shows extensive landscaping already in "The Glenn" and "The Forrest," a complex of curving drives, woods, streams, and ponds leading from the gate lodge at the entrance toward the Haskell and Davis residences high on the ridge. The next year a lithographed promotional plan appeared and showed specific areas laid out as "villa sites." At the same time, a newspaper advertisement announced "Villa Sites of, from 5 to 10 Acres Each," and characterized the community for the first time as a perfect commuter suburb: the site, within an hour of New York City by train, was "selected with special reference to the wants of citizens doing business in the city, and yet wanting accessible, retired, and healthful homes in the country." The community was laid out "in the modern natural style of landscape gardening," with "magnificent" views available, while the privacy of all residents would be protected "by a Lodge and gate-keeper at the entrance."

Landscaped suburban enclaves predated Llewellyn Park in America (e.g., Glendale, Ohio, 1851), and gated communities were already an established paradigm in England (e.g., Victoria Park, Manchester, 1837). Twentieth-century commentators (but few if any nineteenth-century observers) also cite European and American cemeteries as precedents. Fenced, gated, and romantically landscaped cemeteries such as Mount Auburn (Cambridge, Massachusetts, 1831) and Greenwood (Brooklyn, 1838) provided sites for private contemplation and reverie that were, like romantic suburbs, conspicuously detached from the bustle and corruption of urban life.

Illustrations of Llewellyn Park were included in the 1859 posthumous edition of Downing's influential *Treatise on the Theory and Practice of Landscape Gardening Adapted to North America*, thus extending and enhancing its reputation. Gated, fenced, and relatively remote, with no commerce or trade permitted, Llewellyn Park effected an isolation of residence and family in "nature," rendering the domestic domain a distinct and special preserve. In several respects the design of Llewellyn Park became paradigmatic of the modern industrial-era suburb: it was intentionally removed from the city but dependent on mechanized transport for access to and from the city; its plan and landscaping were replete with features antithetical to the city, but economically it was dependent on the fruits of capital investment or professional skills employed in the city; and while the conspicuous embrace of nature emulated Downing's ideal of agrarian republicanism, any productive use of the land was prohibited, in favor of picturesquely composed "scenes" offering pastoral idylls suited for private contemplation.

Nor was Llewellyn Park simply a celebration of rugged individualism. Haskell and a number of early residents appear to have had strong spiritualist and communitarian interests, and community events such as the melodramatic May Day festival necessitated considerable collective effort. Proscription of fences throughout the community and the resulting continuity of vistas across private and common land likewise provided the sense of a commonweal shared among all. The particular sense of "community" thus fostered has remained a characteristic conceit of suburbia throughout the twentieth century: "community" is understood to flourish best if clearly distanced from city, politics, and commerce; likewise it is considered to be enhanced by a landscape contrived to emulate the transcendent ideal of depoliticized, nonproductive "nature."

—*John Archer*

See also
Davis, Alexander Jackson; Downing, Andrew Jackson.
References
Archer, John. "Country and City in the American Romantic Suburb." *Journal of the Society of Architectural Historians* 42 (1983): 139–156.
Davies, Jane B. "Llewellyn Park in West Orange, New Jersey." *Antiques* 107 (1975): 142–158.
Henderson, Susan. "Llewellyn Park, Suburban Idyll." *Journal of Garden History* 7 (1987): 221–243.
Pierson, David Lawrence. *History of the Oranges to 1921.* New York: Lewis Historical Publishing, 1922.
Swift, Samuel. "Llewellyn Park, West Orange, Essex Co., New Jersey, the First American Suburban Community." *House and Garden* 3 (June 1903): 327–335.
Whittemore, Henry. *The Founders and Builders of the Oranges.* Newark, NJ: L. J. Hardham, 1896.
Wilson, Richard Guy. "Idealism and the Origin of the First American Suburb: Llewellyn Park, New Jersey." *American Art Journal* 11 (1979): 79–90.

Lodging, Boarding, and Rooming Houses

Lodging houses, boarding houses, and rooming houses are all variations of single-room housing—businesses that provide rooms (but not necessarily kitchens or private bathrooms) that are an alternative to living in an apartment or in a private house with a family. Since 1800 in some cities, American uses of commercial lodgings have fluctuated with cyclical swings in employment and business opportunities (and the individual income related to them), rapid population increases, and changes in family life and geographic mobility. Historically, rooming and lodging house areas have been located within half a mile of varied jobs. Also, districts of rooming and lodging houses have provided employers with large pools of labor available for short or erratic employment. For at least a century, workers without private transporta-

tion have recognized a major advantage in living near the downtown rather than on a city's periphery. Boarding, rooming, and lodging houses provide the cheapest housing for people who wish to live completely independently, often in neighborhoods with a lively nightlife, services, and social opportunities.

Several social groups provide potential markets for single-room housing. For boarding and rooming houses, the most numerous residents are single adults, steadily employed but not highly paid. Between 1900 and World War II, about half of these people were men and half women. The men most commonly worked as clerks, journeymen carpenters, or in other skilled trades. The women worked as clerks and in low-paying, white-collar office jobs. Since 1950, their work has increasingly been in the service sector of the economy. Couples and entire families have also lived in rooming or boarding houses, occasionally in multiroom suites. Since World War II, retired and elderly tenants have made up an ever larger share of the market. The closing of state mental hospitals after 1960 and the failure to provide as many halfway houses for the mentally ill as were originally promised have greatly increased the number of mentally ill people in inexpensive types of single-room housing.

The uses of the terms *boarding, rooming,* and *lodging* have varied historically as well as regionally. In 1900, what would have been called a rooming house in New York or St. Louis was called a furnished-room house in Philadelphia, while in Boston the same structure might have been called a lodging house. When buildings offer more than six to ten rooms, single-room lodgings are often legally and popularly called hotels and may be liable to collect and pay city taxes and to be inspected as hotels.

At the root of all the various terms are the clients. *Boarders* take their meals with a family. They might rent a place to sleep in the same dwelling or in another location. In *boarding houses,* most common before 1900 but still available, tenants rent rooms from a proprietor who provides family-style breakfasts and evening dinners in a common dining room. *Lodgers* or *roomers* sleep in one house but take their meals elsewhere. Boarding and lodging used to be very common in American cities; in conservative estimates for the years before 1930, one-third to one-half of all urban Americans either boarded or took in boarders at some time in their lives.

By 1900, in most cities, the term *lodging house* was beginning to imply a cheaper variety of single-room housing, those spaces where casual laborers lived. Housing reformers in the Progressive Era typically used the phrase "cheap lodging house" to denote these homes for hobos. By 1950, city planners had come to use the term *SRO* (single room occupancy) for most large and inexpensive downtown rooming houses as well as for the lodging houses on skid row. The rental period for single-room lodgings can be by the day, just as with commercial tourist hotels, although rentals are frequently by the week or month. Tourist accommodations and long-term single-room residence can be mixed in a single building. The structures might be very small, such as converted family houses, or very large commercial operations with hundreds of rooms.

Instead of taking in just one or two boarders at a time (as many families did), old-fashioned family boarding houses provided accommodations for six to ten tenants, sometimes in worker's cottages with four rooms. In a family boarding house, the landlady wielded authority over parlor life, curfews, and guests. After 1900 many people looked back nostalgically to these enterprises when comparing them to later commercial rooming houses. After the Civil War, the number of commercial boarding houses declined sharply, and they were fairly rare by 1900. Proprietors of boarding houses were not quitting the business entirely, but they were no longer providing food and were turning their boarding houses into rooming houses.

By 1900 most rooming houses around downtowns were strictly commercial and often located in a 25- to 40-year-old house, three or four stories high, and originally built for a middle-income family. The owners had moved to the edge of town and leased their house downtown to a woman who rented rooms as her chief source of income. In some cities, old buildings converted to rooming houses have continued in use up to the 1990s.

However, by 1920 rooming houses near a downtown were likely to be in small buildings with commercial space on the ground floor and two or three more stories containing between 15 and 40 rooms for rent. Shared bathrooms were down the hall from the rooms. These accommodations are still common. Their only lobby is usually an area on the second floor near the office and is part of the manager's unit. Larger commercial rooming houses, with at least 60 to 100 rooms, offer elevators, true lobbies, and sometimes a dining room or cafeteria, but upstairs the rooms and baths remain similar to smaller rooming houses.

The reading room of a 10-cent lodging house in the Bowery section of New York City in 1908.

While single-family houses and apartments are largely complete in themselves as domestic environments, daily life is scattered up and down the street for residents of rooming houses. They sleep in one building, eat breakfast in another, have dinner in yet another, and socialize in a corner bar or lunch counter. Thus, rooming house residents need to be in a district of mixed uses with inexpensive retail stores, laundries, bars, and restaurants, as well as pool halls and clubs.

Important alternatives to traditional rooming house life, usually complete with their own rules and curfews, are the dormitories run by charitable organizations. These are often segregated by religion or race, and the best known are those operated by the Young Men's Christian Association (YMCA) and the Young Women's Christian Association (YWCA). Since 1950, residential motels, particularly common along older highways, also operate very much like traditional rooming houses downtown.

Unlike the mixture of genders found in boarding and rooming houses, the residents of cheap lodging houses have overwhelmingly been men. Before the 1950s, these men ranged widely in age and were employed as casual (day-to-day) industrial and transient labor; they often worked as migrant workers and returned to the city between jobs, or when injuries made rough migrant work impossible. Inside lodging houses, room prices have distinguished among three very different options according to how much privacy they afford. In the 1920s, for 25 to 40 cents a night, a man could rent a fully private room. For somewhat less, 15 to 25 cents a night, he got a semiprivate cubicle that the patrons called a "cage" or "crib." These were stalls with partitions about seven feet high and had lockable doors. The partial walls offered visual privacy inside large loft spaces whose ceilings were ten to fourteen feet high. Even cheaper were open dormitory wards—areas crowded with rough homemade bunk beds or cots. In the cheapest flophouses that charged only five or ten cents a night, a tired and nearly broke man got only a dry space on an open floor. Most cheap lodging houses offered a mixture of rooms, cubicles, and wards to compensate for fluctuations in occupancy. Although outsiders often castigated lodging house residents as "homeless men," they were not homeless; they simply had very minimal, inexpensive homes. Thousands of people in almost every large city lived in cubicle and ward hotels for whole seasons, and from year to year. While conditions in urban lodgings could be very unpleasant, they often improved on what employers provided for laborers at distant road projects, farms, or lumber camps. Police lodgings, subsidized missions, and occasional municipal lodging houses have offered other alternatives to commercial lodging houses.

By the 1950s, most Americans had learned to use the pejorative term *skid row* for areas of cheap lodging houses; but before the 1950s these areas were very different places, and the term *single laborer's zone* might be more appropriate for them. A typical single and migrant worker's zone mixed cheap work, cheap rooms, cheap recreation, and cheap clothes. At the heart of this district were multiple employment agencies in rented storefronts. Cheap entertainment and saloons were magnets for workingmen from all over the city. Houses of prostitution or assignation were never far away and were often mixed into cheap rooming house districts, too.

Large cities typically had more than one of these single laborer's zones. African-American and Asian-American ghettos in many cities have had a large number of inexpensive hotel homes. Single sailors and longshoremen often had still another single-room housing area, usually near the docks. For so-called homeless men in single laborer's zones, cheap hotels and the areas around them were more than shelter. They were a significant part of hobo identity, just as suburban houses became important to the middle and upper classes as a source of family identity.

The exceptional and often socially marginal nature of rooming houses and lodging houses have brought them continual negative attention from urban leaders of the dominant culture. The high densities, slumlord-style management, poor health conditions, and fire dangers of some rooming houses and many cheap lodging houses have repeatedly brought them to the attention of city officials. However, other critiques have been more subtle. People who lived in rooming and lodging house areas were leaders in the increasing secularism and decreasing moralism after 1900, changes that showed sharp shifts from Victorian mores. Life in rooming houses and lodging houses plugged individuals directly into the high-voltage currents of the industrial city, offering liberation and personal independence very different from that provided by a room of one's own within a family. These areas thus presented a clear opposition to the family districts of the city—and the people who lived in them.

Critics—from writers of building codes in the 1870s to planners of urban renewal in the 1950s—saw rooming and lodging houses as a source of danger to individual development, gender roles, child rearing, morality, proper material values, and public health. These well-meaning reformers considered single-room housing districts to be public nuisances, not housing resources. Single-room housing not only threatened and undermined middle- and upper-class cultural ideals, but the associated mixture of land uses also endangered hopes for a new city of specialized land uses and separated social groups. As part of their crusade to control the central city, these critics wrote single-room life out of most public housing policy. The results were the construction and remodeling of too few single-room units and the demolition of even well-managed, essential rooming and lodging houses.

Official policies gradually began to change in 1970, but the problems of past neglect and misunderstanding continue to haunt rooming and lodging house life. The undersupply and high cost of the remaining rooming and lodging houses are among the root causes of homelessness in the United States.

—*Paul Groth*

See also
Flophouses; Homelessness; Skid Row.
References
Anderson, Nels. *The Hobo: The Sociology of the Homeless Man.* Chicago: University of Chicago Press, 1923.
Beard, Rick, ed. *On Being Homeless: Historical Perspectives.* New York: Museum of the City of New York, 1987.
Chandler, Margaret. "The Social Organization of Workers in a Rooming House Area." Ph.D. dissertation, University of Chicago, 1948.
Eckert, J. Kevin. *The Unseen Elderly: A Study of Marginally Subsistent Hotel Dwellers.* San Diego, CA: Campanile Press, 1980.
Groth, Paul. *Living Downtown: The History of Residential Hotels in the United States.* Berkeley: University of California Press, 1994.
Hoch, Charles, and Robert A. Slayton. *New Homeless and Old: Community and the Skid Row Hotel.* Philadelphia: Temple University Press, 1989.
Meyerowitz, Joanne J. *Women Adrift: Independent Wage Earners in Chicago, 1880–1930.* Chicago: University of Chicago Press, 1988.
Modell, John, and Tamara K. Hareven. "Urbanization and the Malleable Household: An Examination of Boarding and Lodging in American Families." *Journal of Marriage and the Family* 35 (1975): 467–479.
Peel, Mark. "On the Margins: Lodgers and Boarders in Boston, 1860–1900." *Journal of American History* 72 (1986): 813–834.
Wolfe, Albert Benedict. *The Lodging House Problem in Boston.* Boston: Houghton Mifflin, 1906.

The Loop

The Loop is the oldest, most centrally located of Chicago's 77 neighborhoods. Originally named for the cable cars that circled the area in the 1880s, traction magnate Charles T. Yerkes joined four separate elevated lines into a single loop line in 1897. The traditional boundaries of the five-block by seven-block area are Wabash Avenue (east), Wells Street (west), Lake Street (north), and Van Buren Street (south).

The Loop is world-renowned for its architecture. William Le Baron Jenney's Home Insurance Building (1884–1929) is often considered the world's first skyscraper. Many other noteworthy, innovative architects have also left a memorable legacy here, men such as Daniel Burnham, Louis Sullivan, and Mies van der Rohe. Walking tours offer a unique opportunity to see dramatic changes in architecture from the extensively remodeled Rookery (1888) to the Chicago Title and Trust Building (1992).

A prominent function of the Loop is commerce. For decades, it was the premier shopping district of the Chicago region. State Street set the pace with major department stores like Marshall Field's and Carson Pirie Scott. By the 1970s, two developments had adversely affected retail business in the Loop. Shopping patterns changed with the growing influence of suburban malls. Also, North Michigan Avenue expanded its upscale retail character with the opening of a multistory downtown mall, Water Tower Place, in 1976.

There is cause for confidence in the resurgence of the Loop, especially the part located on State Street. In 1992 Marshall Field's completed a renovation costing $110 million. At the south end of the Loop, the Harold Washington Library Center (1991), the largest city library building in the country, provides a strong anchor. Across the street from it, DePaul University remodeled a former department store for academic and retail use in 1993. In 1996 State Street, which had been closed to automobile traffic in 1979 and reserved for buses and pedestrians, was reopened once again to private vehicular traffic, and major infrastructure projects enhanced the streetscape.

LaSalle Street, on the west side of the Loop, remains the financial center of downtown. The Art Deco Board of Trade Building (1930) and many major banks like Continental, Federal Reserve, Northern Trust, and LaSalle have created a "canyon of finance" here.

The Loop has also been an important part of Chicago's political and governmental history. The City Hall–County Building (1911), the Richard J. Daley Civic Center (1965), and the Mies van der Rohe Federal Center (1964, 1975, 1991) are all located here. For much of its history, the Loop was part of the First Ward, probably the most infamous of Chicago's 50 wards. Many notorious figures in crime and vice operated here, often with the support of elected leaders, or were even elected leaders themselves.

After being a significant residential area for decades, in 1960 the Loop's population declined to its lowest level since Chicago was incorporated in 1837. Efforts have been made to attract residents back to the Loop, and areas like Dearborn Park/South Loop have had considerable success attracting affluent owners and renters. Thus, while changing, the Loop continues to be the vibrant hub of Chicago.

—*Andrew K. Prinz*

See also
Burnham, Daniel H.; Chicago, Illinois; Home Insurance Building; Jenney, William Le Baron; Sullivan, Louis H.
References
Holt, Glen E., and Dominic A. Pacyga. *Chicago: A Historical Guide to the Neighborhoods, The Loop and South Side.* Chicago: Chicago Historical Society, 1979.
Pacyga, Dominic A., and Ellen Skerrett. *Chicago: City of Neighborhoods.* Chicago: Loyola University Press, 1986.
Schnedler, Jack. *Chicago.* Oakland, CA: Compass American Guides, 1993.
Schulze, Franz, and Kevin Harrington, eds. *Chicago's Famous Buildings.* 4th ed. Chicago: University of Chicago Press, 1993.
Sinkevitch, Alice, ed. *AIA Guide to Chicago.* New York: Harcourt, Brace, 1993.

Los Angeles, California

Founded in 1781, Los Angeles today is the second largest city in the United States. By 1990, 3,485,000 people resided within the city itself, and 10 million more lived in the surrounding metropolitan area. Los Angeles has become the largest manufacturing center in the country other than New York, with a harbor second to none. Many ethnic groups reside in the metropolitan region, making it the most multicultural of all American cities. Yet this great metropolis rose to national prominence lacking any significant geographical advantages other than its mild climate. It does not have, for instance, a navigable river, nor does it sit on a historic trade route; and its great harbor is almost wholly artificial. In fact, Los Angeles enjoys none of the physical features that furthered the development of most American cities. Los Angeles exists as it does today largely because of circumstance and its citizens' willingness to combine public and private enterprise to build an urban infrastructure where none previously existed.

El Pueblo de Nuestra Senora la Reina de Los Angeles (The Village of Our Lady the Queen of the Angels) was founded during the late eighteenth century by a small group of settlers subsidized by the Spanish colonial government. The area already served as home to two Catholic missions as well as a presidio charged with defending the area from the expansionist schemes of other European nations. The government established the village as an agricultural settlement to feed the missions and presidio. For their new settlement, the colonizers chose a rather unpromising stretch of land in the middle of a vast semiarid plain several miles inland from the Pacific Ocean. Although the Los Angeles River supplied adequate water for both domestic and agricultural use, it was not even close to being navigable. Transportation therefore consisted of horses, horse-drawn carts, and pedestrian traffic.

Nevertheless, by the time Mexico declared its independence from Spain in 1821, Los Angeles boasted about 1,000 residents, making it the largest settlement in California. The new republic of Mexico subsequently stripped the missions of their landholdings and established a society of large landholders known as rancheros. Because the ranchos were largely self-sufficient and did not require an elaborate urban infrastructure, Los Angeles remained a small village serving the nearby ranchos while it remained a part of Mexico. In 1850, when the U.S. Congress granted California statehood just a few years after its conquest during the war with Mexico, the population of Los Angeles stood at 1,610, a far cry from the rapidly growing city of San Francisco, which housed nearly 35,000 residents 400 miles to the north.

During its first 30 years as an American community, the region surrounding Los Angeles developed a commercial economy. The rancheros initially profited by supplying cattle to the goldfields of northern California, but one of the periodic droughts and the imposition of property taxes soon ended the rancho system in favor of more intensive commercial farming.

Los Angeles might have remained an agricultural community for many years had the owners of the Southern Pacific Railroad not wanted to stifle San Diego's growth. Unlike Los Angeles, San Diego has a fine natural harbor. During the late nineteenth century, San Diego envied San Francisco's dominance; because of the gold rush, San Francisco had emerged as the major city on the West Coast. As San Francisco matured beyond its origins as a boomtown, local businessmen sought to maintain the city's control of the Western economy. The first transcontinental railroad, the Central Pacific, effectively terminated at San Francisco, and its owners wanted to create a transportation net that would tie the entire economy of California to the Bay Area.

San Diego, located 100 miles south of Los Angeles, seemed to be the one city in California that could potentially rival San Francisco. To forestall this, the owners of the Central Pacific wielded their considerable economic and political clout and blocked repeated attempts by San Diego residents to attract another transcontinental railroad that would capitalize on their city's location and magnificent harbor. San Diegans correctly surmised that such a railroad would allow them to tap into the national economy and establish their city as a substantial metropolitan area.

On the other hand, Los Angeles lacked an adequate port and therefore did not appear to threaten San Francisco's dominance of California's economy. As a result, the Southern Pacific Railroad, successor to the Central Pacific, agreed to build a line to Los Angeles after the county government offered it sizable subsidies. Completed shortly thereafter in 1872, the railroad tied Los Angeles into the state and national economies and led to dramatic increases in the area's trade and population. Within a decade, the city's population doubled to 11,138 while the value of its farm products increased more than ninefold.

With the coming of the railroad, Los Angeles businessmen commenced a vigorous publicity campaign during the 1880s to attract trade and residents. The area's proponents cleverly portrayed Los Angeles as an American Eden with a mild and healthful climate. So successful was this public relations campaign that the city and surrounding area grew rapidly throughout the remainder of the nineteenth century despite a series of real estate booms and busts. During the same years, the development of refrigerated railroad cars allowed the area to export what were then exotic fruits—lemons, grapefruits, and navel oranges—to the Midwest. Simultaneously, a major shift in U.S. demographics was gathering momentum as rural residents flocked to cities. Los Angeles benefited greatly from this population movement, particularly after completion of a second transcontinental railroad substantially reduced fares.

The city and its surrounding region could not, however, continue to grow without a new source of water. The Los Angeles basin is semiarid, and nearly all of its rain falls in winter and early spring. As the region grew, local water agencies increasingly tapped into the large aquifer systems that run throughout southern California. By 1900, the city possessed the waterworks to support a population of about 300,000. But it soon became apparent that Los Angeles could not continue to sustain its growth without an even greater water supply. The city government therefore voted to seek a new source of water.

A former mayor of Los Angeles had already anticipated this issue and purchased extensive water rights in the Owens Valley, 150 miles north of the city. Runoff from the snowpack of the Sierra Nevada Mountains provided this thinly populated valley with abundant water all year round. The former mayor hoped to form a private company to divert this water supply to Los Angeles. The city council, however, insisted that any water coming from the Owens Valley be incorporated into the municipal water system. The city subsequently bought out the private investors and prepared to build an aqueduct to deliver the water to the San Fernando Valley. But first, much to the dismay of local farmers, the city had to persuade the federal government to abandon its plan to develop the Owens Valley's water supply to benefit agriculture in that area. Los Angeles also had to convince its voters to pass a $23 million bond issue to pay for the miles of concrete ditches and steel pipes that would carry the water across the Mojave Desert and over the San Gabriel Mountains to reservoirs just north of the city. The electorate overwhelmingly approved the bond issue, and the aqueduct, hailed as an engineering marvel when it was completed in 1913, initially supplied enough water for 1 million residents.

The city, however, refused to sell this water to neighboring communities. Any area that wanted to benefit from the new water supply had to join Los Angeles. With no alternative source of water, many communities did just that. As a consequence, the city limits of Los Angeles expanded rapidly. Nearly the whole of the San Fernando Valley, for instance, annexed itself to the city before 1925. As a result, Los Angeles, unlike many other American cities, now encompassed large areas of suburban communities. But as Los Angeles continued to grow it again threatened to outstrip the water supply. It therefore joined other cities throughout the nearby area to form the Metropolitan Water District. This organization subsequently designed and built an aqueduct from the Colorado River to the metropolitan area during the 1930s.

With an adequate supply of water, the city could sustain rapid growth, but it had also adequate shipping facilities during its formative decades in the nineteenth century. The development of a large artificial harbor in 1912, in combination with existing rail connections, largely resolved this issue. Meanwhile, the discovery of major oil fields in Los Angeles County and the development of new industries such as motion pictures further boosted the area's industrial output. At the same time, the city became one of the nation's largest manufacturing centers with a well-diversified industrial base, including oil refineries, automobile and aircraft factories, motion picture studios, meatpacking houses, garment manufacturing, and many other producers of goods and services.

The resulting growth of the city during the first three decades of the twentieth century was indeed startling. Between 1900 and 1930, the population expanded from 102,000 to 1,238,000. As its population increased, the city became the West Coast location of production facilities for many major corporations. Its explosive growth had allowed Los Angeles to emerge as the premier city in the western United States. It also made the city one of the country's great metropolises.

The city's rapid growth sorely taxed its transportation network and also raised questions about its spatial form. Older cities such as New York and Chicago had experienced much of their growth earlier in the nineteenth century when efficient, mechanized, urban transportation did not yet exist. This necessarily limited the size of most cities to about a two-mile radius, and urban dwellers generally lived within a half-hour walk of their job. Without efficient, inexpensive transportation, these cities grew increasingly dense. Consequently, the larger cities of the earlier nineteenth century, even though vibrant, suffered from public health problems caused by overcrowding.

Before Los Angeles embraced the streetcar and the automobile, it looked much like any other nineteenth-century city, albeit somewhat smaller. Its central business district was the hub of the region and provided manufacturing, retail, and business functions for the entire city, as well as some housing. Heavy industry tended to be located just outside the city center where railroads could conveniently deliver raw materials. Short-haul transportation and distribution, however, continued to rely on carts drawn by horses. The limited speed of these vehicles required a small, tightly packed structure.

The electric streetcar and interurban train promoted decentralization, and the advent of the streetcar, particularly, allowed people to move into suburban housing tracts filled with single-family dwellings. Moreover, city planners in Los Angeles consciously avoided the older form of the city in favor of decentralized growth. By encouraging suburban development, these officials hoped to lower densities, promote healthier living conditions, and ease the burden on the city's sewers and water supplies. The key to such city planning was, of course, improved transportation.

In consequence, Angelenos could live on tree-lined streets in detached houses but still work in the thriving central business district. By 1910 mergers and consolidations within the transportation industry left the Los Angeles region with an extensive streetcar and interurban train system. By the end of the 1920s Los Angeles had a population density that was only one-fourth to one-seventh that of Chicago, Philadelphia, or New York. Nevertheless, most retail, business, and manufacturing activities remained firmly implanted in and around the downtown. Indeed, most streetcar lines converged on the city center, making it a natural hub.

But shortly after 1910 the public transportation system had stopped growing, even at a time when the city's population was doubling every five years. The reason for these seemingly contradictory developments lay in the fact that the city left the construction of transportation facilities, unlike its water and power systems, to private enterprise.

Land developers had built the original streetcar and interurban lines mainly as a way of developing suburban housing tracts. By connecting distant agricultural land with the city center, real estate developers could greatly increase the value of their landholdings. Consequently, most streetcar companies were owned by corporations or individuals more interested in land and housing than transportation. The result was a system of streetcars and interurbans that was poorly designed and lacked coordination. In addition, the streetcars could not operate at a profit once housing tracts had been developed because of high operating and capital costs. Therefore, streetcar development slowed dramatically after 1914 even though population continued to boom. During the first 30 years of the twentieth century, residents of the Los Angeles area constantly complained about the poor quality of rail transit. From their point of view, the railways refused to build badly needed crosstown lines, ran too few cars, provided slow and inadequate service, and bribed public officials.

All of this ultimately led to adoption of the automobile as the primary means of urban transportation. Frustrated by poor rail service, residents used the car to free themselves from railways. The acceptance of the automobile, however, did not come easily. When large numbers of motorists began driving downtown, severe congestion resulted. Like many American cities, Los Angeles had narrow, discontinuous streets that had been constructed years earlier. These roads simply could not handle the influx of automobiles that now flooded the city. In 1920, the city council banned parking on downtown streets to rid the area of congestion, but public protest forced the council to rescind the law after a mere 19 days.

Congestion of the city's streets continued to worsen throughout the 1920s. As more and more residents drove automobiles, per capita ridership declined precipitously on the interurban and streetcar systems. Impatient to solve the transportation problem, property owners and businessmen organized a systematic program to reconstruct streets in the city and county. They hired consultants to design a plan for widening and opening up major thoroughfares leading into the city. Property owners then petitioned the city to assess themselves for constructing the improvements. Using this technique, the city rationalized and rearranged its streets.

The automobile offered residents more flexibility but initially did little to alter the basic city structure. People merely used their automobiles to drive into the city center to shop and work. But with population growth and the use of automobiles booming, downtown traffic became intolerable by the late 1920s despite the extensive street improvements. Rather than abandon their automobiles, people sought to develop commercial outlets in their suburbs. Starting in 1927, many retail chains opened stores in outlying areas that offered convenient parking. Thus began the decentralization for which Los Angeles is so well known.

The invention of the truck also encouraged decentralization. Trucks quickly replaced horse-drawn carts in distributing goods throughout the city. Not only did the truck help establish retail centers outside the city center, it also allowed manufacturers to move to suburbs, avoid the congestion of the central business district, and take advantage of lower land prices.

Los Angeles decentralized quickly. Southern California had vast tracts of cheap, open land. At the same time, the region was the fastest growing in the nation during the first four decades of the twentieth century. Since the city experienced most of its growth during that time, its central business district exerted a relatively weak influence on transportation patterns after suburbanization began. As a result, Los Angeles emerged during the 1920s as a sprawling urban area with huge tracts of suburban housing and many outlying business and industrial centers. The truck and automobile allowed easy access to these various centers, resulting in a city that, by the 1930s, focused not on the central business district but on its suburbs. Eventually, all American cities would decentralize to some extent, but Los Angeles led the way in creating a multicentered region largely dependent on the automobile and truck.

By the 1930s decentralization had already begun to leave signs of urban decay. The movement of industry and retail stores to suburbs had produced a blighted city center. Automobile congestion in the downtown further constricted the flow of goods and people within the city. Poor highway planning and commercial zoning encouraged the development of crowded regional centers, which soon experienced their own transportation problems. By 1937 city engineers were warning that each regional center was leaving behind its own ring of blight.

Aerial view of a freeway interchange just outside the downtown of Los Angeles, California, in 1988.

Planners therefore turned to freeways in an attempt to improve access between outlying areas and the central business district. Downtown merchants and property owners thought that freeways would relieve congestion and stop the decline of the inner city. Suburban interests supported freeway development as a way to ease congestion in outlying shopping centers. Public officials therefore embraced limited access highways as a solution to the development of slums in the inner city. With the help of special state and federal legislation that allocated gasoline taxes and vehicle registration fees to highway development, Los Angeles County developed an extensive freeway system after World War II.

Southern California continued growing after the war. The postwar economic boom benefited Los Angeles and its suburbs as the area continued its development as a preeminent manufacturing center. The motion picture and, later, the television industries expanded, as did garment and furniture making and other manufacturing concerns. In addition, the defense and aerospace industries experienced substantial growth as the Cold War increased the government's demand for weapons systems. Several airplane manufacturers had established themselves in southern California during the 1920s and 1930s because the area's clement weather allowed year-round test flights. World War II turned many of these fledgling companies and their suppliers into some of the largest manufacturing concerns in the country. Later, the government relied on these same companies to produce arms in response to the perceived aggression of the Soviet Union. The result was the creation of thousands of high-paying engineering and manufacturing jobs in Los Angeles.

By the early 1990s the Los Angeles metropolitan area had become the second largest in the United States, behind only New York, with nearly 14 million residents. Furthermore, the area had emerged as the nation's largest manufacturing center other than New York. Its geographical position overlooking the Pacific Ocean had allowed it to dominate American trade with the Pacific Rim. Not surprisingly, its port had established itself as the largest in the United States, with $60 billion of goods passing through it during 1986. Fully 60 percent of the country's trade with the Pacific Rim entered or departed through Los Angeles's harbor. The area also produced $250 billion in goods and services in 1987. Had the metropolitan area been a separate country, it would have ranked as the world's eleventh largest nation in terms of its gross national product, ahead of Austria, Switzerland, and India, just to name a few.

But it is not just the huge volume of its trade that makes the region remarkable. Los Angeles and its environs have emerged as the immigrant's gateway to America. During the 1980s, 25 percent of all immigrants to the United States settled in Los Angeles County. This massive influx of both legal and illegal aliens has dramatically altered the region's ethnic composition. During the earlier part of the twentieth century, Los Angeles was one of the most homogeneous of American cities. In 1930, for instance, 88 percent of the city's population was Anglo. The minority population was small and geographically segregated, with Latinos accounting for 8 percent of the population while blacks and Asians each made up 2 percent of the city's residents.

By 1990 Los Angeles had become the most ethnically diverse metropolitan area in the country. Anglos no longer make up the majority of residents in the city; 41 percent of the city's residents are now Hispanic, 13 percent black, 9 percent Asian, and only 37 percent Anglo. Of the city's residents, 40 percent are foreign-born, while 50 percent speak a language other than English in their homes. Nowhere is the city's ethnic complexion more noticeable than in the public schools, which teach children from 80 different language groups. So large is Los Angeles's ethnic population that some claim the area boasts the largest urban Mexican, Filipino, Korean, and Vietnamese populations outside those respective countries. The area also numbers large Central and South American populations, as well as substantial Chinese and Japanese communities.

In recent years, Los Angeles's many ethnic groups have found themselves competing with each other for a share of the area's resources. On occasion, these tensions have erupted into violence. In 1992, 25 years after the destructive Watts riots, south central Los Angeles became embroiled in the country's worst civil unrest of the twentieth century. The riots were triggered by the acquittal of several Los Angeles police officers accused of beating a black motorist, Rodney King. Nearly three days of uncontrolled violence led to 50 deaths, $750 million of damage, and 500 structures destroyed. As the city recovered from this violence, it tried to create a sense of cooperation among its diverse population.

Los Angeles's experience during the twentieth century has been remarkable. At the beginning of the century, the city existed as a relatively remote urban oasis far removed from the rest of the country. Ninety years later, it had grown into one of the largest, most dynamic metropolitan areas in the world. Along the way, Los Angeles developed a city structure that other cities would later imitate to one degree or another. It was, for instance, the first metropolitan area to decentralize. This initially consisted of residential dispersion into the suburbs, but virtually all of the other economic functions within the city eventually followed suit. This resulted in a city focused not on its central business district but on several regional employment centers.

Other cities experienced similar decentralization as the truck and automobile allowed people and businesses to escape their downtown areas. Some older cities managed to retain a strong central business district because they had experienced substantial growth in the nineteenth century. Nevertheless, even these metropolitan areas decentralized to a large degree. Today, more people throughout the United States commute between suburbs than from suburb to downtown. Los Angeles therefore set the trend in urban development for twentieth-century America.

—Scott L. Bottles

See also
Bradley, Tom; McPherson, Aimee Semple.
References
Bottles, Scott. *Los Angeles and the Automobile: The Making of the Modern City.* Berkeley: University of California Press, 1987.
Brodsly, David. *L.A. Freeway.* Berkeley: University of California Press, 1981.
Fogelson, Robert M. *The Fragmented Metropolis: Los Angeles, 1850–1930.* Cambridge, MA: Harvard University Press, 1967.
Foster, Mark S. "The Model-T, the Hard Sell, and Los Angeles's Urban Growth: The Decentralization of Los Angeles during the 1920s." *Pacific Historical Review* 44 (1974): 459–484.
McWilliams, Carey. *Southern California: An Island in the Sun.* Santa Barbara, CA, and Salt Lake City, UT: Peregrine Smith, 1973.

Lynd, Robert S. (1892–1970) and Helen M. (1896–1982)

Robert S. and Helen M. Lynd are famous primarily for two books that they wrote together, *Middletown: A Study in American Culture* (1929) and *Middletown in Transition: A Study in Cultural Conflicts* (1937).

Robert S. Lynd was born in New Albany, Indiana, in 1892. He graduated from Princeton University in 1914 and became an assistant editor of *Publisher's Weekly.* In 1918, he entered the army where his career interest changed to human service, and after his discharge, he matriculated at Union Theological Seminary. A second transforming experience occurred in 1921 when the Presbyterian Board of Home Missions sent Lynd to Elk Basin, Wyoming, to establish a church.

While in Elk Basin, Lynd worked as a roustabout in the oil fields at the same time that he preached, conducted Bible study groups, taught Sunday school, and began Boy Scout and Girl Scout troops. From these experiences came "Crude-Oil Religion," an article in *Harpers,* and "Done in Oil," in *Survey,* both published in 1922. The second was a slashing attack on the Standard Oil Company of Indiana and John D. Rockefeller, Jr., for the poor quality of life in the oil fields.

Three days after he returned from his short stay in Elk Basin in 1921, Lynd married Helen Merrill, also a midwesterner, who had graduated from Wellesley College in 1919. Before her marriage, she had taught at a girls' college, but after the wedding she went to Columbia University where she earned a master's degree in philosophy.

Although neither of the Lynds had formal training in social science research methods, the Institute for Social and Religious Research selected them to organize and coordinate its Small City Study. This institute was successor to the Interchurch World Movement, which had been founded in 1923 with the goal of unifying all Protestant churches into a single vast social service network. The purpose of the Small City Study was to determine the totality of the religious attitudes and activities in one industrial town.

The Lynds went to Muncie, Indiana, the town that would be known as Middletown, in January 1924 to do fieldwork. When it was completed, Robert became Assistant Director for education research for the Commonwealth Fund in 1926 and Secretary of the Social Science Research Council in 1927. When *Middletown* was published soon after, it proved to be a resounding success, and two universities, the University of Michigan and Columbia University, offered him tenured professorships in their sociology departments even though he had no degree or even any training in that field. He accepted the offer from Columbia, which awarded him a

Ph.D. for *Middletown* after he and Helen excised those portions that she had written.

Meanwhile, Helen had begun a long career teaching social philosophy at Sarah Lawrence College; she earned a Ph.D. in history in 1944 and wrote a dissertation that was published in 1945 as *England in the 1880s: Toward a Social Basis for Freedom.* Robert Lynd remained at Columbia for the remainder of his academic career, becoming increasingly radical because of his alienation from the growing empiricism of sociology and because of his general disillusionment with American society. Although he was unable to complete a projected study of the Depression's impact on selected groups, he served on the Research Committee on Social Trends under President Hoover and the Consumer's Advisory Board of the National Recovery Administration under President Roosevelt. In 1935 he returned to Muncie without Helen to do research for a sequel to *Middletown* called *Middletown in Transition.* In 1940, he published his last book, *Knowledge for What?,* a stinging critique of value-free empirical research. Although he wished to write a study of power in America, he was unable to do so by the time he died in 1970, 12 years before Helen.

—*Dwight Hoover*

See also
Middletown.

References

Fox, Richard Wightman. "Epitaph for Middletown, Robert S. Lynd and the Analysis of Consumer Culture." In Richard Wightman Fox and T. J. Jackson Lears, eds., *The Culture of Consumption,* 101–141. New York: Pantheon, 1983.

Harvey, Charles E. "Robert S. Lynd, John D. Rockefeller, Jr., and Middletown." *Indiana Magazine of History* 79 (1983): 330–354.

Jensen, Richard. "The Lynds Revisited." *Indiana Magazine of History* 75 (1979): 303–319.

Journal of the History of Sociology 2 (1979). The entire issue is devoted to a study of Robert Lynd and his work.

Lynd, Helen M. *Possibilities.* Bronxville, NY: Sarah Lawrence College, 1983.

Shannon, Christopher. *Conspicuous Criticism: American Social Thought from Veblen to Mills.* Baltimore: Johns Hopkins University Press, 1995.

Van Holthoon, F. L. "Robert Lynd's Disenchantment: A Study of Robert Lynd's Cultural Criticism." In Hans Bertens and Theo D'Haen, eds., *The Small Town in America: A Multidisciplinary Revisit,* 30–59. Amsterdam, Netherlands: VU University Press, 1995.